CURRENT
BIOGRAPHY
YEARBOOK
1959

CURRENT
BIOGRAPHY
YEARBOOK

1959

EDITED BY

CHARLES MORITZ

THE H. W. WILSON COMPANY
NEW YORK, N. Y.

TWENTIETH ANNUAL CUMULATION—1959

PRINTED IN THE UNITED STATES OF AMERICA

Copyright © 1959, 1960
by
THE H. W. WILSON COMPANY

International Standard Book Number 0-8242-0125-6

Library of Congress Catalog Card No. (40-27432)

Reasonable quotation is permitted provided due credit is given to **CURRENT BIOGRAPHY**

Preface

The appearance of the twentieth annual volume of Current Biog-RAPHY, cumulating eleven monthly issues in one alphabet, brings to a close its first two decades of publication. During this period it witnessed the entry of the United States into World War II, the end of that armed conflict, and the uneasy peace and "cold war" that followed. It also saw the ushering in of the atomic age and the inauguration of the United Nations. These developments have been reflected in the lives of the celebrities discussed in its pages; now, as the world enters the space age of rocketry and missiles, an increasing number of names of physicists appears in Current Biography.

Ranging over some forty subject fields from archaeology to tech-nology, this twentieth volume of Current Biography Yearbook follows the pattern of its recent predecessors. The twenty sketches of authors originally published in the *Wilson Library Bulletin* that have been included are indicated by (WLB) in the *Cumulated Index* and in the *Literature* classification. Winners of the Nobel Prizes and the Pulitzer Prizes have been accorded biographical treatment. Several persons who appeared in earlier volumes of Current Biography and who continue to find their way into the news have been singled out for revised biographical sketches. They are: George F. Kennan, James R. Killian, Ben Grauer, Henry Drey-fuss, Stanley Kunitz, Archibald MacLeish, and General Lauris Norstad.

Through careful researching by Current Biography writers in newspapers, magazines, authoritative reference books, and the news re-leases of government agencies, all the biographical sketches have been made as accurate and objective as possible. Immediately after their pub-lication in the monthly issues, the articles are submitted to the biographees to give them an opportunity to suggest corrections in time for Current Biography Yearbook. Sketches have also been revised before inclusion in the Yearbook to take account of major changes in the careers of biographees. Although subjects are occasionally interviewed, the question-naire continues to be the main source of direct information.

Heads of veterans, industrial, fraternal, and professional organiza-tions included in this volume can be found in the back under *Organi-zations.* Individuals who are not authors by profession but who have written books are listed under *Nonfiction* or *Literature* in addition to their primary vocational fields.

The pages following contain: *Explanation; Key to Reference Abbre-viations; Key to Pronunciation;* and *Key to Abbreviations.* The indexes at the end of the volume are: *Biographical References (consulted by Current Biography research staff); Periodicals and Newspapers Con-sulted; Necrology* (of persons whose biographies have appeared in pre-vious volumes); *Classification by Professional Field; Cumulated Index. 1951-59).* The 1940-1950 Index is found in the 1950 Yearbook.

Acknowledgement is due to Miss Marjorie Dent Candee, who resigned from the editorship of Current Biography in October 1958 after five years of service.

CHARLES MORITZ

Explanations

Authorities for biographees' full names, with some exceptions, are the bibliographical publications of The Wilson Company. When a biographee prefers a certain name form, that is indicated in the heading of the article: for example, Macmillan, (Maurice) Harold means that he is usually referred to as Harold Macmillan. When a professional name is used in the heading, as, for example, GLENN FORD, the real name, in this case GWYLLYN SAMUEL NEWTON FORD, appears in the article itself.

The heading of each article includes the pronunciation of the name if it is unusual, date of birth (if obtainable), and occupation. The article is supplemented by a list of references to sources of biographical information, in two alphabets: (1) newspapers and periodicals and (2) books. See the section **Biographical References Consulted.**

KEY TO REFERENCE ABBREVIATIONS

References to newspapers and periodicals are listed in abbreviated form; for example, "Sat Eve Post 217:14-15 S 30 '44 por" means **Saturday Evening Post,** volume 217, pages 14-15, September 30, 1944, with portrait. (For full names, see the section **Periodicals and Newspapers Consulted,** found in the rear of this volume.)

January—Ja	July—Jl	Journal—J
February—F	August—Ag	Magazine—Mag
March—Mr	September—S	Monthly—Mo
April—Ap	October—O	Weekly—W
May—My	November—N	Portrait—por
June—Je	December—D	Review—R

KEY TO PRONUNCIATION
(Based on Webster's Guide to Pronunciation)*

ā	āle	N	Not pronounced, but indicates the nasal tone of the preceding vowel, as in the French *bon* (bôN).	û	ûrn; French eu, as in *jeu* (zhû); German ö, oe, as in *schön* (shûn), *Goethe* (gû'tĕ)
â	câre				
ă	ădd				
á	áccount				
ä	ärm			ŭ	tŭb
à	àsk			ŭ̇	circŭs
a̍	sofà		ō	ōld	ü	Pronounced approximately as ē, with rounded lips: French u, as in *menu* (mĕ-nü'); German ü, as in *grün*
			ô	ôrb		
ē	ēve		ŏ	ŏdd		
ĕ	ĕnd		oi	oil		
ẽ	makẽr		o͞o	o͞oze		
			o͝o	fo͝ot		
g	go		ou	out		
ī	īce		th	*then*	zh	azure
ĭ	ĭll		th	thin	′ =	main accent
ᴋ	German ch as in *ich* (ĭᴋ)		ū	cūbe	″ =	secondary accent

(*Exceptions : th in then; main and secondary accents.)

KEY TO ABBREVIATIONS

A.A.A.A.   Amateur Athletic Association of America
A.A.U.   Amateur Athletic Union
A.B.A.   American Bar Association
ABC   American Broadcasting Company
A.C.L.U.   American Civil Liberties Union
ADA   Americans for Democratic Action
AEC   Atomic Energy Commission
AEF   American Expeditionary Force
AFL   American Federation of Labor
AFL-CIO   American Federation of Labor and Congress of Industrial Organizations
ALA   American Library Association
A.M.A.   American Medical Association
A.P.   Associated Press
ASCAP   American Society of Composers, Authors and Publishers
ASNE   American Society of Newspaper Editors
b.   business (address)
B.A.   Bachelor of Arts
BBC   British Broadcasting Corporation
B.D.   Bachelor of Divinity
B.L.S.   Bachelor of Library Science
BMI   Broadcast Music, Inc.
B.S.   Bachelor of Science
CAA   Civil Aeronautics Administration
CAB   Civil Aeronautics Board
C.B.   Companion of the Bath
C.B.E.   Commander of (the Order of) the British Empire
CBS   Columbia Broadcasting System
C.E.   Civil Engineer
CEA   Council of Economic Advisers
C.E.D.   Committee for Economic Development
CENTO   Central Treaty Organization
CIO   Congress of Industrial Organizations
C.M.G.   Companion of (the Order of) St. Michael and St. George
Com.   Commodore
CWA   Civil Works Administration
CWS   Chemical Warfare Service
D.A.R.   Daughters of the American Revolution
D.C.L.   Doctor of Civil Law
D.D.   Doctor of Divinity
D.Eng.   Doctor of Engineering
DEW   Distant Early Warning Line
D.F.C.   Distinguished Flying Cross
D.J.   Doctor of Jurisprudence
D.Lit.   Doctor of Literature
D.Mus.   Doctor of Music
DP   Displaced Person
D.Pol.Sc.   Doctor of Political Science
D.Sc.   Doctor of Science
D.S.C.   Distinguished Service Cross
D.S.M.   Distinguished Service Medal
D.S.O.   Distinguished Service Order
ECA   Economic Cooperation Administration
ECOSOC   Economic and Social Council
EDC   European Defense Community
ERP   European Recovery Program
FAO   Food and Agriculture Organization
FBI   Federal Bureau of Investigation
FCA   Farm Credit Administration
FCC   Federal Communications Commission
FEPC   Fair Employment Practice Committee
FERA   Federal Emergency Relief Administration

FHA   Federal Housing Administration
FOA   Foreign Operations Administration
FPC   Federal Power Commission
FSA   Federal Security Agency
FTC   Federal Trade Commission
G.B.E.   Knight or Dame, Grand Cross Order of the British Empire
G.C.B.   Knight Grand Cross of the Bath
G.O.P.   Grand Old Party
h.   home (address)
H.M.   His Majesty; Her Majesty
ICA   International Cooperation Administration
ICBM   Intercontinental Ballistic Missile
ICC   Interstate Commerce Commission
I.C.F.T.U.   International Confederation of Free Trade Unions
IGY   International Geophysical Year
I.L.A.   International Longshoremen's Association
I.L.G.W.U.   International Ladies' Garment Workers Union
I.L.O.   International Labor Organization
INS   International News Service
IRO   International Refugee Organization
J.D.   Doctor of Jurisprudence
j.g.   junior grade
K.B.E.   Knight of (the Order of) the British Empire
K.C.   King's Counsel
K.C.B.   Knight Commander of the Bath
L.H.D.   Doctor of Humanities
Litt.D.   Doctor of Letters
LL.B.   Bachelor of Laws
LL.D.   Doctor of Laws
M.A.   Master of Arts
M.B.A.   Master of Business Administration
MBS   Mutual Broadcasting System
M.C.E.   Master of Civil Engineering
M.D.   Doctor of Medicine
M.E.   Master of Engineering
METO   Middle East Treaty Organization
MGM   Metro-Goldwyn-Mayer
M.Lit.   Master of Literature
M.P.   Member of Parliament
MRP   Mouvement Républicain Populaire
MSA   Mutual Security Agency
M.Sc.   Master of Science
Msgr.   Monsignor, Monseigneur
NAACP   National Association for the Advancement of Colored People
NAB   National Association of Broadcasters
NAM   National Association of Manufacturers
NATO   North Atlantic Treaty Organization
NBC   National Broadcasting Company
N.E.A.   National Education Association
NLRB   National Labor Relations Board
N.M.U.   National Maritime Union
NRA   National Recovery Administration
NRPB   National Resources Planning Board
NYA   National Youth Administration
O.A.S.   Organization of American States
OBE   Officer of (the Order of) the British Empire
OCD   Office of Civilian Defense
OEEC   Organization for European Economic Cooperation
OPA   Office of Price Administration

OPM   Office of Production Management
OPRD   Office of Production Research and Development
OSRD   Office of Scientific Research and Development
OWI   Office of War Information
P.E.N.   Poets, Playwrights, Editors, Essayists and Novelists (International Association)
Ph.B.   Bachelor of Philosophy
Ph.D.   Doctor of Philosophy
PWA   Public Works Administration
Q.C.   Queen's Counsel
RAF   Royal Air Force
RCA   Radio Corporation of America
REA   Rural Electrification Administration
RFC   Reconstruction Finance Corporation
RKO   Radio-Keith-Orpheum
ROTC   Reserve Officers' Training Corps
SAC   Strategic Air Command
SCAP   Supreme Command for the Allied Powers
SEATO   Southeast Asia Treaty Organization
SEC   Securities and Exchange Commission
s.g.   senior grade
SHAEF   Supreme Headquarters, Allied Expeditionary Force
SHAPE   Supreme Headquarters Allied Powers Europe
S.J.D.   Doctor of Juridical Science
SLA   Special Libraries Association
S.T.B.   Bachelor of Sacred Theology
S.T.D.   Doctor of Sacred Theology
TVA   Tennessee Valley Authority
T.W.U.A.   Textile Workers Union of America
UAR   United Arab Republic
U.A.W.   United Automobile, Aircraft, and Agricultural Implement Workers of America
UMT   Universal Military Training
U.M.W.A.   United Mine Workers of America
U.N.   United Nations
UNESCO   United Nations Educational, Scientific, and Cultural Organization
UNICEF   United Nations Children's Fund
UNRRA   United Nations Relief and Rehabilitation Administration
U.P.I.   United Press and International News Service
USO   United Service Organizations
U.S.S.R.   Union of Soviet Socialist Republics
U.S.W.A.   United Steel Workers of America
VA   Veterans Administration
V.F.W.   Veterans of Foreign Wars
WAA   War Assets Administration
W.A.A.C.   Women's Auxiliary Army Corps
W.C.T.U.   Woman's Christian Temperance Union
W.E.U.   Western European Union
WFA   War Food Administration
W.F.T.U.   World Federation of Trade Unions
WHO   World Health Organization
WMC   War Manpower Commission
WPA   Work Projects Administration
WPB   War Production Board

CURRENT BIOGRAPHY

YEARBOOK

1959

ADKINSON, BURTON W(ILBUR) Mar 5, 1909- United States government official; organization official; librarian
Address: b. National Science Foundation, 1951 Constitution Ave., Washington 25, D.C.; h. 5907 Welborn Dr., Washington 16, D.C.

Serving as president of the Special Libraries Association during its fifty-first year (1959-60) is Dr. Burton W. Adkinson, the head of the Office of Science Information Service of the National Science Foundation, who succeeds Margaret H. Fuller (see *C.B.*, June 1959). Educated as a geographer, with both M.A. and Ph.D. degrees, and originally a teacher in the public school system of the state of Washington, Dr. Adkinson became a librarian purely by accident.

At the onset of World War II, Dr. Adkinson was given the responsibility of supervising a special library in the government. "I have never left the field," says Burton Adkinson, "because of its challenge." In 1945 he joined the staff of the Library of Congress and became chief of the map division two years later. From 1949 to 1957 he was director of the library's reference department.

When Dr. Adkinson was installed as president of the Special Libraries Association at Atlantic City on June 3, 1959, he headed an international organization of professional librarians and information experts who work in the technical and specialized libraries of business, industry, government, the professions, or the various departments of universities or public libraries.

The son of Jason H. and Clara Fannie (Warriner) Adkinson, Burton Wilbur Adkinson was born on March 5, 1909 in Everson, Washington. He has four sisters, three of whom still live in the state of Washington, and a brother, Beecher Harlan Adkinson. The family moved to the town of Maple Falls when Adkinson was still a child. He attended the public schools there and was graduated from Union High School in 1926.

Having shown an interest in teaching as a career, Adkinson matriculated at the Western Washington College of Education in Bellingham. He completed the requirements for elementary school certification in 1929, and immediately accepted his first teaching assignment.

BURTON W. ADKINSON

During the summers of 1932-34 he returned to the teachers college to earn enough credits for a junior high school license. He obtained this in 1934 and for the next five years taught the seventh, eighth, and ninth grades.

During the summer sessions of 1933 to 1936, Adkinson studied at the University of Washington in Seattle; in the latter year he received his Bachelor of Arts degree in education. In 1939 he was granted a master's degree in geography for his thesis on the "Historical Geography of Snohomish River Valley."

After teaching in the public school system of the state of Washington for ten years, Adkinson resigned in 1939 to do postgraduate work in geography at Clark University in Worcester, Massachusetts. At the same time he was visiting lecturer in climatology at Clark University. The Ph.D. degree was conferred on Adkinson in 1942 for a doctoral dissertation devoted to the "Alpine Glaciation in a Section of the Cabinet Mountains."

(Continued next page)

ADKINSON, BURTON W.—*Continued*

Dr. Adkinson was appointed a regional research assistant in the Office of the Geographer of the State Department from 1942-43. The following year he was assistant director of the United States Board on Geographical Names. During the last of the war years 1944-45, Adkinson was the assistant chief of the map intelligence section of the Office of Strategic Services. His affiliation with the Library of Congress dates from late 1945 when he was appointed assistant chief of the map division. Within a short time he was named acting chief and in 1947 he was promoted to the position of chief of the division.

During each year of his administration Dr. Adkinson published a summary report on the progress and accomplishments of his division. These discussions, devoted to the acquisitions of the division through other government agencies, international exchanges, purchases, gifts, and copyright deposit, appeared in the August issues of the *Library of Congress Quarterly Journal of Current Acquisitions* during 1946, 1947, and 1948.

Under Dr. Adkinson's direction, the division established the most comprehensive map collection in the United States. In 1947 more than 100,000 maps were acquired and negotiations were started with foreign governments to ease the international exchange of cartographic items. Though total acquisitions declined in 1948, Dr. Adkinson maintained a good balance between the quantity and quality of both domestic and foreign sources in order to continue his strengthening of the map division.

For eight years beginning in 1949, Dr. Adkinson was director of the reference division of the Library of Congress. In 1957 he was appointed head of the Office of Scientific Information, now the Science Information Service, of the National Science Foundation to succeed Alberto F. Thompson. Established in accordance with a directive from President Eisenhower, the Science Information Service is responsible for collecting scientific data from foreign and domestic sources. This material is then made readily available to researchers, thereby promoting closer co-operation between all available scientific communication facilities in and out of government.

The task of acquiring, organizing, and disseminating the overwhelming number of published materials in the field of scientific research has become complex and cumbersome. Speaking before the documentation division of the Special Libraries Association at the annual convention in Chicago, Illinois in 1958, Dr. Adkinson surveyed the current problem of providing scientific and technical information services. "The tremendous expansion in research and development during and following World War II has produced a veritable flood of published material," he said. "This growth has induced a demand that information be produced and disseminated more speedily, be better organized and be better summarized and indexed. As a result, the inadequacies of present services

have been emphasized" (*Special Libraries,* November, 1958).

Though Adkinson's verdict that "the problems are far outstripping the solutions" is not comforting, the federal government is taking a vital interest in mitigating the situation. The Science Information Service, for example, is conducting studies to determine the amount of money spent by the government for science information services, including libraries. Other analyses "include the methods of improving United States library collections of scientific literature in foreign languages and the information-gathering habits of scientists" (*ALA Bulletin,* March, 1959). The service has granted financial aid for the support of abstracting and indexing sources, prints bibliographies and other reference works, and sponsors experiments in new types of publication methods. All in all, Dr. Adkinson believes that his office under the auspices of the National Science Foundation "will go far toward remedying this country's scientific and technical information ills."

As a special librarian in government, Burton Adkinson readily qualified for membership in the Special Library Association. He has been a diligent worker on its behalf, and his election as the new president for 1959-60 culminates an active career in the association. He has held numerous committee assignments, has "chaired" the geography and map division, and has served as president of the District of Columbia chapter. Before his election as president, Adkinson was treasurer of the association. He is convinced that the Special Libraries Association "must take its place in solving some of the major problems facing librarians and information officers today by initiating studies and projects to improve major bibliographic tools and techniques for information handling" (*Special Libraries,* September 1958).

Of medium stature and heavy-set, Adkinson is five feet seven and one half inches tall and weighs 190 pounds. His hair is gray and his hazel eyes are framed in horn-rimmed glasses. His first marriage to Myra Helen Lewis in 1935 was terminated by her death in August 1937. Married to the former Margaret Louise Klock since September 10, 1942, Adkinson has two daughters, Karen Louise and Margaret Jane. An occasional round of golf and watching the antics of his growing daughters are Dr. Adkinson's sole recreations.

The scope of Dr. Adkinson's research in geography, glaciology, and cartography has been extensive, and his papers on these subjects have appeared in several scientific and professional journals. The librarian has also served on National Research Council committees on geography and on committees of the Pan American Institute of Geography and History.

Other organizations to which Dr. Adkinson belongs are the American Association for the Advancement of Science, the Association of American Geographers, the American Congress on Surveying and Mapping, the Clark University Geographical Society, the Pacific Coast Geographers Association, and the American Documentation Institute. He is also a fellow of the American Geographical Society. In addition to the Special Libraries Association, Burton Adkinson has been active in several other professional societies; he is a member of the Association of College and Reference Libraries, the District of Columbia Library Association, the American Library Association, and the Council of National Libraries Association. His club is the Cosmos.

References

N Y Times p128 N 10 '57
Who's Who in America, 1958-59
Who's Who in Library Service (1955)

ADRIAN, (GILBERT) Mar. 3, 1903-Sept. 13, 1959 American fashion designer; created fashions for MGM and designed custom-made clothes; awarded Circle of New York Fashion Critics' "Winnie" Award in 1945. See *Current Biography* (February) 1941.

Obituary

N Y Times p29 S 14 '59

Consulate General of Japan

CROWN PRINCE AKIHITO OF JAPAN

AKIHITO, CROWN PRINCE OF JAPAN Dec. 23, 1933-

Address: The Imperial Palace, Tokyo, Japan

When Crown Prince Akihito of Japan announced his engagement to Michiko Shoda, the daughter of a wealthy commoner, in November 1958, he broke the imperial tradition of choosing a wife from the court nobility. But Akihito, who will one day be the 125th Emperor of Japan, is used to dispensing with traditions in a westernized and democratized Japan far different from the one into which he was born. As Emperor of Japan, he will have many duties, but none more important than establishing a delicate balance between the new and the old, now that traditional barriers between the throne and the people have broken down. He has determined to remove permanently what he has called "the chrysanthemum curtain" between himself and his subjects.

His Imperial Highness Crown Prince Akihito Tsugunomiya was born on December 23, 1933. He is the fourth child and first son of the Emperor Hirohito and the former Princess Nagako Kuni. According to legend he is the 125th in the dynasty descended directly from the Sun Goddess—the first was the Emperor Jimmu about 660 B.C.

For centuries it has been customary for the Crown Prince to be taken from his parents at the age of two or three and raised by chamberlains in a separate house. So it was with Prince Akihito. He started his formal education at the Gakushuin or Peers' School in 1940 just as his father had done before him. During the latter part of World War II, from March 1944 until November 1945, the Crown Prince lived outside Tokyo at the imperial farm in Chiba Prefecture, at Numazu, and at Nikko.

After World War II, when Japan began to be "democratized" the pattern of the Crown Prince's life and particularly his education be-

gan to differ from that of his predecessors. His father and grandfather had gone through the six elementary grades at the Gakushuin and then continued their studies in special classes with a few selected companions. Akihito moved to a temporary palace at Koganei, the campus of the Gakushuin Junior High School. It was at this time that Mrs. Elizabeth Gray Vining, an American Quaker from Philadelphia, was hired, at the Emperor's request, to tutor the Crown Prince in English. She gave him private lessons—at first once, and later twice a week—and taught several English classes at the school.

Mrs. Vining continuously sought ways to help this young schoolboy have "normal" experiences in his sheltered life. Sometimes she saw to it that his private English lessons included two other classmates; she arranged for him to meet American boys; and she urged the chamberlains to let him keep company with his younger brother, Prince Masahito, more than convention allowed. She tried to help him understand the ideals of the western world and the meaning of democracy.

When the dignity of an imperial court is at stake, change is slow and carefully considered. But during the immediate postwar period many precedents were broken. The climax came when Hirohito renounced his divinity on January 1, 1946 with the words: "The ties between us and our people have always stood upon mutual trust and affection."

After the Crown Prince entered the senior high school course at the Gakushuin he lived part of the time in the boys' dormitory. Later, when Prince Masahito reached high school, both boys spent a part of each week in the dormitory and the rest of the time together in Akihito's palace. The house at Koganei had burned down and the prince now lived in the Tokiwamatsu villa in Tokyo. In 1952 the

AKIHITO, CROWN PRINCE OF JAPAN—*Continued*

prince finished high school and entered the political and economics department at the Gakushuin (Peers') University.

In November 1952, almost a year after he celebrated his eighteenth birthday, Crown Prince Akihito formally came of age. Wearing the robes of the imperial court, he received the Crown of Adulthood and promised his father to ". . . be conscious as ever of my station, cultivate virtue, leaving childlike ways behind, and always carry knowledge into new fields." He was then declared rightful heir to the Japanese throne.

For the coronation of Queen Elizabeth, Prince Akihito was chosen to represent his country. In the spring of 1953 he interrupted his studies to take a six-month tour of fourteen countries, including the United States and Canada. Akihito was the second heir to the Japanese throne to make a grand tour. Thirty-two years before the then Crown Prince Hirohito had visited Great Britain, France, Belgium, the Netherlands, and Italy.

Because the prince had missed about six months of school while on tour he was, at his own request, classified as a "special student" when the new school year started the following spring. He finished his courses with his classmates but was not awarded a degree.

He has also been tutored by some of Japan's leading scholars. One such tutor is Dr. Kotaro Tanaka, Chief Justice of the Supreme Court, who gave him private lessons on the constitution.

On November 27, 1958 the imperial court announced the engagement of the Crown Prince to Miss Michiko Shoda. Akihito chose his own bride, instead of relying on the councilors of the court. Miss Shoda's father is president of the huge Nisshin Flour Milling Company, and the family belongs to the samurai class, not to the peers whose daughters are usually considered the only ones eligible for marriage to a Crown Prince. The marriage on April 10, 1959 symbolized the increasing importance of Japan's business community and the corresponding decline in importance of the peers who are still recognized as such even though the postwar democratization program stripped them of their titles.

The couple have already indicated their intention to break many more precedents. The many formalities surrounding the engagement and marriage were simplified. The Crown Prince has requested that his palace, now being built, provide rooms for children because he does not wish to have his children taken out of the palace when they are still babies.

Crown Prince Akihito is five feet five inches tall and weighs about 120 pounds. He shares his father's enthusiasm for biology, especially ichthyology, and likes riding, tennis, swimming, skiing, and motoring. It was on a tennis court at Kaurizawa, a resort north of Tokyo, that he met Miss Shoda in the summer of 1957. Wearied by the speculation that surrounds a marriageable prince, Akihito showed his sense of humor when, in 1955, he remarked to a classmate: "Don't you think it's a bit too early for me to be tied down with a wife?"

Crown Prince Akihito has adopted many western ways. He sleeps in a western bed and uses an electric shaver. He usually wears one of twenty western suits. He likes to play Latin American rhythms on one of his two high-fidelity sets and offers his classmates whisky and beer in addition to sake. But the Crown Prince is still conscious of the responsibility facing him, and he has not allowed his westernization to erase his appreciation for and understanding of Japan.

References

Life 33:71 D 8 '52; 45:73 D 15 '58
N Y Sunday News p37 N 30 '58
N Y Times p4 N 10 '52; p14 Ja 15 '58; p4 N 26 '58
Time 63:30 Ja 3 '55; 72:26 D 8 '58
Washington (D.C.) Post p7B My 24 '53
International Who's Who, 1958
Gray, E. J. Windows for the Crown Prince (1952)
Japan Biographical Encyclopedia & Who's Who (1958)

ALBERTI, JULES (ROBERT) May 26, 1903- Advertising executive

Address: b. 65 E. 55th St., New York 22; h. 300 E. 57th St., New York 22

"In the past decade," according to Bennett Cerf, "over a half-billion dollars has been spent on testimonial advertisements, and more than 6,000 Grade-A products have been endorsed by the world's outstanding personalities. A major share of the billings as well as much of the credit for turning a chaotic, hit-or-miss practice into a smooth-running, thoroughly respectable enterprise goes to one man. His name is Jules Alberti, and his firm, appropriately enough, is called Endorsements, Incorporated."

The founder and president of this unique "liaison agency between advertisers and celebrities from all walks of life," Jules Robert Alberti was born in Chicago, Illinois on May 26, 1903, the son of Louis and Rose (Talbert) Alberti. His was a theatrical and musical family, and while attending Chicago public schools he became a professional saxophone player. At sixteen he organized his own dance band, and until 1935 received regular assignments to produce musical shows on Chicago radio stations.

During this period, Alberti's band also made several tours of the United States, playing vaudeville and presentation theaters. His vocalist was Benay Venuta. Recognizing her as a talented singer of popular songs, Alberti became her manager and was instrumental in establishing her on network shows over the Columbia Broadcasting System. In 1935 he moved to New York City to produce radio shows there.

Among the celebrities Alberti managed at that time were Elsa Maxwell and Constance Bennett. His experience as a radio producer, master of ceremonies, and manager of celebrities made him a logical choice to head up the American Broadcasting Company's bond solicitation program after the outbreak of World War II. The ABC network named him chairman of its bond committee, and assigned him to the production of a promotion show in April 1942.

For the network's drive, which lasted from 9 P.M. until 4 A.M. on one night, Alberti arranged for the services of such personalities as Orson Welles, and persuaded Western Union to provide free telegraph service for the bond pledges. During the program's seven hours, a total of $19,000,000 was pledged, a success which moved the United States Treasury Department to hire Alberti for full-time bond solicitation work.

With the titles of chief of radio station relations and national coordinator of talent and bookings, Alberti produced bond-drive programs for the Treasury Department's war finance division until late in 1943. In that year he went to work for Twentieth Century-Fox studios as its director of radio advertising. The combination of jobs gave Alberti an acquaintance with many celebrities in the United States.

"When the war ended," Alberti recalls (*Pageant* magazine, December 1955), "I began asking myself just how I could put to use this new experience. The answer came to me from the field of advertising. I discovered that there was no existing liaison agency between the advertising firms and celebrities. Well, why not start one and deal strictly in endorsements by big names?"

The outcome was the firm of Endorsements, Incorporated, which is still the only organization in the United States devoted exclusively to obtaining testimonials for commercial products. It was established in 1945 with a capital of $500; three-quarters of the shares were reserved for Alberti and the remainder for an associate, Hazel McCabe. The firm did not even have a business telephone for the first few months of its existence.

The testimonial field was not exactly reputable when Alberti entered it. The technique had been compromised in the past by such publicity as that created by the titled beauty who endorsed a facial cream, then told newspaper reporters that her complexion was entirely attributable to "fresh air, exercise, and plenty of soap and water." Alberti realized that his first task was to establish credibility.

Advertising executives were at first skeptical of the enterprise, and it was not until the following year that Alberti was assigned by Batten, Barton, Durstine & Osborn, Inc., to obtain endorsements for a Schaefer beer advertising campaign. Alberti's firm ended 1946 with a gross of $6,000. From that beginning, Endorsements, Inc., grew to a volume of $11,800 in 1947 and $67,000 in 1948. Since 1949 its billings have consistently been in the six-figure bracket. Testimonials became a significant part of advertising during the first

Hal Phyfe

JULES ALBERTI

decade of Alberti's venture, representing a ten-year total of $500,000,000. It is estimated that Endorsements, Inc., has figured in half of those billings.

Alberti works exclusively through advertising agencies, and has arranged testimonials for 700 different clients through 100 agencies. Among his more famous endorsers have been General Douglas MacArthur, Cornelia Otis Skinner, Joe Di Maggio, Leopold Stokowski, and Mrs. Eleanor Roosevelt. Nor does he always work with celebrities; he claims that his most difficult assignment was to find ten Southern farmers to endorse a laxative compound.

As an American authority on the techniques of testimonial advertising, Alberti has constantly worked to elevate its reputation. He has written articles for several trade magazines, lectured to professional societies, and is the author of *A Primer of Testimonial Advertising* (1950; revised edition 1955), which stated his firm's working principles in these words:

"It cannot be emphasized too much or too often that testimonials are effective only when they are believable and believable only when: 1. The testimonial is true; 2. The personality and product are logically connected; 3. The testimonial copy is simple, sincere, and honest."

In order to live up to these demands, Endorsements, Inc., maintains a research staff which keeps dossiers on about 7,000 celebrities. When an endorsement is required, the prospect is provided with samples of the product, and months later is asked if he can honestly recommend it. In this manner, more than 3,000 personalities have been recruited by Alberti to endorse products ranging from air purifiers to radios.

(Continued next page)

ALBERTI, JULES—*Continued*

Despite his precautions, Alberti has not been able to prevent some of his campaigns from ricocheting. Once two Hollywood wives appeared in a series of advertisements which praised the brand of cigar smoked by their husbands; shortly after, their marriages ended in the divorce courts. Then, too, critics of the advertising profession are likely to become especially censorious on the subject of testimonials. Such adverse publicity does not seem to have affected Alberti's business. Endorsements, Inc., now has branch offices in Hollywood, Chicago, and Washington, D.C., as well as overseas in London and Paris.

In 1957 Alberti was named National Civilian Coordinator for Special Projects by the Navy Department, and was entrusted with the publicity program to raise funds for the Navy-Marine Corps memorial stadium at Annapolis, Maryland. Because he succeeded in raising $3,000,000 for the project, Alberti was awarded the Navy Meritorious Public Service Citation on September 9, 1958.

In 1959 Alberti was made a special civilian consultant to the Superintendent of the United States Merchant Marine Academy at Kings Point, New York. He was also asked to produce for the United States Navy a one-hour TV "spectacular" entitled *Operation Vigilance*, a documentary story about the Second Fleet. He has acquired motion picture rights for the film biographies of Arthur and Kathryn Murray and of Jack Dempsey.

Alberti has also been honored by the United States Treasury Department, the Navy League, the American Heritage Foundation, and the Sales Executives Club. An enthusiastic joiner, he is active in the Radio and Television Executives Society, the National Better Business Bureau, the Broadcast Pioneers Club, the Sales Executives Club, the Hollywood Stereoscopic Society, the Navy League, and the Friars Club.

Jules Robert Alberti married Maybelle Ross on February 22, 1936; they have one son, Robert Lewis Alberti. The family lives in New York City. Alberti estimates that he devotes eighteen hours a day, seven days a week to his work and to his various civic and professional activities. He has been described as a "dapper, enthusiastic man," and as being "slight, bespectacled, and . . . polite."

Always a devoted spokesman for his profession, Alberti has said: "Do not underestimate the value of a sincere endorsement. Remember that even the British royal family for generations has permitted favored suppliers to advertise 'By Appointment to Their Majesties'!"

References

Am Mag 160:46+ D '55 por
Fortune 52:164+ S '55 por
Nation 182:295+ Ap 14 '56
New Yorker 24:20+ Ja 8 '49
International Year Book and Statesmen's
   Who's Who, 1959
Who's Who in Commerce & Industry,
   1957
Who's Who in the East, 1957

ALESSANDRI (RODRíGUEZ), JORGE

(ä"lä-sän'drē rô-*thrē*'gäs) May 19, 1896-
President of Chile; businessman

Address: b. Presidential Palace, Santiago, Chile; h. Phillips 16, Santiago, Chile

Having won the confidence of Chile's inflation-burdened population with his promise to lead the "country back to economic health through hard work, honesty, and patriotism," Jorge Alessandri was elected to a six-year term as President in September 1958. An independent candidate, Alessandri believes he can solve his nation's difficulties by using the services of competent experts rather than politicians. He campaigned for the betterment of Chile's economic relations with foreign countries and for the increase of foreign and domestic investments. To his duties as chief executive Alessandri brings his experience as a businessman, banker, engineer, and Finance Minister (1948-50). He succeeds General Carlos Ibáñez.

Jorge Alessandri Rodríguez, one of eight children of Arturo Alessandri Palma and the former Ester Rodríguez Velasco, was born in Santiago, Chile on May 19, 1896. His brothers have distinguished themselves in the fields of education, law, medicine, politics, and business. Arturo Alessandri, known as the "Lion of Tarapacá," was President of Chile from 1920 to 1924, for a brief period in 1925, and again from 1932 to 1938. He effected the separation of Church and state and established a social security system.

After his studies at the Instituto Nacional in Santiago, Jorge Alessandri Rodríguez entered the University of Chile in the same city, where he soon displayed exceptional abilities as a mathematician. In 1919, after being graduated with a degree in civil engineering, he was appointed a professor at the university's School of Engineering.

At this time Alessandri also worked as an engineer at the bureaus of public works and railways in the Ministry of Public Works. Later appointed national director of road construction, he was responsible for the planning of roads throughout Chile; this included contracting with private companies for their construction.

For a brief period in 1925 he became active in political life when he was elected a member of the Chamber of Deputies for Santiago as an independent. At that time he sponsored a road construction bill which, when enacted, proved significant in the further development of Chile's transportation network.

After his service in the National Congress, Alessandri held various posts in private industry and in banking, where he earned a reputation for his imagination and administrative abilities. He founded the Paper and Cardboard Manufacturing Company and developed it into the nation's chief supplier of paper products and an important exporter of newsprint. As president of the organization, he supervised the construction of many plants for the manufacture of paper and cellulose, started a commercial reforestation program, and instituted a profit-sharing plan.

Alessandri served as a vice-president of the Bank of South America; president of the Lota Coal Company; a director of the Sugar Refining Company of Viña del Mar; president of the Pizarreño Industrial Society, producers of roofing materials; and president of the Llano del Maipo Railroad, which is now operated by the government.

Before deciding upon a program of action, Alessandri invariably used to consult his subordinates for their views on a problem. For several years he was president of the Confederation for Production and Trade, a private organization of industrialists. While holding this position, he proposed social legislation to the National Congress. In spite of the demands of business affairs upon his time, he has written many articles for the magazines and newspapers of Chile.

Before re-entering politics in 1957, Alessandri held several government positions. He was president of the government-managed Mortgage Credit Bank at a time when inflationary pressures led to frequent nonpayment of mortgages. Later, he assumed the presidency of the Chilean Nitrate and Iodine Sales Corporation, which deals exclusively with foreign sales of nitrates and iodine, two of Chile's exports.

Appointed Minister of Finance in August 1948 by President Gabriel González Videla, Alessandri in the next two years balanced the national budget while avoiding unemployment, eliminated the deficit, and accumulated the first budgetary surplus in twenty years. This enabled Chile to resume payments on her international debts.

As an independent, Alessandri entered the contest for a Senate seat representing Santiago and was elected with a large majority in March 1957. In the following year he was an independent candidate for the Presidency in a race with four other contestants. He won the support of conservative parties, receiving 387,932 votes out of the 1,200,000 votes cast. This gave him a 35,000 vote lead over his nearest opponent, Socialist Salvador Allende.

Since no one received a clear majority, the election was decided by the National Congress which followed the tradition of selecting the candidate who had the largest number of votes. Because of the grave financial problems facing the nation, Alessandri waived all the pomp of the inaugural ceremony when he took office on November 3, 1958 and pledged himself to a program of budgetary austerity.

President Alessandri has been concerned with problems resulting from inflationary pressure: a considerably reduced standard of living, an external debt of $718,000,000, and an unbalanced budget. He is also confronted with a critical housing shortage, with approximately 1,000,000 homeless persons; some 170,000 unemployed out of a labor force of 2,000,000; and a 10 per cent slump in industrial production. The first step that Alessandri took to resolve these difficulties was the appointment of a cabinet which, he believes, is technically competent and unencumbered by political affiliations.

JORGE ALESSANDRI

An integrated economic plan to control inflation by 1960 has been introduced. The purpose of this project is the protection of foreign and domestic investors who provide the capital necessary for the expansion of industry. Alessandri believes that business prosperity will eventually benefit the workers.

To enable the government to meet its financial obligations, the President has proposed programs to reduce government expenditures and to increase its income. He has promised a reform of the tax system with prison terms for evaders, and the overhauling of Chile's social security system which permits some persons to retire with pensions as early as the age of forty-one. Thirty per cent of Chile's annual budget of $400,000,000 is spent for social security.

The economy of Chile largely depends upon the export of copper. When the price of copper decreases 1 per cent per pound on the world market, Chile loses in foreign exchange at the rate of $6,000,000 a year. When copper prices were high, previous administrations used to spend revenues as fast as they were received. Alessandri plans to build a large reserve fund during periods when there is a favorable return on copper.

The President is a bachelor who has chosen to remain in his five-room apartment rather than move into the Presidential Palace. An art collector, he has decorated his home with ivory statuettes, Japanese and Korean *objets d'art,* reproductions of Renaissance painters, and a bust of Apollo. Alessandri avoids an active social life and seeks his relaxation in concerts, art exhibits, and reading in the fields of economics and history.

Six-feet tall, gray-haired, gray-eyed Jorge Alessandri Rodríguez neither smokes nor drinks and eats sparingly. His favorite composer is Beethoven, and his favorite historical figure is

ALESSANDRI, JORGE—*Continued*

George Washington. He is a member of the Union Club in Santiago and an adherent of the Roman Catholic faith. His few intimates agree that "there is a solitude in Señor Alessandri that no one penetrates" (New York *Times,* September 6, 1958).

References

Christian Sci Mon p3 O 14 '58
N Y Times p9 S 8 '58
Who's Who in Latin America Pt 4 (1947)

ALLEN, MARTHA F(RANCES) Oct. 3, 1906- Youth organization director

Address: b. Camp Fire Girls, Inc., 16 E. 48th St., New York 17; h. 434 E. 52d St., New York 22; R.F.D. #2, South Royalton, Vt.

An interest in preventive forms of social work has shaped the career of Martha F. Allen, who as executive vice-president and national director of the Camp Fire Girls, supervises a recreational and educational program of character and health-building activities for some half a million girls in the United States. Prior to joining the staff of the Camp Fire Girls in 1941, two years before she became its chief administrative officer, she had acquired a background of experience in education, social welfare, housing, and community relations.

The only daughter and the oldest of three children, Martha Frances Allen was born to Sam Harrison and Ora Elizabeth (Craig) Allen in Cherokee, Alabama on October 3, 1906. Her English-Irish father, a businessman with land, lumber, and gravel interests, "was too busy enjoying life ever to get rich," Miss Allen recalls. "His combination of humor and temper offset each other. Mother, who was Scottish,

MARTHA F. ALLEN

was as gentle, sweet, and quietly determined as anyone I have ever known."

Identification with her father gave Martha Allen an interest in business and an early religious training which sharpened her concern for people. She notes that in her work with the Camp Fire Girls she has been able "to combine these two sometimes divergent interests." In the small Southern community of Iuka, Mississippi, where she was reared, she attended the local high school; and as "a fragile child," she filled her leisure time with dreaming, reading, and music. The townsfolk of Iuka considered only certain kinds of work appropriate for young women of genteel background; their attitudes helped determine the types of occupation which Miss Allen was encouraged to undertake.

While a student at the Mississippi State College for Women in Columbus, Miss Allen majored in Latin. She belonged to the student council and the YWCA cabinet and served as president of the Honor Society (later called the Mortar Board). After her graduation with the B.A. degree in 1928, she taught English and Latin for a year at McComb High School in Mississippi. Latin was also the subject in which she received her M.A. degree from Columbia University in 1930, having studied under a scholarship from the Mississippi Federation of Women's Clubs. Her thesis, "Value and Significance of Passionless Tranquility," expressed her interest in achieving the balanced way of life advocated by the Roman poet Horace.

From 1930 to 1934 Miss Allen taught Latin and served as adviser to the student council of All Saints' Episcopal College in Vicksburg, Mississippi. Working with young women encouraged her to broaden her scope of activity from teaching to social welfare. In 1934 she moved to Washington to become a social worker on the board of public welfare of the District of Columbia. The following year she joined the staff of the Resettlement Administration and Farm Security Administration of the United States Department of Agriculture.

During her period of employment with the federal government from 1935 to 1939, Miss Allen was especially concerned with housing projects in Greenbelt (Maryland), Westmoreland County (Pennsylvania), and the Green Hills development in Cincinnati (Ohio). She gained firsthand knowledge of problems resulting from unemployment and lack of recreational facilities and took part in organizing community programs in public health, home management, home economics, and handicrafts. Later, from 1939 to 1941, as supervisor of tenant selection and consultant for the Cincinnati Metropolitan Housing Authority, she helped to develop programs of youth and adult activities. For a short time she was associated with the adult educational bureau of the Cincinnati Public Library.

One of the youth-serving groups with which Miss Allen came into contact during her work in community welfare programs was the Camp Fire Girls. This organization appointed her its assistant national director in November 1941, and in April 1943 she succeeded Lester F. Scott as national director and executive vice-president.

She took office during the crucial period when wartime problems, such as increased employment of mothers outside the home, were contributing to juvenile delinquency and when young people needed the help of agencies like the Camp Fire Girls in training for usefulness in the war effort.

Camp Fire Girls, which was founded in 1910 and now has 500,000 members, offers leisure-time co-operative programs of activity in three different age groups: the Blue Birds (seven to ten), Camp Fire Girls (ten to fifteen), and Horizon Clubbers (fifteen to eighteen). The basic religious principles of the organization cover members of the Protestant, Catholic, and Jewish faiths.

Miss Allen has often emphasized in her talks to local groups across the country that the primary purpose of the Camp Fire Girls is to supplement the training of the home, the church, and the school. She has suggested that the organization try to meet the challenge of juvenile delinquency and the need for physical fitness and for character building. Under Miss Allen's guidance, the Camp Fire Girls has given increased attention to the recruitment and training of adult volunteers who co-operate with professional workers of the agency. A successful fund raiser, at a ceremony in 1952 she set fire to the $180,000 mortgage that the Camp Fire Girls had paid off in five years on their seven-story national headquarters building on East 48th Street in New York City.

Much of Miss Allen's achievement in the field of social work has been in the development of groups to provide national planning and centralized action in matters of health and welfare affecting the whole United States. She served as vice-chairman of the National Social Work Council in 1945 and took part in establishing the National Social Welfare Assembly (now consisting of more than seventy voluntary and governmental agencies), of which she was a member of the executive committee from 1946 to 1952.

In order to give young people a chance to participate in community affairs, she helped set up the Associated Youth Serving Organizations, which later became the youth division of the National Social Welfare Assembly. Also for the N.S.W.A. she was chairman of the intergroup relations committee from 1952 to 1957 and chairman of the conference of executives in 1957-1958. She was a member from 1947 to 1954 of the national budget and national quota committees sponsored by the Community Chests and Councils of America and the National Social Welfare Assembly.

In 1956 Miss Allen helped to form a People-to-People youth committee and as chairman of its first workshop gave assistance to the promotion of international understanding among young people throughout the world. For its annual project her own organization, Camp Fire Girls, prepared photographic exhibits to acquaint youths of seventeen foreign countries with life in American communities. Since May 1959 Miss Allen has been chairman of the youth activities committee of People-to-People. As such she is responsible for a program which represents some twenty million young people.

Other important groups that Miss Allen has served are the National Association of Social Workers (1946-1952), National Publicity Council (1950-1953), Advisory Committee on Women's Affairs in Civil Defense (1951-1957), Citizens' Advisory Committee on the Fitness of American Youth (1957), and jury of the National Crumbine Awards for outstanding sanitation programs (1959). She is a member of Zonta International.

Martha F. Allen was recently described by a Dayton, Ohio newspaper writer as having "the youthful grace of one who has been associated with the very young, and . . . the attractive mature look of one continuously, seriously concerned with the problems of these young people." She is five feet six and a half inches tall, weighs 140 pounds, and has light-brown hair and blue eyes. She attends the Unitarian Church. A few years ago she bought a rambling old house in Vermont which she operates as an inn during the summer when she has the opportunity to enjoy her hobbies of farming, landscaping, and cooking. Her other recreations are reading, music, and the theater.

References

Who's Who in America, 1958-59
Who's Who in New York (1952)
Who's Who of American Women (1958-59)
World Biography (1954)

ANDERSON, SIR KENNETH A(R-THUR) N(OEL) Dec. 25, 1891-Apr. 29, 1959

Former Governor of Gibraltar (1947-52); British Army general; knighted (1943) for his exploits in North Africa as commander of First Army. See *Current Biography* (February) 1943.

Obituary

N Y Times p31 Ap 30 '59

ANDERSON, MAXWELL Dec. 15, 1888-Feb. 28, 1959

Playwright; wrote the prize-winning *Winterset, High Tor, Both Your Houses,* and other plays; popularized use of blank verse in modern drama. See *Current Biography* (September) 1953.

Obituary

N Y Times p1+ Mr 1 '59

ANDERSON, WILLIAM R(OBERT) June 17, 1921- United States Navy officer

Address: b. USS Nautilus, FPO, New York; h. 85 High St., Mystic, Conn.

The atomic-powered submarine USS *Nautilus* crossed the geographic North Pole on August 3, 1958 during the first undersea voyage in history from the Pacific to the Atlantic oceans by way of the ice-locked Arctic Regions. The captain of the expedition was Commander William R. Anderson of the United States Navy, who, for completing his mission, was awarded

CAPT. WILLIAM R. ANDERSON

the Legion of Merit. The accompanying citation stated that the trip "points the way for further exploration and possible use of this route by nuclear-powered cargo submarines as a new commercial seaway between the major oceans of the world."

A graduate of Annapolis, Anderson has been in the submarine service for most of his adult life, including World War II and the Korean conflict. He has taught submarine warfare and recently wrote a book, *Nautilus 90 North,* about the historic journey of the atomic-powered submarine. In September 1959 he was promoted to the rank of captain.

William Robert Anderson was born in Bakerville, Tennessee on June 17, 1921. His parents, David Hensely and Mary (McKelvey) Anderson, were farmers. He has two sisters, Josephine and Margaret. Even though he grew up far from the sea, he displayed a yearning for navy life at an early age. When he was ten, he asked for and was promised an appointment to Annapolis by his Representative in the United States Congress.

Upon his graduation from Columbia Military Academy in Tennessee in 1938, Anderson was appointed to the United States Naval Academy in Annapolis, Maryland. His Congressman had kept his promise. He was awarded a B.S. degree in electrical engineering and received a commission as ensign in June 1942. Immediately, he was sent to the Submarine School in New London, Connecticut for special courses.

Having completed this training, Anderson was ordered to active duty and during World War II participated in eleven war patrols. His first sea assignment began in October 1942 as communications officer and first lieutenant aboard the submarine USS *Tarpon.* He was in three war patrols with the *Tarpon* and was given a Letter of Commendation with Ribbon and Combat V Medal. The citation

read in part: "For meritorious conduct in the performance of his duties . . . in the Japanese waters from 10 January to 25 February 1943. As Battle Station Officer of the Deck his skillful navigation of his ship materially assisted his Commanding Officer in conducting successful attacks which resulted in the sinking of 21,000 tons of enemy shipping."

Anderson made six war patrols as gunnery officer and first lieutenant of the submarine USS *Narwhal* in 1943-44. He was then transferred to the submarine USS *Trutta,* on which he served as engineer and diving officer until August 1946. During that time he was awarded the Bronze Star Medal for service during a war patrol in the Yellow Sea. At that time he assisted in sinking seventeen cargo vessels and in rescuing a downed aviator.

Following World War II, Anderson spent three years on the submarine *Sarda,* first as engineer and later as executive officer. Assigned to land duty in September 1949, he became an instructor in the naval unit of the Reserve Officers' Training Corps at the University of Idaho in Moscow.

With the advent of the Korean conflict, he served again on the *Trutta,* as executive officer, from February to September 1951. He was then ordered to take over the same responsibility on the fast attack submarine *Tang.* In May 1953 he received his first full command when he was transferred to the submarine *Wahoo,* which was assigned to the area of Korea from January to May 1954.

Anderson returned to land duty in July 1955 to become head of the tactical department of the Submarine School in New London. He was advanced to the rank of commander on July 1, 1955. In preparation for the eventual command of an atomic submarine, he served in the reactor development division of the Atomic Energy Commission in Washington, D.C. The division was headed by Hyman G. Rickover (see *C.B.,* May 1953), under whose inspiration and direction the first atomic-powered submarine, *Nautilus,* was built.

Assuming command of the *Nautilus* on June 19, 1957, Anderson relieved Eugene Wilkinson, its first captain. Almost immediately, Anderson put into operation the plans and preparations for the arctic expedition. In the summer of 1957 he took the *Nautilus* through three secret exploratory missions underneath the arctic ice pack. When, at one point in these journeys, the *Nautilus* came within 180 miles of the North Pole, it became apparent that a transarctic trip was feasible.

The submarine tried to cross the pole for the first time in June 1958. Entering the Arctic Ocean from the west, the crew discovered that the ice was still too thick in the shallow Chuckchee Sea north of the Bering Strait. The *Nautilus* was forced to return to Pearl Harbor to wait for more favorable conditions. In their preliminary probes the crew carried on scientific research, measuring salinity, temperatures, ice thicknesses, and sounding the depths over 11,000 times.

Once again, on July 23, the *Nautilus* tried to pioneer a submerged sea lane at the top of the world. It passed beneath the North Pole on August 3, traveling deeper than 400 feet beneath the icecap. The submarine had gone under the icecap on August 1 off Point Barrow, Alaska, and surfaced only four days later in the Atlantic at a point between Greenland and Spitsbergen. The new route charted by the *Nautilus* reduces the journey from London to Tokyo by some 4,500 miles.

Commander Anderson, his crew, and his ship were hailed enthusiastically, both in the United States and in Europe. The successful arctic crossing, many observers felt, helped to offset the Soviet Union's Sputnik achievement. The officers and men of the *Nautilus* were awarded the Presidential Unit Citation, the first ever conferred in peacetime. Anderson was awarded the Legion of Merit by President Dwight D. Eisenhower for "foresighted planning, skilled seamanship, and thorough study of the Arctic area."

For the extensive scientific data collected under his leadership, Anderson was awarded an honorary D.Sc. degree by Defiance College in Ohio. For his exploratory achievements, he was given the Christopher Columbus International Award in Genoa, Italy, 1958 Bronze Plaque of Achievement by the Advertising Club of New York City, Gold Medal Award of New York City, Elisha Kent Kane Award of the Geographical Society of Philadelphia, and Patron's Medal of the British Royal Geographical Society. Earlier, the Navy League had conferred upon him the Stephen Decatur Award for his trips under the ice in 1957.

Together with Clay Blair, Jr., Anderson is the author of a series of articles which appeared in the *Saturday Evening Post* in 1957 and 1958. He has also written articles for the *United States Naval Institute Proceedings* (December 1958) and for *National Geographic Magazine* (January 1959). His book, *Nautilus 90 North*, was published by the World Publishing Company in 1959.

William R. Anderson married Yvonne Etzel on June 10, 1943. She is a former air-line stewardess. They have two sons, Michael David and William Robert, Jr. Anderson has blue eyes and brown hair and is of medium build, standing five feet nine inches tall and weighing 160 pounds. He is a member of the American Legion, Amvets, and Junior Chamber of Commerce. His hobbies are reading and woodworking. The New York *Times* said, "An officer who has sailed with him placed him 'at the top of the list,' a man who had his crew behind him despite being a spit-and-polish commanding officer" (August 9, 1958).

References

N Y Journal American p2 Ag 9 '58 por
N Y Post Mag p2 Ag 31 '58 por
Time 73:86+ Ja 5 '59

ANDREWS, (CARVER) DANA Jan. 1, 1909- Actor

Address: b. c/o Actors' Equity Association, 226 W. 47th St., New York 36

Since he began acting in films in 1939 Dana Andrews has appeared in about three motion pictures a year. In dramas, Westerns, comedies,

United Artists Corp.

DANA ANDREWS

and melodramas he has shown his facility in playing a wide variety of characters. After having portrayed youthful movie heroes during most of his career, Andrews made his successful debut on Broadway in 1958 as the middle-aged lawyer from Omaha with marital problems in *Two for the Seesaw*. He returned to Hollywood in 1959 with a new luster conferred by a year of co-starring in the two-character drama. By producing his own film vehicles, Andrews plans to complete his transition into a new and more mature phase of his acting career.

Carver Dana Andrews, who was born on January 1, 1909 in Collins, Mississippi, is the third of seven sons and two daughters of the Reverend Charles Forrest and Annis (Speed) Andrews. His father was a Baptist minister who named Dana after two professors under whom he had studied in theological seminary. Shortly after the boy's birth, his family moved to Louisville, Kentucky, and then to Waelder, San Antonio, Uvalde, and Huntsville, Texas. He graduated from Huntsville High School in 1926 and enrolled at Sam Houston State Teachers College in the same city. There, he majored in business administration, played on the football team, and performed in two undergraduate dramas before he left school in 1929.

At one time Andrews had considered capitalizing on his warm and resonant baritone voice by becoming a lawyer or a concert singer. Instead he went to work for the Gulf Oil Corporation in Austin, Texas as an accountant. Two years later, in 1931, he left his job and hitchhiked to Los Angeles. He made several attempts to become an actor, but after being turned down by the film studios and by the Pasadena Playhouse, he settled for a job in a garage in Van Nuys.

After holding a series of routine jobs for four years, Andrews obtained money from

ANDREWS, DANA—*Continued*

friends for singing lessons. He studied voice for more than a year and was then advised to become an actor. Andrews once more applied for a job at the Pasadena Playhouse, was accepted, and began his stage career by carrying a supernumerary's spear in a Shakespearean drama.

His work at the Playhouse led to a contract with Samuel Goldwyn in December 1938, but to no active roles. He continued his training at Pasadena for another year, acting a total of twenty-four roles, including that of George Washington in Maxwell Anderson's *Valley Forge*. Then he was cast for the minor part of Jed Johnson in *The Westerner* (1940), starring Gary Cooper in a Goldwyn production released through United Artists. Encouraged by this beginning, Andrews married his present wife when the filming was finished.

At the same time Goldwyn temporarily retired from the movie industry, and sold a half-interest in Andrews' contract to Twentieth Century-Fox Film Corporation. For three years he alternated between his two employers, always promised stardom but always assigned to secondary roles. For Goldwyn and Fox he played in *Sailor's Lady* (1940), *Tobacco Road* (1941), *Belle Starr* (1941), *Swamp Water* (1941), *The Ox-Bow Incident* (1943), *Berlin Crisis* (1943), *Crash Dive* (1943), and *The North Star* (1943). He also appeared in RKO's *Ball of Fire* (1941) and in *Kit Carson* (1940), which was released through United Artists.

Then, in 1943, Andrews was simultaneously cast in starring roles by both Goldwyn and Fox. For the former he played the romantic lead in a Danny Kaye musical called *Up in Arms;* for Fox studios he starred in *The Purple Heart,* a fictionalized account of the Jimmy Doolittle raid over Tokyo. The latter established the medium-budget, entertainment type of film in which Andrews was predominantly to star.

After playing the lead in another war movie, *Wing and a Prayer* (1944), Andrews achieved a triumph in the stylish mystery movie, *Laura,* which Fox released in October 1944. The reviewers lauded both the film and Andrews' acting. "In a brief career, Dana Andrews has consistently outdone each of his successive performances," wrote Alton Cook in the New York *World-Telegram* (October 11, 1944). "The smouldering force with which he plays the detective leaves one pretty sure the chain of topping himself will be broken with this picture—unless he turns out to be just about the finest actor of our time."

Andrews did not again receive such unreserved praise for his motion-picture work; he became, however, one of Hollywood's more reliable and popular stars. He made *Fallen Angel* (1945), *State Fair* (1945), *Canyon Passage* (1946), and *A Walk in the Sun* (1946). Then came the enormously successful *The Best Years of Our Lives* (1946).

In this Goldwyn film, which eventually earned nine Motion Picture Academy Awards, Andrews played the romantic lead as an Air Force veteran returning to civilian life. "Dana Andrews," wrote Archer Winsten in the New York *Post* (November 22, 1946), "caught in a role at once glamorous and trite, does his actor's job, as always, with integrity and intelligence."

Returning to his medium-budget stand-bys, Andrews appeared in 1947 in *Boomerang, Night Song,* and *Daisy Kenyon.* In 1948 he starred in *Deep Waters, The Iron Curtain,* and *No Minor Vices.* After playing in *The Forbidden Street* and *Sword in the Desert* in 1949, he acted in *My Foolish Heart, Edge of Doom,* and *Where the Sidewalk Ends,* all of them 1950 releases. He appeared in *Sealed Cargo* and *The Frogmen* in 1951 and in *I Want You* and *Assignment—Paris* in 1952.

In 1952 Andrews ended his motion-picture contracts to become a free lance. In addition to fulfilling an average of two acting assignments a year, he organized an independent movie company called Lawrence Productions. His screen credits in 1954 included *Elephant Walk, Duel in the Jungle,* and *Three Hours to Kill.* In 1955 he appeared in *Smoke Signal* and *Strange Lady in Town;* in 1956 he played in *While the City Sleeps, Comanche, Beyond a Reasonable Doubt,* and *Night of the Demon.* In 1957 motion picture theatre audiences saw him in *Spring Reunion.* In *The Fearmakers,* released through United Artists in 1959, Andrews portrayed a former Korean war prisoner, who, on returning to the United States, finds his public opinion poll business in the hands of a group of ruthless manipulators.

In the late 1950's, Andrews was finding movie roles harder to come by. Typed as the thirty-five-year-old hero, he was becoming too old for his usual roles, and at the same time producers were cutting back on the medium-budget films which were his specialty. "They want top box office names for block busters, and I'm not in that category," he ruefully told one reporter.

He had co-starred with his wife in a summer tour with *The Glass Menagerie* in 1952, but was unable to find a satisfactory script for a Broadway debut. In 1958, after starring in *The Right Hand Man* for the *Playhouse 90* television series, Andrews was offered the role of the Omaha lawyer adrift in New York in *Two for the Seesaw,* then in its sixth month on Broadway. Andrews took over the part from Henry Fonda on June 30, 1958.

"It's about as good a part as a man can have," he told reporter Don Ross (New York *Herald Tribune,* June 22, 1958). "I hope that *Two for the Seesaw* will be a showcase for me." He moved his family to Connecticut, and remained in the play's cast until June 29, 1959. He left to supervise the filming of *11 O'Clock Road* for his independent Lawrence Productions.

Andrews has been married twice. He married Janet Murray on December 31, 1932; she died in 1935. Their son, David Murray Andrews, is now a pianist, organist, and composer. Andrews married Mary Todd, a fellow student at the Pasadena Playhouse, on November 17, 1939. They have two daughters, Catherine and Susan, and one son, Stephen. The family lives in a spacious home in the Toluca Lake district of the San Fernando Valley in California. Andrews owns a fifty-foot yawl, which he views as an investment rather than a luxury, and spends a great deal of his leisure time in sailing.

Youthful in appearance, Andrews has brown eyes and brown hair, is about six feet tall, and has weighed about 175 pounds for the last twenty years. He is a Democrat and a Baptist.

Beginning a stage career when he was nearly fifty was a challenge to Andrews' ability. "On the New York stage, appearance isn't the greatest thing," the actor remarked (New York Herald Tribune, June 22, 1958). "It's technique and voice. In Hollywood, if your voice isn't good they can fix it up with electronic devices but on the stage it's your own voice. Nobody can fix it."

References

N Y Herald Tribune II p4 Je 22 '58 por
N Y Post p40 Jl 23 '58 por
N Y Times II p3 Mr 12 '44
Who's Who in America, 1958-59
Winchester's Screen Encyclopedia (1948)

A. A. MacNair

LOUIS ARCHAMBAULT

ANTHEIL, GEORGE June 8, 1900-Feb. 12, 1959 Composer of avant-garde music for the ballet; experimented with the use of mechanical sound effects in music. See *Current Biography* (July) 1954.

Obituary

N Y Times p17 F 13 '59

ARAKI, EIKICHI Apr. 24, 1891-Feb. 1, 1959 Japanese financial expert; Ambassador to the United States (1952-54). See *Current Biography* (October) 1952.

Obituary

N Y Times p84 F 1 '59

ARCHAMBAULT, LOUIS (DE GONZA-GUE PASCAL) Apr. 4, 1915- Sculptor

Address: 278 Sanford Ave., St. Lambert, Montreal 23, Quebec, Canada

The Canadian sculptor and ceramist Louis Archambault uses a variety of materials, mainly in three-dimensional form, to express his country and its people. His "wonderful" terra cotta wall, representing all of Canada, was a widely praised part of the Canadian Pavilion at the Brussels World's Fair in 1958. Later it was put on permanent display at the new National Gallery in Ottawa. Inclusion of Archambault's work in several important exhibitions in Europe and the United States has extended the reputation he holds at home as a truly significant modern sculptor, whose work symbolizes the endeavor, power, and vastness of his native land.

Of French descent on his father's side and Irish on his mother's, Louis de Gonzague Pascal Archambault was born in Montreal, Canada on Easter Sunday, April 4, 1915, to Anthime Sergius and Annie (Michaud) Archambault. He

was the third of their five children; by a previous marriage his father had two other children. Intending to follow the profession of law, like his father, or of medicine, he studied at the Collège Jean-de-Brébeuf in Montreal and was graduated with the B.A. degree in 1936.

An inclination toward art, however, led Archambault to enroll in 1936 at the École des Beaux-Arts of Montreal, where he took one year of drawing and modeling and two years of pottery. The development of his career, he has explained, was determined by "instinct and constant solitary work." He found himself suited to pottery making and "through pottery, discovered ceramic sculpture and gradually the whole world of three-dimensional inventions."

World War II delayed his full concentration on work of his own. For five years he was employed at a Canadian Marconi factory as plastics foreman. "That was a funny adventure," he has recalled, as quoted in the *Globe Magazine* of the Toronto *Globe and Mail* (July 19, 1958). "I had been at a certain distance from the rough life. It was excellent training to come close to the common struggle, to raw human beings. And I survived inside by drawing and painting."

Since about the end of the war Archambault's work has been seen in more than thirty-five exhibitions, beginning in the spring of 1945 at the Montreal Museum of Fine Arts. Early shows included those at the Dominion Gallery in Montreal (1947); Syracuse (New York) Museum of Fine Arts (1947); and Exhibition of Contemporary Canadian Arts, Art Gallery of Toronto (1950). Exhibiting at Les Concours Artistiques de la Province de Québec, he won the first prize in sculpture in 1948 and the first prize in applied arts in 1950.

Meanwhile, Archambault was also teaching at various local institutions: L'École des Meubles, Montreal Museum of Fine Arts, and L'Institut

ARCHAMBAULT, LOUIS—*Continued*

des Arts Appliqués. For several years he has been an instructor at École des Beaux-Arts of Montreal. Sometime after the war, also, he began to make himself known in the commercial field of ceramics. "In one year," an article in *Studio* (December 1957) noted, "he turned out 300 dishes in various sizes, in fifteen different designs, flat functional plates and platters bearing his personal imprint, inscriptions of primitive abstractions, and he produced a series of five different ceramic figures in small editions, all extraordinarily imaginative." Items such as these, as well as his commercially successful ceramic masks, helped him enough financially so that he could afford to wait for appreciation of his sculpture.

Even in his own country Archambault was hardly well known when in 1950 he was the only Canadian sculptor invited to submit models of his work for display during the 1951 Festival of Britain. His large (ten feet high) mythological bird, *Oiseau de Fer*, made of welded iron plates, became a part of the International Sculpture Exhibition in Battersea Park, London during the festival. As Alan Jarvis, director of the National Gallery of Canada, described it, the iron bird was a "curious combination of primeval strength and formal grace." Archambault built another of his characteristic birds on the shores of a Laurentian lake in 1955. It stood nine feet tall on three curved legs; its body had the form of a huge egg.

As a recipient of the Canadian Government Overseas Award, Archambault spent a year, in 1953-54, in France with his wife and children. He studied Byzantine, Etruscan, and modern French and Italian sculpture. His reputation abroad grew during the next few years as his work was seen at the 10th Milan Triennale (1945), the 28th Venice Biennale (1956), and the 11th Milan Triennale (1957). For the Venice show he had submitted six pieces: two each in bronze, terra cotta, and plaster. Damage to one of his plaster pieces, *La Famille* (1955), broken in shipment back to Canada, convinced the sculptor that he should personally safeguard the delivery and setting up of perhaps his most important contribution so far to international exhibitions—his Canadian wall at the Brussels World's Fair.

Specifications for the free-standing wall of the Canadian Pavilion at the fair had been worked out in 1955 by Charles Greenberg, architect of the pavilion: a portable wall, 125 feet long by ten feet high, which could be built in Canada and shipped in sections to Brussels. The subject matter would be the ten provinces of Canada—one-third of the wall, outside the building, characterizing in bas-relief the people of the country; and two-thirds, inside the building, depicting its natural resources on incised plaques.

Archambault submitted the winning sketches in the closed competition, held in the spring of 1956, to determine the best builder of the wall. He was awarded $25,000 to cover his own fee and that of his collaborator, industrial designer Norman Slater; he also paid for his materials out of that sum. He spent about two years on

the wall, giving up other work. For his large, decorated ceramic tiles inserted in a polished aluminum structure, he had first to find a formula for a strong terra cotta which would be light enough to be held by the aluminum. His tiles keep the texture and color of earth, with other colors forming stylized designs.

Among Archambault's other recent achievements have been two fountains, nineteen feet high and made of welded aluminum plates, for the new Ottawa City Hall. He has also been working on various commissioned works such as a metal screen for the Sun Life Assurance Building in Toronto and on projects for international exhibitions, including the Pittsburgh (Pennsylvania) International Exhibition of Contemporary Painting and Sculpture in December 1958.

Before putting his ideas into three-dimensional form, Archambault works out designs in many experimental drawings on paper. (He said that he made thousands of sketches for his wall for the Brussels fair.) He prefers rough materials, like clay and iron, which, he feels, express power. Steel plates, he finds, have a monumental quality well suited to the Canadian scene. Yet, as Alan Jarvis pointed out, there is "the subtle, lyrical mysticism which pervades his figures." He has been said to represent abstraction in Canadian sculpture, but his pieces resemble natural form.

In 1958 the Royal Architectural Institute of Canada awarded Archambault its Allied Arts Medal for outstanding achievement in an art related to architecture. He was one of the winners in 1959 of the special awards approved by the Canada Council.

Louis Archambault married Mariette Provost on June 7, 1941; they have two teen-age sons, Aubert and Eloi. The quiet, gentle-mannered sculptor has black hair and brown eyes, weighs 140 pounds, and is five feet eight inches tall. Although he is not a party goer or an artist who cares to appear on radio and television, he believes that the artist should not stand apart from the world. "I am terrible solitaire: I always work remotely," he said recently. "I live inwardly, but like to show my work. . . . I have been training for twenty years and now I have a margin of maybe thirty. It's a bit like a cheese, or an old bottle of wine—I hope now to come to my best period. I am full of ideas! There are many, many things ahead. . ."

References

Macleans Mag 71:18+Ja 18 '58 por
Roy Arch Inst Can J 35:216+ Je '58
Studio 154:174+ D '57
Who's Who in American Art (1956)
Who's Who in Art, 1958

ARENDT, HANNAH Oct. 14, 1906- Author; university professor

Address: b. Princeton University, Princeton, N.J.; h. 130 Morningside Drive, New York 27

The distinction of being the first woman ever appointed a full professor at Princeton University falls to Hannah Arendt, author, teacher, political scientist, and philosopher. During the spring semester of 1959, Dr. Arendt was scheduled to teach a co-ordinated program devoted to an analysis of American civilization. Since her arrival in the United States in 1940 as a German political refugee, she has been an organization administrator, chief editor of a publishing firm, and a teacher at the University of Chicago, the University of California at Berkeley, and Brooklyn College. She has also written two books: *The Origins of Totalitarianism*, published in 1951, and *The Human Condition*, which appeared in 1958. Both have established her as an outstanding writer in the fields of philosophy and politics.

The only child of Paul Arendt, an engineer, and his wife, the former Martha Cohn, Hannah Arendt was born in Hanover, Germany on October 14, 1906. Her parents, who were German Jews, lived in Koenigsberg (the present Kaliningrad when that city was a part of East Prussia, and Dr. Arendt was reared and educated there. After completing the requirements for the baccalaureate degree in 1924, she attended the University of Heidelberg, where she majored in philosophy under the renowned Karl Jaspers, and minored in theology and Greek. When only twenty-two years of age, Hannah Arendt received the Ph.D. degree from Heidelberg for a dissertation on St. Augustine. She did postgraduate work on a fellowship (Notgemeinschaft der Deutschen Wissenschaft) which she was awarded in 1928, concentrating on expanding her thesis for publication. *Der Liebesbegriff bei Augustine* (Berlin, 1930) was the published result of her efforts.

When Hitler came to power in 1933, Hannah Arendt fled Germany for Paris where she continued to study and write. She did social work from 1935 to 1939 for the French branch of Youth Aliyah, a relief organization responsible for the placement of Jewish orphan children in Palestine. In 1940, when it became obvious that France would also fall to the Nazis, Dr. Arendt took refuge in the United States.

Hannah Arendt served as research director of the Conference on Jewish Relations from 1944 to 1946. In these years she began to publish in American magazines on subjects which had both an emotional and intellectual meaning for her. "Concerning Minorities" appeared in the *Contemporary Jewish Record* (August 1944), and the *Review of Politics* printed an article on racist thinking (January 1944) as well as an analysis of imperialism, nationalism, and chauvinism (October 1945).

As chief editor of Schocken Books from 1946 to 1948, Miss Arendt was responsible for the publication of several noteworthy classics, including the Max Brod edition of the Kafka diaries. She also collaborated on the translation of the second volume. In 1947 she had published in Heidelberg a group of articles entitled *Sechs Essays*, in which she presented her views and recollections on diverse subjects. From 1949 to 1952 she was executive secretary for Jewish Cultural Reconstruction, Incorporated, an organization which collected and reallocated Jewish writings which the Nazis had seized and dispersed.

HANNAH ARENDT

With the publication of *The Origins of Totalitarianism* (Harcourt, Brace, 1951), Hannah Arendt's reputation as a writer and scholar became firmly established. According to a profile in the *Saturday Review* (March 24, 1951), the book was the result of "long thought and research in the European 'laboratory' and over three years of actual A to Z putting together. . ." The volume analyzed the two most prominent forms of twentieth century totalitarianism — National Socialism (Nazism) and Communism—and sought to establish their origins in the anti-Semitism and imperialism of the nineteenth century. Some reviewers differed with Dr. Arendt's thesis. Hans Kohn, professor of history at the City College of New York, insisted that to him "no clear and convincing pattern of the origins of totalitarianism in anti-Semitism and imperialism emerges," and "the first part of the book dealing with anti-Semitism is inconclusive" (*Saturday Review*, March 24, 1951). However, he praised the professional quality of the book and recommended it highly.

The volume was well received by the critic of the *Annals of the American Academy of Political and Social Science* (September 1951), who called it a work of "academic scholarship." E. H. Carr of the New York *Times* (March 25, 1951) suggested that the book was "written throughout under the stress of deep emotion" and was the "work of one who has thought as well as suffered." The reviewer for the New York *Herald Tribune* (April 8, 1951) predicted that the "book will be read as a brilliantly creative reconstruction."

A Guggenheim fellowship was awarded to Dr. Arendt in 1952. The following year she was invited to lecture at Princeton University. She has also taught at the University of California at Berkeley, the University of Chicago, and Brooklyn College.

(Continued next page)

ARENDT, HANNAH—*Continued*

The Charles R. Walgreen Foundation at the University of Chicago invited Dr. Arendt to deliver its lecture series for the year 1956. Her observations, which were collected and published in a volume entitled *The Human Condition* (University of Chicago Press, 1958), were at once recognized as "subtle and scholarly." Brand Blanshard, in the New York *Times* (February 15, 1959), called it a work "of intense and brooding reflection," and Mary McCarthy suggested that "the combination of tremendous intellectual power with great common sense makes Miss Arendt's insights into history and politics seem both amazing and obvious" (*New Yorker,* October 18, 1958).

It has been Dr. Arendt's contention that three types of human activity—labor, work, and action—have existed throughout history, but that in each culture they have been given greater or less emphasis according to the nature of the society. Labor is the energy expended for acts of simple biological survival; work is defined as the making of objects of some duration; action covers man's relationship with his fellow man. Whereas the ancient Greeks glorified action as the free play of ideas and disdained the first two categories, Dr. Arendt "sees the history of the West as the gradual inversion of this Greek conception of life" (New York *Times,* February 15, 1959). She feels that the "animal laborans" will eventually triumph in contemporary society at the expense of man and his soul.

Beginning with the spring semester of 1959, Hannah Arendt took her place on the faculty of Princeton University as visiting professor of politics. "I'm not at all disturbed about being a woman professor," commented Dr. Arendt about her appointment, "because I am quite used to being a woman" (New York *Herald Tribune,* November 12, 1958). The only woman to hold the rank of a full professor, she has the official titles of Class of 1932 visiting lecturer in the American civilization program and visiting senior fellow of the Council of Humanities. Dr. Arendt is participating with other faculty members in "conducting a special seminar dealing with 'the United States and the Revolutionary Spirit'" (New York *Times,* November 12, 1958).

Since her arrival in the United States, Dr. Arendt has been a frequent contributor to professional and lay periodicals. In 1954 she received a grant of $1,000 from the National Institute of Arts and Letters and the city of Hamburg (Germany) awarded her the Lessing Prize in January 1959. Dr. Arendt is five feet six inches tall, weighs 132 pounds, and has brown eyes and hair. She is a political independent, and though she has worked in Jewish cultural activities, she professes no religious affiliation. Since 1940, she has been known in private life as Mrs. Heinrich Bluecher, wife of a professor of philosophy at Bard College.

A strong undercurrent of pessimism flows through Hannah Arendt's work. Yet to an interviewer from the *Saturday Review* (March 24, 1951) she "conveys absolutely no sense of personal desperation—only wisdom and stability; and the quality of mind responsible for that seems mirrored in a quotation from Karl Jaspers: 'To succumb neither to the past nor the future. What matters is to be entirely present.'"

References

N Y Herald Tribune p2 N 12 '58
Who's Who in World Jewry (1955)

ASHIDA, HITOSHI

Nov. 15, 1887-June 20, 1959 Former Premier of Japan (1948); held various cabinet posts; president, *Japan Times & Mail* (1933-40); author. See *Current Biography* (June) 1948.

Obituary

N Y Times p92 Je 21 '59

AYUB KHAN, MOHAMMAD (ī-yoōb')

1908(?)- President of Pakistan; Army officer
Address: Karachi, Pakistan

Assuming by proclamation the full powers of President of Pakistan on October 27, 1958, General Mohammad Ayub Khan succeeded the Islamic Republic's first President, Iskander Mirza, who had resigned. A former officer in the British Indian Army and Commander in Chief of the Pakistan Army from 1951 to 1958, he had also served as Minister of Defense during a crisis in 1954-55. In international affairs the new President is committed to observance of Pakistan's defense pacts with the Western powers and in domestic matters, to establishment of a type of democracy "the people can understand."

The son of a noncommissioned officer (bugler major) in the British Indian Army, Mohammad Ayub Khan was born about 1908 in Abbottabad in the North-West Frontier Province of what was then the Indian Empire. He comes of Pathan (Indo-Iranian) stock and is a Moslem. His brother, Sardar Bahadur Khan, became a leader in the now defunct Moslem League.

Ayub Khan studied at Aligarh Moslem University and the Royal Military College at Sandhurst in England. He received his officer's commission in 1928 and served for one year with the Royal Fusiliers before being posted to the First Battalion of the Fourteenth Punjab Regiment. During World War II he saw action on the Burma front, and toward the end of the conflict he was one of the comparatively few natives of India to be given a battalion command. Early in 1947, while still an officer of the British Indian Army, he attained the rank of colonel and was appointed president of a services selection board.

By the terms of the Indian Independence Act, effective August 15, 1947, the former Indian Empire was divided into two self-governing dominions within the Commonwealth of Nations. The division was along religious lines, with widely separated Moslem areas roughly to the west and east of Hindu India forming the new dominion of Pakistan, of which Mohammed Ali Jinnah was the first Governor-General.

When the Fourteenth Punjab Regiment became part of the Pakistan Army, Ayub Khan was quickly advanced to brigadier and briefly commanded troops in Waziristan, a troubled area in West Pakistan. He was transferred to East Pakistan and in December 1948, upon being promoted to major general, became the first commander of the new East Pakistan Division.

His next promotion, in mid-1950, gave Ayub Khan the rank of adjutant general. He attended training exercises in West Germany of the North Atlantic Treaty Organization in September and October of that year and visited England, Austria, and Trieste. On January 17, 1951, following the retirement of General Sir Douglas Gracey, he was appointed the first Pakistani Commander in Chief of the Pakistan Army, with the rank of full general.

In the summer of 1953 General Mohammad Ayub Khan and Defense Secretary Iskander Mirza conducted with officials in Ankara the informal talks which led to the Turkey-Pakistan mutual defense treaty signed in February 1954. The Pakistani Commander in Chief visited the United States in October 1953, ostensibly to inspect military installations but also for discussions which resulted in the granting to Pakistan by the United States of millions of dollars in military assistance and supplies.

During the four years beginning 1954, according to the *New Republic* (November 10, 1958), the Pakistan Army received $75,000,000 out of an initial American commitment estimated at $170,000,000, most of the remainder going to the Air Force for jet fighters. To build the 300,000-man Pakistan Army into an efficient fighting force and a key link in the defense chain of the Western powers, General Ayub Khan established a planning board to study problems of equipment, training, and organization. An Army School of Education and Military College at Jhelum and an Army School of Administration were added to the Pakistan Military Academy and the Staff College at Quetta.

Under the government of Prime Minister Liaquat Ali Khan, Pakistan had shown signs of progress. After his assassination in October 1951, the country's internal and economic condition deteriorated, owing to lack of foreign exchange, continuous friction with India over trade barriers and the future of Kashmir, famine, discontent in East Pakistan, and other causes, including widespread corruption. A crisis was reached in October 1954 when Governor-General Ghulam Mohammed declared a state of emergency, dissolved the Constituent Assembly as "no longer representative of the people," and forced Prime Minister Mohammed Ali to accept Mirza as Minister of the Interior and Ayub Khan as Minister of Defense, as well as Commander in Chief of the Army.

By August 1955, when Ayub Khan left the Defense Ministry, Mirza had become Governor-General and elections had been held for the new Assembly. The legislature produced a constitution under which, on March 23, 1956, Pak-

FIELD MARSHAL MOHAMMAD
AYUB KHAN

istan became an Independent Islamic Republic, with Mirza as President. Pakistan retained membership in the British Commonwealth, the United Nations, and the Middle East and South East Asia Treaty Organizations.

A new crisis was reached less than three years later, and on October 7, 1958 President Mirza abrogated the constitution, declared martial law, and called on the Army to "save the country." Ayub Khan was appointed Chief Martial Law Administrator and Supreme Commander of all armed forces. In a radio address he asserted that "a perfectly sound country" had been turned into a laughingstock by the politicians. The "ultimate aim" of the President and himself, he said, was "to restore democracy, but of the type that people can understand and work."

On October 27 Mirza resigned as President of Pakistan, and General Mohammad Ayub Khan assumed the Presidency by proclamation. Later he acknowledged to foreign correspondents that he "had turned President Iskander Mirza out of office because the armed services and the people demanded a clean break with the past" (Elie Abel, New York *Times,* October 31, 1958).

In proclaiming the assumption of all powers, Ayub Khan reaffirmed adherence to the country's various treaty commitments with the Western powers, as well as to a program of economic and social reform. He had earlier referred to the Kashmir dispute with India, adding, "We shall be infinitely glad to have settlement through peaceful means. But if forced to adopt means other than peaceful the blame will surely lie at the doorstep of India" (*Pakistan Affairs,* November 1, 1958). Prime Minister Jawaharlal Nehru of India responded on November 7 by calling the new regime

AYUB KHAN, MOHAMMAD—*Continued*

"naked military dictatorship" (*New York Times,* November 8, 1958).

Regarding internal matters the new President announced in November 1958 that price controls would shortly be imposed as a step toward economic stability. A land reform commission had been appointed to insure higher food production and security for agricultural workers. Toward the end of the month an agreement was signed with the United States officials whereby Pakistan would receive $82,000,000 in surplus American farm products.

In September 1959 Ayub Khan announced the drafting of legislation to provide for a system of "basic democracies." Under this four-tier arrangement, villagers directly elect two-thirds of a village council. In turn, these councils elect chairmen to represent them at the next legislative level, the subdivisions. The other two tiers are district regions and provinces.

Mohammad Ayub Khan is six feet two inches in height and about 210 pounds in weight; he has gray eyes and a clipped, slightly graying mustache. It is said that he possesses both a good sense of humor and a rather quick temper. He enjoys reading, gardening, and shooting and plays tennis and golf. "The Sandhurst influence upon him is strong," noted a biographic sketch in the New York *Herald Tribune* (October 29, 1958), "and his English is 'speckled with reference to 'you chaps.' " He is married and the father of four sons and three daughters. President Ayub Khan was made a field marshal in October 1959.

References

> N Y Times p5 O 20 '58 por; IV p6 N 9 '58
> N Y World-Telegram p5 N 1 '58 por
> Pakistan Affairs 11:1+ N 1 '58 por
> Time 72:39+ N 10 '58 por
> Asia Who's Who, 1958
> International Who's Who, 1958

BACHE, HAROLD L(EOPOLD) (bāch)
June 17, 1894- Financier; stockbroker

Address: b. Bache & Co., 36 Wall St., New York 5; h. 812 Park Ave., New York 21; "Twin Spruce Farm," Washington, Conn.

The brokerage firm of Bache & Company, which celebrates during 1959 the eightieth anniversary of its establishment, is the largest Wall Street firm operating under one management for so long a period of time. Since its reorganization under its present name in 1945, it has been headed by Harold L. Bache, senior partner and a grandnephew of the founder. Bache has particularly encouraged the program of services to small investors for which his company has become famous.

A native New Yorker, Harold Leopold Bache was born in Manhattan on June 17, 1894 to Leopold Semon and Hattie (Stein) Bache. He has one brother, Frank Semon Bache. Harold Bache's grandfather was Semon Bache, a Bavarian glass merchant who had migrated to

New York City in the mid-nineteenth century and whose two sons, Jules Semon and Leopold, became members of the brokerage firm of Leopold Cahn & Company, established by their uncle Leopold Cahn in May 1879. This firm was the forerunner of the present Bache & Company.

For his early education Harold Bache attended the Ethical Culture School in New York City. From 1910 to 1912 he was a pupil at the Gunnery School in Washington, Connecticut, before entering Cornell University, where he studied chemical engineering and the arts for the next two years. He left Cornell in 1914 to work for his uncle, who in 1892 had reorganized Leopold Cahn & Company under the name of J. S. Bache & Company.

Bache's training in the brokerage business included working as a runner at the old outdoor Curb Exchange Association. From October 1914 until the end of the year he was also active in the flour business with Edgar Hess. As a J. S. Bache & Company partner, his father was especially active in the commodity and textile markets. In December 1916 Harold L. Bache also began to acquire special knowledge of this field by joining the New Orleans cotton firm of Julius Weiss & Sons as a trainee.

During the previous summer he had attended the Businessmen's Training Camp at Plattsburg, New York, and on May 12, 1917 he enlisted in the United States Army for World War I service. After graduating from the Plattsburg Officers' Training Camp as a second lieutenant, he was assigned to the 308th Infantry, 77th Division, with which he went overseas in the following April.

Inactivated as a captain in December 1918, he rejoined J. S. Bache & Company for several months before proceeding to Dallas, Texas, as a trainee with Southern Products Company, a cotton subsidiary of the Mitsui enterprises in Japan. From September 1920 to May 1921, when he returned to J. S. Bache & Company, he was active with the firm of Newell & Clayton in Liverpool, England. He was made a partner of J. S. Bache & Company in January 1926.

Under Jules S. Bache, who is remembered as the donor to the Metropolitan Museum of Art of the Bache collection of paintings, the firm of J. S. Bache & Company pioneered in various progressive methods of brokerage. Bache furnished the first stock quotations transmitted by radio and was "an early backer of mutual funds which, in brief, are pools of capital owned mostly by small investors."

J. S. Bache & Company helped to finance many important railroad, automobile, and mining enterprises. It foresaw and survived the 1929 crash by reducing broker's loans previously totaling $200,000,000. Four years later, when banks were closed down, J. S. Bache & Company "made headlines" by extending currency to customers. During World War II it maintained evening office hours as an accommodation to war workers.

Harold L. Bache, who had remained an Army Reserve officer for the ten years following World War I, returned to the Plattsburg Businessmen's Training Camp in the summer of 1940. In December of that year he was named captain commanding Company C of the soon-to-be-activated 17th Regiment of the New York State Guard, and during World War II became regimental executive officer with the rank of lieutenant colonel. He was relieved to the Reserve in August 1946 and since 1947 has been a member of the First Army civilian advisory board.

Upon the death of his uncle in March 1944, Harold L. Bache became senior partner of J. S. Bache & Company, which by June 1, 1945 was reorganized as Bache & Company, with seven new general partners and six limited partners, and a capital of more than $4,000,000. Among the new general partners were the owners of John J. Ryan & Sons, cotton and rayon dealers, who brought the firm enlargement of operations in the commodity field.

In May 1947 Bache & Company sponsored the first financial news program on television, and in April 1949 a syndicate and securities department was instituted. Another Bache innovation was a metals department which is "still largely exclusive" with the firm. An investment company department handles mutual funds and pay-as-you-go accounts; and there are investment supervisory, research, advertising and other departments. Members of a speakers bureau are available to explain the principles of investments and help dispel fallacies about the operations of finance. This bureau is part of the long-range planning of Harold L. Bache, who is said to insist that "Wall Street's case for itself is very poorly made most of the time" and that the "principle of full disclosure" is very useful (New York Times, February 19, 1956).

Active interest of the Ryan family in Bache & Company lasted six years. Late in 1950 the firm entered into an agency arrangement with a Japanese commodities house, and in December 1951, after a two months' visit by Bache to Tokyo, a correspondent arrangement with Nikko Securities Company was announced. Bache & Company also has foreign branches or correspondents in Canada, London, and Paris. It serves a large number of cities in the United States and holds membership on about two dozen securities and commodities exchanges, including four memberships on the New York Stock Exchange.

At the opening of a new Bache office in Beverly Hills, California in January 1956, Harold L. Bache said that he saw increasing recognition that holding stock is "not one of the prerogatives of a wealthy class of privileged individuals" and predicted that the year 1960 would find some 12,000,000 people owning shares of industry (New York Times, January 10, 1956).

In recent years securities transactions by Bache & Company are said to have sometimes exceeded half a million shares a day. By 1956 the number of accounts carried by the firm had reached 75,000. Acting in its advisory capacity, the company made an important innovation in March 1958 by issuing a "shopping list" for investors, covering 396 stocks, with recommendations to buy, sell, or hold.

Fabian Bachrach

HAROLD L. BACHE

Bache has served as a governor of five New York exchanges and four clearing houses, and is a member of numerous out-of-town exchanges. He has been in Big Brother work since 1914, is chairman of Hawthorne-Cedar Knolls School for emotionally disturbed children and in June 1954 was appointed to the New York City Youth Board. Bache is a trustee of the Jewish Federation and a former treasurer of the Jewish Board of Guardians.

Bache's collection of Japanese art is considered one of the finest in the country. Another of his interests is the breeding of prize turkeys and chickens at his 150-acre farm in Washington, Connecticut. After having remained single for the first sixty years of his life, Harold Bache married Mrs. Alice Odenheimer Kay, widow of William de Young Kay on September 5, 1954. She has two children, Ellen and Paul Kay.

References

N Y Herald Tribune p44 D 14 '50 por
N Y Journal-American p36 Jl 18 '54 por
N Y Times p16 S 6 '54 por
Business Executives of America (1950)
National Cyclopædia of American Biography current vol G (1943-46)
Who's Who in America, 1958-59
Who's Who in World Jewry (1955)
World Biography (1954)

BADGER, OSCAR C(HARLES) June 26, 1890-Nov. 30, 1958 Admiral in the United States Navy; commander of the Eastern Sea Frontier and the Atlantic Reserve Fleet (1950-52). See *Current Biography* (May) 1949.

Obituary

N Y Times p29 D 1 '58

BAILAR, JOHN C(HRISTIAN), JR. May 27, 1904- Chemist; university professor
Address: b. University of Illinois, Urbana, Ill.; h. 304 W. Pennsylvania Ave., Urbana, Ill.

The president of the American Chemical Society for 1959 is Dr. John C. Bailar, Jr., professor of inorganic chemistry at the University of Illinois, author, and consultant. He was elected in a nation-wide mail ballot of the society's 86,000 members to succeed Dr. Clifford F. Rassweiler of the Johns-Manville Corporation.

In the scientific world Dr. Bailar is known for his significant contributions to the field of inorganic chemistry. His investigations have dealt principally with substances containing no carbon. This phase of chemistry has become increasingly important during the last decade as a result of the harnessing of atomic energy, wider use of metals, and related developments.

One of the three children of John Christian Bailar and the former Rachel Ella Work, John Christian Bailar, Jr., was born in Golden, Colorado on May 27, 1904. The elder Bailar was a research chemist and professor at the Colorado School of Mines in Golden. As a youngster John often visited his father's laboratory, watched chemical experiments, and discussed points of scientific fact and procedure with his father.

After his graduation from Golden High School in 1920, Bailar majored in chemistry at the University of Colorado in Boulder. He held a four-year state scholarship and earned money as a tutor, clerk in the registrar's office, and switchboard operator. He served on the business staffs of both the college annual and the humor magazine; he was also a member of the cabinet of the university chapter of the Young Men's Christian Association. He was elected to Phi Beta Kappa and Alpha Chi Sigma, a chemical fraternity.

JOHN C. BAILAR, JR.

When he was graduated in 1924, Bailar took his B.A. degree *magna cum laude*.

Remaining at the university as a fellow in chemistry (1924-25), Bailar received the M.A. degree in 1925. He completed further work leading to the doctorate at the University of Michigan in Ann Arbor, where he was a university fellow (1925-26) and a teaching assistant (1926-28). He received the Ph.D. degree in 1928 and was elected to the Sigma Xi and Phi Lambda Upsilon societies. His master's and doctoral theses were entitled "Nitrogen Tetrasulfide and Nitrogen Tetraselenide" and "Halogen-Substituted Aromatic Pinacols and the Formation of Ketyl Radicals" respectively. They were published in the August 1925 and July 1929 issues of the *Journal of the American Chemical Society*.

Since 1928, when he was appointed an instructor of inorganic chemistry, Dr. Bailar has been a faculty member of the University of Illinois. He was promoted to associate in 1930, assistant professor in 1935, associate professor in 1939, and professor in 1943. From 1937 to 1951 he served also as secretary of the chemistry department and more recently has headed the division of inorganic chemistry.

A member of the American Chemical Society since 1927, John C. Bailar has held many positions of responsibility in the local and national organizations. He was appointed treasurer of the section in 1931, a vice-chairman three years later, and chairman in 1937.

In the national organization he has represented his section on the society's council intermittently from 1939 to 1958. He was chairman of the division of chemical education in 1947, chairman of the division of physical and inorganic chemistry in 1950, and the first chairman of the newly established division of inorganic chemistry in 1956-57. Other posts he held were head of the committee on national meetings (1947), divisional officers' group (1949), and national meetings and divisional activities (1955-57). He was also a member of the committee on predoctoral fellowships and nominations and elections. In 1947 he was honored by the Chicago section as one of the ten outstanding inorganic chemists in America. Bailar has been on the board of directors and a life councilor since 1958.

Elected president of the American Chemical Society for 1959, Dr. Bailar succeeded Clifford F. Rassweiler (see *C.B.*, October 1958). The head of the organization during 1960 will be Dr. Albert L. Elder, director of research for the Corn Products Refining Company. Composed of 86,000 chemists and chemical engineers, the American Chemical Society is the largest scientific organization in the world, with chapters in almost every state, the District of Columbia, and Puerto Rico. Since 1937 it has held a national charter from the United States Congress and its phenomenal growth "has paralleled the spectacular evolution of American chemistry from a primarily academic pursuit, carried on by a few hundred scientists, to a flourishing profession and industry which constitute a major force in the life of the nation." The society publishes nine journals and maintains national offices at 1155 16th Street, Washington, D.C.

As the head of the American Chemical Society, Bailar urges the expansion of basic research projects and the support of scientists engaged in this work. He recommended that funds be granted to the individual scientist rather than to the project and to young men as well as the scientists with established reputations if they have "sparkling imagination and a keenness for research" (*Christian Science Monitor,* April 6, 1959).

More than 100 articles written by Dr. Bailar have appeared in scientific and technical journals. These are concerned primarily with the stereochemistry and stereoisomerism of complex inorganic compounds, structures and properties of some metal derivatives of dyes, numbers and structures of isomers of hexacovalent complexes, and studies in the chromammines. He is credited with having found the only two inorganic examples of the Walden inversion. Currently, he is working under an Air Force contract on the co-ordination of polymers in an attempt to discover plastics that can withstand very high temperatures.

Dr. Bailar has served in an editorial capacity on the *Journal of the American Chemical Society, Journal of Chemical Education, Journal of Inorganic and Nuclear Chemistry,* and *Chemical Reviews.* On the editorial board of *Inorganic Syntheses* from 1937 to 1953, Bailar was editor in chief of its fourth volume (McGraw-Hill, 1953). For the American Chemical Society he edited the monograph, *The Chemistry of Coordination Compounds* (Reinhold, 1956), and he is co-author with B. S. Hopkins of *General College Chemistry* (5th edition, 1956) and *Essentials of General Chemistry* (1946), both published by D. C. Heath & Company.

Dr. Bailar was an official investigator on the National Research Committee (1944), directing studies on nerve gases and smoke screens. He has served with the joint research and development board of the Department of Defense (1947-49). With the National Research Council he was on committees dealing with scientific personnel, predoctoral and postdoctoral fellowships, inorganic chemistry, and codification of chemical compounds. Since 1947 he has acted as consultant to several private chemical companies.

Honorary D.Sc. degrees were bestowed on Professor Bailar in June 1959 by the University of Buffalo and the University of Colorado. Besides his affiliation with the American Chemical Society, he belongs to the Electrochemical Society. Professor Bailar also serves as a member of the governing body of Monmouth College in Illinois. His club is the University in Urbana.

Bespectacled and of imposing stature, John C. Bailar, Jr., is six feet three and one half inches tall, weighs 210 pounds, has gray hair and blue eyes. His church is the Presbyterian. He was married on August 8, 1931 to Florence Leota Catherwood. The couple has two sons, John Christian 3d and Benjamin Franklin Bailar.

The mission of chemistry, according to Dr. Bailar, is to foster the scientific method and to encourage its use in many areas of community and individual life. But reason and science need the assistance of the "teachings of religion, or at least a philosophy of life, to guide us in applying the new power that science has given us" (*Christian Science Monitor,* April 6, 1959).

References

Chem & Eng N 37:103 Ja 5 '59 por
American Men of Science vol 1 (1955)
Chemical Who's Who, 1956
Who's Who in America, 1958-59

BALDWIN, JAMES (ARTHUR) Aug. 2, 1924- Author

Address: b. c/o William Morris Agency, Inc., 1740 Broadway, New York 19; h. 81 Horatio St., New York 14

Reprinted from the *Wilson Library Bulletin* Feb. 1959.

In characterizing the work of James Baldwin, critics have noted his poetic sensitivity, his narrative skill, his eloquence, his intensity of feeling. These qualities, which distinguish his novels, short stories, and essays, have won him recognition as one of today's outstanding young writers.

James Arthur Baldwin was born on August 2, 1924 in New York City, the eldest of nine children of David Baldwin, a clergyman, and Berdis Emma (Jones) Baldwin. "Grim" is his terse summary of the poverty and discrimination he experienced as a child in Harlem. Reared entirely in New York, he was graduated in 1942

JAMES BALDWIN

BALDWIN, JAMES—*Continued*

from DeWitt Clinton High School, where he served as a student judge and magazine editor.

After high school Baldwin held a number of jobs, helping to support his family. His only real interest, however, was writing — he can "scarcely remember ever wanting to be anything but a writer." Even in elementary school he had written plays, songs, stories, and poems. In 1945 a Eugene Saxton Fellowship enabled him to devote himself to literary work. His first professional publication was a *Nation* book review in 1946. Since then his articles and stories have appeared in many periodicals (including *Partisan Review, American Mercury, Commentary, Mademoiselle, Reporter, Harper's Magazine* and *New Leader*), and his play *The Amen Corner* has been produced at Howard University.

His first book was *Go Tell It on the Mountain* (Knopf, 1953), a realistic yet poetic story of religious experience in Harlem. Welcomed for its exceptional promise, the novel was one of 350 books chosen by the Carnegie Corporation to represent the United States in Britain. Paul Pickrel, writing in the *Yale Review,* called it "an extraordinarily powerful study," a work of "great force and vigor."

Probably Baldwin's most widely acclaimed book has been *Notes of a Native Son* (Beacon Press, 1955), a collection of personal essays termed "brilliant" by Anthony West in the *New Yorker* and lauded by *Time* for its "bitter clarity and uncommon grace." Ranging from unsparing comments on the novel of protest and the film *Carmen Jones* to acid sketches of the Harlem ghetto and encounters in Europe, the essays probe—to quote Dachine Rainer's *Commonweal* review — "the peculiar dilemma of Northern Negro intellectuals who can legitimately claim neither Western nor African heritage as their own." Baldwin, the same review stresses, "has been enraged into a style; the harshness of his lot, his racial sensitivity, and the sense of alienation and displacement . . . [have] moved him to . . . lyrical, passionate, sometimes violent prose."

Giovanni's Room, his second novel (Dial Press, 1956), the story of an American student in Paris and his involvement with a young Italian barman, received mixed reactions. Several critics were irritated by the appearance of still another new book on the theme of homosexuality; others agreed with Granville Hicks, who, in his New York *Times* review, deplored the "grotesque and repulsive" characters, but affirmed that "even as one is dismayed by Mr. Baldwin's materials, one rejoices in the skill with which he renders them. Nor is there any suspicion that he is . . . [using them] merely for the sake of shocking the reader. On the contrary, his intent is most serious."

Baldwin has traveled in England and on the Continent. Having lived for a long while in France, he hopes to visit the country again. (Paris he calls "the city I love.") He enjoys reading (Dostoevski, Henry James, Dickens, and Proust are his favorites); acting lessons; horseback riding, paddling around the Mediterranean; jazz, live and recorded, and "especially the people who create it." Baldwin is a resident of

Greenwich Village. Recently, he spent some time at the MacDowell Colony in Peterboro, New Hampshire, working on his forthcoming novel, "Another Country." Baldwin is also the author of a play, *Bobo's Blues.* The organizations to which he belongs are the P.E.N. Club, the Dramatists Guild, and the Actors Studio.

Many prizes have followed his first literary award. Among his honors are Rosenwald and Guggenheim fellowships (1948 and 1954) and awards from *Partisan Review* and the National Institute of Arts and Letters (1956). Conflicting judgments have come, too. A number of critics, without denying the impact of his masterful style, have been saddened by the sense of hopelessness revealed in his books—books they find unleavened by humor and filled, as Charles H. Nichols, Jr., (writing in *Commentary,* January 1957) put it, with a Calvinistic, deterministic view of human depravity and doom. But in these very traits others discern the artist impelled by righteous anger—that "savage indignation" roused by cruelty and injustice. Speaking for himself, Baldwin says: "Some people feel that I make too much of being a Negro and others that I do not make enough. My effort is to make real that rare common ground where the differences between human beings do not matter. Sometimes this can only be done by describing the differences, the warfare, and the blood." And of his career as a writer he remarked: "My father, who opposed it most bitterly, . . . taught me something of what it means to have a vocation. I still try to write as he preached, that is, in the sight of God."

References

Lib J 78:364 F 15 '53
N Y Herald Tribune Bk R p3 My 31 '53
N Y Times p8 My 24 '53

BANDARANAIKE, S(OLOMON) W(EST) R(IDGEWAY) D(IAS) Jan. 8, 1899-Sept. 26, 1959 Prime Minister of Ceylon since 1956; had been appointed to cabinet posts; was assassinated. See *Current Biography* (September) 1956.

Obituary

N Y Times p1+ S 26 '59

BANKS, ERNEST *See* Banks, Ernie

BANKS, ERNIE Jan. 31, 1931- Baseball player

Address: b. Chicago Cubs, Wrigley Field, Chicago 13, Ill.

Hard-hitting Chicago Cub shortstop Ernie Banks was named the National League's Most Valuable Player for the 1958 season, during which he established himself as one of the most formidable batsmen in baseball, as well as an excellent fielder. He led both the American and National leagues in home runs with 47 and in runs-batted-in with 129. His batting average was 313. In becoming the sixth Negro National Leaguer to win the award, Banks amassed a total of 283 points in the voting of a twenty-four-man committee of the Baseball Writers Association of America. In 1959 he was again honored with the Most Valuable Player award.

Ernest Banks was born on January 31, 1931, in Dallas, Texas, one of eleven children, some of whom still live with his parents in Dallas. His mother remembers him as an almost model boy who never "prowled" and who was "regular" at Sunday school and church (*Saturday Evening Post,* April 21, 1956). During the depression years his father, Eddie Banks, was employed in cotton picking and construction work and on WPA projects. Eventually he obtained a steady job as a janitor with a wholesale grocery company.

As a youth, Ernie Banks failed to show any special interest in sports but his father, a one-time semiprofessional baseball player, was so insistent that Ernie agreed to try his hand at athletics. He starred as an end on the football team at Booker T. Washington High School in Dallas and averaged 15 to 20 points a game in basketball. In track and field he high jumped 5 feet 11 inches, broad jumped 19 feet, and ran a quarter-mile in 51 seconds.

His first step toward the major leagues was taken in 1948 when the owner of the Amarillo (Texas) Colts spotted Banks playing softball. With his parents' approval, he signed with the summertime baseball troupe that traveled through Texas, New Mexico, Kansas, and Oklahoma. In 1950 Banks was signed by the Kansas City Monarchs of the Negro American League. He reported to the club after his high school graduation.

Recalling his days with the Monarchs, Banks said: "Ten — fifteen — maybe twenty thousand miles a year, and our biggest night was in Hastings, Neb. We got $15 apiece" (*Time,* September 8, 1958). His baseball career was interrupted in March 1951 for a two-year enlistment period in the Army. He saw service in Europe as a private and managed to play a great deal of baseball. Banks rejoined the Monarchs in 1953 after his discharge.

While playing with the Monarchs later in the year Banks so impressed scouts of the Chicago Cubs that the major league team paid $15,000 to obtain him from the Monarchs. The first Negro to wear the Cubs' uniform, he joined the team on September 14, 1953. He played in 10 games before the season ended, managed 11 hits in 35 at-bats, and hit 2 home runs.

Ernie Banks' first full season, 1954, was more than adequate, though not spectacular. He hit 19 home runs, batted in 79 runs, and compiled a .275 batting average. More important, he played in all 154 games, the start of a consecutive-game-playing streak that reached 424, a major league record, before he was stopped by an infected finger in August 1956.

Toward the end of the 1954 season Banks made a change in his hitting style that was to prove invaluable. He had been using a thirty-four ounce bat until that time, but then switched to a lighter thirty-one-ounce bat. "With the heavier bat," Banks explains, "I just couldn't get my bat around. The pitchers were

Wide World

ERNIE BANKS

stopping me on outside pitches. The lighter one whips better, especially for a wrist hitter like me." Since he is rather slightly built for a home run hitter, much of his hitting strength is in his wrists. He throws and bats righthanded.

In 1955 Banks hit 44 home runs, establishing a new major league record for the most home runs in a single season by a shortstop. (This was the record that he improved upon in 1958.) The former record for the highest number of home runs in a single season by a shortstop was 39, set by Vern Stephens in 1949 while with the Boston Red Sox. Banks hit his fortieth home run on September 2 against the St. Louis Cardinals.

Banks also batted .295 in 1955 and drove in 117 runs. He set another major league record by hitting 5 home runs with the bases loaded. His play that season earned him 195 points in the voting for the Most Valuable Player, but he finished third behind Roy Campanella and Duke Snider of the then Brooklyn Dodgers. In 1956 Banks's batting feats were almost as impressive. He managed only 28 home runs that year but ended the season with a .297 average. His hitting tailed off to .285 in 1957, but his home run production increased to 43.

Earlier, his reputation as an infielder had been made secure. In 1955 he was named as shortstop on the *Sporting News* All-Star Major League Team. Arthur Daley wrote in his New York *Times* column for August 24, 1955: "Informed baseball men are agreed that Banks is unquestionably the best shortstop in the business right now. He's a graceful, flowing fielder with wide range, strong arm, and good speed."

Before the 1958 season most baseball experts, in preseason forecasts, picked the Chicago Cubs for eighth place in the National League. The team finished the year in a fifth-place tie with the St. Louis Cardinals, and much of the credit

BANKS, ERNIE—*Continued*

went to Banks, the reason behind his runaway selection in 1958 as Most Valuable Player. He became the second shortstop to win the honor since its inception in 1931. Marty Marion of the St. Louis Cardinals was named in 1944. And he also was only the second player to gain the honor with a second-division team. In 1952 Hank Sauer won it, also with the Cubs. In addition, Banks won the award again in 1959, marking the ninth time a Negro National League player received it since 1949.

Banks's power hitting has proved a boon to attendance. The Chicago team, which has not won a pennant since 1945, saw its attendance dip to 748,183 in 1954 from a postwar high of 1,237,792 in 1948. It has increased steadily since the arrival of Banks and in 1958 was well over the million mark.

While in high school Banks met Mollye Louise Ector, whom he married on April 6, 1953. They make their home in Chicago, but the ball player maintains close ties with members of his family in Dallas. Several of his younger brothers also have ambitions in professional baseball.

Ernie Banks has a quiet manner, and his clothes are well tailored and subdued. He is six feet one inch tall and weighs 180 pounds. He and his wife attend the Methodist Church. They bowl occasionally during the off season and enjoy the movies. Another of Banks's pastimes is swimming. Among Cub fans he rivals the great Chicago players of the past in popularity. In a newspaper poll a few years ago Chicago fans voted him their favorite player by a 5 to 1 margin.

References

N Y Times p33 Ag 24 '55; p33 N 26 '58
Sat Eve Post 228:36+ Ap 21 '56 por
Time 72:36 S 8 '58 por
Baseball Register, 1958

BARROS HURTADO, CÉSAR Aug. 30, 1909- Former Argentine Ambassador to the United States

Address: h. Uruguay 618, Buenos Aires, Argentina

For the first time in nearly three decades Argentina's Ambassador to the United States represents a democratically elected government. From June 1958 to August 1959 this office was held by César Barros Hurtado, a lawyer and sociologist, who has long been a friend of the United States. He resigned the Ambassadorship after President Arturo Frondizi reorganized his government in June 1959.

As a lawyer and scholar, Dr. Barros Hurtado has studied in universities in the United States and has frequently lectured there. He is a member of the National Academy of Sciences in Washington, D.C., and the author of several books on law, political science, and economics. One of his books, *Hacia una democracia orgánica* (Towards an Organic Democracy), compares the legal policies of the political parties in the United States with those in Argentina.

Since 1930 he has been active in the Radical party and its subsequently formed reformist branch, the "Intransigencia."

César Barros Hurtado was born in Tres Arroyos in the province of Buenos Aires on August 30, 1909, the son of Teófilo J. Barros and the former Magdalena Hurtado. He studied at the University of La Plata School of Law. His thesis on a theory of humane sovereignty earned him a doctorate in law and social science. The following year he was a delegate to the academic council of the Law School. The university in 1941 and 1942 asked him to make a good-will tour to other universities in the hemisphere. Following visits to Harvard, Yale, Columbia, Princeton and Rutgers, Dr. Barros Hurtado deplored the lack of student exchange and told the press (New York *Times,* February 1, 1942) that many South American educators admired the university system in the United States and would like to adopt it.

For the past fifteen years Dr. Barros Hurtado has made regular yearly visits to the United States studying and lecturing. He has lectured at the École Libre des Hautes Études in New York and was a member of the council of the Institut de Droit Comparé de l'École Libre des Hautes Études of New York and of the Institute of Comparative Studies on Government and Education of Teachers College at Columbia University. As vice-president of the International Bank of Montevideo, Uruguay, he has represented that institution at conferences in the United States.

Dr. Barros Hurtado has traveled not only in the Western Hemisphere but also in Europe. In 1944 he was appointed a member of the International Academy of Political Science and Constitutional History, and in 1950 he attended its annual meeting in Paris. He served as a

Wide World

CÉSAR BARROS HURTADO

member of the International Congress of Jurists in Prague in 1948.

When Dr. Barros Hurtado ran as candidate for National Deputy for the Federal District in 1946, he shared the Intransigent Radical party ticket with Dr. Arturo Frondizi, his sympathizer and friend.

From the beginning of General Uriburu's regime in 1930 until the fall of Juan Perón in September, 1955, Argentina was governed by one form of military dictatorship or another. General Aramburu headed the interim government which ruled during the transitional period following Perón's fall. The first free elections in more than twenty-five years were held on February 23, 1958. Arturo Frondizi of the Intransigent Radical party was elected President and assumed office on May 1, 1958. On June 23 Dr. César Barros Hurtado presented his credentials to the President of the United States and became his country's Ambassador to the United States replacing Mauricio L. Yadarola. The appointment had been announced in April, before the new government was inaugurated.

A primary task of this new government is to strengthen the national economy. In April, just before he took office, President-elect Frondizi visited five neighboring South American countries—Uruguay, Brazil, Chile, Peru and Ecuador—making an appeal for Latin American unity, particularly a program of common action on economic problems. All of these countries are suffering from falling prices in their exports.

President Frondizi and his government have also tried to attract foreign capital investment. Perón had expropriated approximately 40 per cent of the American & Foreign Power Company's electric power plants, which had originally cost over $100,000,000. Failure to settle this claim discouraged other potential American investors. Within six months after Frondizi took office the general outline of an agreement had been reached and was approved by the Argentine Congress in January 1959. Under this accord the company received compensation for the expropriated properties and sold the remainder of the plants to the government. The proceeds of the sale are to be used for further investment.

Oil is an important resource, and the government was anxious to attract capital for the development of this industry without losing control of it. In October 1958 Ambassador Barros Hurtado signed a memorandum of tentative agreement with a group of American oil companies which could lead to an investment of $790,000,000 in the Argentine oil industry. The final agreement was to have been signed in Buenos Aires on November 12.

Amid talk of a *coup d'état* and disloyalty on the part of some high officials including Vice-President Gómez, Frondizi managed to hold firm—partly because of support from the armed forces. (Alejandro Gómez resigned November 18, 1958.) Individual agreements with various American oil companies were consummated in 1959 and exploration and development activities were begun.

Dr. Barros Hurtado is a member of many political science organizations and institutes not only in his native Argentina but in Colombia, France, and the United States. Guatemala awarded him the Order of Quetzal in 1947 "for his work on behalf of Pan-Americanism," and "for his contribution to the economic development of Brazil" that country presented him the Anchieta Medal in 1957.

César Barros Hurtado is the author of many books and articles on international and constitutional law, political philosophy, and economics. Among his books are *Hacia una democracia orgánica* (1943), *El hombre ante el derecho internacional* (1949), *América; penurias de su libertad* (1950), and *Crisis de la sociedad contemporánea* (1957).

References

N Y Herald Tribune p1 N 13 '58
N Y Times p6 F 1 '42; p27 Ap 22 '58; p28 Je 25 '58
Quien es Quien en la Argentina (1955)

BARRYMORE, ETHEL Aug. 15, 1879-June 18, 1959 Actress; had a vigorous acting career for over fifty years on New York and London stages, on tour, in motion pictures, and on radio and TV; acted with her brothers John and Lionel in movie *Rasputin and the Empress* (1932); awarded 1944 Oscar; tribute paid to her by the building of the Ethel Barrymore Theatre in New York in 1928. See *Current Biography* (March) 1941.

Obituary

N Y Times p1+ Je 19 '59

BARTON, ROBERT B(ROWN) M(ORISON) Aug. 19, 1903- Business executive

Address: b. 190 Bridge St., Salem, Mass.; h. 329 Ocean Ave., Marblehead Neck, Mass.

"An ace in the hole for 1959," said Robert B. M. Barton of a new parlor game which his firm planned to unveil at New York's annual Toy Fair in March 1959. The president of Parker Brothers, games publishers of Salem, Massachusetts, watches his "new models" with as much professional anxiety as any automobile magnate. He probably has a better-than-average idea of how a new parlor game will be received by the unpredictable public. Although trained to be a lawyer, he soon turned to the business of games, and has devoted almost half his life to being an executive of Parker Brothers. From the introduction of Monopoly in 1935 to the more recent crazes for Scrabble and Keyword, his career as a producer of home entertainment was interrupted only by military service in World War II.

Robert Brown Morison Barton was born in Pikesville, Maryland on August 19, 1903 to Randolph and Eleanor (Morison) Barton. His father was a successful Baltimore attorney and trial lawyer. Barton was educated in local schools and at Phillips Exeter Academy in

Fabian Bachrach

ROBERT B. M. BARTON

Exeter, New Hampshire. After completing preparatory school in 1922, he set out to follow his father's profession by enrolling as a prelaw student in Harvard College. He received his B.A. degree in 1926 and in 1929 graduated with an LL.B. degree from Harvard Law School.

After completing his law studies, Barton returned to his native state of Maryland. He passed the state bar examination in 1929 and joined his father's law firm in Baltimore. He was a partner in Barton, Wilmer, Ambler, and Barton from 1930 until 1932, when he was admitted to the Massachusetts bar.

One of Barton's first assignments as junior member of a law firm had been to read and digest five trunkfuls of business documents relating to a case which involved a firm with nationwide distribution. Instead of turning him against corporate law, the task gave Barton a detailed knowledge of business operations. His interest in business was further stimulated when he married Sally Parker, whose father, George S. Parker, was the founder and president of Parker Brothers in Salem, Massachusetts.

The Parker firm had begun in 1883, when George S. Parker became bored with the dull round of checkers and dominoes which constituted American parlor entertainment in the late nineteenth century. At seventeen, he invented and marketed a board game of his own, and the success of his venture ($100 profit on an investment of $40) encouraged him to found the firm which was to become a multimillion-dollar concern. Parker Brothers, which celebrated its diamond anniversary late in 1957, is today the world's leading publisher of board games, and also manufactures kindergarten supplies.

Barton joined his father-in-law's firm in 1932 as assistant treasurer, and was elected president in 1933, succeeding George S. Parker. One of his first tasks as head of the firm was to decide whether or not to purchase a game which had been developed by an unemployed heating engineer of Philadelphia named Charles B. Darrow. Called Monopoly, the new game appeared to be a bad risk, because it violated the industry's cardinal principles that a board game should be simple and have a definite conclusion. After a trial period in Philadelphia, however, Barton decided that Darrow's invention had possibilities.

"So we took it over from Darrow in December of 1935," he recalled (in *Town Journal*, December 1954). "We got along fine until just after Christmas. Then came the deluge. We had so many orders we had people working in three shifts; rented every inch of space we could get—all to make Monopoly."

Because it offered a chance for anybody to earn an imaginary fortune, Monopoly probably owed its initial success to the depression. It has continued to sell as the all-time favorite of parlor games, however, with an estimated 20,000,000 copies having been sold so far.

For a short period after the outbreak of World War II, Barton left the firm to go on active service as a lieutenant in the United States Navy Reserve. Released from duty in November 1944, he returned to his position as president and director of Parker Brothers the following January.

When Barton rejoined the games business, it had changed little since the year when he had first entered the firm; virtually all of the year's business was transacted in the month before Christmas. In the immediate postwar years, however, two new factors changed both the industry and Barton's marketing strategy. One was the trend toward suburban living which made outdoor relaxation—and games—available to more Americans. The other new influence was television, which not only kept people at home but gave them evening hours in which they were free to play family games.

"At first we were afraid television would hurt us," Barton explained to columnist Hal Boyle, "but it has turned out to be a big help. Families stay at home more now. But they can't look at TV all the time—so they play more games."

In developing board games which will catch a share of this new market, Barton himself is an active tester and inventor. When a rival firm put Scrabble on the market, Barton originated the idea for a crossword puzzle game which Parker Brothers published under the name of Keyword in 1953. It sold several million copies during its first year on the market.

Recognizing his leadership in the field, members of the Toy Manufacturers of the U.S.A. elected Barton president of the association in 1953, when the games and toy industries were preparing for a $450,000,000 annual gross. The share earned by board games increased 500 per cent in that year, to $55,000,000, and at least part of the increase was due to the public demand for Keyword.

Barton takes no special credit for the success of his own inventions. "When it comes to this field," he says, "a housewife with a fresh idea may make the oldest professional game inventor look like a beginner. She may be closer to new trends. The main thing about any game is that it must be fun."

As a man who has made his livelihood from manufacturing entertainment for the public, Barton was described by one writer (James J. Canavan in the Boston *Post,* May 10, 1953) as "a tall man, with gray hair and steel-rimmed glasses who gives you the impression of being sorry he ever grew up. He talks about games with all the enthusiasm of a freckled-faced youngster."

Robert B. M. Barton married Sally Parker on October 3, 1931. They have three children, Randolph Parker (an executive in the firm), Sally Bradstreet, and Richard Morison. An active participant in community activities, Barton is a member of the board of directors of the Naumkeag Trust Company in Salem, a trustee of the Salem hospital, and a member of the Harvard clubs of Boston and New York, the Eastern Yacht Club in Marblehead, Massachusetts, where he has his home, and the Metropolitan Club of Washington, D.C. He is an Episcopalian.

After twenty-seven years in the games business, Barton has developed an intensive testing program for his firm's new products before they are put on the market. But he admits he has been unable to find the perfect way of predicting how the public will react to a new offering. "The true test of a good game," he says, "is when the players say, 'Let's play it again.' Then we know we've given them something good."

References

N Y Herald Tribune II p5 D 7 '58
N Y World-Telegram p17 Ja 5 '54
Washington (D.C.) Post p24 D 5 '53
Who's Who in America, 1958-59
Who's Who in Commerce and Industry (1957)

BAZIN, GERMAIN (bȧ-zăɴ′ jȧr-măɴ′)
Sept. 24, 1901-   French museum curator; writer; professor
Address: b. Palais du Louvre, Paris I°, France; h. 29 Avenue Georges-Mandel, Paris XVI°, France

Long a scholar, writer, and teacher of prominence, and a curator in the department of paintings and drawings of the Louvre, Germain Bazin became in 1951 curator in chief, thereby occupying one of the most responsible positions in France. Since that date he has carried out on behalf of his country and his museum many foreign missions, including one to the United States in 1954. He has been in charge of various exhibitions both in France and abroad. His work as secretary of the International Commission on the Restoration of Paintings has brought him into contact with the staffs of museums in many countries.

While most of Bazin's writing and teaching has dealt with historic art, he has also taken a

GERMAIN BAZIN

keen interest in its current developments. In a special 1949 issue of the magazine *L'amour de l'art* which dealt with the cinema he stated his credo: "As the habitual aspects of the world have lost their power of suggestion, their realistic force, the artist who wishes to give an impression of vitality must now take reality by surprise, must snatch from the world some unexpected fragment. To do this he must get away from the ordinary, the normal vision that puts the horizon at the usual level of the eye; he must abandon the centered perspective, that of the theatre, which is conceived for an ideal spectator seated in the middle seat of the balcony. He will rather displace himself spatially in order to get oblique views in perspective, or views from above or below; he will sharply change the scale, make the figures jut forward toward the spectator, or almost lose them in the remoteness of the background,—all in order to discover, as Proust puts it, 'an unusual image of things familiar.'"

Germain Bazin, whose full baptismal name is Germain-René-Michel, was born September 24, 1901 at Suresnes, a western residential suburb of Paris outside the Porte Maillot at the foot of Mont-Valerien. His parents were Charles and Jeanne Laurence (Mounier-Pouthot) Bazin. His father was occupied in industry as an ironmaster, a graduate in engineering of the principal French school of technology, the École Centrale des Arts et Manufactures. Some of Bazin's ancestors had attained a conspicuous place in politics and had been allied with the Bernadotte family.

After his preliminary education at Sainte-Croix de Neuilly and Sainte-Croix d'Orléans, Germain Bazin attended the Collège de Pontlevoy, near Blois, in preparation for the University of Paris. He had always been interested in art, and especially from his childhood on, in painting. At the Sorbonne he studied under the

BAZIN, GERMAIN—*Continued*

prominent professor of art history, Émile Mâle. He was also one of the students of the late Henri Focillon, who was later a visiting professor at Yale. Bazin's studies were, however, varied. Besides working in the Faculty of Letters in which he continued to the baccalaureate and the licentiate, he earned a baccalaureate in sciences and a licentiate under the Faculty of Law. More closely related to his later museum career were his studies at the École du Louvre, leading to the diploma there. His scholarship and publications were finally rewarded by the high degree of Doctor of Letters, a degree for which there is no American counterpart. It ranks above the American Ph.D., but is given exclusively for intellectual attainment, unlike the American honorary degree.

Bazin began his museum career in 1928 as a member of the department of drawings at the École des Beaux-Arts. In 1937 he was appointed curator in the department of paintings and drawings at the Louvre. His work was briefly interrupted by military service in 1939. Serving in the infantry but not at the front, he rose to the rank of captain. When the periodical *L'amour de l'art,* which like many another had been suspended in the spring of 1940, resumed publication in April 1945, Bazin became its director.

In 1951 Bazin succeeded René Huyghe as curator in chief at the Louvre. In 1953 he radically reorganized his department there, substituting for the old arrangement of paintings by national schools a new one in terms of international art currents.

Bazin has varied his museum work with teaching. He was for a time a member of the Faculty of Letters of the University of Brussels, and he has held since 1941 the chair of museology in the École du Louvre. He has lectured extensively at home and abroad, as he did in America in 1954.

It is, however, for his many books that Bazin is most widely known. Although he had published his *Saint Dominique* as early as 1930, it was his book of 1933, *Le Mont-Saint-Michel*—honored by the Academy of Inscriptions and Belles-Lettres—that first laid the foundation for his wider reputation. His other works include *Le Louvre: le palais* (1933), *La peinture italienne aux XIVe et XVe siècles* (1937), *Memling* (1939), *Les trésors de la peinture française* (1939 ff.), *Fra Angelico* (1941), *Corot* (1942), *Le crépuscule des images* (1946), *L'époque impressionniste* (1947), *Les grandes maîtres hollandais* (1950), *Histoire de l'art de la préhistoire à nos jours* (1953), and *L'architecture religieuse baroque au Brésil* (1956-57). He has also collaborated with others as joint author or as editor on various catalogues and other publications, and has written brief texts to accompany volumes of plates. For his interest in writing, as for his career in general, he gives credit to the inspiration of his famous professors, Mâle and Focillon, and to those literary luminaries of his acquaintance, Paul Valéry and Paul Claudel, who in a different way exerted comparable influence upon him.

Among the decorations Germain Bazin has received are those of Officer of the Legion of Honor (1954), Commander of the Belgian Order of Leopold (1956), Officer of the Order of the Belgian Crown, Officer of the Portuguese Order of Santiago, Officer of Merit of the Italian Republic, Knight of the Cruzeiro do Sul (Brazil). He is a corresponding member of the Academy of Portugal.

In Paris Bazin is a member of the Cercle de l'Union and of the Cercle Interallié. He serves on the Council of the Maison de l'Amérique Latine. As these club memberships indicate, Bazin is internationally minded. Like many other French intellectuals, he is interested in the leavening effect of French culture on foreign lands—particularly America. Writing in a special issue devoted to the École de Paris in *L'amour de l'art* for 1945 (volume 25), he says: "While an infamous propaganda daily exerts itself to convince us of our decadence, a group of artists, in which the French are fraternally bound together with the foreigners of the School of Paris who have adopted our culture, maintain the faith of the New World in the creative strength of France. To this modern people our painters and sculptors are transmitting a modern vision of forms and colors, which results, it would seem, in their greater adhesion to French culture now than ever before."

Germain Bazin married Suzanne Heller de Bielotzerkowska on July 7, 1947. They have no children. He has one brother, who is a journalist and a writer of fiction.

Debonair in appearance, with dark eyes and dark hair, Bazin stands five feet eight inches. He weighs about 170 pounds. He was baptized in the Roman Catholic Church, and his political sympathies lie with the French Center, or the Radical-Socialist party. His hobbies are singing and the piano, and he takes a spectator's interest in sports.

References

Dictionnaire Biographique Français Contemporain (1954)
Larousse du XXe Siècle Sup, 1953
Who's Who in France (Paris), 1953-54
Who's Who in France 1957-1958

BEALE, (OLIVER) HOWARD Dec. 10, 1898- Australian Ambassador to the United States; lawyer

Address: Australian Embassy, 3120 Cleveland Ave., N.W., Washington, D.C.

In accepting his first diplomatic post, that of Australian Ambassador to the United States, Howard Beale gave up a ministerial career in which his most important concern had perhaps been the development of atomic weapons and guided missiles. He succeeded Sir Percy Spender in Washington, D.C. in March 1958, soon after having resigned from the Australian cabinet as Minister of Supply and Minister for Defence Production. A Queen's Counsel and a prominent member of the Liberal party, Beale had held a seat in his country's House of Representatives for twelve years.

Oliver Howard Beale was born on December 10, 1898 in Tamworth, New South Wales, Australia to Clara Elizabeth (Vickery) and Joseph Beale, a clergyman and the former head of the Methodist Church in New South Wales. After graduating from Sydney High School, Beale attended the University of Sydney, receiving the B.A. degree in 1921 and the LL.B. degree in 1925. He became a barrister-at-law in New South Wales in 1925, extensively practised common law, and was appointed King's Counsel in 1950.

During World War II Beale served as an officer in the Royal Australian Naval Volunteer Reserve (1941-44) in antisubmarine defense. In the immediate postwar period the Liberal party was organized under the leadership of Robert G. Menzies as a successor to the United Australia party, and Beale was chosen a member of the new party's executive body in 1945 and 1946. Successful in his campaign for a seat in Parliament in the 1946 elections, he became one of seventeen Liberals in the House of Representatives. He was re-elected as a member for Parramatta, New South Wales in 1949, 1951, 1954, and 1955. From 1947 to 1949 he was a member of the Commonwealth Parliamentary Standing Committee on Public Works.

After the December 1949 elections the Liberal party, which had won fifty-two seats in the House of Representatives, joined with the Country party to form a coalition government, thus bringing to an end the eight-year control of the Australian government by the Labour party. The Liberals oppose the Labour party's program of socialization and in international affairs advocate full co-operation within the British Commonwealth and with the United States. Menzies, who was chosen Prime Minister, named Beale as Minister of Information and Minister for Transport. He held these positions in 1949-50 and in 1950 was also chairman of the Australian Transport Advisory Council.

Appointed Minister of Supply in March 1950, Beale took charge of a number of government agencies, including the Australian Contract Board, which buys and distributes supplies for the armed services; the Commonwealth clothing factories which supply uniforms for the services; and the design and inspection branch of the defense services, which tests military equipment.

As Minister of Supply he was also in charge of Australian Defence Science Laboratories and Establishments, the Woomera Guided Missiles Range, and the Maralinga Atomic Weapons Testing Ground. Beale often made public statements in connection with British nuclear explosion tests at Maralinga, and, in August 1956, in defense of the testing he told Australians that atomic weapons were essential to the survival of the British Commonwealth in the event of war. The Woomera range, a 200,000-square-mile area in central Australia, is the headquarters for a British-Australian ballistic-missile research program announced by Beale in May 1956.

Australian News & Inf.
Bureau

HOWARD BEALE

Through a cabinet reorganization in 1956 Beale was given the additional portfolio of Minister for Defence Production and thereby made responsible for the aircraft industry and government plants associated with it. He was also in charge of munitions production, including ordnance, ammunition, explosives, small arms, chemical factories, and government annexes in private industry. His duties included planning and organizing Australian industrial production for mobilization and war, especially in connection with radar, telecommunications, electrical equipment, engineering stores, chemicals, weapons, and other war matériel.

From 1950 to 1958 Beale was Minister in charge of the Australian Aluminium Production Commission, which set up and operated Australia's aluminum ingot industry in Tasmania. As Minister in charge of the Australian Atomic Energy Commission from 1950 to 1956 he controlled production and treatment of uranium in Australia, research and development in industrial atomic energy, and construction of research reactors and laboratories.

Australia, which has large deposits of uranium ore, produces uranium oxide for export to United States atomic energy plants. In 1955 Beale led a mission to the United States to discuss guided missiles and atomic energy matters, including the exchange of information. He announced that the two countries were planning an agreement to develop industrial atomic energy. During 1955 he also headed similar missions to England, other European countries, and Canada; and in 1957 he went to New Zealand to discuss plans for the supply and co-ordination of military equipment.

(Continued next page)

BEALE, HOWARD—*Continued*

Among other government posts held by Beale were Acting Minister for Immigration (1952 and 1954), Acting Minister for National Development (1952-53), Acting Minister for Air (1952-53), and Acting Minister for Defence (1957). He has been a member of the Australian Defence Council, a member of the Cabinet Committee on Defence Preparations, and a member of the Cabinet Committee on Uranium and Atomic Energy.

Beale's appointment as Australian Ambassador to the United States was announced in December 1957; he presented his credentials to President Dwight D. Eisenhower the following March. One of his important tasks as Ambassador, he later said, was to help bring about closer economic ties between the United States and Australia, adding, "American tariff barriers prevent us from increasing our trade with this country" (Washington *Post and Times Herald,* November 2, 1958). He has elsewhere praised certain aspects of economic co-operation between the two nations, such as the increase of United States private investments in Australia since World War II. Of the $250,000,000 that Australia receives yearly from all sources, about 40 per cent ($100,000,000) comes from United States investors.

Speaking at the National Foreign Trade Convention in New York in November 1958, Ambassador Beale urged that an economic conference of all nations be called to discuss multilateral agreements on production and market prices. "We cannot afford to be too rigid on questions of economic doctrine when our future may be at stake; time will not permit," he warned. "It is to be hoped the Communists will join us. In this way we can all move forward toward greater financial stability and economic progress throughout the whole world" (New York *Herald Tribune,* November 18, 1958).

The clubs and associations of which Beale is a member include the Sydney University Club, the Elanora Country Club, the Australasian Pioneers, and the Naval Officers Association, New South Wales. In 1948 he was a delegate to the International Bar Congress at The Hague, the Netherlands.

On December 19, 1927 Howard Beale married Margery Ellen Wood and they have a son, Julian, an engineer. The Ambassador is said to be "tall, friendly, and forthright." Historical reading is one of his hobbies, and he shares several recreational interests with his wife, including golf and yachting. Pictures from their collection of work of contemporary Australian artists hang in the paneled drawing room and other rooms of the Australian Embassy in Washington.

References

International Who's Who, 1958
International Yearbook and Statesmen's Who's Who, 1958
Who's Who in Australia, 1955
World Biography (1954)

BEAM, JACOB D(YNELEY) Mar. 24, 1908-   United States Ambassador to Poland
Address: b. American Embassy, Warsaw, Poland; h. 15 Bayard Lane, Princeton, N.J.

For career diplomat Jacob D. Beam, the position of American Ambassador to Poland has for many months entailed a dual function. He not only represents the United States to the Communist government of Wladyslaw Gomulka in Warsaw, but also negotiates with the Chinese People's Republic through talks with its Ambassador to Poland, Wang Pingnan, whose government is not formally recognized by the United States. Beam replaced Joseph E. Jacobs as Ambassador to Poland in the summer of 1957, after many years of experience had made him a specialist in East European affairs.

The son of a Princeton University professor, Jacob Dyneley Beam was born to Jacob Newton and Mary (Prince) Beam on March 24, 1908 in Princeton, New Jersey. He attended Kent School in Kent, Connecticut for five years and then enrolled at Princeton University, receiving his B.A. degree in 1929. During the following year he studied at Cambridge University, England.

The American consulate at Geneva, Switzerland was the scene of Beam's first post in the Foreign Service. The State Department appointed him a clerk there in June 1931, and about a month later he was promoted to vice-consul. In December of that year, after examination, he became vice-consul of career. His assignment in Geneva consisted largely in observing and reporting on the work of the League of Nations and the International Labor Office.

For a brief period in November 1932, Beam attended the Foreign Service School. Two years later he was sent from Geneva to Berlin as third secretary at the American Embassy. During his six years in Germany, until August 1940, he witnessed the steady growth of Hitler's power and the Nazi aggressions that contributed to World War II. "Coming home from Berlin for a visit to Washington after the war had broken out in Europe," stated a New York *Times* biographical sketch (September 16, 1958), "he shocked Georgetown society with the unmuffled prediction that Hitler's armored divisions would cut the French Army to shreds and drive the British into the Channel."

By the time that this unpopular prediction became a reality, Beam was serving as vice-consul and third secretary at the American Embassy in London, to which he had been assigned in April 1941. He remained here until the fall of 1944, for part of the time in the position of consul and second secretary. From early 1945 to August 1947 he was stationed in Germany, this time as political adviser on German affairs at Supreme Headquarters, Allied Expeditionary Force under General Dwight D. Eisenhower. Then reassigned to the State Department in Washington, he became chief of the division of Central European affairs in October 1947 and acting special assistant in the office of German and Austrian affairs in March 1949.

For the next few years Beam's attention was centered on problems of the Far East. Having gone to Batavia, Java as consul general in October 1949, he served as the United States representative when the sovereignty of that area was transferred in 1950 from the Netherlands to the new government of Indonesia. As soon as a diplomatic mission was established at Indonesia's capital city, Djakarta (formerly Batavia), he assumed the duties of counselor of the American Embassy, and from October 1950 to April 1951 he had the additional responsibilities of the acting United States representative on the United Nations Commission for Indonesia.

Ever since Beam's prewar service in Berlin, he had foreseen the increasing need and importance of diplomatic negotiations between the United States and the Communist world and had prepared himself for a role in coming events "by taking Russian language and history courses and paying for this in-service training out of his own pocket" (New York *Herald Tribune,* September 9, 1958). The first Iron Curtain country to which Beam took his credentials was Yugoslavia, where he held the position of counselor of Embassy in Belgrade from April 1951 to October 1952.

When transferred to the U.S.S.R. in November 1952, Beam was given the title of counselor of Embassy in Moscow with the personal rank of minister. After the United States Ambassador to the Soviet Union, George F. Kennan, was declared *persona non grata* in October 1952, Beam was called upon to serve as chargé d'affaires ad interim until the appointment of Charles E. Bohlen as Ambassador in the spring of 1953. One major event during this critical period was the death of Joseph Stalin in March and the subsequent struggle for power in the Kremlin. "A lot of Washington people," Bill Henry wrote in the Los Angeles *Times* (September 17, 1958), "say that Beam supplied more useful information than either of his bosses."

During his next tour of duty in Washington, beginning in June 1953, Beam continued to be occupied chiefly with events in Communist countries. As deputy director of the policy planning board, he helped to outline long-range diplomatic strategy for the State Department. Then as director of the office of Eastern European affairs, from March to October 1955, he was the member in charge of the United States delegation that met with British and French officials to lay plans for meetings of the "Big Four" Foreign Ministers to discuss plans for German reunification. From October 1955 until July 1957 he was Deputy Assistant Secretary for European Affairs.

In June 1957 President Dwight D. Eisenhower nominated Beam as the United States Ambassador to Poland, and the envoy arrived in Warsaw the following August. In a showdown on one aspect of the East-West conflict, in May 1958 Beam presented Secretary of State John Foster Dulles' note rejecting the Polish proposal for the establishment in Central Europe of a zone free of nuclear weapons

Dept. of State—Whit Keith, Jr.

JACOB D. BEAM

(popularly known as the Rapacki Plan, named after its proponent, Polish Foreign Minister Adam Rapacki).

Ambassador Beam had been in Poland for about a year when it was announced that he would soon meet with Communist China's Ambassador to Poland, Wang Ping-nan, in a resumption of talks between representatives of the United States and Red China that had broken off in December 1957. The negotiations, begun in August 1955, had been held in Geneva between Wang and the United States Ambassador to Czechoslovakia, U. Alexis Johnson.

One urgent reason for resuming the talks was that the Communists had announced their intention of occupying the islands of Quemoy and Matsu, held by the troops of Chiang Kaishek's Chinese Nationalist government on Formosa. Negotiations between Wang Ping-nan and Beam began on September 15, 1958. The Chinese Ambassador insisted upon withdrawal of Chinese Nationalist troops from the islands and of United States forces from the Taiwan area, and the American Ambassador demanded a Communist cease-fire as a preliminary to any settlement of the controversy.

"Never in modern times has so important a conference been covered by so few reporters or in such effective secrecy," Joseph C. Harsch wrote in the *Christian Science Monitor* (September 27, 1958). "American Ambassador Jacob Beam is under orders to disclose nothing of what is said in the second floor back room [of the palace] where he meets with the Chinese." As the weeks passed, the negotiators apparently remained deadlocked in their search for a peaceful solution to the Far East conflict, but tension in the Taiwan Strait gradually lessened.

Newsmen then speculated that Beam and Wang had begun discussing long-standing issues such as the release of American prisoners held

BEAM, JACOB D.—*Continued*

by Communist China. By late March 1959 the two Ambassadors had met for fifteen sessions since mid-September and the intervals between their conferences had lengthened.

While stationed in Belgrade, Jacob D. Beam met Margaret Glassford, an officer in the United States Information Service. They were married in November 1952 and have a son, Jacob Alexander. Ambassador Beam is six feet two inches tall and has graying, crew-cut hair. Calm, patient, and resolute in negotiations, he is said to be "a man who never gets rattled." He belongs to the Metropolitan Club in Washington. An interesting side light on his career, as reported in the New York *Times*, is that during World War II in England he took part in a project to help the London Zoo meet expenses by adopting the social vulture.

References

N Y Herald Tribune p2 S 9 '58 por
N Y Times p10 Je 18 '57; p4 S 16 '58 por
Department of State Biographic Register, 1958
International Who's Who, 1958
Who's Who in America, 1958-59
World Biography (1954)

BEARD, MRS. CHARLES A(USTIN) *See* Beard, Mary

BEARD, MARY Aug. 5, 1876-Aug. 14, 1958 Author; historian; with her husband, Dr. Charles A. Beard, collaborated on many books on American history notably *The Rise of American Civilization.* See *Current Biography* (March) 1941.

Obituary

N Y Times p22 Ag 15 '58

BEINUM, EDUARD (ALEXANDER) VAN Sept. 3, 1900-Apr. 13, 1959 Conductor; musical director of Amsterdam's Concertgebouw Orchestra since 1945; musical director of the Los Angeles Philharmonic Orchestra since 1956. See *Current Biography* (April) 1955.

Obituary

N Y Times p35 Ap 14 '59

BELL, BERNARD IDDINGS, REV. DR. Oct. 13, 1886-Sept. 5, 1958 Clergyman; educator; Canon of Protestant Episcopal Church; author of over twenty books including *Crowd Culture* and *Crisis in Education.* See *Current Biography* (April) 1953.

Obituary

N Y Times p17 S 6 '58

BELL, BERT Feb. 25, 1894-Oct. 11, 1959 Commissioner of National Football League since 1946; member of University of Pennsylvania football team (1916-19). See *Current Biography* (September) 1950.

Obituary

N Y Times p1+ O 12 '59

BELLUSCHI, PIETRO (běl-ū'skĭ) Aug. 18, 1899- Architect

Address: b. School of Architecture and Planning, Massachusetts Institute of Technology, 77 Massachusetts Ave., Cambridge 39, Mass.; h. 1 Fairfield St., Boston, Mass.

On the East coast Pietro Belluschi, since 1951 dean of the School of Architecture and Planning at Massachusetts Institute of Technology, is likely to become best known in the future as the architect of such "American landmark" projects as the Juilliard School at New York City's Lincoln Center for the Performing Arts. In the West, where he practised architecture in Portland, Oregon, he has long been distinguished for his designs of houses particularly suited to the Northwest, public buildings, shopping centers and other commercial constructions, and churches.

"His influence will always be felt in the progress of an indigenous American architecture in the Northwest vernacular." He has left his imprint on many buildings and homes and "younger architects who have caught his spirit of environmental design," editor Jo Stubblebine noted in *The Northwest Architecture of Pietro Belluschi* (F. W. Dodge Corporation, 1953). This volume is a collection of photographs that "show his versatility, his understanding of the character of the land, its people, its materials, and his application of progressive ideas."

Pietro Belluschi was born in Ancona, Italy, on August 18, 1899, the son of Guido and Camilla (Dogliani) Belluschi. When he was six years old, his family moved to Rome, where he spent most of his youth. Of his early years, he has said: "Rebellion against my middle-class environment gave me a stronger motivation for artistic expression than the pervading beauty of Rome. My desire was to differ, not to emulate; so I had no hero but my own self. Drawing was perhaps the only thing I ever did in school with any amount of pleasure. My interest in architecture began in high school, but the inner urge to create came when the ways of rebellion were shown to me" (quoted in *The Northwest Architecture of Pietro Belluschi*).

At the age of seventeen he volunteered for service in the Italian Army and served for three years during World War I in the mountain artillery. After his return to Rome, he attended the university there and received his Doctor of Architectural Engineering degree from the School of Application for Engineers in 1922. He came to the United States in the fall of 1923 on an exchange fellowship to study at Cornell University in Ithaca, New York. "Coming to America," he has commented, "changed my life to a greater extent than I thought possible. From a dreamy, lazy boy I became almost overnight an aggressive and determined man—determined to succeed at all costs as a student, as a person, and as an architect."

Upon receiving a C.E. degree from Cornell in 1924, he traveled out West and was employed as an electrical engineer by the Bunker Hill and Sullivan Mining Company in Kellogg, Idaho. Moving to Portland, Oregon, he became associated with the A.E. Doyle firm, one of the oldest and largest architectural concerns in the Northwest. He started as a draftsman in 1925; two years later he was made chief designer; and in 1932 he became a partner. In 1943 he acquired the firm and changed the name to Pietro Belluschi, Architect.

According to Stubblebine, he was much influenced by Harry Wentz, artist and teacher at the Portland Museum Art School. Among other influences were those of his own Italian background, seen for example in his preference for marble in public buildings and use of loggias and open courts. For his "Oregon house" or "beautiful barns" Belluschi used native timbers, while incorporating such features of Japanese architecture as overhanging roofs and stress upon the house-garden relationship.

One of his early achievements in the field of public buildings is the Portland Art Museum, designed in 1931. Like his Finley's Mortuary, it was included by the committee of education of the American Institute of Architects in its list of the one hundred best buildings in the United States for the years from 1920 to 1940. Among his other public buildings, generally in keeping with the International Style, are the Marion County Court House of Salem, Oregon, the Salem Y.W.C.A. building, and the Equitable Savings and Loan Association building in Portland, designed in 1948, "which anticipates much of what was later done at the U.N. and Lever House [in New York City], though not, like them, a sheath-type curtain-wall" (*Architectural Review*, May 1957).

"Several outstanding churches have come from his drawing board. The first, in 1938, was St. Thomas More chapel [in New Haven, Connecticut], with its spire over the chancel and its straightforward use of wood. After a long lapse, in which Belluschi's philosophy underwent a struggle against the materialism and spiritual poverty of man, have come three churches, full of spiritual feeling and with an elegance of simple interplay of brick, glass, and wood" (*The Northwest Architecture of Pietro Belluschi*). These are the Zion Lutheran Church, the Central Lutheran Church, both in Portland, and the First Presbyterian Church, in Cottage Grove, Oregon, all built in 1951.

In an article for the *Saturday Evening Post* (October 4, 1958) entitled "The Churches Go Modern," Belluschi wrote: "Architecture is, and it always has been, an expression of the human spirit. Church architecture cannot avoid the adventurous path toward self-renewal without decaying, even though the good and the bad may sprout together. The satisfying answers are not alone in the minds of architects and artists, but in the very fabric of our society."

PIETRO BELLUSCHI

In late 1950 it was announced that Belluschi had accepted the position of dean of the School of Architecture and Planning at the Massachusetts Institute of Technology in Cambridge, Massachusetts. He gave up his practice in Oregon and took office in January 1951, succeeding William Wurster. He became associated with the firm Belluschi-Skidmore, Owings & Merrill. One of several architects of Boston's proposed Back Bay Center, he was among those honored in early 1954 by *Progressive Architecture* magazine, which regarded the center as the best designed aggregation of buildings in the United States for 1953. Recently he has served as a consultant for the buildings of the United States Air Force Academy in Colorado Springs. In 1958 he was named the architect for the Juilliard School of Music, to be built at the Lincoln Center for the Performing Arts in New York City, and was designated a collaborator for the design of the new Grand Central City office building in New York City.

In his address "A New Century of Architecture," the closing speech at the centennial convention of the American Institute of Architects in 1957, Belluschi emphasized, "Beauty is not a static quality, not an image to be embalmed, nor a cosmetic to be put on; it is an intrinsic quality of created things, a living quality which respects their nature, their biological and psychological and even practical demands, while reflecting, and in a sense preserving the mystery which is at the base of all created things—the realm of the spirit and the source of its poetry . . . it seems to me that our progress, or if you will, the contribution which our profession may be able to give to mankind in the next hundred years, may well be based on the acceptance of this idea" (*Journal of the American Institute of Architects*, June 1957).

Belluschi has received awards from several architectural associations and magazines. In 1934 he was the American delegate to the

BELLUSCHI, PIETRO—*Continued*

League of Nations' Institute of Intellectual Cooperation in Madrid, and in 1950 United States President Harry S. Truman appointed him to the seven-man National Commission of Fine Arts. He has taught or lectured at numerous American colleges and universities, and was awarded an honorary LL.D. degree from Reed College in Portland in 1950.

Reproductions of his works, and some of his articles, have been published in *American Home, Architect and Engineer, Life, Architectural Forum, Arts & Architecture, Architectural Record, Civil Engineering, House Beautiful, Interiors, Liturgical Arts, Pencil Points,* and *Journal of the American Institute of Architects,* as well as in numerous foreign periodicals. He was made a fellow of the American Institute of Architects in 1948 and was elected in 1955 to the National Institute of Arts and Letters. He is also a fellow of the American Academy of Arts and Sciences and the Danish Royal Academy of Fine Arts, an academician of the National Academy of Design, and an allied member of the National Sculpture Society. He was president of the Oregon Chapter of the American Institute of Architects (1943 and 1944) and president of the Portland Art Museum.

Pietro Belluschi married Helen Hemmila on December 1, 1934; they have two children, Peter and Anthony. He is a Republican and a member of the Roman Catholic Church. He has said, "In architecture, as in art, we cannot be static, but to be truly free (and few of us ever are) it takes more determined courage, introspection, and restraint than to be in shackles."

References

> Arch & Eng 164:21 Mr '46; 200:32 F '55
> Arch Rec 108:9 D '50
> American Architects Directory, 1956
> Stubblebine, J. ed. The Northwest Architecture of Pietro Belluschi (1953)
> Who's Who in America, 1958-59
> Who's Who in the West (1949)

BENOIT-LÉVY, JEAN Apr. 25, 1888-Aug. 2, 1959 French motion picture director; producer; head of U.N. Films and Visual Information Division (1946-49); his documentary *First Steps* won an Academy Award in 1947; author. See *Current Biography* (October) 1947.

Obituary

> N Y Times p27 Ag 4 '59

BERGER, MEYER Sept. 1, 1898-Feb. 8, 1959 Reporter and columnist; on the staff of the New York *Times* for thirty years; won Pulitzer Prize (1950). See *Current Biography* (January) 1943.

Obituary

> N Y Times p29 F 9 '59

BERGGRAV, EIVIND (JOSEF), BISHOP Oct. 25, 1884-Jan. 14, 1959 Former Bishop of Oslo and Primate of the State Lutheran Church of Norway (1937-50). See *Current Biography* (October) 1950.

Obituary

> N Y Times p33 Ja 15 '59

BERKSON, SEYMOUR Jan. 31, 1905-Jan. 4, 1959 Journalist; vice-president and general manager of International News Service (1945-55); publisher of the New York *Journal-American* (since 1955). See *Current Biography* (October) 1949.

Obituary

> N Y Times p29 Ja 5 '59

BETTERIDGE, DON *See* Newman, Bernard

BISSELL, CLAUDE T(HOMAS) (bĭs''l) Feb. 10, 1916- University president; literary critic

Address: b. Simcoe Hall, University of Toronto, Toronto 5, Ontario, Canada; h. 93 Highland Ave., Toronto, Ontario, Canada

Sharing a common intellectual tradition, the university community has become a "great force for world unity," Dr. Claude T. Bissell has stated. As head of the University of Toronto, he hopes that the university will assume the role of "harbinger of a new internationalism" (Toronto *Globe and Mail,* February 25, 1959).

On July 1, 1958 Bissell culminated a long association with the university as student, teacher, and administrator when he became its president. He succeeded Dr. Sidney Smith who had resigned to become Canada's Minister for Foreign Affairs. Earlier, he had headed Carleton University in Ottawa for two years. At the University of Toronto, Canada's largest university, he will meet the problem of increasing enrollments by supervising a $50,000,-000 expansion program to provide facilities for an expected student body of 23,000.

Claude Thomas Bissell was born on February 10, 1916 in Meaford, Ontario to George Thomas and Maggie Editha (Bowen) Bissell. He received his secondary education at Runnymede Collegiate Institute in Toronto. Entering University College of the University of Toronto as a scholarship student, he won four additional scholarships in his undergraduate years.

He was an English and history honors course student, ranking first in these disciplines in his sophomore, junior, and senior years, and achieving first-class standing in all four years. He edited the *Undergraduate,* a literary publication, and played on the lacrosse team. After earning the B.A. degree in 1936, he was a Reuben Wells Leonard Fellow at the university's School of Graduate Studies, where he received the M.A. degree in 1937.

From 1937 to 1940 Bissell studied English and philosophy as a fellow at Cornell University. In 1940 he received a Ph.D. degree from Cornell and began his teaching career as an instructor in English. His thesis, dealing with the evolutionary ethics of Samuel Butler, was awarded the Luana L. Messenger Prize, and was published in part by the Cornell University Press. He left the Cornell faculty in 1941 to return to University College in Toronto as a lecturer in English.

A year later Dr. Bissell obtained a leave of absence and joined the Canadian Army. He was commissioned an infantry lieutenant in March 1943. He served as platoon commander and intelligence officer, then became an adjutant with the rank of captain, serving with the Argyll and Sutherland Highlanders in northwest Europe. At the end of the war he was a faculty member of Khaki College in England for a short time.

Returning to the University of Toronto in 1946, Dr. Bissell resumed his teaching duties and was soon advanced to an assistant professorship of English. That year, at the age of thirty, he was appointed the youngest dean of residence in the history of University College. In 1948 he was given the additional responsibilities of assistant to the president, Dr. Sidney Smith (see *C.B.,* January 1955), and in 1950 he attained the academic rank of associate professor. Two years later Bissell was named to the newly created post of vice-president. In this period he reorganized the School of Graduate Studies, where he had been chairman of the division of humanities and social sciences. He was also acting principal of University College for a brief period.

On July 1, 1956 Dr. Bissell became the third president of Carleton College in Ottawa. On the day that he left Toronto the student newspaper declared a day of mourning. In his brief tenure at Carleton he guided the Dominion's youngest academic institution through an extensive campaign of expansion. Under his presidency Carleton attained the status of a university, adopted a higher scale for faculty salaries, and planned a gradual move to a larger and more extensive campus, to be completed by 1965.

An Institute of Canadian Studies was also established at Carleton, in July 1957. Bissell explained that the institute would "stimulate Canadian studies of an inter-disciplinary nature, with primary emphasis on cultural history" (Toronto *Globe and Mail,* April 30, 1957). He has said that Canada has not fully realized herself as a cultural entity, but it is "beginning to show some of the marks of cultural maturity. . . . Canada is a different nation, with a culture distinct from the United States. . . . There is nothing . . . more disastrous to true understanding than the repetition of the old platitudes about undefended borders, about common traditions and about ease of communication" (Toronto *Globe and Mail,* April 9, 1957).

From Carleton, with a registration of some 1,754 students, Dr. Bissell returned to the University of Toronto and a student body of 13,030. His successor at Carleton is A. David-

CLAUDE T. BISSELL

son Dunton (see *C.B.,* January 1959). On July 1, 1958 he took office as the eighth and youngest president in the Toronto institution's 109-year history.

Canadian universities, like institutions of higher learning in the United States, are now faced with the problems of expanding enrollments and increased costs resulting from inflation. Bissell advocates the financing of education by government, private corporations, and individuals. Such an approach has several advantages, he noted: "It spreads interest in the university; it enables special and unpopular projects to be launched and supported; and by providing many pipers it makes it difficult for any one of them to call the tune" (*Maclean's Magazine,* April 12, 1958).

Regarding the prospect of increasing enrollments in future years, Dr. Bissell has said that "there is no disaster in numbers, provided adequate preparations are made, and provided in the general boom in higher education, we don't convert our universities into social agencies for the relief of the dull" (*Saturday Night,* October 13, 1956).

"On the university level the democratic dilemma can be resolved only if the selection of students is extended in time, certainly back beyond the final year in secondary school, and is based more firmly on intellectual accomplishment." The continuity of a scholarly tradition must be strengthened between high schools and colleges. This is necessary in the forthcoming age not of the common man, but the uncommon man who will guide the world's course "amid frightening hazards and dazzling opportunities" (*Maclean's Magazine,* April 12, 1958).

In literature, which is his field of specialization, Dr. Bissell edited *Our Living Tradition: Seven Canadians* (University of Toronto Press,

1957). Every year since 1947 he has written an annual survey of Canadian fiction for the *University of Toronto Quarterly,* and he has also contributed book reviews to Canadian publications. Bissell believes that the special duty of imaginative writers is to "listen for the sounds of their own country" (Toronto *Globe and Mail,* December 21, 1957). William Arthur Deacon, literary critic of the Toronto *Globe and Mail,* predicted that Bissell's "influence on Canadian writing during the next quarter century may be considerable."

In 1954, as a representative of the Canadian Humanities Research Council, Bissell toured Australian universities, lecturing on Canadian history and literature. He has also explored the common ancestry that Canadian writing shares with Australian literature. When the conference, Canada's Crisis in Higher Education, was held in Ottawa in November 1956, Bissell was chairman of the organizing committee. He later edited *Canada's Crisis in Higher Education* (University of Toronto Press, 1957). Bissell also edited *University College: A Portrait, 1853-1953* (University of Toronto Press, 1953).

Under the auspices of the Carnegie Corporation, Bissell made a comparative study of university administration in Canada, the United States, and Great Britain. As author and speaker, he has brought the problems of Canadian colleges before the public. He has been active in the work of the National Conference of Canadian Universities and has served as the group's finance committee chairman. The organization distributes government funds amounting to $16,000,000 annually to Canadian institutions of higher education.

Dr. Claude T. Bissell was married to Christina Flora Gray of Bothwell, Lanarkshire, Scotland on September 12, 1945. They have a daughter, Deirdre MacFarlane Bissell. The family enjoys classical recordings, color photography, Scottish country dancing, and attending performances of the Stratford Shakespeare Festival, of which Dr. Bissell is a governor. He is a fellow of the Royal Society of Canada and holds the honorary D.Lit. degree from the University of Manitoba (1958) and the LL.D. from McGill University (1958). Bissell is a member of the United Church of Canada.

"It is clear that Bissell's most impressive characteristic is his versatility. In an unusual degree, he combines the abilities of the excellent teacher and the penetrating research scholar with administrative capacities of the highest order. These are the qualities required in a great university president" (John A. Irving, *Saturday Night,* October 13, 1956).

References

N Y Times p19 O 25 '58
Toronto Globe and Mail p1 D 17 '57
por
Canadian Who's Who, 1955-57

BLOCH, ERNEST July 24, 1880-July 15, 1959 Composer; drew upon his Jewish heritage for his music; associated with the Geneva Conservatory, the Mannes School of Music, the Cleveland Institute of Music, and the San Francisco Conservatory; conducted his own works. See *Current Biography* (September) 1953.

Obituary

N Y Times p27 Jl 16 '59

BLÜCHER, FRANZ Mar. 24, 1896-Mar 26, 1959 West German political leader; Vice Chancellor and Minister of European Co-operation (1949-58) ; West German representative on the High Authority of the European Coal and Steel Community since 1958. See *Current Biography* (January) 1956.

Obituary

N Y Times p23 Mr 27 '59

BOLZ, LOTHAR (bôlts) Sept. 3, 1903- Foreign Minister of East Germany; political leader
Address: b. Ministry of Foreign Affairs, Luisenstrasse 56, Berlin N 4, East Germany

As the Foreign Minister of East Germany, Lothar Bolz was chief of his country's advisory delegation to the major powers' Foreign Ministers' conference in Geneva, Switzerland in May and June 1959. There he attempted to enhance the reputation of his government, as the Foreign Ministers of the United States, Great Britain, France, and the Soviet Union discussed the problems of Berlin, reunification of Germany, and European security. Bolz, after several years of practice as a lawyer in Germany, became a Communist and immigrated to the Soviet Union in 1933. After World War II he returned to East Germany and held various positions in the Communist regime established there, becoming Foreign Minister in 1953.

Lothar Bolz, the son of a German watchmaker from Upper Silesia, was born on September 3, 1903 in Gleiwitz, Germany. He attended the Oberrealschule (secondary school) there, and after his graduation, he studied law, literature, and art history at the universities of Munich, Kiel, and Breslau. From the latter university he received a doctor of laws degree. From 1926 to 1929 he served as a barrister at court for training, without receiving any remuneration, and for the next year he acted as an assistant to a judge in a court. From 1930 to 1933 he was a lawyer practising at the Breslau Court of Appeals.

After the Nazis came to power in Germany in 1933, Bolz fled to the Free City of Danzig and joined the Communist party there. He then emigrated to Poland and the Soviet Union, where he worked variously as a lawyer, schoolteacher, and jurist. Evidently he belonged to the hard core of the German Communist leadership in Moscow during World War II, although his name was never mentioned in official party documents.

At the end of the war his homeland was divided into four zones, occupied and governed by the victors, the United States, Great Britain,

France, and the Soviet Union. Berlin was placed under quadripartite Allied government, with free access to the city through the Soviet zone of Germany guaranteed to the three Western Allies. Returning to the eastern zone of Germany occupied by the Russians, Bolz became in 1948 the chairman of the National Democratic party of Germany (NDPD).

During the summer of 1948 the Soviet Union withdrew from the Allied government of Berlin and, on November 30, 1948, established a separate municipal government in its sector of the city. The British, American, and French sectors were formed into an administrative unit, called West Berlin, which came to be considered as simultaneously a province (although not formally incorporated) and a city of the Federal Republic of Germany, the independent government established in West Germany in 1949.

For ten months in 1948-49 the city of Berlin underwent a crisis while the Russians blocked railways and highways, and the Western powers imposed countermeasures and carried on an airlift. This critical situation subsided in May 1949 as the result of a four-power agreement. At the Foreign Ministers' conference in Paris in June 1949 pledges were made to continue this agreement.

In the newly formed East German government during 1949 to 1950, Bolz was Minister of Reconstruction. The constitution for the German Democratic Republic was promulgated on October 7, 1949, and Bolz became a member for Berlin of the People's Chamber. In addition to fulfilling his tasks as Minister of Reconstruction, in November 1950 he was named a Deputy Premier. During a debate held by the U.N. General Assembly's Special Political Committee in Paris in December 1951 about the possibility of holding all-German elections, Bolz declared that such elections would be tantamount to interference in German internal affairs. He continued by saying that East Germany had attempted to arrange free all-German elections with West Germany, which had repeatedly rejected such a proposal (New York *Herald Tribune,* December 12, 1951).

In June 1952 the National Democratic party, of which Bolz is the head, issued an appeal to every German veteran of World War II to support national unity and a pro-Soviet policy. This was regarded as an effort to exploit the traditional view in an important segment of the German military class of favoring a German alliance with the Soviet Union (New York *Times,* June 18, 1952).

The party is composed primarily of former officers and soldiers in Hitler's armies who were captured by the Russians during World War II. Exploiting German nationalism, the Communists had organized the National Democratic party as an extreme right-wing group to serve as an East-West bridge in the event of unification.

While remaining a Deputy Prime Minister in the East German regime, in September 1953 Bolz assumed the additional duties of Minister of Foreign Affairs. Among the various negotiations which Bolz has undertaken were those

Wide World

LOTHAR BOLZ

with Poland in March 1955, when Red leaders discussed joint security measures in case the Paris and London agreements for West German sovereignty and rearmament were ratified. These agreements went into effect on May 5, 1955, and East Germany entered the Warsaw Pact nine days later with the Soviet Union and other Communist states.

By a Soviet-East German treaty signed on September 20, 1955 the Communist regime of Germany was granted full authority to decide its domestic and foreign policies. At the same time a Soviet letter to Bolz stated that henceforth the East German government would have control over the republic's borders and over all civilian traffic across its territory from West Germany to West Berlin. The personnel and supplies of the British, French, and American garrisons in West Berlin would still be controlled by the Soviets in East Germany, as provided by previous four-power agreements, which specified the road, railway, and air routes for the forces.

The Western Allied governments in a note challenged the Soviet Union to maintain its responsibilities for free communications and transportation between Berlin and West Germany. By a subsequent agreement between the Soviet Union and East Germany in the fall of 1955, as reported in the New York *Times* (January 15, 1956), it appeared that the East Germans had been given legal authority over Allied traffic into Berlin, but that the traffic was still being handled by the Russians. Bolz headed the East German mission, accredited to the Soviet delegation, to the Foreign Ministers' conference held in Geneva in the fall of 1955.

In the beginning of 1957 Bolz and leaders of the three other parties used by the Communists to form the National Front, went to Moscow to seek Soviet economic assistance. They were successful in receiving economic aid in the form of a credit of rubles to be

BOLZ, LOTHAR—*Continued*

granted in gold and free currencies and of raising the amount of trade between the two. The right of East Germany to control the air corridor from West Germany to Berlin was reaffirmed, and the Soviet agreement with the three Western Allied governments regarding traffic to the city was described as being of a "temporary and limited nature" (New York *Times,* January 8, 1957).

Soviet Premier Nikita S. Khrushchev in November 1958 stated that the occupation of Berlin must end, and the city must become demilitarized and free. Unless the Western Allies agreed to this, the Soviet Union would transfer its responsibilities in Berlin to the East Germans. The Soviet Union also asked for the conclusion of separate peace treaties for the two Germanys, which would insure the indefinite partition of Germany as neutralized and disarmed areas. The West refuses to grant recognition to East Germany, or to leave West Berlin, and seeks to maintain Germany's reunification as the ultimate goal.

To negotiate these differences, it was agreed to hold another four-power Foreign Ministers' conference in Geneva in 1959. The two Germanys were invited to attend as advisers, and Dr. Bolz headed the East German delegation. His country felt that their delegation's attendance and minor participation in the conference was new proof that the East German regime had acquired international status. After six weeks of discussions, the foreign ministers decided to recess for three weeks, and to reconvene at a later date in the hope that some areas of agreement could then be reached.

Lothar Bolz is reported by Marquis Childs in the Washington *Post and Times Herald* (May 15, 1959) to have been a Soviet citizen and to have married a Russian woman. He has received various awards and decorations from East Germany, North Korea, and Poland.

References

Christian Sci Mon p7 Je 1 '59
Handbuch der Volkskammer der Deutschen Demokratischen Republik (1957)
International Who's Who, 1958
International Year Book and Statesmen's Who's Who, 1959
Wer ist Wer? (1958)
Who's Who in America, 1958-59

BONSAL, PHILIP WILSON (bŏn'säl) May 22, 1903- United States Ambassador to Cuba

Address: United States Embassy, Havana, Cuba

Among the qualifications that make Philip Wilson Bonsal particularly well suited to fill the currently difficult post of United States Ambassador to Cuba are his fluency in Spanish and his knowledge of Latin American problems. Bonsal, a Foreign Service officer, presented his credentials in Havana in February 1959 when he succeeded Ambassador Earl E. T. Smith. In

an earlier diplomatic assignment, in Colombia, Bonsal had acquired a reputation among South Americans for his coolness toward dictators and his preference for democratic movements.

Philip Wilson Bonsal was born in New York City on May 22, 1903, the second of four sons of the late Stephen Bonsal and Henrietta (Morris) Bonsal. The eldest son, Stephen, Jr., a broker and aviator, died in 1950. Stephen Bonsal, Sr., was a famous correspondent and diplomat. He reported many of the major events of his generation for the New York *Herald,* and as a diplomat he served in Madrid, Peking, and Tokyo. During the peace negotiations at Versailles in 1919 he was confidential interpreter for President Woodrow Wilson and Colonel Edward Mandell House. For his book about these negotiations, *Unfinished Business,* he was awarded a Pulitzer Prize in 1945.

Living during his boyhood in various parts of the world, Philip Bonsal was exposed early to many economic and political climates. He started school in the Philippines, where his father served as secretary to the Governor General and then as commissioner of public utilities. Later Philip Bonsal went to Switzerland to study from 1914 to 1916 at the Institute Sillig in Vevey. He attended St. Paul's School in Concord, New Hampshire from 1916 to 1920 in preparation for Yale University, where he was granted a B.A. degree in 1924. During his college years he was a member of the ROTC and was commissioned a second lieutenant in the Field Artillery. He served in the Officers Reserve Corps from 1924 to 1929.

In 1926 Bonsal started his business career with the American Telephone and Telegraph Company and for nine years served with that company in Cuba, Spain, and Chile. From 1935 to 1937 he was a telephone expert with the Federal Communications Commission.

The State Department appointed Bonsal an officer in the diplomatic service on April 6, 1938. Shortly afterward he was assigned to Havana as vice-consul and in August 1938 was named third secretary of the Embassy. He returned to Washington, D.C. to become a division assistant in the State Department in March 1939. Subsequently he served as assistant chief and acting chief of the division of American Republics and in March 1942 was promoted to chief of the division. During 1941 he had been a United States representative to the North American Regional Engineering Meeting in Washington. He was appointed deputy director of the Office of American Republic Affairs on January 15, 1944.

After about two and a half years with the American Embassy in Madrid, where for several months he was chargé d'affaires, Bonsal became first secretary at The Hague in April 1947. Sent to France the following year, he was political adviser to W. Averell Harriman, United States special representative in Europe, at the Economic Cooperation Administration in Paris from 1948 to 1950. He also held a number of positions successively at the United States Embassy in Paris, achieving the rank of minister in November 1950.

On his return to Washington in early 1952, Bonsal was made director of the Office of

Philippine and Southeast Asian Affairs in the State Department. He served as Far Eastern adviser to the United States delegation to the Ninth Session of the United Nations General Assembly, opening in September 1954. Earlier in the year he had been adviser at the Geneva conference dealing with problems in Korea and Indochina.

Philip Bonsal's first post as Ambassador was in Bogotá, Colombia. While in office there, from 1955 to 1957, he took advantage of his fluent Spanish to mingle with the intellectuals and political malcontents, including Alberto Lleras Camargo. Here he earned his reputation among South Americans as a diplomat who can tell the difference between a dictatorship and a democracy, and openly favors the latter. He was cordial to President Gustavo Rojas Pinilla, often criticized for dictatorial policies, but Bonsal's friendliness toward the opposition earned him the President's disfavor. Soon after the Ambassador left the country for another assignment, the Rojas Pinilla regime was overthrown, in May 1957. Bonsal revisited Colombia in August 1958 to attend the inauguration of President Lleras Camargo.

On March 28, 1957 Bonsal was appointed Ambassador to Bolivia, a country struggling with severe economic problems, including inflation and rock-bottom tin prices. The *World-Telegram and Sun* (January 22, 1959) noted that Bonsal has been credited with playing a major role in averting a swing to communism there by associating with oil workers and miners as well as intellectuals.

Philip W. Bonsal was nominated by President Eisenhower on January 21, 1959 to be Ambassador to Cuba. This nomination was approved by the Senate on February 16. Bonsal succeeded Earl E. T. Smith, who resigned shortly after Fidel Castro's rebel forces gained control of the Cuban government during the first few days of 1959, following the overthrow of Fulgencio Batista. Castro, who became Premier in February 1959, had accused Smith of favoring Batista. He found Bonsal "friendly, cordial and knowledgeable about Cuba. A good ambassador" (*Time,* March 16, 1959).

When he arrived at the Havana airport in February 1959, Ambassador Bonsal at once walked up to one of Castro's bearded rebels, shook his hand, and expressed admiration for the courage of the Cubans in their revolution. "It was an act," stated the *Christian Science Monitor* (March 5, 1959), "widely reported in the Cuban press that endeared him immediately to Cubans, as has been demonstrated on several occasions since." Bonsal's father had won the respect of Cuban rebels of another generation when, in 1897, he wrote *The Real Condition of Cuba.*

One cause of friction between the United States and the new Cuban government was that the former had allowed officials of the Batista regime to take refuge in the United States. Bonsal said at a press conference in March 1959 that Cuban requests for extradition of these refugees for trial as war criminals would be considered in accordance with an existing American-Cuban extradition agreement. When Cuban newsmen asked him to comment on the

Dept. of State—Whit Keith, Jr.
PHILIP WILSON BONSAL

revolutionary government's assumption of control of the American-owned Cuban Telephone Company, he replied that it was a matter between the users and suppliers of telephone service.

Philip Wilson Bonsal is a slender man, about six feet tall. He has an engaging manner, and his friends describe him as "cool and smooth—but tough when he needs to be" (New York *World-Telegram and Sun,* January 22, 1959). On April 10, 1929 Bonsal married Margaret Lockett of Knoxville, Tennessee, whom he met in Spain where she was traveling with her mother. Their permanent home is in the old Georgetown section of Washington, D.C. They like pets, especially "Puddin," a golden cocker spaniel, and their hobbies include long walks, horseback riding, and mountain climbing. Bonsal belongs to the Century Club in New York City and the Metropolitan Club in Washington.

References

    N Y Times p7 Ja 22 '59 por
    N Y World-Telegram p20 Ja 22 '59
    Time 73:49 Ja 26 '59 por
    U S News 46:21 Ja 30 '59 por
    Department of State Biographic Register, 1958
    Who's Who in America, 1958-59

BOONE, PAT June 1, 1934- Singer
Address: b. c/o Randy Wood-Jack Spina Agency, 6 W. 57th St., New York 19; General Artists Corp., 640 5th Ave., New York 19

One of the few singing stars idolized not only by millions of American teen-agers but by their parents as well is the youthful and clean-cut Pat Boone. His records have sold more than 20,000,000 copies, he has starred in three suc-

PAT BOONE

cessful motion pictures, and he appears in his own television show, *The Pat Boone Chevy Showroom.* His book, *'Twixt Twelve and Twenty* (Prentice-Hall, 1958), offering advice to the young, ranked high on the nonfiction list of best sellers for 1959.

While recording such jukebox hits as "Love Letters in the Sand" and "Friendly Persuasion," Boone attended Columbia University and was graduated in June 1958. In addition to following a high-pressured career as an entertainer, he is a family man with four daughters and an active evangelical and youth worker in the Church of Christ.

Charles Eugene Boone was born in Jacksonville, Florida on June 1, 1934 to Archie and Margaret Boone, who nicknamed him Pat. He has a younger brother, Nick, and two sisters, Margie and Judy. His father, a descendant of the pioneer woodsman Daniel Boone, moved his family to Donelson, Tennessee in 1936. He is a building contractor. Pat's mother had been a registered nurse. The Boone family moved to Nashville when Pat was six. He began singing in public at the age of ten.

Pat's father bought a cow which the boy learned to milk. "I found the barn with nobody there but Rosemary and me, a fine place to think—and to dream. When my brother decided to be baptized, and my parents asked me if I was ready, I held back," Pat wrote in his book, *'Twixt Twelve and Twenty.* "One evening out in the barn I finally realized that for me the Bible had the answers. That the teachings of Jesus answered all the questions I was asking. . . I was baptized in the Church of Christ shortly before my thirteenth birthday. . . . I didn't become a good Christian overnight. In fact I got my last spanking when I was seventeen."

At David Lipscomb High School Pat Boone was on the baseball, basketball, and track teams and was reporter-cartoonist on the school paper. He became president of the student body, was star of dramatic and musical productions, and was elected "most popular boy." In his junior year he met Shirley Foley, daughter of radio and TV singer Red Foley.

In his book Pat Boone has tried to explain why he and Shirley Foley eloped when they were nineteen. He had his own radio program, *Youth on Parade,* on station WSIX in Nashville. He had made three appearances in New York on *Ted Mack's Amateurs.* He felt that he could finish his studies at David Lipscomb College while supporting a wife. They were married on November 7, 1953.

"We both were twenty years old and waiting for our first child when we went to live in Denton [Texas]," Mrs. Boone wrote in *McCall's* (February 1958). "We owned a Bible, a pair of chinchillas [one of Pat's cheerfully naive ideas for getting rich], and a 1949 Chevy." Pat Boone's job, on the Fort Worth WBAP-TV station, paid $44.50 a week. In addition, he received a gallon of ice cream and two quarts of cottage cheese from the sponsor, a dairy company.

In Denton, Pat Boone enrolled at North Texas State College. His TV fans encouraged him to try his luck with *Arthur Godfrey's Talent Scouts.* He went to New York, won the audition, and then returned to Texas. Randy Wood, head of Dot Records, signed the young college student to a contract. In 1955 Wood launched Pat in the highly competitive record field with a song, "Two Hearts," which reached the top ten on the record seller charts. In August 1955 Boone joined the Godfrey programs on CBS-TV in New York. He also enrolled as a junior at Columbia University, but soon took a leave of absence from college to star in two films, *Bernardine* and *April Love,* for Twentieth Century-Fox Film Corporation.

Commenting on Pat Boone's motion picture debut in *Bernardine* (based on Mary Chase's stage play), the New York *Times* reviewer (July 25, 1957) wrote: "Meet a singing teenage idol—a sunny, clean-cut youth of manly mien and fine voice—with a real screen future, in a wholesome, pleasant comedy about adolescence." Another reviewer also predicted that he would "go far and do much, given half an opportunity" (New York *Post,* July 18). William Peper in the New York *World-Telegram and Sun* (July 25) wrote that Boone "obviously is out to become his generation's Bing Crosby. He has carefully copied the master's elaborately casual manner and his deep-throated purring of a song. Mr. Boone is pretty good at it, in an overly studied way, but it still is an imitation."

Boone's millionth record sale of the title song in his second picture, *April Love,* coincided with the release of the film in November 1957. Appearing opposite Shirley Jones, Pat Boone portrayed a city boy who learns to master harness racing in Kentucky. "Two of the nicest-looking young singers to be found anywhere," observed the New York *Times* (November 28, 1957), "a batch of pleasant tunes . . . but it's high time they gave such a nice lad a picture with a few teeth to it."

When Pat Boone turned down lucrative offers which would have interfered with his college education, he explained, "Too many teen-agers want to quit school. I can't set a bad example. Besides, I'll need an education to support my family if this bubble ever bursts" (*Coronet,* December 1957). He received his B.S. degree from Columbia University in June 1958, graduating *magna cum laude*.

During the summer of 1958 Pat Boone and his family went to California to make his third picture, *Mardi Gras.* "Boone sings in his wholehearted but courteously wholesome manner a great many songs calculated to touch the very young feminine heart," noted the New York *Herald Tribune* reviewer (November 19, 1958).

In January 1957 Boone signed a seven-year $1,000,000 contract with Twentieth Century-Fox Film Corporation and also a $1,000,000-a-year contract with ABC-TV for his weekly *The Pat Boone Chevy Showroom,* owned by his Cooga Mooga, Inc. The corporation also sells a large variety of Pat Boone products, such as shoes, watches, luggage, and lamps.

Other Boone business ventures include two music publishing companies, a restaurant in Denton, and oil wells in the Southwest. In March 1959 Pat Boone joined the Townsend Investment Company in a $1,000,000 transaction involving the purchase of two radio stations, WKDA in Nashville, Tennessee and KNOK in Fort Worth, Texas. The United States Junior Chamber of Commerce selected him as one of the ten outstanding young men of 1958.

With his wife, Shirley, and their four daughters (Cheryl Lynn, Linda Lee, Deborah Ann, and Laura Gene), Pat Boone now lives in a large house in Teaneck, New Jersey. Artist Jon Whitcomb described him in *Cosmopolitan* (November 1957) as "a stocky, sturdily built male with amber-colored eyes, light brown, slightly wavy hair," and added that "his speaking voice is warm and caressing." He is six feet tall and weighs 180 pounds. Although he had never taken singing lessons before he attained fame, he now has a voice coach. He finds that ball playing—pitching and catching backstage—relaxes him for singing. He works out in YMCA gymnasiums while on tour.

In *'Twixt Twelve and Twenty* Pat Boone lists maxims for teen-agers. Some of them are: apply the Golden Rule in your attitude around the house; learn to laugh at yourself. He recommends "dime insurance—calling home to let your parents know where you are and if you are going to be late." He does not approve of smoking or drinking, and he admits in his book that as a teen-ager he "made mistakes."

Pat Boone attends church three times a week. He has preached guest sermons to Church of Christ congregations and he was recently elected to the board of directors for the Northeastern Institute for Christian Education. The idea of teaching still attracts him.

References

Coronet 43:8 D '57 por
Cosmop 143:66 N '57
Life 46:75 F 2 '59 pors
Look 22:81 Ag 5 '58 pors
Parade p8 S 28 '58 pors

Boone, Pat 'Twixt Twelve and Twenty (1958)
International Motion Picture Almanac, 1959
Wood, Carlyle TV Personalities vol 3 (1957)

BOWDITCH, RICHARD L(YON) Oct. 11, 1900-July 31, 1959 Business executive; president, C. H. Sprague and Son Company (1935-54); president, Chamber of Commerce of the United States (1953-54). See *Current Biography* (July) 1953.

Obituary

N Y Times p81 Ag 2 '59

BOWERS, FAUBION (fō'bĭ-ŏn) Jan. 29, 1917- Writer
Address: b. c/o Thomas Nelson & Sons, 19 E. 47th St., New York 17

Much of the current interest of Americans in the dance and theater of Asia can be traced to the books and articles of the widely-traveled and cosmopolitan Faubion Bowers. A former pianist turned writer, he has interpreted for the West such unfamiliar arts of the Orient as Kabuki, the celebrated classical theater of Japan. The survival of Kabuki and its postwar renaissance during the American occupation owed a great deal to the efforts of Bowers, who served first as military aide, then as civilian censor under the administration of General Douglas MacArthur. His *Japanese Theatre* (1952), *Dance in India* (1953), *Theatre in the East* (1956), and *Broadway, U.S.S.R.* (1959) have helped bring about a meeting of minds in the cultural interchange between the East, the Soviet Union, and the West.

Bowers has turned the attention of Western readers to the arts of the dance and the theater in the Orient at a time when they are imperiled. The decline of the caste system under the impact of Western democratization, the infiltration of American mass media, and the relinquishing of patronage on the part of a dwindling aristocracy have threatened traditional forms with extinction.

Of Irish, German, English, and Scottish extraction, Faubion Bowers was born on January 29, 1917 in the cattle-raising and meat-packing town of Miami, Oklahoma, not too far from Bartlesville. His mother taught school in Oklahoma. After he was graduated from the Central High School in Tulsa, Oklahoma in 1933, he entered the University of Oklahoma, where he studied until 1935. Bowers transferred to Columbia University in 1936, and in the following year went to France to study at the University of Poitiers. He received no degree for his college courses.

Helped by a scholarship, Bowers began to groom himself for a career as a concert pianist at the Juilliard School of Music in New York City in 1939. Eventually he became "depressed by the thought of all those little fingers hammering away so fast" and the prospect of a

Frances McLaughlin

FAUBION BOWERS

grimly competitive concert career. Influenced by recordings of Japanese and Javanese music, he lost interest in pianism, bought a ticket for Japan, and set out for that country in 1940.

With some experience in teaching music behind him (he had taught modern harmony at the Groupe Estivale pour la Musique Moderne in Paris in 1937), Bowers was able to secure a post at the Hosei University in Tokyo. Until the rumblings of approaching war forced him to leave for Java in 1941, Bowers devoted himself to further study of the Asian theater and dance. In 1941 he lectured at Taman Siswa in Jogjakarta in Java.

When the United States entered World War II in 1941, Bowers was drafted into the Army as a private. Because of his talent for languages, he became the first person ever to be commissioned as an officer from the ranks on the basis of linguistic ability. He was assigned to Military Intelligence as a Japanese language interrogator and interpreter. A major by 1945, he was the first American soldier to set foot on Japanese soil with the advance party on August 28, 1945. Later, as an aide to General Douglas MacArthur in the American Embassy in Tokyo, Bowers was the first foreigner to greet Emperor Hirohito when he called on the general shortly after the beginning of the occupation.

For his meritorious achievement during the war, Bowers was awarded the Bronze Star, to which an Oak Leaf Cluster was added for his work with the advance party. He was also cited for his achievement as a civilian censor of the Japanese theater.

One of Bowers' duties as an aide to General MacArthur was the suppression of the Kabuki theater, at the command of his superior. American officialdom viewed Kabuki as "feudal" because it praised the virtues of aristocratic ancestral heroes and might undermine the demo-cratic principles that the occupation was trying to impose upon the people from above.

"When the occupation banned Japan's classical theater," Bowers recalls, "I resigned from the Army and took over the civilian job of censor of the theater and reinstated the banned plays." Local wits soon referred to him as "not censor, but sponsor," because he encouraged Americans to attend the plays. Among the other foreigners who came was Santha Rama Rau, daughter of the Ambassador of India to Tokyo, who describes her first encounter with both Kabuki and Bowers in her book, *East of Home* (Harper, 1950). With Santha Rama Rau, an American girl, and an English boy, Bowers hitchhiked through the provinces of northern China after leaving Japan; they went on to Indochina, Siam, and Indonesia. The tour ended in a six-month stay in Bali, where Bowers was pressed into dancing at one of the local village festivals.

His study tours of dance and drama have taken Bowers to diverse corners of the world. Besides France, where he was married to Santha Rama Rau, and Spain, where they honeymooned, his wife and he have at times lived in New York City and in India. On their 1954-55 study tour they traveled in fourteen countries; on their 1957-59 tour they visited the Soviet Union and England. From distant places Bowers sent back articles which appeared in the *New Yorker,* the New York *Herald Tribune, Theatre Arts, Dance,* and *United Nations World;* he also sent back dispatches to Reuters from India. Both Santha Rama Rau and Faubion Bowers wrote books about their three months in the Soviet Union: hers was *My Russian Journey* (Harper, 1959) and his was *Broadway, U.S.S.R.* (Nelson, 1959).

Faubion Bowers' first book, *Japanese Theatre,* was published by Hermitage Press in 1952, and re-issued as a paperback by Hill & Wang in 1959. Reviewing it in the New York *Times* (October 12, 1952), Paul Green stated: "A number of fine critical appraisals and histories of the Japanese theater have been published in France and Germany, but few in America. . . . Faubion Bowers has now brought the subject into fine and living notice again."

In 1953 Columbia University Press published Bowers' *Dance in India,* his attempt to survey the Indian dance of today with the purpose of bringing it nearer the understanding of non-Indians. A critical note in the *United States Quarterly Book Review* (June 1954) declared: "Entirely based on its author's firsthand observations, this study of the Indian dance is remarkably thorough and informative, notwithstanding the modesty of its size and presentation."

Walter Terry, the dance critic of the New York *Herald Tribune,* commended Bowers' third book, *Theatre in the East* (Nelson, 1956) for its superlative reporting, lucid analyses, and its constant awareness of the dance as a mirror of national culture, religion, and ethics. He went on to recommend the book as a helpful text for Congressmen and diplomats (August 5, 1956).

When Terry reviewed Bowers' *Broadway, U.S.S.R.* in the New York *Herald Tribune* of

April 25, 1959, he commented: "He [Bowers] is able to report not only on the theater in the Soviet Union at its best but also at its most trivial. He tells us . . . how fabulous are the feats of circus stars, how enchanting are animal acts, how the Russians themselves poke fun at their own government and system in the satire theater and in variety acts, and . . . how much the theater means to the ordinary Russian, and how the government supports with incredible generosity its arts and its artists." Brooks Atkinson (New York *Times,* April 12, 1959) approved of the felicitous combination of "receptivity and detachment" that generated confidence in the author on the part of the reader.

On October 20, 1951 Faubion Bowers and Santha Rama Rau were married in France. They have one child, a son named Jai Peter. Bowers stands at six feet tall, weighs 185 pounds, and has brown hair and brown eyes. Although he was reared as a Christian, he now disclaims any religious affiliation. He founded the Oklahoma chapter of the Alexander Scriabin Circle, and in 1959 he was working on a study of the Russian composer. In paying tribute to his favorite form of art he once said: "Words can sometimes lie. Only dance tells nothing but the truth."

References

Dance Mag 27:41+ O '53 por

Rama Rau, Santha   East of Home (1950)

BOWERS, MRS. FAUBION   *See* Rama Rau, Santha

BRIGHAM, CLARENCE S(AUNDERS)
Aug. 5, 1877-   Library director; antiquarian; bibliographer; archivist
Address: b. American Antiquarian Society, Salisbury St. and Park Ave., Worcester, Mass.; h. 34 Cedar St., Worcester, Mass.

The upholding of the American Antiquarian Society's pre-eminent position as a library of Americana for the use of advanced researchers has been the responsibility of Clarence S. Brigham for more than a quarter of a century. As its director since 1930 and its president since 1955, the "dean of American antiquarians" has made a notable contribution to the wealth of its resources by exercising a vigilant control over the development of its collections.

Since the publication of his first book in 1900, Brigham has continued to enrich American historical scholarship with his contributions to the study of Americana. His *History and Bibliography of American Newspapers, 1690-1820* remains the primary source for research in the history of early American journalism. Brigham can claim that his association with the American Antiquarian Society actually extends back for more than half a century, for he joined the staff of the society as its librarian in 1908.

Clarence Saunders Brigham was born in Providence, Rhode Island on August 5, 1877, the son of John Olin and Alice (Saunders) Brigham. He has one brother, Herbert Olin

Fabian Bachrach

CLARENCE S. BRIGHAM

Brigham, who is the librarian of the Newport (Rhode Island) Historical Society. After attending the English and Classical School in Providence, Brigham went on to Brown University, from which he was graduated in 1899 with the A.B. degree. In the same year he became an assistant on the staff of the library of Brown University. In 1900 he became the librarian of the Rhode Island Historical Society, and during his eight years there first displayed the devotion to the cause of historical scholarship that later characterized his long tenure with the American Antiquarian Society. In 1908 he joined the staff of the American Antiquarian Society as its librarian.

Since its inception in 1812, the American Antiquarian Society has prided itself on a membership unequaled for distinction in the United States. Its founder and first president, Isaiah Thomas (1749-1831), was the leading publisher and printer of his day. Evidence of its early prestige is the fact that in 1814, by a special act of Congress, the society was made the official recipient of all documents printed and distributed by the government.

Several Presidents of the United States have at one time or another held membership in the society. Among them was Calvin Coolidge, who served as president of the society from 1929 to 1933. He became a close friend of Clarence S. Brigham, who likes to puncture the myth that Coolidge was a man of taciturnity and granitic reserve.

When Brigham became librarian in 1908, the society was entering a critical phase. Clifford K. Shipton, the present librarian, described the situation to a reporter on the Worcester *Sunday Telegram* (January 11, 1959): "By 1900 it [the society] seemed like so many similar organizations to be destined to become a social and antiquarian organization of no significance to the scholarly world. It is due to the vision,

BRIGHAM, CLARENCE S.—*Continued*

the foresight, and the vigorous collecting of Clarence Brigham that the institution has become again a primary organization of the nation in its field."

Brigham's influence soon became evident after he took the position of librarian. He began to define the purposes of the society more rigorously by disposing of items not really pertinent to American history. Many items of anthropological interest or mere local relics were exchanged or sold, and the proceeds were used to buy the printed materials that Brigham judged really important. By 1939 the library had grown from the 99,000 volumes it had possessed in 1908 to 600,000 volumes, plus a half million manuscripts, maps, newspapers, pamphlets, broadsides, and prints. More than twenty miles of continuous shelves contain about seventy-five per cent of all recorded matter printed in North America up to 1820.

In 1913 Brigham began the formidable task of compiling a bibliography of early American newspapers. When he started, he planned to finish the work in five years, but it took him thirty-four years to bring it to completion. This checklist of 2,120 early American newspapers, indicating their location in American libraries, was published in eighteen installments between 1913 and 1927 in the *Proceedings* of the American Antiquarian Society.

For twenty more years publication was delayed; by the time the material was in final form the demands of World War II had cut down book production. It was not until 1947 that the *History and Bibliography of American Newspapers, 1690-1820* was published by the society in two volumes.

In the introduction to his *Journals and Journeymen* (University of Pennsylvania Press, 1950) Brigham stated: "The compilation of the *Bibliography* was a lone undertaking, not a summary of what others had written, but the result of personal research. [It] required travel of about 10,000 miles and examination of files in nearly four hundred towns and cities in thirty different states."

For more than half a century Brigham has continued to write in his elected field of interest, beginning in 1900 with *A Memorial of Amos Perry,* which appeared soon after his graduation from college. In 1902 he wrote a *History of Rhode Island* and a *Bibliography of Rhode Island History. Seventeenth Century Place-names of Providence* followed in 1903; *Report on the Archives of Rhode Island* appeared in 1904, and *The Narragansett Indians* in 1905.

The administrative duties that came with Brigham's appointment as director of the American Antiquarian Society in 1930 did not check his productivity in historical and bibliographical scholarshp. Among the articles and monographs that Brigham wrote after 1930 are *Poe's "Balloon Hoax"* (1932); *Cabon's History of Hayti Journalism* (1940); *David Claypoole Johnston* (1941); *American Booksellers' Catalogues* (1951); and *Paul Revere's Engravings* (1954).

Among the works that Brigham has edited are: *Records of the Town of Portsmouth* (1901); *The Harris Papers* (1902); *Major*

Butler's Fourth Paper (1903); and *Royal Proclamations Concerning America* (1911).

In *Fifty Years of Collecting Americana for the Library of the American Antiquarian Society, 1908-1958* (published by the society in 1958) Brigham discusses the various collections he has developed over the years. He describes fifty-two specialties ranging from early American almanacs and amateur journals through circusiana, first editions, and Hawaiiana to psalmody, watermarks, and Western narratives.

When Brown University conferred an honorary degree on Clarence S. Brigham in 1909, its then president, William Herbert Perry Faunce, described him as a "conscientious explorer of the facts and principles on which our national life is built." Brown honored Brigham a second time in 1934 with a Litt.D.; Clark University awarded him the same degree in 1948. Brigham belongs to the American Historical Association, the Bibliographical Society of America, and the Society for American Archaeology.

Clarence Saunders Brigham married Alice L. Comstock on November 12, 1910. She died in November 1958. His daughter Elizabeth is married to William J. McKee, Jr. of Worcester. Brigham, an inveterate pipe smoker, is always impeccably dressed. Scholars and researchers who visit the American Antiquarian Society have been impressed by its director's prodigious feats of memory.

The American historian Samuel Eliot Morison has said that " 'Brig', like the Canadian Mounties, who always get their man, always gets his fact." Esther Forbes, who has used the resources of the library a great deal, praises him for his "sense of hospitality, scholarship, warmth, and charm."

References

Worcester Sunday Telegram Feature Parade p3 Ja 11 '59 por
Who's Who in America, 1958-59

BRINTON, (CLARENCE) CRANE Feb. 2, 1898- Historian

Address: b. Widener Library 98, Cambridge 38, Mass.; h. 60 Buckingham St., Cambridge 38, Mass.

An authority on the history of ideas and an expert on the theory of revolution, Crane Brinton is McLean Professor of Ancient and Modern History at Harvard University. His many books, including *The Anatomy of Revolution* (1938) *Ideas and Men* (1950), and *A History of Western Morals* (1959), are held in high regard for their originality, ironic outlook, astute analysis, and readability.

Summarizing the history of his own ideas, Brinton wrote on the occasion of the twenty-fifth anniversary of his Harvard class: "While my earlier optimistic rationalism has been tempered by an awareness of the place of prejudices, sentiments, the unconscious and the subconscious, in human life. . . . I think I have kept to the basic belief of my youth in the rightness of human reason."

Born in Winsted, Connecticut on February 2, 1898, Clarence Crane Brinton was the only child of Clarence Hawthorne Brinton, a department store buyer, and Eva Josephine (Crane) Brinton. His ancestors on both sides were New England farmers. At a time, he recalls, "when they still gave a 'classical' education," he was educated in the public schools of Springfield, Massachusetts. At Springfield Central (now Classical) High School, from which he was graduated in 1915, he made debating and journalism his extracurricular activities.

Entering Harvard University in 1915, Brinton came under the "fantastically contradictory influences" of Irving Babbitt and Harold J. Laski. An exceptional student, he received scholarships in each of his four years at Harvard, won the Bowdoin Prize and the Shaw Traveling Fellowship, was elected to Phi Beta Kappa, and was graduated with the B.A. degree *summa cum laude* in 1919. When the United States entered World War I, Brinton served as a private in the Students' Army Training Corps.

Awarded a Rhodes Scholarship, Brinton studied at New College, Oxford University, where he earned the Ph.D. degree in 1923. His dissertation, published by Oxford University Press in 1926 as *The Political Ideas of the English Romanticists,* synthesized the observations of prominent thinkers of the period and analyzed such trends as the rejection of aesthetic canons, the renunciation of rationalism, the loss of power by the landed aristocracy, and the engulfing of rural life by industrial civilization. A reviewer in the London *Times Literary Supplement* (August 19, 1926) found that the book had "none of the tameness and rigidity" which usually characterize doctoral theses.

Since 1923 Brinton has been teaching at Harvard University except for a period he calls "a wartime change of status from professor to bureaucrat," referring to his service as special assistant with the Office of Strategic Services, Theater of European Operations from 1942 to 1945. At Harvard he became an assistant professor in 1927, associate professor in 1934, and full professor in 1942.

In student circles in Cambridge Brinton is considered a genial and popular lecturer, and the casual informality of his morning class has led it to be known as "breakfast with Brinton." As an exchange professor and guest lecturer, Brinton has taught at various American colleges and universities, including Pomona College, University of Virginia, Knox College, and Beloit College.

One of the earliest of Brinton's many books was *A Decade of Revolution* (Harper, 1934), a political and military history of the French Revolution which related the social, economic, and religious tendencies of the period to the larger developments of European civilization. In a review for *Commonweal* (May 1, 1935), George N. Shuster wrote: "In this book American historical writing definitely proves itself to have come of age. The author is not caught in the toils of economist onesidedness, but is as sensitively aware of the march of ideas as the best French and German writers."

John Brook

CRANE BRINTON

In *The Anatomy of Revolution* (Norton, 1938; Prentice-Hall, 1952) Brinton examined the causes, courses, and consequences of four revolutions—the Puritan revolt in England and the American, French, and Russian revolutions. He maintained that revolutions follow similar patterns: structural weaknesses and increasing conflicts within the traditional order leading to the disaffection of the intelligentsia; the awakening of the masses; rule by moderate revolutionaries and their failure; the coming to power of extremists; the reign of terror; the reaction; and the final consolidation of the revolt under a dictatorial figure.

In the preface to a paperback edition of *The Anatomy of Revolution* (Vintage, 1957) Brinton commented that "events in Russia since the death of Stalin surely reinforce the commonplace that the great Russian Revolution is quite over, finished. What is going on now is a working out of what went on from 1917 to 1924, the years of what may be called the Russian Revolution proper. That working out must be very different from the working out of the 'principles of 1776 and 1789.'" Brinton agrees with contemporary writers who have observed that the Russian, American, French, and English rebellions were revolutions from the Left, but that while the first took place in a backward nation, the other upheavals occurred in advanced countries.

World War II and its aftermath next absorbed Brinton's intellectual energies. *Nietzsche* (Harvard University Press, 1941) was not an abstract philosophical analysis, but "an attempt to place Nietzsche's work in the more general currents of 'opinion' in our time," he stated in his preface. *The United States and Britain* (Harvard University Press, 1945; 1948), for which Brinton's two-year war mission in England provided materials, analyzed Anglo-Amer-

BRINTON, CRANE—*Continued*

ican relations and made a plea for increased co-operation.

From Many One; The Progress of Political Integration and the Problem of World Government (Harvard University Press, 1948) is a study of the perplexities involved in developing one world. *The Temper of Western Europe* (Harvard University Press, 1953) surveys the West European scene and its achievements in the postwar era.

With *Ideas and Men; The Story of Western Thought* (Prentice-Hall, 1950), Brinton broadened his field to include Western thought from classical times to the present. Critics agreed that Brinton, with his usual wit, lucidity, and grace, had brought order out of chaos and imposed patterns of meaning on the jumbled complexities of intellectual history. The second half of *Ideas and Men,* covering the period since the Renaissance, has been republished as a paperback under the title, *The Shaping of the Modern Mind* (Mentor, 1953).

In *A History of Western Morals* (Harcourt, 1959) Brinton presents a "moderately hopeful history" of an aspect of the Occidental world which he considers "important, difficult, and relatively neglected." His survey of Western moral development begins with the early Egyptians and ends in the modern age. With characteristic urbanity, Brinton entitles his final chapter "Conclusion: In Which Nothing is Concluded."

Brinton's other books include *The Jacobins; An Essay in the New History* (Macmillan, 1930); *English Political Thought in the Nineteenth Century* (Benn, 1933; Harvard University Press, 1949); and *French Revolutionary Legislation on Illegitimacy, 1789-1804* (Harvard University Press, 1936); and *The Lives of Talleyrand* (Norton, 1936). He edited *The Portable Age of Reason Reader* (Viking, 1956) and has collaborated on other works. From 1936 to 1943 Brinton edited the *American Oxonian,* and from 1939 to 1942 served on the editorial board of the *American Scholar.* Since 1939 he has been on the board of editors of the *Journal of the History of Ideas.*

The historian has been a senior fellow of Harvard's Society of Fellows since 1939 and its chairman since 1942, a fellow of the Royal Historical Society (England), and a member of the American Historical Association, American Philosophical Society, American Academy of Arts and Sciences, and National Institute of Arts and Letters. His clubs are the Harvard and Massachusetts Forest and Park Association (Boston), Century Association (New York), and Green Mountain. From 1936 to 1942 he was director of the Association of American Rhodes Scholars, and in 1950 he was elected vice-president of the Société d'Histoire Politique et Constitutionnelle.

In 1950 Brinton was elected a Chevalier of the French Legion of Honor. He holds honorary degrees from Ripon College (1951) and Kenyon College (1952).

On December 18, 1946 Crane Brinton was married to Mrs. Cecilia Washburn Roberts, a psychologist. He describes his hobbies as the "good academic ones of gardening (summers in Peacham, Vermont), walking, and detective stories." Brinton has blue eyes, white hair, stands five feet eleven inches, and weighs 184 pounds. He has no religious affiliation and usually votes Democratic. He has named Freud a better guide for modern man than Marx, because of the Freudian belief that "the individual must summon from within himself the energies and the wisdom that will free him" (*Saturday Review,* May 5, 1956).

References

Twentieth Century Authors (1942; First Supplement, 1955)
Who's Who in America, 1958-59

BROOKS, JAMES (D.)   Oct. 18, 1906-
Artist

Address: h. 500 W. Broadway, New York 12

The abstract canvases of James Brooks with their curvilinear flow, coursing rhythms, contrasting colors, and well-controlled harmonies have suggested analogues of nature and expressions of the subconscious. In the postwar era Brooks began to explore objectless, complex, abstract art and has since become identified with the New York school. Before that period he had had a career as an historical and allegorical muralist in the 1930's and early 1940's. His murals are in the post office in Little Falls, New Jersey, the Woodside Library in Queens, New York, and the La Guardia Airport in Queens, and his abstract paintings are in the permanent collections of major museums in the United States. Brooks has taught at Columbia University and at Pratt Institute in Brooklyn, New York.

James D. Brooks was born on October 18, 1906 in St. Louis, Missouri to William Rodolphus Brooks and the former Abigail F. Williamson. His father, who was originally from Georgia, and his mother, who was from Tennessee, met at the Louisiana Purchase Exposition at St. Louis in 1904. He has one brother and two sisters. Because William Brooks was a traveling salesman, the family lived in a succession of places in Oklahoma, Colorado, and Texas.

In Dallas James Brooks was graduated from the Oak Cliff High School in 1922 and attended Southern Methodist University, where he majored in art and joined the Kappa Sigma fraternity. After two years at the university, he enrolled at the Art Students League of New York to study with Boardman Robinson and Kimon Nicolaides, earning his tuition by working as a letterer. Later, he continued his art instruction with Wallace Harrison.

During the early 1930's Brooks was an easel painter who based his subjects primarily on the regions where he had grown up. When the Work Projects Administration's Federal Art Project was created, he joined the program at a salary of $22.50 a week. With the WPA he worked as a muralist and decorated various public buildings in the New York area. His mural at the Woodside Library in Queens (1938) depicts the settlement of Long Island.

From 1939 to 1942 Brooks worked on the sketching and painting of the mural *Flight,* which covers an area of about 2,880 square feet around the rotunda of the Marine Air Terminal Building at La Guardia Airport in Queens. The design is intended, Brooks explained, to "re-create the wonder that was and still is felt at the phenomenon of man's leaving the earth and soaring through the air. It utilizes not historical events, but historical attitudes toward flying . . . man's yearning for flight and its final realization" (New York *Times,* June 23, 1940).

Edward Alden Jewell (New York *Times,* September 20, 1942) prophetically commented: "The most effective panels of all seem those filled with a profusion of bright-colored symbols. . . . These essentially abstract shapes are introduced with skill and painted with piquant decorative cunning."

In 1942 Brooks joined the Army as a private and was active until 1945 on detached service with the historical division in the Near East. After his discharge with the rank of technical sergeant, he returned to New York. "With a sense of reawakening and release," Brooks began to experiment in nonobjective painting. On his work in this genre Brooks has commented: "It says little to those occupied with only its peripheral aspects, so interesting to talk and write about. It will not return to nature, as it is a part of nature. Its meaning is carried in its relationships; and the shapes, colors, and things in it exist not as separate entities at all, but as carriers. The impulse they transmit through the painting is its spirit, image, and meaning."

In addition to working as a painter, Brooks was an instructor in drawing at Columbia University, and since 1947 has been an instructor at Pratt Institute in Brooklyn. At Yale University he was a visiting critic of advanced painting from 1955 to 1958.

When the first one-man exhibition of Brooks' abstractions was held in New York's Peridot Gallery in 1949, the artist established himself as a creator of curvilinear forms that gracefully glide, intersect, and flow together. In each successive year through 1953 a one-man show followed at the gallery. The 1953 exhibition contained several pictures concentrating on a single color in which tonal variations created form and space relations. Another solo show was held in 1952 at the Miller-Pollard Gallery in Seattle.

The Grace Borgenicht Gallery exhibited Brooks' paintings and also three hanging scrolls in 1954. Several of the canvases were swirling, eddying areas of exciting color and others were marvels of manipulated space. The reviewer for *Art News* (February 1954) commented: "As in the past, each of his paintings captures a moment of chaos and fixes it, crisply and neatly, in an overall pattern. . . . Brooks offers no footholds for psychological comment or literary analogy. Any trope one might use is simply a measure of desperation to refer the pictures beyond themselves."

JAMES BROOKS

Another one-man show was held at the Stable Gallery during March and April of 1957. *Art News* (April 1957) reported that "his abstractions mostly count as naturalism when one means the nature of the artist. . . . His style is extrovert . . . Brooks seems not to have thought, so much as to have come to terms with his feelings."

The New York *Times* critic noted (March 26, 1957) that he interprets "spring mornings with earth, lake, and sky distilled and expressed. . . . He treats the canvas as a plane surface, yet his compositions seem like landscapes seen from a high vantage point unfolding luxuriously in vertically defined space."

In his "crystal-clear, high-keyed compositions," Dore Ashton (*Arts & Architecture,* May 1957) remarked, he has given "rich colors a weight which achieves a depth others arrive at with texture." The Stable Gallery featured another solo show of Brooks' work in January and February of 1959.

At the International Exhibition of Painting in 1952, sponsored by the Carnegie Institute of Pittsburgh, Pennsylvania, Brooks was the only American artist to be honored when he won the fifth prize. His seven-by-seven-foot picture *R-1953* (a title indicating alphabetically that it was his eighteenth picture of 1953) won second prize ($1,000) and the Logan Medal at the Art Institute of Chicago's sixty-second Exhibition of American Art, in 1957.

Beginning in 1950 Brooks began to contribute his pictures to various exhibitions: the "Vanguard American Painters" show in Japan (1950), University of Minnesota (1951), in Paris (1951), University of Nebraska (1951, 1952), Whitney Museum of American Art (1950, 1951, 1952, 1953, 1955), Brooklyn Museum (1951), Museum of Modern Art (1951), University of Illinois (1952, 1953, 1955), Solomon R. Guggenheim Museum (1954), Carnegie

BROOKS, JAMES—*Continued*

Institute (1955), Bienal of the Museu de Arte Moderna in São Paulo, Brazil (1957), and the judges' show in the City Center Gallery in New York (1958).

James Brooks was married to Mary Mc-Donald, from whom he was divorced in 1939. Charlotte Park became his second wife on December 22, 1947. Brooks has blue eyes and brown hair and is five feet nine inches tall and weighs 160 pounds. He has no religious or political affiliations. In a painting, the artist has said, a man reveals his "richness, nakedness, and poverty" as the case may be, for "nothing can be hidden . . . the least private as well as the most personal of worlds."

The artist's rendezvous with creativity, Brooks believes, is found upon his canvas which combines what he knows with the unknown. "The process of changing formal relations is the painter's method of relieving his self-consciousness as he approaches the mystery . . . his whole life has been a preparation for recognizing and resolving it" (*The New Decade,* Whitney Museum of American Art, edited by John I. H. Baur).

References

> Mag Art 46:24 Ja '53
> Who's Who in America, 1958-59
> Who's Who in American Art (1956)

BROWN, NEWELL June 19, 1917- United States Assistant Secretary of Labor

Address: b. U.S. Department of Labor, Washington, D.C.; h. 3315 Newark St., N.W., Washington, D.C.

Since he took office as Assistant Secretary of Labor in October 1957, Newell Brown has made his special concern the extension of federal unemployment and social security coverage to some 1,300,000 workers in non-profit organizations. He succeeded Rocco C. Siciliano. From 1955 to 1957 Brown served as administrator of the Wage and Hour and Public Contracts Division of the United States Department of Labor. In his native New Hampshire, he directed the Division of Employment Security for five years, published and edited a weekly newspaper, and acted as secretary to Sherman Adams when he was governor of the state.

One in a family of six children, Newell Brown is a great-grandson of the Confederate General John B. Gordon who led the last charge at Appomattox and served as Governor of Georgia from 1886-1890. He is a grandson of the founder of the Brown Company, paper manufacturers of Dublin, New Hampshire, and a son of William Robinson and Hildreth Burton (Smith) Brown of Dublin. Born in Dublin, New Hampshire on June 19, 1917, Newell Brown attended local public schools through his freshman year of high school. He completed his secondary education at Phillips Academy, Andover, Massachusetts, from which he was graduated in 1935. At Princeton University he majored in English, and belonged to the Reserve Officers' Training Corps during his entire undergraduate career.

After receiving his A.B. degree from Princeton in 1939, Brown worked for over a year as a reporter on the Trenton (New Jersey) *Times.* He volunteered for Army duty and was commissioned a second lieutenant on December 1, 1940, a year before the attack on Pearl Harbor. He spent three and a half years in the United States before he was assigned to Burma, where he led guerrillas under the Office of Strategic Services. A lieutenant colonel when discharged in 1946, he was decorated with the Order of Merit and honored with a Presidential Distinguished Combat Unit citation.

When he returned to civilian life, Brown bought the Franklin (New Hampshire) *Journal-Transcript,* a weekly newspaper whose circulation averaged 3,500 copies. From 1946 to 1949 he edited and published the newspaper for the citizens of Franklin, a small industrial city on the Merrimack River.

In 1948 Brown became a delegate to the New Hampshire state constitutional convention. Having supported former United States Representative Sherman Adams in his successful campaign for the governorship of New Hampshire, he sold his country weekly to become secretary to Adams in 1949. He served the governor for ten months, during which time the state's administrative organization was streamlined and the number of departments reduced through consolidations from 83 to 40.

Resigning as the governor's secretary in 1950, Brown became the managing editor of the *Strafford Star,* a newly established afternoon daily newspaper published at Dover, New Hampshire. Within a short time the newspaper folded up for lack of financial support, and Brown returned to the service of the state government in August 1950, when Governor Adams appointed him director of the New Hampshire Division of Employment Security.

Brown kept this post under the successive administrations of Governors Sherman Adams, Hugh Gregg, and Lane Dwinell until he was installed in August 1955 as administrator of the Wage and Hour and Public Contracts Division of the United States Department of Labor. During the five years that Brown lived in New Hampshire's capital city of Concord he championed the city manager form of municipal government and served as chairman of the Concord good government committee.

Although President Dwight D. Eisenhower had sent the nomination of Newell Brown for the Wage and Hour post to the Senate as early as February 4, 1955, it was not until July 1955 that it was referred for hearings to a Senate Labor subcommittee headed by Senator Paul Douglas of Illinois. Both President George Meany of the American Federation of Labor and President Walter Reuther of the Congress of Industrial Organizations protested Brown's appointment to the $15,000 a year position, the chief function of which is to police the minimum wage law under the Fair Labor Standards Act.

Labor leaders charged that, as New Hampshire Employment Security administrator, Brown had allowed Canadian woodsmen to be imported into the state, pushing loggers' wages downward. They also claimed that he had lobbied illegally for the Reed Bill to give states a bigger share of insurance receipts, that he lacked experience for the proposed job, and that he was unsympathetic with the law he had been asked to administer.

Defending himself on July 27, Brown said he not only favored an increase in the minimum wage, but insisted that loggers' wages in New Hampshire had consistently risen since 1951. He also proved that labor criticism of his record was far from unanimous by producing letters of recommendation from four prominent New Hampshire union leaders. Approved by the full Senate committee on July 29 and by the Senate on August 2, Brown was sworn into office on August 15, 1955.

When Rocco C. Siciliano was named special assistant to the President for personnel management, Newell Brown was advanced to be one of four Assistant Secretaries of Labor. President Eisenhower announced Brown's promotion on October 8, 1957. In April 1958 Brown headed a group of four Department of Labor representatives who conferred with the Mexican government on the growing "bracero" problem. (Braceros are agricultural workers who, under an international treaty, are contracted each year by North American planters and fruit growers.) The conferees reached no agreement. Although Brown promised in May that no Mexican farm laborer would be admitted where there was a domestic worker available to take the job, his department endorsed in June a proposal to extend the existing treaty.

In 1957 450,000 Mexicans entered the United States for farm work, and in the spring of 1958 there were 5,200,000 unemployed in the United States. The latter figure, Brown said, was "expected to lessen but not to eliminate the need for foreign labor" in 1958-59. His department was making vigorous attempts to see that farm jobs were offered to unemployed Americans.

At a gathering of representatives of organizations interested in health, education, and welfare legislation in Washington in February 1959 Brown spoke on the critical need to bring workers in non-profit organizations under the protection of social security and unemployment insurance. He called unemployment insurance "a bulwark of individual and community security" and said that it cushioned the impact of unemployment, minimizing the effects of recession on the country's economy.

Brown also revealed that a bill to bring the employees of non-profit organizations under the Unemployment Insurance Act was being drafted by the Administration. "The proposal . . . will have repercussions far beyond its immediate objectives" editorialized the New York Times on February 25, 1959. "But it is high time the issue involved was faced—not only by the Federal but by the state governments as well, and by those whom it affects. . . . About 1.3 million workers in non-profit organizations have the same kind of work as those in industry. . . . They also face the same perils and problems of

NEWELL BROWN

unemployment. It is hard to see why they shouldn't all have the same legal benefits. . ."

Testifying before the Senate Finance Committee on March 20, 1959, Brown assailed as a dole a proposal by eighteen Democratic Senators for a fifteen-month extension of a broadened Federal aid program. He said that the Administration supported a bill, passed by the House, for a three-month extension of the program on a tapering-off basis. On March 31 President Eisenhower signed a bill extending temporary Federal jobless compensation through June 30.

Newell Brown and Alice Dodge Osborn were married on November 1, 1941. They have five children: Rosalind, Alice, Robinson, Christopher, and Hilary. Brown stands at six feet four inches, weighs around 180 pounds, and has blue eyes and brown hair. As befits a native of New Hampshire, he prefers skiing to other sports.

References

N Y Herald Tribune p2 O 9 '57 por
N Y Times p9 F 5 '55; p27 Jl 27 '55; p6 Jl 30 '55
Who's Who in America, 1958-59
Who's Who in New England (1949)

BROWNE, CORAL (EDITH) July 23, 1913- Actress
Address: h. 46 Chester Row, London, S.W. 1, England

Both an accomplished comedienne and a powerful tragic actress, Australian-born Coral Browne has played roles as different as Lady Macbeth in Old Vic productions and Vera Charles, the cynical and tippling actress-friend of Auntie Mame in the motion-picture version of Patrick Dennis' novel. Other Shakespearean

Anthony Buckley, London

CORAL BROWNE

roles that Miss Browne has acted since joining the Old Vic in 1951 include Emilia in *Othello*, Regan in *King Lear*, Helen of Troy in *Troilus and Cressida*, and Queen Gertrude in *Hamlet*. She made her American debut in another Elizabethan drama, Christopher Marlowe's *Tamburlaine the Great*.

On the London stage Miss Browne has appeared in more than twenty plays, including such light comedies as *The Man Who Came to Dinner*, *Simon and Laura*, *The Last of Mrs. Cheyney*, *Affairs of State*, and *My Sister Eileen*. Before joining the Old Vic, she played the leading role opposite Jack Buchanan in the comedy *Castles in the Air*, which ran for over two years in London.

Coral Edith Browne was born on July 23, 1913 in Melbourne, Australia to Leslie Clarence Brown and Victoria Elizabeth (Bennett) Brown. She was educated at Claremont Ladies' College in Melbourne and later studied painting at the Working Men's College in Melbourne. When Coral began her career, there were no professional dramatic schools in Australia; from the age of fifteen on, she learned what she could about acting from amateur productions, and about costumes and set design from the Melbourne Art Gallery.

Miss Browne made her professional debut on May 2, 1931 at Melbourne's Comedy Theatre in the role of Margaret Orme in John Galsworthy's play *Loyalties*. This was followed by such varied parts as Wanda in *The Calendar*, Mimi in *A Warm Corner*, Myra in *Hay Fever*, Madge in *Let Us Be Gay*, Mrs. Murdo Fraser in *The First Mrs. Fraser*, Suzy in *Topaze*, Manuela in *The Command To Love*, Diane in *The Quaker Girl*, Orinthia in *The Apple Cart*, Fräulein von Bernberg in *Children in Uniform*, Hedda in *Hedda Gabler*, and Mrs. Dearth in *Dear Brutus*. She had a total of

twenty-eight plays to her credit before she left for England at the age of twenty-one.

"When a girl is five feet nine inches in heels, with statuesque bearing and a voice both deep and powerful," observed Gertrude P. Lancaster (*Christian Science Monitor*, February 25, 1957), "it is obvious that her progress as an actress will not come through ingenue parts. Coral Browne . . . faced that fact early in her career, listened to her advisers, and left Australia for London."

Her first engagement in London was as understudy to Nora Swinburne as Helen Storer in *Lover's Leap*. When Miss Swinburne became ill, the night after the play opened in the fall of 1934, Miss Browne had the opportunity all young actresses dream about—stepping into the leading lady's shoes. After this she went from one substantial role to another.

Between 1935 and 1950 she appeared in the following London plays: *Mated* (1935), *Basalik* (1935), *This Desirable Residence* (1935), *The Golden Gander* (1936), *Heroes Don't Care* (1936), *Death Asks a Verdict* (1936), *The Taming of the Shrew* (1937), *The Great Romancer* (1937), *The Gusher* (1937), *Emperor of the World* (1939), and *Believe it or Not* (1940). She played Maggie Cutler in the London production of *The Man Who Came to Dinner* (1941), Ruth Sherwood in *My Sister Eileen* (1943), Mrs. Cheyney in *The Last of Mrs. Cheyney* (1944), and Lady Frederick Berolles in Somerset Maugham's *Lady Frederick* (1946). Next she played in *Canaries Sometimes Sing* (1947), *Jonathan* (1948), and the hit musical *Castles in the Air* (1949).

She made her debut with the Old Vic Company in London in October 1951, appearing as Emilia in *Othello*. In March 1952 she played Regan in *King Lear* and in the summer of that year she returned to modern comedy, in the role of Constance Russell in *Affairs of State* at the Cambridge Theatre which ran for eighteen months. In November 1954 she played Laura Foster in *Simon and Laura* at the Strand Theatre, and in July 1955, the title role in *Nina*.

Broadway audiences first saw Miss Browne as Zabina in Christopher Marlowe's *Tamburlaine the Great* at the Winter Garden in January 1956. She was co-starred with Anthony Quayle, who played the title role. Directed by Tyrone Guthrie, the tragedy was presented by the Producers Theater in New York in association with the Stratford Shakespearean Festival Foundation of Canada.

"As the wife of the defeated Emperor of the Turks, Miss Browne makes a deep impression . . . imperious on the throne, pitiless toward herself when she and her husband became the humiliated captives of the invader," commented Brooks Atkinson (New York *Times*, January 20, 1956). Other critics also praised Miss Browne's acting, but the drama closed after a run of less than three weeks.

Immediately after *Tamburlaine* closed Miss Browne returned to London and was asked by the Old Vic Company to play Lady Macbeth.

"I studied for months," she told William Peper (New York *World-Telegram and Sun,* October 29, 1956). "I find Shakespeare very difficult to learn. I mumbled lines everywhere I went and even started to rub the blood off my hands on a bus."

Macbeth opened in London, and Paul Rogers and Coral Browne attracted considerable notice for their torrid performances. "Yes, in London they seemed to think we played it rather heatedly," Miss Browne said later. "And I guess we do. I kick off my heels and we do a bit of kissing before the murders. It isn't sensationalism. It's a perfectly valid way of interpreting the roles. Instead of having Macbeth completely dominated by his wife we have him madly attracted to her. Why not? He's married to her" (New York *World-Telegram and Sun,* October 29, 1956).

The Old Vic production of *Macbeth* opened in New York on October 29, 1956. Brooks Atkinson wrote that "Coral Browne's Lady Macbeth is an extraordinary piece of acting. On her first entrance, her Lady Macbeth is a sensual, baleful woman of grace and authority who sends a shudder through the whole play. . . . By the time of the sleep-walking scene, Miss Browne's Lady Macbeth is a worn, dishevelled, glassy-eyed creature who has tumbled over the brink into madness. . . . This Lady Macbeth is the triumph of the performance" (New York *Times,* October 30, 1956).

In the Old Vic production of *Troilus and Cressida* the following year, Miss Browne had the comic role of Helen of Troy. "Helen, a busty middle-aged bawd," said critic Richard L. Coe, "tinkles on a white piano to her boyish young Paris. . . . Coral Browne's all-too-brief Helen of Troy is a hilarious spoof" (Washington *Post and Times Herald,* February 9, 1957).

During the 1957-58 Old Vic season in London Miss Browne played the Queen of Denmark in *Hamlet.* In the same year she took a comedy assignment in the Warner Brothers motion picture *Auntie Mame,* starring Rosalind Russell. Miss Browne portrayed Mame's worldly friend Vera Charles with a finesse which delighted the reviewers. In April 1959 she joined the cast of the London production of *The Pleasure of His Company.*

Coral Browne and Philip Westrope Pearman, an actors' agent, were married on June 26, 1950. Miss Browne's religious affiliation is Roman Catholic. Her hair is brown, her eyes are hazel, her height is five feet six inches, and her weight is 128 pounds. Her hobby is needlepoint. The Pearmans have three toy French poodles.

With her husband, Miss Browne takes her holidays in Spain. Gertrude P. Lancaster, who interviewed her for the *Christian Science Monitor* (February 25, 1957), said that she has "a pleasing lack of self-consciousness, and her manner of speaking seems neither Australian nor British, but simply cultivated, smooth diction." During the interview, Miss Browne admitted that although she found Old Vic tours valuable and interesting, they took her away from her happy married life at home. She also said that audience response is much the same in the United States as in England, except that Londoners are noisier (they rattle teacups during matinees) and that New Yorkers are inexcusably late in arriving at the theater.

References

Christian Sci Mon p4 F 25 '57
N Y World-Telegram p20 O 29 '56
Who's Who in the Theatre (1957)

BRUHN, ERIK (BELTON EVERS)
Oct. 3, 1928- Ballet dancer
Address: h. 16 Violvej-Gent, Copenhagen, Denmark

For his impeccable technique, fine acting, and ability to pantomime, classic ballet dancer Erik Bruhn has been accorded critical acclaim in the United States and Europe. A Dane by birth, Bruhn danced with the Royal Danish Ballet most of his life and was a full member of the company from 1947 to 1953, when he became a permanent member of the American Ballet Theatre. He has performed with such ballerinas as Alicia Markova, Nora Kaye, Mia Slavenska, Lupe Serrano, and Rosella Hightower. Besides making stage appearances, he has taught ballet and worked as a choreographer. At present, Bruhn has a three-year contract with the Royal Danish Ballet.

Erik Belton Evers Bruhn was born on October 3, 1928 in Copenhagen, Denmark, the son of Ernst Emil and Ellen (Evers) Bruhn. His father was a civil engineer and his mother was a theatrical hairdresser. When he was nine years old, Erik's mother persuaded him to audition for the Royal Theatre. She felt that he would receive a fine academic education as well as ballet instruction. He was chosen to become a student member of the group, one of several children accepted from some 500 applicants.

The Royal Danish Ballet is part of the state-operated Royal Theatre. The members are selected when they are eight or nine years of age by means of competitive auditions. There are no stars in the company; the outstanding dancers become solo dancers. The members of the ballet have a guaranteed lifetime income and a pension after a number of years of membership. The Royal Danish Ballet is over 200 years old and is distinguished for its dramatic characterizations, style of pantomime, and charm of narration. The ballet's dominant principles and training techniques were established by August Bournonville in the nineteenth century.

For ten years Bruhn studied at the Royal Theatre's ballet school, receiving academic and ballet training during the day and appearing in performances at night. In 1947 he was graduated from the school and became a full-fledged member of the Royal Danish Ballet. Two years later he was promoted to the position of solo dancer in the company. During summer vacations Bruhn danced with the now-defunct Metropolitan Ballet in London and studied with Stanislas Idzikowsky.

When the Royal Danish Ballet performed in London in 1949, Blevins Davis, then president

ERIK BRUHN

of the American Ballet Theatre Foundation, saw Bruhn dance. Impressed with Bruhn's talents, Davis invited him to join the Ballet Theatre for its 1949-50 season. Bruhn accepted, and he took a leave of absence from the Danish company, the first of several he was granted. In explaining his decision to appear with another group, he noted that the older solo dancers predominate in the Danish company, and a young artist must often wait many years for the roles he desires. He thought that the Ballet Theatre would broaden his experience (*Theatre Arts,* September 1956).

Commenting on the dancer's 1951 appearances with the Ballet Theatre, John Martin of the New York *Times* stated that Erik Bruhn "indulged in a good deal of unnecessary ictus" (as reported in *Theatre Arts,* September 1956). Bruhn decided to return to Denmark, where he enlisted the aid of the famous ballet teacher Vera Volkova. Bruhn told Emily Coleman (*Theatre Arts,* September 1956): "Volkova made me realize . . . that just a technical approach to ballet was not enough, that technique was a means to an end."

When asked to substitute for Igor Youskevitch during the Ballet Theatre's Hollywood Bowl engagement in 1952, Bruhn took another leave from the Danish Ballet. While he was on the West coast, he appeared in a dance sequence with Renée Jeanmaire in the motion picture *Hans Christian Andersen* (1952).

Since other members of the Royal Danish Ballet wished to emulate Bruhn's numerous excursions abroad, the directors of the company asked Bruhn whether he chose to remain permanently at home or resign from the company and relinquish his pension rights. The dancer decided in 1953 to become a permanent member of the Ballet Theatre. He later appeared with the Danish company, however, in its London performances in 1953 and 1955.

Erik Bruhn first won over the American critics on May 1, 1955, when he interpreted the part of Albrecht in *Giselle* opposite Alicia Markova at the Metropolitan Opera House. John Martin of the New York *Times* (May 2, 1955) said: "It may well be a date to write down in history books, for it was as if the greatest Giselle of today were handing over a sacred trust to the greatest Albrecht of tomorrow. . . . His dancing was like velvet, and his support of Miss Markova was easy, gracious and totally in accord with her, in both mood and technique." During this season Bruhn danced leading roles in *Black Swan Pas de Deux, Swan Lake, Mam'zelle Angot,* and *Nutcracker Pas de Deux.*

In the summer of 1955 Bruhn appeared in the Jacob's Pillow Dance Festival at Lee, Massachusetts with Mary Ellen Moylan in two *grand pas de deux,* the first from Tchaikovsky's *Nutcracker Suite* and the second from *Don Quixote.* The critic for the New York *Herald Tribune* (July 22, 1955) noted that "Bruhn... was close to faultless in both assignments." His performance with Alicia Alonso in *Giselle* and the *Black Swan Pas de Deux* was equally well received.

Participating in the Ballet Theatre's season at the Metropolitan Opera House in the spring of 1956, Erik Bruhn won special approval for his performance in *Theme and Variations* with Rosella Hightower. He was compared to Igor Youskevitch and André Eglevsky as one of the faultless classic male dancers of the present day. After the Ballet Theatre season had ended, Bruhn returned to Copenhagen to dance with the Royal Danish Ballet and then rejoined the American company for an extended tour of Europe under the auspices of the United States Department of State's International Educational Exchange Program.

To give young choreographers a chance to show their work before the public, in 1957 the Ballet Theatre conducted preview and workshop programs featuring new ballets instead of their usual series at the Metropolitan Opera House. Erik Bruhn's ballet *Fiesta* was presented at the Phoenix Theatre in New York in May 1957. The critic for the New York *Herald Tribune* (May 12, 1957) said that it had "charm, lightness, and loveliness of line and pattern." Bruhn had also choreographed a ballet called *Concertette,* which, set to the music of Morton Gould, is now in the repertory of the Royal Danish Ballet.

At the Brussels World's Fair in July 1958, Erik Bruhn appeared with the American Ballet Theatre, dancing the *pas de deux* from *Don Quixote* with Lupe Serrano. Two months later the company began a three-week engagement at the Metropolitan Opera House in New York. Bruhn created roles in several new ballets. He won special praise for his performance in Birgit Cullberg's *Miss Julie* with Violette Verdy. John Martin noted that Bruhn proved himself "once again to be a superb actor-dancer and an artist of the first rank" (New York *Times,* September 19, 1958).

At the end of the autumn 1958 season, the American Ballet Theatre had no definite commitments. Bruhn returned to Denmark, where he signed a three-year contract with the Royal Danish Ballet to choreograph as well as dance. Bruhn was ranked as the first dancer in the classical wing of the American Ballet Theatre.

Erik Bruhn is a member of the Royal Danish Ballet Union, Equity (London), American Guild of Musical Artists, and Screen Actors Guild. He has blond hair and blue eyes. He told Emily Coleman of *Theatre Arts* (September 1956) that his artistic life operates around two maxims: "He does not want people to pay only to see him jump, and he would rather be bad in a good ballet than be great in a bad ballet."

References

Dance Mag 29:40 My '55 por
N Y Mirror Mag p18 N 3 '57 por
N Y World-Telegram p16 Ap 24 '56
Kraks Blaa Bog, 1958
Who's Who in America, 1958-59

BRUNAUER, ESTHER C(AUKIN) July 7, 1901-June 26, 1959 Former United States government official; consultant to Department of State on UNESCO (1947-51); representative to preparatory commission of UNESCO with rank of Minister (1946). See *Current Biography* (November) 1947.

Obituary

N Y Times p23 Je 27 '59

BUECHNER, (CARL) FREDERICK (bĕk'nẽr) July 11, 1926- Author; clergyman; educator

Address: b. c/o Alfred A. Knopf, Inc., 501 Madison Ave., New York 22; Phillips Exeter Academy, Exeter, N.H.

Reprinted from the *Wilson Library Bulletin* Jan. 1959.

The hero of Frederick Buechner's novel *The Return of Ansel Gibbs* is a profoundly civilized man who has all his life followed a course of strict intellectual objectivity and detachment from all deeply emotional involvements. Late in his life, faced with the decision of accepting a political office, with the inevitable publicity and violations of privacy that accompany it, Gibbs goes through a period of intense self-searching and self-discovery. His final choice is commitment, involvement. As he says to his daughter: "You cross your fingers and hold your tongue and do what you can in the time that's left. That is the only holy cause, my dear, ambivalence be damned."

It is significant that Gibbs' conclusion neither rejects the intellect nor in any way compromises his principles. And there is a curious parallel between the development of this fictitious character and the young novelist Buechner himself. At twenty-three, just out of Princeton University, he published a precocious first novel —a highly literate but somewhat studied and self-conscious book. Two years later came a

Elliott Erwitt

FREDERICK BUECHNER

second novel, brilliant in many ways but still heavily academic. *The Return of Ansel Gibbs*, his third novel, marks a distinct departure.

In the years since the publication of the first book Buechner has read, traveled, taught, and studied theology. Now an ordained Presbyterian minister, he combines his writing career with teaching, preaching, and counseling at Phillips Exeter Academy in Exeter, New Hampshire.

Carl Frederick Buechner was born in New York City on July 11, 1926, one of two sons of Carl Frederick and Katherine (Kuhn) Buechner. The family moved about a good deal in Frederick Buechner's childhood, and he attended a different school almost every year of his life until he reached the tenth grade. After graduating from the Lawrenceville School in New Jersey in 1943, he went on to Princeton (with two years, 1944-1946, out for military service), majoring in English and receiving a B.A. degree in 1948. He began work on his first novel while still an undergraduate. But the writing career had really begun earlier—at about six he produced "a spine-tingler about cannibals" called "The Voyage of Mr. and Mrs. Cloth."

The principal influence and inspiration in Buechner's work has been his witty and wise grandmother, whom he calls Naya. She, he writes, "has held me entranced from the time I was a little boy." (She is the prototype of Maroo in his *A Long Day's Dying*.)

Buechner's first poems and stories were published in the *Lawrenceville Literary Magazine*. His first "public" appearance was a group of poems, *The Fat Man's Prescriptions*, in *Poetry*. "Poems were my first love," he writes, "and I wish I could get back to them. For the time being, novels seem to have made me too garrulous."

A Long Day's Dying (1950) was Buechner's first novel. A study of the relationships of a small, sophisticated, and highly articulate group of people — a college student, his widowed

BUECHNER, FREDERICK—*Continued*

mother and grandmother, his mother's several lovers—it won the young author immediate attention. More than one critic, moved no doubt by the somewhat baroque atmosphere and rarified style of the book, compared him to Truman Capote. John W. Aldridge devotes a chapter to the two of them in his *After the Lost Generation.*

The reception of this first novel—the many reviews that called his style "mandarin and derived from Henry James and Elizabeth Bowen" —staggered the young author, for (as Eloise Perry Hazard pointed out in the *Saturday Review of Literature*) Buechner had read little James and no Bowen. But he had steeped himself while at Princeton in seventeenth century English prose, especially Jeremy Taylor and Sir Thomas Browne, and, he remarked, "Reading them so concentratedly you can scarcely fail to absorb something of their style."

The Season's Difference (1952) treated of a mystical experience and the reactions to it of a small group of adults and children. Many reviewers found the book overwritten and too "intellectualized." "It is one of those most tantalizing of all things in writing—a near miss," Oliver La Farge commented in *Saturday Review.*

As Alfred A. Knopf, his publishers, noted on the dust jacket of Buechner's third novel, *The Return of Ansel Gibbs* (1958), this is "indeed a novel that admirers of Frederick Buechner's earlier books could scarcely have predicted." The *Atlantic Monthly* (March 1958) noted with approval that "the style is less ornate, the plot straightforward." While judging it in the main "not a successful book," Elizabeth Janeway in the New York *Times Book Review* found it "worth half a hundred 'successful' and superficial novels that pretend to deal with matters of ethics and religion."

Buechner taught English at the Lawrenceville School from 1948 to 1953 and creative writing at summer sessions at New York University in 1953-54. In 1954-55 he held a Rockefeller Brothers Theological Fellowship at the Union Theological Seminary in New York. During his seminary training he ran an employment clinic at the East Harlem Protestant Parish. He received his B.D. degree and was ordained early in 1958 and is currently chairman of the religion department at Phillips Exeter. Buechner married Judith Merck in April 1956.

References

Sat R Lit 34:10+ F 17 '51 por
Who's Who in America (sup Ap '50)

BUFFET, BERNARD (boo-fā') July 10, 1928- French artist
Address: b. c/o Galerie Drouant-David, 52, faubourg Saint-Honoré, Paris 8e, France

The art of Bernard Buffet has been the voice of the postwar generation of France, "emptied of all illusions, seeing life without rose-colored glasses, viewing the world as a nauseating spectacle" (*Art and Photography,* March 1957). His agonizing canvases of skinned rabbits, emaciated people, and harsh still lifes have made this French artist, an unknown starving youth a decade ago, the "millionaire painter of misery." In 1948 Buffet was honored with the Grand Prix de la Critique, and he has had one-man shows annually since that time at Paris' Drouant-David and Visconti galleries. The Galerie Charpentier in Paris featured a solo retrospective exhibition of his work in 1958.

Bernard Buffet was born in Paris on July 10, 1928. He has an older brother. His father, the son of an army officer, owned a bicycle shop. His mother, to whom he was deeply devoted and who encouraged him to attend art school, died suddenly when he was fourteen. Bernard was educated at the Lycée Carnot and for a short time, in 1944, at the École Nationale Supérieure des Beaux-Arts.

As a youngster, Buffet was a sickly insomniac, who composed his pictures during his sleepless nights. His crippling poverty forced him to paint on bedsheets and use a minimum number of colors. When he had canvases, he worked without an easel, nailing the canvases to the wall. He spent many days studying the great painters at the Louvre, and he soon imagined and created his own spiky, distorted, and monochromatic compositions. His products reflected the era in which he grew up: the defeat of France, the atrocities of the German occupation, and the nihilistic postwar period. Buffet held his debut in 1944 at the Salon des Moins de Trente Ans. Expositions at the Salon des Indépendants and Salon d'Automne followed.

When Buffet entered the contest for the Prix de la Jeune Peinture in 1948, a member of the jury, Dr. Maurice Girardin, appraised Buffet's *The Sitting Drinker* as a work of genius. His colleagues did not agree. Dr. Girardin, a connoisseur and patron of Maurice Utrillo and Georges Rouault, resigned from the jury and purchased four of Buffet's paintings. The repercussions in the art world brought Buffet fame and fortune.

Later that year there were simultaneous exhibitions of Buffet's art: his oils on the right bank of the Seine at the Galerie Drouant-David and his water colors and drawings on the left bank at the Galerie Visconti. Art collectors were attracted by the gigantic portrayals of unadulterated misery, and the critics presented him with the Grand Prix de la Critique. They acclaimed his *The Horrors of War, Hanging from the Gallows, The Angel of Destruction,* and others showing concentration camp victims, drawn with astute draftsmanship and dreadful compactness, "to reveal the very skeleton of war."

In the following years Buffet continued to lead a monastic life and often painted around the clock. "The point of Buffet's art," observed *Time* (February 18, 1952), "seems to be merely that man is miserable." At an exhibition of Buffet's work at the Kleemann Galleries in New York in 1950 there were starving yellow and gray nudes in large, dirty squares and still lifes containing withered fruit and ugly fish on wrinkled tablecloths. *Time* (March 6, 1950) noted that the "positive qualities of Buffet's art were abstract ones, having nothing to do with the pinched and gloomy nature of the subject matter. The spiny silhouettes that dominated his canvases were arranged with deceptive casualness, each in its own flat area, but they struck the eye, separately and together, with maximum force." Products of Buffet's brush have also been displayed at the Knoedler, John Heller, Niveau, and Hutton-Chambard galleries in New York.

Like Picasso, Buffet is interested in the life of the circus. He evidenced his preoccupation with the theme in twenty-six paintings at the Galerie Drouant-David and thirty water colors and drawings at the Galerie Visconti in February 1956. All were sold in a week for $113,000. In reviewing the retrospective show at the Galerie Charpentier in early 1958, Pierre Schneider (*Art News,* March 1958) remarked: "For a contemporary, and a young man of thirty at that, to be given a one-man show at the Galerie Charpentier is as incredible as awarding the Nobel Prize to a teen-ager."

Some critics consider Buffet the leading artist of the second half of the twentieth century, comparing his contribution to that of Goya or Pablo Picasso. Others find his style too limited, but concede his talent for composition. Genêt in the *New Yorker* (February 26, 1956) remarked that his circus characters have the "same sad hatchet faces" that he gave to his war victims, the crucified Jesus, and his self-portraits. Thomas B. Hess in *Art News* (January 1957) described his work as being "as bland and as dehumanized as a Petty girl or an Eames chair. Two landscapes hint that Buffet may have some talent as a scene designer."

Other media besides oils, water colors, and drawings have commanded the attention of Buffet. A skillful lithographer, he issued an edition of *Still Life with White Fruit,* limited to seventy-five copies, one print of which was priced at $80. He painted a gigantic mural of Joan of Arc. He illustrated three books for Jean Giono, the novelist of Provence. When Françoise Sagan wrote the story for the ballet *Le Rendez-vous manqué (The Broken Date),* he designed the décor; it was performed in New York in 1958 and toured Europe. Buffet's work is represented in the permanent collections of the Musée de Petit Palais and Musée National d'Art Moderne, both in Paris, and his pictures were displayed at the Venice Biennale in 1956. He is a member of the Salon d'Automne and Salon des Indépendants.

Shy, retiring, slender, and handsome, Buffet has dark hair and piercing blue eyes. No longer emaciated, he now weighs about 135 pounds. With his affluence, he has acquired several cars, including a chauffeur-driven Rolls-Royce, a yacht, expensive clothes, antique furniture, and several homes. He now paints in the luxury of his mansion in Montmorency.

Working from ten to twelve hours a day, Buffet has in his brief career produced as many paintings as did Auguste Renoir in his entire life. He often completes his compositions in half an hour, and they command from $2,000 to $10,000. In the Communist literary weekly, *Les Lettres Françaises,* Buffet wrote an article

Photo André Ostier
BERNARD BUFFET

entitled "I Am Reproached With Making Too Much Money." He reminded readers that "Van Gogh and Gauguin never had enough to eat. Soutine and Gruber died without having the fame they merited. But art has had its vengeance since: Picasso is not only famous all over the world. He is also a billionaire."

In December 1958 Buffet married Annabel May Schwob de Lure, a model, singer, and writer. He collects pistols, revolvers, and other weapons, and he has bulldogs, ducks, and a monkey. In politics he supports Charles de Gaulle. Explaining his preoccupation with morbidity, Buffet said, "I only paint what I see and feel. You see, poetry and beauty have been killed by the frightful realities" (*Art and Photography,* March 1957).

References

Yale French Stud no 19-20:94+ '57
Bénézit, E. ed. Dictionnaire Peintres, Sculpteurs, Dessinateurs et Graveurs (1948-55)
Bergé, P. Bernard Buffet (1958)
Georges-Michel, M. From Renoir to Picasso (1957)
International Who's Who, 1958
Who's Who in France, 1955-56

CARR, EMMA P(ERRY) July 23, 1880-
University professor; chemist

Address: b. Mount Holyoke College, South Hadley, Mass.; h. 25 Woodbridge St., South Hadley, Mass.

A teacher and researcher who found her work "an exciting adventure," Dr. Emma P. Carr was formerly chairman of the chemistry department at Mount Holyoke College and is now a professor emeritus on the faculty. Her

Vincent S. D'Addario

EMMA P. CARR

outstanding achievements in physical chemistry have placed her in the forefront of women chemists in the United States and abroad. As the recipient of many fellowships and study grants, Dr. Carr did research with several notable professors of chemistry.

After returning in 1930 from a year of study at the University of Zurich, Dr. Carr implemented a joint faculty-student research project at Mount Holyoke which involved "the preparation of a series of highly purified hydrocarbons and the examination of their ultraviolet absorption spectra in liquid and vapor phase." The results of the experiments yielded "a more satisfactory theoretical interpretation of the energy relationships involved in the carbon-carbon double bond of organic chemistry" (*Industrial and Engineering Chemistry,* May 10, 1938).

The daughter of Edmund Cone Carr and his wife, the former Anna Mary Jack, Emma Perry Carr was born in Holmesville, Ohio on July 23, 1880. Her grandfather and father were both doctors who maintained a practice in Coshocton, Ohio, where Emma was reared. A brother, the late James G. Carr, was a physician also and for many years a professor of medicine at the Medical School of Northwestern University.

When she matriculated at Ohio State University in Columbus in 1898, Emma Carr was one of a handful of women students. She studied chemistry with the noted William McPherson, but at the end of her freshman year (1899) she transferred to Mount Holyoke College. Here she completed her requirements as a sophomore and junior, and from 1901 to 1904 she was an assistant in chemistry at the school. Her senior year of undergraduate study was completed at the University of Chicago, where she received the B.S. degree in 1905.

Invited to rejoin the faculty at Mount Holyoke, Miss Carr served as an instructor of chemistry for three years before returning to the University of Chicago, in 1908, for graduate study. She was the recipient of the Mary E. Woolley (1908-09) and the Loewenthal (1909-10) fellowships while she studied and worked on research projects with Professors Alexander Smith and Julius Stieglitz. Her dissertation on physico-organic chemistry, which was written under Stieglitz's direction, qualified her for a Ph.D. degree in chemistry in 1910.

Dr. Carr was appointed an associate professor of chemistry at Mount Holyoke in 1910. Three years later she was raised to the rank of full professor and named chairman of the department. Under her strong and vigorous leadership the chemistry faculty became one of the most outstanding at Mount Holyoke, for she staffed it with some of the finest science instructors in the country. Although Mount Holyoke is essentially a liberal arts college, there has been a strong tradition since its founding by Mary Lyon, herself a teacher of chemistry, of providing advanced scientific training and developing independent research skills.

The textbooks that Dr. Carr used in organizing her first classes were those of her professors at the University of Chicago, Smith and Stieglitz. One of her former students, Dr. C. Pauline Burt, has noted, "The new methodology of these two great teachers she not only shared but transcended. Their approach and hers were to become standard in another generation but it was radical and epoch-making in the early years of this century. A newer approach was not to be possible until after atomic developments in recent years" (*Nucleus,* June 1957).

In a career that always combined research with teaching, Dr. Carr worked on her laboratory investigations as thoroughly as on her classroom preparations. Beginning in 1918 she published her findings in her principal field of research: the application of physical chemistry to organic problems with special emphasis on the absorption spectra of organic compounds in the vacuum ultraviolet.

In 1919 Emma Carr spent one year at Queen's University in Belfast, Northern Ireland doing postgraduate work on spectrographic methods with Dr. A. W. Stewart. A second period of intensive research followed in 1925 when she studied with Victor Henri at the University of Zurich. As the recipient of the Alice Freeman Palmer Fellowship awarded by the American Association of University Women, Dr. Carr returned to Zurich to make a thorough study in 1929-30 of vacuum spectroscopy with Dr. Henri.

Upon her return from Europe in 1930 Dr. Carr received a grant from the National Research Council which enabled her to establish a research project for the investigation of simple unsaturated hydrocarbons. Undergraduate and graduate students as well as professors worked together on this "theoretical study involving the preparation of highly purified hydrocarbons in which the position of the double bond in the molecule was known with certainty and the measurement of the absorption spectra in the far ultraviolet" (Mount Holyoke News Bureau). The spectrographic program continued under Dr. Carr's direction during the 1930's and 1940's with additional financial support from the National Research Council and the Rockefeller Foundation.

Retirement from her official duties as department head came for Dr. Carr in 1946. Although she is now in her late seventies, she is active in the laboratory where the present staff of the chemistry faculty is expanding her work on the spectrographic program. Dr. Carr is now reinterpreting her original conclusions in light of new discoveries made in the field. Recently she has been devoting her energies to the compilation of a punch-card catalogue of all references on the absorption spectra of organic compounds in the vacuum ultraviolet.

Dr. Carr was a cooperating expert in charge of absorption spectra data for the International Critical Tables. On three occasions she served as an official delegate to the conferences of the International Union of Pure and Applied Chemistry: Washington (1926), Bucharest (1935), and Lucerne (1936). The international cultural relations division of the State Department named her a visiting professor to the Institute of Chemistry of the National Autonomous University of Mexico in 1944.

For her research in physical chemistry, Dr. Carr was chosen in 1937 by the American Chemical Society as the first recipient of the Garvan Medal. In 1957 she was named a co-recipient of the James Flack Norris Award of the northeast section of the American Chemical Society. She shared the prize with Mary L. Sherrill, who had been her successor as chairman of the chemistry department at Mount Holyoke. The two women were honored for achievement in the teaching of chemistry.

Honorary degrees have been conferred on Professor Carr by Allegheny College (1939), Russell Sage College (1941) and Mount Holyoke (1952). She also received the alumnae medal of honor of the Mount Holyoke Alumnae Association. Dr. Carr is a fellow of the American Physical Society and a member of the American Association for the Advancement of Science, the American Optical Society, and the American Chemical Society, in which she has served on numerous committees. She was elected to Phi Beta Kappa and Sigma Xi, and she has been given honorary memberships in Sigma Delta Epsilon and Iota Sigma Pi.

Since her retirement Dr. Carr has been a participant in municipal administration and a dedicated civic worker. In 1948 she was selected to represent Precinct D in the South Hadley Town Meeting, a post which she still fills. Formerly her recreation was playing tennis, but this has been replaced by a less active hobby, that of listening to music. Her club is the Cosmopolitan. She is a Methodist.

"A great teacher is known not only by her reputation in the academic world," Professor Burt said in tribute to Emma P. Carr, "but by the example she sets to a rising generation. . . . Throughout the country and in practically

every woman's college and in many great universities [her students] are to be found, the majority of them professors, carrying the torch she lighted for them at Mount Holyoke."

References

Ind & Eng Chem 16:263+ My 10 '38
Nucleus 34:214+, 216+ Je '57 pors
American Men of Science vol I (1955)
American Women, 1939-40
Who's Who in America, 1944-45

CARTER, JOHN (WAYNFLETE) May 10, 1905- Bibliographer; rare book authority
Address: b. 34 New Bond St., London W. 1, England; h. 26 Carlyle Sq., London S.W. 3, England

One of the most distinguished and respected names in bibliographical and book-collecting circles is John Carter, who has had a varied career in the private book business as well as in government service in England and the United States. Since his exposure with Graham Pollard in 1934 of one of the greatest bibliographical scandals of our time, he has maintained his position in the forefront of contemporary bookmen. He has earned such honors as Commander in the Order of the British Empire in 1956 and the Sandars Readership in Bibliography at the University of Cambridge in 1948.

John Waynflete Carter was born on May 10, 1905 in Eton, England, to Thomas Buchanan and Margaret Teresa (Stone) Carter. His father was a clergyman who had earlier practised as an architect. "I come of a respectable upper middle class family with no Welsh or Irish blood and an incapacity, which I have inherited, for making money," he comments. During Carter's childhood his family resided in various places in the Thames Valley. He has one married sister, and his brother Will Carter is a leading British printer.

In 1924 Carter was graduated from Eton College, which his father and grandfather had attended before him. While at Eton he played football until his last year, when an injury to his left leg disqualified him for the game. He took first-class honors in the classical tripos at King's College, Cambridge University, where he received his M.A. degree in 1927. While at Cambridge he became interested in early printing through his godfather, C. H. Turner, the Oxford don. He began also his lifelong hobby of collecting the works of the English lyric poet and classical scholar, A. E. Housman.

Although he had received no previous training in the rare book trade, Carter became assistant director of Charles Scribner's Sons Ltd. of London in 1927. His classical background and knowledge of early printing provided a solid foundation and made it easy for him to learn the business. In September 1928 he made his first trip to the United States to attend the history-making sale of Jerome Kern's book collection.

In 1934 the world of book collecting was shocked by the proof that what had been

Erich Hartmann

JOHN CARTER

considered valuable first editions of such noted Victorian authors as Mrs. Browning, Swinburne, Arnold, and Tennyson were really forgeries. *An Enquiry into the Nature of Certain Nineteenth Century Pamphlets* (Constable, 1934) by John Carter and Graham Pollard proved these editions fakes and established a pattern for checking the authenticity of printed literary works through the application of modern scientific techniques. David Randall wrote in *Publishers' Weekly* (July 7, 1934): "The volume is . . . the bibliographical sensation of the modern book-collecting era, and the story gains added interest by the clever presentation of the evidence, damning with masterly understatement."

It is now established that these forgeries were the work of Thomas J. Wise (1859-1937), a once-revered British bibliographer and book collector. The full story of the fraud and the identity of all of Wise's accomplices are not known and may never be. *The Firm of Charles Ottley, Landon & Co.; Footnote to An Enquiry* (Scribner's, 1948) by John Carter and Graham Pollard contains the results of additional investigations and discoveries.

Of literary forgery, Carter has said (Washington *Star,* August 21, 1955): "Actually in the rare books field, there is less chance of fraud than almost any other field of collecting. It is practically impossible and hardly worth it, financially, to fake a copy of the first edition. It's too easy to compare it with the authentic book and detect the forgery."

"However, in the case of Thomas Wise, he took some well-known work . . . and simply invented an apparently earlier edition. Thus, with no way of comparing it, people were paying vast sums for what they thought was the true first edition."

During World War II, Carter served with the British Ministry of Information in London from 1939 to 1943. He then came to New York City for two years (1944-45), where he worked for the British Information Services.

In 1946 Carter returned to private business in Great Britain as managing director of Scribner's Ltd. of London. One of the most important book finds of his career was his discovery of a copy of the Gutenberg Bible for Scribner's of New York City, which had asked him to keep alert for a copy. Within a few months he had found one that was almost perfect, through a combination of bibliographical detective work and good luck.

"In a volume about rare books, written in 1824, a Gutenberg Bible was described as belonging to Sir George Shuckburgh," Carter told Selwa Roosevelt of the Washington *Star* (August 21, 1955). "This copy never reappeared and therefore was always described as a lost copy. Actually, it had remained intact and in the hands of descendants of Shuckburgh. The lucky owners were quite aware of their valuable possession, but not being particularly bookish or in need of money, they hadn't bothered to notify the book world of its existence."

Carter transported the so-called Shuckburgh copy of the Gutenberg Bible to New York by air, holding the precious cargo in his lap during the flight. For Scribner's he also discovered the original autograph score of Mozart's Symphony Number 35 (K.385), the *Haffner.*

In 1947 John Carter was chosen the Sandars Reader in Bibliography at Cambridge University, the first time that a professional bookman had ever received this high honor. These lectures were later published with the title *Taste and Technique in Book-Collecting; A Study of Recent Developments in Great Britain and the United States* (Bowker, 1948). A reviewer in the San Francisco *Chronicle* (August 9, 1948) stated: "This is a well-rounded consideration of the subject, sensible and sound. As for Mr. Carter's style . . . its familiarity gives the whole book the air of a pleasant stimulating conversation among friends." John Carter was honored once again in 1951 when he was chosen Windsor Lecturer in Bibliography at the University of Illinois.

ABC for Book-Collectors (Knopf, 1952), a glossary of terms used in book collecting, was warmly greeted by the critics in 1952. Carter was praised for his soundness and wit and "individual gift of succinct definition, which loses nothing of its clarity from being phrased elegantly and often epigrammatically" (*New Statesman and Nation,* September 13, 1952). Carter's sense of humor is illustrated by the fact that he wrote a satirical review of his own *ABC for Book-Collectors* in the London *Bookseller* (September 29, 1952).

In 1953 John Carter was recalled to his government's service as Counsellor of Embassy and Personal Assistant to Her Britannic Majesty's Ambassador, Sir Roger Makins, in Washington, D.C. In November 1955 he returned to private business as an associate of Sotheby and Company, London, the famous Bond Street auction house, as its representative for United States operations.

Since the early 1930's John Carter has often contributed to such British publications as the London *Times Literary Supplement,* the *Spectator,* and the *Bookseller*; and to such American periodicals as *Publishers' Weekly,* the *Atlantic Monthly,* and the *Colophon.* In 1957 *Books and Book-Collectors,* a collection of Carter's contributions to periodicals, was published by the World Publishing Company. John Winterich wrote in the *Saturday Review* (March 23, 1957) : " 'What has happened to the literary essay?' one often asks, and pauses vainly for an answer. There will be no need to ask that question as long as John Carter is around."

The day after Christmas in 1936 John Carter and Ernestine Marie Fantl of Savannah, Georgia, were married in the United States. At the time of her marriage Mrs. Carter was curator of the department of architecture and industrial design at the Museum of Modern Art in New York City. Since that time she has been columnist for various newspapers and is at present women's editor of The Sunday *Times* of London.

In politics, John Carter is a Tory. He belongs to the Garrick, Double Crown, and Eton Ramblers clubs in London and to the Grolier Society and the Century Club in New York. He is also vice-president of the Bibliographical Society, and active in the National Book League.

Carter does not himself collect books extensively; he feels that one's professional and personal interests should not conflict. He does still collect works of A. E. Housman and has published bibliographies of the poet. Collecting the Wise forgeries, examples of early printing, and one of his favorite writers, the Latin poet Catullus, rounds out Carter's book-collecting fields.

Two books which may exist somewhere in the world still tantalize Carter's instincts as a rare book sleuth. One is the first book printed in Italy, an edition of Donatus' Latin grammar, the other a perfect copy of the 1603 first quarto of *Hamlet,* of which only two imperfect copies have been found. For bookmen searching for a foolproof definition of a rare book he suggests the following: "A book I want badly, but can't find."

John Carter is six feet tall, weighs 165 pounds, and has brown eyes and gray hair. He lists his favorite recreations as "music, drink, sleep." He says that he deprecates being called an "expert," but William Targ, the vice-president of World Publishing Company, comments: "[John Carter] is one of the most distinguished bibliographers alive, an authority in many areas, including the world of music (manuscripts and books). He has great wit and charm and is in every sense 'a man of the world.' "

References

Pub W 163 :31+ Ja 3 '53 por
Washington (D.C.) Post D2+ Aug 21 '55 por
Altick, R. D. The Scholar Adventurers (1950)
Who's Who, 1958

CHAGLA, MAHOMED ALI CURRIM (chăg′lä) Sept. 30, 1900- Indian Ambassador to the United States
Address: b. Embassy of India, 2107 Massachusetts Ave., Washington, D.C.

Indian democracy has an articulate spokesman in Mahomed Ali Currim Chagla, India's Ambassador to the United States and to Mexico, who was one of his country's most eminent jurists and formerly Chief Justice of the Bombay High Court. Since replacing G. L. Mehta in December 1958 he has concentrated much of his effort on convincing the American people and government of India's need for increased economic aid, often appealing directly to the public.

Mahomed Ali Currim Chagla, the son of Jenab and Currim Chagla, was born in Bombay, India on September 30, 1900. He was educated at St. Xavier's High School and College in Bombay and Lincoln College at Oxford University, England, where he was graduated in the Honours School of Modern History in 1922. While at Oxford he was president of the Oxford Asiatic Society, a political discussion group for Asian students (1921), and of the Indian Majlis (1922). He studied law at the Inner Temple and was called to the bar in 1922.

In the same year Chagla returned to Bombay to set up a law practice which was to flourish until 1941, when he was first appointed to the bench. In reflecting on his career as a lawyer and as a judge, Chagla has decided that he preferred being a lawyer and has explained: "I was more free. I could say what I wanted, do what I liked, accept only the cases I liked" (Washington *Post and Times Herald,* November 28, 1958).

From 1927 to 1930 Chagla was also a professor of constitutional law at the Government Law College in Bombay. In 1933 he was appointed honorary secretary of the bar council of the High Court of Judicature in Bombay, an association of Bombay lawyers. He kept this office until 1941, when he was appointed puisne (junior) judge of the High Court of Bombay State. Six years later he was elevated to the position of Chief Justice which he held until 1958.

An avowed liberal, Chagla used his position as Chief Justice to crusade for the principle that all men are equal before the law. He opposed laws which, in his opinion, infringed on individual liberty and upheld social legislation which he felt would promote the dignity of the individual.

Chagla made headlines when he objected to a section of Bombay's Prohibition Act which permitted members of the armed forces to obtain drinking permits while denying that privilege to Bombay civilians. His assertion that this was discriminatory legislation was rejected by India's Supreme Court in New Delhi, which overruled his decision. He also rendered Bombay's sales tax legislation void when he denied that the state had the power to tax sales made outside of Bombay.

Social legislation that Chagla upheld included a law giving untouchables the right to enter temples and a law enforcing monogamy. Al-

Government of India

MAHOMED ALI CURRIM CHAGLA

though opponents of the latter argued that it interfered with freedom of religion, the Chief Justice maintained its validity in the name of social progress.

Chagla's last major achievement as Chief Justice was a one-man investigation which he conducted into the alleged misuse of funds by a nationalized insurance company. His findings brought about the retirement of two of India's high-level civil servants and the resignation of India's Finance Minister, T. T. Krishnamachari, who was not personally involved but was considered responsible for the action of his subordinates.

In addition to serving on the bench, Chagla has made several contributions to the development of Indian jurisprudence. He wrote two books, *The Indian Constitution* (1929) and *Law, Liberty and Life* (1950), and he served on two government committees designed to improve the state of jurisprudence and legal education in India. As chairman of the Legal Education Committee set up in 1949 he recommended that students be permitted to enter law school after two years of liberal arts college instead of the previously required four. This recommendation was later incorporated into India's educational system. As a member of the Law Commission appointed in 1955, he was delegated to suggest reforms in the administration of India's laws and to find remedies for such impediments to justice as overcrowded court calendars. The commission's report was filed shortly before Chagla left for his present post in the United States.

While a junior judge, Chagla also served as vice-chancellor of Bombay University in 1946. And as Chief Justice, he was interim Governor of Bombay State for two months in 1956.

Before becoming Ambassador to the United States, Chagla had twice represented India on the international scene. In 1946 he was a member of the Indian delegation to the United Nations General Assembly and there made his mark in an impassioned speech defending a resolution condemning South African racism. "If this resolution is defeated," he said, "it would mean that this organization . . . is prepared to connive at the wicked and vicious doctrine of a master race which so many nations victoriously fought in the last war" (Washington *Post and Times Herald,* October 5, 1958).

In 1957 Chagla was appointed India's *ad hoc* judge to the International Court of Justice at The Hague when the court heard arguments in a right-of-way dispute between India and Portugal. The case arose because India refused Portugal the right to cross Indian territory to put down uprisings in Portuguese colonies entirely surrounded by Indian territory.

India's Prime Minister Jawaharlal Nehru personally selected Chagla as Ambassador to the United States in September 1958. Chagla presented his credentials in Washington the following December; he is also Ambassador to Mexico and Minister to Cuba. The fact that Chagla, a Moslem, was appointed to represent a predominantly Hindu nation was generally taken as a sign that Nehru wants to demonstrate the secular nature of the Indian government.

In interpreting his country and its inhabitants to the people of the United States in speeches, interviews, and television appearances, Ambassador Chagla has emphasized the need for greater economic co-operation. He has argued that India is "the only bastion of democracy in Asia," that freedom in his country cannot survive without "economic justice," and that economic co-operation from the United States in the form of increased government aid and private investments will help "the very cause of democracy to survive in the East" by strengthening the largest democracy in the world.

Chagla has criticized United States aid to Pakistan. Only two days after he presented his credentials to President Eisenhower, he made an address to the India League of America in which he stated that the United States, by giving military assistance to "a naked dictatorship" in Pakistan, was forcing India to spend on defense the money which would otherwise be used for economic and social improvements.

As a patron of the arts, Chagla approaches the fine arts with the same liberalism that characterizes his political outlook. "No artist," he has said, "can thrive in a state which seeks to control morals and which denies the individual the right to decide how he shall find his own happiness" (Washington *Post and Times Herald,* October 5, 1958).

In accordance with these views he accepted the chairmanship of a Paul Robeson birthday celebration committee in Bombay. His answer to the critics of this gesture was that he respected Robeson as an artist and as one trying to better the lot of his people. Robeson's political affiliations, Chagla asserted, were of no concern to him.

A collector of mostly contemporary Indian painting and sculpture, Chagla has served as president of the Bombay branch of the Royal Society, which seeks to promote Oriental culture and learning. He is also "passionately devoted" to the theater and believes that the artist is far more representative of his country than the politician. Golf and bridge are also among his recreations.

Mahomed Ali Currim Chagla was married in 1931 to Meherunnissa, daughter of Dharsi Jivraj. They have a daughter, Husnurai; a son, Jehangir, a chemist who lives with his parents; and a son, Iqbal, a student at Cambridge University, England.

References

Christian Sci Mon p9 S 22 '58 por
N Y Herald Tribune p3 D 11 '58 por
Washington (D.C.) Post p2E O 5 '58;
    p3F N 28 '58 por
International Who's Who, 1958
Nalanda Year-Book and Who's Who in
    India and Pakistan, 1951-53
Who's Who, 1958

Milton Mann Studios

DR. FRANCIS L. CHAMBERLAIN

CHAMBERLAIN, FRANCIS L(E CONTE) July 27, 1905- Physician; organization official

Address: b. University of California School of Medicine, San Francisco, Calif.; 490 Post St., San Francisco 2, Calif.

As president of the American Heart Association for 1958-59, Dr. Francis L. Chamberlain heads an organization dedicated to the control and conquest of diseases of the heart and circulatory system that in 1957 caused 53.6 per cent of all deaths in the United States. Dr. Chamberlain, who practises in San Francisco, is associate clinical professor of medicine at the University of California. Entirely supported by voluntary contributions, the 30,000-member AHA conducts its own annual Heart Fund drive and since 1950 has allocated more than $32,000,000 of Heart Fund receipts to research.

Francis Le Conte Chamberlain, a native of Santa Cruz, California, was born to Gregory and Blanche (Clark) Chamberlain on July 27, 1905. He was graduated from the University of California with the A.B. degree in 1930 and served his internship at the Stanford-Lane Hospital of Stanford University in 1933-34. After he received his M.D. degree from the University of California Medical School in 1934, he was for one year assistant resident in pediatrics at the University of California Hospital.

Moving to New York City in 1935 for two years of postgraduate work at Columbia University, Dr. Chamberlain became in that year an assistant resident in medicine at the affiliated Columbia Presbyterian Hospital. While a resident in cardiology at Presbyterian Hospital in 1936-37, Dr. Chamberlain worked under Dr. Dickinson W. Richards and Dr. André F. Cournand. He was a member of the first group in the United States to explore the interior of the heart with a long tube or catheter, a procedure which had an important effect on the development of heart surgery.

The German scientist Dr. Werner Forssmann had first used the catheter in an experiment upon himself in 1929. Richards and Cournand refined Forssmann's method, with the result that "today . . . physicians can determine which heart patients can be treated by surgery, and are able to diagnose cardiac conditions that were undetectable before" (*United States News & World Report,* October 26, 1956). The three shared the Nobel Prize for Medicine and Physiology for 1956.

In collaboration with Drs. Richards, Cournand, and J. L. Caughey, Dr. Chamberlain wrote the report "Intravenous Saline Infusion as Clinical Test for Right-Heart and Left-Heart Failure" (*Transactions of the Association of American Physicians,* 1937). Other early papers which he helped prepare were "Clinical Study of Preparation of Squill (Urginin) in Treatment of Myocardial Insufficiency" (*American Heart Journal,* September 1937) and "Electrocardiographical Changes Associated with Experimental Alterations in Blood Potassium in Cats" (*American Heart Journal,* October 1939).

Dr. Chamberlain was awarded the degree of Doctor of Science in Medicine by Columbia University in 1937. He then went to Boston to serve for one year as cardiology resident at the Massachusetts General Hospital. From 1937 to 1939, furthermore, he worked under the well-known heart specialist, Dr. Paul Dudley White, with whom he collaborated on a number of noteworthy reports. In 1938-39 he held a cardiovascular research fellowship and an instructorship at Harvard University.

Returning to San Francisco in 1939, Dr. Chamberlain was for the next six years a full-time teacher in charge of the heart clinic and electrocardiography laboratory at the University of California Medical School. He was advanced from an instructorship to an assistant professorship of medicine at the University of Cali-

CHAMBERLAIN, FRANCIS L.—*Cont.*

fornia in 1941, became vice-chief of staff at the University of California Hospital, and also held staff appointments at the San Francisco County and Franklin hospitals.

In 1943 Dr. Chamberlain accepted a reserve commission as surgeon in the United States Public Health Service; as such, he still serves as the Veterans Administration's cardiology consultant at Fort Miley, California. His present position as associate clinical professor of medicine at the University of California dates from 1945.

For at least a decade Dr. Chamberlain has been a leader in the American Heart Association and is a past president of both the California and San Francisco heart associations. The national organization, which was established in 1924 and has headquarters in New York City, carries out programs of aid for researchers, of professional education for doctors, and of education for the general public to show how disease may be prevented and heart sufferers helped to lead productive lives.

From a "narrow-based group of medical specialists," the AHA was reorganized in the late 1940's as "a broad-based outfit with national public participation" (*Time*, November 3, 1958). In 1950 the decision was made to earmark one half of the association's funds for research. As a member of the assembly (the policy-making body of AHA) and of the editorial staff of the *American Heart Journal*, Chamberlain has endorsed the association's decision. In October 1958 he credited emphasis on research with having given "force, direction and inspiration to the advancement of cardiovascular medicine" (New York *Times*, October 27, 1958).

Among additional AHA positions that Dr. Chamberlain has held are memberships on the board of directors, the cardiovascular certification examining boards, and the research study committee of the section on clinical cardiology. He began in 1955 two years as chairman of the AHA policy committee and in 1956-57 served as a vice-president of the organization. At the association's annual convention, in Chicago, in October 1957 Dr. Chamberlain was chosen as president-elect to succeed Dr. Robert W. Wilkins, professor of medicine at Boston University, who was installed for a one-year term as president at that time.

Dr. Chamberlain began his own one-year term as president of the American Heart Association on October 28, 1958, the final day of the thirty-fourth annual meeting, held in his home city of San Francisco. His successor, for 1959-60, is Dr. A. Carlton Ernstene, chairman of the division of medicine of the Cleveland Clinic, who was made president-elect at that time.

At a meeting held in Washington, D.C. in February 1959 by the American Heart Association and the National Heart Institute, the New York Heart Association issued what was described as a "box score" on progress against cardiovascular disease. Such ailments as subacute bacterial endocarditis, syphilitic heart disease, diphtheritic heart disease and thyrocarditis were listed as "conquered or largely under control," while congenital heart defects were yielding to surgery and greater under-

standing of their causes. There remained, however, the central problems of atherosclerosis and high blood pressure, which account for 90 per cent of the annual death toll from cardiovascular disease.

In other professional organizations Dr. Chamberlain is a director of the California State Medical Association; a member and former director of both the San Francisco County Medical Society and the San Francisco Tuberculosis Association; and a member of the American Medical Association, the California Academy of Medicine, and the Western Society for Clinical Research.

Francis Le Conte Chamberlain and Marie Louise Moore were married November 16, 1937 and have two sons, Francis Clark and John Walcott. Dr. Chamberlain maintains a private practice in cardiology at his home in San Francisco. His hobby is ranching.

References

American Medical Directory, 1958
Directory of Medical Specialists (1957)
Who's Important in Medicine (1952)

CHANDLER, RAYMOND July 23, 1888-Mar. 26, 1959 Author; wrote mystery stories and novels; also known for his scenarios. See *Current Biography*, 1946.

Obituary

N Y Times p23 Mr 27 '59

CHAPMAN, DANIEL A(HMLING) 1909-
Educator; former diplomat
Address: b. Achimota School, Achimota, Ghana

After the Gold Coast of Africa won its independence on March 6, 1957 and became the new state of Ghana, Daniel A. Chapman was appointed its first Ambassador to the United States and Permanent Representative to the United Nations. In these positions he had advocated the industrialization of Africa and a settlement of the Algerian problem. A geographer, Chapman has written three books on his native country and has served as Secretary to the Prime Minister and the cabinet, as head of the Civil Service, and as an official on the staff of the United Nations Secretariat.

In July 1959 he relinquished his duties as Representative to the U.N. and in the autumn, his Ambassadorship to return to Ghana. There, he became the first African headmaster of Achimota School, a government-subsidized independent institution which has trained most of the country's present leaders.

Born in 1909 in Keta, a seaport of the Gold Coast, Daniel Ahmling Chapman is the son of Jane Atsiamesi (Atriki) and William Henry Nyaho Chapman. He belongs to the Ocloo family, a member of which was chief in Keta until his death in August 1956. Chapman's father had attended school in Cape Coast (formerly Cape Coast Castle) on the Gold Coast and adopted the name of the English family with whom he lived. His brother, C. H.

Chapman, is regional commissioner of Trans-Volta Togoland Region.

Following his schooling at the Bremen Mission School in Keta, Chapman continued his education at Achimota School and was graduated in 1929. From 1930 to 1933 he served as assistant master of Achimota School. After private study, he won a scholarship to Oxford University. He majored in geography, and earned the M.A. degree with honors in 1936. During his postgraduate work at Oxford he specialized in anthropology and archaeology.

Returning to the Gold Coast in 1937, Chapman taught first at the Senior Boys School and then became the senior geography master at Achimota School. Until 1946 he served the school in many capacities: as a member of the school council, librarian, housemaster, and secretary to the principal's advisory committee. At this time he also was examiner in the Ewe language, customs, and institutions for the universities of Cambridge and London. He is the author of three books: *A Regional Geography of South-East Gold Coast, Eweland and Its People,* and *The Natural Resources of the Gold Coast.*

A member of the Ewe tribe, Chapman was the first general secretary of the All-Ewe Conference during 1945-46. He also founded and edited the *Ewe Newsletter.* In 1945 he attended the first Conference of West African Geographers, Naturalists, and Ethnologists, held at Dakar, French West Africa.

For eight years beginning in 1946, Chapman worked in the department of trusteeship and information from non-self-governing territories at the United Nations Secretariat at Lake Success, New York and then in New York City. First he was area specialist, then first officer, and at one time acting chief. While in New York he attended Columbia and New York universities.

After the first native government, headed by Dr. Kwame Nkrumah (see *C.B.,* July 1953), had been in office in the Gold Coast for two years, Chapman was recalled in 1954 to become Secretary to the Prime Minister and the cabinet. As the principal official adviser to Nkrumah from that time until October 1957, Chapman was instrumental in achieving the transfer of governmental control from Great Britain to the Gold Coast.

On March 6, 1957 the new nation of Ghana was formed from the colony of the Gold Coast and British Togoland, held as a U.N. trust territory. Of its own free will it chose to remain in the British Commonwealth of Nations. At that time Chapman assumed the additional post of chief of the Civil Service. On March 8 Ghana was voted a member of the United Nations, and in the following October Chapman was named to represent it in the international body. He was also appointed Ambassador to the United States and submitted his credentials to President Dwight D. Eisenhower on December 13, 1957.

In his first year as Ambassador, Chapman visited the West and Midwest of the United States, and accompanied Prime Minister Nkrumah on his official visit to the United States.

Continental Studios

DANIEL A. CHAPMAN

He also toured the Caribbean and South America, seeking support for a settlement of the Algerian problem.

A member of the Ghana delegation, Chapman attended in 1958 the Conference of Independent African States at Accra, Ghana. At the conference the representatives of Ethiopia, Ghana, Liberia, Libya, Tunisia, Sudan, Morocco, and the United Arab Republic organized a new United Nations bloc to "co-ordinate matters of common concern."

One resolution passed by delegates to the conference urged that the colonial powers set definite dates for granting independence to the subjugated peoples of Africa. Another accorded recognition to the Algerian National Liberation Front as the sole legitimate authority in Algeria and demanded an end to French "military occupation." Ghana also joined the Afro-Asian People's Solidarity Council, formed in January 1958, with a secretariat and headquarters in Cairo.

Ghana is more fortunate than many other undeveloped nations. Although it has a single-commodity economy based on cocoa, it is world's largest producer of that product, the price of which has soared since World War II. Its relatively small population of 5,000,000 does not exert extreme pressure on the food supply. In fact, Ghana has been able to set aside about $700,000,000 for development. But as the people of Ghana become more aware of their needs they are demanding a higher standard of living and more consumer goods. Imports have increased 80 per cent since 1950, and there is a large balance-of-payments deficit.

The future prosperity of Ghana is dependent upon the development of a diversified industrial and agricultural economy. The country has an excellent combination of natural resources; deposits of bauxite and the potential of hydro-electric power could be the foundation of a

CHAPMAN, DANIEL A.—*Continued*

significant aluminum industry. The most urgent need in Ghana's exploitation of its economic possibilities is the assistance of foreign experts.

Ambassador Chapman discussed this problem at Boston University in October 1958. "Money is not what we need," he said. "We don't want dollars. But we do need and want the services of skilled persons who can help us set up the schools and hospitals and enterprises which will broaden the economy of Ghana." At the same time the Ambassador spoke not only of the necessity of carrying out plans for the Volta River project, the potential source of Ghana's hydroelectric power, but also of the need for developing a native textile industry (*Christian Science Monitor,* October 9, 1958).

Following World War I Germany's African colonies became League of Nations mandates administered by the Allied powers. Located between the Gold Coast and French Dahomey, Togoland was arbitrarily divided into two parts and mandated to France and Britain. In 1946 both areas became U.N. trust territories. British Togoland is now part of the state of Ghana, but the eastern or French portion remains separated.

The Ewe people inhabit the southern or coastal portions of both parts of Togoland and the southeastern part of what was until 1957 the Gold Coast. Chapman has been a leading spokesman for his people in their efforts to become citizens of one state. Partition cut across kinship lines and subjected members of the same family to different governments, different languages, and different religions.

Daniel A. Chapman and Jane Abam Quashie were married on December 18, 1941. They have four daughters, Alice Nyamafo, Ruth Novisi, Mary Mawunu, and Jane Atsiamesi, and two sons, David Seloame and William Henry Nyaho.

"We consider the United States our great friend and ally," Chapman has stated, "and we know that if there is a Governor Faubus with whom we cannot agree, we also know that there is a President Eisenhower and a Supreme Court who better represent the feeling of this country."

References

N Y Times p37 Ag 19 '56; p8 O 24 '57
Negro Hist Bul 21:147 Ap '58
Directory of Ghana, 1959

CHEN YI (chŭn'yĕ') 1902 (?)- Foreign Minister of Communist China

Address: b. Ministry of Foreign Affairs, Peiping, China

When he was appointed Foreign Minister of Communist China in 1958, Marshal Chen Yi was deputy premier of his country, deputy chairman of the National Defense Council, member of the Chinese Communist party's Politburo, and mayor of Shanghai. He took over the position from Chou En-lai, who kept his office as Premier. Chen Yi gained prominence as a military leader fighting against the

Japanese during World War II and against Chiang Kai-shek's Nationalist armies during the civil war in China.

Observers predicted that Chen Yi, although no Marxist purist, would carry on the major tenets of his country's foreign policy. These included: solidarity within the Communist bloc of nations; "liberation" of Nationalist Formosa; courting the Afro-Asian group of nations; encouragement of Japanese neutralism; and an attempt to drive a wedge between the United States and Great Britain on issues in the Far East.

It appeared, however, that the highest-ranking leaders of the Chinese and Soviet governments would make the major policy decisions. Although Chen Yi's statements during 1958 and early 1959 indicated that Communist China was increasing her influence in world affairs, observers felt that the suppression of the rebellion in Tibet and the concessions that she had had to make about her communes have lowered the political and economic prestige of Communist China throughout Asia and the world.

Chen Yi was born near Chengtu, Szechwan, China, in 1902 (some sources indicate 1905), the son of a magistrate and a member of the landed aristocracy. He received a classical Chinese education, then attended the University of Communications in Shanghai. Awarded a scholarship from the government, he went to France to study chemistry. When he ran out of money, he went to work in an iron foundry. Chou En-lai was also a student in France at that time; together they helped form the Paris branch of the Chinese Communist party.

After returning to China, Chen Yi formally joined the Communist party in 1923. For brief periods he was an adjutant to a Szechwan warlord, a magistrate, and a journalist (he founded the Chungking newspaper, *Hsin Shu Pao*). In 1927 he joined the political branch of the Chinese Army. When the split between the Nationalists and the Communists occurred in that year, he remained in Central China to harass the Nationalist government with guerilla warfare. Later he went to the Soviet area in Kiangsi.

During the Sino-Japanese war, when Nationalists and Communists both fought against the foreign enemy, Chen Yi became commander of the first detachment of the New Fourth Army in 1938 and acting commander of this army in 1941. Its successes during the early 1940's against Japan won the army a secure foothold for the Communists in East China. After the defeat of Japan in 1945, civil war broke out between the Chinese Nationalists and the Communists.

In 1946 Chen Yi assumed full command of the New Fourth Army, and in the following year he became the head of the People's Liberation Army of Eastern China. He captured Tsinan, the capital of Shantung province, in 1948. To defeat the Nationalists, Chen Yi did not rely upon combat alone. He announced that hungry Nationalist deserters would be fed at Communist reception centers, and persuaded Nationalist generals to turn traitor. Reorganized as the Third Field Army, his forces and the Second Field Army took Nanking and Shanghai in 1949. His military successes once inspired Chen Yi to versify: "When old friends meet you and inquire about me,/ Tell them to look closely at the desolation in the enemy's rear."

The Communists drove the Nationalists off the mainland of China and proclaimed the establishment of the People's Republic of China on October 1, 1949. Chen Yi, remaining in command of the Third Army, was made commanding general of the East China military area, and was also named Mayor of Shanghai. In that city he began to pursue a relatively cautious policy: he retained government officials and workers formerly employed by the Nationalists until they could be screened; he maintained strict discipline over the troops; and he promised private industries that they would be left untouched. He came to be known for his educational work among army troops, and for his skill in persuading members of the gentry, the middle class, and the intellectuals to throw in their lot with the Communist cause.

At this time Chen Yi was a member of the Central Committee of the Chinese Communist party; in 1952 he was also listed as one of the top party personnel in the East China Bureau. He had the reputation of being a "national" Communist, one who had not been trained in Moscow and did not unquestioningly follow Soviet dictates. In 1952 he went to Moscow as a member of the Chinese Communist delegation to the nineteenth Soviet party congress.

Chen Yi first came under the patronage of Premier Chou En-lai in 1955. He was made a marshal, a member of the National People's Congress (parliament), and later a vice-premier of the republic. In 1955 Chen Yi accompanied Chou En-lai to the Afro-Asian conference held in Bandung, Indonesia. There the Chinese Communists made a strong effort to make Peiping the diplomatic capital of the Orient.

During the spring of 1956, Marshal Chen Yi was sent to Tibet to set up a preparatory committee which would pave the way for a Tibetan autonomous region to be included within the national framework of Communist China. Chen Yi announced his government's intention to extend a railway from Northwest China through the Tsaidam Basin and south to Lhasa, the capital of Tibet. At the time of his visit, some sources said that he might have been sent to quell a series of revolts which threatened Peiping's hold over Tibet.

At the eighth party congress of the Chinese Communists, held in September 1956, Chen Yi was chosen to deliver the foreign policy speech which Chou En-lai as Premier and Foreign Minister, had given at other congresses. He maintained in his talk that Communist China would never commit an act of aggression against other countries, and insisted that the question of the Nationalists on Formosa was one that concerned only China. He repeated his country's intention to liberate Formosa, attacked the United States for its war policy, and pledged Communist China's support for the forces of anticolonialism and for the victims of aggression and oppression.

Wide World

CHEN YI

At this congress, Chen Yi was elected a full member of the Politburo of the Chinese Communist party. As such, he has been in on almost all of the party decisions during the crucial period of the first five-year plan. He was also a deputy chairman of the National Defense Council, composed of the most important military men on the mainland. The council appears to have no direct control over the Ministry of Defense, but functions as a policy-making and planning body.

Chou En-lai surrendered the post of Foreign Minister of Communist China in February 1958, although he remained as Premier. Chen Yi was approved as his successor at the closing session of the National People's Congress. Observers did not expect major changes in policy to come with his appointment. During his first year as Foreign Minister, Chen Yi announced that business relations with Japan had been suspended; declared that his country would develop nuclear weapons; predicted that the United States and Great Britain were heading for certain defeat in the Middle East; warned that the temporary suspension of the bombardment of Quemoy and Matsu did not indicate any weakening toward the United States; and asked the United States and Great Britain to prevent the army of Laos from disarming a Communist battalion in the northern part of that country.

Although a world economic survey issued in June 1959 by the United Nations indicated that the rate of economic growth in Communist China exceeded that in any other country of the world, natural disasters in the same month shook the self-confidence of her leading statesmen. The Chinese mainland suffered the severest flood in its recorded history, drought caused crop losses in Manchuria, and a gigantic locust plague devastated 179 counties of five northern and central provinces.

(Continued next page)

CHEN YI—*Continued*

In his addresses Chen Yi has elaborated on the themes of "China for the Chinese" and "revolution is not for export." He became president of the National Association for Eliminating Illiteracy in China in 1956. He is married and has two children. A New York *Herald Tribune* biographical sketch (February 17, 1958) described his figure as "corpulent," and characterized his behavior while Mayor of Shanghai as "blustery and arrogant." He composes poetry, some of which has been quoted in American magazines. A representative sample runs: "I have seen my comrades riding together on horseback. . . Fluttering under the sky are the red flags of October." He likes to play chess.

References

Christian Sci Mon p12 F 12 '58; p7+
    F 13 '58
Manchester Guardian p7 F 12 '58
N Y Herald Tribune p1+ F 12 '58; p6
    F 17 '58
N Y Times p1+ F 12 '58
Time 51:22 Je 28 '48; 52:30 O 4 '48
U S News 28:28 F 10 '50; 44:21 F 21 '58
Washington (D.C.) Post p2 D 8 '48
International Who's Who, 1958
New Century Cyclopedia of Names
    (1954)

CHENEY, BRAINARD (BARTWELL)
June 3, 1900- Author; publicist
Address: h. 112 Oak St., Smyrna, Tenn.

Reprinted from the *Wilson
Library Bulletin* Sept. 1959.

Three novels by Brainard Cheney are detailed dramatizations of his love for south Georgia,

BRAINARD CHENEY

where he finds the lonesome quiet of piney woods and the aching distance of the marshes on Buttermilk Sound the most moving experiences in all nature.

Brainard Bartwell Cheney is descended from prerevolutionary settlers of Scotch, English, and German stock. Cheney's life has numerous ties with the South. Born in Fitzgerald, Georgia, June 3, 1900, he spent his formative years in Lumber City, a small sawmill town on the Ocmulgee River. His father, Brainard Bartwell Cheney, grew up on the family's Georgia plantation and at sixteen was a Confederate soldier. His mother, Mattie Lucy (Mood) Cheney, was the daughter of a Charleston physician. In 1928 Cheney married Frances Neel, well-known librarian and a grandniece of Sam Davis, the boy hero of the Confederacy.

Cheney was educated at The Citadel and at Georgia and Vanderbilt universities. At intervals he has been a bank clerk, high school principal, and manager of a timber camp. For three years he was police reporter and from 1928 to 1942 a political writer on the Nashville *Banner*. From 1942 to 1945 he was executive secretary to United States Senator Tom Stewart of Tennessee, and from 1952 to 1958 he was on the public relations staff of Tennessee's Governor Frank Clement. But the material for his novels has come from his early experiences on the rivers and in the small towns of Georgia.

Lightwood (Houghton, 1939) is a post-Civil War story of the struggle of Georgia farmers against a Yankee-owned corporation's effort to take away their land. E. H. Walton expressed the reservations of some of the reviewers by saying that it "just misses being a first-rate job" because the author overcomplicated his story. However, the reviewer thought it a "superior novel of the South," characterized by "crisp, pungent understatement" (New York *Times Book Review*).

Set in the same period of time and containing some of the same families is *River Rogue* (Houghton, 1942), the story of raftsmen along the Oconee and Altamaha rivers. The central character is Ratliff Sutton, the illegitimate son of a poor white woman and "about the toughest character in modern American fiction," who spends the early years of his life running away from his heritage, and his adult years trying to compensate for the bitterness of his youth.

Critics agreed, as Robert Penn Warren pointed out in the *Saturday Review of Literature*, that it "marks a decided advance over his *Lightwood*." According to a *Time* reviewer, "Brainard Cheney writes with the homely hardness of a grindstone. At his best he is a master at making detail, action, and physical sensation palpable, and almost Homerically fresh. At his worst he is a pedestrian writer, capable of serious lapses of literary judgment, but enormously sensitive to a certain landscape and a certain people."

This Is Adam (McDowell, Obolensky, 1958) is dedicated to the memory of Robin Bess, the Negro overseer of the family farm when Cheney was young, a man whose friendship he says has been a vital influence in his life. It is a fast-paced story of loyalty—the loyalty of a dignified and stubborn Negro who helps a widow hold onto her land when unscrupulous townsmen contrive to cheat her. Cheney presents a perceptive picture of the two races, neither sensational nor sociological, but based on the study of two individuals.

The book "has all the subtlety that a first-class student of 'Negro psychogenetics' and race relations would approve" (New York *Herald Tribune Book Review*). It is "a superior novel," according to Orville Prescott, and Cheney ". . . is expert in his use of a richly flavorsome but easily comprehensible dialect. And he is perceptive and interesting in his characterization of Lucy and Adam." The novel's "serious intention is unquestionable and so is its over-all dignity and impact" (New York *Times*).

A central theme explored in each novel can best be expressed in Cheney's recent statement that "I still am, as I have always been, tormented by the meaning of the individual as against society, the dramatic act as against history."

He has been interested in writing since childhood, when his earliest attempts were animal fantasies and verses about nature. At Vanderbilt he was influenced by John Crowe Ransom, and later by the writings of Caroline Gordon. He has published stories and articles in *Coronet*, the *Georgia Review, Sewanee Review,* and elsewhere. *Strangers in this World*, a musical play, has been produced in Louisville, Kentucky and in Nashville, Tennessee. *River Rogue* was completed on a Guggenheim Fellowship. Work in progress includes two novels, one of them part of a trilogy, of which *This is Adam* is part one.

Cheney is a Democrat, and in religion he says that he has "moved from utopian agnosticism to the Roman Catholic Church." He is a member of the National Press Club, the Serra Club of Nashville, the Knights of Columbus, and the American Legion. He has blue eyes, red hair "now largely gray," and keeps his 150 pounds in shape with swimming, bar bells, and track work. He lives in Smyrna, Tennessee, with his wife, who is professor of library science at George Peabody College for Teachers, Nashville, and editor of "Current Reference Books" in the *Wilson Library Bulletin*.

References

Nashville Banner p29 S 24 '58 por
Who's Who in America (sup O '42)

CLAPP, VERNER W(ARREN) June 3, 1901- Librarian

Address: b. Council on Library Resources, Inc., 1025 Connecticut Ave., N.W., Washington 6, D.C.; h. 4 West Irving St., Chevy Chase 15, Md.

Because American research libraries have been forced to meet "machine-age demands with hand-age methods," the Council on Library Resources, Inc., was founded in September 1956. The council, which has been headed by Verner W. Clapp since its inception, is an independent organization with a grant of $5,000,000 from the Ford Foundation.

VERNER W. CLAPP

According to Verner W. Clapp, the purpose of the Council on Library Resources, Inc., is to initiate and co-ordinate developments that will improve the extent and use of library resources and services. It tries "to identify the problems which now present obstacles to efficient library service and to find methods for overcoming these impediments through the development of new procedures and the applications of technological developments." To accept the council presidency, Clapp resigned his post as Chief Assistant Librarian of Congress, after having served this institution for thirty-three years.

In addition to working at the Library of Congress, Clapp also served as librarian of the United Nations Conference on International Organization in San Francisco in 1945, and undertook the chairmanship of the United States library mission to Japan in 1947-48.

Verner Warren Clapp, the son of George Herbert and Mary Sybil (Helms) Clapp, was born on June 3, 1901 in Johannesburg, Transvaal, Union of South Africa, where his father, an American citizen from Dover, New Hampshire, was engaged in business. After the Boer War the family came back to America to live in Poughkeepsie, New York. Clapp attended the Poughkeepsie public schools until he entered Trinity College in Hartford, Connecticut, where he received the A.B. degree in 1922. While at college, he was captain of the track team and a member of Sigma Nu fraternity; he also was elected to Phi Beta Kappa.

Immediately after his graduation from college, Clapp obtained a summer job at the Library of Congress where, as a cataloger of manuscripts, he worked with the almost illegible papers of Reverdy Johnson, Ambassador to the Court of St. James in 1868-69. He held this position until the autumn of 1922, when he re-

CLAPP, VERNER W.—*Continued*

signed to do graduate work in philosophy at Harvard University.

In the summer of 1923 Verner W. Clapp returned to the Library of Congress for a permanent position. He served for the first five years as a member of the reference staff at the central desk in the main reading room. Later he was (in succession) head of the Congressional unit reading rooms (1928-31); special assistant to the superintendent of the reading rooms (1931-37); assistant superintendent of that division (1937-40) with the special assignment of supervising the work of the division for the blind; administrative assistant to the Librarian of Congress and director of the administrative department (1940-43); and director of the acquisitions department (1943-47).

While director of the acquisitions department, Clapp headed the Cooperative Acquisitions Project which tried to secure European publications produced during World War II. In 1946 he got the Russians to release those German publications which, ordered by American libraries before the war, were being held in the Soviet zone in Germany.

When the United Nations Conference on International Organization took place in San Francisco in 1945, Clapp was asked to set up a library for the conference; from this evolved the present United Nations library which he has served as a consultant. He also contributed to the distribution of information about the conference through the *Documents of the United Nations Conference on International Organization,* a twelve-volume set.

With his appointment as Chief Assistant Librarian of Congress in March 1947, Clapp achieved his first national prominence in American librarianship. In announcing the appointment, Dr. Luther H. Evans, then Librarian of Congress, described the choice as "responsive to a wide popular demand."

In December 1947 Clapp was named chairman of the United States library mission to Japan, to advise on the establishment of a library for the National Diet of that country. Completed in two months, this project assured the setting up of a national library and bibliographic services in Japan.

An active contributor to professional journals, Clapp has written a number of special studies, including a survey of international bibliographic services prepared for UNESCO. He has also taken an important part in library conferences.

In his report, *The Role of Bibliographic Organization in Contemporary Civilization,* which Clapp presented before the fifteenth annual conference of the University of Chicago Graduate Library School in July 1950, he pointed out the importance of easy access to records of communication. Discussing the problem of gaps in bibliographic organization, he urged librarians to "invent devices for making general use of the results of bibliographic work which is now hidden away in particular institutions, offices or files."

Speaking at the bicentennial celebration of the University of Pennsylvania library in May 1951, Clapp emphasized as "one of the unwrit-

ten laws of the universe," the right of the scholar to the materials of his scholarship. "The world may not owe the scholar a living and often does not give him one," he said, "but it does owe him the records on which his researches are based."

When, through a grant of $5,000,000 from the Ford Foundation, the Council on Library Resources, Inc., was established in September 1956, Clapp resigned his post at the Library of Congress, after a thirty-three-year career, to become the first president of the council. Following the organizational meeting of the council, Clapp stated that the aim of the Ford grant, one of the largest ever made for library purposes, and of the council is "to attempt, without losing any of the values which libraries now contribute to our civilization, to make these values more accessible and more effective."

According to its first annual report for the period ending June 30, 1957, the Council on Library Resources is seeking solutions to library problems "through basic research, the development of new techniques and equipment, and through coordination of effort." A study of basic research, under the title *Targets in Library Research,* has been conducted by a staff of experts appointed by Dr. Ralph R. Shaw on a grant of $100,000 to the Rutgers Graduate School of Library Service.

For testing and developing library materials, equipment, and standards a grant of $14,994 was made to the American Library Association to conduct a study of library technology. Other technological research projects include a study of the application of closed circuit television to the use of books at separated parts of a campus, and a study of the deterioration of paper. Numerous grants have been made for studies of methodological improvement and the co-ordination of effort. A council grant has also made possible a study of "cataloging at source."

Clapp is a member of the International Abstracting Board of the International Council of Scientific Unions, American Institute of Graphic Arts, Bibliographic Society of America, American Association for the Advancement of Science, American Library Association, Special Libraries Association, District of Columbia Library Association, and American Documentation Institute. He is also a member of Phi Beta Kappa and Sigma Nu. His club is the Cosmos of Washington, D.C.

Verner W. Clapp married Dorothy Devereux Ladd on August 24, 1929. They have three children, Nancy Priest (Mrs. Joseph H. Rowe), Verner Warren, Jr., and Judith Ladd. His former colleagues at the Library of Congress have admired "his insatiable curiosity and his inexhaustible energies . . . his skill as a diplomat, his inventiveness, his instinct for leadership, and his undaunted spirit."

References

Lib J 72:539+ Ap 1 '47 por
Library of Congress Inf Bul 15:502+ S 17 '56 por
Lib Q 25:127 Ja '55
Who's Who in America, 1958-59
Who's Who in Library Service (1955)

CLARK, CHARLES E(DWARD) Dec. 9, 1889- Federal judge

Address: b. United States Court House, Foley Square, New York 7; 309 Post Office Bldg., New Haven 6, Conn.; h. 36 Laurel Rd., New Haven 11, Conn.

For the last twenty years Charles E. Clark has been a judge on the United States Court of Appeals for the Second Circuit, and in 1954 he was named the chief judge of this court, which is regarded by many as second in importance only to the United States Supreme Court. His earlier achievements as a professor at the Yale University Law School had led to his becoming dean of the school in 1929, a position he held until his appointment to the bench in 1939 by President Franklin D. Roosevelt. Clark's books and articles, as well as his opinions for the court, have been valuable contributions to the understanding of law and its administration in America.

Charles Edward Clark, the son of Samuel Orman and Pauline Caroline (Marquard) Clark, was born in Woodbridge, Connecticut on December 9, 1889. He is a descendant of George Clark, who moved from England to Milford, Connecticut in 1639. His father was a farmer in Woodbridge. He prepared for college at the New Haven High School and then entered Yale College in that city. He was granted the A.B. degree there in 1911, after having been elected to Phi Beta Kappa.

While he continued his studies at the Yale Law School, Clark worked in the office of Judge Livingston W. Cleaveland of New Haven. He was graduated with the LL.B. degree *summa cum laude* in 1913 and admitted to the Connecticut bar in that year. He stayed in the office of Judge Cleaveland until March 1915, when he opened his own offices in New Haven in connection with those of Harrison Hewitt, Ward Church, and Clarence W. Bronson. In the following year he became a junior member of the firm of Hewitt & Clark and in 1918 became associated with the law firm of Watrous & Day in New Haven.

Turning toward a teaching career, he became an assistant professor of law at the Yale Law School in 1919, an associate professor in 1922, professor in 1923, and August E. Lines Professor in 1926. Three years later he was made dean of the law school, succeeding Robert Maynard Hutchins, and also Sterling Professor of Law. He held these positions until 1939.

Under his deanship, the law school reorganized its curriculum in order to emphasize the social functions of the law. Teachers from the fields of commerce, psychology, economics, sociology, and medicine were brought in to supplement the approach of the law professors. In 1933 a combined course in law and business training was established with the co-operation of the Harvard Graduate School of Business Administration.

Meanwhile, Clark had been carrying on several other activities. In 1917-18 he represented the Town of Woodbridge as a Republican member of the Connecticut House of Representatives, where he was selected to serve as chairman of the committee on claims. From

Wide World

JUDGE CHARLES E. CLARK

1927 to 1931 he was a deputy judge in the Hamden (Connecticut) Town Court. He participated in the work of the Connecticut Judicial Council from 1929 to 1931, and in the latter year drafted the Uniform Principal and Income Act for the National Conference of Commissioners on Uniform State Laws. He was a member of the state legislative commission on jails from 1931 to 1939, and from 1935 to 1937 he served as vice-chairman of the Connecticut commission on reorganization of state departments.

Clark acted as a special master in labor litigations, sitting in that capacity in November 1935 for the National Labor Relations Board in the first action to be brought in the New York district under the National Labor Relations Act. He was a special assistant United States attorney general in the antitrust division in 1938. Dean Clark appeared in Washington, D.C. to testify publicly in favor of the bill for the enlargement of the United States Supreme Court, and was known as a supporter of many New Deal measures.

President Franklin D. Roosevelt on January 5, 1939 named Clark to the vacancy on the United States Court of Appeals, Second Circuit. He took office on March 12, 1939. On September 1, 1954 he became the chief judge of this circuit, which comprises New York, Connecticut, and Vermont. The United States Court of Appeals hears cases appealed from the federal district courts and administrative agencies. In recent years it has dealt with cases concerning such problems as civil rights, Communism, admiralty law, copyrights and patents, contracts, criminal law, taxes, antitrust laws, and bankruptcy. *Fortune* (January 1951) described Clark's opinions as "of high quality, lucid, penetrating, and direct."

From 1935 to 1956 Clark served as a member of and reporter to the advisory committee on

CLARK, CHARLES E.—*Continued*

civil procedure of the United States Supreme Court. The committee prepared the Federal Rules of Civil Procedure, which as *Fortune* (January 1951) noted, constitute "this century's major reform of the operation of the legal system." These rules were adopted in all the federal trial courts, are copied by a considerable number of states, and have affected procedure in some degree in nearly all the states. The advisory committee acted as a continuing body and from time to time considered and proposed amendments as experience suggested changes, thus being able to refine the product of its workmanship.

Judge Clark has written a number of books and articles on legal subjects. He collaborated with Livingston W. Cleaveland and Harrison Hewitt on *Probate Law and Practice of Connecticut* (Banks Law Publishing Company, 1915), to which various supplements were added. In 1928 appeared his *Handbook of the Law of Code Pleading* (West Publishing Company). With the assistance of Richard S. Young and Winifred R. Ryan, a second edition of this book appeared in 1947 under the same imprint.

Callaghan and Company published in 1929 his *Real Covenants and Other Interests which 'Run with Land,' including Licenses, Easements, Profits, Equitable Restrictions and Rents;* a second edition appeared in 1947. From 1930 to 1933 the West Publishing Company issued his *Cases on Pleading & Procedure . . . ;* a second edition was printed in 1940. With the assistance of Charles Alan Wright, another edition, entitled *Cases on Modern Pleading,* was brought out in 1952.

In 1932 Clark wrote *Cases on the Law of Partnership, Joint Stock Associations, Business Trusts, and Other Noncorporate Business Organizations* (West), in collaboration with William O. Douglas. With Harry Shulman, Clark produced in 1937 *A Study of Law Administration in Connecticut; A Report of an Investigation of the Activities of Certain Trial Courts of the State* (Yale University Press).

Over the years Clark has held other positions dealing with governmental problems. In 1945 President Harry S. Truman appointed him a member of the Advisory Board on Just Compensation, which prescribed uniform standards of payment to owners of vessels requisitioned by the United States government during World War II. He was chairman of the President's advisory commission on the relation of federal laws to Puerto Rico in 1948-49 and was a consultant-draftsman for the Puerto Rico Judiciary Act of 1951. He was project director of survey unit number eighteen of the judicial department of the commission on state government organization of Connecticut in 1949.

From 1916 to 1923 Clark was secretary of the Connecticut Civil Service Reform Association and later was a member of its executive committee. He served as an adviser on property from 1927 to 1944 for the American Law Institute. He was elected president of the Association of American Law Schools in 1932, and vice-president of the American Judicature Society in 1936 and a director in 1954. He was a member of the executive committee of the

Franklin D. Roosevelt Library from 1938 to 1940.

Judge Clark is a member of various national, federal, state, and local bar associations, and was given the award of merit of the Federal Bar Association of New York, New Jersey, and Connecticut in 1958. He holds honorary degrees from numerous colleges and universities and has been a visiting professor at various universities. He belongs to the New Haven Law Club, the Graduate Club, and the New Haven Country Club, and in New York he is a member of the Yale and Century clubs. He is a Congregationalist.

Charles E. Clark married Dorothy Estelle Gregory of Derby, Connecticut, on October 9, 1915. They have two children: Sarah Ann (Mrs. Marshall Hall, Jr.) and Charles Elias, now a teacher at the Yale Law School.

References

> N Y Times p1+ Ja 6 '39
> Directory of American Judges (1955)
> International Who's Who, 1958
> International Year Book and Statesmen's Who's Who, 1958
> National Cyclopædia of American Biography current vol D (1934)
> Who's Who in America, 1958-59
> World Biography (1954)

CLARK, DICK Nov. 30, 1929- Television personality

Address: b. American Broadcasting Co., 7 W. 66th St., New York 23; h. Drexel Hill, Philadelphia, Pa.

Every weekday afternoon during 1959 an audience estimated at twenty million Americans watched a television program called *American Bandstand.* Consisting only of recorded music and a teen-age dance party, the program derived most of its appeal from its youthful master of ceremonies, Dick Clark, who in less than two years after his appointment as Philadelphia disk jockey, had become an idol of American teen-agers. Because he had the power to establish the success of a song introduced on his program, Clark had also developed into a "dictator" of popular music.

Richard Wagstaff Clark was born on November 30, 1929 in Mount Vernon, New York, the son of Richard Augustus and Julia Clark. He had one older brother, Bradley, who was killed in action during World War II. At the time of Dick's birth, the elder Clark was sales manager for a New York cosmetics company. He later went into radio broadcasting.

Dick Clark was educated at local elementary schools, and at the A. B. Davis High School in Mount Vernon, New York. After receiving his diploma in June 1947, he enrolled at Syracuse University. Father and son entered broadcasting at the same time, Mr. Clark as manager of WRUN in Utica, New York, and Dick as a disk jockey on the Syracuse campus radio station.

During his four years at Syracuse University, Dick held various part-time jobs to help finance his schooling, and during his summer vacations he worked at the Utica radio station managed by his father. In his senior year at Syracuse University, he also worked at WOLF, a commercial radio station near the university. He was graduated with a B.S. degree in business administration in June 1951.

After graduation, Dick went to work for WKTV, a small television station in Utica. As a newscaster, he developed the technique (which he still uses for his *American Bandstand* commercials) of recording the words on tape and playing them back through a hidden earphone. By synchronizing his lips with the recording, the announcer is able to give the impression of spontaneous delivery.

"Dick knew exactly where he was going when he came to us," WKTV manager Michael C. Fusco told reporter Gael Greene (New York *Post,* September 23, 1958). "When I hired him he told me frankly he only intended to stay a year. He was full of ambition. Hours meant nothing. I hated to lose him. But he was much too good for a station our size."

Clark left the Utica station in 1952 for a radio job with WFIL in Philadelphia. Soon he switched to the station's television affiliate, whose studios are still the scene of his nationwide *American Bandstand* program. Clark discovered that because he looked ten years younger than his age, he was unimpressive as a news commentator and announcer in metropolitan broadcasting.

He found his big opportunity, however, four years after he joined the station. In 1956 the then master of ceremonies of WFIL TV's *American Bandstand* program became involved in a series of felonies and misdemeanors which brought the show into disrepute. Seeking a replacement who seemed impeccable, the studio manager assigned the program to Clark.

The *American Bandstand* was (and still is) simply a one-and one-half-hour afternoon program in which local teen-agers danced to recorded music. It was held together by the master of ceremonies, who introduced the records and interspersed them with commercials. Other cities used their afternoon TV time in the same way. Thanks to Clark's magnetic youthfulness, however, the WFIL-TV version became the highest-rated daytime show in any major city.

Within a year the American Broadcasting Company decided to allot ninety minutes of network time to its affiliate's dancing party. The program first appeared on the ABC-TV network on August 5, 1957 from 4 to 5:30 P.M. (EST). On a national basis, Dick Clark's *American Bandstand* continued to exercise its appeal, and teen-agers hitchhiked from as far away as Texas to appear in the Philadelphia studio. Soon its Trendex rating nearly equaled the combined ratings of the two rival networks. In the early months of 1959 the program was broadcast by 101 ABC-TV affiliates and reached an estimated daily audience of 20,000,000 viewers.

It was not long before ABC decided to unleash its new attraction upon the evening hours, and Clark was cast in a new program on

DICK CLARK

Saturday for the half hour from 7:30 to 8 P.M. (EST). Making its debut on February 15, 1958, *The Dick Clark Show* doubled ABC's Trendex rating that night, and had attracted a sponsor before its third airing. The show followed the same records-and-teen-agers formula as the afternoon *American Bandstand* but without the dancing.

The new program was not greeted warmly by the critics. Calling it a "traumatic experience," reviewer Harriet van Horne (New York *World-Telegram and Sun,* February 17, 1958) nevertheless had to concede that "the pony-tailed, side-burned audience loved it." She described the show as follows:

"In general, the music is rude, restless and untamed. The beat is monotonous and insistent. The orchestra . . . seems to consist of a hillbilly 'gee-tar' and a hundred drums, all manned by savages. If there's a piano, it is thumped rather than played. . . . Presiding over this curious concert is Mr. Clark. Astonishingly, he is handsome, clean-cut, and courteous. He is also a rip-roaring success."

Clark's success is indeed phenomenal. His 1959 income is estimated at $500,000 a year. In one ten-day period *American Bandstand* drew 70,000 fan letters. On the afternoon when rock 'n' roll singer Jerry Lee Lewis was introduced on the program, 5,000 of his records were sold in Philadelphia alone. Several new dance steps (the "Stroll," for example) devised by *American Bandstand* teen-agers have become national fads. Even the youngsters who silently shuffle about on the dance floor may become national idols. One fourteen-year-old "regular" (a steady visitor who receives favored attention from the camera) has fourteen fan clubs scattered throughout the country, and receives an average of 350 fan letters and gifts each day.

His powerful influence upon American teen-agers has sometimes made Clark a target for

71

CLARK, DICK—*Continued*

criticism. Harriet van Horne wrote on another occasion (New York *World-Telegram and Sun,* January 14, 1959) : "Since he owns a considerable interest in a music company, Dick's interest in the records he auditions is likely to be more than academic."

Just as often, however, Clark earns praise for his elevating effect upon teen-age manners and behavior. "He has become a symbol for all that's good in America's younger generation,' cording to a writer for *This Week* magazine (November 16, 1958). The publication acted upon this conviction by running a weekly column of advice to teen-agers entitled "Dick Clark Speaking."

Dick Clark married Barbara Mallery, a former schoolteacher, on June 28, 1952. They have one son, Richard Augustus Clark II, born January 9, 1957. The family lives in Drexel Hill, a Philadelphia suburb, from which Clark commutes to New York for his Saturday show. His hobby as well as his profession is music, and he maintains a personal collection of 15,000 records of popular music and jazz, which he plays on an elaborate system of high-fidelity equipment.

Clark has been variously described as "proper," a "gentle, well-spoken man," and a "wholesome, good-looking, junior-executive type." He dresses conservatively and encourages the youngsters who appear on his program to do the same. His success in this respect, as in all others, can probably be attributed to his own statement : "I take teen-agers seriously."

References

N Y Post Mag p2 S 22, 23, 25, 26 '58 pors
N Y Sunday News Mag p4 My 4 '58 por
N Y World-Telegram p12 F 17 '58 ; p27
This Week p8-9+ N 16 '58 por
Time 71 :64 Ap 14 '58 por
Ja 14 '59

CLURMAN, HAROLD (EDGAR) Sept. 18, 1901- Director; author; critic

Address: b. 165 W. 46th St., New York 36; h. 1016 5th Ave., New York 22

Permanent theatrical companies, privately endowed with guaranteed salaries for actors, playwrights, and directors are advocated by Harold Clurman, who has directed more than fifty Broadway plays and is as proud of some of his failures as his successes. His career came full circle in 1956 when he was chosen to direct the American production of Eugene O'Neill's last play, *A Touch of the Poet* (1958), for he had first worked for O'Neill at the Greenwich Village Theatre in 1924 as a $10-a-week extra. In the intervening years Clurman has become "one of the two or three most sought after directors" (New York *World-Telegram and Sun,* October 13, 1958). In the 1958-59 Broadway season he also staged S. N. Behrman's play *The Cold Wind and the Warm.*

Clurman's ideas on the theater are contained in his books *The Fervent Years; The Story of the Group Theatre and the Thirties* (Knopf, 1945), which appeared as a paperback in 1958 (Hill & Wang), and *Lies Like Truth; Theatre Reviews and Essays* (Macmillan, 1958). The latter is a collection of his contributions to *Tomorrow,* the *New Republic,* and the *Nation,* of which he has been dramatic critic since 1953. Clurman was a co-founder of the Group Theatre in 1931, an experimental company which considerably influenced the American stage. From 1941 to 1945 he was a motion picture director and producer.

Harold Edgar Clurman was born in New York City on September 18, 1901 to Samuel Michael and Bertha (Saphir) Clurman. His father was a prosperous physician. Young Harold fell in love with the theater at the age of six when he was taken to see Jacob P. Adler in *Uriel Acosta.* In his early teens he organized neighborhood theatrical ventures. He was educated in the New York public schools, at Columbia University, and at the Sorbonne in Paris, where he received a degree in letters in 1923. His thesis concerned the French drama from 1890 to 1914.

When Clurman returned from Paris in 1924, he was determined to find work in the theater. He became a $10-a-week extra with the new producing company of Kenneth Macgowan, Robert Edmond Jones, Eugene O'Neill, and James Light at the Greenwich Village Theatre in Stark Young's play, *The Saint,* produced in October 1924.

The Theatre Guild appointed Clurman its stage manager for *Garrick Gaieties,* in which Lee Strasberg acted. "From the time of my meeting with Strasberg," Clurman recalls, "my observation of the theater grew more systematic." Cheryl Crawford (see *C.B.,* December 1945), the Guild's assistant stage manager, shared with Clurman and Strasberg the dream of a permanent theater "where plays could be seen as artistic wholes." At this time Clurman played small roles in the Guild production of *Juarez and Maximilian* and enrolled in a course for directors at the Laboratory Theatre given by Richard Boleslavsky and Jacques Copeau.

While working as a play reader for the Theatre Guild (1929-31), Clurman directed *Red Rust* (1929), a play for Guild members who were subscribing to experimental productions given on Sundays. A group of actors began to meet in Clurman's apartment with a view to forming a permanent company.

In the summer of 1931 twenty-eight actors, with Clurman, Cheryl Crawford, and Strasberg as co-directors, hired a barn and some bungalows in Brookfield Center, Connecticut. This was the beginning of the Group Theatre, a noncommercial, experimental acting company, dedicated to the principles of group acting as formulated by Konstantin Stanislavski. The Stanislavski method is "a way of doing something with the actor . . . to enable him to use himself more consciously as an instrument for the attainment of truth on the stage," Clurman has written in *The Fervent Years.* He has also discussed his staging techniques in a chapter in *Directing the Play,* edited by Toby Cole and Helen Krich Chinoy (Bobbs-Merrill, 1953).

Following a mild success with Paul Green's *The House of Connelly,* which opened at the Martin Beck Theatre in New York on September 28, 1931, Clurman told the New York *Times* (December 13, 1931) that O'Neill, Franchot Tone, Maxwell Anderson, the Theatre Guild's board of directors, and others had helped to finance the production. He then appealed to the general public for an endowment of $100,000 so that the Group Theatre might become a permanent establishment, but he could not raise this amount.

The Group's next two productions, *1931-* by Claire and Paul Sifton and *Night Over Taos* by Maxwell Anderson, were failures. Their fourth play, *Success Story* (1932) by John Howard Lawson, brought acclaim to Luther Adler. In the fall of 1933 the Group had its first hit play: *Men in White* by Sidney Kingsley, which won a Pulitzer Prize in 1934. The theater then presented Melvin Levy's *Gold Eagle Guy*; Clifford Odets' plays, *Waiting for Lefty* (1935), *Awake and Sing* (1935), *Paradise Lost* (1935), *Golden Boy* (1937), *Rocket to the Moon* (1938), and *Night Music* (1940); and William Saroyan's *My Heart's in the Highlands* (1939).

The last play produced by the Group Theatre was Irwin Shaw's *Retreat to Pleasure* (1940). Clurman wrote in the New York *Times* (May 18, 1941), "I still believe that the Group type of organization is most conducive to solid, satisfying, and truly representative work in the theater . . . but the basic defect was that the Group tried to maintain a true theater policy artistically, while proceeding economically on a show business basis."

The story of the Group Theatre was told by Clurman in *The Fervent Years.* In his article, "The Passionate Businessman" (*Theatre Arts,* June 1950), Lorenzo Semple, Jr., wrote that "the book is colorful, violently prejudiced, often unfair, and absolutely essential reading for anybody interested in the making of a first-rate theater artist." In the course of its history, the Group was accused of "artiness," "leftism," and "commercialism." None of these charges was valid, in Clurman's opinion.

"Although the Group Theatre never solved its organic problems," Brooks Atkinson, New York *Times* drama critic, observed, "it shook the complacence of the commercial theater, and it is probably more influential now than it was when it was struggling to keep alive. Individual members of the Group have moved into influential positions in the theater as a whole."

Since the Group Theatre disbanded in 1941, Clurman has been co-producer of *All My Sons* (1947) and the director of many notable plays and one musical. These include *The Member of the Wedding* (1950); *The Autumn Garden* (1951); *The Time of the Cuckoo* (1952); *Mademoiselle Colombe* (1954); *Bus Stop* (1955); *Tiger at the Gates* (1955); *Pipe Dream* (1955); *Orpheus Descending* (1957); and *The Waltz of the Toreadors* (1957). He also directed the ANTA (American National Theatre and Academy) revival of O'Neill's *Desire Under the Elms* (1952).

Friedman—Abeles

HAROLD CLURMAN

Clurman was deeply hurt, he told Edward Ellis (New York *World-Telegram and Sun,* October 13, 1958), when the widow of Eugene O'Neill gave *Long Day's Journey into Night* to another director. But Mrs. O'Neill "thought there was another O'Neill play I might direct. This was *A Touch of the Poet.*" It opened on October 2, 1958. Clurman's staging of the drama was called "first-rate" by John Lardner (October 11, 1958). "He makes the play's wordiest and most halting passages fairly gallop along." On December 8, 1958 when S. N. Behrman's play *The Cold Wind and the Warm* had its first performance, Clurman's directing was again approved by the critics. *The Cold Wind and the Warm* ended its run on March 21, 1959 and *A Touch of the Poet,* on June 12, 1959.

The director has maintained that the present New York stage is not as healthy as the theater thirty years ago, primarily because Broadway suffers from a shortage of theaters and high production costs; too many think of the theater only in commercial terms rather than as an art; critics and audiences regard a play as a great hit or great failure, with no room for one that is neither, and yet has merit. Nevertheless there is much that is healthy about the New York theater, and it would survive even the loss of theaters on Broadway—it would reopen in basements, churches, and schools and would always have writers, actors, and audiences (New York *Herald Tribune,* December 29, 1957).

In 1943 Harold Clurman married Group actress Stella Adler, daughter of the noted actor Jacob P. Adler and sister of Luther Adler. He has a stepdaughter, Ellen. In 1950 he received the Donaldson Award for the best direction of the year for *The Member of the Wedding.* Clurman was made a chevalier of the French Legion of Honor. Describing his temperament during rehearsals, Semple wrote of his "superheated volatility . . . he beats his breast, his

CLURMAN, HAROLD—*Continued*

gestures rend the air . . . words pour forth in a torrent. He makes the actors feel they are doing something in the highest and most devoted tradition. An infectious camaraderie grows up."

References

Clurman, Harold The Fervent Years (1958)
Who's Who in America, 1958-59
Who's Who in the Theatre (1957)

COE, FRED(ERICK) Dec. 23, 1914-
Producer

Address: b. c/o The Columbia Broadcasting System, 485 Madison Ave., New York 22; h. East Hampton, N.Y.

Speaking of the men who first "respected television as a unique art form," Jack Gould in the New York *Times* (December 29, 1957) cited Fred Coe as one of the people who lent "a sense of direction and adventure to electronic theater." His remark was based on Coe's decade of achievement as one of the pioneer producers in TV, a man who has engineered and launched over 500 television dramas including *Peter Pan* and *Marty* as well as the first television documentary, *Vincent van Gogh*. He directed the current Broadway stage hit *Two for the Seesaw*.

During the late 1940's and early 1950's of "TV's Golden Age of Drama" many hour-long "live" dramas were produced by Coe for the *Philco Television Playhouse* and *Goodyear Television Playhouse*. He was the winner of the Variety Showmanship Award for 1954, the Peabody Award in 1952 and 1953 (for Wally Cox's *Mr. Peepers* show and for personal

achievement), the Sylvania Award in 1954, and the Christopher Award in 1955.

Frederick Coe was born in Alligator, Mississippi on December 23, 1914, the son of Fred Hayden and Annette (Haroll) Coe. He was an only child; his father was an attorney and his mother a nurse. He was brought up in Buckhorn, Kentucky and Nashville, Tennessee, where he attended the Peabody Demonstration School and made a bold, initial gesture in his future field by writing the class play at the age of twelve. From 1933 to 1938 he attended Peabody College for Teachers in Nashville, going on to Yale University to do graduate work at the Yale Drama School from 1938 to 1940. Coe spent the next five years in Nashville, running community theaters and organizing several dramatic shows over radio station WSM in Nashville.

In 1945 through Jack Davies, a New York theatrical agent, Coe was hired as production manager at NBC. He soon found himself writing, directing, and producing. His diverse chores ranged from interviewing three-year-old tap dancers to helping out with early TV dramas. In *Theatre Arts* (June 1954) Coe wrote in "TV Drama's Declaration of Independence": "When the Playhouse did its first show in October 1948 all of us were convinced it was our mission to bring Broadway to America via the television set. And so we drew our material from the Broadway theater. We took Broadway plays, trimmed them to an hour, and cast them with Broadway players, topped by a Broadway star."

This successful effort on Fred Coe's part "to preserve as much of the original spirit and technique of the theater as can be carried over into a different medium" (N Y *Times*, November 28, 1948) led to such productions as *First Person*, which used the camera as though it were the viewer's eye, *Marty*, *Cyrano de Bergerac*, and *The Trip to Bountiful*, which later served as a vehicle for Lillian Gish on Broadway.

Constantly interested in new and vital effects, as early as 1948 Fred Coe was sending out television cameras "on location" to such places as Grant's Tomb and Rockefeller Center to find human backgrounds for his "live" dramas. He has consistently sought to demonstrate TV's advantage over Hollywood films—the spontaneity of "live" shows.

Fred Coe has also directed Hollywood pictures. In 1957 he produced his first movie for Warner Brothers, *The Left-Handed Gun*, starring Paul Newman, a Western dealing with the career of Billy the Kid which Coe pridefully described as "having a distinctly non-TV quality" (Los Angeles *Times*, August 4, 1957). The reviewer in the *Commonweal* (May 23, 1958) cited *The Left-Handed Gun* as being "beautifully photographed" and "determinedly arty."

As executive producer of the *Television Playhouse* from its inception in October 1948 Fred Coe had produced over 500 dramatic plays, including the adaptation of such novels as F. Scott Fitzgerald's *The Last Tycoon*, Sinclair Lewis' *Bethel Merriday*, and Budd Schulberg's

NBC

FRED COE

What Makes Sammy Run? "When we found no more novels to fulfill the standards we set up, we explored biographies and documentaries," Coe wrote in his *Theatre Arts* article (June 1954).

Other productions that Coe recalled with pleasure were *A Young Lady of Property* by Horton Foote, starring Kim Stanley; Walter Bernstein's adaptation of an F. Scott Fitzgerald short story *The Rich Boy; Rescue* by David Shaw, a re-creation of the Floyd Collins Kentucky cave-in tragedy of the 1920's; *St. Helena* by R. C. Sheriff, adapted from the play by R. C. Sheriff; *The Basket Weaver* by Robert Alan Arthur; and *The Happy Rest* by H. Richard Nash. Grace Kelly was featured in *The Rich Boy* (1952), and Lillian Gish starred in *The Trip to Bountiful*.

"By fostering such word magicians as Paddy Chayefsky, Tad Mosel, Robert Alan Authur, Horton Foote, N. Richard Nash, and J. P. Miller via the old *Philco-Goodyear Playhouse* Coe was able to set dramatic standards which remain unequaled in the fanciful world of video make-believe," commented Marie Torre in the New York *Herald Tribune,* November 13, 1957. A confirmed opponent of the repetitious and the well-worn, Coe once referred to the competing program, *The $64,000 Question,* produced by CBS at the exact time of Fred Coe's *Playwrights '56* as "my most unsophisticated rival." Actually, while *Playhouse '56* originally received a Trendex rating of 13.4 to *The $64,000 Question*'s 45.2, Fred Coe's program eventually won a rating of 20, while the quiz show slipped a bit in popularity as the months went by.

After twelve years on the staff of NBC, Fred Coe in the autumn of 1957 moved to the Columbia Broadcasting System where he is now working under an exclusive contract. His plans for the 1959-60 season include the staging of approximately six shows for *Playhouse 90.* He produced a revival of Victor Herbert's *The Red Mill* for *The Du Pont Show of the Month* on April 19, 1958 on the CBS-TV network.

In an interview with John Crosby in the New York *Herald Tribune* (March 24, 1958) Coe concurred with Crosby's verdict "that TV *must* experiment or it will shrivel into a parlor game." Voicing his own hopes for an experimental, off-Broadway TV repertory theater group, Coe described such an ideal enterprise as follows: "Let us say I would have a night as guest producer, the following week would be John Houseman's, the week after that—maybe Marty Manulis has an idea that wouldn't fit in *Playhouse 90* or maybe a comedian would like to do *Hamlet* in colloquial English with additional dialogue by Goodman Ace."

Fred Coe and Alice Griggs were married on December 28, 1940. They have a son, John Hayden, and a daughter, Laurence Anne. His first marriage ended in divorce, and on August 1, 1952 he married Joyce Beeler, by whom he has a daughter, Sue Ann Coe. His church affiliation is Presbyterian, and he is a member of the Yale Club. He is six feet one inch in height, has hazel eyes and brown hair, and is "absurdly young-looking" (John Crosby, the New York *Herald Tribune,* March 24, 1958).

An article by Fred Coe entitled "Televising Shakespeare" appeared in *Theatre Arts* for April 1951. He is impatient but continuously hopeful about his chosen profession and once said, "On television nothing is impossible. The medium grows as it breathes, every week precedents splinter" *(Theatre Arts,* June 1954). Fred Coe himself says that a TV producer quite simply reads scripts, and hires directors, writers, and actors. "I hold meetings and scream and tear my hair. I try to put on a good show." On the other hand Tad Mosel, a TV writer who has worked with Coe, said that "you always know you have Coe's support. He fights for you. . . . He's the man in the shadows who makes it all possible" (*Newsweek,* January 2, 1956).

References

N Y Times II p11 N 28 '48
Newsweek 47:41 Ja 2 '56; 50:60 D 9 '57
Washington (D.C.) Post p3H D 15 '57
International Television Almanac, 1957
Who's Who in America, 1958-59

COFFIN, FRANK M(OREY) July 11, 1919- United States Representative from Maine; lawyer

Address: h. House Office Bldg., Washington 25, D.C.; h. 26 Mountain Ave., Lewiston, Me.; 3807 Ingomar St., N.W, Washington 15, D.C.

Few freshman legislators have more quickly made a mark in Congress in recent years than Frank M. Coffin of the Second Maine District, the first Democrat to represent a Maine district in Washington, D.C. in twenty-two years. Elected in September 1956, he was re-elected two years later by a greatly increased majority. In the House Foreign Affairs Committee he formed with Representative Brooks Hays of Arkansas the special two-member subcommittee assigned to study Canadian-American relations. In 1954 he managed the successful gubernatorial campaign of Maine's present Senator Edmund S. Muskie and for the next two years was the chairman of the state Democratic committee. Representative Coffin is a lawyer by profession.

Prominence in the Democratic party seems to be a tradition in the family of Frank Morey Coffin, who was born to Herbert Rice and Ruth (Morey) Coffin at Lewiston, Maine on July 11, 1919. His maternal grandfather Frank Morey was four times elected mayor of Lewiston on the Democratic ticket and in 1911 was the speaker of the Maine House of Representatives. His grandmother Maude Morey was a member of the Maine Legislature twenty years later, and his mother served on the state Democratic committee. His father, who died in August 1958, was a restaurateur.

Educated in the Lewiston public schools and at Bates College in his native city, Coffin attracted attention as a debater and long-distance runner. He won the distinction in 1940 of taking his B.A. degree *summa cum laude.* Before his commissioning in 1943 as an ensign in the United States Naval Reserve, Coffin studied

Wide World

FRANK M. COFFIN

industrial administration at Harvard's Graduate School of Business Administration. During the latter part of World War II he saw service in the Pacific theater as a Supply Corps officer, and by the time of his return to civilian life in 1946 he had advanced to lieutenant (s.g.).

Coffin received his LL.B. degree from the Harvard Law School and his admission to the Maine bar in 1947. His honors record brought him an appointment as law clerk to Judge John D. Clifford, Jr., of the United States Circuit Court for the District of Maine. He served as law clerk for the next two years. In 1952, after engaging in private law practice at Lewiston, Coffin joined the Portland law firm of Verrill, Dana, Walker, Philbrick & Whitehouse. His contributions to the law journals have included the papers entitled "Maine Pleadings" and "Lawyer and Political Meddler, or a Jealous Mistress Betrayed" published in the *Portland University Law Review* and the *Harvard Law School Bulletin,* respectively.

Not since the Franklin D. Roosevelt national administration had the state government been out of Republican control. Coffin has said that he first ran for the state Democratic committee in order to help restore two-party government to Maine. He is said, furthermore, to have "had his eye on the governorship." In 1954, when Maine Democrats "closed a desultory, biennial convention . . . without endorsing a single candidate," he was approached by "some leaders . . . to see if he would be the sacrificial lamb" (New York *Times,* September 12, 1956). He declined, and the gubernatorial nomination went to Edmund S. Muskie of Waterville, who chose Coffin to manage the notable campaign which ended on September 13, 1954 with the election of Muskie over the incumbent Republican Governor Burton M. Cross.

The Republicans, however, retained control of the state Legislature as well as all three of Maine's seats in the United States House of Representatives. Coffin was elected chairman of the state Democratic committee in 1954 and remained such until just after his own election to Congress two years later.

In March 1956 Frank Coffin agreed to seek election to Congress in the Second Maine District, which covers seven counties in the south-central part of the state and includes the cities of Auburn, Lewiston, Waterville, and Augusta. The incumbent Republican Representative, Charles P. Nelson, had announced his retirement, and Coffin was opposed in the campaign by state senator James L. Reid of Hallowell.

"Mr. Coffin, in one of his subtle moves, in personal appearances," the New York *Times* (September 12, 1956) has noted, "began to talk of Republican 'rubber stamps' in Congress. As he reached that point, he acquired a habit of drawing a real rubber stamp from his jacket pocket and toying with it, without direct reference to the object. Later, on television, he would reach into a drawer and pull out an oversized caricature of a rubber stamp."

The campaign resulted on September 10, 1956 in a triumph for Coffin over Reid by 55,430 votes to 48,292. "Mr. Coffin's victory," commented John H. Fenton in the New York *Times* (September 16, 1956), "appeared to be due to two factors: (1) some of the Muskie popularity rubbed off on him, and (2) Mr. Coffin also is one of the brighter young Democrats for whom confirmed Yankees could vote with pride." Muskie was re-elected Governor by an increased majority.

Maine's first Democratic Representative in twenty-two years, Frank M. Coffin was seated in the Eighty-fifth Congress in January 1957. In the 1957 session he supported the Eisenhower Administration on 67 per cent of the foreign policy and 62 per cent on domestic policy roll calls. He favored authorization of the President's Middle East Doctrine (January), postponement of seven British debt interest payments (April), and the new Mutual Security Act (July). He opposed reduction of Labor Department and Health, Education and Welfare Department funds (April) and the jury trial amendment to the civil rights bill (June); he voted for the resolution to authorize the House Banking and Currency Committee to investigate national money and credit policies (March).

"Yeas" were cast by Coffin in 1958 for the $2,958,900,000 authorization bill for mutual security (May), statehood for Alaska (May), and a Department of Defense appropriation bill providing an additional $99,000,000 for the Army (June). During this session he opposed a three-year suspension of wool import duties (February) and a bill limiting the power of Congress to nullify laws by enactment of federal statutes (June).

One of the two new legislators assigned on January 7, 1957 to the House Foreign Affairs

Committee, Representative Coffin was a member of a study group which visited Europe in April and submitted a report recommending a new policy toward the Soviet satellite nations. It charged the Eisenhower Administration with having lost "the opportunity of our generation" by failing to act decisively at the time of the anti-Communist revolt in Hungary.

As a member of the subcommittee on foreign economic policy, he formed with Representative Brooks Hays, Democrat of Arkansas, a two-member study group which visited Canada in December 1957 to investigate the causes of "gathering irritations" between the United States and its northern neighbor. In a special report released in May 1958 the two Congressmen found that both countries shared the blame for friction, both having "at times acted arbitrarily and unilaterally" in economic matters.

The Representatives' suggestions for counteracting these irritations included setting up a joint project to compile more detailed authoritative statistics on imports and exports, "a certain amount of forbearance" on the part of the United States in disposing of surplus wheat, tariff changes to encourage expanded trade, and greater United States coverage of Canadian news. About three months later Coffin further called on President Eisenhower to abandon current limits on oil imports, at least so far as these affected Canada.

After revisiting Canada in the fall of 1958 Coffin and Hays submitted a second report, editorially hailed in the Toronto *Globe and Mail* (December 23, 1958) as "a scholarly and statesmanlike document, reflecting . . . a fair and thoughtful approach." The second report, in addition, recommended that Canadian industry be given more opportunity to get United States defense contracts, discussion within the framework of the North Atlantic Treaty Organization of United States lead and zinc quotas, Fulbright scholarships for study in Canada, and other measures.

In his re-election on September 9, 1958 Coffin defeated his Republican opponent, Neil S. Bishop, by 59,698 votes to 37,014, or well over three times his margin over Reid in 1956. On the same date Governor Muskie was elected United States Senator, and Republican Robert Hale was defeated in the First Maine District by Democrat James C. Oliver.

"With law and politics as his principal interests," stated the New York *Times* just after his first election to Congress, "Mr. Coffin also enjoys water-color painting, fishing and boating." The "disarmingly quiet" Congressman from Maine has been married since December 19, 1942 to the former Ruth E. Ulrich. Their children are Douglas, Nancy, Meredith, and Susan. Coffin's church is the Baptist.

References

Christian Sci Mon p4 S 11 '56
N Y Times p23 S 12 '56 por
Congressional Directory (1958)
Who's Who in America, 1958-59

COKER, ELIZABETH BOATWRIGHT

Apr. 21, 1909- Author

Address: b. c/o E. P. Dutton & Co., Inc., 300 4th Ave., New York 10; h. Home Ave., Hartsville, S.C.; Blowing Rock, N.C.

Reprinted from the *Wilson Library Bulletin* Jan. 1959.

Novelist Elizabeth Boatwright Coker finds her plots, her dashing heroes, and pursuable heroines in the legends and artistic family histories of her beloved South Carolina. "My great ambition," she says, "is to compose a truly fine novel of Southern life, featuring a family representative of the real Southerner."

Elizabeth Boatwright was born in Darlington, South Carolina on April 21, 1909, to Bessie (Heard) and Purvis Jenkins Boatwright. "My mother was pure Irish (and typical), my father half Welsh, half English. He was a planter and a banker and a merchant all at the same time."

Her first recognition as a writer came while she was in high school. She won the Charleston Poetry Society's Skylark Prize. At Converse College (Spartanburg, South Carolina), the South Carolina Poetry Society gave her their Carrol Prize; she contributed poems and sketches to *College Humor* magazine; and she wrote for various college anthologies, including *Verse, 1931*, edited by J .C. Rehder (Harper). Miss Boatwright also found time to fulfill the duties of editor in chief of the college literary magazine, *Concept*, and president of the literary club, Wild Thyme.

After college, Elizabeth Boatwright spent a year in New York City. There, she worked on the editorial staff of the Dell Publishing Company and supplemented her income by modeling shoes. Returning to South Carolina, Miss Boatwright on September 27, 1930 was married to James Lide Coker 3d of Hartsville, now president of Sonoco Products Company. They have two children, Penelope and James 4th. "A storyteller by nature, I have never wanted to be anything *but* a writer," Mrs. Coker says. "However, I . . . waited for my youngest child to get in school before I *could* seriously." Also, according to her publisher, Dutton, she "reads completed chapters of a book one by one to husband at night, so he feels a part of the creation. Never reads anything until it's well polished—doesn't want to bore him by repetition."

Daughter of Strangers, her first novel, appeared in 1950. Set on a plantation in South Carolina before the Civil War, it is, according to the *Saturday Review of Literature,* a "serious study of a girl, nearly white, caught in an impossible situation under the racial caste system of the South." The book was described as "extremely readable" by the Chicago *Sunday Tribune,* and "a costume romance of more than usual competence" by the New York *Herald Tribune Book Review. Daughter of Strangers* was a selection of the Fiction Book Club.

Next came *The Day of the Peacock* (1952). It did not receive the critical success accorded its predecessor; the New York *Times Book Review* noted: "Readers who enjoy a happy

ELIZABETH BOATWRIGHT COKER

Among her favorite authors are Siegfried Sassoon, Ernest Hemingway, and William Blake. For recreation she says she is most fond of "walking in the woods, especially in misty weather, swimming, dancing (I take a course each year in modern dance with the college girls at Coker College here). As a hobby, I raise Welsh ponies and small terrier dogs. I have traveled much in Europe with my husband, been to Mexico with him, and many research trips alone to the West Indies."

Work in progress includes a novel with a turn-of-the-century setting. Mrs. Coker is a petite five feet two inches tall, a slim 116 pounds, has blue eyes and light brown hair.

References

Charleston News and Courier p3C Ap 7 '57
Who's Who in America (sup Ap '54)
Who's Who in the South and Southwest (1956)
Who's Who of American Women (1958-59)

ending and don't mind the use of *deus ex machina* will find *The Day of the Peacock* very satisfactory reading."

In 1953 the romantic *India Allan* was welcomed by "readers who like a blending of fact and fiction, of real characters and imaginary ones, and of good ones with evil ones" (New York *Herald Tribune Book Review*). This novel of Civil War and Reconstruction days centers on the daughter of a rich Charleston family and her love for a handsome—but much poorer—young planter from "up country." It was a selection of the Doubleday One Dollar Book Club.

The Big Drum (1957) is an historical novel resulting from Mrs. Coker's researches in London, Barbados, and the Carolinas. The story of Simon Blake, it relates how he is compelled by his enemies to flee England for the dangerous and uncivilized New World. There, he falls in love in Barbados, becomes an early settler of Charles Town (now Charleston, South Carolina), and faces the hazards of the wilderness and its inhabitants.

An historical novel about the Southern beauty, Marie Boozer, *La Belle* (1959) describes the burning of Columbia, South Carolina by Sherman's troops during the Civil War. The volume quotes from daily newspapers, diaries, letters, and other primary sources.

In 1956 the Georgia Writers Association awarded Mrs. Coker their prize for the "best short story of social significance" during that year. Mrs. Coker is a member of American Association of University Women, Camden Hunt, Poetry Society of Georgia, Palmetto Garden Club, Garden Club of America, South Carolina Historical Society, Authors Guild of America, and North Carolina Writers. She is active in local church work. For ten years she has served on the Hartsville public school board. During World War II she was a nurse's aide.

COKER, MRS. JAMES LIDE, 3d *See* Coker, Elizabeth Boatwright

CONRAD, BARNABY, JR. Mar. 27, 1922-
Author; artist; amateur matador; restaurateur
Address: b. c/o Houghton Mifflin Co., 2 Park St., Boston 7, Mass.; h. 18 Leeward Rd., Belvedere, Calif.

An authority on the history, lore, and techniques of bullfighting, Barnaby Conrad, Jr., has devoted most of his writing and painting to that subject. Conrad, an amateur matador as well as an *aficionado* of the sport, was severely injured in the bull ring on two occasions. He has written several fictional and nonfictional works on bullfighting, and his best-selling novel, *Matador*, sold over 2,500,000 copies. His documentary movie, *The Day Manolete Was Killed* (1957), is highly regarded for its poetic sensitivity and its experimentalism. In San Francisco Conrad now owns a bistro appropriately called El Matador.

Barnaby Conrad, Jr., was born in San Francisco on March 27, 1922, the son of Barnaby and Helen Upshur (Hunt) Conrad. He attended the California School of Fine Arts in San Francisco, University of North Carolina in 1940, University of Mexico in 1941, and in 1944 received the B.A. degree from Yale University.

At the age of thirteen Barnaby Conrad saw his first *corrida*, or bullfight; at the University of Mexico he became so interested in the sport that he changed from the study of art to tauromachy. He told Harvey Breit (New York *Times Book Review*, July 6, 1952: "I saw some fights and I said to my friends that it looked very easy. Next thing I knew, I had jumped into the ring with my raincoat for a cape. I didn't know anything. I was really scared when the bull came at me. I made a couple of half-hearted passes at the bull and then leaped over the barrier. A couple of the bullfighters suggested my coming out to learn and so I did. It was terribly difficult and you never learn it all. Look at Manolete, who was supposed to know everything about bulls and got killed."

From 1943 to 1946 Conrad served as United States vice-consul to the Spanish cities of Vigo, Málaga, Seville, and Barcelona. "I guess I was the youngest vice consul that's ever been," he recalls. "I was under 21. I certainly was the worst consul that's ever been. I must've set the foreign service back twenty years" (New York Times Book Review, July 6, 1952).

While in Spain Conrad studied bullfighting with Sidney Franklin and Juan Belmonte. He participated in over thirty amateur fights and was once billed as Bernabé Conrad, El Niño de California. Appearing with Belmonte on the same program in 1945, Conrad was awarded the bull's ears for his performance. He was injured in a later fight and gave up his ambition to become a professional matador because of a disabled leg.

Leaving the foreign service of the United States, in 1946 Conrad went to Lima, Peru, where he fought in the amateur bull ring and played the piano in the city's largest hotel. He then became interested in portrait painting and in late 1946 had a successful show of thirty-five portraits. He has also painted murals in Spain, Mexico, and Peru.

During 1947, when he became secretary and chess companion to Sinclair Lewis in Williamstown, Massachusetts, Conrad began his literary career. At this time he wrote and illustrated his first novel, *The Innocent Villa* (Random House, 1948). The hero of the book is a young American attached to the consul's office in Cordoba, Spain, who loves a beautiful Spanish girl and who is passionately interested in bullfighting. Anne Whitmore in the *Library Journal* (March 15, 1948) pronounced the book "readable, without much plot," but asserted prophetically that the author's description of a bullfight alone "makes the book worthwhile."

His second novel, *Matador* (Houghton, 1952), with illustrations by the author, was a fictionalized account of the life of the great Spanish *torero* Manolete. In the book Pacote, a popular matador, is persuaded to make another appearance, although he has announced his retirement to the public. His destruction is brought on by his alleged friends and his audiences.

The book, which the critics compared to Ernest Hemingway's *The Sun Also Rises* (1926) and Tom Lea's *The Brave Bulls* (1949), became a best seller, was a Book-of-the-Month Club selection for July 1952, and was issued in paper-backed form in the same year by the Western Printing & Lithographing Company.

In *La Fiesta Brava; The Art of the Bull Ring* (Houghton, 1953) Conrad offers a definitive history and analysis of bullfighting. The book contains many photographs depicting the life of the bull, from his early days on the ranch to his death at the hands of the matador. In *Gates of Fear* (Crowell, 1957) he presents the *aficionado* with stories of the great bull rings of the world and the facts or legends on which their reputations are based; he recounts the exploits of the matadors and discusses the

Louise Dahl-Wolfe for
Sports Illustrated

BARNABY CONRAD, JR.

superstitions that circulate in the cafés and around the arenas.

The Death of Manolete (Houghton, 1958) is a requiem in the form of a biography of Conrad's friend and idol, Manuel Laureano Rodríguez Sanchez, better known as Manolete. Venerated by Conrad as the greatest matador of modern times, Manolete was expert in executing the classical passes with cape and muleta. In the book Conrad relates the incidents of August 28, 1947 when Manolete, provoked by the press and the *aficionados,* came out of retirement and entered a contest with a young and arrogant *torero.* Manolete killed the bull by leaping over the horns in the ancient fashion which has all but disappeared, but in the process the bull swerved and Manolete was fatally gored. The book contains over 250 photographs which lend a cinematic quality to the text.

The tragedy of the master among matadors was made into a documentary motion picture, *The Day Manolete Was Killed* (1957). Like an Orson Welles or Charles Chaplin, Barnaby Conrad was producer, composer, writer, co-director, and narrator. The film, made up exclusively of still photographs (the iconographic technique), is valuable both to those interested in the experimental film and to followers of the spectacle. For television's *Omnibus* program Conrad prepared a documentary of the details of Manolete's death, in 1956, and in the following year he wrote a dramatic version for TV's *Playhouse 90.*

A short story by Conrad, "Cayetano the Perfect," was included in *Prize Stories of 1949*; *The O'Henry Awards,* edited by Herschel Brickell. Conrad's writings and illustrations have appeared in *Collier's, Esquire, Reader's Digest, True, Look,* and other magazines. At present he is working on an encyclopedia on bullfighting to be entitled *The Complete Afici-*

CONRAD, BARNABY, JR.—*Continued*

onado and a novel based on the last years of Sinclair Lewis' life.

The best works in English on the fighting of bulls, according to Conrad, are Hemingway's *The Sun Also Rises, Death in the Afternoon* (1932), and "The Undefeated." In an attempt to make more books on the subject available to Americans, Conrad translated from the Spanish and helped to write *My Life as a Matador* (Houghton, 1956), the autobiography of the famous Mexican bullfighter Carlos Arruza, and edited and translated Luis Spota's *Wounds of Hunger* (Houghton, 1957), a novel about a young man who aspires to fight bulls.

In the spring of 1958 Conrad was almost killed in the ring in El Escorial, Spain when he was gored eight inches in his left thigh by a cow. His life was saved by an operation performed by Dr. Luis Giménez Guinea, physician to Spain's outstanding masters of the bull ring. After this experience Conrad concluded: "There is really never anything casual where fighting bovines is concerned. You risk your neck every day you stride into the arena" (*Sports Illustrated*, June 8, 1959).

For several years Conrad has been living in San Francisco, where he has engaged in many activities besides writing. He had a successful exhibition of his paintings, and his canvases have commanded about $1,500 each. Another interest is his bistro, El Matador, which is decorated with photographs of *corridas*, a full-length portrait of Manolete, the beautiful regalia of the ring, and two stuffed bulls' heads. It is also famous for its appetizers, Spanish guitar music, and bullfighting movies shown on Sunday evenings. Sometimes Conrad plays the piano there.

Barnaby Conrad, Jr., was married to Dale Cowgill, a former newspaper columnist, on March 19, 1949. They have two sons, Barnaby, 3d, and Winston Stuart, and a daughter, Tani. Conrad collects tropical fish and flamboyantly colored birds.

References

Newsweek 52:86+ Jl 14 '58
Sports Illus 10:57+ My 4 '59 por
Who's Who in America, 1958-59

COSTELLO, LOU Mar. 6, 1908-Mar. 3, 1959 Film comedian; former partner of Bud Abbott in the Abbott and Costello comedy team. See *Current Biography* (October) 1941.

Obituary

N Y Times p31 Mr 4 '59

CRAIGIE, SIR ROBERT (LESLIE) Dec. 6, 1883-May 16, 1959 Former British Ambassador to Japan (1937-41); career diplomat. See *Current Biography* (July) 1942.

Obituary

N Y Times p84 My 17 '59

CRESAP, MARK W(INFIELD), JR. (krĕs'ŭp) Jan. 3, 1910- Business executive
Address: b. c/o Westinghouse Electric Corp., 3 Gateway Center, Pittsburgh 30, Pa.; h. Backbone Rd., Sewickley, Pa.

By 1970 America will have ultrasonic dishwashers, irradiated foods, TV sets receiving programs from other continents, completely automated factories, and continuous steel casting and direct reduction of ore. These are the predictions of Mark W. Cresap, Jr., president of Westinghouse Electric Corporation. Under his leadership Westinghouse is providing customers with improved electrical appliances, equipping offices and plants with electronic machines, and contributing to the development of submarine, missile, and other defense projects.

Cresap joined Westinghouse in 1951 as vice-president and assistant to the president, Gwilym A. Price, whom he succeeded in December 1957. Before that time he was a management consultant for some ten years, and from 1946 to 1951 he was a partner in the management consultant firm of Cresap, McCormick & Paget.

Born in Chicago, Illinois on January 3, 1910, Mark Winfield Cresap, Jr., is the son of Mark W. and Jessie (Cope) Cresap. His father, who died in 1942, was president of Hart, Schaffner & Marx and negotiated an agreement with Sidney Hillman in 1910 that was one of the first to provide for an arbitration committee. "I heard business and labor talked from the time I was small," Cresap said (New York *Times*, January 19, 1959).

After attending Hill School in Pottstown, Pennsylvania, Cresap studied at Williams College, Williamstown, Massachusetts, where he became president of the Alpha Delta Phi fraternity, worked on the college paper, and earned the B.A. degree in 1932. He then went to the Harvard Graduate School of Business Administration, studied the then relatively new field of management consulting, and received the M.B.A. degree in 1934. In the same year he joined the Chicago management consultant firm of Booz, Fry, Allen & Hamilton.

Named merchandising manager of the John B. Stetson Company, hat manufacturers of Philadelphia, Cresap worked in this position until 1942 when he left to serve in the United States Army. In the rank of colonel he took charge of administrative management for the commanding general, Army Service Forces. He was assigned to the Mediterranean and European theaters and to Washington, D.C.

After his discharge in 1946, Cresap became one of three co-founders of the New York and Chicago management consultant firm of Cresap, McCormick & Paget. Its clients included the Ford Motor Company, Inc., Goldblatt Brothers, a Chicago department store, the American Cyanamid Company, and the New York Public Library. In 1949 Gwilym A. Price, president of Westinghouse Electric Corporation, asked Cresap to study the company's sales organization. Cresap conducted studies which led to an invitation from Price in 1951 to join the organization as vice-president and assistant to the president. Cresap accepted the offer.

Charged with the task of reorganizing the firm's executive structure, Cresap devised a system of staff and line management, with operational decentralization and top-management policy control. To distribute leadership duties further, he set up over sixty-five divisional profit centers. The manager of each of these units is not only responsible for profits but exercises considerable authority over sales, manufacturing, and engineering (*Fortune*, August 1958).

When employees of Westinghouse went on strike for 156 days, starting in October 1955, the firm lost $290,000,000 in business and the workers lost $100,000,000 in wages. The net income of Westinghouse was reduced from $79,900,000 in 1954 to $42,800,000 in 1955.

In August 1955 Cresap was elected executive vice-president of Westinghouse and became a member of the board of directors and of the executive committee. About two and a half years later he became president and chief administrative and operating officer. His predecessor, Gwilym A. Price (see *C.B.*, May 1949), became chairman of the board. When Cresap took on his new duties he said: "With executive vice-president John Hodnette, I will continue to visit all of our manufacturing divisions at least once a year. We have found these visits valuable because they get all Westinghouse people acquainted with management. They improve supervisors' knowledge of company policy. They make all plant personnel feel they are part of the Westinghouse Electric Corporation" (*Electrical World*, January 20, 1958).

Research and education are vital features of Westinghouse policy. Professional workers participate in a unique program called Science Teachers' Day when high school teachers of physics, chemistry, and biology exchange places for one day with Westinghouse scientists and engineers. The teachers tour the laboratory facilities of local Westinghouse plants (there are over 100 factories in the United States) where they become acquainted with current techniques and trends in research and engineering. The Westinghouse Educational Foundation, supported by the corporation, during 1958 awarded $1,590,000 to educational institutions and individual scholars. The George Westinghouse Scholarships were established in honor of the founder of the firm.

Broadening its activities in the atomic age, Westinghouse has developed and supplied nuclear reactors for the atomic-powered submarines of the United States Navy, including *Nautilus*, *Skate*, *Swordfish*, *Sargo*, and *Skipjack*. It has also produced prototypes of new torpedoes and underwater equipment. The company's achievements in the Bomarc and Titan missile programs for the United States Air Force and the Polaris missile project for the Navy were noteworthy achievements of 1958, according to Cresap and Price. The firm also built reactors as prototypes for power plants for surface vessels. On May 26, 1959 the atomic power station of the Duquesne Light Company at Shippingport, Pennsylvania was dedicated, the nuclear aspects of which were produced by Westinghouse.

Fabian Bachrach

MARK W. CRESAP, JR.

The 1958 Westinghouse annual report indicated that net income amounted to $74,772,541, equal to $4.25 a share on 17,180,000 common stock, as compared to $72,652,980, equal to $4.18 a share on 16,943,000 shares of common stock outstanding at the end of 1957. Net sales in 1958 were $1,895,699,358, a decrease of 5.6 per cent from the previous year. Total employee compensation and benefits, when the average number of employees was 114,652, amounted to $765,599,859. Federal, state, local and foreign taxes were $101,144,899.

Planned for the market of tomorrow, the new products for the home that have been demonstrated during the past year by Westinghouse include a bottle cooler-warmer, a hostess cart containing both refrigeration and oven compartments, a full-size thermoelectric refrigerator, dehumidifier, electronic oven, infrared food warmer, and closed-circuit television in the home.

Honors conferred on Westinghouse during 1958 were the Industrial Science Achievement Award of the American Association for the Advancement of Science for developing Opcon, a machine which duplicates the behavior of a person in controlling complicated industrial processes; the Certificate of Merit, awarded to its Bettis Atomic Power Division, the highest industrial award granted by the Navy; and the Peabody Award granted to the Westinghouse Broadcasting Company.

Mark W. Cresap, Jr., and Madeline Reed were married on September 7, 1948. They have two children, Madeline Reed and Mark W. 3d. Cresap likes to cut his own firewood, and he was an enthusiastic gardener at his fieldstone and wood house in Pittsburgh's Sewickley Heights section until he set out 150 plants one day. "That night," he said, "a whole formation of rabbits cleared out every single one. I decided right then and there that I couldn't

CRESAP, MARK W., JR.—*Continued*

fight the whole animal kingdom" (*Newsweek,* April 13, 1959). His favorite exercise is playing soccer with his son. He reads about twenty-five books a year, especially in the fields of history and biography. The Cresap family often spends its vacations at Martha's Vineyard, Massachusetts.

One union official has said of Cresap: "He is a down-to-earth guy who talks our language." He has been described as stocky, energetic, aggressive, personable, and candid. Cresap foresees a period of strong growth for both his company and the electrical industry. "We intend to increase our investment in research," he has said. "Leadership in the nuclear power field is our major aim" (*Electrical World,* January 20, 1958).

As a leader of the business community of Pennsylvania, Cresap is a director of the Pennsylvania Economy League and Pennsylvania State Chamber of Commerce and a member of the Pittsburgh Regional Planning Association and the sponsoring committee of the Allegheny Conference on Community Development. He is a member of the Pennsylvania Governor's State Government Survey Committee and serves on the board of the Allegheny General Hospital. His clubs are the Commercial in Chicago; University, Broad Street, and Williams in New York, Duquesne (Pittsburgh), Allegheny Country (Sewickley), and Rolling Rock. He is a trustee of Williams College. For his services during World War II he was decorated with the Legion of Merit.

References

Who's Who in America, 1958-59
Who's Who in Commerce and Industry (1957)

CURTIS, TONY June 3, 1925- Actor
Address: b. c/o Universal-International Pictures, Universal City, Calif.

Early in 1958 Tony Curtis reached the peak of his popularity when the Hollywood Foreign Press Association, representing fifty-eight countries, named him the "world's favorite movie actor." In his recent roles, such as that of the chain-gang convict in *The Defiant Ones* and the toady of a Broadway columnist in *The Sweet Smell of Success,* he has abandoned the "pretty-boy" assignments which had made him "the bobby-soxer's idol."

As award followed award in 1958 and 1959, Curtis began to be recognized by motion picture critics as a serious, versatile, and dedicated young actor. The New York Film Critics listed *The Defiant Ones,* in which Curtis played opposite Sidney Poitier, among the ten best pictures of 1958. Also in 1958 *Photoplay* magazine named him the most popular star of the year, and in 1959 he was nominated for an Oscar by the Academy of Motion Picture Arts and Sciences.

Tony Curtis, whose real name is Bernard Schwartz, was born on June 3, 1925 to Mr. and Mrs. Mono Schwartz in New York City. His father had been a well-known actor in Budapest, Hungary, but had turned to tailoring because he could not speak sufficient English to procure work on the stage. Bernard grew up, with his younger brother, Robert, in "a tough, rough neighborhood" of the Bronx borough of New York City. He learned to fight with his fists and feet, and by the time he was eleven was a member of one of Manhattan's toughest gangs.

At the age of twelve Tony Curtis became a Boy Scout to try to correct his "near-delinquency" as he later expressed it. He credits a welfare worker named Paul Schwartz with straightening him out. They met when a truant officer took the youth and a few pals to the Jones Memorial Settlement House, where they learned honesty and self-respect.

At the settlement house, Bernie Schwartz, who was already a movie fan, was won over to play-acting. His first role was that of a girl in a play about King Arthur. He attended Seward Park High School in New York, but left it six months before graduation in 1944 to enter the United States Navy. He served as a signalman aboard the submarine USS *Dragonette* until a winch chain snapped and injured him while he was loading torpedoes at Guam. For four weeks he lay in a hospital with his legs paralyzed. After he had recovered, he returned to the United States and completed his schooling at Seward Park High School. He was graduated in 1946.

Deciding to study dramatics on the GI Bill, Bernard Schwartz enrolled at the Dramatic Workshop in New York, and played the idiot son of the lighthouse keeper in *Thunder Rock* at the 92d Street YMCA Playhouse. After a year's study at the Workshop he joined a stock company which toured the "Borsch Circuit" in New York state. He was one of a group which formed the Empire Players; they opened in *Dear Ruth* in Newark, New Jersey and lost money. He next acted with the Cherry Lane players in Greenwich Village and played the title role in *Golden Boy,* in which he was seen by a talent scout for Universal-International Pictures. He was sent to Hollywood and signed a contract for $75 a week.

At the studio Curtis took courses in dramatics, voice, gymnastics, horsemanship, and pantomime. He was finally assigned a bit part in a dancing sequence in *Criss Cross* (1949) which starred Yvonne De Carlo. Although Anthony Curtis (the name he assumed and later shortened to Tony) appeared on less than 100 feet of film, fan mail began to pour in.

Curtis' fan mail increased when he played a more prominent role, as a hoodlum, in *City Across the River* (1949). Then Universal-International costarred him with Piper Laurie (also a newcomer) in a $1,000,000 spectacle, *The Prince Who Was a Thief* (July 1951). The critics were not enthusiastic over the young actor's muscular achievements — scaling high walls, swimming under water, racing through Oriental bazaars—but his fans were delighted with both his acting and athletic prowess.

Over the ensuing eight years Curtis has grown in acting stature by playing a variety of roles. For example, in the *Sweet Smell of Success* (1957) he was a venal, ambitious publicist; in *Kings Go Forth* (1958), a spoiled "rich boy"; in *The Vikings* (1958) a daring marauder; and in *The Defiant Ones* (1958), an embittered convict. He thinks that his career took this turn for the better when he began to free-lance.

Trapeze (1956), in which Tony Curtis played opposite Burt Lancaster had been the "big break" for him, he has said. "It was like the major league." As the young aerialist, "Curtis is earnest and intense, and he is particularly good at the end, when he feels a twinge of fear," observed William K. Zinsser (New York *Herald Tribune,* June 5, 1956). Alton Cook noted: (New York *World-Telegram and Sun,* June 5, 1956). "The surprise is the depth and force of Tony Curtis. He is a jaunty, eager youngster, ecstatic as he works toward mastery of his hard craft. The snarling frenzy with which he meets misfortune is both pathetic and ruthless." On the other hand, Bosley Crowther (New York *Times,* June 5, 1956) dismissed Curtis' acting in *Trapeze* as "simply juvenile."

In reviewing *The Defiant Ones,* a film directed by Stanley Kramer, and costarring Tony Curtis and Sidney Poitier, Arthur Knight wrote in the *Saturday Review* (July 26, 1958): "The real revelation is Tony Curtis . . . he displays a hardness and toughness quite new to him. . . . The spiritual growth of this character, his gradual shedding of false pride and unreasoned resentments, provides the greatest single acting challenge in the film—and Curtis more than meets it."

Among Curtis' recent pictures are: *The Perfect Furlough,* in which he played opposite his wife, Janet Leigh; *Some Like It Hot,* with Marilyn Monroe; and *Operation Petticoat* (filmed on location in Key West, Florida), in which he enacted a Navy submarine officer, costarring with Cary Grant. On television he played the role of David in *The Stone,* presented on the *General Electric Theatre* program on January 18, 1959.

Psychoanalysis, which Curtis began in 1953, has helped him, he believes, in his development both as an actor and a person. "You know where the real trouble lies with a guy like me?" he asked Jesse Zunser (*Cue,* August 2, 1958). "You go too far too fast. So—you begin to think about it. . . . You're on a quick ride and going great, but the question always is: Are you really talented or just dumb lucky? . . . A guy's got to gamble on himself or he gets fat playing it safe," he said. He keeps changing pace. "Don't get typed," he warns, "or you'll get trapped."

Tony Curtis and actress Janet Leigh were married on June 4, 1951. They have two daughters, Kelly Lee and Jamie. Their home is in Beverley Hills, California. Curtis is five feet, ten and one-half inches tall, weighs 160 pounds, and has curly dark hair and blue eyes. His favorite sports are golf, boxing, fishing, and swimming.

He also enjoys photography and oil painting, likes progressive jazz, and is learning to play the flute. He numbers among his closest friends

United Artists Corp.

TONY CURTIS

Jerry Lewis, Frank Sinatra, Marlon Brando, and "anyone Janet likes." He will drive long distances in his Cadillac convertible to see an old Marx Brothers picture. He is a member of the Screen Actors Guild.

References

Cosmop 135 :9 Ag '53
Cue 27 :10 Ag 2 '58 pors
Look 20 :20 N 13 '56
Newsweek 51 :85 Je 30 '58 por
Sat Eve Post 224 :22 F 9 '52

International Motion Picture Almanac, 1958

DALLAS, C(HARLES) DONALD Oct. 24, 1881-Apr. 12, 1959 Industrialist; a founder, president (1931-47), and chairman of the board and chief executive officer (1947-51) of Revere Copper and Brass, Inc. See *Current Biography* (April) 1949.

Obituary

N Y Times p86 Ap 13 '59

DALY, JAMES (FIRMAN) Oct. 23, 1918-
Actor
Address: b. c/o Olga Lee, 113 W. 57th St., New York 19; h. 63 Mile Rd., Suffern, N.Y.

The misfortunes of Job have proved to be the greatest good fortune for James Daly, who succeeded to the title role in Archibald MacLeish's Pulitzer Prize-winning drama *J.B.* in March 1959. He replaced Pat Hingle, who suffered a fractured hip in an elevator accident. A modern version of the Biblical story of Job, the poetic drama maintained its critical and popular success with Daly as its star. He left

Friedman—Abeles

JAMES DALY

the cast on October 10, 1959, shortly before the play ended its New York run, on October 24.

Before his triumphant engagement in *J.B.*, Daly had appeared in short-lived Broadway productions. He had starred in the television show, *Foreign Intrigue*, which was filmed on location in Paris and Stockholm, and had performed in many TV dramas and in the motion pictures *The Court Martial of Billy Mitchell* and *The Young Stranger*.

James Firman Daly, who is descended from Irish immigrants, was born on October 23, 1918 in Wisconsin Rapids, Wisconsin, the son of Percifer Charles and Dorothy Ethelbert (Hogan) Daly. John Daly, his grandfather, operated a lumber raft on the Wisconsin and Mississippi rivers. Daly's father is a fuel merchant, and his mother is an employee of the Central Intelligence Agency in Washington, D.C. His brother, David, works as an agent for the Federal Bureau of Investigation. He has two sisters, Mary Ellen, a captain in the women's branch of the United States Air Force, and Cynthia Ann, a speech pathologist.

While still in high school Daly decided to become an actor. After his graduation from Lincoln High School in Wisconsin Rapids in 1936, he enacted 200 roles in various dramas produced at the three colleges he attended. At the State University of Iowa and the University of Wisconsin he studied dramatics; he then enrolled as an English and drama student at Cornell College in Mount Vernon, Iowa, where he supported himself with part-time jobs which ranged from librarian to hospital orderly. He received his B.A. degree in 1941. Not long after graduation, he enlisted as an infantryman in the United States Army and was later transferred to the Army Air Forces. Before the war ended he was also an ensign in the United States Navy.

Soon after his discharge from the armed services, Daly began his acting career. In his first Broadway assignment he was an understudy for Gary Merrill as the liberal journalist in the comedy, *Born Yesterday*, which opened in early 1946. Daly substituted for Merrill in forty performances of Garson Kanin's play.

After a small role in *Virginia Reel* on Broadway, beginning on April 15, 1947, Daly toured with the Maurice Evans production of Bernard Shaw's *Man and Superman* in 1948 and 1949. Playing the part of Hector Malone, Jr., he won the annual Daniel Blum Award for his performance. The Shavian drama turned out to be his last extended employment for several years. He then appeared in television plays, the legitimate theater, and summer stock.

In the off-Broadway production of Shelley's *The Cenci* in 1950, Daly's interpretation of the role of Count Cenci inspired a *Billboard* (February 18, 1950) reviewer to remark: "James Daly proves that he rates with any classical actor alive today." Later that year Daly understudied Maurice Evans in Shaw's *The Devil's Disciple*. He then won a Theatre World Award for his performance as Bill Walker in Shaw's *Major Barbara*, which was first presented on December 7, 1950, under the auspices of Equity Library Theatre. He next appeared as Talbot, the maintopman, in a Broadway dramatization of Herman Melville's *Billy Budd* on January 24, 1951. In March 1951 he took the part of Harry in Sir James Barrie's *Mary Rose*. Another Shavian assignment came his way in late 1951 when he was cast as Robert de Baudricourt, the cockney soldier, in a Broadway production of *Saint Joan* that starred Uta Hagen.

Devoting most of his energies to television, Daly in 1953 became the star of the popular series *Foreign Intrigue* (later called *Overseas Adventure*). While the show was being filmed, Daly and his family lived in Paris and in Stockholm. On the *Omnibus* television program he took the title roles in *Henry Adams* on April 20, 1955, *The Court Martial of William Mitchell* on April 11, 1956, and in the verse drama *Lee at Gettysburg* on January 20, 1957. On the *Kraft Television Theater* he performed in *No Riders* on April 18, 1956 and in *Death is a Spanish Dancer* on June 9, 1956. For *Studio One* he acted in *The Power* on June 4, 1956 and in *Goodbye Piccadilly* on December 31, 1956. He was also signed in 1956 to deliver TV commercials for Camel cigarettes, a job he has held ever since.

Daly returned to the New York stage to play the role of Jean, the ambitious and sadistic valet, in a revival of Strindberg's *Miss Julie* which began its run at the Phoenix Theatre on February 21, 1956. Walter Kerr in the New York *Herald Tribune* (March 4, 1956) appraised Daly's performance: "There is one emotional hurdle Mr. Daly cannot get over, but only one: this casual, almost unthinking opportunist is once or twice expected to shudder over his own intolerable past, and Mr. Daly seems unable to imagine the precise anguish that stirs in an otherwise perfectly selfish soul. The rest of the time—rocking smugly with his feet on the table, fiercely shining boots as his temperature rises, grimly re-living the events of a terrifying dream —he is a doggedly convincing monster."

In motion pictures Daly made his debut in *The Court Martial of Billy Mitchell* released in December 1955; he later appeared in *The Young Stranger,* which was first exhibited in May 1957. With Helen Hayes he co-starred in a City Center revival of *The Glass Menagerie,* beginning on November 21, 1956. In 1957 Daly went to Berlin, Germany to act in the world première of Thornton Wilder's *Bernice.*

Returning to the United States, Daly starred in *This is Goggle,* which closed in early 1958 on the road in Washington, D.C. He then appeared briefly in *Handful of Fire,* also in Washington, and then took the starring role in the première of Tennessee Williams' *Period of Adjustment* in Miami, Florida. Finally, in March 1959, Daly got what proved to be the break of his career when he was signed to replace the star of *J.B.*

The verse play by Archibald MacLeish brought hyperboles from some critics when it opened in New York on December 11, 1958; it later won the Pulitzer Prize and the Antoinette Perry Award. A typical review ran: "Adjectives pall and superlatives stale in the face of such a drama as this." Recasting the Biblical story of Job in modern terms, *J.B.* has for its setting an enormous tent belonging to a traveling circus "on the roads of the world."

Before Daly could replace Pat Hingle in the title role of *J.B.,* he had to obtain a release from his contract with Otto Preminger to appear in the film version of *Anatomy of a Murder.* Daly first performed the role of J.B. on March 12, 1959.

"Daly is in command of the shifting moods," wrote a *Variety* critic (March 25, 1959), "never over-colored at any point, always a human being in distress, a protagonist but never just a mouthpiece for the interminable questioning to which the Archibald MacLeish text runs. He is convincingly beset, desperately agonized. In short, this is a dimensioned realization by an actor of intelligence and of subtle technique."

In February 1941 James Daly married the actress Mary Hope Newell, who had been his classmate at Cornell College. They have three daughters, Pegeen Michael, Ellen Tyne, and Mary Glynn (whose names are traditional in the Daly family), and one son, James Timothy. The family lives in a remodeled farmhouse in Suffern, New York, where Daly is an auxiliary member of the Tallman Fire Department.

James Daly is five feet eleven inches tall, weighs 170 pounds, and has brown hair and hazel eyes. He belongs to Actors' Equity Association, Screen Actors Guild, and American Federation of Television & Radio Actors. At home, he cultivates his hobbies of breeding sheep and growing roses; he is an enthusiastic swimmer and skater. His political affiliation is Democratic.

"James Daly's *J.B.* will be remembered," predicted one reviewer. With critical success to reinforce the popularity Daly has won from more than 500 television performances, he may well have reached a new point in his career.

He already holds one distinction earned by few in his profession: he is a Doctor of Fine Arts, an honorary degree granted to him by Cornell College in 1957.

Reference

Cedar Rapids (Iowa) Gazette p19+ Mr '59 por

DANIELS, GRACE B(AIRD) Organization official

Address: h. 146 E. Walnut St., Kingston, Pa.

The National Federation of Business and Professional Women's Clubs, which is dedicated to serving the interests of the approximately 25,000,000 working women in the United States, elected Grace B. Daniels as its president for 1958-60. Miss Daniels has been a leader of the federation for many years and has served in a number of social, political, and welfare organizations. In her professional life she has been a cellist, child-guidance teacher, and school director. She now serves as an auditor of Luzerne County, Pennsylvania. As federation president, she is leading its 170,000 members in a concerted effort to place more women in positions of community leadership.

Grace Baird Daniels is the daughter of John F. Daniels and Jessie (Baird) Daniels, a teacher, and the granddaughter of David Baird, a mining engineer. She grew up in Wilkes-Barre, Pennsylvania, and after attending a private girls' school, studied the cello with Emile Hoppe in New York City. Upon her return to Pennsylvania, she played with various musical groups. Later, she turned to child-guidance teaching and she then established a private school in Forty Fort, Pennsylvania, where she worked with children who needed special training in sound and tone work.

Because she has always believed that the individual should make a contribution to the community, Miss Daniels entered government service by accepting an appointment as chief of the division of permanent registration for Luzerne County. In this post she organized the first permanent registration system for voters in the heavily populated county, which is larger in size than the state of Rhode Island. In connection with this task she openly appeared in court to clear up the citizenship status of many individuals who lacked proper credentials.

Now the auditor of the department of costs and accounts of the road and bridge division of Luzerne county, she authorizes final payment for all highway and bridge construction and maintenance. She checks specifications and makes certain that all legal requirements have been met. On the basis of her experience, Miss Daniels believes that women are especially suited for budgetary positions in government. "Women understand well the need for integrity in financial dealings," she has said. "They are good economizers and budget planners. More women managing public funds would be a stabilizing influence in our national economy" (*Christian Science Monitor,* August 25, 1958).

(Continued next page)

GRACE B. DANIELS

Convinced that business, the professions, and government should make greater use of the many talents and abilities of women, Miss Daniels has actively worked toward this goal for over twenty-five years through the National Federation of Business and Professional Women's Clubs. The organization, which has over 3,300 clubs in the United States, is the oldest and largest national association for professional women. Throughout its history it has not only promoted increased opportunities and improved working conditions for women but has also provided special leadership training.

In 1933 Grace B. Daniels and two friends held the first meeting of the Wilkes-Barre Business and Professional Women's Club. Later, Miss Daniels served as first chairman of the bylaws committee; first vice-president; president; membership, news service, and legislative chairman; and parliamentarian. She was instrumental in organizing English classes for adults who could only speak foreign languages. She was secretary, co-chairman, and chairman of district eight in Pennsylvania. Leaving the district office, in rapid succession she was second vice-president and first vice-president of the Pennsylvania BPW.

By unanimous vote Grace B. Daniels was elected president of the Pennsylvania federation and was re-elected for a second term. Under her presidency the BPW carried out a successful campaign for passage by the state legislature of a uniform pay bill; established the federation's first foreign exchange student program; founded the Maxwell School of Political Science for members and other citizens; and phenomenally increased membership.

In 1950 Miss Daniels was appointed to her first major national office—chairman of the membership committee. She became third vice-president in 1952, second vice-president in 1954, and first vice-president in 1956. At the national

convention, held in Seattle, Washington, she was unanimously elected eighteenth president on July 8, 1958. She succeeded Hazel Palmer (see *C.B.,* June 1958). Miss Daniels also serves as president of the board of the Business and Professional Women's Foundation. Established in 1956, it is a clearinghouse and research center on all matters pertaining to professional women.

Beginning in April 1959, Miss Daniels made a three-month tour of various federated conventions and local meetings from the Philippine Islands to Puerto Rico.

As president she initiated programs to aid qualified women to fill more elective and appointive local, state, and national governmental offices. She believes more women should be named to the United States Delegation to the U.N. "If more able American women were serving in U.N. posts, the uncommitted areas of the world where women are seeking status and leadership would turn more and more to America for their leadership" she maintains (*National Business Woman,* August 1958).

Miss Daniels has left the imprint of her personality and influence upon many philanthropic and educational institutions in her region. As a civic leader, she served on the board of the Town Hall Association of Wyoming Valley, which offered public forums and other programs to the community. She was also active in this group when it became the Industrial Relations Committee of Wyoming Valley, the aim of which was to bring other industries to this predominantly anthracite-mining area.

Miss Daniels is a charter president of the Wilkes-Barre Soroptimist Club, a member of the county chapter of the American Red Cross, board of Women's Medical College of Pennsylvania, Wyoming Valley Welfare Association, Luzerne County Republican executive committee, Philadelphia Citizens Committee, and past president of the Wilkes-Barre Serve Your City Club. As an active member of the congregation of her local Episcopal church, she is superintendent of its school and a teacher of an adult Bible class. For her efforts in behalf of national defense during World War II Miss Daniels received a citation for meritorious service from the Governor of Pennsylvania.

The blue-eyed, auburn-haired federation president is "Miss Grace" to two teen-agers, Diane and Jackie, to whom she has been a second mother for ten years. Because their own widowed mother cannot provide for them, Miss Daniels is clothing and educating the girls. In spite of her busy schedule she also finds time for her very feminine avocation—designing hats.

Grace B. Daniels' "quick and efficient grasp of the practical realities of administration are nicely balanced by the warmth and understanding so necessary in human relations and professional achievement." She holds the conviction that the "future hope of the world may well depend on dedicated—intelligent—and courageous women."

References

Christian Sci Mon p4 Ag 25 '58 por
Nat Bsns Woman 37:20 Ag '58 pors

DAVIS, NATHANAEL V(INING) June 26, 1915- Corporation executive

Address: b. Aluminium, Ltd., 1155 Metcalfe St., Montreal 3, Québec, Canada

Included among the largest producers of aluminum in the world, Aluminium, Ltd., is the holding company for the Aluminum Company of Canada (Alcan) and about thirty other subsidiaries in over twenty countries. Its president since 1947 has been Nathanael V. Davis, who succeeded his father, Edward Kirk Davis, organizer and first president of the firm. The company operates in the Canadian provinces of Quebec and British Columbia two of the largest smelters in existence, and in its peak year of 1956 reported production of over 700,000 tons.

The eldest of three sons, Nathanael Vining Davis was born in Pittsburgh, Pennsylvania on June 26, 1915. His father, Edward Kirk Davis, was of an old New England family, and his mother, the former Rhea Ada Reineman, is of Pennsylvania Dutch ancestry. The younger Davis attended Shady Side Academy in Pittsburgh through the sixth grade. His family moved to the Davis family home on Cape Cod, Massachusetts in 1928 when his father became the president of the newly formed Aluminium, Ltd., after having served as vice-president and treasurer of the Aluminum Company of America (Alcoa). (His uncle Arthur Vining Davis is honorary chairman of the board of Alcoa.)

Nathanael Davis continued his education in Massachusetts and following graduation from the Middlesex School in Concord studied at universities in Grenoble and Tours in France. In 1934 he entered Harvard University, majored in international law and economics, and earned his B.A. degree *cum laude* in 1938. This was followed by a year of graduate work abroad at the London School of Economics. While he was a student Davis worked one summer in Aluminium's Italian subsidiary, Società Dell'Alluminio Italiano, at Borgofranco d'Ivrea, as a potman tending a smelting furnace. During other summers he visited various subsidiaries of the parent firm. He became in 1939 a member of the management of Aluminium, Ltd.

In the fall of 1942 Davis was commissioned an ensign in the U.S. Navy and sent to the Aircraft Combat Intelligence School at Quonset Point, Rhode Island. He was assigned to a reconnaissance squadron as intelligence officer and served in the Caribbean and Pacific areas where he saw combat duty. In 1947, after his discharge from the service, he was elected president of Aluminium, Ltd., at the age of thirty-two.

Aluminium, Ltd., was founded in 1928 as a holding company of Alcan and foreign subsidiaries of Alcoa. At its inception, Davis wrote in the *Christian Science Monitor* (October 12, 1956, Aluminium was a "heterogeneous and poorly integrated group of companies. . . . During the difficult depression years aluminum was . . . in small demand, and it was not until 1938 that the company had rounded out its operations by integrating its activities in mining, shipping,

Fabian Bachrach

NATHANAEL V. DAVIS

power generation, smelting, processing, finishing, and delivering aluminum products."

In the following year the outbreak of World War II brought a greatly increased demand for aluminum for airplane construction. The output, which had amounted to only about 85,000 tons in 1938, rose to "109,000 tons in 1940, and, spurred by U.S. contracts, to 214,000 the next year" (*Fortune*, June 1954). Also in 1941 a $55,600,000, twenty-year loan from Britain resulted in the beginning of construction of a second hydroelectric installation at Shipshaw on the Saguenay River in Quebec.

Within eighteen months this plant had been completed and Aluminium had built a giant smelter nearby. During the war years Alcan delivered 680,000 tons to the United States alone.

Under Davis' guidance, Aluminium in the early postwar years launched the largest expansion program ever undertaken in the aluminum industry. Capacity had risen to 400,000 tons by 1948. During the Korean conflict, its sales boomed.

In a speech before shareholders in April 1951 Davis announced that Aluminium would construct a huge power installation of Kemano and a giant smelter at Kitimat in British Columbia. It was reported at the time that the project was completed in 1954 that the Kitimat smelter would produce 91,500 tons of aluminum a year and that the annual capacity would eventually reach 550,000 tons. The Kemano power installation, with its potential hydroelectric capacity of 2,240,000 horsepower, was the largest ever undertaken by private enterprise.

When Aluminium, Ltd., was founded, its ownership of shares was identical with that of Alcoa, but in January 1951 shareholders were directed by Federal Judge John C. Knox to dispose of their holdings in one company or the

DAVIS, NATHANAEL V.—*Continued*

other within ten years. Today (in the words of Davis) Aluminium, Ltd., "is completely independent of Alcoa and, indeed, competes actively with its former sponsor" (*Christian Science Monitor,* October 12, 1956).

Aluminium owns shares in some thirty operating and management companies located in more than twenty different countries and employs about 40,000 persons. Its main mining facilities for bauxite (from which aluminum is chiefly derived) are located in British Guiana, Guinea, and Jamaica, and other deposits are being mined in France, Malaya, and Sarawak. For the year 1957 Aluminium, Ltd., reported a capacity amounting to some 870,000 tons and revenue of $453,000,000.

In March 1958 Davis announced a cut of 2 cents a pound in the price of primary aluminum, the first reduction since 1941. "We believe," Davis explained, "this price reduction at this time, when important segments of the aluminum smelting industry are idle, and when there is a widespread public demand for lower prices, will be a constructive force in improving national and world economy and will be beneficial to consumers, fabricators, and the industry as a whole" (New York *Times,* March 28, 1958).

Unlike his father, Davis conducts much of his business from an office in Montreal. He was elected a director of the New England Mutual Life Insurance Company in 1955 and a trustee of the Committee for Economic Development in 1956. He is also a trustee of the Middlesex School and was active in his church at Chestnut Hill in metropolitan Boston.

It has been said that he is "possessed with excellent judgment and the ability to work easily with people." The young executive finds relaxation in sailing and fishing off Cape Cod. Nathanael V. Davis and Lois Howard Thompson of Jamaica in the British West Indies were married in 1941 and have one son, James Howard Dow, and one daughter, Katharine Vining Davis. Davis' clubs are the University in New York; Somerset in Boston; Country in Brookline, Massachusetts; and Rolling Rock in Ligonier, Pennsylvania.

References

N Y Times p52 S 22 '55 por
N Y World-Telegram p5 My 16 '53 por
Canadian Who's Who, 1955-57
Poor's Register of Directors and Executives, United States and Canada, 1958
Who's Who, 1958
Who's Who in America, 1958-59
Who's Who in Commerce and Industry (1957)

DAVIS, TOBÉ COLLER 1893(?)- Fashion columnist; merchandising consultant

Address: b. Tobé and Associates, Inc., 11 W. 42nd St., New York 36; h. 243 E. 61st St., New York 21

Although her own wardrobe is neither extensive nor particularly fashionable, Tobé Coller Davis has been called "the only recognized oracle of fashion" by the president of Bonwit Teller. As the head of Tobé and Associates, an organization which provides stores with information on trends in the fashion industry, she makes a gross income of almost a million dollars a year.

Putting her oracular gifts to work in journalism, Tobé, as she is known, writes a syndicated fashion column, "Tobé Says," which appears in about forty newspapers. She also undertakes department store consulting, at fees of as much as $1,000 a day. As part of its services, Tobé and Associates publishes several reports, such as *Report from Tobé, Fifth Avenue Windows,* and *The Tobé Guide.* A staff of over thirty writers, fashion consultants, and merchandisers work directly under the supervision of Tobé Coller Davis. With Julia Coburn, Tobé Coller Davis is the co-founder and co-director of the Tobé-Coburn School for Fashion Careers in New York City.

Taube Coller was born in Milwaukee, Wisconsin, the daughter of Oscar and Taube (Silberberg) Coller. Her father was a prosperous clothing merchant who specialized in men's wear. Taube attended school in Milwaukee and then studied home economics at Milwaukee-Downer College in that city. She earned the B.S. degree in either 1912 or 1914. Tobé told a reporter from *Business Week* (January 14, 1956) that she "hated fashion" as a child. But she became interested in fashion and merchandising through the influence of her father. "My stepmother hated to talk business, so my father talked to me."

After Taube was graduated from college, the Coller family moved to New York. When a new business venture of Mr. Coller's failed, Taube decided to get a job. Her first position was with a mail-order house at $12 a week, her second with a man who called himself the "Ostrich Feather King." Then she became a salesgirl at Macy's, and later sold hats at B. Altman & Co. In 1916 she worked as a secretary for a fashion designer, Richard Hickson, from whom she learned a good deal about the fashion world.

Convinced that she could start out on her own, Taube opened her own dressmaking business under the name of Tobé. The dressmaking salon failed in a year, but one of her customers was Franklin Simon, who was so impressed with her business acumen that he offered her a job with his store. From 1918 to 1927 Tobé worked as a stylist (these days known as a fashion co-ordinator) for Franklin Simon. "My job was to see what fashionable people were wearing, then make sure Franklin Simon had it" (*Business Week,* January 14, 1956). Soon she was dispatched to Paris to bring back clothing styles from the Parisian dressmakers, and accessories, perfumes, and cosmetics from the most fashionable *haute couture* houses. Working with New York manufacturers, she translated the Paris fashions into a price and style level acceptable to Americans.

During her nine years with Franklin Simon, Tobé received so many offers from other retailers that she became convinced that she could successfully go into business for herself.

In 1927 she founded Tobé and Associates, Inc., with one assistant and four clients. Within a week her business was "in the black." She had surmised the need for an organization that could give fashion counseling and act as the eyes and ears of the fashion industry for merchandisers throughout the United States. Since then her staff has grown to over thirty persons, and she can claim among her clients some of the most famous names in merchandising.

Tobé and Associates publishes several reports, the most important of which is the *Report from Tobé,* a weekly fifty-to-sixty-page report which analyzes fashion news from all angles. It discusses merchandising trends and promotion techniques in wholesale and retail markets, and often contains fabric swatches and sketches. The report also gives retail and wholesale prices and identifies the manufacturers of designs. Over 250 stores in the United States, Europe, and Asia subscribe to the *Report from Tobé;* the report may cost the subscriber from $750 to $10,000 a year, depending on the volume of his business. Other publications are *Fifth Avenue Windows,* a weekly supplement which advises out-of-town stores about attention-attracting Manhattan displays, and *The Tobé Guide,* a weekly digest, which reports briefly on some of the most important fashion trends. Over 1,000 subscribers in the smaller cities rely on the latter publication.

In addition to releasing the reports, Tobé makes herself available for personal consultation. While visiting a store, she or one of her associates may conduct surveys, check on its operation, survey its stock and display techniques, and make plans for its expansion. Tobé charges $1,000 for a day's consultation at a major department store; she holds a consultation about twenty days a year. Another important service rendered by Tobé and Associates is a series of six annual fashion meetings held throughout the year for buyers and store executives. The staff reports on approaching fashion trends and best-selling ideas and items. On the morning after each meeting Tobé and Associates holds a round-table breakfast meeting for top executives and merchandising experts.

In 1937 Tobé Coller Davis and Julia Coburn, a former fashion editor for *Ladies' Home Journal,* founded the Tobé-Coburn School for Fashion Careers in New York City. Charging $1,350 tuition a year, the school prepares young women for careers in the distribution and promotion of fashions. A student may take either a one-year or a two-year course. To qualify for the one-year course, the student must have completed two full years of college work and preferably be between the ages of nineteen and thirty. For the two-year curriculum, which includes some liberal arts courses, the applicant must be a high school graduate and be between the ages of seventeen and twenty. Since its inception, over 1,500 women have been graduated from the Tobé-Coburn School for Fashion Careers. Miss Coburn is the executive director, while Tobé, a director, gives talks and provides informa-

Dorothy Wilding

TOBÉ COLLER DAVIS

tion for the classes through her own organization.

Millions of women learn of the approaching fashion trends, and receive hints on what to wear and what to buy by reading Tobé's syndicated column, "Tobé Says," which appears each day in the New York *Herald Tribune* and in about forty newspapers throughout the United States and Canada. The columnist chats about interesting and practical fashions she has observed in department stores, chic restaurants, night clubs, and theaters. Tobé takes credit for having popularized car coats, fancy aprons, the Oriental look in fashion, twin sweater sets, short nightgowns, and the chemise dress over the years. *Business Week* (January 14, 1956) notes that through her column she "neatly bolsters her advice to stores by persuading the consumer to go along with that advice."

Two basic principles, according to Tobé, account for her success as a fashion oracle. The first is that fashions reflect daily activities (cars lead to car coats), the second that international news affects fashions (the prominence of the Far East in newspaper headlines has introduced an Oriental influence into styles). Adam Gimbel, the president of Saks Fifth Avenue, has called Tobé the "Ted Williams of fashion." He says: "Nobody's batting average is close to hers in calling the turn on a trend."

Tobé has been married twice. Her first marriage was to Herbert Davis, a real-estate broker, in April 1923. Davis died in 1934, and in August 1940 she was married to newspaper executive David Rosenblum. She was widowed for a second time in 1943. She is five feet, seven inches tall. "If I can wear a style," she says, "the chances are it will look well on most women, because I'm not exactly a sylph."

(Continued next page)

DAVIS, TOBÉ COLLER—*Continued*

Surprisingly, Tobé herself does not dress in designer clothes. "I really don't dress well for someone who's always under scrutiny," she remarks. "I never was crazy about clothes, even as a young girl. I went into the fashion business because it was the only one in which I had some background" (*Saturday Evening Post*, June 27, 1959). She has an extensive collection of hats, however, and one closet filled with about seventy-five pairs of shoes.

Surrounded by servants and pets, Tobé lives in a large brownstone house in Manhattan's East Sixties, where she gives elegant dinner parties for celebrities and her own business associates. She attends the opera, first nights at the theater, and other fashionable events, partly in order to observe what women are wearing.

Among Tobé's many clubs are the Women's National Press Club in Washington, D.C., and the Overseas Press Club. She is a member of the woman's council of the New York State Department of Commerce, and of the business advisory committee of American University in Washington, D.C. She was the first woman to join the board of directors of Allied Stores Corporation in 1955. She is a Chevalier in the French Legion of Honor, and a recipient of the Neiman-Marcus award for distinguished service in the retail field (1941) and the Hall of Fame award in distribution (1953).

In 1943 Tobé established the annual Tobé award to honor an outstanding retailer. In 1948 she established a Tobé award for $1,000 for the French textile industry, in co-operation with the French government and the Economic Cooperation Administration. The award was established to stimulate creative design and the production and export of French textiles to the United States. A group of business associates founded in 1956 an annual series of lectures on retailing in Tobé's name at the Harvard Graduate School of Business Administration, honoring Tobé Coller Davis for her unique contribution to the fashion industry.

References

Bsns W p62+ Ja 14 '56 pors
Cue 18:15 F 5 '49 por
Mlle 11:123 My '40 por
N Y Times III p1 D 19 '54 por
Newsday p63 F 19 '59 por
Sat Eve Post 231:34+ Je 27 '59 pors
Who's Who in America, 1958-59
Who's Who of American Women (1958-59)

DEBRÉ, MICHEL (JEAN PIERRE)

(dĕ-brā') Jan. 15, 1912- Premier of France; lawyer

Address: Hotel Matignon, Paris, France

Forty minutes after he was inaugurated as President of France on January 8, 1959, Charles de Gaulle offered his Minister of Justice, Michel Debré, the post of *Premier Ministre* (Premier) in an administration which pledged itself to economic stability and the restoration of the greatness of France. Debré, a lawyer and jurist who has long been a loyal supporter of de Gaulle, was one of the chief architects of the new constitution which, ratified by referendum in September 1958, was promulgated early in October. Although the constitution does not precisely define the functions of the Premier, most observers believed that under the Fifth Republic de Gaulle would give his most important subordinate powers and responsibilities of his own.

Michel Jean Pierre Debré was born in Paris on January 15, 1912 to Robert Debré and the former Mlle. Debat-Ponsan. His father, a leading pediatrician, is professor at the University of Paris, president of the Academy of Medicine, and a Grand Officer of the Legion of Honor. Originally from Alsace, the Debré family acquired a front rank among the leading families of the intellectual *bourgeoisie* of Paris, and Debré met at the house in which he grew up on the Rue de l'Université many famous artists, scientists, and politicians. Although his paternal grandfather was a noted rabbi, Debré is a practising Roman Catholic.

After attending a *lycée* in Paris, Debré enrolled at the Cavalry School at Saumur, where he completed his military service at the age of twenty with the rank of major. He has maintained his military connections and, at the time of his appointment as Premier, was chief of reserve squadrons. He has earned a degree of doctor of laws and also received a diploma from the École Libre des Sciences Politiques. His liking for history was nurtured by the historian, Élie Halévy, whose knowledge of Victorian England inspired in his protégé an interest in parliamentary government.

In 1934 Debré passed the competitive examination for the Council of State, and received the appointment of *Maître des Requêtes* (a magistrate performing a somewhat similar office to that of a Supreme Court justice's law clerk). He became secretary-general of the commission for customs revision in 1937, and in November 1938 was assigned to a minor position on the staff of the Minister of Finance, Paul Reynaud.

With the outbreak of hostilities in 1939, Debré was immediately mobilized as a lieutenant in the cavalry. Imprisoned in May 1940, he escaped to Morocco, where he joined the French Resistance at Rabat. He returned to France and worked with underground leaders there. One of his chief assignments was the preparation of the list of prefects who were to govern France after the Liberation.

In August 1944 Debré was appointed Special Commissioner of the Republic for the Angers region. At this time he first met General de Gaulle, who was traveling through France on his way to Paris. Debré accompanied de Gaulle as far as Chartres, thus beginning the association which has led to Debré's being referred to as "the most faithful of the faithful" of de Gaulle's followers.

Called to Paris in 1945, Debré was assigned the task of planning reform in public administration. He helped draw up the charters and plan the curricula for political study institutes in Paris, Algiers, Lyons, Grenoble, Strasbourg, and Bordeaux.

After his defeat in the 1946 elections, Debré set to work to plan the new Saar government. In 1947 he was named secretary-general of German and Austrian affairs in the Foreign Ministry. He was elected to the senate in 1948 on the Rassemblement du Peuple Français ticket (Rally of the French People, de Gaulle's party, founded in 1947) for Indre-et-Loire. Debré was elected again in 1955 as a Social Republican, the new name taken by the RPF. At the Council of the Republic, he acted as leader of his party, and served on the committees for foreign affairs and universal suffrage.

Debré has been a member of the Council of Europe, Assembly of the Coal and Steel Community, High Council for Scientific Research and Technical Progress, and the Commission for the Accounts and Budgets of the Nation. In matters of European co-operation, he has earned a reputation of firm opposition to any activities which might imperil the national sovereignty of France.

When General Charles de Gaulle became Premier in June 1958, Debré was named Minister of Justice in his cabinet. He was assigned the task of drawing up a constitution along the lines which the general had proposed at Bayeux in 1946. The new constitution greatly curtails the powers of both Premier and Parliament on the grounds that a stronger executive makes for stability and that the legislature should perform functions only within its domain. Former Presidents had played a primarily ceremonial role. Although the new constitution won popular approval, it caused alarm among leftists, who felt that democratic guarantees and procedures had been impaired. Even its supporters have viewed the constitution as a frankly political document, designed primarily to meet certain concrete political difficulties.

In modern times Michel Debré is the first French statesman to bear his title. The official popularly referred to as "Premier" was formerly called "President of the Council of Ministers," and the new title of *Premier Ministre* indicates his connection with the chief of state, although he is responsible to the National Assembly.

Known for his cultivation, Debré has written several books, including *Refaire la France* (1944) and *Demain la paix* (1945), both in collaboration with Emmanuel Monick; *La mort de l'état républicain* (1947), *La république et son pouvoir* (1951), *La république et ses problèmes* (1953), *Ces princes qui nous gouvernent* (1957), and *Refaire une démocratie, un état, un pouvoir* (1958). He has been a tireless contributor to magazines and newspapers, especially to the Gaullist weekly, *Carrefour*, and to *L'écho de Touraine*, the weekly paper of his constituency, which has been outspoken in its criticism of the excesses of government and diplomacy. Founded some months before de Gaulle's 1958 cabinet was formed, Debré's own weekly was originally named *The Messenger of Anger* and later renamed *The Messenger of the Nation*.

Debré's fervid patriotism has been assailed in the French press as nationalism and even as unabashed chauvinism. He has defended himself

French Embassy Press
& Inf. Division

MICHEL DEBRÉ

against such charges by claiming that he is free from nationalism as he conceives it: "An excessive sentiment manifested by a desire for superiority or disdain with regard to foreign countries." Often hostile toward foreign countries, Debré has sometimes made the United States a target for his criticism.

In *Ces princes qui nous gouvernent* Debré had declared that "the establishment of a government program, its presentation and its defense, must respond at least in part to the need for hope and for illusion which the human heart feels." After de Gaulle's accession to power in 1958, Debré found himself in a position to put his theories into practice in the face of complex problems before which others had failed.

Foremost among these problems was the ending of the hostilities in Algeria and the urgent need to assign Algeria a place in the new French community. Debré's somewhat debatable position was that if Algeria could be said to have any personality at all, it was French rather than North African. Other problems included the role of France in the North Atlantic Treaty Organization, the European Atomic Energy Community (Euratom), and the European Market (Euromarket). The imposition of the austerity regime and the implementation of the new constitution also called for immediate consideration.

In 1936 Michel Debré married Anne-Marie Lemaresquier, the daughter of Charles Lemaresquier of the Académie des Beaux-Arts, who is the chief architect of the French national palaces. They have four sons: Bernard, Vincent, François, and Jean-Louis. Debré stands at five feet, five inches, dresses elegantly, and is given to impassioned invective, especially against the Fourth Republic. An aide has said

DEBRÉ, MICHEL—*Continued*

of Debré: "When he relaxes he just changes the kind of work he is doing." He is an officer of the Legion of Honor and has received the Croix de Guerre, the Rosette of the Resistance, and the Medal of Escaped Prisoners.

References

Carrefour Ja 7 '59 pors
Christian Sci Mon p10 Ja 9 '59
N Y Times p10 S 5 '58 por; p2 Ja 16 '59
Washington (D.C.) Post p6A Ja 12 '59
Dictionnaire Biographique Français Contemporain (1954)
Who's Who in France, 1955-1956

DE HEVESY, GEORGE *See* Hevesy, George de

DE MILLE, CECIL B(LOUNT) Aug. 12, 1881-Jan. 21, 1959 Motion picture producer and director; pioneered in the production of multi-million-dollar movie spectacles based on Biblical subjects. See *Current Biography* (May) 1942.

Obituary

N Y Times p1+ Ja 22 '59

DENNIS, PATRICK *See* Tanner, Edward Everett, 3d

DERWENT, CLARENCE Mar. 23, 1884-Aug. 6, 1959 Actor; appeared in about 500 plays on London and New York stages; acted in Hollywood films; president of Actors' Equity Association (1946-52); president of American National Theatre and Academy since 1952. See *Current Biography* (November) 1947.

Obituary

N Y Times p23 Ag 7 '59

DE VRIES, PETER Feb. 27, 1910- Author; journalist

Address: b. c/o New Yorker, 25 W. 43d St., New York 36; h. 170 Cross Highway, Westport, Conn.

Reprinted from the *Wilson Library Bulletin* Mar. 1959.

Satirist Peter De Vries has been called the "funniest serious writer to be found either side of the Atlantic" by British author Kingsley Amis. In his books De Vries has displayed his humorous appreciation of life, his skill in imagining characters and situations comical in themselves, his ability to create verbal jokes, and a social consciousness.

His best-selling novel, *The Tunnel of Love*, was adapted for the Broadway stage, where it had a long run, and for the movies. An editor of *Poetry* magazine for six years, De Vries is now on the staff of the *New Yorker*.

Peter De Vries was born on February 27, 1910 in Chicago, Illinois. His parents were Joost De Vries and the former Henrietta Eldersveld, Dutch immigrants who settled in a tightly knit Dutch Calvinist community on Chicago's South Side. De Vries' father went into business as a furniture mover, beginning with a "one-horse outfit which he gradually built up to a sizeable warehouse business."

At Chicago Christian High School (operated by the Reformed Church in America and the Christian Reformed Church) Peter participated in basketball, debating, and public speaking. After his graduation in 1927, he enrolled at Calvin College in Grand Rapids, Michigan.

There he worked hard to prepare for the Michigan intercollegiate extemporaneous speaking championship contest—and won it in 1931. He states: "Possible psychological explanation: stuttered in childhood. Determined to show 'em. Showed 'em. Quit." To prove that he quit, he adds: "Now wouldn't go near lecture platform for $10,000 fee."

After graduation from college in 1931 with a B.A. degree in English, De Vries worked for his neighborhood newspaper. Then he began free-lancing. He also operated a flock of candy vending machines in Chicago, peddled taffy apples, and was a radio actor.

In 1939 he was hired as associate editor by *Poetry* magazine. His first novel, *But Who Wakes the Bugler?* with illustrations by Charles Addams, was published in 1940 (Houghton). The *Saturday Review of Literature* said: "It may well be that this book will become known . . . as the first wild bleat of a young voice which was soon to blossom...." There was no quick blossoming, however. His next two novels, *Handsome Heart* (Coward-McCann, 1943) and *Angels Can't Do Better* (Coward-McCann, 1944), had only a small public and a dubious critical reception.

PETER DE VRIES

His personal life was faring better. "Two events," writes De Vries. "Published writer named Katinka Loeser, met and married her (October 1943). Second: got Thurber to lecture for *Poetry* benefit. He decided I should write for *New Yorker*. I did, and moved to New York."

A long bookless period followed. Then came *No But I Saw the Movie* (Little, 1952), a collection of his best stories, all but one from the *New Yorker*. Aware of De Vries' development, the New York *Times Book Review* wrote: ". . . There is evidence that Mr. De Vries is a writing man with something beyond cleverness. . . . There's the meat of social satire here." Until this time, De Vries claimed his readers comprised a "small but undiscerning band." This was no longer true after *The Tunnel of Love* appeared (Little, 1954). It was selected by the Atlantic Book Club and became a best seller. "This," said the *Saturday Review,* "is the incredible story of Augie Poole, an unsuccessful cartoonist who cultivates sedulously all the vices of the great artist in the hope that somewhere along the way, talent may rub off on him."

The Theatre Guild commissioned him to write a play based on the book, and he did so in collaboration with Joseph Fields. The stage comedy, which opened on Broadway on February 13, 1957, received rave reviews, ran for a year, and was published in book form by Little, Brown in 1957. The story was also made into a motion picture, released in 1958.

Comfort Me With Apples was issued in 1956 by Little, Brown. In general, critics agreed with the *Atlantic Monthly* that this book "did not seem quite as hilarious" as *The Tunnel of Love.*

The Mackerel Plaza (Little, 1958) lived up to the bright future predicted for him. "Ruefully," observed *Time,* "author De Vries has picked his targets, among them the more ludicrous foibles of suburbia. . . ." The hero of the story is Reverend Andrew Mackerel, who leads the People's Liberal Church, the "first split-level church in America." A recent widower, he falls in love with a former bit-part actress. He finds it difficult to marry her when the community plans a monument, Mackerel Plaza, to his wife's memory.

A sequel to *Comfort Me With Apples* was published by Little, Brown in 1959 as *The Tents of Wickedness*. In this book De Vries satirizes the upper-class conformists of revolt who have become more stereotyped than the conformists of so-called respectability and decency. He also parodies the literary mannerisms of Marquand, Faulkner, Proust, James, and others. The book was a dual midsummer selection of the Book-of-the-Month Club.

De Vries has four children: Jan, Peter Jon, Emily, and Derek. He is six feet two inches tall and weighs 190 lbs. His eyes are blue and his hair is brown, thick, and wavy.

At present, he is employed part-time by the art department of the *New Yorker*. De Vries is a Democrat. His favorite contemporary author is Anthony Powell. Among his awards is a $1,000 grant from the American Academy of Arts and Letters and the National Institute of Arts and Letters.

References

N Y Times Bk R p28 Ap 29 '56 por
N Y World-Telegram p9 F 9 '57
Time 74:100 Jl 20 '59 por
Who's Who in America, 1958-59

DODD, THOMAS J(OSEPH) May 15, 1907- United States Senator from Connecticut; lawyer

Address: b. Senate Office Bldg., Washington, 25, D.C.; h. 1576 33d St., N.W., Washington, D.C.; 63 Concord St., West Hartford, Conn.

A supporter of integration in the public schools and of federal assistance to economically depressed regions, Thomas J. Dodd, Democrat of Connecticut, was elected for a six-year senatorial term in November 1958. He defeated the incumbent, William A. Purtell, by 554,561 to 408,506 votes. Two years earlier, after two terms as United States Representative from the First Connecticut District, he had lost a senatorial race to Republican Prescott S. Bush.

Dodd, who has been a member of a Hartford, Connecticut law firm since 1947, began his career as an agent of the Federal Bureau of Investigation and later served as special assistant to several successive Attorneys General. He was executive trial counsel for the United States at the Nuremberg war crimes tribunal in 1945-46.

A grandson of Thomas Dodd, who migrated from Ireland to Connecticut, Thomas Joseph Dodd was born in Norwich, Connecticut on May 15, 1907. His parents were Thomas Joseph Dodd, a contractor, and the former Abigail Margaret O'Sullivan. After attending Norwich Free Academy and St. Anselm's Academy, he majored in philosophy at Providence College in Rhode Island, receiving the Ph.B. degree in 1930.

In preparation for a career in law, Dodd studied at Yale University School of Law, where he was president of the Democratic Club. After earning the LL.B. degree in 1933, he was a special agent with the FBI for two years. He returned to Connecticut in 1935 and organized the National Youth Administration programs which provided educational and employment opportunities for young people adversely affected by the depression. Dodd's work as director of the program was used as a model in many other states.

From 1938 to 1954 Dodd served in the Department of Justice as a special assistant to five successive Attorneys General. He helped to establish the Department's first civil rights section, was its first assistant director, and prosecuted cases involving the Ku Klux Klan in South Carolina. He also worked on cases concerned with the right to form labor unions and to bargain collectively in Georgia. During World War II he exposed industrial sabotage and subversion in several cases that set precedents.

(Continued next page)

THOMAS J. DODD

After a London conference in 1945 which created an International Military Tribunal to bring war criminals to trial, Supreme Court Justice Robert H. Jackson was appointed chief prosecutor for the United States. At Jackson's request Dodd was named executive trial counsel. Dodd was prominent in the planning and directing of courtroom strategy at the trials, which were held in Nuremberg, Germany. He especially distinguished himself when he examined Dr. Alfred Rosenberg, the Nazi editor and journalist, who was found guilty and hanged. In August 1946 Dodd replaced Jackson temporarily as the chief United States prosecutor.

For his work at Nuremberg Dodd was honored with a Presidential Citation, Medal of Freedom, and Czechoslovakian Order of the White Lion. In April 1949 he publicly declined the Officer's Cross of the Order of Polonia Restituta because he could see no difference between the Communist tyranny in Poland and that which prevailed during the German occupation. When he returned from Germany, he joined the Hartford law firm of Pelgrift, Dodd, Blumenfeld & Nair.

Dodd has long been interested in the affairs of the Connecticut Democratic party, and he has held several posts in the organization. In 1936, 1948, and 1956 he was a delegate to the Democratic National Convention, and in 1956 he was chosen to present the foreign policy plank of the party's platform to the meeting.

In 1946 and 1948 Dodd unsuccessfully sought the Democratic gubernatorial nomination. Four years later he was his party's candidate for United States Representative for the First Connecticut District, composed of Hartford County. In spite of the Eisenhower landslide, he was elected in November by a plurality of 23,540 votes. Re-elected in November 1954, Dodd increased his plurality to over 36,409 votes. He

was the only Connecticut Democrat in either the Eighty-third or Eighty-fourth Congresses.

In his first year in Congress Dodd was assigned to the Government Operations Committee and to a Select Committee to Investigate Incorporation of Lithuania, Latvia, and Estonia into the U.S.S.R. From 1954 until the end of his second term Dodd served only on the Foreign Affairs Committee, but was a member of its subcommittees on Europe, Inter-American Affairs, and National Security, a member of study missions to Latin America and the Middle East, and chairman of a special subcommittee to investigate imprisonment and mistreatment of American citizens in Communist China. In retaliation for Chinese abuse of Americans, Dodd recommended that the United States ask all free nations to join in a trade embargo against Red China (New York *Times,* December 1, 1954).

In June 1953 Dodd strongly opposed the Department of Defense reorganization bill as an attempt by a military clique to gain additional power. He introduced a proposal in 1955 to establish a committee on unethical financial practices to investigate attempts by financiers to gain control of certain defense industries. In May of 1955 he offered an amendment to the Public Utility Holding Company Act to remove any obstacle to atomic power development. Dodd also sponsored a bill in July 1956 to establish a federal $3 billion, five-year flood insurance program.

During his four years as a House member, Dodd cast votes in favor of private power development on the Niagara River in New York (July 1953), relaxation of immigration laws to admit refugees from Communism (July 1953), the wiretapping bill (April 1954), St. Lawrence Seaway bill (May 1954), postal pay raises (April 1955), Colorado River project (March 1956), Powell amendment to the school construction assistance bill and for the bill itself (July 1956), and civil rights bill (July 1956). He opposed restoration of rigid farm price supports (May 1955) and Natural Gas Act exemptions (July 1955).

In the election year of 1956 Dodd was the senatorial candidate of the Democratic party, opposing the incumbent, Republican Prescott S. Bush. Dodd was defeated in November by 479,460 to 610,829 votes. Less than a year later he announced his candidacy for the Senate seat held by William A. Purtell.

On the first ballot at the Democratic state convention at Hartford on June 28, 1958, he defeated both former Governor Chester Bowles and former Senator William Benton for the nomination.

At a press conference during his election campaign, Dodd stated that the major issues were unemployment, inflation, and a war threat. He said that the United States should increase its military budgets to make it invincible; Communist China's military action against Quemoy and Matsu should be referred to the U.N.; corporation taxes should be decreased; down payment requirements in the field of housing should be reduced; the FBI should not be granted more authority to tap telephone conversations; and the Democratic party should adhere to its principles and platforms (New York *Herald Tribune,* October 23, 1958).

Victorious over Purtell by 144,219 votes at the November election, Dodd was assigned in the Eighty-sixth Congress to the Senate Appropriations, Judiciary and Aeronautical and Space Sciences committees and was named acting chairman of the internal security subcommittee of the Judiciary Committee.

As one of a bipartisan group of fifteen Senators, in January 1959 Dodd sponsored a bill for the implementation by the federal government of the Supreme Court's public school desegregation decisions. Another bill of which Dodd is a co-sponsor proposes a constitutional amendment which prohibits states from taxing out-of-state residents.

The 1959 roll call of the Senate reveals that Dodd favored the housing bill (February), extending the draft (March), statehood for Hawaii (March), authorizing federal loans and grants of $389,500,000 for the redevelopment of economically depressed areas (March), extending the Temporary Unemployment Compensation Act (March), labor-management reporting and disclosure bill (April), and authorizing $485,-300,000 for the National Aeronautics and Space Administration (June).

Thomas J. Dodd is five feet eight and a half inches in height and 160 pounds in weight, has hazel eyes, and white hair. If he wore a toga he would "look the perfect picture of a Roman senator," because "his features are as sculptured as a bust of Caesar, and his resonant voice would lend itself well to Latin" (*Newsweek,* October 22, 1956). Dodd holds memberships in the International, Connecticut, and American bar associations, is a past vice-president of the International Penal Law Society, and has been active in many civic organizations. In 1948 he received the honorary LL.D. degree from Rollins College. He was created a Commander of the Italian Order of Merit in 1958 for his advice and assistance to the Italian government during the period when it was struggling against Communist attempts to gain control of that nation.

Married to Mary Grace Murphy on May 19, 1934, Dodd is the father of four sons, Thomas Joseph, Jr., Jeremy, Christopher, and Nicholas Owen, and two daughters, Carolyn and Martha. He is a Roman Catholic. For relaxation he enjoys deep-sea fishing, horseback riding, and the theater.

References

N Y Herald Tribune p13 Jl 6 '58 por; p16 N 5 '58 por
N Y Post Mag p2 My 18 '58 por
N Y Times p24 N 6 '58 por
Washington (D.C.) Post p27 Ja 20 '53 por
American Catholic Who's Who, 1958 and 1959
Congressional Directory (1959)
Who's Who in America, 1956-57
World Biography (1954)

DONNER, FREDERIC G(ARRETT) 1902-
Corporation executive

Address: b. General Motors Corp., 1775 Broadway, New York 19; h. 9 North Court, Port Washington, N.Y.

Becoming head of the General Motors Corporation on September 1, 1958, Frederic G. Donner succeeded Harlow H. Curtice as chief executive officer and Albert Bradley as chairman of the board. Since 1946 Donner had been a member of the corporation's financial and operations policy committees and as such was largely responsible for the financing of post-World War II expansion and operations. He had joined the corporation's financial staff in 1926 and became vice-president in charge of that staff in 1941. In his present position he shares responsibility with John F. Gordon, who is president of G.M., a post previously held by Curtice. Acknowledged as "the biggest manufacturing company in the world," General Motors reported earnings of $844,000,000 and sales of $10,990,000,000 in 1957. In 1958 it spent half a billion dollars "to produce completely new 1959 models in all lines for the first time in its history" (New York *Herald Tribune,* October 15, 1958).

Frederic Garrett Donner was born in 1902 at Three Oaks, Michigan, where his father was the accountant for a featherbone plant. He was brought up in this small rural community in the southwestern part of the state and there "went regularly to the Congregational Sunday School, shied from athletics, read voraciously, mostly history" (*Time,* September 8, 1958). He early developed a routine, devoting (a boyhood friend recalls) "so much time for work, so much for play and so much for study." Graduated from the Three Oaks High School in 1919, Donner entered the University of Michigan, majored in economics, won the Phi Beta Kappa key, and received his B.A. degree with honors in 1923.

For nearly three years Donner worked in the Chicago accountancy firm of Reckitt, Benington and LeClear. In March 1926 he joined the financial staff of the New York City offices of the General Motors Corporation as an accountant. "His early assignments," according to a company biographical sketch, "included helping to prepare monthly forecasts and annual pricing studies. Another important phase of his work in the late 1920's and early 1930's related to various benefit plans that were under consideration. This work brought him into contact with the late Edward R. Stettinius, Jr., who served as vice-president in charge of personnel from 1931 to 1933."

Named assistant treasurer of General Motors on January 1, 1934 and general assistant treasurer on June 15, 1937, Donner took part in a number of studies relating to dealer relations policies and directed much of the preparation of the material presented to the Senate Temporary National Economic Committee (TNEC) in 1939. He became vice-president in charge of the financial staff and a member of the administration committee on July 7, 1941, and on

Richard N. Cassar

FREDERIC G. DONNER

January 5, 1942 was elected to the board of directors.

During World War II Donner's duties included supervising the preparation of reports for presentation to the War Department adjustment board and setting up one of the first bank credit arrangements under the "V-loan" procedure that made funds available for expanding war production. Approximately 400 banks in the United States participated in the $1,000,-000,000 General Motors revolving credit, the largest ever extended to one corporation.

The credit plan in part made possible an expansion of G.M.'s working capital from a prewar $434,173,000 to about $950,000,000 in the middle of 1945. This growth took place under Alfred P. Sloan, Jr., who had become chairman of the board and chief executive officer in 1937, and Charles E. Wilson, who had succeeded William S. Knudsen as president in January 1941.

Reconversion to peacetime industry of the corporation's various operating divisions (Chevrolet, Pontiac, Oldsmobile, Cadillac, Frigidaire, Fisher Body, Allison engines, Truck and Coach, and about two dozen others) was initiated in June 1946. At that time "the responsibility of chief executive officer (which at G.M. means policy formation) was moved back to the presidency because the postwar problems were centered in the plants" (*Business Week,* August 30, 1958). Simultaneously, the functions of the old policy committee were transferred to two new bodies, the financial policy and operations policy committees, to both of which Donner was elected.

Raising new capital for conversion accordingly became a major concern of Donner. Some 1,000,000 G.M. preferred stocks were sold in December 1946 to a nation-wide group of underwriters, thus supplementing the sale of

$125,000,000 promissory notes to eight insurance companies a few months earlier. In 1948 Donner was one of a group of G.M. executives who visited West Germany to determine whether control of Adam Opel A.G. (a German subsidiary seized by Hitler), should be resumed, and this was done, local funds being raised for rehabilitating the property.

Improvement in the capital position of General Motors by 1949 resulted in the decision to retire the $125,000,000 note issue. In 1950 Donner's staff was assigned to carry out a two-for-one stock split to "broaden the market for the common stock of the corporation." Donner and his staff also had major responsibility for preparing and putting into effect the revised pension plan covering hourly as well as salaried G.M. workers, which was approved in the same year.

Harlow H. Curtice succeeded Wilson as G.M.'s president and chairman of the two committees in February 1953, after Wilson had been named Secretary of Defense in the Eisenhower administration. Capital needs for rapidly expanding production were met by the financial policy committee in the following December through a new $300,000,000 public offering of debentures. G.M. sales reached an all-time high of almost $12,500,000,000 in 1955, a year in which the corporation added $350,000,000 to its invested capital through the sale of additional common stock, in what was said to be the largest industrial financing ever undertaken.

On April 2, 1956, when Sloan retired as chairman, he was succeeded by Albert Bradley, formerly chairman of the financial policy committee, a position taken over by Donner who was at that time elected executive vice-president of General Motors. Donner also succeeded Bradley as group executive in charge of five General Motors subsidiaries and served as a director of the Ethyl Corporation, in which General Motors has a stock interest.

Both Curtice and Bradley announced their retirement in the summer of 1958. Frederic G. Donner was elected on August 23, 1958 to take office in September as board chairman and chief executive officer. John F. Gordon, formerly head of the Cadillac division, replaced Curtice as president. At the same time the board announced a realignment of its governing committees through the creation of a new finance committee and an executive committee (Robert E. Bedingfield, New York *Times,* August 26, 1958). Gordon was named to head the executive committee and Donner, the financial committee in an action seen as marking a reversion to the division of authority existing before the Sloan-Wilson era.

Business Week (August 30, 1958) quoted observers as saying, "Donner's job is going to be to plan distribution policies . . . and to plan for the day that may well come when some court or government agency gets really serious about breaking up General Motors." On November 6, 1958 the antitrust and monopoly subcommittee of the Senate Judiciary Committee proposed that the Justice Department consider court action to break up the General Motors Corporation. The next day Donner said that the subcommittee report had reflected "speculative, conjectural, and partisan opinion" (New York *Times,* November 8, 1958).

Donner's associates describe him as a quiet, serious man "who is brilliant without ostentation." He avoids publicity and interviews. He is five feet eight inches in height and has gray hair. He likes to travel and to play an occasional game of golf, and he is "a rapid . . . reader with a partiality to books on the Civil War and detective stories." Donner's wife is a former high school teacher whom he married in the late 1920's. They have two grown children.

Frederic G. Donner is a member of the University Club in New York, the Recess and Detroit clubs in Detroit, and the Creek and North Hempstead Country clubs on Long Island. He is an honorary member of Beta Gamma Sigma, the commerce society. *Life* (October 13, 1958) registered Donner's conviction that " 'most people have a false idea of what the financial end is. At G.M. it can mean personnel, engineering, research, sales, even styling—and for me it now means all of them.' "

References

N Y Herald Tribune III p5 Ag 26 '58;
    III p4 Ag 27 '58
N Y Times p20 Ag 9 '58 por
Newsweek 52:81 S 8 '58 por
Time 72:79 S 22 '58 por
U S News 45:60+ S 5 '58 por
Who's Who in America, 1958-59

DONOVAN, WILLIAM J(OSEPH) Jan. 1, 1883-Feb. 8, 1959 Lawyer; major general in the United States Army; directed Office of Strategic Services in World War II; Ambassador to Thailand (1953-54). See *Current Biography* (September) 1954.

Obituary

N Y Times p1+ F 9 '59

DREYFUSS, HENRY (drā'fŭs) Mar. 2, 1904- Industrial designer
Address: b. 4 W. 58th St., New York 19; b. and h. 500 Columbia St., South Pasadena, Calif.

> NOTE: This biography supersedes the article which appeared in *Current Biography* in 1948.

During the thirty years since industrial design began to change the shape, color, and performance of mass-produced goods in the United States, Henry Dreyfuss has emerged as an undisputed leader of his profession. With Walter Dorwin Teague and Raymond Loewy he is often considered one of the three pioneering giants who have applied to American manufacturing the maxim that form follows function.

Dreyfuss views design as "a silent salesman" which goes along with the product to extol its utility and other values; he believes that the primary function of the industrial designer is to help increase sales for clients. Thousands of items, from kitchen utensils to jet transport planes, have been affected by his efforts to increase safety, comfort, efficiency, and beauty. Many designs still on his drawing board will probably influence daily living for some years to come.

The son and grandson of theatrical costume designers, Henry Dreyfuss was born in New York City on March 2, 1904 to Louis and Elsie (Gorge) Dreyfuss. His one brother, Arnold, is deceased. At the age of sixteen Henry Dreyfuss was graduated from the Ethical Culture Fine Arts School in New York, and soon afterward he became an apprentice to stage designer Norman Bel Geddes, with whom he worked on sets for *The Miracle,* produced on Broadway beginning January 16, 1924.

The theater was Dreyfuss' training ground for industrial design. He gained much of his experience as a designer of stage presentations for the Strand motion picture theater in New York, a job which he secured as a result of writing a brash letter of criticism to the theater manager. For 260 weeks he prepared six new stage settings weekly. At twenty-three he was in considerable demand by theaters trying to withstand the onslaught of talking pictures against stage presentations. He left Broadway, however, for a visit to Paris and from there went to Tunis and Algeria, where he was employed as a guide for American Express.

Commissioned by R. H. Macy & Company, Dreyfuss returned to New York in 1927 to examine the department store's merchandise with the purpose of redesigning the unattractive items. After a two-day survey of the store's products, he decided to reject the offer because he felt that the cost of retooling to make the necessary improvements would be too high. "A fundamental premise was involved in my refusal —one from which I have never retreated," he later wrote. "An honest job of design should flow from the inside out, not from the outside in" (*Designing for People,* Simon and Schuster, 1955).

After Dreyfuss opened his first industrial design office in New York, on Fifth Avenue, in 1929, he helped meet expenses by designing sets for elaborate Broadway shows like *The Last Mile* (1930) and *The Cat and the Fiddle* (1931). Gradually attracting clients in industry, he worked on a variety of assignments that included hinges, pianos, cigarette lighters, jewels, and tractors.

The depression of the 1930's tended to further Dreyfuss' career because manufacturers came to realize that they could increase the sale of their products through designs that would make them more attractive and more efficient. Also Dreyfuss and other early industrial designers were fighting on the winning side in the contest of the period between decoration and generic design. He has always favored clean-cut lines over fancy ornamentation.

One of the first household products to come under the Dreyfuss influence was the Mason jar, which he redesigned to occupy less space by making it square with a rounded top. As early as 1930 he acquired Bell Telephone Laboratories

Sarra, Inc.

HENRY DREYFUSS

as one of his clients, and he has since worked with the company's engineers in evolving the present-day telephone set and a variety of related products. For General Electric in 1933 he designed a refrigerator that had its motor unit in the bottom instead of the top, enclosed in an easy-to-clean-construction. Toward the end of the decade he planned the interior of the perisphere at the New York World's Fair (1939-40), a scale model of the "city of tomorrow."

During the 1930's Dreyfuss designed two trains for New York Central, the *Mercury* and the *Century,* introducing a number of comforts and luxury features in train travel. His innovations in redesigning *McCall's* had an effect on almost all magazine publishing. "It's hard to pick up a magazine today that does not show the Dreyfuss influence," *Forbes* reported (May 1, 1951). "Among others, *Time* and *Reader's Digest* have been Dreyfuss-influenced."

Long-standing clients of Dreyfuss include Crane Company (his work for that firm led the trend toward built-in plumbing fixtures); John Deere & Company, whose extensive line of farm machinery required research into problems of safety and maintenance; Minneapolis-Honeywell Regulator Company; and Mergenthaler Linotype Company. He has designed vacuum cleaners of the Hoover Company, Eversharp pens, Royal typewriters, Warner and Swazey lathes, gas stations for Cities Service Company, bowling balls for American Machine & Foundry Company, and equipment for dental offices. Among his most widely publicized designs in the field of transportation were airplane interiors for Lockheed Aircraft Corporation and ship interiors of the S.S. *Independence* and S.S. *Constitution* for the American Export Lines.

An interesting commission that Dreyfuss undertook for the United States government during World War II was the planning of a suite of strategy rooms to be used by the Joint Chiefs of Staff in Washington. He was called in by

the Navy "to improve the habitability" of a certain class of destroyer; in assignments for the Army he has worked on the Nike in cooperation with Western Electric Company and other companies.

Dreyfuss restricts his list of clients to about fifteen at a time. His organization, headed by six partners, has a staff of about fifty specialists and office workers in New York and South Pasadena, California. Dreyfuss divides his time between the two offices. He puts much stress upon teamwork and research, believing that an industrial designer must have firsthand knowledge of all operations and problems involved in the making and merchandising of a product. In judging public taste, according to Dreyfuss, the designer must be cautious about timing; he must offer change and development without moving forward too fast. Yet long-range planning for his client requires him to think twenty or thirty years ahead. To every design problem Dreyfuss applies a five-point yardstick: utility and safety, maintenance, cost, sales appeal, and appearance.

A forthright opponent of artificial or planned obsolescence, Dreyfuss criticizes the practice of some manufacturers, especially in the automobile industry, of maintaining a market by making superficial changes that do not actually improve the product or reduce costs. Besides confusing and deceiving the customer, Dreyfuss asserts, artificial obsolescence is unnecessary because "we're going to see products become *functionally* obsolete so fast that it will seem absurd to think up ways of making them *stylistically* obsolete."

"Everything—absolutely everything—I know about industrial design is in these papers," Dreyfuss remarked when he finished writing *Designing for People,* in which he discusses his life, his work, and his theories. The book has been praised for its vitality and gusto, professional simplicity, and entertaining style. A series of pictorial records of his designs has been privately printed: *Ten Years of Industrial Design* (1939), *A Record of Industrial Design* (1947), *Industrial Design—A Progress Report* (1952), and *Industrial Design—A Pictorial Accounting* (1957).

Since 1947 Dreyfuss has been an associate in industrial design at the California Institute of Technology and since 1952 a lecturer in engineering at the University of California at Los Angeles. He is a member of the visiting committee of Harvard University Graduate School of Design and has lectured at Harvard, Yale, Massachusetts Institute of Technology and other universities as well as before many professional groups. In 1953 he was appointed a member of the Governor's Citizens Advisory Committee on Educational TV in California.

One of the founders of the American Society of Industrial Designers, Dreyfuss also served as president of that organization and is now a Fellow. He belongs to the American Society of Agricultural Engineers, Architectural League of New York, Society of Automotive Engineers, Academy of Political Sciences, and American Ordnance Association. His honors include the Gold Medal Award of the Architectural League of New York (1951), Order of Orange-Nassau, presented by Queen Juliana of the Netherlands (1952), and the D.Sc. degree from Occidental College (1953).

When Dreyfuss opened his office in New York in 1929, one of his first employees was Doris Marks, whom he married on July 26, 1930. She has remained active in the company, handling many of the business transactions in the California office. The Dreyfuss children are John Alan, Gail, and Ann.

Henry Dreyfuss is a tall, sturdy man with brown hair and brown eyes. Brown is also his favorite color for his suits and office décor. He is said to have an urbane, and sometimes sardonic, wit. "There is no obvious evidence in his life of any hobbies except that of an abiding and intensive interest in the daily lives of his fellow Americans," Richard L. Simon wrote of Dreyfuss in the publisher's introduction to *Designing for People*. Other exceptions are his love for the theater and his delight in unusual gadgets.

References

Am Artist 15 :52+ S '51 por
Forbes 67 :18+ My 1 '51 por
N Y Times III p3 Je 18 '50 por
Ptr Ink 262:58+ F 21 '58 por
International Who's Who, 1959
Who's Who in America, 1958-59
Who's Who in World Jewry (1955)

DRYDEN, HUGH L(ATIMER) July 2, 1898- United States government official; physicist
Address: b. National Aeronautics and Space Administration, Washington 25, D.C.; h. 5606 Overlea Rd., Washington 16, D.C.

With the establishment of the United States government's National Aeronautics and Space Administration in mid-1958, Dr. Hugh L. Dryden moved from his position as director of the National Advisory Committee for Aeronautics to become deputy administrator of this civilian space agency, which has the NACA as its nucleus. During some forty years of government service, much of it with the National Bureau of Standards, he has worked on a number of technical projects for the armed forces and various government agencies. Dryden's own research has centered on aerodynamics.

Born on July 2, 1898 to Samuel Isaac and Nova Hill (Culver) Dryden, Hugh Latimer Dryden is a native of Pocomoke City, Maryland and was reared in Baltimore. He attended Johns Hopkins University on a scholarship, was elected to Phi Beta Kappa, and received the B.A. degree with honors in 1916, after three years' study. His postgraduate work at Johns Hopkins was influenced by Dr. Joseph S. Ames, who guided him into aeronautical research. He earned his M.A. degree in 1918 and his Ph.D. degree in 1919. Very much interested in flying, he made his first airplane trip while a university student in a Curtis Eagle, whose speed of 107 miles an hour was the ultimate in air travel at that time.

Wide World

HUGH L. DRYDEN

The laboratory work accepted for his doctorate had been done at the National Bureau of Standards in Washington, D.C., where Dryden had taken a summer position in 1918 to conduct research in fluid mechanics. He remained at the bureau while completing graduate study and in 1920 was made chief of the aerodynamics section. Here he pioneered in aerodynamics of high speed. In collaboration with Dr. Lyman J. Briggs, in 1924 he made some of the first studies of the flow around airplane wings at speeds near and above the speed of sound.

At the Bureau of Standards, where he was advanced to chief of the mechanics and sound division in 1934, Dryden was also responsible for nonaeronautical work such as testing the efficiency of roof ventilators and investigating the pressures exerted by wind on building materials and structures. Simultaneously, he continued his studies of aerodynamics, concentrating on turbulence and control of the boundary layer, the subject that he chose when invited to deliver the 1938 Wright Brothers Lecture before the Institute of the Aeronautical Sciences. Also in 1938 he was made head physicist at the Bureau of Standards.

During World War II Dryden served on committees advising the Joint Chiefs of Staff, National Advisory Committee for Aeronautics, Army Ordnance Department, and Army Air Forces on aeronautical matters and guided missiles. For heading the Washington Project of the National Defense Research Committee in the development of "Bat," the United States' first guided missile successfully used in combat, he won the Presidential Certificate of Merit in 1948. As deputy scientific director of the scientific advisory group of the Army Air Forces, Dr. Dryden traveled to Germany, France, England, and Switzerland in 1945 to

DRYDEN, HUGH L.—*Continued*

study the scientific efforts these countries had made in the development of aeronautics and guided missiles.

In January 1946 Dryden was appointed assistant director of the National Bureau of Standards and six months later advanced to associate director. He left the bureau in 1947, however, to become director of aeronautical research of the National Advisory Committee for Aeronautics. Two years afterward he was made director of the entire organization, which had about 8,000 employees, three large laboratory centers, and two smaller field stations. "Under Dryden's direction," as noted in the New York *Times* (November 4, 1958), "the National Advisory Committee for Aeronautics gained widespread respect for its advanced aeronautical research, such as the development of the Marilyn Monroe fuselage shape, which made possible modern supersonic interceptors and bombers."

The House of Representatives Select Committee on Astronautics and Space Exploration held hearings in April 1958 for the purpose of deciding on the kind of organization needed to lead the United States' space efforts. Dr. Dryden presented the administration's proposal of using the National Advisory Committee for Aeronautics as the nucleus for the new space agency. He explained that since its establishment in 1915 the NACA had been co-ordinating aeronautical research in the United States and further testified, "Since the end of World War II, NACA has been engaged increasingly in research applicable to the problems of space flight. It has designed and constructed special aerodynamic, propulsion and structures research facilities required for this work".

After considerable debate in Congress, much of it concerning civilian-versus-military responsibility in space and the form and composition of the federal agency to handle space projects, the NASA was established in July 1958 as a civilian agency under the control of the President with the advice of an eight-man council. Many observers expected Hugh L. Dryden to head the agency, but presumably because of some Congressional opposition to Dryden, President Eisenhower nominated T. Keith Glennan as space administrator. Dryden was named deputy administrator, a position which allows him to concentrate on the technical problems of space research.

At a meeting of the American Astronautical Society in December 1958 Dryden stated that scientists would soon work out propulsion systems to rocket men into space. Before these systems could be used, however, difficulties such as those regarding guidance and recovery would have to be overcome. Since space problems are so great, he suggested, "it may be well to enlist the skills and cooperation of other nations" (Washington *Post and Times Herald,* December 28, 1958).

The results of Dryden's research in aeronautics, well over a hundred papers, have been published in various professional journals. He wrote seventeen technical reports for the NACA. From 1941 to 1956 he was editor of the *Journal for the Institute of the Aeronautical Sciences.* He is on the board of editors of the *Quarterly of Applied Mathematics* and the Aeronautical Publications Program of Princeton University.

Dryden represented the United States at the sixth International Congress for Applied Mechanics, in Paris in 1946, and at the seventh congress, in Istanbul in 1952. He has been a vice-president since 1956 of the International Union of Theoretical and Applied Mechanics, of which he was formerly president. He belongs to a large number of other professional organizations, including the National Academy of Sciences (home secretary since 1955), Royal Aeronautical Society (fellow), Institute of the Aeronautical Sciences (president in 1943), and Washington Academy of Sciences (president in 1946). He is a member of the advisory council of the Daniel and Florence Guggenheim Institute of Air Flight Structures.

His many awards have included the Daniel Guggenheim Medal (1950) and the Wright Brothers Memorial Trophy (1955). He was appointed an honorary officer, civil division, of the Order of the British Empire in 1948. In 1958 he was elected to the Baltimore City College Hall of Fame and was awarded the Career Service Award by the National Civil Service League. He holds seven honorary degrees.

Married to Mary Libbie Travers on January 29, 1920, Dryden has three children: a son, Hugh Latimer, Jr., a chemist, and two daughters, Nancy Travers Dryden and Mrs. Andrew Van Tuyl. Dr. Hugh L. Dryden leads a men's Bible class at Washington's Calvary Methodist Church. Since college days he has held a local preacher's license and occasionally he gives sermons. He is a Democrat.

In a talk to the Cosmos Club in November 1954 on the theme of the scientist in contemporary life, Dr. Dryden, a past president of the club, contended: "Scientific knowledge is power, but it is power to be used for good or for evil as men choose. . . . I am not one of those few who believe that we can yet abolish the use of force in the world . . . such strength is a greater contribution to the peace of the world than military weakness is."

References

Aero Digest 61:26+ N '50 por
Aviation W 48:12+ Mr 8 '48 por
Sci Mo 78:289+ My '54
Science 128:582+ S 12 '58
American Men of Science vol I (1955)
Who Knows—and What (1954)
Who's Who in America, 1958-59
World Biography (1954)

DULLES, JOHN FOSTER Feb. 25, 1888- May 24, 1959 Former Secretary of State of the United States; lawyer; served as Secretary of State from January 1953 to April 1959; attended Hague Convention in 1907, Versailles Peace Conference in 1919 and the San Francisco organizational conference for the United Nations in 1945; negotiated peace treaty with

Japan in 1951; authority on international law; had been senior partner of Sullivan & Cromwell law firm; influential Presbyterian layman; interim United States Senator (1949); advocated bipartisan foreign policy. See *Current Biography* (September) 1953.

Obituary

N Y Times p1+ My 25 '59

DUNTON, A(RNOLD) DAVIDSON July 4, 1912- Canadian university president

Address: b. Carleton University, Ottawa 1, Ontario, Canada; h. 410 Maple Lane, Rockcliffe, Ottawa, Ontario, Canada

When A. Davidson Dunton resigned as chairman of the board of governors of the Canadian Broadcasting Corporation in July 1958 to become president of Carleton University in Ottawa, newspapers pointed out that his new position brought a change of emphasis rather than of professional field. At the CBC since 1945, he had been "an outstanding Canadian figure in the field of public education in the widest sense of the term," J. E. Coyne, chairman of the board of governors of Carleton University, noted.

The university, which started as Carleton College in 1942 and became the seat of the Institute of Canadian Studies in 1957, is at present undergoing a period of expansion, and moving gradually to an extensive new campus. Before he joined the CBC, Dunton had served as general manager of Canada's Wartime Information Board.

Arnold Davidson Dunton was born on July 4, 1912 in Montreal, Ontario, Canada to Robert Andrew and Elizabeth (Davidson) Dunton, both natives of that city. He was two years old when his lawyer father died. Graduating at fifteen from Montreal High School and Lower Canada College, he was too young to go on to a Canadian university. In 1928 he spent a year at the University of Grenoble in France, studying French literature and history. In 1930 and 1931, at McGill University in Montreal, he studied economics and history and also played football. He entered Trinity College, Cambridge University, England in the fall of 1931 for further study of economics. During his year at Trinity he was a member of a Cambridge hockey team which made a European tour and he worked in his free time as a reporter on the London *Daily Express*. At the University of Munich he studied economics and German in 1932-33.

After working briefly for a Montreal advertising agency, Dunton spent a year in Mexico as a private tutor. In 1934 he "talked his way into a summer reporting job on the Montreal *Star*" and in 1935 became a "full-time legman" (Alan Phillips in *Maclean's Magazine*, April 2, 1955). "An ardent competitor in Laurentian ski meets and Montreal squash tournaments," Dunton started the *Star*'s first ski column. By 1937 he was writing editorials and had been advanced to associate editor. A year later, when J. W. McConnell, the sugar magnate, added to his

A. DAVIDSON DUNTON

newspaper holdings the Montreal *Standard,* he made Davidson Dunton the editor of this once widely circulated but then moribund "week-end" paper.

Under Dunton's editorship, the *Standard* tripled its circulation. "A broken eardrum kept him out of the armed services in World War II," Harvey Hickey noted in the Toronto *Globe and Mail* (July 5, 1958). "While still editing the *Standard,* he carried on an information service for the RAF Atlantic Ferry Command." On leave of absence from the *Standard,* Dunton joined the Wartime Information Board at Ottawa in 1942, became assistant general manager in 1943, and general manager in 1944. While holding the latter position he organized all press and radio coverage of the two Quebec Conferences and was responsible for Canadian coverage of the United Nations Conference on International Organization at San Francisco.

The Canadian Broadcasting Corporation was "created under provisions of the Canadian Broadcasting Act of 1936 to be a single national authority to control, for purposes of coordination, all broadcasts in Canada and to carry on a national broadcasting service within the nation" (*Canadian Almanac and Directory*). Commercially operated radio stations were permitted, in addition to the federal network, but were required to conform with rules set down by the CBC. In operation, this dual function showed various defects, and in July 1944 a federal Parliamentary committee recommended a division of authority through appointment of a full-time chairman of the board of governors, who should act as an interpreter of policy and be responsible for public relations, and a general manager. Dunton's work for the Wartime Information Board had attracted the attention of Canada's Prime Minister William Lyon Mackenzie King, and on October 23, 1945 his ap-

DUNTON, A. DAVIDSON—*Continued*

pointment for three years as chairman of the CBC was announced. He was reappointed in 1948 and 1951, and in 1952 his term was extended to ten years.

"They All Throw Rocks at Davy Dunton" was the title of an article in *Maclean's Magazine* of April 2, 1955 by Alan Phillips, who discussed the many problems confronting the CBC chairman in his first seven years. Among them was the charge, aired as early as June 1946 at a Parliamentary Radio Committee hearing, that the CBC favored the Liberals in the allotment of political broadcasting time. The quality of CBC broadcasts was also assailed, a result being the institution in 1947 of the highly rated *Wednesday Night* radio series. The Canadian Association of Broadcasters, representing commercial stations, opposed the corporation's determination to retain telecasting in its own hands and criticized the system of financing. Like the BBC, the CBC had been supported by a license fee for receiving sets, but in 1951 Parliament approved in its place an annual grant to the CBC of $6,250,000 for the next five years, with the corporation receiving 15 per cent of the excise tax on sale of sets.

Early in 1956 a Royal Commission on Broadcasting headed by R. M. Fowler began a new study of the financing and operation of the CBC. The Fowler commission, reporting in March 1957, recommended among other measures that a new fifteen-member board of governors, distinct from the CBC board, be established to supervise all broadcasting in Canada and that the CBC have a president and board chairman. Such was the situation when on July 4, 1958 Dunton resigned from the CBC to accept the position of fourth president of Carleton University. A factor in making the decision, he stated, "was that the set up was going to change, necessarily leaving me in a changed position and so if I was going to move, now would be the time." (In November 1958 these recommendations went into effect.)

An outgrowth of the work of a committee on college-level education formed by the Ottawa Young Men's Christian Association in 1938, Carleton College was chartered in 1942 and in September of that year offered its first classes. In the summer of 1947 the college announced complete four-year courses and five-year honours courses leading to the bachelor's degrees in arts, science, and commerce, the first of which were conferred in 1948. By act of the Ontario legislature, Carleton College became Carleton University in February 1957; in April an Institute of Canadian Studies was founded.

By the end of the academic year 1957-58 Carleton had awarded 1,078 bachelor's degrees and ten master's degrees, and its enrolment had reached a total of 1,754 full-time and part-time students. It was planned that in 1958-59 first units of the university would be moved from Ottawa's Glebe district to an extensive new campus at the confluence of the Rideau River and the Rideau Canal. Transfer of the entire college is expected to be completed by 1965. Installed as president of Carleton as of July 16, 1958 Dunton succeeded Claude Thomas Bissell, who had held the office for two years before accepting an appointment as president of the University of Toronto.

Kathleen Barry Bingay of Vancouver, British Columbia, a constitutional lawyer who had served in the Department of External Affairs, became the wife of A. Davidson Dunton on June 30, 1944. "The Duntons," William Boss wrote, "have two children, daughters Darcy, nine, and Deborah, six, and the whole family likes nothing better than to go out . . . and ski on Saturday and Sunday winter afternoons" (*Saturday Night,* August 2, 1958). Another of Dunton's favorite sports is tennis. He is five feet eight inches tall, weighs 162 pounds, and has blue eyes and dark-brown hair.

He holds an honorary D.Sc. degree (1946) from Laval University and an honorary LL.D. degree (1954) from the University of Saskatchewan. He is a member of the United Church of Canada and belongs to Delta Upsilon fraternity, the Rideau Club (Ottawa), Le Cercle Universitaire d'Ottawa, and the Montreal Racket Club.

References

Toronto Globe and Mail p1 Jl 5 '58 por
Canadian Who's Who, 1955-57
International Who's Who, 1958
Who's Who in America, 1958-59
Who's Who in Canada, 1956-57
World Biography (1954)

DUPLESSIS, MAURICE (LE NOBLET)

Apr. 20, 1890-Sept. 7, 1959 Prime Minister of Quebec from 1936 to 1939 and since 1944; formed National Union party in 1936; lawyer.

See *Current Biography* (October) 1948.

Obituary

N Y Times p15 S 7 '59

DÜRRENMATT, FRIEDRICH Jan. 5, 1921- Swiss playwright

Address: b. c/o Kurt Hellmer, 52 Vanderbilt Ave., New York 17

One of the most stimulating plays of the 1958 theatrical season in New York was *The Visit* by the Swiss dramatist Friedrich Dürrenmatt. The play, featuring Alfred Lunt and Lynn Fontanne in the starring roles, opened on May 5, 1958 and ran (with a six-week summer vacation) through November 30, 1958. Variously described as a tragedy, a tragi-comedy, a tragical farce, a satire, a "satiric parable," a "black morality," and a "grisly fable," *The Visit* marked Dürrenmatt's first appearance on the Broadway stage. The critics were divided in their reception and interpretation of the play, but they were agreed on one thing—that Dürrenmatt was a dramatist of genuine significance in the modern theater.

Friedrich Dürrenmatt was born on January 5, 1921 in Konolfingen, in the Canton of Bern, Switzerland, the son of Pastor Reinhold and Hulda (Zimmermann) Dürrenmatt. His grandfather, Ulrich Dürrenmatt, was a well-known

Swiss satirist and political poet. At thirteen the boy moved with his family to Bern, where he attended the Gymnasium. After graduation he entered the University of Bern, where he studied theology, philosophy, German literature, and the natural sciences. Later he studied art and philosophy at the University of Zürich.

Dürrenmatt had originally planned to become a painter. Then, as he explained to Joseph Morgenstern (New York *Times,* May 25, 1958), ". . . all of a sudden I began to write, and I just had no time to finish my university degree." Painting then became only an avocation, and Dürrenmatt now describes himself as a "Sunday painter."

His first play, *Es steht geschrieben,* was, in the author's words, "a wild story of German Anabaptists during the Reformation." Its first production, at the Schauspielhaus in Zürich on April 19, 1947, caused a minor theatrical scandal because of its somewhat unorthodox religious sentiments; but, as Dürrenmatt comments, "after the scandal subsided they gave me a prize for it."

Playwriting has remained Dürrenmatt's primary interest, but he has also written radio scripts, motion picture scenarios, novels, and criticism. For a time he was drama critic for *Die Weltwoche,* published in Zürich. His first novel to be translated into English was *Die Richter und sein Henker* (1952) translated by Therese Pol as *The Judge and His Hangman,* and published by Harper in 1955. A cleverly plotted detective story, the book was favorably received by American critics. Anthony Boucher, writing in the New York *Times* (July 17, 1955), praised its "amusing satire on Swiss culture and politics," and the *Saturday Review's* Sergeant Cuff called it "urbane and crisp" (July 23, 1955). Another novel, *The Pledge,* is planned for publication by Alfred A. Knopf in the spring of 1959.

Other works of fiction by Dürrenmatt are *Pilatus* (1949); *Der Nihilist* (1950); *Die Stadt* (The Town, 1952); another detective story, *Der Verdacht,* (Suspicion, 1953); *Griechin Sucht Griechin* (Greek Man Seeks Greek Woman, 1955), a book which, Dürrenmatt acknowledges, "the critics panned unanimously. It was a completely logical book but they couldn't see it that way"; and *Die Panne* (The Breakdown, 1956).

This last work, a mystery melodrama, was adapted for television in the United States by James Yaffee under the title *The Deadly Game* and performed on NBC's *Suspicion* in December 1957 with Boris Karloff and Gary Merrill in the leading roles. In October 1958 it was announced that an expanded version of the story would be produced on Broadway as a play.

Dürrenmatt's first really successful play was a comedy, *Die Ehe des Herrn Mississippi* (The Marriage of Mr. Mississippi), produced first in Munich in 1952. Two earlier plays, *Der Blinde* and *Romulus der Grosse,* had been produced in Basel in 1948 and 1949 respectively. With *Die Ehe des Herrn Mississippi* Dürrenmatt became established as one of the most popular contemporary European dramatists; and his style, with

B. Herbold, Zurich

FRIEDRICH DÜRRENMATT

its peculiar mixture of the comic and the grotesque, was recognized as a unique and distinguishing feature of his work. "People say I am a cynic because I show things that are harsh and funny at the same time," he has said. "I try to show the world as it is, and if people say I am a cynic it is a public defense."

Die Ehe des Herrn Mississippi was adapted for American production by Maximilian Slater with the title *Fools Are Passing Through.* It played briefly off-Broadway in April 1958. The play has been described as "a bizarre dance of death with four very different men contending for the possession of one woman." Given a spirited and imaginative production, it struck most of the New York critics as an interesting and provocative play. Brooks Atkinson (New York *Times,* April 3, 1958) found, however, that once the novelty of the production wore off "the intricacies within intricacies become tedious; the crises become tepid and the philosophy, hollow." Walter Kerr (New York *Herald Tribune,* April 3, 1958) agreed that "we are asked to listen well beyond our interest, and beyond the actual requirements of a cynical parable's essential point." But, he concluded, "Even so, the craftsmanship is curious and promising." And Richard Watts, Jr. (New York *Post,* April 13, 1958) commented on Dürrenmatt: "That he has a striking and ironic mind, a sardonic sense of humor, and a feeling for vivid theatrical images was made clear in the ingenious off-Broadway production."

Two other plays by Dürrenmatt which have had European but not American productions are *Nächtliches Gespräch mit einem verachteten Menschen* (Nocturnal Conversation with a Scorned Man), produced in Munich in 1952, and *Ein Engel kommt nach Babylon* (An Angel Comes to Babylon), produced in Munich in 1953. The latter play has been described as "a kind of parable" that "represents a variation on

DÜRRENMATT, FRIEDRICH—*Continued*

the age-old theme of the heavenly emissary who brings confusion instead of happiness."

On January 29, 1956 Dürrenmatt's *Der Besuch der alten Dame* (The Old Lady's Visit) had its première at the Zürich Schauspielhaus. An immediate success, the play soon was produced in Germany and in France. In an English adaptation by Maurice Valency (on which Dürrenmatt himself collaborated), the play was done by the Lunts in England, but it was not produced in London. The explanation offered for this is that British audiences were so shocked by the harshness and horror of the play that the producers hesitated to bring it to London—this in spite of the fact that Valency's adaptation had subdued much of "the macabre gallows-humor of the original (in which the heroine wore a wig and an artificial leg). . . ."

The scene of the play is a drab, provincial European town to which the heroine (played by Lynn Fontanne) returns after an absence of many years. Now enormously wealthy, she has come back to get revenge on a villager (Alfred Lunt) who had seduced her many years before. Gradually and relentlessly she buys up the entire town, corrupting even the most respected citizens, until they accede to her wishes and cold-bloodedly execute her former lover. Her mission accomplished, she then leaves the town.

The Visit (its title shortened from the original) opened in New York on May 5, 1958 in the newly refurbished Lunt-Fontanne Theatre. It was offered under the sponsorship of the Producers Theatre and staged by Peter Brook. The New York drama critics agreed unanimously that the play was a stunning theatrical work, though they disagreed in their interpretations of its meaning. Brooks Atkinson (New York *Times,* May 6, 1958) wrote: "Dürrenmatt is a sufficiently powerful dramatist to make an unpalatable theme acceptable. He writes with wit and humor when he is setting his snares. But he writes with cold fury when he gets to the core of his theme."

Henry Hewes in the *Saturday Review* (May 24, 1958) found the play "one of the most extraordinary theatrical works of our time. It is very possible that with it . . . Dürrenmatt has arrived at a new dramatic form for modern tragedy." Valency, the adapter of the play, considers it a tragedy, "perhaps the first that the modern theatre has produced" (*Theatre Arts,* May 1958), but he adds that it is "a tragedy that ends in satire." In the ruthless destruction of the hero, the cold and remorseless satisfaction of the heroine as she leaves the town with his coffin, there is revealed, as Valency observes, not so much the greatness of the human spirit "as the pathetic nature of the human animal with his endless talent for rationalization, his sorry pompousness and his mouse-like fury."

Dürrenmatt himself offers no easy explanation of his play. "When you write a play," he has said, "you don't do it to teach a lesson or prove a point or build a philosophy because you can never force art to do anything." He says about his "message": "The World for me stands as something monstrous, an enigma of

calamity that has to be accepted but to which there must be no surrender."

A heavy, stocky man (he weighs 230 pounds), much given to smoking long cigars, he is witty and genial; but, according to Valency, "his manner is grave and impressive. It is only when he takes off his glasses for a moment that you realize he is still a young man." Dürrenmatt has been married since 1947 to Lotti Geissler, formerly a German actress. They live in Neuchâtel with their three children, three dogs, and numerous cats.

References

N Y Times II p 1+ My 25 '58
Theatre Arts 42:17+ My '58
Time 71:83 My 19 '58
Who's Who in Switzerland (1955)

EGAN, WILLIAM ALLEN Oct. 8, 1914-
Governor of Alaska; merchant

Address: b. State Capitol, Juneau, Alaska; Valdez Supply, Valdez, Alaska; h. Valdez, Alaska

After having led the movement which culminated in statehood for Alaska in 1959, William Allen Egan became the first Governor of the forty-ninth state of the Union when he was inaugurated for a four-year term on January 3, 1959. Egan, a Democrat, served as speaker of the territorial House of Representatives, was a territorial senator, and presided in 1955-56 over the convention which drafted Alaska's present constitution.

As Governor, Egan is faced with the problems of setting up an effective state government for Alaska and solving its economic problems. Alaska, the largest state in the Union, has vast natural resources which are largely unexploited; only 20,000 acres are under cultivation, and 95 per cent of its food supply comes from out of the state.

Revenues in 1958-59 fell far short of estimated needs for 1959-60, but the Egan administration was able to present in March 1959 a balanced budget of $26,500,000 without resorting to new taxes. Thus it is offering $126 worth of services to each of its 210,000 residents.

Sixth child in a family of five boys and two girls, William Allen Egan was born to the late William Edward Egan and Cora (Allen) Egan at Valdez, Alaska on October 8, 1914. His father, a gold miner who came to the territory from Butte, Montana, was killed by a snowslide in 1924. William attended Valdez High School, from which he was graduated in 1932. For a while, he worked in a cannery, then drove trucks for a living. Finally he bought and enlarged the general store, which he still operates as the Valdez Supply. His habit of giving candy away in the store made him popular with the children of Valdez.

Elected as a Democrat to Alaska's territorial House of Representatives, Egan began in January 1941 the first of five sessions in the legislative body, which met only in odd-numbered years. He co-sponsored in 1941 the first bill to submit the issue of statehood to Alaska's voters, but it was not approved. In 1943 he wrote the territory's first measure providing funds for hospitalizing tuberculous patients.

From 1943 to 1946, Egan served in the United States infantry and later became an officer in the Army Air Forces. Returned to the House of Representatives in 1947, he drew up the measure which offered construction aid to small hospitals. He was re-elected to the 1949 and 1951 sessions, and in 1951 was named speaker. In 1953 and 1955 he was elected territorial speaker.

In the referendum of 1946, most of Alaska's citizens indicated their desire to make their territory a state. In 1950 the United States House of Representatives passed an Alaska statehood bill, but it was shelved in the Senate. The situation went into reverse in 1954 when a combined Alaska-Hawaii bill granting both areas status as states was approved by the Senate, but it was killed in the House. In 1955 the House again refused to vote on the Alaska bill.

In 1955 the territorial legislature decided to follow the precedent set by the territory of Tennessee in 1796, when it prepared a constitution and elected federal representatives and senators as if statehood were already a reality. A constitutional convention, composed of fifty-five delegates, met for deliberations at the University of Alaska for seventy-five days from late 1955 to early 1956. Senator Egan, who was president of this convention, has been called the principal architect of the charter signed on February 5, 1956 and ratified by Alaska's voters on April 24 by 17,447 to 7,180 votes.

The constitution of 1956 went into effect when President Eisenhower proclaimed statehood for Alaska on January 3, 1959. It provides for only two elected executive officers, a Governor and a Secretary of State empowered to serve as a Lieutenant Governor. The Governor appoints all department heads, subject to approval by the Legislature, and all judges, from lists provided by a judicial council. Membership in the House of Representatives is increased from twenty-four to forty, and that of the Senate from sixteen to twenty. Both chambers meet annually (*Book of the States*, 1958-59).

The Democratic territorial convention chose Egan in June 1956 as a candidate for one of the two Tennessee Plan senatorships. He was elected in October. With Ernest J. Gruening, a Democrat, elected as "Senator" and Ralph J. Rivers, another Democrat, elected as "Representative," Egan went to Washington, D.C. to work for statehood.

The United States House of Representatives on May 28, 1958, and the Senate on June 30, sanctioned the entrance of Alaska into the Union as a state. President Eisenhower signed the enacting bill on July 7. The measure required Alaska to disclaim all rights to land and property not granted under the act; these were reserved for the federal government. Alaskans approved the conditions of their statehood in a referendum on August 26, when primary elections were held and Egan was selected as the Democratic nominee.

In the Democratic landslide at the general election of November 25, the majority party

WILLIAM ALLEN EGAN

won all but about six seats in the Legislature, two United States Senate seats, to be filled by Ernest Gruening and E. L. Bartlett, and Alaska's only seat in the House, to be filled by Ralph J. Rivers. Egan defeated his Republican opponent, John Butrovich, Jr., by some 6,000 votes.

Sworn into office on January 3, 1959, a few minutes after statehood was proclaimed, Egan was unable to assume his full duties as Alaska's first elected chief executive until April 20. At his inauguration he looked haggard and thin from an operation he had undergone in December 1958. He collapsed shortly after the ceremony, was rushed to a hospital, and in the next four months underwent two more major abdominal operations. At one time hospital authorities gave him only a 50 per cent chance of recovering. In May 1959 he underwent surgery for the fourth time.

While in the hospital in January, Egan fulfilled a campaign pledge when he ended the issuance of licenses for salmon traps. Egan believed that the traps depleted the salmon crop and favored big business against independent fishermen. In the weeks after his election, furthermore, Egan had closely studied the fiscal problem with advisers from the federal Bureau of the Budget. When the administration budget for 1959-60 was presented on March 14 it was balanced at $26,500,000, and no new taxes were requested. It allocated increases, over preceding budgets, for education, health, welfare, and the Fish and Game Department.

During Egan's enforced absences, Secretary of State Hugh J. Wade acted as Governor. In June 1959 Congress passed the Alaska omnibus bill designed to give that region equal status with the other states of the Union.

William Allen Egan is five feet eight inches tall, weighs about 165 pounds, has brown hair, and gray eyes. He is an eloquent public speaker. On November 16, 1940 he married Neva Mc-

EGAN, WILLIAM ALLEN—Continued

Kittrick, a teacher. Their son is Dennis William; a daughter, Elin Carol, is deceased. Organizations to which Egan belongs are the Pioneers of Alaska, Fraternal Order of Eagles, Veterans of Foreign Wars, and American Legion.

References

N Y Times p54 Ja 4 '59 por
N Y World-Telegram p4 Jl 12 '58 por
U S News 45:74+ D 26 '58 por

EGHBAL, MANOUCHEHR (ăk'băl) 1909-
Prime Minister of Iran; physician

Address: b. Presidence du Conseil des Ministres, Ave. Kakh Carrefour, Tehran, Iran; h. Ave. Djalalieh, Tehran, Iran

Among the anti-Communist allies of the United States in the Middle East, oil-rich Iran is thought by some Western observers to be the strongest both economically and politically. Iran's pro-Western Prime Minister, Dr. Manouchehr Eghbal, was named by Mohammed Riza Shah Pahlevi to succeed Hussein Ala in April 1957. A physician by training, Dr. Eghbal had earlier specialized in infectious diseases, and as rector of the University of Tehran from 1954 to 1956 he had become one of his country's leading educators. Although he is the youngest Prime Minister in Iran's recent history, he has had long and wide experience in government administration.

Manouchehr Eghbal was born in 1909 in Meshed, the department of Khurasan, in northeastern Iran and received his primary and secondary school education in Iran. In 1926 he went to France, where he attended first the University of Montpellier and then the University of Paris. He studied medicine in Paris for more than five years, specializing in tropical and infectious diseases, and was granted his Doctor of Medicine degree from the University of Paris in July 1933.

Later in the year Eghbal returned to Tehran and joined the army to fulfill his military service. During 1935 he was employed as head of the health department in his home city of Meshed and as chief physician of infectious diseases at Shah Reza Hospital in Meshed. The following year he became chief of the department of infectious diseases at Razi Hospital in Tehran and in 1939 was appointed to an equivalent position at Pahlevi Hospital in Tehran.

For a period of almost fifteen years, beginning in 1939, Dr. Eghbal was professor of infectious diseases on the faculty of medicine at the University of Tehran. Much of his time was given to various social, educational, and medical activities arising from his membership in the high council of the Pasteur Organization, the council of administration of the Iranian Red Lion and Sun Organization, council of administration of the Imperial Social Services, and the High Council for Health and Education.

The Iranian government called upon Dr. Eghbal to fill a number of increasingly important administrative offices: Under Secretary of State for Public Health in 1942, Acting Minister of Public Health in 1946, Minister of Posts and Telegraphs in 1947, Minister of National Education in 1948, and Minister of Roads and Communications and Minister of the Interior in 1949. He was appointed governor-general of Azerbaijan, a northwest province of Iran, in 1950. During the fourteen months that he held this position he was also rector and professor at the University of Tabriz, in the capital of Azerbaijan.

As governor-general of Azerbaijan, Dr. Eghbal had a key post because the province borders on the Soviet Union, which once claimed it. The Communists had gained control of the area in 1945, and after their loss of power Azerbaijan had been troubled by political and economic problems. In his administration during 1950-51 Eghbal came to be regarded as a firm enemy of Communism.

After his return to Tehran, Eghbal served in 1953 as a member of the Iranian Senate. He was elected in 1954 as rector of the University of Tehran and in 1955 was appointed dean of the university's faculty of medicine. His first undertaking as rector was to remove the armed security guards that had been set up to prevent political demonstrations. Yet he was able to quell Communist agitation among the students and restore normal campus life.

Dr. Eghbal made a three-month tour of the United States in the spring of 1956. Soon after his return to Tehran, he was appointed by Mohammed Riza Shah Pahlevi, who is his close friend, as Minister of the Imperial Court—the significant position of liaison officer between the Shah and the cabinet. He was in this office when a political crisis arose in March 1957 as a result of the slaying by Iranian bandits of three Americans engaged in United States economic aid work in a desert in southeast Iran.

Iran's seventy-four-year-old Prime Minister Hussein Ala resigned in the belief, according to Western newspapers, that the government needed a younger and stronger hand at the helm. On April 3, 1957 the Shah appointed Dr. Eghbal as Prime Minister and assigned Ala to Eghbal's position as Minister of the Imperial Court. A few days earlier, when Eghbal had been offered the office of Prime Minister, he had stated that he would accept on the condition that martial law, in effect almost continuously since World War II, would be removed from all parts of Iran. Dissolution of martial law was announced on April 4.

Lifting of martial law would allow, Prime Minister Eghbal promised, the formation of political parties for all except the Communists. In May 1957 an Opposition People's party was formed, and in February 1958 Eghbal announced the establishment under his leadership of a government majority party called the Nation, thus in effect setting up a two-party system.

When he became Prime Minister, Eghbal had assured his countrymen that he would try to raise the standard of living in Iran. While advances in social reform and economic development have been reported from time to time in the Western press, some observers have expressed misgivings over the slowness of the country's ruling class to move against corruption and to change Iran's system of feudal landholding. Acting for the Shah, Dr. Eghbal introduced a bill in Parliament in October 1958 forbidding all government officials and members of the royal family from dealing with companies holding or seeking contracts with the government.

Since Iran's economy largely depends upon oil royalties, it is significant that in April 1958 Prime Minister Eghbal presented to Parliament an agreement between the National Iranian Oil Company and the Pan American Oil Company, a subsidiary of a United States firm, which would allow Iran 75 per cent of net profit. A large part of the government's oil revenues is used to finance its $1 billion Plan Organization for building dams, electric power lines, irrigation projects, bridges, and roads. The agency for this vast development program formerly had independent status in the government, but in February 1959 it was put under the personal charge of Prime Minister Eghbal.

At present Iran relies considerably also upon the United States to maintain its economic stability. The New York *Times* of June 8, 1957 stated: "In the last three years the United States has supplied grants of emergency aid and budgetary assistance totaling $108,000,000 in addition to loans of $40,000,000."

In international affairs Iran has been partly guided since 1955 by its membership in the Baghdad Pact, made up of Iran, Iraq, Pakistan, Turkey, and England and sponsored by the United States, which participates in the work of some of its committees. Since taking office as Prime Minister, Eghbal has represented his country at the meetings of the council of ministers of the pact and has endorsed the purpose of answering the threat of Communist aggression against the pact nations. He has urged full participation of the United States in the pact.

Acting as chief spokesman for the Middle East nations at the Baghdad Pact council meeting in Karachi, Pakistan in January 1959, Dr. Eghbal stated that the pact had not yet achieved its most important tasks. As reported by the New York *Times* (January 27, 1959), Eghbal "mentioned the slowness of progress toward the establishment of a common defense system and the lag in fulfillment of economic plans for the areas protected by the Baghdad treaty."

At this time, however, in an effort to bolster the Baghdad Pact, the United States was conducting economic and defense negotiations with Iran, Turkey, and Pakistan to reaffirm existing security agreements. When the Soviet Union warned that Iran would become an enemy of the U.S.S.R. if it signed a bilateral defense agreement with the United States, Eghbal replied, "We are not afraid of any threats. Let them shout and abuse us until they get tired. If they think they can intimidate us and force us by these means to relinquish our rights and interests they are sadly mistaken" (New York *Herald Tribune,* February 29, 1959). The United

Universal, Tehran

MANOUCHEHR EGHBAL

States-Iranian pact was signed on March 5, 1959.

Iraq officially withdrew from the Baghdad Pact on March 24, 1959. After this action, the member nations in August changed the name of the alliance, which had been known as the Middle East Treaty Organization (METO), to the Central Treaty Organization (CENTO).

Dr. Manouchehr Eghbal became a member of the Academy of Medicine in Paris in 1952, and while visiting the United States in 1956 he was awarded an honorary doctor's degree by Lafayette College. Among his many Iranian decorations are First Class Homayoun and First Class Tadj (the highest decoration in Iran). His foreign decorations include the Grand Cordon du Cèdre Libanais, the French Légion d'Honneur, the German Grosses Verdienstkreuz mit Schulterband, and Ordre du Mérite du Royaume d'Iraq. He is married and has three children.

References

N Y Times p3 My 28 '57
Newsweek 47:110+ My 21 '56 por
U S News 42:22 Ap 12 '57
International Who's Who, 1958
Middle East, 1958
World Biography (1954)

ENCKELL, CARL J(OHAN) A(LEXIS)
June 7, 1876-Mar. 26, 1959 Finnish statesman; businessman; first Finnish Minister to the U.S.S.R.; Foreign Minister (1918-19, 1922, 1924, 1944-50). See *Current Biography* (April) 1950.

Obituary

N Y Times p80 Mr 29 '59

ENDELEY, E(MMANUEL M(BELA) L(IFAFFE) Oct. 4, 1916- British Cameroons political leader; physician
Address: Buea, British Cameroons, West Africa

When the United Nations General Assembly met in February and March of 1959 to pave the way for the independence of U.N. trust territories in West Africa, Dr. E. M. L. Endeley appeared before the trusteeship committee to speak for one of the diverse views emerging in the British-administered Cameroons on the political future of the country. He was the first Prime Minister (1957-59) of the Southern Cameroons, which is now a quasi-federal territory within Nigeria.

At present, as head of the Kamerun National Congress party, Dr. Endeley leads the opposition in the Southern Cameroons House of Assembly. He believes that the Southern Cameroons should remain with Nigeria when that country becomes independent in 1960. Since Prime Minister John N. Foncha, head of the Kamerun National Democratic party, favors a merger with the adjacent French Cameroons, the U.N. plans to conduct a plebiscite to decide the issue.

Emmanuel Mbela Lifaffe Endeley was born on October 4, 1916 at Buea in what was then Germany's Kameruns colony, which was to be divided into British and French Cameroons four years later. A Bantu, he is a member of the Bakwiri tribe, of which his father, Mathias Lifaffe Endeley, was the first literate chief. His mother was the former Mariana Mojoko Liombe.

Beginning his education at a new British Government School in Buea, Emmanuel Endeley also went to a Roman Catholic Mission School at Bojongo before he attended the Government Secondary School at Umuahia in Nigeria. In 1934 he entered the Yaba Higher College at Lagos, Nigeria with the intention of studying agriculture. He soon turned his attention to medicine and in 1935 was one of four students granted scholarships to the Nigeria School of Medicine. "I was influenced," he has explained, "by the needs of my people for better facilities and by the scarcity of doctors in the country."

Soon after he received his L.S.M. (Licentiate of Surgery and Medicine) degree in 1943, Dr. Endeley was assigned to his own district as an assistant medical officer of the Nigerian Medical Service. He served at Buea, Port Harcourt, and Lagos in Nigeria until 1946, when a professional charge was brought against him and his name was erased from the Register of Practitioners. It was restored in 1950, and since then Dr. Endeley has engaged in private practice at Buea.

Meanwhile, in 1946, the recently formed United Nations approved a British trusteeship for eastern Cameroons (in 1922 the League of Nations had made that territory a British mandate). Also in 1946 the Cameroons Development Corporation was established for the production of bananas, rubber, cocoa, and other products on 250,000 acres of leased land in the fertile region of the southern part of British Cameroons. All corporation profits were to be used for the benefit of the people of the trust territory.

A Cameroons Development Corporation Workers' Union was formed, and when Dr. Endeley returned from Lagos to Buea in 1947 he became its secretary. According to the London weekly *West Africa* (August 18, 1951), he "knew nothing about unions and little about the Cameroons Development Corporation," but nevertheless set himself to study labor regulations, address meetings and enforce collection of dues, build membership up to over 19,000, and obtain bargaining-agency recognition. He was made general president of the union in 1949.

For several weeks during the fall of 1949 Endeley led a successful strike for better working conditions. The strike coincided with a visit of the United Nations Trusteeship Mission, headed by Dr. Ralph Bunche, to Togoland and French and British Cameroons. Deeply impressed by the orderliness of the strike, Dr. Bunche recommended that the African representation on the corporation's board of directors be enlarged. In March 1950 Dr. Endeley resigned his presidency of the workers' union to accept, from the Nigerian government, a Development Corporation directorship which he was to hold through 1954.

As organizer and president of the Cameroons National Federation (later known as Kamerun National Congress), Dr. Endeley had spoken for various political movements at the time of the first United Nations Visiting Mission. He had also been a delegate to the conferences on the Nigerian constitution held at Enugu in 1949 and Ibadan in January 1950. The outcome of the Ibadan conference was the promulgation on June 29, 1951 of a new constitution which recognized a central Council of Ministers as the principal policy-making body for Nigeria and the trust territory. Legislative authority was vested in a central House of Representatives and three regional Houses of Assembly—western, northern and eastern. The Southern Cameroons were part of the eastern region.

At the election held in the same summer Dr. Endeley's Kamerun National Congress party won most of the Southern Cameroon seats in both the eastern regional House of Assembly and the central legislature. In accordance with the provision of the 1951 constitution that one member of the Nigerian Council of Ministers must come from the trust territory, Dr. Endeley was named to the council in January 1952. He served as Minister without Portfolio in 1952-53 and as Minister of Labor in 1953-54.

When conferences for restudy of the Nigerian constitution were called at London in the summer of 1953, Dr. Endeley as head of the Cameroons delegation presented a petition asking "autonomy for the trust territory, with direct representation at the centre in the Nigerian Government." He expressed the view that the Southern Cameroons, after fifteen months of trial, had come to the conclusion that the eastern House of Assembly was "too unstable to be a suitable organ for an underdeveloped territory." Colonial Secretary Oliver Lyttelton deferred decision on the Southern Cameroons until a pending election in the eastern region had established that Dr. Endeley's party voiced the majority opinion.

The Kamerun National Congress Party made a clean sweep of Southern Cameroons at the December 1953 election. In the following month constitutional discussions were resumed at Lagos in Nigeria. As a result, on October 1, 1954 British Cameroons became "quasi-federal territory within the Federation of Nigeria, with its own legislature (known as the Southern Cameroons House of Assembly) and Executive Council, competent, subject to the assent of the Governor-General of Nigeria, in all matters reserved to the Region by the Federal constitution of Nigeria" (*Whitaker's Almanac*, 1959).

Until the election of March 1957, Dr. Endeley had the title of Leader of Government Business. The Kamerun National Congress party won the majority of seats in the House of Assembly, and Endeley took office as the first Prime Minister of Southern Cameroons. He served until the election of January 1959. At that time the Kamerun National Democratic party, which advocates secession from the Nigerian federation and unification with French Cameroons, defeated Endeley's party. John N. Foncha then became Prime Minister.

During 1958 the French government announced that the French Cameroons would be granted independence on January 1, 1960 and the British government announced that Nigeria would become an independent member of the British Commonwealth on October 1, 1960. At the U.N. General Assembly session held in early 1959 to arrange for terminating the trusteeship agreements, the most controversial issue concerned the Southern Cameroons. (The northern section of British Cameroons presented less of a problem because it is almost indistinguishable from northern Nigeria.)

Arguing against Foncha's proposal for secession, Dr. Endeley maintained that economic progress in the Southern Cameroons was entirely dependent upon a policy of association with Nigeria. The General Assembly voted in March to hold a plebiscite in Northern Cameroons in November 1959 and in Southern Cameroons between December 1959 and April 1960. Decision on the questions to be put in the Southern Cameroons plebiscite was deferred until the next session of the General Assembly.

When the General Assembly reconvened in the fall of 1959, Endeley and Foncha requested that the plebisicite be postponed. On October 16 the General Assembly voted to recommend that the future of the Southern Cameroons be decided by popular election not later than March 1961. The two questions to be presented to the electorate will be whether the inhabitants wish to join Nigeria or the French Cameroons.

"Mountaineering on the 13,500-foot Cameroon Mountain is my favorite and occasional pastime," Dr. Endeley has said. "I also enjoy gardening and hiking." In his pen portrait in *Our Council of Ministers* (1952) Ernest Ikoli has further noted that "Dr. Endeley did a little water color painting when in school" and that bookbinding is another of his hobbies.

DR. E. M. L. ENDELEY

On October 4, 1945 Dr. E. M. L. Endeley married Ethel Mina Green, a registered nurse in the Nigerian Medical Service. His sons are William Ngembo, Ernest Ikome, and Eman Moka. He is six feet one inch tall and weighs about 200 pounds. He was awarded the Queen's Coronation Medal in 1953 and has also been honored with the Order of the British Empire.

References

West Africa p749 Ag 18 '51 por
International Who's Who, 1958
International Year Book and Statesmen's Who's Who, 1958
Who's Who in Nigeria (1956)

EPSTEIN, SIR JACOB Nov. 10, 1880-Aug. 19, 1959 Sculptor; artist; born in United States and became a British subject; knighted in 1954; known for his nude statues, religious figures, and bronze portraits. See *Current Biography* (July) 1945.

Obituary

N Y Times p1+ Ag 22 '59

EVANS, HERBERT M(CLEAN) Sept. 23, 1882- Anatomist; physiologist; former university professor
Address: b. Institute of Experimental Biology, University of California, Berkeley 4, Calif.; h. 511 Coventry Rd., Berkeley, Calif.

Classic contributions to endocrinology and vitamin studies have been made by Dr. Herbert M. Evans, who, as a physiologist and anatomist, has probed all the interrelated factors influencing the process of life. A leading authority on the pituitary gland, he has isolated in purified form four hormones of this master endocrine gland. Other experiments have yielded informa-

DR. HERBERT M. EVANS

tion on still another pituitary hormone, the erythropoietic, which Dr. Evans recognized as governing the production of red blood cells.

Dr. Evans is one of the few individuals who has worked with both hormones and vitamins. In 1922 he discovered vitamin E and found that it is an essential factor in the reproduction of higher animals. Dr. Evans is emeritus professor of anatomy and emeritus Hertzstein professor of biology at the University of California at Berkeley. Since 1953 he has been director emeritus of its Institute of Experimental Biology.

Born in Modesto, California on September 23, 1882, Herbert McLean Evans is the son of Dr. C. W. Evans and the former Bessie McLean. His father was a surgeon for the Pacific Railway and his uncle, Robert A. McLean, was the first master surgeon in California. Herbert often accompanied his father to attend victims of train wrecks, and at an early age he decided to follow medicine as a career. He worked his way through the University of California as a laboratory assistant, was elected to Phi Beta Kappa, and graduated in 1904 with a B.S. degree. He pursued his medical education at Johns Hopkins University, where he was influenced by Dr. Franklin P. Mall, professor of physiological anatomy.

After receiving the M.D. degree in 1908, Evans turned to research over the objections of his father who had hoped he would be a surgeon. He accepted an assistantship in the department of anatomy at Johns Hopkins in 1908, and during the next seven years he was promoted through the ranks of instructor, associate, and associate professor. From 1913 to 1915 Dr. Evans also served as a research associate with the Carnegie Institution of Washington.

Professor Evans proved himself an able anatomist as early as 1909 when he demonstrated the origin of body vascular trunks from capillary plexuses, the networks of minute blood

vessels between the ends of the arteries and the beginnings of the veins. His explanation of the physiological behavior of vital stains of the benzidine series was announced in 1915. In the same year Dr. Evans was appointed professor of anatomy at the University of California in Berkeley, where he continued his research on azo dyes, especially Evans Blue. In 1917 he introduced the use of these dyes to estimate blood volume in the body. The following year Dr. Evans started to outline and describe the forty-eight chromosomes in man, a project completed in 1929.

From anatomy Dr. Evans moved into the fields of embryology and endocrinology. With Joseph A. Long he studied the oestrous cycle in rats, that period of sexual activity which coincides with the discharge of ova. Their findings, published in 1921, established and described a regular sexual cycle in rodents.

About this time Dr. Evans had begun a research project to which he has devoted the greater part of his career. The studies concerned the hypophysis cerebri, or pituitary gland. Lodged at the base of the brain, this organ secretes some twelve different hormones directly into the blood stream and is the principal coordinator of all other endocrine glands. Seeking to discover whether the pituitary secreted a hormone which controlled growth, he started experiments in 1920 involving the oral administration of pituitary extract.

These were largely unsuccessful but in 1922 he administered parenterally pituitary extracts into baby rats and produced giant rodents. When the injections were stopped, growth ceased. Furthermore, the injection of pituitary extracts into rats dwarfed by the removal of their pituitaries permitted the animals to regain normal size. However, Evans' studies demonstrated that the extract did not restimulate the other functions besides growth, such as sex functions, normally controlled by the pituitary gland. After this hormone was discovered, growth in underdeveloped children was induced by treatment based on Evans' findings. However, the cost of producing this secretion is still prohibitive.

Another aspect of Evans' research during the 1920's was his study of vitamins and nutrition. In 1922 he detected a criterion of vitamin A deficiency in continuous vaginal cornification. His work on the oestrous cycle of rats prompted a study on the importance of diet and vitamin intake on sterility and fecundity. Evans began a search for foods which contained elements essential to the normal development of the embryo. By December 1922 he announced the discovery of vitamin E, which was found to be necessary for reproduction in higher animals. With Oliver H. and Gladys Anderson Emerson, Evans determined the empirical constitution of vitamin E and obtained it in pure chemical form in 1935. In 1932 he produced permanent diabetes by chronic administration of anterior pituitary extracts.

Dr. Evans completed the separation of the growth-producing hormone in 1939, and with Dr. Choh Hao Li he succeeded in obtaining it in purified form in 1944. When the impurities were removed, scientists could determine the amount of the pure form needed by the body for normal growth. Evans' experiments proved conclusively that injections of pure hormone restimulated growth in normal animals as well as animals whose pituitaries had been removed.

During the early 1940's Evans, Dr. Li, and Dr. Miriam E. Simpson obtained in pure form the adrenocorticotropic hormone (or ACTH). This is a secretion of the pituitary's anterior lobe which stimulates the adrenal cortex to produce more of its own hormone, cortisone. By 1949 ACTH and cortisone were being administered to sufferers from rheumatic fever and rheumatoid arthritis. Evans, Li, and their associates also reported that ACTH could counteract the effect of the growth hormone. Other pituitary secretions, the anterior-hypophyseal interstitial-cell-stimulating hormone and the follicle-stimulating hormone, were first purified by Evans, Li, and Simpson.

The existence of still another distinct secretion of the pituitary was suggested by Evans in 1953. Working co-operatively with other scientists at Berkeley, Dr. Evans showed that the erythropoietic hormone governed the production of red blood cells and that it alone prevented anemia in newborn rats.

Since 1953 Dr. Evans has been professor emeritus at the University of California and director emeritus of the institute. Working with Dr. Marjorie M. Nelson, Evans gathered new information in 1956 on the relationship between diet and hormones in maintaining normal pregnancy and achieving live births. Evans and Dr. Nelson also announced that research had demonstrated that severe deficiencies of several of the B vitamins, such as folic acid, pantothenic acid, and riboflavin caused congenital abnormalities in rats.

During his career Dr. Evans has published over 500 papers in scientific journals. He served as joint editor of *American Anatomical Memoirs* (1918-38) and the *Journal of Nutrition* (1928-33). He has been in demand as a lecturer at universities and medical schools in the United States and abroad. He served as a delegate to the third International Conference on Standardization of Hormones in 1938 and the second Pan American Congress of Endocrinology in 1941.

Honorary degrees have been conferred on Evans by the Albert-Ludwigs-Universität in Freiburg im Breisgau, Germany (1930), Universidad Nacional Mayor de San Marcos de Lima, Peru (1941), Catholic University of Chile (1941), University of Paris (1946), Birmingham University (1950), Universidad Central del Ecuador (1954), University of California (1955), University of Geneva (1956), and Johns Hopkins University (1957). In 1941 he was appointed an honorary professor at the University of Chile and the Universidad Central del Ecuador, and he was named Charles Mickle Fellow of the University of Toronto in 1949.

Awards bestowed on Evans include the John Scott Medal (1928), Banting Medal (1949), Squibb Award of the Association for the Study of Internal Secretions (1949), and Passano Foundation Award (1952). The magazine *Modern Medicine* selected Evans in 1954 as one of ten scientists to receive the Award for Distinguished Achievement for work on the pituitary gland.

Professional organizations to which Dr. Evans belongs are the National Academy of Sciences, American Physiological Society, Society for Experimental Biology and Medicine, and American Association of Anatomists (president, 1930-32). He is also a fellow of the American Academy of Arts and Sciences. His honorary foreign memberships include the medical societies in Budapest, Buenos Aires, and Santiago (Chile), Biological Society of Argentina, and endocrinology societies of Portugal and Italy. His clubs are the University of California, the Faculty (of the university), Roxburghe, and Bohemian (San Francisco).

Dr. Herbert M. Evans was married to Dorothy Frances Atkinson on June 14, 1945. He had two previous marriages. By his first marriage, to Anabel Tulloch on September 17, 1905, he became the father of Marian McLean Evans. On June 28, 1932 he was married to Marjorie E. Sadler, and they had another daughter, Gail Bayne Evans. Dr. Evans has white hair and is distinguished in appearance. For relaxation he has enjoyed mountain climbing, studying the botany of the Sierra Nevada arctic alpine zone, and collecting books on Western Americana and the history of medicine.

References

American Men of Science vol 2 (1955)
International Who's Who, 1958
Jaffe, B. Men of Science in America (1958)
Who's Who, 1959
Who's Who in America, 1958-59
World Biography (1954)

EVATT, HARRIET (TORREY) (ĕv'ăt)
June 24, 1895- Author; illustrator
Address: b. Bobbs-Merrill Co., Inc., 724-730 N. Meridian St., Indianapolis 7, Ind.; h. 74 E. Kanawha Ave., Worthington, Ohio

Reprinted from the *Wilson Library Bulletin* Oct. 1959.

In Knoxville, Tennessee, Mrs. Harriet Torrey Evatt was born on June 24, 1895. She was brought up in that state, in North Carolina, and in Ohio. She had two sisters, and their father was John McCullough Torrey, a mural painter of a pioneer Ohio family and their mother, Lenna Van Meter (Richardson) Torrey, a Virginian of Knickerbocker Dutch ancestry. The future author was a niece and the namesake of Harriet Hawley, who also wrote for children.

"I always wanted to be a writer and artist," Mrs. Evatt says, "and I finally combined the two in writing and illustrating children's books. Perhaps a poem published on the contributors' page of *St. Nicholas* when I was about nine decided me."

In 1924 she married William S. Evatt, former State Tax Commissioner of Ohio, an attorney in Columbus, and a talented violinist. The year of their marriage the Evatts built a red brick house in Columbus, where they have lived ever

HARRIET EVATT

since, filling it with antiques, a hobby of Mrs. Evatt's.

Mrs. Evatt's first book was *The Red Canoe* (1940). Her second was *Suzette's Family* (1941), about a French-Canadian girl, living on an island in the St. Lawrence River, who had four brothers, but yearned for a sister. The reviews contained some reservations. The *Commonweal* said: "Much of it is authentic, though she mixes the old and new in a strange manner, and has her French Canadians conversing with English-speaking people without any language difficulties—which is quite a feat." The *Library Journal* said: "It is difficult to believe that so trite a plot could provide such a fresh, unpretentious, and natural picture of pleasant home life as it does. Written without apparent intent to inform, it succeeds better in doing so than many stories with unfamiliar backgrounds. . . . Indifferently illustrated with black-and-white drawings by the author."

These two were followed by *The Secret of the Ruby Locket* (1943) and *The Mystery of the Creaking Windmill* (1945), in which Virginia Kirkus saw "charm and humor," while the New York *Times Book Review* said, "there is warmth in it." The Chicago *Tribune* found it to be "a book of genuine merit." *The Snow Owl's Secret,* also illustrated by Mrs. Evatt, won the Ohioana Award for the best juvenile book written in 1946.

"For more than twenty-five years," Mrs. Evatt said in 1954, "my husband and I have gone to the Temagami Forest Preserve in the North Country, 'the icebox of Canada,' three hundred miles north of Toronto . . . [to] fish, canoe, sketch, and camp. Bear Island is the Ojibway reservation, where I got to know the daily life of the North Woods Indian. . . . Here I met Danny Whiteduck, son of our guide."

Danny was the hero of *The Red Canoe,* and another small Indian from this part of North America appears in *The Snow Owl's Secret,* recovering the lost treasure of the Ojibways.

Still other titles written from Mrs. Evatt's knowledge of these Indians are her three picture books—*The Papoose Who Wouldn't Keep Her Stockings On* (1954), *Big Indian and Little Bear* (1954), and *Davy Crockett, Big Indian and Little Bear* (1955).

The Mystery of the Old Merchant's House (1947) the Chicago *Tribune* felt had "a pleasant old-fashioned, New England flavor." This was followed by *The Secret of the Whispering Willow* (1950). About this last title there was a division of critical opinion, the *Library Journal* calling it "a mystery that girls will enjoy . . . delightful picture . . . of French Canada," while the New York *Herald Tribune Book Review* said it was not easy reading for those under twelve and the pictures were much too childish, yet "the story is worth while, the family atmosphere is excellent." The New York *Times Book Review* said: "The situations are of a routine variety, so are the characters; and Ninon is just a little too good to be true. Yet there is a disarming warmth in this story and a lively pace sustains the interest." Her next book was *The Mystery of the Alpine Castle* (1951).

The Secret of the Singing Tower (1953) grew out of a visit to Holland. "I have never written a book about a country I have not visited," Mrs. Evatt declares, "although I often give a town or a village a fictitious name. Most of my research work is done on location whether it be the United States, Canada, or Europe."

Mrs. Evatt regards her husband as the chief influence in her writing and painting and has dedicated all her books to him. She has written many short stories and serials for children magazines, as well as verse, with illustrations. She had a period of being a theatrical press agent.

In 1946 she received the Don Casto Award offered by the Columbus Art League, of which she is a member, for the best portrait in oils. She is also a member of the Ohio Water Color Society, the Columbus Art Gallery, and an honorary member of Theta Sigma Phi, the journalism fraternity for women. She is active in Nightingale Cottage, the Children's Hospital in Columbus, and in the women's auxiliary of St. John's Episcopal Church there. Her favorite authors are Dickens, Colette, and Ludwig Bemelmans. She is five feet two inches tall and weighs 135 pounds; she has hazel eyes and brown hair.

The Evatts are Republicans, attend the theater as often as possible, and like travel of all kinds, especially in Europe. They have three female cats—two Persian Smokes and a sapphire-eyed Siamese—that their friends call the "wrecking crew." The Siamese was one of the main characters in *The Mystery of the Alpine Castle.*

Bobbs-Merrill Company, Inc., who has published all of Mrs. Evatt's books, issued her thirteenth title in October 1959, *The Secret of the Old Coach Inn.*

References

Columbus Dispatch p18C My 19 '57 por
Who's Who in America (sup D 1 '51)
Who's Who in American Art (1956)
Who's Who of American Women (1958-59)

EVATT, MRS. WILLIAM S(TEINWE-DELL) *See* Evatt, Harriet

FELDMANN, MARKUS May 21, 1897-Nov. 3, 1958 Minister of Justice and Police in the Swiss Federal Council; President of the Confederation of Switzerland in 1956. See *Current Biography* (June) 1956.

Obituary

N Y Times p27 N 4 '58

FELS, WILLIAM C(ARL) Oct. 31, 1916-
College president

Address: b. Bennington College, Bennington, Vt.

Known best in the United States for his special knowledge of school administration and educational finance, William C. Fels became on May 12, 1958 the fourth president of Bennington College, a leading experimental and progressive college for women. Before coming to Bennington, Fels had served as associate provost of Columbia University, executive secretary of the Ford Foundation college grants program, and as associate director of the College Entrance Examination Board. Some of the innovations that president Fels proposed during his inaugural address were state tuition awards, group insurance prepayment plans to finance college education, and the use of social security machinery to enable students to obtain a higher education.

Bennington College continues to live up to its reputation for being an "educational maverick." Since its founding in 1932 it has advocated small classes and personalized instruction for its students. Its campus still consists largely of a barn and a few white clapboard houses sheltering a youthful faculty and a small student body. An experimental atmosphere still prevails at Bennington as it did in the 1930's, when "no marks, no exams, no academic requirements in the then accepted sense" were the rules of the day. Lacking large endowments, the college still relies mainly upon high student tuition for its income, and stresses an arts program which will prevent the graduation of the "aesthetic illiterate."

William Carl Fels was born in New York City on October 31, 1916, the only child of Carl Schurz and Aimee (Hess) Fels. He spent his boyhood in New York, where his father was a dress manufacturer. After attending elementary school in New York, he prepared for college at Bordentown Military Institute, Bordentown, New Jersey. He graduated in 1933. When he graduated from Columbia College in the class of 1937, Fels received the Brainerd Memorial Prize for being "the most worthy of distinction on the ground of his qualities of mind and character."

For his postgraduate work Fels chose to remain in Morningside Heights. From 1937 to 1939 he studied at the Columbia Law School, and from 1939 to 1941 at the Columbia Graduate Faculties, where he received the M.A.

WILLIAM C. FELS

degree. He was an instructor in the humanities at Cooper Union in New York City from 1941 to 1942, when he entered the United States Army as a private. By the time of his discharge in 1946, Fels had risen to the rank of captain in the Ordnance Corps. During his military career he served as public relations officer at the Ordnance School in Aberdeen, Maryland.

Columbia University not only provided Fels with his formal education, but also gave him his first experience in educational administration. After his Army discharge, Fels worked at Columbia University from 1946 to 1948, first as veterans' counselor, then as assistant to the general secretary. When Fels resigned his post as associate provost of Columbia in 1957, Dr. Grayson L. Kirk, its president, said that Fels was "admirably equipped for his new position." He also expressed his regret and said that he felt a "keen sense of loss" over Fels' departure.

Work with the College Entrance Examination Board further broadened Fels' experience in educational administration. From 1948 until 1952 he served as its secretary, and from 1952 until 1955 as its associate director. He also arranged the College Scholarship Service in which 150 colleges participated in order to increase the efficiency of the administration of scholarship funds.

The problem of guaranteeing the financial stability of small, independent colleges without huge endowments such as Bennington has been one of Fels' primary concerns. To insure their future, Fels has proposed that both state and independent institutions charge the same realistic levels of tuition, that the states provide ample tuition awards, and that families insure themselves against the expenses of higher education just as they do against the costs of illness.

(Continued next page)

FELS, WILLIAM C.—*Continued*

In his inaugural address of May 12, 1958 Fels charged some critics of American education with looking for the path to Sparta rather than to Athens. "The failure I speak of in education," he said, "is not a failure to transmit knowledge, but a failure to infect humanity with virtue." He declared that his "constant concern" would be the preservation of the "living reform" that Bennington College represents in the "cloudy future."

Aware that low faculty salaries in the past have too often served as a form of hidden tuition subsidy for students, Fels has been greatly preoccupied with efforts to raise faculty salaries —through boosting tuition rates, if necessary. In February 1958 he announced a "cost of education plan" for the fall of 1959, which increased tuition fees at Bennington by $400, but which also gave the students' families the opportunity of paying the tuition on a monthly basis. He also offered some parents an arrangement of interest-free loans. According to Terry Ferrer in the New York *Herald Tribune* (February 17, 1958), Fels believed that the plan would bring the college more income and would benefit middle-income families in particular.

William C. Fels was a frequent contributor of articles to both general and professional publications. His articles in educational journals have voiced his concern over such matters as educational testing, college admissions standards, the administration of scholarships, and faculty salaries. From 1948 until 1951 he was editor of the *College Board Review*.

Since the end of World War II William C. Fels has taken on many community responsibilities. He has been a member of the board of trustees of the Riverdale Country School, and the board of directors of Encampment for Citizenship. He has served on the national advisory committee of the National Merit Scholarship Corporation and of the education committee of the Museum of the City of New York. In 1955 he served as consultant to the college grants program of the Ford Foundation. He advised the Commission on Instruction and Evaluation of the American Council on Education and was chairman of a committee of the Fund for the Advancement of Education which tried to evaluate experiments in the better utilization of teaching resources. He has also served on the George F. Baker Trust.

On January 7, 1945 William C. Fels was married to Harriet Sloane. They have two children, Thomas Weston and Ann O'Conor Sloane Fels. The new president of Bennington College stands six feet three inches in height and has brown eyes and brown hair and weighs 160 pounds. He has written of himself: "I am a product of general education and I believe in it, but I am not so bemused by it that I do not realize that every man is perforce a specialist" (*Educational Record*, April 1958).

References

N Y Times p29 Je 10 '57

Who's Who in America, 1958-59

FELT, HARRY D(ONALD) June 21, 1902- United States Navy officer

Address: Headquarters, Commander, U.S. Forces, Pacific, Pearl Harbor, Hawaii

Succeeding Admiral Felix B. Stump as Commander in Chief, United States Forces in the Pacific and Far East, Admiral Harry D. Felt assumed his command on August 1, 1958. He has authority over all United States Army, Navy, and Air Forces in the area, including the Seventh Fleet defending the supply lines to the Chinese offshore islands of Quemoy and Matsu. He is also a military leader of the Southeast Asia Treaty Organization.

Before assuming his command, Felt had served for nearly two years as Vice-Chief of Naval Operations. An Annapolis graduate of 1923 and a naval flyer since 1929, Felt served in the Pacific in World War II as a commandant of carrier-based aircraft and won two decorations for heroism.

Harry Donald Felt was born to Harry Victor and Grace Greenwood (Johnson) Felt in Topeka, Kansas on June 21, 1902. He attended public school in Goodland, Kansas before moving to Washington, D.C., at the age of ten. After his graduation from a Washington high school, he was appointed to the United States Naval Academy at Annapolis, Maryland. He received his B.S. degree from Annapolis on June 8, 1923 and was commissioned an ensign. Before reporting in August 1928 for flight training at Pensacola, Florida, he served as ensign and as lieutenant (junior grade) on the battleship *Mississippi* and the destroyer *Farenholt*. Named a naval aviator one year later, he flew naval aircraft with the Battle Fleet. In October 1931 he was assigned as instructor at the Naval Academy, with the rank of lieutenant. Two and a half years of "normal tours of aviation duty both aboard ship and ashore" followed, and in June 1938 he was advanced to lieutenant commander.

At the time of the attack on Pearl Harbor, he was commanding a dive-bombing squadron which operated from the carrier *Lexington*. After the United States entered World War II, he was immediately reassigned as commander of the air group aboard the carrier *Saratoga*, and in January 1942 was advanced in rank to commander. In the South Pacific he won the Distinguished Flying Cross "for heroism and extraordinary achievement . . . during action against enemy ground forces in the Guadalcanal-Tulagi area on August 7-8, 1942."

On August 24, 1942, while leading a bomb and torpedo air group northeast of the Solomon Islands, Felt "eyed the Japanese light carrier *Ryujo* with cruiser and destroyer escort from 14,000 feet" and "just after *Ryujo* turned into the wind to launch fighters . . . pushed over his first wave of bombers." He then "went down with the second wave in a screaming dive through flak and fighters to score one out of his group's four to ten 1,000-lb.-bomb hits on the carrier" (*Time*, June 9, 1958). For his "extraordinary heroism and distinguished service" in this action, which resulted in the damaging or sinking of the carrier, the damaging of the cruiser, and the sinking of the destroyer, Felt was awarded the Navy Cross.

Returning to shore duty in January 1943 Felt served first as commanding officer of the naval air station at Daytona Beach, then of the Naval Air Station at Miami, Florida. He was advanced to captain in July 1943. In March 1944 he began a year of membership in the United States Military Mission to the Soviet Union, as "the first naval aviator to serve in this capacity."

Reassigned in February 1945 as commanding officer of the light carrier *Chenango*, Felt returned to the Pacific and "for exceptionally meritorious conduct . . . during operations against enemy Japanese forces near the Ryukyu Islands from May 2 to June 14, 1945" was awarded the Legion of Merit with Combat "V." The accompanying citation credited him with having "contributed materially to the conquest of Okinawa." The officers and men of the *Chenango* also won a Navy Unit Commendation for a "notable record of service and aggressiveness in combat."

From January 1946 until July 1947, when he entered the National War College at Washington, D.C., Captain Felt was on duty in the office of the Chief of Naval Operations. For a year after graduation from the National War College in June 1948, he held the command of the carrier *Franklin D. Roosevelt*. In July 1949 Felt joined the staff of the Naval War College at Newport, Rhode Island. In April 1950 the commandant, Vice-Admiral Donald B. Bearns, named Felt his chief of staff and aide. After being promoted to Rear Admiral on January 1, 1951, Felt was detached from the Naval War College in the following March to take over a "secret sea command" which turned out to be that of the Middle East Force operating in the area of the Persian Gulf.

Felt returned to the Naval Operations Office at Washington for nearly two years beginning October 1951. Then, as a flag officer, he commanded the Anti-Submarine Carrier Division 15 and the Attack Carrier Division 5. He was appointed Assistant Chief of Naval Operations (Fleet Readiness) in July 1954 and promoted to Vice-Admiral in February 1956, commanding the "mobile and strategically powerful" Sixth Fleet in the Mediterranean. In August 1956 he was called back to Washington to serve under Admiral Arleigh Burke as Vice-Chief of Naval Operations. He was promoted to full Admiral on September 1, 1956, and served as Vice-Chief of Naval Operations for about twenty months. As a global strategist, Felt tended to agree with Army Chief of Staff General Maxwell D. Taylor, who claimed that "the mutually destructive nuclear power of the United States and Russia made general war far less likely than limited war" (New York *Herald Tribune*, April 25, 1958).

President Eisenhower appointed Felt on May 26, 1958 to succeed the retiring Admiral Felix B. Stump as Commander, United States Forces in the Pacific and Far East. Felt took over on August 1, 1958 what has been described as "the largest unified command in the U.S. de-

U. S. Navy

ADM. HARRY D. FELT

fense setup" (*United States News & World Report*). It takes in all United States forces in the area, including 500,000 men, 400 ships, and 2,500 planes.

After a quick tour of inspection, Felt reported on his return late in August that the United States Seventh Fleet was "armed and ready for any eventuality" in the Quemoy crisis. He was later understood to have questioned the wisdom of defending Quemoy and Matsu and the effectiveness of the Chinese Nationalist forces in a series of reports to the Pentagon, but asserted shortly afterward that he had "never questioned United States policy."

At Taipei, Formosa on September 21, after having attended a Southeast Asia Treaty Organization conference at Bangkok, the United States commander in the Pacific called the Quemoy situation "very serious" but maintained that the Seventh Fleet and -the Air Force were very strong in the area as the result of a huge build-up of planes, ships, and missiles since August 23, when the intensive shelling of Quemoy by the Communists began.

General Laurence S. Kuter, the Pacific Air Force commander, and Felt conferred for three hours on September 24 with Generalissimo Chiang Kai-shek, studying ways of improving the convoying of supplies to Quemoy. Ten days later, while in Washington to attend an ANZUS (Australia, New Zealand, United States) Treaty Council meeting, the Admiral praised the "amazing" progress of the Chinese Nationalist forces, and declared that he was "very optimistic" about the Quemoy supply situation.

Harry Donald Felt and Kathryn Cowley of Mobile, Alabama were married on August 3, 1929 and have one son, Lieutenant Donald Linn Felt, a naval aviator and jet pilot. Admiral Felt is five feet seven inches in height, his son, six feet four. ("He makes me feel like

FELT, HARRY D.—*Continued*

a runt," the father has been quoted as saying.) "I love the Navy," Admiral Felt says, citing the attack on the *Ryujo* as his "most memorable experience" and claiming that all his career "has been plain fun."

References

Gen Army 3:6+ Ja '56 por
N Y Herald Tribune p11 Ap 24 '58 por; p5 My 27 '58 por
N Y Times p9 My 27 '58 por
N Y World-Telegram p5 Jl 5 '58 por
Time 71:17 Je 9 '58 por
U S News 44:19 Je 6 '58
Navy Register, 1958
Who's Who in America, 1958-59

FIELD, BETTY Feb. 8, 1918- Actress

Address: b. c/o Actors' Equity Association, 226 W. 47th St., New York 36

During an acting career of twenty-six years Betty Field has proved herself a skilled, poised, and luminous actress in a wide range of child, ingénue, and character roles. On the Broadway stage she interpreted several leading parts in plays by Elmer Rice, her former husband, and for her role in Rice's *Dream Girl* she won the New York Drama Critics Circle Award for 1945-46. In the 1958-59 season Miss Field played the witty Yankee patrician in the first American production of Eugene O'Neill's *A Touch of the Poet*. She has also appeared in many Hollywood films and on television.

Betty Field was born in Boston, Massachusetts on February 8, 1918, the only child of Katherine Francis (Lynch) and George Baldwin Field. She is a descendant of Priscilla and John Alden. Her parents were divorced when she was very young, and she lived with her mother and stepfather in Newton, Massachu-

BETTY FIELD

setts, Morristown, New Jersey, and Forest Hills, Long Island.

At an early age Betty Field wanted to become an actress, and she entered the American Academy of Dramatic Arts in New York in October 1932. The first in her class to obtain an acting assignment outside, she made her debut in 1933 as a maid in *The First Mrs. Fraser* at a Stockbridge, Massachusetts summer theater. Before her graduation from the academy in April 1934, she was engaged by Gilbert Miller for his London production of *She Loves Me Not* (1934). Miller had to rewrite the role of Frances Arbuthnot, the debutante, changing her into a sub-debutante, because of Betty's childlike appearance.

Her first Broadway play was *Page Miss Glory* (1934), in which she played a reporter with one line to speak. Then in November 1935 she succeeded Katherine Squire as Audrey in *Three Men on a Horse*. She replaced Joyce Arling as Susie in *Boy Meets Girl* in July 1936 and also toured in this part from the fall of 1936 to March 1937. In the next few years she portrayed Hilda Manney in *Room Service*, which opened on May 19, 1937; Nora in *If I Were You*, January 24, 1938; Barbara Pearson in *What A Life*, April 13, 1938; Clare Wallace in *The Primrose Path*, January 4, 1939; and Rose Romero in *Ring Two*, November 22, 1939.

After the playwright Elmer Rice saw Betty Field in *Ring Two*, he chose her for the feminine lead in his new comedy, *Two On an Island*, which opened in New York on January 22, 1940. In reviewing her performance in the role of Mary Ward, Brooks Atkinson (New York *Times*, January 23, 1940) commented on the "modest sunniness of Betty Field's personality" and the "grace of her acting. She gives the whole play a captivating radiance."

Miss Field's next vehicle was Elmer Rice's *Flight to the West*, which opened on December 30, 1940. In this argumentative drama about a flight from Lisbon to the United States Miss Field interpreted the part of Hope Nathan. In Rice's *A New Life*, which had its première on September 15, 1943, she achieved stardom as Edith. She then succeeded Margaret Sullavan as the lead in *The Voice of the Turtle* in December 1944.

It was not until Elmer Rice's *Dream Girl*, which ran for 348 performances after it opened on December 14, 1945, that Miss Field achieved her first genuine triumph. As Georgina Allerton she was on the stage, either in reality or in her dreams, for all but three minutes of the total playing time. In its taxing physical demands, the part rivaled that of Hamlet, usually looked upon as the longest speaking role in the stage repertory. For her performance Betty Field received the New York Drama Critics Circle Award for the best performance by an actress for 1945-46. Lewis Nichols in the New York *Times* (December 15, 1945) wrote: "As Georgina Allerton she is wistful . . . fierce . . . amicably tough . . . amicably stately . . . and always a heroine."

Cast as Helen Brown, Betty Field played in *The Rat Race*, beginning on December 22, 1949; Peter in *Peter Pan* in August 1950; and Theodora in Rice's *Not for Children,* which was first presented on February 13, 1951. She replaced Jessica Tandy as Agnes in *The Fourposter* in June 1952.

Another highly acclaimed role created by Miss Field was that of Mildred Tynan in Dorothy Parker's and Arnaud d'Usseau's *The Ladies of the Corridor,* which began its run on October 21, 1953. Acting an alcoholic, Miss Field brilliantly played a scene berating herself for her ill-starred marriage before a mirror. Ultimately she commits suicide by flinging herself outside of an apartment hotel window.

In *Festival,* a comedy about musical prodigies, she was seen as the music teacher, Sally Ann Peters. The play opened on January 18, 1955. In it "she spoofs the innocent character she is playing as neatly as she does the raging sophistication about her," William Hawkins noted (New York *World-Telegram and Sun,* January 19, 1955).

When David Ross staged an off-Broadway production of Anton Chekhov's *The Sea Gull* in 1956, he selected Miss Field to play Madame Treplev. "She strikes a lively modern note," wrote Tom Donnelly (New York *World-Telegram and Sun,* October 23, 1956), "but there are quite a few flats in among the sharps. . . . She doesn't seem to be playing Chekhov at all. In its way, her performance is consistent. It is light, quick, and controlled . . . in going resolutely after every conceivable laugh, she makes Madame Treplev seem not so much the mercurial artist of some magnitude, and of some personal involvement, but a giddy entertainer from the Moscow music halls."

In a revival of *The Waltz of the Toreadors* which opened on March 4, 1958 Betty Field portrayed Mlle. de Ste-Euverte, playing opposite Melvyn Douglas. She was "altogether delightful," Walter Kerr wrote, "a deeply satisfying blend of innocence and idiocy in a welcome revival of a brilliant play" (New York *Herald Tribune,* March 5, 1958).

Signed to co-star with Helen Hayes, Kim Stanley, and Eric Portman in *A Touch of the Poet,* Betty Field played a blue-blooded Yankee of the nineteenth century. In this last play of Eugene O'Neill, which opened on October 2, 1958 and closed on June 13, 1959, she acted her part with stateliness, grandeur, and calm distinction. Miss Field played the role of the spinster in an April 28, 1959 TV version of O'Neill's comedy, *Ah Wilderness!*

Throughout her long career Miss Field has appeared in many Hollywood motion pictures. She displayed her versatility in *Of Mice and Men* (1939) as the discontented wife of a rancher who fell victim to the innocent but mentally retarded Lennie, the migratory farm worker. In *Kings Row* (1942) she enacted the role of Cassie, who tried to escape from small-town reality into madness. In *Tomorrow the World* (1944) she was confronted with the problem of democratizing a German boy indoctrinated with Nazism.

Other movies in which Betty Field appeared were *What a Life* (1939), *Seventeen* (1940), *Blues in the Night* (1941), *The Shepherd of the Hills* (1941), *Are Husbands Necessary?* (1942), *Flesh and Fantasy* (1943), *The Great Moment* (1944), *The Southerner* (1945), *The Great Gatsby* (1949), *Bus Stop* (1956), and *Picnic* (1956).

Betty Field and Elmer Rice were married on January 12, 1942 and have three children, John Alden, Judith, and Paul. Her two sons and daughter have acted with Miss Field in summer theaters. The couple were divorced in 1956, and in 1957 Miss Field was married to Edwin J. Lukas. She is five feet five inches tall, has blue eyes, and very light brown hair. Off stage she uses very little make-up. She talks in a leisurely manner and has an acute sense of humor.

Miss Field dislikes night clubs, jewelry, card-playing, and all forms of transportation except horses and taxicabs. She likes art galleries, steaks, snow, highly seasoned food, opera, concerts, the zoo, painting, reading, walking, and going to the theater. Her favorite roles are Georgina Allerton in *Dream Girl* and Hedvig in Henrik Ibsen's *The Wild Duck.*

References

Colliers 118:14+ Ag 31 '46
N Y Times Mag p20 Mr 3 '46 por; p18 Ja 12 '47 por
Blum, D. Great Stars of the American Stage (1952)
International Motion Picture Almanac, 1959
Who's Who in America, 1958-59
Who's Who in the Theatre (1957)

FINNEGAN, JOSEPH F(RANCIS) Sept. 12, 1904- United States government official; lawyer

Address: b. Federal Mediation and Conciliation Service, 14th St. and Constitution Ave., Washington 25, D.C.; h. 2510 N. Nelson St., Arlington 7, Va.

When the Senate confirmed President Dwight D. Eisenhower's nomination of Joseph F. Finnegan to be director of the Federal Mediation and Conciliation Service, the late Senator Matthew M. Neely, Democrat from West Virginia, remarked that Finnegan was the first nominee in his experience against whom there had not been a single protest. One of the reasons for the absence of opposition was Finnegan's obvious qualification for the assignment. He had twenty years of experience in labor law and, as *Time* pointed out, he had "done an impressive amount of arbitration work, approved by both labor and management." He took over as head of FMCS on February 7, 1955, succeeding Whitley P. McCoy, who had resigned the previous December.

Joseph Francis Finnegan was born to Dennis J. and Elizabeth (Flanagan) Finnegan in North Adams, Massachusetts on September 12, 1904. His father was a newspaperman. Educated in New York City, Joseph Finnegan attended St. Francis Xavier High School and Columbia College. After he was graduated from Columbia in 1928 with an B.A. degree, he went to Fordham University Law School at night and received his law degree in 1931. He helped to pay his way through school by working days

Wide World

JOSEPH F. FINNEGAN

as a cargo checker on Brooklyn piers and by writing a question-and-answer column for investors in the *Wall Street Journal*.

Finnegan was admitted to the New York state bar in 1931. In the same year he became an assistant United States attorney in the Southern District of New York and worked under Thomas E. Dewey until 1934, when he joined the law firm of Lauterstein & Conroy. Later he became a partner in the successor firm, Lauterstein, Spiller, Bergerman & Dannett. In 1948 he founded his own law firm in New York City.

Like a large number of other lawyers in the mid-1930's, Finnegan entered the field of labor law when the Wagner Act, passed in 1935, guaranteed labor the right to bargain collectively. Clients of Finnegan's law firm—including R.H. Macy & Company and the Metropolitan Opera Association—needed legal advice on labor relations. "I became an expert awfully fast," Finnegan has remarked (*Business Week,* November 23, 1957).

World War II interrupted his work in labor law. Finnegan entered the Air Transport Command of the United States Army Air Forces as a first lieutenant in 1942 and rose to major. As assistant chief of the military personnel division, he had the assignment of persuading unsatisfactory generals and other high-ranking officers to retire.

A short time after returning to his law practice at the end of the war, Finnegan met James P. Mitchell, who was then handling personnel matters for R.H. Macy & Company. The two men frequently worked together. This was to be an important association for Finnegan. In January 1955, when President Eisenhower wanted someone to fill the post of director of the Federal Mediation and Conciliation Service,

Secretary of Labor Mitchell suggested his former colleague, who by that time had his own law firm specializing in labor and arbitration cases. Finnegan had served on panels of the FMCS and with the National Mediation Board, the New York Mediation Board, and the American Arbitration Association.

Finnegan is the seventh director of the Federal Mediation and Conciliation Service since its foundation in 1913 as part of the Labor Department, and the fourth man to fill the post since the Taft-Hartley Law (Labor-Management Relations Act) established the service as an independent agency.

Business Week (November 23, 1957) commented that Finnegan has more power over his staff of 200 mediators—or commissioners, as they are officially called—than any comparable government official. He appoints all staff members, who do not have Civil Service status, and he can fire them whenever he sees fit.

Since taking office on February 7, 1955 Finnegan has followed the policy laid down by President Eisenhower which calls for the federal government to stay out of industrial disputes as long as possible. He promised that his staff would not try to "tell either labor or management what kind of a settlement they should agree on." And he added: "That is a matter resting squarely between the parties, and is of the very heart and essence of collective bargaining under our free enterprise system. To hold otherwise would be to invite a totalitarian approach to the solution of labor problems" (*United States News & World Report,* July 22, 1955).

This policy was strictly adhered to in the momentous automobile and steel negotiations of 1955, although the threat of strikes in both those key industries was ever present. That was the year that Walter Reuther, president of the United Automobile Workers union, was pressing for his now-famous "guaranteed annual wage" and there had been dire predictions of industrial turmoil and work stoppages. Despite the strike threat, Finnegan and his aides stayed away from the bargaining sessions between the companies and the U.A.W. and both sides were notified that they had to find their own solution. This they did without any prolonged shutdowns. A similar hands-off policy was followed by the government and the mediation service in the 1955 steel negotiations, even after the steelworkers went on strike. A settlement was reached only twelve hours after the strike began.

The long Westinghouse Electric Corporation strike, which lasted 156 days and cost hundreds of millions of dollars in lost wages and production, provided a far sterner test of the approach to mediation procedures favored by Finnegan, who once summed up his task as being "to bring in light and remove heat" (*Reader's Digest,* January 1959). The Mediation Service had worked on the Westinghouse case for a week before the strike began on October 17, 1955, making idle some 55,000 workers at Westinghouse plants across the country. Finnegan himself played a key role in the drawn-out, and often seemingly hopeless, efforts to arrange a settlement between the company and the International Union of Electrical Workers. Time and again he and his aides persuaded the two sides back to the bargaining table.

A proposal made personally by Finnegan on the 112th day of the strike—that the most controversial issue in the strike be shelved while agreement was worked out on other points—removed some of the heat and kept negotiations alive. There were further deadlocks, however, and finally the company and the union asked the mediators to recommend a settlement.

Soon after an agreement was reached in March 1956, Finnegan said in a speech that he had resisted heavy pressure to "lower the boom" on management or labor during the Westinghouse strike. He added that the long walkout, ended by voluntary collective bargaining, had "vindicated adherence to the basic philosophy of volunteerism" in labor negotiations (New York Times, March 30, 1956). He has elsewhere emphasized the importance of faith in the integrity of the mediators.

In the nation-wide steel strike that threw some 650,000 workers out of work for a month in July 1956, the Federal Mediation and Conciliation Service played a pivotal role in achieving a settlement. The costly (an estimated $50,000,000) nineteen-day strike of New York newspaper deliverers during December 1958 was also settled with Finnegan's help. The New York Times (December 29, 1958) report on the settlement stated that "the final agreement was reached . . . in the offices of the mediation service. . . . Negotiating committees of both sides had been meeting there with Federal mediators since before the strike."

Joseph F. Finnegan is a member of the Bar Association of the City of New York, the Catholic Lawyers Guild, and the New York Athletic Club, and the Phi Kappa Sigma fraternity. He is a Republican. He was married to Maurine C. Schooler on November 14, 1947.

In "Unsung Heroes of the Labor Front" (Reader's Digest, January 1959) Irwin Ross pictured Finnegan as a "beefy, nimble-witted lawyer with an earthy vocabulary." He is five feet ten and a half inches tall, weighs 200 pounds, and has gray hair and gray eyes. He prefers gardening and reading as his recreations. In May 1957 he received the Berlin Award from Holy Cross College; in September 1957, the St. John Francis Regis Award from the University of San Francisco; and in February 1956, the annual Scroll of Honor awarded by the Columbia College Class of 1928. The scroll called him a "dynamic diplomat of the troubled industrial arena."

References

Bsns W p143+ N 23 '57 por
N Y Herald Tribune II p2 Jl 22 '56 por
N Y Times p6 F 18 '56 por
Time 65:82 Ja 24 '55
U S News 41:20 Jl 13 '56 por
Who's Who in America, 1958-59

FISCHER, CARLOS L. 1903- Uruguayan political leader

Address: b. Legislative Palace, Montevideo, Uruguay

In South America the smallest country in area is República Oriental del Uruguay, which paradoxically enjoys the highest standard of living on the continent. Only Uruguay among its neighbors has peacefully developed successive forms of democratic government over the past 130 years. It is currently governed by a nine-member National Council, the President of which for 1958-59 is Dr. Carlos L. Fischer.

A member of the moderately socialist Colorado party, Fischer was elected to Parliament in 1943, was appointed to several cabinet posts, and became national councilor in 1953. After having been the majority party for ninety-three years, his party was defeated in the countrywide elections of November 30, 1958. Martín R. Echegoyen, a Nationalist, is scheduled to succeed Fischer as President of the council on March 1, 1959. At that time the latter will complete his tenure on that body as its members are ineligible for re-election. Fischer continues his career in government, however. In November 1958 a majority of voters chose him to serve as Senator for a four-year term.

The elections signaled a victory for the forces of conservatism in Uruguay, since the Colorado party has always favored social welfare programs, public ownership of utilities, and close inter-American co-operation. The National party may threaten the existence of the present council system itself.

Carlos L. Fischer was born in 1903 in Fray Bentos, Uruguay. This was the year in which José Batlle y Ordóñez, the "father" of modern Uruguayan progressivism and the innovator of the plural executive in Uruguay, came into power. It was not until 1919 that this South American nation first adopted a collegiate executive, by means of which a nine-member National Administrative Council shared authority with a President. This bifurcated arrangement remained in effect until 1934, when a new constitution abolished the council and restored full administrative powers to the Presidency.

Following the death of Batlle y Ordóñez in 1929 the Colorado party split into two factions, one headed by the sons of Batlle y Ordóñez and the other by his nephew, Batlle Berres. Carlos Fischer, who worked as a newspaperman in the 1920's and 1930's, became closely associated with the latter group. In 1943 he was sent to Parliament, representing the department of Rio Negro. He was re-elected in November 1946.

In 1947 Fischer was appointed Minister of Livestock and Agriculture, a position he retained until February 1951. In this office he directed several studies for the improvement of the rural economy, in cooperation with the International Bank for Reconstruction and Development and the United States Technical Cooperation Administration (now International Cooperation Administration). He also sent a

FISCHER, CARLOS L.—*Continued*

technical mission to New Zealand to observe modern agricultural methods in operation.

In March 1951 Andrés Martínez Trueba (see *C.B.*, November 1954) took office as President of Uruguay. In the tradition of Batlle y Ordóñez, Martínez Trueba announced his intention to restore a collegiate executive form of government with the office of President eliminated. A constitutional amendment embodying this proposal was adopted by plebiscite in December. It was stipulated that Martínez Trueba should be President of the new nine-member council until the expiration of his elective term, after which the President would be chosen annually from the members of the major political party. The Opposition was always guaranteed three seats on the council.

Soon after the new governmental system was instituted on March 1, 1952, Carlos L. Fischer was appointed Minister of Public Works. When Antonio Rubio died in November 1953, Fischer was named to succeed him as a member of the National Council. One year later he resigned to campaign for election to that body.

Victorious on November 28, 1954, Fischer became a member of the council on March 1, 1955 for a four-year term. At that time former President Batlle Berres was inaugurated as council President. Subsequently, this office was held by Alberto F. Zubiría (see *C.B.*, December 1956) and Arturo Lezama. On March 1, 1958 the council elected Fischer as its President.

Uruguay has an area of only 68,369 square miles and a population estimated in 1956 to be around 2,650,000. It has the highest standard of living and the lowest rate of illiteracy in South America. Education is compulsory through the elementary grades and free even at the university level. All adults who can read and write are obliged to vote, and political candidates are elected by proportional representation.

The present constitution, adopted in 1934 and amended in 1951, provides for "old-age pensions, child welfare, state care of mothers, free medical attention for the poor . . . an eight-hour day and a six-day week, a minimum wage, and special consideration for employed women and minors" (*World Almanac, 1958*).

Uruguay's two major political parties, the Colorado and the National, trace their origins back to the civil war of the 1830's. At present the National party includes most of the large landowners and is strongest in interior towns and rural areas. Its "policy is conservative almost to the point of reaction" (*Political Handbook of the World, 1958*). The Colorado party is supported principally by laborers and the urban population. It advocates government ownership and operation of public utilities and continued separation of Church and State.

Carlos L. Fischer and his fellow members of the National Council were confronted with the problems of inflation and a treasury overburdened by the costs of an unwieldy bureaucracy, social welfare projects, and subsidies for industries and consumers. Other critical aspects of the economic situation were inflation-engendered strikes that occurred in almost every industry and the decline in the export trading of wool,

beef, and wheat. Uruguay's trade deficit with the United States, the largest purchaser of Uruguayan products, reached $50,000,000 in 1957. In August 1957 the government tried to stabilize the currency by slightly devaluating the peso and by relaxing trade restrictions.

Relations with the United States were not improved when the Uruguay government closed down meat-packing plants owned by Armour & Company and Swift & Company, Inc. in April 1958. But when United States Vice-President Richard M. Nixon visited the country only a few days later he was cheered by many Uruguayans. In October 1958 Armour and Swift, which had been losing money on their Uruguayan plants, turned these businesses over to workers' associations.

The voters of Uruguay expressed their dissatisfaction with the economic crisis of their country in the general elections of November 30, 1958. The Colorado party lost its ninety-three-year-old position as majority party by nearly 90,000 votes to the National party. A constitutional amendment calling for the restoration of a single executive was, however, defeated, although it had been supported by the National party and a faction of the Colorado party.

FISK, JAMES BROWN   Aug. 30, 1910-
Physicist

Address: b. Bell Telephone Laboratories, Murray Hill, N.J.; h. Lee's Hill Rd., R.F.D. 1, Basking Ridge, N.J.

When the conference on detecting violations of a nuclear test ban was held in Geneva, Switzerland during July and August 1958, Dr. James Brown Fisk, executive vice-president of the Bell Telephone Laboratories, served as chairman of the delegation of United States scientists. A noted physicist, Dr. Fisk has acted as government adviser on defense and disarmament and is one of the two chief deputies of Dr. George Bogdan Kistiakowsky, the President's special science adviser.

Under Dr. Fisk's direction negotiations with the Soviet bloc were completed in an atmosphere of mutual understanding. "In negotiations," Dr. Fisk "is inclined to sit back and let the other side express its views before coming in with his arguments" (New York *Times,* July 4, 1958). This technique may have been responsible for the success achieved by the conference. The scientists agreed that international control of nuclear tests was possible; that it was "technically feasible" to establish a control system to detect violations of nuclear test suspensions; and that a control system should be directed by an international body.

The son of Henry James and Bertha (Brown) Fisk, James Brown Fisk was born on August 30, 1910 in West Warwick, Rhode Island. He was educated in the local public schools and the Massachusetts Institute of Technology. Fisk was awarded the Proctor Traveling Fellowship to Cambridge University, England (1932-1934), and it was there that he gave up his interest in aeronautical engineering for nuclear physics.

When he returned to the United States, Fisk completed his doctoral dissertation in theoretical physics at Massachusetts Institute of Technology in 1935.

Dr. Fisk taught physics at M.I.T. and was a junior fellow in the Society of Fellows at Harvard from 1936 to 1938. In the following year he served as an associate professor of physics at the University of North Carolina. He joined the staff of the Bell Telephone Laboratories as an electronic research engineer in 1939. During World War II he supervised work on the development of the microwave magnetron for use in high frequency radar. In another important project Fisk and Dr. William Shockley, another Bell Laboratories scientist, devised "one of the first complete mathematical computations for an atomic pile." The New York *Times* (July 4, 1958) quoted a British nuclear physicist's description of this job "as 'one of the finest pieces of scientific work' he had ever seen."

When the war ended Dr. Fisk was appointed head of the electronics and solid state research division at Bell Laboratories. In 1947 Fisk was offered a teaching position at Harvard University, which he refused in face of a "draft" from officials of the Atomic Energy Commission. Beginning January 1947, he served as the first director of the division of research at the agency. Dr. Fisk introduced several programs in theoretical research, urging that this field of study be separated from reactor development.

Because of his prior commitment to Harvard, Dr. Fisk resigned from the commission in August 1948 to accept the Gordon McKay Professorship of Applied Physics at Harvard. "He is remembered [there] as much for his dry humor and impromptu stories as for his lectures in physics" (New York *Times,* July 4, 1958).

In June 1949 Fisk returned to the Bell Laboratories to direct research in the physical sciences. He was appointed vice-president in charge of research in March 1954, and in the following year became a director of the laboratories and executive vice-president responsible for all technical activities.

After the London disarmament talks in the fall of 1957 failed, Premier Nikita S. Khrushchev and President Eisenhower exchanged correspondence on the subject of disarmament and nuclear test suspension. Not until early May 1958, however, did the Russians agree to the appointment of experts "to study methods of detecting violations of an agreement on test suspension" (*Christian Science Monitor,* May 26, 1958). President Eisenhower declared that the United States experts would be chosen on the basis of scientific competence, and he suggested that the Russians select their delegation in the same manner. Dr. Fisk headed the United States delegation which also included Dr. Ernest O. Lawrence, Nobel Prize laureate and director of the Radiation Laboratory of the University of California and Dr. Robert F Bacher, of the physics department of the California Institute of Technology. Representatives from Britain, France and Canada were asked to participate and a panel of scientific and political advisers was named to assist the group.

JAMES BROWN FISK

Czechoslovakia, Poland and Romania joined Russia at the conference table in Geneva.

From the start the conference was conducted in a spirit of co-operation. The subject to be considered was the feasibility of establishing a "control system to detect violations of an agreement on the world-wide suspension of nuclear weapons tests" (New York *Times,* August 31, 1958). The scientists agreed that surface or near-surface explosions of some volume would not be difficult to observe. The most complicated problem was the detection of underground and high-altitude explosions of only a few kilotons. (A kiloton is a measure of nuclear power with one kiloton equal to 1,000 tons of TNT.) Experts from East and West were in total disagreement as to whether it was possible to devise a reasonable control system to detect these explosions.

The scientists opened their discussions with a consideration of the acoustical system. By this method the "sound, or airwaves, generated by an atomic explosion are recorded by sensitive microbarometers, thus giving a precise indication of the location and size of the explosion" (New York *Times,* July 8, 1958). Within ten days of the start of the talks, Dr. Fisk and Dr. Yevgeny K. Fedorov, chairman of the Soviet group, had endorsed the method of registering acoustic waves "for the detection of nuclear explosions at considerable distances . . . with the aid of a network of control posts" (New York *Times,* July 11, 1958).

A second major area of agreement concerned the radiological method of detecting nuclear explosions. This involves the "collection of radioactive debris scattered into the atmosphere by above-the-surface atomic explosions" (New York *Times,* July 24, 1958). Early in the talks the Western scientists had called for the use of planes and the Soviet scientists had insisted that ground collection stations were adequate to gather the fall-out. Their agreement on air

FISK, JAMES BROWN—*Continued*

sampling attested to the remarkable negotiating skill of Dr. Fisk and Dr. Fedorov, the Soviet chairman, and the desire of both groups to compromise.

The most controversial method for detecting atomic explosions involved the installation of seismic stations. After several sessions of hard bargaining, Dr. Fisk and Dr. Fedorov agreed on the number of stations and their sites, and the equipment to be used for detection. Dr. Fisk showed his reputation for skilful negotiating was justified, for he forced the Soviet bloc to accept a greater number of control posts than they had deemed necessary. In the final report the conferees suggested the establishment of 180 detection centers to "identify virtually all nuclear explosions except those below the equivalent of 1,000 tons of TNT" (New York *Times,* August 31, 1958).

Dr. Fisk has been a frequent contributor to the scientific journals and his laboratory work has been fully documented and described in those periodicals. He also served as associate editor of *Physical Review* from 1945 to 1948. His membership in numerous professional and scientific societies includes Tau Beta Pi and the National Academy of Sciences and he is a fellow of the American Physical Society, American Academy of Arts and Sciences and the Institute of Radio Engineers. Since 1952, Fisk has sat with the general advisory committee of the Atomic Energy Committee and the President's Science Advisory Committee. He has also served as an adviser to the Office of Scientific Research and Development of the United States Navy. Honorary degrees have been bestowed on Fisk by Harvard (1947) and Carnegie Institute of Technology (1956).

Tall and spare, pipe-smoking James Fisk appears more like a mild college professor than a hard-hitting, keen-minded negotiator of atomic disarmament. Married since June 10, 1938 to the former Cynthia Hoar, Dr. Fisk has three sons, ranging in age from thirteen to eighteen. For relaxation he tends the five acres of ground surrounding his farmhouse in New Jersey.

References

N Y Herald Tribune p12 Je 29 '58 por
N Y Times p2 Jl 4 '58 por
U S News 44:20 Je 13 '58 por
American Men of Science vol I (1955)
Who's Who in America, 1958-59

FLEESON, DORIS Journalist

Address: b. c/o United Feature Syndicate, Inc., 220 E. 42d St., New York 17; h. 3344 P Street, N.W., Washington 7, D.C.

In nearly 100 of the United States' leading newspapers, five times a week, there appears a column of political commentary by a liberal, hard-hitting reporter named Doris Fleeson. The number, the scope, and the reliability of her "personal pipe-lines" to Congressional and administration news sources have amazed and sometimes annoyed official Washington for years.

Doris Fleeson was born in Sterling, Kansas, the daughter of William and Helen (Tebbe) Fleeson. She left the small city, where her father operated a clothing store, to attend the University of Kansas in Lawrence and received the B.A. degree in 1923.

First employed as a reporter for the Pittsburg (Kansas) *Sun,* she moved rapidly from there to the Evanston (Illinois) *News-Index* as society editor, the Great Neck (Long Island) *News* as city editor, and eventually, in 1927, to the New York *Daily News,* for which she covered city news on general assignment. "There we learned to hit 'em in the eye," she later said.

In time she was assigned to the *Daily News* Albany bureau, where she began the political reporting that was to become her specialty. On September 28, 1930 she was married to John O'Donnell, a *Daily News* political reporter. Two years later their daughter Doris was born. At about that time Miss Fleeson was in the midst of her coverage of Judge Samuel Seabury's investigation of official corruption in New York.

In 1933 Miss Fleeson was one of the leaders in the founding of the American Newspaper Guild. At a mass meeting that established the Guild of New York Newspaper Men and Women—forerunner of the American Newspaper Guild—she was named to a committee to go to Washington, D.C. and urge the National Recovery Administration to adopt a code providing a minimum wage of $35 a week for reporters.

At the Washington hearing that followed she protested a provision in the code, submitted by the Newspaper Publishers Association, that would have exempted those making more than $35 a week from the regulations of the National Recovery Administration on the ground they were "professionals." Newsmen, she said, objected to being classified as professionals in order to "deprive them of the benefits of the N.R.A."

When Franklin Delano Roosevelt moved from Albany to Washington in 1933, Miss Fleeson and her husband John O'Donnell also went to the nation's capital, to work at the *Daily News*' newly opened Washington bureau. With O'Donnell she wrote the newspaper's *Capitol Stuff* column. She was the one permanent woman member of the press entourage that accompanied President Roosevelt on his campaign tours.

A liberal before she went to Washington, through her closeness to the Roosevelt administration she became more firm in her convictions in both the foreign and domestic sphere. With war brewing in Europe, Miss Fleeson found herself drifting away from the editorial opinions of her newspaper. At the same time there arose domestic difficulties with her husband.

They were divorced in 1942, and Miss Fleeson went abroad to do a series of articles for the *Daily News* about wartime conditions in Germany. Later, while her former husband continued as Washington columnist, she was assigned to desk editing, radio news, and Albany coverage. On May 15, 1943 she announced that she was resigning from the

Daily News to become a war correspondent for the *Woman's Home Companion.*

For that magazine Miss Fleeson covered the war on the Italian and French fronts in 1943 and 1944, writing ten articles beginning with "650 Wacs Defy the Subs" (*Woman's Home Companion,* October 1943) and ending with "Into the Heart of France" (October 1944). While covering the war she also made trips back to the United States and kept up her contacts in Washington.

In February 1944, at one of Mrs. Eleanor Roosevelt's press conferences at the White House, she was called upon to describe her experiences on the Italian front. And in August of that year, while a luncheon guest of Mrs. Roosevelt at Hyde Park, New York, she gave her impression of conditions in France.

After the war, in 1945, Miss Fleeson returned to Washington and launched a column on political affairs for the Washington *Evening Star* and The Boston *Globe.* One of her early columns, published May 16, 1946, became front page news when it blasted into the open a feud between Supreme Court Justices Robert H. Jackson and Hugo Black.

The column revealed that Justice Black "regarded as an open and gratuitous insult, a slur upon his personal and judicial honor" a statement Justice Jackson had included in a dissent to the court's portal-to-portal pay decision of 1945. The import of the statement was that Justice Black should have disqualified himself because his former law partner was an attorney for the winning side in the case. The column was reprinted in various papers.

Such journalistic coups brought more and more newspapers as subscribers to her column, which was soon being distributed through the Bell Syndicate. In 1954 she dropped her affiliation with the Bell Syndicate and became associated with the United Feature Syndicate, which presently distributes her column.

The New York Newspaper Women's Club, in 1937, gave Miss Fleeson its first of what became an annual award for outstanding reporting, for her coverage of the 1936 Republican National Convention. She received another award from the club in 1943—this time for a story about Wendell L. Willkie's world trip. In 1950 Miss Fleeson was one of four newspaperwomen given "headliner awards" for "distinguished service in the field of journalism" by Theta Sigma Phi, national fraternity of newspaperwomen. The next year she was honored by the ladies auxiliary of the Veterans of Foreign Wars, and in 1953 she received a medal of honor from the University of Missouri School of Journalism.

Among her other honors are the Raymond Clapper Award of $500 for "exceptionally meritorious work," given to her in 1954 at the annual convention of the American Society of Newspaper Editors. And in the same year she received a distinguished alumna citation from the University of Kansas. She has honorary Doctor of Humane Letters degrees from Culver-Stockton College and Russell Sage College.

Although Miss Fleeson considers herself a nonpartisan liberal, some readers feel that she

DORIS FLEESON

favors the Democrats. She is often outspokenly critical, as well as lively and witty, believing that people toward whom her candor is directed will accept her remarks because she treats everyone in the same manner. "There is, in fact, almost no Washington figure, Republican or Democrat," *Newsweek* (October 7, 1957) noted, "who has not felt the sharp edge of her typewriter." Democratic Senator Patrick V. McNamara praised her in July 1956 for trying "to skim the whipped cream off the propaganda" in reporting on the health of President Dwight D. Eisenhower (New York *Times,* July 19, 1956).

On Edward R. Murrow's *Person to Person* CBS TV program on May 23, 1958, Miss Fleeson spoke of her concept of politics as a "creative art." When asked what she found the greatest deterrent to reporting, she answered, "I think perhaps the press agent; the explosive growth of public relations is rather alarming to an old police court type like myself, who likes to see the whites of their eyes, who likes to study the demeanor of the witness. . . . I think reporters need to use their legs always, and see the people and talk with the people."

Doris Fleeson has brown hair and green eyes, is five feet two inches tall, and weighs 110 pounds. She talks in a rapid, straightforward manner. In August 1958 she was married for a second time, to Dan A. Kimball, president of the Aerojet-General Corporation of Sacramento, California, and former Secretary of the Navy. She divides her time between Sacramento and Washington, where she has a 100-year-old home in Georgetown. Her daughter, Doris, is now Mrs. Richard W. Anthony. Miss Fleeson is an Episcopalian.

References

Newsweek 50:72+ O 7 '57 por
N Y Post Mag p61 S 16 '49 por
Time 58:55 Jl 9 '51; 59:57 Ap 21 '52
Who's Who in America, 1958-59

FLEMING, DONALD M(ETHUEN) May 23, 1905- Canadian Minister of Finance; lawyer

Address: b. Confederation Bldg., Ottawa, Ontario, Canada; h. 259 Glencairn Ave., Toronto 12, Ontario, Canada; 555 Maple Lane E., Ottawa 2, Ontario, Canada

The Canadian Minister of Finance, Donald M. Fleming, is trying to eliminate "discrimination" by the United Kingdom against Canadian products by making sterling freely convertible into dollars. He is also working to balance the import-export ratio of the United States and Canada. Fleming was first assigned to his present responsibilities in June 1957, when the Progressive Conservative party organized its first cabinet in twenty-two years, and was reappointed in April 1958. Since 1945 he has represented the Eglinton-Toronto riding in Parliament, where he has earned a reputation as a competent debater, astute critic of Liberal party policies, and expert on financial matters. For many years he has been a successful lawyer in Toronto.

Of Scottish, English, and French ancestry on his father's side, and Irish on his mother's, Donald Methuen Fleming was born to the late Louis Charles Fleming and the late Maud Margaret (Wright) Fleming on May 23, 1905. He is a native of Exeter, Ontario and was brought up at Galt, Ontario, where his father taught mathematics at the Collegiate Institute. At sixteen Fleming was graduated from the institute and continued his education at the University of Toronto, where he held political science scholarships. He won the Breuls Gold Medal in political science and the Governor General's Gold Medal for proficiency, and earned the B.A. degree in 1925.

To prepare for a career in law, Fleming studied at Osgoode Hall Law School in Toronto. He was awarded the Christopher Robinson Memorial Scholarship and the Silver Medal before his graduation in 1928. He received the LL.B. degree from the University of Toronto in 1930. Admitted to the bar of Ontario in 1928, he read law with S. H. Bradford and has been a partner since 1929 in the Toronto firm of Kingsmill, Mills, Price & Fleming. In this period Fleming contributed many articles to Canadian law journals and digests. He was created a King's Counsel in 1944.

Active in Toronto municipal affairs from 1938 to 1944, Fleming was an alderman (1939-44), representing ward nine, and served as chairman of the Civic Property (1940), Civic Works (1942), and Public Welfare (1944) committees and was a member of the City Planning Board (1942-44). He was also a Toronto school trustee in 1938 and a board director of the annual Canadian National Exhibition in 1941.

Elected to Canada's House of Commons on June 11, 1945 as a Progressive Conservative, he unseated the incumbent Liberal member for the Eglinton division of Toronto by a majority of 7,940. He was re-elected in the general elections of June 27, 1949, August 10, 1953 (with the largest plurality received by any candidate in his party), June 10, 1957 (with a record vote of over 25,000), and March 30, 1958.

In Parliament Fleming became a party spokesman for the criticism of government ministries. The "industrious preparation" and "forceful exposition" of his arguments brought him widespread attention (John A. Stevenson, *Saturday Night,* July 5, 1958). By 1948 he had received enough support within his party to seek election as leader of the Progressive Conservatives at their convention, but was defeated by Premier George A. Drew of Ontario.

In the following years Fleming became "a competent specialist on financial problems" (John A. Stevenson). During a debate in 1956 on the propriety of a government loan for an oil pipeline, he defied the Speaker's order to remain seated and was the first member of the Commons in twelve years to be suspended for part of a sitting. Fleming was a delegate to the Commonwealth Parliamentary Conferences at London, Ottawa, and Nairobi (Kenya) in 1948, 1952, and 1954, respectively; attended the coronation of Queen Elizabeth II in 1953; and in the same year was decorated by King Paul I of Greece with the Red Cross Medal.

When George A. Drew resigned as leader of the Progressive Conservatives in September 1956, Fleming announced his candidacy as his successor. At the convention in December he was defeated by Diefenbaker, because of a widespread reluctance to choose another Ontarian as standard-bearer.

At the general election of June 10, 1957 the Progressive Conservatives won 110 seats in the Commons to 103 for the Liberals. Other parties took fifty seats. Thus Diefenbaker formed his country's first Progressive Conservative government in twenty-two years. Named Minister of Finance and Receiver-General of Canada, Fleming was sworn in on June 21, 1957. He became at the same time a member of the Privy Council. Six days later he was also named a governor of the International Bank of Reconstruction and Development and the International Monetary Fund.

The Progressive Conservative government called a general election on March 30, 1958 and was returned to power with the largest majority any party has ever commanded in the Commons. Diefenbaker reappointed Fleming to the responsibilities he had held in the former Progressive Conservative cabinet.

During the 1957 campaign the Progressive Conservatives had attacked the United States "giveaway" of surplus grain to foreign countries; American control of various Canadian corporations; and the Liberal party's "lenient dealings with the United States over Canada's national resources" (*Business Week,* June 29, 1957). On July 6, 1957 Diefenbaker said that his government intended to divert 15 per cent of Canada's imports from the United States to the United Kingdom (*Manchester Guardian,* November 11, 1957).

At a conference of British Commonwealth finance ministers at Mont Tremblant, Quebec in the fall of 1957, over which Fleming presided, the then British Chancellor of the Exchequer, Peter Thorneycroft, proposed that Canada and the United Kingdom establish the "basis of a free-trade area to link Canada with the sterling bloc." In commenting on Thorneycroft's plan, Fleming told Parliament that it was not a part of Canada's 15 per cent proposal to divert to the "United Kingdom purchases by Canadians of Canadian products" (*Manchester Guardian*, November 11, 1957).

When the Commonwealth Conference on Trade and Economics opened in Montreal in September 1958, with Fleming as chairman, he attacked the unjustified discrimination by the United Kingdom and the rest of the sterling bloc against Canadian and other dollar goods. His nation, he asserted, had accepted quotas, embargoes, and currency restrictions, which make up dollar discrimination, as necessary to postwar sterling recovery. This end had been achieved, and, therefore, he invited Great Britain to make its currency freely exchangeable for dollars.

One result of the meeting was an agreement by Britain to reduce import controls on Canadian products in exchange for a Canadian pledge to continue duty-free entry of British aircraft, automobiles, and other commodities. (This arrangement enabled Britain to sell $150,000,000 worth of such items to Canada in 1957.) Fleming also announced at the conference a Canadian plan to grant $550,000,000 to underdeveloped Commonwealth countries (*Saturday Night,* October 11, 1958).

On June 17, 1958 Fleming presented to Parliament a budget for the fiscal year of 1958 of $5.1 billion, of which $1.7 billion was designated for defense. Its estimated deficit was $648,000,000. At that time the Finance Minister emphasized that United States-Canadian trade showed a "chronic massive imbalance" of $1 billion annually and was in need of "energetic corrective measures" (Toronto *Globe and Mail,* June 18, 1958). Because of "shrinking revenues and party commitments" the budget "ruled out any serious reduction of taxation" (John A. Stevenson). To meet past and future deficits, Fleming announced on July 14 the largest refunding program in Canada's history, involving the offer of new bonds for old ones amounting to $6.4 billion (Raymond Daniell, New York *Times,* July 15, 1958).

Donald M. Fleming and Alice Mildred Watson were married on May 13, 1933 and have three children, David William, Mary Louise, and Donald Watson Fleming. Among his community responsibilities are the positions of elder and Sunday school superintendent of the United Church of Canada's Bloor Street Church in Toronto, president of two Bible societies, official of the Y.M.C.A., trustee of Toronto General Hospital (1939-44), director of United Welfare Chest (1944-45), and senator of the University of Toronto (1945-49). He is a member of the Royal Canadian Institute, Canadian Political Science Association, and Canadian Bar Association.

His clubs are the Canadian, Empire, National, and Albany in Toronto and the Ottawa Country and Rideau in Ottawa, and he belongs to the Ancient Free and Accepted Masons, Ancient and Accepted Scottish Rite, Independent Order of Foresters, and Canadian Legion (honorary). He is a former commodore of the Island Aquat-

Capital Press Service, Ottawa

DONALD M. FLEMING

ic Association (1935-37). His favorite sports are long-distance swimming and tennis. For his fluency in the French language he was made a Chevalier of the Société du Bon Parler Français of Montreal in 1948.

References

Can Bsns 22:48+ Ja '49 por
Toronto Globe and Mail p1 O 19; p11 O 20 '56
Britannica Book of the Year, 1958
Canadian Parliamentary Guide (1958)
Canadian Who's Who, 1955-57
Canadiana vol IV (1958)
International Who's Who, 1958
Who's Who in America (sup S-N '58)
Who's Who in Canada, 1956-57

FLEXNER, ABRAHAM Nov. 13, 1866-Sept. 21, 1959 Former educator; founder (1930) and director (1930-39) of Institute for Advanced Study in Princeton, New Jersey; instrumental in reforming medical education (1917-28); author. See *Current Biography* (June) 1941.

Obituary

N Y Times p1+ S 22 '59

FORD, GLENN May 1, 1916- Actor

Address: b. c/o MGM Studios, Culver City, Calif.

In the annual exhibitors' poll conducted by the *Motion Picture Herald* in December 1958, Glenn Ford was named "Number One Box Office Star in America." In 1956 he had occupied fifth place in the poll and in 1955 the twelfth. Among the fifty-odd films Glenn Ford has made for

Columbia Pictures Corp.

GLENN FORD

Columbia Pictures or for Metro-Goldwyn-Mayer are: *Gilda, The Blackboard Jungle, Don't Go Near the Water, Imitation General, Torpedo Run, Trial,* and *The Teahouse of the August Moon.*

Of Welsh descent, Gwyllyn Samuel Newton Ford was born in Quebec, Canada on May 1, 1916, the only child of Newton and Hannah Ford. His father was a railroad executive, manufacturer, and mill owner, the nephew of Sir John MacDonald, former Prime Minister of Canada, and a descendant of Martin Van Buren, eighth president of the United States.

Ford spent much of his childhood in Glenford, the site of his family's paper mill; the town later supplied him with the name he chose for his motion picture career. He made his acting debut at the age of four, when, dressed in a Lord Fauntleroy suit, he appeared in *Tom Thumb's Wedding.* The role required him to consume a large dish of chocolate ice cream. "That," he told Theodore Strauss of the New York *Times* (March 22, 1942), "sold me on becoming an actor."

When Ford was seven, his family moved to Santa Monica, California, where he received his entire formal education. His father never objected to his theatrical ambitions, but did insist that he learn how to work with his hands in case he should prove unsuccessful as an actor. Ford has said that "learning to work with my hands has given me a way of life most actors don't have. It tided me over during the years I was trying to crash the theater" (*Saturday Evening Post,* January 4, 1958).

In Santa Monica High School Ford excelled in English, participated in football, track, and lacrosse, and served as the school commissioner of entertainment. He devoted his nights to working with little theater groups and his weekends to operating the searchlight on top of the Wilshire Theater. By the time he was graduated from high school in 1934, he had been promoted to stage manager at the theater.

In 1935 Ford was assigned the three-line role of the grocery boy in *The Children's Hour* because he could also function as the stage manager. After that he was stage manager and actor (with one line) in *Golden Boy,* starring Francis Lederer. In 1938 he toured the West coast in *Soliloquy* with John Beal. The play failed in San Francisco, made another attempt in New York, and then expired, leaving Ford stranded after its three-day run. He returned to the West on borrowed train fare, hoping that he might be able to take a screen test in Hollywood.

Between acting assignments Ford shingled roofs, installed plate glass windows, and joined a little theater group. Tom Moore of Twentieth Century-Fox arranged a screen test for Ford; it turned out to be a fiasco. A year later, he was called back for another test. It succeeded, and the next day Ford was cast in his first movie role in *Heaven with a Barbed Wire Fence* (1939).

Columbia Pictures Corporation put Ford under contract in 1939 and assigned him to a string of "B" pictures. Usually, as in *Texas* (1941) and *The Desperadoes* (1943), he was the hero who gave and took a considerable amount of pummeling. In *Destroyer* (1943) he was a tough chief boatswain's mate.

On December 13, 1942 Ford entered the United States Marine Corps. Looking back on the years he spent in military service, Ford calls them three of the best of his life. He remembers that a grudging tribute from his platoon sergeant, Red Murphy, who was determined not to like movie actors, meant more to him than any Oscar.

Returning to motion pictures in 1945, Ford was cast with Bette Davis in *A Stolen Life* (1946) and with Rita Hayworth in *Gilda* (1946). After pronouncing the plot of *Gilda* incredibly bad, Howard Barnes of the New York *Herald Tribune* (March 15, 1946) went on to say: "Glenn Ford is excellent as a stumble-bum who runs a casino in Buenos Aires without any notion of the score." A reviewer for *Variety* (March 20, 1946) commented: "Glenn Ford is a far better actor than the tale permits."

For his performances in the starring roles that followed, he received equally high praise. He appeared as an unemployed mining engineer involved with an adventuress in the melodrama *Framed* (1947) and as a professor of psychology in the farce *The Return of October* (1948).

In 1953 Ford's contract with Columbia Pictures was rewritten, and he was permitted to free lance in films for Warner Brothers, Universal International, and RKO Radio Pictures. MGM decided to try him in the role of the doctor-husband in *Interrupted Melody* (1955), based on the story of Marjorie Lawrence, the opera star, whose career was interrupted by infantile paralysis. More than pleased with the results, the studio awarded him a long-term contract.

Without using mannerisms or special make-up, Ford has successfully enacted a wide variety of roles. Reviewing *The Blackboard Jungle*

(1955), in which Ford was a sorely tried teacher of a class of delinquents, William K. Zinsser said in the New York *Herald Tribune* (March 21, 1955): "Ford's performance is excellent. There is something about him that is immensely appealing." Cast as the father of a kidnapped boy in *Ransom* (1956) with Donna Reed, he gave, according to John Beaufort (*Christian Science Monitor,* January 17, 1956), "another of his recent mature and thoughtful performances." In his review of *Don't Go Near the Water* (1957) in the New York *World-Telegram and Sun* (November 15, 1957) Alton Cook remarked: "Glenn Ford is a sly and adept comedian."

For his recent roles in such military and Western films as *Cowboy* (1958), *The Sheepman* (1958), *Imitation General* (1958), and *Torpedo Run* (1958) Ford is especially well equipped. He served in the United States Marines for a number of years, and he now owns a small ranch. This is important to Ford, who takes his acting assignments very seriously. "The minute you have a script in your mind," he says, "you start living it" (*Saturday Evening Post,* January 4, 1958). A new contract with MGM takes effect in December 1959 when the old one expires.

Glenn Ford and Eleanor Powell, the dancer, were married in Beverly Hills, California on October 23, 1943. The couple were divorced on November 23, 1959. Their only son, Peter Newton, shares his father's enthusiasm for how-to-do-it hobbies. Ford installed the plumbing, electrical wiring, and air conditioning system in his home. He enjoys reading, swimming, mountain climbing, and the serious study of movie scripts.

References

Sat Eve Post 230:18+ Ja 4 '58 por
International Motion Picture Almanac, 1959

FOX, GENEVIEVE (MAY) July 14, 1888-Oct. 6, 1959 Author of books for young people, including *Mountain Girl* (1932) and *Sir Wilfred Grenfell* (1942). See *Current Biography* (Yearbook) 1949.

Obituary

N Y Times p21 O 10 '59

FRANCIS, FRANK (CHALTON) Oct. 5, 1901- Librarian; museum director

Address: British Museum, Great Russell St., London, W.C. 1

In 1959—the year which marked the two hundredth anniversary of its opening—Frank Chalton Francis became the Director and Principal Librarian of the British Museum. When he took over its highest administrative position, Francis had been in the service of the British Museum for more than three decades, most of the time in the Department of Printed Books.

The belief that has governed Francis during his career is the conviction that librarianship should be furthered through international friendship and co-operation. Like the great Sir Anthony Panizzi (1797-1879), Francis

British Inf. Services

FRANK FRANCIS

served as Keeper of Printed Books before he became Principal Librarian. He has published widely on bibliographical subjects and has translated works from the German. He has been an active force in promoting the publication of the photoprinted edition of the British Museum catalogue of printed books.

Frank Chalton Francis was born on October 5, 1901 in Liverpool, England, the only son of F. W. Francis and Elizabeth (Chalton) Francis. After introductory studies at the Liverpool Institute, one of the city's larger schools, he attended the University of Liverpool, where he received his B.A. degree in classics. For his postgraduate work he went on to Emmanuel College, Cambridge University, where he received his M.A. While at Cambridge, Francis studied ancient Greek philosophy, especially that of Posidonius, the Greek Stoic philosopher of the early first century B.C.

During the academic year of 1925-26 Francis was an assistant master at Holyhead County School, where he taught Latin and Greek. In 1926 he accepted an appointment to the staff of the British Museum. For the first three months of World War II he lived in the Museum and during the entire course of the war he was responsible for protecting it against fire from enemy air raids and for carrying on salvage operations.

Except for 1946-47, when he served as Secretary of the British Museum, Francis has seen unbroken service with its library. In 1948 he returned to the library as Keeper in the Department of Printed Books, one of two such posts under the Principal Keeper. One keeper is responsible for the reading rooms and the information and "public relations" aspect of the library's activities, the other for the maintenance of the catalogue and the organization of the cataloguing.

(Continued next page)

FRANCIS, FRANK—*Continued*

The library of the British Museum is one of the most famous in the world and, with holdings numbering more than 6,000,000 volumes, the largest library in Great Britain. Entitled as a "copyright" library to receive one copy of every book published in Great Britain, it contains the largest collection of English books to be found anywhere. Opened in January 1759, the library built its collections upon the benefactions of Sir Hans Sloane, Sir Robert Cotton, the First and Second Earls of Oxford, and the royal libraries of George II and George III.

Sir Frederic G. Kenyon, a former Director and Principal Librarian, said: "The British Museum is, next to the British Navy, the national institution which is held in most respect abroad. A visit to it is almost obligatory on travellers to this country; and foreign scholars regard it with a reverence which they sometimes extend to the temporary custodians of its treasures."

The objectives of such an institution as the library of the British Museum had been envisioned as early as 1650 by John Durie in the following terms: "To keep the publick stock of Learning, which is in Books and Manuscripts, to increas it, and to propose it to others in the waie which may be most helpful unto all." Sir Anthony Panizzi, generally regarded as the most important administrative genius in the history of the Museum, said in 1836: "I want a poor student to have the same means of indulging his learned curiosity, of following his rational pursuits, of consulting the same authorities, of fathoming the most intricate enquiry, as the richest man in the kingdom."

Under present conditions, the library of the British Museum is overcrowded. But plans now underway for a building to be erected opposite the main body of the Museum on the other side of Great Russell Street in Bloomsbury should relieve the crowding. There Francis hopes to provide for the general public many conveniences now extended only to the scholars who use the overtaxed facilities.

In recent years Francis has been responsible for the cataloguing of new books and for filling in gaps in the collections through the acquisition of new books. He has made a special effort to acquire materials about the new nationalism in Africa and the East. He has inaugurated the photoprinted edition of the British Museum catalogue of printed books, which will consist of over 300 volumes, to be published during the next six years at the rate of about one volume per week. Each volume consists of approximately 20,000 entries covering 500 pages. Libraries all over the world have subscribed to this ambitious undertaking.

In spite of many commitments, Francis has found time to make a number of contributions to the world of library service, both on a national and an international level. He has frequently contributed articles on bibliographical subjects to professional periodicals. At various times he has been concerned with the *Journal of Documentation* (joint editor, 1947), *The Library* (1936-53), *Library Quarterly* (advisory editor), and *Libri* (associate editor). He has edited several volumes on bibliographical subjects and has translated several books from the German, among them William Cohn's *Chinese Art* (Studio, 1930).

On the national level, Frank Francis has been honorary secretary to the Bibliographical Society since 1940. Before this time—from 1938 through 1940—he was joint honorary secretary with Ronald B. McKerrow, the famous bibliographer. He was vice-president (1954) and president (1957-58) of the Association of Special Libraries and Information Bureaux. From 1949 to 1959 he was head of the Council of British National Bibliography.

On the international level Frank Francis has been equally active. He has been vice-president of UNESCO's International Advisory Committee on Bibliography since 1954 and has been active on this important committee since 1951. These contacts with colleagues from many countries have proved invaluable for him. "One can do so much by friendship that one cannot do by formal business contacts," says Francis.

Other international committees on which Francis has served or is now serving are: the academic libraries section of the International Federation of Library Associations (chairman); International Committee of Library Experts, U.N. (1948); and UNESCO Provisional International Committee on Bibliography (1952).

At the present time many sets of rules are used in various countries for the cataloguing of books. Francis helped to organize a preliminary international conference held in London in July 1959; another is planned for 1960. These conferences will try to formulate basic principles for cataloguing in various countries, in order to make their catalogues more mutually useful.

In 1927 Frank Chalton Francis married Katrina McClennon of Liverpool. They have two sons and one daughter. The elder son, a Cambridge graduate, is articled to a solicitor and the younger is a student at Trinity College, Cambridge. Their daughter is assistant librarian at the Institution of Mining and Metallurgy.

The Francis' new residence, an apartment known as the Director's house, is located in the west wing of the British Museum. Although Francis regrets his having had to leave Morden Lodge in Surrey, especially its large garden, he will now be able to entertain many friends from other professions.

Francis was chosen the David Murray Lecturer at the University of Glasgow in 1957. He has lectured in bibliography at the School of Librarianship, University College, London since 1945. He belongs to the Bibliographical Society of America and similar societies. He is a Fellow of the Society of Antiquaries and since 1958 has been a Companion of the Bath. His club is the Athenaeum in London.

A "big, energetic, and enthusiastic man," Francis likes to motor, play golf, and walk in his leisure moments. He has built up a personal book collection on the history of bibliography, printing, papermaking, book illustration, and libraries.

The new Director and Principal Librarian of the British Museum has defined the task of the national library which he now heads as follows: "To maintain its own collections at the highest pitch of efficiency and to act as the co-ordinator of all complementary library services. To do this means a greatly developed machinery of collaboration."

Reference
Who's Who, 1959

FRANKE, WILLIAM B(IRRELL)
(frăngk'ē) Apr. 15, 1894- Secretary of the Navy; accountant

Address: b. Department of the Navy, Washington 25, D.C.; h. 3410 Q St., N.W., Washington, D.C.; Benson, Vt.

The man who is responsible for converting the United States Navy's fleet into nuclear-powered craft capable of discharging missiles is the reticent and limelight-shunning William B. Franke, who has been Secretary of the Navy since June 8, 1959. He succeeded Thomas S. Gates, Jr., who in late 1959 became Secretary of Defense. Franke has been in government service for nine years and has held such posts as Under Secretary of the Navy and Assistant Secretary of the Navy. Regarded as a financial genius who "knows how to chart a course through a sea of figures," Franke was a member of the New York accountancy firm of Franke, Hannon & Withey before entering the government.

William Birrell Franke was born in Troy, New York on April 15, 1894, the son of William G. and Helena E. (Birrell) Franke. He received his early education in Troy and New York City. Since his parents could not afford to send him to college, Franke earned his tuition by holding jobs with Cluett, Peabody and Company of Troy and the General Electric Company of Schenectady. Graduated from Pace Institute (now Pace College) in New York City, he became a certified public accountant and in 1924 was elected to the American Institute of Certified Public Accountants and the New York State Society of CPA.

After graduation Franke worked with the firm of Touche, Niven & Company of New York City and later with Naramore, Niles and Company in Rochester, New York. Having formed his own accounting firm in 1929, he continued as a senior partner in the firm, Franke, Hannon & Withey of New York City, until 1954.

Franke has served as an officer or director of many companies. These positions include: chairman of the board and director of John Simmons Company, Newark, New Jersey; General Shale Products Corporation, Johnson City, Tennessee; Key-James Brick Company, Chattanooga, Tennessee; Appalachian Shale Products Company; Appalachian Block Company, Marion, Virginia; and Elizabethton Cinder Block Company; vice-president and di-

WILLIAM B. FRANKE

rector of the J. H. Day Company, Inc., Cincinnati, Ohio; treasurer and director of Telanserphone Company and Air Call Radio Paging, both of New York City; and director of Julius Kayser & Company; Wenonah Development Company; Carolina, Clinchfield & Ohio Railway; and Securities Company.

It is reported that government officials first became aware of Franke's unusual abilities when he audited and exposed inconsistencies in the records of the Louisiana State University and Agricultural and Mechanical College in Baton Rouge after the assassination of Huey P. Long in 1935. From 1948 to 1951 Franke was a member of the United States Army Comptrollers Civilian Panel. During 1951 and 1952 he served a year as a special assistant to the Secretary of Defense. For these services he was awarded the Patriotic Civilian Service Commendation from the Army in 1951 and the Distinguished Service Award from the Department of Defense in 1952.

Appointed by President Eisenhower, on October 4, 1954 Franke took the oath of office as Assistant Secretary of the Navy concerned with financial management. Three years later, on March 29, Eisenhower nominated him as Under Secretary, to succeed Thomas S. Gates, Jr. The Senate Armed Services Committee recommended confirmation and acting chairman John C. Stennis commented that Franke had "satisfied the committee" that there would be no conflict between his securities holdings and his post (New York *Times*, April 12, 1957). He was sworn in several days later.

After the death of Deputy Secretary of Defense Donald A. Quarles, in May 1959 Gates was appointed to succeed Quarles, and Franke to succeed Secretary of the Navy Gates. The Senate confirmed the Franke nomination on June 2, and he assumed his new duties on June 8.

While serving as Assistant Secretary of the Navy, Franke was appointed, in October 1954,

FRANKE, WILLIAM B.—*Continued*

a member of the "Doolittle Group," which was charged with examining the operations of the Central Intelligence Agency. Headed by Lieutenant General James H. Doolittle (retired), the group made public their over-all analysis that the CIA was doing "a creditable job."

Under the leadership of Franke the Navy is trying to adjust its functions to the requirements of the space age and a modern defense system. It has as its goal a nuclear-powered, missile-launching fleet. Several atomic submarines, such as the *Nautilus* and *Seawolf,* are now in operation. The first atomic-powered surface craft is also being developed. At the same time, the Navy is gradually eliminating older craft. On February 24, 1959 it announced plans to discard forty-three ships, including five battleships.

In the coming era the Polaris submarine will be more and more significant. The first craft in this class, the *George Washington,* was launched on June 9, 1959, after an expenditure of $100,000,000. The vessel can fire the Polaris intermediate range (1,500 miles) ballistic missile while submerged. Franke has called the Polaris submarine the "virtually invulnerable deterrent" against war (New York *Times,* June 14, 1959).

When the United States Navy's third nuclear submarine, the *Skate,* was christened on May 16, 1957, Franke said that the launching "marks the end of the era of research and prototype development." Another nuclear submarine, the *Skipjack,* was commissioned on April 15, 1959. The 252 foot-long vessel, which cost $40,000,000 to build, cruises at over twenty knots in water deeper than 400 feet. During August and September 1958 the Navy successfully carried out Project Argus. This operation, which involved eight ships including the missile-test vessel, *Norton Sound,* fired three rockets, each with a nuclear warhead, into outer space.

Other aspects of the Navy's modernization program aim at expanding its abilities to engage in antisubmarine warfare and to land Marines by launches and helicopters. Franke believes that the Navy's facilities must reflect the most recent advances in technology. What disbursements are needed should be viewed as premiums on an insurance policy for a peaceful world (New York *Herald Tribune,* May 17, 1957).

William B. Franke was married to the former Bertha Irene Reedy on June 28, 1919. Their three daughters are Phyllis Birrell (Mrs. Harding Hall Fowler), Anne Tallmadge (Mrs. John Anthony Ulinski, Jr.), and Patricia Wendell (Mrs. W. Sherman Kouns). In religion Franke is a Presbyterian and in politics a Republican. His clubs are the Union League (New York City), Army & Navy (Washington, D.C.), Army Navy Country (Arlington, Virginia), Rutland Country (Rutland, Vermont), and Rhode Island Country (Barrington, Rhode Island). He maintains a summer home at Benson, Vermont.

Franke is a slightly stoop-shouldered man, whose favorite sports are swimming and golf.

He works twelve to fourteen hours a day. In Washington he has earned a reputation for modesty, taciturnity, and conscientiousness. In spite of his retiring nature, he has been willing to keep his office open to his subordinates and others. He holds an honorary D.Sc. degree from the University of Louisville (1948) and a D.C.L. degree from Pace College (1955).

References

> N Y Times p5 F 4 '59 por; p12 Je 4 '59 por
>
> Who's Who in America, 1958-59

FREDENTHAL, DAVID Apr. 28, 1914-Nov. 13, 1958 Artist; noted for sketches of World War II battles and news events. See *Current Biography* (Sept.) 1942.

Obituary

> N Y Times p11 N 14 '58

FRENCH, ROBERT W(ARREN) May 8, 1911- Economist; government official

Address: b. Board of Commissioners of the Port of New Orleans, 2 Canal St., New Orleans 6, La; h. 1828 Calhoun St., New Orleans, La.

The Port of New Orleans, gateway to the 12,000-mile Mississippi River system, the Gulf of Mexico, and the Gulf Intracoastal Waterway, has had Dr. Robert W. French as its director since 1956. He has earned a distinguished reputation as an economist, administrator, educator, and authority on the problems of foreign trade. For six years French served as dean of the School of Business Administration of Tulane University in New Orleans and taught at Tulane, at Louisiana State University, and at the University of Texas. He has also worked for federal, state, and local agencies on special assignments as tax consultant and adviser on federal regulations.

Of English, Scottish, Irish, and Welsh ancestry, Robert Warren French was born on May 8, 1911 in South Bend, Indiana to Lura Minnie (Keller) and Robert Warren French, a salesman. He has one sister, Ruth Everingham. French attended high school in Buchanan, Michigan, where he won letters in basketball, tennis, and track, and was active in dramatics and in the glee club. When he was graduated in 1928, he was valedictorian of his class.

While a student at the University of Michigan, French supported himself by working as a grocery clerk, window trimmer, waiter, cook, apprentice tool and die maker, and construction worker. At one time he also held a research assistantship in economics. He was elected to Phi Kappa Phi honorary society and awarded the B.A. degree *magna cum laude* in 1932. Although he had concentrated on prelaw courses as an undergraduate, he studied economics in graduate school, and in 1933 he received his M.A. degree. His thesis discussed "The Economic Relationship of Detroit to Border Cities of Canada."

From 1932 to 1934 French continued his studies at the University of Michigan as an Earhart Fellow in social sciences. In 1934-35 he was the first scholar to hold the University of Michigan Fellowship at Brookings Institution in Washington, D.C. Returning to the University of Michigan, he received a Rackham research grant in 1936-37 in order to study border crossing between Canada and the United States. After having submitted a doctoral dissertation on the subject of American direct investments in Canada, French earned the Ph.D. degree in 1937. While at the University of Michigan, French was influenced in deciding upon an academic career by Professors Charles F. Remer, Lawrence Preuss, Roderick McKenzie, and Max Handman.

In 1935 French was appointed a teaching fellow in economics at the University of Michigan. Two years later he became a junior partner with Johnson-Smith Company, his family's department store in Sparta, Michigan. Leaving this position in 1941, he received an appointment as assistant professor of business administration, College of Commerce, Louisiana State University in Baton Rouge. He held this post while he served at the same time as assistant director of the university's bureau of business research. From 1941 to 1946 he edited the *Louisiana Business Review*.

As a professor at the University of Texas in Austin from 1946-49, French taught business administration, directed the bureau of business research, and edited the *Texas Business Review*. At both Texas and Louisiana State he taught undergraduate and graduate courses in foreign trade.

Dr. French became professor of economics and business administration at Tulane University in New Orleans in 1949 and also dean of its School of Business Administration. On November 1, 1953 he was appointed vice-president for development of the university. He also helped to initiate the annual institutes on taxation, foreign transportation, and port operations in which specialists have regularly participated.

Early in his career Dr. French began to serve on government agencies. For two years beginning in 1943 he was a member of the advisory committee of the Economic Committee of Louisiana. In 1950 he organized the Public Affairs Research Council of Louisiana, a research and information agency which he headed as executive director until 1954. It has been widely praised for its studies and reports on improving state government.

Another body on which French served was the committee on Southwest economy of the President's Council of Economic Advisors. As chairman, French organized it, selected its personnel, and prepared a report on the economic potential of eight Southwestern states. He also headed the study committee on federal aid to welfare (1954-55), appointed by the federal Committee on Intergovernmental Relations. He was a member of the study committee on Louisiana economy for the Louisiana Commission on Higher Education in 1955-56.

Dr. French's authoritative studies have been published in professional journals and in the yearbooks of the *American Peoples Encyclo-*

Blackstone Studios

ROBERT W. FRENCH

pedia. He supervised a survey of eighty-five counties lying between New Orleans and El Paso, Texas, and an investigation of the economic aspects of the tidewater channel from New Orleans to the Gulf of Mexico, now under construction.

Succeeding Walter J. Amoss, French was appointed director of the Port of New Orleans in 1956. The port has twelve miles of wharves which service over 4,000 freighters each year. In 1957 it enjoyed a world traffic totaling $2 billion, of which 75 per cent was with Latin-American countries. The port facilities include a huge vacuum cleaner that snuffs grain from barges at the rate of two tons every minute, cranes for lifting locomotives, and devices to pack, sort, and weigh numerous commodities. The port can also claim the fastest turn-around time (slightly over two days) of any port in the country, low insurance rates, little racketeering and pilfering, and two reliable unions (*Reader's Digest,* June 1958).

The city of New Orleans is undergoing a great industrial transformation largely because of its advantages of transportation, plentiful water supply, and vast natural resources such as gas and oil. It is the site of Esso Standard Oil Company's refinery, the largest in the United States, and it is a center of the chemical industry. To keep pace with growth of the area French is guiding a ten-year, $72,000,000 plan to expand and modernize the port. Part of this project provides for converting almost all the wooden docks to steel and concrete.

Robert W. French and Dorothy Louise Smith were married on July 8, 1934. Mrs. French was a musician and a schoolteacher. They have two daughters, Nancy Alice and Judith Kay. Dr. French is five feet nine inches tall, weighs 168 pounds, and has blue eyes and brown hair. His political affiliation is Democratic. He is an active layman in the Carrollton Avenue Methodist Church in New Orleans, as a member of

FRENCH, ROBERT W.—Continued

the board of stewards and chairman of its policy committee. His favorite active sport is tennis, and he enjoys choral singing. His fraternity memberships include Pi Gamma Mu, Beta Gamma Sigma, Phi Eta Sigma, Omicron Delta Kappa, Delta Sigma, and Sigma Iota Epsilon. He also belongs to the Propeller Club of the United States, and Export Managers' Club and Rotary Club of New Orleans.

Besides fulfilling his duties as director of the port, French is the president of the Louisiana Ports Association and a director of the Mississippi Valley Association and of the Mississippi Valley World Trade Conference. He is also on the boards of Centenary College of Louisiana at Shreveport, Dillard University in New Orleans, and Flint-Goodridge Hospital of Dillard University, and a member of the development council of the University of Michigan.

His professional organizations are the Foreign Policy Association, Council on Foreign Relations, National Foreign Trade Council, Gulf Ports Association, American Society of Public Administration, American Marketing Association, American Economic Association, American Statistical Association, and American Academy of Political and Social Science.

References

Directory of American Scholars (1951)
Who's Who in America, 1958-59
Who's Who in Commerce and Industry (1957)

FRESNAY, PIERRE (frĕ-nā′) Apr. 4, 1897- Actor; director

Address: b. 4 rue de la Michodière, Paris 2ᵉ, France; h. 8 rue Saint-James, Neuilly-sur-Seine, France

In a career of over forty years on stage and screen, the French actor Pierre Fresnay has played a wide range of characters. He is internationally known for his performances in the films *La Grande Illusion, Marius, Fanny, César,* and *Monsieur Vincent.* With the Comédie Française he appeared in French classical and modern repertory for eleven years, and has starred on the British and American stage. In 1937 Fresnay became the leading actor and co-manager of the Théâtre de la Michodière in Paris. He has often been named the best French actor, and in 1949 received the Prix Féminin du Cinéma.

Pierre Fresnay was born Pierre-Jules Laudenbach in Paris, France on April 4, 1897. His mother was the former Claire Dietz and his father, Henri Laudenbach, was an Alsatian who immigrated to Paris after the Franco-Prussian War of 1870-71 and became a professor of languages at the University of Paris. It was his father who taught Fresnay how to become fluent in the English language. After studying at the Lycée Montaigne and the Lycée Henri-IV, he earned a bachelor's degree at the Conservatoire National d'Art Dramatique in Paris.

Encouraged by his uncle Claude Garry, the actor, to pursue a career on the stage, Fresnay made his debut with the Comédie Française as Mario in *Le Jeu de l'amour et du hasard* in January 1915. He next appeared in Molière's *Le Tartuffe* and *Le Misanthrope* and Racine's *Les Plaideurs.* The Comédie named him a *pensionnaire* (pensioner) in July 1915.

During World War I Fresnay served in the army from 1916 to 1919, rising through the ranks to second lieutenant. When he returned to the Comédie, he acted Clitandre in *Les Femmes savantes* in October 1919. In the next year he made his first appearance on the London stage, with the Comédie, as Clitandre in *Le Misanthrope.*

Advanced to *sociétaire* (associate) by the company in 1923, Fresnay later appeared in the casts of over eighty plays, classical and modern, comedy and tragedy. From 1924 to 1926 he toured in Great Britain, performing in French classics.

After eleven years with the Comédie, Fresnay resigned because "it is a state-controlled theater and is frankly political in its management. I began to feel that and wanted to leave" (New York *Post,* October 25, 1934). Such a step was difficult; as *sociétaire* and life member, he was not permitted to act on any other stage. The company sued him and, ultimately, he was free to act elsewhere, but before obtaining his freedom, he had to pay the Comédie 200,000 francs.

After his association with the Comédie Française had ended, Fresnay played the title role in Rostand's *Cyrano de Bergerac* and starred in Sacha Guitry's *Un Miracle* and *Franz Hals, Marius, L'Amour gai,* among many others.

Returning to England in 1927, Fresnay performed in English in *The Game as He Played It* at Huddersfield. Back in Paris, he played the title role in *Noé,* in a performance that was much praised by the critics. With the Compagnie des Quinze, he starred in *Don Juan* at the Globe Theatre in London on February 26, 1934. In one of the great successes of his career he appeared as the Duc de Chaucigny-Varennes in Noel Coward's *Conversation Piece* at His Majesty's Theatre in London in April 1934. In that play Pierre Fresnay performed in English, as a replacement for Mr. Coward, who had been forced to abandon the role because of illness. The show was imported into New York with Fresnay as its star in October 1934.

When Fresnay appeared on Broadway in André Obey's *Noah* in February 1935, Burns Mantle wrote (New York *Daily News,* February 14, 1935): "Pierre Fresnay's hero was magnificently robust and deliciously comic. . . . As Noah he reveals his rare gift of impersonation, his accurate command of a wide range of moods, and a voice of uncommon beauty and flexibility."

His following stage appearances were as Henri III in *Margot* in Paris in November 1935; Max in *O Mistress Mine* in London in December 1936; and in *Les trois valses* in Paris in 1937. With his wife Yvonne Printemps, the actress, Fresnay took over the management of the Théâtre de la Michodière in Paris in 1937, establishing both a classical and contemporary repertory.

At his own theater Fresnay took the leading roles in *Léocadia* (1940) by Jean Anouilh; *Comédie en trois actes* (1941); Édouard Bourdet's *Père* (1942) and *Vient de paraître* (1945), a satire on the venality of modern literature; *Auprès de ma blonde* (1946); *Si je voulais* (1946); and *Moulin de la galette* (1951). In the comedy *Les Œufs de l'autruche* (1948) Fresnay enacted the role of a boorish bourgeois who suddenly realizes his pigheaded blindness to his family's needs. As an air corps officer in *Les Cyclones* (1954) set in a future era, he portrayed an individual faced with a choice between sacrificing his men and perfecting an air machine.

Since 1915 Fresnay has performed in over fifty motion pictures. In the Marcel Pagnol trilogy, *Marius, Fanny,* and *César,* which captured the provincial color of water front life in Marseilles, Fresnay co-starred with Jules Raimu. Fresnay played Marius, whose love for the sea conflicted with his love for Fanny. Harold Hobson (*Christian Science Monitor,* March 20, 1951) commented that the "idiosyncratic force of character inherent in the people in the films, and the power of Pierre Fresnay's acting, as the self-justifying Marius, are such that the audience is swept into admiration." Other memorable films in which Fresnay appeared were *La Dame aux camélias* and *SOS Mediterranean,* which won the Grand Prix du Cinéma in 1939.

In *La Grande Illusion* (1937), one of the most overpowering of all pacifist films, Fresnay was given a starring role. The theme of the movie is the ability of human beings to find a common ground through a similarity of temperament that transcends national differences. Fresnay played the young French officer and Erich von Stroheim the German martinet who finally come to understand and respect each other.

In 1958 *La Grande Illusion* was voted one of the twelve best films of all time in a poll taken of 117 film historians from twenty-six nations. A jury of distinguished directors also named it as one of the six best films.

For the film *La Valse de Paris* (1950), a biography of Offenbach, Pierre Fresnay, who has styled himself the "least musical of men," learned to sing and to conduct an orchestra; he also learned how to handle the 'cello well enough to play eight bars of a waltz. The role of Offenbach, differing from any part he had so far portrayed, suited his desire never to play the same type more than once.

In the film biography *Monsieur Vincent* (1948) Fresnay portrayed the seventeenth century French humanitarian priest, St. Vincent de Paul. He received the Grand Prix Internationale at the Venice International Film Festival as the best actor, and the movie won an Oscar from the Academy of Motion Picture Arts and Sciences as the best foreign film.

Dieu a besoin des hommes (God Needs Men) is the story of some islanders off the coast of Brittany who have been deprived by the Church of a priest because of their sinful ways. Fresnay enacts the part of a man who takes upon

Harcourt, Paris

PIERRE FRESNAY

himself the functions of a priest without first being ordained. *Time* (April 16, 1951) called it a "masterly picture" that "explores the struggle within the layman-priest . . . and the authority of a church jealous of its sacred functions." The film took a grand prize at the Venice International Film Festival and won a special award from the International Catholic Film Office.

In *Les Aristocrates* (1955) Fresnay starred as an aging marquis, left over from another era, who is content to stay in his crumbling homestead among his children who have modern ideas. In 1957 Fresnay appeared in the screen version of *Les Œufs de l'autruche*. On the stage of the Michodière he acted in *Père* in late 1958.

Pierre Fresnay and Yvonne Printemps were married in 1932. Two earlier marriages, to Rachel Berendt and to Berthe Bovy, ended in divorce. He is by birth a Protestant. To relax, Fresnay gardens, collects books, and reads scripts. With Maurice Sachs he adapted Terence Rattigan's comedy *French Without Tears* for the French stage.

Fresnay's credo is: "Change personalities as often as possible. Those actors who continually typify a single character, however varied it may be, are usually capitalizing on an initial success. . . . I feel that the true personality of the actor should have to be divined from the several different characters he portrays."

References

N Y Herald Tribune V p4 Ag 20 '50
N Y Post Mr 16 '35; p17 Ja 31 '49
Dictionnaire Biographique Français Contemporain (1954)
Who's Who, 1958
Who's Who in France, 1955-56
Who's Who in the Theatre (1957)

FROEHLICH, JACK E(DWARD) (frō'-lĭk) May 7, 1921- Engineer

Address: b. Jet Propulsion Laboratory, California Institute of Technology, 4800 Oak Grove Dr., Pasadena, Calif.; h. 2555 Tanoble Dr., Altadena, Calif.

The Pioneer IV space missile was successfully hurtled past the moon and into lasting orbit around the sun by the United States on March 3, 1959. One of the scientists responsible for this achievement was Jack E. Froehlich, chief of design and power plants and satellite project director at the Jet Propulsion Laboratory in Pasadena, California. Now only thirty-eight, he was a member of the team that launched into outer space Explorers I, III, and IV and Pioneer III, which tried to reach the area surrounding the moon. Dr. Froehlich is also project director of the National Aeronautics and Space Agency's Vega program.

Jack Edward Froehlich was born on May 7, 1921 at Stockton, California to Adolph Henry and Maude Leone (Gillespie) Froehlich. A few years later, his family moved to Burbank, California. At Burbank High School Jack excelled in mathematics, became a cheer leader, and served as vice-president of the student body. Before he was graduated in 1939 he had learned to pilot a plane.

After studying for one semester at the University of California at Los Angeles, he transferred to the California Institute of Technology in Pasadena. When World War II interrupted his education, he spent four years as a test pilot in the United States Marine Corps. Discharged in February 1946 with the rank of captain, Froehlich resumed his studies at the California Institute of Technology. He was elected to the Sigma Xi honorary scientific society, and received the B.S. degree in 1947. He earned an M.S. degree in aeronautical engi-

neering in 1948 and a Ph.D. in aeronautical engineering in 1950.

In 1949 Froehlich was appointed a research engineer on the staff of the newly organized Jet Propulsion Laboratory, which is owned by the government and operated by the California Institute of Technology. His duties included supervising the design of rocket vehicles, liquid-propulsion research, development materials, and studies in aeroballistics. He was advanced to chief of the guided missiles engineering division in 1953 and to head of the design and power plants department in 1955.

One break-through in missile development, Froehlich has said, was the development of solid-fuel rockets, with which the Jet Propulsion Laboratory began experimenting in 1950. The innovation of the internal-burning charge permits the use of a light, thin-walled combustion chamber instead of the heavy-pressure vessel previously required.

The Jet Propulsion Laboratory also developed the key technique to make it possible to fire rocket systems in stages, without which it would have been impossible to put satellites into orbit around the earth or to probe the moon. A Los Angeles *Times* reporter, Graham Berry, wrote (April 27, 1957) that Jet Propulsion Laboratory scientists under Froehlich's direction adapted the idea of the lock used to link a bayonet with a rifle. "Acceleration at take-off," Froehlich explained, "loosened the lock, so that at burnout the spring gently pushed apart the burned-out stage and the next forward stage as it ignited."

The four-stage Jupiter C rocket propelled the United States' first earth satellite, Explorer I, into its orbit in outer space on January 31, 1958. Froehlich and other Jet Propulsion Laboratory scientists had worked on the last three stages of the rocket.

Explorer I enabled scientists to measure the earth's bulge at the equator, the amount of meteoric dust in space, and the density of the atmosphere at various altitudes. The satellite also transmitted valuable data about its own temperature. What was perhaps most significant, Explorer I and other earth satellites confirmed the existence of a region around the earth of high-intensity corpuscular radiation due to natural geophysical causes.

When Explorer I was successfully fired, Froehlich predicted that a similar rocket could be sent to the moon (Miami *Herald,* February 2, 1958). He said that it could be accomplished by mounting a heavier payload on a Jupiter intermediate-range ballistic missile.

At White Sands Proving Grounds in New Mexico Froehlich conducted countless tests in the behavior of the small Loki rockets. He studied their behavior in a cross-wind and discovered that if a rocket is spun too fast, it tends to vibrate instead of being stabilized in flight.

Explorer III was put into orbit by the Jet Propulsion Laboratory-Army team on March 26, 1958. (Explorer II did not go into orbit.)

At a meeting in Los Angeles in July 1958 Froehlich said the intense radiation in certain areas of outer space, revealed by the satellites, indicated that man-carrying rockets in pro-

JACK E. FROEHLICH

longed flight around the earth would require a shield of lead to protect human space-travelers. The radiation achieved an intensity of 2,800 kilometers at the highest altitudes reached.

About two weeks after Froehlich spoke, Explorer IV was put into orbit on July 26, 1958. It provided information on America's Project Argus, the nuclear detonations 300 miles above the earth on August 27, 30, and September 6, 1958. These nuclear blasts injected artificial radiation into outer space, which Explorer IV was able to trace, and then relay to scientists on earth. Scientists also gained much new information about the earth's magnetic field.

Meanwhile, Air Force scientists tried to send Pioneer I to probe in the vicinity of the moon on October 11, 1958. Pioneer I traveled some 71,300 of the 223,700 miles to the moon, revealing that radiation intensity decreased at extremely high altitudes.

On December 6, 1958 Froehlich and others attempted a similar moon probe and managed to push Pioneer III some 65,000 miles into the heavens. Froehlich had been responsible for Juno II, a launching device which had sent Pioneer III aloft. Juno is a sixty-ton, four-stage system based on an elongated version of the Army's Jupiter intermediate-range ballistic missile.

The last three stages functioned perfectly. But the engine of the first stage stopped burning less than four seconds too soon, robbing the missile of sufficient velocity to allow it to escape the earth's gravitational pull. Later, it was reported that Pioneer III had proved that cosmic radiation would not prevent manned space flights.

The engineering shortcomings of Pioneer III were overcome on March 3, 1959, when Froehlich and his associates successfully shot Pioneer IV past the moon at a distance of about 37,000 miles and into orbit around the sun. It was said that the Jet Propulsion Laboratory team had developed the second and third stages, and the fourth stage tip, or payload, and that they had worked "night and day" to do so.

Using equipment developed at the Jet Propulsion Laboratory, Pioneer IV established a record for long-distance radio communication. Its signal was heard clearly on earth when it was 400,000 miles away, a "scientific accomplishment" and an "important advance in the new and growing technology of astronautics" (John W. Finney, New York *Times*, March 7, 1959). Pioneer IV is the second man-made planet circling the sun. The Soviet Union launched a successful rocket on January 2 which passed within 4,660 miles of the moon before it was placed in its orbit around the sun.

Jack E. Froehlich was married to Marian Louise Crofts on June 22, 1946. Before their marriage, Mrs. Froehlich was a kindergarten teacher. They have two sons, John Howard and Mark Edward. Froehlich is five feet eight inches tall, weighs 157 pounds, and has brown eyes and black hair.

Although Froehlich lists flying, golf, and photography among his favorite recreations, he says that "in this business, your job is pretty much your hobby. I try to divide my time between my job and my family." Nevertheless, the pressure of work kept Froehlich away from home about nine weeks during the first four months of 1958. He cannot recall the last time he worked a forty-hour week.

References

Los Angeles Times II p1 Ap 27 '58 por
N Y World-Telegram p3 Mr '59 por

FROST, FRANCES MARY Aug. 3, 1905-Feb. 11, 1959 Poet; novelist; writer of children's books. See *Current Biography* (Yearbook) 1950.

Obituary

N Y Times p27 F 13 '59

FROTHINGHAM, CHANNING May 10, 1881-Aug. 11, 1959 Physician; served as chairman of the Committee for the Nation's Health; helped to organize Peter Bent Brigham Hospital in Boston; specialized in internal medicine. See *Current Biography* (March) 1948.

Obituary

N Y Times p29 Ag 12 '59

FRYE, JACK Mar. 18, 1904-Feb. 3, 1959 Business executive; former head of Trans World Airlines and General Aniline & Film Corporation. See *Current Biography* (April) 1945.

Obituary

N Y Times p1+ F 4 '59

FULLER, JOHN L(ANGWORTHY) July 22, 1910- Biologist
Address: b. Roscoe B. Jackson Memorial Laboratory, Bar Harbor, Me.; h. 6 Snow St., Bar Harbor, Me.

A specialist in genetics and animal behavior, John L. Fuller of the Roscoe B. Jackson Memorial Laboratory in Bar Harbor, Maine has studied the reactions of dogs to natural rather than controlled conditions. His other studies have been concerned with the genetics and dietary habits of rats. His *Nature and Nurture, a Modern Synthesis,* written for the general reader, was published by Random House in 1954. He has also written books dealing with motivation and with genetics.

John Langworthy Fuller was born on July 22, 1910 at Brandon, Vermont, the son of John Harold and Oliata Joyce (Langworthy) Fuller. He has a sister, Mary, and two brothers, Robert and Samuel. His father, a New England educator, wrote poems and essays about outdoor life for publications in the region.

At Kennett High School in Conway, New Hampshire, John Fuller played football and basketball and was graduated in 1927 as vale-

JOHN L. FULLER

dictorian of his class. He continued his education at Bates College in Lewiston, Maine. He majored in biology, wrote for the college newspaper, helped to edit the yearbook, and was elected to Phi Beta Kappa and Sigma XI. As a class poet named to the all-state football team, he became something of an academic rarity. In 1931 he earned the B.A. degree.

Although Fuller had first intended to enter the field of public health, he later chose a career in scientific research. Important in this decision was the encouragement he received from Dr. J. W. M. Bunker of Massachusetts Institute of Technology, where Fuller took his graduate work on a fellowship. After submitting his thesis which explored the relationship between the physiology and habitat selection of seven species of land isopods, he received the Ph.D. degree.

In 1935 Fuller became a biology instructor at Sarah Lawrence College in Bronxville, New York and in 1936 he taught zoology at Clark University in Worcester, Massachusetts. He joined the faculty of the University of Maine as an instructor in 1937, was promoted to an assistant professorship in 1941, and to an associate professorship in 1945. During this period he was also a summer Fellow at the Woods Hole Oceanographic Institution in Falmouth, Massachusetts (1935, 1936), biologist with the New Hampshire Fish and Game Department (1937-38), and biologist with the Maine Department of Fisheries and Game (1940-45). He studied the food cycle of marine plankton and conducted research on the ecology and growth rates of fresh-water fishes and marine fouling organisms.

While teaching an honors course at the University of Maine on the nervous system, Fuller became interested in psychobiology, the study of mental life and behavior and its relation to other biological processes. "The

establishment of the Division of Behavior Studies at the Jackson Memorial Laboratory gave me an opportunity to participate actively in this work," Fuller recalls, "and I joined the staff . . . in 1947." At that time he was appointed a research associate, and from 1951 to 1954 he served as staff scientific director. The laboratory is one of the largest in the world devoted to the study of cancer and animal behavior.

In order to understand the genetic and physiological bases of psychological temperaments, Fuller centered his research on the differences between "strains of purebred dogs and their hybrids." To make investigation easier, he and his staff developed the radio inductograph, "a compact short-wave radio set through which a dog can broadcast his emotions and physiological experiences while free and leading a normal existence" (*Science News Letter*, July 2, 1949).

In these experiments with the dogs, who "live luxuriously" and are "never submitted to surgical experience" (*Coronet*, August 1949), Fuller examined them under basal conditions and situations of stress. He also carried out tests in spatial orientation, discrimination learning, and delayed response. He discovered that the effects of heredity are more clearly shown when one deals with simple motor behavior rather than complex attributes such as intelligence and emotional make-up. Fuller also concluded that no single breed is consistently superior on all tests. Instead there are characteristic ability patterns which seem to depend on heredity (*Science Digest*, March 1957).

While working with puppies, Fuller discovered that three weeks is the earliest age at which stable conditioned avoidance reflexes can be established. He correlated this fact with developmental changes recorded on an electroencephalogram (an apparatus which registers action potentials of the cerebral cortex). On the basis of his observations of rats, Fuller set forth a multifactorial threshold hypothesis in order to explain the inheritance of audiogenic seizure susceptibility. This hypothesis may also serve as a model for clarifying the inheritance of other functional aberrations of the nervous system.

Fuller also related audiogenic seizure susceptibility to the relative rates of facilitation and inhibition in the nervous system. This he deduced from experiments in which methods similar to those of classical neurophysiology were applied to the entire organism. Another aspect of Fuller's work has been his examination of "situational analysis" as a systematic approach to the study of individual behavior.

In an address before the National Academy of Sciences in 1955 Fuller described some of his dietary experiments with mice at the Jackson Laboratory. In one of these, overweight mice whose progenitors had also been overweight were transformed into streamlined specimens on a diet of food which they did not like. This research convinced him that both normal and obese mice enjoy the taste of food, but differ in their ability to control how much of it they eat.

During his scientific career John Fuller has written *Nature and Nurture, a Modern Synthesis* (Random House, 1954) and some fifty papers and articles reporting his work for various scientific publications. In 1954 he received a fellowship from the John Simon Guggenheim Foundation. For his Guggenheim project he summarized the findings on the relationship of human and animal genetics to psychology. Another aspect of his Guggenheim work was observing physiological techniques in their application to the problem of how genes produce their effects upon behavior.

Among the scientific societies to which Dr. Fuller belongs are the American Society of Zoologists, American Society of Physiologists, American Genetics Society, American Psychological Association, Committee for the Study of Animal Societies under Natural Conditions, and American Society of Naturalists. He is a trustee of Bates College and active in the American Red Cross.

John L. Fuller and Ruth Irene Parsons, a public school teacher, were married on September 2, 1933. They have three children. He is five feet eleven inches tall, weighs 185 pounds, and has brown eyes and gray-brown hair. For recreation the scientist enjoys tennis, hiking, listening to music, and playing the piano.

References

American Men of Science vol II (1955)
Who Knows—and What (1954)

FULLER, MARGARET H(ARTWELL)

July 19, 1904- Librarian; organization official

Address: b. American Iron and Steel Institute, 150 E. 42d St., New York 17; h. 8 Peter Cooper Rd., New York 10

For its fiftieth anniversary year (1958-59) the Special Libraries Association has had for its president Mrs. Margaret H. Fuller, librarian of the American Iron and Steel Institute, an organization of companies in the steel industry. Mrs. Fuller, who followed Alberta L. Brown as president (see *C.B.*, May 1958), will be succeeded in office by Dr. Burton W. Adkinson (see *C.B.*, June 1959). During her administration Mrs. Fuller has concentrated on raising professional standards in the organization by introducing new membership requirements. She feels that this is a "strong step forward in the development of special librarianship."

In her presidential acceptance speech, Mrs. Fuller told her associates to "have the courage at this time to give real meaning to the words 'special librarian.'" Founded in 1909, the Special Libraries Association has about 5,000 members in the United States, Canada, and Europe. It seeks to "promote the collection, organization, and dissemination of information in specialized fields of knowledge and to adapt information resources to the needs of a particular institution or clientele."

Trained as a business statistician, Mrs. Fuller came to library work "through the back door," as she phrases it. She rose from library as-

Ira L. Hill

MARGARET H. FULLER

sistant with the American Telephone and Telegraph Company to librarian with the George S. Armstrong Company, consulting engineers. Since 1949 she has supervised the library of the American Iron and Steel Institute. Her outstanding contributions to the work of the Institute have done much to aid, develop, and promote both library service and library support within the industry (*Special Libraries*, September 1958).

Descended from early New England settlers, Mrs. Fuller was born Margaret Hartwell Peck on July 19, 1904 in Providence, Rhode Island, the oldest daughter of William Burgess and Lucy King (Hartwell) Peck. Her mother is still living and her father, who was a manufacturing jeweler, died in October 1958. Mrs. Fuller's paternal grandfather, William T. Peck, was principal of the Providence, Rhode Island Classical High School and a trustee of Brown University. Her sisters are Mrs. David C. Salmon, the wife of an attorney, and Mrs. Theron R. Stinchfield, whose husband is a high school principal.

After completing her elementary school education in Providence, Margaret and her family moved to Mountain Lakes, New Jersey. Here she attended St. John's School, a small private school, from which she was graduated in 1921. At Wheaton College (Norton, Massachusetts), she majored in mathematics and statistics, and was active in the science club. Her school sports included hockey and basketball.

Upon receiving her B.A. degree in 1925, Miss Peck came to New York City to work with Moody's Investors Service. She resigned three years later to take a job as library assistant in the general business library of the Western Electric Company. When the depression struck the firm in 1932, she was laid off for a period of three years. She returned to New Jersey where she took a part-time job as field captain

FULLER, MARGARET H.—*Continued*

for the Morris Area Girl Scouts, assisting the director in organizing girl scout troops and volunteer committees. From 1933 to 1935 she was employed as a cashier with the Jersey Central Power and Light Company.

Recalled by the Western Electric Company in 1935, Margaret Peck worked as a business research statistician. Three years later, she returned to library work as an assistant in the information center of the American Telephone and Telegraph Company. Here she did research as well as reading, clipping, and indexing newspaper and magazine articles. "Pretty soon," she relates, "I began relieving our librarian at noon so she could go for lunch. I found I liked it and started going to Columbia at night for some library science work" (Milwaukee *Journal*, November 11, 1958).

Her formal education at Columbia University School of Library Service, begun in 1939, was not completed until 1943. In that year she became a "one-man" librarian with the George S. Armstrong Company, a management engineering firm. Six years later she resigned to become the librarian of the American Iron and Steel Institute, a trade association of iron and steel companies. She presides over a staff of five persons who maintain a library containing 80,000 books and more than 100 file drawers of clippings and pamphlets. The library serves staff members and is open to the general public.

Mrs. Fuller has greatly expanded the activities of her library. She introduced a program of co-operation and communication between the librarians of the institute's member companies. She has issued an annual directory of the company libraries, circulated newsletters, directed biennial two-day meetings at the institute's offices, and continued publishing the Index of the American Iron and Steel Institute Yearbooks. Mrs. Fuller also serves as an editorial assistant on the institute's bimonthly publication, *Steelways*.

A member of the Special Libraries Association since 1941, Margaret Fuller has been an outstanding worker on behalf of the organization. She edited the New York *Chapter News* before ascending to the vice-presidency of the chapter (1951-52) and presidency (1952-53). She has been active in the metals division of the association, serving as chairman (1954-55), member of the executive committee (1955-56), and chairman of the procedure committee (1956-57). In the association itself, Mrs. Fuller's activities include membership on the headquarters personnel committee (1953-54; 1957-58), chairman of the committee on *Special Libraries* (1955-57), awards committee (1957-58), convention advisory committee (1957-58), fiftieth anniversary committee (1957-58), and first vice-president and president-elect (1957-58). At the annual meeting of the association in Chicago in June 1958 Mrs. Fuller was installed as president.

During her year's term as president of the Special Libraries Association Margaret Fuller has visited fifteen of the thirty-one member chapters. One of her chief assignments has been the discussion of a new set of membership

standards for the group. She says: "An active member will have to have her degree in library science plus three years of experience. I think it will do a lot to make membership mean something to industry" (Milwaukee *Journal*, November 11, 1958).

Besides fulfilling professional duties and speaking engagements, Mrs. Fuller has written several articles. "Publications and Services Offered by American Iron and Steel Institute" was printed in the *Transactions* of the forty-first annual convention of the Special Libraries Association in 1950. For the *Wheaton Alumnae Quarterly* (October 1953) she wrote "Create Your Own Job," which discussed the activities of a special librarian. Her own library at the American Iron and Steel Institute was reviewed by Mrs. Fuller for the New York *Chapter News* (December 1956) of the Special Libraries Association.

Other organizations to which Mrs. Fuller belongs are the American Woman's Association and the Wheaton Club of New York. She is still a participant in Girl Scouts' activities. She is affiliated with the Baptist Church and is a voting Republican. Horseback riding is her favorite recreation.

An attractive woman with light hair and blue eyes, Margaret Fuller is four feet eleven inches tall and weighs 120 pounds. She has been married to Francis A. Fuller, a Wall Street insurance underwriter, since July 12, 1946. The couple's New York home, an apartment in Peter Cooper Village, is filled with family heirlooms, antiques, and Mrs. Fuller's favorite fresh flowers. Vacations are spent at Maplelm, their farm in the mountains of Phillips, Maine.

A disarming manner, an interest in people, an innate sense of tact and diplomacy, and an ability "to think straight and to the point" characterize Mrs. Fuller. "In her business and social contacts," according to *Special Libraries* (September 1958), "she has added to the stature of the library profession by the conduct of her job, the enthusiasm she displays for her work, the contributions and sincere helpfulness which she so generously offers."

References

Milwaukee Journal p3 N 11 '58 por
Special Libraries 49:285+ S '58 por
Who's Who in Library Service (1955)
Who's Who of American Women, 1958-59

FULTON, E(DMUND) D(AVIE) Mar. 10, 1916- Canadian Minister of Justice and Attorney General; lawyer

Address: b. Justice Bldg., Ottawa, Ontario, Canada; h. 157 Battle St. West, Kamloops, British Columbia, Canada; 94 Driveway, Ottawa, Ontario, Canada

In the Progressive Conservative governments formed in 1957 and 1958 E. D. Fulton was chosen by Canadian Prime Minister John G. Diefenbaker to be Minister of Justice and Attorney General. Fulton, a lawyer from Brit·

ish Columbia, who has been described as a "forceful and colorful orator," has been a member of the House of Commons since 1945. At forty-three years of age, he has gone farther in Canadian national politics than anybody in his age bracket since Mackenzie King.

Edmund Davie Fulton was born in Kamloops, British Columbia on March 10, 1916 into a family whose eminence in Canadian government had been established for several generations. He is the fourth son of Frederick John Fulton, a lawyer who had been in succession Provincial Secretary, Attorney General, and Minister of Lands and Works in the British Columbia government from 1901 to 1909, and from 1917 to 1921 represented, as a Conservative Unionist, the Cariboo riding in Canada's Parliament. Edmund's mother, Winifred M. (Davie) Fulton, was the daughter of A. E. B. Davie, the eighth Premier of British Columbia.

Even as a pupil at St. Michael's School in Victoria, British Columbia, Edmund Fulton reportedly had an ambition to make his career in government service. After his graduation from Kamloops High School, he entered the University of British Columbia, where he rowed, took part in theatricals, and received his B.A. degree in general arts in 1936. Fulton was then elected to a Rhodes Scholarship which enabled him to attend St. John's College, Oxford University, England from 1937 to 1939 and to take there a second class in jurisprudence and the B.A. degree.

Called to the British Columbia bar in January 1940 Fulton practised as a barrister and solicitor with his father's law firm of Fulton, Morley, Verchere & Rogers in Kamloops until his enlistment in July in the Seaforth Highlanders of Canada for World War II service. He went overseas in October, commanded an infantry company in Italy, and later, as deputy assistant adjutant general of the First Canadian Division, served also in northwest Europe.

Major Fulton was still on active duty when in October 1944 he was named by the Kamloops Progressive Conservative Association to be the party's candidate for the Kamloops riding in the federal House of Commons at the next general election. This riding, created in 1935, had been continuously represented by a Liberal, T. J. (Tip) O'Neill, an Irish locomotive driver with strong labor support. Twenty-eight days before the election of June 11, 1945, Fulton flew home to conduct his campaign. He won over O'Neill by 177 votes. A month later he was transferred to the Reserve of Officers.

During his first week in the House of Commons, Fulton made an impression on Liberal Prime Minister William Lyon Mackenzie King when he not only "became the first English-speaking Conservative MP to give part of his maiden speech in French" but "attacked King's policies with such vigor that he was interrupted eleven times by three angry Liberal cabinet ministers" (*Maclean's Magazine*, January 4, 1958). Within his first three months Fulton addressed Parliament forty-two times on subjects ranging from the blueberry problem to governmental extravagance.

Ashley & Crippen, Toronto

E. D. FULTON

Fulton was president of the Young Progressive Conservative Association of Canada for three years beginning in 1946. He was re-elected by the Kamloops riding in 1949 by 1,283 votes, and in the same year, although a minority member, he won a two-year fight to ban the circulation of crime comics in Canada. In 1953, when Fulton won re-election by 3,798 votes, he had the Food and Drugs Act changed to force bacon packagers to use transparent wrappings.

Following the resignation of George Drew of Ontario as leader of the Progressive Conservatives in September 1956, Fulton announced his candidacy for the party leadership. A Roman Catholic fluent in French, he went to the convention at Ottawa in December with strong support by the Quebec delegation, but John G. Diefenbaker of Saskatchewan was elected leader on the first ballot with 774 votes. Donald Fleming of Toronto, now Finance Minister, polled 393, and Fulton, 117. Diefenbaker and Fulton remained good friends, and in the 1957 campaign Fulton went to Diefenbaker's constituency to deliver speeches in French.

At the general election of June 10, 1957 Fulton's majority in Kamloops rose to 4,171, while in the country at large the Conservatives won 110 seats in Commons to 103 for the Liberals. Other parties won fifty seats. Canada's first Conservative government in twenty-two years accordingly took office on June 21, 1957 with John G. Diefenbaker as Prime Minister and E. D. Fulton as Minister of Justice and Attorney General. (Fulton had previously declined the Speaker's chair in Commons and the Ministry of External Affairs.) Fulton was sworn into the Privy Council on the same day and made a Queen's Counsel in July.

Having established a reputation in Parliament as a specialist in immigration as well as

FULTON, E. D.—*Continued*

legal matters, he was also named Acting Minister of Citizenship and Immigration. As such, he announced on July 26, a decision to curb immigration for the balance of the year, in view of an expected influx of between 350,000 and 400,000 persons and the likelihood of considerable seasonal unemployment. In March 1958 Fulton told a press federation that the slowdown in immigration represented a temporary policy only and would be "reviewed in the light of economic prospects." In the following month he declared that the government was "quite adamant" in barring immigrants entering through the United States.

In contributing a commendatory preface to the late John C. Farthing's book *Freedom Wears a Crown* (1957), Justice Minister Fulton "by implication" questioned the right of a government taking office after one dissolution of Parliament to seek another at its "own convenience" (John A. Stevenson in *Saturday Night,* November 23, 1957). Hopeful of increasing the Conservative majority, Diefenbaker nevertheless decided to "go to the country" in 1958. In the campaign preceding the general election of March 30, Fulton was one of seven cabinet ministers who stumped Quebec in an all-out effort to capture that Liberal stronghold. The election produced a landslide for the Conservatives, who obtained the largest majority in Parliament any Canadian party had ever enjoyed.

In a pre-election address before the student body at Kingston, Ontario the Justice Minister had stated that the government was "discussing clinics as the means of treating and rehabilitating drug addicts so that they won't become criminals." *Saturday Night* noted on May 10, 1958 that the Diefenbaker government had "clearly been testing public opinion on capital punishment" and that there was "little doubt" that both Fulton and Diefenbaker favored modification or abolition. In August 1958 Fulton announced a joint offer by the federal and British Columbia governments to pay the transportation expenses of some 3,000 radical members of the Dukhobors sect who wish to settle in the Soviet Union.

In November 1958 journalists speculated about the stand that Fulton might take on the controversial issue of "loss selling" and retail price-fixing, wondering whether the law against the latter might be repealed.

"Rusty-haired" "Davie" Fulton is six feet tall and "speaks with a snipped Oxford accent" (Peter C. Newman). In his early years in Parliament he "spent many off hours . . . playing polo and throwing darts" and earlier still had riding, fishing and shooting as favorite recreations. He belongs to the Vancouver Club and the Kamloops Golf and Country Club. He is an active member of St. Theresa's Roman Catholic parish in Ottawa. Mrs. Fulton is the former Patricia Mary Macrae of Winnipeg, Manitoba. The Fultons were married on September 7, 1946 and have three daughters, Catherine Mary, Patricia, and Cynthia Ann.

References

Can Bsns 21 :8-10+ Ja '48 por
Macleans Mag 71 :17-18+ Ja 4 '58 pors
Monetary Times (Toronto) 126 :22-23 Jl '58 por

Canadian Parliamentary Guide, 1958
Canadian Who's Who, 1955-57
Catholic Who's Who, 1952
International Who's Who, 1958
Who's Who in America (sup S-N 1958)

FUOSS, ROBERT M(ARTIN) (fōōs) Dec. 16, 1912- Editor

Address: b. The Saturday Evening Post, Curtis Publishing Co., Independence Sq., Philadelphia 5, Pa.; h. Wayne, Pa.

In the magazine publishing business where editorial executives have been known to regard their advertising and promotion departments as "necessary evils," Robert Fuoss, executive editor of the *Saturday Evening Post,* has scored something of a coup. After about eight years in advertising and promotion, four of them with the Curtis Publishing Company, he was named on March 17, 1942 as managing editor of the *Post,* a brand-new position which had been created by newly appointed editor, Ben Hibbs (see *C.B.,* July 1946). An executive who worked with Fuoss at the time has said, "For anyone to go into the number two job on the editorial board of the *Saturday Evening Post,* from the advertising side, and make himself liked by the associate editors, was a terrific feat." Through the years, Fuoss has closely shared with Hibbs the satisfaction of seeing the *Post* climb in average net paid circulation to about 5,800,000 in 1958. Fuoss was named executive editor in 1955. "His life has been a typical *Post* success story," observed Jack Pollack, former president of the Society of Magazine Writers, "and he has become a most influential guy in the U.S. magazine business."

Robert Martin Fuoss was born on December 16, 1912 in Saline, Michigan, the son of Martin and Edith (Mattison) Fuoss. He attended the University of Michigan High School in Ann Arbor and received the B.A. degree in 1933 at the University of Michigan. Almost immediately he started work as editor of a weekly newspaper, the Saline *Observer,* writing sports articles and pulp fiction on the side.

After a year, Fuoss decided to try his luck in New York City, but the newspaper job he was after eluded him, and he worked for a while as a salesman for the Vick Chemical Company. He became associated with Batten, Barton, Durstine & Osborn, Inc., working on the U.S. Steel account in Pittsburgh, and then moved into the advertising firm's promotion department. Later he joined the promotion department of *Liberty* magazine.

A. J. Gallagher, who in 1937 was organizing the promotion department at Curtis Publishing Company and consequently was on the alert for likely young men, met Fuoss and "put him over all the hurdles." But he adds, "I had practically decided to hire him almost the minute I laid eyes on him," because he felt that for a young man, Fuoss was "far and away ahead of his age."

As promotion manager for *Country Gentleman* from 1937 to 1939, Fuoss worked closely with its editor, Ben Hibbs, the man who would later become *Post* editor, and once again his boss. Some time after he moved over to the *Post* as promotion manager in 1939, Fuoss caused a stir in the publishing world for his ingenious and lively promotions.

One of these occurred during the War Bond campaign. The promotion was built around a Chinese, wearing mandarin robes, who was pictured on billboards and elsewhere uttering "Confucius-say" maxims urging the purchase of War Bonds and, indirectly, the *Post*. Fuoss also sent an actor, dressed in the mandarin costume, to Detroit where he went to ball games and hotels, doing nothing but carrying the *Post* under his arm, and occasionally sitting down and reading it.

In 1942 the *Post* was languishing. Its circulation had dropped, and its editor, Wesley Winans Stout, having encountered several points of "strong disagreement" on policy, resigned. Walter D. Fuller, president of Curtis Publishing Company, chose as his successor editor Ben Hibbs, former editor of the *Country Gentleman*. Hibbs immediately created the new position of managing editor and appointed twenty-nine-year-old Robert Fuoss, "because he had good ideas on visual stuff" (*Business Week*, March 15, 1952). According to promotion chief A. J. Gallagher, Hibbs had done an unusual thing, but Fuoss had exhibited a remarkable grasp of the publishing business from the editing as well as promotion and advertising point of view.

While Hibbs' predecessors, notably the great George Horace Lorimer and, later, Wesley Stout, had operated under a one-man rule, Hibbs has delegated heavy responsibilities to Fuoss. He reportedly has authority to give pay raises and rate increases, and does, "although not without telling Ben right away" (*Writer's Digest*, May 1950). Hibbs has depended upon Fuoss' reactions to medical and sports articles in particular because "Bob knows more about those subjects." Between them, the two men ordinarily read between 30,000 and 80,000 words a day after hours. This is the cream of the day's manuscript catch which they take home. Fuoss has said, "In this job . . . today's work always gets done today." In April 1946, Fuoss was among fourteen newsmen to visit Austria in order to study the United States military government there.

In its issue of March 12, 1955, the *Post* made this announcement: "Robert Fuoss, who has been managing editor for the past thirteen years, moves up to the newly created post of executive editor, and Robert Sherrod takes his place as managing editor." Hibbs explained that "the complexities of magazine editing and publishing have increased to such an extent during the past ten years that the load of executive duties has simply become too heavy for two men."

The *Post*, established in 1728, asserts that it is the first magazine in America as well as

ROBERT M. FUOSS

the oldest, and that it was founded by Benjamin Franklin. In its early days, it struggled through good and bad conditions, until Cyrus H. K. Curtis bought it for $1,000 in 1897. Publisher of the extremely successful *Ladies' Home Journal*, a general magazine for women, Curtis saw in the *Post* the *Journal*'s counterpart in the men's field. Curtis named Lorimer as editor and in ten years the magazine jumped from a circulation of 97,000 to 1,242,000 and advertising climbed from $59,000 to $3,056,000. Those were the days when the *Post* offered stories by authors such as Booth Tarkington, O. Henry, Sinclair Lewis, J. P. Marquand and Mary Roberts Rinehart. By 1927, the *Post* had a circulation of 2,818,000 and a gross advertising income of $53,145,000, an earnings record it was not to equal for another twenty years.

Hibbs, with Fuoss at his side as managing editor, modernized type faces and layout, trimmed the writing, emphasized personalities and human interest; in short, made the *Post* into a general family magazine and at the same time opened wider avenues for the promotion and sales departments. By 1952, according to *Business Week*, circulation had increased about 1,000,000 and advertising nearly tripled. The *N.W. Ayer Directory of Newspapers and Periodicals* lists *Post* circulation for 1958 at 5,152,891 at 15 cents a copy, and a company spokesman claimed at the end of 1958 that the circulation was approaching the six million mark.

In addition to the *Saturday Evening Post*, the Curtis Publishing Company publishes *Ladies' Home Journal*, *Holiday*, the *American Home*, and *Jack and Jill*. Selections from the *Saturday Evening Post* are frequently anthologized, and a collection of its short stories is published annually by Random House.

On August 30, 1936, Robert M. Fuoss married Mary Holton Leckner and they have one

FUOSS, ROBERT M.—*Continued*

daughter, Mary Marshall Fuoss. For recreation the editor likes to play golf and pool, and "just sit and talk." He is a member of the Down Town Club in Philadelphia, Theta Chi and Sigma Delta Chi fraternities.

References

N Y Times p66 Mr 18 '42 por; p25 Ap
    14 '46
Time 39:40 Mr 23 '42 por
Who's Who in America, 1958-59

FUREY, WARREN W(ILLIAM) Jan. 8, 1898-Nov. 19, 1958 Physician; educator; president of the Radiological Society of North America (1949-50). See *Current Biography* (May) 1950.

Obituary

N Y Times p35 N 20 '58

GALBRAITH, JOHN KENNETH Oct. 15, 1908- Economist; educator; author
Address: b. Harvard University, Cambridge, Mass.; h. 30 Francis Ave., Cambridge, Mass.

A professor of economics at Harvard University since 1949, John Kenneth Galbraith does not consider himself an "ivory tower economist." His positions and publications confirm his practical interest in the interplay of economics and politics in American life. He has served in government posts, written nontechnical books for the lay public, helped to edit *Fortune* magazine, and was a key figure in the Presidential campaigns of Adlai E. Stevenson.

Born on a farm at Iona Station, Ontario, Canada on October 15, 1908, John Kenneth Galbraith is the son of William Archibald and Catherine (Kendall) Galbraith. He did his undergraduate work at the University of Toronto, where he received a B.S. degree in 1931. He studied economics on a scholarship at the University of California at Berkeley, earning his M.S. degree in 1933 and his Ph.D. degree in 1934. From 1934 to 1939 Galbraith taught as an instructor and tutor at Harvard University. He was a Social Science Research Fellow in 1937, studying at Cambridge University, England, and in 1939 he became assistant professor of economics at Princeton University.

After a year at Princeton, Galbraith entered government service. His first position was that of economic adviser and assistant to Chester Davis, agricultural member of the National Defense Advisory Committee. He became an assistant administrator of the Office of Price Administration as director in charge of price controls in 1941 and in 1942 became the deputy administrator. He soon came under attack from Congressional and business leaders. "We started with no controls in 1941 and by 1943 we had virtually everything under control," Galbraith has said. "I reached the point that all price fixers reach—my enemies outnumbered my friends."

The fact that there was some basis to Galbraith's remarks was indicated by statements of several businessmen before a House Interstate Commerce Committee on May 27, 1943, openly demanding his ouster. The controversy that engulfed him brought about his resignation on May 31, 1943.

After his OPA experience, Galbraith held other government positions. As director of the United States Strategic Bombing Survey in 1945, he investigated the effect of air attacks on the economies of Germany and Japan. When World War II ended, he was appointed director of the State Department's Office of Economic Security Policy, which took charge of the economic affairs of the two defeated countries.

As a member of the board of editors of *Fortune* magazine from 1943 to 1948, Galbraith was given a chance to use his trenchant writing and caustic wit, talents not too common among professional economists.

A seventeen-page report called *Beyond the Marshall Plan*, prepared by Galbraith for the National Planning Association in 1949, proposed needed reforms in the Marshall Plan. This paper expressed satisfaction and confidence in the Marshall Plan, but warned the American government that it must tolerate social and political tensions in European countries and allow them to embark on political and economic experiments of their own choosing.

John Kenneth Galbraith has also served as consultant to the Department of Agriculture, the National Resources Planning Board, the Council of Economic Advisors, the National Security Resources Board, the Selective Service Administration, and the American Farm Bureau Federation.

In 1949 Galbraith returned to Harvard as professor of economics. As an economic thinker, he admits that he is influenced by John Maynard Keynes, the British economist and financial expert who advocated government spending to fight unemployment, and by John Black, a fellow economist at Harvard.

When the Senate Banking and Currency Committee was engaged in investigating the stock market in March 1955, Professor Galbraith was called in to testify. He told the committee that there was overspeculation in the market and other disturbing resemblances to 1929. He recommended that the margin requirement on stock buying be raised—perhaps gradually—from 60 per cent to 100 per cent, so that trading would be on a cash basis.

Since Galbraith's testimony greatly differed from the opinions expressed by the stock exchange presidents who had preceded him, it created a controversy within the Senate. Republican Senator Homer E. Capehart of Indiana charged Galbraith with disliking the American economy and "praising Communism." According to the economist, Capehart's accusations were based on incomplete quotations out of context from Galbraith's report, *Beyond the Marshall Plan* (New York *Herald Tribune*, March 21, 1955).

Against these accusations Galbraith was defended by Democratic Senators J. William Fulbright of Arkansas and A.S. ("Mike") Monroney of Oklahoma, and others. In a telegram to the New York *Times* (March 21, 1955) Galbraith said: "I would think the consequences of reading these two paragraphs out of context would be more unfortunate for the Senator than for me. My position on Communism is part of the intellectual history of our time. The pamphlet warns of the dangers of Communism."

The thesis Galbraith presents in his *American Capitalism; The Concept of Countervailing Power* (Houghton Mifflin, 1951; revised edition, 1956) is that when too much power concentrates in the hands of one or more companies, other companies or groups arise to counterbalance it. He therefore sees no harm in bigness itself, because it is the equilibrium established between power and countervailing power that makes the American economy stable and prosperous.

The Great Crash: 1929 (Houghton Mifflin, 1955) won much critical approval. C. J. Rolo, reviewing it in the *Atlantic Monthly* (June 1955), observed that "Mr. Galbraith's prose has grace and wit, and he distills a good deal of sardonic fun from the whopping errors of the nation's oracles and the wondrous antics of the financial community." The book tells what happened in the twelve months leading up to the big crash and what took place immediately thereafter.

In *The Affluent Society* (Houghton Mifflin, 1958) John Kenneth Galbraith again deviates from orthodox economic thought. He maintains that the American economy has reached a point where "urgency of production" is a myth. Increased production does not satisfy genuine needs, but only gratifies wants that have been manufactured by advertising. He feels that much more should be expended for public services, which are far from affluent.

Journey to Poland and Yugoslavia (Harvard University Press, 1958) grew out of an informal journal that Galbraith kept while lecturing behind the Iron Curtain in the spring of 1958. He was the first Western economist to discuss the capitalistic economy in a Communist country since the Russian Revolution.

In addition to these books for the general reader, Galbraith has written works of more limited scholarly appeal that have been published by university presses. He has contributed book reviews and articles to magazines, and has appeared as a panelist on television.

During the Presidential campaigns of 1952 and 1956 Galbraith worked as a ghost writer and adviser on key issues for Adlai E. Stevenson. Among his recommendations during the latter campaign was a standstill on price increases to combat the rising cost of living.

For his work with the OPA John Kenneth Galbraith received the President's Certificate of Merit, and for his services as director of the United States Strategic Bombing Survey he was awarded the Medal of Freedom. He won a Guggenheim Fellowship in 1955 and the

JOHN KENNETH GALBRAITH

Tamiment Book Award in 1958 for *The Affluent Society*. An honorary membership on the University of Chile's faculty of economics was bestowed on him in July 1958.

In September 1937 John Kenneth Galbraith was married to the former Catherine P. Atwater, daughter of a New York attorney. They have three sons. Skiing is a favorite form of recreation for him, although he considers himself only a "retarded novice." When free of other engagements, he spends his summers with his family on their "unfarmed farm" in southern Vermont.

His colleagues look upon Galbraith as an unorthodox and challenging thinker who has an acute sense of humor. Standing six feet eight inches, he is one of the tallest men in American academic life. He is a Fellow of the American Academy of Arts and Sciences and belongs to the Harvard Club in New York and the Cosmos Club in Washington.

References

Christian Sci Mon p12 Mr 22 '55 por
Life 19:18+ O 22 '45
Time 65:88 Mr 21 '55 por
Washington (D.C.) Post p6C Ja 21 '57

American Men of Science vol III (1956)
Who's Who in America, 1958-59

GAMBLE, RALPH A(BERNETHY) May 6, 1885-Mar. 3, 1959 Former Republican United States Representative from New York (1937-57); served as assistant party whip and member of the Banking and Currency Committee. See *Current Biography* (January) 1953.

Obituary

N Y Times p31 Mr 5 '59

GANDHI, INDIRA (NEHRU) Nov. 19,
1917- Indian political party official
Address: b. Indian National Congress, New
Delhi, India; h. Allahabad, India

Fulfilling both her own political career and a
family tradition, Mrs. Indira Gandhi, the only
child of Prime Minister Jawaharlal Nehru, was
elected on February 2, 1959 as president of the
country's ruling party, the Indian National
Congress. The post was previously held by her
grandfather, Motilal Nehru, and her father. In
this office, corresponding to the party chairmanship in the United States, she succeeded U.N.
Dhebar, who resigned midway in his second
two-year term. Mrs. Gandhi, the wife of member of Parliament Feroze Gandhi (no relation
to Mohandas Gandhi), has been her father's
official hostess since 1947. In her own right she
has become influential in politics through her
work in social welfare and cultural programs
throughout India.

Shrimati Indira Nehru was born to Jawaharlal and Kamala (Atal) Nehru on November 19,
1917 at Allahabad, northern India, into a
wealthy family of Kashmiri origin. During her
childhood, she recalls, all her games mimicked
the political affairs of grownups. Anand Bhawan,
the mansion of the Nehrus, became a center of
National Congress agitation in Allahabad after
her lawyer grandfather, Motilal Nehru, and her
father joined Mohandas Gandhi's crusade for
India's freedom from British rule. Other members of the Nehru family, including her aunt,
Vijaya Lakshmi Pandit, were also drawn into
the struggle. (For articles on Mrs. Pandit and
Jawaharlal Nehru see *C.B.*, January 1946 and
April 1947, respectively.)

At the age of twelve, when politics was no
longer a game, Indira Nehru formed an organization of school children, a "monkey
brigade," to carry messages past British soldiers

Information Service of India
INDIRA GANDHI

to and from leaders of the National Congress
movement. Earlier, in 1926-27, she had spent
some twenty months with her mother and father
in Switzerland, where Mrs. Nehru received
medical treatment (she died in 1936 after a
long illness).

After attending boarding schools in Switzerland and India, Indira Nehru went to Visvab-
harati and Santiniketan universities in India.
She then studied history for a year at Somerville College, Oxford University, England,
where she was active in student movements.
The informal part of her education, and perhaps the more important, she received from her
father, who wrote to her frequently from British prisons in India about his political views.
The letters have been published in some of
Nehru's books, including *Glimpses of World
History* (1939).

As a disciple of Gandhi, Indira Nehru had
worked during her later girlhood among untouchables in slum areas to promote projects
for hand-spun cloth and Indian-made goods.
Becoming a member of the Indian National
Congress in 1938, she took a more active and
dangerous role in the independence movement.
In 1942 she married Feroze Gandhi, a lawyer,
and after their return from a honeymoon in
Kashmir, both she and her husband were arrested on charges of subversion by the British
and sent to jail. While serving a thirteen-
month prison term, she taught illiterate prisoners to read and write.

On August 15, 1947 the Indian Empire was
partitioned into the dominions of India and
Pakistan, which became members of the British
Commonwealth of Nations. In preparation for
India's assumption of sovereignty Mrs. Gandhi
had been active in elections and in contacts with
villagers, especially the women. During 1947
she worked under Gandhi's direction in areas in
New Delhi affected by the Hindu-Moslem rioting that followed the partition. The Mahatma,
who opposed demonstrations of violence, was
assassinated in January 1948.

With the establishment of India as an independent state, Nehru was made Prime Minister, and Indira Gandhi became his official
hostess and housekeeper in New Delhi. She
accompanied her father on many of his visits
abroad, including trips to Communist China and
the Soviet Union and, in 1949 and 1956, to the
United States. She explained in Washington
in December 1956 that her purpose on these
visits was to try to establish contacts with
people on nonpolitical levels—social welfare,
educational, and cultural.

Gradually Mrs. Gandhi gained a political
stature of her own. In 1955 she was appointed
to the twenty-one member working committee
of the National Congress, the party's executive group. Later in the year she was chosen,
with more votes than any other candidate, to
become the first woman member of the Congress
party's eleven-member central elections committee, which selects the party's candidates for
Parliament. She was also then president of the
women's division of the Congress and a member of the All-India Social Welfare Committee,
which operates under the supervision of the
government's Planning Commission.

One of Mrs. Gandhi's tasks in late 1955 was to serve as chairman of a special government committee to welcome the Soviet Union's Premier Nikolai A. Bulganin and Communist party Secretary Nikita S. Khrushchev on their much-publicized visit to India. At that time some observers in the Western press suggested that in her political leanings she was somewhat to the left of her father, who adheres to a policy of co-existence.

In January 1959 a fifteen-member group of party leaders, known as the Ginger Group, to which Mrs. Gandhi belonged, charged the Indian National Congress with complacency in facing such challenges as its long-range goal of establishing a truly democratic socialist society. The call for more vigorous party action was again heard the following month in the unanimous election of Mrs. Gandhi as president of the National Congress. Her father, who was first elected in 1929 when he succeeded his own father, had held this position for many years. Mrs. Gandhi is the Congress' fifty-sixth president and the fourth woman to fill the office.

Although Nehru had not opposed his daughter's candidacy, he later stated in reply to questions from newsmen that he thought her election was not a fortunate precedent for India. He pointed out, however, that her election represented an effort to make use of the abilities of the younger generation in party leadership. Many of her opponents expressed misgivings about growing nepotism in the government, since the executive branch of the party would be controlled by the father and the organizational branch, by the daughter. Her supporters called attention to the appeal that she could make to the women voters in the elections scheduled for January 1961 and to the younger members of the party.

Addressing the All-India Congress Committee (the 400-member policy-making body of the party) in May 1959, Mrs. Gandhi reported on her recent tour of the Communist-governed state of Kerala in southwest India. She openly criticized the Communists for advancing the interests of their party rather than of the people, and she urged Congress members to oppose the Communists in a political campaign exposing the "dangers" of their rule in Kerala. On July 31, 1959 Indian President Rajendra Prasad dismissed the Communist government of Kerala because of its inability to govern peacefully and according to the national constitution.

In her social service work Mrs. Gandhi devotes particular attention to the problems of children. She is vice-president and chairman of the standing committee of the Indian Council for Child Welfare, member of the Children's Book Trust, and vice-president of the Children's Film Society. Under her direction a large group of volunteer workers has been formed to co-operate with UNICEF and Indian government agencies in teaching child care in the villages. She is the convener of Bharat Sewak Samaj, a social service body.

A patron of the arts, Indira Gandhi helps organize the festivals, pageants, and folk dances for Republic Day and other national celebrations. She is a member of the All-India Handicrafts Board and vice-president of the Delhi Music Society, formed to promote an appreciation of Western classical music. Her interests in reading range from fashion articles to philosophy.

Mrs. Gandhi, a slim, dignified "fragile-looking" woman whose taste in dress is simple yet elegant, resembles her father in facial appearance. Observers disagree as to how close she is to him in temperament. She is the mother of two boys, Rajiv and Sanjaya; and many of her hobbies are those that she can share with her family, such as riding, trekking in the mountains, swimming, and skiing. She has domestic interests like interior decorating and gardening, and she believes that for all women there should be a balance between home life and social service.

References

Christian Sci Mon O 1 '58; F 3 '59 por
Indian News p3 S 15 '56 por
N Y Times p13 F 3 '59 por
Time 66:28 N 21 '55 por
Washington (D.C.) Post p23A D 13 '56
Times of India Directory and Year Book, 1958-59

GARNER, ERROLL (LOUIS) June 15, 1921- Jazz pianist; composer
Address: b. 520 5th Ave., New York 36

As one of the most popular jazz pianists in the world, self-schooled Erroll Garner has received accolades not usually given a jazz instrumentalist. He came up from the night-club circuit to perform his own compositions with the Cleveland Symphony in 1956, and on a 1958-59 tour under the auspices of impresario Sol Hurok he displayed his talents to almost every segment of the American public, including some Navajo Indians at Window Rock, Arizona.

Unable to read music and innocent of formal musical training, Garner has been one of the few jazz artists to come under the dignity of concert sponsorship. His bouncy style with its overtones of French impressionism, its insistent bass, and its lagging beat have delighted his followers, who have bought more of his records that those of any other jazz pianist. Many critics and connoisseurs of jazz accord him first place among the keyboard artists of today.

Erroll Louis Garner was born in the East Liberty section of Pittsburgh, Pennsylvania on June 15, 1921, the son of Ernest and Estella Garner. He was the youngest of six children. Four of his brothers and sisters were amateur musicians; the oldest, Linton, is now a professional pianist and arranger. His father was a Westinghouse plant employee who played the guitar and mandolin as a hobby.

In this musical atmosphere the boy soon displayed a precocious ability to pick out tunes from music he had heard on the family phonograph. His family recalls that he began to play before he was three years old; at six he enrolled for formal piano lessons.

Bruno of Hollywood

ERROLL GARNER

His teacher dropped him, however, when she discovered that Erroll was repeating her examples from memory rather than learning to read musical notations.

That was the only formal training Erroll ever received, but his keyboard proficiency developed so quickly that he made his professional debut the following year, when he was seven. He appeared regularly over Pittsburgh radio station KDKA with an ensemble called the Candy Kids. While still an elementary-school pupil, he worked as a substitute pianist on the Allegheny river boats.

At Westinghouse High School in Pittsburgh, Garner was barred from playing the piano because he could not read sheet music. He played a tuba in the school marching band instead. After school hours, he found regular employment as a pianist in local taverns, night clubs, and restaurants. If he played with a band, he was forced to memorize the musical score, or to improvise as he went along. "I think that's how I developed my style," he remarked later. "Not being able to read, I could only play with a band by listening carefully to the arrangements. Gradually, out of that, I began to play as if I were a full band myself."

Garner abandoned his high school studies in favor of a job with a local dance orchestra. In 1939, when he was eighteen, he went to New York as accompanist for a singer named Ann Lewis, and later toured with her for almost a year. Then he was hired briefly to play the organ at children's matinees at a cinema in Glen Falls, New York. He left to take his Army physical examination and to prepare for induction.

Inducted in 1942, Garner served in the United States Army for less than a year, then was medically discharged because of an asthmatic condition. A few months later he was back in New York City, performing at Tondelayo's night club on West 52nd Street, then called "Swing Alley." His style had matured, and Garner was so much in demand that he sometimes found himself working at three jobs at the same time.

With recognition and encouragement from jazz notables, Garner joined with bass player "Slam" Stewart and guitarist "Tiny" Grimes. The trio toured the East Coast and in 1946 returned to New York for an engagement at the Strand Theater. While playing there, Garner was asked by the Savoy Record Company to a recording session which was to make him a national figure in the field of jazz.

An elevator strike obliged Garner to walk up fifteen flights of stairs to the studio, and although asked to play "something bouncy" he felt too tired for anything more lively than ballad music. One of the numbers he recorded that day was "Laura." Later, while playing at a Los Angeles night club called the Suzy Q, Garner learned that "Laura" was a best seller. The record eventually sold a half-million copies.

For the next two years Garner played at night clubs across the United States, making records under several different labels. In 1948 he was invited with "Slim" Stewart and other jazz musicians to a festival in Paris, where he played at the theater Les Ambassadeurs. Returning to the United States, he was engaged by a small New York night club called the Three Deuces. While there he received his first mention in a mass-circulation magazine. Calling him "Mr. Piano," a *Newsweek* story remarked (August 1, 1949): "His name means nothing to most people. But to many true jazz aficionados he is just about the man for whom the piano was invented."

As Garner's reputation grew, his audience became more diversified. On March 27, 1950 at the Music Hall in Cleveland he became the first modern jazz instrumentalist to give a solo recital in the United States. In December 1950 Erroll Garner gave a concert at the Town Hall in New York. He signed an exclusive contract with Columbia Records that year, after having recorded under more than thirty different labels.

In the following years, recitals and recording sessions became more important than night-club engagements in Garner's career. He found it easy to make the logical step forward from his famous improvisations into composition. Much of his music was lost because it was not written down; finally he developed a system of keyboard composition while an assistant made notations.

This system was used when Garner gave a recital of his compositions with the Cleveland Symphony Orchestra in August 1957. Garner played his ideas to arranger Nat Pierce, who jotted them down and expanded them into an orchestral score. While the orchestra members played from the score, Garner played from memory throughout the concert. Drawing more than 7,000 listeners, the concert was generally well received; one newspaper critic called it a "noble and delightful experiment." Columbia recorded the compositions and released the album under the title of *Other Voices*.

Shortly after the Cleveland concert, Garner returned to Paris, where he was awarded the French Prix du Disque for the year's best jazz recording (*Jazz for Everyone*). The same year he received a Brazilian award for his *Concert by the Sea* album, and he was chosen the year's best pianist in *Down Beat* magazine's International Jazz Critics' Poll. He has since received awards from periodicals in four nations.

In June 1958 Garner signed with impresario Sol Hurok as his exclusive representative, the first jazz musician to appear under Hurok's management on a national tour. Since then, Garner has cut his night-club engagements to a minimum, devoting his time to composing scores for the ballet, movies, and Broadway shows, to concerts, recording sessions, and television appearances. From these activities he earns an estimated $250,000 a year.

"Two qualities of Garner's playing contribute to his wide popularity," wrote Don Nelsen in the New York *Sunday News* (February 22, 1959). "The first is his heavy emphasis on the melody of a tune, from which he rarely strays very far. The second is an infectious rhythmic swing. . . . You'd have to be unconscious not to be affected by the insistent, uninhibited, romping pulsation he lays down. His being left-handed may account in part for the powerful striding effect he gets from the bass register of his instrument."

Erroll Garner affects a small moustache and an even smaller goatee; he is five feet two inches tall and weighs 168 pounds. Unmarried, he lives in a studio apartment equipped with a seven-foot Baldwin piano in the Carnegie Hall building, New York City. He designed the furnishings and decorations himself. He occasionally designs his own wardrobe. He is a Roman Catholic, lists no political affiliation, relaxes with golf, photography, and spectator sports. Recently he began to collect art objects. Because he is small in stature, he uses a battered copy of a Manhattan telephone directory for a cushion on his piano stool.

Each of Garner's hands is insured for $100,000. His gift of improvisation is mainly a link between these hands and his musical instinct. Garner himself once wrote: "All I know is, for every note—there is another note that melts it. I just hear a sound coming into my head, and hope to catch it with my hands."

References

Compact 8:68+ por
N Y Sunday News Mag p4 F 22 '59 por
Newsweek 34:56 Ag 1 '49; 50:71 Ag 26 '57 pors
Sat Eve Post 230:25+ My 17 '58 por

GHEERBRANT, ALAIN   Dec. 27, 1920-
Explorer; author

Address: h. 179 rue de la Pompe, Paris 16, France

The fascinating account of his exploration of South America's Serra Parima that Alain Gheerbrant gave in *L'Expédition Orénogue-*

ALAIN GHEERBRANT

Amazone (Journey to the Far Amazon) brought the French author international attention. During the period from 1952 to 1954 the book was translated into eleven languages, and it has been regarded as one of the best travel and adventure books of our times. In 1953 he explored the "jungle of misunderstanding" in the Belgian Congo, later presenting his findings in *Congo noir et blanc* (1956), which drew an enthusiastic response from European critics for its poetic and humanitarian ideas.

The Gheerbrant family, of Flemish origin, settled in France in 1704. Since that time, Gheerbrants have been prominent in French government, politics, and letters. Alain Gheerbrant was born in Paris on December 27, 1920, the second son of Jean-Laurent and Alice (Arambourg) Gheerbrant. His father was formerly director of the Institute of Colonial France and is now honorary director of the Central Committee of Overseas France. He is also technical consultant for *La Nouvelle revue Française d'Outre-Mer* and is the author of *Notre Empire, un univers, un idéal* and *Pavie, le grand humain de l'Indochine.* Alain's older brother, Bernard, is a specialist in modern art and literature and editor of a book club, Club des Librairies de France.

Reared in his native city, Alain Gheerbrant attended the University of Paris, where his professor of philosophy was the then unknown Jean-Paul Sartre. He has said that he was influenced in his choice of career by "all the authors of good books, from Plato to Jules Verne and from Hans Arp to Hemingway." In 1938 he completed his studies for his baccalaureate. He entered the Cavalry School of Saumur in Morocco in 1940 and in the early part of World War II served in the French Army with the third regiment of Moroccan Spahis in North Africa.

Upon learning that the Nazis had overrun France, Gheerbrant returned to Paris, resigned

GHEERBRANT, ALAIN—*Continued*

from Henri Philippe Pétain's "Army of the Armistice," and joined the Resistance forces. He was able in 1942 to pass his examinations for the degree of law and letters from the Sorbonne. From 1942 to 1944 he worked with the underground, distributing leaflets, but not writing political tracts. During the long periods of time when he was forced to remain in hiding to evade the man hunt organized by the S.S. (*Schutzstaffel*), he wrote poetry and essays and gradually in "the great prison created by the Nazi occupation," crystallized his ideas of life and his philosophical values.

Gheerbrant's first volume of poems was entitled *L'Homme ouvert* (Fontaine, 1945). His work also began appearing in various little magazines such as *Fontaine, Les quatres vents, Gazette des lettres* (published in France) and *Formes et couleurs* (Switzerland). In 1944 he and his brother Bernard opened a bookshop-gallery called La Hune, which his brother still operates successfully. Alain became editor of a magazine, *Editions "K,"* that published contemporary poetry, philosophy, and art and brought together a group of writers and artists "who felt the urge to express a philosophy of hope and good will." Becoming interested in primitive art and spontaneous art expression, Gheerbrant compiled with Camille Bryen *Anthologie de la poésie naturelle* (1949) containing poems by children, charwomen, hairdressers, pastry cooks, and other nonprofessional writers. It even included a section of the Paris city directory—a listing of different kinds of machine shops that reads like free verse.

It was this interest in "naïve poetic expression" that aroused Gheerbrant's desire to find a "culture untouched by ours" and to explore unknown territory. For many years he had been preparing himself for such an undertaking by studying anthropology, ethnology, and medicine. Finally an opportunity arose through Luis Saenz, a Colombian coffee plantation owner whom Gheerbrant had met in Sartre's classes. With two French companions—Pierre Gaisseau and Jean Fichter—who handled camera and sound equipment, the party of four set out on May 6, 1949 from Bogotá, Colombia. All were under thirty years of age. They started their 2000-mile journey by truck, but soon met with an accident that wrecked part of their equipment. While awaiting repairs, they witnessed the initiation ceremonies of the Piaroa Indians. Continuing mostly by canoe, they advanced through jungles and llanos to the Orinoco River on which they descended, coming at last to the unexplored Serra Parima, a region lying between the jungles of the Orinoco and the upper Amazon valley.

Their observations made, the explorers found it difficult to get out of the jungle. Most of their equipment and all of their film and recordings were lost in the violent Maraca rapids, but Gheerbrant managed to save his 2000 pages of notes by rolling them into a can and tying it around his neck. Exhausted, sick, and half-starved, they reached Boa Vista on July 2, 1950.

Upon his return to civilization, Gheerbrant wrote two books: *Des Hommes qu'on appelle*

sauvages (R. Marin) and *L'Expédition Oré-noque-Amazone* (Gallimard), both published in 1952. The latter book won the 1952 Prix des Vikings, a Franco-Norwegian literary award. French critics were enthusiastic, calling the expedition a "tremendous adventure" and extolling the four explorers as doing "honor to the race of man." The critic of *Ce Soir* (Paris) wrote: "Great understanding of people and of life shines forth from the pages. . . . The author is not only a scholar, he is a writer of talent who reports what he has seen (and he knows what to look for) without romanticism, without frills, without stooping to literary tricks." The critic of *Paris-Presse* declared: "It is not only an extraordinary physical achievement. The scientific and ethnological results are even more important. Thanks to them an immense territory will be identified and mapped, and the highly mysterious habits of a most primitive people made known."

L'Expédition Orénoque-Amazone found numerous readers in England, Denmark, Norway, Sweden, and Switzerland. It was published in the United States in 1954 by Simon & Schuster under the title *Journey to the Far Amazon: An Expedition into Unknown Territory*, in a translation by Edward Fitzgerald. The critic of England's Newcastle *Journal* stated: "The book is like a tone poem of rising excitement in which the predominant notes are those of compassion and wonder. What fascinates most about this modern Odyssey is its affirmation of man's triumph over nature, so that civilized human and savage are seen as but two stages of the victory. . . . The four men are a living proof that sympathy, tolerance and courage can win from the most sinister part of nature's realm a great reward." *Atlantic Monthly's* critic wrote: "The author is not only an intrepid spirit; a knowledgeable student of ethnology and anthropology; a modest, human and perceptive personality—he is also a poet whose writing does justice to his great adventure." Critics in Brussels, Copenhagen and Dublin declared the book to be one of the best contemporary travel stories. In February 1955 *Journey to the Far Amazon* was chosen as one of the "Notable Books of 1954" by the American Library Association, making the selection in terms of "quality, authenticity, honesty of purpose, and potential contribution to the resources of the reader as a citizen and as an individual."

Still in search of primitive art and culture, Gheerbrant in 1953 journeyed to the Belgian Congo to study the inter-relation of white civilization and black traditional society. This time he went alone. Upon his return in 1954 he devoted himself to writing *Congo noir et blanc* and giving lectures in England, Sweden, Belgium, Denmark, Finland, and North Africa. Published in France in January 1956, *Congo noir et blanc* (Gallimard) posed the question: Can self-centered Western peoples with their narrow ideas of culture and civilization still communicate with peoples of a primitive society? According to Gheerbrant, the black men seem to have "safeguarded their whole being" to a greater extent than the white men who, though they possess the secrets of uranium, "expose the emptiness of their inner lives."

Critics for such politically divergent reviews as the Communist *L'Humanité* and the conservative *Figaro* found the book and its ideas praiseworthy. "Gheerbrant went to find a road through the jungle of misunderstanding in the Congo," wrote *Figaro*'s critic. "His final message is that there is hope, that there are great possibilities for men of good will if they act quickly enough." Adrien Jans of *Le Soir* (Brussels) declared: "This man has clear ideas. He is convinced of what he thinks and of what he says. . . . His book cannot fail to be discussed. . . . He pleads for the need and duty of understanding and respecting other races, of guiding and helping them without destroying their individual character—all that comes of their being themselves. To cut a man away from himself and from the earth that bore him is the greatest crime we could commit."

In 1956 the Club des Libraires de France published *Voyages du Père Labat aux isles de l'Amérique,* edited by Gheerbrant. He has lectured extensively in Europe and North Africa on exploration, especially on his South American and Congo expeditions.

Alain Gheerbrant has no political affiliations. His religion is Christian. He is a member of the Explorers' Club of France and has worked closely with the Musée de l'Homme in Paris. He was married in 1943 and divorced in 1953; he has one son, Michael. A handsome man with blue eyes and black hair, he wore a beard during his Amazon trip but is now clean-shaven. He weighs 150 pounds and is five feet six inches tall. Horseback riding, sailing and underwater hunting are his favorite sports and for other recreation he turns to all the arts, including the art of cooking. His chief interest is to continue his ethnological research in China, the Far East, Central America, and in the United States.

GIFFORD, CHLOE   Organization official; educator

Address: b. General Federation of Women's Clubs, 1734 N St., N.W., Washington 6, D.C.; h. 345 Woodland Ave., Lexington, Ky.

Heading the world's largest international organization of women, Miss Chloe Gifford was elected president of the General Federation of Women's Clubs on June 5, 1958 for a two-year term. She succeeded Mrs. Robert I. C. Prout to this office. Miss Gifford, who calls herself a "professional educationist," has been since 1940 an assistant in charge of the department of community services of the College of Adult and Extension Education of the University of Kentucky. During her G.F.W.C. administration she is emphasizing programs for both community development and international affairs—helping to perfect democracy in the United States and supporting the United Nations.

Chloe Gifford was born in Mount Olivet, Kentucky, the only child of John S. and Lida (Sledd) Gifford. After attending Sayre School in Lexington, she enrolled at the University of Kentucky in Lexington, where she studied political science and sociology. She earned the

CHLOE GIFFORD

LL.B. degree in 1923, the A.B. degree in 1924, and the M.A. degree in 1944. Ambitious to become a children's court judge, she prepared for the bench, but was given little encouragement because of her youth. She was admitted to the Kentucky bar in 1926.

In 1929 Miss Gifford was appointed dean of girls at Sayre School. She held this post until 1940, when she joined the faculty of the University of Kentucky, where she taught political science. She also helped in the adult education department of the university and served on scholarship committees. She later became a member of the national advisory committee for General Mills scholarship awards, the President's Citizens Advisory Committee on the Fitness of American Youth, and the citizens committee of the United States Office of Education.

The University of Kentucky named Chloe Gifford director of its bureau of clubs and community service. Through these activities she became a member of the General Federation of Women's Clubs, president of the Kentucky division of the American Association of University Women and the G.F.W.C., president of the Kentucky Welfare Association, founder and president of the President's Council of Kentucky (an organization of the presidents of all women's clubs in the state). At one time she served on the boards of sixteen state organizations.

With her experience in education, Miss Gifford was the logical choice as chairman of the G.F.W.C.'s education committee in 1950. She made many speeches to groups in forty-eight states in which she urged increased citizen interest in public school needs. "Our country has provided education for *more* people than any other country throughout the years," she said later. "We do not have a *class* education, and to offer a curriculum that will stimulate the bright student and coax from him his maximum

GIFFORD, CHLOE—*Continued*

as well as provide for the less apt student an adequate education, is no minute task that can be accomplished quickly and without any error" (*Clubwoman*, November 1958).

As third vice-president of the General Federation of Women's Clubs in 1952, Miss Gifford was asked to recruit 100,000 new members. Traveling from coast to coast, she earned a reputation for completing each assignment with energy and efficiency, while maintaining a keen sense of humor. After her election as first vice-president of the G.F.W.C. in June 1957, she spoke of the need for "an educated citizenry." "Let us, I beg of you, no longer eye the educator with suspicion or refer to the intelligent individual as an egghead or a highbrow," she said. "The march of science, amazing economic growth, needs of national defense, the complexity of the world in which we live—all demand that we have trained and skilled leadership" (New York *Times,* June 5, 1957).

At the sixty-seventh convention of the federation, held in Detroit in June 1958, Miss Gifford was unanimously chosen president by some 2,800 voting delegates. During her two-year term of office as president of the G.F.W.C. her duties require her membership in some thirty committees and councils, and officiating at public ceremonies.

The General Federation of Women's Clubs, founded in 1890, has a membership of more than 11,000,000 women in fifty countries. This includes 850,000 members who pay per capita dues in 15,500 clubs in the United States. The federation functions through eight departments: American home, communications, community affairs, conservation of natural resources, education, fine arts, international affairs and international clubs, and public affairs. Members have sponsored a series of community improvement contests (first in co-operation with the Kroger Foundation and for the past five years with the Sears Roebuck Foundation). The clubwomen have "achieved remarkable results in their rural and urban communities," noted the *Christian Science Monitor* (September 30, 1958), "establishing youth centers, playgrounds, libraries, hospitals, nurseries, and generally cleaning up their towns and cities."

One of the G.F.W.C. projects close to Miss Gifford's heart is its foreign policy program which emphasizes the exchange of foreign students and teachers and the value of having them live in homes and on campuses. She also is stressing the study of international issues by women. In the spring of 1958 she was a guest of the West German government, and in October she went to Munich with the Crusade for Freedom group to report on Radio Free Europe. She attended the international convention of the General Federation in Geneva, Switzerland in 1955 and will head the first General Federation Asiatic Convention, to be held in Manila, June 20-26, 1959.

The G.F.W.C. has recently urged the establishment of a United Nations police force; the recruitment of science teachers and the encouragement of students to take science courses; the renewal of the United States reciprocal trade agreements "at five-year instead of three-year intervals and without crippling amendments"; and equal pay for comparable work for men and women.

Referring to certain other issues, Miss Gifford deplored the action of some clubwomen in introducing "inconsequential resolutions" to the G.F.W.C. conventions and told them, "I'm a lobbyist now. I want resolutions I can go up to the 'Hill' and really fight for."

For many years Miss Gifford taught Sunday School at the Woodland Christian Church in Lexington. She is a member of Kappa Delta Pi and Kappa Beta Pi societies, among others. Appointed a Kentucky Colonel in 1955, she serves on many state organizations for health, safety, civil defense, education, and the sale of defense bonds. She is also a member of the Atlantic Union Committee, National Farm-City Week, and Action Committee. In February 1958 she attended a White House Conference on National Security. She is a Democrat.

Chloe Gifford has brown eyes and steel-gray curly hair and is five feet eight inches tall. Her husky voice is pleasing. Associates speak of her vivacity and her flair for making friends. She is the first full-time career woman and the first unmarried woman to hold the presidency of the G.F.W.C. She makes her home in Washington, D.C. with her mother while on leave of absence from her university position.

References

Christian Sci Mon p4A S 30 '58 por
Who's Who in America, 1958-59

GOLDEN, HARRY (LEWIS) May 6, 1902- Editor; publisher

Address: Carolina Israelite, 1312 Elizabeth Ave., Charlotte, N.C.

One of the best-selling books of 1958 was a collection of essays called *Only In America,* written by a South Carolina editor named Harry Golden. A man with a rare combination of erudition, literary style, and wit, Golden has been publishing since 1941 a monthly newspaper, the *Carolina Israelite,* from which most of the essays in his book were drawn. Long before the book appeared he had attracted the attention of prominent people in political and literary circles, both Jews and Gentiles, who, because they enjoy his flair for nostalgia and irreverence, have become faithful subscribers. When *For 2c Plain,* adopting the same formula of humor as *Only in America,* was published by the World Publishing Company in 1959, it also became an immediate best seller.

Harry Lewis Golden (originally Goldenhurst) was born in New York City's Lower East Side on May 6, 1902, one of five children of Leib and Nuchama (Klein) Goldenhurst. His parents were immigrants from Austria-Hungary; his father became an editor on the *Jewish Daily Forward.* Golden was graduated in 1918 from the East Side Evening High School. He studied English and literature at City College of the City of New York, but left in the early 1920's without completing work for a degree.

"I majored in America—in books and history and literature—with no attempt to pinpoint anything in particular or to become anything in particular," he has said since. "I just wanted to become what my father would call a learned man." At this time he held a number of jobs in New York: a blocker of ladies' straw hats, hotel clerk, and newspaper reporter. But his principal activity was as a speaker and pamphleteer for the Socialists and the Henry George single-tax movement.

Following the widespread publicity concerning Golden after his book, *Only in America,* became a best seller in 1958 it came to light that he had served a Federal prison term in the 1930's under the name of Harry L. Goldhurst. He was convicted of using the mails to defraud in connection with stock purchases on margin. He pleaded guilty and served most of a five-year term with time off for good behavior.

Reactions to news of Golden's prison record were chiefly friendly, as exemplified in Adlai E. Stevenson's comment: "The story of Harry Golden reminds me of the story of O. Henry, who spent three years in prison. I suspect that this experience deepened Harry Golden's understanding, lengthened his vision, and enlarged his heart. His subsequent life and work is best evidence of this." Carl Sandburg, who wrote the foreword to *Only in America,* said: "This story ties me closer to him" (New York *Times,* September 20, 1958).

As Harry L. Golden he made a new start. After stints as a schoolteacher and work on a number of newspapers, including the New York *Post* and the New York *Mirror,* he moved to North Carolina in 1939. There he worked first for the Charlotte *Observer* and then the Hendersonville *Times-News.* Along the way he found time to write what he describes as "a million pamphlets and articles for the Zionists, the New Deal, the Socialists and the Democratic party." He was also asked to write a history of the Presbyterian Church.

In 1941 he returned to Charlotte, and with the assistance of a couple of financial supporters started a monthly newspaper, the *Carolina Israelite.* (The backers soon ended their relationship with the publication.) "I wanted to publish a liberal newspaper in North Carolina," he said, "but I was a Jew, a liberal, and a northerner. The odds were too much. So I insulated myself. I called the paper the *Carolina Israelite.* My critics could say, 'This is another Jew paper,' and perhaps, I thought, sooner or later the non-Jews would get acquainted with it."

His initial circulation was only 800. But Golden kept working, publishing what one editor described as a Yiddish newspaper translated into English. It came out somewhat irregularly, in a sixteen-page, five-column tabloid format, that soon came to consist chiefly of 25,000 words of essays by Golden surrounded by some 100 advertisements. There were no big headlines, no pictures, no social notes, no obituaries.

"When I feel like writing, I write," Golden said. "I put it in a barrel, and when it comes time to bring out the *Israelite,* I reach in the

HARRY GOLDEN

barrel." The diverse contents of each issue indicated his wide interests, for the essays were ranged over such subjects as: "It Was Better When Papa Was the Boss," "Dr. Johnson's Recipe for Oysters," "Where are the Knishes of the East Side When I Was a Boy?" "Cato's Hangover Cure," and "A Plan to Solve the Problems of the White Citizens' Council."

Golden soon came to have nearly as many non-Jews as Jews among his subscribers; he found his newspaper going into the hands of North Carolina farmers, mill workers, teachers, editors, and housewives. Among his readers came to be such prominent and varied personages as Harry Truman, Earl Warren, Adlai E. Stevenson, Thomas E. Dewey, Fannie Hurst, William Faulkner, and Carl Sandburg.

Golden also published a number of his own more serious studies: *Jews in American History, Their Contribution to the United States of America* (1950, with Martin Rywell); *Jews in the South* (1951); *Jewish Roots in the Carolinas* (1954), and *A Pattern of American Philo-Semitism* (1955). Beginning in 1953 he also contributed occasional articles about the South to the magazines *Commentary* and the *Nation.*

What really brought Golden to national attention were the three satiric proposals he put forward in 1956 and 1957 for solving the problems of integration. The Golden Vertical Negro Plan was to install stand-up desks in the public schools, since Southerners seemed to object only to sitting, not standing, beside Negroes. The Golden Out-of-Order Plan reported his observation that Southern whites would use colored drinking fountains without objection providing they thought the separate white facilities were out of order. He suggested the continuance of separate facilities, but keeping them "out-of-order" until whites got used to the idea. The Golden Borrow-a-Child Plan reported his discovery that Negro maids were permitted to sit

GOLDEN, HARRY—*Continued*

in the white sections of theatres, providing they were escorting a white child. He suggested that white parents could save baby-sitter fees by depositing their children at centers where Negroes who wished to attend a movie could borrow them.

Accounts of these jests were widely reprinted, appearing in *Time* magazine (April 1, 1957) and in the New York *Times* (September 8, 1957). In November of that year the World Publishing Company in New York contracted with Golden to publish a collection of his essays.

In February 1958 the frame house in Charlotte, which was Golden's combination home and office, was completely destroyed by fire, including his subscription list of about 16,000 names. Newspaper friends throughout the country wrote stories about the loss, urging these subscribers to write to him. Their efforts brought him national publicity and even more subscribers.

Golden's book was published on July 18, 1958, under the title *Only in America*—drawn from a stock headline, "It Could Happen Only in America," which he uses for his occasional essays on success. It won wide critical acclaim and soon appeared on the leading best-seller lists.

"What makes the whole potpourri so stimulating," William Du Bois wrote in the New York *Times* (July 18, 1958), "is his serene knowledge that what he has to say is worth saying." Maurice Dolbier wrote in the New York *Herald Tribune* (July 18, 1958): "It's nice to live in the same country with him." Robert C. Bergenheim said in the *Christian Science Monitor* (July 21, 1958): "If you enjoy nonconformists who lean on logic for their independent ideas you'd appreciate Harry Golden."

A Southern newspaper editor once summed up Harry Golden as "a pleasant myth." Although he has many friends, he stays aloof, sitting for hours before a typewriter listening to classical music, laboring over his essays. But whatever others may say about him, "one thing they can't say," Golden himself says, "is that Harry Golden is not an interesting so-and-so."

On March 17, 1926 he was married to an Irish girl, Genevieve Gallagher, a former schoolteacher. Golden has been separated from his wife for many years. He has three grown sons —one a reporter, another a university instructor, and the third an art director. A fourth son died in the summer of 1957 of muscular dystrophy.

Harry Golden is a Democrat, and a member of Charlotte's Temple Israel (Conservative), the Shakespeare Society of America, Inter-Racial Society of Charlotte, Southern Regional Council, and National Association for the Advancement of Colored People.

References

Coronet 44:46 S '58
N Y Herald Tribune p8 My 31 '58
N Y World-Telegram Mag p1 S 13 '58
    por
Time 69:62 Ap 1 '57
Who's Who in World Jewry, 1955

GORDIMER, NADINE Nov. 20, 1923-
Author

Address: b. P.O. Box 55, Denver, Transvaal, South Africa; h. 7 Frere Rd., Parktown, Johannesburg, South Africa

Reprinted from the *Wilson Library Bulletin* May 1959.

The title of Nadine Gordimer's book *A World of Strangers* expresses a theme which pervades her fiction. Discussing one of her earlier books, William Peden commented in *Saturday Review*: "Most of Miss Gordimer's people are 'eternal foreigners' in their own countries; the theme of exile, alienation, and aloneness are as much a part of her work as they are of James Joyce's." With the feeling of personal alienation there is always present, since she is a South African, the alienation of the races. As a member of the white minority, she writes with sensitivity and compassion of the issue by which her country is torn.

Nor has she confined her probing of race conscience to fiction. Speaking directly, in a *Holiday* magazine travel sketch about Lourenço Marques—the Portuguese resort near the Union of South Africa known as "the South African Riviera"—she reveals how tourists from Johannesburg enjoy the relaxed Latin atmosphere of a place without a color bar, without apartheid, relieved of the guit and unease they feel at home.

Nadine Gordimer, the daughter of Isidore Gordimer, a jeweler, and Nan (Myers) Gordimer, was born November 20, 1923, in a small town in the rich gold-mining area of South Africa. Reared in the same town, she received part of her education at a convent and was later graduated from the University of the Witwatersrand in Johannesburg.

Her early life had a definite influence on her career. "A solitary sort of childhood made me bookish," she explains, "and an adolescence

NADINE GORDIMER

and youth among people who didn't share my tastes acted as a stimulus to make me express myself privately—on paper." A writer since the age of nine, she began publishing her stories at fifteen.

American readers were introduced to Miss Gordimer with the publication of her stories in the *New Yorker, the Virginia Quarterly Review,* the *Yale Review, Harper's Magazine, Charm,* and *Mademoiselle.* A collection of twenty-one stories, most of them having a South African background, was published as *The Soft Voice of the Serpent, and Other Stories* (Simon & Schuster, 1952).

Critics saw great promise in this book. In his *Commonweal* review, Richard Hayes, despite some reservations, admired her "intensely perceptive observation," as well as the "spatial and material authenticity" of the South African stories. Miss Gordimer, he concluded, "is ... so much a mistress of this time and place, so verbally dexterous, so mercilessly accurate in her sensory responses, that one anticipates the performance of a potentially major writer."

Her first novel was *The Lying Days* (Simon & Schuster, 1955), a narrative in autobiographical form of the childhood and adolescence of a white girl in a mining suburb of Johannesburg. One reviewer found fault with the structural organization and another with the characterization; but all recognized her deftness with words and her mastery of emotional nuance. Bestowing praise without qualification, James Stern, in the New York *Times Book Review,* made an impressive comparison: "Her book is in many respects as mature, as packed with insight into human nature, as void of conceit and banality, as original and as beautifully written as a novel by Virginia Woolf. ... I can think of no modern first novel superior to Miss Gordimer's."

Fifteen of her short stories appeared in a second collection under the title *Six Feet of the Country* (Simon & Schuster, 1956). The book received exceptionally good notices and was recommended by the Book Society in England. Walter Allen, in the *New Statesman and Nation,* lauded her as a writer of great gifts, adding: "She can illuminate life, and not merely South African life; yet it is when her material is specifically South African that she has most to offer."

A World of Strangers (Simon & Schuster, 1958) is her second novel, an account of a young English intellectual, a stranger in Johannesburg, determined to remain a passive observer—uncommitted in the conflict between the races, aloof from the tensions between British South Africans and Dutch Afrikaners. In the loneliness of South Africa he feels curiously at home, a "stranger among people who were strangers to each other."

A number of critics cited flaws in the novel —structural defects, excessively convoluted language, evidence of a feminine viewpoint in the hero's first-person narration. Others, however, dismissing the imperfections as minor, found in the work the urgency of today's headlines and artistry, as well. In the opinion of *Time* magazine's reviewer, Miss Gordimer "not only tells the truth about her countrymen, but she tells it so well that she has become at once their goad

and their best writer. . . . She proves in ... [her] excellent new novel that the faces of evil and arrogance have an endless variety of expressions for one who can bear to look at them."

A small, slim, attractive young woman, Nadine Gordimer is the wife of Reinhold Cassirer, a company director, whom she married in 1954. She and her husband live in Johannesburg with their son, her husband's daughter by a previous marriage, and her own daughter by a previous marriage. Though reticent about her personal interests and recreations, she has disclosed some of her literary favorites: "E. M. Forster—anything he's written—and numbers of others, including J. D. Salinger's stories, Charles Finney's *The Circus of Dr. Lao,* and Malraux's *Man's Fate."*

References

Lib J 78:1139+ Je 15 '53 por
N Y Herald Tribune Bk R p20 O 11 '53
N Y Times Bk R p8 Ap 5 '59

GORDON, THOMAS S(YLVY) Dec. 17, 1893-Jan. 22, 1959 United States Democratic Representative from Illinois; chairman of the House Foreign Affairs Committee (1957-58). See *Current Biography* (April) 1957.

Obituary

N Y Times p25+ Ja 23 '59

GOREN, CHARLES H(ENRY) Mar. 4, 1901- Bridge expert; author

Address: b. 710 50th St., Miami Beach, Fla; h. 544 Susquehanna, Huntingdon Valley, Pa.

The system of point-count bidding which Charles H. Goren popularized has made him the world's top contract bridge player. His books on bridge have sold nearly 4,000,000 copies in the United States and have been translated into eight foreign languages. His daily bridge column is syndicated in over 200 newspapers and he holds top honors in master tournaments (5,791 points) and has won some 2,000 trophies. Nine out of ten bridge teachers use his bidding system. He also conducts a regular column in *Sports Illustrated* and lectures widely, both in the United States and abroad. He has been National Bridge Champion thirty-one times. A recent award was the Life Masters Pair Gold Cup, which he won in August 1958 in Miami with Mrs. Helen Sobel as his partner.

Charles Henry Goren was born in Philadelphia, Pennsylvania on March 4, 1901 to Jacob and Rebecca Goren, Russian-born Jewish immigrants. He has a brother, Edward. His father was a writer. Charles Goren attended Central High School in his native city, attained an excellent scholastic record, and was active on the school paper and in sports and debating. After his graduation in 1918 he worked as department store furniture salesman until a cousin in Montreal, Canada offered to help him go through college.

(Continued next page)

Moffett Chicago

CHARLES H. GOREN

Accordingly, he enrolled at McGill University in Montreal, planning to become a lawyer. While at the university he was sports editor of the paper, and he won the Alexander Prize for scholarship achievement in 1922. Returning to Philadelphia after graduating from McGill University with the LL.B. degree in 1922 and the LL.M. degree in 1923, Goren passed the Pennsylvania bar examinations. In his thirteen years of law practice as Goren admits, he never made more than $5,000 a year. "I didn't give up the law," he said. "It gave me up" (*Time,* September 29, 1958).

In his first attempt to play bridge, when still a law student, Goren had been thoroughly defeated by his opponents. Determined to master the game, he bought a copy of Milton Work's book on auction bridge and studied it for several months. "He was soon winning local tournaments and rounding out his skimpy law income with bridge winnings," *Time* noted. "But as soon as he could afford to, Goren gave up playing for money. He saw that the road to bridgedom's peak lay in teaching and writing."

By 1931 Goren was competing in major tournaments. His first book, *Winning Bridge Made Easy,* was published by Telegraph Press in 1936. In suit bids Goren generally followed Ely Culbertson's "honor-trick" count, but he adopted Milton Work's method for no-trump bidding whereby a hand is evaluated by a point count: four points for an ace, three for a king, two for a queen, and one for a jack. Fascinated by the simplicity of the point-count system, Goren devoted much time to expanding the idea into a general bidding method and to popularizing it in his books.

During the past decade the honor-trick method of determining the value of a bridge hand has been generally supplanted by the point-count method. Experts had used point count

for years, but Goren's books have made it possible for even beginners in bridge to use the high-card point count without difficulty. "With balanced hands—hands without a void or singleton—the high-card point count is both practical and accurate and reflects essentially the true value of a hand," observed B. Jay Becker in his article "Contract Bridge" in *Information Please Almanac, 1959.*

"Beyond its tremendous advantage of simplicity," *Time* (September 29, 1958) pointed out, "the Goren method is more reliable than Culbertson's. Ely's honor-trick count tended to undervalue kings, queens, and jacks, overvalue the ace and the A-K combination." Goren speaks of his point-count bidding as a "back to nature movement," meaning that it makes scant use of artificial conventions, relies on "natural" bids that are naturally related to the cards in the hand.

Contract bridge was devised by Harold S. Vanderbilt in 1925 and soon replaced auction bridge, which had developed from whist, a more than 200-year-old game. Ely Culbertson popularized contract bridge and his own system in 1931 when he won a simulated grudge match against Sidney Lenz, a promoter of the "Official System." Various systems of bidding have been developed. The system now used in tournaments conducted by the American Contract Bridge League, the governing body of bridge, evolved through the efforts of Culbertson, Work, Goren, and others.

After *Winning Bridge Made Easy* was published, Goren gave up the practice of law to write other books, teach bridge, and play in tournaments. In 1944 he succeeded Culbertson as the Chicago *Tribune*'s bridge columnist, when Culbertson became the Chicago *Sun*'s columnist. In 1951 *Goren's New Contract Bridge Complete* was published by Doubleday & Company and became a best seller. A revised edition of the book, which appeared in October 1957, contained several important changes in his system, improvements that he was able to recommend because of the increase in the level of bridge skill in the United States during the preceding six years. *Publishers' Weekly* (November 25, 1957) reported that within a month after publication the revised edition was in its third printing and was selling 1,000 copies a day.

Goren has a talent for gentle, whimsical humor, commented one critic who admired the "bright touches" in the bridge expert's writing. His books, besides those already mentioned, include the *Standard Book of Bidding, Point Count Bidding at a Glance, Contract Bridge for Beginners, Contract Bridge in a Nutshell,* and *Contract Made Easy.* Doubleday's *Goren Presents the Italian Bridge System* appeared in January 1958. In August 1958 Simon & Schuster published a paperback *New Way to Better Bridge* by Goren, which includes a deck of marked cards that may be dealt into twenty-four different bridge hands.

Among recent magazine articles that explain Goren's method are those in *Good Housekeeping* (July and August 1957) and *Woman's Home Companion* (January 1957). Since Sep tember 1957 he has been a special correspondent for *Sports Illustrated,* writing a weekly column on bridge and other card games.

Charles H. Goren, who is a bachelor, is five feet eight and a half inches tall, weighs 175 pounds, and has brown eyes and brown hair. Although once a chain cigar smoker, he now refrains from smoking. He is an avid golfer and a patron of the theater and symphony. When he plays in bridge tournaments he wears horn-rimmed glasses. His manner at the bridge table is dramatic. He is much in demand socially, and his bridge partners have included such famous enthusiasts as the author Somerset Maugham, who wrote a preface to Goren's series in *Sports Illustrated.* Goren is exceptionally tolerant of kibitzers at card games. He says: "Today's kibitzer may be buying my books tomorrow."

References

Sports Illus p14 S 16 '57 por
Time 72:56+ S 29 '58 pors
Who's Who in America, 1958-59

Andre Emmerich Gallery
—Lee Boltin

ADOLPH GOTTLIEB

GOTTLIEB, ADOLPH Mar. 14, 1903-
Artist

Address: b. c/o André Emmerich Gallery, 17 E. 64th St., New York 21; h. 27 W. 96 St., New York 25

Adolph Gottlieb is one of the leading members of the so-called New York school of abstract expressionists. Largely self-taught, except for two brief periods of study at the Art Students League of New York, he began as a representational painter and had his first one-man show in 1930. Early in the 1940's he arrived at his characteristic "pictograph" style, in which symbolic forms were presented segmentally, as in archaic or primitive art. Introducing Gottlieb's retrospective exhibition in November 1957, Clement Greenberg stated: "Until about six or seven years ago—when he triumphantly broadened, before relinquishing forever, the 'pictograph' style that had become his signature —he seemed a rather narrow if tremendously competent painter. Since then he has become the most adventurous artist in the country." In addition to his easel painting, Gottlieb has won acclaim for his decorations for synagogues and the stained-glass façade he designed for the Milton Steinberg Memorial Center in New York.

Born in New York City on March 14, 1903, Adolph Gottlieb is the son of Emil and Elsie (Berger) Gottlieb. His father was a merchant. Young Gottlieb left high school in 1920 to study painting under John Sloan and Robert Henri at the Art Students League. The following year he worked his passage to Europe, where he attended sketch classes without instruction at the Grand Chaumière and other studio schools in Paris and later visited Berlin and Munich. Returning to New York in 1923, he finished high school and studied at the Parsons School of Design and again at the Art Students League. He continued to paint during the next five years

while supporting himself by odd jobs, such as sign painting and teaching at settlement houses and summer camps.

Gottlieb first achieved recognition by winning second prize in the national competition sponsored by the Dudensing Galleries in the summer of 1929. In May of the next year that gallery presented a joint exhibition of the work of Gottlieb and the first-prize winner, Konrad Cramer. The critic for *Art News* wrote of Gottlieb's pictures: "At present there is a wide range of variety in his interests—figures, still lifes, landscapes, and street scenes. In the majority of these, the artist's enthusiasm appears to have somewhat outdistanced his technical equipment." During 1934 Gottlieb's oils were displayed at the Uptown Gallery in February and his water colors at the offices of Theodore A. Kohn & Son in May.

In the summer of 1935 Gottlieb returned to Europe for two months. Between 1935 and 1939 he exhibited annually with "The Ten," an independent group of painters working in a more or less expressionist idiom. It included such now well-known artists as Mark Rothko, Ilya Bolotowsky, Ben-Zion, and Lee Gatch. Gottlieb was employed as an easel painter on the WPA Federal Art Project in 1936. The following year he left the project and lived in the desert near Tucson, Arizona, painting semiabstract still lifes and landscapes. He was commissioned to execute a mural in the Yerrington (Nevada) Post Office in 1940, as a result of winning a nation-wide competition sponsored by the United States Treasury. Reviewing Gottlieb's one-man show at the Artists Gallery in April 1940, Emily Genauer observed in the *World-Telegram* that the painter was "a romantic, working in deep and somber tones sometimes organized into quiet austere arrangements of

GOTTLIEB, ADOLPH—*Continued*

still life, and sometimes into landscapes that have an imaginative, unworldly air."

Around 1941 Gottlieb began to evolve what he called the "pictograph" style, with which he was to be closely identified for the next decade. The canvas was divided into a number of rectangular compartments and the spaces within the box outlines filled with enigmatic, archaeological, and totemic symbols—such as human eyes and noses, circles, crosses, dots, arrows, serpents, suns and moons. Myth and fable supplied Gottlieb with a number of his themes, and he favored earth, clay, and mineral hues. Among the better-known paintings in this idiom were *Eyes of Oedipus, Pursuer and Pursued, Terrors of Tranquility, Black and Tan Fantasy,* and *Romanesque Façade.* The works of this period were seen in one-man shows at the Artists Gallery (1942), Wakefield Gallery (1944), Gallery 67 and Nierendorf Gallery (1945), Jacques Seligmann Gallery (1949), and the Kootz Gallery (1947, 1950, 1951).

When asked why his pictures were compartmentalized, Gottlieb replied: "I am like a man with a large family and must have many rooms. The children of my imagination occupy the various compartments of my painting, each independent and occupying its own space. At the same time they have the proper atmosphere in which to function together, in harmony and as a unified group. One can say that my paintings are like a house, in which each occupant has a room of his own" (*Arts & Architecture,* September 1951).

Gottlieb was one of the three avant-garde abstractionists selected in 1951 by architect Percival Goodman to provide the decorations for the new synagogue, school, and center for Congregation B'nai Israel, in Millburn, New Jersey. It was his task to design the Ark Curtain, nineteen feet high and eight feet wide, which incorporated stylized representations of traditional Jewish religious symbols. So successful was the result that two years later Goodman again called on him to design the Ark Curtain for the new synagogue for Congregation Beth El, in Springfield, Massachusetts. This time his design was converted into wool, in a sort of hooked rug technique, with Gottlieb using the craftsman "as if he were his paint brush," directing him to change colors and textures as their work together progressed.

His most ambitious architectural commission was to design the 1,300-square-foot stained-glass façade of the Milton Steinberg Memorial Center in New York (1952-54). For this project he devised a kind of checkerboard pattern comprised of ninety-one individual window panels and covering four floors. One-third of the surface was designed and painted in twenty-one different abstract compositions, each one foot tall and three feet wide, of stylized motifs derived from traditional, religious iconography pertaining to Jewish holidays and ritual. "It's a satisfaction to reach a larger audience than normally sees modern paintings," the artist stated after the façade was completed. "Work of this kind has to be more intellectual, less subjective than easel painting. Its effect on my

oils will probably be to lead me, in reaction, to more subjective abstraction than ever" (New York *Herald Tribune,* September 19, 1954).

Meanwhile, critics had observed a change in direction in Gottlieb's style. Gradually breaking through the rigid formula of the pictograph framework in the early 1950's, he achieved a new freedom of spatial depth, enlarged the scale of his work, and enriched the range of color. As one critic described his *Ancestral Image,* the single totem had been lifted out of the pictograph context and the symbol magnified so that it became a picture on its own. Among the key works in this transition were *Frozen Sounds, Armature, Chromatic Game, Figurations of Clangor,* and *Blue at Noon.*

A retrospective exhibition of thirty-one of Gottlieb's paintings dating from 1941 to 1957 was held at the Jewish Museum in New York in November-December 1957. In his review of the show for *Arts,* Carl Baldwin noted that the artist's mature output fell into one of three categories: "powerful, heavy lines which form entanglements or cages, often with connotations of monstrosity" (*Unstill-Life* of 1952, *Unstill-Life No. 3* of 1954-56); "an over-all calligraphy or 'pictography' where a repertoire of signs and symbols are scattered over the entire field" (*Sounds at Night* of 1948, *Hot Horizon* of 1956); and "pictures which are divided strictly in two with a polemical opposition of the iconic upper part and the activated lower part" (*Groundscape* of 1954-56, *Burst* of 1957). As an immediate follow-up to this exhibition, nine large canvases by Gottlieb were displayed at the André Emmerich Gallery in January 1958.

Outside New York, Gottlieb has exhibited at the Arts Club of Chicago, Walker Art Center in Minneapolis, Area Arts in San Francisco, and the Galerie Maeght in Paris. A ten-year retrospective exhibition of his work was shown at Bennington College and Williams College in 1954. He has participated in a number of national and international group shows.

The painter won the $100 first prize at the 1944 annual exhibition of the Brooklyn Society of Artists for his canvas *Symbols of the Desert,* and in 1951 he received the purchase award of the University of Illinois. He is a member of the College Art Association and the National Society of Mural Painters, and in 1944-45 served as president of the Federation of Modern Painters and Sculptors. During 1958 he taught at Pratt Institute in Brooklyn. Gottlieb was married to Esther Dick on June 12, 1932. As a hobby, he collects African, South Sea, and pre-Columbian art. Selden Rodman (*Conversations with Artists*) has quoted Gottlieb: "We're going to have perhaps a thousand years of nonrepresentational painting now."

References

Art N 54:42+ Mr '55

Baur, John I. H. Nature in Abstraction (1958)

Seuphor, M. Dictionary of Abstract Painting (1957)

Who's Who in America, 1958-59

Who's Who in American Art, 1956

GRANAHAN, KATHRYN E(LIZA-BETH) United States Representative from Pennsylvania

Address: b. Room 1220, House Office Bldg., Washington 25, D.C.; Federal Court House Bldg., Philadelphia 31, Pa.; h. 2491 N. 50th St., Philadelphia 31, Pa.; The Mayflower, Washington 6, D.C.

The first woman to represent a Philadelphia district in the Congress of the United States, Kathryn E. Granahan was elected to the House of Representatives on November 6, 1956 to fill out the unexpired term of her husband, the late William T. Granahan, in the Eighty-fourth Congress. On the same date she was elected to the Eighty-fifth Congress for the term expiring January 1959; in November 1958 she was re-elected, to the Eighty-sixth Congress. Mrs. Granahan, a Democrat, represents the Second Pennsylvania District, which covers seven Philadelphia wards. She is a member of the Government Operations and Post Office and Civil Service Committees. As chairman of the Postal Operations Subcommittee, she began in the spring of 1959 an investigation into the distribution of obscene photographs and motion pictures.

Philadelphia's first Congresswoman was born Kathryn Elizabeth O'Hay, the daughter of James B. and Julia (Reilly) O'Hay; she is a native of Easton, Pennsylvania, where she attended local public schools. A graduate of Easton High School and of Mount St. Joseph College in Chestnut Hill, Philadelphia, Kathryn O'Hay worked in the social welfare field before she married William T. Granahan. She began her public career as supervisor of public assistance in the auditor general's department of the Commonwealth of Pennsylvania. She was also a liaison officer between that department and the Department of Public Assistance at Harrisburg, where in 1941 William T. Granahan became chief disbursing officer for the Commonwealth treasury. They were married on November 20, 1943.

A veteran of World War I, William T. Granahan had worked in the building business before he became supervisor for the inheritance tax of the Commonwealth of Pennsylvania. At the time of his marriage he was already recognized as a Democratic leader in Philadelphia's 52nd Ward. As Democratic candidate for United States Representative from the Second Pennsylvania District, he was elected to the Seventy-ninth Congress on November 7, 1944.

In his freshman term in Congress, Representative Granahan created something of a stir. He not only joined a union line in November 1945 that was picketing the American Tobacco Company, but defied custom by holding on to the Democratic leadership of his home ward in west Philadelphia.

Granahan did not get to be a member of the Eightieth Congress. He was defeated in November 1946 by Robert N. McGarvey, but won back his seat in 1948. He was re-elected in 1950, 1952, and 1954. During his five terms in Congress, Mrs. Granahan worked closely with her husband, who became one of the

Wide World

KATHRYN E. GRANAHAN

ranking members of the House of Representatives Interstate and Foreign Commerce Committee. He co-sponsored a bill in 1954 to increase unemployment benefits by about fifty per cent, and introduced a bill to increase the salary of postal workers and other government employees by $800 a year. In 1956, he introduced a bill to make Good Friday a national holiday.

Representative Granahan died on May 25, 1956, a month after he had been renominated by local Democrats for a sixth term in Congress. Early in June his widow was named to succeed him as Democratic leader of Philadelphia's 52nd Ward. On June 11 Mrs. Granahan was nominated by Democratic leaders of the Second Pennsylvania district as the party candidate to fill out her husband's term expiring in January 1957, and for the new Congressional term beginning at that time. Mrs. Granahan's name therefore appeared twice on the ballots on November 6, 1956. She defeated her Republican opponent, Robert F. Frankenfield, by 95,567 votes to 57,773, and became the first woman to represent a Philadelphia district in Congress. She was re-elected in November 1958 by 84,058 votes to 42,759 for Maurice L. Green, her Republican opponent.

Following the precedent set by her late husband, Mrs. Granahan retained her ward leadership after her first Congressional campaign. She is anxious to erase the unsavory impression of ward leaders which the general public entertains; in her campaign to alter this stereotype, Congresswoman Granahan has refused to provide the traditional barrel of beer for her ward meetings. Instead, she serves cookies and tea. The seventy-two district committeemen who attend these meetings, according to George Dixon of the Washington *Post and Times Herald* (May 18, 1957), "are reconciled." Mrs. Granahan told Dixon in an interview that "only the highest type of people

GRANAHAN, KATHRYN E.—*Cont.*

should be in politics—even in the lowest echelons."

Mrs. Granahan believes that it is poor strategy to change her hats in the middle of a campaign; throughout her 1956 campaign she wore the same beige satin beret. For her first appearance in the House of Representatives, Mrs. Granahan donned a new flowered hat, only to be told by the House parliamentarian that a rule in the House manual forbids the wearing of hats during sessions. She commented: "When the rule was adopted in 1831, it was inconceivable that a woman would ever be a member of Congress" (Washington *Post and Times Herald,* April 16, 1957).

Officially a member of Congress since November 7, 1956, Mrs. Granahan enjoyed seniority over other newcomers to the House of Representatives in January 1957. She had already expressed a desire to replace her husband on the Interstate and Foreign Commerce Committee, but no woman has yet been named to that committee. Mrs. Granahan was assigned to the Post Office and Civil Service and the District of Columbia committees.

Since then Mrs. Granahan has been appointed to the Government Operations Committee and has become chairman of the Postal Operations Subcommittee. Not long after she was first elected, Mrs. Granahan said she would like to see the passage of civil rights legislation, repeal of the "union-busting provisions of the Taft-Hartley law," and some solution to the problem of the high cost of living (New York *Herald Tribune,* December 2, 1956). Accordingly, in June 1957 she supported the civil rights bill, while opposing the proposed "jury trial" amendment.

The voting record of Mrs. Granahan indicates that she supported the Patman resolution, rejected by the House, calling for a House study of national monetary and credit policies (March 1957); an increase in funds for a study of federal regulatory agencies (April 1957); an 11 per cent pay increase for federal employees (August 1957); extension of the government security program to all federal workers (July 1958); and the veterans housing bill (February 1959).

The Congresswoman from Philadelphia favored freezing of farm price supports (March 1958) and a $1,077,827,200 public works appropriation (June 1959). She voted for both the Alaska and Hawaii statehood bills, and in the field of foreign relations favored postponement of the British debt payments in April 1957 and the Mutual Security Acts of 1957, 1958, and 1959. She approved making the Small Business Administration a permanent agency (June 1957); amendment of the Atomic Energy Act to permit freer exchange of information with allied nations (June 1958); and authorization for the construction of a cultural center in Washington (August 1958).

As chairman of the Post Office and Civil Service Committee's Subcommittee on Postal Operations, Mrs. Granahan announced in April 1959 her plans to hold a series of open hearings on the growing problem of unsolicited mail, advertising obscene photographs and movies. She declared that she might promote a bill authorizing the government to seize pornographic material at the delivery point. She was reported to have said that the Post Office Department had been "lax in halting the circulation of pornography," and to have announced that she would call Postmaster General Arthur Summerfield as a witness. "If he hasn't got the power to do it," she was quoted as saying, "let's give it to him" (New York *Sunday News,* April 12, 1959).

Later in April, Mrs. Granahan's subcommittee visited the Post Office Department and examined some of the materials which had been seized as obscene by the department. Summerfield testified at one of the first hearings that mail order pornography and obscenity is a still growing business of $500,000,000 a year. He also said that the serious increase in juvenile delinquency is partly due to "defiant barons of obscenity" (New York *Times,* April 2, 1959).

In May, Mrs. Granahan urged parents and "decent-minded citizens" to form a national campaign against the sale of "smut and filth," and said that her committee would make suggestions for possible moves to be made against obscene literature by private citizens and organizations. She said, "The peddling of smut to children is a heinous crime that must be stopped" (New York *Times,* May 19, 1959). A few days later, Dr. Clyde Taylor, public affairs secretary for the National Association of Evangelicals, testified before her subcommittee that there was evidence that Communists might be circulating obscene literature, deliberately trying "to morally sabotage American youth." Mrs. Granahan agreed that the situation called for immediate action (New York *Times,* May 23, 1959).

"Like most ladies in public life," George Dixon wrote in the Washington *Post and Times Herald* (April 16, 1957) "Representative Granahan withholds her age even from the *Congressional Directory,* but I would guess her for the middle forties." A Roman Catholic, Mrs. Granahan is a member of the Philadelphia Circle of the International Federation of Catholic Alumnae and of the Father John McGarrity Post of the Ladies of Charity. She is the vice-president of the board of the St. Francis Country House for Convalescents, and chairman of the board of governors of the Women's Democratic Club of Philadelphia. She belongs to the Catholic War Veterans and American Legion Auxiliaries, and Emergency Aid of Philadelphia. She likes to play golf for recreation.

References

N Y Sunday News p76 Ap 12 '59 por
Washington (D.C.) Post pA19 Ap 16 '57; pA13 My 18 '57
Congressional Directory, 1959
Who's Who in America, 1958-59
Who's Who of American Women, 1958-59

GRANT, HILDA KAY *See* Hilliard, Jan

GRAU, SHIRLEY ANN   July 8, 1929-
Author

Address: b. c/o Brandt & Brandt, 101 Park Ave., New York 17; h. 12 Nassau Dr., Metairie, La.

Reprinted from the *Wilson Library Bulletin* Dec. 1959.

"Southerner though she is she has no truck with Southern Gothic," said Granville Hicks of Shirley Ann Grau in the *Saturday Review*. "Neither in the stories [*The Black Prince, and other Stories*] nor in the novel [*The Hard Blue Sky*] does one find echoes of William Faulkner or Eudora Welty or any others of the distinguished writers of the Southern revival." "To one who has long since wearied of the 'Literary South' these stories [*The Black Prince*] are as welcome as a hot shower to a garbage collector," wrote Harriette Simpson Arnow, forcefully if not elegantly, in a letter to Miss Grau's publisher, Alfred A. Knopf.

Shirley Ann Grau, one of the two daughters of Adolph E. Grau and Katherine (Onions) Grau, was born in New Orleans on July 8, 1929. Her ancestry is German, Scottish, and Louisiana Creole (her two grandmothers were of mixed French and Spanish blood). A paternal grandfather who disapproved of militarism left Prussia for this country in the 1870's; the other grandfather, an Indianan, came from a family of Scottish farmers and river-boat men.

Shirley Ann attended the Booth School in Montgomery, Alabama, a city which she found to be "a wonderful place," though she had expected to be homesick. At Newcomb College (the women's college of Tulane University) in her own city of New Orleans she had "a splendid, if not intellectual time," joining no organizations and participating in no athletics, which always struck her as being very dull. After receiving her B.A. degree in 1950 with honors in English, she spent a year in graduate work at Tulane University of Louisiana in New Orleans, doing research in English literature of the Renaissance and seventeenth century. In 1955 she married James Kern Feibleman, a teacher (they have a son, Ian James).

Alfred A. Knopf published her first book, *The Black Prince, and other Stories* in 1955. Its hero, Stanley Albert Thompson, is a half-legendary Negro. Only three of the stories had previously appeared in print: one in *New World Writing* (New American Library of World Literature, 1953), another in the *New Mexico Quarterly,* and the other in the *New Yorker.*

To the *Time* reviewer, *The Black Prince* seemed "the most impressive U.S. short story debut between hard covers since J. D. Salinger's *Nine Stories*" (Little, 1953), but William Peden in the *Saturday Review* thought that "few of her stories quite measure up to the promises so feverishly proclaimed on the dust jacket."

"In all of these stories," wrote Riley Hughes in *Catholic World,* "she has caught the authentic slur of speech, the slant of shadow on a blue night, and the random, spiraling move-

SHIRLEY ANN GRAU

ment of life." The book was published by William Heinemann, Ltd., in London and S. Fischer-Verlag in Germany.

Miss Grau, who once announced that her "ambition is to write an even dozen novels," discarded her first attempt. When *The Hard Blue Sky* appeared in 1958, several reviewers suggested that she should have continued writing short stories. They also objected to an almost total absence of plot. A long book, it described the life of a community of present-day French-Spanish descendants of Louisiana pioneers "on the tiny Isle aux Chiens in the coastal curve just east of the tripartite mouth of the Mississippi" (*Library Journal*).

"This island world, alien and apart and tempered by the whims of the sea and the sky, has a somnolent fascination; the vitality and the violence of the lives it shapes are retained and reflected with a very realistic but unquestionable lyricism," said Virginia Kirkus. "If this novel lacks a compelling organization and seems at times fragmentary and discursive, it is yet a notable achievement, for its interest remains unfailing," wrote Gene Baro in the New York *Herald Tribune Book Review.*

Believing that an artist must fulfill his own standards and goals, Miss Grau does not "read reviews or even results of interviews" regarding her work. "I have seen people ruined," she has explained, "by undue attention to what is said about them and/or their books. A writer has to go his own way, and other opinions are confusing." Having "no cause and no message," she writes, "I've always thought writing was lots of fun, and I still do. It also fits beautifully with my housewifely duties, which would make a regular job quite impossible."

For enjoyment Miss Grau swims, sails, fishes, hunts, and listens to music. She whistles "constantly and off-key," plays the violin, and is especially interested in folk songs.

(Continued next page)

GRAU, SHIRLEY ANN—*Continued*

The Feiblemans have "a fair record collection, a better collection of modern painting and sculpture," to which both husband and wife are devoted. They have a winter home in Metairie, a suburb of New Orleans, and a summer place on Martha's Vineyard, Massachusetts. They entertain a steady stream of welcome guests at both places.

The writer, green-eyed and black-haired, is of medium height (five feet seven inches) and weight (125 pounds). Her church affiliation is Unitarian, and she is a Democrat.

References

Mlle 40:85 Ja '55 por

Who's Who of American Women (1958-59)

GRAUER, BEN(JAMIN FRANKLIN)

June 2, 1908- Radio and television personality

Address: b. c/o National Broadcasting Company, 30 Rockefeller Plaza, New York 20; h. 29 E. 63d St., New York 21

> NOTE: This biography supersedes the article which appeared in *Current Biography* in 1941.

For three decades, Ben Grauer, the NBC announcer and commentator, has broadcast special news events and covered international crises, political conventions, and major sporting incidents. He has narrated documentary dramas, introduced musical programs, and conducted quiz and interview shows. The National Academy of Vocal Arts has called Grauer's voice "the most authoritative in the world." A talented extemporaneous speaker, Grauer has ad-libbed for over fifty minutes on one occasion and has been known to sustain conversations on radio during emergencies. Grauer is also a bibliophile and typophile, an aspect of his life discussed by Lewis Felix White in *A Brief Account of the Between-Hours Press, Ben Grauer, Proprietor* (1952).

Benjamin Franklin Grauer was born on Staten Island, New York on June 2, 1908 to Adolph and Ida Kunstler (Goldberg) Grauer. His father was a surveyor, a civil engineer, and owner of an antique shop. The Grauer family moved to Manhattan when Ben was six, and he attended the public schools in New York City. A motion picture scout saw him when he was about seven years old, and shortly thereafter he began appearing in movies, including *The Town that Forgot God* (1920). In Broadway theatrical productions he created the role of Georgie Bassett in *Penrod* (1918), in which there appeared an ingénue named Helen Hayes; enacted the leading part of Tyltyl in Maurice Maeterlinck's *The Blue Bird* (1923), and performed in *Processional* (1925). During World War I Ben entertained military personnel and sold $1,000,000 worth of Liberty Bonds.

Ben's parents decided that his education was being neglected and in 1925 took him out of the theater world. He attended the Town-send Harris Hall High School in New York and he then enrolled at the City College of the City of New York. While in college he almost failed a course in public speaking, but then won the George Sandham Extemporaneous Speaking Prize in his senior year. He majored in English and received the bachelor's degree in 1930.

When he was graduated, Grauer, who had become a bibliophile, opened a bookshop in New York and conducted a mail-order business. This venture proved financially unsuccessful, and he returned to acting, this time on radio. He then applied for a job as an announcer at NBC and since 1930 has served on its announcing staff.

For NBC he has covered every type of news event from the 1932 Olympic Games in Los Angeles to meetings of the United Nations, including the United Nations Conference on International Organization at San Francisco in 1945.

Since 1937 Grauer has been broadcasting the events of every Presidential inauguration; since 1944 he has covered every national Democratic and Republican convention. He has served as host and moderator on quiz shows, panel discussions, musical programs, and melodramas. During World War II he was host on a radio program which gave British children who found refuge in the United States a chance to talk with their parents in England. Grauer also sold defense and war savings bonds totaling $15,000,000.

Among the important news events Ben Grauer has covered are the Lindbergh baby kidnaping case (1932), the maiden flight of the dirigible *Akron* (1933), the Paris Conference of Allied Foreign Ministers (1946), the solar eclipse in Brazil (1947), the Berlin airlift (1948), the war between Israel and the Arab states (1948), the coronation of Queen Elizabeth II of Great Britain (1953), and the opening of the Brussels World's Fair (1958). From U.N. headquarters in New York he reported on developments during the Suez Canal crisis (1956), the Hungarian revolt (1956), and the Lebanese rebellion (1958).

Ben Grauer has scored several "scoops" or "firsts" in the broadcasting industry. He interviewed the first survivor ashore when the SS *Morro Castle* burned near the coast of Asbury Park, New Jersey in 1934; he was the commentator for NBC-TV's first special event, the opening of the New York World's Fair in 1939; and he made the first on-the-scene news broadcast of the assassination of Count Folke Bernadotte in Israel in 1948.

The commentator has been a host or an announcer on many NBC radio and television programs. Among them are: *Information Please; Walter Winchell for Jergen's Lotion; Kay Kyser's College of Musical Knowledge; Living; Big Story; Citizen's Searchlight,* and the NBC Symphony Orchestra broadcasts under the late Arturo Toscanini (1940-1954).

During the summer of 1958 Ben Grauer was host on a television program called *The Reason Why.* It was a local half-hour interview show which explored in depth the reasons why certain celebrities chose their respective professional fields. Among the famous people Grauer interviewed were Alicia Markova, William Benton, Carmine G. De Sapio, Peter Ustinov, and Elsa Maxwell. He explained that his purpose was not to "badger" but to "win their confidence" in order to get a provocative interview.

In 1959 Grauer announced regularly on *Monitor* and had a Monday through Thursday five-minute radio show with his wife, interior decorator Melanie Kahane (see *C.B.*, July 1959). It was called *Decorating Wavelengths*. He also played host on *Tactic*, a series of six television programs on cancer control which were kinescoped for distribution throughout the United States.

In an article about Ben Grauer in the *American Magazine* (January 1948) Clarence Woodbury called him the "little guy who can do anything." Most of his broadcasts are spontaneous, and he prefers commenting on special events rather than straight announcing and news reporting. *Time* magazine (March 15, 1948) called him "one of the glibbest ad-libbers on the air."

When asked in an interview if television and radio commentators should express their personal views while broadcasting, Grauer replied that most of them do editorialize. He implied that the element of subjectivity is always present, both in the selection of programs and materials, and in the words used. He feels that next to books radio is the most intellectual medium of communication.

One of Ben Grauer's hobbies is printing. In recognition of his love for fine printing, his friend Lewis Felix White wrote *A Brief Account of the Between-Hours Press, Ben Grauer, Proprietor* (Privy Council Press, 1952). The book tells of the commentator's adventures with his hand printing press, his experiments with techniques, and his demonstration of the craft in January 1952 on NBC-TV's *Seeing is Believing*. When Grauer pulled the first proof (which came out perfectly) "all concerned gave a long sigh of relief." This was the first television program to demonstrate the art of hand printing. Commending Grauer's talent for printing, White has said: "Though he has produced but a few printed items, his zeal entitles him to full membership in the fellowship of printers."

An admirer of fine press books and of rare books, Grauer has collected a library of some 5,000 volumes. Among his treasures are Galileo's *Historia e dimostrazioni . . . intorno alle macchie solari* (Rome, 1613) and a collection of first editions by D. H. Lawrence that is as complete as he can make it. He also collects old playing cards, studies archaeology, and has purchased works of art and antiques during his many trips abroad. He prizes an autographed photograph of Arturo Toscanini which hangs in his living room.

On September 25, 1954 Ben Grauer married Melanie Kahane, the interior designer. They share an interest in the decorative arts. The broadcaster is five feet six inches tall and has brown eyes and dark hair. He is a wit, a raconteur, and a gourmet.

The awards which Grauer has received include: the H. P. Davis Announcers Award (1944); Silver Medal, United States Treasury;

NBC

BEN GRAUER

Alumni Service Medal, City College (1949); Civilian Service Citation, United States Army (1951); and Man of the Year Award, National Federation of Temple Brotherhoods (1955). He is a chevalier of the French Legion of Honor.

Ben Grauer belongs to the American Institute of Graphic Arts, Bibliographical Society of America, Laboratory of Anthropology, Tau Delta Phi, and Sigma Delta Chi. His clubs are the Overseas Press (he is the vice-president) and the Grolier. An independent in politics, he free-lances when elections come around. Writing in the *Saturday Review of Literature* (February 17, 1951), Bennett Cerf said: "If we must have commercials on radio and television . . . let us at least have them delivered by a man like Ben Grauer."

References

Am Mag 145:50 Ja '48 por
Newsweek 32:48 Jl 19 '48 por
Time 51:82+ Mr 15 '48
Who's Who in America, 1958-59
Who's Who in Foreign Correspondence, 1956-57
Wood, C. TV Personalities vol III (1957)

GRAUER, MRS. BEN(JAMIN FRANKLIN) *See* Kahane, Malanie

GRISWOLD, OSCAR W(OOLVERTON) Oct. 22, 1886-Oct. 5, 1959 Retired lieutenant general of the United States Army; commanded troops in the Pacific during World War II. See *Current Biography* (September) 1943.

Obituary

N Y Times p43 O 7 '59

GROSZ, GEORGE July 26, 1893-July 6, 1959 Artist; represented in world's principal museums and private collections; taught at Art Students League of New York since 1932. See *Current Biography* (April) 1942.

Obituary

N Y Times p33 Jl 7 '59

GRUEN, VICTOR (DAVID) July 18, 1903- Architect

Address: b. 135 S. Doheny Dr., Beverly Hills, Calif.; h. 321 Fordyce, West Los Angeles, Calif.; 31-33 W. 12th St., New York 11

A "practical visionary," architect Victor Gruen has tried to counteract the congestion of urban areas and the "scatteration in suburbia" with bold ideas. He is widely known for the planning of Northland, near Detroit, Michigan, which has been called "a classic in shopping center design." The senior partner of Victor Gruen Associates, with offices in six major American cities, Gruen has guided his firm in planning projects ranging in cost from $50,000 to $100,000,000. These include commercial, industrial, residential, cultural, and civic buildings, as well as master planning and urban redevelopment.

Victor David Gruenbaum, who shortened his name to Gruen during World War II, was born on July 18, 1903 in Vienna, Austria, the son of Adolf and Elizabeth Lea (Levy) Gruenbaum. His father was a lawyer.

At the end of World War I Victor Gruen became aware of the inadequate houses in which many people lived, and he "dreamed of new and better cities." As a practical step toward realizing these dreams, he entered the State Vocational School for Building located in Vienna after he had completed his studies at the Realgymnasium.

VICTOR GRUEN

In 1923 Gruen was employed by Melcher & Steiner, an architectural firm belonging to a friend of his father. He first worked as a brickmason but was soon advanced to duties in designing, supervising, and co-ordinating. At the same time he studied at Vienna's Master School for Architecture of the Academy of Fine Arts, under Professor Peter Behrens. During these years he was strongly influenced by the work of architects Adolf Loos and Le Corbusier, and on hiking trips through Austria and Germany he was much impressed by such medieval cities as Rothenburg ob der Tauber and Lübeck.

Nine years after he went to work for Melcher & Steiner, Gruen resigned and opened his own architectural office in Vienna. Together with two friends he won a prize in a public housing competition. He designed and supervised some residential and commercial structures in Austria, Germany, and Czechoslovakia. However, this was a period of economic depression and his work was largely limited to furniture design, apartment interiors, and stores.

Victor Gruen had just received his largest commission for a store building when Hitler's troops arrived in Vienna. After three "terrorizing" months during which he lost most of his friends and also his office, he obtained a visa for the United States. When he arrived with his family at his destination in July 1938, he had $8 in his pocket. He brought with him only his drafting table, his T square, and his books.

Gruen's first jobs in the United States included helping with the scenic design of two Broadway shows, work for a display company, an assignment for the Futurama building of the New York World's Fair (1939-40), and the design for his first American store, Lederer de Paris on Fifth Avenue. From small shops his commissions progressed to chain store design for Barton's Bonbonnière and Grayson-Robinson Stores, Inc., and to part of the work on the new Macy's stores in Kansas City and San Francisco. Thus, after a critical period of "much hard work, with some setbacks," Gruen had earned a reputation in the United States as a store architect.

By 1951 he had organized an architectural firm called Victor Gruen Associates. In 1958 it had five partners, thirty-two associates, and employed about 200 persons, including structural, mechanical, electrical, and civil engineers; interior and graphic designers; and specialists in traffic planning and landscaping.

In the same year Victor Gruen Associates had two production offices, in Los Angeles and Detroit, and four smaller co-ordinating offices, in New York, San Francisco, Minneapolis, and Miami. Gruen and his partners believe: "Specialization is an enemy of creative work and ... only work in the entire sphere of the man-made environment will keep us steadily in contact with all problems and will enable us to solve specific problems well."

Begun in 1952 and opened in 1954, Northland, which is probably the best known of all American shopping centers, was the first of a succession of large-scale building projects by the firm. Spreading over 160 acres just outside Detroit, the J.L. Hudson Company's Northland contains a compact cluster of some eighty stores within a pedestrian island landscaped with benches, trees, gardens, and modern sculpture. It includes an auditorium for the use of civic groups. Parking areas for 7,500 cars and a route for motor traffic are provided. The center is an example of the successful integration of architecture, art, and landscape.

Southdale, the second suburban shopping center planned by Gruen, opened on October 8, 1956, in Edina, Minnesota, seven miles from Minneapolis. This $20,000,000 center was developed by the Dayton Company on an eighty-four-acre site, with some seventy stores grouped in an enclosed garden court. Southdale introduced two new concepts: controlled temperatures throughout the whole center, inside and outside the stores, of seventy degrees, and the development of some 400 acres of surrounding land with office buildings, apartment houses, and parks to be integrated with the project.

The Gruen organization also drafted plans for other shopping centers: Eastland in the Detroit area; Bay Fair in Oakland, California; Valley Fair in San José, California; and Glendale near Indianapolis. It also prepared city planning programs for Kalamazoo, Michigan, Green Bay, Wisconsin, and St. Petersburg, Florida. It designed the regional health center near Southdale; the Tishman office buildings; the Wilshire Building, Civic Center Parking Garage, Pacoima Housing Project, and Palos Verdes Development in Los Angeles; and the Charles River Park Urban Redevelopment in Boston, Massachusetts.

Commissioned by private enterprise, Gruen's revitalization plan for Fort Worth, Texas was proposed in March 1956. It was a bold scheme to combat traffic congestion in 300 acres of downtown Fort Worth and convert streets into beautiful pedestrian malls. It was temporarily shelved in mid-1958 because of lack of support, but has inspired similar plans for other cities.

In the Fort Worth plan Gruen had applied the principles he first developed for his shopping centers. He believes that the business districts of large cities should be rebuilt along the original concepts of the city as a market place. Once people arrive within the market place they should walk—not ride—and shops should be arranged in logical patterns. (See *Harvard Business Review,* November and December, 1954.)

The architect has promoted his ideas in many speeches and in many articles for professional and consumer magazines. *How to Live with Your Architect* (Store Modernization Institute), a pamphlet by Gruen, appeared in 1949, and his book, *New Shopping Towns, U.S.A., The Planning of Shopping Centers* (Reinhold), is scheduled for publication in 1960.

Victor Gruen belongs to the American Institute of Architects (A.I.A.), Architectural League of New York, Illuminating Engineering Society, Urban Land Institute, Detroit Eco-

nomic Club, Lambda Alpha, and other professional groups. He is a director of the Citizens' Housing and Planning Council of New York, Inc., and an honorary trustee of Harvard University Graduate School of Business Administration.

He has received numerous awards and honors from the A.I.A., *Progressive Architecture, Institutions Magazine,* the Store Modernization Institute, and the Avenue of the Americas Association, Inc. His work has been exhibited at the National Gallery, Washington, D.C.; the Brussels World's Fair of 1958; the Eighth Pan-American Congress of Architects in Mexico City; and leading museums of the United States, Canada, and Australia.

The architect is a busy and restless man. He is five feet six inches in height and has green eyes and brown hair. On September 28, 1951 he was married to Lazette McCormick Van Houten, a journalist. He has two children by a former marriage; they are Michael Stephen and Margaret. Gruen became a United States citizen in 1943.

Viewing the future with optimism and faith, Gruen believes that city planners will make the "long overdue adjustment of the urban pattern to the facts of modern technology" and that architects will provide an order in which both the automobile and human beings will have an adequate habitat.

References

American Architects Directory, 1956
Who's Who in America, 1958-59

GUERRERO, JOSÉ GUSTAVO June 26, 1876-Oct. 27, 1958 International jurist; member of Permanent Court of International Justice and later of International Court of Justice (president in 1946). See *Current Biography* (January) 1947.

Obituary

N Y Times p35 O 28 '58

GUEST, EDGAR A(LBERT) Aug. 20, 1881-Aug. 5, 1959 Writer of verse; his work was syndicated in some 300 American newspapers; wrote many volumes of inspirational verse that eulogized the simple and folksy virtues. See *Current Biography* (September) 1941.

Obituary

N Y Times p27 Ag 6 '59

GUFFEY, JOSEPH F. Dec. 29, 1875-Mar. 6, 1959 Former Democratic Senator from Pennsylvania (1935-47); supported New Deal legislation and other liberal measures. See *Current Biography* (March) 1944.

Obituary

N Y Times p21 Mr 7 '59

GUNDERSEN, GUNNAR Apr. 6, 1897-
Physician; organization official

Address: b. 1836 South Ave., La Crosse, Wis.;
h. R.F.D. 2 La Crosse, Wis.

Throughout almost forty years of practice as
a physician and surgeon, Dr. Gunnar Gundersen
has been very much concerned with state and
national medical affairs and has participated in
the work of a number of professional organizations. He was installed in June 1958 as the
112th president of the 170,000-member American Medical Association, to serve for one year.
He will be succeeded by president-elect Louis
M. Orr of Orlando, Florida. In his home city
of La Crosse, Wisconsin, Dr. Gundersen helps
direct the Gundersen Clinic and the Adolf
Gundersen Medical Foundation.

The eldest son of a Norwegian surgeon who
moved to the United States in 1891, Gunnar
Gundersen was born to Dr. Adolf and Helga
(Isakaetre) Gundersen on April 6, 1897 in
La Crosse, Wisconsin, where his father later
established the Gundersen Clinic. Since the
death of Dr. Adolf Gundersen in 1938 this
clinic has been operated by four of his sons,
Drs. Gunnar, Sigurd Bjarne, Alf Helge, and
Thorolf Egil Gundersen. Two other sons, Drs.
Trygve and Sven Martin Gundersen, practise
in Boston, Massachusetts and Hanover, New
Hampshire, respectively.

Gunnar Gundersen, who "never had any other
idea" than to enter his father's profession, received his preparatory school education in Oslo,
Norway. He returned to the United States to
attend the University of Wisconsin in Madison,
where he was graduated with the B.S. degree
in 1917. He received his M.D. degree from the
College of Physicians and Surgeons at Columbia University in 1920.

Fabian Bachrach
DR. GUNNAR GUNDERSEN

After a two-year internship at the Lutheran
Hospital in La Crosse, he began private practice as an associate of his father. Dr. Gunnar
Gundersen is still an attending surgeon at
the Lutheran Hospital. In 1927 the Gundersen
Clinic was established. Operated in conjunction
with the Lutheran Hospital next door, the clinic
today handles from 3,000 to 4,000 patients a
year.

In memory of their father, the Gundersen
brothers established the Adolf Gundersen Medical Foundation in 1945. "This nonprofit organization grants fellowships to young doctors for
advanced study in specialized fields, provides
facilities and modern equipment for such studies, conducts investigations into many unsolved
problems of medicine and surgery, and provides
free diagnostic services to indigents with complex medical problems."

Dr. Gundersen was named by President Harry
S. Truman on December 29, 1951 to a fifteen-
member commission headed by the Chicago
orthopedic surgeon Dr. Paul B. Magnuson.
Members were charged to study the nation's
total health needs and to recommend ways for
meeting them. The commission included not only
members of the medical profession, but also
representatives of labor unions and other laymen. A day later Dr. Gundersen asked that his
name be removed because of his belief that the
commission was designed "as an instrument of
practical politics to relieve President Truman
from an embarrassing position as an unsuccessful advocate of compulsory health insurance"
(New York *Times,* December 31, 1951).

In April 1952, however, Dr. Gundersen appeared before the commission as "a private
physician speaking for group medical practice"
and termed panel discussions such as the commission was holding, "the only way to get
at" the nation's needs. At the same time he told
reporters that he "headed the Gundersen Clinic
of twenty physicians operating in the free
enterprise system" and "believed in that type of
service to the public."

The American College of Surgeons announced in 1952 that Dr. Gundersen was chairman of a new joint commission on hospital
accreditation formed to prepare the 1952 list of
approved hospitals. The commission was composed of representatives of a number of American and Canadian medical associations. In 1953
he took his place on the council of the World
Medical Association, which has members in
fifty-three countries. (For its publication he
wrote, during the next two years, articles entitled "Control of Advertising in Medical Publications" and "Medical Aspects of Social Security." He also contributed "The Influence of
Norwegian Medicine in the United States" to a
Norwegian publication.)

The Wisconsin physician became chairman in
1955 of the American Medical Association's
board of trustees, of which he had been a member since 1948. The association, which has its
headquarters at 535 N. Dearborn St. in Chicago, elects its president one year in advance
of his installation for a one-year term of office.
At the association's annual convention in New

York City in June 1957 when Dr. David B. Allman of Atlantic City, New Jersey, took office as president, Dr. Gundersen was named président-elect.

As president-elect he visited the Soviet Union and on his return was interviewed for the May 1958 number of *Today's Health,* an A.M.A. publication. He found no evidence he said, that the Russians were "ahead of us in the medical race," and felt that the equipment of their hospitals and laboratories was "not up to our standards." On the other hand, he stated, "A good physician in Russia is as good as a physician in this country," and it was Dr. Gundersen's belief that the Russians concur in American views on sharing medical knowledge.

Shortly before his installation at San Francisco on June 24, 1958, as president of the American Medical Association, Dr. Gundersen told an interviewer for a doctors' publication that he "agreed the country was moving in the direction of prepaid group practice and that 'up to a point' he considered the trend 'a good thing'" (reported by Helen Dudar, New York *Post Magazine,* June 23, 1958). At the convention a joint committee of the A.M.A. and the American Bar Association recommended the setting up in Washington, D.C. of a small experimental clinic to supply free drugs on a controlled basis to drug addicts.

In an address delivered late in October, Dr. Gundersen urged physicians and insurance men to join forces "to ward off any government inroads into the free enterprise system" of insurance and medicine. Speaking before the National Gerontological Society early in November, he called for an end to compulsory retirement plans. In Chicago later in the month he suggested that mental illness may be a communicable disease somewhat like tuberculosis. "We know," he told the Conference of Mental Health Representatives, "that healthy ideas can be communicated to persons in the mass, and we must therefore suspect that sick ideas can be similarly communicated."

Other professional organizations in which Gundersen has been active are the Wisconsin State Medical Society, American Board of Surgery, American College of Surgeons, International College of Surgeons, and American Public Health Association. He is a past president of the Wisconsin State Board of Health (1943-49) and a former regent of the University of Wisconsin (1931-37). He has been a member of the board of directors of the La Crosse Trust Company since 1942.

Gunnar Gundersen and Mary Baldwin were married on June 23, 1923 and have two sons, a daughter, and several grandchildren. The elder son, Gunnar Adolf, is a doctor and radiologist associated with the Gundersen Clinic; the younger, Cameron B., is a captain in the Air Force Medical Corps. The daughter, Mary, is the wife of F. M. Bugge, an Oslo lawyer. The "big, easy-mannered" Wisconsin physician is six feet tall and weighs around 190 pounds. Vegetable gardening occupies much of his spare time, and he is also interested in reforestation projects.

References

J Am Med Assn 164:876+ Je 22 '57 por
Los Angeles Times I p8 Jl 25 '58 por
American Medical Directory, 1958
Directory of Medical Specialists (1957)
Who's Important in Medicine (1952)
Who's Who in America, 1958-59
World Biography (1954)

GWENN, EDMUND Sept. 26, 1875-Sept. 6, 1959 Actor; performed on London and New York stages; made many Hollywood films; won 1948 Academy Award as best supporting actor. See *Current Biography* (September) 1943.

Obituary

N Y Times p15 S 7 '59

HALSEY, WILLIAM F(REDERICK), JR. Oct. 30, 1882-Aug. 16, 1959 United States Navy Fleet Admiral (ret.); commander of Navy forces in South Pacific (1942-44); commander of Third Fleet (1944-45); president of International Telecommunications Laboratories (1951-57). See *Current Biography* (December) 1942.

Obituary

N Y Times p1+ Ag 17 '59

HANSBERRY, LORRAINE May 19, 1930-
Playwright

Address: b. Raisin in the Sun Co., 157 W. 57th St., New York 19; h. 337 Bleecker St., New York 14

When Lorraine Hansberry's *A Raisin in the Sun* opened at the Barrymore Theatre in New York on March 11, 1959, it represented several important "firsts" as a landmark in American drama. It was the first play written by a Negro woman to be produced on Broadway, the first to be presented by its producers, and the first to be directed by a Negro in over half a century. On April 7, 1959 the play became the first written by a Negro to receive the New York Drama Critics Circle Award, winning over entries by Tennessee Williams, Eugene O'Neill, and Archibald MacLeish. In *A Raisin in the Sun* Sidney Poitier made his first attempt at success as a star on Broadway.

Heralded as a young American playwright of major talent, Lorraine Hansberry had been writing since she was a teen-ager, but had never gotten around to getting her short stories or plays published or produced. In her work she is trying to break down the racial stereotype of the Negro (which she considers "bad art") by writing plays about people who "happen to be Negroes" rather than "Negro plays." After the triumphal opening of *A Raisin in the Sun,* Miss Hansberry said: "I like to think—I hope—that it will now be easier for other Negroes." In June 1959 the *Variety* poll of New York drama critics named Miss Hansberry the "most promising playwright" of the season.

(Continued next page)

HANSBERRY, LORRAINE—*Continued*

Lorraine Hansberry was born in Chicago, Illinois on May 19, 1930, the youngest daughter of Carl Augustus Hansberry and Nannie (Perry) Hansberry. Her father, a prosperous real estate broker, founded one of the first banks for Negroes in Chicago. She has two brothers, Carl, Jr., and Perry, and a sister, Mamie.

"My father had fought a very famous civil-rights case on restricted covenants," Miss Hansberry told an interviewer for the *New Yorker* (May 9, 1959), "which he fought all the way up to the Supreme Court, and which he won after the expenditure of a great deal of money and emotional strength." Her father died in Mexico in 1945, where he was making preparations to move his family. "Daddy felt he still didn't have his freedom in this country. . . . One of the reasons I feel so free is that I feel I belong to a world majority, and a very assertive one."

Although her parents could have afforded to send her to private schools, Miss Hansberry attended, she said, mostly "Jim Crow schools, on the South Side of Chicago, which meant half-day schools. . ." She went to three grade schools, then Englewood High School where she was graduated in 1948. While in high school, Miss Hansberry succumbed to the "theater magic" of *The Tempest, Othello, Dark of the Moon,* and other plays. "I was intrigued by the theatre," she has said. "Mine was the same old story—sort of hanging around little acting groups, and developing the feeling that the theatre embraces everything I like all at one time."

Miss Hansberry attended the University of Wisconsin for two years, where she took a course in stage design and saw the plays of Strindberg and Ibsen for the first time. Later, when she came around to reading Sean O'Casey's work, she agreed with him that real drama "has to do with emotional involvement and achieving the emotional transformation of people on the stage." She has often paid tribute to O'Casey for his ability to exhibit the nobility and complexity of mankind.

After having studied painting at the Art Institute of Chicago, Roosevelt College, and Guadalajara, Mexico, Miss Hansberry decided she had no talent, and moved to New York City in 1950. She wrote three plays (which she never finished) and some short stories. She studied for a short time at the New School for Social Research, working on and off as clerk in a department store, tag girl in a fur shop, and aide to a theatrical producer. She worked from time to time as waitress, hostess, and cashier in a restaurant in Greenwich Village run by the family of Robert Nemiroff, the music publisher and song writer. (In 1953 she married Mr. Nemiroff.)

One night in the fall of 1957, Lorraine Hansberry and her husband read a scene from her first version of *A Raisin in the Sun* to some friends assembled for a small dinner party at their home. Among them was Philip Rose, a music publisher. "We stayed up very late, reading and arguing about the play," she recalls, "and suddenly I realized that it had taken on a life of its own."

It took over a year to get enough money to put the play into rehearsal; most of the backing came in small amounts from many "angels." Philip Rose and David J. Cogan, a tax consultant, became co-producers. They assigned the leading role to Sidney Poitier, an old friend of Miss Hansberry, and chose Lloyd Richards, a young Negro actor and director, to direct the play. Since 1907, when Jesse Shipp directed *Abyssinia,* no Negro had directed a Broadway production. *A Raisin in the Sun* drew high critical praise in its New Haven, Philadelphia, and Chicago tryouts.

A *Variety* critic (January 28, 1959), commenting on the New Haven try-out, predicted that the play would "ripen into substantial Broadway tenancy. There is just enough down-to-earth humor to lighten the occasionally heavy pressure." When the play opened at the Ethel Barrymore Theatre, Walter Kerr in the New York *Herald Tribune* called it "an impressive first play, beautifully acted . . . relieving and wonderfully caustic comedy."

Brooks Atkinson in the New York *Times* (March 12, 1959) admired the play because Miss Hansberry discussed serious problems without writing a thesis drama. "She has told the inner as well as the outer truth about a Negro family in Chicago," Atkinson wrote. "The play has vigor as well as veracity and is likely to destroy the complacency of anyone who sees it."

"The thing I tried to show," Miss Hansberry explained to Ted Poston of the New York *Post* (March 22, 1959), "was the many gradations in even one Negro family, the clash of the old and the new, but most of all the unbelievable courage of the Negro people." The title of the play comes from Langston Hughes's poem, "Harlem": "What happens to a dream deferred,/Does it dry up like a raisin in the sun,/Does it fester like a sore and then run . . . or/Does it explode?"

Lorraine Hansberry is five feet four inches tall, weighs 118 pounds, and has dark-brown tousled hair. An interviewer for the *New Yorker*'s "Talk of the Town" (May 9, 1959) was impressed by her "dark brown eyes, so dark and so deep that you get lost in them," and went on to characterize her as a "relaxed, soft-voiced young lady with an intelligent and pretty face."

Television viewers have seen Miss Hansberry on David Susskind's program, *Open End,* and on Irving Kupcinet's program, *At Random,* where she carried on a brisk discussion with Otto Preminger, producer of the motion-picture version of *Porgy and Bess.* She told Preminger that she deplored *Porgy and Bess* as being "stereotyped" and "bad art." "We've had great wounds from good intentions," she said. "Even the most sympathetic novel for the Negro . . . happens to have been built around the most offensive character in American literature—who is Uncle Tom. That doesn't mean we Negroes don't understand Harriet Beecher Stowe's motives."

On June 20, 1953 Lorraine Hansberry married Robert Nemiroff. They live in a book-lined Greenwich Village walkup apartment above Joe's Hand Laundry with Spice, who is "sort of a collie." Miss Hansberry's main form of relaxation is to invite friends in for long conversations, with movie and play-going as close competitors. Both she and her husband enjoy skiing and ping-pong. She does her own housework and likes to cook.

William Shakespeare and Sean O'Casey rank high among Miss Hansberry's intellectual idols. Since the success of her first play she has begun work on the book for a modern opera based on the life of Toussaint L'Ouverture, the Negro slave who liberated Haiti from the France of Napoleon. As for the reason why so many Negro writers of the present day are young, she says: "Maybe because we have so much to say, we start earlier."

References

Cue 28 :20 F 28 '59 por
N Y Post Mag p2 Mr 22 '59 por
N Y Times II p3 Mr 8 '59; p37 Ap
   9 '59 por
New Yorker 35 :33 My 9 '59

Louise Barker, Chicago

REV. DR. WALTER HARRELSON

HARRELSON, WALTER (JOSEPH), REV. DR. Nov. 28, 1919- Clergyman; educator

Address: b. University of Chicago, Chicago 37, Ill.; h. 5321 S. Greenwood Ave., Chicago 15, Ill.

In keeping with the Baptist tradition that "the Church's ministry must be a learned ministry," the Divinity School of the University of Chicago has been training men and women of all Protestant denominations for the ministry since 1890. In 1955 the Reverend Dr. Walter Harrelson, clergyman, Biblical scholar, educator, and author, became dean of the school, succeeding the Reverend William N. Hawley. Harrelson, who was ordained in the Baptist ministry, had been an instructor at Andover Newton Theological School in Newton Center, Massachusetts.

Walter Joseph Harrelson was born on November 28, 1919 in Winnabow, North Carolina to Isham Danvis and Mae (Rich) Harrelson. His father was a local merchant and a man of broad sympathies and human understanding who took an active interest in the movement to improve race relationships in his community. Harrelson is one of four brothers and four sisters, all reared on a farm in Winnabow. He attended grammar school there and Bolivia High School in a nearby town. In high school he played basketball and completed his studies in 1935.

Several years after graduation he attended Mars Hill College in North Carolina for a year and a half. His education was interrupted by service in the supply branch of the United States Navy (1941-45). He entered with the rank of storekeeper, 3d class, and was discharged as a chief storekeeper. Thereupon, he became a student at the University of North Carolina in Chapel Hill. For his outstanding

academic work, he won honors in his major subject, philosophy, received a Phi Beta Kappa key, and was an instructor in philosophy in his last year. For relaxation, he participated in Y.M.C.A. activities and sang in the choir. He earned the B.A. degree in 1947.

At Union Theological Seminary in New York from 1947 to 1950, Harrelson pursued graduate study in the Old Testament and was awarded a traveling fellowship in 1949. He received the B.D. degree *summa cum laude* in 1949 and the Th.D. degree in 1953. His dissertation was an analysis of the history and importance of the ancient city of Shechem. For his postdoctoral work he attended the University of Basel in Switzerland as an exchange fellow (1950-51) and Harvard University (1951-53). Dr. Harrelson credits two of his professors with having encouraged him to become a theological educator: Helmut Kuhn of the University of Munich and James Muilenburg of Union Theological Seminary.

Dr. Harrelson was ordained as a Baptist minister in 1949, following eighteen months of work as a student minister in the slum areas embraced by the East Harlem Protestant Parish in New York City. At the same time that he tried to bring the Christian faith to its inhabitants he made every effort to improve the deplorable conditions in which they lived.

Beginning his career in education in 1951, Harrelson was appointed an instructor in the Old Testament at Andover Newton Theological School in Newton Center, Massachusetts. He remained at this post until 1955, when he became associate professor and dean of the Divinity School at the University of Chicago. Harrelson succeeded Dean William N. Hawley.

The Divinity School was originally founded in 1866 as the Baptist Seminary; in 1890, after having assumed the name of the Baptist Union Theological Seminary, it became the Divinity School of the newly incorporated University

HARRELSON, WALTER, REV. DR.—
Continued

of Chicago. Its leaders believe that only in organic relationship to a university engaged in general education and following the disciplines of advanced study can Baptist energies be oriented to the dynamics of American society.

The Divinity School is now one of the four parts of the Federated Theological Faculty of the University of Chicago. During the 1920's three denominations established centers of learning adjacent to the university: the Chicago Theological Seminary (Congregational), the Disciples Divinity House (Disciples of Christ), and the Meadville Theological School (Unitarian). After fifteen years of co-operation, the four theological institutions became formally affiliated in 1943 as the Federated Theological Faculty of the University of Chicago. It offers a single curriculum and a single unified program of study under one faculty. However, each school retains independence over its financial matters, student body, and relations with its church constituency. The Divinity School is dedicated to educating and training men and women for the pastoral ministries, as well as for the academic ministries.

Dr. Harrelson has written *I Met a Man Named Jesus* (1957) and *The Family Studies the Old Testament* (1958), both issued by the Pilgrim Press. *The Prophetic Tradition* is being prepared for publication by Doubleday & Company. In explaining the purpose of this book, Dr. Harrelson has stated: "I have attempted to re-examine certain facts. The Prophets of Israel were mysterious figures in their own right. The accepted analogies of Christian social belief no longer stand up." Harrelson has also contributed to the *Encyclopædia Britannica*, *Encyclopedia Americana*, Biblical dictionaries, and various religous journals.

On the lecture platform Dr. Harrelson delivered a series of addresses on the Book of Acts at the Seattle convention of the American Baptists and spoke on the Bible at the North American Conference on Faith and Order, held at Oberlin, Ohio in 1957. He was Clark Lecturer at Pomona College, Claremont, California in March 1959.

Dr. Harrelson has long been active in national Baptist work as well as ecumenical affairs. He is also a member of two special commissions of the Commission on Faith and Order of the World Council of Churches, the Society of Biblical Literature and Exegesis, American Schools of Oriental Research, Biblical Colloquium, Society for Theological Discussion, National Council on Religion in Higher Education, and the Chicago Society for Biblical Research. He was a fellow of the National Council on Religion in Higher Education (1949) and the American Council of Learned Societies (1950-51).

Dr. Walter Harrelson was married to Idella Aydlett on September 20, 1942. They have three children: Marianne, David Aydlett, and Robert Joseph. Harrelson is five feet eleven inches tall, weighs 185 pounds, and has brown hair and gray eyes. His hobbies are bridge and bowling. He is a Democrat.

References

Who's Who in America, 1958-59
Who's Who in American Education, 1957-58

HARRIS, MARK Nov. 19, 1922- Author; educator

Address: b. c/o San Francisco State College, San Francisco, Calif.; h. 4606 19th St., San Francisco 14, Calif.

Reprinted from the *Wilson Library Bulletin* June 1959.

"I am a storyteller," says Mark Harris, who has written novels about soldiers and ballplayers, and an impressionistic biography of the poet Vachel Lindsay, "not a sociologist or linguist or psychologist. I do not educate or reform. When I am writing my novels I leave my morality in the other room. . . . I do not think I am of those writers who, *Life* says, 'feel surrounded by sinister, hostile forces, even a Philistine conspiracy to control their thoughts.' My books have regularly been published by capitalists and read by Philistines, and one of them has even been beamed to the nation on television at considerable expense, by the United States Steel Corporation."

The family of Mark Harris originated in middle Europe; his "grandparents on both sides slugged things out in lower Manhattan." He was born in Mount Vernon, New York on November 19, 1922, the son of Carlyle Finkelstein, a lawyer, and Ruth (Klausner) Finkelstein. A sister, Martha, now lives in Minneapolis, and a brother, Henry, in New York City.

After graduating in 1940 from A. B. Davis High School in Mount Vernon, Mark Harris did a hitch in the Army (1943-44). He at-

Mike Blass

MARK HARRIS

tended Clemson Agricultural College in South Carolina, the University of New Mexico in Albuquerque, and the University of Denver, where he received his B.A. degree and a Phi Beta Kappa key. He also took an M.A. degree in English at Denver. He has worked as a newspaper reporter in New York, St. Louis, and Albuquerque. The University of Minnesota granted Harris his Ph.D. degree in American studies for a dissertation titled "Randolph Bourne: a Study in Immiscibility," and he taught at the university from 1951 to 1954, when he moved to San Francisco State College. There he is an assistant professor in the language arts division.

Like the subject of his dissertation, Randolph Bourne, Mark Harris is immiscible—he doesn't mix well. At one time he wanted to be so famous that people would send him questionnaires; now, when he does receive them, he does not like to fill them out. Conversation he finds very difficult. "There is nothing I can say which will explain myself," he says. "To some extent I have said what I know in my books." He contends that the kind of writing he likes to do is economical and subtle. "The more economical and the more subtle one becomes, the fewer people there are to talk to." The books, therefore, are, to Harris, the thing.

Trumpet to the World (Reynal, 1946) was written in South Carolina and Georgia. It is the story of a young Negro who marries a well-to-do white girl. Hodding Carter (New York *Herald Tribune Weekly Book Review*) wrote of this that "in the field of protest literature, Mr. Harris's compact, sympathetic, but essentially shadowy tale is notable principally for its easy, reportorially clear and restrained narration."

The *United States Quarterly Book Review* called *City of Discontent* (Bobbs, 1952) "interpretive, and to quite an extent fictional. [This] biography of Vachel Lindsay does not appraise the man, it fashions his likeness. . . . The reader will witness through this bard and mountebank, this troubadour and sponger, this wild and adolescent evangelist what it costs to crusade against Mammon."

The Southpaw (Bobbs, 1953) is the first of the baseball novels about Henry W. Wiggen, the young pitcher on the New York Mammoths team. Harry Sylvester in the New York *Times Book Review* called it "a distinguished and unusual book . . . badly flawed by Mr. Harris' opinions on the war in Korea."

Bang the Drum Slowly (Knopf, 1956), is narrated by Wiggen. Robin Gottlieb in the New York *Herald Tribune Book Review* thought it "more than just another novel about baseball. It is about friendship, about the lives of a group of men as one by one they learn that a teammate is dying." Wiggen fans were lukewarm about *A Ticket for a Seamstitch* (Knopf, 1957). William Hogan wrote in San Francisco *Chronicle* that "the story about a seamstress from out West who catches up with her idols, the Mammoths, might have been written as a television script."

Something About a Soldier (Macmillan, 1957), another short novel, on the other hand, seemed to Hogan "a beguiling little work of art. In it, Harris proves again he is one of the most imaginative and talented young novelists in America." The soldier Pvt. Jacob Epp (*né* Epstein) becomes a conscientious objector. J. P. Sisk in *Commonweal* found it "full of humor, sympathy and a relish of language."

The photograph of Harris shows a compactly built (135-pound), young man with hazel eyes behind glasses, and brown hair coming to a widow's peak on his forehead. He is five feet eight inches tall, and is a Democrat. He married Josephine Horen on March 17, 1946. The Harrises have a daughter, Hester Jill, and son, Anthony Wynn. His latest novel, *Wake Up, Stupid,* a satire in the form of correspondence, was published by Knopf in 1959 as a paperback original.

Reference

Who's Who in America (sup Ag '46)

HART, PHILIP A(LOYSIUS) Dec. 10, 1912- United States Senator from Michigan; lawyer

Address: b. Senate Office Bldg., Washington 25, D.C.; h. 2812 Calvert St., N.W., Washington, D.C.; Lansing, Mich.

On election day in 1958 Philip A. Hart, a Democrat, won a resounding victory over the Republican incumbent, Charles E. Potter, as United States Senator from Michigan. Hart, a political protégé of Governor G. Mennen ("Soapy") Williams of Michigan, had served for two terms as his state's Lieutenant Governor. An attorney by profession, he was a member of a Detroit law firm and was United States District Attorney for the Eastern District of Michigan. Hart supports foreign aid programs, favors tax relief to those with low incomes, and opposes political censorship of art.

Philip Aloysius Hart, Jr., was born in Bryn Mawr, Pennsylvania on December 10, 1912 to Philip Aloysius and Ann (Clyde) Hart. His grandfather was an Irish immigrant, and his father was president of a Bryn Mawr bank. Philip studied at Waldron Academy and West Philadelphia Catholic High School. He got his first taste of politics when he attended the 1924 Democratic National Convention with his father.

At Georgetown University Hart was president of the student body and earned the B.A. degree *cum laude* in 1934. He continued his education at the University of Michigan Law School, where one of his fellow students and friends was to become his political mentor, the present Democratic governor of Michigan, G. Mennen Williams. Hart received his J.D. degree in 1937.

Admitted to the Michigan bar in 1938, Hart began his legal career at that time as an associate in the Detroit firm of Beaumont, Smith & Harris. Three years later he was commissioned a second lieutenant in the United States Army and was assigned to the 4th Infantry Division. During the D-Day invasion of Normandy, on June 6, 1944, his right arm was wounded. In

Fabian Bachrach

PHILIP A. HART

December Hart rejoined his division and was discharged in 1946 with the rank of lieutenant colonel. He was decorated with the Bronze Star with clusters, Invasion Arrowhead, Purple Heart, and French Croix de Guerre.

When he returned to Detroit in 1946 he entered the general law practice of Monaghan, Hart & Crawmer. He stayed with this firm until 1949 when he received his first political appointment as Michigan's corporation securities commissioner. His duties included the approving of stock issues of corporations in the state, licensing real estate brokers and builders, and collecting real estate taxes.

After two years as corporation securities commissioner he was appointed federal director of the Michigan Office of Price Stabilization. For his execution of the price control program he was named Outstanding Federal Administrator for the Year 1952 by the Federal Business Association. He was then appointed in 1952 United States District Attorney for the Eastern District of Michigan. In this post he gained some fame when six Michigan Communist leaders were indicted on September 22, 1953 for conspiracy to teach or advocate violent overthrow of the United States government. The six were convicted on February 16, 1954.

In 1953 Hart became the legal adviser to Governor G. Mennen Williams, and the following year he was elected Lieutenant Governor after he won the Democratic primary by a 5 to 1 margin. His re-election in 1956 made him the first Democrat to serve two terms as Lieutenant Governor.

A large private income enabled Hart to fulfill a campaign pledge to devote full time to this post which until then had been a part-time position. As Lieutenant Governor he served as president of the Senate, Acting Governor during the absence of the Governor, and as a member of the state administrative board, which supervised the activities of all the state agencies.

On November 4, 1958 Hart was elected to the United States Senate for a six-year term, defeating Charles E. Potter. His plurality of 170,003 votes exceeded that of Governor Williams, who was re-elected to an unprecedented sixth term. Hart's candidacy had been supported by labor unions. During his campaign he had visited many parts of the state in a helicopter piloted by his wife.

Several weeks after his election Hart stated that the most important tasks confronting Congress are to build an America that is strong in the eyes of the world, appealing in the eyes of the world, and one which achieves the aspirations of Americans here at home (*United States News & World Report,* December 26, 1958).

Insisting that "equal opportunities for employment, for education, and for voting are basic premises in the picture that America tells the world we represent," Hart feels that everything possible should be done by the federal government to "eliminate discrimination and insure a vote to all our citizens."

Foreign aid, he believes, is "one of the major devices that is available to us to contest with the Soviets for the emerging half of the world." Taxes, Hart has pointed out, cannot be substantially cut, but the national legislature can eliminate "as many inequities in the tax structure" as possible and "lighten the burden for those least able to pay." Hart pledged support for the Kennedy labor reform bill, but believes that legislation must prevent corrupt practices by the "tempter as well as the tempted" (New York *Times,* November 23, 1958).

After taking his seat in the Senate, Hart was assigned to the Committee on Agriculture and Forestry and the Committee on Judiciary. He was also named to a three-member Judiciary subcommittee charged with undertaking a study of the administrative practices of departments and agencies of the federal government. In April 1959 Hart was one of twelve Senators appointed to a special committee to study the nation's water supply.

In his first year in the Senate Hart introduced measures which would give states financial assistance for school construction; authorize temporary unemployment benefits for individuals who have exhausted their benefit rights and for those who are not eligible; and which would eliminate the thirty-acre ceiling on wheat grown for the farmer's own use.

When controversy arose over the selection of paintings to be displayed at the American National Exhibition in Moscow in the summer of 1959, Senator Hart took a firm stand against the judgment of art by government. The show was assailed because it included the works of artists who have "records of affiliations with Communist fronts and causes." Hart declared: "I believe that it is the Soviet Union which has lost face by attempting political censorship of its artists. We do not want to get ourselves into that situation. There are a great many people in the world who think one can judge a civilization and the soul of a people more clearly by looking at its painting and sculpture than by counting its plumbing and automobiles. The sooner we understand that fact the better it will be for us" (New York *Times,* June 14, 1959).

On roll call votes in 1959 Senator Hart supported the housing bill (February); the appropriation of $465,000,000 for airport construction (February); a grant of $389,500,000 for redevelopment of economically depressed areas (March); extension of some provisions of the Temporary Unemployment Compensation Act (March); continuation of the draft (March); Hawaii statehood (March); increasing the United States subscription to the International Monetary Fund and the International Bank for Reconstruction and Development (March); the Kennedy labor bill (April); and authorizing $485,300,000 for the National Aeronautics and Space Administration (June).

Philip A. Hart married Jane Cameron Briggs, daughter of the late Walter O. Briggs, a leading Detroit industrialist and owner of the Tigers, on June 19, 1943. They have four daughters, Ann Clyde, Jane Cameron, Mary Catherine, and Laura Elizabeth, and four sons, Walter Briggs, James Cox, Michael Patrick, and Clyde William. The Senator is a former vice-president and director of the Detroit Baseball Company (Tigers) and a former director of the Detroit Lions Football Company.

From 1950 to 1958 Hart was the Michigan chairman of the American Christian Palestine Committee which aims to further the development of Israel as a state. Hart has made generous contributions to that country, which has named a forest in his honor. He served as a director of the Boys Republic of Farmington, Michigan and Bosco House of Detroit, both Catholic homes for delinquent boys, and as a director of the Urban League of Pontiac, Michigan. He is a trustee and past president (1953) of the Michigan State Bar Foundation.

Senator Hart received the Citation Award from the Disabled Veterans of Michigan and a Citizen of the Year award from the Jewish War Veterans of Michigan. He is a member of the American Judicature Society; American Society of International Law; Michigan State, Ingham County, Oakland County, and Detroit bar associations; Phi Delta Phi legal fraternity; and Detroit Committee on Foreign Relations. Hart is also an Eagle, Elk, Moose, Knight of Columbus, American Legionnaire, Veteran of Foreign Wars, AMVET, Disabled War Veteran, and Catholic War Veteran. He is an adherent of the Roman Catholic Church. In his free time he enjoys reading.

References

New Repub 139:7+ O 27 '58
N Y Times p24 N 6 '58
Congressional Directory (1959)
Who's Who in America, 1958-59

HARTFORD, (GEORGE) HUNTINGTON, 2D Apr. 18, 1911- Businessman; patron of the arts
Address: b. 420 Lexington Ave., New York 17; h. 1 Beekman Place, New York, 22

When Huntington Hartford 2d decided that much modern art was too extreme, he characteristically took action. One of the results is a new art gallery which will be built in New York City. As an heir to the Great Atlantic and Pacific Tea Company (A & P) fortune, he has not been hindered by lack of funds for this project, nor for any of the other business and artistic ventures which have caught his interest.

Although sometimes erroneously called "the 3d," he is the only Hartford to be named after the founder of the A & P chain. He was born George Huntington Hartford 2d on April 18, 1911, in New York City, the son of Edward V. and Henrietta (Guerard) Hartford. He has one sister, Josephine. His father, who did not take an active part in the A & P management, accumulated a personal fortune as an inventor.

On the death of his grandfather, the boy received 10 per cent of the chain store firm's stock (all of which was then within the Hartford family) in trust. In addition, much of his father's stock and personal fortune reverted to him after his mother's death in 1948. When A & P moved to place its stock on the market in 1958, his share was estimated at $95,000,000. His fortune has been valued at $500,000,000.

Educated at private schools, Hartford was graduated from St. Paul's preparatory school in Concord, New Hampshire in June 1930. At Harvard, where he enrolled the following September, he majored in English literature, and played on the tennis team for three years. He also played on the squash team. He was graduated with a B.A. degree in June 1934.

Although he seems to have devoted most of his time from graduation until the outbreak of World War II to the enjoyment of his wealth, Hartford did hold several jobs. In 1935-36 he worked as an A & P clerk; in 1940 he was a reporter for the new defunct *PM* in New York; and for a short time he was employed by the Harvell Die Casting Company in California.

In 1942 Hartford was commissioned as an ensign in the Coast Guard and was assigned as an admiral's aide in Greenland and the North Atlantic area of operations. Later he was transferred to the Pacific area, where he served as commander of a Navy cargo vessel. He was discharged with the rank of lieutenant in 1945.

After the war, Hartford began the business and artistic ventures which have made him a public figure. The first of these was the Hartford Model Agency, which he founded in 1947; it was the first agency to pay its models on a weekly basis and the first to have a "built-in" screen test for those with acting ability. The agency is prospering with branches in New York City and Hollywood.

Perhaps as an extension of his new business, Hartford became interested in motion picture production at this time. While in Hollywood he met and married Marjorie Sue Steele, a

John Engstead

HUNTINGTON HARTFORD 2d

nineteen-year-old dramatics student and amateur painter. Hartford credits his wife with influencing him in the two areas, art and theater, which have taken a considerable part of his time and money since his marriage in 1949.

In that year he created the Huntington Hartford Foundation near Los Angeles. A $600,000 retreat for artists, writers, and composers who are selected by a seven-man advisory board, the foundation is at present under the direction of Professor John Vincent of the University of California at Los Angeles. The Fellows receive food, lodging, and working facilities while at the retreat.

After taking a financial part in several motion pictures, Hartford made a personal entry into movie production in 1950. His plan was to produce a series of episodic films, each consisting of two or three short stories. The first of these was released in 1953 under the title of *Face to Face,* consisting of Joseph Conrad's "The Secret Sharer" and Stephen Crane's "The Bride Comes to Yellow Sky."

The latter story featured Mrs. Hartford in the feminine lead, but the critics accepted her acting on its own merits. A New York *Times* (January 14, 1953) reviewer called it an "off-beat serving of Americana . . . a gem of its kind," and the *New Yorker* (January 24, 1953) remarked that Hartford "has emerged as a movie producer who deserves the congratulations of all of us."

Hartford used the same approach to enter legitimate theater. After helping to finance several Broadway shows (including *The Seven Year Itch*), he purchased Hollywood's Vine Street Theatre in 1953. It was turned into a showplace theater at a cost of $1,000,000, renamed the Huntington Hartford Theatre, and opened in September 1954 with Helen Hayes starring in Barrie's *What Every Woman Knows.*

As a patron of the fine arts, Hartford is not willing to accept what he terms its "vulgar" and "meaningless" extremes. In 1951 he had rejected two applicants for his retreat because he considered their work too abstract, and he followed the action by publishing a tract entitled "Has God Been Insulted Here?"

All seven advisers to the foundation resigned at that time, but Hartford appointed a new advisory board and there the controversy rested until 1955. Then he wrote an article for the *American Mercury* (March 1955) in which he condemned "obscurity, confusion, immorality, violence" in contemporary painting. To ensure wide readership, he reprinted the article in full-page advertisements in six New York newspapers.

Putting his views into tangible form, Hartford in 1956 began plans for a new art gallery in New York City. A $2,000,000 structure on Columbus Circle, it was to have been called the Gallery of Modern Art, but the Museum of Modern Art in January 1959 filed suit against Hartford to restrain him from using a name which might cause public confusion between the two galleries.

The most recent of Hartford's artistic projects was the stage production of Charlotte Brontë's *Jane Eyre.* He adapted the novel in 1951 and after several postponements managed to sign Errol Flynn for the male lead in 1957. The show opened, and closed, on the road in March 1958, and later had an unsuccessful six-week run in New York City, with a cost to Hartford of about $500,000.

Hartford is currently planning a sculpture garden for Hollywood and has various other interests, both commercial and avocational. He is the founder and president of the Handwriting Institute in New York, devoted to his interest in graphology. An amateur student of neurology, he was a research associate at Columbia University in 1957 and 1958 in that field.

Hartford is chairman of the board for the Oil Shale Corporation, a research firm engaged in studying means for extracting petroleum from low-grade shale. He also owns the patent for a fully automatic parking system called Speed Park, and in collaboration with the Otis Elevator Company he plans to erect a one-attendant, 276-car garage in downtown New York City.

Huntington Hartford 2d has been twice married. The first marriage, to Mary Lee Epling on April 18, 1931, was terminated by divorce eight years later. He married Marjorie Sue Steele on September 10, 1949. They have two children, John and Catherine.

A tall, well-built man (six feet, 175 pounds), Hartford is still boyish looking and surprisingly shy in his rare public appearances. His hair and eyes are brown; he wears spectacles for close work such as writing. Since among his announced future plans are an autobiography, a play about Byron, and a biography of British poetess Laurence Hope, it appears that writing will be the next art to feel the impact of Hartford's fortune and many-sided interest.

References

Cosmop 141:78+ S '56
Life 32:76+ F 4 '52
N Y Sunday News p32+ Je 8 '58 por
N Y Times IV p3 S 26 '54 por; II p19
    F 1 '59
Sat R 41:7 Ag 2 '58 por

HATFIELD, MARK O(DOM) July 12, 1922- Governor of Oregon; educator

Address: b. State Capitol, Salem, Ore.; h. 833 High St. S., Salem, Ore.

In the Oregon election for governor in November 1958, victorious Mark O. Hatfield was one of the few Republican candidates for a major office who withstood a national Democratic landslide. He was quickly recognized as a leader among the liberals of his party in the West. At the age of thirty-six, in January 1959, he took office as the youngest governor in the history of Oregon, succeeding Democrat Robert D. Holmes, in whose administration he held the post of Secretary of State. While serving earlier in the state legislature for six years, Hatfield had worked as a teacher of political science and dean of students at Willamette University, Salem, Oregon, principally from 1950 to 1956.

Mark Odom Hatfield was born in Dallas, Oregon on July 12, 1922, the only son of Charles Dolen and Dovie (Odom) Hatfield. His father, now a retired railroad construction blacksmith, was employed for thirty-five years with the Southern Pacific Railroad. When Mark Hatfield was about eleven years old, the family moved to Salem, the capital of Oregon, where his mother taught in a junior high school. She later worked for the state income tax department. Originally from a Republican stronghold in eastern Tennessee, Mrs. Hatfield probably inspired much of her son's early interest in politics, as Milton MacKaye suggested in his *Saturday Evening Post* article, "Oregon's Golden Boy" (May 9, 1959).

At Salem (now North Salem) High School, Hatfield played the clarinet in the band, joined the debating team, and acted in school plays. In 1940 he entered Willamette University in Salem, and while majoring in political science he kept up his interest in debating and music. He was president of a fraternity which later became Beta Theta Pi. He worked at the State Capitol as a guide, in a grocery stock room, in the post office during the Christmas rush, and in the state automobile office when extra help was needed.

Completing his academic course in three years, Hatfield was graduated with the B.A. degree in 1943. He was immediately called into the United States Navy as a midshipman and sent to Amphibious Attack School in Coronado Beach, California and then to Midshipman School in Plattsburgh, New York. Aboard the U.S.S. *Whiteside* he saw action during World

Don Lee Studio

MARK O. HATFIELD

War II at Iwo Jima and Okinawa; he commanded landing craft to and from beaches to carry troops ashore and return with the wounded.

During part of his thirty-one months in the Navy, Hatfield was engaged in the postwar transport of Chiang Kai-shek's troops from Indochina to northern China. Before his discharge with the rank of lieutenant (j.g.) in 1946, he also served with the Shore Patrol in San Francisco. "Let's face it," he said, as quoted in the *Saturday Evening Post* (May 9, 1959), "I went into the Navy a small-town boy and a convinced isolationist. That was before I saw the want and waste in the world, before I saw men and women in Asian streets literally dying of hunger. I knew I could never be an isolationist again, and it was a painful awakening."

For a year, in 1946-47, Hatfield took law courses at Willamette University. Then deciding to study political science further, he entered Stanford University in California, where he helped meet expenses by working as a counselor to freshmen. For his M.A. degree, conferred in 1948, he submitted a thesis on the labor policies of Herbert Hoover from 1898 to 1928. He returned to Willamette University in 1949 as instructor in political science. The following year he was advanced to dean of students and assistant and then associate professor, positions that he held until 1956.

Meanwhile, as a Young Republican who attributed many of his political ideals to the 1940 Republican Presidential nominee, Wendell Willkie, Hatfield began to take a more active interest in politics. The favorable response to a radio discussion series that he conducted, *The Political Pulse,* led him to campaign for a seat in the state legislature. He served as a representative from 1950 to 1954 and as a senator from 1954 to 1956. He co-sponsored a bill in 1953 to guarantee Negroes equal access to pub-

HATFIELD, MARK O.—*Continued*

lic places and was author also of Oregon's minimum-wage law for teachers.

In national politics Hatfield had become an early supporter of Dwight D. Eisenhower. He was among the first to circulate petitions for Eisenhower's candidacy for President and he served as executive secretary of Oregon Citizens for Eisenhower. He was chosen in preference to Senator Wayne Morse, now a Democrat but then a Republican, as a member of the platform committee at the 1952 Republican National Convention, a position that he also filled during the 1956 convention.

Running for the post of Secretary of State in 1956, Hatfield was the only Republican candidate for an Oregon state office to survive a Democratic sweep that elected Robert D. Holmes as governor to fill out the unexpired term of Paul Patterson. Hatfield won by a margin of 19,000, while Holmes's margin was 6,000. In January 1958 Hatfield announced his candidacy for the Republican nomination for governor. Victorious in the May primary election, he went on to defeat Holmes by about 65,000 votes the following November. The Democrats kept their majority in the legislature.

"When I first ran for office in 1950, I broke away from the traditional rut of a Republican campaign," Hatfield explained in accounting in part for his success at the polls. "It seemed to be time for the Republican party to get acquainted with the people. I had a lot of coffee hours. I never appealed for support on the basis of prejudice for my party or against the Democrats. I appealed on the basis of a program for action" (New York *Herald Tribune*, November 16, 1958). After his 1958 victory Hatfield was compared in the press with New York Governor Nelson A. Rockefeller, also one of the few important successful Republican candidates of the year, as a "bright hope" of the party.

Hatfield resigned his post as Secretary of State and took office as governor in January 1959, in Oregon's centennial year, which the state celebrated with a Centennial Exposition and Trade Fair, opening in June in Portland. In matters of social reform and civil rights he belongs to the liberal wing of his party. He opposes "right-to-work" laws and has called for the repeal of the antipicketing law of 1953. On the issue of public-versus-private power he supports the principle of a federal regional corporation to develop the Columbia Basin hydroelectric power system.

Throughout his life Hatfield has been active in church affairs. He served as moderator of the First Baptist Church in Salem for three terms and is a member of the board of the Western Baptist Theological Seminary in Portland. He is also interested in the work of Youth for Christ, Campus Crusade, World Vision, and International Christian Leadership. During a visit to New York in June 1959 he addressed a meeting of the Christian Businessmen's Committee of New York City and delivered a layman's sermon at the Marble Collegiate Church.

Hatfield was named Junior First Citizen of Salem for 1954 and holds honorary degrees from Willamette University (1958), Lafayette College (1959), and Houghton College (1959). He is a Mason and belongs to the Rotary Club and the American Legion, among other organizations.

During the summer of 1954 Hatfield conducted students on a political science tour in Europe under the auspices of the Student International Travel Association. One of the members of the group was Antoinette Marie Kuzmanich, who later became a teacher and counselor for women at Portland State College. She and Hatfield were married on July 8, 1958.

An experienced public speaker, Governor Hatfield expresses his convictions in a crisp and forceful manner. He is well-groomed and personable, stands six feet tall, weighs 175 pounds, and has brown hair and green eyes. One of his recreations is playing the piano, and he is an avid spectator of most sports.

References

Christian Sci Mon p5 N 10 '58; p3 Je 1 '59 por
N Y Herald Tribune p30 N 16 '58 por
Sat Eve Post 231:32+ My 9 '59 por
Who's Who in America (sup Mr '56)

HATOYAMA, ICHIRO Jan. 1, 1883-Mar. 7, 1959 Former Premier of Japan (1954-56); Minister of Education (1931-34); chief secretary of Tanaka cabinet (1927-29). See *Current Biography* (May) 1955.

Obituary

N Y Times p21 Mr 7 '59

HAWKINS, JACK Sept. 14, 1910- Actor
Address: b. William Morris Agency, 1740 Broadway, New York 19; h. Westmead, Roehampton, S.W. 15, England

Often cast as a rugged and resolute military man, Jack Hawkins is one of Great Britain's leading movie box-office attractions. He began his career as a child actor in London at the age of thirteen, toured with Dame Sybil Thorndike and Sir Laurence Olivier, and starred in West End plays before World War II. He appeared in Broadway productions of *Journey's End, Dear Octopus,* and *Romeo and Juliet* and played in Shaw's *Caesar and Cleopatra* on NBC-TV's *Producers' Showcase.* To such films as *The Cruel Sea, The Prisoner,* and *The Bridge on the River Kwai* he contributed performances that explain why a *Variety* critic called Hawkins "one of the most reliable, convincing, and solid British actors."

Jack Hawkins was born in London, England, on September 14, 1910, to Thomas George Hawkins and Phoebe (Goodman) Hawkins. His father was a public works contractor. He was educated at the Trinity County School, Middlesex. Two things pointed the way to his future career. As a boy chorister at St. Michael's church, Wood Green, he developed an excellent voice. Family friends sent him to Miss Italia Conti, principal of a school for child actors.

who needed some boys for a London production of a children's play, *Where the Rainbow Ends.* Jack became a pupil at the school and made his theatrical debut as a frog at the Holborn Empire Theatre on December 26, 1923 at the age of thirteen. The next year, at the New Theatre, in March, he played the role of Dunois' page in *Saint Joan,* having won the approval of George Bernard Shaw when he auditioned for the part.

By the time Hawkins was eighteen, he was playing regularly in West End shows. He also toured in *Saint Joan* and in *Interference.* In 1928 he acted the role of Ainger in *Young Woodley* and in 1929 he appeared with Laurence Olivier in *Beau Geste.*

Making his Broadway debut at the Henry Miller Theater on March 22, 1929, Hawkins portrayed Lieutenant Hibbert in the war play, *Journey's End.* He returned to England in 1930 to play the role of Patrick Battle in *The Breadwinner* in London, followed by the part of Alaric Craven in *Autumn Crocus* in 1931. During the run of *Autumn Crocus* he celebrated his twenty-first birthday; he also met Jessica Tandy, another member of the cast, whom he married in 1932. (The marriage was terminated by divorce in 1940.)

Although he began his motion picture career in 1932, Jack Hawkins did not at first take motion pictures seriously, but considered himself primarily a stage actor. "My first picture bit was for Alfred Hitchcock," he told Howard Thompson (New York *Times,* April 4, 1954), "in *The Lodger.* That performance as a newspaper reporter was something I prefer to draw a veil over. During my early years—those impressionable ones—I managed to pick up a good bit of stage know-how in Sybil Thorndike's company, in John Gielgud's original outfit, and later under one of our great directors, Basil Dean. Then I began commuting to the studios and found myself in a ghastly series of what we called 'quota quickies'."

From 1931 until World War II broke out, Hawkins appeared in some fifty plays on the London stage and on tour and in fifteen motion pictures. He acted in many plays with the Repertory Players and in Shakespearean productions with the Open Air Theatre. He returned to Broadway in January 1939 to play the part of Nicholas Randolph in Dodie Smith's tenuous comedy, *Dear Octopus,* which starred Lillian Gish. Turning to classic comedy, he enacted Algernon Moncrieffe in *The Importance of Being Earnest* at the Globe Theatre in London in August 1939. At the Old Vic Theatre in April 1940 he played Edmund in *King Lear* and Caliban in *The Tempest.*

Joining the ranks of the Royal Welsh Fusiliers in 1940, he earned a commission as a second lieutenant and after five months he took charge of ENSA (equivalent to the American USO) in India and the South East Asia Command. One of the ENSA companies under his supervision starred a young actress named Doreen Lawrence, whom Hawkins later married. In 1943 he played the role of a brigade major in a British propaganda film, *Next of Kin,* which warned against loose talk in war-

JACK HAWKINS

time. He became a colonel in 1944, and was discharged two years later.

In August 1946 Hawkins made his first postwar appearance on the London stage as King Magnus in Shaw's *The Apple Cart.* For the British Council he toured the Continent in 1946 and 1947 as King Claudius in *Hamlet,* as Othello, and as Reverend Morell in Shaw's *Candida.* He also resumed his film career, acting in *The Fallen Idol, The Small Back Room, State Secret, No Highway,* and many others. He won particular notice for his portrayal of the Iron Curtain police chief in *State Secret.*

The actor moved on to more rewarding assignments, including roles in the films *The Elusive Pimpernel, The Black Rose,* and *The Story of Mandy,* which elevated him to full stardom. Hawkins also likes to direct, and intends to continue in this phase of theatrical production. He directed Christopher Fry's verse play, *The Lady's Not For Burning,* and Michael Pearson's *Against the Tide,* both in 1948, in London.

Playing Mercutio in Dwight Deere Wiman's 1951 Broadway production of *Romeo and Juliet,* starring Olivia de Havilland, Hawkins was singled out for praise for his interpretation of Romeo's lusty familiar. "He is romantic, cynical, and bawdy," wrote William Hawkins in the New York *World-Telegram and Sun* (March 12, 1951). "[He] dies cursing both the warring houses in a performance which is satisfactory with flashes of distinction."

While on contract with J. Arthur Rank to do two pictures a year, Hawkins appeared in *Outpost in Malaya* opposite Claudette Colbert (1952); *Malta Story* (1954) with Alec Guinness; *Land of Fury* (1955); *Touch and Go* (1956); *The Third Key* (1957) and others. He received exceptional notices for his performance as Lieutenant Commander Ericson in *The Cruel Sea* (1953). "As the harried captain," noted the New York *Times* reviewer (August 11, 1953),

"Hawkins projects with conviction and polish the picture of a man ready to accept the staggering burden of command." Alton Cook (New York *World-Telegram and Sun,* August 11, 1953) commented: "Jack Hawkins brings a performance of great strength to add a full realization of the captain's solid qualities."

The Cruel Sea won the David O. Selznick Golden Laurel Award for 1953. "For me, this film was far and away the most realistic picture of my career," Hawkins wrote in an article in the New York *World-Telegram and Sun* (August 1, 1953). "When I look back on the long hours we spent at sea, it seems that for a time I was no longer an actor, but a sailor. . . . The days of the drawing-room comedy have almost disappeared, and the actor who goes into films must expect to put up with just as many hardships as the characters he portrays."

A poll of British movie theaters in 1954 and in 1955 named Hawkins the top box-office attraction in England. Since he had played almost no romantic parts, the selection was somewhat surprising. Hawkins, however, insisted modestly: "I have no illusions about myself. . . . It happened because I had good stories. Some people can make bricks without straw. I can't" (New York *Herald Tribune,* March 11, 1956).

In the 1955 Warner Brothers spectacle called *Land of the Pharaohs* Hawkins played the Pharaoh with a rampaging vigor, but in spite of a screenplay by William Faulkner, the film was generally reviled by the critics. In *The Prisoner,* the 1955 motion picture about the Communist brainwashing of a cardinal in the Balkans, Alec Guinness and Jack Hawkins were co-starred as the cardinal and his interrogator. Reviewers were enthusiastic about both actors, calling Hawkins' performance a brilliant and powerful one.

Two years later, Hawkins again acted with Alec Guinness, this time in the prize-winning *The Bridge on the River Kwai,* which was concerned with conflicting loyalties in a Japanese prison camp in Ceylon during World War II. Hawkins played a dedicated British army major, who, when given a job to blow up an enemy bridge, finds himself pitted against another military fanatic, the British colonel (Guinness), who had built the bridge as a prisoner of war. William Holden and Sessue Hayakawa played the other two leading roles. Hawkins was acclaimed for his subtle, forceful, and often humorous characterization of the major. Richard L. Coe (Washington *Post and Times Herald,* March 14, 1958) said: "Jack Hawkins, probably one of England's most overlooked greats, gets to the heart of a professorial type forced into action." *The Bridge on the River Kwai* won seven Academy awards.

In England Hawkins has been active in television, and for NBC-TV he played in a ninety-minute presentation of Shaw's *Caesar and Cleopatra* on March 5, 1956. Although the production drew mixed reactions from the reviewers, Hawkins was generally applauded. "Jack Hawkins as Rufio rang true at all times" remarked a *Variety* critic (March 7, 1956).

When Hawkins made his first visit to Hollywood in 1957, to promote *The Bridge on the River Kwai,* he discovered to his surprise that he liked the film capital. "I can only believe that those who have a tough time in Hollywood and complain so much about it must be slightly deficient in talent" he told Joe Hyams of the New York *Herald Tribune* (December 13, 1957). Considering himself now primarily a movie actor, he has nothing but contempt for stage actors who look down on screen acting.

Jack Hawkins and actress Doreen Lawrence were married in 1947. They have three children. (By his first marriage, to Jessica Tandy, he has a daughter, Susan.) Hawkins belongs to the Garrick, Savage, and Royal Automobile clubs, and enjoys riding, fishing, and music. He was made a Commander of the Order of the British Empire in 1958.

References

    N Y Herald Tribune IV p3 Mr 11 '56
      por; p15 D 13 '57 por
    N Y Times II p5 Ap 4 '54
    Who's Who, 1959
    Who's Who in the Theatre (1957)

HAYAKAWA, S(AMUEL) I(CHIYE)

July 18, 1906- Philologist; author; psychologist; teacher

Address: b. 1600 Holloway Ave., San Francisco 27, Calif.; h. 225 Eldridge Ave., Mill Valley, Calif.

For some twenty years, S. I. Hayakawa, currently professor of language arts at San Francisco State College, has been provoking comment with his lectures, books, articles, and television talks on language habits in relation to the common phenomena of contemporary civilization. His uncommon common sense and individual tricks of expression are trademarks that have become familiar to increasing numbers of readers, students, and lecture audiences since his *Language in Action* was published in 1941. In this Book-of-the-Month Club selection Hayakawa explained the principles of general semantics, a system based chiefly on the theories of Alfred Korzybski and recently defined by Hayakawa as "a comparative study of the kinds of responses people make to the symbols and signs around them."

In speaking of those unconscious assumptions known in the language of general semantics as "identification reactions," Hayakawa often uses an illustration derived from his own background. Because of his Japanese name and appearance he finds that he is often expected to speak and write Japanese (he does not) and to "have an Oriental mind."

Samuel Ichiye Hayakawa was born in Vancouver, British Columbia, on July 18, 1906, to Ichiro and Tora (Isono) Hayakawa, and, like his younger brother Fred and sisters Ruth and Grace, was educated in the various Canadian cities where his father had his import and export business. He has been in Japan only once, in August-September 1953, when he visited his parents, who had returned to Japan. He also delivered lectures in several Japanese cities at the invitation of the Tokyo *Manichi* and the Japan Language Society.

He attended St. John's High School in Winnipeg, Manitoba, graduating in 1923, and went on to the University of Manitoba, where he received his A.B. degree in 1927. The following year he was awarded an M.A. degree from McGill University, Montreal; his thesis was entitled "Literary Criticism of Matthew Arnold." He had majored in English because he had always wanted to be a writer, and had strong leanings toward poetry. In 1930 he went to the University of Wisconsin as a graduate assistant in English, and received his Ph.D. in 1935 with the thesis "The Writings of Oliver Wendell Holmes."

In 1936 Hayakawa was appointed instructor in English in the University of Wisconsin Extension Division, a post which he occupied until 1939 when he became first instructor, then assistant professor, and later associate professor of English at the Illinois Institute of Technology in Chicago. Although *Language in Action* (Harcourt, 1941) appeared after he moved to Chicago, the book actually grew, he states, "directly out of my teaching experience in Wisconsin and the conviction that somehow or other my interest in Middle English, linguistics, modern poetry, Elizabethan lyric, etc., had a bearing on the problems of the average citizen in a democracy. Extension Division teaching, which forces one to consider relationships of academic subject matter with problems of day-to-day life in an average community, was really responsible for compelling me to formulate my linguistic principles in ways understandable to nonspecialists in language and literature."

A meeting with Stuart Chase, who was also concerned with problems relating to language habits, led in 1938 to an introduction to Alfred Korzybski and his theories which he had named general semantics, and eventually to Hayakawa's popular interpretation and adaptation of General Korzybski's ideas in *Language in Action.*

After eight years of teaching and practising the principles stated in *Language in Action* the author concluded that it was embarrassingly inadequate. He rewrote it under the title *Language in Thought and Action* (Harcourt, 1949). It has since been translated into Swedish, Japanese, Korean, and Chinese, and is one of the fifteen books included in the publisher's "Classroom Library," composed of titles selected "from forty years of publishing, that because of their excellence, timelessness, and appeal, have become classics."

Before going to his present position in San Francisco State College, Hayakawa was, from 1950 to 1955, Lecturer in the University College, University of Chicago. In addition to teaching and writing, he is in much demand as a lecturer, and has produced for National Educational Television a series of thirteen half-hour film presentations on general semantics, also entitled *Language in Action.* He has conducted a series of informal lecture-demonstrations on jazz over FM radio station WFMT in Chicago, and another series at the University of Chicago on the social significance of jazz, with musical illustrations by Bob Scobey.

In January 1959 Hayakawa delivered the Claude Bernard Lectures at the Institute of

S. I. HAYAKAWA

Experimental Medicine and Surgery at the University of Montreal, speaking on problems of scientific creativity and on the semantic causes of stress, in connection with the institute's researches on these subjects under Dr. Hans Selye. This is the first occasion on which a lecturer not qualified in the physical sciences has been designated Claude Bernard Professor by the institute.

In addition to the books already mentioned, Hayakawa has edited *Language, Meaning and Maturity* (Harper, 1954) and *Our Language and Our World* (Harper, 1959), two collections of representative articles from the magazine *ETC., a Review of General Semantics,* of which he is founder (1943) and editor. He has also contributed numerous articles, columns, and reviews to various periodicals including the Chicago *Defender,* Chicago *Sun (Book Week), New Republic, Harper's Magazine, Poetry, Public Opinion Quarterly, Sewanee Review, Asia, Saturday Evening Post,* and *ETC.*

Hayakawa's contributions to psychology, psychosomatic medicine, and the arts, the by-products of his teaching and writing on general semantics, have been recognized by his election as a Fellow of the American Association for the Advancement of Science, and of the American Psychological Association. He has received the degree of D.F.A. (honoris causa) conferred by the California College of Arts and Crafts and the Claude Bernard Medal conferred by the Institute of Experimental Medicine and Surgery of the University of Montreal.

The many organizations to which Hayakawa belongs indicate the wide span of his interests. They include the Press and Union League Club of San Francisco; Commonwealth Club of California; American Anthropological Association; American Psychological Association; American Sociological Society; International Society for General Semantics (of which he was president in 1949-50); Modern Language Association;

HAYAKAWA, S. I.—*Continued*

and Institute of Jazz Studies. He was recently elected to the board of the Society for the Psychological Study of Social Issues. He also belongs to the Linguistic Society of America, American Dialect Society, and Society for Contemporary American Art. He is a past director of the Consumers Union. His political affiliation is Democratic.

While at the University of Wisconsin Hayakawa frequently contributed to the *Rocking-Horse,* an independent literary magazine edited by Margedant Peters, whom he married on May 29, 1937. They have three children: Alan Romer, Mark, and Carol Wynne.

Brown-eyed and black-haired Hayakawa is five feet seven inches tall, and weighs 140 pounds. He has a ready smile, an alert, interested manner, and wide-ranging interests. At the moment he prefers fishing and collecting jazz records, but he also takes a connoisseur's interest in modern and early Chinese art, and has been a fencer. Typical of the variety and extent of his activities is this list included in the foreword of *Language in Thought and Action* as contributing to his reasons for revision: a period of study and observation at the Menninger Clinic and Foundation in Topeka, Kansas; the study of art under László Moholy-Nagy; serving on the board of directors of a co-operative wholesale; president of a small chain of co-operative grocery stores; and first-hand research on folk music and jazz with the co-operation of self-taught folk musicians of the Negro community.

References

Sat Eve Post 231:22+ D 27 '58 por
Twentieth Century Authors (First Supplement, 1955)
Who's Who in America, 1958-59

HAYES, PETER LIND June 25, 1915-
Actor; comedian
Address: b. American Broadcasting Company, 7 W. 66th St., New York 22; h. 103 Mt. Tom Rd., New Rochelle, N.Y.

"ABC has a winner," reported the New York *Herald Tribune* when Peter Lind Hayes began his variety television program in October 1958. Described as an "easy-going, happy grab-bag with imaginative touches and deft production," the *Peter Lind Hayes Show* brought prestige to both Hayes and daytime television until the program was discontinued in April 1959.

It took a long time for nation-wide recognition to come to Hayes, who began his career in 1924 with a summertime role in his mother's vaudeville act. Before achieving his first notable reviews in 1946 as a night club mimic, he had acted small parts in several Hollywood movies and toured the South Pacific as an Air Corps entertainer in World War II. His wife, Mary Healy, has shared in most of his stage and screen successes since 1947.

Peter Lind Hayes was born Joseph Conrad Lind in San Francisco on June 25, 1915, the son of Joseph Conrad and Grace Dolores (Hayes)

Lind. Later the family moved to Cairo, Illinois, where Mr. Lind died when Peter was two years old. The boy attended Roman Catholic parochial schools there and in New Rochelle, New York.

Under her maiden name of Grace Hayes, Mrs. Lind was a well-known vaudeville entertainer. During the school year Peter lived with relatives in Cairo and during the summer months joined his mother on tour. He first appeared on stage in one of her skits at the age of nine. From that time until he was sixteen, he combined his studies with occasional appearances on the stage. While a secondary school pupil at the Iona Irish Christian Brothers School in New Rochelle, he wrote a vaudeville skit for his mother. He abandoned his studies to make his professional debut in the show when it opened at New York's Palace Theatre. That ended his formal schooling and began his career as Peter Lind Hayes. Under his new name, he shared vaudeville billing with his mother during 1932 and 1933.

Those years were the last ones for vaudeville, which was being replaced by the talking motion picture as the country's favored medium of entertainment, and in 1933 the family moved to Hollywood. After appearing in several films, including Paul Whiteman's *King of Jazz,* Grace Hayes opened her own night club, the Grace Hayes Lodge in San Fernando Valley in 1939. Hayes regularly performed at the night club with his mother and guest entertainers. His reputation for mimicking soon earned him bookings at other night clubs and eventually minor roles in the movies.

Peter Lind Hayes made his first screen appearance in Republic's *Outside of Paradise* in 1940. During his one-year contract with Paramount Pictures which followed, he made three films. He played supporting roles in a total of fifteen pictures in the three years of his screen career, continuing at the same time his night club routines at the Grace Hayes Lodge.

When Hayes was twenty-four years old he met starlet Mary Healy, who was then under contract to Twentieth Century-Fox studios. She had appeared in several musical comedies, including Rudy Vallee's *Second Fiddle.* Introduced to each other on a publicity tour sponsored by Dick Fidler, Hayes and Miss Healy were married in Yuma, Arizona on December 19, 1940.

The day after he finished a movie about military life, on July 28, 1942, Hayes enlisted in the Army Air Corps. Assigned to entertainment duty, he appeared in the movie *Winged Victory* and performed in a touring variety show which featured eleven performers called "The Winged Pigeons." While serving as a technical sergeant on Guam, Hayes appeared in 620 shows in the South Pacific theater of operations, and was awarded the bronze star and two battle stars for his service. He was discharged on Christmas day of 1945.

While her husband was in the military service, Mary Healy went to New York to star in three Broadway shows, including Orson Welles' stage production of *Around the World in 80 Days.*

After his discharge from the Air Corps, Hayes opened in the Downtown Theatre in Detroit with a vaudeville skit which proved so successful that he took it on tour. It brought him featured billing at the Copacabana night club in New York City, where he opened on May 30, 1946 with his character impersonations. His gift for mimicking was soon recognized by critics.

"A few weeks ago," wrote *Life* magazine (August 12, 1946), "a young man with a crew cut, large eyes and an apologetic air wandered out on the floor of the Copacabana night club in New York City and began his impersonations. Five minutes later, night club comedy had reached its highest level in years. . . Hayes' comedy, like Charlie Chaplin's, is sadly and shrewdly human."

When Hayes terminated his contract at the Copacabana, Mary Healy was also free of her stage commitments, and until 1949 the couple toured the night clubs of the United States with a singing and comedy act. They made their debut on television as a team in that year, and on July 29, 1951 began producing their own CBS-TV series, *The Star of the Family.* Arthur Godfrey retained them in 1953 as his permanent substitutes for the *Arthur Godfrey Show.* By signing the contract, Hayes and his wife barred themselves from television except as "stand-ins," when their employer was ill or on furlough.

For the next five years, Peter Lind Hayes and Mary Healy performed on stage, in motion pictures, and on the radio to fill gaps in their schedule. In 1953 they played the adult leads in the movie fantasy *The 5,000 Fingers of Dr. T.* For CBS radio they launched a daily program called *The Peter and Mary Show,* which in 1959 was transferred to the ABC radio network, and in 1958 were teamed as the husband-and-wife stars of *Who Was That Lady I Saw You With?* at the Martin Beck Theatre on Broadway. Opening March 3, 1958, the play ran for six months in spite of only lukewarm notices from the critics, with the exception of Walter Kerr of the New York *Herald Tribune.*

Believing that the royalty checks which come in the mail are the best form of economic security, Hayes has also tried his hand at commercial writing. While in the Air Corps he had written two songs for his entertainment troupe which later became hits, and he also wrote several articles which appeared in national magazines. He has collaborated with Robert J. Crean to write melodramas for TV. The first of these, *Come to Me,* was produced by the *Kraft Television Theater* in December 1957. Written by Hayes, the title song of the show sold about half a million copies.

During the run of his Broadway show Hayes ended his contract with Arthur Godfrey and began to plan a television show of his own. According to critic John Crosby, television had little to offer during the daylight hours of 1958. In the New York *Herald Tribune* (May 16, 1958) he wrote: "Parlor games. Quizzes. Giveaways. That is the shape of daytime TV." He deplored the fact that Hayes was leaving the Godfrey show.

PETER LIND HAYES

But the critics were delighted when they saw the *Peter Lind Hayes Show,* which made its debut on October 13, 1958. Jack Gould in the New York *Times* (October 14, 1958) commented that Hayes "is quick and amusing of tongue, chats with his guests in leisurely fashion, and has a slight suggestion of agreeable weariness." The fact that Hayes was drawing upon his famous impersonations to brighten the program did not escape the notice of the critics.

Mary Healy often appeared with her husband on the *Peter Lind Hayes Show.* Their rapport on and off the stage has made them favorite entertainers. They have two children, Peter Michael and Cathy Lind. A religious family (Roman Catholic), they believe that families on stage should follow the same standards as those watching the performance.

"Anything Mary and I do on TV could be done in a church," Hayes told one interviewer (New York *World-Telegram and Sun,* June 7, 1958). "There's an old saying," he told another writer (*Pageant* magazine, November 1958), "that the family that prays together, stays together. Well, we believe that the family that *plays* together stays together too."

References

Life 21 :60+ Ag 12 '46 por
Pageant 14 :110+ N '58 por
Sat Eve Post 231 :26+ D 27 '58 pors
Time 47 :74 Je 24 '46
Who's Who in America, 1958-59

HEES, GEORGE (HARRIS) June 17, 1910- Canadian Minister of Transport
Address: b. Parliament Bldg., Ottawa, Ontario, Canada; h. 21 Dunvegan Rd., Toronto, Ontario, Canada

As Minister of Transport in the Canadian Conservative government that took office in

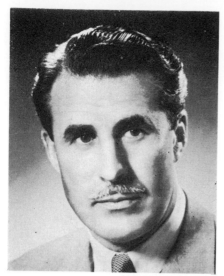

Herb Nott & Co., Ltd.,
Toronto

GEORGE HEES

June 1957 and April 1958, George Hees has for the past two years headed a department which covers not only the nationally-owned railroads and airlines and other means of transportation, but also the St. Lawrence Seaway Authority. An early supporter of Prime Minister John Diefenbaker, he is said to run the most efficient department in the Diefenbaker government, and is regarded as a possible future prime minister.

Grandson and namesake of the founder of Canada's largest firm for the manufacture of window furnishings, George Harris Hees was born in Toronto, Ontario on June 17, 1910. His father was Harris Lincoln Hees, his mother the former Mabel Mills Good of New York. Prepared at Trinity College School, Port Hope, Ontario for the Royal Military College of Canada, Kingston, Ontario, he matriculated there in 1927. At his graduation in 1931 he was one of the top ten in his class.

After studying political science at the University of Toronto for two years, he went to England in 1933 for a year at Cambridge University. At Toronto Hees had played Rugby and was center on the 1932 intercollegiate championship Toronto Varsity Blues. He also won the Canadian intercollegiate heavy-weight championship. At Cambridge he knocked out his Oxford opponent in the annual boxing tournament, and went on to defeat the Imperial Services heavy-weight titleholder. In 1938 he starred on the Toronto Argonauts, a championship Rugby team.

Joining the family business, George H. Hees, Son & Company, Ltd. at Toronto in 1934, Hees subsequently became a director and the vice-president. He gave up his active connection with the firm when he was first elected to Parliament, and the business was later sold for three million dollars.

When World War II broke out in 1939, Hees, who had earlier joined the Toronto militia,

was called to active duty as a lieutenant in Canada's 3d Anti-Tank Regiment. He took part with distinction in the Normandy landings, and later became the brigade major of the 5th Canadian Infantry Brigade. On November 2, 1944 he was wounded by a sniper when his unit was engaged in the capture of the Walcheren island causeway in the Netherlands. He was retired with the rank of major in 1945.

Becoming interested in politics, Hees campaigned in the Grey North by-election of February 1945, on behalf of Conservative candidate Garfield Case, who was running against General Andrew McNaughton, the Minister of National Defense. On convalescent leave at the time, Hees gave eye-witness accounts of the shortage of troops abroad. McNaughton, who was badly beaten in the election, demanded that Hees be court-martialed for participating in politics while still in uniform.

The Liberal Prime Minister, W. L. Mackenzie King, believed that this would make Hees a martyr. With a general election impending, he decided to permit the military services to grant leave to officers and men who wanted to take an active part in the political campaign. At the general election of June 11, 1945 Hees was a candidate for the Toronto-Spadina riding. He was decisively defeated. At a by-election in May 1950 he was elected to Parliament by Toronto-Broadview voters and has represented the latter district continuously since that time.

As a minority party member in the federal legislature, Hees attacked Liberal defense and housing policies, and introduced several legislative proposals which some observers considered trivial. The Liberals looked upon him as a lightweight; the Conservatives "never allotted him any higher parliamentary duty than deputy leader of the public-works caucus" (*Maclean's Magazine,* June 20, 1959). In 1953, however, he proved to be a popular campaign speaker, and in March 1954 he was elected to succeed George Nowlan of Nova Scotia as president of the National Progressive Conservative Association. In 1954-55 Hees made a number of cross-country trips, reorganizing the party and giving lectures on (as he put it) "political charm." "It's about time we realized that people would rather be entertained than educated," he said.

Some members of his party deplored Hees' fondness for using advertising techniques in campaigning, but they had to admit that his methods succeeded. When George Drew of Ontario retired as Conservative party leader in 1956, Hees for a short time considered himself as a possible candidate for the position. He soon decided, however, to throw his weight behind John G. Diefenbaker of Saskatchewan, who easily won the election.

After the general election of June 10, 1957, Prime Minister John G. Diefenbaker formed Canada's first federal Conservative government in over twenty years. Appointed Minister of Transport, George Hees was sworn into office on June 21. He took charge of the Air Transport Board, the Board of Transport Commissioners, the Canadian Maritime Commission, and the National Harbours Board. The Canadian Overseas Telecommunications Corporation, Canadian National Railways, and Canadian National West Indies Steamships Limited reported to Parliament through him. In July Hees also became responsible for the St. Lawrence Seaway Authority and Trans-Canada Airlines.

The Liberals expected to find Hees an easy target for ridicule. They continued to regard him as a political dilettante without experience in the transportation field, but they were soon disappointed. "By long hours of work, often from 7 a.m. to midnight, he mastered the operations of his sprawling department" and "under fire in the House. . . proved a sharp politician, a quick thinker, a man with a good sense of humor, impossible to disconcert or anger" (*Newsweek*, November 11, 1957).

A crisis which early confronted the new Transport Minister arose from a strike that the Seafarers' International Union started on July 4, 1957 against the government-owned Canadian National Steamships, Ltd. Since the dispute was still deadlocked in November, Hees approved the transfer to the Trinidad registry of the eight West Indies vessels of the steamship service. The union continued to block operation of the ships. In May 1958 Hees had the fleet put up for sale; in August he faced a barrage of criticism from Liberals in the Commons when he announced that the eight ships had been sold to the Cuban State Export Bank for $2,800,000. The sale left only ten cargo ships and eight tankers in Canada's ocean-going merchant fleet.

Another problem that has vexed Hees since 1957 is the question of piloting on the St. Lawrence Seaway and the Great Lakes. Hees maintained in 1958 that pilots are needed only at certain points along the route and that piloting throughout the entire area would impose a large and unnecessary financial burden on the shipping industry. Legislation has been proposed in the United States Congress, however, which would make such piloting mandatory for all overseas ships.

Early in November 1957 Transport Minister Hees announced that tolls would be charged on the entire St. Lawrence Seaway, including the Welland Canal, which was then toll-free. He made the statement in answer to a set of questions from Lionel Chevrier, the former Transport Minister and ex-president of the St. Lawrence Seaway Authority. The proposed program encountered considerable opposition from vested interests in both Canada and the United States, but in March 1959 the two countries were able to agree upon and make public an intricate toll structure covering the entire seaway route, including the Welland Canal.

Transportation by water has not been George Hees' only concern. In February 1958 he revealed that the government was planning to introduce competition gradually into domestic transcontinental air travel, in which the government-owned Trans-Canada Airlines had held a monopoly since about 1938. In January 1959 Canadian Pacific Airlines was granted permission to make a daily round-trip flight between Vancouver and Montreal.

In still another area of transportation, Hees reported in May 1959 the formation of a Royal Commission on Railway Transportation. The board was appointed to analyze a number of railroad problems, especially freight rates. The ministry also planned to set up a Royal Commission on Transportation to deal with all forms of transportation: sea, air, roads, and railroads.

In the general election of March 31, 1958 Hees was returned to Parliament by Toronto-Broadview with a record majority. As he approaches the age of fifty he "still looks much more like an athlete than a politician. His two-hundred-pound, six-foot-two-and-a-half inch body is planted on the ground with a permanent backward lean. . . . A meticulously trimmed, now white-sprinkled mustache camouflages the firm set of his lips, just as his tufted brows shield the stubbornness of his direct brown eyes" (*Maclean's Magazine*, June 20, 1959).

Hees continues to be fond of sports; he walks four miles a day and has a daily swim after work. He plays squash, tennis, and golf, and is an ardent skier. He does not smoke or gamble, and he drinks only moderately. He is, however, an inveterate gum-chewer. He is an Anglican. Mrs. Hees is the former Mabel Ferguson Dunlop. The couple, who were married on June 30, 1934, have three daughters, Catherine Mabel, Martha Ann, and Roslyn Georgia.

Although Hees has been quoted as saying by *Maclean's Magazine* (June 20, 1959) that "when you have as good a Prime Minister as John Diefenbaker you just don't think in terms of any other leader," his industry, efficiency, and charm make him one of the more likely candidates to succeed the man he so much admires.

References

Can Bsns 24:58-9+ Ap '51 por; 25: 38+ My '52 por
Macleans Mag 67:6+ My 1 '54; 72: 18+ Je 20 '59 pors
Newsweek 50:69 N 11 '57

Canadian Parliamentary Guide (1959)
Canadian Who's Who, 1955-57
Encyclopedia Canadiana (1958)
International Who's Who, 1958
Who's Who in Canada, 1958-59

HEISS, CAROL E(LIZABETH) January 20, 1940-   Figure Skater
Address: h. 107-41 105th St., Ozone Park, N.Y.

At nineteen years of age, petite and blonde Carol Heiss ranks as the top women's figure skater in the world. She has won the world championship four consecutive times, the national championship for three consecutive years, and the North American title two times in a row. Miss Heiss is favored to win the Olympic championship in 1960, and in the 1956 Olympics she finished second to another American, Tenley Albright (see *C.B.*, September 1956).

When she is not ice skating, Miss Heiss is a full-time student at New York University, from which she is scheduled to graduate in 1961.

CAROL E. HEISS

Since the death of her mother in 1956, she has spent a good deal of time taking care of her younger sister and brother, Nancy, seventeen, and Bruce, fifteen. Nancy placed second to Carol in the 1959 national competition; Bruce is Middle Atlantic Senior Men's champion.

When she won the world's championship in 1956, Carol Heiss, who was then sixteen, became the youngest international titlist since Sonja Henie captured the crown at fifteen. Two years earlier, Carol's skating career had been threatened after a collision with Nancy during a practice session. Her sister's skate inflicted a deep gash in Carol's left leg and severed a tendon below the calf. At the time it had seemed doubtful that she would ever compete again.

Carol Elizabeth Heiss was born on January 20, 1940 in New York City, the first child of Edward and Marie (Gademann) Heiss. Both of her parents came to America from Germany in the late 1920's, and met and were married in the United States. Carol's father is a baker, and her mother was a textile designer. Carol was raised in Ozone Park, which forms a part of the Borough of Queens in New York City, in a seven-room white stucco house where the Heiss family still lives.

Carol's career was actually launched on her fourth birthday when she received a pair of roller skates, although it was not until Christmas of that year that she received a pair of ice skates. "The first memory I really have of being on skates," Miss Heiss told Frank Graham, Jr., (*Saturday Evening Post*, January 31, 1959) "was at the Brooklyn Ice Palace. I was five years old and had long blond curls."

Local ice skaters who watched the youngster whirl gracefully about the ice urged Mrs. Heiss to get in touch with Pierre and Andrée Brunet, former Olympic and World Pairs champions who were then teaching the art of skating. Mrs. Brunet gave lessons to Carol

until she was seven. At that point she turned Carol over to Pierre Brunet, who called in Mrs. Heiss and asked her if she wanted him to take over Carol's instruction. He warned that Carol would have to practise five to eight hours a day. When Mrs. Heiss asked Brunet if Carol could become a champion and he predicted that she would be "on top" in ten years, Mrs. Heiss gave her approval for Carol to go ahead.

Miss Heiss has never regretted that decision, but she is aware of the many sacrifices it cost her parents. "My parents were never well off financially," she explains. "My training to become a champion figure-skater is quite expensive what with skates, costumes, rink fees for practice sessions and other incidentals. . . Without their help, understanding and encouragement I never could have gotten started" (New York *Sunday News Magazine*, April 26, 1959).

Carol won her first championship, the National Novice title, when she was eleven. The next year she won the National Junior Championship, and became the youngest member of the United States team competing for world championships at Davos, Switzerland. She placed fourth. The collision with her sister just before the world competition at Oslo, Norway, in 1954 kept her off skates for many months, but she came back in 1955 to place second to Miss Albright at the World Championships in Vienna.

The Olympics took place the following year, and Miss Heiss was often mentioned as Miss Albright's chief competitor. Although the contest was close, Miss Albright won by a margin of 169.6 points to Miss Heiss' 168.1. "The victory of the two American girls climaxed the most brilliant demonstration in the fancy skating art the United States ever has presented to an Olympic audience," Barrett McGunn wrote in the New York *Herald Tribune* (February 3, 1956). "Carol, a pretty little blonde with hair done up in a pony tail, put on a striking performance, crowded with high leaps, spins in the air and even dizzier spins on the ice in a vain attempt to overtake her teammate."

Reports followed of a feud between the two girls when Miss Heiss neglected to congratulate Miss Albright on her brilliant victory and refused to pose with her for photographers. Both girls denied any bitterness, but the stories, true or not, added to the drama of their next meeting later in February at Garmisch-Partenkirchen, Germany, the scene of the world competition. When it was over, Carol Heiss had won her first major victory.

Championship skating is divided into two phases—compulsory (school) figures, which count 60 per cent of the total score, and free skating, which counts 40 per cent. There are 68 basic figures, and the contestant must perform six of these, picked by lot. In reporting the championships, the New York *Herald Tribune* noted (February 19, 1956): "Going into tonight's free program Miss Heiss held the narrowest of leads after the completion of the school figures earlier in the day. That in itself was a terrific upset as never before had she defeated Miss Albright in this phase of the event. . . Carol . . . put on a terrific show in the final, given over to the free skating. The tiny blonde skated flawlessly, and her performance featured double axels, double flips and loops."

The victory was what Miss Heiss had been aiming at for ten years of continuous practice and sacrifice. "The tears she never shed when time and again she lost to her perennial rival, Tenley Albright, finally slid down Carol Heiss's cheeks at Garmisch-Partenkirchen, Germany, where she became the new world's figure-skating champion" (*Life*, March 5, 1956).

When Miss Heiss and Miss Albright met in Philadelphia for the national championships in March, Miss Heiss was once more relegated to second place. Miss Albright, however, retired before the start of the following season, and Carol Heiss' pre-eminence has not been in serious jeopardy since. She has added three more consecutive world titles, has won the national championships in 1957, 1958, and 1959, and the North American crowns in 1958 and 1959.

In spite of her many titles, Miss Heiss has no intention of turning professional. Her mother, who died of cancer in October 1956, made her daughter promise not to become a professional skater until she won an Olympic gold medal.

Carol Heiss, a hazel-eyed blonde, is five feet two inches tall and weighs 109 pounds. At New York University, where she studies on a full scholarship, she is working toward a Bachelor of Arts degree. Her typical day starts at 5 in the morning. By 7 her sister and she are skating under the watchful eye of Brunet, and they continue practising until noon. Then Miss Heiss goes to classes, returns home, prepares dinner, studies, and goes to bed. This constitutes her routine six days a week, every month of the year except August, when she takes a month off for water skiing and a few dates. Her activities off the ice are also athletic. She likes swimming, tennis, water-skiing, and fencing, but also likes to read and listen to classical and semi-classical music. She is a Roman Catholic.

At New York University Miss Heiss was named Queen of the Lambda Gamma Phi fraternity, and in May 1959 she became the first undergraduate ever to receive the university's presidential citation. Pretty though she is, Miss Heiss spares but little time for dates. "Romance does not go well with any sport," she says (New York *World-Telegram and Sun*, March 21, 1957). For that reason, she has indicated that she will retire from competition after the 1960 Olympics. "I want to get an education and marry and have a family," Miss Heiss says. "Skating is for now. Education and marriage are for always."

References

Life 40:141+ Mr 5 '56 pors
Look 22:68+ Ap 1 '58 pors
N Y Herald Tribune III pl F 3 '56; III pl F 19 '56
N Y Sunday News Mag p4 Ap 26 '59 pors

N Y World-Telegram p17 Mr 21 '57
Read Digest 74:190+ Ap '59
Sat Eve Post 231:24+ Ja 31 '59 pors
Washington (D.C.) Post pC-1 F 19 '56

HELBURN, THERESA 1887(?)-Aug. 18, 1959 Theatrical producer; director; author; a founder (1919), executive director (1919-32), and administrative director (1933-58) of Theatre Guild in New York. See *Current Biography* (September) 1944.

Obituary

N Y Times p29 Ag 19 '59

HEROLD, J(EAN) CHRISTOPHER May 11, 1919- Author; editor
Address: b. c/o Stanford University Press, Stanford, Calif.; h. 684 Paco Dr., Los Altos, Calif.

Reprinted from the *Wilson Library Bulletin* May 1959.

The winner of the 1958 National Book Award for nonfiction has a cosmopolitan background. Jean Christopher Herold was born on May 11, 1919, in Brünn (Brno), Czechoslovakia, of Austrian parentage. His father, Dr. Carl Herold, a psychoanalyst, was the son of Carl M. Herold, an industrialist and inventor; his mother, Elisabeth (Rostra-Schnabel) Herold, was a musician like her father, the famous pianist Artur Schnabel. Jean Christopher's early schooling was "desultory": half a year at a German school in Brünn, then a period with a tutor. In his tenth year he attended a village school near Vienna. From 1929 to 1932 he lived in Berlin and attended the Realgymnasium of Berlin-Zehlendorf.

In 1932, since the situation in Germany looked unpropitious, the boy stayed at the Herold's Austrian country place, sharing with his fifteen-year-old aunt a tutor who taught them to play bridge and "a splendid three-handed card game named Préférence." For lessons in French, they read Beaumarchais' *The Marriage of Figaro*.

When Hitler came to power young Herold continued his studies at the College de Genève. Geneva, to him, was not the city of Calvin, but the city of Voltaire and Rousseau; "the city, also of Madame de Staël, who tried to bridge the chasm between French Classicism and German Romanticism." Summers were spent at Tremezzo, on Lake Como, Italy, where Artur Schnabel had a villa. Here Herold practised his English with some young American female pianists and a Church of England clergyman who corrected his enunciation. He matriculated at the University of Geneva in the Faculty of Letters in the autumn of 1938.

Grandfather Schnabel ("to whom I owe virtually everything") recommended his immigration to the United States. In April 1939 he boarded the *Champlain* — his first choice, the *Paris,* having burned — and arrived in New York two weeks before his twentieth birthday. Staying with friends in New York, he met his future wife, Barbara Anne Chapman, whom he

J. CHRISTOPHER HEROLD

married January 3, 1943, in Richmond, Virginia. In May of that year he was naturalized as a United States citizen.

In 1942 Herold received an M.A. degree in political science from Columbia for a thesis entitled "Political Economy in Diderot's *Encyclopédie*," then entered the Army for training in the antiaircraft artillery. Transferred to the Military Intelligence Service, he was temporarily an interpreter with the Second French Armored Division in Yorkshire, England. In 1944 he went to Paris for a reunion with his mother from whom he had not heard for three years. He then interrogated civilian and military spies, saboteurs, counterspies, and suspects for the First Army Interrogation Center in Belgium and Germany. After the war he joined the Columbia University Press as assistant editor in 1946, staying ten years before becoming editor in chief of the Stanford University Press, his present post.

At Columbia Herold was in charge of the European historical and geographical articles in the second edition of *The Columbia Encyclopedia* (1950), which he described as "gruelling work." Aside from "about ten million articles" in the *Encyclopedia*, he wrote *The Swiss Without Halos* (Columbia University Press, 1948). Virginia Kirkus called the book "scholarly without being pedantic in style," and Felix E. Hirsch, in *Library Journal*, a "delightful background book for college students who are sick of dull textbooks."

Joan, Maid of France (1952), an Aladdin Book for the nine-to-sixteen group (or eleven-to-fourteen, according to some critics), was to the *Christian Science Monitor* "a fresh and devout statement of the story of Joan of Arc." The *New Yorker* called it "clear, movingly written." A compilation, *The Mind of Napoleon* —a personage whom Madame de Staël drove to

distraction — appeared in 1955 (Columbia University Press).

In 1953, when Mr. Herold began his affair with Germaine (Necker) de Staël, he "knew little of her as a person. I think I know her pretty well now, and I am glad I came to know her only 140 years after her death." The actual writing of *Mistress of an Age; a Life of Madame de Staël* (Bobbs, 1958) took two years. It was a November choice of the Book-of-the-Month Club and a selection of the Book Society of England. Clifton Fadiman (*Book-of-the-Month Club News*) wrote that "her fascination exerted in a remote period . . . comes almost uproariously alive in Mr. Herold's packed pages, filled with almost as much life as must have run and leaped in Germaine's dumpy body and electric brain." It was selected by the National Book Awards jury as its nonfiction winner on March 3, 1959.

Francis Steegmuller in the New York *Times Book Review* said it is "long, detailed, full of color, movement, great names, and lively incident. Mr. Herold recounts this passionate, crowded existence with verve, humor, and irony." R. F. Deen in *Commonweal* pointed out that Herold "tries to remain sympathetic to her thought, but detached from her passions. The effort to stay aloof involves a considerable expense of irony, some of it patronizing."

The author has brown eyes, dark hair, stands five feet nine and a half inches tall, and weighs 145 pounds. He has no political preferences, and is a (nonpractising) Roman Catholic. He writes in longhand, and preferably under pressure, facing deadlines, "in a state of exhaustion mitigated by thousands of cups of tea." His favorite recreations are "music and *far niente*." Cervantes is his favorite author.

The Herolds live in Los Altos, California. Their son, Christopher David, is star pitcher on his Little League Baseball team and uses "Madame de Staël" as a "term of insult and derision, no doubt wisely so," Herold remarks.

References

Book-of-the-Month Club N O '58 por
Sat R 41:15 O 25 '58 por
Washington (D.C.) Post p17C Mr 19 '58
Saerchinger, César Artur Schnabel; A Biography (1958)

HERZOG, ISAAC HALEVI, RABBI Nov. 1888- Chief Rabbi of Israel

Address: b. The Chief Rabbinate, Jerusalem, Israel; h. Chief Rabbi's Residence, 4 Ibn Ezrah St., Jerusalem, Israel

Bulletin: Rabbi Isaac Halevi Herzog died on July 25, 1959.

A lifelong dream of Rabbi Isaac Halevi Herzog achieved reality on May 14, 1948 when the state of Israel was established. As Israel's Chief Rabbi and a leading spokesman for the Orthodox position, he is now striving to realize another dream—the restoration of Israel as a *religious* state. With a population ranging from the ultra-Orthodox to nonpractising or "secular" Jews, Israel has been torn by violent religious disputes. Rabbi Herzog contends that religious questions must be resolved in accordance with Talmudic law. He also believes that Israel can achieve her destiny within the framework of modern political liberalism.

Rabbi Herzog came to Israel from Ireland, where he served as spiritual leader of the Jewish communities of Belfast and Dublin before becoming Chief Rabbi of Eire (Irish Free State). In 1936 he succeeded Abraham I. Hacohen Kook as Chief Rabbi of Palestine. Throughout his active life, which has included two trips to the United States, Rabbi Herzog has pursued his Talmudic studies. His major work, *Main Institutions of Jewish Law,* is a five-volume analysis of the evolution of the Jewish legal system.

The only son of Joel and Liba (Cirowitz) Herzog, Isaac Halevi Herzog was born in Lomza, Poland in November 1888. He was first educated by his father, a learned Talmudist, who was rabbi of the community of Russian and Polish Jews living in Paris. In 1905 Herzog entered the University of London, where he studied classical and modern languages and mathematics. After receiving a B.A. degree in 1909, he remained at the university to earn an M.A. degree in Semitics in 1911 and a D.Lit. degree in 1914. He also studied at the University of Leeds and at the École des Langues Orientales in Paris.

Ordained in 1910, Herzog accepted his first religious appointment as rabbi of the Jewish community of Belfast in 1915. He then served as Chief Rabbi of Dublin from 1919 to 1925, when he was appointed Chief Rabbi of all Eire. Twice he declined positions outside Ireland: in 1932, when the post of Chief Rabbi of Salonika and the whole of Greece was offered him, and again in 1935, when he was invited to head the Union of Orthodox Jewish Congregations in Paris.

In 1936 Herzog accepted the call of Palestine's Ashkenazic community to serve as their spiritual leader, thus becoming the second Chief Rabbi since the British mandate. (The Ashkenazim, or north Europe's Jews, differ in ritual and interpretation from the Sephardim, or south Europe's Jews. The Sephardim have a separate Chief Rabbi in Jerusalem.)

As Chief Rabbi during Hitler's campaign of extermination of the Jews, Rabbi Herzog devoted himself not only to matters within Palestine, but also to the needs of Jews throughout the world. He entered diplomatic negotiations, broadcast personal appeals, and led public prayers for the relief of Jews persecuted by the Nazis.

In 1941 Rabbi Herzog toured the United States in an effort to raise funds for the transfer of 1500 students and 200 teachers from the Talmudic academy of Lithuania to Palestine. The tour was cut short when Nazi forces in North Africa reached El Alamein and Rabbi Herzog returned to Palestine in order to be with members of his congregation during the crisis.

A lifelong Zionist who even during his student years in England had been active in the

Wide World
RABBI ISAAC HALEVI HERZOG

religious party of Zionism, Rabbi Herzog used his influence as Chief Rabbi to gain the support of world leaders for the establishment of the state of Israel. Statehood changed his own role. "I was the Chief Rabbi of Palestine," he said in 1949. "Now I am the Chief Rabbi of Israel. I am the same man, but there is a big difference."

Rabbi Herzog has summed up his political beliefs with the statement: "True democracy does not mean a spiritless, godless state. Although the state will not interfere with the freedom of the individual, it must bear the specific impress of a God-conscious people."

One outgrowth of statehood has been an intense effort to revive Jerusalem as the center of Talmudic learning. The Chief Rabbi presides over a group of scholars who are now engaged in revising the sixty-three books of the Talmud. He is also chief editor for *Otzar Haposkim,* a collection of answers which leading rabbis have given to practical questions raised by the Talmud.

Rabbi Herzog has also been a leader in efforts to restore Jerusalem as the seat of Jewish religious authority. In 1949 he called a World Rabbinical Conference as a first step toward establishing a central religious authority in the Chief Rabbinate of Jerusalem. Since Judaism is congregational rather than hierarchical, the acceptance of such authority would be purely voluntary. The Chief Rabbi would, according to Rabbi Herzog, "act as a guiding light to all Jewish communities that seek religious instruction in the light of the Torah and its oral tradition."

In 1949 Rabbi Herzog toured the United States and European countries on behalf of the United Jewish Appeal. While in the United States he visited President Truman. They read the Bible together, and the Chief Rabbi found

HERZOG, ISAAC HALEVI, RABBI—
Continued

the President a truly religious man. "I felt it at once," he told reporters. "It was like two sparks meeting as one."

For the Orthodox Jew the study of the Bible and the Talmud is far more than a pleasant intellectual exercise; it is a means of communion with God. Despite many other responsibilities, Rabbi Herzog has pursued this form of spiritual communion throughout his life, finding time to publish important legal works in Hebrew and English. His major work, *Main Institutions of Jewish Law* (Soncino, 1936-39), is a five-volume study of the methods as well as the conclusions of Talmudic jurisprudence. It was written in English first and then translated into Hebrew.

Rabbi Herzog's first published work, a treatise on the Talmudic discussions of two learned rabbis, appeared as an appendix to his father's *Imrei Yoel* (The Sayings of Joel). In 1920 he wrote *Divrei Itzhak* (The Words of Isaac), which deals with the laws of sacred objects and purification. *Ohel Torah* (The Tabernacle of Torah), published in 1948, received the Rav Kook prize for rabbinical literature from the city of Tel-Aviv. In addition, Rabbi Herzog has contributed to the memorial volumes honoring Maimonides and to scholarly periodicals.

As Chief Rabbi, Herzog presides over the Rabbinical High Court of Appeals. He is a member of the Board of Yeshivot, the Institute for Research in Talmudic Law, the Academy for Biblical Study and Research, and the Institute of Torah Jurisprudence. He is a Fellow of the Jewish Academy of Arts, Science and Letters of America.

Isaac Halevi Herzog was married in 1917 to Sarah Hillman, daughter of the assessor to the Chief Rabbi of the British Empire. They have three sons, Hyman, Jacob, and David. Fluent in ten languages, Rabbi Herzog speaks English with a slight trace of Irish accent. As befits an Orthodox Jew, he has a full, flaring beard. He is short in stature and has twinkling blue eyes.

The Chief Rabbi is firm in his belief that Israel must be governed by religious law. The law of marriage and divorce and the law of rabbinical courts are examples of the sort of legislation, inspired by the Torah, that he wants to see the Knesset (Israeli parliament) pass in all areas. Commenting on these laws for *Jewish Horizon* (February 1955), he said: "They are landmarks in the fortification of the Torah's position in the frame of the state. But they are merely partial achievements, because our Torah embraces all aspects of life." To see Israel embrace the Torah is his dream, his desire, and the inspiration of his efforts.

References

Time 53:75+ My 23 '49 por

Universal Jewish Encyclopedia (1948)
Who's Who, 1958
Who's Who in World Jewry (1955)
Who's Who Israel, 1958

HEVESY, GEORGE (CHARLES) DE
Aug. 1, 1885- Chemist

Address: b. Stockholms Högskola, 2 Sandås gatan, Stockholm, Sweden; h. 18 N. Mälarstrand, Stockholm, Sweden

For his "discovery and development of tracer techniques in chemistry, biology, and medicine," Dr. George de Hevesy received the 1958 Atoms for Peace Award. The Hungarian-born scientist, who is a professor at the Research Institute for Organic Chemistry at the University of Stockholm, is also the holder of the 1943 Nobel Prize in chemistry and other awards.

As the first scientist to use radioactive isotopes as indicators in the study of the physical and chemical processes of plants and animals, de Hevesy introduced a new era in the field of biochemistry. He was the first to employ a stable isotope as a tracer in biology and the "first to explore the possibility of creating radioactive substances within the system being studied by means of neutron bombardment." He has contributed to the research on the separation of isotopes and he was a codiscoverer of the element hafnium.

One of the eight children of Louis de Hevesy, a farmer, and his wife, the former Baroness Eugenie Schosberger, George Charles de Hevesy was born in Budapest, Hungary on August 1, 1885. After graduating from the Gymnasium of the Piarist Order in Budapest in 1903, he attended the University of Budapest for two years. He continued his researches at the University of Freiburg (Germany), which awarded him the doctor's degree in natural philosophy in 1908. Until 1910 he studied in Germany and Switzerland and from 1908 to 1910 was employed as an assistant at the Technical High School in Zurich.

An honorary research fellowship to study at the University of Manchester with Ernest Rutherford, winner of the Nobel Prize in chemistry for investigations in the field of radioactivity, was awarded to de Hevesy in 1911. One of the first projects he attempted in Rutherford's laboratory was the separation of Radium D, a radioactive degradation product of radium, from a sample of lead chloride. Despite repeated efforts during his two-year stay in Manchester, de Hevesy was unable to accomplish the separation. Later discoveries showed that Radium D and lead are isotopes (atoms of the same chemical element with different weights) and thus not separable by chemical means. Physical means for separating Radium D from lead were developed in the 1940's by United States scientists working on the atomic bomb project.

Failure to separate Radium D from lead proved to be a beginning rather than an end for de Hevesy. In 1912-13, working with Professor Friedrich Adolf Paneth at the Vienna Institute of Radium Research, he began a series of investigations using labeled lead as a tracer. By adding small quantities of Radium D to lead in its compounds, de Hevesy traced the lead through its chemical processes by measuring the radioactivity. In effect, his studies had shown that "the identity in the chemical properties of Radium D, and other radioactive isotopes of lead, with ordinary lead, made it possible to use these radioactive isotopes as indicators to follow the behavior of lead in its chemical processes" (*Nature,* December 17, 1949).

De Hevesy returned to Budapest in 1913 to accept an appointment as lecturer at the university. Though he worked for the Hungarian government during World War I, he did not neglect his experiments with lead tracers. When the war was concluded in 1918, he was named a full professor. Two years later he joined the staff of the Institute for Theoretical Physics at the University of Copenhagen.

During his early years in Denmark, de Hevesy perfected his work on radioactive isotopes. In 1923 he succeeded in applying the tracer technique to determine the intake and distribution of lead in bean plants. These investigations established a pattern for numerous similar researches. With Professor Johannes Nicolaus Brönsted, de Hevesy tackled the problems dealing with the separation of isotopes. Their joint accomplishments on the separation of mercury and chlorine isotopes by diffusion has become classical. Also in 1923, de Hevesy and the physicist D. Coster announced the discovery of the element hafnium by means of the X-ray spectrum method. Dr. de Hevesy completed the chemical separation of hafnium from zirconium of which it is an analogue and analyzed the properties of hafnium compounds. The X-ray technique which de Hevesy introduced was extended and developed further for use in quantitative analysis of the geochemical frequency and distribution of many other elements.

De Hevesy resigned from the institute in 1926 to accept an appointment as a professor of physical chemistry at the University of Freiburg. In 1930 he was Baker Lecturer at Cornell University (Ithaca, New York). He returned to Copenhagen in 1934, the same year in which he initiated a series of tracer experiments based on Harold Urey's discovery of deuterium. By placing goldfish in a solution of heavy water de Hevesy and his colleague Professor Hofer "showed a rapid exchange between the environmental water and that in the body." His studies on the presence of deuterium in human beings showed that the body did not distinguish between ordinary and heavy water (*Nature,* December 17, 1949).

The field of radioactivity was enriched by de Hevesy's use of phosphorus isotopes as tracers in the metabolism of phosphate compounds. Dr. de Hevesy also analyzed the phosphorus-bearing compounds in brain tissue, cancerous cells, and the nucleic acids which constitute the genes. His tracer techniques were widely used in making direct studies in living organisms, where previously such studies had been impossible.

Moving to Sweden in 1943, de Hevesy was appointed a professor at the Research Institute for Organic Chemistry at the University of Stockholm. In the same year he was awarded the Nobel Prize in chemistry "for his work on the use of isotopes as tracer elements in researches on chemical processes." As noted in *Nobel, the Man and his Prizes* (by H. Schück

American—Swedish News Exchange
GEORGE DE HEVESY

and others, 1951), de Hevesy's "method for studying the mechanism of biological processes has revolutionized research in physiological chemistry. In organic chemistry, too, the importance of his method in elucidating the course of a reaction can scarcely be overestimated."

Since World War II, Professor de Hevesy's research activities have continued undiminished. His basic discovery of tracing radioactive atoms through physical processes has been compared in significance with the invention of the microscope, and Dr. Detlev W. Bronk, president of the Rockefeller Institute, has ranked de Hevesy's contributions "among the most important advances in the peaceful use of atomic energy in our time."

In a recent interview at the Rockefeller Institute Dr. de Hevesy said that the most important research project in which he is now involved deals with the formation and life span of red corpuscles in patients suffering from cancer.

The Atoms for Peace Award was conferred on Dr. de Hevesy in January 1959. Designated as the second recipient of the honor by a group of distinguished scientists, de Hevesy was selected from a list of more than one hundred nominees representing some twenty countries. (The first award was made to Niels Bohr in October 1957.) The prize, which was established as a memorial to Henry and Edsel Ford, consists of a gold medal and a cash award of $75,000.

A prolific author, Dr. de Hevesy has been contributing articles to scientific journals for over thirty years. Since 1950 he has produced more than fifty papers on such varied subjects as blood chemistry, iron metabolism, and radiation effects in biochemistry. With Paneth, he wrote the *Manual of Radioactivity* (Oxford University Press, 1926). De Hevesy is also the author of *Das Element Hafnium* (Julius Springer, Berlin, 1927); *Quantitative Analysis*

HEVESY, GEORGE DE—*Continued*
by X Rays (McGraw-Hill, 1932); *Praktikum der Röntgenspektroskopischen Analyse* (Akademischer Verlag, Leipzig, 1932); *Radioactive Indicators* (Interscience Publishers, 1948).

Honorary degrees have been bestowed on de Hevesy by the universities of Cape Town (1929), Uppsala (1945), Freiburg (1948), and Copenhagen (1950). He received honorary M.D. degrees from the universities of São Paulo (1952), Rio de Janeiro (1953), and Turin (1956). Besides the Nobel Prize, de Hevesy has been the recipient of the Canizzaro Prize of the Academy of Sciences of Rome (1929), the Copley Medal of the Royal Society (1950), Faraday Medal (1951), Bailey Medal of the London College of Physicians (1952), and the Silvanus Thompson Medal of the British Institute of Radiology (1956). De Hevesy holds honorary membership in the chemical societies of London and Helsinki, the Royal Institute of London, the Royal Society, and the scientific academies of Copenhagen, Göteborg, Stockholm, Brussels, Rome, and Heidelberg.

George de Hevesy is of medium height and weight; he has brown eyes, brown hair, and a thick mustache. Hiking and skiing are his sports. His religion is Catholic. The scientist married Pia Riis on September 26, 1924 and has one son George Louis, and three daughters, Jenny, Ingrid, and Pia. The family fled from the Nazis in 1943 and sought refuge in Sweden, where de Hevesy adopted citizenship two years later.

References

N Y Times p17 N 27 '58 por

International Who's Who, 1958
Vem är Det, 1957
Who's Who in America, 1958-59

HILALY, AHMED NAGUIB 1891-Dec. 11, 1958 Premier of Egypt at the time of the overthrow of King Farouk in 1952. See *Current Biography* (July) 1952.

Obituary

N Y Times p2A D 12 '58

HILL, ROBERT C(HARLES) Sept. 17, 1917- United States Ambassador to Mexico

Address: b. American Embassy, Mexico, D.F., Mexico; h. Embassy Residence, Londres 102, Mexico, D.F., Mexico; 244 Main St., Littleton, N.H.

United States Ambassador to Mexico Robert C. Hill, whose appointment was confirmed by the Senate on May 20, 1957, is regarded as "one of America's top young diplomats." He had earlier served as envoy to Costa Rica and El Salvador, and at the time of his appointment to Costa Rica, in 1953, he was "the youngest American ever sent abroad with the full rank of Ambassador." In 1956-57 Hill was the Assistant Secretary of State for Congressional Relations. He had been an executive

with the Todd Shipbuilding Corporation and from 1949 to 1953 with W. R. Grace and Company.

Robert Charles Hill was born to Dr. Frank Allen Hill, a physician, and Catherine Lyle (Morse) Hill at Littleton, New Hampshire on September 17, 1917. He spent his boyhood in Littleton and prepared for college at the Taft School, Watertown, Connecticut, where he was president of the Gamma Society and captain of the baseball team. Graduated in 1938, he entered Dartmouth College, Hanover, New Hampshire with the class of 1942, and as a left halfback captained the freshman football team until an injury "put him out of play" (New York *Times,* November 18, 1957).

Beginning his career as a junior executive with the Todd Shipbuilding Corporation, Hill was sent to Washington, D.C. as the national Capital representative of this New England shipbuilding concern. His first association with the State Department was as an officer of the Foreign Service Auxiliary in 1943, the second year of United States involvement in World War II.

After receiving an appointment as clerk in that service in October 1944, Hill was assigned in December as a vice-consul at Calcutta, India. In February 1945 he was assigned to United States Army Headquarters in the China-Burma-India Theatre at New Delhi, as a State Department representative with the rank of captain. In addition, he was put in charge of consular activities at New Delhi.

He studied with the class of 1946 at Boston University Law School, and in 1946-47, his wartime attachment to the Foreign Service having come to an end, he was employed in Washington, D.C. as clerk to the United States Senate Committee on Banking and Currency. For about four years beginning in 1949 he was assistant vice-president at the New York City headquarters of W. R. Grace and Company, operators of a steamship line and aviation subsidiaries serving South and Central America.

On October 24, 1953 Hill was appointed United States Ambassador to Costa Rica, and while in that country he officiated, at the suggestion of President José Figueres Ferrer, as official "observer" in the renegotiation of a contract between the Costa Rican government and the United Fruit Company's local subsidiary. In September 1954 Hill was named Ambassador to El Salvador.

In March 1954, partly "to increase his knowledge of . . . the people of the countries on the route," Ambassador Hill drove his car over the Inter-American Highway from San Salvador to Laredo, Texas. The motion pictures which he took along the way were used by the United States Information Agency, and he later published an account of the trip in the travel section of the New York *Times* (April 17, 1955).

"I was criticized by friends when I was in El Salvador and Costa Rica," Hill told the Senate committee considering his appointment as Ambassador to Mexico two years later, "because I traveled over practically every foot of ground in the country. I slept out in the country in tents that the United States Army provided. . . . I traveled with the United States Information Agency groups often in the countries that I was accredited to. . . . There is no substitute for the Ambassador meeting the people. . . . It is terribly important." Hill also said: "I speak Spanish so that I can get along socially. I would never attempt to negotiate in the language of the country to which I was accredited. . . ."

Early in September 1955 Ambassador Hill was named special assistant to Herbert Hoover, Jr., the Under Secretary of State for Mutual Security Affairs. This appointment was confirmed in October and during the next five months Hill worked in Washington, D.C., coordinating the foreign assistance programs authorized by the Mutual Security Act and preparing and presenting to Congress legislative proposals for the mutual security program. He specialized in aid for underdeveloped countries.

His success was conspicuous, and in February 1956, at a time when foreign policy seemed likely to be a major issue in the coming election campaign, Hill was named to succeed Thruston B. Morton, who resigned to run for the United States Senate, as Assistant Secretary of State for Congressional Relations. This appointment, confirmed on March 7, called for "a very special talent." It effected "a liaison between the executive and legislative branches" and entailed direction of "the strategy of the presentation to Congress of all legislative proposals bearing on foreign relations" (New York Times, July 16, 1956).

As reported in the Times, "key officials" were saying that if it had not been for Hill's knowledge of "how to talk to the legislators," the "showing of foreign aid—and in particular aid to Yugoslavia—would probably have been far worse." In letters to Senators during 1957 Hill recorded that the State Department was trying to "create a climate favorable to eventual Spanish participation in NATO" and believed that "statehood for Alaska and Hawaii . . . should be viewed in a favorable light by the great majority of United Nations members." He expressed "special concern over restrictions on the admission of persons of the Jewish faith into Saudi Arabia."

During the Senate Foreign Relations Committee hearing on May 17, 1957 on the nomination of Robert Hill to succeed Francis White as Ambassador to Mexico, a Democratic Senator, Mike Mansfield of Oklahoma, paid tribute to the work of Hill, a Republican, as Assistant Secretary of State. "I think the record ought to show," Mansfield declared, "that he has performed his tasks superbly, that he has been impartial, nonpartisan."

At this hearing, which was followed quickly by Senate confirmation, Hill stated that he "did not think the United States government should enter into grant programs in Latin America to any great extent." He believed "the situation in Mexico from an economic and industrial point of view is excellent," while keeping "an open mind on the oil problem." He was sworn in as Ambassador to Mexico on May 20, 1957.

Harris & Ewing

ROBERT C. HILL

In seeking to win the good will of the people, Hill visited "every large newspaper and television plant in Mexico City." When he served the opening kickoff in a football game between a Mexican and United States university, he "booted the ball sixty yards. It was by far the best kick of the game and the crowd kept yelling, 'Bring back the Ambassador'" (New York Times, January 3, 1958).

On October 18, during an international film festival at Mexico City, Hill helped the United States to achieve a diplomatic victory when he introduced from the stage Willie Mays, Roy Sievers, and Bobby Avila, who were playing exhibition baseball in Mexico. Their appearance, coming immediately after the screening of The Defiant Ones, helped to curb the anti-American feeling that had previously troubled the festival.

He has "declined to be overoptimistic" about the favorable impression he has made. The New York Times (January 3, 1958) observed that "for one thing, the imposition of a tariff on lead and zinc could make Hill one of the most unpopular Ambassadors in Mexico overnight." Hill has "repeatedly said that this will be his last diplomatic tour and that he will return to private business."

The honorary Doctor of Laws degree was conferred on Robert Hill by New England College at Henniker, New Hampshire in May 1957. He stands six feet three inches tall, weighs around 220 pounds, and has brown eyes and brown hair. His church is the Episcopal; his political affiliation is Republican; and his fraternity is the Alpha Delta Phi. His clubs are the Metropolitan, Chevy Chase, and University in Washington, the Elkridge in Baltimore, and the Dartmouth in New York City. Robert Charles Hill and Cecelia Gordon Bowdoin were married on December 1, 1945 and

HILL, ROBERT C.—*Continued*

have two sons, William Graham Bowdoin Hill and James Bowdoin Hill.

References

Christian Sci Mon p14 O 12 '57
N Y Herald Tribune p3 Ap 20 '57 por; p8 D 15 '57 por
N Y Times p16 Ap 2 '57; p16 N 18 '57 por; p7 Ja 3 '58 por
U S News 40:20 Mr 9 '56; 41:125 Jl 20 56 por; 42:22 My 3 '57 por
Department of State Biographic Register (1957)
International Who's Who, 1958
Who's Who in America, 1958-59

HILLIARD, JAN Nov. 28, 1910- Author

Address: h. Richview & Royal York, R.R. #1, Weston, Ontario, Canada

Reprinted from the *Wilson Library Bulletin* Mar. 1959.

All who have visited and loved the Maritime Provinces of Canada, particularly Nova Scotia, will welcome the novels of Jan Hilliard, a Nova Scotian who has set the action of her first two books in that lovely region. *The Salt-Box* (Norton, 1951) deals with memories of her youth: from the upstairs window of the salt-box house her father "could see the lighthouse on the point and hear the grating voice of the foghorn. He saw old ships leaning on the wind, coming in with sugar and molasses from Barbados or outward bound with lumber; and tankers trailing smoky feathers against the sky; and all the little fishing boats, like white moths caught in the restless waters." Again and again the story evokes the life of harbor dwellers.

Jan Hilliard was born Hilda Kay in Yarmouth, Nova Scotia, a small seaport of the

Peggy Todd

JAN HILLIARD

south shore, on November 28, 1910. Her father, Leonard Kay, was an Englishman who married a Nova Scotian girl, Dorcas Batten. On her death he left his family to wander through western Canada in the gold-rush days, but with no success. This story is delightfully told in *The Salt-Box* which won the Canadian Stephen Leacock award for humor in the year of its publication.

Jan Hilliard attended Yarmouth Academy. From the age of eleven she had written verse and short fantasies, but what she really wanted to do was to draw and paint. After high school, she went to New York where she enrolled in the Grand Central School of Art. But presently she discovered that her portraits were better painted with a pen and that lack of funds would curtail her art studies. She soon returned to Canada to work as a secretary, first in Montreal and later in Toronto.

Each of Miss Hilliard's books has a character who paints, but not very successfully. She has herself continued sketching and painting as a hobby, and she is secretary of an amateur art group. Of her own work she likes best her ink sketches on wet paper.

Jan Hilliard is a keen admirer of the women writers Virginia Woolf, Rosamond Lehmann, Elizabeth Bowen, and Colette. But she admires also some work of Dylan Thomas, Truman Capote, and all of James Thurber—"Bless him," she says. Two of her favorite books are *The Sea Around Us* (Oxford, 1951) by Rachel Carson and *The Importance of Living* (Reynal, 1937) by Lin Yu-t'ang.

Her first published work was a long short story. Since then she has concentrated on the novel. In between times, she adds to a "journal of events (not world events, but such things as the war against stray cats in our garden), opinions, random thoughts, reminiscences, people, ideas for books." This she hopes to winnow and publish on some more leisurely day.

Jan Hilliard's husband, Joseph Howe Grant, is a former Bluenose (Nova Scotian to the initiated) whose ancestors came from Scotland in the 1770's. Although this is the only resemblance, so did the forebears of the Mackays in her second work, *A View of the Town* (Abelard-Schuman, 1954).

Of it her publishers said, "This is a quiet small-town comedy about life in a Nova Scotia community, with a nice gallery of eccentric characters"—Simon Ward, who has spent a leisured lifetime compiling a local history and who would never have completed it alone; Mary Mackay, a brandy-bibbing matriarch wielding power with ill-concealed cruelty. The long struggle between these two affects all about them, not least Simon's unhappily married younger daughter. Regarding her search for freedom and happiness, John Gould of the New York *Times Book Review* said, "It is fair to note that Canadian divorce laws are stringent and that we southerners must accept that fact as a sufficiently motivating condition for this story. We may be obliged, too, to accept some of the other wee Down-East orts without carping; for Miss Hilliard writes a lively prose, does well with her characterizations and conversations."

Miss Hilliard's third novel, *The Jameson Girls* (Abelard-Schuman, 1956), is set in a colonial mansion, perched on a high precipice above the swift-flowing Niagara River, much like a castle of the robber barons of old. This is the domain of King Jameson, the wicked and domineering rumrunner king, who made his fortune in prohibition days. The story tells of his death and of the women surrounding him as he slowly dies. Walter O'Hearn of the New York *Times Book Review* declared that "the Niagara valley small town lives in these pages, gables, dust and all, but King Jameson is only a carnival goblin." Her next novel was *Dove Cottage* (Abelard-Schuman, 1959).

Jan Hilliard and her husband have a dog, Gina Lollobrigida, a "beautiful and devoted black terrier of questionable origin" who firmly believes she is a member of the family—"Gina is not people, but don't tell her," says Miss Hilliard. These three live on the borders of the city of Toronto in "an elderly sort of house surrounded by trees," where our author keeps busy, adding to her writing, housework, gardening, stargazing, sketching, and painting. Her days are full; as she says, "There's never enough time!" Her portrait shows a blonde woman with hazel-green eyes and a mouth ready to smile easily at the humor she sees in all the world around her.

References

Canadian Who's Who, 1955-57
Hilliard, Jan The Salt-Box (1951)

HINES, DUNCAN Mar. 26, 1880-Mar. 15, 1959 Author; publisher; gourmet; compiled guides to American restaurants and hotels. See *Current Biography* (May) 1946.

Obituary

N Y Times p31 Mr 16 '59

HOARE, SIR SAMUEL JOHN GURNEY, 2D BARONET *See* Templewood, Samuel John Gurney Hoare, 1st Viscount

HODES, HENRY I(RVING) (hō'dēs) Mar. 19, 1899- Former United States Army officer
Address: b. c/o Adjutant General, Department of the Army, Washington 25, D.C.

When a group of nine American soldiers were being held in East Germany in 1958, the man responsible for the first negotiations for their release was not a trained Foreign Service diplomat. He was General Henry I. Hodes, Commander in Chief of the United States Army in Europe. The exigencies of the "cold war" had forced many roles upon General Hodes, who commanded what has been called the world's "most modern combat-ready army." He retired from the Army on March 31, 1959.

After graduating from West Point, Hodes had performed military duty on three continents. As a colonel, he was twice wounded

U. S. Army

GEN. HENRY I. HODES (RET.)

while leading a regimental combat team in World War II. Hodes joined the fighting in Korea as assistant commander of the Seventh Infantry Division three months after the conflict began, and later figured prominently in the truce negotiations between the United Nations and the Chinese forces.

Henry Irving Hodes was born to Harry Ketcham and Mary Sophia (Shaw) Hodes in Washington, D.C., on March 19, 1899. After graduating from the United States Military Academy on July 2, 1920, he was commissioned a second lieutenant in the infantry. He was promoted immediately to the grade of first lieutenant and sent to the Cavalry School at Fort Riley, Kansas, where he completed the basic course. For the next seven years he served with the Fourth Cavalry at Fort Brown, Fort Sam Houston, and Fort McIntosh in Texas, a period of service interrupted only by an uncompleted flight-training course with the Air Service from September 1923 to April 1924.

As a cavalry lieutenant and later captain (August 1, 1935), Hodes also served with the 6th Cavalry at Fort Oglethorpe, Ga., the 26th Cavalry at Fort Stotsenburg, Philippine Islands, the 13th Cavalry at Fort Riley, and the 8th Cavalry at Fort Bliss, Texas. During this period he was regarded as "one of the Army's top horsemen," according to *Time* magazine (July 16, 1951). He completed the advanced equitation course at the Cavalry School in Fort Riley, and later was graduated from the Command and General Staff School at Fort Leavenworth, Kansas (June 1937).

In September 1939 Captain Hodes began a new phase of his military career by entering the Army War College. After graduating in June 1940, he was assigned to the War Department General Staff and promoted to major (July 1, 1940). He served with the General Staff as a member, later as Assistant to the Chief of the

HODES, HENRY I.—*Continued*

Operations Branch, and then as Chief of the Troop Movement Section, Theater Group, Operations Division. He was promoted to lieutenant colonel on December 24, 1941 and to colonel on February 1, 1942.

Colonel Hodes left Washington in November 1943 for duty as a field commander. He assumed command of the 112th Infantry Regiment in January 1944, and served with it in France, Luxembourg, and Germany. After having been awarded the Silver Star for gallantry in action, he was hospitalized by his second combat wound on September 20, 1944.

Two months later, Hodes was returned to the United States to rejoin the General Staff, Operations Branch. After being promoted to brigadier general (January 8, 1945), he became Assistant Deputy Chief of Staff. From September 1947 to February 1949 he was Chief of Staff for the United States Fourth Army.

In May 1949 Brigadier General Hodes was transferred to Japan for duty as Assistant Commander of the 1st Cavalry. A year later (June 1950) he was moved to the Seventh Infantry Division in the same capacity, and went with his new outfit for its first combat mission in Korea. Beginning in September 1950, and lasting until January 1952, his Korean assignment involved more and more responsible duties, and he was promoted to major general February 13, 1951. Hodes first became a public figure when he was named to the United Nations Armistice Delegation. He attended the first conference, on July 10, and later became the senior delegate for the U.N. team. At that time, Murray Schumach in the New York *Times* (October 26, 1951) remarked that "probably every general who was in Korea when [Hodes] first arrived has been rotated, or, in a few cases, killed."

Before joining the negotiations, whose primary task was the establishment of a cease-fire and a neutral belt between South and North Korea, Hodes had seen the conflict at first hand. He participated in the amphibious landing at Inchon and won his second Silver Star for gallantry in the fight for Seoul, the South Korean capital. His only son, a West Point graduate, was seriously injured in action in Korea.

Perhaps this helps explain his firmness during the truce negotiations, when he was characterized as a "stern taskmaster" who regarded the Korean fighting as "almost a crusade." An American news magazine described him at one point in the negotiations as "wearing a green nylon flight jacket, with a frayed cigar clamped in his teeth and an expression of grim satisfaction on his face" (*Time*, December 3, 1951). His stern quips with the Chinese delegation were more than once featured in the American press. During this time, Hodes was Chief of Staff and later Deputy Commander of the Eighth Army. On December 17, 1951, just before the negotiators became involved with the repatriation of prisoners of war, he left the U.N. team to assume command of the 24th Infantry Division.

In March 1953 Hodes began a short assignment as commandant of the Command and General Staff College at Fort Leavenworth, Kansas. He was transferred to Europe the following February, when he assumed command of the Seventh Corps in Stuttgart, Germany. As commanding general of one of the two Army corps headquarters in Europe, Hodes was head of the 5th and 9th Infantry Divisions. He spent "four days in the office and three in the field during a normal work week," according to correspondent Cecil Neth of the Army newspaper *Stars and Stripes*.

In December 1954 Hodes was moved up to the post of commanding general of the Seventh Army, with headquarters also in Stuttgart. In his new assignment, Hodes was responsible not only for the two combat divisions in Seventh Corps, but also for the three divisions in Fifth Corps at Frankfurt. He was promoted to lieutenant general on August 18, 1954. During his command, the Seventh Army reached its present peak of combat strength.

"The United States Seventh Army in Europe —chief United States cog in the NATO 'power for peace' program—has quietly emerged during the past year as the largest and most modern combat-ready army command in the world," said an Army review for 1955 (as quoted in the New York *Times,* January 3, 1956). "Today it is the only American field army equipped with the full range of nuclear weapons possessed by the United States for ground force use. All year these new weapons and equally important new combat techniques have been integrated into the Seventh Army, making it one of the world's key deterrent forces against war."

The following year, Hodes was given command of the United States Army, Europe, with responsibility for all ground forces on the Continent. He was named to the post by President Eisenhower to succeed General Anthony C. McAuliffe, who retired as USAREUR Commander in Chief on May 31, 1956. Two days after assuming formal command in Heidelberg, Hodes was promoted to the four-star rank of general (June 1, 1956).

"In taking over in Europe," commented *U.S. News & World Report* (March 16, 1956), "General Hodes will inherit a U.S. command that has been strengthened with the latest in atomic weapons; is ready—as General McAuliffe said recently—to fight 'for every inch of the ground we hold.' It could make aggression against Western Germany a costly venture."

How costly it might prove was indicated by General Hodes in a Berlin press conference on November 30, 1958 as tension grew over Russian demands that the Western powers withdraw from their sector of the city. "If West Berlin is attacked in any way," said the General, "it is a military problem and I know what I will do" (Los Angeles *Times*, December 1, 1958). He made it clear that he considered any new Communist blockade of West Berlin an attack on the United States.

General Hodes is a veteran soldier. Among his decorations are the Distinguished Service Medal, the Legion of Merit, the Silver Star, and the Purple Heart, all with oak leaf cluster; the Bronze Star and the Combat Infantryman's Badge; and the Distinguished Service Order (Great Britain) and the Order of Military Merit Taiguk (Korea). He has been described as "a tall, impressive soldier [with] the sort of piercing glance that's been the bane of second lieutenants since the first gold bar was minted."

Hodes married Laura Celeste Taylor on July 9, 1925. They have one son, John Taylor, himself an Army officer and a combat veteran of Korea, and two daughters, Jean Marie and Laura Celeste.

References

N Y Times p3 O 26 '51; p4 Ja 3 '56
Time 58:26 D 3 '51
U S News 40:16 Mr 16 '56
Who's Who in America, 1958-59

HOPE, STANLEY C. 1893- Organization official; industrial executive

Address: b. SoundScriber Corp., 8 Middletown Ave., North Haven, Conn.; h. 435 E. 52d St., New York 22

President of the National Association of Manufacturers for the year 1959, Stanley C. Hope was elected to his one-year term of office in December 1958 to succeed Milton C. Lightner, now chairman of the board. The 21,329 member companies of NAM are said to represent about 85 per cent of the manufacturing output of the United States. Most of Hope's business career has been in the oil industry, and from 1949 to 1958 he was president of Esso Standard Oil company. He is now president of SoundScriber Corporation.

Stanley C. Hope was born in Springfield, Massachusetts in 1893. Toward the end of World War I he began an association with the Standard Oil (New Jersey) family of companies which continued for forty years. First appointed sales manager in the New York office of the Gilbert & Barker Manufacturing Company, a New Jersey Standard affiliate, he was named the company's European sales manager in 1919.

"From 1922 to 1927," stated the New York *Herald Tribune* (September 25, 1950), he "worked abroad for G. & B. and other Jersey companies . . . changed the system of selling gasoline in Europe and North Africa to a bulk from can basis . . . a tough job to convince skeptical Europeans that bulk storage and pump deliveries were safe." Hope returned to the United States in 1927 to assume the vice-presidency of Gilbert & Barker, and two years later he was, in addition, named vice-president of the Atlas Supply Company, another affiliate. He was elected president of Gilbert & Barker in 1932 and became chairman of the Atlas Supply Company in 1956.

In the World War II defense effort Hope's firm, Gilbert & Barker, made artillery components for the armed forces. Hope himself served on New Jersey's Coordination Committee, and as chairman of a remote control systems group for the War Department, he co-

Fabian Bachrach

STANLEY C. HOPE

ordinated the activities of some twenty-five companies making devices for automatic sighting and firing mechanisms for antiaircraft guns. For his achievement Hope received a citation from the Army Ordnance Department. After the war he served as head of the Hartford-Springfield post of Army Ordnance Association and chairman of its fire control instrument division.

Hope was named president of Stanco, another Jersey Standard subsidiary, in 1946, and in the summer of 1948 became the executive vice-president, as well as a director, of Esso Standard Oil Company, the principal domestic manufacturing and marketing affiliate of the Standard Oil Company (New Jersey). On October 22, 1949 Stanley C. Hope was elected president of Esso Standard Oil Company, and filled this position until his mandatory retirement from Standard oil in July 1958, at the age of sixty-five. He succeeded Monroe J. Rathbone, who went to the parent Standard Oil Company (New Jersey) as a director and in December 1953 became its president.

When the first catalytic cracking plant in New England was dedicated at Esso's refinery in Everett, Massachusetts in October 1953, Hope declared that in one day this 24,000-barrel unit could turn out enough fuel to keep 4,000 cars in continuous operation for twenty-four hours and heat 42,000 homes. Announcing in April 1955 a physical capital budget for Esso Standard of $133,000,000 for new and improved marketing facilities in eighteen states, Hope noted that among new units to be installed were fluid hydroforming, fluid coking, and hydrorefining devices developed by Esso Research & Engineering Company, as the former Standard Oil Development Company had recently been renamed. Esso's 1956 capital expenditure budget of $126,600,000 contained sizeable items for refinery improvement and expansion, service station building, and capacity

HOPE, STANLEY C.—*Continued*

enlargement in the growing field of petro-chemicals.

Not long after leaving the petroleum business, Hope accepted the presidency in 1958 of SoundScriber Corporation, replacing William C. Less. SoundScriber, which employs about 370 workers and owns a 56,000-square-foot plant in North Haven, Connecticut, manufactures electronic dictation and transcribing machines, remote control microphones, dual recorders, and tape recorders. Earlier, in March 1958, he had become a director and member of the executive committee of S. H. Kress & Company.

On December 5, 1957, during its sixty-second annual Congress of American Industry in New York City, the National Association of Manufacturers elected Milton C. Lightner as its president for 1958 and Stanley C. Hope as its national vice-president. NAM presidents serve for one year only and are customarily succeeded by the national vice-president.

At a press conference following his expected election to the presidency at the 1958 NAM convention, Hope said that he thought American labor laws were "in pretty good shape," but he indicated that the NAM would continue to press for "right-to-work" legislation. Inflation, he believed, would stay for a long time, though "nobody, least of all the manufacturers, wants it to continue" (New York *World-Telegram and Sun,* December 5, 1958). Hope further indicated that an NAM decision limiting directors to three consecutive terms would bring more "realistic" executives into the association's policy making. "The quicker we convince the public we are not a reactionary organization," he declared, "the better it will be" (*Time,* December 15, 1958).

In a "year-end" statement issued early in January, the NAM president called himself a "restrained optimist" about business in 1959. "The economy," he asserted, "hit the bottom of the 1957-58 downturn last April. . . . The gross national product is at a new high and will continue to advance" (New York *World-Telegram and Sun,* January 12, 1959). Hope also belongs to the Advertising Council and the American Management Association.

Civic interests have occupied much of Hope's time. In November 1952 he was sworn in as an honorary deputy commissioner of the New York City department of commerce, and in April 1953 he accepted the chairmanship of the steering committee for the new federal civil defense establishment headed by Val Peterson. This steering committee outlined an "industry program" for the protection of plants and workers against atomic attack, and chose Hartford, Connecticut as the site of a pilot operation.

Through the years Hope has served with the National Safety Council and the Esso Safety Foundation, and in October 1958 he became chairman of the Automotive Safety Foundation. Early in October 1955 he was named a trustee of the Esso Education Foundation organized by the Standard Oil Company (New Jersey) and a group of affiliates "to assist the nation's privately supported colleges and universities." This foundation received pledges for 1956 of $1,300,000.

In March 1955 Hope was appointed to the New York State Business Advisory Council and in the following month was one of nine prominent businessmen added to the board of directors of the New York Council of the Navy League of the United States. Hope is a director of Williamsburg Restoration, Inc. During 1954 he was chairman of the campaign for United Cerebral Palsy of New York City. The March of Dimes, United Negro College Fund, Girl Scouts, and Boy Scouts are other organizations whose causes he has helped.

Stanley C. Hope is married and makes his home in New York City. Boating and skiing have been mentioned as his favorite outdoor relaxations. He is a keen yacht-racing competitor and was one of the organizers of the Mont Tremblant Ski Club in Quebec.

References

> N Y Herald Tribune p24 S 25 '50 por
> Time 72:68 D 15 '58 por
>
> Business Executives of America (1950)
> Who's Who in America, 1958-59

HOPPE, WILLIE Oct. 11, 1887-Feb. 1, 1959 Billiard champion; winner of fifty-one world titles. See *Current Biography* (June) 1947.

Obituary

> N Y Times p1+ F 2 '59

HOUSEMAN, JOHN Sept. 22, 1902- Producer; director; writer

Address: b. c/o Columbia Broadcasting System, Inc., 485 Madison Ave., New York 22

To present Shakespeare's plays "unencumbered by pedagogical clichés and theatrical fustian" has been the aim of producer and director John Houseman, who for three years was artistic director of the American Shakespeare Festival Theatre and Academy in Stratford, Connecticut. "To the actor, Shakespeare's plays bring richer and better parts than anything else ever written," he has stated. "They are a field day for producer or director, and when they are done in an original, vital way, they should be even more of a field day for the audience." In 1956 he was appointed artistic director of the Festival and he served in that post until his resignation on August 29, 1959.

The success of the Stratford venture has convinced Houseman that a classical repertory theater can someday become a reality in the United States. Eventually he would like to maintain a classical repertory theater the year-round, giving actors fairly consistent employment and providing an atmosphere hospitable to creative effort.

To his assignments he brings a rich fund of experience as director, producer, and writer. With Orson Welles he founded the Mercury Theatre in New York in 1937. He directed

New York productions of *King Lear, Coriolanus, Lute Song,* and *Four Saints in Three Acts.* Among his many motion-picture credits are *Lust for Life, Executive Suite,* and *Julius Caesar.* He has also directed radio and television programs and is currently one of the executive producers of *Playhouse 90.* He has lectured on the drama at Vassar and at Barnard.

John Houseman (whose surname has been Anglicized) was born on September 22, 1902 in Bucharest, Rumania to Georges and May Haussmann. His father was a French grain merchant; his mother was Welsh-Irish. He received his education in private schools in Paris and at Clifton College in Bristol, England. From 1923 to 1925 Houseman was a prosperous grain broker in Argentina, England, Canada, and the United States. He began to write and adapt plays from the French and German as a hobby, then moved to theatrical production and direction, when the export market dropped out from under him.

Houseman first achieved theatrical recognition in New York in 1934 when he staged *Four Saints in Three Acts,* an opera by Virgil Thomson with text by Gertrude Stein. It aimed at complete simplicity in libretto and music, was performed by an all-Negro cast against scenery of cellophane, and ran for forty-eight performances.

For the Theatre Guild Houseman directed Ibsen's *Lady from the Sea* and Maxwell Anderson's *Valley Forge* in 1934. In 1935 he produced *Panic,* with Orson Welles in the leading role. This marked the first association of the two men who were to do so much to revitalize the New York theater. In the next year Houseman directed Leslie Howard in a Broadway revival of *Hamlet,* and directed the WPA Negro Theatre, a subdivision of the Federal Theatre. He produced Marlowe's *Dr. Faustus* (directed by Welles) and Shakespeare's *Macbeth.*

In November 1937 Houseman and Welles founded the Mercury Theatre and met with spectacular success. They introduced to New York audiences such new actors as Joseph Cotten and Agnes Moorehead in productions of *Julius Caesar* in modern dress, *The Shoemaker's Holiday, Heartbreak House, The Cradle Will Rock,* and *Danton's Death.* When the Columbia Broadcasting System brought the Mercury Theatre to radio audiences, the group gained world-wide attention with its broadcast in October 1938 of *The War of the Worlds.* The show stampeded some listeners into panic, when they interpreted it as an actual invasion of the United States by men from Mars.

After two seasons with the Mercury Theatre, Houseman directed *The Devil and Daniel Webster,* and produced *Liberty Jones* and *Native Son* on Broadway. He also wrote dramatizations for the Helen Hayes radio show. He first went to Hollywood in 1941, as vice-president of David O. Selznick productions. After Pearl Harbor, however, he resigned to join the Office of War Information as chief of the radio program bureau of the Overseas Branch where he produced the "Voice of America" programs.

JOHN HOUSEMAN

Returning to Hollywood in late 1943, Houseman became a producer for Paramount Pictures, and later for Radio-Keith-Orpheum, Rampart, and Metro-Goldwyn-Mayer film companies. Among the films he produced are: *The Unseen* and *Miss Susie Slagle's* (associate producer), 1945; *The Blue Dahlia,* 1946; *Letter From An Unknown Woman,* 1947; *They Live By Night,* 1948; *Man With Much Heart,* 1949; *Holiday for Sinners,* 1952; *The Bad and the Beautiful,* 1952; *Julius Caesar,* 1952; *Executive Suite,* 1954; *Her Twelve Men,* 1954; *Moonfleet,* 1954; and *Lust for Life,* 1956.

Several of the films he produced or directed won honors. *Julius Caesar* and *The Bad and the Beautiful* were nominees for the "best picture" award of the Academy of Motion Picture Arts and Sciences. *Julius Caesar,* an MGM production, directed by Joseph L. Mankiewicz and produced by John Houseman, starred John Gielgud as Cassius, Marlon Brando as Mark Antony, Louis Calhern as Julius Caesar, and James Mason as Brutus.

For MGM Houseman also produced *Executive Suite,* starring Fredric March, William Holden, and eight other stars. Based on Cameron Hawley's best-selling novel, the film was directed by Robert Wise. Alton Cook called it "a searching and dramatic study of modern business warfare" (New York *World-Telegram and Sun,* May 7, 1954).

Based on Irving Stone's novelized biography of Vincent Van Gogh, *Lust for Life,* starring Kirk Douglas, had its world première on September 17, 1956 in New York. Bosley Crowther of the New York *Times* wrote (September 18, 1956): "It is gratifying to see that MGM in the persons of producer John Houseman and a crew of superb technicians has consciously made the flow of color and the interplay of compositions and hues the most forceful devices for conveying a motion pic-

HOUSEMAN, JOHN—*Continued*

ture comprehension of Vincent Van Gogh." The film was directed by Vincente Minelli, who in 1959 won an Academy award for his direction of *Gigi*.

Between motion-picture assignments, Houseman has written and produced various shows for the Columbia Broadcasting System, among them the early experimental television show, *Sorry, Wrong Number*. For the television program *Playhouse 90* he recently directed *Wings of the Dove* and *Face of a Hero*. In 1959 he produced the documentary crime series, *The Law Breakers*.

From time to time Houseman returned to New York to direct plays: *Lute Song* (1946), *King Lear* (1950), and *Coriolanus* (1954). For his skill in directing *Lute Song*, an adaptation of the Chinese classic, *Pi-Pa-Ki*, Houseman was praised by Howard Barnes (New York *Herald Tribune*, February 17, 1946) for keeping "the action surprisingly fluid in his staging [resulting] in a lovely and eloquent fantasy . . . a piece of enchanting stagecraft."

Until John Houseman's production of the Shakespearean tragedy appeared on Broadway in December 1950 (starring Louis Calhern), Brooks Atkinson of The New York *Times* had agreed with Charles Lamb's contention that *King Lear* could not be acted. But in his column of December 26, 1950 Atkinson confessed that Calhern and Houseman had forced him to change his mind.

When Houseman staged one of Shakespeare's more controversial plays, *Coriolanus,* at the Phoenix Theatre in New York in January 1954, it ran for fifty performances and won acclaim from the critics. Most of them extolled the vitality, clarity, and sprightliness of this production of a classic too seldom performed in the United States.

After becoming artistic director of the American Shakespeare Festival Theatre and Academy in Stratford, Connecticut in 1956, John Houseman directed several of the plays that were produced; others were staged by Jack Landau, now the major director. Attendance at the Stratford Festival has increased each year since it was founded in 1955 by Lawrence Langner until in 1958 it reached 165,000 for the season. Its acting company (trained in its Academy) has presented the plays of Shakespeare in six major American cities. The Academy is a year-round institution enrolling a student body of about one hundred.

The Festival presents a series of pre-season performances at Stratford at reduced rates for schools which bring their pupils to the shores of the Housatonic River by the busload. Houseman announced that its 1959 series (which began on May 19) was a sell-out. The fifth season of the Festival began on June 12, 1959 with *Romeo and Juliet. The Merry Wives of Windsor, All's Well That Ends Well,* and *A Midsummer Night's Dream* are also in its 1959 repertory.

In collaboration with Jack Landau, Houseman has written a narrative and pictorial history entitled *The American Shakespeare Festival; the Birth of a Theatre.* Its publication

in June 1959 by Simon & Schuster coincided with the beginning of the fifth season of the Festival.

John Houseman is married to the former Joan Courtney. They have one son, John Michael. Houseman is six feet tall, weighs about 200 pounds, and has brown hair and blue eyes. He has been described by various observers as "erudite," "elegantly gray-flanneled," and as having a "slightly incongruous cherub's face." "There is no one way to do Shakespeare," Houseman told Lambert Jester (*Cue,* June 14, 1958). "By lending characteristic American energy, vividness, and imagination to the Bard's works, maybe we can come closer to the Renaissance spirit."

References

Good H 145:60 Jl '57
Sat R 37:33 My 1 '54
International Motion Picture Almanac, 1959

HUMPHREY, DORIS Oct. 17, 1895-Dec. 29, 1958 Dancer and choreographer; pioneered in techniques of modern dance. See *Current Biography* (April) 1942.

Obituary

N Y Times p32 D 30 '58

HUNTER, KERMIT (HOUSTON) Oct. 3, 1910- Playwright

Address: b. c/o University of North Carolina, Chapel Hill, N.C.

Regarded as one of the leading contemporary American authors of outdoor historical plays, Kermit Hunter has written some eight "symphonic dramas" of the type that Paul Green introduced to the South. Hunter also composes the incidental music for his plays. At least two of his dramas, *Unto These Hills,* performed annually at Cherokee, North Carolina, and *Horn in the West,* produced each year at Boone, North Carolina, seem to have established themselves as classics of the outdoor summer theater.

Kermit Houston Hunter, a native of McDowell County in southern West Virginia, was born on October 3, 1910. In the autobiographical sketch that he contributed to *North Carolina Authors* (University of North Carolina Library, 1952), he stated that he was born "in the coalfields [section] of an average middle-class Protestant family." In high school he wrote poems, essays, and plays. At Ohio State University in Columbus, to which he transferred from Emory and Henry College in Emory, Virginia, he wrote several plays and won the Vandewater Poetry Prize in 1931. Also in 1931 he received the B.A. degree.

After traveling in Europe, he concentrated his attention mainly on music for the next seven years. He taught for a brief time, won the West Virginia Young Artists' Contest in piano in 1933, and then studied at the Juilliard School of Music in New York City. "Also between 1931 and 1940," he wrote in *North Carolina*

Authors, "I worked on two newspapers, was secretary of two chambers of commerce, business manager of a professional baseball team, and organist and choir director of a Methodist church."

During five years in the Army, beginning in 1940, Hunter rose to lieutenant colonel, became assistant chief of staff of the Caribbean Defense Command, and was awarded the Legion of Merit. After World War II he was for two years (1945-47) the first business manager of the North Carolina Symphony Society, the pioneer state-supported symphony orchestra in America.

Although Hunter had continued to write plays, even during his military service, he did not begin to study playwriting seriously until he enrolled in 1947 at the University of North Carolina in Chapel Hill for graduate work. There he studied under Samuel Selden, chairman of the department of dramatic art and director of the Carolina Playmakers, the troupe organized by the late Frederick H. Koch in the 1920's to create a regional drama. Three one-act plays by Hunter were produced by the Carolina Playmakers, and in 1948, when the Cherokee Historical Association was seeking an author to write a play about the history of the Cherokee Indians for presentation at the Mountainside Theatre then under construction at Cherokee, North Carolina, Professor Selden recommended Hunter for the commission.

Completing the play, *Unto These Hills,* early in 1949, Hunter offered it as his M.A. thesis and won the Joseph Feldman Playwriting Award for the same year. Also in 1949 the North Carolina Legislature appropriated $35,000 for the production of *Unto These Hills* which opened the Mountainside Theatre on July 1, 1950.

The earliest and the most famous of annually revived American outdoor historical spectacles, Paul Green's *The Lost Colony,* was first staged on Roanoke Island in 1937 to commemorate the 350th anniversary of Sir Walter Raleigh's ill-fated settlement. As Bernadette Hoyle pointed out in *Tar Heel Writers I Know* (Blair, 1956), in writing *Unto These Hills,* Kermit Hunter "had the problem of depicting the whole history of the Cherokee in North Carolina." But "instead of trying to show four hundred years in detail," he followed the pattern of *The Lost Colony* by confining the main action to a brief period (1828-40) and concentrating on the theme of the brotherhood of man.

Hunter has called Samuel Selden the "spiritual father" of *Unto These Hills,* which had a cast of 140 (of which seventy were Cherokees) and was staged by Harry Davis, the associate director of the Carolina Playmakers. *Unto These Hills,* which was published by the University of North Carolina Press in 1951, has been produced every succeeding summer for a two-month run and by 1954 was attracting audiences totaling 150,000 to the Mountainside Theatre.

Forever This Land, Hunter's second outdoor drama, was commissioned by the New Salem Lincoln League for production in 1951 at New Salem, Illinois, where Abraham Lincoln spent

KERMIT HUNTER

his young manhood. The play was (in the author's words) "an effort to show . . . Lincoln emerging as a product of the land and its people." Nevertheless, when Professor John T. Flanagan of the University of Illinois visited the Kelso Hollow Theatre in the New Salem State Park he found that "the main story of *Forever This Land* is not primarily the Lincoln story, but rather the tale . . . of a town" (*New York Times,* July 29, 1951).

Brooks Atkinson thought it "about the best" of the outdoor historical dramas he had seen (New York *Times,* July 6, 1952). In two seasons it drew some 85,000 persons; then it closed because of what Hunter has called "the shakiness of the local organization" (*Variety,* March 2, 1955).

A third outdoor drama, *Horn in the West,* first presented at the Daniel Boone Theatre, Boone, North Carolina in 1952, was commissioned by the Southern Appalachian Historical Association with the stipulation that "the story should exemplify the religious, economic, political and social life of . . . some early period, preferably the time of Daniel Boone."

"So I took a loyal British subject in the New World," Bernadette Hoyle quoted Hunter as saying, "and showed how he changed from an aristocrat to a democrat, from . . . [an advocate of a] State church to religious freedom." *Horn in the West* has been revived each year for a ten-week season, drawing an average summer audience of around 42,000. Hunter's fourth outdoor drama, *The Bell and the Plow,* dealing with the life of Father Eusebio Kino, the Jesuit missionary explorer of the Southwest, was presented at Tucson, Arizona in 1954 as part of the Tohono Festival.

Remaining at the University of North Carolina as an instructor in English while studying for a Ph.D. degree, Hunter wrote regular drama, poetry, and fiction, as well as outdoor plays. Bernadette Hoyle noted that he received

HUNTER, KERMIT—*Continued*

a Guggenheim Fellowship for the twelve months beginning June 1, 1955 to enable him to work on "a sociological novel laid in the background of the soft-coal industry in southern West Virginia."

A fifth outdoor drama, *Voices in the Wind,* dealing with the history of Florida, was completed in 1955 for presentation in February 1956. During 1956 *Chucky Jack* was produced at Gatlinburg, Tennessee and *The Eleventh Hour* at Staunton, Virginia. *Chucky Jack* which was repeated in 1957, concerned John Sevier, the first governor of Tennessee. *The Eleventh Hour,* sponsored by the Virginia Woodrow Wilson Centennial Commission and the Staunton-Augusta Chamber of Commerce, dealt with the life of President Wilson, who was born in Staunton.

Hunter's eighth outdoor drama, *Thy Kingdom Come,* was based on the life of Saint Paul. It was first presented at the Sherwood Amphitheatre, Roanoke, Virginia on June 25, 1957 for a summer run. Among the high lights in the drama, which was repeated in 1958, were the stoning of Saint Stephen, the conversion on the road to Damascus, and the final meeting of Peter and Paul.

"I share . . . the idea," Kermit Hunter has stated, "that the outdoor drama represents the greatest challenge today, in that the American theatre should be a strong and growing thing not confined to Broadway, that out of the urge of local areas for expression can come a new era in American drama" (*North Carolina Authors*).

References

Hoyle, B. Tar Heel Writers I Know (1956)
North Carolina Authors (1952)
Walser, R. G. Picturebook of Tar Heel Authors (1957)

HURTADO, CÉSAR BARROS *See* Barros Hurtado, César

INNOCENTI, FERDINANDO (ēn-ō-chĕn'tĭ) Sept. 1, 1891- Italian industrialist

Address: b. Innocenti Società Generale per l'Industria Metallurgica e Meccanica S.p.A., Via Senato, 19, Milan, Italy; h. Piazza San Babila, 4d, Milan, Italy

Fifty years ago Ferdinando Innocenti, president of the Innocenti corporation of Milan, opened a small machine shop which grew into a vast industrial enterprise, making its founder one of Italy's leading producers of heavy machinery, a builder of steel mills in many countries, and the world's second largest motor scooter manufacturer. An innovator all his life, he perfected tubular steel scaffolding early in his career and later developed a special process for manufacturing seamless steel tubes. The motor scooter is an adaptation of his tube production for the frame, and the low-priced automobile which is reported to be his next venture

in low-cost transportation is a similar adaptation for the chassis.

Ferdinando Innocenti was born in humble circumstances in Pescia, in northern Italy, on September 1, 1891, the only son of Dante and Chiti (Zelinda) Innocenti. He has one sister, Bianca Innocenti Fusaia. He received early schooling in his native town, but for the most part he was self-taught in principles of mechanical engineering. In place of formal technical training, Innocenti had an enthusiasm for machinery. At the age of sixteen, in order to support himself at school, he worked in a machine shop, and he is reported also to have been at one time a plumber's helper. At eighteen he established his own machine shop.

In 1922 he abandoned his shop in his home town to go to Rome, where he set up his first plant and experimented with structural steel tubing for bolting together horizontal and vertical sections to form scaffolding, pontoons, bridges, and removable grandstands. The idea soon brought him recognition in Italy and abroad, and in time the name Innocenti became identified with structural tube assemblies commonly seen as temporary scaffolding on buildings under construction. He specialized in furnishing steel pipe of every size and industrial application.

Less than ten years after moving to Rome, Innocenti again changed his base of operations, transferring in 1931 to Milan, in Italy's fast-growing industrial north. At this time and until 1933 his company was called Innocenti Steel Tube, Inc. He specialized in the production of seamless steel tubes based on a special hot-piercing process of ingots or billets, not requiring the special specifications for steel needed in other seamless methods. His enormous factory, named Dalmine, is still widely known in the industry as the Italian producer of seamless tubes for Italy and for export.

Black Star

FERDINANDO INNOCENTI

When Italy began to reconstruct its economy at the end of World War II, Innocenti decided to strike out anew instead of rebuilding plants that had been extensively damaged in the war. His new project, which included retooling, was carried out on so vast a scale that Innocenti was soon able to enter world markets and meet international competition in two new sectors of the machinery industry: heavy equipment and transportation. His basic product in the latter is the Lambretta, a popular, low-cost, two-wheel passenger scooter, attaining a fuel mileage of 120 miles a gallon. There has been a series of models of the three-wheel commercial version.

The heavy machinery plants, the realization of which had long been an ambition of Innocenti, soon were receiving orders for equipment for steel mills and seamless tube manufacturing plants, as well as for heavy machine tools. Production grew rapidly and won preferred standing in many countries for Innocenti design and construction of steel mills and tube plants.

The Lambretta sales for 1956 were reported at $43,000,000, with exports to ninety-six countries, including 6000 scooters for the United States. The heavy machinery sector earned another $19,000,000 in an expanding world market. *Time* (December 23, 1957) reported, "Now the world's No. 2 scooter producer (170,000 a year behind Italy's Vespa), Ferdinando Innocenti has raised his sights to four wheels. Occasion: a deal to produce a Lambretta version of West Germany's four-passenger, four-wheel Goggomobil. . . . Innocenti's tubing will form the framework of the new Lambretta Goggomobil. He will have to dress it up for the Italian market, since Italians demand more flair to body style than the functional-minded Germans. But he still hopes to charge only $500 for his Lambretta Goggo, half the price of the cheapest Fiat."

Innocenti's network of plants in Milan expresses the most advanced technical design and modern construction, ranking in range of productive capacity and up-to-date methods with the leading plants of its kind in the world. In an area where work stoppage and political strikes are not uncommon, the industrialists' labor relations are marked by an almost strike-free record. Labor benefits are numerous. Lunches are provided to all workers below cost on company premises. An entire building is set aside for workers' meetings and activities. Management is excluded from it and the workers are in charge, promulgating their own house rules and regulations through committees of their own choice. Adjacent to it are a soccer field and swimming pool. The company provides free schooling for apprentices in mechanics and courses leading to specialization and higher paid categories in the plants.

In 1957 the Venezuelan government granted Innocenti a contract to plan, design and construct a $400,000,000 steel complex. This complex, now in the course of construction, will range from the mining of the iron ore to production of finished steel along a five-mile strip at the head of the Orinoco River. By the end of 1957 Innocenti was employing some 100 engineers in Venezuela. He had set up a three-year training program for several hundred Venezuelans at his plants in Milan and other plants in Italy and Germany to be the technical cadre for the enterprise on the Orinoco, which is scheduled for completion in 1962. Other important installations built by the Innocenti corporation are in Argentina, Mexico, the United States, Canada, Belgium, Germany, France, England, Switzerland, Poland, Yugoslavia, Czechoslovakia, and India.

Innocenti received an honorary degree in engineering from the Politecnico in Milan (1953). His decorations include Cavaliere del Lavoro, Gran Ufficiale Repubblica Italiana, and Cavaliere di Colombo.

Ferdinando Innocenti married Anita Boccarini on March 31, 1923. He has one son, Luigi, a mechanical engineer, who is vice-president of the firm. Innocenti, a quiet, energetic man, is five feet four inches tall, weighs 143 pounds, and has blue eyes and brown hair. He is a Roman Catholic. As a hobby he collects antiques with which, in rooms of his own design, he decorated an elaborate penthouse in Rome and a mansion in Milan. During the summer he vacations on his yacht in the Mediterranean.

References

Time 25:66+ D 23 '57 por
International Who's Who, 1958
Panorama Biografico degli Italiani d'Oggi (1956)

IONESCO, EUGÈNE Nov. 26, 1912- Playwright
Address: b. c/o Grove Press, Inc., 195 Broadway, New York 3; c/o Société des Auteurs Dramatiques, 9 et 11 rue Ballu, Paris (IX) France

Europe's most controversial *avant-garde* playwright, Eugène Ionesco, was, by his own admission, "a resounding failure" in Paris in 1950; in 1958 he became "a dumbfounded success" in Paris, London, and New York. His plays, *The Chairs, The Lesson, The Bald Soprano, Jack,* and *Amédée* have also been performed in Italy, Germany, Israel, Switzerland, Poland, Yugoslavia, Brazil, and other countries.

Ionesco's eccentric and grotesque characters have provoked critics to write: "These odd, elliptical fantastifications are amusing and provocative" (Brooks Atkinson, New York *Times*) and "hollow and pretentious fakery" (Richard Watts, Jr., New York *Post*). "Thus Ionesco has maintained his controversial status by splitting reviewers down the middle," observed *Theatre Arts* (March 1958). "It is just possible that his place in the theatre is analogous to that of so-called pure dance in ballet, which concentrates on abstract impressions rather than narrative." Although critics may differ over the merits of Ionesco as a playwright, most of them agree that he is preoccupied with one theme: the futility of human communication.

Eugène Ionesco was born in Bucharest, Romania on November 26, 1912 of Romanian par-

EUGÈNE IONESCO

ents. He lived in France from the age of one until he was thirteen, then moved to Romania, where, at twenty-four, he became a professor of French. Three years later he returned to France and worked for a publishing house. He is now a French citizen.

"For a long time he was extremely poor," according to Muriel Reed (*Réalités,* December 1957). "Rodika, his wife, worked in a lawyer's office . . . his writings did not interest any publishers, but they [the Ionescos] laughed about it. They rapidly made a host of friends whom Ionesco entertained hugely by relating all his failures." His first recorded publication, *No!*, was a "fragmentary meditation on the general absurdity of life, the inanity of culture and the uselessness of language as a means of communication," noted Richard Roud (*Commonweal,* August 29, 1958).

When interviewed by Edouard Roditi for *Harper's Bazaar* (May 1958), Ionesco said that in his first play, *The Bald Soprano (La Cantatrice Chauve)* he culled "absurd sentences from a popular foreign-language manual. The play . . . is a kind of spoken pantomime and acquires its meaning from the tone and gestures of the actors, who can transform it into a comedy, a farce, or even a melodrama."

Seeing his first play produced on the stage of a small Paris theatre (Théâtre des Noctambules) had been "a prodigious, irreplaceable, unheard-of adventure" for him. Although two of the three critics present at the première on May 11, 1950 dismissed the play as dull and worthless, Ionesco began writing plays as fast as he could.

The Lesson (La Leçon) was first produced at the tiny Théâtre de Poche on February 20, 1951. A few young critics dared to applaud his work, and when *The Chairs* was presented on April 22, 1952 at the 350-seat Théâtre Nouveau Lancry, writers rallied to defend the play. Samuel Beckett (author of *Waiting for Godot*) was among those who praised Ionesco's fresh approach. Dramatist Jean Anouilh, who went on record as saying that he preferred the play to the dramas of Strindberg, compared its combination of drollery and gloominess to the atmosphere prevailing in the comedies of Molière.

The Chairs also received praise from some of the Broadway critics when it opened at the Phoenix Theatre in New York City on January 9, 1958. The central character, an aged man (played by Eli Wallach), is determined to leave his "message to mankind" before he dies. He and his aged wife (played by Joan Plowright) invite a varied group of notables who are invisible to the audience. They line the stage with chairs for their guests. The climax comes when the Orator, who is visible, arrives to deliver the old man's message, but he speaks only gibberish.

The Lesson concerns a homicidal professor who kills his young students. "The play perhaps symbolized how pedantry destroys individuality," commented *Time* (January 20, 1958). "Ionesco's seems an agreeable but thin talent, with a kind of philosophic-puppet show appeal."

William Saroyan, in his introduction to *The Chairs* and *The Lesson (Theatre Arts,* July 1958), said of Ionesco: "He seems to find the world entirely laughable. His plays . . . bewilder, delight, annoy, astonish, amaze, and amuse me. . . . Who told him to transform lunacy into a thing of greater beauty than mathematics itself? What triggered this Rumanian in Paris, at the age of forty-five? Ionesco most likely would prefer people to laugh. Laugh all you like, but just try to forget what you saw and how it made you feel. You can't. It was art. It was new art."

"Ionesco has been compared to Lewis Carroll," observed Euphemia Van Rensselaer Wyatt in *Catholic World* (March 1958), "but his macabre cheerfulness is closer to *Cautionary Tales* of Hilaire Belloc, with, however, an undercurrent of dramatic tension. He seems to have a natural showman's gift for the dramatic idiom." Henry Hewes in *Saturday Review* (January 25, 1958) remarked: "The ridicule in *The Chairs* is not subtle, but it has an effective dramatic suddenness . . . actors fluctuate quickly between the intensely tragic and the hysterically comic." Ionesco has explained that *The Chairs* is based on the theme of absence, and *The Lesson* on the taking possession of one being by another.

His next play, *Jack, or the Submission (Jacques, ou la Submission)*, was first produced in October 1955 at the Théâtre de la Huchette. Jacques is a young man whose family wants him to marry. He chooses for his fiancée a girl with three noses. Some of the Paris audience shouted its disapproval, and there were fist fights in the lobby. By this time Ionesco's name had become celebrated in Paris. In 1956 *The Chairs* was revived, and audiences were not lacking at the Studio des Champs Elysées. In 1957 the double bill of *The Bald Soprano* and *The Lesson* accumulated a total of 300 performances in Paris. Ionesco can no longer tell witty stories about his failures, but he still quotes the opinion of his daughter who once said: "Just between the two of us, papa, I won't repeat it, naturally, but won't you admit that your plays are rather silly and a little childish?"

When *The Bald Soprano* and *Jack, or the Submission* were presented in New York at the Sullivan Street Playhouse in June 1958, Richard Watts, Jr., wrote in the New York *Post* (June 4): "Ionesco's art is the spiritual kin of the Royal Nonesuch with which the Duke and the King fooled the gullible townspeople in *Huckleberry Finn.* . . . There is no denying him a certain comic gift. . . ."

Ionesco's other plays include *Amédée, or How to Get Rid of It,* in which he places a corpse on the stage, symbolizing the dead love of an old couple—a corpse that grows and grows until it finally invades the entire space. In *Le Nouveau Locataire* (*The New Tenant*) a man rents a flat in Paris and then a procession of furniture fills the stage and hems him in. "In this new dramaturgy," said Jean Paris (*Reporter,* October 4, 1956), "objects supersede words. It is the inanimate that points to our failure in this universe. We suffocate in materialism where objects take precedence over thoughts."

In *L'Impromptu de l'Alma,* Ionesco appeared as himself, and named his three critics Bartholomaeus I, II, and III. He claims that their remarks were borrowed from the published reviews of Ionesco's plays by French critics. The play makes a plea for the artist to free himself from the interference of pressure groups of the Right or the Left.

With his wife Rodika, and daughter, Marie-France, Ionesco lives in a Paris flat crowded with furniture and decorated with theater bills. "I am not a political critic," he says. "I spoof the so-called bourgeois world much as Flaubert . . . or as Congreve and Sheridan made fun of the ridiculous aspects of their society. . . . Still, I'm not a moralist as were Pascal and Molière. . . . It is often difficult to invent anything as absurd as what we hear as we go about our daily business. . . . In all my plays I try to present a critique of some form of conformist thought and phony verbiage" (*Harper's Bazaar,* May 1958).

Eugène Ionesco is "round and short, shy and apologetic," according to Josette Lazar (New York *Times,* January 5, 1958). Edouard Roditi in *Harper's Bazaar* (May 1958) described him as having the sadness and weariness of a clown . . . whose serious purposes . . . are always concealed beneath a mask of comedy." Muriel Reed in *Réalités* (December 1957) wrote that he is "gentle, mischievous, and good-natured . . . stubborn and independent . . . an insomniac . . . chain smoker. . . . He is both a sociable and worried man."

In the United States Ionesco's plays have been made available in English translation by Grove Press in both paper-backed and hardcover editions published in 1958. One volume includes *Amédée; The New Tenant;* and *Victims of Duty,* translated by Donald Watson, and the other, entitled *Four Plays,* includes *The Bald Soprano; The Lesson; Jack; or, the*

Submission; and *The Chairs,* translated by Donald M. Allen.

References

N Y Times II p1 Ja 5 '58
Réalités p45 D '57 por
Theatre Arts 42:14 Mr '58; 42:25 Jl '58

IRONS, ERNEST E(DWARD) Feb. 17, 1877-Jan. 18, 1959 Chicago physician; president of the American Medical Association (1949-50). See *Current Biography* (October) 1949.

Obituary

N Y Times p27 Ja 19 '59

IRONSIDE, WILLIAM EDMUND IRONSIDE, 1ST BARON May 6, 1880-Sept. 22, 1959 British army officer; served as Chief of Imperial General Staff (1939-40); was Commander in Chief of Home Forces (1940); received rank of field marshal (1940). See *Current Biography* (May) 1940.

Obituary

N Y Times p39 S 23 '59

JACOPI, GIULIO Sep. 7, 1898- Archaeologist

Address: b. Piazza delle Finanze 1, Rome, Italy; h. Via Gaeta, 87, Rome, Italy

Among the finds in the archaeological excavations currently in progress at Sperlonga, Italy may be the original Greek Laocoön group, proving that the famous statue which has been the pride of the Vatican Museum in Rome for over three centuries is only a copy, according to Professor Giulio Jacopi, archaeologist in charge. Under his direction, experts are now piecing together over 12,000 fragments found in a cave believed to have been a banquet hall of the Emperor Tiberius in the first century B.C., in which they also expect to find sculptural groups depicting such legendary figures as Scylla and Ganymede. The project has resulted in what has been described by *Life* (December 2, 1957) as possibly "one of the most important modern finds of ancient art."

Professor Jacopi, who has been superintendent of antiquities in Rome since 1956, previously directed important excavations at Rhodes, Anatolia, Caria, Reggio Calabria, and Ostia. He has taught archaeology at the universities of Bologna and Messina and is the author of over 100 books and articles in his field.

Giulio Jacopi was born on September 7, 1898 in Trieste, then an Austrian crownland. His father, Giuseppe Jacopi, was secretary-general of the municipality of Trieste, and his mother was the former Luciana Anzulovich. He spent a harried youth from the outbreak of World War I, when his father, a member of the Italian National Liberal party of Trieste, was arrested on a charge of sedition and plotting against Austria. Brought before a military tri-

GIULIO JACOPI

bunal, he was saved from execution by the sudden suicide of his accuser, but was nevertheless deported to a political internment camp at Gödersdorf, near Vienna. Giulio Jacopi's mother, unable to endure the anxiety, committed suicide.

In Austria during the war years, young Giulio enrolled in the University of Graz in 1916. He studied at the University of Vienna in 1918 and graduated from the University of Rome in 1920. For the next three years he traveled extensively in Greece and the Aegean Islands and did postgraduate studies in Athens and at the School of Italian Archaeology in Rome. He received a diploma from the latter school in 1923.

He was appointed superintendent of monuments and excavations for the Italian islands of the Aegean, at Rhodes, in 1924 and remained in that post until 1933. During that time he founded the Institute of Archaeological History at Rhodes and directed important excavations there. Discoveries included the acropolis of the Homeric city of Camirus and over 1,000 tombs which Jacopi felt demonstrated the "evolution of civilization and of funeral rites from Homeric times to those of Alexander, with equipment of unsuspected wealth and variety" (*Illustrated London News,* May 20, 1933).

Also unearthed was the marble funeral monument of Crito and Timarista, which Jacopi considers perhaps the most beautiful example of Attic art of the fifth century B.C. Important documents on festivals, the history of Camirus, its political and sacred institutions, and its monuments were recovered.

In 1933 Jacopi was director of the Roman Society of Antiquities (Antichita de Roma). From 1935 to 1938 he headed the Italian archaeological mission in Anatolia, where he discovered an arch dedicated to Augustus, the local Jupiter, Tiberius and Livia. The monument, perhaps a part of the forum of the city of Aphrodisias, was decorated with a marble frieze depicting a festival. His discoveries there led to important documentation on the famous Aphrodisian school of sculpture and on the city itself, built in the fourth century B.C. He received special recognition from the Italian Academy in 1937 for his discoveries at Aphrodisias.

During World War II Jacopi rescued from danger the archaeological remains in many museums located in combat areas, including Bologna, Ferrara, Parma, Modena, Reggio Emilia, Piacenza, Rimini, and Ravenna. He acted as secretary to the Italian Institute of Ancient History from 1939 to 1942 and for the next four years was superintendent of antiquities for the provinces of Emilia and Romagna. He served in a similar position in Reggio Calabria from 1946 to 1954, was in charge of the excavations at Ostia from 1954 to 1956, and became superintendent of the major division of antiquities in Rome in the latter year. In addition, he held the chair in archaeology at the University of Bologna in 1944-1945 and at the University of Messina from 1946 to 1956.

Since the fall of 1957 Professor Jacopi has been in charge of the excavations carried on in the cave of Tiberius at Sperlonga, a tiny village near Gaeta. Remains had lain hidden until Erno Bellante, an engineer and amateur archaeologist in charge of building a road nearby, started digging in the long-unused cave in his spare time and began to unearth its treasures.

The discovery of fragments bearing the signatures of Athenodorus and Agesander, two of the three sculptors from Rhodes mentioned by the Roman historian Pliny as responsible for the Laocoön, led Professor Jacopi to make a tentative identification of the statue on September 25, 1957. When two days later, a fourth fragment gave the last five letters of Polydorus, the third artist listed by Pliny, Jacopi became more certain of his thesis.

Other archaeologists have, however, disputed his claim on the grounds that there are discrepancies between the fragments at Sperlonga and available information about the original group. The former is too large, they claim, to have been carved from a single block of marble, as Pliny stated.

The Laocoön group depicts a bearded priest of Apollo with his two sons, agonizing in the coils of a serpent as punishment, according to Virgil, for warning the Trojans against bringing the wooden horse into their city. The unsigned Vatican statue was also discovered by accident in a cave. A peasant came across fragments in the Baths of Titus (now called Baths of Trajan), Rome in 1506. Michelangelo identified it as the statue mentioned by Pliny, but there has long been a suspicion that it was a copy of an earlier work.

In addition to the Laocoön, twenty-two marble heads, corresponding to Greek statues of various sizes, have been found at Sperlonga. Another group of statuary, when finally pieced together, may show Zeus carrying off Ganymede to Olympus to become cupbearer of the gods. A third seems to depict Ulysses and six sailors fighting off Scylla the sea monster.

The fragments are being put together in a workshop in the cave, which is 150 feet wide by 180 feet deep and is at the foot of a rock rising from the sea. A protecting wall was built to keep out the tides. Both Suetonius and Tacitus refer to a villa that Tiberius occupied on that part of the seacoast, and it is thought that the cave was his banqueting hall which he deserted after narrowly escaping death when the roof fell in.

Giulio Jacopi was married to Marica Monte Santo on April 19, 1929. He has gray eyes and brownish hair, is five feet eleven inches tall and weighs 180 pounds. He is a Roman Catholic. He is a member of the German Archaeological Institute and the Institute of Etruscan Studies. Since 1933 he has been an authorized private tutor in archaeology and history at the University of Rome. He was made a Knight Professor of the Sovereign Military Order of Malta in 1931, a Knight of the Crown of Italy in 1942, and a Cavaliere Ufficiale al Merito of the Republic of Italy in 1953.

Chief among Jacopi's books, for which he does much of the photography himself, are *Clara Rhodos* (Bergamo, 1927-33), *Rodi* (Bergamo, 1933), *Patmo, Coo e le Minori Isole Italiane dell'Egeo* (Bergamo, 1937) and *Scavi in Prossimita del Porto Fluviale di S. Paolo* (Milan, 1943). In reviewing the first of these, W. van Ingen (*American Journal of Archaeology*, October 1936) praised its wide appeal and usefulness to experts in various fields and described it as "a monument to its author's versatility and thoroughness."

References

Chi è? (1957)
Panorama Biografico degli Italiani d'Oggi (1956)

JANSSENS, JEAN BAPTISTE, VERY REV. *See* Janssens, John Baptist, Very Rev.

JANSSENS, JOHN BAPTIST, VERY REV. Dec. 22, 1889- Superior General of the Jesuit Order

Address: 5 Borgo Santo Spirito, Rome, Italy

His distinguished background in linguistics, jurisprudence, and educational administration makes the Very Reverend John Baptist Janssens, Superior General of the Society of Jesus, eminently qualified to head one of the most scholarly and well-disciplined orders in the Roman Catholic Church. Leadership of the Jesuit Order is considered one of the most important offices in the Church, and the Superior General is elected to it for life. When delegates from the fifty world-wide provinces of the Society of Jesus met in Rome to elect a new head in 1946, their choice of Belgian-born Father Janssens as Superior General was unanimous. He succeeded the Very Reverend Vladimir Ledochowski, who died in 1942.

Wide World

VERY REV. JOHN BAPTIST JANSSENS

Born in the ancient town of Mechlin or Malines, Belgium on December 22, 1889, John Baptist Janssens was one of four children born to Charles and Christina (Kockerols) Janssens. A number of his uncles and great-uncles belonged to religious orders. Before his death in 1952, his brother was a Benedictine monk in the Abbey of Mont César, Louvain, Belgium.

In 1899 Janssens left his home town, long the ecclesiastical capital of Belgium, and entered Hasselt College, a secondary school. For the next few years he studied the classics and distinguished himself in rhetoric by placing first in the course. After graduating from Hasselt in 1905, he entered St. Louis College in Brussels where he studied classical philology, philosophy, and law. On September 23, 1907, he entered the Jesuit novitiate at Tronchiennes, Belgium.

After two years at Tronchiennes, Janssens was sent to the Jesuit College of Theology and Philosophy at Louvain. When he completed this two-year preparation in 1911, he entered the University of Louvain to study civil law, at the instigation of Father Vermeersch, whose aid and successor he was eventually to become. In 1914 he earned his doctorate in Civil Law.

In the long and arduous spiritual preparation that leads up to ordination in the Society of Jesus, Janssen had before him four more years of theological studies. However, after one year at the theologate (a Jesuit house of theological studies) he was assigned to teaching Latin in the College of Our Lady of Antwerp, a secondary school. In 1917 he returned to Louvain to finish his studies in theology. While he was there, his father died.

In 1919, at the age of thirty, John Baptist Janssens was ordained to the priesthood. After his ordination, he returned to Louvain once more to finish his final year of theology. In 1920, while serving his tertianship (a third period of novitiate after ordination) at Tronchi-

JANSSENS, J. B., VERY REV.—*Continued*

ennes, he served as assistant to the Master of Novices. The next year he left for Rome, where he entered the Gregorian University to take a biennium (two-year course) in Canon Law. He received a doctorate in that subject in 1923.

While attending Gregorian University, Father Janssens took a leave of absence in 1922 in order to go to Constantinople to work among White Russians who had escaped from the Russian Revolution. Associating with the refugees, he learned to speak Russian, but he does not consider himself as fluent in it as he is in Flemish, French, German, Italian, and Latin.

Returning to Belgium from Rome, Father Janssens became professor of Canon Law on the Jesuit Theological Faculty at Louvain. There he taught for the next ten years. On August 17, 1929 he became Rector of the Jesuit Theological Institute at Louvain. During his years there he helped found the collection of works on theology, philosophy, and allied subjects which became known as the Museum Lessianum, and for a time served as its director. He led a group of theologians interested in catechetical work, and was rewarded by seeing the Centre de Documentation Catéchétique, now known as the International Center for Studies in Religious Education, established in Brussels.

After a decade of teaching Canon Law at Louvain, Father Janssens was chosen to represent the Belgian provinces at a Procurators' Congregation in Rome, where, as rector administrator, he met delegates who administered the Society's far-flung provinces. When he returned to Louvain he continued as Rector for two more years, until in 1935 he became instructor of Tertians at Tronchiennes. In this capacity he was responsible for guiding young priests in their final year of spiritual formation. He was able to converse with the Tertians in their own language, whether it was Dutch, French, German, English, Italian, Spanish, or Russian.

In 1938 Father Janssens represented the Northern Belgium province at a General Congregation of the Society of Jesus in Rome, summoned by Superior General Vladimir Ledochowski, the man he was destined to succeed. When the congregation disbanded, Father Janssens did not return to teaching. The geographical area of his administration expanded beyond the Jesuit Theological Institute at Louvain, when he was appointed Provincial of Northern Belgium. In 1939 he visited his province's mission of Kisantu in the Belgian Congo. The administrative ability he displayed in the Congo led to his appointment as president of the general council of Congo mission superiors.

The days of World War II were trying ones for the Jesuit Order. In 1942 Superior General Ledochowski died, leaving the "spiritual shock battalion" of the Roman Catholic Church without a General. Conceived by the soldier-saint, Ignatius of Loyola, along military lines, this "light cavalry" of the Church has the same supreme commander as all Roman Catholics— the Pope. At his command, the Jesuits are geared for immediate action in any sector of the world.

Although he was ready, like his fellow Jesuits, for any assignment anywhere, Father Janssens was assigned to his own homeland. In 1943 he was named Pro-Vicar General of Holland and Belgium. Agents from the Gestapo often visited the Jesuit House in Brussels during World War II. Father Janssens gave them a dignified reception at the same time that he skilfully protected his fellow priests. Many Jesuits in his province had joined the underground movement and Father Janssens knew it, but with his usual astuteness he guarded his secrets as he escorted the Gestapo agents around the premises. With the adroitness of a diplomat he showed them only what he wanted them to see. It is said that he helped elicit the declaration of one Nazi that "we'd rather fight a whole division than argue with one Jesuit."

On September 15, 1946, Father Janssens was elected Superior General of the Jesuit Order. Twenty-sixth in the line of successors of St. Ignatius, Father Janssens is the spiritual leader of 34,000 Jesuits (of whom 7,500 are Americans) in the Ignatian apostolate of teachers, preachers, missionaries, and leaders of social action.

In September 1957, the Superior General, who was suffering from asthma and who a few months earlier had admitted that his health was not equal to the tasks demanded of him, called an "extraordinary" General Congregation, to which 180 priests came from thirty-three countries. Conclaves of the General Congregation, the highest legislative agency of the order, are usually called on the death of the Superior General. This "extraordinary" session was only the fifth summoned in the four and one-quarter centuries of the existence of the Society of Jesus.

Observers believed that the conclave was summoned to revise the administrative leadership, thus relieving the ailing General, but the only announced change after a session of nine weeks was the addition of three aides to represent India-East Asia, South America, and Africa.

With the creation of the India-East Asia assistancy, the Society of Jesus now has nine assistancies, or geographic regions, into which it is divided for administrative purposes. Each assistancy is represented at Jesuit headquarters in Rome by an "assistant" who is a member of the Superior General's cabinet of advisers. With the addition of the three aides, the fundamental, one-man rule of the Society of Jesus appeared to remain unchanged.

Although Father Janssens has never visited the United States, he is known for his knowledge of American life and affairs, and is reported to be concerned with the growth of materialism in that country. Forming the largest national group in the Jesuit Order, the American Jesuits, who have long been famous for their colleges and universities, are now holding key positions in Jesuit headquarters in Rome. Father Vincent A. McCormick, who heads the American assistancy, is a member of the Superior General's cabinet.

Father Janssens is a thin man, medium in height, with sparse, light brown hair. Gentle but alert, and with a dry sense of humor, he shows intense interest in any person who happens to be speaking to him. He does everything he can to promote straight and logical thinking, both in himself and in his subordinates. His simplicity as a Jesuit is reflected in his surroundings. A Jesuit acquaintance says his office contains only a desk, three bookshelves, two straightbacked chairs, and one religious picture on the wall. His desk is reported to be "completely clean, like that of a man who has got his business all done."

References

N Y Times p7 S 6 '57 por
Newsweek 28:83 S 23 '46

JENSEN, JACK EUGENE *See* Jensen, Jackie

JENSEN, JACKIE Mar. 9, 1927- Baseball player

Address: b. Boston American League Baseball Company, Boston 15, Mass.; h. Crystal Bay, Nev.

JACKIE JENSEN

Since 1954 Boston Red Sox outfielder Jackie Jensen had played beneath the long shadow of greatness cast by Ted Williams. He had been traded twice by other American League teams. But in 1958 Jackie Jensen emerged as the American League's Most Valuable Player. He scored 233 points in the poll of the twenty-four man committee of the Baseball Writers Association of America, winning on the strength of a 1958 record that included 122 runs batted in, the league's highest total, 35 home runs, and a .286 batting average. Further, he played in all of Boston's 155 games.

The award established Jensen as a figure of national prominence in a major sport for a second time. In 1948 he had been named an All-American fullback while playing football on the University of California team.

Jack Eugene Jensen was born on March 9, 1927 in San Francisco, California to parents who became divorced when he was five years old. To support Jackie and his older brothers, his mother worked eleven hours a day in a warehouse. While a pupil in high school, he took jobs in restaurants, manufacturing plants, and freight yards.

Growing up included for Jackie Jensen a large variety of sports. Red Smith wrote in *Collier's* (July 8, 1950): "Jackie Jensen couldn't remember a time when he hadn't been active in sports, hadn't dreamed of playing professional ball. As a high-school junior in Oakland, California [in the Bay area around San Francisco where he was raised], he had been chosen on the all-city teams in baseball, football and basketball. As a senior he had repeated in all sports. As a junior in the University of California, he'd been All-American fullback, had run 67 yards for a touchdown in the Rose Bowl." During World War II Jensen served briefly in the Navy. Still in training when the war ended, he was assigned for a time to Far-

ragut, Idaho as athletic instructor for court-martial prisoners.

At the end of his junior year in college, in June 1949, Jensen joined the Oakland team of the Pacific Coast League. His contract called for a payment of $25,000 a year over a three-year period. He proved disappointing, both at bat and in the field. His baseball experience had been limited to college, where he divided his time between pitching and the outfield. He had been a good college player, having led California to the national collegiate championship in 1948, but the competition was a great deal stiffer in the Pacific Coast League.

In 125 games in 1949 Jensen hit only .261. He hit nine home runs and made 16 errors afield for a fielding average of .942, a mediocre record for an outfielder. He was not ready for the major leagues, but because of a "bonus rule" then in effect, any ballplayer who received more than $6,000 for signing with a team could spend only one season in the minors. He was bought from Oakland by the New York Yankees and reported to that team for spring training in 1950.

During his first season with the Yankees, Jensen had the low batting average of .171; he played in 45 games and hit only one home run. He divided the 1951 season between Kansas City, then a minor league team in the American Association, and the Yankees, with which he hit .298 in 56 games.

The New York Yankees traded Jensen, along with pitcher Frank Shea and outfielder Archie Wilson, to the Washington Senators for outfielder Irv Noren in the spring of 1952. Arthur Daley wrote of the trade in the New York *Times* (May 6, 1952): "It is quite possible Jackie will develop into a star. Branch Rickey, as shrewd a judge of ball players as ever lived, always asks two questions about any prospect.

JENSEN, JACKIE—*Continued*

Can he run? Can he throw? . . . Jensen can run and he can throw."

In 144 games with the Senators in 1952, Jensen batted .286, drove in 80 runs and hit 10 home runs. It was a satisfactory season, but Jensen tailed off in 1953. He again hit 10 home runs, and batted in 84 runs, but his average dipped to .266. In December 1953 he was traded to the Red Sox for pitcher Maurice McDermott and outfielder Tom Umphlett.

"Jensen's contributions to the Red Sox have been outstanding," a writer for the *Christian Science Monitor* (February 27, 1959) pointed out. "He has been a regular who is wonderfully dependable—a good hitter and base runner and an ever-improving fielder. . . . On a team where the brilliant Ted Williams starred, Jensen never failed to be a valuable asset. He has worked his way up in baseball to the point of being a key member of a big-league team. . . . Partly because of Williams' brilliance, Jensen never had the spotlight with the Red Sox the way he did as a college football star. He has been content with the knowledge of his own steady improvement and the contributions to the team which made it possible."

Jensen's record with the Red Sox shows that only in 1956 did he fail to bat in more than 100 runs for Boston and that season he had 97. He hit 25 home runs in 1954, 26 in 1955, 20 in 1956 and 23 in 1957. He had a .315 batting average with the Red Sox in 1956, and his lowest average with the Boston club was .275 in 1955. In 1954 he led the league in stolen bases with 22 and in 1956 he led the league in triples with 11. His 116 runs batted in during 1955 also was a league high score.

When Jackie Jensen was named the American League's Most Valuable Player in 1958, he became the first member of a non-pennant-winning team to be given the award since 1954, the year in which Yogi Berra of the Yankees had been the recipient. The Red Sox finished in third place in 1958.

In January 1959 Jensen received another honor. He was named winner of the Clark Griffith Memorial Award for the year's outstanding contribution to baseball. In late February 1959 he signed a contract with the Red Sox for $40,000, a boost of $11,500 over his 1958 salary (New York *Times,* February 28, 1959).

Jackie Jensen is married to the former Zoe Ann Olsen, who was an Olympic diving star in the late 1940's. They met when Jensen was a lifeguard at the swimming pool of the Athens Athletic Club in Oakland and were married on October 16, 1949. The Jensens have a daughter, Jan, and a son, Jon. Jensen spends his winters at his home in Crystal Bay, Nevada. He is also part owner of the Bow and Bell Restaurant in Oakland.

The husky, blue-eyed baseball player has curly blond hair, is five feet eleven inches tall, and weighs 190 pounds. He throws and bats righthanded. His "pet peeve" is flying, which terrifies him. His hobbies are gardening and reading. Sports writers find him accessible and forthright.

References

Colliers 126:30+ Jl 8 '50 por; 129:24+ Je 21 '52 por
Sat Eve Post 231:31+ Ap 4 '59 por
Sport Illus 8:40+ Je 23 '58 por
Baseball Register, 1958

JERNEGAN, JOHN D(URNFORD) June 12, 1911- United States Ambassador to Iraq

Address: American Embassy, Baghdad, Iraq

An urgent search by Secretary of State John Foster Dulles for an outstanding diplomat to head the American Embassy in Communist-infiltrated Iraq resulted in the appointment in November 1958 of John D. Jernegan, a career diplomat. The new ambassador, who has specialized in Mediterranean and Middle Eastern affairs for twenty-one of his twenty-three years in the Foreign Service, replaced Waldemar J. Gallman, who became the director general of the Foreign Service.

John Durnford Jernegan, the only child of Edward Skinner and Ida (Hollingsworth) Jernegan, was born on June 12, 1911 in Los Angeles. His father was a banker. He was educated in Salt Lake City and in Palo Alto, California. At Palo Alto High School, from which he was graduated in 1929, he joined the debating team and worked for the school newspaper.

Majoring in political science at Stanford University, Jernegan was graduated in 1933 "with great distinction" and as a member of Phi Beta Kappa. At Stanford he continued his interest in journalism, serving as a reporter, night editor, and associate editor of the Stanford *Daily*. He also worked part time as a sports writer for the San Francisco *Chronicle* and as a correspondent for the Oakland *Tribune*.

After his graduation from Stanford, Jernegan spent a year at the Georgetown University School of Foreign Service and another year at Stanford University where, in 1935, he received a Master of Arts degree in political science. His thesis topic was "The International Law of Contraband and Blockade."

In 1936 Jernegan worked for a short time as a sports reporter for the Oakland *Tribune,* but soon left the staff to enter the Foreign Service. He attributes his choice of career to his parents' interest in foreign affairs and to the Rogers Act of 1924, which completely reorganized the Foreign Service to grant diplomatic officers promotion on a merit basis.

In Mexico City, where he served as vice-consul from 1936 to 1938, Jernegan began his diplomatic career in a milieu of relative calm. From then on he found himself caught in situations of political, military, and economic turmoil. In 1938 he was sent as a vice-consul to Spain, where a civil war, a prelude to World War II, was in progress. This conflict, on which the United States government took no official stand, ended in March 1939 with the victory of the insurgent General Francisco Franco.

Six months after the United States entered World War II, Jernegan returned to the Department of State in Washington, where he worked as a desk officer in the Division of Near Eastern Affairs. At that time the division was responsible for the general conduct of foreign relations with Afghanistan, Burma, Greece, India, Iran, Iraq, Palestine, Transjordan, Saudi Arabia, Syria, Lebanon, Turkey, and all territory in Africa except the Union of South Africa and Algeria.

In 1942 Jernegan was promoted to Foreign Service grade 8, and in 1943 he was sent to Iran, where he was third Secretary, then Second Secretary of the Embassy in Teheran. While holding this position he accompanied Secretary of State Cordell Hull to the first Moscow Conference of Foreign Ministers in October 1943. Anthony Eden of Great Britain and Viacheslav Molotov of the Soviet Union also attended the conference. In 1945 Jernegan went with Secretary of State James F. Byrnes to the second Moscow Conference of Foreign Ministers, in which Ernest Bevin of Great Britain and Molotov also participated.

The next year, as a grade 4 Foreign Service officer, Jernegan returned to the Division of Near Eastern Affairs as Assistant Chief. The Division in 1946 was responsible for relations with Egypt, Greece, Iraq, Lebanon, Palestine and Transjordan, Saudi Arabia, Syria, and Turkey.

In June 1947 Jernegan wrote a startlingly strong speech that United States Ambassador to the United Nations Warren Austin delivered to the Security Council. It condemned Yugoslavia, Albania, and Bulgaria for "committing the very kind of acts which the United Nations was designed to prevent" by aiding the Greek Communist guerrillas in their attempt to overthrow the Greek government (*Newsweek,* July 7, 1947). The speech urged the United Nations to use economic and diplomatic sanctions and even military force if a settlement were not made. With the help of the United States military aid program the Greek government defeated the guerrillas two years later.

Having been promoted to grade 3, Jernegan in 1948 became the director of the Office of Greek, Turkish, and Iranian Affairs. In this post he dealt with United States military and technical aid programs established to insure the international security of these countries. More specifically, these programs, set up under the Truman Doctrine, were designed to contain the Soviets on the Iranian and Turkish borders and to help the Greek government defeat the native Communist rebels. It was also part of Jernegan's job to justify the cost of these programs to the Congress of the United States.

Leaving the United States again in 1950, Jernegan became the Consul General in Tunis, where he witnessed Tunisia's struggles against France for internal autonomy. As a grade 2 Foreign Service officer, he returned to the State Department two years later, this time as Deputy Assistant Secretary of State for Near Eastern, South Asian, and African affairs.

In his new position Jernegan became responsible for United States relations with the Arabian Peninsula, Lebanon, Syria, Iraq, Egypt,

Dept. of State—
Whit Keith, Jr.

JOHN D. JERNEGAN

Israel, Egyptian Sudan, Jordan, Greece, Cyprus, Turkey, Iran, Afghanistan, Pakistan, Ceylon, India, Nepal, and other African nations. At this time he was especially concerned with the deteriorating relations between Israel and her Arab neighbors. "Every act of violence across the frontiers," he told a group of American Jewish leaders, "is a setback to progress" (New York *Times,* March 7, 1955). He expressed confidence, however, that a solution could eventually be found, and said that he did not foresee any imminent aggression against Israel by her neighbors.

By 1955 Jernegan had achieved grade 1 in the Foreign Service ratings. He left Middle Eastern affairs for a time in that year, and went to Rome to serve as Minister Counselor and Deputy Chief of Mission of the American Embassy. Three years later, however, he was recalled to the troubled Middle East and appointed Ambassador to Iraq. Sworn in on December 18, 1958, he took charge of the Embassy in Baghdad on January 7, 1959.

President Dwight D. Eisenhower nominated a career diplomat rather than a political appointee because he hoped that an expert could help to improve American-Iraqi relations and put a halt to the growing power of the Communists in the government of Iraq's Premier Abdul Karim Kassem. Installed after a successful coup in July 1958, Kassem had accepted Soviet arms and was fostering trade ties with the Soviet Union, Communist China, and the Communist nations of Eastern Europe. At the same time he had allowed Iraqi Communists to infiltrate his government. When Jernegan arrived, the United States Embassy in Baghdad was being kept under strict surveillance by Kassem's government. The new Ambassador found his freedom of action severely limited as a consequence.

Shortly after he took his post, Jernegan participated in what was described as a "friendly

JERNEGAN, JOHN D.—Continued

and cordial" meeting with the Premier (New York *Herald Tribune*, January 20, 1959). But in May 1959, after less than four months in Iraq, the Ambassador came home to consult with the Secretary of State and the President on the steady advance of communism in Iraq, exemplified by a large-scale purge of conservatives in the army and government. In July 1959, however, Kassem faced serious uprisings allegedly inspired by the Communists.

In June 1948 John D. Jernegan married Mary Margaret Brownrigg. They have three sons, Jeffrey Latham, John Brownrigg, and Jeremy Hollingsworth, and one daughter, Joan Andersen. The tall, brown-haired diplomat speaks French and Italian; he used to know Spanish, and "once could manage in Persian." He spends his leisure reading, swimming, and going on picnics with his family. In keeping with his position as a career diplomat, Jernegan has no political party affiliation.

References

N Y Herald Tribune p18 D 1 '58
Department of State Biographic Register, 1959
Who's Who in America, 1958-59

JOHANSSON, INGEMAR   Sept. 22, 1932-
Boxer

Address: c/o Edwin Ahlqvist, Kungsportsavenyn 29, Göteborg, Sweden

When Ingemar Johansson defeated Floyd Patterson to win the world heavyweight boxing championship on June 26, 1959, his victory brought new life to a sport that had fallen into disrepute. A personal triumph for the young Swede, the bout helped to wipe out the disgrace which ended Johansson's amateur boxing career in 1952 when he was eliminated from the Olympic trials at Helsinki for "not fighting."

In August 1959 a widespread suspicion that the American underworld had helped to promote the match was justified when an investigation by New York District Attorney Frank S. Hogan revealed the complicity of racketeers. Arthur Daley of the New York *Times* was moved by the scandal to call boxing a "sports slum." Surviving the disclosures with his own integrity intact, Johansson signed a contract with Jack Dempsey to fight a return bout with Patterson in the United States in the spring of 1960.

The new champion was born on September 22, 1932, in Göteborg, Sweden, the son of Jens and Ebba Johansson. His current nickname of "Ingo" is an American headline-writers' abbreviation. He has two brothers (one of whom, Rolf, is an amateur boxer) and one sister. His father was a stone-cutter in Göteborg, a seaport which is Sweden's second largest city; he is now Ingemar's official manager.

After a rough-and-tumble boyhood, Johansson left school when he was fifteen. He went to work as a street laborer, and later as a dock worker. Inspired by stories of a cousin named Ring Larson who had fought as a light-heavyweight in the United States, Johansson had begun to train as a fighter at thirteen. He was encouraged by Edwin Ahlqvist, Swedish magazine publisher and boxing promoter.

At his first serious amateur bout, in 1947, Johansson already weighed about 180 pounds. He fought as a heavyweight, and the following year won the junior championship of Göteborg. Then followed fifteen months in the Swedish Royal Navy to fulfill his military obligation. By 1950 he had fought his way to the amateur heavyweight championship of Sweden, and was ready for international competition.

In the United States in 1951 as Europe's "Golden Glove" representative, Johansson knocked out Ernest Fann at the Chicago Stadium. The eighteen-year-old Swede bruised his hand in the fight. A more permanent effect of his tour was admiration for the counter-punching style of Rocky Marciano, whose fights were models for Johansson from then on.

At nineteen, with eighty victories in eighty-eight fights, Johansson went into his last amateur fight in 1952 at the Olympic trials in Helsinki, Finland. "The only sour note came in the heavyweight bout when (Eddie) Sanders won a second-round disqualification over frightened Ingemar Johansson of Sweden," reported a New York *Herald Tribune* correspondent. "The officials were so disgusted with the Swede's actions —the cause of a piercing din of whistles and boos—that they declared there would be no second place and Johansson would not get a silver medal."

The disqualification was considered a national disgrace in Sweden, where newspaper headlines read "Ingemar, For Shame," and ended Johansson's amateur career. Only after he won the championship from Floyd Patterson (who had won the middleweight title during the same Helsinki Olympics) did Johansson's version of the fiasco get much attention. He explained that he was in poor condition at the Olympics, and that he had been cautioned by his team leader to let Sanders expose himself first.

Ahlqvist had faith in his protégé, however, and advised Johansson to redeem his reputation in the professional ranks. He matched the young fighter against Robert Masson for a purse of $2,000; Johansson won by a knockout in the fourth round on December 5, 1952, in Göteborg. In the following year he knocked out Emile Bentz and Raymond Degl'Innocenti, and won decisions from Lloyd Barnett and Erik Jensen.

Moving cautiously up the ranks of European heavyweights, Johansson in 1954 knocked out Werner Wiegand. In 1955 he knocked out Kurt Schiegl, Gunter Nurnberg, and Hein Ten Hoff; took decisions from Ansel Adams, Uber Bacilieri, and Joe Bygraves; and won after a foul by Aldo Pellegrini. Johansson says of the latter fight, which saw him knocked down for the only time in his professional career: "He was a wild one. Three times I have beat him as an amateur before we meet as professionals. He is so angry when I am beating him the third time that he bites my shoulder. The marks of the tooth are there for several days later. . . . It is clear that he knows he will lose and wants to be disqualified" (New York *Mirror*, June 28, 1959).

As a reward for a busy year, Ahlqvist brought Johansson to the United States in late

1955, and again the young Swede studied the tactics of Rocky Marciano, who was then champion. The following year he won a decision from Hans Friedrich of Stockholm, and then went to Bologna, Italy, where he won the European heavyweight crown by knocking out Franco Cavicchi in the fifth round. He also knocked out Peter Bates that year.

In 1957 Johansson knocked out Henry Cooper and won a decision from Archie McBride, both veteran American boxers. By 1958 the Swede was without a competitor in Europe. He defeated the British Empire champion, Joe Erskine, when the Welshman was unable to go out for the fourteenth round; then, after a knockout victory over Heinz Neuhaus, Johansson was matched against Eddie Machen of the United States.

Machen was at that time considered to be the leading contender for Patterson's heavyweight crown. The bout, staged in Göteborg on September 14, 1958, lasted two minutes and sixteen seconds. In that brief period Johansson earned a purse of $77,000 and the guarantee that he could fight Patterson. *Ring* magazine named him "Fighter of the Year"; he was the first European since Max Schmeling to be thus honored.

Johansson flew to the United States in November 1958, and again in January and April 1959, before the Patterson match was finally arranged. The fight received more publicity both before and after it took place than any contest in recent ring history. "In the current heavyweight market," wrote Jesse Abramson in the New York *Herald Tribune* (June 21, 1959), "Johansson is as attractive a challenger as could be found. He provides international glamor, and there is the chance, remote though it may be, that his beloved right will be the destructive weapon he claims it to be."

Johansson describes his right hand punch as "something mystic." "There is something strange about my right hand, something very hard to explain," he has said (New York *Post Magazine*, June 28, 1959). "The arm works by itself. It is faster than the eye and I cannot even see. Without my telling it to, the right goes and when it hits, there is this good feeling all down my arm and down through my body."

The Swede shocked sports writers by his unorthodox training methods. He established his training camp at a $100,000 estate in the Catskills at Grossinger, New York, where he installed his fiancée, Birgit Lundgren, and several members of his family; he frequently went to New York City to dine, to dance, and even to make television appearances.

Patterson, meanwhile, was training with traditional Spartan severity, and at fight time, 9:30 p.m. on June 26, was a five-to-one favorite to defeat Johansson. The first two rounds were uneventful, but in the third round Johansson opened up Patterson's defense with a left hook, then floored the champion with his publicized right hand.

Patterson was knocked down six more times before the referee stopped the fight after two minutes and three seconds of the third round. Johansson was proclaimed the new heavyweight champion of the world. He is the first Euro-

Wide World

INGEMAR JOHANSSON

pean in a quarter of a century to hold the title, and the first Scandinavian ever to do so.

Johansson did not immediately receive his estimated $250,000 share of the fight's revenue. It was tied up by a lawsuit with Eddie Machen, who claimed he had a contract for a return match with the Swede. With the money from previous bouts Johansson has engaged in several business ventures, including a 100-ton fishing boat and a construction and landscaping firm.

Remarkably handsome for his profession, Johansson is six feet tall and weighed 196 pounds for the fight; he has brown hair and blue eyes. Columbia Pictures recognized these attributes when they signed him to a film contract in the fall of 1959. At home his working day is a combination of business management and physical training. He likes to play golf, drive sports cars, and watch American movies. He was married at seventeen and divorced at twenty; his two children, Jane and Thomas, are in the custody of their mother.

Whatever Johansson's championship crown holds for him, he has earned a place in sports history. "Johansson's tremendous punch against Patterson," wrote *Time* magazine (July 6, 1959) "had already become as much a part of boxing lore as the 'long count' that saved the championship for Gene Tunney in his 1927 fight with Jack Dempsey. And by any standard, Johansson's right hand is the biggest thing to hit boxing in years."

References

N Y Herald Tribune III p1 Je 19 '59
N Y Times p42 Ap 28 '59; V p3 Je 21 '59 pors
N Y World-Telegram p25 Jl 1; p22 Jl 2; p20 Jl 3 '59
Sat Eve Post 231:26+ Je 20 '59 por
Sports Illus 11:14+ Jl 6 '59 por
Time 74:33+ Jl 6 '59 por

JOHN XXIII, POPE Nov. 25, 1881- Supreme Pontiff of the Roman Catholic Church

Address: Vatican City

The approximately half a billion Roman Catholics throughout the world acknowledge as their spiritual leader His Holiness John XXIII, who succeeded Pope Pius XII on October 28, 1958, to become the 262d Supreme Pontiff of the Church. Angelo Giuseppe Roncalli had spent much of his life outside his native Italy, in the papal diplomatic service, before being named a Cardinal and the Patriarch of Venice in January 1953. In the sermon preceding his coronation on November 4, 1958 Pope John XXIII emphasized his conception of the papacy's mission as essentially pastoral. Earlier, in an address broadcast by the Vatican radio in thirty-six languages to leaders of all countries, he pleaded that nations direct their resources to improvement of the welfare of humanity rather than to the preparation of armaments.

For five centuries the Roncalli family had lived on the farm in Sotto il Monte, near Bergamo in northern Italy, where Angelo Giuseppe Roncalli was born on November 25, 1881. He was the eldest son and the third of the thirteen children of Giovanni Battista and Marianna (Mazzola) Roncalli. In his boyhood he helped his father, a sharecropper, to work the fields and gather fuel in the woods. Fond of study, he became known in the community as a bookworm and walked daily eight miles each way to attend school at Celana. Throughout his life he retained close contact with his native Lombardy village and its people, often spending his vacations at Sotto il Monte.

At the age of eleven, having decided to become a priest, Angelo Roncalli entered the seminary at Bergamo, where he was a pupil from 1892 to 1900. He then studied at the Pontifical Seminary in Rome, received a laureate in theology, and was ordained a priest on August 10, 1904 in the Church of Santa Maria in Monte Santo. During that year he officiated at his first mass in Saint Peter's Basilica in Rome.

Father Roncalli served from 1905 to 1914 as secretary to Monsignor Giacomo Radini-Tedeschi, Bishop of Bergamo. In these early, formative years of his priesthood he organized Catholic Action groups, taught at the Bergamo seminary, and helped initiate the now widespread practice of publishing regular parish news bulletins. His interest in historical research led to his discovery at the Ambrosian Library in Milan of documents concerning Saint Charles Borromeo, who had visited Bergamo in the sixteenth century. Eventually, between 1936 and 1952, Roncalli's five-volume history of the saint was published, one of his several historical studies.

Drafted into the Italian Army at the outbreak of World War I, he served first as a sergeant in the Medical Corps and then, with the rank of lieutenant, as a chaplain in various hospitals. Briefly after the war Father Roncalli was spiritual director of the Bergamo seminary, before Pope Benedict XV called him to Rome in 1921 to reorganize the Society for the Propagation of the Faith.

His visits to European Catholic centers in behalf of the missionary work of this association helped prepare him for the long period of Vatican diplomatic service which began in 1925 when Pope Pius XI elevated him to titular Archbishop of Aeropolis and appointed him apostolic visitor to Bulgaria. Ten years later he was given the title of Archbishop of Mesembria and promoted to the dual post of apostolic delegate to Turkey and to Greece.

Somewhat characteristically, since his secretary happened to be momentarily absent, Roncalli decoded the Vatican cable to the Istanbul headquarters announcing his own appointment in December 1944 as Papal Nuncio to France. In answer to his subsequent protest that he could not handle so difficult an assignment, he was told that he was the personal choice of Pope Pius XII. Relations between the Vatican and the French government, then under General Charles de Gaulle, had become strained because the Vatican had sent a nuncio to the Nazi-dominated Vichy government during the German occupation of France in World War II. According to Bernard Wall in the London *Observer* (November 2, 1958), Roncalli's "worst problem as Nuncio to France was how to contain the radicalism of the younger French clergy and their spearhead, the French Dominican Order. Here his point of view seems to have been much that of the higher clergy, his friends. With them, he helped to soft-pedal the fulminations against worker-priests and other Gallic innovations prepared sulphurously by [certain] Roman Curia Cardinals. . ."

"During his eight years' stay, Nuncio Roncalli became one of the most popular men in Paris," *Time* (November 10, 1958) reported. ". . . In addition to respecting his ability, the French also liked his cuisine." In 1952 he was made permanent observer of the Holy See to UNESCO. When Pope Pius XII nominated Archbishop Roncalli a Cardinal in 1953, Socialist French President Vincent Auriol claimed the customary privilege of a head of a Catholic state to award the red biretta to the new Prince of the Church, to whom he also gave the grand cross of the Legion of Honor.

A few days after being named Cardinal, Roncalli was appointed Patriarch of Venice to succeed Carlo Agostini. "Here I have a new chance to be entirely a pastor," Roncalli said at the time. "I am convinced that the ministry of the pastor is the most fascinating, the finest that a man can be offered in his life." He still had an opportunity to travel, serving as papal legate to a Marian congress in Lebanon in 1954 and to a centenary celebration at the French shrine of Lourdes in 1958.

As Cardinal Patriarch of Venice he expressed his views on several occasions on the role of the Catholic Church in Italian politics. In a pastoral letter in 1956 he opposed a suggestion that the Christian Democrats in Venice form a city government in alliance with the leftist Socialist party of Pietro Nenni. The following year when the Socialists held their national convention in Venice, he was cordial to the delegates, but later made it clear that "a dialogue between Catholic and Marxist forces was never opened and never could be opened at Venice" (*United States News & World Report,* November 7, 1958).

Pope Pius XII died on October 9, 1958. Angelo Giuseppe Cardinal Roncalli was one of fifty-one Cardinals who met in the Sistine Chapel at the Vatican on October 25 to vote for his successor. Three days later, on the twelfth ballot, Roncalli was elected the 262d occupant of the Chair of Saint Peter. He announced at once that he wished to be known as Pope John (Giovanni) XXIII. Among the many reasons that he gave for his choice was that "John" was both the name of his father and of the patron saint of Sotto il Monte. He was crowned at Saint Peter's Basilica in Rome on November 4 in a colorful five-hour televised liturgical ceremony that is probably more impressive and complex than any other in the Catholic Church.

Other titles that Pope John XXIII holds include Vicar of Jesus Christ, Supreme Pontiff of the Universal Church, Patriarch of the West, and Bishop of Rome (his church in Rome is the Basilica of Saint John Lateran). He is also Sovereign of the State of Vatican City, the world's smallest independent state, comprising about 1,000 occupants in a 108-acre area in Rome.

Almost immediately after his election Pope John stated his belief that his reign would not be a "continuity" of that of Pope Pius XII. He early demonstrated his capacity for independent action by resuming after an interval of several years the Audiences of Tabella—audiences granted by the Pope on fixed days of the week to Cardinals and certain other prelates. To fulfill the most pressing duty of his office, in November 1958 he created twenty-three new Cardinals, raising membership in the Sacred College of Cardinals to seventy-five, higher than it had been since the sixteenth century.

Partly because of his advanced age (Pope John became seventy-eight years old in November 1959), the new Pontiff has been generally regarded as a "compromise" or "interim" Pope. In reply to many speculations reported in the newspapers, he said, "Some people have made a picture for themselves of a political Pope, others of a learned Pope, others of a diplomatic Pope. But instead the Pope is just the Pope; he is the Good Shepherd who tries by all means to reach the souls of men and to spread and defend truth and goodness" (New York *Times,* November 7, 1958).

Like his predecessor, Pope John XXIII is a linguist. He speaks Italian, Latin, Greek, French, and Turkish and has some familiarity with German, Spanish, Romanian, Bulgarian, English, and Russian. More often in the press John XXIII has been contrasted, rather than compared, with Pius XII. The new Pope is

Wide World

POPE JOHN XXIII

short, white-haired, and stout, weighing 205 pounds. He prides himself on his peasant background and on the fact that some of his near relatives till the soil in the Po valley. He is noted for his wit, joviality, warm-heartedness, and for his ability to administer with a firm hand. "Although he is a master of the protocol of diplomacy, Pope John doesn't go in for encumbering formality as far as his own person is concerned," the New York *Herald Tribune* (November 5, 1958) noted. "He instructed *L'Osservatore romano,* the Vatican newspaper, to discontinue use of the traditional awed phrases such as 'illuminated discourse' and 'words of wisdom' to describe the papal utterances and to write merely that the Pope 'said.' "

References

N Y Herald Tribune p2 O 29 '58; p4 N 7 '58 por
N Y Times p14 O 29 '58 por
N Y World-Telegram p3 O 28 '58 por
Newsweek 52:36+ N 10 '58 por

Chi è? (1958)
International Who's Who, 1958
Panorama Biografico degli Italiani d'Oggi (1956)
Who's Who in Italy, 1957-58
World Biography (1954)

JOHNSON, EDWARD Aug. 22, 1878(?)-Apr. 20, 1959 Former general manager of the Metropolitan Opera (1935-50); promoted importance of American singers through *Metropolitan Opera Auditions of the Air*; began career as Canadian-American operatic tenor. See *Current Biography* (March) 1943.

Obituary

N Y Times p35 Ap 21 '59

JOHNSON, WENDELL (ANDREW LE-ROY) Apr. 16, 1906- Speech pathologist; educator; writer

Address: b. East Hall, State University of Iowa, Iowa City, Iowa; h. 508 Melrose Court, Iowa City, Iowa

During the past thirty or more years many misconceptions regarding speech problems have been dispelled, and many enlightening facts have been revealed, through the work of the speech clinic at the State University of Iowa, with which Dr. Wendell Johnson has been associated since its founding in the mid-1920's. He directed the clinic from 1943 to 1955 and continues to carry on investigations in speech pathology in connection with educational, governmental, and private projects. From early childhood until about the age of forty Johnson was troubled by the problem of his stuttering. In seeking to overcome his own difficulty he was brought to help other people and gradually extended his concern to the broader areas of semantics, personality adjustment, and related subjects. "The study of one communication disorder," he says, "has led me to an interest in the process of communication comprehensively considered."

Wendell Andrew Leroy Johnson was born in Roxbury, Kansas on April 16, 1906 to Andrew R. and Mary (Tarnstrom) Johnson, both of whom had come to the United States from Sweden in their childhood. The youngest in a family of six children, he has three brothers, Leonard, Wilbert, and Marion, and two sisters, Myrtle and Edna. His father was a cowboy who rode horseback from Denver to Seattle to Los Angeles and worked on ranches along the way, before settling down to develop his own cattle business and wheat farm in Kansas.

"I grew up on a horse myself," Johnson recalls. "I herded cattle quite a lot as a boy and rode horseback the two and a half miles to school at Roxbury every day all through grade and high school." Outstanding in sports, he was captain of the basketball and baseball teams and played football and tennis. He also took part in the high school's literary activities, having wanted since boyhood to become a writer. This ambition, he feels, may have been influenced by the fact that he had great difficulty in talking because of severe stuttering.

In 1924 Johnson was graduated from Roxbury High School as valedictorian of his class. During the next two years he attended McPherson College in Kansas, but in 1926 he entered the State University of Iowa, where a program of research on stuttering was being started. While participating in the first experiments of the speech clinic, he worked as part-time assistant to Dr. George D. Stoddard, then professor of education and psychology, and majored in English to earn the B.A. degree in 1928. He also helped to edit the *Iowa Literary Magazine* and won election to Phi Beta Kappa.

Having decided to remain at the State University of Iowa for graduate study, Johnson held several scholarships and assistantships in education and psychology that enabled him to study for the M.A. degree, received in 1929, and the Ph.D. degree, received in 1931. His master's thesis, published as a book by Appleton-Century in 1930, was entitled *Because I Stutter;* and his doctoral thesis, published as a State University of Iowa Monograph in Child Welfare in 1932, was entitled *The Influence of Stuttering on the Personality.*

Some of Johnson's research as a graduate student had been done in the university's speech clinic, then under the direction of Dr. Lee Edward Travis, and in 1931 he was appointed a research associate of that laboratory, in charge of clinical work with stutterers. "I ended up specializing in my own defect," he has remarked, "and it can be said that I became a speech pathologist because I needed one. I am like the fellow who when asked, 'Why did you come to fall in the lake?' replied, 'I didn't. I came to fish.'"

From 1937 to 1939 Johnson was assistant professor jointly in the departments of psychology, speech, and child welfare at the State University of Iowa. He was associate professor in the same departments from 1939 until he was appointed professor of speech and pathology in 1945. Meanwhile, from 1939 to 1942, he was also technical director of the Iowa remedial education program, a diagnostic survey and re-educational demonstration project sponsored by the Iowa Child Welfare Research Station and the Iowa State Department of Public Instruction.

Johnson became the director of the University of Iowa speech clinic in 1943 and also chairman of the council on speech pathology and audiology. These positions entailed responsibility for general supervision of clinical services, a large part of graduate research, and the professional training in speech pathology. Because of a mild heart attack in May 1955 he gave up his administrative duties, but has con-

WENDELL JOHNSON

tinued his work in clinical, research, and training programs in the areas of stuttering, symbolic processes, and semantic problems in communication. He was visiting professor at the University of Southern California in the summer of 1948 and at the University of Colorado in the summer of 1956.

An important part of Johnson's research has concerned the onset of stuttering, and his personal experiences have figured in much of his writing. In an article for the *Saturday Evening Post* (January 5, 1957) he made the significant observation, "My own problem began in first grade, when my teacher got the idea that I was beginning to stutter." When investigating the causes of stuttering, he examined the traditional theories that stuttering is due to organic imperfection or personality flaw. This led to his challenging the supposition that the problem exists only or principally in the speaker.

His considerations were summarized in the *Handbook of Speech Pathology,* edited by Lee Edward Travis (Appleton, 1957): "The problem of stuttering appears to arise primarily in an authoritative listener's perception of the child's speech fluency as unacceptable, and as the speaker interiorizes this evaluative orientation toward his own speech he becomes his own most disabling listener." Consequently, Johnson believes, much of the therapy of the speech clinic should be directed toward the parent rather than the child and should concern personality disturbances.

Johnson is prolific both as an author and a lecturer. Among his books are *People in Quandaries* (Harper, 1946), *Your Most Enchanted Listener* (Harper, 1956), and *The Onset of Stuttering* (University of Minnesota Press, 1959). He has written about 100 published papers, thirty magazine articles, and 100 book reviews. His editorial experience has included work on the *Journal of Speech and Hearing Disorders* (1943-48) and the *Quarterly Journal of Speech* (1950-56). He has delivered hundreds of lectures before organizational and university audiences, and his series of forty classroom lectures in general semantics are recorded on tapes available from the State University of Iowa Bureau of Audio-Visual Instruction. His appearances on radio and television have also been numerous.

Often called upon by the United States government to serve in an advisory capacity, Johnson has been consultant to the Department of Health, Education and Welfare and to the Walter Reed Army Hospital (audiology and speech center), among other agencies. He is an active member of many professional organizations, notably the American Speech and Hearing Association, of which he was president in 1950 and subsequently member of various committees.

He also belongs to the American Psychological Association, the Institute of General Semantics, the Speech Association of America, the American Association for the Advancement of Science, and several Iowa groups. His clubs are the Cosmos in Washington, D.C., the Triangle at the State University of Iowa, and the Optimist International. He attends the Uni-

tarian Church in Iowa City, of which he is a past member of the board of directors.

As an undergraduate at the State University of Iowa, Wendell Johnson met Edna Bockwoldt, whom he later married, on May 31, 1929. Their children are Nicholas and Katherine Louise. Johnson has brown hair and brown eyes, weighs 190 pounds, and is six feet one and a half inches tall. He now has a spectator interest in baseball and other games that he played in his boyhood. He is active, though "not much good," at fishing. Also he finds recreational pleasure in reading the books that he reviews for the New York *Times* and other publications. In his *Saturday Evening Post* article he told of being saddened throughout his childhood by the "unnerving mysteriousness" of his speech difficulty and of his eventual realization that "the more one knows about a thing, the less afraid of it one becomes."

References

Sat Eve Post 229:26+ Ja 5 '57 pors
American Men of Science vol III (1956)
Leaders in Education (1948)
Who's Who in America, 1958-59

JONES, ROGER W(ARREN) Feb. 3, 1908- United States government official

Address: United States Civil Service Commission, 8th St. and F St., N.W., Washington 25, D.C.; h. 3912 Leland St., Chevy Chase 15, Md.

For the more than 2,000,000 United States government employees covered by Civil Service regulations, the appointment of Roger W. Jones to the Civil Service Commission in January 1959 promised a strengthening of the merit system that has tried to encourage integrity and efficiency in the executive branch of the government. Jones took office in March 1959 for a six-year term as chairman of the commission, designated by President Dwight D. Eisenhower to succeed Harris Ellsworth who retired. Most of Jones's twenty-six years in civil service has been spent in the Bureau of the Budget. His various positions, culminating in the office of the bureau's deputy director held during 1958, have given him a knowledge of government personnel matters and of administrative and legislative problems that is perhaps unexcelled by any other federal employee.

Of old New England stock on both sides of his family, Roger Warren Jones was born to Henry Roger and Eleanor (Drake) Jones in New Hartford, Connecticut on February 3, 1908. He has one sister, now Mrs. Elbert Manchester. His father was an attorney who also published a weekly newspaper, the New Hartford *Tribune*.

In preparation for college Roger Jones studied at the Gilbert School in Winsted, Connecticut, where basketball was his favorite sport. Graduating in 1924, he entered Cornell University, majored in English, and became battalion commander in the ROTC. He was also manager of Cornell Musical Clubs and attended most of the organ recitals at the university.

(Continued next page)

ROGER W. JONES

After receiving his B.A. degree from Cornell in 1928, Jones spent a year as an instructor at Miami Military Academy in Coral Gables, Florida. He then moved to New York City, where from 1929 to 1931 he was employed as assistant manager and clerk in Doubleday, Doran Book Shops. He also took courses at Columbia University, presented a thesis on William Cullen Bryant as a journalist, and was awarded the M.A. degree in English in 1931.

For a year or so afterward he worked as a tutor while studying for a doctorate. His special interest was in American democratic institutions and their history and the literature of American politics from the Mayflower Compact to the first inaugural address of President Franklin D. Roosevelt. "I didn't think anyone had properly evaluated the impact of American political writing on our letters," he has stated (Washington Evening Star, March 15, 1959).

Jones went to Washington, D.C. in the fall of 1933 to do research for his dissertation at the Library of Congress. He was, however, diverted from his goal when he accepted a temporary government assignment to prepare a report for the Central Statistical Board. Other temporary appointments followed, at the regular starting salary for college graduates of $2,000 a year. Eventually, after taking civil service examinations, he rose through the grades to assistant executive officer. In 1939, when the Central Statistical Board became part of the Bureau of the Budget, he agreed to continue his work under the new setup as an administrative officer at a salary of $4,600.

During the period just before the United States entered World War II, Jones helped organize some of the defense agencies, including the Office of Facts and Figures. Most of his military service, from 1942 to 1945, was with the Munitions Assignments Board, where he worked for the Combined Chiefs of Staff with United States and British officers on munitions pooling. He advanced from the rank of captain in the Army to that of colonel and was awarded the Legion of Merit, the Army Commendation Ribbon, and the Order of the British Empire.

When Jones returned to the Bureau of the Budget after the war, his first task was to help liquidate war agencies. In 1946 he worked on special assignments for the estimates division of the bureau; the following year he became assistant to the director for legislative liaison, charged with handling contacts between the bureau and Congress.

Jones's experience in this position, requiring a knowledge of the work of the various committees of the Senate and House of Representatives, prepared him further for the important post of assistant director for legislative reference of the Bureau of the Budget, to which he was appointed in February 1949. A detailed discussion of his duties in this office, and his notable competence in carrying them out, was given in an article by Katharine Hamill, "This is a Bureaucrat," in Fortune (November 1953). In general, he was responsible for reviewing all bills before and after Congressional action to see whether they conformed to the President's policies and fiscal programs and to prepare an appraisal of the bills to help guide the President in approving or vetoing them.

"In a normal year," Katharine Hamill wrote, "Jones and his staff process some 5,500 requests and reports from Congress and the agencies, about 1,000 enrolled bills (legislation passed by Congress), and 100 Executive Orders and Proclamations. The processing is sometimes long-drawn and involved, with dozens of memoranda and letters written in formidable federalese."

From March to September 1958 Jones was one of three statutory assistant directors of the Bureau of the Budget. He then became deputy director of the bureau and was serving as such when President Eisenhower nominated him a member of the three-man Civil Service Commission in January 1959. After Senate approval he was sworn into office on March 9, at which time Eisenhower designated him chairman of the commission.

The appointment was praised as nonpolitical. Although Jones is a Republican, he had served without partisanship under Presidents Roosevelt and Truman, as well as under Eisenhower. The Washington Evening Star (January 19, 1959) commented that the selection was "a morale booster for the Federal career service," since Jones was chosen "for special competence for the task of building a stronger merit system."

The Civil Service Commission commemorated the formal establishment of the principle of merit in federal employment with its celebration during 1958 of the seventy-fifth anniversary of the signing of the Civil Service Act. As the personnel agency of the United States government, the commission has the primary task of hiring and retaining "an effective and loyal work force" for the executive branch of the government. It furnishes examinations to test the fitness of job applicants and sets standards as a basis for reinstatement, promotion, and transfer of employees. Together with the

President and the federal departments, the commission shares responsibility for the management of employees skilled in hundreds of major occupations. During World War II the number of government employees reached 3,816,000. At present the figure is about 2,500,000—more than the total number of people employed by the eight largest corporations in the United States. Only about 10 per cent work in or near Washington, D.C.

Believing that "public recognition of achievements is a valuable asset" in maintaining a climate in which federal employees are encouraged to do their best work, in January 1958 President Eisenhower announced the establishment of the President's Awards for Distinguished Federal Civilian Service. Jones was one of the first five career employees to receive an award. His citation read: "Has with exceptional objectivity and constructiveness made outstanding contributions to the development of Federal legislation." Jones also holds the Career Service Award of the National Civil Service League, conferred in 1955.

Jones is vice-president of the Washington Institute of Mental Hygiene and of the United Givers Fund for the Washington area. He belongs to the Cornell Club of Washington and to Sigma Phi Epsilon and Delta Theta Phi societies. An Episcopalian, he is a member and former vestryman of All Saints Church in Chevy Chase, Maryland.

On February 1, 1930 Roger W. Jones married Dorothy Heyl, whom he had known at Cornell University and had met again in New York when she was studying for a degree in library science at Columbia University. Mrs. Jones now holds a part-time position with the Montgomery County Public Library in Maryland. The Joneses have a daughter, Cynthia Alice (Mrs. John Hodges), and two sons, Roger Heyl and Edward Chapman.

Straightforward in manner, Jones is said to have won the respect and confidence of members of Congress by his frankness during hearings on impending legislation. He has blue eyes and gray hair, weighs 160 pounds, and is five feet ten and a half inches tall. Away from the office, he finds recreation in Civil War history and his old favorites in literature, especially poetry. For exercise he enjoys walking and gardening. He outlined to Michael Mok of the Washington *Evening Star* some guides for the civil service employee, emphasizing the need for a feeling of dedication as a public servant. "The good staff man—bureaucrat if you like—must develop a lot of expertise about the programs he carries out," Jones said. "Regardless of the political direction of the administration, its leaders should be able to expect a loyal, capable staff."

References

Fortune 48:156+ N '53
N Y Herald Tribune p14 Ja 18 '59
U S News 46:22 Ja 30 '59
Washington (D.C.) Evening Star p27A
    Mr 15 '59 por
American Men in Government (1949)

JORDAN, B(ENJAMIN) EVERETT Sept. 8, 1896- United States Senator from North Carolina

Address: b. Senate Office Bldg., Washington, D.C.; h. Saxaphaw, N.C.

After his interim appointment as United States Senator from North Carolina by Governor Luther Hodges to succeed the late Senator W. Kerr Scott, B. Everett Jordan was elected to the position on November 4, 1958 by the citizens of his state and will complete Scott's term in Congress, which expires on January 3, 1961. Jordan, a textile manufacturer, had never sought an elective office before this, but had been active in the Democratic party in North Carolina since 1935. He had been successful as a fund raiser, and was chairman of the North Carolina Democratic executive committee from 1949 to 1954, and Democratic National Committeeman from North Carolina from 1954 to 1958.

In 1927 Jordan organized the Sellers Manufacturing Company in Saxaphaw, North Carolina, and later became the owner of two other textile firms in the Saxaphaw area, the Jordan Spinning Company and the Royal Cotton Mill Company. Jordan has also been active in various religious, philanthropic, and educational work in his state.

Benjamin Everett Jordan, the son of the Reverend Henry Harrison and Annie Elizabeth (Sellers) Jordan, was born in Ramseur, North Carolina, on September 8, 1896. He was the eldest of the six children of the Methodist minister. From 1912 to 1913 he attended the Rutherford College Preparatory School in North Carolina, and then entered Trinity College (now Duke University) in Durham, North Carolina. He served with the Tank Corps of the United States Army during World War I, from 1918 to 1919, and with the occupation forces in Germany in 1919.

When Jordan returned from overseas, he continued with the work he had done as a mill hand for various textile manufacturers in North Carolina before he entered the service. He became the plant superintendent of the Gastonia Textile Company in Gastonia, North Carolina, in 1923. Several years later one of his uncles suggested that he buy an abandoned mill in Saxaphaw, North Carolina. This he did, and in 1927 he organized the Sellers Manufacturing Company, of which he became general manager, secretary-treasurer, and director.

The principal products of this firm are mercerized cotton yarns, and blends of cotton and nylon, and cotton and orlon. Its sales range is between $3 to $6,000,000 a year, and it employs about 350 workers. Jordan and the firm have tried to improve the living conditions of the Saxaphaw villagers, many of whom work for the firm, and to make the town a model community. Recently a community center for the company's employees has been built.

Within a fifty-mile radius of Saxaphaw are two other textile plants which Jordan owns. Since 1939 he has been the general manager, secretary-treasurer, and director of the Jordan

Harris & Ewing

B. EVERETT JORDAN

Spinning Company in Cedar Falls; since 1945 he has been president, treasurer, general manager, and director of the Royal Cotton Mill Company in Wake Forest. The latter firm produces cotton combed yarns; it employs 275 workers, and has an annual sales range of $3 to $6,000,000. Jordan has been the secretary-treasurer of the National Processing Company in Burlington, North Carolina, since 1945.

In addition to his business interests, Jordan has been active in Democratic state politics since 1935. Although he gained a reputation as a money raiser for the party, for many years he never sought an elective office. He supported W. Kerr Scott, whose wife was his first cousin, when the latter ran for governor of North Carolina in the bitter campaign of 1948; Scott was elected. From 1949 to 1954 Jordan served as the chairman of the Democratic state executive committee. In 1952 he supported William B. Umstead in the gubernatorial race against Scott's candidate, and Umstead won. Two years later, Jordan became the Democratic National Committeeman from North Carolina. Scott had been elected a United States Senator from North Carolina, but died in 1958 before he had finished out his six-year term.

Governor Luther Hodges of North Carolina announced on April 19, 1958 his appointment of B. Everett Jordan to the United States Senate to succeed Scott. The Governor also said that Jordan would serve until a general election in November 1958, and that he would ask the state's Democratic committee to nominate Jordan as the party's candidate in the election. His request was granted, and Jordan was elected on November 4, 1958 to complete Scott's term, which expires on January 3, 1961.

The new Senator is reported to be a conservative, whereas Scott was generally regarded as a Southern liberal. Jordan was expected to work closely with North Carolina's senior Senator, Sam J. Ervin, Jr. During the Eighty-sixth Congress, first session (1959), Jordan served on the Senate committees for agriculture and forestry, post office and civil service, and rules and administration, and on the Joint Congressional Committee on the Library.

Over the years, Jordan has taken part in various religious, educational, and philanthropic activities. From 1927 to 1958, he was a Methodist adult Bible class teacher; for the twenty years from 1930 to 1950 he served as chairman of the Methodist Board of Stewards. During the period of 1935 to 1940 he was a Methodist lay leader, and from 1952 to 1956 he acted as vice-president of the Board of Methodist Colleges. He is a trustee of Duke University and Elon College in North Carolina.

From 1943 to 1958 Jordan served as a member of the North Carolina Peace Officers Benefit and Retirement Commission, and for the six years from 1945 to 1951 he was a member of the North Carolina Medical Care Commission. He has been the president and a director of the Alamance County Tuberculosis Association, and a director of the Alamance County Red Cross, and of the Cherokee Council of the Boy Scouts of America. He also has served as chairman of the board of trustees of the Alamance County General Hospital.

Jordan has been a director of the Wachovia Bank and the Highland Container Company in Jamestown, North Carolina. He was at one time a director of the Cotton Textile Institute of the United States, and of the North Carolina Cotton Manufacturers Association. He also served as vice-president of the Durene Association of America. He is a Mason, and acted as president and a director of the Rotary Club in Burlington, North Carolina. He is a member of the Sons of the American Revolution, and Omicron Delta Kappa. In recognition of his achievements, he received an honorary degree from Duke University in 1940, and was elected Alamance County man of the year in 1955.

Benjamin Everett Jordan married Katherine McLean of Gastonia, North Carolina on November 29, 1924. They have three children: Benjamin Everett (who works in his father's business), Rose Ann (Mrs. Roger Gant, Jr.), and John McLean. Mrs. Jordan, who takes a personal interest in roadside beautification, works through the county branch of the North Carolina Highway Commission to plant lawns and dogwood trees along the roads. When not residing in Washington, D.C., the Jordans live in a rambling country house on a farm outside Saxaphaw, North Carolina. Senator Jordan's main hobby is reported to be work.

References

N Y Herald Tribune p17 Ap 20 '58
N Y Times p75 Ap 20 '58
U S News 44:20 My 16 '58
Washington (D.C.) Post pF23 My 25 '58

Congressional Directory, 1959
Who's Who in America, 1958-59

JOYCE, J(AMES) AVERY May 24, 1902-
Author; barrister; lecturer

Address: b. 3 King's Bench Walk, Temple, London, England; c/o American Friends Service Committee, 130 Brattle St., Cambridge, Mass.

"Arising on the East River is a rudimentary but evolving pattern of parliamentary activity and a radically new form of world-based democracy"—this is a description of the United Nations by British author, lecturer, and barrister J. Avery Joyce. His book *Revolution on East River; The Twilight of National Sovereignty* (Abelard-Schuman, 1957) expounds his conviction that the U.N. has really been moving toward an effective "parliament of man." National sovereignty, he believes, is "on the way out."

Recognized as an authority on constitutional and international law, Joyce is a barrister of the Inner Temple, London, and practises common and criminal law on the South-Eastern Circuit and before the High Court in London. He has conducted courses in law, political science, and international relations at the University of London and Queen's College, and in the United States at the University of Denver, Grinnell College, and other schools. For more than two decades he has been a popular lecturer. A seasoned Parliamentary candidate, he several times contested marginal seats in Lancashire and in London.

James Avery Joyce was born in London, England on May 24, 1902 to George Thomas Simeon Joyce and Elizabeth Mary (Leng) Joyce. He has a brother, Leonard Edward, and a sister, Dora Mary. His father is now retired after a career in the Civil Service. James left elementary school at the age of fourteen. In order to attend the London School of Economics, he financed his own education, and earned the B.S. degree with Good Honours. He later gained a degree in law and a postgraduate diploma in history at the University of London by part-time study.

Joyce began his career in public life in 1919 as a lay speaker in the Methodist Church. He attributes his interest in social reform to the influence of three men: Lord Robert Cecil, formerly chief British delegate to the League of Nations; Lord John Boyd Orr, active in the Parliamentary group for world government, with whom J. Avery Joyce has worked closely; and Dr. Fridtjof Nansen of Norway.

For several years Joyce studied at the School of International Studies at Geneva, following its organization in 1923 under the League of Nations. While there, he organized the Youth Movement of the League. His first book, *Youth Faces the New World* (1931), describes the work of young peoples' organizations concerned with international studies.

In 1938 he became the founder and chairman of the International Forum, London, to promote discussions on world affairs. As a special correspondent, he held a permanent press seat and attended the League of Nations assemblies between 1929 and 1937. In the 1930's, he lectured on industrial law, economics, and government to adult education groups in London,

Universal Pictorial Press & Agency, London

J. AVERY JOYCE

including the Workers Educational Association, and worked to promote International Labor Office Conventions.

When World War II broke out, Joyce gave his services as a "poor man's lawyer" at citizens' advice bureaus in London and taught lecture courses in central air raid shelters. He increased his attention to the adult education movement, which he calls in his book *Justice at Work* "the very core of any modern democracy." For nearly ten years he lectured on everyday law and problems of states at Morley College and City Literary Institute. He gave more advanced courses at Goldsmiths' College, University of London and at the Sussex branch of the Law Society. He also lectured on public administration at King's College of Household and Social Science, University of London and gave broadcasts on everyday law and social science over the British Broadcasting Corporation system.

Joyce was chairman of a public round table discussion on "World Organization: Federal or Functional?" held in 1944 in London under the auspices of the International Forum. The purpose of the round table was to "discuss how to organize a peaceful world after World War II." Joyce edited a verbatim report of this discussion, published in 1945. In 1944 he was selected as vice-chairman of the World Airways Committee in order to investigate the relationship between world unity and civil aviation. He served in the late 1940's as chairman of the World Citizenship Movement (British section) and was president in 1950.

At a World Citizens Conference in Woodstock, Illinois on May 22, 1948, Joyce stated that in order to be effective "world citizenship must rest on a charter of human rights that will guarantee the four freedoms to each member of the world community" (*New York Times*, May 23, 1948). He advocated a world

JOYCE, J. AVERY—*Continued*

government with its own parliament, police force, and supreme court and the abolition of national armaments.

On lecture tours under the auspices of the American Friends Service Committee, Joyce has spoken on world economic and social problems at many universities. Herbert H. Rosenthal, director of the Institute of International Administration at the University of Denver, described Joyce as "a first-rate scholar, an excellent public speaker, and an intelligent and objective observer."

When Joyce ran as Labour party Parliamentary candidate in the British general election in 1951 for the Oldham East constituency, he was defeated by I. M. Horobin, Conservative, by about 2,000 votes. From 1952 to 1955 he was Labour Parliamentary candidate for Lambeth (Norwood division), London. He is a frequent visitor to United Nations assemblies and other meetings at U.N. headquarters and is a consultant to ECOSOC.

Among his articles on current affairs in leading English and American journals is "Liberty or Fear: the Final Choice" (*Survey,* January 1951), in which he stated: "Human loyalty can no longer be confined within the boundaries of the nation-state but must express itself toward all mankind."

In his guest editorial, published in the *Saturday Review* (January 4, 1958) and entitled "A Citizenship of Space?" he discussed the legal points that will be involved when a nation first reaches the moon. He suggested that some sort of United Nations "sovereignty" be conferred on all space craft, and that, beyond a point (say twenty miles from the earth's surface), the freedom of outer space should prevail by international agreement.

Joyce's books include *Three Peace Classics: Erasmus, Sully, Grotius* (1938), *Rearmament Debunked* (1939), *Education for a World Society* (1946), *World Law* (1948), *Now Is the Time* (1950), *Justice at Work* (1952), *World in the Making* (1953), and *Revolution on East River* (1957). Commenting on *Justice at Work,* a reviewer for *John O'London's Weekly* stated, "Joyce writes in a human and concise style, rare in books about the law, and in his manner is easy and colloquial." *World in the Making* traces the constant effort of man, through discovery, invention, travel, communication, and organizations to reach out toward all the people of the earth.

Reviewing *Revolution on East River* in the New York *Times Book Review* (February 3, 1957), R. L. Duffus observed that Joyce "may be completely right in pointing out that if we do not have some kind of world government sooner or later there may not be any civilized world to govern; or, as he says, 'Utopia has become the only practical politics.' But although he gives excellent advice as to how the people of the free countries could behave better and more wisely, he doesn't touch the real problem—that is to say, the Russian Communist problem." The London *Times Literary Supplement* (June 21, 1957) noted: "Joyce gives us the pure gospel of the liberal idealist." In 1959 J. Avery Joyce's *Red Cross International; And the Strategy of Peace* (Oceana), was issued.

Organizations to which he belongs are the Fabian Society, the International Law Association, the British Institute for Adult Education, the World Calendar Association, and the Howard League for Penal Reform. His Church is the Methodist. Joyce stands five feet eleven inches tall, weighs 180 pounds, and has brown eyes and gray hair. He was formerly a cricket player and a runner.

Reference

Oldham Voice O '51

KAHANE, MELANIE (kŭ-hān') Nov. 26, 1910- Interior designer; industrial designer

Address: b. Melanie Kahane Associates, 32 E. 57th St., New York 22; h. 29 E. 63d St., New York 21

Internationally known for her inventiveness and creative use of colors, materials, and textures, Melanie Kahane has introduced many innovations in the decoration of homes and offices. As president of Melanie Kahane Associates, an interior decorating and industrial designing firm, Miss Kahane has anticipated trends in style and has applied merchandising principles to decorating and designing.

In addition to having planned the interiors of many homes and offices, Miss Kahane has devised furniture, lighting fixtures, fabrics, and home appliances. Design, she believes, is a "way of living." She is married to NBC commentator Ben Grauer (see *C.B.,* July 1959). They have a radio show together on which they discuss decorating problems.

Melanie Kahane was born in New York City on November 26, 1910 to Morris and Rose (Roth) Kahane. Her father was an architect and electrical engineer. She has one brother, William. Melanie spent her childhood in Sioux Falls, South Dakota, where she attended the Hawthorne School. By the age of nine, she had developed an interest in painting and architecture because her father had "exposed her to the beauty and refinements of architecture." During her childhood Melanie designed and made all of her dolls' clothing and furniture. She also studied ballet for eight years and when she was fifteen taught ballet classes.

Upon her graduation from Hackettstown High School in New Jersey in 1928, Melanie Kahane decided to enroll at the Parsons School of Design in New York City to study costume design and commercial illustration. While at Parsons she designed theater sets, costumes, and window displays. After completing her course, Miss Kahane was awarded a scholarship to study in France at the Paris School of Parsons. There, she also did free-lance work.

Returning to New York, Miss Kahane was employed as an illustrator for Tobias Green & Company (1931-32), catalogue illustrator with Shearer & Patrick (1933), a sketcher for dress designer Maurice Rentner (1933-35), and women's wear designer with Gross-Sidney (1933-35). In 1936 Melanie Kahane went into business for herself as an interior and industrial design consultant.

According to a profile of Miss Kahane in *Interiors* (June 1954), she often "starts from scratch, with space" and her ideas involve basic structural work. In "one apartment . . . her plan called for thousands of dollars of architectural work—set down by her staff architect in twenty-seven pages of specifications!" Her decorating ideas draw upon both modern and traditional furniture styles.

Among the many prominent people whose homes Miss Kahane has decorated are Dr. Robert F. Goheen, president of Princeton University, Billy Rose, and William T. Grant. She also created the décor of the Governor's mansion in Austin, Texas. Her extensive list of clients includes the Radio Corporation of America, International Silver Company, Youngstown Kitchen Corporation, Charles of the Ritz, *Life* magazine, and General Electric Company.

Miss Kahane has designed fabrics, lighting fixtures, home appliances, "package kitchens," a collapsible cabana, wrought-iron furniture, modular office furniture, and airplane interiors. Upon the invitation of the governments of Sweden and Denmark, Miss Kahane traveled in both countries and produced a motion picture on contemporary Scandinavian interior design, which has been shown on television in the United States.

The widespread style of hard-surface flooring, such as vinyl tiles, in the major rooms of a house has been credited to the efforts of Melanie Kahane. Her unusual color combinations are famous throughout the design industry. In 1949 Miss Kahane created a black, white, and pumpkin French provincial bedroom which became the most photographed room in the history of decorating. Her use of pink and orange as the color scheme for *House & Garden* magazine's "House of Ideas" (January 1953) was another color innovation. The introduction of colored lamp bulbs in homes and offices resulted from Miss Kahane's studies for the Westinghouse Electric Corporation.

Melanie Kahane believes that the discovery of the living habits and interests of the client is an important task of the interior decorator. The décor of a home should reflect the personality of the family and express what they would like their "home to say" (New York *Times,* July 3, 1958).

The current rise in interest in interior decorating among families of middle and lower incomes Miss Kahane attributes to the increased concern that men have for the home. Men have come to realize that the home can be an investment which, like a stock ownership, yields a return over a period of years.

While attending a meeting of the Miami Fashion Group in Florida, the interior decorator discussed the problem of budgets in decorating. She claims that "everybody follows a budget." No matter how wealthy a client may be, he still does not have a bottomless purse for house decoration, she explains. She recommends a more courageous approach to the employment of color and to furniture placement (Miami *Herald,* October 31, 1958).

Marcus Blechman
MELANIE KAHANE

Miss Kahane exhibited a room at the National Home Furnishings Show in New York City in September 1958 and displayed sketched plans for furnishing a room at the Design Center for Interiors, New York City, in 1959. She was a committee member for the interior design of the United States Pavilion at the Brussels World's Fair in 1958.

Discussing the fair at the Architectural League in New York in June 1958, she said that there "was no evidence of anything new in the design of home furnishings. . . . The barriers between countries in the design of furniture and architecture seemed to be lost . . . which threatens a certain feeling of sterility."

The Grauers live in their own brownstone house (repainted white), on the east side of New York City. They have decorated their rooms with modern furniture and antiques, original paintings, sculpture, a modern tapestry, and curios collected on trips around the world. The living room is furnished in off-white, with such accents of blue as a huge eighteenth-century Austrian porcelain stove. Ben Grauer houses part of his collection of 5,000 books in the dining room-den.

Melanie Kahane and her husband, Ben Grauer, began in January 1959 an NBC network radio program *Decorating Wavelengths,* which is broadcast Monday through Thursday for five minutes. The program offers furnishing hints and news. Miss Kahane was not only the first decorator to appear on CBS-TV's *Omnibus* but was also the first of her profession to work and appear on color television.

Melanie Kahane was married to Theodore Earl Ebenstein, an insurance broker, in 1934, and they were divorced in 1945. They have one daughter, Joan Lynn Ebenstein. Miss Kahane was married to Ben Grauer on September 25, 1954. The slender, attractive, and vivacious decorator has brown hair, brown eyes, is five feet six inches tall, and weighs 120 pounds. One of the best-dressed women in the decorating business, she prefers simple, tailored clothing for daily wear and more dramatic apparel for formal wear. She is a skilled rifle woman and swimmer. She has taken extension courses in philosophy and psychology, and has an excellent command of French. She has a French poodle, Dufy.

In professional associations Miss Kahane has served as national secretary of the American Institute of Decorators and as president of its New York chapter. She belongs to the Municipal Art Society, Architectural League, Decorator's Club, Inter-Society Color Council, and the Illuminating Engineering Society. In 1953 she received the decorator of the year award from the National Association of Carpet Retailers. She served on the American Theatre Wing from 1939 to 1945 and worked on the board of directors of the Merchant Seaman's Canteen.

References

Miami Herald p1 D O 31 '58 por
Who's Who of American Women (1958-59)

KARAMI, RASHID 1921- Prime Minister of Lebanon; lawyer

Address: b. Office of Prime Minister, Beirut, Lebanon

Bounded on the north and east by Syria and on the south by Israel, the Republic of Lebanon has a population of about 1,500,000, which is approximately 54 per cent Christian, 44 per cent Moslem. To protect the interests of religious groups, a 1943 constitutional agreement stipulates that the President must always be a Christian, the Prime Minister always a Moslem. The Prime Minister since September 1958 has been Rashid Karami, who held this post in 1955 and who led an anti-Western revolt which lasted for some five months in 1958. An admirer of Gamal Abdel Nasser of the United Arab Republic, Karami has proclaimed a policy of "neutrality" between East and West. In December 1958, however, he declared that his country would no longer feel bound by the terms of the Eisenhower Doctrine, which had become "outdated."

Rashid Karami, a Sunni (orthodox) Moslem, was born in 1921 at Tripoli, the second largest city of Lebanon, where members of his family had been political leaders for many years. His father, Abdel Hamid Karami, was not only the Grand Mufti, or Moslem spiritual leader in Lebanon, but also served as a Premier of Lebanon. The semi-autonomous state was created in 1920 out of five districts of the former Ottoman Empire and administered by France under a League of Nations mandate.

In his native city Rashid Karami received his elementary and secondary schooling. He was about twenty years old when the Free French displaced the Vichy French in Lebanon in November 1941 and declared that country an independent republic. Parliamentary elections were held in 1943, and after a gradual transference of power, the French withdrew the last of their troops from Lebanon late in 1946. Rashid Karami was at that time a law student at Fuad al-Awal University in Cairo, Egypt. Graduated in 1947, he practised law for two years at Beirut, the capital of Lebanon, and then spent a year in France and Britain.

Upon the death of his father in 1950, Rashid Karami became head of the family and the natural political leader of Tripoli, a predominantly Moslem city. Elected in 1951 to the Lebanese Parliament as a deputy from Tripoli, he was in the same year appointed Minister of Justice. Re-elected in 1953, Karami became Minister of National Economy and Social Affairs, and in September 1955, following the resignation of Prime Minister Sami Solh (or Sami Bey es-Solh), he was appointed Prime Minister and Minister of the Interior. At thirty-four, he was the youngest Prime Minister in the history of Lebanon. He served until March 15 of the following year, when he submitted the resignation of his cabinet to Parliament, an action taken for the first time in Lebanon.

Although the immediate cause of Karami's resignation was a dispute about school subsidies, the Premier had been out of favor with the Lebanese Chamber of Deputies ever since the cessation of negotiations about a new pipeline contract with the Iraq Petroleum Company. The Chamber felt that Karami should have brought pressure on the oil company to continue the negotiations. Another source of discontent had been Karami's attempt, in January, to make a defensive alliance with anti-Western Syria.

"For emotional and commercial reasons," the New York *Times* observed (September 26, 1958), "Tripoli has always wanted to become a part of Syria. Thus, a student of politics in Tripoli explained once, if Mr. Karami ever stops promoting the union of Tripoli and Syria, he will stop being elected as Deputy from Tripoli." Karami had supported a union movement as early as 1952.

Sami Solh became Prime Minister for the sixth time in November 1956. On March 16, 1957 his government concluded an agreement with the United States providing for the supply of certain equipment to the Lebanese army and for a policy of co-operation, under the Eisenhower Doctrine, for mutual defense. When on April 5, 1957 this policy won an overwhelming vote of confidence in Lebanon's unicameral legislature, Karami resigned his seat in protest. He was, however, re-elected in the summer of the same year, as was Premier Solh, who proceeded to form his seventh pro-Western government.

Proclamation on February 1, 1958 of the United Arab Republic merging Syria with Egypt was followed in Lebanon on March 14 by the formation under Sami Solh of a new coalition government representing all pro-Western parties. Arab nationalist opponents charged, and the government denied, that Premier Solh planned to push through a constitutional amendment to permit the pro-Western President Camille Chamoun, elected for a six-year term in 1952, to succeed himself.

In the same month rioting broke out in Beirut. At Tripoli in May the citizens forcibly opposed a government order to take down portraits of Nasser, and Karami, still a member of Parliament, led a resistance movement which spread over the country and lasted 140 days. "I consider Nasser a superman," he is reported to have said (*Time*, October 6, 1958). On March 13 Foreign Minister Charles Malik accused the United Arab Republic of "massive interference" in Lebanon's affairs, and on June 11 the United Nations Security Council approved a resolution calling for the stationing of "observers" to check on alleged infiltration of men and arms from Syria. (The U.N. team later reported that no "massive infiltration" could be proved, although admittedly there were Syrian "volunteers" in the rebel forces at Tripoli and elsewhere.)

Alarmed by the coup that overthrew the pro-Western regime in Iraq on July 14, President Chamoun called on the United States for help. On the next day American marines, soon augmented by paratroopers, were landing in Lebanon. On July 31 the Lebanon Chamber of Deputies elected General Fouad Chehab, the army Chief of Staff, to succeed Chamoun as President. Karami supported the candidacy of Chehab who, on September 24, the day after he took office, named the rebel leader as Prime Minister, Minister of the Interior, and Minister of National Defense. Meanwhile the departure of one battalion of marines in August had initiated a gradual withdrawal of United States forces.

As early as March 1958, Karami had expressed to an interviewer his belief that Lebanon, with its Christian majority, should not at at the moment align herself with either the United Arab Republic or the Western-sponsored Federation of Iraq and Jordan. He did not, however, oppose a future union of all Arabs which, he said, might come "sooner than you think" (New York *Times*, March 23, 1958).

Taking office as Prime Minister, he named a cabinet of eight (four Christians, three Moslems, and one Druse), pledged himself to maintain the independence and territorial integrity of Lebanon, and advocated "positive neutrality" between East and West. ("Positive neutrality" is the phrase Nasser uses to describe his own position.) When the United States promptly offered his government full support, the new Premier said that Lebanon would welcome American military and economic aid, if offered "without strings." Subsequently, his government accepted an outright grant of $10,000,000 from the United States International Cooperation Administration, but not without considering the possibility of aid from the Soviet bloc.

Members of the extremist Christian Phalange, supporters of ex-President Chamoun, anticipated the appointment of Karami as Prime Minister, and violently opposed it. On the day that he was appointed there were riots in Beirut which resulted in nineteen deaths. About a week later the Phalangists called a general strike to protest Karami's appointment. By October 8, after being a Premier for only seventeen days, Karami had threatened to resign in order to prepare the way for a military government.

Wide World

RASHID KARAMI

Efforts to form such a government came to nothing. On October 14 Karami formed a compromise cabinet of only four members, two Moslem and two Christian, with the Phalangist leader, Pierre Gemayel, as his Deputy Premier. The new government, which received a unanimous vote of confidence from Parliament, demanded emergency powers to facilitate the disarming of the civilian population. These were voted on November 12, giving Karami's cabinet the right to govern by decree for the next six months, but before the vote, the Chamoun bloc had left the parliamentary chamber in protest. Later, on October 8, 1959 Karami enlarged his four-man cabinet to eight members.

"The Americans," the Lebanese Prime Minister declared on December 10, 1958, "now consider the Eisenhower Doctrine a unilateral declaration which is *dépassé*. We also consider it out of date and we no longer feel bound by the terms of this declaration." At the time of this announcement Karami also said that he had proposed to the United States a "U.N. partition of Palestine into Arab and Israeli states" (Washington *Post and Times Herald*, December 11, 1958).

Early in January 1959 Karami paid a ten-day visit to Egypt, partly to confer with Nasser on the ironing out of any lingering Syrian-Lebanese disagreements about tariffs and trade, and partly to preside over the Arab League economic council meetings. One outcome of the council meetings was an agreement that Lebanon should participate in an Arab Development Bank with an initial capitalization of about $57,400,000.

To finance the Arab Development Bank, Lebanon recommended at an international oil conference in April 1959 that each nation earmark 5 per cent of its oil profits for the bank's activities. The conference, which was attended by representatives of nine Arab states and

KARAMI, RASHID—*Continued*

emirates and Venezuela, urged greater Arab participation in oil refining and marketing.

Karami announced in April 1959 an early resumption of negotiations, suspended in 1956, between Lebanon and the Iraq Petroleum Company, for increased oil transit royalties. The company has a pipeline terminus at Tripoli. On June 4 Karami and the oil company signed an agreement profitable to Lebanon. Three days later, at Cairo, the Lebanese Prime Minister concluded a major trade pact with President Nasser of the United Arab Republic. Continuing his role in directly carrying out his own foreign policies, Karami came to the United States in September 1959 to head the Lebanese delegation to the U.N.

Prime Minister Karami, according to a biographical sketch in the New York *Times* (September 26, 1958), is "handsome in a Levantine way with liquid brown eyes and black hair and mustache." Ordinarily "well-dressed and calm," he can be "as adroit and flexible on an issue as he is suave and graceful in his drawing room." Karami is a bachelor. His home is a mansion on a rocky headland overlooking the sea at Tripoli.

References

Christian Sci Mon p4 N 1 '58
N Y Times p8 S 26 '58 por

KASSEM, ABDUL KARIM (EL-) Nov. 21, 1914- Premier of Iraq

Address: b. c/o Ministry of Defense, Baghdad, Iraq; h. Alwaiyah, Baghdad, Iraq

In the strategic Middle East, Abdul Karim Kassem, the Premier of Iraq, has maintained his own position and the independence of his country ever since he led a successful revolution in July 1958 against its pro-Western monarchy. A man with no political experience, Kassem had risen in the Iraqi army to the rank of brigadier, but ever since his early training at military college, he had wanted to lead a revolution in his country. He has dedicated himself to the cause of Arab nationalism, and advocates neutralism between the Soviet Union and the West.

In the political sphere, Kassem has several urgent problems to confront: his struggle with President Gamal Abdel Nasser of the United Arab Republic for leadership of the Arab world; his difficulties with pro-Nasser adherents in Iraq; his fight to contain the Communists in his country, who are infiltrating the civil government, the police, and the press; and his search for a foreign policy to adopt toward the Soviet Union. In the social and economic spheres he faces the problems of trying to raise the standard of living of the workers and farmers.

Abdul Karim el-Kassem was born on November 21, 1914, in Baghdad, Iraq, at the home of his grandfather, a skin and hide merchant. His father, Kassim Mohammed el-Bakr, a Sunnite, or orthodox Moslem, owned a small corn and barley farm on the Tigris River, south of Baghdad. His mother belonged to the Shiite non-orthodox sect of Islam, the largest religious group in Iraq. According to Richard P. Hunt in the New York *Times Magazine* (June 28, 1959), he was brought up in his grandfather's house, along with his cousin, Fadhil Abbas al-Mahdawi, who since the 1958 revolution has presided in the brutal trials of the High Military Court.

He attended a school in Baghdad, where one report described him as "a better than average student, but inclined to be dreamy and visionary." At the age of seventeen, he enrolled in the Iraqi Military College in Baghdad, and after his graduation two years later in 1934, he was commissioned a second lieutenant. Several years of routine military service in the infantry followed, and then in 1939 he was assigned to the military college as a first lieutenant and instructor.

In 1941 he was graduated from the Iraq Staff College with high honors. The New York *Times* (July 16, 1958) reported a Syrian news release which said that as a lieutenant, he took part in a pro-German revolt in Iraq in 1941. He became a staff officer serving with various army headquarters, and was then advanced to the rank of major, in command of a battalion. After a campaign against Kurdish tribesmen in northern Iraq, Kassem was awarded the highest Iraqi military decoration.

During the war of the Arab states in 1948 to prevent the establishment of a Jewish homeland in Palestine, he commanded a battalion and distinguished himself for front-line bravery. He reportedly refused a decoration because he disliked the way the war had been conducted. In May 1948, when Iraqi troops were ordered to observe a cease-fire in the war, Kassem, according to the New York *Herald Tribune* (July 15, 1958), was among those who refused to obey. His troops continued fighting until June 11, 1948, when a coordinated cease-fire was negotiated through the Arab League.

Kassem then attended a school for senior officers for six months in Great Britain, where he was regarded as little better than a mediocre officer. Upon his return to Iraq, he was advanced to the rank of colonel and made a deputy director of Iraqi army ordnance. In 1955 he became a brigadier (the equivalent of an American brigadier general), and was a member of a military mission which went to Turkey to observe army maneuvers. During Israel's Sinai campaign against Egypt in 1956, in the so-called "Suez crisis," Kassem commanded his country's troops in Jordan.

Kassem's most recent command was that of the Nineteenth Infantry Brigade of the Third Division, one of the country's few well-equipped units. In 1957 it was sent to Jordan to help King Hussein with trouble in his army. Kassem claims that he began to make plans for this revolt about the time that he was made commander of the Nineteenth Infantry Brigade, although he had thought about revolution ever since his graduation from the military college.

By the time he received that command, he had formed a Free Officers' Movement; after that he began sounding out other officers and constructing a revolutionary organization, all in strictest secrecy. The appropriate moment came when his brigade and other army units were ordered to march through Baghdad on their way to Lebanon to crush an uprising there. Instead, Kassem, with the help of Colonel Abdul Salam Aref, marched into the city on the night of July 13, 1958, killed King Faisal II, Crown Prince Abdul Illah, and Premier Nuri as-Said, and proclaimed a republic. Kassem has attributed the success of the revolution to his study of the causes of failure of other Iraqi uprisings, and of the successful experience of Gamal Abdel Nasser of Egypt.

Kassem became Premier and acting Defense Minister in the new government; Aref was named Deputy Premier. A cabinet was chosen, and a three-man sovereignty council, to exercise the prerogatives of chief of state, was formed. The most important task for the country, Kassem felt, was to improve the living standard of the people and to prevent them from living in the slums. The problems of internal politics in the aftermath of revolutionary chaos, and foreign policies, however, became dominant.

Later in 1958, Aref was convicted of plotting to assassinate Kassem, but the Premier refused to have his former deputy executed. Kassem is "neither vindictive nor bloodthirsty", in the opinion of Richard P. Hunt (New York *Times Magazine*, June 28, 1959). "I will not hang traitors just because you or some other group demands it!" Kassem is reported to have told Communist hecklers who were calling for more executions of pro-Westerners (*Life*, August 3, 1959).

Kassem has announced that his foreign policy will be based on the idea of friendship to all countries, without becoming a vassal to any. His country withdrew from the Western-oriented defense organization under the Baghdad Pact, but the oil agreements with the Western concerns are still in force. (After Iraq renounced the alliance, the Baghdad Pact, which had been known as the Middle East Treaty Organization, changed its name to the Central Treaty Organization.) Though some observers feared that Communists in Iraq might become too strong, Kassem successfully quelled a pro-Communist uprising in Kirkuk in July 1959, and has taken other steps to limit Communist infiltration of the government. He has, however, accepted economic and military aid from the Soviet Union.

He has also held in check the Arab nationalists in Iraq who favor close co-operation with President Nasser of the United Arab Republic. Kassem stopped an army mutiny by pro-Nasserists in Mosul in March 1959, and has taken other steps to keep their influence in the government under control. During the celebrations of the first anniversary of the revolution, the Premier felt so secure that he promised the formation of political parties in early 1960.

The problem of balancing the internal and foreign forces in Iraq has left Kassem little time to carry through the reforms for raising the standard of living which he had envisaged. As the revolutionary government feels more secure, however, it seems likely that further steps will be taken to legalize the redistribution of land, to industrialize the country, and to provide better housing and medical facilities.

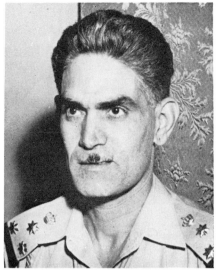

Wide World

ABDUL KARIM KASSEM

Kassem has never married because he has said he feared that a domestic life might cause conflicts that would deter him from his purpose of revolution. He rents a white and tan brick house in the suburb of Alwaiyah, but often eats and sleeps in his office in the Ministry of Defense. He keeps a number of hunting dogs as his pets, and enjoys playing sports, particularly soccer and basketball. In addition to his native Arabic, he speaks Kurdish, Turkish, and English. He is probably either a Shiite or a Sunnite Moslem.

Richard Hunt has written in the New York *Times* magazine (June 28, 1959) that the Iraqi Premier is "something of an oddity in the Arab world, because he is not a leader by reason of the force of a powerful personality. He is an indifferent speaker, high-voiced and ill at ease on the platform. What he does have is a vision . . . an air of being above it all and fair to all. In Iraq the public has trusted no one for very long; Kassem is trying to become the one man that everybody can trust."

References

Christian Sci Mon p2 Jl 25 '58 por
Life 46:38B Mr 23 '59 por; 47:78 Ag 3 '59 por
N Y Herald Tribune p7 Jl 15 '58
N Y Times p14 Jl 16 '58; p10 Jl 23 '58 por
N Y Times Mag p9+ Je 28 '59 por
N Y World-Telegram p5 F 9 '59 por
Time 73:32+ Ap 13 '59 por

KELLY, JOE May 31, 1901-May 26, 1959
Radio and TV entertainer; quiz-master on radio's *Quiz Kids*; appeared on radio's *National Barn Dance* and TV's *Totem Club*. See *Current Biography* (June) 1945.

Obituary

N Y Times p35 My 27 '59

KENNAN, GEORGE F(ROST) Feb. 16, 1904- Historian; writer

Address: b. Institute for Advanced Study, Princeton, N.J.

> NOTE: This biography supersedes the article which appeared in *Current Biography* in 1947.

In seeking to answer the questions of how to end the East-West "cold war" and how to prevent a global atomic war, George F. Kennan can apply more than twenty-five years of experience as a United States career diplomat and the lifelong study that has made him an undisputed authority on Russia. His series of lectures heard over the British Broadcasting Corporation in the fall of 1957 and subsequently published in *Russia, the Atom and the West* (1958) urged a new approach in dealing with the Soviet Union. And his suggestions, especially his proposal for "disengagement"—withdrawal of United States troops from Europe—have aroused a continuing stir of controversy in many world capitals. Much of the current United States strategy which he now finds outmoded for meeting the Soviet threat is founded upon policies which Kennan himself helped formulate as a top State Department adviser during the Truman administration.

Since 1956 Kennan has been a permanent professor at the school of historical studies at the Institute for Advanced Study in Princeton, New Jersey, having become a member of the institute upon his retirement from the Foreign Service in 1953. Briefly during the preceding year he had been United States Ambassador to the Soviet Union. He is probably otherwise chiefly known to Americans as the author of *Russia Leaves the War* (1956), which won the Pulitzer Prize in history for 1957.

George Frost Kennan, a descendant of Scotch-Irish settlers in pre-Revolutionary America, was born in Kossuth Kent and Florence (James) Kennan in Milwaukee, Wisconsin on February 16, 1904. He has a brother, Kent Kennan, a musician. His uncle, George Kennan, was an expert on Czarist Russia who wrote *Siberia and the Exile System,* an abridgment of which from the first edition of 1891 was published in 1957 with an introduction by George F. Kennan.

For his college preparatory training Kennan attended St. John's Military Academy in Delafield, Wisconsin. He then enrolled at Princeton University, chose history as his major subject, and received the B.A. degree in 1925. The following year, in September, he entered the United States Foreign Service and subsequently was assigned as vice-consul to Geneva in 1927, to Hamburg in 1927, to Berlin in 1928, and to Tallin (Estonia) in 1928. During part of the year 1929 he served as third secretary in Riga (Latvia), Kaunas (Lithuania), and Tallin. These cities were regarded as "listening posts" for the Soviet Union, where the United States then had no diplomatic mission.

In anticipation of eventually extending recognition to the Soviet Union, the State Department opened a division of Russian studies to train selected Foreign Service officers in the Russian language, literature, history, and political theory. From 1929 to 1931 Kennan studied under this program at the Berlin Seminar for Oriental Languages and the University of Berlin. When the United States reopened its embassy in Moscow in 1933, he was called from his third secretaryship at Riga to accompany Ambassador William C. Bullitt to the Soviet capital.

The posts that Kennan filled during the next few years included vice-consul in Vienna (1935), second secretary in Moscow (1935-36), second secretary and later consul in Prague (1938-39). At the outbreak of World War II, in 1939, he was sent as second secretary to Berlin, where he became first secretary the following year. When the United States joined the war, in December 1941, he was interned by the Nazis at Bad Nauheim. Repatriated in June 1942, a few months later he took up the new assignment of counselor at Lisbon in neutral Portugal. During late 1943 and early 1944 he was counselor of the American delegation to the European Advisory Commission, which met in London to prepare recommendations on policy in Europe for the United States, Great Britain, and the Soviet Union.

Serving first under Ambassador W. Averell Harriman and then under General Walter Bedell Smith, Kennan was minister-counselor in Moscow from May 1944 to April 1946. The State Department next appointed him as its deputy for foreign affairs at the National War College in Washington, D.C., where he was lecturer for almost a year on foreign policy and international relations.

In the spring of 1947 Secretary of State George C. Marshall named Kennan director of the policy planning staff of the Department of State and charged him with responsibility for long-range planning of United States action in foreign affairs. His appointment helped to bring about an important change in policy toward the Soviet Union. Turning from its immediate postwar attitude of appeasement and compromise, the United States adopted the policy of "containment" of the expansionist tendencies of the U.S.S.R. through application of "counterforce" wherever Soviet imperialism might make itself felt. Kennan laid the foundations for this new program in an article in *Foreign Affairs* for July 1947, signed by Mr. "X."

After Dean Acheson became Secretary of State in 1949, he chose Kennan as one of his principal advisers, with the title of counselor of the Department of State. Kennan returned to Moscow in May 1952, as Ambassador to the U.S.S.R., but remained there only until the following October when the Russians declared him *persona non grata*—ostensibly because of critical comments on Soviet treatment of Western diplomats that Kennan made while on a visit to Berlin.

While serving as State Department counselor, Kennan had taken a leave of absence in 1950, to carry on research in problems on foreign policy at the Institute for Advanced Study. Leaving the Foreign Service in 1953, he became a member of the institute, and since January 1956 he has been professor at its school of historical studies.

Many of Kennan's observations on United States foreign policy first became generally known through lectures which later appeared in book form. His lectures in 1951 for the Charles R. Walgreen Foundation at the University of Chicago were published in *American Diplomacy, 1900-1950* (University of Chicago Press, 1951), which began with a chapter on the war with Spain and carried its review of the fifty-year period up to a consideration of America and the Russian future. The book, which won the Freedom House Award, was praised by critics for clarity of thought and phrasing.

Similar favorable reception was given to *Realities of American Foreign Policy* (Princeton University Press, 1954), a series of four lectures which Kennan delivered as the Stafford Little Lecturer at Princeton during 1954. Another book by Kennan published in 1954 was *Das Amerikanisch-Russische Verhältnis* (Deutsche Verlags-Anstalt, Stuttgart).

A major area of exploration for Kennan has been the origins of present Soviet conduct in world affairs. *Russia Leaves the War* (Princeton University Press, 1956) was the first volume in a projected series on Soviet-American relations from 1917 to 1920. The second volume, *The Decision to Intervene,* was published in 1958.

Besides winning the Pulitzer Prize, *Russia Leaves the War* received the National Book Award, the Bancroft Prize, and the Francis Parkman Prize of the Society of American Historians. Reviewers were much impressed both by the thoroughness and integrity of Kennan's scholarship and the literary quality of his writing. Commenting in *Political Science Quarterly* (June 1957), F. C. Barghoom stated, "This work of historical reconstruction and criticism possesses great power, subtlety, integrity, and charm. . . . One of the finest qualities of Ambassador Kennan's account is its charitable spirit. While the author finds much to criticize or to deplore and frequently gives expression to wry irony regarding the follies and frailties of statesmen, he is never harsh, intolerant, or dogmatic."

On a leave of absence from the Institute for Advanced Study, Kennan held the George Eastman Visiting Professorship at Balliol College, Oxford University, England, in 1957-58 and lectured there on the subject of Soviet-Western relations during the period from 1918 to 1939. For six Sundays in late 1957 he gave radio addresses on the British Broadcasting Corporation which attracted world-wide attention. Excerpts were printed in many newspapers in the United States and abroad; the lectures formed the bases of two articles by Kennan in *Harper's Magazine* (February and March 1958); and they were published in the book *Russia, the Atom and the West* (Harper, 1958).

Kennan's BBC addresses, the Reith Lectures, offered a number of ideas for governments to "think about," including the proposals that the United States withdraw its forces from Europe while the U.S.S.R. withdraw from the Euro-

GEORGE F. KENNAN

pean satellite nations, and that Germany be reunited and neutralized. He questioned whether arming the NATO countries with atomic missiles would succeed in maintaining peace and whether the United Nations could resolve the deep-seated conflict between the U.S.S.R. and the West. He expressed his belief that the U.S.S.R. does not want a general war: the Russians present "a combined military-political threat," but "with accent on the political."

Among those disagreeing with Kennan was Dean Acheson, who in January 1958 issued a statement that Kennan's opinions, especially regarding troop withdrawal, did not represent the views of the Democratic party. He said that when Kennan had advanced the same proposals in 1949, the Democratic Administration had rejected them. While acknowledging Kennan's authority in the field of Russian history, Acheson stated, "Kennan has never, in my judgment, grasped the realities of power relationships, but takes a rather mystical attitude toward them" (*United States News & World Report,* January 17, 1958). Months after his BBC broadcasts, however, Kennan's suggestions were still being debated in European and other government circles.

In another important contribution to the continuing debate on foreign policy, Kennan declared in October 1959 that the conscience of the nation balks at a policy of basing security on weapons of "indiscriminate mass destruction." He proposed that the United States develop "conventional forces" and at conferences between East and West foster the abolishment of nuclear weapons (*Christian Science Monitor,* October 23, 1959).

According to *Newsweek* (August 27, 1956), Kennan was "originally a moderate Republican . . . he became an active Democrat out of strong disagreement with John Foster Dulles' foreign policy." He has several honorary LL.D. degrees, including those from Yale, Princeton,

KENNAN, GEORGE F.—*Continued*

and Northwestern universities. He belongs to the American Academy of Political and Social Science, among other professional organizations, and to the Century Club in New York.

George F. Kennan married Annelise Sorenson on September 11, 1931 and is the father of Grace, Joan Elizabeth, Christopher James, and Wendy Antonia. He is tall and slender and has blue eyes. For recreation he plays the piano and guitar and he reads extensively in English, American, Russian, and German literatures.

References

Directory of American Scholars (1957)
Robinson, Donald   The 100 Most Important People in the World Today (1952)
Who's Who in America, 1958-59
World Biography (1954)

KEROUAC, JACK   March 12, 1922- Author

Address: b. c/o Viking Press, 625 Madison Avenue, New York 22

To the American reading public, the writer Jack Kerouac is the standard-bearer and leading novelist of the much-publicized "beat generation." The "beat" movement that he captains has not only given the English vocabulary a new adjective and the young a new fad but has also furnished columns of copy for hard-pressed feature writers. Kerouac first became prominent when his *On the Road* was published in 1957. He followed it with four others in quick succession, and in the process became one of the more controversial novelists of recent years.

Usually called Jack or John, Kerouac was christened Jean; he was born in Lowell, Massachusetts, on March 12, 1922, the son of Leo Alcide and Gabrielle (LeVesque) Kerouac. His father was a job printer in Lowell; his mother was of French-Canadian extraction. Jack attended local Catholic parochial schools, then went to New York City to prepare for college at the Horace Mann School.

Having won an academic and athletic scholarship to Columbia University, Kerouac matriculated there in September 1940. He played football in the freshman backfield, and although he broke a leg in the season's third game, he showed enough promise to be chosen for the varsity team in 1941. But Kerouac was even then restless with the wanderlust he was later to celebrate in his novels. He left Columbia in the fall of 1941.

First he went south to Virginia "to become a big poet," as he remarked later, then he enlisted briefly in the United States Navy. He served two months in uniform before he was given a psychiatric discharge. He did odd jobs in automobile service stations, and served for a while in the Merchant Marine in the North Atlantic. He returned to the United States—and Columbia—in October 1942.

His second sojourn at college was even shorter than the first; he quit both the football team and his classes that same autumn. He established an apartment near the Columbia campus which became a gathering place for the university's young intellectuals. Among the students Kerouac met that winter was Allen Ginsberg, who later became the poet of the "beat generation" just as Kerouac became its novelist.

Kerouac apparently devoted the years from 1943 to 1950 to roaming through the United States and Mexico. He made at least one more voyage as a merchant sailor, spent a summer as a forest-fire lookout in Washington's Mount Baker National Forest, and returned from time to time to his mother's home to work on a novel about his Lowell boyhood. The book was published in 1950 by Harcourt, Brace.

Showing little kinship to his later books, *The Town and The City* was favorably regarded by the reviewers. "In many respects, John Kerouac, now 28, is the best and most promising of the young novelists whose first works have recently appeared," wrote a *Newsweek* critic in a review (March 13, 1950) which was illustrated by a photograph of Kerouac as a serious and well-groomed young man wearing a sedate jacket and tie.

The book displayed all of Kerouac's warmth and enthusiasm for detail. "Kerouac has as keen an eye for externals as Sinclair Lewis had in his early novels, but he has none of his sarcasm or mockery," the same critic wrote; "he has the ability to infuse . . . grandeur into simple doings that marked Thomas Wolfe's first books, but he is more balanced than Wolfe. He has a zest for the ordinary."

But even while his first novel was being reviewed, Kerouac was working on a new one. He abandoned the process of write-and-rewrite in favor of a spontaneous composition that could capture the emotions and personalities of his seven-year odyssey. He had spent three years writing *The Town and the City*, but he wrote *On the Road* in a period of three weeks in 1951. He bought art paper in twenty-foot rolls, pasted the ends together, and typed virtually non-stop until he had completed his epic.

Segments of the novel were printed in the *Paris Review, New World Writing* and elsewhere, but not until 1957 did Viking Press publish the complete novel. Although it flirted only briefly with the best-seller lists, *On the Road* was certainly one of the most controversial books of recent years. Together with Ginsberg's poem *Howl*, it has been accepted as the literary expression of youth's current revolt against the adult world (or "Squaresville"); on its own merits it has been welcomed as counterpoint to the self-conscious formalism of much of America's university-based writing.

The word "beat," Kerouac explains, originated with Herbert Huncke, one of Kerouac's innumerable friends. "To me, it meant being poor, like sleeping in the subways, like Huncke used to do, and yet being illuminated and having illuminated ideas about apocalypse and all that. . . . 'The Beat Generation', that was supposed to be the title of 'On the Road' (New York *Post*, March 10, 1959). Later, Kerouac decided that "beat" stood for "beatific."

On the Road recounts the adventures of Kerouac (Sal Paradise), Ginsberg (Carlo Marx), a frenetic hipster named Neal Cassady (Dean Moriarty), and their friends both on the road and at way stations across the continent. An example of the style and general attitude of the novel is the passage in which Sal, the narrator, describes the first meeting of Carlo and Dean: ". . . they danced down the streets like dingle-dodies, and I shambled after as I've been doing all my life after people who interest me, because the only people for me are the mad ones, the ones who are mad to live, mad to talk, mad to be saved, desirous of everything at the same time, the ones who never yawn or say a commonplace thing, but burn, burn, burn like fabulous yellow roman candles exploding like spiders across the stars and in the middle you see the blue centerlight pop and everybody goes 'Awww!'"

On the Road eventually sold 20,000 copies in its hard-bound edition, and 500,000 in soft covers. Kerouac's third published novel, *The Dharma Bums,* was published by Viking in October 1958. Indebted to Buddhist philosophy and Japanese *haiku* poetry, the novel covers the developments in Kerouac's life and outlook during the six years between the writing and the publishing of *On the Road.* Zen Buddhism, an enthusiasm of many members of the "beat" movement, plays a major part in the novel, which is about two young men who try to find Dharma (truth) through poverty, rejection of society, and union with nature in the Western mountains.

At the time *The Dharma Bums* was published, Kerouac reportedly had six more novels already written. Several have been released: *The Subterraneans* (Grove Press, 1958) deals with a Negro-white love affair in San Francisco, while *Doctor Sax* (Viking Press and Grove Press, 1959) returns to Lowell, Massachusetts, and Kerouac's boyhood; *Maggie Cassidy,* (Avon, 1959) is a sequel to *Doctor Sax.*

In the future Kerouac may bring to light several more novels that he wrote in the lean years before *On the Road* was published. The ones released so far have met with similar reviews: some critics have maintained that his is an extraordinary and refreshing talent; others have agreed with Eugene Burdick that "Kerouac is a bad writer and often a silly one. . . . He is like a sensitive eyeball that sweeps and perceives but is not connected to a brain" (*Reporter,* April 3, 1958).

A number of articulate young Americans have adopted the way of life that Kerouac celebrates in his novels as an ideal, transforming a cult into a national movement. The originators of the cult have complained, however, that their ideas are being corrupted by the disciples. "Lately the vision has been invaded, mauled, overstudied, imitated," commented Eugene Burdick (*Reporter,* April 3, 1958). "The ring of bemused spectators has pressed in close with the inevitable result: the vision has suffocated. Some of the originals, like Kerouac, want out."

Married at twenty-two and again at twenty-eight, Kerouac now lives with his mother in Northport, New York. Each of his marriages was dissolved after about six months. "I was his benefactor all my life," Kerouac's mother has said (New York *Post,* March 10, 1959). "He always lives with me, outside of when he travels. . . . But when he did travel, there was

Keith W. Jennison

JACK KEROUAC

always money for him. I used to send it any time he needed it, for food, clothes. I was working in a factory, I was making good money. You know, he's really a nice boy." Mrs. Kerouac has read thirty-four pages of *On the Road,* and plans to finish it some day.

References

N Y Post p4+ Mr 10 '59 por
Reporter 18:30+ Ap 3 '58
Who's Who in America (sup Je-Ag '58)

KERR, JAMES W(INSLOW) March 11, 1914- Canadian business executive

Address: b. Trans-Canada Pipe Lines, Ltd., 92 King St. E., Toronto 1, Ontario, Canada; h. 15 Forsythe Place, Hamilton, Ontario, Canada

Trans-Canada Pipe Lines, Ltd., the world's longest natural gas pipe line, running 2,290 miles from Alberta to Quebec, went into operation in October 1958. Its president and chief executive officer is James W. Kerr, who was appointed in December 1958, succeeding Charles S. Coates, who supervised the design, engineering, and construction of the pipe line.

Kerr came to his new position after a successful career in Canadian Westinghouse Company, Ltd., during which he became the firm's vice-president and general manager of the apparatus products group. As a native Canadian, he should find more favor with the "Canada-First" elements in the Conservative Parliament than did his predecessor, Charles S. Coates, a Texan.

His rapid rise to the vice-presidency of Westinghouse after completing his training as an electrical engineer testified to Kerr's skill in combining technical knowledge, salesmanship, and managerial talent. Now that the major

JAMES W. KERR

construction of Trans-Canada Pipe Lines, Ltd., has been completed, the new president faces the task of directing its operation. The natural gas line will greatly aid Canada's industrial expansion, thus helping to rectify the country's adverse balance of international trade.

James Winslow Kerr, the son of George Robert and Helen Robertson (Bews) Kerr, was born in the industrial city of Hamilton, Ontario, Canada, on March 11, 1914. His father was a vice-president and treasurer of the Canadian Westinghouse Company, Ltd. He attended the public schools and Delta Collegiate Institute in Hamilton, and then entered the School of Applied Science at the University of Toronto, Canada. He was graduated with a Bachelor of Science degree in electrical engineering in 1937.

During the summers from 1931 to 1936 Kerr had worked at the main plant of the Canadian Westinghouse Company, Ltd., in Hamilton. This firm produces electrical appliances, foundry goods, generators, transformers, lighting fixtures and lamps, electric motors, and equipment for air conditioning, railroads, radios, television, and other communications media. From 1937 to 1938 Kerr served the company as an engineering apprentice, and then was an apparatus correspondent.

After two years in the training course, Kerr entered the company's office in Toronto, Ontario, in 1941 as a sales engineer. During World War II he served in the Royal Canadian Air Force, and rose to the rank of squadron leader. In 1945 he accepted a position in the transformer sales department of Westinghouse in Hamilton. He was made assistant manager of central station sales in 1947, and the manager in 1948. He assumed new responsibilities in the following year when

he became the manager of both central station and transportation sales.

During the three years from 1949 to 1952 Kerr was manager of apparatus sales, and in the latter year accepted the title and duties of general manager of the power products division. He became general manager of the apparatus products group in 1954, and two years later, vice-president and general manager of the apparatus group. During his years with the company, Kerr was closely associated with many important power and industrial developments. He took part in the negotiations of such projects as the Des Joachims, Sir Adam Beck, St. Lawrence Seaway, and Kitimat hydroelectric power developments.

Offered the presidency of Trans-Canada Pipe Lines, Ltd., Kerr accepted, he has said, because he could not resist the "challenge of change" and the "opportunity for broader participation in the development of Canada's energy resources and industrial potential" (New York Times, January 14, 1959). At the time of his appointment, in December 1958, when it was announced that he would succeed Charles S. Coates, who had been the president since 1957, it was reported that Trans-Canada was going through a complete reorganization at the executive level. With the completion of the pipe line in October 1958, the main responsibilities of the firm's officers would no longer be construction, but operation.

The company, according to the Atlantic Monthly (November 1956), was originally the idea of Clint Murchison, the Texas oil promoter, who in 1951 persuaded the Canadian government to allow a 34-inch natural gas pipe line to be constructed from Alberta through wilderness regions to Ontario and Quebec. The company was incorporated in a special act of the Canadian Parliament in March 1951. Then a group of Canadians asked for the right to build a line from Alberta to Winnipeg and into the United States. The questions of whether or not the gas could be exported to the United States, and whether or not the northern route was feasible, were debated at length.

Finally, in early 1954, the Canadian government sponsored the merger of the Canadian group, Western Pipe Lines, Ltd., with Trans-Canada Pipe Lines, Ltd., with Nathan E. Tanner as president. Shortly thereafter, the Alberta provincial government agreed to allow the export of its natural gas. The firm's next problem was to arrange contracts for the purchase and sale of gas, for without them it could not borrow the money with which to build the pipe line, but without the line it found it could not get the contracts.

In the latter part of 1954 the company was allowed to build a natural gas pipe line from Niagara, New York, to Toronto, under an agreement with the Tennessee Gas Transmission Company; thus it was able to establish a market for itself in the Toronto area. Later it negotiated a contract whereby Tennessee would take its Canadian gas at the Manitoba-Minnesota boundary for sale in Chicago. The initial opposition of Tennessee's American competitors to this threat of importation of

Canadian gas coincided with the time when Trans-Canada was unable to finance the building of the portion of pipe line through northern Ontario.

Because the issue involved Canadian national pride, the national and Ontario provincial governments agreed to lend Trans-Canada $125,000,000 to build the 600-mile link. The Conservatives in Parliament opposed this, fearing the extent of American ownership in Canadian resources and industry. They later said if Trans-Canada could not fulfill its promises, the government itself should build the pipe line. The Liberals' position, however, won out. Further economic difficulties beset Trans-Canada, due partly to the reluctance of American bankers to finance the line, but the Liberals were again successful, after bitter debate, in getting the Canadian Parliament to pass a bill to lend the company more money, this time $80,000,000.

Soon it was reported that the company had firm commitments for all the gas it could move to eastern Canada. The natural gas line, extending from Alberta to Montreal at a cost of about $375,000,000, has been delivering its product since the autumn of 1958 to homes and industries in an area which covers three-fifths of Canada's population. The question of exporting natural gas to the United States is still undecided; it depends on the approval of the new Conservative government in Canada and of the Alberta provincial government.

In order to stay abreast of advances in scientific techniques, Kerr visited the Soviet Union in the spring of 1958 with a group of Canadian businessmen. He has made a number of speeches based on his observations during this trip. He reported that Russia is planning to construct 25,000 miles of gas transmission lines within the next ten years, over ten times the length of the Trans-Canada operation he directs.

Kerr is a member of many professional and business associations, including the Engineering Institute of Canada, the Association of Professional Engineers of Canada, and the American Institute of Electrical Engineers. He has served as vice-president of the engineering alumni association of the University of Toronto, and as a member of the board of governors of the Hamilton and District Officers' Institute, the Hamilton General Hospital, and the Stratford Shakespearean Festival Foundation of Canada. He also has been vice-chairman of Hamilton's United Appeal. He is active in church life as an elder of the Westdale United Church. His political affiliation is with the Conservatives.

James Winslow Kerr married Ruth Eleanor Marrs of Hamilton, Ontario, on October 5, 1940. They have two children, David and Barbara. His clubs are the Hamilton, and the Hamilton Golf and Country. He is a member of Theta Delta Chi. For recreation the business executive enjoys playing golf, curling, gardening, and woodworking.

References

N Y Times p56 Ja 14 '59
Canadian Who's Who, 1955-57

KETTERING, CHARLES FRANKLIN

Aug. 29, 1876-Nov. 25, 1958 Electrical engineer; inventor; vice-president and head of the research division of the General Motors Corporation. See *Current Biography* (December) 1951.

Obituary

N Y Times p1+ N 26 '58

KEY, WILLIAM S(HAFFER) Oct. 6,

1889-Jan. 5, 1959 Major General in the United States Army; Oklahoma civic and business leader. See *Current Biography* (July) 1943.

Obituary

N Y Times p33 Ja 7 '59

KHAN, MOHAMMAD AYUB *See* Ayub Khan, Mohammad

KILLIAN, JAMES R(HYNE), JR. July

24, 1904- Educator; former United States government official

Address: h. 111 Memorial Drive, Cambridge 42, Mass.

> NOTE: This biography supersedes the article which appeared in *Current Biography* in 1949.

As special assistant for science and technology to the President of the United States, James R. Killian, Jr., brought to his post many successful years of scientific and administrative experience. At the time of his appointment by President Dwight D. Eisenhower in 1957, he had been president of Massachusetts Institute of Technology in Cambridge, Massachusetts for almost a decade. Previously he had held other administrative posts in the institute and had been editor of the scientific journal, *The Technology Review*. He is now chairman of the M.I.T. corporation. On May 28, 1959 he resigned as the President's special assistant for science and technology.

Over the years Killian had served the United States government in various advisory capacities, and when Eisenhower felt a need for a personal scientific adviser in view of Soviet advances in missiles and other areas of technology, he chose Killian. Although the educator has never been a practising scientist, he has been held in high esteem by the scientific community whose views and conclusions he has effectively communicated to the President.

James Rhyne Killian, Jr., was born in Blacksburg, South Carolina, on July 24, 1904, the son of James Robert and Jeannette (Rhyne) Killian. He is of German, Scottish, and Irish descent. He was raised in Concord, North Carolina, where his father was in the textile business, but entered high school in Thomson, Georgia in 1918. Two years later he enrolled in the McCallie School in Chattanooga, Tennessee, where he played in the band and was active in the debating society. He was graduated from the school in 1921.

(Continued next page)

Wide World

JAMES R. KILLIAN, JR.

Having been awarded a freshman scholarship, Killian became a student at Trinity College (now Duke University) in Durham, North Carolina. He transferred to the Massachusetts Institute of Technology in Cambridge, Massachusetts in 1923, where he majored in engineering and business administration. His extracurricular activities included track and editing the *Tech,* M.I.T.'s student newspaper. He was awarded the B.S. degree in 1926.

Killian then became assistant managing editor of the *Technology Review,* a scientific journal published by the alumni association of M.I.T. After one year, he was made managing editor, and in 1930, the editor. When Dr. Karl T. Compton, president of M.I.T., was looking for an executive assistant in 1939, he chose Killian. After four years in this position, Killian accepted the title of executive vice-president of the institute in 1943. During World War II, when the number of scientists at M.I.T. rose into the thousands under the research and training program, he was often the ranking administrative officer and acting president. From 1945 to 1948 he was vice-president of M.I.T.

When Compton resigned as president of M.I.T. in 1948 to become chairman of the National Research and Development Board in Washington, D.C., Killian was named to succeed him. At his inauguration in 1949, he said: "We must continue to muster the democratic ranks of American scientists into invincible battalions. We must again be able to beat the enemy to the draw as we did in developing the atomic bomb. Our schools of science and engineering, if they are strong, are a powerful fleet-in-being, a striking force that can be thrown instantly into action if needed."

During the years of his presidency, Killian promoted the expansion of M.I.T., with its ties to private business, radiation research, radar,

computation, and missile guidance systems, and the whole range of weapons technology. His administration was also marked by a greater emphasis on the humanities and social sciences in the education of scientists and engineers. A School of Humanities and Social Studies, and a Center of International Studies were established.

Convinced that engineers should become leaders as well as specialists, Killian stressed a broader liberal arts training. As an educator, he spoke out also for better public schools, modernized science training in secondary schools, special provisions for gifted pupils, and greater attention to basic research. He has said: "Our preoccupation in America with the common man should not let us forget that our advancement depends upon the uncommon man. This is particularly true in education."

In addition to his office at M.I.T., Killian held a number of positions in the United States government. He was a member of President Harry S. Truman's Communications Policy Board from 1950 to 1951, and of the President's Advisory Commission on Management from 1950 to 1952. He became a member of the Science Advisory Committee of the Office of Defense Mobilization in 1951. From 1953 to 1955 he was on the board of visitors of the United States Naval Academy, and from 1954 to 1955 he was chairman of a study group which compared American and Soviet scientific programs at the request of the National Security Council. He has been chairman of the President's Technological Capabilities Panel, member of the Committee for the White House Conference on Education, and chairman of the President's Board of Consultants on Foreign Intelligence Activities.

In the fall of 1957, the Russians placed into orbit the first artificial earth satellite, thus causing the United States to re-evaluate its scientific and military position. On November 7, 1957 President Dwight D. Eisenhower announced the selection of Killian as his special assistant for science and technology. In his work, Killian was directly responsible to President Eisenhower and his tasks included studying the missile and other military programs, advising on priorities in research, and helping to iron out rivalries between the various services.

Commenting on the appointment, *Business Week* (November 16, 1957) wrote: "Perhaps Killian's finest attribute for his job is his ability to understand scientists. His thirty years at M.I.T. have taught him how to mold into a productive group hundreds of brilliant specialists, all of whom were apt to be going in different directions at once. Because he understands these people, where each is going, and what is the relationship of each project to the whole, he is genuinely respected. This means that scientists now have somebody at the top they can turn to who will be receptive to their ideas."

As scientific adviser, Killian delivered speeches urging better science education in America and stating the country's need for more scientists and engineers. He aided in studies on the feasibility of an international ban on nuclear weapons testing and disarmament inspection, on science and public policy, on outer space, and on the possibility of building an atomic-powered airplane. Killian was actively concerned in the decision to let the United States Army use Jupiter-C to orbit a satellite; the release of research funds held back by the Budget Bureau; steps toward greater scientific co-operation with Allied governments; and the return to the policy of staffing United States embassies with scientific attachés. A Science Information Service and a Federal Council for Science and Technology, with Killian at its head, also was authorized.

With Harold E. Edgerton, Killian wrote *Flash! Seeing the Unseen by Ultra High-Speed Photography,* published by Hale, Cushman & Flint in Boston in 1939. His speeches have been published in many newspapers, periodicals, and books. He has received honorary degrees from twenty colleges and universities, and was awarded the President's Certificate of Merit in 1948, the Army Department's Certificate of Appreciation in 1953 and Exceptional Civilian Service Award in 1957, the rank of officer of the French Legion of Honor in 1957, and the Public Welfare Medal of the National Academy of Sciences in 1957.

Killian is a Fellow of the American Academy of Arts and Sciences, and a member of Sigma Chi, Phi Beta Kappa, and Tau Beta Pi. He has been a director or a member of the board of trustees of numerous organizations, including the Carnegie Foundation for the Advancement of Teaching, Atoms for Peace Awards, Inc., and the Federal Reserve Bank of Boston. He belongs to clubs in New York City, Boston, and Washington, D.C.

On August 21, 1929 James Rhyne Killian, Jr., married Elizabeth Parks of Asheboro, North Carolina. They have two children: Carolyn Makepeace (Mrs. Paul Staley) and Rhyne Meredith. Killian is six feet tall and weighs 175 pounds; he has brown hair and brown eyes. For recreation he enjoys painting, gardening, camping, mountain climbing, and hiking. He is an amateur ornithologist and photographer. He collects first editions of George Meredith.

References

Bsns W p142 N 16 '57
Chem & Eng N 35:26 N 18 '57
N Y Herald Tribune p1 N 8 '57
N Y Times p10 N 8 '57
Newsweek 50:42 N 18 '57
Sat R 40:54 D 14 '57
Time 70:20 N 18 '57; 72:20 Jl 14 '58
International Who's Who, 1958
Who's Who, 1958
Who's Who in America, 1958-59

KING, SAMUEL WILDER Dec. 17, 1886-Mar. 24, 1959 Former Governor of Hawaii (1953-57); Republican delegate to the United States Congress (1935-42). See *Current Biography* (October) 1953.

Obituary

N Y Times p31 Mr 26 '59

KITSON, HARRY DEXTER Aug. 11, 1886-Sept. 25, 1959 Psychologist; professor, Teachers College, Columbia University (1925-51); wrote books on vocational guidance and psychology. See *Current Biography* (April) 1951.

Obituary

N Y Times p23 S 26 '59

KLOPSTEG, PAUL E(RNEST) May 30, 1889- Scientist; educator; organization official

Address: h. 828 Apple Tree Lane, Glenview, Ill.

Experience in education, government, and industrial scientific work has given Dr. Paul E. Klopsteg an unusually comprehensive knowledge of the problems of the branches of service represented by the ninety-one scientific organizations that make up the American Association for the Advancement of Science. He is serving as president of the A.A.A.S. during 1959, in succession to Dr. Wallace R. Brode. For more than thirty years he was associated with the Central Scientific Company in Chicago and has an equally impressive record of achievement as a university professor. In government service he has held positions with the National Science Foundation and many other important organizations.

Paul Ernest Klopsteg, the only son of the Reverend Julius and Magdalene (Kuesthardt) Klopsteg, was born on May 30, 1889 in Henderson, Minnesota. He had five older sisters, four of whom are living. From childhood he had shown a liking for science, and although his parents had wanted him to be a clergyman, they encouraged him to choose a subject of study in accordance with his own interests.

His family, however, could offer him little financial help. After his graduation from Henderson High School in 1905, therefore, Paul Klopsteg spent two years learning the printing trade. He entered the University of Minnesota in 1907 and used this skill to work his way through college. As a journeyman printer, he was employed for twenty to twenty-five hours a week by the H. W. Wilson Company, then located in Minneapolis. Much of his work was on *Readers' Guide to Periodical Literature* and *Cumulative Book Index.* In his senior year he obtained an assistantship in electrical engineering, his major subject.

In 1911, upon receiving his B.S. degree, Klopsteg was awarded a scholarship that enabled him to study at the University of Minnesota for his M.A. degree, conferred in 1913. He remained at the university to take his Ph.D. degree in physics in 1916, specializing in measurement and instruments, particularly electrical measuring instruments.

During World War I Klopsteg, who had been promoted to assistant professor, left the University of Minnesota to serve from 1917 through 1918 as a development engineer with the Ordnance Department of the United States Army at Aberdeen Proving Grounds in Maryland. At the end of the war he became head of technical advertising at the Leeds & Northrup

PAUL E. KLOPSTEG

Company in Philadelphia, manufacturers of electrical measuring instruments.

Moving to Central Scientific Company in Chicago in 1921, Klopsteg was employed first as manager of manufacturing and development, and after being made director in 1922, he was elected president of the company in 1930. He remained in this position until 1944 and retained his directorship until 1955. George R. Harrison wrote in *Science* (February 21, 1958) that he "made an immense contribution to American science by sponsoring and aiding in the development of a large number of new instruments and by improving many basic types of apparatus needed for teaching and research. Of particular importance was his contribution to the development of the Cenco series of mechanical vacuum pumps, including the Hyvac and the Hypervac." Klopsteg was granted some forty-five patents, mostly in connection with scientific apparatus.

When the National Defense Research Committee was formed in 1940, Klopsteg was named vice-chairman of the instruments section. With the reorganization of this group after the attack on Pearl Harbor in World War II, he became chief of the physics division of the superseding agency, the Office of Scientific Research and Development, and served in that capacity until the end of the war. In early 1944 he was given the additional assignment of assistant chief of the office of field service, which in general had the function of facilitating communication between the O.S.R.D. and the military commanders in the theaters of operation. For his war work, which included service in the Hawaiian Islands and at General Douglas MacArthur's headquarters in Brisbane, Australia and New Guinea, Klopsteg was awarded the Presidential Medal for Merit in 1948.

Dr. Klopsteg had resigned from the presidency of the Central Scientific Company in 1944 to accept an appointment as professor of applied science at Northwestern University in

Evanston, Illinois. As an adviser to the dean of the newly established Northwestern Technological Institute, he directed research and graduate studies there until his retirement from the university in 1954.

Meanwhile, in his work for the government Klopsteg was in part responsible in 1945 for the establishment by the National Academy of Sciences of the committee on prosthetic devices, on which he served as chairman for eleven years. Since 1956 he has been a member of its succeeding group, the prosthetics research board. Also for the National Academy of Sciences he has been chairman since November 1957 of the committee on atmospheric sciences. In 1949-50 he was a member of the board of directors and chairman of the Argonne National Laboratory, and since 1953 he has been a member of the personnel security review board of the Atomic Energy Commission.

For several years a close adviser to Dr. Alan T. Waterman, director of the National Science Foundation, Klopsteg had become assistant director for physical sciences of the foundation upon its establishment in 1951. He was made an associate director in 1952 and an associate director for research in 1957. At present he has the position of special consultant to the director.

In his nongovernmental associations, also, Klopsteg has long been interested in the work of scientific groups, having been the principal founder of the American Association of Physics Teachers in 1930 (president in 1953-54). With Dr. Karl T. Compton and other prominent scientists he joined in 1931 in establishing the American Institute of Physics, which now has a membership of about 20,000 physicists and publishes nine journals. From 1930 to 1945 he was a member of its governing board and from 1938 to 1945 was its chairman and chief policy officer.

Klopsteg's offices in the American Association for the Advancement of Science have included member of the board of directors since 1949, member of the executive committee since 1953, and chairman of the committee on public information and science since 1957. In December 1957 he was chosen president-elect of the A.A.A.S., and on January 15, 1959 he took office as president.

During the last six days of December 1958 the association held its 125th annual meeting, in Washington, D.C., at which reports covering all branches of science from astronomy to zoology were presented. Emphasis was given to contemporary scientific problems such as space medicine. A resolution passed by the A.A.A.S. council at this session expressed "profound hope" that an East-West agreement would be reached to ban nuclear weapons tests.

One of Klopsteg's special subjects of research has concerned the technical aspects of bows and the flight of arrows, and he has collected an extensive library on archery, which is also his hobby. During the war he conducted a project designed to produce "silent, flashless weapons" for the Office of Strategic Services. Although he tried to have his reports declassified in 1949, information about the bow-and-arrow weapons that he developed was not released until 1958. He is the author of *Turkish Archery and the Composite Bow* (privately printed, 1934; second edition, 1947) and co-author, with C. N. Hickman and F. Nagler, of *Archery: The Technical Side* (National Field Archery Association, 1947).

Another of Klopsteg's books is *Human Limbs and Their Substitutes* (McGraw-Hill, 1954), written with Dr. Philip D. Wilson and others. He has contributed numerous papers to the *Physical Review,* the *American Journal of Physics, Science,* and other professional journals. One of his recent articles, "The Bright Young Men in Science," appeared in *Esquire* (August 1958).

Dr. Klopsteg's awards include the Maurice Thompson Medal of Honor of the National Archery Association (1939) and honorary Sc.D. degrees from Northwestern University (1942) and Wesleyan University (1948). He belongs to the University Club in Evanston and the Cosmos Club in Washington, D.C. He attends the Covenant Methodist Church in Evanston. He is a Republican.

On June 11, 1914 Paul E. Klopsteg married Amanda Marie Toedt, a schoolteacher. They had three daughters: Marie (Mrs. J. M. Graffis, Jr.), Ruth (Mrs. H. L. Drake), and Irma Louise (deceased). Dr. Klopsteg is five feet eleven inches tall, weighs 190 pounds, and has blue eyes and gray hair. He is a seasoned traveler and enjoys outdoor living, especially in the north woods. He also spends his leisure time in gem cutting and woodworking.

References

Field & S 61:44+ O '56 por
Science 126:618 S 27 '57 por; 127:395+ F 21 '58 por
American Men of Science vol I (1955)
Who's Who in Chicago and Illinois (1950)
Who's Who in America, 1958-59

KNUTH-WINTERFELDT, KIELD GUSTAV, COUNT Feb. 17, 1908- Danish Ambassador to the United States

Address: Embassy of Denmark, Washington, D.C.

Since the autumn of 1958, Count Kield Gustav Knuth-Winterfeldt, a career diplomat, has been in Washington, D.C. as Denmark's Ambassador to the United States. At the age of fifty, he was the youngest Danish diplomat ever appointed to such a high post, although he brought with him to the United States a broad background of experience in South America, Japan, and Germany. He succeeded the popular Henrik Kauffmann, who served as Danish Ambassador to the United States from 1947 to 1958.

Before coming to the Danish Embassy in Washington, Count Winterfeldt had occupied prominent posts in the Danish Foreign Ministry in Copenhagen. He had also served as Danish Minister to Argentina. In the United States he is representing a small and democratic nation which is a key country in the North Atlantic

COUNT KNUTH-WINTERFELDT

Treaty Organization and which owns, in Greenland, an important link in the Atlantic and Arctic defense systems.

Count Kield Gustav Knuth-Winterfeldt was born in Copenhagen, Denmark on February 17, 1908. He is the son of Count Viggo Christian Knuth-Winterfeldt, an officer in the Danish Army, and Clara Augusta Ingeborg (Grüner) Knuth-Winterfeldt. His two brothers are Count Preben Knuth-Winterfeldt, a painter, and Count Eggert Knuth-Winterfeldt, a professor at Copenhagen's Technical High School. His sister, Mrs. Xenia Bang, also lives in Copenhagen.

Count Knuth-Winterfeldt first became acquainted with the United States during his childhood. His father owned a farm near New Orleans and before World War I his family lived both there and in California. Count Knuth-Winterfeldt had begun his education in the United States when the family had to return to Denmark. He attended the Cathedral School in Roskilde, from which he was graduated in 1926. He received his Doctor of Laws degree from the University of Copenhagen in 1931.

Soon after his graduation in 1931 the Count entered the Danish Ministry for Foreign Affairs as a secretary. In 1935 he was appointed Danish vice-consul in Hamburg and in 1938 he became secretary of the Danish Legation in Tokyo. After serving twenty months in Copenhagen as secretary in the Ministry, Knuth-Winterfeldt was again assigned to Hamburg on January 6, 1941 as vice-consul. A year and several bombings later he returned to the Ministry for Foreign Affairs in Copenhagen, where he served for eight years.

On August 1, 1950 Count Knuth-Winterfeldt was appointed Envoy Extraordinary and Minister Plenipotentiary to Buenos Aires, Montevideo, La Paz, Santiago de Chile, and Asuncion. In 1954 he became the head of the trade and industries department, Ministry for Foreign Af-

KNUTH-WINTERFELDT, COUNT
—Continued

fairs. From 1956 to 1958 he served as Deputy Director in the Ministry for Foreign Affairs.

On many occasions Knuth-Winterfeldt has represented his country at special conferences and events. In 1957 he was the leader of the Danish trade delegation to India and Ceylon and of a similar delegation to Peking. He was the Danish Ambassador to Ghana when that country celebrated its new nationhood in March 1957. In July and August 1958 he was the leader of the Danish trade delegation to Moscow.

On October 6, 1958 Count Knuth-Winterfeldt and his family arrived in Washington, D.C. to take up his duties as Danish Ambassador to the United States. He succeeded Henrik Kauffmann, who, having retired from public service, still lives in Washington.

Ever since the North Atlantic Treaty Organization was formed on April 4, 1949, Denmark has been an essential part of the alliance. Her willingness to tolerate American air bases in Greenland remains vital to the Atlantic and Arctic defense networks. Since jets from Russia's nearest bases can reach Denmark in ten or fifteen minutes, Denmark's geographic position in the event of war is an exposed and vulnerable one.

Denmark has decided to remain circumspect in her relations with the Soviet Union. Remaining firmly aligned with the West, she has taken care not to allow the Soviets to create any inflammable incidents. The Danish island of Bornholm in the Baltic Sea lies close to Poland and to East Germany, and refugees fleeing to the island could give the Communists an excuse to raid or occupy the island. Furthermore, there are no NATO air or missile bases in Denmark, except for the Danish possession of Greenland.

As is true with most small coastal countries, trade constitutes Denmark's most important source of economic support. As convinced free traders, the Danes have been apprehensive about the development of the European Common Market in 1958. They favored the seventeen-nation free trade area which would have included Britain, their best customer for bacon, butter, and other agricultural products. It is too early to analyze the effects on Denmark of the European Common Market which began to operate on January 1, 1959. But the increased convertibility of currencies may offset some of the difficulties.

Count Knuth-Winterfeldt owns Rosendal Castle, forty miles south of Copenhagen, Margretelund Manor, and Godthaab, the home farm near Faxe, Denmark. Rosendal Castle is the scene of an annual garden party to which 400 guests are invited; Faxe is the locale for the count's experiments with seeds and cattle. He and the countess hope to use a grass seed which he developed for the lawn of the new Danish Embassy in Washington scheduled for completion in 1959.

Count Kield Gustav Knuth-Winterfeldt married Gertrud Lina Baumann on December 8, 1938. The daughter of the late Adolf Baumann,

president of the Schweizerischer Bankverein, the countess has aroused enthusiasm from American society reporters for her wit, candor, graciousness, good grooming, and fluency in six languages. She maintains a chalet at Grindelwald in her native Switzerland so that her children will have a home there as well as in Denmark. The Knuth-Winterfeldt children are Axel-Ivar, Ditlev Helge, and Isabel Suzanne.

The tall and ruddy-blond diplomat enjoys tennis and at one time showed promise as an amateur sculptor. He is a Lutheran. In Washington the Knuth-Winterfeldts live, in 1959, in the temporary Danish Embassy, which was once occupied by Perle Mesta, the former U.S. Ambassador to Luxembourg. They have brought with them to the United States a quantity of Danish silver and portraits of the count's ancestors. Although cramped for space in their temporary quarters, they have found room for two large Afghan dogs, Mogambo and India, and eight parakeets.

Count Knuth-Winterfeldt has received many decorations. He is a grand officer of the Argentine Order of Merit, a grand officer of the Chilean Order of Merit, officer of the Greek George I Order, officer of the Swedish Order of the North Star, and officer of the Danish Order of the Dannebrog.

References

Christian Sci Mon p6 O 7 '58 pors
N Y Herald Tribune p2 Je 21 '58
Washington (D.C.) Post p1D O 8 '58; p1B O 15 '58
International Who's Who, 1957
International Year Book and Statesmen's Who's Who, 1958

KOZLOV, FROL R(OMANOVICH)

(kŭs-lôf', frōl) August 17, 1908- Soviet Communist party leader and government official

Address: Council of Ministers of the Union of Soviet Socialist Republics, Moscow, U.S.S.R.

From the day he became a First Deputy Premier of the Council of Ministers of the Union of Soviet Socialist Republics, on March 31, 1958, Frol R. Kozlov has been regarded in the West as a probable heir apparent to Nikita S. Khrushchev, who heads both the government and the Communist party in that country. That impression was considerably strengthened in the summer of 1959 when Kozlov toured the United States in connection with the opening of a Soviet exhibit of science, technology, and culture in New York City.

Frol Romanovich Kozlov, one of the youngest Soviet leaders, was born August 17, 1908, in the village of Loshchinino, about 150 miles southeast of Moscow in European Russia. His parents were poor peasants who owned their own land, but had to supplement their living by working in a textile factory in the nearby city of Kasimov. He was one of nine children, five of whom died in childhood from starvation. In 1923, when he was 15 years old, Kozlov also began to work in the Kasimov textile factory, which was known as the Red Textile Workers' Plant. In time he became an assistant foreman.

Kozlov joined the Young Communist League in the year he began to work in the factory. Three years later he joined the Communist party. In 1926 he was also elected secretary of the Young Communist League committee in the factory, and he then advanced to director of the League's economic department for the entire Kasimov district.

The Young Communist League sent him to Leningrad in 1928 to study in a workers' school run by the Mining Institute. After graduation he went on to study at the Leningrad Polytechnical Institute, from which he received a degree in metallurgical engineering in 1936.

Kozlov was assigned as an engineer to the steel plant in Izhevsk, a city in the foothills of the Ural Mountains 600 miles east of Moscow that is one of the oldest metallurgical centers in the country. Here he became superintendent of the blooming mill.

In 1939 Kozlov was elected secretary of the Communist party committee in the plant where he worked, and the following year he became secretary of the party's city committee. In that position he played, during the crucial years of World War II, an active part in organizing the production and supply of arms for the Russian front. Two of his brothers were killed in the war.

In 1944, when the worst of the war was over, Kozlov was transferred to Moscow where he spent three years in responsible posts on the staff of the party's Central Committee. Then he was sent to Kuibyshev, a Volga River port and industrial center 500 miles southeast of Moscow, as second secretary of the party's regional committee.

In 1949, when the city of Leningrad was in the midst of a purge of the followers of the recently-deceased Andrei A. Zhdanov, Kozlov was sent to that city as a Central Committee organizer in the Kirov machine tool plant—the largest and politically most important enterprise in the city.

Kozlov, in October 1949, became secretary of the party's city committee in Leningrad; in 1952 he became second secretary for the regional committee. His role between those dates, however, is uncertain. Another man, A. I. Alekseyev, is reported to have become first secretary of the party's city organization in June 1950. Kozlov was a delegate to the Nineteenth Congress of the Communist Party of the Soviet Union in October 1952, and at its close was elected as one of the 125 members of the party's Central Committee.

He first came to the attention of the world outside the Soviet Union in January 1953, when he wrote a 7,000 word article on political vigilance for the theoretical journal, *Kommunist*. Although the article was not explicit in its accusations, its publication coincided with the announced discovery of a conspiracy by a group of doctors, most of them Jewish, to murder Soviet leaders. Among the leaders they allegedly murdered was Zhdanov.

Stalin died March 5, 1953, and on April 4 it was announced that the alleged doctors' plot had

Wide World

FROL R. KOZLOV

been a fabrication. Shortly after the disclosure, Kozlov was replaced as second secretary of the Leningrad regional party organization. In September, however, Khrushchev became first secretary of the Central Committee; in November he traveled to Leningrad to install Kozlov as the regional party secretary.

Kozlov had already become a member of the Supreme Soviet of the Russian Republic, and in the elections of March 1954, he was named a deputy to the Council of the Union, one of the two houses of the U.S.S.R. Supreme Soviet, from the Smolny election district in the city of Leningrad. He later became, until he received a government post, a member of the presidium (or executive committee) of the U.S.S.R. Supreme Soviet.

In December 1954, it was announced that a former Soviet Minister of State Security and some of his subordinates had been executed for framing innocent persons in what was called the "Leningrad Case." No such case had ever before been announced, but observers outside the Soviet Union deduced that it referred to the purge that had taken place in 1949 when Kozlov was sent to Leningrad.

At the Twentieth Congress of the Communist party in February 1956, Kozlov expressed "deep gratitude" for the exposure of those who had framed the "Leningrad Case." At the close of the Congress he was again elected to the Central Committee, and at the end of the month, when Khrushchev established a ten-man bureau to co-ordinate local party organizations in the Russian Republic, Kozlov was made a member.

At the February 1957 meeting of the party's Central Committee, when Khrushchev was battling setbacks because of the Hungarian revolt, Kozlov was named an alternate member of the party's presidium, or executive committee. At the meeting of the committee in June 1957 that removed Georgi M. Malenkov, Viacheslav M.

KOZLOV, FROL R.—*Continued*

Molotov, and Lazar M. Kaganovich from the presidium Kozlov was named to fill one of the vacancies as a full member.

Immediately after the Central Committee meeting Khrushchev accompanied Kozlov to Leningrad to speak at ceremonies marking the 250th anniversary of the city. In his speech he declared that Malenkov "was one of the most important organizers of the so-called Leningrad Case." At another rally Kozlov denounced those removed by the Central Committee as "dogmatists and Talmudists."

Observers outside the Soviet Union suggested, long after the event, that in the crucial struggle within the Central Committee in June 1957, he may have done much to line up Khrushchev's majority. In any event, Kozlov was promoted in December of that year to chairman of the Council of Ministers of the Russian Republic— the first government position he had ever held. Three months later, at the end of March 1958, when Khrushchev became chairman of the Council of Ministers of the Soviet Union, he named Kozlov as one of his two First Vice-Chairman (or First Deputy Premiers). In the official reports Kozlov's name was listed first, ahead of the other First Vice-Chairman, Anastas I. Mikoyan.

Some observers—among them was Whitman Bassow, Moscow correspondent for the Washington *Post and Times Herald* (April 2, 1958)— took this to mean that Kozlov was "the heir apparent to Khrushchev." Others, however— among them Harry Schwartz of the New York *Times* (April 6, 1958)—pointed out that the source of power in the Soviet Union was the party secretariat, where Kozlov held no position, and not the government.

Immediately after being named First Vice-Chairman of the Council of Ministers, Kozlov accompanied Khrushchev on an official visit to Hungary. Later in the year he visited the World's Fair in Brussels, Belgium. On May 26, 1959, it was announced in Moscow that he would come to the United States in June to open the Soviet Exhibition in New York. The exhibit, and its United States counterpart in Moscow, were the result of a cultural exchange agreement between the United States and the Soviet Union.

Kozlov arrived in the United States on June 28, 1959, and departed on July 13. While in the country he visited New York, Washington, San Francisco, Detroit, Chicago, and Pittsburgh. The purposes of his tour, according to observers in the United States, were threefold: to depict the Soviet Union as an advocate of peace, to encourage a meeting between Khrushchev and President Dwight D. Eisenhower, and to stimulate Soviet-American trade.

Many observers felt, afterwards, that in his attempt to win friends and influence Americans Kozlov had failed. "Kozlov just didn't get across to Americans," wrote Francis B. Stevens in *United States News & World Report* (July 20, 1959). "He stirred up very little antagonism —but, likewise, he stirred up very little interest."

Kozlov is a handsome, stocky, round-faced man with curly, iron-gray hair, blue-gray eyes, and a broad smile. He is five feet eight inches tall and weighs 176 pounds. He has what Russians call the "Leningrad manner"—meaning the air of a sophisticate with a veneer of Western European culture. He is married, and has a daughter, Olga, for whom he brought home a doll from a United States toy factory, and an older son Oleg, for whom he accepted a volleyball. He has one surviving sister.

Kozlov was described, in *United States News & World Report* (July 6, 1959), as "a new type of Soviet leader—a man who combines the toughness of a top Communist with the affability of a successful business executive. . . ." President Eisenhower said, after they met: "I found a man that was very friendly, and frankly I enjoyed the visit I had with him." Vice-President Nixon said he was "a fine diplomat." Senator Frank Church, Idaho Democrat, described him as "a kind of bourgeois Bolshevik." Governor G. Mennen Williams of Michigan said he was both "shrewd and tough" and "a very urbane, gracious man." San Francisco's Mayor George Christopher found him "a very humorous man," and a businessman in that city said: "He's a hell of a salesman; I wish we were working for me."

For his services to the Communist Party and the Soviet government Kozlov has been awarded three Orders of Lenin, two Orders of the Red Banner of Labor, the Order of the Great Patriotic War Second Class, the Order of the Red Star, and several medals.

References

Christian Sci Mon p10 Je 26 '59; p7 Je 29 '59
Cur Digest of the Soviet Press 9:16,24 Ja 29 '58 por
N Y Herald Tribune p6 Ja 11 '59 por
N Y Times p12 Ap 1 '58 por
N Y World-Telegram p2 Mr 31 '58 por; p5 Je 29 '59
Time 71:24 Ap 14 '58; 74:10 Jl 13 '59
U S News 47:20 Jl 13 '59 por

KRUTCH, JOSEPH WOOD (krōoch)

Nov. 25, 1893-   Writer; naturalist

Address: 5041 E. Grant Rd., Tucson, Ariz.

The perceptiveness and lucidity that have distinguished the literary criticism and scholarship of Joseph Wood Krutch since the mid-1920's are evident in his recent writings as a naturalist. Krutch is the author of twenty books published between 1924 and 1959. Since his retirement in 1950 as Brander Matthews Professor of Dramatic Literature at Columbia University, he has been mainly concerned with natural history, in such books as *The Great Chain of Life* (Houghton, 1957).

For many years the drama critic of the *Nation*, Krutch still contributes frequent articles on the theater, as well as on other subjects, to various periodicals. In his mastery of the contemplative essay, he has become known for his grace of style, reasonableness, humor, wisdom, and humanistic philosophy.

Joseph Wood Krutch, the son of Edward Waldemore and Adelaide (Wood) Krutch, was born in Knoxville, Tennessee on November 25, 1893. His father was a merchant whose parents had moved to the United States from Germany in the middle of the nineteenth century, and his mother was of Scottish and English descent. He had two brothers, Frederick (deceased) and Charles Edward, still living in Knoxville. Also reared in Knoxville, Krutch attended the University of Tennessee after graduating from the local high school in 1911. At college he distinguished himself in oratory and edited the literary monthly.

He was interested in science from an early age and majored in mathematics at the University of Tennessee, which awarded him a B.S. degree in 1915. He decided, however, to do graduate work in the humanities and in 1916 took his M.A. degree at Columbia University. The following year he became an instructor in English at Columbia. Then in 1918 he interrupted both his teaching career and graduate research to serve in the Psychological Corps of the United States Army, where he advanced in rank from private to sergeant.

As a Cutting Traveling Fellow in 1919-20, Krutch resumed study for his Ph.D. degree, which he received from Columbia in 1924. His doctoral thesis, *Comedy and Conscience After the Restoration* (Columbia University Press, 1924), was his first published work. Meanwhile, from 1920 to 1923, he had taught at the Polytechnic Institute of Brooklyn as associate professor of English. During 1924-25 he was a special lecturer in English at Vassar College in Poughkeepsie, New York with the rank of professor, and in 1925 he was appointed associate professor in the Graduate School of Journalism at Columbia.

Upon his return from a year of study in Europe on a Guggenheim Fellowship in 1930-31, Krutch became a lecturer at the New School for Social Research in New York City. He went back to Columbia University in 1937 as professor of English and in 1943 was named Brander Matthews Professor of Dramatic Literature.

Krutch's reputation as a scholar grew with publication of his books on English literature, including *Edgar Allan Poe: A Study in Genius* (Knopf, 1926), notable for its thorough literary and psychological analysis; *Five Masters; A Study in the Mutations of the Novel* (H. Smith, 1930), which treated the lives and works of Boccaccio, Cervantes, Richardson, Stendhal, and Proust; and *Samuel Johnson* (Holt, 1944).

In this early period his most widely discussed book was *The Modern Temper; A Study and a Confession* (Harcourt, 1929). In it Krutch declares that the reality revealed by science is incompatible with the human spirit, which only reaches its full potential if it perceives and lives by the ultimate values. When applied to society, the scientific method rejects as delusions the values and beliefs upon which Western culture is founded.

Krutch also asserted that all great civilizations decay eventually, and are rejuvenated by primitive peoples who have an "animal acceptance of life for life's sake." Some reviewers found Krutch unduly pessimistic in his assess-

JOSEPH WOOD KRUTCH

ment of the contemporary rejection of the moral, aesthetic, and other values of the past.

Pessimism also seemed to his fellow critics to prevail at times in Krutch's treatment of contemporary drama, although his reviews have been praised for their discernment and literary excellence. He had joined the staff of the *Nation* magazine in 1924 as drama critic and associate editor. Beginning in 1932 he served for five years as a member of the editorial board and in 1937 returned to the position of drama critic. He was president of the New York Drama Critics Circle in 1940-41.

Among Krutch's other contributions in the field of the drama are *The American Drama since 1918* (Random House, 1939; revised edition, Braziller, 1957) and *"Modernism" in Modern Drama, A Definition and an Estimate* (Cornell University Press, 1953). He has also edited plays of William Congreve and Eugene O'Neill.

The influence of Krutch's scientific interests has always been considerable in his writing. His hobby, natural history, began to assume an important place in his work with the publication in 1948 of *Henry David Thoreau* (Sloane) and in 1949 of a collection of contemplative essays on nature and man's relation to the universe, *The Twelve Seasons; A Perpetual Calendar for the Country* (Sloane).

After retiring from teaching in 1950 and leaving the staff of the *Nation*, Krutch devoted himself almost exclusively to writing, with emphasis on natural history. One of his books, *The Best of Two Worlds* (Sloane, 1953), like his earlier *The Twelve Seasons*, concerns New England and in general expresses his belief that "all nature to some extent participates in the joy of life."

Several of Krutch's recent books deal with the Southwest, where he now lives. Among them are *The Desert Year* (1952), *The Voice of the Desert; A Naturalist's Interpretation* (1955), and *The Grand Canyon: Today and All*

KRUTCH, JOSEPH WOOD—*Continued*

its Yesterdays (1958)—all three published by Sloane. Commenting on *The Voice of the Desert* in the *Saturday Review* (November 26, 1955), T. E. Cooney pointed out, "Mr. Krutch's style is almost exactly that style which students remember so well from his professorial days: clear, reasonable, free from flamboyance, and unobtrusively studded with appropriate literary quotations and allusions. It is, as is the spirit of the whole book, humanistic."

"Man's humanity," Krutch believes, "is threatened by the almost exclusively technological approach in social, political, and philosophical thought." He presents this point of view in *The Measure of Man: On Freedom, Human Values, Survival and the Modern Temper* (Bobbs, 1954), which won the National Book Award for nonfiction in 1955. In this reassessment of the subject that he had considered many years before in *The Modern Temper* Krutch adduced his reasons for "no longer believing that the mechanistic, materialistic, and deterministic conclusions of science do have to be accepted as fact and hence as the premises upon which any philosophy of life or any estimate of man and his future must be based."

Krutch also registers his objection to the deterministic contentions of modern culture in Edward R. Murrow's *This I Believe*: "The difference between a totalitarian and a democratic society is the difference between those who believe the individual man capable of being the captain of his soul and those who believe that he is merely the creature of the society in which he lives. I believe that we cannot set the world free until we believe that the individual himself is free."

In *Human Nature and the Human Condition* (Random House, 1959) Krutch examines certain contemporary problems: an economy based upon waste; the "permissive exploitation" of the public by advertisers who cater to the "lowest tastes and vulgarest appetites"; and the appearance upon the educational scene of teachers whose aims resemble those of the advertisers. He contends that modern men should be concerned not only with raising the standard of living, but with achieving the good life. Science cannot create values, but must be founded upon a system of values whose end is man.

A large number of articles by Krutch, many of them on natural history and the drama, have been published in periodicals like *Theatre Arts, Atlantic Monthly, Harper's Magazine, Natural History, New York Times Magazine,* and *American Scholar.* He also writes book reviews for the *Saturday Review,* the *Reporter,* and other magazines and has contributed essays to several anthologies.

Since 1953 Krutch has been secretary of the Arizona Sonora Desert Museum, a nonprofit organization of Tucson devoted to conservation and to public education in the value of the disappearing natural world. He is a member of the American Academy of Arts and Letters, was a founder of the Literary Guild, and belongs to the American Philosophical Society and the Century Club. He won the Burroughs Medal for Nature Writing in 1953 and was awarded

an honorary Litt.D. degree from Columbia University in 1954 and the D.H.L. degree from Northwestern University in 1957.

Joseph Wood Krutch married Marcelle Leguia, a trained nurse of Hendaye, France, on February 9, 1923. He is described as reserved and dignified, has brown eyes and blond hair, stands five feet eleven and a half inches tall, and weighs 170 pounds. Appropriately for a writer sensitive to minute details in his observations on man and nature, one of his hobbies is photography. Joseph Henry Jackson, in reviewing *The Best of Two Worlds,* wrote of Krutch as "a thoughtful man, a civilized man, and, best of all, a balanced man" (San Francisco *Chronicle,* November 4, 1953).

References

International Who's Who, 1958
Living Authors (1931)
Twentieth Century Authors (1942; First Supplement, 1955)
Who's Who in America, 1958-59
World Biography (1954)

KUBLY, HERBERT (OSWALD) Apr. 26, 1915- Writer

Address: b. c/o Brandt & Brandt, 101 Park Ave., New York 17

The American reading public knows Herbert Kubly best as the author of two books on contemporary Italy—*American in Italy* (Simon & Schuster, 1955) and *Easter in Sicily* (Simon & Schuster, 1956). The first of these won the 1956 National Book Award for nonfiction. Travel writing, however, is only one side of Kubly's literary career. He is also a playwright, a journalist, and an author of fiction. *Varieties of Love* (Simon & Schuster, 1958) is a collection of his short stories.

Herbert Oswald Kubly's ancestors left their home in the Swiss village of Elm, canton of Glarus in the mid-nineteenth century to settle in New Glarus, Wisconsin, where Herbert (known to his friends as Nick) was born on April 26, 1915, to Nicholas Heinrich Kubly, a farmer, and Alda Sabina (Ott) Kubly. "Though I was a fourth-generation American, my childhood could not have been more Swiss if my peasant ancestors had never left Switzerland," Herbert Kubly wrote in *House & Garden* (October 1957). "In New Glarus we observed Swiss holidays, ate Swiss food, played Swiss games, yodeled, and spoke only *Muttersprache,* the Schweizer-Deutsch patois of Elm." He has one sister, Mrs. Robert Dibble.

At New Glarus High School he was editor of the school paper, *Old Guard.* As Kubly related in *Holiday* (September 1958), from childhood he had shown more interest in books than in cows. His father's permission to enter the University of Wisconsin, following his graduation from high school in 1933, was "granted only when it was apparent that [Herbert] would be a failure as a farmer."

Journalism and philosophy were his major subjects at the university in Madison. He was a columnist on the university's newspaper,

Daily Cardinal, editor of the yearbook, *The Badger,* and active in dramatics and in Theta Chi, a social fraternity. Kubly's lively interest in writing was encouraged first by a high school English teacher, Nina Kennedy, and at the University of Wisconsin by Professor Helen C. White.

Upon graduating from the university with the B.A. degree in 1937, he took a job as a police reporter on the Pittsburgh *Sun-Telegraph.* In 1939 he became art critic for the paper, a post he held until 1942 when he was hired as a reporter on the New York *Herald Tribune.* From 1945 to 1947 he was an editor and music critic of *Time* magazine.

Meanwhile, Kubly had begun to write plays. The first of these was *Men to the Sea,* which was produced on Broadway under the direction of Eddie Dowling in 1944. The play dealt with the problems of war wives whose husbands were overseas. It received mixed reviews from the New York critics. Burton Rascoe in the New York *World-Telegram* (October 16, 1944) found it "a tensely dramatic and compassionate handling of a human problem." Louis Kronenberger, on the other hand, writing in *PM* (October 4, 1944) thought the play pretentious and diffuse. "The author," he commented, "seems to have thought up situations rather than studied human beings." Ward Morehouse concluded his review in the New York *Sun*: "It is not a good play, strictly speaking. But it reveals some strong writing and scenes of great feeling and brings forth Mr. Kubly as a writer of definite promise."

Other plays by Kubly are *Inherit the Wind* (not to be confused with the play of the same title about the Scopes trial, produced on Broadway in 1956), which was performed in London in 1948, *The Cocoon* (1954), and *Beautiful Dreamer* (1956). In 1947 and again in 1948 the National Theatre Conference, through its New Playwrights Committee, awarded Kubly a fellowship. During this same period he held a Rockefeller grant for creative writing and fellowships at the MacDowell Colony in Peterboro, New Hampshire.

From 1949 to 1955 Kubly was associate professor of speech and director of the Playwrights' Workshop at the University of Illinois in Urbana. In 1950 he received a Fulbright scholarship to go to Italy "for study of the use of the humanities in the democratization of a former totalitarian people." More specifically, his project was to study the use of the theater in international communications. Out of this Fulbright grant and the fourteen months which it enabled him to spend in Italy, Kubly wrote his first book, *American in Italy.*

He stated in the opening pages of the book, "The routine of a midwestern university had begun to pall on me, and I needed the stimulation of new people and new places." *American in Italy* is not a conventional travel book but, as Virginia Kirkus pointed out in her review of it (November 15, 1954) "an exciting record of the kind of conversations and relationships . . . that are rich groundwork for the broader implications to which they lead."

These "broader implications" are based on Kubly's view that the United States is losing

Benedict Frenkel Studios

HERBERT KUBLY

its friendship with Italy through a lack of understanding of that country and its people. The judges of the National Book Award, who selected *American in Italy* as the best work of nonfiction published in 1955, described it as "the story of the author's love affair with the Italian people. . . . It has a fine balance of humor, pathos, and understanding of the people of another nation."

Since 1950 Kubly has traveled extensively in Europe, reporting on some of his experiences in *Esquire, Holiday, House & Garden,* and other magazines. Italy has remained his major interest, and in 1956 he published a second volume, *Easter in Sicily.* As in the first book he concentrates here primarily upon colorful personalities. C. J. Rolo (*Atlantic Monthly,* December 1956) found it "sprightly reading throughout. In a somewhat patchy way it does achieve an image of the moral and physical landscape of Sicily."

In *Varieties of Love* Kubly collected sixteen of his short stories. The background of these ranges widely—Italy, France, Switzerland, Germany, New York, North Carolina, and a transatlantic liner. He explains in the foreword to the volume that the stories were written over a ten-year period with no relationship between them intended. But on collecting them he discovered that they shared a common theme— "the terrible loneliness of human beings and their pathetic efforts to find love."

Reviewers were generally impressed by the variety of tone in the volume, ranging from light humor to grim tragedy. William Peden in the New York *Times Book Review* (June 22, 1958) called them "provocative and exciting stories," the only flaw being the author's "occasional fondness for caricature and the inevitable oversimplification of dilemmas." In the New York *Herald Tribune Book Review* (June 22, 1958) Clyde S. Kilby observed that although

KUBLY, HERBERT—*Continued*

from time to time the reader feels that Kubly "has striven a little too hard for his effects," most of the stories "show an excellent insight into the nature of the human make-up, and a quiet ability to depict what has been observed." A more recent story by Kubly, "Good Fortune, Signora," appeared in *Vogue,* September 1, 1958.

In the summer of 1958 Kubly returned to the MacDowell Colony to work on a novel. He is a member of the Edward A. MacDowell Association. His other memberships include the professional speech fraternity Pi Epsilon Delta and the Dramatists Guild of America, of which he was national secretary from 1947 to 1949. His political preference is Democratic. He is a member of the United Church of Christ. He is six feet tall, weighs 165 pounds, and has green-blue eyes and brown hair. For recreation Kubly enjoys swimming, boating, travel, photography, and square dancing.

References

Esquire 46:639+ D '56 por
Holiday 24:20+ S '58
House & Gard 112:71+ O '57 por
Who's Who in America, 1958-59

KUIPER, GERARD P(ETER) (koi'pēr)
Dec. 7, 1905- Astronomer; university professor; author
Address: b. Yerkes Observatory, Williams Bay, Wis.

"One of the most brilliant of present-day astronomers," Dr. Gerard P. Kuiper is the director of the Yerkes Observatory in Wisconsin and the McDonald Observatory in Texas. His observations of planets have upset established hypotheses in astronomy and introduced several startling and original theories. In 1949 Dr. Kuiper presented an explanation of the origin of the earth and planets which has been well received by fellow scientists. His intensive observations of the planet Mars to discover whether life exists there and his explanations of its climatic and atmospheric conditions, volcanic eruptions, and polar icecaps have been widely publicized.

Dr. Kuiper has also added to man's knowledge of the universe with his discovery of satellites to the planets Uranus and Neptune, his accurate calculations of Pluto, and his explanations of the craters on the moon's surface. He has recently suggested that the earth will be destroyed by fire, water, ice, or snow within five to ten billion years (Los Angeles *Times,* March 30, 1958).

One of the four children of Gerard and Anna (de Vries) Kuiper, Gerard Peter Kuiper was born on December 7, 1905 in Harencarspel, the Netherlands. He was graduated from the Gymnasium in Haarlem in 1924 and studied astronomy and physics at the University of Leiden, receiving the bachelor's degree three years later. In 1928 he served as a research assistant and the next year Kuiper went to Sumatra as a member of the Dutch solar eclipse expedition. In 1933 the University of Leiden granted

him the Ph.D. degree for his thesis on special investigations of binary stars.

Dr. Kuiper came to the United States in 1933 as the recipient of a research fellowship at the Lick Observatory of the University of California. Harvard University appointed him a lecturer in astronomy in 1935 and the next year he was named assistant professor at the University of Chicago. Kuiper was made an associate in 1937 and given the rank of full professor in 1943.

Harvard University invited Dr. Kuiper to serve as a research associate at its radio research laboratory from 1943 to 1945. During World War II, Kuiper served as a civilian with the Office of Scientific Research and Development (1943-44), as a consultant to the operational analysis section of the Eighth Air Force in England (1944) and as a member of the War Department Mission to Europe (1945). Since 1947 Dr. Kuiper has been the director of the Yerkes Observatory of the University of Chicago (at Williams Bay, Wisconsin) and the McDonald Observatory (at Fort Davis, Texas), operated jointly by the universities of Chicago and Texas.

In February 1948 the planet Mars was 63,000,000 miles from earth and in a favorable position for study. Using an infrared spectrograph which he helped to develop and a photoconductive lead-sulphite cell, Kuiper observed the green Martian spots for evidence of life. There was no indication that higher plant and animal life thrived on Mars, since the existence of water or vegetation containing water would have appeared black on infrared photographs. Dr. Kuiper believed the green spots were low-order plants such as lichens and mosses which "act like sponges and suck up water vapor present in the air" (*Christian Science Monitor,* February 18, 1948). Other arguments against the existence of higher life on Mars, according to the astronomer, were the low oxygen content, the variations in climate, and the absence of a gaseous agent to filter out ultraviolet rays from the sun.

When Mars came within 35,000,000 miles of the earth on September 7, 1956, a distance it reaches only once every fifteen years, Dr. Kuiper was one of the astronomers who conducted intensive investigations of the planet. He could now verify his conclusions on the make-up of the Martian polar icecaps which scientists had once believed were composed of carbon dioxide. According to a report by Earl Ubell (Washington *Post and Times Herald,* September 16, 1956), Kuiper "laid to rest the idea that the cap could be frozen carbon dioxide or dry ice." The polar caps were rather "ice crystals spread a fraction of an inch thick over a maximum of four million square miles in the winter and receding to a white knob in summer."

In March 1948 Kuiper announced his discovery of a new satellite to the planet Uranus. It was 300 miles in diameter and 75,000 miles away from its parent. In May of the following year Kuiper discovered a second satellite to the planet Neptune. This satellite was 200 miles in diameter and "of magnitude 19.5, which made it the faintest moon observed to date" (*Christian Science Monitor*, August 22, 1949).

In addition to being an experimental scientist and investigator, Kuiper has made his mark as a theorist. In October 1949 he delivered a paper in which he propounded a new theory of the origin of the earth and other planets of the solar system.

Dr. Kuiper's theory refuted the widely accepted explanation propounded by the German astrophysicist Dr. Carl F. von Weizsäcker. Working with mathematical-physical formulae which combined theories of the formation of vortices or whirlpools with astronomical data (New York *World-Telegram*, October 15, 1949), Kuiper suggested that the solar system originated from a nebula or cloud of gas and dust rotating around the sun some three billion years ago. This sphere contracted into a thin pancake, like the rings of Saturn, in the plane of the present planetary orbits. "When the density of the pancake reached a critical value, it would then have broken into a number of whirling eddies or 'proto-planets'. These would have continued to shrink and finally condense into planets and their satellites" (*Christian Science Monitor*, January 14, 1950). In this way were created the satellites or globes as we have them today. Kuiper's theory also explained the masses of the planets, their composition, planetary rotation and the formation of the moons. He considered the planets to have grown in a few thousand years and the satellites in a century.

A significant achievement in Dr. Kuiper's career was his first accurate measurement of the planet Pluto. Using the giant 200-inch reflecting telescope at the Palomar Observatory, Dr. Kuiper calculated Pluto's diameter at 3,550 miles (45 per cent that of the earth's) with a mass about one-tenth as great as the earth. This was "ten times smaller than previous estimates made on the basis of deviations in the movements of Pluto's closest neighboring planet, Neptune" (*Christian Science Monitor*, June 3, 1950).

Astronomers had formerly attributed Neptune's deviations to the gravitational pull of Pluto, the outermost object in our solar system. But Professor Kuiper suggested in 1956 "that the reported variations in the motion of Neptune that led in the 1920's to forecasts of another, outside planet (Pluto), were in fact observational errors" (*Christian Science Monitor*, February 21, 1956). He reclassified Pluto from the ninth planet to an unrecaptured moon of a once-larger Neptune. Kuiper's conclusions were based on the smallness of Pluto, the relative slowness of its rotation, and the eccentric pattern of its orbit.

As part of his long-range program "to determine the detailed nature of the sun's family of planets," Dr. Kuiper has investigated Saturn, Jupiter, the asteroids, and Venus. In 1948 he announced that the rings of Saturn were particles of ice covered with thin hoarfrost. Studies also revealed that Jupiter's rings were also covered with snow. During the summer of 1958, Kuiper detected volcanic eruptions on Jupiter, probably caused "by the release of large amounts of heat energy on the planet's

GERARD P. KUIPER

surface" (New York *Times*, July 14, 1958). Kuiper's observations of the asteroids, or minor planets, found them to be of irregular shape, moving in rapid rotation, and having a density much like that of the moon. His hypothesis that the asteroids were originally satellites of Jupiter which were lost in its formative stage was supported by the mathematical calculations of Dr. E. K. Rabe of the University of Cincinnati Observatory. Kuiper also charted Venus' equator, the position of the poles and the axis of rotation that passes through them.

Besides publishing numerous articles in scientific and professional journals, Gerard Kuiper has edited *The Atmospheres of the Earth and Planets* (University of Chicago Press, 1949). *The Solar System* (University of Chicago Press, 1953-58) is devoted to the celestial bodies. Kuiper is also editor in chief of *Stars and Stellar Systems,* to be published by the University of Chicago Press during the next few years.

The astronomer has brown hair and blue eyes, stands five feet eleven inches and weighs 185 pounds. He married Sarah Parker Fuller on June 20, 1936 and has two children, Paul and Lucy. Kuiper has been honored with the Order of Orange Nassau (the Netherlands), the Janssen Prize and the Rittenhouse Medal. His memberships include the American Astronomical Society, the National Academy of Sciences, and the American Academy of Arts and Sciences and he has been elected to the astronomical societies of France, Holland, and London. His clubs are Innominates and Quadrangle.

References

N Y World-Telegram p14 O 15 '49; p22 S 5 '50

American Men of Science vol I (1955)
International Who's Who, 1958
Who's Who in America, 1958-59

KUNITZ, STANLEY (JASSPON) July 29, 1905- Poet; teacher; editor

Address: 157 W. 12th St., New York 11

NOTE: This biography supersedes the article which appeared in *Current Biography* in 1943.

In reviewing Stanley Kunitz's *Selected Poems, 1928-58* in September 1958, John Ciardi, the poetry editor of the *Saturday Review*, wrote that "Kunitz is certainly the most neglected good poet of the last quarter-century." Robert Lowell told Little, Brown & Company, which published the collection: "He has been one of the masters for years, and yet so unrecognized that his *Selected Poems* make him the poet of the hour." The neglect was atoned for in 1959 when Kunitz received the National Institute of Arts and Letters grant in poetry, a two-year grant from the Ford Foundation, and the 1959 Pulitzer Prize for Poetry.

In collaboration with Howard Haycraft, Kunitz has edited a series of biographical dictionaries of authors for the H. W. Wilson Company. He has taught English and creative writing at Bennington College, the New School for Social Research, and other institutions, and currently teaches the craft of poetry at the Poetry Center of the Young Men's Hebrew Association in New York City.

Stanley Jasspon Kunitz was born on July 29, 1905 in Worcester, Massachusetts. ·His father, Solomon Kunitz, a dress manufacturer, committed suicide shortly before Stanley was born, leaving behind him a business made bankrupt by an associate's misappropriation of funds, and a book collection in which his son was later "passionately to burrow." His mother, Yetta Helen (Jasspon) Kunitz, was of Russian descent. To support her daughters and infant son and to repay the debts left behind by the collapse of the Parisian Wrapper Company, Mrs. Kunitz opened a dry-goods store in Worcester. Throughout most of his childhood, Stanley Kunitz was cared for by his two older sisters and a succession of servants.

Educated in the public schools of Worcester, at Classical High School Kunitz edited the school magazine, played on the tennis team, won several debating prizes, and became valedictorian of his class upon his graduation in 1922. At Harvard University, to which he won a scholarship, he elected English as his major. He began to write poetry at the suggestion of Professor Robert Gay, and was awarded the Lloyd McKim Garrison Medal for Poetry. He was graduated *summa cum laude* in 1926, and was elected to Phi Beta Kappa. In 1927 he received the M.A. degree from Harvard. During his summer vacations he had worked for the Worcester *Telegram,* and after he finished his studies at Harvard, he became a Sunday feature writer for that newspaper. At that time he completed a novel which he later "heroically destroyed."

In 1927 Stanley Kunitz joined the H. W. Wilson Company as an editor. Encouraged by H. W. Wilson, he became editor of the *Wilson Bulletin,* a publication for and about the library world (now known as the *Wilson Library Bulletin*). Under the pseudonym of Dilly Tante, he edited a book of biographies entitled *Living Authors* (H. W. Wilson, 1931). With Howard Haycraft, Kunitz edited a series of biographical reference books for the H. W. Wilson Company, including: *Authors Today and Yesterday* (1933); *The Junior Book of Authors* (1934); *British Authors of the Nineteenth Century* (1936); *American Authors: 1600-1900* (1938); *Twentieth Century Authors* (1942); and *British Authors Before 1800* (1952). In 1955 the H. W. Wilson Company published *Twentieth Century Authors: First Supplement,* edited by Stanley Kunitz with Vineta Colby as assistant editor. In 1959 Kunitz was working on *European Authors,* a projected volume of biographies to be published by the H. W. Wilson Company.

His first volume of poetry, *Intellectual Things* (Doubleday, Doran, 1930), was cordially received by most of the book reviewers. William Rose Benét called it "modern and yet very old, intricate and metaphysical and yet undeniably full of the true seer, the poet born . . . his words sorcerize . . . Mr. Kunitz has gained the front rank of contemporary verse in a single stride" (*Saturday Review of Literature,* July 19, 1930).

Leaving the H. W. Wilson Company when his career was interrupted by World War II, Kunitz entered the United States Army as a private in 1943 and was discharged as a staff sergeant in 1945. In the service he edited a weekly Army news magazine called *Ten Minute Break,* and was a non-commissioned officer in charge of information and education in the Air Transport Command.

In 1945 Kunitz was awarded a Guggenheim Fellowship for creative writing. From 1946 to 1949 he taught English at Bennington College, where he organized a literary workshop. As visiting professor of English at the New York State Teachers College in Potsdam, New York, from 1949 to 1950, Kunitz tried to adapt creative literary workshop techniques to a teacher-training situation. For four summers (1949 to 1953), he directed a seminar at the Summer Workshop in the Creative Arts at Potsdam.

Discussing his approach to teaching for *Education* magazine (November 1952), Kunitz wrote: "Essentially what I try to do is to help each person rediscover the poet within himself. I say 'rediscover' because I am convinced that it is a universal human attribute to want to play with words, to beat out rhythms, to fashion images, to tell a story, to construct forms. . . . The key is always in his possession: what prevents him from using it is mainly inertia, the stultification of the senses as a result of our one-sided educational conditioning and the fear of being made ridiculous or ashamed by the exposure of his feelings."

The New School for Social Research in New York City named Kunitz director of its Poetry Workshop in 1950. He received an Amy Lowell Poetry Traveling Fellowship in 1953, and spent the next year in Europe. On leave of absence from the New School, Kunitz was a visiting professor at the University of Washington (1955-56), Queens College (1956-57), and Brandeis University (1958-59). During the summers of 1957 and 1958 he directed a poetry workshop at the New York City Writers' Conference at Wagner College in Staten Island, New York. For the Poetry Center of the Young Men's Hebrew Association, he acted as chairman of an "Introductions" program in 1957-1958, in which fifteen young poets were introduced in readings from their works.

Stanley Kunitz's second volume of poetry *Passport to the War* was published by Holt in 1944. The reviewer for the New York *Times* March 26, 1944) noted: "Kunitz has now (it seems) every instrument necessary to the poetic analysis of modern experience. Time and time again in his new poems he achieves, with precision and fullness, his aim."

Fourteen years later his *Selected Poems, 1928-1958* (Little, Brown, 1958) appeared. Paul Engle, reviewing it for the Chicago *Sunday Tribune,* said: "Every poem has a sudden moment of achieved imagination. He is best in the quick, finely achieved brief lyric." John Ciardi wrote in the *Saturday Review* (September 27, 1958): "At times one must labor to follow the subtleties of his perception. The point is that the labor will not be in vain."

During 1959 Stanley Kunitz received several high honors. He was one of the first group of eleven writers to receive a two-year Ford Foundation grant designed to "give artists at the peak of their creative lives the freedom to concentrate on their work without interruption from side activities." In May 1959 he was awarded the Pulitzer Prize for Poetry. In 1959 he also won a grant from the National Institute of Arts and Letters.

As recently as 1957, Kunitz has pointed out, many publishers in the United States were wary of publishing a book of poems. Three publishers refused to read the manuscript of his own Pulitzer Prize-winning collection; five rejected it. The outlook for poets has been brightening lately, thanks to paperback publishing and an increased number of foundation grants for poetry.

Replying to the criticism that his poems are obscure, Kunitz has said: "A poet cannot concern himself with being fair to the reader. Time will tell. All poems contain a degree of mystery, as poetry is a discovery of one's hidden self. . . . Poetry is not concerned with communication; it has roots in magic, incantation, and spell-casting." Poets are "gayer than other writers," Kunitz believes, because they are less burdened by commerce, by the need to entertain, or by the desire to please. Accordingly, the poet should be both selfish and idealistic, independent of his audience, but "true to language—true to man himself."

Among the many awards that Kunitz has received are: the Oscar Blumenthal Prize from *Poetry* magazine (1941); the Harriet Monroe award for distinguished poetry granted by the University of Chicago (1957); the Levinson

Brandeis Univ. News Bureau
STANLEY KUNITZ

Prize from *Poetry* magazine (1958); and the *Saturday Review* award (1957).

Stanley Jasspon Kunitz was married to Helen Pearce in 1930 and was divorced in 1937. His second marriage, in 1939, was to Eleanor Evans, a former actress, by whom he has a daughter, Gretchen. This marriage was dissolved in 1958. In the same year he was married to the former Elise Asher, a painter and poet. The Kunitzes live in a brownstone house, filled with paintings and books, in New York's Greenwich Village.

Because he prefers to be close to nature, Kunitz has spent much of his life in the Connecticut and Pennsylvania countryside. His hobbies are playing tennis and "making things grow." He has brown eyes, black hair sprinkled with gray, is five feet eight inches tall, and weighs 140 pounds. A liberal, he considers himself a "political person," and feels that the poet is "a citizen of the world."

Stanley Kunitz lists as his favorite poets Donne, Marvell, Blake, Milton, Hopkins, Baudelaire, Rimbaud, and Yeats. Influenced most by the lyric poets, he has "vigorously tried to make his own furrow" instead of following his contemporaries. In "The Summing Up" Kunitz provides an autobiographical footnote to his career:

"When young I scribbled, boasting, on my wall,
No Love, No Property, No Wages.
In youth's good time I somehow bought them all,
And cheap, you'd think, for maybe a hundred pages.
Now in my prime, disburdened of my gear,
My trophies ransomed, broken, lost,
I carve again on the lintel of the year
My sign: Mobility—and damn the cost!"

References

N Y Times p36 My 5 '59 por
Newsweek 52:79 Jl 28 '58

KUZMIN, IOSIF I(OSIFOVICH) 1910-
Soviet government official; Communist party
official
Address: b. Scientific-Economic Council of the
U.S.S.R., Moscow, U.S.S.R.

When Nikita S. Khrushchev, First Secretary
of the Communist party, started out in 1957 to
give the economy of the Soviet Union its most
thorough overhauling since the Communist
Revolution of 1917, the man he chose to put
his plans into operation was a forty-seven-year-
old "engineer-turned-politician" named Iosif I.
Kuzmin. Although scarcely known to the public at the time of his appointment, in May 1957,
as chairman of the U.S.S.R. State Planning
Committee (Gosplan), he had for several years
worked directly under Khrushchev in government and party posts. He served as head of the
State Planning Committee until March 20, 1959,
when he also left his position as Deputy Premier and became chief of the Scientific-Economic Council with the rank of a cabinet
minister.

Iosif Iosifovich Kuzmin was born in 1910
in the Caspian Sea port of Astrakhan. At sixteen he went to work in a furniture factory,
later was employed in the municipal power
plant, and in 1930 joined the Communist party.
Moving to Leningrad, he worked there as a
lathe operator and machinist, and studied for
a year at the institute for ship engineers and
then for five years at the Budenny military
electrical engineering academy, also in Leningrad.

Upon his graduation in 1937 Kuzmin was assigned to work in Moscow's Proyektor Factory,
a searchlight-producing plant, where he became
an assistant director of the experimental division. He headed the Communist party unit in
the factory and was an organizer for the party's
Central Committee. Beginning in 1939 he advanced in the ranks of the party's Control Commission, responsible for party discipline, and
from 1940 to 1946 held the position of deputy
chairman. In 1947 he became a member of a
special government board dealing with agricultural problems, the bureau of agriculture and
storage. When Khrushchev launched a reorganization of the Soviet agricultural program in
1950, Kuzmin was made deputy chairman of the
board.

Kuzmin joined the staff of the Central Committee in 1952. As chief of the departments
that directed machine building and industry and
transportation, he worked directly under
Khrushchev, who became First Secretary of the
Central Committee in September 1953.

At the Twentieth Congress of the Communist
party in February 1956, Kuzmin was named a
member of the party's central auditing commission, which keeps track of party accounts. Two
months later he was a member of the group
that accompanied Khrushchev and the then
Premier Nikolai A. Bulganin on their visit to
Great Britain.

On May 4, 1957 Kuzmin was propelled from
relative obscurity into the upper reaches of the
Soviet hierarchy when he was named chairman
of the U.S.S.R. State Planning Committee and
a First Deputy Premier in the Council of Min-

isters—a rank making him one of the members
of the government Presidium alongside the
most powerful leaders in the Soviet Union.
"Kuzmin's sudden elevation seems to be the
most striking change in the Soviet government
in years," wrote Harry Schwartz, commentator
on Soviet affairs for the New York *Times* (May
6, 1957). It seemed to have resulted, Schwartz
pointed out, from a struggle in Moscow over
proposals put forward by Khrushchev for the
decentralization of Soviet industry.

Four days after the appointment Khrushchev
presented his proposals to the Supreme Soviet.
They called for the elimination of half the economic ministries and reorganization of others.
The direction of Soviet production and construction would be transferred to ninety-two
regional councils throughout the country that
would be under the direction of Kuzmin's committee. The Supreme Soviet approved the proposals May 10.

The power struggle continued, however, and
culminated in July with the removal of Viacheslav M. Molotov, Lazar M. Kaganovich, Georgi
M. Malenkov, and Dmitri Trofimovitch Shepilov
from their party and government posts. As an
aftermath of that struggle the title of First
Deputy Premier was abolished and Kuzmin
became one of three Deputy Premiers.

The Soviet government announced in September 1957 that it was abandoning at the end
of 1958 the five-year plan of economic development. The plan, adopted in February 1956, was
to have run through 1960. The government
explained that it was necessary to scrap the
plan because of the decentralization of industry
and the discovery of new mineral and power
resources. In its place, the government stated,
a seven-year plan would be drafted covering
1959 through 1965.

In 1957 Kuzmin was elected to fill a vacancy
in the Council of Nationalities, representing
Dzherzhinsky Election District No. 153 in
Baku, an oil port on the Caspian near his native
Astrakhan. When the Supreme Soviet convened
in December, Kuzmin reported on the operations under the 1957 economic plan and on
proposals for the 1958 plan.

Partly because of the industrial reorganization, he disclosed Soviet industrial output had
increased during 1957 by 10 per cent, as compared with the 7.1 per cent that had been
planned. The increase included an 11 per cent
increase in the production of means of production and an 8 per cent increase in consumption
goods.

The 1958 plan, according to Kuzmin, had
been drawn up to conform to the new decentralized management system and would provide for more efficient use of republic resources and co-ordination of economic
relations between republics. Goals would be
set only for major indices, with republics to
work out other goals for themselves within
that framework. It also had been geared, he
said, to conform to the seven-year plan that
was being drafted. The plan called for a 7.6
per cent increase in gross industrial output
in 1958, to include an 8.3 per cent increase

in production of means of production and a 6.1 per cent increase in production of consumption goods. Maximum effort, he noted, would be concentrated in expanding the chemical, oil, gas, and metallurgical industries.

When the Soviet cabinet was reorganized in April 1958, the title of First Deputy Premier was revived. Kuzmin, however, was not restored to that rank and remained as one of four Deputy Premiers. The Supreme Soviet, which approved that change in the government, also approved Khrushchev's proposal to liquidate the machine and tractor stations. Kuzmin reported that the economic reorganization had abolished 141 ministries and released 56,000 white-collar employees for other work.

Reporting in July 1958 on the first six months' operation of the 1958 plan, Kuzmin made known that gross production had increased 10.5 per cent over the first half of 1957, or 4 per cent more than the planned increase. However, failures to achieve the planned goals were noted in such items as metallurgical equipment, oil equipment, and prefabricated houses.

One of the major problems in Soviet economic planning, it was becoming clear, was a shortage of investment capital. In his July 1958 report Kuzmin noted that capital investment, though larger than in 1957, was only 93 per cent of the amount planned.

The loudly heralded seven-year plan of economic development was made public on November 14, 1958, after it had been presented to the Central Committee, which ordered it submitted for nation-wide discussion. It called for a capital investment program "almost equal" to total investments since the revolution in 1917 in order to attain a gross industrial production increase by 1965 of 80 per cent over 1958.

This was to include an 85 to 88 per cent increase in production of means of production and a 62 to 65 per cent increase in production of consumer goods. It called for the Soviet Union to have the highest per capita production in Europe by 1965 and in the world by 1970. The Soviet people were told that by 1970 they would enjoy the highest standard of living in the world.

Harry Schwartz, writing in the New York *Times* (November 16, 1958), called the plan "the most ambitious such document ever unveiled by the Kremlin." He continued, "The full extent of Khrushchev's audacity can be summed up simply: If the targets outlined by him for 1965 and 1970 are actually attained on schedule, then in the next decade or so the Communist world will clearly have won the economic competition with the West and, quite possibly, the political and propaganda contest for the allegiance of the uncommitted, underdeveloped nations of Asia, Africa, and Latin America as well."

Kuzmin is a man of stocky build, about five feet eight inches tall, with curly graying black hair. At receptions his manner is pleasant, but quiet, giving the impression

Sovphoto

IOSIF I. KUZMIN

that he prefers to remain in the background. He appears to be studious and well informed about economic statistics. As is usual with many Soviet officials, little is known about his private life.

References

N Y Herald Tribune p16 My 7 '57
N Y Times p11 My 7 '57; p14 O 21 '58
International Who's Who, 1958

LANDOWSKA, WANDA July 5, 1877- Aug. 16, 1959 Harpsichordist; pianist; known for her technique and interpretation of early keyboard music; through her teaching, concertizing, and writings fostered appreciation of this music. See *Current Biography* (November) 1945.

Obituary

N Y Times p23 Ag 17 '59

LASKER, MRS. ALBERT D(AVIS) Nov. 30, 1900- Philanthropist; organization official

Address: b. 405 Lexington Ave., New York 17; h. 29 Beekman Place, New York 22; Amenia, N.Y.

The Albert and Mary Lasker Foundation has made a major contribution to the advancement of medical knowledge through its awards for research in heart disease, mental illness, and cancer. Since the death of her husband, the advertising pioneer, Mrs. Mary Lasker has been president of the Albert and Mary Lasker Foundation. According to Edward R. Murrow, who spoke with her on his May 22, 1959 *Person to Person* television program, she is "a woman of many and varied interests: flowers and philanthropy, cancer research and community

MRS. ALBERT D. LASKER

welfare, art, and the ailments of the heart." Her name has become associated with many of the large organizations that fight disease, and with expanded health programs. It has also become associated with one of the world's finest private collections of French impressionist and modern art.

Mary Woodard Lasker was born on November 30, 1900 in Watertown, Wisconsin, the daughter of Frank Elwin and Sara (Johnson) Woodard. Her father was a banker with holdings in lumber, and her mother was an active civic leader who did a great deal of independent thinking. Her mother's books on psychology and psychiatry were her first reading materials. Now "it almost embarrasses Mrs. Lasker to recall that, at 12, her favorite reading was Hudson's 'Law of Psychic Phenomena'" (New York *Post*, June 12, 1944). Mary attended school in Watertown and then studied fine arts at the University of Wisconsin from 1918 to 1920. She transferred to Radcliffe, taking her A.B. degree *cum laude* in 1923. Following her graduation, Mary "read English" at Oxford University for one semester.

Upon her return to the United States in 1924, Mary Woodard became associated with the Reinhardt Galleries, selling paintings to museums and collectors, arranging exhibitions of the old and modern masters, and handling artists' publicity. After spending seven years as an art dealer, Miss Woodard left the art field. "I was tired of being in a business where numerically few things were sold. I wanted to sell masses of things to masses of people. I found out that the things which people still bought in a depression were paper patterns" (New York *Post*, June 12, 1944). In 1932 she originated Hollywood Patterns, which later became a subsidiary company of Condé Nast.

When Mary Woodard married Albert D. Lasker on June 21, 1940, he was president and

sole owner of Lord and Thomas, one of the largest and oldest advertising agencies in the United States. Lasker wrote in his memoirs: "I made more money out of advertising than any man who ever lived." Even while he was active in business, he gave prodigal amounts of money to philanthropies in medicine and education. To the University of Chicago he donated over $1,000,000 as well as his estate at Lake Forest, Illinois, which was valued at more than $3,000,000. He also contributed millions to promote cancer research.

In 1938 Lasker announced his retirement from the advertising world to devote himself exclusively to public life and to philanthropic activities, and in 1942 Lord and Thomas was dissolved. Albert and Mary Lasker established their foundation to aid and encourage medical research and public health administration. The foundation "underwrites pilot projects in basic research related to the major illnesses—now principally heart diseases, cancer, and mental illness—and also fosters dissemination of public information on the needs of medical research" (New York *Herald Tribune*, May 2, 1958).

Since her husband's death in 1952, Mary Lasker has been the driving force behind the Foundation. Her intelligence, vigor, and perhaps most important of all, her imagination, have stimulated the Foundation's work of continued service. The Foundation's annual award, consisting of a cash prize and a reproduction of the *Winged Victory of Samothrace*, has become recognized as one of the most significant honors bestowed in American medicine. Some of the recipients have been Dr. Selman Waksman, who discovered streptomycin; Dr. Jonas Salk, who developed the polio vaccine; and Dr. Henry H. Kessler, who worked in rehabilitating the crippled and disabled. Ten Lasker Award recipients have later won the Nobel Prize. The awards are more than significant honors; they have aroused public and professional interest in supporting medical research.

"Not only can she grasp an idea quickly when it is presented to her," Mrs. Franklin D. Roosevelt said of Mary Lasker, "but she sees where you can go with it" (New York *Herald Tribune*, May 2, 1958). This ability has enabled Mrs. Lasker to expand her interests and engage in other activities of a medical nature besides those supported by the Foundation. In 1944 she became secretary of the National Committee for Mental Hygiene. She took the assignment because she recognized the importance of removing the stigma of mental illness by educating the public. The Committee has also enlarged facilities for treatment, established a vocational adjustment bureau, and granted funds for research.

The study and analysis of health problems in American life today and the dissemination of information to the public have always proved difficult. Mrs. Lasker has helped to solve these problems through the National Health Education Committee, of which she is presiding chairman. A study of the Veterans Administration hospital case-load for 1957 revealed that of the $745,000,000 spent in medical care for veterans only $9,000,000 were spent in medical research.

This sum compared unfavorably with a total of $121,000,000 spent for research on plant and animal diseases by the Department of Agriculture. "The key to reversing the steadily increasing medical care costs for our aging veterans," according to Mary Lasker, "is an enlarged research budget, which places human needs at least on a level with those of farm animals" (New York *Times*, March 23, 1958).

The Committe has also planned a "life-saving" educational effort during 1959 to combat death from heart attacks and strokes. A report issued by the Committee in April 1959 indicated that the American life span has been increased by 6.3 years since 1943, with women gaining more than men. Mrs. Lasker foresees three-fourths of the nation living long enough to become great-grandparents, provided that money is forthcoming for medical research (New York *Herald Tribune,* April 24, 1959).

Mary and Albert Lasker collected some of the finest examples of French impressionist and modern painting. Some of these works were shown on television when Mrs. Lasker was interviewed on *Person to Person* by Edward R. Murrow in 1959. Simon & Schuster published a book of color reproductions of the paintings called *The Albert D. Lasker Collection: Renoir to Matisse,* by Wallace Brockway.

Her love of visual beauty influenced Mrs. Lasker's decision to initiate semiannual plantings of greens and flowers around New York public buildings. These plantings, dedicated to her mother, the late Mrs. Sara J. Woodard, led New York City to establish a program of "Salute to the Seasons," which plants seasonal flowers and trees and illuminates some of the city's more attractive buildings. "Beauty pays," Mrs. Lasker told Edward R. Murrow on *Person to Person.* "I think that more people should take advantage of this way of getting visitors."

Mrs. Lasker is a member of the board of trustees of the Menninger Foundation and of the Institute of Psychoanalysis, a teaching and research organization in Chicago. She is also a vice-president of the Planned Parenthood Federation and secretary of the Health Insurance Plan of greater New York. She sits on the executive board of the New York City Board of Hospitals, the advisory council of the National Cancer Institute of the United States Public Health Service, the American Heart Association, the National Advisory Heart Council of the National Heart Institute, and the American Cancer Society. Her nonmedical interests include the American Committee on United Europe and the Museum of Modern Art in New York. She has received numerous awards, including honorary degrees from Bard College and the University of Wisconsin.

Her dark hair and violet-blue eyes help make Mary Lasker a strikingly beautiful woman. Her first marriage, to Paul Reinhardt, the art dealer, took place on May 23, 1926 and was dissolved in 1934. She has no children of her own, but she maintains a strong family relationship with Mr. Lasker's children by a previous marriage. At her town house, which is furnished in a white and neutral color scheme to offset the great Lasker collection, she is an active hostess. Mrs. Lasker says she likes "to supply a calm but interesting setting for people."

References

N Y Herald Tribune p9 My 2 '58 por
N Y Post p29 Je 12 '44 por
Who's Who in America, 1958-59
Who's Who of American Women (1958-59)

LASKER, MARY WOODARD *See* Lasker, Mrs. Albert D.

LATHAM, DANA July 7, 1898- United States government official; lawyer
Address: b. Internal Revenue Service, 12th St. and Constitution Ave., N.W., Washington 25, D.C.; h. 9460 Sierra Mar Place, Los Angeles 46, Calif.

The responsibility for collecting the largest amount of taxes in the world belongs to Dana Latham, who as the United States Commissioner of Internal Revenue supervises the collection of more than $80 billion each year. President Dwight D. Eisenhower appointed Latham to the top tax position on October 9, 1958, to succeed Russell C. Harrington, a Rhode Island accounting executive.

The new Commissioner heads an agency that employed him briefly in the early part of his career as a special attorney for the Bureau of Internal Revenue in Washington, D.C., and San Francisco. He has also been an executive for a California finance company and, for more than twenty-four years, a partner in a Los Angeles legal firm specializing in taxation.

Dana Latham was born in Galesburg, Illinois on July 7, 1898 to Harry S. and Margaret (Dobyns) Latham. His father was a schoolteacher who, Dana Latham says, "hardly made enough to eat" (Los Angeles *Times,* October 31, 1958). As a consequence, the family moved to Delaware, Ohio, the home of Ohio Weslyan University, where the elder Latham gradually got into the book business by canvassing the fraternities for used books, which he rebound and resold. Eventually his father's business became one of the leading book stores in town.

During his high school years in the town of Delaware, Dana Latham helped the family budget by framing pictures and raising vegetables in the home garden. Later at Ohio Wesleyan University, he helped to defray expenses by working in his father's book store. His studies interrupted by World War I, he entered the Army and trained as a field artillery officer, but the war ended before he saw active duty.

Returning to Ohio Wesleyan, he won academic honors, received a Phi Beta Kappa key and was graduated *magna cum laude* with a B.A. degree in 1920. He then attended the University of Chicago Law School for a short time, but transferred to Harvard University, which awarded him the law degree in 1922. He worked his way through Harvard as a private tutor.

(Continued next page)

DANA LATHAM

Meanwhile, his family had moved to California because of his father's failing health, but Dana Latham returned to Illinois to take the state bar examination. After being admitted to the bar, he worked as law clerk and associate in the Chicago firm of Hopkins, Starr & Hopkins. His being sent to Washington, D.C. on tax cases led to his first interest in taxation.

In 1926 he left the firm for his first government position, as a $3,900 special attorney for the Bureau of Internal Revenue, operating out of Washington and San Francisco. The job took him through the eleven Western states and gave him further background in income taxes, which at the time was a relatively new field of taxation with few specialists.

After nearly two years with the government, he was asked by a Washington tax law firm to open an office in Los Angeles. From 1927 to 1929 he practised in that office as a member of the Miller, Chevalier & Latham tax law firm. In 1929 he gave up the practice of law for an administrative position with Pacific Finance Corporation in Los Angeles. He served Pacific as a vice-president and director until 1934 and helped to take the company through the depression years.

In 1934, together with Paul Watkins, then head of the legal department at Pacific Finance, he organized the law partnership of Latham & Watkins in Los Angeles. The firm lasted for nearly a quarter of a century, until Latham accepted the Internal Revenue post in 1958. In the years after 1934 the Latham & Watkins firm handled many of the income tax cases in the Western states. In addition to advising on taxes, the firm set up and represented corporations and handled estate, trust, and other legal cases. According to the Los Angeles *Times,* the Latham-Watkins partnership grew to be "one of the city's big law firms," and Latham was "sought out not only for his knowledge of

taxes, but for his general wisdom" (October 31, 1958).

Persuaded by Herbert Hoover, Jr., to return to government service, he acted as a special adviser to the State Department, working with Under Secretary of State Hoover in 1954-55. He later said that his attitude toward accepting government appointments was changed by Hoover's remarking that executives themselves are to blame if they criticize the government but reject the opportunity to do the needed work.

When Russell C. Harrington resigned as Commissioner of Internal Revenue to return to private business in the fall of 1958, President Eisenhower named Latham to the post. He was sworn into office in November 1958, although his appointment was subject to confirmation by Congress, which reconvened in January 1959.

The New York *Herald Tribune* noted that Latham brought with him to the Internal Revenue "an impressive knowledge of the nation's tax laws," having served "on both sides of the tax fence," the government and private industry. In his private practice "he became known by the bureau he now heads as a 'difficult' but respected adversary'" (November 10, 1958).

As the head of the Internal Revenue Service, Latham supervises the assessment and collection of all taxes imposed by any law providing internal revenue. He also has the responsibility of protecting the revenue and of administrating and enforcing the laws and regulations relating to alcohol, alcoholic beverages, tobacco, and firearms.

The headquarters of the Internal Revenue Service is located in Washington, D.C., but the organization is decentralized with regional offices across the country. According to the *Government Organization Manual 1957-58,* the function of the Washington office is "to develop national policies and programs for the administration of internal revenue laws and to provide over-all direction to the field organization." The Commissioner is under the general direction of the Secretary of the Treasury.

In discussing his new office and plans for it, Latham said, "The primary problems, it seems to me, are to treat the taxpayer right, to simplify the process of tax collection and simplify the laws concerning collection, eliminating the inequities as we go" (New York *Herald Tribune,* November 10, 1958).

In keeping with this policy, by mid-January 1959 Latham had extended the use of the simple punch-card form for filing tax returns from taxable incomes below $5,000 to those below $10,000. He also studied these possibilities: the use of the simple punch-card form for incomes below $15,000; further simplification of tax forms; "a more human approach" to form letters; speedier handling of correspondence and tax disputes; and quicker preparation of new regulations and less delay in announcing them.

Latham has served as a trustee of Ohio Wesleyan University, Occidental College, and the John Tracy Clinic. He is past president of the Los Angeles Bar Association, the Los Angeles Traffic Association, and the Harvard Law

School Association of Southern California. He is a member of the American, International, California, and Los Angeles bar associations, the American Law Institute, and the Phi Kappa Psi fraternity. His social clubs are the Los Angeles Club and the Los Angeles Country Club. He has written articles on tax and other legal problems for law journals.

While a university student in Chicago, Dana Latham met Olive Eames, who was working at the Marshall Field department store. They were married on June 16, 1923, and they have three daughters, Jeanne (Mrs. Richard Alden), Corinne (Mrs. Kenneth W. Cooper), and Polly (Mrs. Robert A. Barley), and several grandchildren. Latham is a tall, husky man with brown eyes, balding gray hair, and a soft voice. "There is absolutely nothing unusual about my life," he is fond of telling reporters. For relaxation he plays golf, shooting in the high eighties, and bridge. He is a Methodist and a Republican.

References

Los Angeles Times II p 1 O 31 '58 por
N Y Herald Tribune p6 N 10 '58 por
U S News 45:21 O 10 '58 por
Who's Who in America, 1958-59

Wide World

DAVID L. LAWRENCE

LAWRENCE, DAVID L(EO) June 18, 1889- Governor of Pennsylvania

Address: b. State Capitol, Harrisburg, Pa.; h. 355 S. Aiken Ave., Pittsburgh, Pa.

During most of his seventy years, David L. Lawrence has been a Democratic political leader who often preferred to use his power behind the scenes to help select state and national candidates than to run for high office himself. He was elected in 1958 to succeed George M. Leader as Governor of Pennsylvania for a four-year term, becoming the first Pennsylvania Democrat to succeed another Democrat in about 100 years. He is also his state's first Roman Catholic Governor, and the oldest man ever to win the office. As mayor of Pittsburgh from 1946 to 1958, he was responsible for much of the remarkable postwar progress of the city.

Of Scotch-Irish ancestry, David Leo Lawrence was born in a working-class section of Pittsburgh on June 18, 1889, the son of Charles B. and Catherine (Conwell) Lawrence. He was involved in politics almost from childhood, since his father, a teamster, was a precinct leader who held a county job in Pittsburgh. David Lawrence was educated in parochial schools and took a two-year commercial course instead of completing high school.

At the age of fourteen, he left school to become an office boy for William J. Brennen, Democratic party leader of Pittsburgh. According to the *Saturday Evening Post* (March 14, 1959), "He sat in on political meetings; he listened and he learned. Equipped with a feel for politics, he rose from ward worker" to Allegheny County Democratic chairman in 1920. During World War I he had served as an enlisted man in the office of the Judge Advocate General in Washington, D.C.

On the national level Lawrence gained his first political experience when he worked as a page boy in behalf of Woodrow Wilson at the Democratic National Convention in 1912. He has served in some official capacity at every National Convention since then and has been a delegate to every convention since 1924. Locally, he was a member of the Pittsburgh registration commission from 1914 to 1924. After the victory of Franklin D. Roosevelt and his inauguration as President in 1933, Lawrence became collector of internal revenue for the Western District of Pennsylvania. He resigned this position in 1934 to assume the chairmanship of the Democratic State Committee, a post that he held until his election as mayor of Pittsburgh, except for an interval of two years.

As reported in *Time* (November 4, 1957), when Roosevelt "rolled into the White House, Democrat Dave Lawrence rolled into statewide power, dragging with him his own candidate for governor, Businessman George H. Earle." During Earle's term in office, 1935-39, Lawrence served as secretary of the commonwealth and "was considered the real ruler of Pennsylvania" (*Christian Science Monitor,* September 5, 1958).

Toward the end of the term, disunity in the party led to an indictment of Lawrence by a grand jury on charges of graft and corruption for passing out illegal contracts and "macing" state employees for political funds. But he was acquitted on all counts in two lengthy trials before Republican juries.

After 1939 Lawrence returned to Pittsburgh to head the Harris-Lawrence Company, Inc., an insurance firm, and to continue as Pittsburgh Democratic party leader. He was influential in selecting and mustering support for Democratic candidates for mayor of Pittsburgh and in 1945 decided to run for the office himself. He was

LAWRENCE, DAVID L.—*Continued*

elected to an unprecedented four terms as mayor of Pittsburgh. In 1945 he won the office by a margin of 14,000 votes, and by his fourth-term election in 1957 his majority was nearly 60,000 votes. As mayor, Lawrence embarked on a program of rejuvenation that turned Pittsburgh into one of the best cities in the country.

The *Christian Science Monitor* (September 5, 1958) described the change in the city: "Its soot was once so heavy that housewives washed their curtains once a week, office lights were turned on at noon, property values in the golden triangle dwindled, and business firms found it hard to recruit executives who would consent to live in Pittsburgh.

"Today, a sparkling constellation of modern skyscrapers stands in its center. The air is smog free. Century-old slums are being razed. New bridges and expressways have been built, and a one billion dollar industrial expansion program is under way."

A survey by the editors of *Fortune* magazine in 1958 put Pittsburgh among the eight best-administered cities in America. It gave the city a high rating for various municipal services, including traffic engineering, air-pollution control, and low traffic-accident death rates. It also cited the city for its rebuilding and long-range planning programs.

Lawrence has been called the last of the big city "bosses" as well as the dean of a new kind of city "boss"—the modern reformer. His rejuvenation program won him the respect of Pittsburgh's business community and the title of the most powerful big-city mayor in the United States. He was elected vice-president of the United States Conference of Mayors in 1948 and served as president of the conference from 1950 to 1952.

His long activity in the Democratic party has given Lawrence considerable power at Democratic conventions in choosing Presidential candidates. He was an ardent supporter of Adlai E. Stevenson in 1952 and 1956, and he regards Stevenson as still one of the top statesmen in the party. Although a Roman Catholic himself, Lawrence would probably not back a Catholic Presidential candidate in 1960 unless other issues were larger. "When I think of a national campaign," he has said, "I'm sure a Catholic running for the Presidency must have an issue so big, so strong, so completely overriding that his religion is never thought of.... It's got to be something that touches the people's hearts—an appeal to the passions" (*Saturday Evening Post,* March 14, 1959).

When Pennsylvania party leaders were unable to decide upon a Democratic candidate for Governor in 1958, Lawrence agreed to accept a "draft." He won a three-to-one edge in the primary. On November 4, 1958 he won the election by a slim margin over Arthur T. McGonigle, while another Democratic candidate, then Governor George M. Leader, lost the United States Senate race to Republican Hugh Scott.

Campaigning on a bipartisan platform of building up the state, Lawrence had made little mention of political distinctions. In his in-

augural address on January 20, 1959, he said that his goal for the next four years was to lead business, labor, and government in a joint effort to help the state recover from the recession. "Pennsylvania's problems are not political. They are economic," he said (*Christian Science Monitor,* January 22, 1959). One of the first things he did in office was to adopt a Republican suggestion that the budget be balanced and state spending be "cut to the bone." He is a member of the Democratic Advisory Council, which in April 1959 issued a statement on unemployment calling for the development of an expanding economy.

In 1957 Lawrence was selected as one of the nine best mayors in the nation. The United States Conference of Mayors gave him its Distinguished Service Award for "outstanding contributions to his City, his State, and his Nation." He was the first mayor so honored, and the only previous American recipient was General George C. Marshall. In February 1959 the University of Pennsylvania awarded Lawrence an honorary degree of Doctor of Laws.

He is a trustee of the University of Pittsburgh and the Carnegie Institute of Technology, a member of the advisory board of Duquesne University, and a director of the Roselia Foundling Asylum. He has been a lifelong member of St. Mary of Mercy Catholic Church in Pittsburgh.

David L. Lawrence was married to Alice Golden on June 8, 1921. They have three children living—two married daughters, Mary and Anna May, and a son, Gerald, who is a student at La Salle College. Two other sons were killed in an automobile accident in 1942.

Joseph Alsop has described Lawrence as "a large, solid, quiet-spoken man with a large, deeply lined, intelligent face" (*New York Herald Tribune,* October 21, 1956). He likes to talk to young people, especially to college groups. He occasionally plays gin rummy and two-handed pinochle, but bridge, poker, golf, and country-club life do not interest him. He belongs to the Pittsburgh Athletic Association. One of his favorite books is said to be Edwin O'Connor's *The Last Hurrah.*

References

Christian Sci Mon p1 S 5 '58 por
Harper 213:55+ Ag '56
New Republic 139:10 N 3 '58
N Y Herald Tribune p8 Je 5 '58 por
Sat Eve Post 231:28+ Mr 14 '59 por
Time 70:20 N 4 '57 por

Who's Who in America, 1958-59

LEAHY, WILLIAM D(ANIEL) May 6, 1875-July 20, 1959 Fleet Admiral; Chief of Staff to Presidents Franklin D. Roosevelt and Harry S. Truman during World War II; Ambassador to France during the Vichy regime; senior adviser to President Roosevelt at the Yalta meeting. See *Current Biography* (January) 1941.

Obituary

N Y Times p1 Jl 21 '59

LEDERBERG, JOSHUA May 23, 1925-
Geneticist; university professor
Address: b. Department of Genetics, Stanford
University Medical School, Palo Alto, Calif.

One of the three American scientists to receive the 1958 Nobel Prize in medicine, Dr.
Joshua Lederberg, formerly of the University
of Wisconsin and now chairman of the genetics
department at the Stanford University Medical
School, was honored "for his discoveries concerning genetic recombination and the organization of the genetic material of bacteria." He
will share the award with Dr. G. W. Beadle
of the California Institute of Technology and
Dr. Edward L. Tatum of the Rockefeller Institute for Medical Research.

Genetic recombination is the term used to
define the process of sexual fertilization (mat-
ing) in bacteria, which, as one-celled organisms, usually reproduce by simple cell division.
Lederberg's efforts to breed bacteria to gain
new insight into their genetic mechanism has
expanded the entire field of research, thereby
making "possible the rapid development of a
branch of knowledge by which cancer research
'will be strongly influenced'" (New York
Times, October 31, 1958). The Nobel Prize
committee also acknowledged Lederberg's discovery of a method of artificially introducing
new genes into bacteria, thus making easier the
investigation of hereditary substance.

Frequently referred to as a young "genius"
by his fellow scientists, Joshua Lederberg was
born on May 23, 1925 in Montclair, New Jersey to Zwi H. and Esther (Goldenbaum) Lederberg. When Joshua was still a child his parents moved to New York City and settled in the
Washington Heights neighborhood. He attended
Stuyvesant High School, one of the finest science secondary schools in the city. When he
was graduated in 1941, he ranked among the
first five students in a class of several hundred.

At Columbia College, where he was enrolled
as a student in the premedical curriculum in
1941, Joshua Lederberg received intensive training in the techniques of scientific research. He
served as a laboratory assistant to Professor
F. J. Ryan, of the zoology department, and
helped conduct several noteworthy experiments
on the mutation and adaptation of Neurospora,
or bread mold fungi. After receiving his bachelor's degree with honors in 1944, he matriculated at the College of Physicians and Surgeons
at Columbia University. At the end of his second year (1946), Lederberg was invited to
work with Dr. Edward L. Tatum at Yale
University . "My ultimate goal was research,"
says Lederberg, "and at the time I was interested in biochemical genetics. Tatum had pioneered in some studies in this field. . . . Originally, I had intended to take just three months
away from my medical education to complete
experiments that Tatum had set up. But I
never got back to Columbia."

At Yale Joshua Lederberg was awarded a
research fellowship to continue his graduate
studies with Dr. Tatum. He concentrated on
an analysis of sexual reproduction in bacteria,
in particular, the species known as Escherichia

JOSHUA LEDERBERG

coli. Scientists had accepted the established biological fact that bacteria reproduced by simple
cell division, whereby each cell split into two
cells, each containing a complete set of chromosomes. The experiments conducted by Lederberg and Tatum showed that certain strains of
Escherichia coli possessed the mechanism for
sexual or genetic recombination, which, according to Lederberg, "corresponds exactly to the
normal sexual fertilization in the higher organism" (New York *Herald Tribune,* October 31,
1958).

By 1947 Lederberg had definitely proved
"that bacteria have a sex life of a sort, *i.e.*
reproduce by the union of two organisms with
a consequent exchange of genes" (*Time,* November 10, 1958). By uniting two wholly different strains in a culture, Lederberg was able
to show that a third strain was produced
which possessed the characteristics of the two
parent cells. His discovery of the process of
sexual recombination not only expanded the
field of experiment but was a significant step
forward in "developing bacterial genetics into
a comprehensive field of research" (New York
Times, October 31, 1958).

After receiving the Ph.D. degree in microbiology from Yale University in 1948, Joshua
Lederberg accepted an appointment as assistant
professor of genetics at the University of Wisconsin. In 1950 he was named an associate
professor, and four years later, when he was
only twenty-nine, he was promoted to the rank
of full professor. Lederberg organized the department of medical genetics in 1957 and
served as its first chairman. In February 1959
Dr. Lederberg assumed the chairmanship of a
newly created department of genetics at Stanford University.

Studies of the genetic mechanism of the bacteria, which had been pioneered jointly by
Tatum and Lederberg, were continued by

LEDERBERG, JOSHUA—*Continued*

Lederberg in the laboratories of the University of Wisconsin. With the assistance of his wife, also a geneticist, and a doctoral candidate Norton D. Zinder (now of the Rockefeller Institute), Lederberg demonstrated that genetic material was exchanged either by *conjugation,* "in which an entire complement of chromosomes is transferred from one bacterial cell to another, or by *transduction,* in which hereditary fragments only are transferred" (University of Wisconsin news release). Lederberg showed how, by means of the transduction process, a bacterial virus could carry hereditary material from one cell to another.

After a virus has attacked a bacterium, it "breaks it up and reorganizes its material into hundreds of new virus particles. If these particles in turn infect another bacterium and it survives, they sometimes change it into a new strain. Apparently the viruses, acting somewhat like submicroscopic spermatozoa, take hereditary material from the first bacterium and transfer it to the second" (*Time,* November 10, 1958).

More startling than the research on transduction has been Lederberg's work on the breeding and cross breeding of viruses. The investigations of the behavior of viruses which may culminate eventually in the control of virus diseases "may lead," in the words of a New York *Times* (October 31, 1958) editorial, "to discoveries alongside of which even the discovery of atomic energy may seem relatively small."

In the process of breeding microbes and viruses in cultures, Dr. Lederberg has produced new strains which bear little resemblance to their parentage. Specifically, by pairing bacteria resistant to penicillin with those resistant to streptomycin, Lederberg obtained new generations of bacteria resistant to both drugs. His experiments proved that "the disease-producing power of germs can be increased by genetic processes, or a virulent organism may be made comparatively weak by this means" (New York *Herald Tribune,* August 14, 1953).

Though it has been difficult to evaluate the practical aspects of Lederberg's theoretical investigations, the Nobel Prize committee recognized the significance of his research in the control of all virus diseases, and also in cancer. This perplexing illness "is caused by genetic change in human cells that makes them multiply irresponsibly. Increased knowledge of genetics," states *Time* (November 10, 1958), "may eventually cure or prevent cancer."

As a geneticist, Dr. Lederberg has been concerned with the "contamination" of the moon by lunar rockets. He and Dean B. Cowie, a physicist with the Carnegie Institution of Washington, told a symposium dealing with the possible uses of earth satellites that nonsterile rockets reaching the moon could destroy or materially distort the picture of the biochemical evolution of life as recorded in the surface of the moon.

The biochemical origin of life, according to Lederberg and Cowie, was based on carbon, hydrogen, and oxygen built into complex organic molecules by the action of ultraviolet light, atomic radiation, or other natural sources of energy. They have maintained that evidence of this origin might be found on the moon's surface since this body lacks an atmosphere; hence, the importance of preserving intact the moon and planets and of prohibiting the transport of genes from one planet to another. "Even a fragment of an organism," reported the two scientists, "might short circuit an otherwise tortuous history of evolutionary progress" (*Science,* June 27, 1958).

Short and husky, Joshua Lederberg has achieved much for a scientist his age. He has written extensively, both singly and with co-authors, and has published in *Science, Nature,* and the *Proceedings of the National Academy of Science.* In 1953 he received a $1,000 award from the Eli Lilly Company for outstanding work by a scientist under thirty-five years of age.

The wife of the Nobel Prize winner is Dr. Esther Marilyn Lederberg, an outstanding experimental geneticist in her own right. She has degrees from Hunter College (B.A.), Stanford University (M.A.), and the University of Wisconsin (Ph.D.), and has received a United States Public Health Service fellowship for research. The origin of this husband and wife research team goes back to 1946 when both of them served as assistants to Dr. Edward L. Tatum.

References

N Y Herald Tribune p2 O 31 '58
N Y Times p11 O 31 '58
N Y World-Telegram p2 O 30 '58
American Men of Science vol I (1955)
Jews in the World of Science (1956)

LEE KUAN YEW Sept. 16, 1923- Prime Minister of Singapore; lawyer

Address: City Hall, Singapore

The first Prime Minister of the new State of Singapore, Lee Kuan Yew, is a paradoxical figure. On the one hand, Lee, who is from a wealthy Singapore family, has a law degree from Cambridge University, plays golf, and speaks English much better than Chinese. On the other, as a politician, he is anti-British and a radical socialist, campaigned in shirtsleeves to "fight against the white man," and heads the People's Action party, which contains followers of the Communist line. Lee's cabinet, advocating eventual union with the Federation of Malaya, has started a Five Year Plan for industrial development, but already faces serious financial problems.

Speaking of his Cambridge education, Lee Kuan Yew has said: "They wanted me to become an educated man, the equal of an Englishman, the model of perfection. I cry with Nehru when I think I cannot speak my mother tongue as well as I speak English" (Toronto *Globe and Mail,* June 1, 1959). Lee Kuan Yew (also written Lee Kuan-yew or Lee Kwan Yew) is of Chinese ancestry, and, like his wealthy grandfather and father, is a native of Singapore, the British colony founded by Sir Thomas Stamford Raffles in 1819. Born on September 16, 1923, Lee Kuan Yew received his secondary education at Raffles Institution, the preparatory school for Raffles College, now a part of the University of Malaya. In the Cambridge School Certificate in 1939, Lee received the best grades in all of Malaya. Winning the Anderson scholarship, he went to Raffles College. He then went to England to read law at Cambridge, where he took a double first and headed the honors list, with a star for distinction. While a university student, he became a socialist.

He was admitted to the English bar in 1950, but returned to Singapore, where he became legal advisor to the Postal Union. His counseling helped the postal employees to win a pay raise, and soon Lee was negotiating industrial disputes for several other unions.

Singapore has an area of about 220 square miles and a population of about 1½ million, about 80 per cent of whom are Chinese. The island is separated from the Federation of Malaya on the Asiatic mainland by a mile-wide, causeway-spanned strait. It has an excellent natural harbor but no natural resources; as a result, Singapore's economy is based on trade, largely with Malaya and Indonesia. The island is also Great Britain's principal Far Eastern naval base.

During World War II, the Japanese occupied Singapore, but when the British reoccupied the area in 1945, Singapore became a crown colony, administered by a Governor assisted by a legislative council, only a few of whose members were elected. A step toward self-rule was taken in 1951 when a Singapore City Council with a majority of elected members came into being; then in 1954 the Rendel Commission drew up a new constitution for the crown colony. Effective February 1955, this constitution created a legislative assembly of thirty-two members, twenty-five of them elected.

Under the limited franchise which existed before 1955, the elective seats in the legislative council had been held by the Progressives, a party dominated by wealthy, English-speaking, conservative Chinese businessmen. With a greater degree of self-government in prospect, three leaders of other interests decided to unite and break this British-fostered political monopoly. They were David Saul Marshall, a former Progressive, who is considered the colony's outstanding criminal lawyer, Lim Yew Hock, a right-wing Chinese trade union organizer, and Lee Kuan Yew.

More radical than the others, Lee soon broke away to form the People's Action party, of which he became secretary general. Marshall and Lim combined to found the Labour Front, which won thirteen of the elective seats in the Legislative Assembly at the first election under the new constitution on April 2, 1955. The People's Action party won three seats, with Lee Kuan Yew easily victorious in Tanjong Pagar, a constituency in the western section of the island, which includes many of the poorest Chinese citizens. Campaigning in English, Lee called for immediate self-government in Singapore; it was not until some time later that he mastered Mandarin enough to address Chinese

Wide World

LEE KUAN YEW

audiences in that tongue. He still speaks Chinese haltingly, but is fluent in Malay.

Becoming the first chief minister of Singapore as the result of the 1955 election, David Marshall headed a delegation to London in April 1956 to negotiate with British officials on the island's desire for self-rule. The negotiations failed, and Marshall, who had quarreled not only with the British but with his own delegation which included Lim Yew Hock and Lee Kuan Yew, resigned as chief minister in June, and was succeeded by Lim Yew Hock. Marshall organized the Workers' party, which has not gained much of a following. That year witnessed increased activity by Communist front organizations, led among others by certain members of the People's Action party. It culminated in a students' strike and riots resulting in thirteen deaths, over 500 arrests, and the imprisonment of several leaders of the People's Action party.

In 1957, Lee Kuan Yew accompanied Lim Yew Hock to London for conferences. These meetings resulted in the signing, on April 11, of a constitutional agreement providing for a Singapore citizenship, a native head of state, an elected council, consisting of nine members, presided over by the Prime Minister, and a fully elective legislative assembly of 51 members. A British High Commissioner was to remain responsible for defense and external affairs outside of cultural and commercial matters.

Seeking endorsement of his position on Singapore's independence, Lee resigned his seat in the legislative assembly on April 29, 1957 in order to contest in an individual by-election at Tanjong Pagar on June 29. He was returned by an overwhelming majority. On August 13, however, he was ousted from his party's secretary-generalship by extreme leftist elements, but regained his leadership on October 26. In the spring of 1958 Lee again accom-

LEE KUAN YEW—*Continued*

panied Lim Yew Hock to London for the signing of a further constitutional agreement whereby the colony would be transformed into a self-governing state of the British Commonwealth by March 1959.

The first election under the new constitution was held on May 30, 1959, when Lee Kuan Yew campaigned as an anti-colonial non-Communist, demanding social reform and advocating eventual union with Malaya. The less radical parties failed to agree on a united front, and the People's Action party won decisively, capturing forty-three of the fifty-one seats in the new legislative assembly.

The British governor, Sir William Goode (now temporary head of state), called on Lee to form a government. In keeping with a campaign promise, Lee refused to do it "as a matter of honor" until eight left-wing party members, jailed since 1956, had been granted release. His request was granted. Sworn in as Prime Minister on June 5, Lee announced a cabinet of impressive intellectual and professional caliber that became known as the "cabinet of dons." It includes former Mayor Ong Eng Guan, who became Minister of National Development, and Dr. Toh Chin Chye, a research physiologist, who was named Deputy Prime Minister. The program of the new cabinet includes a Five Year Plan for the development of industry, agriculture, and fisheries, a reorganization of city administration, increased liberal and technical education, and the emancipation of women.

Sentiment in Singapore has always been strong for union with the Federation of Malaya, but Malaya, with a ratio of three Malayans to two Chinese, has been well aware of the problems that stand in the way of the merger. The population of Singapore is about 80 per cent Chinese, with more than its share of Chinese Communists. Lee, however, has emphasized that he is an old friend of Dato Abdul Razak, the Malayan Prime Minister, and that perhaps a union economically advantageous to both sides can be worked out.

By the middle of June the Lee government had begun a cleanup campaign which suppressed pornographic newspapers, and banned pinball machines and jukebox saloons. The government is also trying to abolish polygamy, except for Moslems, and concubinage, a common local Chinese practice. In the same month, under Development Minister Ong, workmen began to clear ground for "Queenstown," a new suburban city to house 53,000 slum dwellers.

The People's Action party in the middle of 1959 had such grave problems to face as a treasury deficit of $4,700,000, a rapidly expanding population, growing unemployment, and the presence of the British naval base in spite of native pressures to have it removed. Another major problem is Communism. The People's Action party depends to some extent on Communist support, and Lee has to try to appease extremists in his own party at the same time that he tries to persuade possible foreign investors that his regime is sound and stable.

"It's the only hope," Lee has said of radical social and economic reform. "If we don't try,

Singapore will become Communist. If we try and fail, it will become Communist. The important thing is for us to try" (*Reporter*, May 14, 1959).

Lee has been described as "a witty conversationalist and a charming luncheon companion" (*Reporter*, May 14, 1959). Vernon Bartlett, correspondent for the Manchester *Guardian*, has discerned in the Premier "an occasional intellectual intolerance that leads him to treat too many people as knaves or fools" (June 3, 1959). Bartlett continued: "I have seldom met a politician, and never another Asian one, who seems so at home discussing world problems with European journalists." Lee plays golf and is called "Harry Lee" by his friends.

References

Guardian (Manchester) p7 Je 3 '59
Reporter 20:27+ My 14 '59
Time 73:34 Je 8 '59 por; 73:36 Je 15 '59 por
Asia Who's Who (1958)

LEMKIN, RAPHAEL June 24, 1901-Aug. 28, 1959 Lawyer; author; taught law at Duke, Yale, Rutgers, and Princeton universities; served on American staff at Nuremberg war crimes tribunal; helped to draft U.N. genocide convention of 1948. See *Current Biography* (May) 1950.

Obituary

N Y Times p82 Ag 30 '59

LENYA, LOTTE Actress; singer

Address: b. c/o Columbia Records, 799 7th Ave., New York 19; h. South Mountain Rd., New City, N.Y.

As the principal exponent of the music of Berlin's pre-Hitler days and particularly of the earlier music of Kurt Weill, Lotte Lenya has earned a unique reputation in the American theater and also in the recording industry. Although she had been a star in Germany in the late 1920's and 1930's, Lenya remained in comparative obscurity in the United States until the death of her husband, Kurt Weill, in 1950.

Because of her desire to acquaint Americans with the early compositions of her late husband, Miss Lenya returned to the stage to take over her original role of Jenny in an off-Broadway production of *The Threepenny Opera* in 1954. She scored a tremendous success in the role and went on to make numerous recordings and concert appearances. Recently Miss Lenya went back to her first love, ballet, when she participated (as a singer-actress) in the New York City Ballet's production of the Kurt Weill-Bertolt Brecht ballet *The Seven Deadly Sins*.

Karoline Blamauer, now known as Lotte Lenya, was born in Hitzing, a working-class quarter of Vienna, Austria. Her mother was a laundress and her father one of Vienna's coachmen. Near the family's home was a small permanent circus, and it was there that the youngster made her first professional appearance as a dancer at the age of six. At eight she had learned to walk the tightrope.

During World War I, Karoline was sent to live with an aunt in Zurich, Switzerland, where she enrolled in the ballet classes of the Stadttheater. Soon she became a member of the *corps de ballet* and also played small parts in pantomimes and operettas. She told Jay S. Harrison of the New York *Herald Tribune* (July 27, 1958): "I played all the important modern authors and the Greeks. Then I went to Berlin with my teacher—as a performer you 'arrived' only if Berlin accepted you." (Berlin during the Weimar Republic was the theatrical capital of Europe, attracting such notables as Erwin Piscator, Max Reinhardt, Alexander Moissi, and Elisabeth Bergner.)

Her first audition was for a children's ballet, *Die Zaubernacht* (The Magic Night), the music for which was composed by Kurt Weill. Although the young actress-dancer was hired, she refused the part because her teacher, who had applied for a post as director, was not given a position. For several years Lotte Lenya appeared in Shakespearean roles and various kinds of acting parts. Leopold Jessner, general manager of the Berlin State Theatre, discovered her playing in a suburb of Berlin and featured her in his production of *Oedipus.*

In the summer of 1925, while Lenya (as she prefers to be called) was visiting her friends, playwright Georg Kaiser and his wife, she met Kurt Weill, a young composer. Weill and Kaiser were collaborating on an opera, *Die Protagonist.* By the end of the summer Kurt Weill and Lotte Lenya had fallen in love and were married in 1926. Lenya told Jay S. Harrison of the New York *Herald Tribune* (July 27, 1958): "We were so poor that he [Kurt Weill] had to rent a tuxedo to appear at the opening of his first big success, *Die Protagonist.*" At about that time Weill met the poet Bertolt Brecht, and the two decided to collaborate on operas and operettas.

The first joint work by Brecht and Weill was *The Little Mahagonny,* a dramatic narrative set to music. Lenya was given the principal singing role, and she and the work created a sensation when it was presented at a Baden-Baden music festival. She introduced what was to become one of her most famous songs, "Alabama Song," which was written by Brecht in his version of Tin Pan Alley English. Lenya was taught the lyrics phonetically.

In 1928 Brecht and Weill finished work on their version of John Gay's *The Beggar's Opera,* entitled *Die Dreigroschenoper* (*The Threepenny Opera*). Lenya was given the important role of Jenny. In an article she wrote for *Theatre Arts* (May 1956), Lenya described the difficulty they had in producing the work and how many friends predicted the operetta would be a resounding failure. However, their friends were wrong, and *The Threepenny Opera* brought acclaim to almost everyone involved. It ran for five years in Berlin and was presented throughout Germany and in the capitals of Europe. John McLain of the New York *Journal-American* (January 6, 1956) stated

LOTTE LENYA

that "Lenya in the role of the calculating, underworld tart, Jenny, skyrocketed to a peak of popular adulation." Her name became a household word throughout Germany.

During the long run of *The Threepenny Opera* Lenya left the show to appear in non-singing dramatic roles, from time to time returning as Jenny. Lotte Lenya appeared as another Jenny in Brecht and Weill's *The Rise and Fall of the City of Mahagonny* in 1930. This controversial opera set off a riot when it was presented in Leipzig, Germany. Some critics have called Lenya's role her greatest triumph in the Berlin theater.

By 1933 the Nazi party had become firmly entrenched in Germany, and Lenya and Kurt Weill, who had been warned that their names appeared on the Gestapo blacklists, fled the country to Paris. There they performed concert versions of Weill's works, and two years later the Weills came to the United States. Lenya appeared with Helen Hayes in *Candle in the Wind* in October 1944 as Cissy, but the play ran for only ninety-five performances. The following year she played the duchess in *The Firebrand of Florence,* for which her husband wrote the score. Handicapped by a feeble libretto, the show closed about a month after its March 1945 première. After this, Lenya decided to forego any further attempts to gain a foothold in the American theater and retired from the stage. She continued to act as her husband's adviser when he wrote the music for such Broadway shows as *Lost in the Stars, Down in the Valley,* and *Street Scene.*

After Kurt Weill's death in 1950, Lenya was persuaded to appear in a concert version of *The Threepenny Opera* at a Kurt Weill memorial concert. Then in October 1951 she played the role of Socrates' wife in Maxwell Anderson's *Barefoot in Athens,* which closed after thirty performances. In 1952 Marc Blitzstein's newly translated version of *The Threepenny Opera*

LENYA, LOTTE—*Continued*

was given in concert form at Brandeis University in Waltham, Massachusetts. Although she had had many offers to produce the latter work, Miss Lenya had turned them down because she felt that everyone wanted to overproduce it. Finally, Lenya accepted Stanley Chase's and Carmen Capalbo's bid, and the show opened in Greenwich Village on March 10, 1954. During its twelve-week off-Broadway run (with Lotte Lenya in her original role of Jenny) the theater was filled to capacity for each performance, but the play had to end its engagement because the theater was booked for another production at the end of the three months.

On September 20, 1955 *The Threepenny Opera* reopened at the Theatre de Lys in Greenwich Village with Lenya again playing the role of Jenny. The show has enjoyed the longest run of any off-Broadway production to date. Walter Kerr commented in the New York *Herald Tribune* (September 21, 1955): "Lotte Lenya makes a visit worth while on her own." The critic for the New York *Times* (September 21, 1955) said: "Miss Lenya is full of strength in this bitter role, bringing to it the vigor and pathos it embodies."

Taking a short leave from the show at the Theatre de Lys, Lenya returned to Germany in December 1955 to attend the openings of two Kurt Weill shows. She sang in *The Threepenny Opera* after she came back, but in April 1956 left the cast permanently. She received a "Tony" award for her performance on April 1, 1956. Since her departure from the show Lenya has busied herself with working on a definitive biography of Kurt Weill upon which she began collaborating with George Davis. She has also made many recordings, among them *The Threepenny Opera* (Theatre de Lys version) on the MGM label and *Lotte Lenya Sings Berlin Theatre Songs of Kurt Weill* (1955), *The Seven Deadly Sins* (1957), and *September Song* (1957) for Columbia Records. In 1958 she recorded *The Threepenny Opera* (complete original German version) and *The Rise and Fall of the City of Mahagonny* (in German) for Columbia.

At New York's Lewisohn Stadium Lotte Lenya participated in a Kurt Weill concert on August 1, 1958. Harold C. Schonberg of the New York *Times* (August 2, 1958) said that "she has a rasping voice that could sandpaper sandpaper, and half the time she does not even attempt to sing. But she can put into a song like 'Pirate Jenny' an intensity that becomes almost terrifying." On February 15, 1959, when she appeared in another memorial tribute to Kurt Weill at Carnegie Hall, she received an ovation from the audience.

As Annie in the Brecht-Weill ballet *The Seven Deadly Sins* Lotte Lenya impressed ballet devotees with her acting ability in the New York City Ballet's production during the 1958-59 season. *Time* magazine (December 29, 1958) said, "Singer Lotte Lenya chanted the English lyrics . . . with the shrugging mock quavers and smoky, wistful quality that she commands as gracefully as ever."

Lotte Lenya was married to Kurt Weill in 1926. A year after his death in 1950, she married George Davis, an editor. Davis died in 1958. Lenya is slender and is five feet two and a half inches tall. She has blue eyes and carrot-blonde hair. She has a home in New City, Rockland County, New York. Of her singing she says: "I am a straight actress, not a songstress."

References

N Y Herald Tribune IV p1 Jl 27 '58 por
N Y Sunday News II p4 Ap 11 '54 por
Newsweek 46:53 D 26 '55
Theatre Arts 4:78+ My '56 pors
Time 72:42 Ag 11 '58 por

L'ESPERANCE, ELISE (DEPEW STRANG) 1879(?)-Jan. 21, 1959 Physician; founder of the Strang Cancer Prevention Clinic and other clinics in New York. See *Current Biography* (November) 1950.

Obituary

N Y Times p31 Ja 22 '59

LEVENSON, SAM(UEL) Dec. 28, 1911- Television performer; lecturer

Address: b. c/o Nat Fields, 730 5th Ave., New York 19; h. 1380 Union St., Brooklyn 13, N.Y.

"Don't call me a comedian—I'm not," insists Sam Levenson, television performer, lecturer, and American humorist. His reminiscences of his boyhood and his comments on the problems of youth and of family life have delighted TV and night club audiences for some ten years. A former teacher in the New York City public schools, Levenson began his own television program early in 1951.

He has been a regular panelist on *This Is Show Business* and *Masquerade Party*. He stirred widespread interest and controversy when he gave a series of talks to parents about children on CBS-TV's morning program, *Arthur Godfrey Time* in February 1959. *The Sam Levenson Show* was chosen to replace this program, beginning in April 1959, when Godfrey became ill. Levenson's show was discontinued in September 1959.

Samuel Levenson was born on December 28, 1911 in New York City (some sources indicate Russia) to Rebecca (Fishelman) and Hyman Levenson. He was the youngest of eight children: seven boys and one girl. His father was a tailor, who made no more than $20 a week. But the children had a wholesome and happy upbringing, thanks in large measure to their mother, whose tolerant yet firm philosophy Sam Levenson has often extolled in telecasts. In his article "A Brooklyn Bedtime Story" (*Collier's*, October 20, 1951) he said: "My earliest memories are of a time when we were living in New York, on East 2nd Street. . . . I was already twelve years old when Papa's pursuit of happiness led up to Brooklyn and a two-family house." At eight

Sam began studying the violin, and music has remained a principal interest throughout his life.

After his graduation from Brooklyn's Franklin K. Lane High School in 1929, Levenson majored in Spanish at Brooklyn College. There he was influenced in the choice of his lifework by the magnetic personality and unorthodox teaching methods of Maír J. Benardete, his instructor in Romance languages, whom he has called the "most inspiring and eccentric teacher I have ever known" (*Coronet,* April 1959). Benardete not only "could make books come alive with Broadway flourishes" but "taught life itself." It was he who first gave Levenson the idea of keeping card files on characters, which were later the source of most of his television monologues.

Beginning his career as a teacher of Spanish, after receiving the B.A. degree in 1934, Levenson was given a permanent appointment at Abraham Lincoln High School in Brooklyn in 1937. In the following year he was reassigned to Brooklyn's Samuel J. Tilden High School and continued there for the next eight years.

Meanwhile, he had undertaken postgraduate work at Columbia University, where he studied with Federico de Onis, and earned the M.A. degree in Romance languages in 1938. His master's thesis was entitled "Ideas on Art, Music, and Literature in the Writings of José Ortega y Gasset." In this period Levenson contributed articles to the Board of Education periodical *High Points* on such subjects as anti-Latin American propaganda and peace education. For *School and Society* (March 15, 1941) he wrote a piece called "J'Accuse," which urged a teachers' crusade against Hollywood's "colossal barrage of mediocrity that sells."

Levenson broke into show business in 1940 when a group of teachers, who had formed an orchestra to perform at a Catskill hotel, took Levenson along as a master of ceremonies. His pay was room and board for his wife and himself. The next summer he received $50 in addition to room and board. During these engagements Levenson learned the art of timing and perfected his own style of delivery. He became an entertainer after school and on weekends.

Gradually depending less on jokes than on such personal recollections as those of his first "trip to the mountains," he began about 1942 to advertise himself as a "folk humorist" willing to entertain at luncheons, teas, fund-raising projects, and organizational functions. Within two years he was overwhelmed by engagements.

By 1946 Levenson had to choose between being a part-time performer or becoming a full-fledged entertainer. Since he had little confidence in his ability as a comedian, he took a five-year leave of absence from the school system, so that if his plans in show business did not materialize, he could return to teaching without losing his status.

Night club bookings followed, and in the spring of 1949 he was seen by Marlo Lewis, co-producer of Ed Sullivan's TV program, *Toast of the Town.* Lewis immediately signed

SAM LEVENSON

him for the show. During the next eighteen months Levenson made four successful appearances on Sullivan's program, and was a guest entertainer on the *Cavalcade of Stars,* the Milton Berle and Rudy Vallee shows, and *This Is Show Business.*

When Jack Benny began his CBS-TV series in October 1950, Levenson was engaged to fill in for a quarter of an hour on each show. He simply talked informally about such situations as sending a child to summer camp and the chaos resulting in a home that risks both a child and a TV set.

"The critics raved," declared Maurice Zolotow (*Saturday Evening Post,* August 23, 1952) and Levenson soon had "his own sponsor, his own thirty-minute program, and his own personal gold mine." This program, *The Sam Levenson Show,* first seen on CBS-TV on January 27, 1951, introduced a new kind of humor to television: a "kids'" show with a sense of humor. With it, he established his reputation as a shrewd observer of the American domestic scene. This program ran until June 10, 1952.

From 1951 to 1954 Levenson was a regular panelist on *This Is Show Business.* In the summer of 1955 he was hired for ten weeks to substitute for the Hoosier humorist Herb Shriner on *Two for the Money.* "What Herb Shriner does about the kid from Indiana I want to do about the city boy," he explained. His efforts for the urban child were so successful that he continued with *Two for the Money* in 1956.

In the next two years Levenson busied himself with night club and lecture commitments, sometimes at meetings of Parent-Teachers' Associations and Rotary Clubs, rather than with television. "I've been offered a [TV] series," he revealed in 1958, "but I've turned it down, mainly because I refuse to play the part of an idiot father who is saved

LEVENSON, SAM—*Continued*

from danger by his kids. I prefer intelligent comedy that gives me an opportunity to say something about the American scene." He also said that it was difficult for a comedian to meet a weekly schedule without tiring the audience (New York *World-Telegram and Sun,* August 6, 1958).

Reviewing one of Levenson's cabaret appearances a *Variety* (October 1, 1958) correspondent observed: "Levenson's family chronicles strike a familiar chord with audiences of any background. Although his family was orbited around Brooklyn and Coney Island, it is pure and delightful Americana, as native to Long Beach, Calif. as Long Beach, N.Y. . . . Far from being deadpan . . . he laughs heartily, infectiously at his own jokes."

During the latter part of 1958 Levenson rejected offers for educational TV programs extended him by NBC and CBS. "Television is being criminally wasted as an aid to education," he told Marie Torre (New York *Herald Tribune,* January 2, 1959), "because nobody is willing to put up a little money and treat education as excitingly, at least, as it treats a box of cereal."

In 1959 Levenson acted as a regular panelist on NBC-TV's *Masquerade Party,* an identity contest, and appeared on *The Ed Sullivan Show.* On *Arthur Godfrey Time,* a daily TV show, he made several telecasts, discussing children and their problems. His views were widely reprinted and provoked an avalanche of letters. Beginning on April 29, 1959 *The Sam Levenson Show* was selected to succeed *Arthur Godfrey Time* when Godfrey underwent treatment for lung cancer.

Sam Levenson takes exception to the theories which advocate the unfettered development of children. He has said: "Kids don't want freedom. They want protection. They want someone to sit down and tell them what they need to be told. . . . The kid who won't listen to anyone is the one who never learned that people who love him are the ones who say 'No' " (*Pageant,* June 1958).

Levenson's book, *Meet the Folks; A Session of American-Jewish Humor,* was published by the Citadel Press in 1948. It is an ingratiating compilation of his original anecdotes and jokes about life in American-Jewish households.

Brooklyn College named Sam Levenson Alumnus of the Year in 1952; four years later he received the Brooklyn College Alumni Association's Outstanding Achievement Award. Levenson, who has donated his services gratis to public and parochial schools and many organizations, is a member of B'nai B'rith and of the congregation of Union Temple of Brooklyn.

Samuel Levenson and Esther Levine were married on December 27, 1936 and have one son, Conrad Lee, and one daughter, Emily Sue. Levenson, who stands at five feet nine inches, weighs around 195 pounds and has brown eyes and brown hair. He mentions music and books as favorite relaxations.

References

Commentary 20:255+ S '55
N Y Times Mag p14+ D 17 '50 pors
N Y World-Telegram Mag p3+ D 7 '57 pors
Allen, S. Funny Men (1956)
Who's Who in America, 1958-59
Who's Who in World Jewry (1955)
Wood, C. TV Personalities vol II (1956)
World Biography (1954)

LEVINE, IRVING R. Aug. 26, 1922- News correspondent; author

Address: b. c/o National Broadcasting Co., 30 Rockefeller Plaza, New York 20

Now covering the Mediterranean area at the Rome bureau of NBC News, Irving R. Levine is well known to a large radio and television audience in the United States for his firsthand reporting of news and backgrounds of current events from countries overseas. He was NBC's correspondent in Moscow from mid-1955 to April 1959, when he went to Rome to replace Joseph Michaels, who in turn was assigned to the Soviet Union. Besides broadcasting regularly and shooting thousands of feet of film for television, while in Russia Levine wrote a popular report on contemporary living there called *Mainstreet, U.S.S.R.* (1959).

Irving R. Levine was born on August 26, 1922 in Pawtucket, Rhode Island. Early interested in news reporting, he worked during his high school years for a local newspaper. Later as a student at Brown University in Providence, he was employed part time on the Providence *Journal* and *Bulletin.* He was elected to Phi Beta Kappa at Brown and was graduated in 1944.

As a lieutenant in the Army Signal Corps during World War II and for a short time afterward, Levine gained experience in motion picture photography by heading a news photo group in Japan and the Philippine Islands. Then in further preparation for a career as a news correspondent he attended Columbia University's Graduate School of Journalism, which granted him the M.Sc. degree in 1947.

International News Service employed Levine in 1947 as a foreign news editor in New York City. The following year he was assigned to Austria to head the INS bureau in Vienna, and during the period from 1948 to 1950 he covered assignments in France, Italy, England, Ireland, Germany, Czechoslovakia, and Bulgaria, as well as Austria. With the outbreak of the Korean war in the summer of 1950, he was sent to the Far East. He accompanied United States paratroopers on airborne invasions of enemy territory to dispatch firsthand reports of battlefield developments and interviewed generals and privates in the service.

Later in 1950 Levine joined the National Broadcasting Company news staff. For more than a year, during part of the Korean fighting and the truce negotiations, he broadcast regularly from Korea and Japan. Awarded a fellowship by the Council on Foreign Relations, he returned to the United States in September

1952 for a year of specialized study at Columbia University. During the next few years he spent some time again in the Far East reporting on events in Hong Kong, Formosa, Indochina, and Thailand and some time in New York as a NBC news reporter contributing to the radio programs *World News Roundup, News of the World,* and *Monitor.*

After waiting two years for a visa to the U.S.S.R., in 1955 Levine sent a radiogram to Moscow addressed to Nikita Khrushchev asking for permission to accompany a group of American agriculturalists on a five-week tour of Soviet farms. Successful in this application, he went to Russia with the delegation in July and before the end of the visit appealed to Khrushchev to be allowed to remain in the Soviet Union as NBC's permanent news correspondent.

Levine was the first American television correspondent to be granted accreditation in the U.S.S.R. and the first radio correspondent since 1948. For some months, before Daniel Schorr was accredited in December 1955 to report from Moscow for the Columbia Broadcasting System, he was the only American correspondent with permanent accreditation in the country. Levine was also the correspondent in Moscow for *Variety* magazine and special correspondent for *The Times* of London.

During nearly four years in the U.S.S.R., Levine traveled in Central Asia, Siberia, and the Ukraine, among other regions, and visited hundreds of cities and farms while making films for the National Broadcasting Company. He was the first American to photograph for television the Volga-Don Canal and the inside of a Soviet factory. His feature films shown on NBC-TV include *Look at Russia* and *Religion in Russia.* He has also prepared film and commentaries for programs like *NBC News—the Huntley Brinkley Report.* In March 1957 he appeared on *Today* with films and records showing the impact of jazz on the Russian people.

For radio, Levine launched in September 1955 a ten-minute regular series program, *This is Moscow,* and in June 1958 he gave three "Primer on Russia" broadcasts, discussing wages in the Soviet Union, culture, progress in satellite research, and other topics. He also contributed to *World News Roundup,* transmitted spot news stories for various programs, and answered questions about Russia sent in by listeners for a section of the weekend program, *Monitor.*

One of Levine's "firsts" in Russia was achieved in April 1956 when he became the first American correspondent to receive replies from Premier Nikolai A. Bulganin to a list of questions submitted in writing. Some of the questions concerned the forthcoming trip, in May, of Bulganin and Khrushchev to Great Britain. Levine accompanied the Soviet leaders on this visit and also on their visit to Finland in June 1957.

Since Levine's broadcasts from Moscow were censored, he experienced occasional difficulties with the Soviet authorities. In December 1958 he was notified that he would be barred temporarily from radio broadcasting because of alleged censorship violations. He was, however,

IRVING R. LEVINE

permitted to use cable and telephone facilities to transmit news. One specific charge was that Levine had tried to circumvent censorship rules on December 2 by not submitting to the censor his script on his interview with visiting United States Senator Hubert Humphrey. The ban against Levine was, however, lifted before his departure from Moscow in the spring of 1959 when he was transferred to Rome as NBC's Mediterranean newsman.

Main Street, U.S.S.R. (Doubleday, 1959) had its origin in the questions that Levine's American audiences asked him about the Soviet Union, covering a large variety of subjects from matters of everyday life to details about the structure of the Soviet government and the Communist party. Both anecdotal and factual, Levine's book is based mainly on his personal observations and his examination of contemporary Russian publications. Each of the twenty-six chapters discusses an important aspect of Russian society such as education, housing, medicine, transportation, and entertainment. Levine has also contributed to *This Week, Collier's,* and other magazines. Recent articles include "I Settled My Bride in Moscow" (*Saturday Evening Post,* February 7, 1959), "The 10 Most Influential Women in Russia" (*Ladies' Home Journal,* April 1959), and "A View of Soviet Libraries" (*Saturday Review,* April 11, 1959).

The National Junior Chamber of Commerce selected Levine as one of the Ten Most Outstanding Young Men in America for 1956. Other awards that he has received include the 1957 Headliners Award, the 1957 Overseas Press Club honor for the best radio and television reporting from abroad, and the 1959 Columbia Journalism Alumni Award for distinguished service to journalism.

When Irving R. Levine was interviewed in New York on Dave Garroway's *Today* show,

LEVINE, IRVING R.—*Continued*

he met Garroway's secretary, Nancy Cartmell Jones, whom he married in July 1957. Levine is five feet eleven and a half inches tall and weighs 160 pounds. His hobbies, appropriately, are photography and stamp collecting.

Reference

N Y Times II p11 Mr 10 '57 por

LINDT, AUGUSTE R(UDOLPHE) Aug. 5, 1905- U.N. official; Swiss diplomat

Address: b. Office of the High Commissioner for Refugees, Palais de Nations, Geneva, Switzerland; h. 86 route de Florissant, Geneva, Switzerland

The World Refugee Year, 1959-60, a project of the United Nations to focus world attention on the plight of refugees and to encourage governments to permit their resettlement, is being guided in part by Auguste R. Lindt. The General Assembly elected Lindt by acclamation in 1956 and re-elected him in 1958 as High Commissioner for Refugees to succeed the late Dr. G. J. van Heuven Goedhart. In this post Lindt extends assistance and protection to some 1,500,000 persons in various parts of the world, including those who fled from Hungarian Communism. Before filling his present post, Dr. Lindt, a Swiss citizen, served as a foreign correspondent, army information officer, diplomat, and Swiss Permanent Observer to the U.N.

The son of Auguste and Lina (Rüfenacht) Lindt, Auguste Rudolphe Lindt was born on August 5, 1905 in Bern, Switzerland. He studied law at the University of Geneva in 1924-25 and then continued his education at the University of Bern, where he received the LL.D. degree in 1927. Instead of entering the field of

United Nations

AUGUSTE R. LINDT

law, he turned to journalism and became a contributor to leading Swiss and German newspapers. In 1932, as a foreign correspondent, he began the first of a series of trips to cover the crises that led up to World War II, in such places as Manchuria, Liberia, Finland, Palestine, Romania, the Persian Gulf area, Tunisia, and Jordan. Later, he was assigned to London.

During his *Wanderjahre,* Lindt contributed hundreds of articles to newspapers, and somehow found time to write a book. Called *Special Correspondent; With Bandit and General in Manchuria,* it was published in England by Cobden-Sanderson in 1933 and in Germany by F. A. Brockhaus in 1934. The book, which was dedicated to "Dsheilali—companion of future adventures," reports on Manchuria during the Sino-Japanese War, and tells of Lindt's frequent brushes with danger. In Manchuria he was once mistaken for a secret agent, and, on another and prophetic occasion, for a member of the commission of inquiry of the League of Nations, which investigated Japanese aggression in the region.

During World War II, Switzerland maintained a state of armed neutrality. To help his nation carry out its policies, Lindt joined the Swiss army in 1940 and put his journalistic talents to work as the head of the army information section. The five years that Dr. Lindt spent in military service marked his transition from newspaper work to diplomacy.

Demobilized in 1945, Lindt was sent by the Swiss government on a special political mission to London. In the autumn he was appointed to the International Committee of the Red Cross. His first diplomatic assignment came at the end of 1946 when he was made press attaché at the Swiss Legation in London. Three years later he was promoted to the post of counselor and held this post until 1953.

Meanwhile, Lindt was gradually becoming more concerned with activities of the U.N. As early as 1948 he had been elected to the program committee of the U.N. International Children's Emergency Fund (UNICEF). In 1953 he also assumed the posts of chairman of the executive board of UNICEF (officially renamed U.N. Children's Fund in that year), president of the opium conference, and Permanent Observer of Switzerland to the U.N. (Switzerland has not joined the U.N. because membership would be incompatible with its neutral position.)

The Swiss government in 1955 bestowed on Dr. Lindt the rank of a Minister Plenipotentiary. In the following year he headed the Swiss delegation to the United States for the Conference on the Statute of the International Atomic Energy Agency. This agency was established July 29, 1957 to promote the peaceful uses of atomic energy.

On December 10, 1956 the General Assembly elected Dr. Lindt by acclamation as U.N. High Commissioner for Refugees. When he was re-elected in November 1958, he said that he would serve only for another two years. Successor to the U.N. International Refugee Organization, the Office of the High Commissioner for Refugees was created by the U.N. by the resolution of December 14, 1950. It provides legal and political protection for the many displaced and homeless persons uprooted by Nazism, persecution, and the devastation of wars.

By statute, the U.N. defines a refugee as "any person outside his country of nationality, or, if he has no nationality, the country of his habitual residence, because he has or had fear of persecution for reason of race, religion, nationality, or political opinion, and is unable, or because of such fear, is unwilling to avail himself of the country of his nationality or to return to the country of his former habitual residence." A refugee remains under the protection of the Office of the High Commissioner until he becomes a naturalized citizen where he has permanently resettled or voluntarily returns to his country of origin.

In 1954 the General Assembly and the Economic and Social Council made the Office of the High Commissioner for Refugees responsible for a four-year plan to assist refugees in making permanent adjustments and to obtain funds. Because it has aided 2,000,000 people in the first four years of its existence, the High Commissioner's office received the Nobel Peace Prize of 1954; the sum of $35,066 accompanying the award was used to resettle refugees in Tinos Camp, Greece and to close that camp.

The Office of the High Commissioner for Refugees is scheduled to operate until January 1, 1964. It should be distinguished from the U.N. Relief and Works Agency for Palestine Refugees in the Near East, which administers relief to Arab refugees who fled their homes when the state of Israel was created in 1948.

Within a few days after his appointment, Dr. Lindt left for Austria to visit the camps set up to receive the refugees who left Hungary during the revolt that began in October 1956. In Vienna Lindt discussed with Vice-President Richard M. Nixon the problem of resettling these escapees. By March 1957 over 120,000 Hungarian refugees had been placed in permanent homes in twenty-nine nations; by November 1957 88 per cent of the Hungarians who managed to escape during the political upheaval had found new places to live.

In recent years, the Office of the High Commissioner has been centering its efforts on refugees quartered in Austria and Germany. From 1955 to July 1958 $5,500,000 of the approximate total of $15,000,000 were allotted to refugees in these countries. About sixteen refugee camps on the Continent have been evacuated, and one of Dr. Lindt's immediate goals is to empty the remainder at the earliest possible date. The most urgent tasks facing Lindt's staff in 1959 were to assist refugees in Greece, homeless Europeans on the mainland of China and Hong Kong, Algerians in Morocco and Tunisia, and displaced handicapped persons living outside camps in Europe.

Dr. Lindt and his staff have the responsibility of assisting in the celebration of World Refugee Year, which began on June 30, 1959. This world-wide information program encourages larger financial contributions, increased immigration quotas, and extension of the office's protective activities. The High Commissioner especially wants to reach "permanent refugee solutions, through voluntary repatriations, resettlement or integration, on a purely humanitarian basis and in accordance with the freely expressed wishes of the refugees themselves" (*United Nations Review,* March 1959). For leading the World Refugee Year the American Association for the United Nations honored Lindt with its 1959 award.

The determined and energetic Auguste R. Lindt is five feet eleven inches tall and weighs about 185 pounds. He has light brown hair and a ruddy complexion. Although he likes camping in the Swiss Alps more than any other form of recreation, he also enjoys sailing, gardening, and collecting pipes. He is extremely fond of dogs.

Lindt's clubs are the Society of Swiss Writers and the Royal Central Asian Society. He is the father of two daughters, Caroline, his official hostess, and Gillian (Mrs. Albert Edwin Gollin), and a son, Michael. When Lindt was re-elected High Commissioner, the New York *Times* (November 16, 1958) took notice of the fact that "even the stubborn nine votes of the Iron Curtain countries were not recorded against this good and humane man."

References

N Y Herald Tribune II p2 D 16 '56 por
International Year Book and Statesmen's Who's Who, 1959
Who's Who, 1959
Who's Who in America, 1958-59
Who's Who in the United Nations (1951)

LIPSKY ELEAZAR (lĭp'skĭ ĕl"ē-ā'zĕr) Sept. 6, 1911- Author; lawyer

Address: b. 292 Madison Ave., New York 17; h. 607 West End Ave., New York 24

Reprinted from the *Wilson Library Bulletin* Sept. 1959.

"A high-minded novelist in whom glows that passion for justice which lawyers without exception acquire along with the diploma entitling them to toy with torts and writs," was John K. Hutchens' characterization of Eleazar Lipsky when he reviewed his novel *The Scientists* (1959), a selection of the Book-of-the-Month Club, in his weekday book department in the New York *Herald Tribune*. "In Mr. Lipsky, a graduate of Columbia Law School and District Attorney Frank Hogan's office, it must gleam with a special luster, since he continues to be a practicing attorney even while collecting his considerable royalties as a successful author."

Eleazar Lipsky was born in New York City on September 6, 1911. His parents are Louis Lipsky and Charlotte (Schacht) Lipsky. Louis Lipsky founded the American Zionist movement in this country and wrote plays and essays. Eleazar had two brothers: David, a publicist, and Joel, a linguist and translator.

After graduation in 1928 from James Monroe High School in the Bronx, where he won an oratorical medal, young Lipsky entered Columbia College on a state scholarship and won an-

ELEAZAR LIPSKY

other medal, the Curtis, for oratory, as a member of the debating team. He was also a member of the Columbia Laboratory Players, Philolexian, and Beta Sigma Rho, contributed to the Columbia *Spectator* and *Morningside* (the literary publication), and found time to write a syndicated newspaper column.

Lipsky received his B.A. degree in 1932 and an LL.B. degree from Columbia Law School two years later, when he became a member (later a partner) of the law firm of Daru, Hellman, and Winters. An interlude followed, 1938-39, as editor of *The New Palestine,* a political journal devoted to the Near East, and field representative for the United Palestine Appeal and the United Jewish Appeal "during the darkening crisis in Europe." Interested, like his father, in the Zionist movement, he spent much time and energy as speaker and writer for the movement and was president of Masada, the Youth Zionist Organization of America, later discontinued. Resuming the practice of law, he became an assistant district attorney for New York County under Frank S. Hogan, working most actively in the homicide bureau.

In this "empty cavernous office" then recently vacated by Thomas E. Dewey, he found material for his book *Lincoln McKeever.* Back in private practice (1946), he was asked to speak before the Mystery Writers of America (he later became that society's legal counsel). His subject was the legal absurdities in certain current motion pictures. Under the influence of Liam O'Flaherty's *The Informer,* Lipsky had written about 100 pages on the life of a stool pigeon, and these he turned over to an MWA member who happened to be an employee of Twentieth Century-Fox Film Corporation.

He sent them to the West Coast, where they were placed on the desk of Darryl Zanuck, who bought the scenario almost at once. As *The Kiss of Death* the film featured Victor Mature,

and brought Richard Widmark attention as the laughing hyena who pushed an old lady in a wheel chair down a flight of stairs to her death. It was published by Penguin Books as a novel in 1947 and followed by *Murder One* (Doubleday, 1948) about a homicide by an alleged prostitute, which was a selection of the now defunct Unicorn Book Club.

The People Against O'Hara (Doubleday, 1950), a choice of the Mystery Guild, is described by the author as a story about "an honest man forced by circumstances and desperation to commit an illegal act to save his client's life." The New York *Herald Tribune Book Review* stated that "once again [the author] recreates factually and convincingly the squalor of the underworld, the impersonality of the law courts, and the general mixture of cynicism and humanity which make up New York's world of crime." Metro-Goldwyn-Mayer made a movie of it, with Spencer Tracy, Pat O'Brien, and the late John Hodiak as stars.

Lipsky began his next novel as a thirty-page screen original, but found himself "in the anguish of creating a major novel"—*Lincoln McKeever* (Appleton), a selection of the Literary Guild for December 1953. The author had traveled through the Southwest on a speaking tour, covering the length of the Rio Grande Valley and noting the clash of civilizations from Brownsville to Tijuana. All the legal facts about the murder of Judge Douglas Hanna, the illicit extradition of Don Carlos from Mexico, and the trial were based upon the record. Critic Paul Engle (Chicago *Sunday Tribune*) called it "a diverting and in many instances consuming story"; W. R. Burnett (*Saturday Review*) praised the scenes of suspense and violence, but thought that Lipsky "handles women as if they were so many hot potatoes."

Four years of writing, in evenings, on weekends, and during summers at Fire Island, New York went into the writing of *The Scientists* (Appleton, 1959) a novel about the controversy which developed in an imaginary university over the discovery of a profitable drug known as biocin. Orville Prescott (New York *Times*) considered the novel "readable and adequately entertaining. It achieves a high level of competence." But, he concluded, "it lacks any quality or distinction that can make it stick in the memory or touch the emotions."

Lipsky, once seen, is not soon forgotten. As Gerold Frank (*Book-of-the-Month Club News*) has said, he "bears a striking resemblance to George Sanders, the actor. He has a handsome face, brown hair, penetrating gray eyes under black brows, and the eloquence you might expect." Lipsky married, Hannah Kohn, a social worker, on July 5, 1935, and they have three sons, Michael, Jonathan, and David.

References

Book-of-the-Month Club N p4 Ja '59 por
N Y Herald Tribune p19 Ja 26 '59
N Y Herald Tribune Bk R p2 Ja 10 '54 por
Martindale-Hubbell Law Directory, 1952
Who's Who in America (sup Ap '54)

LITCHFIELD, P(AUL) W(EEKS) July 26, 1875-Mar. 18, 1959 Industrialist; former chairman of the board and chief executive officer of the Goodyear Tire and Rubber Company. See *Current Biography* (December) 1950.

Obituary

N Y Times p31 Mr 20 '59

LIVINGSTON, JOHN W(ILLIAM) Aug. 17, 1908- Labor leader

Address: b. American Federation of Labor and Congress of Industrial Organizations, 815 16th St., N.W., Washington, D.C.; h. 5772 Guildord Ave., Washington, D.C.

As the director of the organization department of the merged labor group, the American Federation of Labor and the Congress of Industrial Organizations, John W. Livingston has been responsible since 1955 for increasing the federation's membership to 13,100,000, for helping the many member unions in their efforts, and for supervising the organization's twenty-two regions and their staffs. He had served as vice-president of the international union of the United Auto Workers-CIO since 1947 and became director of the UAW-CIO General Motors department in 1952. Known as a negotiator as well as an organizer, Livingston participated in virtually all UAW contract negotiations with the General Motors Corporation from 1942 to 1955.

John William Livingston, the son of Richard Monroe and Mary Alice (Burks) Livingston, was born in Iberia, Missouri, on August 17, 1908. His father farmed the land there in the foothills of the Ozarks. Livingston grew up in the area and attended high school at Iberia Academy for two years. In December 1927 he was employed by the Fisher Body Division of the General Motors Corporation in St. Louis, Missouri, where he worked in the trim department.

Beginning his union activity in June 1933, Livingston was one of the moving spirits behind a secret meeting of Fisher workers summoned to talk over the various techniques of organizing a union to fight speed-up, low wages, and favoritism. This meeting brought about the establishment of the AFL Federal Local No. 18386, which later became Local 25 of the UAW-CIO. He was elected president of the local in 1934 and played an important role in a strike which took place in the Fisher Body and Chevrolet plants in 1934.

For a brief period Livingston was out of office, but he then returned as president of the local and chairman of the strike committee during successful strikes for recognition against the General Motors Corporation in 1936 and 1937. He continued as president until April 1939, when he became employed as a UAW-CIO international representative in the General Motors department. After three years in this post—during which time he served successively as vice-chairman and chairman of the national UAW-GM negotiating committee—Livingston was elected during the 1942 UAW-CIO convention in Chicago as the di-

Chase Photo

JOHN W. LIVINGSTON

rector of UAW-CIO region 5 and a member of the international executive board.

Region 5 was composed of eight states: Missouri, Kansas, Texas, Colorado, Louisiana, Oklahoma, Arkansas, and New Mexico. During the first eighteen months of Livingston's directorship, the UAW-CIO membership in this region was increased thirteen-fold. He was active in many other organization campaigns, including the one at the Caterpillar Tractor Plant in Peoria, Illinois in 1948. In 1946 he was made co-director, with UAW-CIO President Walter P. Reuther, of the union's General Motors department. In 1952 Livingston assumed sole responsibility for this post.

Meanwhile, at the Atlantic City convention in 1947, Livingston was first elected as one of the two international union UAW-CIO vice-presidents; he also became director of the UAW-CIO aircraft, airline, McQuay-Norris, and piston ring departments. Late in 1948 he became director of the agricultural implement department of the UAW-CIO and participated in the campaign to bring all farm implement workers in the UAW-CIO ranks. He co-ordinated the UAW-Political Action Committee campaign drive for the 1948 national Presidential election.

Beginning in May 1951, Livingston served for a year on the National Wage Stabilization Board in Washington. He played an important part in establishing a policy free from most of the limitations of its World War II counterpart—the War Labor Board. After Livingston was named director of the UAW-CIO national General Motors department in April 1952, he resigned from his government post and later from the directorship of the national agricultural implement department. For three years, however, he kept the directorship of the national aircraft department.

Over the years Livingston has had a great deal of negotiating experience. He was the

LIVINGSTON, JOHN W.—*Continued*

chief international officer assigned in 1948 to the General Motors wage and contract negotiations, in which the annual wage improvement and cost-of-living escalation were introduced into the contract. He took part in the 1950 talks between the UAW and General Motors Corporation, which resulted in an unprecedented five-year agreement later used as the model for agreements in many other industries. He presided over the UAW's bargaining team during the 1955 General Motors negotiations. They led to the establishment there for the first time of a full union shop and to the victory of the principle of guaranteeing wages to laid-off industrial workers.

Contracts have been secured in the aircraft industry which have almost abolished "merit systems" and have substituted systems of automatic wage progression. Once opposed to sound union security provisions, the aircraft industry now provides union shop provisions in most UAW contracts. During recent years long strikes have characterized major wage negotiations in the aircraft and agricultural implement industries, but usually these strikes have been used as a basis to establish wage and contract patterns in those industries.

During the summer of 1950 Livingston was chairman of a twelve-man UAW-CIO delegation which visited England, France, Italy, and West Germany, and was the guest of the British Amalgamated Engineering Union. In Paris, he presided over the first conference of the automotive and truck department of the International Metalworkers Federation. He conferred with many European trade union officials and with representatives of the Economic Cooperation Administration in an effort to contribute toward the building of trade unions capable of benefiting European workers and remaining free from Communist domination. On his return to America, he laid before the ECA, which had sponsored the European tour, a program for implementing the Marshall Plan so that it would benefit people from all economic levels.

At the first constitutional convention of the American Federation of Labor and Congress of Industrial Organizations in December 1955, Livingston was appointed the director of organization of the merged labor movement. In this position he has the responsibility for launching the biggest organizing drive in American labor history with the objective of bringing into the ranks of organized labor those workers who are not yet unionized.

The merged federation hopes to enlist 26,000,000 more members, and Livingston is concentrating his attention on unorganized workers in the chemical, oil, textile, paper, wood, furniture, shoe, and leather industries, and white-collar workers. Some observers have seen three obstacles in the way to this goal: the intractability of the unorganized labor force (particularly the white-collar workers), the advancing years and diminished spirit of the organizing staffs, and the conflicting jurisdictional claims of rival unions. Over the last three years, from 1955 to 1958, the AFL-CIO unions have organized 1,000,000 nonunion workers, but the recession and automation have more than offset the gain.

John William Livingston married Rubye Britt on May 9, 1931. He is known to his friends as Jack. In his leisure hours he enjoys hunting and fishing. *Business Week* (November 19, 1955) noted that he has "a jovial, likable personality; he is scrupulously honest and fair. His staff members swear by him." Most observers agree that he is a determined negotiator, who has thoroughly mastered trade union principles.

References

Bsns W p170+ N 19 '55 por
Fortune 52:57+ D '55 por
Who's Who in America, 1958-59
Who's Who in Labor (1946)

LÓPEZ MATEOS, ADOLFO (lō'päs mä-tä'ōs) May 26, 1910- President of Mexico

Address: Palacio Presidencial, Mexico City, D.F., Mexico

The responsibility of leading the impressive industrial and social revolution taking place in Mexico has been given to Adolfo López Mateos. He was elected to a six-year term as President on July 6, 1958, as successor to Adolfo Ruiz Cortines. To this office López Mateos brings his varied experience as politician, Senator, Minister of Labor, lawyer, scholar, and educator. A one-time Socialist, he is now the head of Mexico's dominant political organization, the Party of Revolutionary Institutions, and advocates further industrialization of the country by government, domestic companies, and foreign investors.

The youngest of the five children of Dr. Mariano López and Elena López de Mateos, Adolfo López Mateos was born on May 26, 1910 in Atizapán de Zaragoza, near Mexico City, Mexico. His father, an orthodontist, died before he was a year old. His mother was descended from Francisco Zarco Mateos, a writer and Foreign Minister and chief of cabinet under President Benito Pablo Juárez; José Perfecto Mateos, a hero in the struggle against the French intervention; and Juan A. Mateos, a novelist.

After pursuing his elementary studies in Mexico City, López Mateos received his secondary education at the Scientific and Literary Institute of Toluca. To earn his expenses, he worked as a librarian, acquiring what he calls the "vice" of reading and becoming familiar with Spanish, French, English, and American literature. While at Toluca he sometimes walked forty miles over mountains to visit his mother and later hiked 850 miles to Guatemala in forty-six days. He also boxed and played soccer.

At the National Autonomous University of Mexico in Mexico City, López Mateos won first prize in an oratorical contest and became a student leader in the unsuccessful movement to elect the educator José Vasconcelos as President of Mexico. He received the B.A. degree from the university. Later, he served as secretary to Filiberto Gómez, Governor of the state of Mexico, whose niece he married. In 1931 he became secretary to Carlos Riva Palacio, head of the National Revolutionary party, a precursor of the Party of Revolutionary Institutions (P.R.I.). In the evenings López Mateos studied law at the National Autonomous University.

Earning his law degree in 1934, he worked briefly in the District Attorney's office in Toluca. He also became auditor of the Workers' National Development Bank. In federal government service he was chairman of the editorial commission of the Ministry of Education and then assistant director of the Department of Fine Arts. In the latter post, López Mateos promoted symphony concerts and ballet productions at Mexico City's Palace of Fine Arts.

At the Scientific and Literary Institute of Toluca he taught Spanish-American literature and world history and later became its director. He was one of the founders of the School of Economics at the National Autonomous University. López Mateos was also secretary general of the National Union of Educational Workers.

During the 1946 general elections, he was one of the chief campaign speakers for the P.R.I. standard-bearer, Miguel Alemán, who won at the polls in July. At that time López Mateos was elected to a six-year term as a federal Senator for the state of Mexico. Shortly thereafter he was appointed secretary general of the P.R.I. and chairman of the Senate Foreign Relations Committee. As chairman he headed in 1951 the Mexican delegation to the United Nations Economic and Social Council meeting at Geneva, Switzerland. In 1951 he also had a hand in writing the United States-Mexican migrant labor treaty.

In the Presidential election year of 1952, López Mateos represented his party on the Federal Election Commission and managed the campaign of the P.R.I. candidate, Adolfo Ruiz Cortines. After he was elected and installed in office, President Ruiz Cortines appointed López Mateos as Minister of Labor and Social Welfare. "His ability as a conciliator," Marion Wilhelm observed (*Christian Science Monitor*, November 11, 1957), "soon became apparent after the 1954 peso devaluation when the United Labor Bloc, worried about the price squeeze, threatened to call a general strike. With tact and skill, he resolved the crisis through a round of moderate wage increases. . . . He favors what he calls a 'modern concept' of productivity based on national cooperation for a just distribution of income, arguing that the worker should be strong enough to bargain freely and that employers should be enlightened." Of the 13,382 labor disputes which the department handled during his ministerial career, only thirteen developed into strikes. While in this post, López Mateos co-operated with the United States technical assistance program.

Having been groomed for the presidency by Ruiz Cortines and endorsed by former Presidents Alemán and Lázaro Cárdenas, López

Wide World

ADOLFO LÓPEZ MATEOS

Mateos was nominated by acclamation at the P.R.I. convention in November 1957. He then resigned as Minister of Labor to campaign and won the support of employers' groups, the Confederation of Mexican Workers, and the National Confederation of Peasants.

Since the P.R.I. or its predecessors have controlled the Presidency for five decades and at this time held 150 of 162 seats in the lower chamber of the federal legislature as well as the entire Senate, it was a foregone conclusion that López Mateos would be elected. In his speech accepting the nomination, he said that "our fundamental economic objective is industrialization" (New York *Times*, November 18, 1957). He called for expansion of the nationalized oil industry through domestic investment and discussed the need for collaboration by private interests and the state. "We shall always keep our doors open to foreign capital as long as it obeys the laws," he said (quoted by Daniel James, New York *Times Magazine*, June 8, 1958).

While campaigning, López Mateos advocated the nationalization of electric resources in southern Mexico and the building of highways, irrigation systems, and other public works. He supported the harnessing of the Grijalva and Usumacinta rivers. Together they discharge enough water to double Mexico's present 2,000,000 kilowatts of energy and her current agricultural production. Experts believe that if the area between the rivers were developed it would become a great agricultural-industrial complex, partly because the region contains large deposits of vital minerals.

On July 6, 1958 the P.R.I. candidate received about 85 per cent of the ballots. This was the first Presidential election in which women were eligible to vote. The President-elect met with United States Senator Lyndon B. Johnson of Texas in November to discuss

LÓPEZ MATEOS, ADOLFO—*Continued*

the possibility of eliminating some trade barriers between their two countries and increasing capital investment in Mexico by the United States government and private American businesses.

Installed as President on December 1, 1958, López Mateos stressed in his inaugural address the need for increased educational facilities, as well as achieving "abundance" for all. "Liberty is fruitful only when it is accompanied by order," he remarked (New York *Times*, December 2, 1958).

These words were interpreted as a warning to the leaders of a series of strikes which had plagued Mexico steadily since February 1958 and had culminated in serious rioting in August. Some observers believed that these strikes were led by dissident labor leaders and in some instances were Communist inspired and were in part motivated by the wish to impress the incoming President with labor's strength.

Confronting the President is the problem of inflation: the increasing costs and ever-growing number of government services, an empty treasury, and the menacing spiral of prices.

Adolfo López Mateos and Eva Zamano were married in 1937 and have one daughter, who is named after her mother. A former schoolteacher, Doña Eva is "deeply interested in social work" and as first lady of Mexico "is expected to devote much time to the problem of infant malnutrition" (Daniel James, New York *Times Magazine*, June 8, 1958).

The President is five feet ten inches in height, about 170 pounds in weight, has wavy black hair and black eyes. He is an inspiring and effective orator. For hobbies he collects classical records, paintings by contemporary Mexican artists, and Spanish, French, and English books. He also enjoys watching boxing matches and playing canasta. "I was raised in a Roman Catholic background," he has said, "but I practise no religion" (*Time*, December 8, 1958).

References

Christian Sci Mon p12 Jl 21 '58
N Y Herald Tribune p6,14 Jl 9 '58; p5 D 2 '58 por
N Y Times p20 D 2 '58 por
N Y World-Telegram p5 Je 14 '58
Washington (D.C.) Post p21A Jl 10 '58
International Who's Who, 1958

LOREN, SOPHIA Sept. 20, 1934- Actress

Address: Paramount Pictures, Hollywood, Calif.

When she was awarded an acting trophy at the Venice Film Festival in September 1958, Sophia Loren was secure in a niche longed for by every foreign movie actress who ever looked toward Hollywood. As a star, Miss Loren was playing opposite America's most popular movie idols, had earned more than a million dollars from her Hollywood films, and was beginning to win serious attention for her acting ability.

Wealth and popularity have lent a fairy tale touch to Miss Loren's life. Her childhood was spent in a Naples industrial suburb, surrounded by poverty and war; she began her climb to stardom by winning a beauty contest prize when she was fifteen. After several years as an extra and a model in Rome, she was signed for the female lead in an Italian documentary film, and made more than twenty movies before starring in her first American production in 1956.

Sophia Loren was born in Rome on September 20, 1934, the daughter of Ricardo Scicolone and Romilda Villani. Her parents never married, although Scicolone later granted Sophia and her younger sister, Maria, the legal right to use his surname. Not long after Sophia's birth, the mother moved to Pozzuoli, an industrial town near Naples where the family lived with Sophia's maternal grandparents. The child was educated in a Catholic parochial school there.

Today, Miss Loren recalls her childhood in Pozzuoli as an Ugly Duckling story. She claims that the schoolgirl Sophia Scicolone was plain and thin enough to earn the nickname of *stecchetto* ("the stick"). Already poor, the family lived even more meagerly when the ports and factories of Naples made the area a military target for Allied bombs in World War II.

"A scarecrow of a girl buried in poverty," is the way Miss Loren describes herself (*American Weekly*, September 28, 1958) at the age of twelve, when she enrolled in the local Teachers' Institute. She trained for teaching for the next three years. By that time she had developed the physical attributes that were to make her famous. "It became a pleasure to saunter down the street," she recalls.

Equipped with these attributes and a dress made from pink window curtains, she entered a Naples beauty contest for "Queen of the Sea" in 1949 at the insistence of her mother. She won second place in the contest. Shortly after, she left school in the hope of becoming a film star, and went with her mother to Rome.

The mother and daughter worked as extras in the movie *Quo Vadis* for a combined income of $33. They found few other acting jobs, however, and Sophia went to work as a model for Italy's popular *fumetti*—magazines in which models act out a melodrama in a sequence of still photographs. Sophia alternated this work with occasional small movie roles for the next two and one-half years. Her "break" came when she met Carlo Ponti, the Italian movie producer who was later to become her husband.

Carlo Ponti helped the girl to lose her Neapolitan dialect, enroll for acting lessons, and obtain her first starring role. The film was *Africa Under the Sea*, a semidocumentary underwater movie. It was in this production that she adopted the name of Loren. Even before the movie was released, she found herself in demand for other roles, among them the female lead in *Aïda*. Although the singing voice was provided by somebody else, Miss Loren achieved recognition of a kind for her role as the Ethiopian slave girl. Little of it, however, was reserved for her acting ability.

In the next three years Sophia Loren made more than twenty films, often working on three different movies at the same time. Her most common role was that of a young working girl or a wife faced with a problem. Enough of these films were exported to make Sophia familiar to moviegoers all over Europe. She achieved her first real renown in 1955, a year which Italian publicity men christened "The Year of Sophia."

By 1955 Miss Loren had become enough of a celebrity to be presented to Queen Elizabeth II, and to make her first appearance on the cover of an American magazine (*Life*, August 22, 1955). Her climb to fame paralleled that of other foreign-born actresses and gave a new topic of debate to the American press: European charms as opposed to native ones.

Vittorio de Sica, director and producer of *The Bicycle Thief*, contributed to Miss Loren's international reputation when he engaged her for several films. Her last Italian movie was *The Luck of Being a Woman*, in which she starred with Charles Boyer. She was also signed in 1955 for the female lead in Stanley Kramer's *The Pride and the Passion*. Miss Loren knew almost no English when she was hired for the part. What she did not learn before filming began in Spain the following year was supplied to her by phonetic cue cards, with the English words rendered in Italian spelling.

The Pride and the Passion, with Cary Grant and Frank Sinatra, was the first of four movies Miss Loren made for American studios for an estimated $800,000. *Boy on a Dolphin* with Alan Ladd, *Legend of the Lost* with John Wayne, and *The Key* with William Holden were also filmed in Europe.

In 1957 Miss Loren arrived in Hollywood amid a tumult of publicity. Since then she has starred in *Desire Under the Elms, Houseboat* (the first of seven movies she is making for Paramount studios under a $2,000,000 contract), *The Black Orchid*, and *That Kind of Woman*.

The film version of O'Neill's *Desire Under the Elms* was the first movie to win serious critical attention for Miss Loren. "An honest, pulsing picture," wrote Bosley Crowther of her performance (New York *Times*, March 16, 1958). Delbert Mann, her director, remarked that "she has had little or no formal training in acting, but her instinct is faultless" (New York *Times*, February 16, 1958).

With Miss Loren when she came to Hollywood was Carlo Ponti, who had guided her success ever since her first movie. They were married by a proxy ceremony in Mexico on September 17, 1957. The couple spend much of their free time in Switzerland.

Many writers have tried to appraise Miss Loren's attractions. "She is a tall, strong, big-framed, wide-hipped healthy girl of distinctively European style," wrote John Reese in the *Saturday Evening Post* (October 20, 1956). "Her face, with its wide, high forehead, high cheekbones, and slanted almond

Columbia Pictures Corp

SOPHIA LOREN

eyes, is striking rather than pretty." A *Vogue* writer (September 15, 1958) was content to remark that "after Loren, bones are boring." She is five feet eight inches tall and weighs 134 pounds.

Now that she has achieved stardom, Sophia Loren would like to concentrate on becoming an actress. Winning an acting trophy at the Venice Film Festival of 1958 for her performance in *The Black Orchid* was perhaps her first step toward achieving this ambition. "The seven-man international jury of critics and directors," wrote Robert Hawkins in the New York *Times* (September 14, 1958), "was saluting a tour de force accomplishment by an actress who only recently was known mainly for her physique."

References

Am W p8+ S 28 '58; p14+ O 5 '58
  pors
Cosmop 144:76+ F '58 por
Life 42:137+ My 6 '57 por
Newsweek 46:53+ Ag 15 '55 por
Sat Eve Post 229:24+ O 20 '56 por
This Week p10+ N 9 '58 por
Chi è? (1957)

LORGE, IRVING (DANIEL) Apr. 19, 1905- Psychologist; university professor; educator

Address: b. Teachers College, Columbia University, New York 27; h. 390 Riverside Dr., New York 25

An authority on the psychology of learning and the problems of communication, Dr. Irving Lorge has devised intelligence tests and readability measurements and has theorized on human intelligence and the abilities of the aged. He has also made one of his special concerns

IRVING LORGE

the education of gifted children. Associated with Teachers College of Columbia University throughout his career, he is now the executive officer of its Institute of Psychological Research.

Irving Daniel Lorge was born in New York City on April 19, 1905 to Frieda (Katz) and Solomon Lorge, a retail butcher. He grew up in a family of four children: two boys and two girls. Educated in the school system of New York City, he studied at Townsend Harris Hall High School, a secondary institution for gifted students. He then entered the City College of the City of New York and became a Fellow in its School of Education.

Encouraged by the late Paul Klapper, who was then dean of the School of Education at City College, Lorge decided to make education his career. He was elected to Phi Beta Kappa and received the B.S. degree in 1926. At Teachers College of Columbia University, he earned the M.A. degree in 1927 and the Ph.D. in 1930. In 1927 he became a research assistant in the psychology division of the Institute of Educational Research, where he was urged by the head of the institute, the late Edward L. Thorndike, to enter the field of research in psychology. Lorge was advanced to research associate in 1931, associate professor of education in 1938, and professor in 1946. In 1939 he succeeded Thorndike as executive officer, and seven years later moved to the Institute of Psychological Research as its executive officer.

One of the research problems to which Lorge early addressed himself was the readability of writings familiar to everyone. They all tested high in readability—the reason, Lorge decided, why they are both popular and familiar. He discovered that the 23d Psalm, beginning "The Lord is my Shepherd," could be readily understood by anyone with seven and a half years of schooling. Seventh graders could grasp the language of Lincoln's Gettysburg Address; sixth graders could handle fifteen selected excerpts from *Alice in Wonderland*.

During World War II the Office of Price Administration summoned Lorge to Washington to test the readability of the agency's regulations. He concluded that OPA regulations were written in language too difficult for most people to understand, and the rules were rewritten in accord with the readability standards Lorge had developed over a period of ten years.

From 1942 to 1944 Lorge served as consultant to the Army special training division. Applying his readability yardstick, he discovered that the books used to teach reading and writing to illiterates were actually more appropriate for men with a fourth or fifth grade education. The division switched over to more simplified texts.

During World War II and the early postwar years Lorge served as a consultant to several other government agencies: the Office of the Air Surgeon (1941), chief of the Corps of Engineers (1941-46), and Adjutant General's Office (1944-48). Recognizing his contribution to the problems of military personnel, the War Department conferred on him its Award for Patriotic Service.

Since 1947 Lorge has spent his summers working with the Superior Educational Council of the University of Puerto Rico on the development of a readability formula in Spanish. The project has involved the setting up of reading tests for Puerto Rican students from the third grade through college. Lorge has also tested some 1,000 writings in Spanish for comprehension difficulty.

Dr. Lorge has conducted extensive research in such areas as intelligence testing, the gifted child, and the psychology of the aged. With Professor Thorndike he helped develop the Logic-Thorndike Intelligence Test, and with G. Burgemuster he devised the Columbia-Mental Opportunity Scale.

On the basis of his studies, Dr. Lorge has seriously questioned the theory that the intelligence quotient remains the same, with slight variations, throughout life. He has found that the IQ is related to the schooling an individual receives and that it can be raised as much as twenty points. His conclusions resulted from a twenty-year research project.

In his studies of the psychology of the aged, Lorge has called attention to the highhandedness of establishing sixty-five as a compulsory retirement age. He believes that retirement should be based on "functional" rather than on "chronological" considerations. "People do not suddenly become unproductive at a given age," he maintains. "Some people should be retired at 40 because they can't pull their share of the job load, while others may still be able to work effectively at 90" (New York *Times,* September 10, 1953).

According to Lorge, men and women approaching sixty are entering a "golden age" and should take advantage of retirement as a period of developing new interests and pursuits. An adult at any age can learn the same things he was able to learn at twenty. Although an older adult slows down physically, his mental abilities undergo little, if any, loss. Only the speed at which he can learn will, in general, be decreased (New York *Herald Tribune,* January 5, 1951).

Together with seventeen other social scientists, in 1956 Lorge took the position that racial background does not determine inborn psychological characteristics in men. The group issued the joint statement to refute claims made by supporters of public school segregation that white children are inherently brighter than colored children (*United States News & World Report,* October 26, 1956). Lorge later reaffirmed his contention that "intellectual performance is a direct outgrowth of educational opportunity" (*Daily Columbia Spectator,* October 31, 1956).

A frequent contributor to scientific journals and professional publications, Lorge has written articles on many subjects, ranging from sugar to vocational aptitudes. He has also written articles of general interest which have appeared in newspapers. He serves, at present, as consulting editor to the *Journal of Applied Psychology, Psychometrika,* and the *Journal of Experimental Education.*

His books include *Influence of Regularly Interpolated Time Intervals upon Subsequent Learning* (Teachers College, 1930); *American Agricultural Villages: 1930, An Analysis of Census Data* (American Statistical Association, 1933); *Rural Trends in Depression Years; A Survey of Village-Centered Agricultural Communities* (Columbia University Press, 1937) with Edmund de S. Brunner; *A Semantic Count of English Words* (Teachers College, 1938) and *The Teachers Word Book of 30,000 Words* (Teachers College, 1944), both with Thorndike; *The Semantic Count of the 570 Commonest English Words* (Teachers College, 1949); and *Retirement and the Industrial Worker* (Teachers College, 1953), with Jacob Tuckman.

Active in many professional societies, Lorge is a Fellow of the American Association for the Advancement of Science, American Statistical Association, American Psychological Association (chairman, division of maturity and old age and division of educational psychology, 1953-54), Psychometric Society, Gerontological Society, and the New York Academy of Sciences (chairman of the psychology section and a past vice-president). His Greek letter societies are Phi Delta Kappa, Sigma Xi, and Kappa Delta Pi, and his fraternal affiliation is with the Free and Accepted Masons.

On August 13, 1939 Irving Lorge married Sarah Wolfson, who is now a language consultant to the New York City Board of Education. They have two daughters, Paula Lee and Beatrice Susan. Dr. Lorge stands six feet tall and weighs 220 pounds. He has brown eyes and auburn hair. He is Jewish and a member of the Democratic party. His avocational interests are the theater, reading, and his research.

References

American Men of Science vol 3 (1956)
Who's Who in America, 1958-59

LOVELL, (ALFRED CHARLES) BERNARD Aug. 31, 1913- Scientist; university professor; author

Address: b. Jodrell Bank Experimental Station, Jodrell Bank, Cheshire, England; h. The Quinta, Swettenham, Cheshire, England

The first holder of a chair in radio astronomy at the University of Manchester and director of the Jodrell Bank Experimental Station, Dr. Bernard Lovell is recognized as one of the foremost authorities in his field. At Jodrell Bank he supervises the world's largest radio telescope, which owes its existence to his foresight and zeal. Dr. Lovell has used this unique instrument to track the Russian and American earth satellites, to chart radio signals giving data on the existence of cosmic explosions, to observe the activity of the mysterious aurora, and to obtain climatic and topographical information about the planets.

Dr. Lovell's most recent achievement has been the transmission of radio signals between Jodrell Bank and the United States via the moon. These experiments may lead to the possibility of using the moon, or artificial satellites, for direct, high-frequency radio communication between continents.

The son of Gilbert and Emily (Adams) Lovell, Alfred Charles Bernard Lovell was born on August 31, 1913 in a village on the borders of Somerset and Gloucestershire. His father managed a petrol station and radio repair business and also served as a local Free Church preacher. Bernard received his education at the Kingswood Grammar School in Bristol and Bristol University where he was a physics major. He took a Bachelor of Science degree in 1933 and a Ph.D. degree three years later. In 1936 Lovell was appointed an assistant lecturer in physics at the University of Manchester, and the following year he was named an assistant to Professor Patrick Maynard Stuart Blackett, with whom he worked on cosmic ray research.

When Great Britain entered World War II in 1939, Lovell abandoned his peace-time investigations to serve with the Telecommunications Research Establishment on a project devoted to radar development. Dr. Lovell's contributions to research on blind-bombing devices, to the use of microwaves for detecting ships and aircraft with greater precision, and to the development of radar television for navigation were recognized when he was named an Officer of the Order of the British Empire in 1946.

Appointed a lecturer at the University of Manchester when he returned there in 1945, Lovell immediately set about applying his military experience with radar techniques to the study of cosmic rays. He was promoted to senior lecturer in 1947 and two years later he was named a reader in physics. When his experiments in the detection of cosmic ray bursts by radar began to suffer from interference in the city of Manchester, Lovell received permission to establish a laboratory at Jodrell Bank. At this open field in Cheshire, which had belonged to the botany department of the University, Lovell constructed a new radio tele-

BERNARD LOVELL

scope with a diameter of 218 feet. This instrument assisted Dr. Lovell in his investigation of meteors and his discovery of new data on radio stars and emissions from the Milky Way and other galaxies. In 1951 Lovell was appointed Professor of Radio Astronomy at the University and director of the Jodrell Bank laboratory.

A major drawback of the Jodrell Bank telescope was its fixed structure. To overcome this difficulty, Dr. Lovell announced early in 1952 that the University of Manchester would build a giant radio telescope which would be movable in its mountings. Financed jointly by the British government and the Nuffield Foundation at a cost of about £700,000, the telescope was planned to surpass the range of the great optical telescopes at Mount Wilson and Mount Palomar in the United States. The radio telescope, which was designed by engineer H. C. Husband, has the added advantage of operating in daylight and in cloudy skies. Construction was started in 1953 and completed in the autumn of 1957, in time for Professor Lovell and his staff to participate in collecting data for the International Geophysical Year.

The radio telescope's receiving antenna which looks like a large radar scanner has a reflecting surface 250 feet in diameter. The reflector is cradled in a bowl of structural steelwork weighing some 800 tons. It is held erect by two steel lattice towers 180 feet high which rise from a system of deep-trussed girders. Delicate receiving and recording instruments and electronic controls are housed in a control building and in a small cabin beneath the great reflector. This unique instrument, weighing altogether 2,000 tons, rotates horizontally on steel rails. A vertical rotation can be made at the rate of twenty-four degrees a minute and a horizontal rotation at twenty degrees a minute. The extent of its pick-up range depends upon the strength of the space signals being received. Dr. Lovell believes that the antenna could identify radio-

wave sources one billion to two billion light-years away.

The radio telescope has already yielded information on the solar system which Dr. Lovell believes "might well give us the key to unlock the secrets of the evolution of the entire universe" (Manchester Guardian, November 24, 1958). Dr. Lovell has made elaborate observations of auroral activity, establishing that auroras occur simultaneously over the Northern and Southern hemispheres. An important service performed by the radio telescope was the tracking of Russian and American satellites in orbit; Lovell and his staff worked closely with American scientists in tracking all the moon rocket launchings, including Pioneer IV, which has established an orbit around the sun. By tuning in on a satellite's radio signal, the telescope has been able to pinpoint the satellite's exact location at any given time and has collected essential data transmitted by the satellite's measuring instruments.

Experiments now being conducted at Jodrell Bank by Dr. Lovell and his associates may be "a great step forward in world communications —including television and radio-telephony" (Manchester Guardian, May 16, 1959). The scientists have been relaying vocal transmissions from Jodrell Bank to pick-up stations in the United States by "bouncing them off the moon." "These messages," according to Professor Lovell, "were received quite intelligibly by the Americans, who telephoned us soon afterwards to say that the messages had been understood" (Manchester Guardian, May 16, 1959). Dr. Lovell believes there are "tremendous" commercial possibilities in using the moon as a space relay for transatlantic radio communications without the usual interference of the ionosphere.

In 1959 Professor Lovell was planning to repeat his lunar radio experiments, using code signals, with the planet Venus when that planet was to come close to earth. As early as August 1957 he announced that he would try to make radar contact with Venus, but improvements in the long-range transmission equipment at Jodrell Bank were necessary. By using a new transmitter with a power output three thousand times greater than the average radar installation, Lovell planned to measure the orbit of Venus and the rotation of the planet on its axis with greater accuracy than had been done before.

An educator and philosopher as well as an astronomer, Dr. Lovell was invited to deliver the Reith Lectures on the British Broadcasting Corporation Home Service in the fall of 1958. This series of talks was collected in The Individual and the Universe (Harper, 1959). The book surveys the contributions of the great astronomers through the ages and discusses the achievements of modern astronomy.

Dr. Lovell believes that scientists may soon be able to decide between the two leading scientific theories of the nature and origin of the universe by using giant radio telescopes. According to the "evolutionary" theory, all matter in the universe was once concentrated in a relatively small mass, which exploded at some definite point of time and formed the galaxies as we know them. These galaxies are flying apart at a constant rate; therefore the universe is thinning out as it gets older.

The second theory proposes a "steady state universe," in which matter is constantly being created in space in the form of hydrogen gas. As the old galaxies fly apart, new ones are created in the spaces between them; the world will always be about as dense as it is now. By observing the distances between galaxies as they were billions of years ago, radio astronomers may soon be able to end the dispute between the two theories.

Other books that Dr. Lovell has written are *Science and Civilization* (Nelson, 1939), *Radio Astronomy* (Chapman, 1951), *Meteor Astronomy* (Oxford, 1954), and *The Exploration of Space by Radio* (Chapman, 1957). He has also written many articles for astronomical journals.

Dr. Lovell was elected a Fellow of the Royal Society in 1955. The year before, he was presented with the Duddell Medal of the Physical Society. The American Academy of Arts and Sciences has honored Lovell with honorary foreign membership.

Mrs. Lovell, the former Mary Joyce Chesterman, was a teacher before she married the professor in 1937. The Lovells have two sons and three daughters. In his free time away from the Jodrell Bank laboratory Dr. Lovell enjoys cricket, plays the piano, and grows prize gooseberries.

References

International Who's Who, 1958
Who's Who, 1959

MCCALL, DUKE K(IMBROUGH), REV. DR. Sept. 1, 1914- Clergyman; educator

Address: b. The Southern Baptist Theological Seminary, 2825 Lexington Rd., Louisville 6, Ky.; h. 1042 Alta Vista Rd., Louisville 5, Ky.

A Southern church leader, Duke K. McCall since 1951 has been president of the Southern Baptist Theological Seminary in Louisville, Kentucky. Previously he had held the highest administrative position in the Southern Baptist Convention, whose headquarters are in Nashville, Tennessee. He also served as president, from 1943 to 1946, of the Baptist Bible Institute in New Orleans, Louisiana, now known as the New Orleans Baptist Theological Seminary.

The seminary president has also been the head of the National Temperance League since 1953. He is the author or editor of several books, and has been awarded honorary degrees by several colleges and universities. He was graduated from Furman University in Greenville, South Carolina in 1935, and later received Th.M. and Ph.D. degrees from the Southern Baptist Theological Seminary.

Duke Kimbrough McCall, the son of John William and Lizette (Kimbrough) McCall, was born on September 1, 1914 in Meridian, Mississippi. His father was a lawyer, and he has two sisters, and two brothers, both of whom are doctors. He was brought up in Memphis, Tennessee, and was graduated in 1931 from the Central High School, where his extracurricular activities included playing football, debating, and editing the yearbook.

He then entered Furman University in Greenville, South Carolina, where he majored in English. He won the oratorical medal and the general excellence medal, and was granted the B.A. degree in 1935 *summa cum laude* and as valedictorian of his class. The Southern Baptist Theological Seminary in Louisville, Kentucky, awarded him the Th.M. degree in 1938, and the Ph.D. degree in 1942; his thesis for the latter degree was entitled, "Date and Authorship of Zechariah 9-14."

Meanwhile, in 1940, McCall had accepted the pastorship of the Broadway Baptist Church in Louisville, Kentucky. Three years later he became the president of the Baptist Bible Institute in New Orleans, Louisiana. In 1946 he was appointed to the top administrative position, that of executive secretary of the executive committee, of the Southern Baptist Convention, in Nashville, Tennessee. The Convention, which has a membership close to 9,000,000, is the largest Baptist group in the United States.

In 1950 McCall went on a trip around the world to see the Southern Baptist mission fields. In Africa, he found that no white missionaries were pastors of churches, but served as superintendents of schools, supervisors of farms, nurses, and attendants at orphanages. The Africans are the pastors of the churches, he discovered, and the leaders; the missionaries serve in the ranks (*Time*, October 9, 1950).

He assumed the position of president of the Southern Baptist Theological Seminary in Louisville, Kentucky on September 15, 1951, after the death of Dr. Ellis A. Fuller. At the age of thirty-seven, McCall was the youngest man ever to assume the presidency in the ninety-two year history of the seminary. It was

Walton Jones

REV. DR. DUKE K. MCCALL

MCCALL, DUKE K., REV. DR.—*Continued*
founded in 1859, has about sixty-five teachers, and an enrollment of about 1,500 students, both men and women. Racial segregation was ended at the seminary in 1951.

In a speech before the Southern Baptist Convention in Kansas City, Missouri in May 1956, President McCall declared that "too many spiritually immature, emotionally and morally unstable people" are being prepared at the present time for the Christian ministry by the churches. He called on the churches to make more careful selection of candidates for the ministry and to demand that those chosen be better trained (Washington *Post and Times Herald,* June 1, 1956).

The board of trustees of the seminary dismissed thirteen professors in June 1958, apparently because of an insoluble disagreement about administration between these faculty members and Reverend McCall. The trustees said that the dispute had originated in a change in the legal structure of the seminary in 1942, which had placed administrative power in the hands of the president rather than in the hands of the faculty.

According to *Newsweek* (December 15, 1958), the teachers had charged that after seven years of trying to establish a relationship with him, they were forced to conclude that "working" with the president was "distressingly identical" to "agreeing" with him. Reverend McCall asked for decisive action to avoid further crises and "ultimate anarchy" in the seminary's affairs. The New York *Times* reported (December 9, 1958) that the teachers wanted to stress scholarly and traditional disciplines, whereas Dr. McCall was more interested in modern aspects of the ministry, such as radio and television.

In investigating the dismissal, the American Association of Theological Schools (of which McCall was then vice-president and a member of the accrediting commission) found signs of mismanagement, but let the seminary remain fully accredited if its board of trustees would take steps to repair the damage to the seminary and the dismissed professors. The AATS said that McCall should resign his association positions immediately. In April 1959, the board of trustees announced that in order to end the dispute, it had asked the thirteen professors to resign, and the teachers had agreed to do so. The official statement on the rift said: "We are not enemies who are fighting, we are brethren who do not agree" (New York *Times,* April 5, 1959).

Since 1953 McCall has been president of the National Temperance League, which in 1958, at a conference in Cleveland, reaffirmed the league's determination to oppose the serving of liquor in airplanes and the advertising of alcoholic beverages in national magazines.

The Broadman Press of Nashville, Tennessee, published McCall's *God's Hurry* in 1949. With W. A. Criswell he wrote *Passport to the World* (Broadman, 1951), and with E. F. Haight he wrote the Sunday school lesson annual, *Broadman Comments on the International Bible Lessons for Christian Teaching, Uniform Series, 1958-1959,* in two volumes (Broadman, 1957 and 1958). McCall edited for Broadman in 1958 a book entitled *What is the Church? A Symposium of Baptist Thought.*

Reverend McCall has been a member at large of the National Council of the Boy Scouts of America since 1954, and a member of the executive board of the Old Kentucky Home Council of Boy Scouts since 1956. As a member of the United States Civilian Committee on Training for the Chaplaincy in 1954 and 1955, he visited military installations in Europe and Korea. For the four years from 1955 to 1959, McCall served as a member of the board of visitors of the United States Air Force Air University in Maxwell Field in Alabama. He participated as one of seven Southern church leaders in a round-table discussion on the morality of segregation, reprinted in *Life* (October 1, 1956). In the discussion, McCall said: "If you want to believe in enforced segregation, you may do so. But do not use the Bible to support your arguments. Such use is misuse."

He was awarded an honorary LL.D. degree in 1945 by Baylor University in Waco, Texas; an honorary D.D. degree in 1949 by Furman University in Greenville, South Carolina; and an honorary Litt.D. degree in 1955 by Shurtleff College in Alton, Illinois.

Duke Kimbrough McCall married Marguerite Mullinnix, who was then a student, on September 1, 1936. They have four sons: Duke Kimbrough, Jr., Douglas Henry, John Richard, and Michael William. The seminary president has brown eyes and light brown hair; he is five feet ten inches tall, and weighs 185 pounds.

References

The Southerner (1945)
Who's Who in American Education, 1957-58

MCCONE, JOHN A(LEX) Jan. 4, 1902-
Businessman; United States government official
Address: b. Atomic Energy Commission, Washington 25, D.C.; h. 1100 Oak Grove Ave., San Marino, Calif.

The chairman of the Atomic Energy Commission has become a key man in the planning of nuclear projects for peace and defense, as the United States moves further into the atomic age. The new chairman is John Alex McCone, appointed to a five-year term in June 1958 to succeed Admiral Lewis L. Strauss. An Eisenhower Republican, he has won the approval of the Democrats and has been able to compromise with the Joint Congressional Committee on Atomic Energy on many controversial points.

McCone is a former California engineer and industrialist with much experience in key government advisory capacities. As a businessman he has headed West coast engineering and shipping firms. In government he has served as an adviser to President Truman, as Under Secretary of the Air Force, and as special representative for President Eisenhower.

John Alex McCone was born in San Francisco on January 4, 1902 to Alexander J. and Margaret (Enright) McCone. His ancestors had been in the machinery and manufacturing business since 1860, when his grandfather who bore the same name started a small iron foundry in Nevada.

After graduating from Los Angeles High School, John McCone went to the University of California at Berkeley, where he graduated from the College of Engineering in 1922. In his first job he worked as a riveter and boilermaker for the Llewellyn Iron Works in Los Angeles. Later, he became superintendent of the concern. During the depression his company merged with Consolidated Steel Corporation, but he stayed on. He served the firm as a construction manager and vice-president in charge of sales, and in 1933, before his thirty-second birthday, he was named executive vice-president and director.

In 1937 McCone left Consolidated Steel Corporation to organize his own firm, Bechtel-McCone, of which he was president and director. His company designed, engineered, and constructed petroleum refineries, power plants, and process plants throughout the United States, South America, and Arabia. During World War II the firm built and maintained the Birmingham Aircraft Modification Center in Alabama. The largest American plant of its kind, it modified B-24 and B-29 bombers and other military aircraft.

During World War II McCone became president and director of the California Shipbuilding Corporation. He "set production goals higher than anyone thought could be met, and then he made sure they were met," said the New York *Herald Tribune* (November 6, 1957). As a result, his company produced 467 ships during the war. He also served as director of the Marinship Corporation in California and the Oregon Shipbuilding Corporation.

After the war McCone took over the Joshua Hendy Iron Works in California as its president and sole owner. That company, now known as the Joshua Hendy Corporation, operates a fleet of tankers and cargo ships in the Pacific. In 1948 McCone also became chairman of the board of Pacific Far East Line, Inc., one of the largest American steamship lines in the Pacific.

As a member of President Truman's Air Policy Commission in 1947, McCone helped to write the report *Survival in the Air Age,* a document which helped bring air defense policies up to date. In 1948 he served as a special deputy to Secretary of Defense James V. Forrestal, when he became responsible for preparing the first and second budgets of the newly formed Department of Defense.

Appointed Under Secretary of the Air Force in June, 1950, McCone fought constantly for a larger share of the defense budget for the Air Force. By the time he resigned in October, 1951, production of military planes had doubled. Air Force Secretary Thomas K. Finletter gave him the Exceptional Civilian Service Award.

While with the Air Force in 1951, McCone sent a memorandum to President Truman recommending an embryo missiles program under someone "with full authority and control of

U. S. Air Force

JOHN A. MCCONE

funds to exercise absolute power over the entire effort." In 1958 the New York *Herald Tribune* referred to this memorandum, calling McCone a "prophet with honor" and saying that if his recommendation had been carried out, the United States might not be behind the Soviets in guided missiles (July 10, 1958).

Although he returned to private business after 1951, McCone came back to serve the government on several occasions. In 1954 Secretary of State Dulles appointed him to sit on the Public Committee on Personnel, the purpose of which was to survey the diplomatic corps and recommend proposals for strengthening and modernizing it. As a leading Roman Catholic layman, McCone represented the United States at the seventeenth anniversary of Pope Pius XII's coronation in 1956, and in October 1958 he was one of three United States representatives sent to the Pope's funeral in Rome.

President Eisenhower nominated McCone to the Atomic Energy Commission on June 6, 1958. The Senate unanimously confirmed his appointment on July 9, and he was sworn in and named chairman on July 15. "Congressmen from both sides of the political aisle welcomed the nomination of McCone," said Warren Unna in the Washington *Post,* adding that McCone would bring new "harmony for the A.E.C. internally, as well as for the commission's relations with the Joint Congressional Committee" (June 7, 1958).

The question of private-versus-public development of peacetime atomic power programs had been one of the problems that had beset Admiral Strauss' chairmanship of the A.E.C. The Admiral favored private development. Edwin Dale, Jr., of the New York *Times* spoke for most observers when he wrote of McCone that he "is a conservative, like Strauss. . . .

MCCONE, JOHN A.—*Continued*

However, he will probably be by nature a more flexible man than Mr. Strauss. . ." (July 20, 1958).

On another controversial issue—the banning of nuclear tests—McCone has often maintained that stopping the tests would hinder valuable peacetime research. Nevertheless, he supported Eisenhower's August 1958 proposal to suspend nuclear tests for one year conditional upon Soviet agreement.

On still another controversial issue—secrecy —the *Christian Science Monitor* noted that "a gradual, unofficial, and unannounced about-face by the Atomic Energy Commission has all but dropped the veil of secrecy surrounding the A.E.C.'s spectacular experiments at its Nevada Test Site" (October 27, 1958). In September, the A.E.C. had lifted its censorship of one of its most vital phases—making sure that bombs do not go off accidentally.

At his first press conference, in October, 1958, McCone said that the United States would go ahead with nuclear tests if the Geneva conferences failed to produce Soviet agreement on the initial one-year test ban. He said that stopping U.S. tests "would delay and probably prevent the development of small, clean weapons" (Los Angeles *Times*, October 30, 1958). Although there was no East-West agreement on the one-year test ban, the United States announced in August 1959 that it would not resume tests during 1959.

McCone was one of the signers in November 1958 of an agreement between the United States and the six-nation European Atomic Energy Community (Euratom), comprising West Germany, France, Italy, Belgium, the Netherlands, and Luxembourg. The agreement is a "joint nuclear power and research development program" to be carried out in Europe and to include the building of atomic reactors.

Before taking on his new position, McCone had been director of several companies, a trustee of the California Institute of Technology and a regent of Loyola University in Los Angeles. A director of the Stanford Research Institute, he was also president and one of the founders of the Los Angeles World Affairs Council. All these he relinquished when he assumed the post with A.E.C.

On June 21, 1938 John McCone married the former Rosemary Cooper of Idaho, who often accompanies him on his world travels.

Described as a "man with a slide-rule mind" but one "who never forgets that he is dealing with human beings," McCone is a professorial-looking man with gray hair and rimless glasses. Among his many clubs is the Burning Tree Country Club, where he has frequently played golf with his close friend, the President. A Washington *Star* editorial said of McCone: "He is the very model of a model 'modern' Republican" (July 15, 1958).

References

Bsns W p31+ Je 14 '58 por
Newsweek 52:52 Jl 14 '58 por
Time 71:16 Je 16 '58 por
Who's Who in America, 1958-59

MCDEVITT, JAMES L(AWRENCE) Nov. 3, 1898- Labor union official
Address: b. 815 16th St., N.W., Washington 6, D.C.; h. 5901 Goldsboro Rd., Bethesda, Md.

Director of the AFL-CIO Committee on Political Education since March 1957, James L. McDevitt was given a major share of credit for the sweeping victories of labor-backed Democratic candidates in the Congressional elections of November 1958. From 1951 to the end of 1955 he had served as director of the AFL's Labor's League for Political Education. He was also president of the Pennsylvania State Federation of Labor from 1938 to 1954.

Born to William Paul and Sarah Margaret (Hickey) McDevitt on November 3, 1898, James Lawrence McDevitt is a native of Philadelphia, Pennsylvania. He attended local Roman Catholic parochial schools. Apprenticed in 1916, after two years of high school, to his father's craft of plasterer, he learned his trade under the guidance of Local 8 of the Operative Plasterers' and Cement Masons International Association of the United States and Canada, an American Federation of Labor union.

In 1918 he enlisted in the United States Army for World War I service and went to France with the American Expeditionary Force. After being discharged in July 1919 he resumed his apprenticeship and became a journeyman plasterer a year later. In 1925 he was made business manager of his union, a position that he occupied for the next ten years. In the course of his career he also served the union as recording secretary, vice-president, and president.

While serving as his union's business manager, McDevitt became president of the Philadelphia Building Trades Council, and thereafter was a member of the city's Building Code Commission and Housing Authority. In 1935 he was named area labor relations director of the Works Progress Administration and was appointed to the Philadelphia Regional Labor Board.

Elected president of the Pennsylvania Federation of Labor for the first time in 1938, McDevitt remained for the next sixteen years the chief executive of the organization, one of the largest state federations in the country. At the time of the 1938 primaries in Pennsylvania his organization, composed mainly of craft unions, supported the candidacy of Governor George Earle for the United States Senate in opposition to Joseph F. Guffey, who was favored by John L. Lewis.

In the same year Governor Earle appointed McDevitt to the State Unemployment Compensation Board of Review. In July 1939 McDevitt threatened to lead a state-wide strike of WPA workers unless Congress eliminated from the relief bill sections calling for longer work hours without increase in pay. Pledged to the ticket of Franklin D. Roosevelt and Henry A. Wallace, McDevitt was a member of the Electoral College of 1940.

During World War II McDevitt was chairman of the labor division of the Philadelphia War Chest; he also led labor drives for the

Community Chest and the Red Cross. Among the state agencies on which McDevitt served were the Displaced Persons Commission, State Planning Commission, Advisory Council for Private Trade Schools, Advisory Committee on Public Utility Arbitration Law, Advisory Committee on the Physically Handicapped, and the Advisory Council on the Governor's Highway Safety Council. On the national level, he was appointed to the national advisory committee of the Bureau of Employment Security and to the Committee for the Extension of Labor Education.

Largely in consequence of the enactment of the Taft-Hartley Law in 1947, the American Federation of Labor decided in October of that year to form a "political arm" to be known as Labor's League for Political Education. Joseph D. Keenan was named as its national director. The AFL had not formally endorsed a Presidential candidate since 1924, when it backed Senator Robert M. La Follette on a third party ticket. In 1948 there was a strong movement to endorse President Harry S. Truman for re-election, but this effort was frustrated.

After Keenan resigned as director of Labor's League for Political Education, on September 17, 1951 the administrative committee announced the appointment of McDevitt as his successor. Again in 1952 the AFL did not directly endorse a candidate. McDevitt, whose organization was financed by $1 voluntary contributions, denied that it controlled any votes, and stated that it merely provided "material to enable voters to cast their ballots intelligently for candidates in their own best interests." Some observers felt that its organ, the *Political Reporter,* which had been established in 1949 and attained a circulation of 100,000, clearly favored Democratic candidates.

With the merging of the American Federation of Labor and the Congress of Industrial Organizations on December 5, 1955, Labor's League for Political Education was supplanted by the present Committee on Political Education (COPE), with Jack Kroll and McDevitt as co-directors. (The former had headed the CIO Political Action Committee since the death of Sidney Hillman.)

In June 1956 the co-directors of COPE announced the forthcoming distribution to AFL-CIO members of some 16,000,000 to 17,000,000 copies of what amounted to a "political blacklist" of antilabor Congressmen and others (New York *Herald Tribune,* June 7, 1956). Interviewed shortly after the November 1956 election, McDevitt noted that President Eisenhower, although re-elected, had failed to "carry the legislative candidates of his party" in general. "I would say," he added, "we have actually added to the number of friendly members on the Republican and Democratic sides. . . . We have certainly had a victory legislatively" (*United States News & World Report,* November 16, 1956).

Appointed sole director of COPE on March 6, 1957, following the resignation of Jack Kroll, McDevitt set to work to prepare in 1958 for what was to be labor's biggest campaign. At

Harris & Ewing

JAMES L. MCDEVITT

eight regional conferences organized by COPE it was stressed that this campaign would be a "showdown" between the union movement and "reactionary forces . . . out to destroy the American labor movement." Particular targets were fifteen Republican Senate seats at stake in November, and the so-called "right to work" referenda on the ballots in six states. (These referenda were defeated in all states except Kansas.)

In a "private post-mortem on the Democratic landslide in Maine" in September, the Republican National Committee admitted that "COPE's relatively small $1 million campaign kitty and paid manpower have assumed an unusually important role" and gave McDevitt's committee "full credit" (New York *Herald Tribune,* October 20, 1958). At the November election Democrats gained Republican-held Senate seats in nine states and labor-backed Democrats took numerous House seats. Expenditures of $659,121 by COPE for the Senate and House campaigns were later reported to Congress. "The figure," remarked *United States News & World Report* (November 28, 1958), "represents only half the money collected by COPE, since half is left with the State AFL-CIO organizations."

Honors conferred on James L. McDevitt include the Silver Congress Medal awarded him by La Salle College at Philadelphia in 1943, and a Page One Award by the Newspaper Guild of Greater Philadelphia in 1954 for his work in the labor field. McDevitt has been prominent in such groups as the American Council for Christians and Jews, the National Trade Council for Palestine, and the National Association for the Advancement of Colored People. He has been a member of the executive committee of the state council for the Fair Employment Practices Commission. His service organizations are the American Legion and Veterans of

MCDEVITT, JAMES L.—*Continued*

Foreign Wars. Golf is his favorite outdoor recreation.

McDevitt has been married twice, first on January 25, 1921 to Margaret Winifred Murphy (now deceased). He married Margaret Mary Toole on January 3, 1953. He has one daughter, Margaret (Mrs. Thomas R. Byrne), and two sons, James Lawrence, Jr., and William Patrick, by the first marriage. McDevitt is a Roman Catholic and a Democrat.

References

N Y Herald Tribune II p9 Mr 7 '57
Who's Who in America, 1958-59
Who's Who in Labor (1946)

MCDONNELL, WILLIAM A(RCHIE)
Nov. 20, 1894- Banker; organization official

Address: b. First National Bank in St. Louis, 305 N. Broadway, St. Louis 2, Mo.; h. 33 W. Brentmoor, St. Louis 5, Mo.

Chairman of the board and chief executive officer of the First National Bank in St. Louis, Missouri, William A. McDonnell is the first banker in thirty years to have become president of the Chamber of Commerce of the United States. He was installed on April 29, 1958 for a one-year term, succeeding the Washington, D.C. department store executive Philip M. Talbott.

"I am of Scottish descent. My branch of the 'McDonnells of Glengarry' came to America before the Revolutionary War, settled eventually in Alabama," William A. McDonnell has related. "My father, a University of Alabama graduate, came to Arkansas in 1881, set up an old-fashioned general store on $3,000 borrowed capital. My mother was a proficient painter and

Wide World
WILLIAM A. MCDONNELL

pianist, and deeply devoted to the Southern Methodist Church." He is one of the four children of James Smith and Susie Belle (Hunter) McDonnell. His brother, James Smith McDonnell, is head of the McDonnell Aircraft Corporation.

Born on November 20, 1894 in Altheimer, Arkansas, William Archie McDonnell grew up in Altheimer, Denver, Colorado, and Little Rock, Arkansas. He is a graduate of the Little Rock High School and of the Vanderbilt University School of Law at Nashville, Tennessee, where he received his LL.B. degree *summa cum laude* in 1917 and won the Founders' Medal, the highest award in the graduating class. He was admitted to the Arkansas bar in 1917 but instead of starting practice, he enlisted in the Army for World War I service, entering as a private and rising to the rank of captain, with duty as operations officer of the 6th Field Artillery Brigade. He was in France for fourteen months and saw action in the Saint-Mihiel, Argonne, and other engagements.

After his discharge from the Army in 1919, McDonnell joined the Little Rock law firm headed by former Congressman Charles C. Reid and Lawrence B. Burrow, and became a junior partner. "We had a general practice—no criminal law," he told Sidney Shalett when interviewed for *Nation's Business* (May 1958). "I found myself leaning to office work and the preparation of briefs rather than jury appearances. . . . Eventually, I became general counsel for the Federal Bank & Trust Company of Little Rock, which our firm represented, and went into banking on a full-time basis."

A year later, in 1928, McDonnell moved to the larger Bankers Trust Company of Little Rock as a vice-president. In 1933, when it was renamed the Commercial National Bank, he became its executive vice-president. During the next eleven years McDonnell was active in the Little Rock Chamber of Commerce, serving as director, president, and national councilor. He was president of the Arkansas Bankers Association in 1940, director of the executive committee of the Arkansas Public Expenditures Council in 1941-42, and director and treasurer of the Arkansas state committee of the National War Fund in 1943-44.

McDonnell moved to St. Louis in 1944, when he was appointed vice-president of that city's Mercantile-Commerce Bank & Trust Company. Joining the First National Bank in St. Louis in 1947 as executive vice-president, he was made president the following year and chairman of the board and chief executive officer in 1957. The bank that he heads is among the forty largest in the United States. "It occupies," Sidney Shalett reported, "nearly an entire downtown city block and recently completed a five-year $7,500,000 remodeling program. . . . It carries on a correspondent banking business with approximately 1,000 banking institutions in thirty-two states and eleven foreign countries" and has "year-end assets of more than $664,000,000."

In 1950 McDonnell was named a "Class A" director of the Federal Reserve Bank of St.

Louis, and he is a member of the advisory council of the Federal Reserve Board. He is also a director of his brother's McDonnell Aircraft Corporation, the St. Louis and San Francisco Railroad, the Southwestern Bell Telephone Company, and three insurance companies.

In St. Louis, as he had done earlier in Little Rock, McDonnell takes an active part in business organizations, including the American Bankers Association and the Association of Reserve City Bankers. Among the many offices that he has held in the Chamber of Commerce of the United States were vice-president (1954-57), treasurer (1957-58), and chairman of several committees. He was elected president on March 14, 1958 and was installed in office the following month.

The Chamber of Commerce of the United States, established in 1912 at the suggestion of President William Howard Taft, has as its purpose "to provide the organizational means by which businessmen of America can work together to make their views, opinions, thoughts and judgment count in national affairs." Its "underlying membership" of more than 2,500,000 businessmen comprises more than 3,400 organization members (local, state and regional chambers of commerce, and trade and professional associations) and more than 22,000 business members (firms, corporations, and businessmen). It has headquarters in Washington, D.C. at 1615 H Street, N.W., and there are regional offices in six key cities across the country.

A week after becoming president of the Chamber of Commerce, McDonnell told the House of Representatives banking committee that "tax revision" to produce "higher real income" was more important than an "across-the-board" tax cut. The Chamber of Commerce supported a five-year extension of the Reciprocal Trade Law in June. In the following month its president "spearheaded" opposition to the Kennedy-Ives labor bill because of various "omissions"—including the outlawing of organizational and recognition picketing.

At the beginning of October the Chamber announced plans for establishing, in January 1959, a training program "to get businessmen into politics at the precinct level," while refraining from endorsing candidates or parties. "The schooling is a long-range approach to the theme that the chamber's president, William A. McDonnell, has been sounding in recent speeches," Richard E. Mooney noted in the New York Times (October 3, 1958). "He has said that labor unions are politically powerful because they are 'organized politically at every level.' Also, he has said, 'business has a right to protect its interest and we intend to do so.'"

Some of the civic organizations to which McDonnell has given special attention are the United Fund Campaign of Greater St. Louis, the Missouri Public Expenditure Survey, the St. Louis Symphony Society, Civic Progress, Inc., and the Boy Scouts.

William A. McDonnell and Carolyn Vandergrift Cherry of Little Rock were married on October 26, 1921 and have one daughter, Cherry (Mrs. David W. Black), and one son, Sanford

Noyes. The gray-haired banker attends a Methodist church, and he describes himself as an "independent" in politics. He belongs to the Sigma Chi fraternity and is a member of the St. Louis Country, Noonday, Racquet, Missouri Athletic, and Stack clubs. Golf, duck hunting, and swimming are his sports.

References

N Y Times p1+ Mr 15 '58 por
Nations Bsns 46:38+ My '58 pors
St. Louis Commerce 32:7 Ap '58 por
Time 71:97 Mr 24 '58 por
Washington (D.C.) Post p12C Mr 16 '58 por
Business Executives of America (1950)
Who's Who in America, 1958-59
World Biography (1954)

MCKAY, DOUGLAS June 24, 1893-July 22, 1959 United States Secretary of the Interior (1953-56); Governor of Oregon (1948-52); Oregon State Senator (1935-37; 1939-41; 1945-47). See *Current Biography* (May) 1949.

Obituary

N Y Times p27 Jl 23 '59

MACLAINE, SHIRLEY Apr. 24, 1934- Actress; dancer
Address: b. c/o Twentieth Century-Fox Film Corporation, Beverly Hills, Calif.

Since appearing in her first motion picture four years ago, Shirley MacLaine has become one of the most popular and widely applauded of the newer Hollywood stars. Her appeal to the public has raised her earning power from the $6,000 paid her in 1954 for her film debut in *The Trouble With Harry* to $250,000 for her tenth film, *Can-Can*. Her acting ability has already gained her the Silver Bear award of the International Berlin Film Festival.

Of Scotch-Irish descent, Shirley MacLaine was born Shirley MacLean Beaty in Richmond, Virginia on April 24, 1934. Although neither of her parents was in the entertainment field at the time of her birth, her father, Ira O. Beaty, now in the real estate business, has included leading a band among his earlier occupations. Her mother, Kathlyn (MacLean) Beaty, whose maiden name was altered by Shirley into her own professional name, had acted in little theaters and taught college dramatics. Shirley has a younger brother, Warren Beatty, who has appeared in television roles and on Broadway.

At the age of two and a half Shirley began studying ballet. "Otherwise," she remembers, "I was a tomboy. I couldn't *stand* dolls" (*Look,* September 15, 1959). While attending Washington and Lee High School in Arlington, Virginia, she spent summers in New York dancing in the choruses of *Kiss Me Kate* and the revival of *Oklahoma!* After graduating, she moved to New York in order to pursue her dancing career.

(Continued next page)

MGM

SHIRLEY MACLAINE

It was in the chorus of the Rodgers and Hammerstein musical *Me and Juliet,* which began its New York run on May 28, 1953, that Shirley MacLaine participated in her first Broadway opening. She left this production a year later to join the cast of *The Pajama Game,* in which she not only appeared in the chorus but also acted as understudy to Carol Haney, the leading dancer. A few days after the première of the show, which took place on May 13, 1954, Miss Haney injured her leg and was unable to appear for a month. Shirley MacLaine replaced her.

Among those who saw Miss MacLaine in Carol Haney's role during this and a later replacement were film producer Hal B. Wallis, who later signed her to a long-term motion-picture contract, and Alfred Hitchcock, under whose direction she made her film debut in *The Trouble with Harry.*

In this ghoulish comedy, released in 1955, Miss MacLaine played a widow who helps to dig up and rebury the corpse of her recently departed husband. Reviewing *The Trouble with Harry,* Bosley Crowther (New York *Times,* October 18, 1955) remarked that "there's an especially disarming screwball blandness about the manner of Miss MacLaine." Her talent as a comedienne was further exploited in *Artists and Models* (1955), a film starring Dean Martin and Jerry Lewis. In this Greenwich Village harlequinade, she gained more attention as Bessie Sparrowbush.

Shirley MacLaine's third film role marked a complete change of pace, when she portrayed an Indian princess in Michael Todd's *Around the World in 80 Days* (1956). Although reviewers agreed that she handled the role well, some felt that it did not take advantage of her elfin personality. Criticizing S. J. Perelman, the author of the screenplay, John Beaufort suggested in the *Christian Science Monitor*

(October 23, 1956) that "had Mr. Perelman seen Miss MacLaine's comedy performance in 'The Trouble with Harry,' he probably would have thought up something more rewarding for her to do than look decorative."

No fewer than four films in which Shirley MacLaine was featured were premièred in 1958. Two were comedies: a mock-Western called *The Sheepman,* in which she played a saucy cowgirl, and a screen version of Thornton Wilder's farce *The Matchmaker,* in which she took the role of a young milliner bent on matrimony. In the brooding *Hot Spell,* she played the daughter of a disintegrating Southern family.

When the motion-picture adaptation of James Jones's novel *Some Came Running* was first exhibited in 1958, Shirley MacLaine's interpretation of the loose-living Ginny Moorhead was not universally well received. The critic for *Time* magazine (January 12, 1959), for example, thought it showed only "occasional flashes of brilliant overacting." Hollywood entertained no such reservations. For the same performance Miss MacLaine was nominated for the 1958 Academy of Motion Picture Arts and Sciences Award, which went, however, to Susan Hayward.

Although films have taken up most of Shirley MacLaine's time since 1954, she has also made several television appearances. The circumstances of her first important TV assignment early in 1955, paralleled those of her first important stage appearance: Betty Grable injured her ankle shortly before her scheduled appearance in a musical "spectacular," and Miss MacLaine replaced her. TV has provided Miss MacLaine with a showcase for her talents as a singer and a dancer. She now has a five-year contract with NBC-TV to make five guest appearances each year.

Miss MacLaine's first film to be shown in 1959 was the comedy *Ask Any Girl,* in which she co-starred with David Niven. The high praise given by American reviewers for her acting in this farce was echoed in Europe, where she won the Silver Bear of the International Berlin Film Festival as the best actress of the year.

A far less favorable reaction greeted Miss MacLaine's second 1959 motion picture, *Career.* Certain reviewers found fault both with the film and with her acting. Among the faultfinders was Bosley Crowther of the New York *Times* (October 9, 1959), who called her "as soggy as a dishrag as a semi-professional dipsomaniac." But Paul V. Beckley of the New York *Herald Tribune* (October 9, 1959) commended her portrayal of the drink-sodden daughter of a Broadway director.

In September 1959 Shirley MacLaine became the center of a minor international incident after Soviet Premier Nikita S. Khrushchev visited the set of her first musical film, *Can-Can.* When the Soviet leader later registered his moral protest to the cancan that she and a company of dancers had performed for him, Miss MacLaine protested: "Our dance is not nearly as risqué as the can-can was originally" (New York *Times,* September 22, 1959).

Shirley MacLaine and Steve Parker, now a film producer in Japan who travels frequently to Hollywood, were married on September 17, 1954. They have a daughter, Stephanie Sachiko, whose middle name means "happy child" in Japanese. The family occupies a modest ranch house in a section of the San Fernando Valley where few movie stars make their homes.

Both in appearance and in personality, Shirley MacLaine departs somewhat from the traditional Hollywood film queen. She stands five feet six inches and usually weighs about 118 pounds. Her figure resembles that of a dancer rather than that of a voluptuous siren. Her face, while exceedingly mobile, is by no means classical. She has a fair, freckled complexion, slanting blue eyes, and auburn hair, which is irregularly cut and, according to Miss MacLaine, subject to no fixed schedule of combing. For hobbies she enjoys cooking and carpentry, and for a pet she has a boxer. She prefers casual clothes.

Moreover, Miss MacLaine's pixyish appearance accurately reflects an offbeat personality which has been the subject of much publicity and commentary. Columnist Hedda Hopper, voicing the reaction of the Hollywood old guard, has called her "embarrassingly honest." Shirley MacLaine has said, "If I don't like something or someone, then I say so and that clears everything up" (New York *Times,* May 24, 1959).

In training for a role, Miss MacLaine governs herself by no set method. "I wait for the other actor to speak his lines, then I say mine" is her own description of her dramatic technique. Film producers and directors have remarked upon her versatility and ability to make whatever she does seem free from pretense.

The success of unconventional Shirley MacLaine has been analyzed by *Time* magazine (June 22, 1959): "The surprise is not that Shirley has moved to the top, but that she has been able to do it on her own terms . . . without studio-supervised romances, even without a swimming pool. It could have happened only in the new Hollywood, which has found that kookiness [eccentricity] can be more appealing than yesterday's gilded glamour."

References

N Y Sunday News Mag p2 Ag 6 '58 pors
Newsweek 52:91 Ag 18 '58 por
International Motion Picture Almanac, 1959

MACLEISH, ARCHIBALD (mak-lēsh')
May 7, 1892-   Poet; university professor; former librarian

Address: b. Harvard University, Cambridge 38, Mass.; h. Willard St., Cambridge, Mass.

NOTE: This biography supersedes the article which appeared in *Current Biography* in 1940.

Although he dates the beginning of his life from the year he retired from the practice of law to devote his full time to poetry, Archibald MacLeish has perhaps taken a more active part

Friedman—Abeles
ARCHIBALD MACLEISH

in public life than any other living poet. "The nature of art," he believes, "is action, and there is no part of human experience, public or private, on which it cannot act or should not" (*Atlantic Monthly,* January 1958).

MacLeish has at various times been a soldier, lawyer, staff writer for *Fortune* magazine, Librarian of Congress, assistant director of the Office of War Information, Assistant Secretary of State, and a founder of the United Nations Educational, Scientific, and Cultural Organization. At present he is Boylston Professor of Rhetoric and Oratory at Harvard University. For his creative achievement he has received three Pulitzer Prizes: the first in 1933 for the long narrative poem *Conquistador,* the second in 1953 for his *Collected Poems 1917-1952,* and the third in 1959 for *J.B.,* a verse play, which the *Saturday Review* predicted "may well become one of the lasting achievements of art and mind in our time" (September 1, 1956).

Archibald MacLeish was born on May 7, 1892 in Glencoe, Illinois, the son of Andrew and Martha (Hillard) MacLeish. His father, described by MacLeish as a "cold, tall, rigorous man of very beautiful speech," was born in Glasgow, Scotland, was an early settler of Chicago, and became a partner in Carson, Pirie, Scott and Company, the Chicago department store.

After attending Glencoe public schools, MacLeish went to Lakeville, Connecticut to study at the Hotchkiss School, and "hated it," then entered Yale University. As an undergraduate he was on the football and swimming teams, was editor of the literary magazine, and a member of the senior society. He was elected to Phi Beta Kappa and graduated with the B.A. degree in 1915. He entered Harvard Law School, he says, "to avoid going to work." In spite of his assertion that he "could never be-

MACLEISH, ARCHIBALD—*Continued*

lieve in the law," MacLeish was the head of his class by the time he received his LL.B. in 1919.

World War I interrupted MacLeish's law training. He served first in a hospital unit overseas, then in the field artillery, and advanced in rank from private to captain. His brother Kenneth, an aviator, was killed in action during the war. After his discharge MacLeish taught at Harvard for a year. His first book of verse, written as an undergraduate, *Tower of Ivory,* had been published by Yale University Press in 1917.

From 1920 to 1923 MacLeish practised law in Boston, with the firm of Charles F. Choate, Jr. Finding that it interfered with his writing, he gave up the law and in the winter of 1923 went to France with his wife and two children. "[I] date the beginning of my life," he says, "from that year." He spent the next six years reading T. S. Eliot, Ezra Pound, and various French poets, and writing poetry.

He returned to the United States in 1928 and spent part of the following year in Mexico, retracing by mule pack the route of Hernando Cortes from San Juan de Ulúa to Tenochtitlán. The result of this trip was the long poem *Conquistador* (Houghton, 1932) which narrates in *terza rima* (the rhyme scheme of Dante's *Divine Comedy*) the conquest of Mexico by Cortes. *Conquistador* won MacLeish a wide audience and his first Pulitzer Prize, in 1932.

During the 1930's MacLeish's poetry often reflected the social and political awareness of a people caught in the depression. *Panic; A Play in Verse* (Houghton, 1936), concerned with the bank crisis, was staged before a group composed mainly of laborers and unemployed workers, who responded so enthusiastically that MacLeish said: "Now I have found my audience."

Beginning in 1930, MacLeish had been supporting his family by writing for Henry Luce's *Fortune* magazine, where, according to an associate, he wrote "graceful, forceful prose until five in the afternoon." In 1937 he served as chairman of the congress of the League of American Writers, and in 1938 he was named curator of the Nieman Collection of Contemporary Journalism by Harvard University.

President Franklin D. Roosevelt appointed MacLeish Librarian of Congress in 1939, to succeed Herbert Putnam. The appointment occasioned some controversy: the American Library Association deplored the poet's lack of professional library experience, and a few Congressmen suspected his political views. Most scholars and writers favored the choice, and MacLeish, who remained in the post until 1944, proved an able and industrious Librarian of Congress. He acquired a number of valuable manuscripts, began a permanent film collection, and established a Slavic collection.

Another controversy arose in May 1940, when MacLeish made a speech before the American Association for Adult Education. In his address he condemned the pacifistic tendencies of American youth, blaming writers of his own generation, whose antiwar books were, he thought, dangerous "as education for a generation which would be obliged to face the threat of Fascism in its adult years."

In an article in the *Nation* (May 18, 1940) called "The Irresponsibles," reprinted as a book by Duell, Sloan & Pearce in 1940, MacLeish again chastised the intellectuals—this time for not participating in public affairs. Offended by this attack, several writers accused MacLeish of having made an unjustifiable and undignified about-face in his views. By implying a need for censorship, they said, he gave aid and comfort to the reactionaries who had fought his appointment as Librarian of Congress.

During World War II, MacLeish served as director of the Office of Facts and Figures, an agency charged with disseminating data on the defense effort (1941-42). He was also assistant director of the Office of War Information (1942-43), and Assistant Secretary of State (1944-45). In the latter post he helped to plan and publicize the need for a world organization.

At the end of the war MacLeish played an important part in organizing the United Nations Educational, Scientific, and Cultural Organization. He attended the London conference of 1945 that drafted the body's constitution, served as chairman of the American delegation to its first general conference in Paris in 1946, and was an executive member of its general council.

In 1949 Harvard University invited MacLeish to become the Boylston Professor of Rhetoric and Oratory. He has remained in that position until to the present day, teaching creative writing and English literature. Although he finds teaching strenuous, he likes the long summer vacations that afford him the leisure he needs in which to write.

When his *Collected Poems, 1917-1952* (Houghton) appeared in 1952, Richard Eberhart called the volume a "major achievement in American letters. . . . There is something basically lithe, wiry, direct and clear-seeing about his talent" (New York *Times Book Review,* November 23, 1952). For the collection, the poet won the Bollingen Prize, a National Book Award, and his second Pulitzer Prize.

During 1957 MacLeish lectured on American culture throughout Europe under the auspices of the United States Department of State. In an essay for the *Atlantic Monthly* (January 1958) he pointed out that Europeans and Asians resent American materialism which, they feel, has forced the artist into isolation. Correcting this impression, MacLeish wrote that the artist sometimes voluntarily chooses his isolation, the better to devote himself to his art.

The text of MacLeish's *J.B.; A Play in Verse* was published in 1958 by Houghton, Mifflin Company and became a best seller. Based on the Old Testament story of Job, the drama was first produced at Yale and opened on Broadway on December 11, 1958. When it terminated its New York run on October 24, 1959 it went on tour across the nation. *J.B.* won for MacLeish his third Pulitzer Prize and an Antoinette Perry Award.

Why should one love a God who permits unjust suffering? This is the question from the Book of Job which MacLeish re-examines in the light of the abysmal suffering of mankind in the twentieth century. The answer of Mac-Leish is that man can rise above the outrages of his situation and forgive God and love Him in spite of the unjust universe He has created.

J.B. was called "great poetry, great drama, and . . . great stagecraft" by John Ciardi (*Saturday Review,* March 8, 1958), who asserted that until MacLeish's version of Job no great poetic drama had been written since Shakespeare. Not all the reviewers, however, praised *J.B.* Kenneth Tynan (*New Yorker,* December 20, 1958) found that the play was flawed by some "pompously hollow lines" and a muddled conclusion. The critic wrote: "I was bored to exasperation by the lack of any recognizable human response to calamity."

In the forty years between *Tower of Ivory* and *J.B.,* Archibald MacLeish has produced twenty-nine books, including five verse plays, a verse ballet, and seven books of prose. In spite of the criticism directed at him on and off throughout his career, he has become, as Morton Dauwen Zabel observed in 1941, "a major American prophet."

Archibald MacLeish and Ada Hitchcock, a singer, were married on June 21, 1916. They have had four children, Kenneth, Brewster Hitchcock (now deceased), Mary Hillard, and William. MacLeish holds over fifteen honorary degrees, has been president of the American Academy of Arts and Letters (in 1953), and is a member of the National Committee for an Effective Congress. He belongs to the Century Club of New York and the Tavern Club in Boston. He is tall and grey-haired.

References

N Y Times p36 My 5 '59
Living Authors (1931)
National Cyclopædia of American Biography current vol F (1939-42)
Twentieth Century Authors (1942; First Supplement, 1955)
Who's Who in America, 1958-59

MCMINNIES, MARY (JACKSON) June 13, 1920- Author

Address: Thainerbauer, Reith bei Kitzbühel, Tirol, Austria

Reprinted from the *Wilson Library Bulletin* Nov. 1959.

Author of two brilliant, sardonic novels of life in the British diplomatic service, which were based on direct observation, Mary McMinnies is now living in comparatively peaceful Austria. She and her husband, John Gordon McMinnies, who is employed by Her Majesty's Foreign Service but is not a career diplomat, had previously gone from one diplomatic crisis to another.

Mrs. McMinnies was born Mary Jackson on June 13, 1920, in Madras, India. Her brother, David Stuart Jackson, a pilot officer in the R.A.F.V.R., was killed at the age of twenty-one in operations over Germany in 1944. Her sister, Sylvia, is a painter. Their parents were Yorkshire Quakers. Herbert Guy Jackson, an

MARY MCMINNIES

engineer in government employ in India from 1914 to 1943, was a conscientious objector (for which he was penalized two years' seniority) during World War I; instead of active duty he served in a Friends' ambulance unit in Iraq. Mrs. Jackson, nee Emily Stuart, took a B.A. degree at the University of Leeds with first class honors in English, wrote articles for the *Manchester Guardian* on social problems in India under the name Julia Foresight, and was socially ostracized for some years for inviting Eurasian ladies into her home. "This was at a time when *Passage to India* conditions existed, of course," explains Mary McMinnies.

Mary was sent to England at the age of seven, living during both terms and holidays with her brother at a small school in Buckinghamshire and returning there for holidays even after she entered the Friends' School at Saffron Walden, Essex, at thirteen. At sixteen she went to Munich to perfect her German. (Her German master in England used to bawl at her, "Be *ganz objectiv*, child, *ganz objectiv*," and she feels that she has profited by this advice.) A year of acute boredom followed, studying French in the home of a dentist's family at Aix-en-Provence.

After that, says Milton Waldman, in an article in the *Book-of-the-Month Club News,* there "followed in rapid succession marriage, motherhood, and, the war having broken out, enlistment in the Wrens, the British equivalent of the Waves. All three ventures, she affirms without amplification, proved unsuccessful." (In 1939 she had married Gordon Winter, assistant editor of *Country Life,* and was "a wife and mother 1939-1942." A son, William, is now eighteen.)

In 1945 she went to Vienna as an interpreter for the Allied Commission to Austria; in 1946 she went on her own to Cairo, then to Beirut to fill a job with the British Legation news department. In the autumn she left for Athens

MCMINNIES, MARY—*Continued*

to work again for H.M.G. at the Embassy, and on September 15, 1947 she married John McMinnies, then third secretary.

"In 1949 we were posted to Cracow in Poland," she wrote, "where he was in charge of a British newspaper. In 1950 the paper was closed down by the Polish Government and we were posted to Warsaw. In late 1950 he was posted as vice-consul to Bologna, Italy where we stayed two years. In 1953 he was posted to Malaya, as one of General Templer's 'information team' to attack 'the hearts and minds of the people.' We had hoped for a cushy spot, e.g., Kuala Lumpur, instead were given central Johore."

Here Mrs. McMinnies was considered "quite dotty" by the other English *mem-sahibs,* for, apart from painting the respectable government bungalow (cream and chocolate) sea-green and decorating it with fishing nets and also breeding turkeys, she went to China with her husband, staying in villages overnight.

On a hilltop in Johore she wrote her first published novel, *The Flying Fox* (Harcourt, 1957). (Her first, written at twenty-one, was summarily rejected; Hutchinson & Company's reader considered it "pornographic.") "The author of this pungent, well-written first novel [*The Flying Fox*] has etched with first-hand knowledge a study of tragic interplay among the regrettable types she portrays," said the *Christian Science Monitor.* The types were Europeans in Malaya, especially one British ne'er-do-well. "Its pace, excitement, and construction are those of a veteran," according to Margaret Parton (New York *Herald Tribune Book Review*).

The Visitors (Harcourt, 1958) was written in an eight-by-ten-foot bedroom in London. "For ten months she went out socially with nobody but her agent once and her publisher once," says Waldman. "Food consumption, she reports, was negligible, but the toll of cigarettes and cider, terrific." The 1956 Anglo-French invasion of Suez kept her husband busy at the Foreign Office, meanwhile. Critics, with some reservations, also praised this story of Milly Purdoe, the beautiful, amoral wife of a diplomat stationed in a Communist satellite country, immediately recognizable as Poland. "Poor Milly is merely a kind of woman's magazine Bovary," stated the *Times* (London) *Literary Supplement,* but Kay Boyle (*Saturday Review*) wrote that "the dialogue is bright and entertaining, the plot moves at a disciplined gallop, the delineation of scene and character is highly professional." The novel was a December 1958 selection of the Book-of-the-Month Club.

Mary McMinnies is "a tall, fair, handsome woman, whose outward demeanor suggests placidity rather than intensity" (Waldman). She describes herself as hazel-eyed, five feet seven inches in height, and 115 pounds in weight. Not interested in politics, she would, however, "vote Labour rather than see the Tories win." Her recreations are "eating and drinking queer things; overhearing conversations—this is a mania: will follow any pair of people anywhere."

Reference

Book-of-the-Month Club News N '58 por

MAHAN, JOHN W(ILLIAM) June 24, 1923- Lawyer; organization official

Address: b. Mahan and Mahan, 28½ N. Last Chance Gulch, Helena, Mont.; h. 620 Madison Ave., Helena, Mont.

Second largest of the American veteran's organizations, the Veterans of Foreign Wars of the United States has some 1,200,000 members in many posts throughout the country. At its fifty-ninth annual encampment, in New York City in August 1958, John W. Mahan, a Montana lawyer and former state V.F.W. commander, was elected commander in chief for 1958-59. The V.F.W. not only maintains a program for the benefit of veterans, but also carries out a number of activities in the public interest, such as vigilance in combating subversion. Its national headquarters are in Kansas City, Missouri.

A native and lifelong resident of Montana, John William Mahan was born in Missoula on June 24, 1923 to John William and Iola C. (Morgan) Mahan. His father, an attorney who had served overseas with the Army in World War I, was an active member of the Veterans of Foreign Wars, a national commander of the Disabled American Veterans (1924-25), and at the age of forty-one became the youngest brigadier general and adjutant general in the history of the Montana National Guard. John Mahan has a younger brother, Tom, at present his law partner, and one sister, now Mrs. Lucile Foot of Washington, D.C.

In high school in Helena, Montana, Mahan was president of the freshman class and of the student body in his senior year (1940-41). He was also prominent in debating. Later he was president of the freshman class at Montana State University in Missoula, where his undergraduate work was interrupted in the summer of 1942 by enlistment in the Marine Corps for World War II service.

Entering as a seaman second class at the Naval Flight School, John W. Mahan trained at St. Mary's College in California and at Pasco in the state of Washington before taking the preadvanced flight course in Corpus Christi, Texas. He was graduated with a second lieutenant's commission. He also trained at the Daytona Beach Dive Bomber School in Florida and saw further stateside duty at Cherry Point, North Carolina and in the Mojave Desert, California. He then fought in the Pacific as a pilot in Dive Bomber Squadron 332 of the 3rd Marine Air Wing until his return to the United States in April 1945.

When he was discharged from the United States Marine Corps in January 1946, Mahan held the rank of captain. He resumed his studies at Montana State University, majoring in law, and in 1949 received his LL.B. degree and admission to the state bar. During the period from 1950 to 1952 he served the State of Montana as a special assistant attorney general and as a police judge. Since 1952 he has engaged in private practice as a partner in the law firm of Mahan and Mahan, which was established at Helena by his father and which now includes his younger brother, Tom, a West Point graduate and a Korean War veteran. Considered one of the best-known young trial counsels of the Pacific Northwest, Mahan pleads cases in federal as well as the higher state courts, and has served as counsel for various state boards.

Immediately after being relieved from active duty in the Marine Corps in 1945, Mahan had joined the Veterans of Foreign Wars. During the next five years he held various offices at Post 116 in Helena, including junior and senior vice-commander. In 1950-51, the year in which he served as its commander, the post earned the highest state V.F.W. community service award. Also during that year he co-sponsored the state honorarium for World War II veterans which provided a $21,000,000 bonus for Montana ex-servicemen.

The Helena attorney served as state commander of the V.F.W. in 1952-53. Then in 1954 he was elected to represent District 16 on the national council of administration for a two-year term. At the encampment, in Dallas, Texas in August 1956, he was unopposed for election as junior vice-commander in chief. Next year, when Richard L. Roudebush of Indianapolis, Indiana, was elected commander in chief, Mahan was elevated to senior vice-commander in chief.

Later in 1957 Commander Roudebush designated Mahan to serve as a special observer for the V.F.W. at the trial in a Japanese court of Specialist 3/c William S. Girard for causing the death of a Japanese woman at an American firing range about sixty miles from Tokyo. There was much dispute as to whether Girard should be tried in a Japanese court or by court martial, and it is said that "demands of the V.F.W. for a revision of the 'status of forces' treaties were strengthened during [Mahan's] assignment" (*V.F.W. Magazine,* October 1958).

Unopposed for election as V.F.W. commander in chief for 1958-59, John W. Mahan took office on August 22, 1958, the final day of the annual encampment in New York City. Delegates to the convention heard addresses by Francis Cardinal Spellman, Mayor Robert Wagner of New York City, Governor Averell Harriman of New York, and Secretary of State John Foster Dulles, who was awarded the organization's Bernard Baruch Medal for the "greatest contribution to the cause of American security, unity, and world peace." (Former President Harry S. Truman has also received the award.)

The convention adopted resolutions urging that a tax-free Federal bonus up to $4,500 each be paid to veterans of World War II and the Korean War and that the pension system for World War I veterans be liberalized. The veterans advocated severance of diplomatic relations with the Soviet Union and its expulsion from the United Nations. They opposed world

JOHN W. MAHAN

government, the Atlantic Union, and the "weakening" of such "basic security laws" as the Smith Act, Internal Security Act, Immigration and Nationality Act, and the Communist Control Act (New York *Times,* August 22, 1958).

"We, as an organization, fight each and every day for veterans' legislation to help the hospital program, the widows, and the orphans," Commander Mahan said in his acceptance speech. "During my term, we will fight even harder to see that the one hundred forty-four millions of dollars now available for hospital construction and re-modernization are used now for that purpose." He urged the enlargement of the Marine Corps and an increase in the National Guard from 400,000 men to at least double that number, so that the United States would have "a force large enough to handle immediately any limited war" in which it might find itself. He said that we need to prepare for limited conflict in order to avoid nuclear war, which would destroy our civilization.

Addressing veterans of New Mexico about a month later, Commander Mahan advocated cabinet rank for the director of the Veterans Administration and the formation of a veterans committee in the United States Senate, where seventeen veterans measures died in the last session of Congress. At a meeting of the Illinois V.F.W. he promised that World War I pension legislation would be reintroduced in the Eighty-sixth Congress. "I would like to suggest," he said, "that all of you contact your Senate and congressional candidates and see how they feel about such legislation. I am sure that you will know what to do with those who do not favor a World War I pension plan."

Commander Mahan is also a member of the American Legion, the Disabled American Veterans, and the Jaycees. He is an Elk and an Eagle and is active in the Chamber of Commerce and the Exchange Club in Helena. He is

MAHAN, JOHN W.—*Continued*

an Episcopalian and a Democrat. Mahan, who mentions golf and swimming as favorite recreations, stands six feet three inches tall and weighs about 175 pounds; he has blue eyes and black hair. John W. Mahan and Shirley Tuohy were married August 4, 1943. They have three daughters, Kim Iola, Shelley, and Bartley.

Mahan believes that "the greatest test of loyalty—of love for country—is your day-to-day respect of the rights of your fellow man. Your neighbor's right to voice his own opinion, his right to privacy, his right to his own property— these basic freedoms are the heart of our loyalty to the great American ideals of Washington, Jefferson, and Lincoln."

References

N Y Times p3 Ag 23 '58 por
V.F.W. 46:12 O '58

MALAN, DANIEL FRANÇOIS May 22, 1874-Feb. 7, 1959 Prime Minister of the Union of South Africa (1948-54); an Afrikaner and an advocate of apartheid. See *Current Biography* (April) 1949.

Obituary

N Y Times p20 F 7 '59

MALBIN, ELAINE May 24, 1932- Singer
Address: b. c/o Coppicus & Schang, 113 W. 57th St., New York 19; h. 925 Fifth Ave., New York 21

The lyric soprano voice of Elaine Malbin has helped to make opera a more familiar form of art to millions of Americans. Her performances in televised operas have won her the title of "prima donna of television." Since 1950 she has often sung starring roles

ELAINE MALBIN

over the CBS and NBC television networks. She has also appeared on Broadway in such productions as *My Darlin' Aida* and *Kismet* and has performed with the New York City Opera Company.

Since her debut in New York's Town Hall Elaine Malbin has accumulated a wealth of musical experience. The young soprano has sung over the radio, in concert halls, and at music festivals throughout the United States. She has appeared on the *Ed Sullivan Show* and the *Voice of Firestone* and has recorded for RCA Victor. In April 1956 she was chosen to sing the leading role in the world première of Norman Dello Joio's opera, *The Trial at Rouen,* over NBC-TV.

Born on May 24, 1932 in New York City, Elaine Malbin is the daughter of Irving and Dorothy (Biales) Malbin. She was brought up in Brooklyn, where she attended the local public schools. When Elaine was in the sixth grade, one of her music teachers recognized that she had unusual vocal ability and recommended formal musical training. Her parents borrowed money on their household furniture to buy a piano and help to finance her lessons. While Elaine attended James Madison High School in Brooklyn, she did baby-sitting in the evenings to help defray her music expenses.

When Elaine Malbin made her debut at Town Hall in New York City on March 31, 1945 the concert aroused considerable interest because of her precocity. The music critic of the New York *Times* (April 1, 1945) noted: "Her work left no doubt as to her possession of decided talents and innate musicality. . . . But the fact remained that despite her gifts she was not as yet ready for public hearing or critical appraisal."

By doubling up her courses, Miss Malbin completed her high school education in three years and was graduated in 1948 at the age of sixteen. During that year she became a staff singer with the National Broadcasting Company, appearing regularly on the radio programs *Serenade to America, Music for Tomorrow,* and *Saturday Matinee.*

She also appeared in five Carnegie Hall Pops concerts and in 1949 sang with a Broadway Gilbert and Sullivan company. She played leading roles in *The Chocolate Soldier* in St. Louis and Dallas, and in *Naughty Marietta* with the Detroit Civic Opera Company.

Perhaps Elaine Malbin took the biggest step forward in her career when she was selected to sing opposite Lawrence Tibbett in a CBS-TV production of *La Traviata* in March 1950. Shortly afterwards the young soprano received offers from the Metropolitan Opera Association and the New York City Opera Company. Miss Malbin felt that she could gain more experience by singing the leading roles offered her by the New York City Opera Company than in the minor ones offered by the Metropolitan. For the next two seasons (1951-1952) she appeared in *Carmen, Turandot, La Bohème,* and many other operas with the New York City Opera Company. She devoted her summers to concert appearances at Robin Hood Dell in

Philadelphia and at Lewisohn Stadium in New York.

In the fall of 1952 Miss Malbin appeared in the title role in the sumptuous Broadway musical *My Darlin' Aida*, based rather remotely upon the opera by Verdi. Brooks Atkinson of the New York *Times* (October 28, 1952) called her performance "brilliant" and stated: "She has put the music and the character together in a fiery and accomplished performance that is completely captivating." The show, however, was not unanimously welcomed by the critics, and closed on January 11, after a run of only eighty-nine performances.

After her Broadway engagement, the young soprano starred in an NBC-TV production of Puccini's *Sister Angelica*, and then, during her first trip to Europe, was heard over the British Broadcasting Corporation in Gian-Carlo Menotti's *The Medium*. While in England she sang at the famous Glyndebourne Opera Festival in Ferruccio Busoni's *Arlecchino*.

When she sang the title role in the *NBC Television Opera Theatre*'s production of Richard Strauss' *Salome* in May 1954, Miss Malbin earned new compliments from the critics. Howard Taubman of the New York *Times* (May 9, 1954) wrote: "Miss Malbin sang the difficult title role with style, control, and beauty of tone." The following year she returned to Broadway as a replacement for Doretta Morrow in the starring role in *Kismet*.

After singing in *Kismet* on Broadway from January to March in 1955 she went on tour with the show to the West coast. William Hawkins of the New York *World-Telegram and Sun* (January 29, 1955) remarked: "Miss Malbin has a clear and quite lovely soprano voice... When she steps toward the footlights and lavishes her breath on a high finish, there is a tingling grandeur about the sound that our musical theatre lacks too much."

On December 4, 1955 Elaine Malbin was again seen on the television screen with the *NBC Television Opera Theatre* in her first appearance as Cio-Cio San in *Madama Butterfly*. Louis Biancolli of the New York *World-Telegram and Sun* (December 5, 1955) observed: "Miss Malbin rates an operatic acting Oscar for her Cio-Cio San and vocally she wasn't far behind," while Ronald Eyer of *Musical America* (December 15, 1955) called the performance "a great personal triumph for the young soprano."

Another landmark in Elaine Malbin's career was her performance as Joan of Arc in *The Trial at Rouen* by Norman Dello Joio, given its world première on April 8, 1956 on NBC-TV. *Time* magazine reported (April 16, 1956): "Soprano Elaine Malbin not only sang beautifully, but turned out to be an actress of imposing ability." Howard Taubman of the New York *Times* (April 9, 1956) noted that Miss Malbin "sang Joan with sweetness and strength that illuminated the character."

During the 1957 television opera season Elaine Malbin sang the role of Violetta in the *NBC*

Television Opera Theatre's production of *La Traviata*. While most of the critics praised her performance, Irving Kolodin of the *Saturday Review* (May 4, 1957) felt that she was "the one bit of questionable casting . . . only acquiring dramatic truth in the pathetic ending." Ross Parmenter of the New York *Times* (April 22, 1957) stated that "a few high notes . . . were a little edgy, but for the most part her singing was fresh, clear and agile and quite often the tone was lovely enough to be affecting."

Another important assignment was given to Elaine Malbin when she sang in the television première of Francis Poulenc's *Dialogues of the Carmelites* in December 1957. Paul Henry Lang of the New York *Herald Tribune* (December 9, 1957) commented: "Elaine Malbin, the heroine, is a dependable singer and an earnest actress, but, at least through the loud-speaker, her voice is somewhat lacking in variety."

In between her appearances on TV Miss Malbin has sung in concert halls in leading American cities and in numerous night clubs. In July 1957 she portrayed Cio-Cio San at the Empire State Music Festival in Ellenville, New York. She has recorded several albums for the RCA Victor label, including *Naughty Marietta, The Firefly, The Merry Widow,* and *A Connecticut Yankee.*

Brown-eyed and brunette Elaine Malbin is five feet tall and weighs 112 pounds. To shed tensions, develop stamina, and remain in trim, she works out daily in a gymnasium. A profile of the singer in *Vogue* (October 15, 1956) described her as "serious and disciplined." A fashionable dresser, she was named one of the ten best-dressed women in America in 1956. She is a member of Actors' Equity Association and the American Federation of TV and Radio Artists.

In an article "Opera—On a Silver Platter" which she wrote for the New York *Herald Tribune* (August 26, 1956) Elaine Malbin said: "Gradually, thanks to TV, Americans are beginning to appreciate that Rhinegold isn't necessarily Ballantine's big competition, that Parsifal isn't a vegetable, that Mignon doesn't have to be eaten with onions. . . ."

References

Cue 26:14 D 7 '57 por
Down Beat 21:9 O 6 '54
N Y Sun News Mag p4 Ja 22 '56 por
N Y World-Telegram Mag p20 Ap 20 '57
Who's Who in America, 1958-59

MALLORY, C(ASSIUS) C(HESTER) Oct. 18, 1890-Jan. 2, 1959 Steamship company executive; president of the Grace Line (1953-55) and chairman (1955-57). See *Current Biography* (February) 1956.

Obituary

N Y Times p17 Ja 3 '59

MALONE, ROSS(ER) L(YNN, JR.) Sept. 9, 1910- Attorney; organization official

Address: b. Roswell Petroleum Building, Roswell, N.M.; h. 1511 W. Seventh St., Roswell, N.M.

One of the youngest lawyers to head the American Bar Association since its founding in 1878, Ross L. Malone took office on August 29, 1958 during its eighty-first annual meeting at the Hotel Statler-Hilton in Los Angeles. The eighty-second president of the national organization of the legal profession, who is an au-

Gittings

ROSS L. MALONE

thority on oil and gas legislation, was Deputy Attorney General of the United States from 1952 to 1953.

In his native city of Roswell, New Mexico, Malone has been a practising attorney for more than twenty-five years. An active member of the American Bar Association for more than two decades, he has served on various committees and as a member of its board of governors from 1951 to 1954. During 1954 and 1955 he served under Herbert Hoover as a member of the task force on legal services and procedures of the Commission on Organization of the Executive Branch of the Government (Hoover Commission). He has written a number of professional articles and has lectured at legal institutes throughout the United States.

Rosser Lynn Malone, Jr., was born on September 9, 1910 to Rosser Lynn and Edna (Littlefield) Malone in Roswell, New Mexico. He was educated in the public school system of Roswell and received his LL.B. degree from Washington and Lee University in Lexington, Virginia in 1932.

After his graduation from Washington and Lee University, Malone returned to Roswell, and was admitted to the bar in Chaves County,

New Mexico in 1932. He joined a law firm that later became known as Atwood & Malone. In 1936 he became city attorney for Roswell, a post that he held until World War II, when he was appointed a lieutenant (j.g.) in the United States Navy. He saw active duty afloat in the Pacific area and, upon his discharge in 1946, held the rank of lieutenant commander, USNR. In 1941, shortly before entering the service, Malone served as chairman of the New Mexico Alien Enemy Hearing Board.

From 1946 to 1951 Malone served on the legal committee of the interstate oil compact commission, an assignment which drew heavily upon his specialized knowledge of the legal problems of oil resources.

While serving on the board of governors of the American Bar Association in 1952, Malone was chosen by James P. McGranery, United States Attorney General under President Truman, to succeed A. Devitt Vanech as Deputy Attorney General. He was sworn into office in August 1952 as one of McGranery's "three key men." McGranery said he looked upon Malone's appointment as "a real step in carrying out the promise I made when I assumed office, that the business of the department would be discharged with dignity and dispatch" (New York *Times*, August 13, 1952).

During his appointment as Deputy Attorney General, Malone made an important contribution to the improvement of federal judiciary procedure. He originated "the arrangement whereby the Department of Justice submits to the American Bar Association the names of lawyers under consideration for appointment to the federal judiciary for recommendation as to their professional qualifications."

As a member of the Hoover Commission in 1954 and 1955, Malone studied the legal services and procedures of federal agencies. In August 1954 he was a member of the American Bar Association committee that urged Congress to end abuses of its investigatory powers and protect the rights of witnesses.

Malone began his service with the American Bar Association in 1938 as a member of the junior bar conference; he was state chairman for New Mexico. He became state delegate from New Mexico to the association's policy-making body, the house of delegates, in 1946. He has been a member of more than a dozen working committees of the American Bar Association, and in 1951 he became a member of its board of governors. From 1951 until 1954 he served on the board of directors of the American Bar Foundation (the research group of the association) and belonged to the executive and building committee which was responsible for planning, financing, and building the American Bar Center, the national headquarters of the association in Chicago.

When Malone accepted the silver gavel of office as president of the American Bar Association from his predecessor, Charles S. Rhyne, on August 29, 1958, he made the keynote of his address "world peace through world law." Other objectives in his four-point program were elimination of what Chief Justice Earl Warren has called the "interminable and unjustifiable delays in our courts which are today compromising the basic legal rights of countless thousands of Americans"; closer co-operation between the practising profession and the law schools and law students; and accelerated legal education through a well-planned national and state program.

According to Malone, the American Bar Association planned to conduct lawyer conferences in selected cities throughout the United States, which would "provide a pilot project for a world conference of lawyers envisioned for a later date."

One of the important achievements of the eighty-first annual meeting of the American Bar Association was the formation of a permanent Conference of State Trial Court Judges, a first move toward the national organization of state judges. The legal aspects of school segregation and the legal status of outer space also received much publicity during the meeting.

Ross L. Malone is much concerned with the fact that the legal profession is losing many of its potential recruits to engineering and the sciences. In a speech before the Indianapolis Bar Association in the fall of 1958 he pointed out that among a group of national merit scholarship winners only 3 per cent planned careers in law, while 50 per cent were intending to enter engineering and the sciences. Admissions to the bar, he said, had dropped from 13,641 in 1950 to 9,450 in 1956.

Ross L. Malone has always taken an active interest in civic and regional affairs. In his native Southwest he has been a trustee of the Southwestern Legal Foundation in Dallas, Texas, and a member of the Board of Bar Examiners for New Mexico. He is former president of the Roswell Chamber of Commerce and of the Chaves County Bar Association.

On October 10, 1934 Ross L. Malone was married to Elizabeth L. Amis, also of Roswell, New Mexico. In 1956 he received the Hatton W. Sumners Award of the Southwestern Legal Foundation for his contribution "to the improvement of the administration of justice." Washington and Lee University gave him an honorary Doctor of Laws degree in June 1958. He is a member of the American Law Institute, a fellow of the American College of Trial Lawyers, and belongs to Phi Delta Phi, Sigma Nu, and Omicron Delta Kappa fraternities. His religion is Methodist.

References

U S News 44:20 Mr 7 '58
Who's Who in America, 1958-59

MALRAUX, ANDRÉ (mäl-rō') Nov. 3, 1901- French cabinet member; author
Address: b. Hotel Matignon, 57 rue Varennes, Paris 7ᵉ, France; h. 19 avenue Victor-Hugo, Boulogne-sur-Seine (Seine), France

Few famous writers have ever attained so high a place in government as has the many-sided French author André Malraux. Appointed Minister of Information by General Charles de Gaulle in June 1958, Malraux resigned a month later from that post, but on January 8, 1959 became a Minister of State in the new French cabinet. In French government he has taken responsibility for youth, cultural, and scientific affairs. Called de Gaulle's "one-man brain truster," he is, according to Ernest O. Hauser (*Saturday Evening Post*, September 13, 1958), "the second most important member of the team."

André Malraux was born on November 3, 1901 in Paris, son of Fernand-Georges and Berthe (Lamy) Malraux. André's father, a wealthy banker, had his business at Suresnes, near Paris. André was not brought up by his mother, since his parents separated while he was still a child. He went to the Lycée Condorcet and, after obtaining his baccalaureate, entered the School of Oriental Languages where he studied Sanskrit, Chinese, and archaeology.

After completing his studies, Malraux began working in the art department of the Kra publishing house where he remained until 1924. In 1921 he married Clara Goldschmidt, of German-Jewish origin, who became a writer. Two years later he went with her to Cambodia to look for the remains of some Khmerian sculpture along the "royal road" and found them around Banteai-srey. After difficulties with the colonial government over his right to transport the statues, Malraux returned to France in the autumn of 1924, but two months later was back again in Indochina. In Saigon he collaborated with the nationalistic Young Annam League and took part in publishing the newspaper *L'Indochine*. Later he went to China, where he may have taken part in the Chinese civil war of 1925-27 in Canton. In 1926 he published *La Tentation de l'Occident*, an epistolary novel.

Malraux returned finally to Paris in 1927. In the next few years appeared his novels *The Conquerors* (1928), *The Royal Way* (1930), and *Man's Fate* (1933). During that time he was an editor at the Gallimard publishing house and undertook more archaeological expeditions, including one in China and one in southern Arabia. He divorced his wife in 1930.

Man's Fate, which won Malraux the Goncourt Prize in 1933, made him a prominent figure in the world of letters. It was a forceful novel of heroes engaged in the Chinese Revolution of 1924. The revolutionists learn that man's destiny is one of greatness and of misery: greatness in his disregard for death and in his decision to act in behalf of a common ideal, and misery in the humiliating discovery of his final solitude and self-centeredness.

In 1934 Malraux attended the Writers' Congress in Moscow where his speech on the freedom necessary for the artist was most unwelcome. In the same year he and André Gide petitioned Hitler against the trial of Georgi Dimitrov, the Bulgarian Communist leader, who was accused of having participated in the Reichstag fire. In 1935 he attended in Paris the Congress of Writers in Defense of Culture where he again defended the claim of the artist. In the same year he wrote *Days of Wrath*, his only novel that has circulated freely in the

ANDRÉ MALRAUX

Soviet Union; the other novels were banned there in spite of their strongly anti-Fascist character.

At the outbreak of the Spanish Civil War in 1936, Malraux joined forces with the Loyalists. He helped to organize their air force, in which he also flew as a machine-gunner, and he served as an adviser to the Spanish Republican leaders. In 1938 he lectured in America in order to obtain funds for the Spanish Republicans. Against the background of the Spanish Civil War he wrote his third major novel, *Man's Hope* (1937), which exalts the brotherhood of men confronted with the constant possibility of death. *Man's Hope* was also produced by Malraux as a motion picture, winning him the Louis-Delhuc Prize in 1945.

Man's Hope closed the first chapter of Malraux's life, the one of revolutionary experience. The revolution was for him, in Pierre de Boisdeffre's words, "only one form, among others, of that 'struggle with the angel,' that conquest of the absolute which all his works attempt to illustrate while he is looking for *a fundamental idea upon which the concept of man could be based.*" In his search for this idea, Communism seemed to him, as to many intellectuals of the time, a possible step toward a practical humanism. According to de Boisdeffre, Malraux broke with Communism at the beginning of World War II when he saw the Soviet collaboration with Nazi Germany leading to the invasion of Finland, Poland, and the Baltic States.

When World War II broke out, Malraux enlisted in the Tank Corps, and was wounded and captured by the Germans in June 1940. He managed to escape to the unoccupied zone of France where he joined the resistance movement and participated, under the name of "Colonel Berger," in the underground fight of the Maquis against the Germans. Shortly be-

fore the liberation in 1944, he was captured again by the Germans and moved from one prison to another until he was finally freed by the French Forces in Toulouse.

While fighting on the Alsatian front Malraux met General Charles de Gaulle who, after the meeting, is said to have exclaimed: "At last! I have met the man!" The meeting began an intimate friendship. In de Gaulle's provisional government Malraux served as Minister of Information from November 1945 until de Gaulle's resignation in January 1946. In the next decade, except for acting as the national propaganda chief of the Gaullist Rassemblement du Peuple Français, he confined himself to his writing.

During this period he wrote the monumental study *Psychology of Art* (1948-50). The work is a passionate and lyrical search for the transcendental in man. The idea of the grandeur and permanence of man, which in his novels Malraux had tried to find in individual or social action, is, in *The Voices of Silence*, sought exclusively in the world of art. Five years spent in the study of painting and sculpture had convinced Malraux that only art can assure man of his reality. Viewed in the perspective of history, masterpieces possess an intrinsic and everlasting value. Thus art, taking the place of a religious humanism, attests that through genius there exists a universal man, independent of time and space, who can attain the liberty and eternity so completely denied to man as an individual.

In spite of his devotion to art, Malraux has always tried to be a man committed to a cause (*l'homme engagé*) and, consequently, a man of action. An opportunity for action presented itself again as a result of the Algerian rebellion of May 1958 which brought de Gaulle into power. Appointed Minister of Information in June 1958, Malraux, who was interested chiefly in "great issues," apparently was not too happy until he was replaced by Jacques Soustelle a month later. Then he was able to devote himself entirely to the production of ideas, even though he remained a cabinet member in charge of youth, cultural and scientific affairs. When the new cabinet for France was announced on January 8, 1959, the name of André Malraux appeared on the list as Minister of State (with no party affiliation).

According to André Malraux, France needs a stable government able to insure "the rebirth of the country" and the restoration of its former grandeur. An anti-Communist and anti-Fascist, Malraux considers himself a leftist with a great interest in social action. "Malraux admits," C. L. Sulzberger noted (New York *Times*, June 23, 1958), "[that] de Gaulle must save the country from extremes of both Right and Left."

Malraux's second wife, Josette Clotis, a writer, was killed in a railroad accident in 1945. He married on March 13, 1948, Marie-Madeleine Malraux, née Lioux, a concert pianist, widow of his half-brother Roland Malraux. They have four children; he has three from his previous marriage and she one from hers. Malraux has been described as "pale," "slender," "an intensely nervous man," but the most "compulsive, stimulating conversationalist in French intellectual circles." He is an officer of the Légion d'Honneur, a Compagnon de la Libération, and holds the Médaille de la Résistance and the Croix de Guerre (1939-45).

References

N Y Herald Tribune p2 Je '58 por
N Y Times p9 Je 3 '58
N Y Times Mag p9+ Jl 6 '58 por
Columbia Dictionary of Modern Literature (1947)
Dictionnaire Biographique Français Contemporain (1954)
Picon, Gaëtan Malraux par lui-même (1958)
Talvert, H. & Place, J. Bibliographie des auteurs modernes de langue française (1801-1956) vol 13 (1956)
Twentieth Century Authors (1942; First Supplement, 1955)
Untermeyer, Louis Makers of the Modern World (1955)
Who's Who, 1958
Who's Who in America, 1958-59
World Biography (1948)

Ralph Tornberg

NORMAN W. MANLEY

MANLEY, NORMAN W(ASHINGTON)
July 4, 1893- Chief Minister of Jamaica; lawyer
Address: b. Headquarters House, Duke St., Kingston, Jamaica, B.W.I.; h. "Drumblair," Old Church Rd., Constant Spring, Jamaica, B.W.I.

Generally recognized as the "dean of West Indian statesmen," Norman W. Manley has been the Chief Minister of Jamaica since 1955. A former Rhodes scholar and one of the most prominent lawyers in the Caribbean, Manley is the founder and head of Jamaica's moderately socialistic People's National party, which greatly increased its majority in Jamaica's most recent election, held in July 1959. The People's National party government, in the wake of the election, took office on August 14, 1959.

Norman Washington Manley, the son of Margaret Ann (Shearer) and Thomas Albert Samuel Manley, was born July 4, 1893 in Jamaica at Roxburg in the parish of Manchester where his father was a produce merchant. Norman Manley is of Irish and Negro descent. He was raised in rural Jamaica, was educated at the local elementary schools and at the main secondary school, Jamaica College. In high school he won distinction as a scholar and an athlete. In the Jamaica Inter-scholastic Competition he ran the 100 yard dash in ten seconds, a local record which held until the track was rebuilt forty years later.

After his graduation in 1912 Manley taught in an agricultural vocational school until 1914, when he received a Rhodes Scholarship to study law at Jesus College, Oxford. But World War I interrupted his plans, and in 1915 he joined the Royal Field Artillery. For his service he was awarded the Military Medal. At the conclusion of World War I, he returned to Oxford where he received a B.A. degree in 1920 and a B.C.L. degree the following year. At Oxford Manley won the Lee Essay Prize, passed his bar examinations with the Certificate of Honour, and was called to the bar from Gray's Inn in 1921. He then returned to his native island where he was admitted to the bar in 1922.

Manley's success as a commercial and criminal lawyer has become legendary in the Caribbean. He has participated in virtually every major case in Jamaica since 1923, and some of his cases are considered "classics in the art of quiet pleading" (New York *Times*, March 10, 1959). He first appeared in an English court in 1946, when he gained an acquittal for a Jamaican accused of murder. Five years later he returned to England as the first Jamaican lawyer to appear before the Judicial Committee of the Privy Council. At that time he defended a United States chemical company in a trademark case.

Manley turned to politics because he felt it was the best way to help ameliorate the poverty and social disruptions which prevailed in Jamaica in the 1930's and 1940's. The island, only 500 miles from Miami, imported virtually all its necessities of life and drew its income from the export of sugar and bananas. This income became insufficient when Jamaica found itself unable to meet competition from other markets. A shipping shortage during the war years also contributed to the economic slump.

To help ease the situation Manley founded, in 1937, a rural betterment and social welfare organization, Jamaica Welfare Ltd., whose immediate task was to deal with the disruption resulting from the breakdown of the banana co-operatives. The work of this group has been the subject of a UNESCO study. The following year, when Jamaica was paralyzed by a

MANLEY, NORMAN W.—*Continued*

general strike, Manley established the People's National party, a left-wing group with aims similar to those of Britain's Labour party.

In 1944, when a new Jamaican constitution granting limited self-government and universal suffrage was adopted, Manley stood as a candidate for the assembly, the island's legislative body which served under a British-appointed governor. Manley and his young party lost this contest, but in 1949 he was elected to the assembly as a representative from East St. Andrew.

It was not until 1955, however, that his party gained a majority in the assembly, which until then had been controlled by the Jamaica Labor party, the conservative group headed by Sir Alexander Bustamante, Manley's cousin and long time political foe. Manley replaced Bustamante as Chief Minister and also took the job of Minister of Agriculture.

When he took the island's top office, Manley hoped to develop industry and diversify agriculture in an effort to end the economic slump which had put 20 per cent of the working force out of jobs. He was also pledged to win wider self-government and to promote a West Indies Federation.

The new government instituted tax holdings to attract foreign capital for the development of Jamaica's industry. Under an agrarian reform program the government bought land from large estate holders to distribute acreage among the peasants, and irrigated formerly untillable land in the hope that Jamaica would eventually have, in Manley's words, "for every man an acre and for every acre a man."

Considerable progress was made during Manley's first term in office. Industrial growth was impressive, and the construction of new hotels gave a big boost to the tourist trade. Renegotiation, conducted by Manley in 1957 with the one Canadian and two American aluminum companies mining Jamaica's bauxite, gave the government's treasury much needed additional revenues. The Jamaicans for the first time were able to produce their own staple, rice.

The bauxite industry created over 4,000 new jobs, and the aluminum companies agreed to restore all mined-out land to agricultural productivity. "The companies," said Manley, "have done an impressive job in the agricultural field. Their policy as to agricultural tenants has been enlightened and beneficial" (*Saturday Evening Post*, July 19, 1958). Bauxite has brought a prosperity to Jamaica which the island has never enjoyed before.

In November 1957, Jamaica was granted full home rule. According to the amended constitution, the conduct of domestic affairs was placed entirely in the hands of the Jamaican assembly and council of ministers, with Britain still determining foreign and defense policies. The island will eventually obtain complete independence as a member of the West Indies Federation, when the Federation achieves dominion status in the British Commonwealth.

The Federation, for which Manley pioneered, was established in 1958. The plan is to make it a customs and trade union with freedom of movement of peoples and goods among the British islands in the Caribbean. The islands included in addition to Jamaica are Barbados, Antigua, Montserrat, St. Christopher-Nevis-Anguilla, Trinidad-Tobago, Dominica, Grenada, St. Lucia, and St. Vincent.

Paradoxically, Manley, who is known as the "father" of the Federation, has recently found himself in the position of defending Jamaica's interests against those of the Federation. Although it had been expected that Manley would take a Federation office, he preferred to remain in Jamaican political life. In Jamaica's 1959 election campaign, Manley, whose party won the contest, pledged to work for a revision of the Federation's constitution to protect Jamaica's economic interests. In his speeches, the Chief Minister reflected the fears of the Jamaicans that their island, now the most prosperous of the union, would be taxed to support the smaller islands unable to pay their own way. The Jamaicans also resented the fact that their island did not have representation in the Federation's parliament commensurate with its population and the money it contributed to the federal government.

In addition to his work as the island's Chief Minister, Manley has maintained an interest in the welfare of Jamaicans who have emigrated to Great Britain. When race riots flared in London in the fall of 1958, Manley immediately flew to England to help his people and forestall British action to limit immigration. As a solution to the race problem created by the immigration of West Indians to Great Britain, Manley has proposed a "grass roots plan" of integration, involving the training of local leaders and social workers for communities with large colored sections.

In 1921 Norman W. Manley married British sculptress Edna Swithenbank. They have two sons, Douglas Ralph, a college professor, and Michael Norman, a journalist and trade union worker.

Manley, restrained, intellectual, and logical, with a tendency toward the ascetic, neither drinks nor smokes and has recently become a vegetarian. A Queen's Counsel and president of the Jamaica Bar Council, he has in the past served as a member of the Central Board of Health, the Advisory Board under the Agricultural Produce Law, the Marketing and Industries Board, the Agricultural Policy Committee, the Social Security Committee, the Award Committee for the Issa Scholarship, the Award Committee for the Rhodes Scholarship, and the Caribbean Commission. He is a past president of the Jamaica Boxing Board of Control and of the Jamaica Olympic Association and a past chairman of the Jamaica Co-operative Development Council. Manley holds an honorary Doctor of Civil Law degree from Howard University in the United States.

The erudite statesman has written articles on music, literary criticism, agriculture, and politics. He is five feet eleven inches tall and weighs 180 pounds. He is a Methodist. His recreations are music, reading, and farming.

References

Guardian (Manchester) p4 S 20 '58 por
Time 67:38 Mr 12 '56 por

MANNES, MARYA Nov. 14, 1904- Writer
Address: b. 136 E. 57th St., New York 22

With the publication of *More in Anger* in 1958, Marya Mannes did more than satirize a few prominent features of the American scene. She also summed up her career as gadfly, an occupation to which she has devoted most of her writing since she went to work for the *Reporter* magazine in 1952.

Writing has always been Miss Mannes' main preoccupation, although she has gone through several phases in her art. She ventured into the magazine field as reviewer for an art magazine. Later she did editorial work for two national mass-circulation magazines, until she went into government work in World War II. She has written poetry, essays, stories, and articles for national publications. She has also written three books, all of them outlets for her conscience which, she says, "strenuously resists the numerous efforts I have made throughout my life to still it."

Marya Mannes was born in New York City on November 14, 1904, the daughter of David and Clara (Damrosch) Mannes. Her grandparents emigrated from Germany and Poland during the nineteenth century. Her father, born in the United States, was a violinist, and her mother, who came to the United States as an infant, was a pianist. Both of them were founders of and teachers at the Mannes College of Music in New York. Miss Mannes is the niece of Dr. Walter Damrosch, the distinguished orchestra conductor and pioneer in teaching music appreciation. She is proud of her older brother, Leopold, who with Leopold Godowsky, Jr., helped to perfect Kodachrome color film and who has been president of the Mannes College of Music since 1951.

At Miss Veltin's School for Girls in New York City, from which she graduated in 1923, Miss Mannes indulged her extracurricular activities of "reading, fantasy, play-acting, writing poetry, and worshiping heroes, living and dead." She credits the school, which went out of existence in 1924, with having given her important disciplines. These included, she says, "a solid acquaintance with Latin and French, an attitude towards the English language compounded equally of respect and love, and an abiding aversion towards sloppiness and obscurity."

When she was eighteen, Miss Mannes received a modest inheritance which could finance either a college education or a trip to Europe. She chose the latter and spent a year in England after her graduation. After her return to the United States, she made an unsuccessful attempt to become an actress. desiring stage experience to pursue ambitions as a dramatist. (She wrote at least ten playscripts.)

"I tried out for the Guild's production of 'Antony and Cleopatra' once," she told reporter Betsy Luce (New York *Post,* December 27, 1944). "They weeded me out from forty girls because they thought I looked Egyptian. But when I stood up—they said I wouldn't do. They said I'd make two of Helen Hayes, who was starring in it."

MARYA MANNES

Instead she turned to writing. *Theatre Arts* magazine published two of her stories and an article between 1926 and 1928. The first of these was illustrated by Miss Mannes, while the others where illustrated by her husband, Jo Mielziner, the scenic designer, whom she married in 1926. She also worked as a reviewer for *Creative Art,* a short-lived magazine edited by Rockwell Kent during the 1920's.

During this period Miss Mannes was also a frequent contributor to *International Studio* magazine and wrote a play called *Café,* which reached Broadway in 1930. She has characterized the play as a "disastrous flop." One of her short stories appeared in *Harper's Magazine* in 1932, and several of her poems were also published.

Her marriage to Mielziner had ended in divorce in 1930. She went to work as feature editor for *Vogue* magazine three years later, and worked for the Condé Nast firm until 1936, when she married artist Richard Blow. The couple lived in Florence, where Blow had his studio in a villa. During this time she turned from writing to portrait sculpture as her favorite mode of expression.

Shortly before Pearl Harbor, Miss Mannes was employed by a firm called Short-Wave Research. With the help of a staff of four, she directed the work of the short wave research bureau, which screened about 2,000 aliens as prospective foreign-language broadcasters for the OWI. When the bureau was disbanded in 1943, she joined the Office of Strategic Services as an intelligence analyst.

Her government work ended in 1945. She had earlier, in 1944, gone abroad to research and write extensive articles about the belligerent neutrality of Spain and Portugal. The tour, which lasted four months, resulted in articles for the *New Yorker* and other magazines. After the war she

MANNES, MARYA—*Continued*

continued to write as a free lance and went to Jerusalem in 1946.

In the same year Miss Mannes went to work as feature editor of *Glamour* magazine. In 1947 she left *Glamour* to write a novel, *Message From a Stranger,* which was published in 1948 by Viking Press. It was essentially a story of immortality based on the premise that the dead live in the memory of the living, who—in effect—summon their presence. The book received mixed reviews.

"The best compendium I know of the most approved social, political, sexual, and domestic attitudes of modern educated women," said Diana Trilling in the *Nation* (February 21, 1948). The New York *Herald Tribune* (February 22, 1948) termed it "elementary, over-simplified political talk and a somewhat naïve metaphysic." The New York *Times* (February 15, 1948) remarked that the book "has flaws, but . . . the virtues of a well-furnished mind and an understanding sensibility are of far more importance than any minor flaws in structure and diction."

Since 1952 Miss Mannes has been a staff writer for the liberal fortnightly magazine, the *Reporter.* Each issue has contained a generous amount of her facts and opinions, incorporated in essays, articles, television reviews, and satirical verse written under the pseudonym of "Sec."

It was from her *Reporter* magazine essays, that she drew about a third of *More in Anger.* Published by Lippincott late in 1958, the book attracted much critical attention. One of the few unenthusiastic reviews was written by Harry Golden in the *Saturday Review* (November 15, 1958). After describing the volume as a "series of loosely-jointed essays which criticize modern American complacency, weakness, self-satisfaction, fat-dripping prosperity, and lack of discipline," Golden remarked that "her book is legitimately criticism, but it can be called just as honestly a series of grips. . . Miss Mannes' argument disappoints us because she is not after any of the whys."

William du Bois in the New York *Times* (October 30, 1958) took a more favorable stand. "Whether or not you can accept all she says without a sudden rush of blood to the brain," he wrote, "this book is guaranteed to shock you into awareness of its author as an original thinker. You may even have the time of your life at her intellectual, razzle-dazzle vaudeville if you remember to check your prejudices at the door."

In addition to her collection of essays, Miss Mannes prepared a collection of satirical verses, illustrated by Robert Osborn, which was published by Braziller in January 1959. Almost all of the poems were originally published in the *Reporter* under the pseudonym of "Sec."

Throughout her career, Miss Mannes has steadily contributed verse to well-known magazines. Besides her poems for the *Reporter,* she has published verses in the *New Yorker* and the *Literary Digest.* More recently, she has written broadcasts for the NBC network in the United States and the BBC Third Programme in England.

Miss Mannes has been married three times. The first marriage, to Jo Mielziner, ended in divorce in 1930; the second, to Richard Blow, ended the same way in 1943. She has one son, David Jeremy Blow (who is now attending college), by her second husband. She married Christopher Clarkson on April 2, 1948, and is presently living in New York City.

The political allegiance of Marya Mannes is outspokenly Democratic. She belongs to no organized religion or clubs. Her recreations are swimming and beachcombing, and she says that she has "no hobbies, but if I ever stopped writing I would return to portrait sculpture." Considering her current rate of production, it seems unlikely that she ever will. Instead she will probably continue to write in order to achieve her declared purpose to "communicate clearly and honestly what I see and what I believe about the world I live in."

MANNING, ERNEST (CHARLES) Sept. 20, 1908- Premier of Alberta

Address: b. Legislative Bldg., Edmonton, Alberta, Canada; h. P.O. Box 2317, Edmonton, Alberta, Canada

Heading what *Time* magazine has called "the nearest approach to a theocracy in the Western Hemisphere," Ernest Manning has been Premier of the province of Alberta in Canada since 1943. He has also been a leader of the Social Credit party since its inception under the evangelist William Aberhart in 1934. Although the Social Credit party originated in the radical monetary theories of Major C. H. Douglas, it has for many years been frankly conservative. Much of Premier Manning's popularity can be attributed to his government's sound and realistic handling of the recent oil boom in Alberta.

Ernest Charles Manning is the second of the three sons of George Henry and Elisabeth Mara (Dickson) Manning, both of whom came from England. Ernest was born on a farm at Carnduff in Saskatchewan on September 20, 1908. A year later the family moved to a homestead near Rosetown in the same province, to start what later developed into a 640-acre wheat farm. The boy attended the nearby one-room Glenpayne school and, later, the high school at Rosetown. He was much interested in mechanics, and his favorite possession was a Model T Ford.

At sixteen, Manning accidentally tuned in on a broadcast from Calgary, Alberta of the Prophetic Bible Conference. He became entranced by the speaker, William ("Bible Bill") Aberhart, a fundamentalist preacher who was also a high school teacher. Aberhart was raising funds for a Prophetic Bible Institute to teach young people about the prophetic nature of the Scriptures, and when the school opened in the fall of 1927, Ernest Manning was one of its first students. For two years, he lived with the Aberhart family; in his final year at the institute he joined the teaching staff. After completing his studies in 1930, he remained at Calgary as secretary to Aberhart and manager of the institute, and also took part in evangelical radio broadcasting.

With its agricultural economy, Alberta was hard hit by the depression. Mortgage foreclosures on farms were frequent, jobs for young people were almost nonexistent. Aberhart began to study the problem, and in 1932 he came upon the Social Credit theory of Major C. H. Douglas, a Scottish engineer, who blamed wars, depressions, and revolutions largely on a conspiracy of bankers (mostly Jewish) who wanted to dominate the world. Douglas maintained that the "real" wealth of a nation (based on factors like raw materials and labor force) is always greater than its financial wealth, but that the people receive none of the benefits of this wealth. He recommended that the government eliminate the dictatorship of the bankers' money by issuing a "national dividend" to every citizen.

On his Sunday radio broadcasts, Aberhart discussed Social Credit, and when in 1934 the Alberta government ridiculed proposals by Aberhart and Manning that it adopt the theory, the two men formed their own party. They featured prayers and hymns at Social Credit rallies throughout the province. At the election in August 1935 the Social Credit party won fifty-one of the fifty-seven seats in the provincial Assembly, and Manning was elected from Calgary.

Installed as Premier of Alberta in the fall of 1935, Aberhart named Manning to his cabinet as Provincial Secretary. Manning became the second youngest cabinet minister in the history of British parliaments. He also became Minister of Trade and Industry, mediated several labor disputes, and promoted many of the acts passed by the new Assembly in its 1936 session. No action during the first session, however, could be referred to the principles of Social Credit. Early in 1937, at a special session, the Alberta legislature passed a Credit House Act to prepare the way for fulfillment of a campaign pledge to pay a $25 monthly dividend to all adults. This and twelve other acts to implement monetary reform were disallowed by the courts or by the Canadian government.

In 1936 Manning had contracted tuberculosis, but had recovered. When the regular Canadian Army rejected him for World War II service because of scars on his lungs, Manning joined the Reserve Army as a lieutenant. He had risen to captain when Premier Aberhart died in 1943.

Named to succeed Aberhart in May of 1943, Manning called for a new election for 1944. Booming wartime farm prices and a demand for Alberta coal had meanwhile revived the provincial economy, and Manning, playing down "dividends," declared that the significant issue was the threat of Socialism. He promoted Social Credit theory as a way to "make Capitalism work." Thousands of voters who had opposed the "radical" Social Credit party in 1935 and 1940 began to support it. In the 1944 election the party recaptured all the Assembly seats lost four years before, and won all the Alberta seats in the Federal House of Commons in Ottawa.

Alberta Government

ERNEST MANNING

A rift in the party had been developing ever since 1937, when orthodox Douglasites set up a Social Credit Board to review the progress of the Alberta government in achieving monetary reform. The board began, after 1941, to devote more and more attention to criticism of democracy and to attacks on the "Judaic world conspiracy." The Social Credit party gradually split into two factions, the Douglasites and the "realists" led by Manning, who wanted to forget about the antidemocratic and anti-Semitic aspects of Douglas' teaching. In the autumn of 1947 Manning began to rid the party of Douglasites, removing from office or power every member of the faction who opposed him. The purge was successful: in 1948 the Social Credit Board was disbanded.

The Social Credit party won another landslide in 1948, mainly because of promise of prosperity from exploitation of Alberta's oil resources begun in the previous year. The provincial government, controlling 93 per cent of all oil rights, adopted a policy of leasing large tracts to big companies on a "checkerboard" plan. Alternate blocks of land on which oil was discovered reverted to the government, which then auctioned them off to smaller companies. The policy was profitable. In 1949 Manning recalled $113,000,000 of the province's debts, and initiated a program for building roads, schools, and libraries.

Following elections in 1952, in which the Social Credit party not only won forty-nine out of fifty-six seats in the Assembly, but also proved victorious in British Columbia, Premier Manning took over the Ministry of Mines and Minerals. He added another portfolio—that of Attorney General—in 1955. An election in 1955 gave the "Socreds" their first genuine opposition in some time. By the middle of 1957, however, the oil boom had poured more than $600,000,000 into the provincial treasury, and Manning ear-

MANNING, ERNEST—*Continued*

marked $11,000,000 for a Social Credit dividend. He also reduced the provincial debt by 60 per cent. In 1957 the oil boom was on the wane, and in the following year payments of citizens' oil and gas royalty dividends were temporarily suspended.

The fortunes of the Social Credit party hit rock bottom at the federal election of March 31, 1958, when the Progressive Conservatives won all seventeen of Alberta's seats in the House of Commons. A provincial by-election, however, encouraged Premier Manning to call a provincial general election for June 18 of that year. The result was the biggest victory in the history of the party. Social Credit captured sixty-two of the sixty-five seats in the Assembly, reducing the opposition to three. "We don't need an opposition," Manning had said earlier (*Time,* September 24, 1951). "They're just a hindrance to us. You don't hire a man to do a job and then hire another man to hinder him."

Manning received an honorary LL.D. degree from the University of Alberta in 1948. He is still a Baptist lay preacher, and throughout his political career has continued to direct the Prophetic Bible Conference and to broadcast Sundays on the *Back to the Bible Hour.* "I abhor the word politician," he has said (*Time,* January 2, 1950). "I would much rather concentrate on my Bible work."

Retiring in manner, Ernest Manning has blue eyes and fair hair, is five feet eleven inches tall and slender in build. Only the members of his immediate family call him Ernie. Mrs. Manning, who was the pianist and organist of the Prophetic Bible Conference, is the former Muriel Aileen Preston of Calgary. The Mannings were married on April 14, 1936 and have two sons, William Keith and Ernest Preston. They live on a large dairy farm near Edmonton. Manning does not drink, smoke, or play cards. He plays the violin for relaxation, and likes to read mystery stories and books about yachting and the sea.

References

Macleans Mag 68:24-5+ Je 25 '55 pors
Sat Night 63:11+ F 28 '48 por; 68:11+ Ja 31 '53 por
Time 55:25 Ja 2 '50 por; 58:47 S 24 '51 por; 60:30 Ag 18 '52
Toronto Globe and Mail p7 Ap 18 '59 por
Adair, J. R., ed. Saints Alive (1951)
Canadian Who's Who, 1955-57
International Who's Who, 1958
Who's Who in America, 1958-59
Who's Who in Canada, 1958-59
World Biography (1954)

MANUILSKY, DMITRI Z(AKHAROVICH) 1883-Feb. 22, 1959 Former Ukrainian Foreign Minister (1944-52); served as United Nations delegate from the Ukraine; long a powerful force in the Comintern. See *Current Biography* (December) 1948.

Obituary

N Y Times p23 F 23 '59

MARSHALL, GEORGE C(ATLETT) Dec. 31, 1880-Oct. 16, 1959 United States Army officer since 1902; General of the Army since 1944; Army Chief of Staff during World War II; Secretary of State (1947-49); Secretary of Defense (1950-51); winner of the Nobel Peace Prize (1953), presumably for authorship of the Marshall Plan (European Recovery Program). See *Current Biography* (March) 1947.

Obituary

N Y Times p1+ O 17 '59

MARTIN, HARRY (LELAND, JR.) Oct. 28, 1908-Dec. 22, 1958 Journalist; president of American Newspaper Guild (1947-53); information director of American Red Cross (since 1955). See *Current Biography* (June) 1948.

Obituary

N Y Times p2M D 24 '58

MARTINU, BOHUSLAV Dec. 8, 1890-Aug. 28, 1959 Composer; violinist; born in Bohemia; wrote symphonies, operas, choral works, ballets, concerti, and chamber music; taught at Princeton University and Mannes College of Music. See *Current Biography* (November) 1944.

Obituary

N Y Times p83 Ag 30 '59

MASON, NORMAN P(EIRCE) Dec. 24, 1896- United States government official; business executive

Address: b. Housing and Home Finance Agency, 1626 K St., N.W., Washington 25, D.C.; h. 3015 Orchard Lane, Washington, D.C.; 4 Delwood Rd., Chelmsford, Mass.

A champion of the Republican administration's proposed housing legislation of 1959, Norman P. Mason has been administrator of the Housing and Home Finance Agency since January 1959. For five years before that time, he was commissioner of its subsidiary, the Federal Housing Administration. Until he entered government service in 1954, Mason had a long career in business as head of the William P. Proctor Company, a lumber firm in Chelmsford, Massachusetts and the Sowles Hardware Company in Plattsburgh, New York. In his present post he succeeded Albert M. Cole.

Norman Peirce Mason was born on December 24, 1896 in Willsboro, New York to Anne (Bebb) and Robert Lew Preston Mason. He has two sisters, Margaret (Mrs. George F. James) and Alice Huntington Mason, an accountant in Chelmsford. His mother, of Welsh stock, was descended from a Governor of Illinois and Michael Bebb, the botanist. His father built and operated the Willsboro pulp mill for the New York & Pennsylvania Company, Inc., and later owned the Sowles Hardware Company, a wholesale firm.

From Plattsburgh High School, where he was a member of the debating society, Norman Mason was graduated in June 1912. Almost immediately, he went to work in his father's hardware business, first as a stock boy and eventually as clerk, purchasing agent, and employee at large. During these years he developed an interest in what he remembers as the "newest thing on the horizon—radio." Mason recalls, "I had my own short-wave radio station. My call letters were 8-O-R, and I received my amateur operator's license." About this time he volunteered for one month's military training at a camp in upstate New York which was supervised by General Leonard Wood.

In February 1918 Mason enlisted in the United States Navy as a 3d class petty officer, attended radio school, and became a radio operator. Assigned to the S S *Manchuria,* he was a member of a crew that transported many thousands of American troops to Brest, France.

Discharged in September 1919, Mason returned to Plattsburgh and operated the Sowles Hardware Company until his father's death in November 1922. When the business was sold, he became the president of the William P. Proctor Company, a lumber concern in Chelmsford owned by his wife's family. Primarily a manufacturer of wooden boxes, the firm had lost many customers when textile firms began to move from New England to the South and fiber boxes began to replace wooden boxes in industrial uses. From 1937 until he resigned in 1954 Mason held the posts of treasurer and chief executive officer. As the head of the firm, he doubled the number of its employees and considerably expanded its activities into new areas such as lumber dealers' supplies.

Other business positions held by Mason have been board member of the Central Savings Bank of Lowell, Massachusetts and founder and president (1950-54) of the Cooperative Reserve Supply Corporation of Cambridge, Massachusetts, a co-operative warehouse for lumber dealers. He also found time to participate in trade associations. After holding local and regional posts in such organizations, Mason became a director in 1944 of the National Retail Lumber Dealers Association and served as its president in 1947 and 1948. He was also a director of the Chamber of Commerce of the United States from 1949 to 1954 and was president of its construction and civic development committee.

During World War II Mason served on the lumber industry's advisory committee to the Office of Price Administration and as an adviser to the War Production Board. In 1945 he was a committee member of the housing conference of the National Housing Agency, a government body. Later, at the time of the Korean conflict, Mason was a consultant to the Office of Price Stabilization. During the Eisenhower administration he was on the President's Advisory Committee on Housing Policies and Programs.

When the Federal Housing Administration was charged with alleged abuses in early 1954, Mason was summoned to Washington in April as acting administrator to institute new policies.

NORMAN P. MASON

The administration ordered an investigation into reported corruptions: apartment project builders had obtained government-insured loans for far more than construction costs and kept the excess as "windfall" profits; and home owners were persuaded to borrow excessively, and given shoddy materials and workmanship on new housing and improvements. The Senate Banking and Currency Committee also conducted an investigation into the agency's policies and practices.

President Eisenhower nominated Mason to be FHA administrator on June 7. His appointment was unanimously approved by both the Senate Banking and Currency Committee and the Senate. At this time, Mason has said, "my task was two-fold. First, to clean up the personnel, which had become shiftless and careless, to say the least, in the top echelons. Second, to revise the agency's regulations and practices so as to minimize the possibilities of abuses." Twenty-two officials were dismissed, and the government obtained 200 indictments against agency employees.

Regulations were revised to eliminate the possibility of windfall profits, premium loan rates to banks were reduced, and FHA field directors were clearly warned by Mason not to accept any gifts or gratuities. He also was instrumental in guiding through Congress the housing bill of 1954 which provided for guarantees against fraud.

Rules were issued forbidding FHA loans under the controversial Title I program for such "luxury" items as tennis courts, exterior steam cleaning, lawn sprinkling systems, outdoor barbecue pits, fireplaces, and television antennae. Mason also expanded the agency's lending facilities, introduced a housing program for the aged, and worked for urban renewal and higher quality homes for purchasers.

(Continued next page)

MASON, NORMAN P.—*Continued*

On January 14, 1959 Mason was named administrator of the Housing and Home Finance Agency. The Senate Banking and Currency Committee and the full Senate again unanimously confirmed the nomination. His agency has an estimated $1 billion budget for the fiscal year of 1959 and has jurisdiction over the FHA, Community Facilities Administration, Urban Renewal Administration, Public Housing Administration, and Federal National Mortgage Association.

At present Mason is working for the enactment by Congress of the administration's 1959 housing bill. It would remove the prevailing ceiling on the amount of private home mortgages the FHA can insure, terminate the public housing program, and require cities and states to pay for one half, instead of one third, of the costs of slum clearance projects.

Norman P. Mason and Helen C. Proctor were married on August 25, 1920 and have two children, David Holmes and Nancy (Mrs. Charles Svenson). Thickset, Mason is five feet five inches tall, weighs 165 pounds, has thinning gray hair, and brown eyes. His favorite avocations are gardening, golfing, skiing, and photography. He is an Episcopalian and a Republican.

For many years Mason was chairman of his local Selective Service Board and served as vice-president of the Lowell Community Chest. For the National Academy of Sciences he was chairman of its Building Research Institute and executive committee member of its research advisory board.

The Masons have four homes: one in the fashionable Georgetown section of Washington, the family home at Chelmsford, a summer home on Cape Cod, and a log cabin at Dunstable, Massachusetts.

References

N Y Times p10 Je 5 '54; p17 Ja 15 '59 por
N Y World-Telegram p7 Ag 7 '54 por
U S News 36:24 Ja 23 '59
Who's Who in America, 1958-59

MATEOS, ADOLFO LÓPEZ *See* López Mateos, Adolfo

MATTEI, ENRICO (mà-tā'ē) Apr. 29, 1906- Italian government official

Address: b. Ente Nazionale Idrocarburi, Via Lombardi, 43, Rome, Italy; h. Via del Tritone, 181, Rome, Italy; Via Fatebenefratelli, 13, Milan, Italy

Since 1955 Italy has become important in the competition for the control of oil in the Middle East largely through the efforts of Enrico Mattei. As president of Ente Nazionale Idrocarburi, Mattei heads a multibillion-dollar state-owned combination employing some 75,000 workers. It monopolizes the methane and gasoline resources in northern Italy, operates important businesses, and holds extensive foreign concessions.

Agreements with Iran and Morocco provide for a 75-25 division of profits, thus undermining the standard 50-50 formula long in force between foreign oil companies and countries in the Middle East. Mattei had a long career as an industrialist, was a member of Parliament, and was a leader of the underground resistance movement during World War II.

One of five boys, Enrico Mattei was born on April 29, 1906 at Acqualagna in Pesaro e Urbino province, Italy to Angela (Galvani) and Antonio Mattei, a warrant officer of the *carabinieri,* Italy's military police. At fourteen Mattei began working as a varnisher and messenger for a tannery, and later became its manager after he had acquired a diploma in accounting. At twenty-seven he established his own small chemical business, the beginning of what grew into a prosperous industrial enterprise in Milan.

When Italy entered World War II, Mattei joined the underground movement. He was twice captured by the Fascists, but escaped from prison on both occasions. Although he had no military training, this modern *condottiere* helped to organize 82,000 partisans in northern Italy. He finally became general commandant of this partisan force, the only non-Communist one of any size in Italy.

"We lost one out of three men," C. L. Sulzberger has quoted him as saying (New York *Times,* November 29, 1958). At Rome in October 1945 Mattei was decorated by the American General Mark W. Clark for "heroic activity in leadership of the Italian underground during the German occupation."

Toward the end of the war Mattei served on the Christian Democratic party executive committee for northern Italy. In 1945-46 he was a member of the national council of the Christian Democratic party. He was elected a deputy to the first Italian republican Parliament.

When the Christian Democratic leader Alcide de Gasperi formed a government in 1945, Mattei was named northern commissioner of the Italian General Petroleum Agency (Azienda Generale Italiana Petroli). Under the Mussolini regime this agency had "spent millions of dollars and achieved negligible results in the search for oil in the Po Valley and elsewhere" (Leo Wollemborg, Washington *Post and Times Herald,* August 31, 1958).

Charged with the task of selling the assets of the agency, Mattei, who soon became head of A.G.I.P., offered the properties for sale at $1,000,000, but there were no bidders. He also continued searching for oil. In 1946 explorations resulted in the discovery of methane (natural gas) in the region southeast of Milan and the finding of oil in commercial quantities in a twenty-five-square-mile area in Lombardy. The methane gas deposits had an initial production in excess of all other Italian fields. By 1953 the wells were producing an annual amount of 71 billion cubic feet, enabling Italy to save over

$32,000,000 on foreign purchases of coal and oil (*Time,* November 29, 1954).

Following his appointment in February 1953 as president of the newly formed Ente Nazionale Idrocarburi (E.N.I.), Mattei resigned his seat in the national legislature. The agency was created with the approval of all political parties and granted capital amounting to $50,000,000.

When the E.N.I., supplanting the former A.G.I.P., was given exclusive control over the fuel resources in northern Italy, the Standard Oil Company of New Jersey lost its research rights there. Both the Gulf Oil Corporation and the Anglo-Iranian Oil Company, Ltd., kept their wells in Sicily, however.

In July 1956 a new oil law was enacted which not only reaffirmed the E.N.I. monopoly in the Po Valley, but limited the exploration rights of any company elsewhere in Italy to 740,000 acres and empowered E.N.I. to purchase tracts around each newly discovered well. This legislation was an outcome of Mattei's implacable opposition to foreign oil investments in his country.

Meanwhile Italy's natural gas production was steadily mounting from 64,000,000 cubic meters in 1946 to 5 billion in 1958. This output, distributed by a 2,500-mile network of pipelines, has brought a profit of some $75,000,000 yearly. Much of this wealth has been used to finance the building of a government-owned industrial empire of vast proportions. E.N.I. and its subsidiaries control a "180,000-ton tanker fleet, a nationwide chain of gasoline stations, a string of new motels, some large oil refineries, a gas-operated thermoelectric plant, soap and margarine factories, heavy engineering and metal works and a giant chemical plant which utilizes natural gas for the production of 60,000 tons of synthetic rubber and 750,000 tons of nitrogenous fertilizers a year" (Leo Wollemborg, Washington *Post and Times Herald,* August 31, 1958).

Despite oil finds in Sicily and Abruzzi e Molise, Italy's demand for fuel is still far greater than domestic production can provide. Therefore, Mattei has sought to control oil resources in other countries. When, in April 1954, the eight company Anglo-American-Franco-Dutch consortium began discussing with the government of Iran the reactivation of its oil industry, Mattei requested a modest partnership for Italy. The consortium countered with what he called a "humiliating" rejection.

When Gamal Abdel Nasser came to power in Egypt, Mattei saw his opportunity (according to Leo Wollemborg). In partnership with the Nasser regime, the E.N.I. tapped an important oil field in the Sinai peninsula in 1955. From this deposit Italy is now receiving 500,000 tons of crude oil a year.

Mattei's major triumph in the international petroleum contest came in 1957 when, as the result of discovery of new oil fields near Qum, Iran, he "persuaded the Shah of Iran to give him three highly promising concessions, covering 8,800 square miles, on terms that shocked the international consortium" (Claire Sterling, *Reporter,* March 20, 1958).

The agreement stipulates that 75 per cent of the profits will go to Iran and the remaining

Wide World

ENRICO MATTEI

25 per cent to an E.N.I. subsidiary, as contrasted with the 50-50 split which had long been the basis of agreements between the consortium and Middle Eastern countries. As provided by the agreement, Iran is not merely a passive recipient of royalties, but an active partner in the technical and financial aspects of oil development.

In contrast with his Iranian coup, Mattei suffered a serious setback when he attempted to acquire oil resources in Libya. With Libyan Premier Mustafa Ben Halim he drafted an agreement in 1957, but Libya refused to sign it after the Ben Halim government fell. Eventually, the concession was awarded to American Overseas Petroleum, Ltd., a joint subsidiary of the Texas Company and the Standard Oil Company of California.

In July 1958 Mattei concluded an agreement with the government of Morocco under which an E.N.I. subsidiary would be granted exploration rights in a 10,000-square-mile tract on the fringe of the Sahara desert. Under this arrangement, Morocco receives 75 per cent of the profits from exploitation of possible deposits. In December 1958 the United Arab Republic granted thirteen new large oil concessions in the Sinai desert to E.N.I.'s Egyptian subsidiary. The combination also has interests in Spain, France, and Somaliland.

"More is at stake than the split in profits between the sovereign state and the producing company from abroad," noted *Business Week* (September 28, 1957). "Before atomic energy becomes cheaply and plentifully available, oil will be the lifeblood of the industrialized nations of the free world. . . . For almost a decade, international oil has enjoyed a period of stable development, partly because the oil companies and the major oil countries agreed on the so-called 50-50 formula."

(Continued next page)

MATTEI, ENRICO—*Continued*

According to Mattei, the major oil companies pursue a policy of limited output and high prices for their international holdings. They sell crude oil to Europe at a price level which would cover the cost of production in the United States, in order to protect the home industry. The aim of E.N.I. is to achieve maximum production at low prices. The present competition could result in economic recession or political instability for some of the nations involved. As a solution, he suggests an agreement between the Organization for European Economic Cooperation and the Arab League to establish a fund from oil revenue to develop industry and mechanization in the Middle East (Toronto *Globe and Mail,* January 23, 1959).

In his column in the New York *Times* of November 29, 1958, C. L. Sulzberger referred to Mattei as "unofficially speaking" the "Gray Eminence" of the Italian government. "Some say he controls a bloc of Parliamentary deputies variously estimated at between fifty and one hundred. . . . Some say that in his search for Arab petroleum, he prods Italian foreign policy along a pro-Nasser and neutralist line."

Enrico Mattei is lean, tall, and attractive. Independently wealthy, he donates his salary to an orphanage. His favorite form of recreation is fishing for trout. He married the former Margherita Paulas in 1936.

References

Christian Sci Mon p9 N 18 '58 por
N Y Herald Tribune p4 D 13 '57
N Y Times p5 Ja 6 '58 por

Ascoli, M. ed. Reporter Reader (1956)
Chi è? (1957)
Dizionario Enciclopedico Italiana (1957)
Panorama Biografico degli Italiani d'Oggi (1956)
Who's Who in Italy, 1957-58

MAY, ANDREW JACKSON   June 24, 1875-Sept. 6, 1959 Former United States Representative from Kentucky (1931-47); chairman of House Military Affairs Committee (1938-47); Democrat; lawyer. See *Current Biography* (April) 1941.

Obituary

N Y Times p15 S 7 '59

MBOYA, THOMAS JOSEPH *See* Mboya, Tom

MBOYA, TOM ('m-boi'ā) Aug. 15, 1930-Kenya nationalist leader

Address: b. Kenya Federation of Labor, Nairobi, Kenya

In the nationalist movement for self-government by black-skinned Africans, Tom Mboya has become recognized as an articulate and resourceful political leader. Not yet thirty years old, he is general secretary of the Kenya Federation of Labor, a member of the Kenya Legislative Council (parliament), and president of the Nairobi People's Convention party. A spokesman, too, for the African cause outside the British crown colony, he was chosen chairman of the All-African Peoples' Conference, held in Ghana in December 1958, a focal point of the movement for independence and Pan-Africanism that has been sweeping through large parts of the vast continent in the last few years.

Tom Mboya was born on August 15, 1930 on a hemp estate on Rusinga Island in Lake Victoria. This is in Kenya's White Highlands—the European-settled area. He is a member of the Luo tribe, the second largest in Kenya. His parents, illiterate natives who had been converted to Roman Catholicism, had their son baptized Thomas Joseph. They also gave him the name Odhiambo, which signifies the time of his birth, and the second clan name of Mboya. "I was brought up a Catholic," Mboya has said, "but today I don't follow those things" (*Newsweek,* May 12, 1958). He received his early education in Catholic mission schools, learning to write in the sand, and for two years (1946 and 1947) he attended Holy Ghost College, a Catholic high school near Nairobi. School fees were high, however, and since Tom was the oldest of six children, he had to help meet the cost of educating his brothers.

Instead, therefore, of trying to qualify for a Cambridge School Certificate, in 1948 he entered the Royal Sanitary Institute's Medical Training School for Sanitary Inspectors in Nairobi. From there he went to Jeanes School near Nairobi. In 1950 he qualified as a sanitary inspector and the following year was appointed to the staff of the Nairobi City Council. He notes in an autobiographical sketch that he earned less than one-fifth of the salary of the European inspector on the staff.

Interested in improving the conditions of laborers, Mboya joined the African Staff Association in 1951. He was elected president the next year and worked to convert the association into a trade union, the Kenya Local Government Workers' Union. Also in 1952 he joined the Kenya African Union, a Negro political group which was outlawed by the government in 1953 following the outbreak of the Mau Mau uprising. He served as director of information services and briefly as treasurer of the Kenya African Union after some of the other leaders had been arrested.

Mboya's political activities resulted in a notice of dismissal from his job as a sanitary inspector; rather than fight the case, he resigned. He was then elected national general secretary of the Kenya Local Government Workers' Union, for which at first he had to work without salary. His union affiliated with the Kenya Federation of Labor in 1953, and in October of that year Mboya was elected general secretary of the federation, which is said to be Socialist-inclined but anti-Communist.

During 1954 Mboya visited Geneva, Brussels, and London, presenting his views on the Kenya situation to the International Confederation of

Free Trade Unions and to the British Trades Union Congress. He also studied workers' education in Calcutta, India and visited Pakistan.

In March 1955 Mboya was catapulted to considerable fame by settling a strike of 4,000 dock workers at Mombasa. He persuaded the strikers to return to work and then negotiated a 33 per cent wage increase for them along with other benefits. It was the first time an African had successfully represented a union in a strike situation. Mboya is a member of the Kenya Labor Advisory Board, the Wages Advisory Board, and the Rural Wages Committee.

Awarded a British Workers Travel Association Scholarship, Mboya spent a year (1955-56) studying industrial relations, political institutions, and international politics at Ruskin College, Oxford University. While in England, he associated with British Labourites interested in colonial affairs. He made a brief visit to the United States in the fall of 1956 and returned to Kenya with a gift of $35,000 from leaders of the AFL-CIO for construction of a trade union headquarters. He has been in the center of political developments in Kenya ever since.

The situation that existed there when Mboya returned was ready-made for this "extraordinary young man," as Robert Coughlan called him in *Life* magazine (February 2, 1959). The Mau Mau uprising had been crushed by the British. Jomo Kenyatta, the alleged Mau Mau leader, had been jailed. Some 750,000 Kikuyu tribesmen, supporters or members of Mau Mau, were undergoing "rehabilitation." No other important African leader had appeared on the scene.

Moreover, a new constitution, introduced in 1954 at the height of the Mau Mau revolt by the then Colonial Secretary Oliver Lyttelton, had gone into effect. Hailed in 1954 as a great advance by some, it provided for a multiracial government, with members of the Legislative Council to be elected by the three racial communities in Kenya—Europeans, Asians, and Africans.

The first direct elections of African members of the Legislative Council were scheduled for March 1957, as part of the Lyttelton Plan for a gradually increasing role for the Africans in Kenya's government. (Until 1957, six African members of the Legislative Council had been appointed by the British Governor.) Eight Africans were to be elected by some 100,000 of their race who could qualify as voters.

Mboya, though determined to run, was nevertheless on record against the multiracial, gradualistic Lyttelton constitution. He was elected by a narrow margin, in a hotly contested campaign in Nairobi. So were seven other likeminded Africans, whom Mboya promptly welded into a solid bloc. All eight refused to accept posts reserved for them on the Council of Ministers. In addition, they lost no time in demanding fifteen additional seats in the Legislative Council, or a total of twenty-three—enough to provide a single-vote majority over the European and Asian members combined.

A subsequent British plan made African and European elected representation equal at four-

TOM MBOYA

teen seats each, with the fourteen Africans representing some 6,000,000 and the fourteen Europeans, some 60,000. Mboya opposed the plan but could not block it. Six additional Africans were elected in March 1958, all of whom were his firm followers. Thus, the political deadlock continued, with all fourteen African members now boycotting the constitution under which they were elected.

"We reject a government which is based on an imposed constitution," Mboya shouted to 4,000 cheering Africans at Nairobi's Makadara Hall, shortly after the 1958 elections. "No one will hand us freedom on a silver platter. We must be prepared to use our power—not guns and *pangas*—to achieve it!" (*Time*, April 7, 1958). In an interview with Elspeth Huxley (New York *Times Magazine*, April 27, 1958) Mboya stated, "Our aim is undiluted democracy —a vote for every adult on full universal suffrage, and on a common roll with Europeans and Asians. We want to abolish all privileges for minorities. Their rights as individuals will be respected, but they must submit to the rule of the majority, and claim no privilege because of their race, or their supposed advanced level of civilization."

With Africans outnumbering Europeans 100 to 1, Tom Mboya's "undiluted democracy" in effect means African rule in Kenya. To the argument that the Africans in Kenya are not ready to govern, Mboya replied at the All-African Peoples' Conference, of which he was chairman and which was held in December 1958 at Accra, Ghana: "Civilized or not civilized, ignorant or illiterate, rich or poor, we, the African states, deserve a government of our own choice. Let us make our own mistakes, but let us take comfort in the knowledge that they are our own mistakes."

Like Prime Minister Kwame Nkrumah of Ghana, whom he greatly admires, Mboya pre-

MBOYA, TOM—*Continued*

fers not to use violence as a means of achieving these aims. He favors using all other methods —political, economic, passive resistance, boycott. If force is made necessary by the policies of the colonial powers, he argued at Accra, the blame will be on them, not on the Africans.

As chairman since July 1958 of the eastern, central and southern African subregional organization of the International Confederation of Free Trade Unions, Mboya spends a substantial part of his time in travel. He attended the ICFTU board meetings in Brussels in November 1958 and, on behalf of the ICFTU, the inaugural session of the United Nations Economic Commission for Africa in December 1958. During 1959 he conducted a world-wide Africa Freedom Fund campaign, beginning in April with a lecture tour in the United States under the auspices of the American Committee on Africa.

Tom Mboya is an imposing figure with distinctive almond-shaped eyes. He is a brilliant orator in both Swahili and English. Robert Coughlan of *Life* believes him to be "intellectually quick, courageous, dedicated and vain." His library includes the works of Plato, Tom Paine, and Mark Twain.

References

> Christian Sci Mon p9 Ap 9 '58
> N Y Herald Tribune p6 Ja 20 '59 por
> N Y Times p12 O 25 '55; p9 Ag 19 '56
> N Y Times Mag p114+ Ap 27 '58
> Newsweek 51:50 My 12 '58 por

MEYER, EUGENE Oct. 31, 1875-July 17, 1959

Chairman of the board of the Washington *Post and Times Herald* (1947-59); editor and publisher of the Washington *Post* (1940-46); first chairman of the Reconstruction Finance Corporation (1932); first president of the International Bank for Reconstruction and Development (1946); governor of the Federal Reserve Board (1930-33). See *Current Biography* (September) 1941.

Obituary

> N Y Times p1 Jl 18 '59

MILLE, CECIL B. DE. *See* De Mille, Cecil B.

MILLER, LEE P(FEIFFER) Nov. 7, 1891-

Banker

Address: b. Citizens Fidelity Bank and Trust Co., Fifth and Jefferson Sts., Louisville, Ky.; h. 2238 Village Drive, Louisville, Ky.

The American Bankers Association, which has a membership of 17,603 banks and branches, elected Lee P. Miller as its president for 1958-59. Miller, who succeeds Joseph C. Welman, serves a one-year term. President of the Citizens Fidelity Bank and Trust Company of Louisville since 1949, Miller has been active in

the affairs of the A.B.A. and the Kentucky Bankers Association for many years.

The only son in a family of two children, Lee Pfeiffer Miller was born to George and Catherine (Pfeiffer) Miller on November 7, 1891 in Louisville, Kentucky. He was graduated from the Louisville Male High School in 1909. The elder Miller was a banker, and in 1911 Lee became an employee of the Fidelity Trust Company.

He first worked as a bank messenger, but was soon advanced to bookkeeping clerk and later to assistant auditor. Military service during World War I interrupted his banking career. He entered the Army as a private on January 1, 1918 and by the time of his discharge on March 25, 1919 had attained the rank of sergeant first class.

Returning to the Fidelity Trust Company, he held during the next twenty-five years a series of increasingly responsible positions, culminating in that of executive vice-president. When the Fidelity Trust Company and the Citizens Bank merged in 1944 to become the Citizens Fidelity Bank and Trust Company, Miller was elected secretary and vice-president of the new organization. In October 1949 he became president and was able to carry out many new policies. He is credited with being one of the first bankers to practise the open-door policy, making himself available to all customers and employees.

During the first nine years of Miller's presidency, the number of accounts in the bank doubled, the deposits had climbed from $145,-000,000 to $246,000,000 and the loans advanced from $43,000,000 to $116,000,000.

A member of the Kentucky Bankers Association, an affiliate of the A.B.A., Miller was on the Kentucky association's jurisprudence committee for nineteen years and was its president from 1937 to 1951. He then served for three years as chairman of the tax research committee. On the Kentucky Bankers Association executive committee for three years beginning in 1938, Miller was its chairman in 1940-41.

Lee P. Miller has also been an active participant in the affairs of the American Bankers Association. Founded in 1875, it is principally a service organization to enhance the usefulness of banks. The various phases of its activities include government relations and the promotion of legislation, studies of monetary policy and the issuing of reports and informative bulletins, and publication of the magazine *Banking; Journal of the American Bankers Association*.

The educational section of the A.B.A. is the American Institute of Banking, which conducts courses in 503 cities and towns throughout the nation and through correspondence study. The association also maintains a Graduate School of Banking at Rutgers, the State University of New Jersey, in New Brunswick. The A.B.A. has its headquarters at 12 East 36th Street in New York City.

For twenty years a member of both the A.B.A.'s committee on federal legislation and its subcommittee on taxation, Lee P. Miller was for several of these years the chairman of the subcommittee and from 1955 to 1957 served as chairman of the whole committee. During these years he began to conduct research on his theory that the reserve for "bad debts" for banks should be placed "on a countrywide basis." From 1952 to 1954 he was also a member of the A.B.A. special committee on the excess profits tax. In the A.B.A. trust division he served on the taxation committee for eleven years and was committee chairman for four years. He was vice-president of the division's executive committee in 1957-58.

When Joseph C. Welman (see *C.B.*, May 1958) was elected A.B.A. president in September 1957, Lee P. Miller became vice-president for a one-year term. He was elected president for 1958-59 on September 23, 1958 during the eighty-fourth annual convention, held in Chicago.

The meeting was marked by a stormy debate on a motion, submitted by Arthur T. Roth, president of the Franklin National Bank of Long Island, to expel mutual savings banks from the association. The crux of the matter was that "the savings banks and loan associations are permitted to channel income tax-free into reserves until these reach 12 per cent of savings accounts," while "commercial banks follow a different formula in establishing tax-free bad debt reserves" (Albert L. Kraus, New York *Times*, September 22, 1958).

Roth claimed that the savings banks had prevented the A.B.A. from effectively representing commercial banking before the United States Congress. Before the open debate on the Roth proposal, the executive council of the A.B.A. had "recommended that the delegates vote against the amendment" (*Business Week*, September 27, 1958). They did so on September 24 by 1,520 to 1,445.

Commenting on the election of Lee P. Miller, the New York *Times* (September 25, 1958) observed that the new A.B.A. president "steps into a job that few of his fellows would envy. Before Congress convenes in January, he must attempt to give an appearance of unity to an industry torn by perhaps the most bitter conflict in its history." At stake is the recodification of federal banking laws for the first time in a quarter of a century. A measure to this effect was approved by Congress and signed by the President in 1959.

Before debate on the Roth amendment began, Miller had promised to call a conference of savings bank and A.B.A. officials for the discussion of differences, if the amendment were defeated. On September 26 William A. Lyon, president of the National Association of Mutual Savings Banks, was authorized to name a committee for this purpose.

In connection with Congressional legislative action in December 1958, the A.B.A. economic policy commission recommended "a broad tax increase if the next budget cannot be balanced by cuts in Federal spending." In March 1959 the association endorsed legislation that would require advance approval of bank mergers by three federal agencies.

Walton Jones

LEE P. MILLER

In addition to being president of the Citizens Fidelity and Trust Company, Miller is president and a director of the Citizens Fidelity Insurance Company and a director of the Louisville Investment Company, Louisville Transit Company, Jefferson Island Salt Company, and other concerns. He is also a director of the Associated Industries of Kentucky and the Kentucky Chamber of Commerce, chairman of the board of trustees of the University of Louisville, and a trustee of the Masonic Widows and Orphans Home.

Miller is an avid fan of the basketball teams of the University of Louisville and the University of Kentucky. Before the establishment of little league baseball teams, he was active in setting up a similar organization among Louisville boys. He names horse racing, basketball, cards, and golf as favorite recreations. He has been honored by election to the Newcomen Society. His clubs are the Pendennis, Filson, Audubon Country, Frankfort Country, Wildwood Country, Harmon Landing Country, and Metropolitan (Washington, D.C.).

Lee P. Miller and Lucille Curd were married on June 26, 1919. They have one son, Lee Curd Miller, a lawyer. Blue-eyed and silver-haired, Lee P. Miller stands at five feet eleven inches and weighs about 190 pounds.

References

Banking 51:44+ O '58 pors
Poor's Register of Directors and Executives, 1959
Who's Who in America, 1958-59
Who's Who in Commerce and Industry (1957)
Who's Who in the South and Southwest (1956)

MITCHELL, WILLIAM L(LOYD) Sept. 4, 1900- United States government official

Address: b. Social Security Administration, 330 Independence Ave., S.W., Washington 25, D.C.; h. 6669 Barnaby St., N.W., Washington 15, D.C.

The multibillion-dollar, poverty-prevention program directed by United States Commissioner of Social Security William L. Mitchell is the world's largest social-insurance and social-welfare operation of its kind. As head of the Social Security Administration, now a part of the Department of Health, Education and Welfare, he is responsible for four bureaus handling old-age and survivors insurance, federal-state

Dept. of Health, Education &
Welfare—S. Stanton Singer

WILLIAM L. MITCHELL

assistance to the needy, children's health and welfare, and Federal Credit Unions. The nomination of Mitchell in December 1958 was a nonpolitical appointment based upon his record of more than thirty-five years in government service, the last thirteen of which were spent as Deputy Commissioner of Social Security. He succeeded Charles I. Schottland.

William Lloyd Mitchell was born in Newark, New Jersey on September 4, 1900 to William Augustus and Mary Ellen (Sweeney) Mitchell. His brother, Everitt Mitchell, works in advertising for a New York combustion engineering firm. His sister, Eleanor Mitchell, is deceased. On his mother's side of the family he is of Irish descent. For several generations his father's family had lived on Long Island.

When William L. Mitchell was less than a year old, his father moved from Newark, where he had been employed in the shoe business, returned to Long Island, and in 1905 became a contractor in Port Washington. He later went into the coal and feed business. The boy attended public schools in Port Washington, won the Amherst Cup in oratorical contests, and

played on several high school athletic teams. Also active in church affairs, he was an altar boy and choir singer at St. Peter of Alcantara Roman Catholic Church.

Upon his graduation from Port Washington High School, Mitchell worked for the Great American Insurance Company in New York City. In February 1922 he entered Georgetown University School of Foreign Service in Washington, D.C. For about a year he attended classes in the evening and was employed during the day as a chain man on a surveying team for the Department of Public Buildings and Grounds.

In April 1923 Mitchell joined the staff of the bureau of foreign and domestic commerce of the Department of Commerce, where his first assignment was to decode cables relating to the government's foreign commercial relations. Later transferred from Washington, he served for a time as commercial agent in the New York district office of the bureau and in 1929 moved to Louisville, Kentucky as assistant manager to open a district office there. He subsequently held the post of district manager for the bureau in Norfolk, Virginia and then in Atlanta, Georgia.

With the political change in the administration of the federal government in 1933, a number of positions were removed from Civil Service and filled by patronage employees. Mitchell's office was one of those affected. He was transferred to the National Recovery Administration as executive assistant to the state director for Georgia and soon afterward became state director for Georgia. He was later appointed regional NRA director for the Southeast, with headquarters in Atlanta, and remained in this post until the dissolution of NRA, which the United States Supreme Court declared unconstitutional in 1935. Meanwhile, in 1934, he had also been made regional director of the National Emergency Council, which furnished commercial information for President Franklin D. Roosevelt during the depression.

Mitchell moved in March 1936 from NRA to the Social Security Board in Washington. The board was established in accordance with the Social Security Act passed by Congress in 1935 to give some assurance of financial help to all citizens in meeting their basic needs when old age or other circumstances should reduce their earnings. As director of the bureau of personnel and business management of the Social Security Board, Mitchell supervised hiring of the staff and was responsible for the acquisition of space and other physical properties necessary in carrying out the new program. From 1938 to 1941 he was also associate director of the bureau of employment security of the Social Security Board, a bureau transferred to the Department of Labor in 1949.

After the Social Security Board was abolished in 1946 and replaced by the Social Security Administration, Mitchell was named Deputy Commissioner of the agency. While in this post, Mitchell spent two months during 1948 as a special consultant to the American Mission for Aid to Greece, studying the Greek social security system and making recommendations for its reorganization. In 1955 he led the United States delegation at the Inter-American Conference on Social Security in Caracas, Venezuela. He headed his country's delegation to the International Conference of Social Work in Toronto, Canada in 1954 and to a meeting of the same organization in Tokyo, Japan in 1958. Also in 1958 he was chairman of the United States delegation to the International Social Security Association Conference in London, and he has since become a member of the executive committee of that association.

In December 1958 President Dwight D. Eisenhower named Mitchell to succeed Charles I. Schottland (see *C.B.,* December 1956), whose resignation as Commissioner of Social Security became effective in January 1959. The large-scale program that Mitchell supervises is carried out under four bureaus: the bureau of old-age and survivors insurance; the bureau of public assistance, which is responsible for grants-in-aid to the states to help finance their programs for the needy; the children's bureau, while helps to provide for maternal and child health and welfare services and benefits for crippled children; and the bureau of Federal Credit Unions, which charters and supervises voluntary co-operative associations to encourage thrift among members and provide for loans.

The best known of these bureaus is the bureau of old-age and survivors insurance, which is itself often popularly called Social Security. Originally old-age protection was given to some 33,000,000 workers. Various amendments to the 1935 act extended coverage so that by 1955 more than double that number were insured. A revision passed by Congress in 1956 brought military personnel into the system, and a major amendment in 1958 raised old-age, survivors, and disability insurance benefits and increased the Social Security tax rate.

For the fiscal year ending June 30, 1958, before these changes in the law were reflected, the Old-Age and Survivors Trust Fund had taken in $7,267,000,000 in revenue and $557,000,000 in interest on investments. It paid out $7,875,-000,000 in benefits and $166,000,000 for administrative costs (New York *Times,* June 23, 1959). In early 1959 more than 12,500,000 recipients of old-age, survivors, and disability insurance were mailed Social Security checks, at a monthly expenditure of about $740,000,000.

Mitchell holds the Distinguished Service Award of the Department of Health, Education and Welfare, the highest honor that the department confers. For several years he has been a member of the American Public Welfare Association and has devoted time to the work of its committees. He serves on the advisory committee for the *Social Work Yearbook.* He is also on the advisory board of the family life council of the National Catholic Welfare Conference and is a trustee of the William J. Kerby Foundation, which seeks to perpetuate the ideas of Monsignor Kerby of Catholic University on democracy and the dignity of the individual.

Since 1922 Mitchell has been a member, and on occasion an officer, of Delta Phi Epsilon, a professional foreign service fraternity. He belongs to the Georgetown Alumni Association and the Georgetown Club of Washington, which presented him with its annual merit award for foreign service students in March 1959. He is a member also of the Kenwood Country Club in Washington.

On June 17, 1926 William L. Mitchell married Jessie M. Henderson, at that time a secretary to Will H. Hays, the motion picture executive. The Mitchells have a daughter, Marilyn M. Tercero, and three sons, William L., Jr., John Henderson, and Brian Edward. They also have several grandchildren. Commissioner Mitchell is five feet eleven inches tall, weighs 184 pounds, and has hazel eyes and gray hair. He likes outdoor sports, particularly golf and fishing. Another of his favorite diversions is sketching.

References

Christian Sci Mon p10 D 30 '58
Who's Who in America, 1958-59

MONROE, MARILYN June 1, 1926- Actress

Address: b. Marilyn Monroe Productions, 598 Madison Ave., New York 22

When Marilyn Monroe made her widely publicized return to Hollywood in 1958, after a two-year absence, critics wondered if she could recapture the standing she had once held in the world of make-believe. The release of *Some Like It Hot* in January 1959 demonstrated that (to critics, at least), Miss Monroe still radiates appeal, and may even have managed the difficult transition from star to actress.

Marilyn Monroe was born Norma Jean Mortenson (or Baker) on June 1, 1926, in Los Angeles. Published accounts of her childhood are contradictory, but it appears that her mother

Warner Bros.

MARILYN MONROE

MONROE, MARILYN—*Continued*

was hospitalized by a mental breakdown soon after Norma Jean's birth, and that the child was reared in a succession of foster homes. The mother has been variously identified as Gladys (Monroe) Mortenson and Gladys Pearl Baker.

After twelve sets of foster parents and at least one stay in a Los Angeles orphanage, where she worked in the dining room and pantry, Norma Jean remembered her mother only as "the woman with the red hair" who sometimes visited her. The child received a sketchy education at various public schools; the last was Van Nuys High School in the San Fernando Valley.

"Looking back," she told Pete Martin in an interview (*Saturday Evening Post*, May 5, 1956), "I guess I used to play-act all the time. For one thing, it meant I could live in a more interesting world than the one around me." She was also confused by the shifting sets of moral values she encountered as she moved from one set of foster parents to the other.

Shortly after her sixteenth birthday, her latest foster family had to leave California, and to avoid returning to an orphanage or another set of foster parents, Norma Jean married James Dougherty. The relationship broke up in 1943 when Dougherty joined the United States Merchant Marine, and ended in divorce shortly after the end of World War II. During the war years, Norma found employment first as a parachute inspector, then as a paint sprayer in a Los Angeles aircraft factory.

Already possessing the physical opulence which was to make her famous, she was induced by a local photographer to take lessons at a charm school. She worked on and off as a photographer's model, and by the summer of 1946 had appeared on the covers of several men's magazines. As a result, she received bids from Howard Hughes and Twentieth Century-Fox Film Corporation.

Christened Marilyn Monroe by a talent scout, she signed a one-year contract with Twentieth Century-Fox Film Corporation at $125 a week. She appeared briefly in *Scudda Hoo, Scudda Hay,* but the episode landed on the cutting room floor before the film was released. She received no other roles, and the studio failed to renew her contract when it expired in 1947. Then she was hired for six months by Columbia Pictures, playing a small part in *Ladies of the Chorus.*

As a free lance, supporting herself by once again working as a photographer's model, she played an infinitesimal part in a Marx Brothers' comedy, and in 1950 was signed by John Huston for *Asphalt Jungle.* Although she was not mentioned in the screen credits, Miss Monroe received so much fan mail for her performance as a kittenish cocotte that she was rehired by Twentieth Century-Fox for *All About Eve.*

On the strength of her brief appearance as a brassy Lorelei in *All About Eve* Twentieth Century-Fox Film Corporation signed her to a seven-year contract with options up to $3,500

a week. In the following year she was cast in small roles in such indifferent movies as *The Fireball, Let's Make It Legal, Love Nest,* and *As Young As You Feel.* She appeared on the screen for a total of fifty minutes in all of them, but she did gain some acting experience. Meanwhile, the studio launched an elaborate publicity campaign for its new starlet.

The campaign succeeded, and in 1952 she shared star billing in *Don't Bother to Knock, Full House, Clash by Night* (for RKO), *We're Not Married, Niagara,* and *Monkey Business.* Columnist Hedda Hopper called her Hollywood's "most promising star," and *Photoplay* magazine gave her its "most popular actress" award. By the end of 1953, Miss Monroe had earned more money for her studio than any other Hollywood star.

Until she broke her Twentieth Century-Fox contract at the end of 1954, Miss Monroe and her studio experienced a tidal wave of popularity unequaled by any other film actress since Jean Harlow. She starred in *Gentlemen Prefer Blondes, How to Marry a Millionaire, River of No Return* (a Monroe song from the film sold 75,000 records in three weeks), *There's No Business Like Show Business,* and *The Seven Year Itch.*

Although these films earned some critical acclaim in addition to popular adulation, Miss Monroe was far from satisfied with the progress of her career. Her marriage to former Yankee outfielder Joe Di Maggio had foundered after nine months. She was upset by the divorce and by her inability to win the more serious roles she coveted, such as that of Grushenka in *The Brothers Karamazov.* She left Hollywood to study under the Lee Strasbergs at their Actors Studio in New York City.

In January 1955, Miss Monroe announced that she had formed her own production company with fashion photographer Milton H. Greene. A year later, Marilyn Monroe Productions announced that it had purchased the rights to a Terence Rattigan play (later filmed as *The Prince and the Show Girl*). Meanwhile, Twentieth Century-Fox signed her to a new contract calling for four films in seven years.

The first of these, *Bus Stop,* moved a *Life* writer to remark (August 3, 1956) that "all this intellectual activity has done Marilyn absolutely no harm. . . . She shows that she has learned a great deal about her trade, developing a sure satiric touch as a comedienne." Co-starring Don Murray, the film won generally favorable reviews. Just before its release, Miss Monroe was married to playwright Arthur Miller.

After her marriage, she flew to London with her husband to begin work on *The Prince and the Show Girl* with Sir Laurence Olivier as her co-star and director. The Monroe-Olivier production, which one journalist called "the most improbable show business combination of the decade," was released in June 1957 by Warner Brothers. Don Ross in the New York *Herald Tribune* (June 9, 1957) wrote: "Admirers of Miss Monroe need not fear that her sojourn in England, where the film was made, has changed her. To be sure, she conquered the English press and had a command audience with Queen Elizabeth. But she is the same Marilyn, the love goddess that millions of American men have dreamed of sharing a small island with."

Although the movie was not cheered by the critics, few blamed Miss Monroe. "Whatever may be her destiny as an actress of serious dramatic roles," said a reviewer for the *Christian Science Monitor* (June 18, 1957), "there appears not to be the slightest doubt at this writing that Marilyn Monroe is a sparkling light comedienne."

For almost two years Miss Monroe did not try to exploit her new success. She lived quietly with her husband in New York and Connecticut, occasionally sitting in as an observer at the Actors Studio. During this period, Arthur Miller was appealing the contempt-of-Congress conviction which resulted from his refusal to answer two questions for the House Un-American Activities Committee. The verdict was reversed in 1958.

The same year, in the midst of a barrage of publicity, Miss Monroe returned to Hollywood to star in Billy Wilder's production of *Some Like It Hot*. Released early in 1959 by United Artists, it was pronounced "probably the funniest picture of recent memory" by *Variety* (February 25, 1959), which added that Miss Monroe's performance had a "deliciously naive quality."

Having achieved at least a grudging recognition of her claims to acting ability, Miss Monroe also seems to have found a successful marriage. Her first, to James Dougherty on June 19, 1942, legally ended in divorce in 1946. Her second, to Joe Di Maggio on January 14, 1954, ended in divorce nine months later. She married Mr. Miller in a Jewish ceremony on July 1, 1956.

A blue-eyed blonde with a soft voice, a breathless way of speaking, and a tremulous way of walking, Miss Monroe is five feet, five and one-half inches tall. It is reported that she now weighs slightly more than her former 118 pounds, but she insists that "I measure the same as I did five years ago" (thirty-seven and one-half, twenty-three, and thirty-six). These physical assets have without doubt contributed to her success, but producer Billy Wilder said after *Some Like It Hot* was released: "I don't deprecate Marilyn's measurements, but they aren't [everything]. . . . Her appeal stems from many things, including voice, grace of movement, and personality. She's an actress who keeps improving all the time." Marilyn Monroe received Italy's David di Donatello Award as the "best foreign actress of 1958."

References

Colliers 128:15+ S 8 '51 por
Cosmop 134:38+ My '53 por
Life 32:101+ Ap 7 '52 pors
Sat Eve Post 228:25+ My 5, 28+ My 12, 42+ My 19 '56 por
Time 67:74+ My 14 '56 por
Martin, W.T. Will Acting Spoil Marilyn Monroe? (1956)
Who's Who in America, 1958-59

MOONEY, EDWARD, CARDINAL May 9, 1882-Oct. 25, 1958 Roman Catholic prelate; ordained a priest in 1909; apostolic delegate to India (1926-31); became Archbishop of Detroit in 1937; proclaimed Cardinal in 1946. See *Current Biography* (Apr.) 1946.

Obituary

N Y Times p 1+ O 26 '58

MOORE, PRESTON J. Feb. 7, 1920- Organization official; lawyer
Address: b. c/o American Legion, 1608 K St., N.W., Washington 6, D.C.; P.O. Box 671, Stillwater, Okla.; h. 803 Blakeley St., Stillwater, Okla.

The forty-year-old American Legion has as its national commander for the year 1958-59 the Stillwater, Oklahoma lawyer Preston J. Moore, who was elected in September 1958 to succeed John S. Gleason, Jr., of Chicago. The Legion, which has been described as the largest organization of war veterans in history, had in 1957 a membership of 2,749,778 in 17,026 posts.

Born to Charles Felix Moore and Leta (Townsend) Moore on February 7, 1920, Preston J. Moore is a native of Colton, Oklahoma. He was brought up at Bartlesville in the northern part of the state, where his father, a disabled veteran of World War I and a member of James H. Teel Post 105 of the American Legion, was occupied as a salesman. (The elder Moore died in 1945; his widow is today a specialist in family relations with the Extension Division of Oklahoma State University.)

For one semester after his graduation from Bartlesville High School in 1937, Preston Moore attended Oklahoma Agricultural and Mechanical College (now Oklahoma State University) in Stillwater. He left college to work for the Phillips Petroleum Company in Indianapolis, Indiana. Later returning to Oklahoma A. and M., he completed two years of college before joining the Army on July 7, 1941.

Moore entered the Army as an infantry private, but later transferred to the Air Force and trained to be a medical administration officer. He was commissioned a second lieutenant on January 27, 1943, later becoming executive officer of the 222d Airborne Medical Company. With the 5th Bomb Group, 13th Air Force he saw service in New Guinea, at Wakde and Morotai (where the 5th Bomb Group won a distinguished unit citation), and on Samar in the Philippines and elsewhere. While on terminal leave in 1945 just before his discharge in the rank of first lieutenant, he joined his late father's American Legion post at Bartlesville.

The G.I. Bill of Rights enabled Moore to attend the University of Oklahoma for completion of his college course and the study of law. He transferred to Thomas C. Reynolds American Legion Post 303 on the campus at Norman, Oklahoma, becoming for 1946-47 its service officer and for 1947-48 its commander. In 1946 he became chairman of the Oklahoma American Legion foreign relations committee and attended the national convention at San Francisco. Under his commandership the Reynolds post not only

Chase Studios, Ltd.

PRESTON J. MOORE

increased in membership from 300 to over 1,000 but spent $12,000 on community playgrounds. His leadership brought him in 1948 the distinction of being the first World War II veteran to be elected state commander of the American Legion in Oklahoma.

In January 1949 Moore received his LL.B. degree and his admission to the Oklahoma bar. His uncle, Brown Moore, a prominent Oklahoma attorney, immediately took him into partnership in Stillwater. At present Moore's law partner is Robert M. Murphy of Stillwater. Moore is vice-president and general counsel of the American Life Insurance Company.

Since moving to Stillwater, Moore has been a member of Hanner Sharpe Post 129. He served the Oklahoma American Legion as department judge advocate in 1950 and as alternate national executive committeeman from 1950 to 1954. He was commander of the Hanner Sharpe post in 1953-54.

Other positions that Moore held were national executive committeeman from Oklahoma (1955-58), member of the national commander's advisory committee (1956-57), and member of the national executive committee's liaison committee on national security (1956-58). He has also served on the national executive committee's subcommittee on revision of constitution and bylaws.

Since its establishment in 1919 the Legion has exerted a strong political influence. The setting up of the Veterans' Bureau (a forerunner of the Veterans Administration) was in considerable measure the result of its pressure upon Congress, as later was the enactment of the G.I. and Korean veterans' bills of rights. A countersubversive section of the Americanization division does research on subversive activity. Since the early 1920's a national child welfare division has expended over $132,000,000 to aid children of deceased and disabled veter-

ans. The monthly *American Legion Magazine* ranks fifteenth in circulation among the country's periodicals.

"The purposes of the American Legion," observed former President Harry S. Truman at its fortieth national convention at Chicago in September 1958, "are set out in the preamble of its constitution and in its Congressional charter. When I joined the Legion those purposes were 'to promote peace and good will among the peoples of the United States and all the nations of the earth,' and 'to preserve the memories and incidents of the Great War of 1917-1918.' Since that time it has been necessary to amend this statement of purposes so that it now reads 'to preserve the memories and incidents of two world wars and the Korean hostilities fought to uphold democracy'" (New York *Times,* September 4, 1958).

The convention also heard addresses by Ambassador Henry Cabot Lodge, Jr., Defense Secretary Neil H. McElroy, Madame Chiang Kaishek, and others. It approved a resolution urging Congress to overturn by corrective legislation any United States Supreme Court decisions in which the justices "improperly assumed the role of legislative policy-maker." Other resolutions adopted opposed recognition of Communist China, called for investigation of the American Civil Liberties Union, urged Congress to resist attempts to "weaken, destroy, or repeal" the McCarran-Walter Immigration and Nationality Act, and extolled the late Senator Joseph R. McCarthy as "a real American whose vindication is brought about by the events of our own era" (Washington *Post and Times Herald,* September 5, 1958).

On September 4, 1958, toward the end of the American Legion's national convention in Chicago, Preston Moore was elected on the first ballot to a one-year term as national commander. "Moore," a New York *Herald Tribune* (September 5, 1958) report observed, "had traveled 100,000 miles to Legion posts throughout the country to win the $18,000-a-year post."

In his first major address since taking office, Commander Moore recommended on November 11, 1958 that civil defense be placed under the Defense Department, and called on the federal government to "start the national shelter program." On December 3 he expressed his determination to lead a strong Legion drive for higher veterans' pensions. Speaking in Los Angeles on January 5, 1959, he predicted a $41.2 billion defense budget. "I could safely say we would need $5 billion more," he declared.

Moore has been active in Boy Scouts and Young Men's Christian Association work at Stillwater, where he is a member of the official board of the Methodist church. He belongs to the Oklahoma and American bar associations and the Kiwanis and American Business Men's Club. A thirty-second degree Mason, he received from the Order of De Molay for Boys in Milwaukee, Wisconsin in 1958 the De Molay National Legion of Honor in recognition of his civic leadership. He is also a member and trustee of the Elks.

Another organization to which he belongs is the Izaak Walton League, fishing being among his favorite forms of recreation. He also likes golf. He stands at six feet two inches, weighs 205 pounds, and has hazel eyes and brown hair. His political affiliation is with the Democratic party. Mrs. Moore, a secretary before her marriage on August 29, 1941, is the former Nella Mae Reinhardt. The couple have two sons, Preston, Jr., and Brown.

Reference

American Legion Mag 65:12+ D '58 pors

MORGAN, LUCY (CALISTA) Sept. 20, 1889- Educational director

Address: Penland School of Handicrafts, Penland, N.C.

Every year for almost thirty years, students, teachers, and visitors from all parts of the United States and from many foreign countries have been welcomed in increasing numbers at the world-famed Penland School of Handicrafts, whose establishment and development have been the life-long work of Lucy Morgan. The school that she founded in 1929 grew out of a community project she had begun a few years earlier in an isolated section of the North Carolina mountains to revive the dying craft of hand weaving.

Now the Penland School, which was incorporated as a nonprofit institution in 1938, offers instruction in some fifty types of handicrafts, while retaining its special reputation in teaching the folk arts of dyeing, spinning, and weaving yarn. In collaboration with LeGette Blythe, Miss Morgan told the full story of Penland School in *Gift from the Hills* (Bobbs-Merrill, 1958).

The sixth of nine children of Alfred and Fannie Eugenia (Siler) Morgan, Lucy Calista Morgan was born on September 20, 1889 in a log cabin near Franklin in North Carolina. She is a descendant of Patrick Henry and Revolutionary War heroes; and David Swain, an ancestor on her mother's side of the family, was a Governor of North Carolina and a president of the University of North Carolina. Reared in the Southern Appalachians, where many inhabitants are of pure English and Scottish lineage, Lucy Morgan had what she calls an "Anglo-Saxon upbringing," in which readings from Dickens, community singing, and activity centered about the local Episcopal church were long-lasting influences.

Although she has spent almost all of her life in the North Carolina mountains, Lucy Morgan received her teacher training outside her home state. She was graduated with a life certificate from Central State Normal School in Mount Pleasant, Michigan in 1915 and during several summers took courses at the University of Chicago. Her early experience as an educator was also acquired in the Midwest—in public schools in Farwell, Michigan (1915); Traverse City, Michigan (1916); and Berwyn, Illinois (1917). After being employed at the Children's

LUCY MORGAN

Bureau in Chicago in 1918-19, she taught for a year in public schools in Havre, Montana.

In June 1920 Miss Morgan returned to the Blue Ridge Mountains—to Penland, North Carolina—to become a teacher and the principal of Appalachian School, founded some years earlier by her brother, the Reverend Rufus Morgan, an Episcopal minister. For recreation she often visited people in their mountain cabins, finding a few who still knew the old crafts of yarn dyeing and hand weaving. She became more and more inspired to try to fulfill a two-fold goal—to revive hand weaving in her community and thereby to increase living standards by providing mothers with the opportunity to add to their income without having to leave their remote homes.

During her vacation from January to March in 1923 she took a course in hand weaving at Berea College in Kentucky. When she returned to Appalachian School, she had three looms sent from Berea to use in teaching weaving in Penland. Soon afterward she bought twelve more looms, which were set up in homes in the community. Every day Lucy Morgan went out on foot or horseback to instruct potential weavers in using the looms.

The cost of materials and the prices she paid to weavers for finished products soon consumed her savings. She had, however, gradually won the backing of Episcopal Bishop Junius Horner, who suggested that she try to sell some of the products at the General Convention of the Episcopal Church, held in New Orleans. Success at the convention encouraged her to seek markets at similar gatherings and at vacation resorts and fairs. Penland crafts eventually became widely known. (Later, an exhibit at the 1933 Chicago World's Fair helped the handicraft project to survive the depression years.)

(Continued next page)

MORGAN, LUCY—Continued

In order to qualify for financial aid under a state vocational education program, Miss Morgan had to provide a central place in which to teach weaving. With the help of her neighbors who contributed logs, stones, and labor, she built Weavers' Cabin, the first of the picturesque buildings which now house the school. In December 1928 representatives of craft schools and other groups from several states met in Weavers' Cabin to plan the founding of the Southern Highland Guild (as related by Allen Eaton in *Handicrafts of the Southern Highlands*, Russell Sage Foundation, 1937).

Lucy Morgan had begun her community handicrafts program in 1924. However, she dates the founding of Penland School of Handicrafts from August 1929, when Edward F. Worst of Chicago spent his vacation teaching weaving, free of charge, to Penland pupils, some of whom were from outside the mountains. An authority on hand weaving, Worst had been a weaving instructor of Miss Morgan and was the author of the only books then available on the craft.

As Penland School grew in reputation, other teachers volunteered their services or accepted the small salaries that the school could afford to pay. One teacher explained why he gave up a $1,200 offer to work at Penland for $150: "It's worth the difference just to be in a place like this where there are no requirements, grades, papers to correct, or rules, and where students don't have to be urged but are there because they want what we have to offer. It's an interesting place to be, with interesting and congenial people to be with" (quoted in *Gift from the Hills*).

Penland's building program, which is still in progress, has been helped substantially by gifts of students to a school that has charged them minimal fees. Local and other business interests have also contributed, notably Lily Mills at Shelby, North Carolina. Within twenty-five years the school has acquired a thirty-three-acre campus and about ten buildings. In time it offered courses in ceramics, metal work, painting, wood carving, and other arts and crafts, as well as weaving.

Many of Penland's foreign students, teachers, and visitors come from northern Europe, where handicrafts are highly valued. In 1949 Lucy Morgan established periodic craft study tours to Scandinavian countries and a system of student exchange between Finland and Penland School. On two occasions she made trips abroad to visit craft schools and meet people who might be interested in her school.

One of Penland School's recent achievements was reproducing 113 yards of eighteenth century green baize cloth for the tables in Independence Hall, Philadelphia. When describing this and other challenges met by the school, particularly the construction of its buildings, Miss Morgan is less concerned in *Gift from the Hills* with tangible achievement than with the happy effect of co-operative efforts in arts and crafts upon the people who have shared in the projects.

Besides writing articles for craft magazines and for her school's own occasional publications,

Lucy Morgan has lectured in the United States and Canada, and she has served as adviser to the United States Office of Education on art in public schools and as judge for the Army's handicrafts contest for servicemen. She is a member of Alpha Sigma Tau, Delta Kappa Gamma (honorary), Southern Highland Handicraft Guild, Colonial Coverlet Guild, North Carolina Recreation Commission, and the Business and Professional Women's Club of Spruce Pine, North Carolina. She holds an honorary Doctor of Humanities degree from Central Michigan College of Education (formerly Central State Normal School) and an honorary Doctor of Humane Letters degree from Women's College of the University of North Carolina, among other awards. She is a Democrat.

Lucy Morgan has been pictured as "a hearty, active ninety pounder," with an excellent sense of humor, the courage of a gambler, and the "gift for calling out human goodness." For a change from her work and handicraft hobbies, she enjoys the ocean.

References

Ind Woman 32:324+ S '53

American Women, 1939-40

Who's Who in American Art (1956)

Who's Who in the South and Southwest (1956)

Who's Who of American Women (1958-59)

MORGAN, THOMAS E(LLSWORTH)

Oct. 13, 1906- United States Representative from Pennsylvania; physician

Address: b. House Office Bldg., Washington 25, D.C.; h. Fredericktown, Pa.

A United States Representative from Pennsylvania since 1945, Thomas E. Morgan, a Democrat, has been chairman of the Foreign Affairs Committee since February 1958, when he succeeded Thomas S. Gordon. In his home town of Fredericktown, Pennsylvania, where he is known as "Doc" Morgan, he practises medicine part time. He is an advocate of a bipartisan foreign policy, anti-recession measures, and civil rights legislation.

Thomas Ellsworth Morgan, one of eight children of William and Mary (Lawson) Morgan, was born October 13, 1906 in Ellsworth, Washington County, Pennsylvania. His father was a coal miner who lost his job during a strike in 1927 for his activities with the United Mine Workers of America. He attended public schools in Washington County and East Bethlehem Township High School in Fredericktown.

Morgan received the B.S. degree in 1930 from Waynesburg College in Pennsylvania, a Bachelor of Medicine degree from the Detroit College of Medicine and Surgery in 1933, and the M.D. degree in 1934 from the Wayne University College of Medicine in Detroit, where he had been president of his class. After an internship at Grace Hospital in Detroit, Morgan established a medical and surgical practice in Fredericktown and became affiliated with Waynesburg Hospital.

Interested in politics since his student days, Morgan had worked for the election of Al Smith in the Presidential campaign of 1928. After his return to Fredericktown, he was active in local Democratic politics and by 1939 assumed leadership of the local Democratic organization.

In the election of November 7, 1944 Morgan was selected to represent the Twenty-fourth District of Pennsylvania. He was re-elected in each succeeding Congressional election. In 1952, after the state had been reapportioned, he was chosen as Congressman of the Twenty-sixth District, which includes Fayette, Greene, and Washington counties and has a population of some 450,000.

Morgan, who carries on a handshaking campaign between elections, has built up a solid following through the years and won his most recent contest by 40,000 votes. He is probably the only Congressman who can claim that he helped bring many of his constituents into the world.

In his first year in Congress Morgan served as a member of the committees on Census, Flood Control, Invalid Pensions, Mines and Mining, and Enrolled Bills. In May 1946 he was assigned to the Foreign Affairs Committee. Three years later President Harry S. Truman appointed him chairman of the Advisory Committee on Management Improvement to Assist in Improving Government Organization. As chairman of the Foreign Affairs subcommittee on the Near East, in 1956 Morgan presided over an investigation of a United States shipment of tanks to Saudi Arabia, which had taken place in spite of the protests of Israel.

Although he has voted for reductions in various foreign aid measures before his committee, Morgan has consistently supported the Truman and Eisenhower foreign aid programs. He voted "yea" on a bill giving assistance to Greece and Turkey (May 1947), a $6 billion foreign aid authorization bill (March 1948), the extension of the Marshall Plan (April 1949), aid to Korea and Formosa (February 1950), a $7.5 billion foreign aid bill (August 1951), President Eisenhower's Middle East Doctrine (January 1957), and the mutual security bill (May 1958). He opposed a three-year extension of the reciprocal trade program (February 1955).

An advocate of more liberal immigration policies, Morgan voted to sustain Truman's veto of the McCarran-Walter immigration bill (June 1952) and favored the admission of 217,000 refugees from Communist nations (July 1953). He is a consistent supporter of civil rights legislation, having favored the anti-poll tax measure (July 1949), the Powell amendment to the school construction bill (July 1956) and after the amendment was passed, the bill itself (July 1956), and the civil rights bill (July 1956). He opposed what he considered to be a limited voluntary Fair Employment Practice Commission bill (February 1950).

As a friend of labor, Morgan supported the full employment bill (February 1946), Tru-

Wide World

DR. THOMAS E. MORGAN

man's veto of the Taft-Hartley bill (June 1947), the veto of a limited Social Security extension measure (June 1948), a proposal to raise income tax exemptions by $100 (March 1954), a bill to raise unemployment benefits (July 1954), a move to increase the minimum wage to one dollar an hour (July 1955), and the temporary unemployment compensation bill (May 1958).

On other domestic issues he has voted for a long-range housing bill (June 1949), Alaskan statehood (May 1958), the Department of Defense reorganization bill (June 1958), and Hawaiian statehood (March 1959). He was against the setting up of a permanent Committee on Un-American Activities (January 1945), the subversive activities control bill (May 1948), the St. Lawrence Seaway bill (May 1954), and the Eisenhower highway construction bill (July 1955).

On February 8, 1958 Morgan became chairman of the House Foreign Affairs Committee, as successor to Thomas S. Gordon, Democrat of Illinois, who resigned because of illness and died on January 22, 1959. Morgan supports a bipartisan foreign policy, as enunciated by the late Senator Arthur H. Vandenberg, and therefore advocates the Eisenhower foreign policy. Bills concerning the Department of State introduced by Morgan include a proposal to authorize the appointment of an Assistant Secretary for African Affairs (March 1957) and an amendment to the Foreign Service Act of 1946 to grant salary increases for Foreign Service personnel (February 1958).

After President Eisenhower proposed $3.9 billion for military, economic, and technical aid abroad, a bill to this effect came before the House Foreign Affairs Committee in March 1959. The usual Congressional opposition to foreign aid was intensified by findings of a

MORGAN, THOMAS E.—*Continued*

Foreign Affairs subcommittee, also headed by Morgan. In a unanimous report submitted in March, the group charged that there was mismanagement in the foreign aid program and cited examples of "pilferage of military supplies . . . provided by the United States and the diversion of such items either to civilian or other use different from that intended" (Washington *Post and Times Herald,* March 2, 1959). A compromise $3.5 billion foreign aid bill was passed and signed into law in July 1959.

Aside from foreign affairs, Morgan's main interest is anti-recession legislation. He represents a coal mining area where the depletion of bituminous coal deposits and technical innovations in mining have left thousands unemployed. He therefore introduced an area redevelopment bill in January 1957 to grant federal aid to alleviate unemployment in depressed areas and to retrain the technologically unemployed.

In January 1957 Morgan presented a measure to establish quota limitations on imports of foreign residual oils. In 1958 he proposed to amend the Federal Coal Mine Safety Act in an attempt to reduce further the accidents in coal mines. Another measure Morgan submitted in January 1957 was an amendment to the Social Security Act to provide that the retirement age be lowered to sixty years for the purpose of old-age and survivors insurance benefits.

Congressman Morgan is the first doctor to serve as head of the Foreign Affairs Committee since it was established and the only practising physician in the House. Although he has given up his activities as a surgeon, he continues his general practice on weekends with the help of an associate and when Congress is not in session. He applied a tourniquet to the wound of Representative Kenneth A. Roberts, who had been hit by a bullet fired by Puerto Rican nationalists in the House in March 1954.

Thomas Morgan met Winifred Strait at Grace Hospital, where she was a nurse. They were married on August 26, 1937 and have one daughter, Mary Ann. The Congressman is one of the largest men in the House; he stands six feet four inches and weighs 240 pounds. His favorite sports are golfing, boating, and flying. He is president of the board of commissioners of the East Bethlehem Township Board, and belongs to the American Medical Association and the Pennsylvania State Medical Society. He also belongs to the Benevolent and Protective Order of Elks, the Loyal Order of Moose, and the Order of Owls. He speaks on the floor of the House only on rare occasions.

References

N Y Times p17 O 30 '57
Uniontown (Pa.) Standard O 30 '56
Washington (D.C.) Post p11A F 9 '58
Biographical Directory of the American Congress, 1774-1949 (1950)
Congressional Directory (1959)
Who's Who in America, 1958-59

MORSE, TRUE D(ELBERT) Jan. 21, 1896-
Under Secretary of Agriculture; agricultural consultant

Address: b. U.S. Dept. of Agriculture, Washington 25, D.C.; h. 5207 Westwood Dr., Washington 16, D.C.

Second in command to Secretary of Agriculture Ezra Taft Benson, True D. Morse, the Under Secretary of Agriculture, has served in the post since January 1953. He has also been president of the Commodity Credit Corporation, heading since February 1954 the organization responsible for the direct price support program, and for such related activities of the Department of Agriculture as the soil bank payments. The corporation is authorized by Congress to borrow up to $14.5 billion of United States funds. Morse, who has been a successful farmer, farm appraiser and consultant, teacher of agriculture, and writer about farm problems, belongs to the President's Advisory Board on Economic Growth and Stability and the Committee on Government Activities Affecting Prices and Costs.

In one way or another, True Delbert Morse has been associated with agriculture all his life. The son of Delbert Lewis and Olive (Lawrence) Morse, he was born on a farm near Carthage, Missouri on January 21, 1896. He has a sister, Helen Morse, a home agent in Cass County, Missouri, and a brother, L. Glen Morse, who was formerly with the United States Fish and Wildlife Service. At Neosho High School in rural southwestern Missouri, from which he was graduated in 1916, Morse was active in athletics and debating, and was elected president of the senior class.

To support himself at the College of Agriculture of the University of Missouri, Morse operated a 400-acre farm and dairy for about five years, and in 1920 he was made the executive secretary of the Missouri Federation, Cooperative Livestock Shipping Association. At the University of Missouri, where he received his B.S. in Agriculture in 1924, Morse also studied in the School of Business and Commerce, and in his last two years was a part-time extension assistant in livestock marketing. He was elected to the honorary fraternities Alpha Zeta, Gamma Sigma Delta and Alpha Phi Zeta, and to the social professional fraternity, Alpha Gamma Rho. For a year after graduation Morse served as a specialist in agricultural economics in the University of Missouri Extension Service.

Morse joined the Doane Agricultural Service in 1925, and remained with the organization until he was nominated Under Secretary of Agriculture in December 1952. Founded by D. Howard Doane, the Doane Agricultural Service, in St. Louis, Missouri, is engaged in farm management, agricultural research, and farm appraisal. For about ten years it made studies of various states and areas, trained appraisers, and advised insurance companies planning to make farm loans. The organization furnishes a business service for agricultural groups, first published in 1938, called the *Doane Agricultural Digest,* which in 1952 had a circulation of about 40,000. A Doane editorial service supplies features to about a dozen magazines, including *Progressive Farmer, Successful Farming,* and *Farm Journal*; Morse not only contributed to such periodicals but wrote appraisal and farm loan handbooks and university bulletins. He has been a faculty member of the School of Banking of the University of Wisconsin, and has lectured in the United States and Canada.

When the Doane Agricultural Service was incorporated in 1943, Morse was elected president. A little less than ten years later he was made chairman of the board. Although it is capitalized at a modest $35,000 in common stock, the Doane Agricultural Service had in 1952 an income of more than a million dollars. In that year the service was managing about a thousand farms in fourteen states, and was being described in the press as "the nation's largest farm management, appraisal, and farm research organization."

From La Salle Extension University in Chicago, Morse received his LL.B. in 1932. He was admitted to the Missouri bar in 1932, and is also a member of the bar of the Supreme Court of the United States. Morse served as president of the American Society of Farm Managers and Rural Appraisers in 1941; he was vice-president of the American Farm Economists Association in 1952. He is a trustee and secretary of the National Council for Community Improvement; a director of the Foundation for American Agriculture; an executive secretary and trustee of the Agricultural Institute; and a director of the Mutual Savings Life Insurance Company.

Originally a Democrat like his father, True D. Morse switched his political allegiance when he became convinced that the Republicans were "offering the best for the country." "I voted for Hoover," he told a New York *Times* reporter (December 25, 1952), "and I've voted for the Republican candidate for President ever since." Morse headed the National Republican Farm Committee for Dewey in 1948, and in 1952 he contributed some suggestions for the Republican platform's farm plank. He had not yet met General Eisenhower at that time, but he was at least casually acquainted with Ezra Taft Benson, Eisenhower's choice for Secretary of Agriculture. The two chatted about agricultural problems, and on December 24, 1952, on Benson's recommendation, the incoming President announced the appointment of Morse as Under Secretary of Agriculture.

Confirmed by the Senate as Under Secretary of Agriculture on January 29, 1953 and as a director of the Commodity Credit Corporation a few days later, Morse became president of the C.C.C. in February 1954. He was the chief United States delegate in the negotiations that resulted in the renewal of the International Wheat Agreement in April 1953 and the adoption of an International Sugar Agreement at London later in the year.

During the Senate hearing on his appointment, Under Secretary Morse said that he agreed with "90 per cent supports of basic commodities." At an emergency conference at Des Moines, Iowa in June 1953, Morse said that grain storage should not be run by the government, but stored on the farm and handled by

U. S. Dept. of Agriculture

TRUE D. MORSE

commercial interests. The government bins would soon be looked upon as "monuments to the failure of free enterprise" (*Time,* June 15, 1953). In an address in Chicago in February 1954, Morse predicted that a failure to put into operation the administration's flexible price support program would turn the country "back to the philosophy of scarcity . . . tried and found wanting in the 1930's."

Morse signed an official report, released in October 1955, in which the administration rejected as "too costly and complex" Senator Hubert Humphrey's proposal to pay farmers for taking land out of production voluntarily. In January 1956 the President called for the creation of a $1,000,000,000 soil bank that would pay farmers for growing smaller crops and improving soil fertility. This was included in the Agricultural Act which was vetoed in April because it restored rigid price supports. A $1,200,000,000 soil bank authorization became a part of the compromise legislation enacted and signed by the President in May 1956. The response from farmers did not, however, live up to expectations, although by the end of 1957 farmers had retired over 21,000,000 acres of land under the soil bank plan. The Department of Agriculture later predicted that farmers would produce record crops in 1958 in spite of soil bank payments.

The Commodity Credit Corporation also carries out price support programs. Early in February 1959 the Department of Agriculture reported that its investment in surplus farm commodities had grown to more than $9,000,000,000 and indicated that the administration would recommend abandonment of the parity concept and a change to supports based on open market prices. Nevertheless, in May the House of Representatives adopted a farm program that failed to change the existing price support program. In a special

MORSE, TRUE D.—*Continued*

statement to Congress on June 1, President Eisenhower said that "continuation of this legislation another year leads the wheat program one step closer to disaster." The protests of the administration were overridden. In the middle of June a House and Senate conference committee agreed on a bill aimed at cutting wheat surpluses by increasing price supports and reducing planting allotments. In August the President announced that he would appeal to the American people by radio and television in an effort to get support for the proposals of the administration.

Under Secretary Morse received in 1956 the University of Missouri Alumni Association's "Citation of Merit for outstanding achievement and meritorious service in agriculture." He is an honorary member of St. Louis Rotary. A member of the Disciples of Christ Church, he served as president of the St. Louis Christian Missionary Society in 1935-40, as president of his local church in 1941-43, and as vice-president of the Missouri Christian Churches in 1943. He is a trustee of the non-denominational Bible College of Columbia, Missouri; a member of the board of the Council of Churches, National Capital Area, and of the board of National City Christian Church Corporation; and a member of the National Capital Area Council, Boy Scouts of America.

True Delbert Morse and Mary Louise Hopkins of Sedalia, Missouri were married on November 20, 1927. They have a son, James Buckner Morse, a construction engineer in St. Louis, and a daughter, Rebecca Jane Leonard. Morse has bluish-gray eyes and brown hair; he stands six feet one inches tall, and weighs 190 pounds. Fishing, travel, and outdoor activities are his favorite recreations.

References

Christian Sci Mon p3 D 24 '52
Farm J 77:32 F '53 por
N Y Times p23 D 25 '52 por
Newsweek 41:19 Ja 12 '53 por
Rural Electrification N 18:3 F '53
U S News 34:51 Ja 16 '53 por
Washington (D.C.) Post p21 Ja 29 '53 por
Who's Who in America, 1958-59
Who's Who in Commerce and Industry (1957)
World Biography (1954)

MOSHER, A(ARON ALEXANDER) R(OLAND) May 10, 1881-Sept. 26, 1959

Labor union official; president of Canadian Congress of Labour (1940-51); president of Canadian Brotherhood of Railway Employees (1908-52); served on Canada Labour Relations Board. See *Current Biography* (December) 1950.

Obituary

N Y Times p86 S 27 '59

MUELLER, FREDERICK H(ENRY)

(mül'ĕr) Nov. 22, 1893- United States Secretary of Commerce

Address: b. United States Department of Commerce, Washington 25, D.C.; h. 4301 Massachusetts Ave., N.W., Washington 16, D.C.

In a ceremony at the White House on August 10, 1959, Frederick H. Mueller was sworn in as Secretary of Commerce, succeeding Lewis L. Strauss, who had failed to receive Senate confirmation. A furniture manufacturer from Grand Rapids, Michigan and an expert on oil imports, Mueller served as Assistant Secretary of Commerce from 1955 to 1958; in November 1958 he became Under Secretary. During World War II he directed a group of companies that manufactured troop-carrying gliders, and helped to set up the Civil Air Patrol in Michigan. As Secretary of Commerce, Mueller heads a permanent staff of 32,000, in addition to an army of 100,000 temporary census takers who will be employed when the federal census is taken in 1960.

Frederick Henry Mueller was born in Grand Rapids, Michigan on November 22, 1893 to John Frederick and Emma (Oesterle) Mueller. His father, a German immigrant, landed in Baltimore at the age of three on a ship that had successfully run the Confederate blockade. When he was twelve years old, he moved to Grand Rapids to learn furniture making. A skilled cabinetmaker, he established his own business in Grand Rapids a year before Frederick Henry Mueller was born.

While attending the public schools of Grand Rapids, Mueller began an apprenticeship at his father's company at the age of thirteen. He entered Michigan State University at East Lansing, and earned a bachelor's degree in mechanical engineering in 1914. Becoming a partner in his father's firm in the same year, he mastered the technical and administrative aspects of the business so successfully within nine years that he was made general manager at the age of twenty-nine. Later named president of the company, he guided it as top executive until he retired in 1955. While a furniture manufacturer, he was associated with the Grand Rapids Furniture Makers Guild, the National Association of Furniture Manufacturers, and the Furniture Mutual Insurance Company. He was also a director of the People's National Bank of Grand Rapids.

During World War II, Mueller was president and general manager of Grand Rapids Industries, a group of woodworking manufacturers who pooled facilities to make troop-carrying gliders and aircraft components. Given a private plane as a Christmas present from his wife in 1944, Mueller qualified for a pilot's license, survived a crash, and organized Michigan's Civil Air Patrol, with which he served as a group commander. A lover of flying, he logged up 1,400 hours in light planes, and still holds a private pilot's license, although he gave up piloting in 1951. "Flying is like playing the piano," Mueller has said. "You have to keep taking lessons and practising if you hope to be any good at it."

To fill the vacancy created by the resignation of Lothair Teetor, President Dwight D. Eisenhower on November 22, 1955 named Mueller Assistant Secretary of Commerce for Domestic Affairs. A "small businessman at heart" by his own description, Mueller brought to his post his long years of experience of running a business employing about 100 persons. He wrote in an article for *Fortune* magazine (July 1957) that "the best thing for the vitality of small business is the maintenance of a healthy economic climate." Although he expressed his opposition to the "coddling" of small business in the same article, he pleaded for a change in the tax structure that would give small businessmen an opportunity to reinvest a greater percentage of profits in their enterprises. He attributed the failure of small businesses to a lack of managerial ability on the part of small businessmen themselves.

A vigorous opponent of government "interference" (by which he means federal efforts to aid business by subsidies) except for defense needs, Mueller does recognize the need for certain governmental regulations in behalf of the public interest. He believes that research promises the greatest opportunity for growth and that if a company is too small to spend a large amount for research on its own, it should pool its resources with similar firms.

Although he is considered an ultraconservative in some quarters, Mueller has become known in the Department of Commerce for his accessibility to his subordinates and for his disregard of ceremony and bureaucratic routine. During his years as Assistant Secretary he became the department's expert on the problems of oil imports, and was instrumental in the investigation that led to the voluntary and mandatory quota control program.

When Admiral Lewis L. Strauss was named Secretary of Commerce in a recess appointment in November 1958, Mueller was promoted to Under Secretary of Commerce. After Strauss resigned in June 1959, Mueller was appointed Acting Secretary. Three weeks later he was named Secretary of Commerce, and was confirmed in the appointment by the Senate on August 8. Mueller learned of his nomination from Mrs. Dwight D. Eisenhower on July 21, when she received a telegram from the President to that effect while she and Mueller were traveling from Washington, D.C. to Camden, New Jersey for the christening of the world's first atomic merchant ship, the *Savannah*.

As Secretary of Commerce, Mueller heads one of the most complex bureaucratic structures in the United States government. He is responsible for the operation of the Business and Defense Services Administration, Patent Office, Bureau of the Census, Office of Business Economics, Bureau of Foreign Commerce, National Bureau of Standards, Coast and Geodetic Survey, Weather Bureau, Maritime Administration, Bureau of Public Roads, St. Lawrence Seaway Development Corporation, and other offices and agencies.

Addressing the graduating class of the United States Merchant Marine Academy on August

FREDERICK H. MUELLER

7, Mueller outlined his initial declaration of trade policy. "I am neither a free trader nor a protectionist," he said. "I go forward in the middle-of-the-road course." He announced that he approved of expanding commerce with the Soviet Union but only on terms that would prove "mutually advantageous." Indicating that his policy would closely follow that of his predecessor, Lewis L. Strauss, whose recent appointment had been rejected by the Senate, Mueller challenged the Soviet Union to advance some "realistic proposals" if it wanted to increase its trade with the United States (New York *Times*, August 8, 1959).

In the event of a serious business decline, Mueller prefers tax reduction to raising expenditures for unproductive public works that are, he feels, primarily the responsibility of the states. He believes, however, that interstate and defense highway building *is* the responsibility of the federal government, and that they would provide economic stimulus in a time of recession. In his opinion, reduction of the national debt should precede tax reduction.

Frederick Henry Mueller was married in 1915 to Mary Darrah of Grand Rapids. She died in 1958. Mueller lives in a large Washington apartment with his daughter Marcia, an artist, poet, and publicist, who has been successful in her fight to overcome cerebral palsy. Since the death of her mother, she has become the hostess and housekeeper for her father. His only other offspring is a son, Frederick, who is a furniture manufacturer.

Known as "Fritz" to his intimates, Mueller is a trim and handsome man whose bristling white crew cut makes him look younger than his age. According to one of his associates in the cabinet, "he behaves like a tackle, never like an end." He relaxes with golf, bridge, and books on economics. He is a past president of the East Grand Rapids Board of Education

MUELLER, FREDERICK H.—*Continued*
and a former member of the governing board
of Michigan State University. He belongs to
the Rotary Club, Kent Country Club, and the
Peninsular Club in Grand Rapids. He is a
32d degree Mason and Shriner, and a member
of the national honorary engineering fraternity,
Tau Beta Pi. In June 1959 Michigan State
University conferred on him an honorary LL.D.
degree for his distinguished service to nation,
state, and community. Mueller attends the
Episcopal Church.

"Conservatism is no longer in the doghouse,"
Mueller told the Economic Club of Detroit on
October 19, 1959. "It has won massive public
acclaim and support. . . . [The public] has
learned from bitter experience that the road
to the extreme left always leads to less freedom and less jobs and to more taxes, bigger
national debt, and greater income-robbing inflation" (New York *Times,* October 20, 1959).

References

N Y Herald Tribune p1+ Jl 22 '59 por
N Y Post Mag p2 Ag 30 '59
N Y Times p15 Jl 22 '59 por; p7 Jl 28
'59
N Y World-Telegram p9 Jl 22 '59 por
Nations Bsns 47:64+ S '59 por
Newsweek 54:64 Ag 3 '59 por
Time 74:16 Ag 3 '59 por
U S News 47:21 Ag 3 '59 por
Washington (D.C.) Post p1F Jl 26 '59
Who's Who in America, 1958-59

MÜNNICH, FERENC (mün'ĭk) 1886- Premier of Hungary
Address: Parliament Bldg., Budapest, Hungary

When Ferenc Münnich became Premier in
the Communist government of Hungary on January 28, 1958, the New York *Times* commented
that for "forty years Münnich has been a faithful follower of the dominant Moscow line. He
is not expected to change." Although Münnich
is a native of Hungary, he has spent many
years of his life in the Soviet Union, where he
became a Communist in 1917. After World
War II he helped to establish the Communist
regime in Hungary and filled various posts in
the diplomatic service. He became a member of
the Hungarian cabinet during the 1956 revolt
and was made First Deputy Premier in February 1957. In addition to holding the premiership
in the Hungarian government, he is a member
of the Central Committee and Politburo of the
Hungarian Socialist Workers' (Communist)
party.

Ferenc Münnich was born in Hungary in
1886. Little is known of his early life except
that he was graduated from Cluj University
(now in Romania) and holds a doctoral degree
in law. At the outbreak of World War I in
1914 he was mobilized into the Austro-Hun-
garian Army; he served on the Russian front
and soon fell into captivity. Becoming a Communist during his imprisonment in Russia, he

helped overthrow Czar Nicholas II in March
1917 and participated in the Bolshevik coup of
November 1917.

Upon his return to Hungary in 1918 he joined
Béla Kun in helping to found the Hungarian
Communist party and participated in establishing the Béla Kun Communist regime. At the
time of the Hungarian Soviet Republic, in 1919,
he was commander of the Budapest militia and
later political commissar of the Hungarian Red
Army. When Kun's regime came to an end in
late 1919, he went back to Russia.

In Moscow, Münnich worked in the Comin-
tern, carried out secret police assignments, and
received military training. When the Spanish
Civil War broke out in 1936, he was picked as
a trusted police agent and sent to Spain to fight
for the Republican government. He was the
leader of one of the revolutionary divisions and
eventually was made brigadier general of the
Ninth International Brigade. After the defeat
of the Loyalists' forces in 1939, he was deported
to France and from there he returned to the
Soviet Union.

During World War II Münnich fought with
the Red Army in the battle of Stalingrad and
elsewhere and served as a political commissar
and secret police agent. In 1945 he went back
to Hungary. First he was high commissioner of
the city of Pécs, and later he became chief of
police in Budapest, where he helped to restore
order in the aftermath of the war.

By leaving Budapest to fill assignments in the
Hungarian diplomatic service, Münnich was able
to avoid the danger of intraparty conflicts at
home and Stalinist purges of leadership in the
European satellite countries. For a time he
represented his government in Finland and was
minister to Bulgaria from 1951 to 1954 and
Ambassador to Bulgaria in 1954. He became
Ambassador to the Soviet Union later in 1954,
and, after two years there, in 1956 he was sent
to Belgrade as Ambassador to Yugoslavia.

Demonstrations against the Communist regime
in Budapest developed into open revolution in
October 1956. Münnich left Yugoslavia for
Hungary and on October 27 became Minister
of the Interior in the cabinet of Imre Nagy,
who replaced András Hegedüs as Premier.
Nagy protested the Soviet Army's suppression
of the revolt, and as soon as it became apparent
that his government had incurred the disapproval
of the Soviet Union, Münnich and a group of
men including János Kádár withdrew their support of Nagy.

Leslie B. Bain wrote in the *Reporter* on
March 21, 1957 that "like Kadar, Münnich
began by believing that the original Nagy program must be kept to pacify the country. Immediately after the return of the Soviet forces
on November 4 and the dismissal of Nagy,
Münnich said to me: 'We are not crazy; we
know that the Nagy program is a must for
Hungary.' But the drift of events pushed Münnich toward open terror and he became the
nemesis of 'deviationists.' " On November 4,
when the Kádár government had been installed
by the Soviet Union, Münnich had joined the
cabinet as Minister of Armed Forces and Public Security, and as a Deputy Premier.

In early December 1956 Münnich broadcast an order declaring the dissolution of revolutionary committees formed during the revolt in factories, government offices, and other establishments. "Experience shows," he said, "that the committees are not carrying out any action in the public interest and, on the contrary, where they exist their operation is hampering the work of the state authorities and the carrying out of tasks in the public interest." The New York *Times* (December 5, 1956) commented that "the significant thing in his order was the acknowledgement that the committees still existed in some places and apparently were attempting to function."

Two months after the revolution, according to *Time* magazine (February 10, 1958), Münnich's "new police and army apparatus was working so smoothly that Russian troops could retire to rural barracks." In late February 1957 Münnich was elevated to the post of First Deputy Premier of Hungary. While Premier János Kádár was visiting Communist China in the fall of 1957, Münnich served as Acting Premier of his country.

In a report in the New York *Times* (October 6, 1957), Harrison E. Salisbury described the feeling of some observers that Premier Kádár was engaged in an almost constant battle to hold his own "moderate" course against a "hard-line" Stalinist faction which was advocating a tougher program, principally in the treatment of those arrested for their role in the revolt. Salisbury reported that Münnich at that time "was said to be a fence sitter, ready to come down on the winning side."

Premier Kádár resigned his government position in January 1958, but retained his role of First Secretary of the ruling Socialist Workers' (Communist) party. On January 28 Münnich was unanimously approved by the National Assembly of Hungary as Premier. After he was sworn into office, he promised there would be no revolutionary changes in Hungarian policy. The new government, he said, "will follow the same road as that chosen by the Kadar government. We in the government always supported him and were always in agreement with him." He added that since the end of the 1956 revolt, "a unity was created in this party and government that . . . never existed before—not even after the liberation. This will remain in the future, too" (Washington *Post and Times Herald,* January 29, 1958).

After elections to parliament on November 16, 1958, when voters ratified a single list of 338 candidates, the new assembly unanimously voted to continue Münnich as Premier of Hungary. In a note handed to the United States chargé d'affaires in Budapest on January 28, 1959, the Hungarian government proposed diplomatic talks to put relations with America on a normal basis. Since before the revolt in 1956, the United States had not been represented in Hungary by an accredited minister. When the American government returned the note as inacceptable on the grounds that it was offensive in language and contained a veiled threat, Hungary warned that it might curtail the activities of the American legation in Budapest.

FERENC MÜNNICH

As Leslie B. Bain pictured Münnich in the *Reporter*: "He is a cultural, clever man with a hearty appetite for the good things of life." Other descriptions in the Western press note his portliness and habit of smoking small cigars. He holds both Hungarian and Russian citizenship.

References

N Y Herald Tribune p3 Ag 24 '57
N Y Times p2 Ag 24 '57; p1+ Ja 28 '58; p6 Ja 29 '58
Reporter 16:25+ Mr 21 '57
Time 71:29 F 10 '58
International Who's Who, 1958

MURRAY, DON(ALD PATRICK) July 31, 1929- Actor

Address: b. c/o Twentieth Century-Fox Film Corp., 444 W. 56th St., New York 19

By playing a variety of roles such as the rambunctious cowboy in *Bus Stop,* the worried bookkeeper in *The Bachelor Party,* and the harried drug addict in *A Hatful of Rain,* thirty-year-old Don Murray has won a reputation as a versatile and gifted Hollywood actor. But success in films, on the stage, and over TV has not blunted Murray's sense of social mission. He founded HELP (Homeless European Land Program), which aids European war refugees, and continues to take a leading part in its activities. In 1957 he was a winner of the *Motion Picture Herald*-Fame Poll.

Of Irish ancestry, Donald Patrick Murray was born on July 31, 1929 in Hollywood, California, the son of Dennis and Ethel (Cook) Murray. Both parents were theatrical people; his mother was a Ziegfeld girl and his father was a dance director and later a stage manager. Don's elementary education took place at vari-

DON MURRAY

ous public schools in Long Island, Cleveland, and Texas, while his parents moved from theater to theater.

Already determined to make his career as an actor, Murray, instead of going to high school, enrolled at the American Academy of Dramatic Arts in New York City in October 1946 and was graduated in April 1948. During his vacations from the academy he performed in repertory plays at several summer stock theaters. He acted on the New York stage, but it was not until he was cast in Tennessee Williams' *The Rose Tattoo* that he was assigned his first important role: that of Jack Hunter, the young sailor having his first fling at sexual adventure.

The Rose Tattoo opened at the Erlanger Theatre in Chicago on December 29, 1950 and moved to the Martin Beck Theatre in New York City on February 3, 1951. Critics characterized Murray's supporting role as "a touching performance," "completely disarming," and one of "notable skill." One critic for the weekly *Variety* (February 7, 1951) maintained that the play's three relative newcomers "all register as future prospects, Murray and Miss [Phyllis] Love especially, as film possibilities."

While the play was running on Broadway in 1951, Murray was arrested for refusing to bear arms in the Korean conflict. A religious youth, he had registered as a conscientious objector when he was eighteen, after having met stage director Paton Price, a pacifist, in summer stock. Murray spent a day in prison and the following month on bail, but was able to convince the authorities of the sincerity of his beliefs.

After *The Rose Tattoo* completed its run on Broadway and on tour, Murray enrolled in 1952 for "alternative service," a method of fulfilling a military obligation by working with a social service group. With the Church of the Brethren, he served in a German refugee camp, as-

sisted lawless Italian street children, and then led recreational activities in an Italian camp for refugees from Communism. He remained in the Italian camp for six month as a volunteer after his obligatory two years were finished. It was during this time that he conceived the idea which later came to fruition: that of relocating the refugees to a farming community where they would be self-supporting.

Unable to implement his dream, since his salary as a volunteer worker was less than $10 a month, Murray returned to New York and his stage career in 1955. He was cast in a revival of Thornton Wilder's *The Skin of our Teeth* which was staged in Paris in June 1955 as a part of the State Department's "Salute to France" program. The play later appeared for short runs in Washington, Chicago, and New York.

After a color television performance of the play on September 11, 1955, Murray received a prominent role in the baseball farce *The Hot Corner*. It opened in Philadelphia on December 27, 1955, then moved to the John Golden Theatre in New York, where it closed on January 28, 1956, after five performances.

At that time, director Joshua Logan was searching for an actor to play the cowboy suitor of Marilyn Monroe in the film version of William Inge's comedy, *Bus Stop*. On the strength of his screen test, Murray was signed for a long-term contract. Also cast for the movie was actress Hope Lange, Murray's fiancée; they were married while *Bus Stop* was being filmed in Hollywood.

Although veterans of the stage, both husband and wife were termed "discoveries" when the movie was released in 1956. A New York *Post* critic wrote (September 2, 1956): "The new boy is Don Murray . . . very lively, and a fresh welcome talent. The new girl is Hope Lange, a sincere charmer." Almost immediately, Murray was cast in Paddy Chayefsky's *The Bachelor Party*, which was released by United Artists the following year.

In this study of lonely and restless New Yorkers, Murray played a young accountant who, while out on a spree with his office mates, tries to mask his worries about his wife's pregnancy and his economic future. He followed this performance by co-starring in *A Hatful of Rain*, the Twentieth Century-Fox film about drug addiction which was released in 1957.

By then firmly established as movie stars, both Murray and Miss Lange were contributing 10 per cent of their incomes to HELP, which Murray had founded in conjunction with Dr. Belden Paulson of the Congregational Christian Service Committee. Assisted by a $33,000 grant from the U.N. High Commissioner for Refugees, they purchased 130 acres of land in Sardinia, Italy, for their resettlement program which gives refugees land they can till as their own. "By working the land," Murray said, "these people are creating jobs for themselves and others in the area" (*Coronet*, July 1957).

To help finance the project, and to dramatize the plight of the displaced persons, Murray wrote a story entitled "For I Have Loved Strangers," based on his experiences in Italy. It was performed on TV's *Playhouse 90* on December 19, 1957. Murray and his wife co-starred in the play, and contributed their earnings, estimated at $20,000, to the refugee community.

Returning to Hollywood, Murray starred as the "saddle tramp" relentlessly pursued for a murder he has not committed in *From Hell to Texas* (Fox, 1958). He next appeared in another western *These Thousand Hills* (Fox, 1959). Movie audiences also saw Murray in 1959 in *Shake Hands with the Devil*, a United Artists release filmed in Ireland, which dealt with the 1921 Irish rebellion.

Some of Murray's important TV parts have been Lachie in *The Hasty Heart* on *Show of the Month*, December 18, 1958 and the title role in *Billy Budd* on the same program on May 25, 1959. Both in films and in television plays Murray tries to lose his identity in the character he is playing. "I guess you'd call me a Method actor," he has said (*Coronet*, May 1959). "I try to immerse myself in the parts, so that I vanish and the parts come out." He says he is distressed when movie fans recognize him as an individual. The fictional character which Murray would most like to portray is Jean-Christophe Krafft, in Romain Rolland's long novel about a Franco-German musical genius, *Jean-Christophe*.

Don Murray married Hope Lange on April 16, 1956. They have two children, Christopher Paton and Patricia Elda, and live in a simple home in Beverly Hills. Their favorite recreation is listening to popular music at home. Miss Lange, who appeared in the play *The Hot Corner* with Murray, has recently made the pictures *The Young Lions*, *Jesse James*, *Peyton Place*, and *The Best of Everything*.

Lean and boyish, Murray stands six feet one inch, weighs 175 pounds, and has thick brown hair and green eyes. Characterized as "a sensitive and religious man," he rarely smokes or drinks, avoids Beverly Hills parties, and still devotes much of his time and money to his refugee venture, which has its headquarters in Elgin, Illinois. He was baptized in 1955 as a member of the Church of the Brethren. "Being a CO (conscientious objector) has finally lost its sting," Murray has said. "The government realizes the help such people can give in non-violent activities" (New York *Mirror*, January 26, 1958).

Certainly, Murray's pacifism has had a long-reaching effect and has created a double career for him. "Although helping the refugees is his first concern," remarked writer Richard Gehman in *Coronet* (May 1959), "Don still is intensely serious about his acting—if only because he realizes that without it he would be unable to finance his humanitarian work."

References

Life 42:82 Ap 29 '57 pors
Look 21:99+ D 10 '57 pors
Los Angeles Times VII p3 D 15 '57 por
International Motion Picture Almanac, 1959

NELSON, DONALD M(ARR) Nov. 17. 1888-Sept. 29, 1959 Business executive; former United States government official; chairman of the War Production Board during World War II. See *Current Biography* (March) 1941.

Obituary

N Y Times p37 S 30 '59

NEVILLE, JOHN May 2, 1925- British actor
Address: 92 Hadley Rd., New Barnet, Hertfordshire, England

By portraying Hamlet with the Old Vic Company on a tour of major American and Canadian cities as well as on the London and Broadway stage, John Neville has reached the pinnacle of a Shakespearean actor's career. Critics everywhere have acclaimed him for his interpretation of this role during the 1958-59 season. After a six-year apprenticeship in Brit-

JOHN NEVILLE

ish repertory theatres, he became associated with the Old Vic in 1953. He has since played stellar roles in *Macbeth*, *Othello*, *Romeo and Juliet*, *Richard II*, and *Troilus and Cressida*.

Television audiences saw Neville as Romeo in the *Producers' Showcase* presentation of *Romeo and Juliet* on NBC-TV on March 4, 1957. He was praised by TV critic Jack Gould (New York *Times*) for his "perceptive artistry." The Old Vic Company's production, with John Neville and Claire Bloom, was "a work of art, alive with vitality and filled with tenderness . . . brought before the cameras with impeccable craftsmanship."

John Neville was born on May 2, 1925 in Willesden, London, England to Reginald Daniel and Mabel Lillian (Fry) Neville. He was educated at Willesden and at Chiswick county

NEVILLE, JOHN—*Continued*

schools, where he played football and was active in dramatics. Later, he played professional football. After service in the Royal Navy during World War II, Neville entered the Royal Academy of Dramatic Art in London.

On completion of his dramatic training in 1947 he appeared at the New Theatre, London on April 23 in a walk-on part in *Richard II* and later in the season made his professional debut with Robert Atkins at the Open Air Theatre in Regent's Park. He portrayed Lysander in *A Midsummer Night's Dream* and Chatillon in *King John*. During 1948 he toured Norway with a production of John Galsworthy's *Justice*, and then acted in repertory at Lowestoft, England for nine months. This was followed by fifteen months with the Birmingham Repertory Theatre in Birmingham, England.

His press notices were so favorable that in 1950 he was invited to join the Bristol (England) Old Vic Company, where he played for three consecutive seasons. During this period he enacted such parts as Richard in *The Lady's Not For Burning*, Dunois in *Saint Joan*, Edgar in *Venus Observed*, Valentine in *The Two Gentlemen of Verona* (this production twice visited the Old Vic Theatre in London), the twins Hugo and Frederick in *Ring Round the Moon*, the Duke in *Measure for Measure*, and Gregers in *The Wild Duck*.

When the Bristol Old Vic Company brought their production of *Henry V* to the Old Vic Theatre in London for the coronation year (1953), Neville played the title role. In the following season he joined the London Old Vic. Favorable reviews of his performances as Fortinbras in *Hamlet*, the Dauphin in *King John*, Bertram in *All's Well That Ends Well*, Orsino in *Twelfth Night*, Cominius in *Coriolanus*, and Ferdinand in *The Tempest*, prompted the Old Vic officials to cast him in the title role in *Richard II* in the 1954-55 London season. Neville has since been seen in many Old Vic productions, most notably as Mark Antony in *Julius Caesar* and as both Othello and Iago in *Othello* (alternating the roles with Richard Burton).

On Broadway in the 1956-57 season the Old Vic Company appeared under the management of Sol Hurok and was presented by the Old Vic Trust, Ltd., and the Arts Council of Great Britain. John Neville played Macduff in *Macbeth*, Thersites in *Troilus and Cressida*, the title role in *Richard II*, and Romeo, opposite Claire Bloom, in *Romeo and Juliet*. "Although the Old Vic eschews the star system in theory," noted *Cue* (October 20, 1956), "there are stars in practice. John Neville and Paul Rogers have emerged as top British actors within the past few years. . . . Neville has been widely hailed as the successor to [John] Gielgud as a consummate stylist in classic roles."

Commenting on Neville's interpretations of Romeo and of Richard II, the late Wolcott Gibbs wrote in the *New Yorker* (November 3, 1956): "Neville is a young Englishman who reminds me, physically, quite a lot of the late Leslie Howard. This means that he is a delicately romantic figure, with a remarkably sensitive face and a graceful carriage, and to this extent admirably equipped to play either a ruined king or a doomed lover. In both roles he speaks with beautiful precision and with proper reverence for the sacred rhythms; his mobile features are faithful mirrors of his moods . . . his gestures are eloquent, and if at times the air around him seems overfull of hands, they are agreeable hands to watch. But the final effect [in *Richard II*] is pathetic rather than tragic . . . as Romeo it is an exercise in declamation."

Brooks Atkinson, on the other hand, praised Neville's interpretation of Romeo as ideal. "He is handsome, lean and sensitive. He moves with unconscious grace. He speaks verse easily without losing the impetuosity of the character. It is romantic acting that, by taste again, avoids the excesses of gesture, speech and posing . . . he has assimilated the ardor, imagery and extravagance of the drama in a pithy, pulsing character portrait" (New York *Times*, October 25, 1956).

Switching from the poetic ardor of Romeo to the decisive action of Macduff, Neville was acclaimed for his role in *Macbeth*, also presented on Broadway and on tour. Richard L. Coe, reviewing the production in the Washington *Post and Times Herald* (February 2, 1957), wrote: "I relished the rich variety of Neville's voice. Now Richard II has become Macduff, whom he reads affectingly, though I wish he used more force—natural horror—for his discovery of Duncan's murder. This actor seems to have great gifts except inner conviction." Herbert Whittaker in the Toronto *Globe and Mail* (October 3, 1956) noted that, after "last week's sad Romeo, [he] is a revelation in this week's Macduff. In this role he struck three grand moments, with ascending power. . ."

Broadway critics were divided in their appraisal of Neville's acting in *Richard II*. Walter Kerr in the New York *Herald Tribune* (October 24, 1956) mentioned the "occasional flashes of brittle despairing cynicism" in which Neville's Richard "comes most trenchantly alive," but thought that his "inner resources do not expand with the increasing melody of the lines." Richard Watts, Jr., in the New York *Post* (November 11), compared Neville's interpretation with that of Maurice Evans in the same role. "Both characterizations were brilliant, but the play seems less a star's vehicle and more an integrated drama in Neville's hands." Tom Donnelly in the New York *World-Telegram and Sun* (October 24) praised Neville's portrayal in the early scenes but later on, he contended, "all semblance of solid imperial humanity vanishes. The king becomes pure grease paint and bombast."

John Beaufort in the *Christian Science Monitor* (October 27, 1956) considered that Richard was acted "with authority and stirring eloquence. . . . Neville reveals many of the complex facets and motives of the monarch who emerges as a human being while he is failing as a king." Brooks Atkinson in the New York *Times*

(October 24) regarded Neville's Richard as "a brilliant portrait."

On December 26, 1956 the Old Vic Company presented *Troilus and Cressida* in New York. Neville, who had played Troilus in the London production, changed to the part of Thersites. "Neville, no longer Richard or Romeo, becomes a stunning character actor as cynical Thersites, ambling down an orchestra aisle muttering guileful phrases in west county accents," observed Richard L. Coe (Washington *Post and Times Herald*) when the production was given in Washington, D.C. at the National Theatre on February 8, 1957.

Although Neville had no desire to play Hamlet, he was persuaded to study the part by director Michael Benthall. "I always thought I was more suited to character parts," Neville has said. "In Hamlet, you've nowhere to hide. You can't hide behind a beard or makeup. . . . But once you begin to study this prince, you can't get away from him. He is the most fascinating character in all drama. . . . As I see him, he's a young man—very young—as young as I can make him. And he's constantly being disillusioned" (Los Angeles *Times,* October 12, 1958).

Making his American debut as Hamlet in San Francisco in September 1958, Neville was given a resounding welcome by the critics. His portrayal drew such tributes as "tremendous authority," "sensitive," and "extremely moving." New Yorkers, meanwhile, awaited his first appearance in the role on Broadway, scheduled for the evening of December 9, 1958.

John Neville is married to Caroline Hooper, a former actress. They have five children, two of them adopted. Neville's acting in Shakespearean dramas at the Old Vic in London has won for him the title "heartthrob of Britain's bobby-sox set." He has blond hair and "a lean, hawk face in repose with deep-set [blue] eyes," according to Cecil Smith of the Los Angeles *Times,* to whom he told his plans to abandon Shakespeare at the end of the 1959 season. "It's exciting. I don't know what I'm going to do—what sort of acting," Neville said. He enjoys jazz music as well as opera.

References

Los Angeles Times V p1 O 12 '58
Who's Who in the Theatre (1957)

NEWMAN, BERNARD (CHARLES) May 8, 1897- Author; lecturer

Address: h. 3 Gerard Rd., Harrow-on-the-Hill, Middlesex, England

World-traveled British author and lecturer Bernard Newman has written about 100 books—detective novels, stories of espionage, accounts of his travels, and discussions on international affairs—and has addressed audiences estimated at a quarter of a million people a year. Having visited and lived in many parts of Europe, Africa, Asia, and America, he is noted for his firsthand knowledge of world affairs, the tone of human sympathy in his approach, and the varied practical experience that serves as a back-

BERNARD NEWMAN

ground for all his work, whether serious considerations of political problems or spy tales.

In the United States Newman is possibly best known for *Balkan Background* (Macmillan, 1945), *The Flying Saucer* (Macmillan, 1950), and *Report on Indo-China* (Praeger, 1954). He writes some of his detective and spy stories under the pseudonym of Don Betteridge, one of the most recent being *Spies of Peenemünde* (Hale, 1958).

One of six children (five boys and a girl) in a farming family in England's Leicestershire, Bernard Charles Newman was born on May 8, 1897 in Ibstock, to William Betteridge and Annie (Garner) Newman. He is a grand-nephew of the famous nineteenth century novelist George Eliot, and a cousin of Maurice Evans, the actor. His mother being Alsatian, the boy learned to speak German and French as well as English. He was educated at Market Bosworth Grammar School (1908-14) and received early training in acting.

When war broke out in 1914, Bernard Newman, then seventeen, joined the British Army and during World War I, in which he was mentioned for gallantry, was attached for a time to the American 33d Division. According to Orville Prescott (New York *Times,* January 9, 1945), he was sent to Germany as a spy, an assignment he won through his convincing impersonation of a German officer, and spent three years in the German Intelligence Service. His service in the war, Newman has said, did most to influence the course of his career because it directed his attention to foreign affairs.

In 1919 Newman entered the British Civil Service as staff officer in His Majesty's Office of Work. While in this post (until 1937) and for many years afterward, he spent his summers traveling throughout Europe, mainly on a bicycle that became known to his readers as "George." He interviewed a number of heads of state (including Hitler in 1933), was banned from Italy

NEWMAN, BERNARD—*Continued*

by Mussolini, and lived at times among peasants and Balkan gypsies, for the most part speaking the native tongue wherever he went. His adventures also included activities in political and military intelligence work in various European countries, touring as a strong man in a Polish circus, appearing in grand opera in Paris, and living on a Russian communal farm.

Meanwhile, since the publication of *Round About Andorra* in 1928 and the *Cavalry Went Through* in 1930—which reportedly inspired the German panzer divisions and later the British commandos—Bernard Newman had been building a reputation as a prolific writer of travel books and of novels dealing mainly with espionage. Before World War II he had written more than twenty books, among them several accounts of his travels in Europe, including *Cycling in France* (1936) and *Ride to Russia* (1938), both published by Herbert Jenkins.

Some of the titles of Newman's early novels are *Armoured Doves* (1931), *The Mussolini Murder Plot* (1936), *Lady Doctor—Woman Spy* (1937), and *Death Under Gibraltar* (1938). The Boston *Transcript* (October 10, 1936) found that the "fresh ideas" in Newman's *German Spy* "set it apart from the common spy-fiction grist"; while W. A. Roberts in the New York *Herald Tribune* (October 4, 1936) commented, "He knows the jargon, as well as the technique of espionage. The average detective story is not half so true to police procedure as this author's books are to the methods of those who wield invisible weapons in time of war." One of Newman's spy stories is said to have been used in Russia as a textbook on military espionage.

At the beginning of the hostilities of World War II Newman served with the British Expeditionary Force as a lecturer. He was later transferred to the French Army, to which he was attached when the Germans made their attack in May 1940. Having escaped to England, he was employed for five years (1940-45) as staff lecturer by the Ministry of War Information, charged with maintenance of public morale. During 1942 he visited the United States, for the first time, on a tour for this agency. He afterward lectured for Army Education in Europe and the Middle East (1945-46); India, South East Asia, and Japan (1947); and the Mediterranean and North Africa (1948).

In his books during and following World War II Newman turned more and more to commentaries on world affairs and international political developments, writing among some twenty similar publications *The Story of Poland* (1940), *British Journey* (1945), *The Red Spider Web* (1947), and *Morocco Today* (1953). The result of about twelve years of study of problems concerning postwar boundaries, *New Europe* (1942) was regarded by most critics as a highly informative, readable, and thought-provoking book for the layman. The author's hope for peace lay in a federation of Europe, following a period of population exchange based upon similarity of cultures, to ease tension in troubled areas.

Well received and widely reviewed in the United States, Newman's *Balkan Background* was called by Orville Prescott, "a clear, authoritative and extraordinarily detached guide to chaos" (New York *Times,* January 9, 1945). As a solution to the minority questions of the Balkans, Newman suggested wholesale transfers of population, according to plebiscites, and looked forward to the establishment of a Balkan federation coupling local autonomy with a central government to control matters of defense and foreign affairs.

Turkish Crossroads (Hale, 1951) was described in the *Saturday Review* (December 13, 1952) as "a report which combines the charm of personal exploration with skilful research and solid appraisal of up-to-date information." Personal exploration is also the keynote of a large number of Newman's other books of travel and description, such as *Middle Eastern Journey* (Gollancz, 1947) and *North African Journey* (Hale, 1955) and the Jenkins' publications *Both Sides of the Pyrenees* (1952), *Spain on a Shoestring* (1957), and *Unknown Germany* (1958).

Newman was meanwhile also gaining in popularity as a novelist. His *Papa Pontivy and the Maginot Murder* (1940) was praised in the New York *Times* (August 4, 1940) as "one of the best tales of espionage and counter-espionage that we have yet encountered." Other novels are *Black Market* (1942), *Spy Catchers* (1945), *Dead Man Murder* (1946), *Moscow Murder* (1948), *Cup Final Murder* (1950), and *Death at Lord's* (1952). A science-fiction tale which was also a comment on world affairs, *The Flying Saucer* was reviewed in the Springfield *Republican* (January 15, 1950) as "an adult, intelligent and plausible yarn, written with considerable humor and satire."

Under the pseudonym of Don Betteridge, Newman has also written a series of detective stories, some of which are *Scotland Yard Alibi* (1938), *The Escape of General Gerard* (1944), *Dictator's Destiny* (1945), *The Potsdam Murder Plot* (1947), and *Spies Left* (1950). Newman's books, in all classifications, have been published in some twelve countries, from Russia to Mexico, and have sold more than a million copies. He is the author also of magazine articles.

As a lecturer, Newman has addressed groups in China, India, Malay, Burma, Japan, Turkey, Egypt, the Sudan, North America, and many European countries. During his travels abroad he has acted as correspondent for several journals, including *European Digest,* and has broadcast from European radio stations. He has been described as "the Oscar-holder of the lecture world" (London *Daily Express*) and as a speaker who is "as informative as he is amusing" (*News Chronicle*). Many of Newman's lectures echo the subject matter of his books, with titles like "Spies in Fact and Fiction," "Alsace-Lorraine Today," "The Cold War," and "Far Eastern Journey." One of his lectures, "Making a Book," tells how to plan, write, and sell a book.

On August 23, 1923 Bernard Newman married Marjorie Edith Donald, a former teacher. They have three daughters: Margaret, Hilary, and Lauriston. He is five feet ten inches tall, weighs 220 pounds, and has blue-gray eyes and brown hair. He belongs to the Royal Institute of International Affairs, the P.E.N., the Society of Authors, and the Royal Society of Arts. In 1954 he was made a Chevalier in the Légion d'Honneur. In the words of David Cleghorn Thomson on a British Broadcasting Corporation program, "He has an uncanny knack for getting on rapidly with everybody, a terrifying energy, and an absolutely unconquerable patience and cheerfulness; moreover his sense of humour and endurance are insuperable."

References

N Y Times p17 Ja 9 '45
International Who's Who, 1958
Who's Who, 1958
World Biography (1954)

NEWMAN, PAUL Jan. 26, 1925- Actor
Address: b. Warner Brothers Pictures, Inc., 666 5th Ave., New York 19

A serious young actor who believes that study and self-discipline are responsible for his achievement, Paul Newman has reached stardom in screen, stage, and television with a background of training in college theater, drama workshop, and summer stock. He still approaches his acting assignments as if they were study sessions. For his performance in *The Long, Hot Summer* Newman won the Best Actor of the Year award at the Cannes film festival of 1958. During 1959 he co-starred with Geraldine Page in Tennessee Williams' *Sweet Bird of Youth*, playing the blackmailing gigolo, Chance Wayne.

Paul Newman was born in Cleveland, Ohio on January 26, 1925, the son of Arthur Newman. His father owned a large sporting-goods store in Cleveland; his uncle, Joe Newman, is a well-known Ohio journalist and poet. The boy was educated at local elementary schools and at Shaker Heights High School from which he was graduated early in World War II. He then enrolled at Kenyon College in Gambier, Ohio.

Newman left college about 1944 to enlist in the United States Navy, which assigned him to its V-12 education program at Yale University. After four months, however, Newman was eliminated from the program because of color blindness. He served during the following two years as a radioman, third class, on naval torpedo planes in the Pacific Theater of Operations.

Discharged in April 1946, Newman returned to Kenyon College to major in economics and dramatics. He played on the football team, operated the student laundry, and acted in ten undergraduate plays. Soon after his graduation in 1949 he appeared in *The Glass Menagerie, Suspect,* and *The Candlestick Maker* in summer stock in Williams Bay, Wisconsin. In the autumn of 1949 Newman joined the Woodstock Players in Woodstock, Illinois, with whom he performed in sixteen plays. When his father's death interrupted his theatrical career, he returned to Cleveland.

Warner Bros.

PAUL NEWMAN

Until 1951, when he turned the management over to his brother, Newman ran the family sporting-goods business. Still determined to become an actor, he entered the department of drama at Yale University. After he had studied for a year, with the encouragement of his instructors he went to New York, where he found employment in television almost immediately.

After such video dramas as *The Web, The Mask,* and *You Are There,* Newman undertook the role of Alan Seymour in William Inge's *Picnic.* Joanne Woodward, whom Newman later married, was the understudy of the leading feminine roles. Opening on Broadway on February 19, 1953, *Picnic* concentrated on a group of frustrated and sex-starved women in a small Kansas town who become reconciled to the shortcomings of their existence. The play won the Pulitzer Prize and the New York Drama Critics Circle Award, and Newman received his share of the critics' praise.

"Paul Newman as a college lad infatuated with pretty faces . . . [helps] to bring to life all the cross-currents of Mr. Inge's sensitive writing," said Brooks Atkinson (New York *Times,* February 20, 1953). Newman left the cast of *Picnic* before it went on tour, having been signed to a long-term contract with Warner Brothers Pictures studios. His first film vehicle was *The Silver Chalice* (1955) based on the novel by Thomas B. Costain.

Borrowed by Metro-Goldwyn-Mayer for *The Rack* (1956), Newman played a Korean war veteran on trial for collaboration with the enemy. "He is so convincing as the boy-man caught in the trap of war that one squirms in his theater seat as Mr. Newman answers the court martial attorneys," wrote Joe Pihodna (New York *Herald Tribune,* November 6, 1956).

In Joseph Hayes' *The Desperate Hours,* a melodrama about a trio of escaped convicts who

NEWMAN, PAUL—*Continued*

take over a suburban home and make hostages out of its inhabitants, Newman played Glenn Griffin, a psychotic gunman. The thriller began its Broadway run on February 10, 1955. John Beaufort in the *Christian Science Monitor* (February 19, 1955) described Newman's performance as "an enormously effective portrayal." Extending his range, Newman was next seen as a fifty-five-year-old fighter in *The Battler*, a TV adaptation of a short story by Ernest Hemingway that was presented in October 1955.

In *Somebody Up There Likes Me* (MGM, 1957), Newman was cast as Rocky Graziano, who fought his way from the slums to the heavyweight boxing championship of the world. This role promoted Newman from a relatively unknown actor to one of the "hottest properties" in Hollywood, and made him a box-office star. In quick succession, he made *The Helen Morgan Story* (Warner, 1957), *Until They Sail* (MGM, 1957), and *The Left-Handed Gun* (Warner, 1958).

Two films with Southern settings tested Newman's versatility in 1958. Co-starring with Joanne Woodward, he appeared as Ben Quick in *The Long, Hot Summer* (Fox), a free adaptation of William Faulkner's novel *The Hamlet* and several of Faulkner's short stories. To prepare himself for the picture, Newman lived unrecognized for three days in Clinton, Mississippi, where he lounged in the bars and pool parlors to observe the customs and speech patterns of the local inhabitants. In this story of a bullying father who chooses the vagrant Ben Quick as his successor, Newman was "as mean and keen as a cackle-eyed scythe" (*Time*, March 29, 1958).

Newman next won distinction for his sensitive interpretation of Brick in Tennessee Williams' *Cat on a Hot Tin Roof*. He played the ex-athlete who drinks himself into stupefaction because he falls short of the hopes of both his wife and his father. For his performance in *The Long, Hot Summer* Newman was voted the best actor at the 1958 Cannes film festival, and for his acting in *Cat on a Hot Tin Roof* he was nominated for an award of the Academy of Motion Picture Arts and Sciences.

Motion-picture audiences next saw Newman in *Rally 'Round the Flag, Boys!* (Fox, 1958) with Joanne Woodward, and *The Young Philadelphians* (Warner, 1959). In the summer of 1959 he succeeded in getting a release from his contract with Warner Brothers before it was to expire. Returning to Broadway, he took the leading male assignment in Tennessee Williams' *Sweet Bird of Youth*, which was considered such a foregone success that Newman and other members of the cast signed contracts that committed them through January 1960. The drama opened on March 10, 1959.

In this latest Tennessee Williams excursion into moral decay, Newman played Chance Wayne, a spiritually bankrupt gigolo, who has become the lover of a fading motion-picture actress whom he hopes to blackmail. When the alcoholic, hashish-smoking actress makes a successful Hollywood comeback, she leaves her escort behind in his home town, resigned to being maimed by his enemies, and facing "time—the enemy in us all." Walter Kerr (New York *Herald Tribune*, March 22, 1959) applauded Newman's "ambiguous figure—half vulgar greed, half yearning idealism—recklessly balanced on the slopes of Hell."

Paul Newman and his first wife, Jackie Witte, have three children: Scott, Susan, and Stephanie. After his divorce from Jackie Witte, he married Joanne Woodward, winner of a 1957 Academy Award, on January 29, 1958. They are the parents of a daughter, Elinor Theresa.

In appearance Newman has often been compared with actor Marlon Brando, a comparison Newman does not appreciate: "I wonder if anyone ever mistakes him for Paul Newman," he once said. "I'd like that." He is five feet eleven inches tall, weighs 160 pounds and has blue eyes and light brown hair. Among his hobbies are fishing, tennis, and skiing.

"The theater is my true love," Newman has said. "I know it sounds corny, but that's how it is" (New York *Post Magazine*, August 11, 1957). He believes, however, that an actor should not limit himself to one medium, but enrich his skills in a variety of media. He is co-operative during rehearsals, and examines the intellectual and emotional problems of each character he plays before every performance. "It's a painful experience," Newman has remarked. "I worry about acting and constantly complain to myself about my own performances." Newman has also noted that an actor learns by acting and that "every new role is a study session." To advance his development, he often attends sessions of the Actors Studio, of which he is a graduate. One of his ambitions is to become a director.

References

Christian Sci Mon p6 O 8 '57
Los Angeles Times IV p3 Ja 4 '59
N Y Post Mag p3 Ag 11 '57 por; p3 Je 8 '59 por
International Motion Picture Almanac, 1959

NICKERSON, ALBERT L(INDSAY) Jan. 17, 1911- Petroleum executive
Address: b. Socony Mobil Oil Company, Inc., 150 E. 42nd St., New York 17, N.Y.; h. 431 Grace Church St., Rye, N.Y.

The Socony Mobil Oil Company, Inc. is the second largest of the Standard Oil enterprises, ranking only after Standard Oil of New Jersey in importance. Albert L. Nickerson has been president of the corporation since July 1955 and its chief executive officer since February 1958. Originally the Standard Oil Company of New York and later known as Socony-Vacuum, the corporation adopted its present name in April 1955.

Socony Mobil Oil had in 1958 some 202,000 stockholders and more than 77,000 employees. Its most profitable year was 1956, when the net income was $249,503,667. Among its wholly owned affiliates in the United States are Magnolia Petroleum Company, General Petroleum Corporation, and the Mobil Producing Company. Under normal conditions, about a third of the corporation's crude oil supply comes from the Middle East, where Socony Mobil owns stock in the Arabian American Oil Company and Iraq Petroleum Company, Ltd., and has an interest in production in Iran. Providing about one-tenth of the total spent for research by the entire United States oil industry, Socony Mobil maintains research centers at Dallas, Brooklyn, and Paulsboro, New Jersey.

In 1911, the year in which the old Standard Oil trust was broken up, Albert Lindsay Nickerson was born on January 17 in Dedham, Massachusetts, the son of Albert Lindsay and Christine (Atkinson) Nickerson. Graduated in 1929 from the Noble and Greenough School, Albert Nickerson went on to Harvard College, where he made average grades, and rowed for three years on the junior varsity crew. After his father died in 1932, his mother started an antique shop in Dedham, and Nickerson, after taking his B.S. degree at Harvard in 1933, decided to remain in New England, to be near his family. He looked for promising openings in the steel, timber, and aluminum businesses, but this was the depth of the depression. He began his working career as a $19-a-week "grease monkey" in a Brookline, Massachusetts, Mobilgas filling station.

"When I started out . . . there was only one way to go, if one was willing to work like the dickens," Nickerson has said (New York *Times,* September 23, 1956). He displayed notable initiative in making sales and in giving service. "We barbershopped the customers to death," he told a *Fortune* writer (April 1958). One day a supervisor stopped into the service station and noticed the special treatment the young Harvard graduate was giving to customers. Nickerson was promoted—to service station manager in 1934, to supervisor in 1935. The following year the Standard Oil Company of New York made him a general salesman for the Boston area.

At about the same time, Socony started a management training program, and selected the young gas and oil salesman to be a member of the first class. For the next four years, Nickerson has commented, "it was simply a question of progression, working as hard as I could and being lucky" (New York *Times,* September 23, 1956).

In April 1940 Nickerson was given his first executive position when he was made district sales manager at Brockton, Massachusetts. A year later, after sales in his district had been higher in proportion to expectations than in any other New England district, he was promoted to New England division manager for Socony. Through most of 1943 he was on leave of absence for World War II civilian service, as director of the placement bureau of the War Manpower Commission. When he returned to Socony at the end of the year he was named assistant general manager of the company's Eastern Marketing Division, extending from Maine to South Carolina. He held this position

Frank H. Bauer

ALBERT L. NICKERSON

for less than two years; soon after the war ended he was sent to England to become chairman of the affiliated Vacuum Oil Company, Ltd.

Nickerson had been sent to London to give the British company temporary American technical aid in re-establishing its markets. Although he expected to remain at least five years, the parent company in the United States decided that the reopening of foreign markets needed close attention. "They selected the domestic director for the job," Nickerson recalls, "and I got his." Sent back to New York in November 1946 to become director in charge of domestic marketing for Socony-Vacuum Oil Company, Nickerson announced in May 1947 that the company was reorganizing its sales staff and setting up an intensive training program for salesmen that would be geared to "buyer's market" conditions. When the director of foreign marketing operations suffered a stroke in 1951, Nickerson was again promoted: he was elected a vice-president of the company, in charge of foreign trade and refining.

The Vacuum Oil Company, founded in 1866, had joined the old Standard Oil group in 1879. In 1931 it merged with the Standard Oil Company of New York to form the Socony-Vacuum Oil Company. The word "Mobil" was first used by Vacuum, and in April 1955 the stockholders voted to change the corporation's name to Socony Mobil Oil Company, Inc., to provide a clearer identification with such products as Mobiloil, Mobilgas, Mobil Tires, Mobil Batteries and other accessories. The decision preceded major management changes, effective in July 1955, whereby George V. Horton retired as chairman of the board and was succeeded by B. Brewster Jennings, president of the Company since 1944.

(Continued next page)

NICKERSON, ALBERT L.—*Continued*

Albert Nickerson was elected to succeed Jennings as president, but Jennings continued as chief executive officer until 1958. At the time of his election as president at a salary of $102,500 a year, Nickerson said, "I've had an uneventful life."

In the twenty-two years before he was named Socony's president, Nickerson had seen the company grow from sales of $459,000,000 and a net of $22,545,600 in 1933 to sales in 1955 of $1,839,000,000 and profits of $207,434,000. He felt that the most important development in marketing had been "the trend away from company-operated stations that led the independent business man to play a greater role at the service station and distributor level" (*National Petroleum News,* August 1955), and predicted that turbine engines for automobiles would not affect the industry seriously.

Addressing a meeting at Dallas, Texas, early in October 1955, Nickerson viewed the threat of atomic power to the oil industry without any discernible alarm. He declared that an expected gradual shift to nuclear fuels would not decrease but would increase the need for oil, because the resulting rise in international living standards would create new uses for petroleum. He predicted that by 1965 world demand for oil would increase by 65 per cent.

When B. Brewster Jennings retired on February 1, 1958, Albert L. Nickerson became chief executive officer as well as president of Socony Mobil Oil, Inc. Fred W. Bartlett, vice-president for production, succeeded Jennings as chairman of the board. In 1956 the company had made a record profit of $249,503,667, but for various reasons, notably the recurrent crises in the Middle East, the earnings fell to $220,432,894 in 1957. They dropped still lower, to $156,786,000 in 1958. Earnings for 1959 were expected to pick up, although, as Nickerson pointed out at the annual meeting in May, the oil industry faces growing problems abroad, in spite of a better level of business in the United States. He cited as some of these problems an oversupply of oil products, increasing costs, and difficult relations with foreign governments.

A co-worker of the president of Socony Mobil Oil has credited Nickerson with having "the temperament of a judge who can withhold his decision until he has heard all the argument." To Robert E. Bedingfield of the New York *Times* (September 13, 1956) he appeared "a low-pressure salesman who gets a great deal more out of an hour's work than some other people who outwardly show great energy." Six feet two inches tall and 180 pounds in weight, the former Harvard oarsman often takes a one-man scull out on Long Island Sound early in the morning. Nickerson also likes to vacation off the coast of Maine in his 34-foot sloop. He also enjoys bird-hunting and golf, which he took up about five years ago. Before taking up golf, he used to garden next to his old-fashioned frame house in Rye, New York, where he is a trustee of the Country Day School.

Nickerson is a director of the City Bank Farmers Trust Company and the United States Chamber of Commerce. He is a member of the American Management Association and the International Management Association, Inc., of which he was appointed the planning council chairman in 1956. In 1958 he was elected to trusteeships for both the American Museum of Natural History and the Rockefeller Institute. He is also a trustee of International House. He belongs to the Manursing Island and Apawamis Clubs in Rye, and the Harvard and Pinnacle Clubs in New York.

On June 13, 1936 Albert Lindsay Nickerson married Elizabeth Perkins, daughter of James H. Perkins, who was chairman of the board of the National City Bank of New York. They have four children: Christine, Albert W., Elizabeth, and Victoria. Nickerson is a Republican and an Episcopalian.

References

Bsns W p59+ Jl 2 '55 por; p101 Ja 18 '58 por
Fortune 57:69 Ap '58 por
N Y Herald Tribune p30 Je 29 '55 por; IIp7 Jl 10 '55 por
N Y Times p43 Je 29 '55 por; IIIp3 S 23 '56 por; p47 Ja 14 '58 por; p14 N 6 '58 por
N Y World-Telegram p30 Je 28 '55 por
Nat Petroleum N 47:180+ Ag '55 por
Printer's Ink 252:68 S 16 '55 por
Poor's Register of Directors and Executives (1959)
Who's Who in America, 1958-59
Who's Who in Commerce and Industry (1957)

NILES, JOHN JACOB Apr. 28, 1892- Folk singer; folklorist; composer
Address: h. Boot Hill Farm, RFD #7, Lexington, Ky.

For almost half a century, John Jacob Niles, the folklorist and folk singer, has been collecting and arranging early American folk songs, ballads, and carols, and performing them throughout the United States and Europe. With John and Alan Lomax, he has been largely responsible for the quickening of interest in American folk music; in some respects he has brought to that music the same talents that Cecil Sharp brought to the folk music of Great Britain.

A composer as well as a collector and arranger of music, Niles has written some of the "folk" songs he sings, and has composed an ambitious oratorio, *Lamentation.* He has also written several books, including *One Man's War* (Holt, 1929), and has edited numerous song collections. The advent of the long-playing record broadened his already extensive audience, and he can be heard on the Camden, Tradition, and Boone-Tolliver labels.

John Jacob Niles was born on April 28, 1892 in Louisville, Kentucky, the son of John Thomas and Lula Sarah (Reisch) Niles. His father was a farmer and a contractor. Music played an important part in his childhood. His father loved ballads, and taught the boy many of the songs he knew. His mother, who schooled John in the fundamentals of music, played the organ in church and was an accomplished pianist.

Reminiscing about his childhood, John Jacob Niles says: "We made our own fun; we made our own music. We also made our own instruments. When I was quite small, my father bought me a three-string dulcimer. But when I was up in my teens and wanted a bigger and better dulcimer, my father told me to get busy and make one. I've been making my own dulcimers ever since." The dulcimer, one of the most ancient of musical instruments, has a flat wooden sounding board. The dulcimers that Niles uses have from three to eight strings. Niles also makes his own lutes.

Niles attended the local public schools in Jefferson County and DuPont Manual High School in Louisville. In school he taught himself a system of musical shorthand and began to keep a notebook of the folk music he heard. After he was graduated from high school in 1909, he worked as a surveyor in the mountain counties of Kentucky, where he took advantage of his opportunities to hear and write down Southern Appalachian folk songs.

Soon after the United States entered World War I, Niles enlisted as a private in the United States Army Air Corps. While serving as a ferry pilot in Europe, he took notes on the singing of the officers and men in the fighting units he visited. In October 1918 a plane crash left Niles partly paralyzed because of a back injury. For the next seven years he walked with only the greatest difficulty, but he gradually learned to walk again without crutches or a cane. In 1918 he was discharged with the rank of first lieutenant.

Instead of coming back to the United States at the end of the war, Niles decided to stay in France and study music. He took courses at the Université de Lyon and at the Schola Cantorum in Paris. In 1919 he returned to the United States and entered the Cincinnati Conservatory of Music, where he studied for two years. In Cincinnati he began to organize and arrange the vast body of music he had collected since his 'teens.

In 1921 Niles left the Cincinnati Conservatory of Music and came to New York. He worked for a while as a master of ceremonies at the Silver Slipper night club, groomed the horses that appeared in the *Ziegfeld Follies,* and worked as a rose gardener on Long Island. At a concert he gave in Princeton, New Jersey he met a contralto Marion Kerby, who shared his interest in American folk songs. The two became a team and concertized throughout the United States and Europe. Niles adapted all the songs that they performed in their repertoire. During the summers he acted as a chauffeur and guide for a New York photographer, Doris Ulmann, who was photographing native American types in the Southwest. These summer journeys gave Niles a chance to gather more folk songs, and by 1934 he had the largest private collection in the English-speaking world.

He devoted much of his time to writing. *Singing Soldiers* (Scribner, 1927) and *Songs My Mother Never Taught Me* (Macaulay,

JOHN JACOB NILES

1929) came out of Niles' war experiences. Both books are collections of songs the soldiers sang in World War I, along with the anecdotes and incidents that caused some of these songs to be written. Niles wrote the latter book with Douglas S. Moore. He was also co-author with Lieutenant Bert Hall of *One Man's War* (Holt, 1929), the story of the Lafayette Escadrille, a squadron of American fighter pilots who fought under the French flag before the United States entered World War I. For *Scribner's Magazine* the folk singer wrote several short stories dealing with life in the American South. Among them were: "Hedge-hoppers" (March 1929), "The Passing of the Street Cry" (September 1929), and "Eleven A.M." (January 1930)

Since the 1930's John Jacob Niles has appeared as a solo concert artist, accompanying himself on the dulcimer, and singing his folk songs, ballads, and carols in village auditoriums, school houses, churches, college auditoriums and large cities throughout the United States and Europe. Wearing the bright-colored shirts and corduroy trousers that have become his trademarks, he sings traditional folk songs in his own arrangements and his own compositions.

In October 1946, Niles appeared in a midnight concert at the Town Hall in New York, presenting a program that included such staples of his repertory as "Black is the Color of My True Love's Hair," "The Seven Joys of Mary," and "I Wonder as I Wander." A New York *Times* critic commented: "In appearance, manner, and dress, the 54-year-old singer suggested an itinerant preacher. . . Mr. Niles is not a singer of the conventional type. His voice is like an organ with several stops. . . . The lower tones are hoarse and lack body, but the upper ones, that resemble falsetto, grow increasingly lyric, sweet, and poignant the higher they go." In September 1959, Niles performed in another concert at Town Hall, before an audience composed largely of teen-

NILES, JOHN JACOB—*Continued*

agers. Dressed in formal tie and tails, he made a striking contrast to the informally attired folk singers with whom he shared the bill.

Alarmed by the rise of totalitarian states in the modern world, Niles began in 1940 to write a choral work that would present the dilemma faced by the democracies. His oratorio, *Lamentation*, which was finished ten years later, deals with the Babylonian captivity of the Jews, as related in the Old Testament. He told William Mootz of the Louisville *Courier-Journal* (October 12, 1952) that he draws a parallel between "the situation the Jews faced before the fall of Babylon and the situation the democracies of the free world today face in their fight against Communism." *Lamentation* had its première on March 14, 1951 at Indiana State Teachers College, Terre Haute, Indiana, and was performed with the Louisville Philharmonic Chorus in Louisville in March 1953.

Much of Niles' singing has been recorded. For the RCA Victor label he recorded *Early American Ballads* (1939), *Early American Carols and Folk Songs* (1940) and *American Folk Lore* (1941). With a few changes, these were re-issued under the Camden label, in 1954. When the Camden album *John Jacob Niles, Fiftieth Anniversary Album* was released in 1957, the reviewer for the New York *Times* (February 17, 1957) wrote that "As an artist and as a man, who conveys intense drama, Mr. Niles, with his small, almost weirdly high voice, can sing rings around most of his successors." He credited Niles with having "done much to set the other singer-guitarists or banjoists off on their travels." For Tradition Records he recorded *I Wonder As I Wander* in 1958. He has also recorded under his own label, Boone-Tolliver.

In the album notes for his Boone-Tolliver recordings, Niles has admitted that some of his "authentic" folk songs are not at all authentic. Like Brahms, he has presented as folk material music he had written himself. Reviewing the Boone-Tolliver albums in the *Saturday Review* (August 29, 1953), Oscar Brand said: "The weird, hoarse falsetto of John Jacob Niles adds a strange power to some of his renditions. . . . In a few of the songs the queer delivery often overpowers the material. . . . Yet listening to Niles is a fascinating experience; certainly no one will be bored." Niles has also been heard on a series of broadcasts over the University of Kentucky station entitled: *John Jacob Niles' Salute to the Hills.*

Many of Niles' collections have been published by George Schirmer, Inc. Among them are: *Seven Kentucky Mountain Songs* (1929), *Songs of the Hill-Folk* (1934), *More Songs of the Hill-Folk* (1936), *Ballads, Carols, and Tragic Legends from the Southern Appalachian Mountains* (1937), *The Anglo-American Ballad Study Book* (1945), and *The Shape-Note Study Book* (1950). His magnum opus, *The Ballad Book of John Jacob Niles,* will be published by the Houghton Mifflin Company. Many of his choral arrangements and original compositions have been published by Carl Fischer, Inc.

John Jacob Niles married Rena Lipetz, a writer and editor, on March 21, 1936. They have two sons, Thomas Michael Tolliver and John Edward. The folk singer has blue eyes and gray hair, weighs 155 pounds and is five feet nine inches tall. Farming, gardening, wood-carving, painting, and foxhunting are his favorite recreations.

On June 2, 1949 Niles received an honorary Doctor of Music degree from the Cincinnati Conservatory of Music. He belongs to the American Society of Composers, Authors, and Publishers (ASCAP), the American Folklore Society, and the American Dialect Society. His political affiliation is Republican; his religious affiliation is Episcopalian.

References

> Life 15:57 S 6 '43 pors
> Baker's Biographical Dictionary of Musicians (1958)
> Who is Who in Music (1951)
> Who Knows and What (1954)

NOBLE, EDWARD J(OHN) Aug. 8, 1882-Dec. 28, 1958

Financier; manufacturer; former chairman of the Blue Network and American Broadcasting Company; chairman of Beech-Nut Life Savers, Inc. See *Current Biography* (January) 1944.

Obituary

N Y Times p15 D 29 '58

NORSTAD, LAURIS Mar. 24, 1907- NATO

commander; United States Air Force officer
Address: b. APO 55, New York; h. Villa Saint-Pierre, Marnes-la-Coquette, France

> NOTE: This biography supersedes the article which appeared in *Current Biography* in 1948.

The Supreme Commander of the North Atlantic Treaty Organization's military forces since November 1956, General Lauris Norstad believes that his primary tasks are to "deter aggression, to prevent war" and to maintain sufficient military strength along the iron curtain in order to "defend the forward areas of the NATO countries" (*U.S. News & World Report,* July 5, 1957). He also has been the head of the United States European Command since September 1958.

Norstad is the youngest American Air Force officer to become a four-star general, a rank he attained in July 1952. During World War II, he planned Allied air operations in the Mediterranean area and the atomic bombings of Japan. He also participated in the writing of the National Security Act of 1947, which unified the military services.

Of Norwegian-Swedish ancestry, Lauris Norstad was born on March 24, 1907 in Minneapolis, Minnesota. He was reared in Red Wing, Minnesota, where his father, the Reverend Martin Norstad, was pastor of a Lutheran church. His mother's maiden name was Marie Johnson. Norstad was graduated from Red

Wing High School. He had originally planned to study law, but becoming interested in the Army, secured an appointment to the United States Military Academy at West Point, New York.

After earning the B.S. degree and a commission as second lieutenant of cavalry in 1930, he took flight training. In 1931 he was transferred to the Air Corps. Later assigned to the Eighteenth Pursuit Group at Schofield Barracks, Hawaii, Norstad was placed in command of that group in July 1933.

In September 1939, following three and a half years as adjutant of the Ninth Bombardment Group, he entered the Air Corps Tactical School at Maxwell Field, Alabama. Graduating three months later, he was named officer in charge of the Ninth Bombardment Group Navigation School at Mitchel Field, New York. When the United States entered World War II in December 1941 Norstad was assistant chief of staff for intelligence of Air Force command headquarters at Langley Field, Virginia and at Bolling Field, District of Columbia.

Impressed by Norstad's leadership abilities, the Commanding General of the Army Air Forces, General Henry N. ("Hap") Arnold named Norstad to his advisory council at Washington in February 1942. There Norstad made studies upon which Air Forces policies were based. In August he became assistant chief of staff for operations of the Twelfth Air Force, and he was sent to North Africa in October to plan the air strategy for the Allied invasion. In this capacity he was under the command of General Dwight D. Eisenhower, who was later to write of him that his "alertness, grasp of problems, and personality" were so unusual that "I never thereafter lost sight of him" (*Newsweek,* October 1, 1951). In the summer of 1943 Norstad planned the air operations that accompanied the Allied land attacks in Sicily and Italy.

One of the youngest brigadier generals of the Air Forces when advanced to that rank in March 1943 at the age of thirty-six, Norstad was appointed director of operations of the Mediterranean Allied Air Forces in the following December. He recommended that the Allies attempt to seal off Germany from the Soviet Union, instead of embarking on an invasion of southern France. "I felt," he later told C. L. Sulzberger (New York *Times,* June 25, 1956), "that if we moved across the Ljubljana gap [in Yugoslavia] into the Vienna and Budapest plain . . . we could push up . . . across east Germany and west Poland."

Transferred to Washington in August 1944, Norstad was assigned as chief of staff of the global Twentieth Force, whose B-29 bombers "rained destruction on the Japanese nation, ruining its economic capacity to wage war, and culminated its activities with the successful atomic bombing of Hiroshima and Nagasaki." The quoted phrases are from the citation accompanying the award to Norstad of an oak leaf cluster to the Distinguished Service Medal he had won in the Mediterranean theater. Norstad, who was promoted to major general in

U. S. Air Force
GEN. LAURIS NORSTAD

June 1945, has been credited with planning the Twenty-first Bomber Command's missions, including the incendiary raids on Tokyo.

At the request of General Eisenhower, then Army Chief of Staff, Norstad was appointed director of the plans and operations division of the War Department General Staff in June 1946 to plan the size, composition, and utilization of the postwar Air Forces. One of four Army-Navy negotiators of the services agreement upon which the National Security Act was based, he was largely responsible for securing equal status of the Air Force with the Army and Navy in the new defense establishment. With Vice-Admiral Forrest P. Sherman, he drafted the enabling legislation, passed in 1947.

Advanced to lieutenant general on October 1, 1947, Norstad served for three years as acting vice-chief of staff for operations of the Air Force and was held responsible, in the event of war, for translating into action any over-all plan for aerial defense or attack. He also helped to write the Finletter report, which "urged a seventy-group Air Force long before the Korean war, at a time when Harry S. Truman insisted that forty-eight groups were enough" (*Newsweek,* October 1, 1951).

Reassigned in October 1950 as Commander in Chief, United States Air Forces in Europe, with headquarters at Wiesbaden, Germany, Norstad on April 2, 1951 assumed additional duty as Commander of the Allied Air Forces in Central Europe under the Supreme Headquarters of the Allied Powers in Europe (SHAPE). His mission called for full and continuous support of Allied army forces in this sector and gaining and maintaining air superiority.

On July 5, 1952 Norstad was promoted to the rank of full general, becoming at forty-five the youngest American to wear the four-star

NORSTAD, LAURIS—*Continued*

insignia, and on July 27, 1953 he was named Air Deputy to the Supreme Allied Commander, Europe. Serving during the next three years under both Generals M. B. Ridgway and Alfred M. Gruenther, he "shaped atomic strategy, built up the air base network-communications system and radar-warning service" (*Time*, April 23, 1956).

Succeeding Gruenther, Norstad became Supreme Allied Commander, Europe on November 20, 1956. When his appointment had been announced, *U.S. News & World Report* (May 4, 1956) remarked that "Norstad is known to feel that, on the ground or in the air, he lacks sufficient strength to defend Europe for very long east of the Rhine. He and NATO remain dependent upon the deterrent effect of the ever-ready United States Strategic Air Command."

NATO strategy was defined by its commander in March 1958 as that of preventing "less-than-ultimatum incidents with less-than-ultimatum means." He believes that the organization must maintain its "ground shield" concept of keeping sufficient strength in central Europe, with tactical atomic weapons (Frank Kelley, New York *Herald Tribune*, May 11, 1958), so that it has an "absolute power to devastate the Soviet Union regardless of what offensive surprise action she takes" (Hanson W. Baldwin, *Reader's Digest*, May 1958). At a press conference on November 3, Norstad revealed that the number of NATO battalions in Europe equipped with short-range tactical missiles would be expanded from thirty to 100 by 1963, with the consequent elimination of thirty to forty conventional aircraft squadrons (W. Granger Blair, New York *Times*, November 4, 1958).

During the Berlin crises of 1958-59, West Germany was equipped with antiaircraft rockets capable of carrying atomic warheads. However, the control of the warheads was delegated to Supreme Commander Norstad. Besides serving as Supreme Allied Commander in Europe, Norstad became on September 15, 1958 the head of the new United States European Command, the first of eight unified commands organized by the Defense Department.

Among Norstad's military decorations are the Silver Star, Legion of Merit, and Air Medal, and he holds the ratings of command pilot, combat observer, and technical observer. He was made an honorary commander of the Order of the British Empire, grand officer of the Ordre du Ouissam Alaouite Cherifien (Morocco), commander of the French Legion of Honor, and was awarded the French Croix de Guerre avec palme.

General Norstad, Alfred M. Gruenther has said, "has one of the keenest strategic minds in the world today." Another associate has remarked that "his mind is like a precision instrument," and he has been characterized as "a philosopher in uniform." He is handsome, slim, six feet tall, and has graying-blond hair. The general rarely smokes, but "keeps a rack of thirteen pipes on his desk, often chewing on the end of a cold briar while concentrating"

(*Newsweek*, December 17, 1956). His hobbies include golf, fishing, croquet, shooting, photography, reading, listening to music, and conversation. Lauris Norstad and Isabell Helen Jenkins were married on April 27, 1935 and have one daughter, Kristin.

References

Gen Army 2:18+ My '54 por
N Y Herald Tribune p4 Je 4 '58 por
Britannica Book of the Year, 1957
International Who's Who, 1958
Robinson, D. The 100 Most Important People in the World Today (1952)
Who's Who, 1958
Who's Who in America, 1958-59
World Biography (1954)

NORTON, MARY T(ERESA HOPKINS) Mar. 7, 1875-Aug. 2, 1959 Former United States Representative from New Jersey (1925-49); Democrat; first woman to head a Congressional committee. See *Current Biography* (November) 1944.

Obituary

N Y Times p25 Ag 3 '59

OBOLENSKY, SERGE Oct. 3, 1890-
Address: Hotel Astor, Times Square, New York 36

The inquisitive who consult the fourteen-line biography of Serge Obolensky in *Who's Who in America* for 1956-57 will find his profession listed as hotel administrator. But Obolensky has had a career more suitable for the hero of a picaresque novel than for an hotel executive. He has been a Russian cavalryman and an American paratrooper, a socialite and a gentleman farmer, a husband to a princess, a counter-revolutionary, a refugee, businessman, and author.

In living his checkered and romantic life, Obolensky has tried to obey his father who used to exhort him: "Learn, do things, but when you do, remember you must always put your country first, your family second, and yourself third." In 1958 American readers had an opportunity to discover how well Obolensky had put these precepts into practice when his autobiography *One Man in His Time* was published by the new firm of McDowell, Obolensky in New York.

Born on October 3, 1890 in Tsarkoe Selo (now called Pushkin) Russia, Serge Obolensky was the son of Platon S. and Marie (Narischkine) Obolensky. As a member of the Czarist royalty, his full title was Prince Serge Platonovich Obolensky-Neledinsky-Meletsky. His father was a wealthy landowner, whose estates included 60,000 acres of farmland in addition to seven houses in St. Petersburg.

Serge was educated at the St. Petersburg secondary school, and was graduated with honors in 1910. For the next two years he studied agriculture at St. Petersburg University. In 1912 he went to England to study political economy at Christ Church College, Oxford. He left the university at the outbreak of World War I in 1914 and returned to Russia.

Enlisting as a private in the Chevalier Guards regiment of the Imperial Army in 1914, Obolensky subsequently reached the rank of major. He fought as a cavalryman in East Prussia, participated in the 1915 retreat to Daugavpils (Latvia), then was transferred to the south. He was awarded the crosses of St. George (2nd, 3rd, and 4th degrees), St. Stanislav (3rd degree), and St. Anne (3rd and 4th degrees). On October 9, 1916 Obolensky married Princess Catherine Yourievsky Bariatinsky, a young widow who was the daughter of Czar Alexander II.

After the Bolshevik Revolution in 1917, Obolensky joined White Russian forces fighting in the Crimea; then, using a dead man's passport, he lived in disguise in Moscow for about seven months. Finally becoming discouraged with the counterrevolutionary cause, Obolensky and his wife escaped through the Ukraine to Austria and Switzerland. In 1919 they arrived in London.

Obolensky's first employment in Britain was with a manufacturer of agricultural machinery; he spent a year in Australia as the firm's agent. Returning to London, he went to work for the brokerage house of Byng Foley. He was divorced from his first wife in 1924, and was married in June of the same year to Alice Muriel Astor, who had inherited $5,000,000 from John Jacob Astor, her father.

In 1926 the Obolenskys moved to the United States, where he began a successful career as businessman and hotel administrator. From 1928 to 1930 he worked for the Chase Security Corporation, for the Chase Harris Forbes Corporation, and for the foreign department of the Chase National Bank. In 1931, the year in which he became a United States citizen, he joined the Vincent Astor Real Estate Office. In 1932 his marriage with Alice Astor Obolensky ended in divorce. He continued, however, to be associated with his former brother-in-law until 1942, and during this period he was also one of the executives of the St. Regis Hotel, one of the Astor properties.

In February 1941, after an unsuccessful attempt to join the United States Army in anticipation of war, Obolensky enlisted in the New York State Guard as a private. He served in its 17th Regiment until 1942, having been commissioned and promoted to captain. On July 25, 1942, his unit was federalized, and Obolensky was assigned to the Office of Strategic Services (OSS) with the rank of major.

Assigned as training officer for a unit of commando-trained paratroopers whose mission was to bolster resistance fighters in occupied Europe, Major Obolensky was the oldest combat paratrooper in the United States Army. After five qualifying jumps, he led a four-man team into Sardinia to establish liaison between Italian and Allied forces. The jump was made on September 13, 1943, when Obolensky was almost fifty-three years old.

Obolensky was awarded the Bronze Star for this mission, which entailed carrying dispatches

Irwin Dribben

SERGE OBOLENSKY

from General Dwight D. Eisenhower. His second combat mission was to lead OSS men into France in front of the Allied invasion armies in 1944. He served behind German lines for one month, and was awarded the French Croix de Guerre. He was discharged from the Army in January 1945 with the rank of lieutenant colonel.

After the war, Obolensky began his present career as an administrator and refurbisher of luxury hotels. He joined the Hilton Hotels firm in 1945 as promotion director, and when the Hilton Hotels International, Inc., was formed in May 1948, Obolensky was made a director and vice-president. He resigned the following year.

Upon his resignation he founded Serge Obolensky & Associates, an independent firm of promotion consultants. In April 1949 he was named president of the Sherneth Corporation, which operated the Sherry-Netherland Hotel in New York City. He left that firm in 1954 to become president of the Ambassador Hotel, and the following year was named vice-chairman of the board of the Ambassador International Corporation.

His most recent move was made in March 1957, when the Ambassador was sold to the Zeckendorf Hotels Corporation. Obolensky joined Zeckendorf as vice-chairman of the board. His mission with this firm, as with the earlier ones, has been to modernize old hotels.

"My associates and I have done this with the Plaza, the Sherry-Netherland, and the Ambassador," he explained (in the *New Yorker*, October 25, 1958). "The people I work with are generally interested in capital gains. First, I go behind the house, to see if the plumbing, the electric wiring, the refrigeration, the kitchen, and so forth, are in order. Then I bring a certain touch of good taste into the rooms, including the public rooms. . . . It takes at least six

OBOLENSKY, SERGE—Continued

or eight months to what I call deliver the goods."

In association with William Zeckendorf, Obolensky has already "delivered the goods" at the Astor, and plans to do the same at other hotels in New York City. The Zeckendorf Hotels Corporation is a subsidiary of Webb & Knapp, which owns the Astor and the Manhattan on the west side, and the Drake, the Commodore, and the Chatham on the east side of the city.

Even as a hotel man, Obolensky still follows a military regimen in his daily life. He arises at seven and goes to work after performing yoga exercises, and although he enjoys night life, he is usually in bed before midnight. An ardent sportsman and a joiner, he belongs to some eighteen clubs and associations. Among his activities is the Air Force Reserve, which he joined in 1949 and serves as a colonel.

In 1958 Obolensky's memoirs, *One Man in His Time* (McDowell, Obolensky) were published. The critics found the contents of the book absorbing, but had some reservations about its literary style. The New York *Times* reviewer Orville Prescott remarked (November 21, 1958): "All this material is interesting, but Colonel Obolensky does not make the most of it." Dissenters included Harry W. Baehr in the New York *Herald Tribune* (December 7, 1958) who called the book one of "considerable charm and exceptional interest," and Igor Cassini in the *Saturday Review* (January 17, 1959) who judged it "a rare treat."

Obolensky married Alice Muriel Astor (now deceased) on June 24, 1924. The marriage ended in divorce in 1932 after the birth of two children, Sylvia Guirey and Ivan Obolensky. The son is the junior partner of McDowell, Obolensky, the firm which published *One Man in His Time.*

Serge Obolensky still wears the mustache he once sported as a young cavalry officer. He treasures a portrait done in 1917 by Saveli Sorine, who wanted to preserve Obolensky's features for posterity as an aristocratic type soon to be extinct. The painting, recovered after the revolution, is riddled with Bolshevik bullet holes. The man depicted does not much differ from the hotel man of today, who at sixty-nine is as tall (six feet three inches) and as slender (154 pounds) as when he enlisted in the Czar's army. Ten years ago Jinx Falkenburg rated him as "easily the best non-professional dancer of the Viennese waltz in America." Altogether, as Igor Cassini wrote in the *Saturday Review* (January 17, 1959), Obolensky "has always seemed to be the epitome of the patrician, dashing man-of-the-world."

References

N Y Herald Tribune p29 O 20 '49 por
N Y Sunday News Mag p21 Mr 1 '59 por
New Yorker 34:36+ O 25 '58
Obolensky, Serge One Man in His Time (1958)
Who's Who in America, 1956-57

O'BRIEN, LEO W(ILLIAM) Sept. 21, 1900- United States Representative from New York; journalist

Address: b. House Office Bldg., Washington, D.C.; 116 Washington Ave., Albany, N.Y.; h. 99 Hawthorne Ave., Albany, N.Y.

In the United States House of Representatives, Leo W. O'Brien, a Democrat, led the fight which resulted in the passing of bills granting Alaska and Hawaii status as the forty-ninth and fiftieth states of the Union. A former reporter for International News Service and the New York *Times,* O'Brien has represented voters in Albany and Rensselaer counties in Congress since April 1952. He is a member of the Interstate and Foreign Commerce Committee and Interior and Insular Affairs Committee and the chairman of the latter's subcommittee on territorial and insular affairs.

Leo William O'Brien was born on September 21, 1900 in Buffalo, New York. He has a sister, Irene, now a Sister of Mercy. After attending St. Joseph's Collegiate Institute and Mount St. Joseph Academy, O'Brien studied at Niagara University in Niagara Falls, New York, where he earned the B.A. degree in 1922.

Moving to Albany, O'Brien joined the staff of the Albany *Times-Herald* as a reporter. He wrote "stories ranging from hot politics to torch murder" (George Dixon, Washington *Post and Times Herald,* April 23, 1958). Later, he became his paper's principal writer on state politics and also covered the Albany capitol for International News Service and the New York *Times* (1943-50). For distinguished newspaper work he received the New York State Legislative Correspondents Association award in 1950.

For his work as a radio and television commentator, Leo O'Brien in May 1951 received with Howard Maschmeier the Sigma Delta Chi's "distinguished service to American journalism" medallion for their radio news program at Station WPTR in Albany. As early as 1935 O'Brien became a member of the Albany Port District Commission, which supervises the operation of the port of Albany for the cities of Albany and Rensselaer. He continued to serve on this commission until 1952 and for a period was its secretary.

Early in February 1952, after the death of United States Representative William T. Byrne, a Democrat, of the Thirty-second New York District, the Albany County Democratic committee chose O'Brien to complete Byrne's unexpired term. The Liberal party also endorsed O'Brien. Since the district is predominantly Democratic, O'Brien won over his Republican opponent by 66,883 to 27,274 votes at the special election of April 1. He took his seat in the Eighty-second Congress on April 9.

Through the reapportionment based on the 1950 census, New York's Thirty-second District became the Thirtieth when O'Brien won election to the Eighty-third Congress in November 1952. His district comprises all of Albany county and parts of Rensselaer county, including most of the city of Troy. During his years in Congress O'Brien has served on the

House Interior and Insular Affairs Committee and the Interstate and Foreign Commerce Committee, and early in 1958 he was appointed to the House Select Committee on Astronautics and Space Exploration.

Opposed to the McCarran-Walter Immigration and Nationality Act, in 1953 O'Brien and twenty-three other Representatives joined Emanuel Celler, Democrat of New York, in urging the rewriting of the act. They proposed the abolition of the national-origins quota system and the admission of 251,000 refugees yearly. Two years later, in May, O'Brien was one of the sixteen New York Democrats who suggested changes in the law and called for the removal of Scott McLeod, administrator of the bureau of security and consular affairs, which enforces the act.

Interested in the future of the Foreign Service, O'Brien in the summer of 1953 recommended that the Department of State create a career bureau to provide college graduates with on-the-job training as diplomats. In the Eighty-fifth Congress he sponsored a proposal to create a commission for studying methods of modernizing and expanding the Foreign Service. His purpose, he stated, was to achieve "a massive transfusion of Main Street" into the "arteries" of the service.

In order to simplify the wording of legislation, O'Brien introduced a House resolution in March 1954 for a special study of this matter. He also wrote a book containing incidents in the life of a freshman Congressman, which was never published because the author's attitudes toward House traditions and practices have continuously changed. In an article written for the International News Service in May 1955, he stated that the "establishment of a 'school' for freshman Congressmen, operated two nights a week during the first month of each new Congress, would pay dividends."

As chairman of the House Interior and Insular Affairs subcommittee on territorial and insular affairs, in March 1956 O'Brien championed a measure to finance a mental hospital in Alaska through a grant of government land. The measure was passed by the House. For several years he favored, with leaders of both parties, concurrent consideration of Alaskan and Hawaiian statehood. When the Alaska statehood bill was "bottled up" in the House Rules Committee in May 1957, its advocates decided to consider each state separately. They believed that opposition came from different sources and that each measure would attract more support standing by itself. Therefore, on July 25, O'Brien announced that the House would not consider Hawaiian statehood until 1958.

In 1957 the Alaska bill was reported to the House of Representatives in June and to the Senate in August, but no further action was taken before adjournment. It was reintroduced in the second session of the Eighty-fifth Congress. Opponents of Alaskan statehood cited the territory's strategic importance and its sparse population; the Southern bloc envisioned

Wide World

LEO W. O'BRIEN

increased support for civil rights legislation in the Senate. In spite of their arguments, the Alaska bill was passed by both houses and on July 7, 1958 was enacted into law. Alaska officially became a state on January 3, 1959.

Re-elected to the Eighty-sixth Congress in November 1958, Representative O'Brien became in January 1959 the second Democrat in rank on the House Interior and Insular Affairs Committee. The chairman of a three-member subcommittee which visited Hawaii in late 1958, O'Brien reported to Congress in January that "Hawaii is entitled to statehood by every fair test and precedent." The subcommittee countered the argument that Hawaiian labor unions were infiltrated by Communists with the contention that the territory's inhabitants "abhor it [Communism] as we do."

A Hawaii statehood bill managed by O'Brien cleared the full Interior Committee on February 4 by a 25-to-4 vote, but not before an amendment had been adopted which reduced Hawaii's representation in the House from two seats to one. The bill was officially approved by the Senate on March 11, by the House on March 12, and by the President on March 18.

On key issues in the Eighty-second Congress O'Brien voted "nay" on a $46 billion ceiling on military spending (April) and "yea" on the 1952 mutual security bill (June). In the 1953 session he cast his first vote for Hawaiian statehood (March) and favored increased funds for public power (April) and private power development on the Niagara River (July)

In 1954 Representative O'Brien supported increasing unemployment compensation (July), 140,000 public housing units (July), and revision of the Atomic Energy Act (July). He disapproved the St. Lawrence Seaway project (May) and the combined postal pay and post-

O'BRIEN, LEO W.—*Continued*

age increase (July). In the following year he favored raising Congressional salaries (February).

On major legislation in 1956 he supported the Colorado River project (March), Eisenhower highway construction bill (April), Powell amendment to the school construction bill (July), school construction bill (July), and civil rights bill (July). He favored in 1957 the Eisenhower Middle East Doctrine (January), postponement of seven British debt payments (April), revision of the immigration laws to relieve certain hardship cases (August), and approving the construction of a power project at Niagara Falls by the New York State Power Authority (August).

The voting record indicates that in 1958 O'Brien was against a five-year extension of the trade agreements act (June) and a proposal providing that no Congressional act shall be construed as nullifying state laws unless Congress so specifies or unless there is an irreconcilable conflict between a state and federal law (July). He voted for a measure to prevent reduction in price supports and acreage allotments (March). In 1959 he favored extension of the Federal Airport Construction Act (March) and increasing United States subscriptions to the International Monetary Fund and the International Bank for Reconstruction and Development (March).

O'Brien is a small man with gray hair. His wife is the former Mabel Jean of Cambridge, Massachusetts. The O'Briens have one son, Robert, and one daughter, Mary. Their five-year-old grandson, Terence, now shares with his grandfather the distinction of having a lake named after him in Alaska. In January 1957 O'Brien was named to the Alaska International Railway and Highway Board.

References

> N Y Times p27 F 8 '52; p12 Mr 13 '59 por
>
> Congressional Directory, 1959
> Who's Who in America, 1958-59
> Who's Who in the East (1957)

OGBURN, WILLIAM F(IELDING) June 29, 1886-Apr. 27, 1959 Sociologist; professor at Columbia (1919-27), Chicago (1927-51), Florida State (since 1953) universities; held many posts in federal government; author. See *Current Biography* (February) 1955.

Obituary

> N Y Times p33 Ap 29 '59

OLIVETTI, ADRIANO Apr. 11, 1901- Business executive

Address: b. Ing. C. Olivetti & Co., Via G. Jervis, 11/13, Ivrea, Italy; h. Villa Belliboschi, Ivrea, Italy

Italian industrialist Adriano Olivetti is a new kind of Continental businessman who has successfully pioneered in the employee-management field for twenty years without sacrificing any of the growth of his firm from a small typewriter factory to the largest manufacturer of its kind in Europe, with plants and agencies around the world. In 1952 Olivetti was honored by an exhibition of his industrial and architectural designs at the Museum of Modern Art in New York.

While making Olivetti a standard for modern design in business and office machinery, he has created a complete welfare state from cradle-to-the-grave for several thousand workers at the company's Ivrea plant. He has also begun a town and country redevelopment plan for all Italy to brace sagging local economies and foster culture and political action at the community level. He was elected to the Italian Parliament in May 1958 on the ticket of the Comunità party, named for the Comunità movement, which he founded.

Adriano Olivetti, whose father, Camillo Olivetti, established the Olivetti Company in 1908, was born on April 11, 1901 in Ivrea, near Turin, Italy. He was the eldest of six children. His mother, the former Luiga Revel, was a Waldensian. Adriano attended the Politecnico di Torino, from which he was graduated in 1924 with a degree in industrial chemistry. The same year he joined the Olivetti Company as an apprentice.

At the request of his father, an electrical engineer who had visited the United States and had lectured at Stanford University in California, Adriano Olivetti went to America in 1925 to study plant management and industrial methods. Following his return to Italy in February 1926, he radically changed the organizational structure of the plant and instituted new procedures, with emphasis on teams of scientifically trained young men engaged in design and research. Costs were cut and output rose significantly without increasing the number of workers. In the early 1930's the company initiated a bold policy of penetration into highly competitive and protected markets abroad, and a new typewriter was launched, the M-40, which became a leader in the field.

In 1933 young Olivetti was made managing director. The next twenty-five years, especially those following World War II, saw the development of the company on a huge scale both at home and abroad. Olivetti now manufactures eighteen different office and business machines, which are produced in eleven factories in six countries. New plants, including a machine tool plant in Naples, were built in Italy, Scotland, Spain, Argentina, South Africa, and India. The number of employees increased from 1,200 in 1932 to 22,000 in 1956, with distributors in 106 countries and sales subsidiaries in sixteen. The Olivetti Company became Italy's biggest dollar earner for mechanical exports ($2,400,000 in 1953) after the Necchi sewing machine. Annual sales passed the $40,000,000 mark in 1956, more than 60 per cent of which represented exports, with the United States taking 16 per cent.

The company grew to be Europe's largest manufacturer of typewriters and business machines. The M-40 typewriter was followed by the Lexikon 80, the Lexikon Elettrica, the neat, lightweight portable Lettera 22, and the Studio 44, in a complete renewal of its typewriter line. Olivetti later added the teleprinter, a line of printing calculators and adding machines, and an office dictaphone. For high level of industrial design and quality the Lettera 22 won the Compasso d'Oro in 1954 and Adriano Olivetti was awarded the Gran Premio Nazionale Compasso d'Oro in 1955.

The plants, products, and advertising have won recognition for artistic, modern design. *Fortune* (June 1951) observed: "At every point of contact the basic harmony of workmanship and design reflects the unique Olivetti personality. . . . One standard of taste guides every visual aspect of the company's operations—from factory architecture to product design to advertisements, showrooms, workers' housing, and community planning." Olivetti received the Grand Prix d'Architecture (1956) from the Cercle d'Études Architecturales of Paris. He was awarded the Palma d'Oro (1950) for high quality of advertising style and copy.

Adriano Olivetti demonstrated his keen interest in social welfare early in life. After becoming president of the firm in 1938, on the retirement of his father, he became interested in Ivrea and began developing company responsibility for both workers and community. "Today Olivetti employee benefit programs are among the most comprehensive in the world" (*Saturday Review*, January 18, 1958). The benefits include camps for children, tuition for higher education, apprentice schools, workers' transportation system, and help to workers to finance, design, and build their own homes. He also gives workers a share in management.

After World War II, as an extension of the Ivrea experiment, Olivetti undertook a project of town planning to aid indigent communities crippled by war. He established the National Institute of Town Planning (Instituto Nazionale di Urbanistica), which aids in the planning and setting up of small factories in rural areas to stop the drift of agricultural populations into cities and to strengthen local economies.

To Olivetti the idea of town and country redevelopment has the factory at its center. Around it and closely integrated with it are the farmers and the economists, sociologists, and town planners who blueprint its growth toward a high standard of living. The factory, as the nucleus, he believes should not belong to any man or group. About sixty-five communities have benefited so far and the movement is spreading throughout north and central Italy and towns in Sardinia. Locating his machine tool plant in Naples rather than in the industrial north of Italy is also part of his plan for achieving permanent economic recovery in the depressed southern region.

In 1948 Olivetti launched the Comunità movement, to which he devotes much of his spare time and a good part of his income. The movement, also at the town planning level, is dedicated to social, cultural, and political betterment in the democratic tradition. In ten years he has created some seventy-one community

Blackstone Studios, Inc.

ADRIANO OLIVETTI

assistance centers in towns and villages. Each center is provided with a library, courses in political and labor problems, a curriculum in elementary studies, and lecturers. He also has lectured at these centers.

As head of the movement, Olivetti became founder and leader of the Italian Institute of Community Centers. The New York *Times* (November 7, 1956) noted: "In one sense they resemble the New England town hall meetings, but are further afield in their concept to improve the living standards and economic status of the residents."

In the local election of 1956 about sixty of Olivetti's followers ran for community offices and some forty were successful. That same year Olivetti was elected mayor of Ivrea. In 1958 he announced that the Comunità movement—now officially called Community of Culture of the Workers and of the Peasants—was sufficiently advanced to present candidates in the national elections for Parliament. Olivetti, who had been unsuccessful in the 1953 campaign, was elected to Parliament in May 1958.

Strongly anti-Communist, Olivetti explained in January 1958, "Free, autonomous, let us say Christian, socialism—that is what we want" (New York *Times*, January 23, 1958). He had some years earlier warned, "Democracy, liberalism, and socialism must find a new, vital, and harmonious language. Otherwise, our society will passively accept an omnipotent state, whether Communist or Fascist, within ten years" (*Time*, February 8, 1954).

Olivetti has served on the Upper Council of Public Works; the UNRRA-Housing Board, Rome; the Technical Advisory Committee for Increasing Employment; Workers' Housing, Rome (1949); and the board of directors of the Institute of Economic Studies, Milan. He

OLIVETTI, ADRIANO—*Continued*

is president of the National Institute of Town Planning, Rome and corresponding member of the Academy of Science, Turin.

Books written by Olivetti include *L'ordine politico della comunità* and *Società, stato, comunità*. He is owner of the nonprofit Edizioni di Comunità (Community Publications) in Milan, which publishes the magazine *Comunità* and volumes on politics, philosophy, art, and other subjects.

Adriano Olivetti is unpretentious in appearance and manner; he has a shy, pleasant smile, blue eyes, and graying hair. He is of medium height and robust. He is married to the former Maria Grazia Galletti and has a son and three daughters. In 1957 the National Management Association (Dayton, Ohio) presented him with its Edward O. Seits Memorial Award for international management and free enterprise leadership. He is a Cavaliere del Lavoro (1952) and Officer de la Legion d'Honneur (1954).

References

N Y Times Mag p28 Je 19 '55
New Yorker 38:93+ S 27 '58
Read Digest 70:169+ Ja '57 por
Time 63:84 F 8 '54 por
Chi è? (1957)
Dizionario Enciclopedico Labor (1950)
Panorama Biografico degli Italiani d'Oggi (1956)

OLMEDO, ALEX (ôl-mä'thō) Mar. 24, 1936- Tennis player
Address: c/o University of Southern California, Los Angeles, Calif.

American sport fans and the tennis world at large were startled a few days after Christmas in 1958 when the young and handsome Alex Olmedo led the United States to a smashing upset victory over Australia in the Davis Cup matches, symbolic of world tennis supremacy. All but unknown before the Cup play, Olmedo, who comes from Peru, also won the United States indoor and Wimbledon, England, championships during the first seven months of 1959, and established himself as the world's finest amateur tennis player.

For all his brilliance, Olmedo still proved erratic in performance and at times became the center of controversy. His almost single-handed triumph in the Davis Cup play was clouded by widespread criticism of the United States for using a native of Peru. In July 1959 Olmedo was censured for his lackluster play against and loss to an inferior opponent in the National Clay Courts tournament at Chicago, but in September he redeemed himself when he and Neale Fraser scored a victory in the United States Amateur championships at Forest Hills.

Alejandro Olmedo y Rodríguez was born March 24, 1936 in Arequipa, one of the largest cities in Peru. His mother, whose maiden name was Fortunata Rodríguez, is Spanish,

and his father Salvador Olmedo is one-fourth Inca Indian. Olmedo was the second oldest of seven children and as a youngster liked all sports and engaged in most of them— soccer, cycling, track and field, and weightlifting. But because his father was the caretaker of a local tennis club, Alex was naturally drawn to tennis. He first held a racket at the age of seven, but played very little until he was older.

Olmedo played tennis with his brother, Mario, who was two years older. Both were coached by their father, who offered movie tickets and candy money as a prize for the matches. "I was fourteen before I got good enough to win one of those movie tickets," Olmedo told Will Grimsley (*Saturday Evening Post,* June 27, 1959). But he improved rapidly. That same year he borrowed his father's favorite racket, and, entering the men's tournament at the club, won the title without too much trouble. He then represented Arequipa in the South Peruvian championships, which he also won.

When he was fifteen, Olmedo's play was good enough to attract the attention of Jorge Harten, president of the Peruvian Tennis Association. Harten subsequently asked an American professional tennis player, Stanley Singer, then living in Peru, to appraise the youngster's talents. Singer's verdict was: "I've never seen more natural ability." Harten arranged for Olmedo to attend school in Lima, the capital of Peru. Having moved into the Singer household, he began year-round practice sessions.

When Olmedo reached the age of eighteen he was ready to come to the United States. First he attended night school to learn English, then enrolled at Modesto Junior College in Modesto, California. His trip to the United States was financed through donations from friends of Singer. "I came here with two purposes," Olmedo has said. "One, to improve my tennis. Two, to get an education" (New York *Post,* February 22, 1959).

The Pacific Southwest Tennis Association had been briefed in advance about Olmedo. Soon after he arrived in the United States he was taken in tow by Perry Jones, the president of the association and the man generally recognized as the dean of West Coast tennis.

"Olmedo," said Jones, who served as non-playing captain of the 1958 Davis Cup team, "can be superb, simply superb. His coaches have been telling him so for years. But they have to keep pushing, pushing. He tends to relax when he should drive himself. The eternal vigilance of tournament tennis has been a hard lesson for Olmedo to learn" (*Christian Science Monitor,* February 13, 1959).

Jones' words are substantiated by Olmedo's tournament record, which was unimpressive before the Davis Cup play. He won the national collegiate championships in 1956 and 1958, after transferring from Modesto to the University of Southern California. In his first Wimbledon appearance, in 1957, he was beaten in the first round. During his play at Forest Hills, New York, for the United States national outdoor championships, Olmedo never progressed far enough to rate even passing notice.

The turning point for Olmedo came in August 1958. Playing in the national doubles championships at Brookline, Massachusetts, Olmedo and Hamilton Richardson of New Orleans beat Australia's crack combination of Ashley Cooper and Neale Fraser 7-9, 7-5, 6-3, 6-4. Allison Danzig, writing in the New York *Times* (August 24, 1958), predicted that Olmedo and Richardson "could well develop into one of the best teams in amateur tennis."

The following month at Forest Hills, Olmedo carried Fraser to five sets before losing, in a quarter-final match. In October, he was chosen as one of the five Davis Cup team members. The others were Earl Buchholz, Jr., of St. Louis, Chris Crawford of Piedmont, California, Barry MacKay of Dayton, Ohio, and Richardson. Buchholz was eighteen and Crawford was nineteen. It was a young and fairly inexperienced team. Jim Moffet, chairman of the selection committee, sounded far from hopeful as he commented: "They are the best players available with great potential" (New York *Herald Tribune*, October 3, 1958).

When the question of Olmedo's Peruvian citizenship came up, officials noted that he had been a resident of the United States for five years, two more than necessary under Davis Cup rules. Moffet also said at that time: "The Peruvian Government wired that the country was honored and proud we selected Olmedo."

Davis Cup play began a few days after Christmas, and the American team was a decided underdog. The United States had won the Cup only once in the previous eight years, and there seemed little likelihood the young team could break Australia's supremacy. But the United States turned a startling upset, due almost entirely to Olmedo.

He won the opening match from Mal Anderson 8-6, 2-6, 9-7, 8-6. MacKay lost his match to Cooper, but the following day Olmedo and Richardson teamed to beat Anderson and Fraser in a four-hour struggle, 10-12, 3-6, 16-14, 6-3, 7-5, to give the Americans a 2-1 lead in the best three of five matches. Olmedo won the Cup for the United States the following day by beating Cooper, 6-3, 4-6, 6-4, 8-6. MacKay subsequently lost to Anderson.

The victory, however, was somewhat marred by the criticism from the English, Australians, and some Americans of Olmedo's inclusion on the Cup team. Olmedo said of the furor: "It hurts me, but I am not going to let it get me down. . . . All the tennis I learned I picked up in the United States" (Los Angeles *Times*, January 7, 1959).

Olmedo scored another triumph in July 1959, when he won the Wimbledon singles title, defeating Rod Laver of Australia, 6-3, 6-4, 6-3. A few weeks later, however, he was under heavy fire for losing to the lightly regarded Abe Segal of South Africa, 6-2, 6-1, 6-0, in the National Clay Court championships in Chicago. "Angry officials threw the Wimbledon champion, Alex Olmedo out . . . after he had disappointed spectators with a sloppy, listless performance. . ." (New York *Times*,

Wide World

ALEX OLMEDO

July 17, 1959). He was disqualified in the tournament, but escaped suspension, and a few weeks later won the Eastern Grass Courts title at South Orange, New Jersey.

At an exciting match in Brookline, Massachusetts, the Australian team of Neale Fraser and Roy Emerson defeated Olmedo and Earl Buchholz for the national doubles championship in August, 1959. The scores were 3-6, 6-3, 5-7, 6-4, and 7-5, and Al Laney of the New York *Herald Tribune* (August 24, 1959) commented: "If Olmedo had played the game of which he is capable but which we have not yet seen in this country, there is little doubt that the result could have been reversed."

A week later, the Davis Cup was returned to Australia. On August 28 Olmedo was beaten 8-6, 6-8, 6-4, 8-6 by Neale Fraser, although the American Barry MacKay upset Rodney Laver. The next day, Olmedo and Earl Buchholz lost the doubles match to Fraser and Roy Emerson in straight sets. Olmedo's play was disappointing in both matches, but he redeemed himself to some extent the third day, when he won a brilliant, 66-game singles match from Laver, 9-7, 4-6, 10-8, 12-10. MacKay later lost to Fraser, giving the 3-2 tennis victory to the Australian team.

Richard ("Pancho") Gonzales, professional tennis champion and a good friend of Olmedo, predicted in 1959 that Olmedo would replace him as pro champion by 1962. According to Gonzales, however, Olmedo is lazy, careless in minor tournaments, and a little too fond of late parties for his own good (Washington *Post and Times Herald,* August 23, 1959).

A friend once asked Olmedo what he had been thinking of when he lost a set of an important match through carelessness. Olmedo explained, "I start thinking out there, 'What am I doing here in front of all these people like a monkey in a cage? . . . Here it is one

OLMEDO, ALEX—*Continued*

hundred degrees in the shade and I run myself dizzy chasing a little white ball' " (*Saturday Evening Post,* June 27, 1959).

An even six feet tall and weighing 165 pounds, Olmedo, who is nicknamed "the Chief" because of his Indian ancestry, presents a striking appearance, with copper-colored skin, black hair, and chiseled features. His off-court relaxations include chess, music, reading, and Western movies, which, he says, he always leaves before the end, "while the Indians are still ahead" (*Saturday Evening Post,* June 27, 1959). Olmedo admits he would like to get married and may find the way to build a tidy nest egg by turning professional.

References

Christian Sci Mon F 13 '59 por
N Y Post Mag p5 F 22 '59 por
Newsweek 53:60 Ja 12 '59
Sat Eve Post 231:22+ Je 27 '59 por
Sport Illus 10:11 Ja 12 '59 por
Time 73:51 Ja 12 '59

Washington (D.C.) Post p14 Ag 23 '59 por

OLMEDO Y RODRÍGUEZ, ALEJANDRO *See* Olmedo, Alex

OSBORN, ROBERT C(HESLEY) Oct. 26, 1904- Cartoonist
Address: h. R.F.D. Salisbury, Conn.

Today one of the best-known cartoonists in America, Robert C. Osborn did not take up his pen as a graphic critic of twentieth century frailties until he was forty-two years old. He spent his early years in disappointment as a serious artist. Service in the Navy as a wartime creator of safety posters shaped his cartooning genius and led to a career as satirist with pen-and-ink.

Robert Chesley Osborn was born on October 26, 1904 in Oshkosh, Wisconsin, the town whose name has become a symbol for rural Midwestern America. He is the son of Albert Leroy and Alice Lydia (Wyckoff) Osborn, and has one brother, Chandler. His father was a prosperous lumberman. Robert Osborn attended local schools, graduating from Oshkosh High School in June 1922.

After a brief period at the University of Wisconsin in Madison, he transferred to Yale University, where he majored in English literature. His primary extracurricular interest was the development of his undoubted ability to draw. He was art editor of the undergraduate *Yale Record* and also a member of the Yale Dramatic club during his years in New Haven, Connecticut.

Graduating from Yale with a Ph.B. degree in 1928, Osborn went to Europe to study painting. He studied at the British Academy in Rome that year and in 1929 attended the Académie Scandinav in Paris. When he returned to the United States he found employment as a teacher of art and Greek philosophy at the Hotchkiss School in Lakeville, Connecticut, where he also coached the football team and taught trap shooting.

It was his last full-time position. He returned to Europe after leaving Hotchkiss in 1935 and traveled in Austria, Germany, Spain, and Portugal. During these years Osborn's efforts as a painter of landscapes and still lifes failed to attract critical approval. The only exception in this period of failure occurred in 1936 when the *Yale Associates Bulletin* published a portfolio of his work.

Osborn first tried his talent at lighter work in 1939. He produced a series of satirical "how-to" books with text and line drawings (which he called caricatures rather than cartoons), each thirty-two pages in length. *How to Shoot Ducks, How to Shoot Quail,* and *How to Catch Trout* were published by Coward-McCann in 1941, and *How to Ski* followed them in 1942. The New York *Times* (October 18, 1941) termed them "Lear with a leer . . . brief and hilariously to the point."

Oddly enough, the war gave Osborn the chance to develop this aspect of his talent. After becoming a member of the civilian training camp at Fort Devens, Mass. in 1940, he went on active duty as a Navy lieutenant (reserve) in 1941. His ability with a drawing pen won him an assignment to the Bureau of Aeronautics, drawing posters and safety pamphlets for Naval aviators.

Transferred to the Pacific area of operations, Osborn expanded his cartoon character, "Dilbert," into a series of "Sense" posters which stressed the need for caution in flying and maintenance. The cartoons became so famous that flyers incorporated "Dilbert" into their vocabularies as a synonym for "blunder," and Dilbert panels were reproduced by the New York *Times* and *Life* magazine.

After the war Osborn was awarded the Legion of Merit for his contribution to flying safety. "His cartoon characters formed a cornerstone for the . . . training programs of Naval Aviation in World War II," the citation read in part, "and his loyal and enthusiastic labors contributed materially to the effectiveness and survival in combat of Navy pilots and air crewmen."

Released from active duty in 1946, Osborn decided to pursue cartooning as a full-time occupation. He settled in Salisbury, Connecticut and celebrated his return to civilian life by producing *War is No Damn Good* (Doubleday, 1946), in which "strutted a wonderful, viciously funny parade of balloon-shaped generals and admirals, gorilla-faced noncoms and forlorn, tortured G.I.s" (*Time,* April 6, 1953).

Osborn's drawings first began to appear in national publications, including *Harper's Magazine* and *Fortune,* in 1947. Most of them were published as illustrations or solitary cartoons. He was also commissioned to illustrate books, the first being *If You Want to Build a House* (1947) for the Museum of Modern Art. In 1948 he arranged an exhibition of cartoons for the museum.

Beginning in 1953 Osborn's work began to appear regularly in magazines as self-sustained cartoon panels, sometimes accompanied by his own text. He satirized such aspects of American life as ulcers (*Fortune,* April 1954) and the "income ax" (*Look,* March 10, 1953). Since 1956 he been a frequent contributor to the liberal *New Republic,* for which he has parodied topics from "Brinkmanship" to modern automobiles.

Just as he had earlier done for military life, Osborn summarized his opinions of the civilian community in *Low & Inside* (Farrar, Straus, 1953). "If anything," remarked *Time* magazine (April 6, 1953) "the sequel is even deadlier and more acidly humorous than the original." His most recent book was *Osborn on Leisure,* issued by Simon & Schuster in 1957, an essay (with cartoons) on the pressures of modern living and the creative use of leisure that provides a release from them.

Principal books that Osborn has illustrated include *The Exurbanites* by A. C. Spectorsky (Lippincott, 1955), *Trial by Television* by Michael Straight (Beacon Press, 1955), *Parkinson's Law* by C. Northcote Parkinson (Houghton, 1957), *The Insolent Chariots* by John Keats (Lippincott, 1958), and *Subverse* by Marya Mannes (Braziller, 1959). Another of Osborn's recent achievements is a series of caricatures commissioned in 1957 by the Museum of Natural History in New York for its cafeteria walls.

In his relatively short career as the cartoon critic of twentieth century folkways, Osborn has established himself in art as he probably could never have hoped to do with the serious painting which occupied his early years. His work can be recognized even without the signature by many literate Americans. His position as a creative artist has likewise been recognized by the critics.

"The bold, smooth, generous sweep of the line makes you say 'It's an Osborn,'" remarked a writer for *Print* (October 1956). "Next you find yourself screwing your face into the countenance in the drawing, twisting your body into its gesture. . . . This, in a sense, is the secret of every good cartoonist. . . . But, even in his easiest advertising illustration (where compromise is like water in the wine), Osborn goes much deeper, close to the core of art. He expresses *himself.* Each drawing carries his enthusiastic vitality, his moral sense (so Wisconsin), his optimism, his sense of belonging (so American). When you say 'It's an Osborn,' you recognize too, beyond the mechanical character of the line, these qualities. You say, in effect 'It's Osborn.'"

Since receiving his Navy Legion of Merit, Osborn has earned many tributes to his work, including the Gold Medal of the Society of Illustrators in 1959 and several Art Directors Club awards. He has continued to help the Navy with its safety program and for this work was given the Distinguished Public Service Award in 1958. He was a Fellow at Berkeley College, Yale in the same year.

Osborn lives on his Connecticut farm with his wife, the former Elodie Courter, whom he

ROBERT C. OSBORN

married on March 18, 1944, and his two children, Nicolas Courter and Eliot Wyckoff. In the local community, he is a member of the Salisbury school board. He is also active as a Yale alumnus, serving as chairman of the university's committee on the arts, and is a member of the Elizabethan and Scroll and Key clubs.

A big man (six feet two inches tall, weighing 180 pounds), Osborn has been described as "buoyant" in bearing in contrast to the snapping-turtle character of his drawings. His eyes and hair are both brown, although the latter is now mixed with white. Politically he is registered as a Democrat, surprising no one who has seen his work in the *New Republic.*

Whether he is expressing graphic opinions of American foreign policy or satirizing the civilian equivalents of his wartime Dilbert, there is a unity to Osborn's work. "This," he wrote in the preface to *Low & Inside,* "is about the steady plight of man; the anarchy of his laughter and the terrifying lawfulness of his tragedies." It is as the recorder of that plight that Osborn has found his career.

References

PM p19 D 20 '45
Print 10:25+ O '56
Time 61:80 Ap 6 '53
Who's Who in America (sup S-N '58)

OSBORNE, JOHN (JAMES) Dec. 12, 1929-
British playwright; actor

Address: b. John Osborne Productions, Ltd., 23, Albemarle St., Piccadilly, London, W.1, England; h. 15, Woodfall St., Chelsea, London, S.W. 3, England

A caustic and unpitying critic of contemporary British social institutions, John Osborne has expressed his corrosive ideas in dramas suc-

International News Photos,
London

JOHN OSBORNE

cessfully presented on the New York and London stages. His *Look Back in Anger* won the New York Critics Circle Award as the best foreign play of 1957; *The Entertainer* served as a vehicle for Sir Laurence Olivier; and *Epitaph for George Dillon,* which closed after three weeks on Broadway, had an unprecedented reopening several weeks later.

Regarded as a leader of the present generation's "angry young men," Osborne has said that to "become angry is to care." His acrid invective speaks for the disgruntled working-class intellectuals brought up by the welfare state: their teeth are fixed, their education is provided, but they have few challenges and opportunities. Osborne advises his countrymen to "feel now, think later." He has been a busy actor as well as a dramatist, specializing in characterizations of old men.

John James Osborne was born in London on December 12, 1929 to Nellie Beatrice (Grove) and Thomas Godfrey Osborne, a commercial artist. His family, of middle- and working-class origins, "used to own a pub but lost it," and Osborne remembers a "boyhood in the midst of a brawling, laughing, drinking, moaning" environment (New York *Post,* February 23, 1958).

For his secondary education Osborne studied at Belmont College in Devonshire and received the general certificate of education. He did not attend a university. For a short time he worked on trade journals: the *Gas World* and the *Miller.* Then, he was a tutor to a group of juvenile actors who were touring the English provinces in *No Room at the Inn.* At the Lyceum Theatre in Sheffield he made his debut as a player in 1948.

While on tour Osborne wrote verse, which he has called a "useful discipline," and a play, *The Devil Inside,* which was produced. With a

friend he managed a small theatrical company at seaside resorts. After he completed *On the Pier at Morecambe* (since renamed *Look Back in Anger*), he sent it to London producers, all of whom rejected it.

Finally, Osborne prevailed upon the English Stage Company to present his play, and its première, in May 1956, at the Royal Court Theatre "had spectacular results." When interviewed by David Dempsey (New York *Times Magazine,* October 20, 1957), Osborne said that the play ran for eighteen months in London "in spite of an almost uniformly bad press. . . . The reviewers thought it a social outrage. . . but the people recognized it as something real, something that was happening to them." New Yorkers, too, were impressed when it opened on October 1, 1957 at the John Golden Theatre. It ran for 408 performances, had a second Broadway production at the Forty-first Street Theatre beginning in November 1958, and toured the United States and Canada.

Look Back in Anger attacks the snobbery and decay of "the Establishment," including the British aristocracy, untouched by the welfare state. The main character, Jimmy Porter, has a state-subsidized education, but because he did not attend Oxford or Cambridge, he cannot "reach the top." By marrying into the middle class and yet refusing to subscribe to its values, he only compounds his troubles. "He is a young man who is anxious to give a great deal," Osborne wrote in his introduction to the play (published in 1957 by Faber in London and Criterion Books, Inc., in New York) "and is hurt because no one seems interested."

The British poet Stephen Spender cited Osborne's work as "containing great promise of sustained high performance." *Vogue* magazine (April 1, 1957) commented: "Young people delight in *Look Back in Anger;* British critics call it, one way or another, the play of its decade. . . . With hilarious accuracy Osborne shows a non-U husband and a U wife, living drearily in a Midlands bed-sitter, destroying their marriage with an emotional neuroticism reminiscent of those battlers of another era, Frieda and D. H. Lawrence."

Osborne's next play, *The Entertainer,* was produced in London in May 1957 and in New York in February 1958. It starred Sir Laurence Olivier as Archie Rice, a middle-aged music hall entertainer, who, resigned to a bleak existence in an exhausted England, warns his audience, "Don't clap too hard, it's a very old building." John Beaufort (*Christian Science Monitor,* February 24, 1958) wrote that the three generations of the Rice family symbolize certain periods in recent British history: Archie's father with his "memories of the glories and standards of the golden Edwardian age when he was a great star; Archie and his generation, the generation of two wars, the decline of the empire, and the decadence of a social structure; Archie's children, the helpless victims of political muddling and the equally helpless 'beneficiaries' of a suffocating welfare state."

Reviewing *The Entertainer,* Walter Kerr (New York *Herald Tribune,* February 13, 1958) wrote: "He is not dealing this time with the fiery intellectuality of his earlier [characters] but with the commonplace chaos of near-illiterate deadbeats. His language is, therefore, commonplace; the sting and variety and whiplash excitement of the first play are absent.... The play has its problems, serious ones. But it comes to a final image that is truly moving." *The Entertainer* was produced in Prague in 1958 and in Toronto in 1959.

Epitaph for George Dillon, written in collaboration with Anthony Creighton, was first presented in London on February 11, 1958 and opened at New York's John Golden Theatre on November 4, 1958. It deals with a young playwright who cadges his room and board from a middle-class London family he despises, but not much more than he despises himself. The ending finds him about to be married to the sluttish daughter of the house. Although it was applauded by most reviewers, Brooks Atkinson of the New York *Times* (November 5, 1958) found that the play lacked the vitality of Osborne's other dramas and tended to grow monotonous. The Broadway production closed about three weeks later, but reopened in January 1959 after the producers released it to other managers at the urging of Marlene Dietrich, Moss Hart, William Inge, and Tennessee Williams. The second presentation of *Epitaph for George Dillon* ran at the Henry Miller Theatre for forty-eight performances.

Henry Hewes reported in the *Saturday Review* (November 22, 1958) that *Epitaph for George Dillon* was written by Osborne and Creighton in 1953, when they were both unemployed, a biographical fact that helps explain the embittered mood that prevails throughout the drama. Once more the hero belongs to the "cad" tradition of the other Osborne plays.

In his political essay, "And They Call It Cricket" (*Encounter,* October 1957), Osborne assailed Britain's explosion of the nuclear bomb as "the most debased criminal swindle in British history." He called royalty the "gold filling in a mouthful of decay" and said its "meaningless" symbolism is a bar to the socialist education of the masses. The article was included in *Declaration* (Dutton, 1958), a symposium edited by Tom Maschler.

Osborne's plays have appeared in book form under the imprints of Faber & Faber in London and Criterion Books, Inc., in the United States. The playwright has organized a film company called Woodfall Productions, which has filmed *Look Back in Anger* and his musical, *The World of Paul Slickey.*

John Osborne and Mary Eileen Ure were married on November 8, 1957. They met shortly before Miss Ure played the leading feminine role in *Look Back in Anger.* His first marriage, to actress Pamela Elizabeth Lane, ended on April 9, 1957. The playwright is six feet two inches tall, slight in build, has blue eyes and brown hair, and dresses conservatively. He belongs to the Savile Club in London.

For recreation, Osborne likes "motoring, reading, listening to music, good company... and occasionally television." He has called the drama critics "pretty tired old men." After the success of *Look Back in Anger,* Osborne bought his first automobile; when his license plates arrived, they bore the initials AYM (Angry Young Man).

"In America, I can enjoy myself enormously," declared John Osborne (New York *Post,* February 23, 1958). "I don't have to get mad at anything—because, you know, I'm not involved.... But in England, I really have a very deep feeling for my country and I am outraged by injustice."

Osborne deeply admires the work of D. H. Lawrence, Jean Anouilh, and Tennessee Williams. "The confounded fellow can write," observed Beverley Baxter in *Maclean's Magazine* (December 7, 1957), "and even his discordance creates a harsh beauty.... Somehow, perhaps reluctantly, playwright Osborne touches the emotions though we do not know why. In short, he has genius."

References

Cue 26:10 O 26 '57 por
N Y Herald Tribune IV p1 F 9 '58
N Y Mirror Mag p2 Je 8 '58 por
N Y Times II p1 S 29 '57
New Yorker 33:36+ O 26 '57
Sat R 40:9 Jl 27 '57 por; 41:25 N 22 '58 por
Who's Who, 1959

OTT, MEL(VIN THOMAS) Mar. 2, 1909-Nov. 21, 1958 Baseball player; manager of the New York Giants (1942-48). See *Current Biography* (July) 1941.

Obituary

N Y Times p1 N 22 '58

PAAR, JACK (HAROLD) May 1, 1918-Television personality
Address: b. c/o National Broadcasting Co., 30 Rockefeller Plaza, New York 20

For the first time, after some twenty-three years of "near misses" on radio and then television, Jack Paar met with undisputed resounding success as the star of *Tonight* (later the *Jack Paar Show*), a late-hour presentation of the NBC-TV network. Since July 1957, when he first appeared on the program, he has attracted an audience of several million from coast to coast "with his strange mélange of chatter, music and tom-foolery" (*Look,* January 21, 1958).

Paar is "a remarkably sophisticated man, rather in the style of Will Rogers," commented Gilbert Millstein (New York *Times Magazine,* November 10, 1957), "with an acerbic wit oriented in the direction of the Midwest, from which he sprang, and, of course, a gift for verbal improvisation that permits him to run on and on without boring people." With such talented "ad-libbers" as Elsa Maxwell, Dody Goodman, Hans Conried, Genevieve, and Cliff Arquette, he made his program both popular with viewers and profitable for sponsors.

(Continued next page)

N B C

JACK PAAR

Jack Harold Paar was born in Canton, Ohio on May 1, 1918 to Howard and Lillian Paar. He has a brother, Howard, Jr., and a sister, Flora. Another brother died at a very early age. His father, who was a New York Central Railroad division superintendent, died in 1956. The family lived successively in Canton, Jackson (Michigan), and Detroit. In boyhood Jack Paar cured himself of stuttering by putting buttons in his mouth and reading aloud. At the age of fourteen he contracted tuberculosis. His father, who was interested in building radios, installed a workbench at the boy's bedside and taught Jack as much as he knew about electronics.

In a twelve-part series, "Jack Paar," in the New York *Post Magazine* beginning on September 29, 1958, Dave Gelman quoted Paar's mother as saying: "He could never sit still long enough to fish with his father. He spent most of his time sealed up in his room, reading biographies of great men." After he was cured of tuberculosis he worked in a railroad gang in freezing weather to harden himself. In high school he was a champion wrestler for a time. He left school at the age of sixteen and obtained a job as a radio announcer. He broadcast from stations in Indianapolis, Youngstown, Pittsburgh, Cleveland, and Buffalo, eventually performing as a comic disc jockey.

In World War II Paar was a noncombatant soldier in the United States Army with the 28th Special Service Company. He entertained the troops in the South Pacific for two years, and for part of that time he was tent mate with actor Jackie Cooper at Guadalcanal. He earned his reputation as a comedian by making fun of officers before highly amused audiences of enlisted men on various islands.

Hired by Howard Hughes, head of RKO Pictures, Paar made his screen debut in *Walk Softly, Stranger* (1950), starring Joseph Cotten.

He played minor roles in four other films, including *Love Nest* (1951), which featured a young starlet, Marilyn Monroe, and *Down Among the Sheltering Palms* (1953)—both for Twentieth Century-Fox.

On radio Paar was a temporary replacement for Don McNeill on the *Breakfast Club* program and filled in for Phil Baker on the original *$64 Question* show. For a while he was at liberty. In 1947 he was Jack Benny's summer replacement on radio, and a magazine poll chose him as "the most promising star of tomorrow." He was also a replacement for Arthur Godfrey for a short time.

He continued to appear on one radio or television show after another, and finally, in 1952, he was given a television show of his own, *Up to Paar*, on NBC-TV, but it failed. His most notable critical success was on the CBS-TV *Morning Show,* in 1954, but it did not attract sponsors. An afternoon CBS-TV show also did not succeed. In 1957 there was an ABC radio program which "fizzled." On July 29, 1957 he was given the *Tonight* show on NBC-TV.

From the start, audiences liked Paar's Monday-through-Friday night show. "His Nielsen rating is respectable," *Printers' Ink* pointed out a few months later (October 18, 1957), adding that the show had four sponsors. A year after its première it had as many as thirty-eight. Paar credited Jack Douglas, for the fifteen minutes of script used each night (the rest was largely impromptu), and pianist José Melis, with whom he has worked for many years. Some critics believe that informality, unpredictability, and Paar's skill in choosing guest performers are among the principal reasons for the program's popularity.

"Paar has given valuable service as a collector and exhibitor of fragments of true comedy," noted John Lardner (*New Yorker,* April 19, 1958), but he criticized his sometimes "unaccountably sullen, tired, and arrogant tone." Paar's feuds with Walter Winchell, Dody Goodman, and others have made much "copy" for columnists, for Paar can "counterpunch," observed *Time* (August 18, 1958). "A caustic remark, a misconstrued question, a real or fancied attack in or out of the studio can provoke stinging repartee."

Among awards that Paar has won for his show are those given by *Radio-TV Daily,* which named him Man of the Year in television for 1957 and 1958, and Sylvania, which chose *Tonight* as the outstanding comedy series for 1957. *Look* magazine honored it as "the best novelty show of the year." In February 1958 NBC's president, Robert W. Sarnoff, changed the program's name to the *Jack Paar Show.* Beginning in July 1959, the series was seen Monday through Thursday evenings. The Friday night spot was filled by *The Best of Paar,* filmed high lights of previous performances.

As guest columnist for John Crosby's column (New York *Herald Tribune,* June 13, 1958), Jack Paar wrote: "I have said we don't rehearse our show. We defend ourselves. And after over 500 hours of show (or what would equal the lifetime of Jack Benny's radio and

TV career) my defenses still stand. . . . I hope that my theories—and my own role on television —have merit. (Perhaps, even, at long last, they have a future.) . . . I make my money through comedy. Yet, I like to think of myself not as a comic but as a humorist. To me, a comic says funny things. A humorist thinks funny things."

In the late 1930's Jack Paar married a girl named Irene from whom he was soon divorced. They were later married and divorced again. He married Miriam Wagner in October 1943. They have a daughter, Randy. Interviewed by Edward R. Murrow on his *Person to Person* program on November 22, 1957, Paar said that his interest in electronics, oil painting, and his campaign against crab grass were his chief hobbies.

He and his family lead a quiet life in their red house in Bronxville, New York, where he has a high-fidelity system throughout. The grounds, which he and his wife landscaped, include a swimming pool. Paar is six feet tall and has a dimpled chin and a shy smile. He reportedly dislikes answering mail, worries about his work, and views his success cautiously.

References

Am Weekly p8 Ap 20 '58 pors
Look 22:76+ Ja 21 '58 pors
N Y Post Mag p1+ S 29 '58
N Y Times Mag p58+ N 10 '57
Time 72:52+ Ag 18 '58 pors

PAIGE, JANIS Sept. 16, 1923- Actress; singer
Address: b. c/o Actors Equity Association, 226 W. 47th St., New York 36

Comedienne and singer Janis Paige has in recent years entertained stage, television, motion picture, and night club audiences across the United States. She played leading roles in the Broadway musical comedy *The Pajama Game,* which won an Antoinette Perry Award in 1955, and in the motion picture *Silk Stockings* (1957). During 1955 and 1956 she starred in the television situation comedy, *It's Always Jan,* and has since made frequent guest appearances on some of TV's most popular shows.

Born Donna Mae Jaden in Tacoma, Washington on September 16, 1923, Janis Paige adopted the surname Paige from a grandparent, after moving to Hollywood, and took her first name, Janis, from the popular World War I personality Elsie Janis. She was reared by her grandparents, while her mother worked outside the home.

Her childhood ambition was to be a Metropolitan Opera singer, and while attending Stadium High School in Tacoma she studied singing and sang lead roles in student productions of *The Merry Widow* and *The Desert Song.* After graduation she moved to Seattle, where she continued vocal training for a year and worked in a plumbing supply shop to earn money.

She then went to California, resumed her voice study, and worked at the Hollywood Canteen. While pouring coffee and preparing sand-

JANIS PAIGE

wiches for servicemen at the canteen, she was invited to fill in for an absent singing star. The response of the G.I.'s and a movie talent scout to her singing of George Gershwin's "The Man I Love" and "One Fine Day" from *Madama Butterfly* was enthusiastic. Janis Paige received a contract from Metro-Goldwyn-Mayer Studios and then, as she has said, "sat around for a whole year, doing absolutely nothing" except taking voice lessons (New York *Post,* November 30, 1946). Eventually she obtained a release from MGM and signed a contract with Warner Brothers.

Miss Paige's first role was in *Hollywood Canteen* (1944) as a pigtailed messenger girl who helps a wounded soldier regain his health. Her performance led to her being selected for the part of Sally in Somerset Maugham's *Of Human Bondage* (1946). Before appearing in this picture, she was seen in a short film *I Won't Play* (1945) and portrayed a gangster's "moll" and night club singer in the melodrama *Her Kind of Man* (1946).

"What fascinated me" in *Her Kind of Man,* wrote the reviewer for *PM* (May 5, 1946), "was, first, Janis Paige's voice, which seems to me to be really something to holler 'Encore!' about." Eileen Creelman, in the New York *Sun* (May 4, 1946), found Janis "a newcomer with a pretty face and a pretty way with some of Broadway's old torch songs."

After being featured in *Two Guys from Milwaukee* (1946), the actress-singer "blossomed right into stardom" in the musical comedy *The Time, the Place and the Girl* (1946), adding "a touch of elfin spirit" and being "the main reason for things going as well as they do in this musical" (New York *World-Telegram,* December 26, 1946). Subsequently she had important parts in *Love and Learn* (1947), *Cheyenne* (1947), *Winter Meeting* (1948), *Wallflower* (1948). *Romance on the High Seas*

PAIGE, JANIS—*Continued*

(1948), and *The Younger Brothers* (1949), among others. For Republic Pictures she made *Fugitive Lady* (1951) and for United Artists, *Two Gals and a Guy* (1951).

During this Hollywood period Miss Paige received more than fifty honorary titles, including "Puritan Maid of 1944," "Trailer Queen of 1947," "Best Table Decoration of 1946," and "Miss America of Pin Up Girls." She learned "to talk extemporaneously on any subject" (*Collier's,* March 27, 1948). In the *Motion Picture Herald*-Fame Poll for 1947, she was voted one of the Stars of Tomorrow.

In 1950 an important change began in Miss Paige's career. "April to August 1950 was the low point of my life," she has stated. "I was ill, I was broke, and I couldn't get a job" (*Theatre Arts,* January 1952). With the help of Ruth Aarons, her agent, she worked out a night club singing act and began at the Statler Hotel in Detroit a series of night club engagements that "clicked."

In July 1951, while in New York City appearing at the Paramount Theatre, she competed with more than two hundred actresses for the part of Jody in the Howard Lindsay-Russel Crouse stage play, *Remains to Be Seen,* and won the role. When the mystery-comedy opened on Broadway, to run for 198 performances, Brooks Atkinson wrote in the New York *Times* (October 4, 1951) that "Janis Paige plays the part of the Middle Western singer with a lot of energetic clowning, but with no apparent talent." William Hawkins in the New York *World-Telegram and Sun* (October 4, 1951), however, commented that "Miss Paige is one of the most refreshing sights in ages" with "youth and fire and energy and kindness and determination in a crazy mixture."

After the closing of *Remains to Be Seen,* Janis Paige fulfilled an engagement at the Copacabana night club in Manhattan, played the lead role in *Annie Get Your Gun* at the Starlight Theatre in Kansas City, and made a television appearance with Bob Hope in Hollywood. Then she co-starred in the musical comedy hit *The Pajama Game,* which opened on May 13, 1954. As Babe, a machine operator in a pajama factory and head of the union's grievance committee, she won applause from both Broadway critics and audiences. Brooks Atkinson described her appearance and her singing as "exhilarating."

Janis Paige remained in the cast of *The Pajama Game* until June 1955, when she left for Hollywood to film her own television situation comedy series, *It's Always Jan,* written for her by Arthur Stander. In this series, which was seen on CBS-TV in 1955-56, she played the part of a widowed career woman and night club singer with a small daughter, living in a crowded apartment with a young model and a secretary. The New York *Times* called the show "another Hollywood potboiler— stereotyped plot characterizations and gags . . . outmoded TV, in short" (September 13, 1955). *TV* magazine (January 1956) regarded it as "one of the best situation comedies to hit" in the fall of 1955.

Among the many other television programs on which Janis Paige has performed are *Salute to Baseball* (NBC, April 1957), Jack Benny's *Shower of Stars* (CBS, April 1958), and the *Garry Moore Show* (CBS, October 1958). She had one of the leading parts in the televised version of *Roberta* (NBC, September 1958), which starred Bob Hope.

To some moviegoers, Miss Paige's most successful role was that in *Silk Stockings* (1957), an MGM musical starring Fred Astaire. Alton Cook observed, "A big share of the bountiful mirth is in charge of Janis Paige with her hilarious travesty of a fancy, flouncing movie star. Even Fred himself loses the attention when this girl is allowed on the screen" (New York *World-Telegram and Sun,* July 19, 1957).

On December 27, 1947 Miss Paige married Frank Martinelli, Jr., whom she later divorced. She married Arthur Stander on January 18, 1956 and was granted a divorce on June 4, 1957. She is described as "a trim, green-eyed, auburn-haired five-five." "One of the most deft and engaging of our girl clowns" (as Alton Cook remarked), she has recently announced her ambition to become also a dramatic actress.

References

Cosmop 139:118+ S '55 pors
N Y Herald Tribune IV p3 O 3 '54
International Motion Picture Almanac, 1957
Wood, Carlyle TV Personalities Biographical Sketch Book (1956)

PANT, GOVIND BALLABH Sept. 10, 1887- Indian Minister for Home Affairs

Address: b. Ministry for Home Affairs, New Delhi, India

"The massive, ever-patient-toward-all" Home Minister of India, Pandit Govind Ballabh Pant, has played a crucial role in coping with the problems of the nation during its first years of independent statehood. Since he assumed his present post in January 1955, he has helped to reorganize some of India's princely states and has held steadfastly to the experiment of a bilingual state in Bombay. This septuagenarian leader is a Bharat Rata (gem of Bharat), the highest honor conferred by the nation for outstanding services.

Sri Pant has been a member of the Congress working committee (the chief executive body of the Congress party) since 1931. He was Chief Minister of the United Provinces from 1937 to 1939 and again between 1946 and 1954. On May 1, 1958 he was elected Deputy Leader of the Congress party in Parliament, succeeding the late Maulana Abul Kalam Azad. He is also the leader of the Rajya Sabba, the upper house of the Indian Parliament.

Govind Ballabh Pant was born on September 10, 1887 in Khunt in the Almora district of the United Provinces of Agra and Oudh. He attained a brilliant scholastic record at Muir Central College in Almora, where he earned the B.A. degree, and at the Faculty of Law,

University of Allahabad, which granted him the LL.B. degree. In 1919 he became an advocate of the Allahabad High Court and a member of the bar at Naini Tal, United Provinces.

Active in politics since 1916, he organized in that year the Kumaun Parishad to consider local problems. He was elected to the United Provinces Legislative Council (1923). As head of the Swarajist party in the Legislative Council for seven years, he functioned as the leader of the Opposition. In 1927 Govind Ballabh Pant was elected president of the United Provinces Congress committee and presided over its Aligarh session.

He took part in the demonstrations in 1928 against the Royal Statutory (Simon) Commission which had been appointed by the British government to ascertain whether India was ready for a greater degree of self-government. During these demonstrations he sustained serious injuries which have partly disabled him to this day. Between 1930 and 1932 he was twice imprisoned for participating in the civil disobedience movement. He became the general secretary of the All-India Parliamentary Board in 1934 and was elected to the Central Legislative Assembly, becoming its deputy leader of the Congress party. In 1931 he was elected a member of the Congress working committee.

Pant formed the first Congress cabinet of the United Provinces in 1937, and he remained in the post of Prime Minister until his resignation in 1939. In the following year he was imprisoned in connection with the *Satyagraha* (passive resistance) movement of Mohandas Gandhi. During the "quit India" campaign Pant was detained from 1942 to 1945 at Ahmadnagar Fort. From 1946 to 1949 he was a member of the Constituent Assembly. He again served as chief minister of the United Provinces for eight years, beginning in 1946.

Prime Minister Jawaharlal Nehru appointed Pant Home Minister of the national government and the latter took office in January 1955. In this post he has been concerned with many controversial and significant problems, including the Kashmir question, the Naga rebellion in the Assam region, the reorganization of states on a linguistic basis, and the agitation of the Bhooswamis Sangh (ex-landlords' league) in Rajasthan. In September 1955 Pant was given the additional portfolio of Heavy Industries, but he relinquished it in November. In 1956-57 he served on a four-man committee which approved of all Congress candidates running in the 1957 national elections. (The Congress party won a preponderant majority of the seats in Parliament in March.)

At a press conference in the summer of 1955 Pant explained the reasons which made it impossible for the Indian government to carry out its pledge of 1949 to hold a plebiscite on the Kashmir issue: "We made a certain statement at the time when Kashmir acceded to India—a fact which cannot be denied. But at the time we made that statement circumstances were different from what they are now. The time factor is important; many things have happened during the last seven or eight years.

GOVIND BALLABH PANT

"Firstly, Kashmir has been following a certain policy for her advancement and many development schemes are in progress. Secondly, Pakistan has entered into a military alliance with America. Thirdly, the Constituent Assembly of Kashmir which was elected by adult franchise has taken a definite decision." (The Kashmiri Constituent Assembly in February 1954 ratified the state's accession to India and in November 1956 adopted an act to make Kashmir-Jammu an integral part of India.)

Pandit Pant has been called the architect of the bilingual state of Bombay which was organized in November 1956. It has an area of 190,919 square miles and a population of 48,000,000 (of whom two-thirds are Marathi-speaking and one-third are Gujarati-speaking people), and is the largest state in India in respect to area. It comprises Saurashtra, Kutch, Vidarbha (Marathi areas of former Madhya Pradesh), and Marathawada (Marathi areas of former princely state of Hyderabad).

The creation of the state of Bombay was part of the national reorganization of Indian states on a linguistic basis, reducing them in number from twenty-seven to fourteen. In addition, there are six centrally administered territories. Sri Pant created five zonal councils composed of representatives of contiguous states to promote greater co-ordination between the various state administrations in the development of waterways, trade, and welfare programs. For a national language, India adopted Hindi.

Pant has also drafted plans for making the administration of Delhi state work more efficiently. Under his scheme heads of departments will have immediate contact with the chief commissioner who directs the administration without the interposition of secretaries. In attempting to satisfy ethnic group feeling, the Indian government granted an amnesty to Naga tribes-

PANT, GOVIND BALLABH—*Continued*

men who had carried on a rebellion for two years. Nagaland, a new state, was established on December 1, 1957.

Pandit Pant approved of the policy of quelling disorders in the south of India towards the end of 1957 led by E. V. Ramaswamy Naicker (known as E.V.R.). E.V.R. held that the fair-skinned Aryans (Brahmins) tyrannized over the dark-skinned Dravidians or Sudras. Anthropologists claim that the mixture of races has been very great. Membership of India in the British Commonwealth of Nations is regarded by Pant as no more than an idea and only indicates the need for a wider fellowship of nations. It does not in any case impose any liabilities or obligations on India.

Govind Ballabh Pant was married in 1918 to Kala Pande. They have one son and two daughters. Nehru paid tribute to Pant's work at an observance of the Home Minister's seventy-first birthday in September 1958. Nehru said: "His has been a dedicated life and he has towered above the people of our generation by not only his ability and integrity, but also his calmness in the face of difficulty and crisis. The country owes a debt of gratitude to him. To those who have worked with him as colleagues and comrades he has been a tower of strength."

References

> Asia Who's Who, 1958
> International Who's Who, 1958
> International Year Book and Statesmen's Who's Who, 1958
> Nalanda Year-Book and Who's Who in India and Pakistan, 1951-53

PARKINSON, THOMAS I(GNATIUS)
Nov. 27, 1881-June 17, 1959 Former president (1927-53) and chairman (1953-54), Equitable Life Assurance Society of the United States; dean, Columbia University School of Law (1923-24). See *Current Biography* (April) 1949.

Obituary

N Y Times p31 Je 18 '59

PARSONS, ROSE PEABODY *See* Parsons, Mrs. William Barclay

PARSONS, MRS. WILLIAM BARCLAY
Oct. 11, 1891- Women's organization official; civic worker
Address: b. National Council of Women of the United States, 345 E. 46th St., New York 17; h. 149 E. 73d St., New York 21

The exchange of ideas and information among women throughout the world to promote international understanding and peace has been a major objective of Mrs. William Barclay Parsons in her leadership of a number of volunteer groups working for human betterment. From 1956 to 1959 she was head of the Na-

tional Council of Women of the United States, an affiliate of the International Council of Women, of which she is a vice-president and member of the executive committee. She has also contributed to the cause of peace as chairman of the women's committee of the People to People Foundation. In late 1959 she became honorary president of the National Council of Women and remains on its executive committee.

Born in Groton, Massachusetts on October 11, 1891, Rose Peabody Parsons was one of six children of Endicott and Fanny Peabody. Her father and mother, whose maiden name was Peabody also, were cousins. Her father founded and became headmaster of Groton School, the well-known New England preparatory school, where one of her three surviving sisters teaches. Her only brother is Bishop Peabody of the Central New York Episcopal Church.

From 1908 to 1910 Rose Peabody attended St. Timothy's School in Catonsville, Maryland. After graduation she went to Europe and lived for a year with a French family in Paris. In 1913 she made a world tour, returning from the Far East via the Trans-Siberian Railroad. On her return to the United States she began a lifelong career of volunteer work dedicated to helping people. She cared for the needy in hospital clinics, attended children of the poor in settlement houses, and took a six-month training course at Presbyterian Hospital in New York City.

A month after America entered World War I, Rose Peabody went to France and was assigned to the care of afflicted French war orphans. Later she joined the United States Mobile Hospital unit as a Red Cross representative and saw service in all the major campaigns. On July 14, 1918 she was awarded the Croix de Guerre Militaire by the French government for bravery under fire. She remained with the Red Cross until February 1919. The following month, on March 22, 1919, she married Dr. William Barclay Parsons of New York, who had been a captain in the American Ambulance Field Service and who had served with the Mobile Hospital unit.

During the school years of their three children, Mrs. Parsons took an active part in parent-school work. From 1930 to 1933 she served as president of the Parents League of Independent Schools of New York and directed her organizing abilities toward the programing of better films and radio shows for children. She helped start the Schools Motion Picture Weekend List of programs for movie houses in scheduling pictures for good family entertainment. She was appointed also to the Columbia Broadcasting System's radio committee for selection of better programs for the young. In the field of music she was chosen the first vice-president of the Metropolitan Opera Guild in 1935 and worked as such until 1941 to provide opera performances for young people and students.

After the outbreak of World War II, Mrs. Parsons returned to Red Cross work. In 1941 she was appointed administrator of volunteer services of the North Atlantic area and spent the next five years organizing, directing, and coordinating volunteer activities for the American Red Cross.

Having seen the disastrous effects of two World Wars on nations and family life within nations, Mrs. Parsons looked toward the establishment of machinery for peace and its promotion through women's contributions to the rebuilding of a peaceful world. In 1946 she founded Women United for the United Nations, which is composed of some thirty affiliating women's organizations, and for the next six years served as its chairman. The group became a sponsor of the volunteer, nonprofit Information Center for the United Nations, also conceived by Mrs. Parsons and established in New York City in January 1948 to broaden the public's understanding of the U.N. Its work was so effective that it became recognized as an unofficial arm of the U.N. During its first two and three-quarter years more than 100,000 persons from over 100 countries stopped at the center to inquire about the U.N.

Mrs. Parsons was also concerned with the United Nations as U.N. chairman of the National Council of Women of the United States. The latter organization, founded in 1888, represents about twenty national and local groups and operates as a clearinghouse for information of interest to women, on such subjects as international relations, child welfare, status of women, and education.

In 1953 Mrs. Parsons founded and was chosen chairman of the committee of correspondence of the National Council of Women and the same year became chairman of the council's newly established Women's Center. Located across from the U.N. in the Carnegie Endowment International Center, the Women's Center has enabled the council to offer expanded services to similar-minded American organizations and to women leaders in other countries.

As part of her work on the committee of correspondence, Mrs. Parsons established a monthly bulletin to disseminate information about women's activities in the United States to interested organizations abroad. The bulletin, now an official monthly publication of the council, provides the intimate touch that Mrs. Parsons feels is badly needed in the reporting of women's activities. "People abroad don't want U.S. thought pushed down their throats any more than we do Russian," she has explained. "Nor do they often believe U.S. propaganda any more than we do Communist propaganda" (New York *World-Telegram and Sun,* November 18, 1953).

When she was elected president of the National Council of Women in October 1956, Mrs. Parsons automatically became a member of the executive committee of the International Council of Women, of which the United States council is one of forty-four affiliates. She had earlier been appointed consultant at the U.N. for the I.C.W. and a vice-convener of the peace and international relations committee, and in 1954 she was made vice-president of the I.C.W., an office that she still holds. The international organization, which has its headquarters in

MRS. WILLIAM BARCLAY PARSONS

Paris, brings together women from all over the world to discuss what action should be taken on various problems affecting human welfare.

In February 1957 Mrs. Parsons was chosen chairman of the women's committee of the newly organized People to People Foundation, established to promote world peace through international contacts between individuals. Stemming from a proposal made by President Eisenhower in September 1956, the foundation is based on the belief that the people of the world can understand each other despite the disagreements of their governments.

By arranging for affiliation of the foundation with the National Council of Women, Mrs. Parsons helped place the organizational strength of hundreds of local women's clubs behind the movement. Allied in their aim to promote understanding through correspondence between American women and those in foreign lands, especially between those of similar personal and vocational interests, the foundation has the use of the council's Letters Abroad program, which has been a clearinghouse of international correspondence since 1952. Mrs. Parsons' women's committee of People to People has established a visitors' exchange program and has urged the study of foreign languages in the United States and the study of English abroad and the setting up of women's clubs programs to study foreign culture and customs. Mrs. Parsons is also a director of the Common Council for American Unity and People to People.

As president of the National Council of Women, Mrs. Parsons traveled extensively. In July 1958 while on a trip to see her son, a missionary, and his family in Japan, she represented the International Council of Women at the Conference of the Asia-African Women held in Ceylon. Reporting on this in the article "Around the World in 70 Days" in the *Bulletin of the National Council* (July 1958), Mrs. Par-

PARSONS, MRS. WILLIAM BARCLAY
—Continued

sons stated: "My third trip around the world convinced me more than ever of the importance of close cooperation among women in all parts of the free world. We all have very much the same interests and see the necessity for the betterment of peoples everywhere and the importance of moral and spiritual forces to make life worth living."

Besides their missionary son, William Barclay Parsons, Jr., Dr. and Mrs. Parsons have two daughters, Rose (Mrs. R. V. Lynch) and Anne Barclay (Mrs. H. A. Priest, Jr.), and several grandchildren. Mrs. Parsons has blue eyes and brown hair, weighs 154 pounds, and is five feet seven and a half inches tall. Her many hobbies include golf, sailing, choral singing, painting, and tapestry work. In her younger days she played the violin. She belongs to the League of Women Voters and the Cosmopolitan Club and is on the board of the United Church Women. She is an Episcopalian and a Republican.

Reference

> Who's Who of American Women (1958-59)

PASTERNAK, BORIS (LEONIDO-VICH) (päs-tyir-näk′) Feb. 10, 1890- Russian author

Address: Peredelkino, U.S.S.R.

For Boris Pasternak's "important achievement both in contemporary lyrical poetry and in the field of the great Russian epic tradition," he was awarded the Nobel Prize for Literature in 1958. He abstained from accepting it, "in view of the meaning given to this honor in the community to which I belong." Although his novel, *Doctor Zhivago,* has been translated into eighteen languages, it has not been published in the Soviet Union, where Pasternak has lived all his life, except for several short trips abroad. In the "motherland" he has written his poetry, short stories, an autobiography, a novel, and made translations into Russian of Shakespeare and other writers.

Boris Leonidovich Pasternak was born in Moscow on February 10, 1890, the eldest of the four children of Leonid Osipovich and Roza (Kaufmann) Pasternak. He is of Jewish descent. He was raised, according to *Time* magazine (December 15, 1958), in a "gracious, leisurely, art-saturated world." His father was a celebrated painter who had done portraits of Tolstoy, Chaliapin, Rilke, Rachmaninoff, and Lenin. His mother was a concert pianist, and one of the family friends who greatly influenced Pasternak was the composer Scriabin. His brother, Alexander, is now an architect in Moscow, and his two sisters, Lydia and Josephine, have lived in England for many years.

His lack of absolute pitch forced Boris Pasternak to give up his adolescent ambition to become a musician. After graduation from a Moscow Gymnasium, he entered Moscow University in 1910. In 1912 he enrolled as a philosophy major in the University of Marburg in Germany, studying under Professor Hermann

Cohen, a disciple of Hegel and Kant. After traveling in Italy, he returned to Moscow in the winter of 1913-14 and settled down to his major interest, the writing of poetry. When an old leg injury disqualified him from military service during World War I, he worked in a chemical factory in the Urals. After the Bolshevik Revolution, he was employed in the library of the Soviet Commissariat of Education, and became further identified with the symbolist and futurist movements in poetry, led by his friend, Vladimir Mayakovsky.

Critics were impressed by his freshness of vision, his audacious use of imagery, freedom of invention, and terseness of style. Pasternak stressed the importance of images because he believed that only they could keep pace with the fecundity and change of nature itself.

During the purge trials in the Soviet Union during the late 1930's, Pasternak was asked to sign an approval of the execution of Red Army generals. He later told an interviewer: "My wife was pregnant. She cried and begged me to sign, but I couldn't. That day I examined the pros and cons of my own survival. I was convinced that I would be arrested—my turn had now come! I was prepared for it. I abhorred all this blood. I couldn't stand things any longer. But nothing happened. It was, I was told later, my colleagues who saved me indirectly. No one dared to report to the hierarchy that I hadn't signed." Some critics believe that Stalin was lenient toward Pasternak because of his translations into Russian of Georgian poets.

Over the years Pasternak has also translated into Russian works by Goethe, Kleist, Verlaine, Ben Jonson, Swinburne, and Shelley. He has translated Shakespeare's *Hamlet, Henry IV, Romeo and Juliet, Antony and Cleopatra,* and *Othello,* and has written several articles dealing with the significance of Shakespeare.

In 1949 New Directions in New York published Pasternak's *Selected Writings,* which contained his autobiography, "Safe Conduct," written in 1931, short stories, and poems. This edition was reprinted in 1958 under the title: *Safe Conduct; An Autobiography and Other Writings.* Marc Slonim wrote in the *Saturday Review* (December 13, 1958) that in these works Pasternak "looks at history from the heights of fate and imagination; he tries to establish the link between man and the universe, and he defends his right to dream and to create, to enjoy life or to experience 'this fit of sadness which rattles and rises like the quicksilver in Torricelli's tube.'"

Other English translations of his poems have appeared in *A Second Book of Russian Verse* (Macmillan, 1948), edited and translated by C. M. Bowra, and in *A Treasury of Russian Verse* (Macmillan, 1949), edited by Avrahm Yarmolinsky, and in such magazines as *Poetry* (August 1947), *Reporter* (September 4, 1958), *New Republic* (November 3, 1958), *Saturday Review* (December 13, 1958), and *Partisan Review* (winter, 1958). Representative collections of Pasternak's poetry first appeared in English in 1959; they were Eugene M. Kayden's translation of *Poems* (University of Michigan Press) and George Reavey's translation of *The Poetry of Boris Pasternak* (Putnam).

For a number of years Pasternak had been writing a novel. "I always dreamt of a novel," he has said, "in which, as in an explosion, I would erupt with all the wonderful things I saw and understood in this world." It was accepted after Stalin's death by the State Publishing House, but following a closer examination of the manuscript, the work was barred (for the rejection letter, see the New York *Times Book Review,* December 7, 1958). In the meantime Pasternak had sold the foreign rights to Feltrinelli, a publisher in Milan, Italy, who refused to return the manuscript "for revisions" and published it in Italian in September 1957.

Translations into most European languages followed, and the American edition, *Doctor Zhivago,* was published by Pantheon Books, Inc., in September 1958. By November 1958 the novel had been translated into eighteen languages. Marc Slonim wrote of the novel and its hero in the New York *Times Book Review* (September 7, 1958) : "His quarrel with the epoch is not political but philosophical and moral. He believes in human virtues formulated by the Christian dream, and he asserts the value of life, of beauty, of love and of nature. He rejects violence, especially when justified by abstract formulas and sectarian rhetoric. . . ."

A central theme of the novel is Pasternak's conviction that "what has for centuries raised man above the beast is not the cudgel, but the irresistible power of unarmed truth." He has said of his book: "This is not politics. . . . I am not a politician. But every poet, every artist must somehow grope for the trends of his time."

The Royal Swedish Academy of Literature announced on October 23, 1958 that Boris Pasternak had been awarded the 1958 Nobel Prize for Literature. He immediately cabled the Nobel committee that he was "immensely thankful, touched, proud, astonished, abashed" by the award. Writers in the Soviet *Literary Gazette* and *Pravda* called him a "traitor," a "malevolent Philistine," a "libeler," a "Judas," and an "extraneous smudge in our Socialist country," and *Pravda* stated that he would reject the prize if there were "a spark of Soviet dignity left in him." He was expelled from the Soviet Writers' Union.

Several days later Pasternak declined the award, and in a personal letter to the Soviet leader Nikita S. Khrushchev asked to be allowed to remain in Russia. "Leaving the motherland will equal death for me," he stated. "I am tied to Russia by birth, by life and work." When the Nobel awards were presented in Stockholm on December 10, 1958 Anders Oesterling of the Royal Swedish Academy paid an unscheduled tribute to Pasternak *in absentia* near the close of the ceremony. The poet's $41,420, heavy gold medal and leather-bound scroll are being held in trust for him in case he will have a chance to accept them in the future.

Boris Pasternak is married to the former Zinaida Nikolaevna Neuhaus. She is his second wife; he divorced his first wife, Eugenia, in

wide World

BORIS PASTERNAK

1931. He has three sons: one is a pianist, one an engineer, and one a physics student. For many years he has lived in his house in the writers' colony in Peredelkino, a suburb of Moscow. There he enjoys gardening and talking with friends about philosophy and literature. He has said: "It is in our power to do but one thing, and that is not to distort the living voice of life."

References

Dublin R 232:49+ Spring '58
N Y Times p6 O 24 '58
Sat R 41:20+ S 6 '58
Time 72:80+ D 15 '58

International Who's Who, 1958
Pasternak, B. Safe Conduct (1958)
Smith, H. ed. Columbia Dictionary of Modern European Literature (1947)
Twentieth Century Authors (First Supplement, 1955)
Yarmolinsky, A. ed. A Treasury of Russian Verse (1949)

PAULI, WOLFGANG Apr. 25, 1900-Dec. 15, 1958 Winner of Nobel Prize in physics (1945) for research on atomic structure. See *Current Biography* (June) 1946.

Obituary

N Y Times p15 D 29 '58

PAXTON, ROBERT Jan. 19, 1902- Industrialist

Address: b. General Electric Co., 570 Lexington Ave., New York 22; h. 165 Palmer Lane, Thornwood, N. Y.

The General Electric Company, whose business volume exceeds $4 billion a year, has as its president Robert Paxton. He was elected

Burns Photography, Inc.

ROBERT PAXTON

on April 23, 1958 to succeed Ralph J. Cordiner, who became chairman of the board and retained the title of chief executive officer. Paxton believes that for its future success General Electric requires employees who are capable of initiative and independent action in the areas of their responsibility. An engineer, Paxton joined a General Electric training program in 1923 and afterward held increasingly important posts in the manufacturing and administrative phases of the company's operations.

Born to Robert Wilson and Annie Gordon (Johnson) Paxton on January 19, 1902 in Edinburgh, Scotland, Robert Paxton was brought to the United States by his parents at the age of two. He was raised in Troy, New York. As a preadolescent he was fascinated by electrical textbooks from the International Correspondence Schools. This interest led to his enrollment at Rensselaer Polytechnic Institute in Troy when he was ready for college.

Finding the money to pay for his academic expenses was difficult. Paxton's father, a carpenter in upstate NewYork, had won a Carnegie Medal and $1,000 for saving the life of a man who had fallen into the Hudson River. He used this to help put his son through school. Bob Paxton won a scholarship and held part-time jobs while studying to be an engineer.

After his graduation from Rensselaer with the E.E. degree in 1923, Paxton was accepted by General Electric for its engineers' training program. One year later he was assigned to the switchgear department in Schenectady, New York. Beginning in 1927, he worked at the switchgear works in Philadelphia and gained important experience in manufacturing, engineering, and managerial operations.

In 1940 he was promoted to the job of assistant to the manager of the Philadelphia works; manager in 1941; and head of the

Pittsfield, Massachusetts apparatus works in 1945. In the key position of manager of the transformer and allied products division (1948-50), Paxton was responsible for plants in Pittsfield and Holyoke, Massachusetts; Fort Edward, New York; and Oakland, California.

General Electric appointed Paxton manager of manufacturing policy for the company in 1950, and in September of that year he was elected a vice-president. His next advancement was to the post of executive vice-president with responsibility for the industrial products and lamp group. With the reorganization of the company's top echelon in 1954, Paxton became the director of the apparatus group. This included Canadian General Electric Company, Ltd., product divisions, apparatus sales division, and the commercial vice-presidents.

A major reorganization was carried out in 1957, and at that time Paxton was advanced to the newly created post of executive vice-president of operations and to the board of directors. One year later he was elevated to the presidency. His predecessor, Cordiner, became chairman and remained in the post of chief executive officer.

General Electric is America's largest electrical-equipment manufacturer; it produces over 200,000 different items in more than 170 plants in thirty-one states and several countries. Its scientists conducted the research that led from Edison's lamp to the incandescent bulb. They made important discoveries in the science of electronics, developed the X-ray tube, and were the first to seed clouds for weather control. They were also the first to produce man-made diamonds.

Cordiner and Paxton believe that self-development and independent thinking on the part of the company's 260,000 employees are basic factors in the company's future prosperity. This conviction was reflected in General Electric's policies between 1950 and 1958 when it decentralized its functions into over 100 departments. Delegated to each was the authority to make its own decisions and to conduct its affairs on a profit-making basis.

"More than that, there has been a deliberate, formal effort to move the responsibility . . .to each individual person," Paxton said on November 12, 1958 in an address to the Grocery Manufacturers of America. To aid its staff to meet job requirements and qualify for advancement, General Electric offers thousands of courses in factory skills, over 500 courses to professional, technical, and semitechnical employees, and advanced management training for executives.

A major concern of Paxton during his first six months as president was Operation Upturn, a plan to meet the 1957-58 economic recession. In the first quarter of 1958 profits had declined by 23 per cent. The new plan was a company-wide attempt to bring to the consumer the quality services and products already available. "Translated into operating terms," commented *Business Week* (May 17, 1958), "this means that all functions of GE—manufacturing, engineering, finance, public and employee relations, and not just marketing—are getting the job of making sure the customers are being satisfied." For the third quarter of 1958 earnings had increased 6 per cent over the same period in 1957, despite a 4 per cent decrease in sales.

Another major problem of Paxton's has been labor relations. Although the company's major labor contracts are effective until October 1960, discussion of employment security issues has been taking place since 1958. The two largest unions representing General Electric workers, the International Union of Electrical Workers (AFL-CIO) and the independent United Electrical, Radio & Machine Workers of America, asked for supplemental unemployment benefits, a guaranteed wage, or a decreased work week.

The company rejected these demands and in August 1958 offered its employees a stock-savings program in which GE would match any employee's savings up to 6 per cent of his regular earnings. The two unions opposed the plan. In his speech to the Grocery Manufacturers of America, Paxton remarked that the unions were against the savings offer "because it increases the financial independence of our employees, and these unions seem to prefer the collective approach where all employees contribute to a fund, but only a few of them ever draw out any benefits."

At that time Paxton asserted that the union movement has been transformed "from an idealistic, popularly supported activity into a well-heeled special interest which has achieved monopoly power over large segments of the labor force." He continued: "General Electric believes all employees should decide for themselves—individually—whether they should join or not join a union, stay in or get out, or pay dues or not to a union."

In order to maintain its position in the future, General Electric has entered many newly developing areas of science. It has built and operated a test reactor and a power reactor in Vallecito, California. An all-nuclear power station was constructed at Dresden, Ohio for the Commonwealth Edison Company, and a $19,500,000 reactor was erected at Eureka, California for the Pacific Gas & Electric Company. At present, General Electric plans to produce boiling-water nuclear plants for utility companies and to develop five boiling-water plants to provide "knowledge required to produce competitive atomic power" (New York *Herald Tribune,* January 9, 1959).

For the government General Electric operates the Hanford plutonium works at Richland, Washington, is carrying out research on the atomic-powered airplane, and is designing a twin-reactor with a pressurized-water system for the submarine *Triton.*

In the field of jet aircraft, General Electric produced the engine for the first United States jet fighter in 1942, the world's first Mach 2 bomber, and the world's first Mach 2 operational fighter. It now ranks with Pratt & Whitney Company, Inc., as the leading jet engine manufacturer. From its work in jets General Electric entered missile production and has achieved second place after General Dynamics Corpora-

tion in defense contracts. General Electric also developed a sodium-cooled reactor which was used in the atomic submarine *Seawolf.*

On June 23, 1947 Robert Paxton was married to S. Louise Bloom. She is a cousin of the first Mrs. Paxton, who died some years ago. For relaxation he and his wife like to garden at their Thornwood home. Paxton is a director of the Canadian General Electric Company, Ltd., and the National Association of Manufacturers, a limited life trustee of Rensselaer Polytechnic Institute, and a member of the American Institute of Electrical Engineers and the Rensselaer Polytechnic Institute Alumni Association (president, 1951-52). He is five feet ten and one-half inches in height, weighs 182 pounds, has blue eyes and iron-gray hair. His church is the Presbyterian of Pleasantville, New York. On each working day Paxton arises at 5 A.M. and is at his desk in New York at 8 A.M.

In June 1958 Paxton stated: "The progress we all seek as Americans compels a high degree of organization in society, and some may assume that that fact requires the extension of authority over the thoughts and actions of men. On the contrary, a prerequisite to progress . . . rests in the encouragement . . . of the differences in men, of their individualities, their freedom, and their dignity."

References

N Y Times p45+ Ap 24 '58
N Y World-Telegram p44+ S 3 '58
Time 71:78 My 5 '58
Wall St J Ap 24 '58
Poor's Register of Directors and Executives, 1958
Who's Who in America, 1958-59
Who's Who in Commerce and Industry (1957)

PEARE, CATHERINE OWENS Feb. 4, 1911- Author
Address: h. 295 St. Johns Pl., Brooklyn 13, N.Y.

Reprinted from the *Wilson Library Bulletin* Oct. 1959.

In accurate and readable biographies Catherine Owens Peare has brought the lives and times of such important figures as Mahatma Gandhi, Robert Louis Stevenson, and Charles Dickens to younger readers. She is also the author of the definitive biography *William Penn* (1957), written for an adult audience. Based upon thorough research, including a study of newly discovered documents, the book presents various aspects of Penn's career: as a religious and political leader, martyr, spokesman, and administrator.

Catherine Owens Peare was born on February 4, 1911 to Eugene J. and Georgie (Owens) Peare in Perth Amboy, New Jersey. Her grandparents came from France, Scotland, England, and Germany. There were early signs that Catherine would express her inherent gifts by writing. In her senior year in high school at Tenafly, New Jersey, she was editor of the

CATHERINE OWENS PEARE

school paper. In college she wrote plays, two of which were produced, and from time to time she contributed verse to the campus paper.

Catherine Peare was graduated from New Jersey State Teachers College at Montclair in 1933 when there were few jobs to be had for new applicants anywhere and no teaching posts open to recent science majors. Typing had been one of her high school courses, to which she added a short course in stenography with a view to a business job and for its utility in doing research.

There followed a Wall Street job, with a good grounding in investments, during which Miss Peare wrote in the evenings and weekends, publishing a bit here and there. During summer vacations she traveled, to Costa Rica and Cuba and Spain and France. Out of these journeys there grew an ideal for factual writing on smaller nations, which the hopeful author presented to Siri Andrews, then editor of juveniles at Henry Holt and Company. Miss Andrews listened and said, "You can write. What about biography instead of geography for young people?"

That was how the continually growing Peare list of biographies began for Henry Holt with the first title, fittingly for a science major become writer, *Albert Einstein* (1949). There are now thirteen. In reviewing the Einstein volume, a reviewer for the Springfield *Republican* wrote: "A better understanding of the man may be had by anyone who reads this book. Here is the background for the marvels in science which have been revealed in a lifetime of study and experimentation."

There followed *Mahatma Gandhi* (1950); then a group of eleven titles for nine-to-twelve-year olds: *Stephen Foster* (1952), *John James Audubon* (1953), *Henry Wadsworth Longfellow* (1953), *Louisa May Alcott* (1954), *Mark Twain* (1954), which was a selection of the Junior Literary Guild, *Robert Louis Stevenson* (1955), *Jules Verne* (1956), *Rosa Bonheur* (1956), *Washington Irving* (1957), *Charles Dickens* (1959), and in April 1958 a junior edition of the adult biography of *William Penn* which J. B. Lippincott Company had published in the fall of 1957. Miss Peare has also done two biographies for young adults for the Vanguard Press—*Mary McLeod Bethune* (1951) and *John Woolman, Child of Light* (1954).

About the Woolman book T. M. Longstreth said in the *Christian Science Monitor*: "Miss Peare has succeeded admirably in presenting John Woolman's gradual progress under divine guidance without estranging young readers from him because of his piety." The *Saturday Review* went farther: "It is extremely difficult to interpret the life and times of a religious leader to young people, but Miss Peare, herself a Quaker, has told this story with competence and deep understanding. John Woolman emerges as a figure of strength and wisdom, a rightful leader of a great religious movement, a man whose life should be an inspiration to young people today."

While gathering the material for the book on John Woolman Miss Peare found there had been no recent, complete story written about William Penn. That led to the publication by Lippincott, three years later, of her biography *William Penn*. Edmund Fuller wrote enthusiastically of it in the New York *Times*: "Catherine Peare's full scale adult biography is probably the finest available. Because of her skill and experience in writing for younger readers, one could be certain that her *William Penn* would be a worthwhile book; and so it is."

A. C. Ames said in the Chicago *Sunday Tribune*: "A thorough, scholarly life of William Penn is a valuable thing to have and that is what Miss Peare has provided us with. Hers is a rewarding and many sided subject, important in American history, in the 17th century religious ferment in England, and in plain, human interest."

Carl Bridenbaugh, in the New York *Times Book Review* added: "This is certainly the finest biography of William Penn yet to appear. . . . This was a man possessed of boundless physical and intellectual energy who gave his all to his faith, the oppressed of all nations and universal peace. This was a man, too, who went to his grave poor, rejected and badgered. It is a tragic story and a moving one."

In 1958 Lippincott published *Scientist of Two Worlds: Louis Agassiz,* Catherine Peare's biography of the Swiss-American zoologist and geologist. In the following year *The Helen Keller Story* (Crowell) was issued.

Miss Peare is a hazel-eyed blonde, slender, with a ready smile and a good sense of humor. Travel, needlework, and swimming are her favorite leisure pastimes, though the travel is more often than not devoted to tracking down material for the next book.

References

ALA Bul 53:309+ Ap '59 por
Who's Who of American Women (1958-59)

PENNARIO, LEONARD (JOSEPH)
July 9, 1924- Concert pianist

Address: c/o Columbia Artists Management, Inc., 113 W. 57th St., New York 19

A former child prodigy who made his debut at the age of twelve, Leonard Pennario has continued to mature as a pianist who has displayed his technical dexterity in both the concert hall and on long-playing records. His popularity with concert audiences throughout the United States once led a music critic for the Cincinnati *Post* to nominate him "the people's choice."

Since 1942 Pennario has played with almost every major orchestra in the United States, has given recitals in American music centers, and has concertized extensively in Europe and the Far East. His recordings on the Capitol label have appeared regularly in *Billboard* magazine's list of the "most popular classical recordings." Pennario has given a request recital at the White House for President Dwight D. Eisenhower. He has often played on radio and television, and has performed on the sound tracks of the motion pictures *September Affair* and *Julie*.

Leonard Joseph Pennario was born in Buffalo, New York on July 9, 1924, the oldest son of Mary (Chiarello) and John D. Pennario. His father was a salesman. Leonard has a younger brother, Joseph, who is studying medicine. When Leonard was a child at the Holy Angels Parochial School in Buffalo, he showed such one-finger dexterity on the school piano that he attracted the attention of one of his teachers who recommended that he be given piano lessons. Soon after he began his lessons with Elwood G. Fischer, Leonard made his first public appearance in Buffalo in the auditorium of a local department store. He was seven years of age.

Leonard Pennario first decided to become a concert pianist when, at the age of eight, he attended a performance by Sergei Rachmaninoff. That year, in Buffalo, he gave his first full-scale recital. When Leonard was ten, the Pennario family moved to Los Angeles, where he completed his elementary school education. In 1934 he won the William Daniels Memorial Scholarship for piano and theory.

In Los Angeles, Leonard continued to study the piano, first under Olga Steeb, then under Samuel Ball. In October 1936 he made his debut with the Dallas Symphony Orchestra under the baton of Paul van Katwijk, playing the Grieg Piano Concerto in A Minor. Two years later he added to his growing reputation when he performed with the Los Angeles Philharmonic Orchestra, Otto Klemperer conducting.

Although he spent much of his free time in practising and concertizing, Leonard was active in extracurricular activities at Los Angeles High School. He belonged to the Periclean Society, the California Scholarship Federation, and the Ephebian Society. An excellent linguist, he earned the Spanish language medal.

After his graduation from high school in 1942, Pennario entered the University of Southern California in Los Angeles as a music

LEONARD PENNARIO

major. He studied under Guy Maier and learned composition under Ernst Toch and orchestration under Lucien Cailliet. During the concert season of 1942-43 he appeared with the Chicago Symphony Orchestra and the Minneapolis Symphony Orchestra.

In the spring of 1943 a call from the United States Army Air Force interrupted Pennario's college education. Assigned to the Special Services Division, he performed his concert engagements in uniform. The proceeds were turned over to the Air Force Relief Fund and the Army Emergency Relief Fund. It was also in uniform that Pennario made his debut at Carnegie Hall on November 17, 1943, where he was the featured soloist with Artur Rodzinski and the New York Philharmonic Symphony Orchestra. Virgil Thomson, writing in the New York *Herald Tribune* (November 18, 1943), called him "a sensationally brilliant pianist. . . . Last night in the Liszt E-Flat Concerto [No. 1] he took over the conduct of the work with a sweep and a power . . . that left the orchestra and its conductor panting behind him. . . ."

Sent overseas to the China-Burma-India theater of operations, Pennario performed at hospitals, Red Cross clubs, and Army bases. He not only gave concerts and fulfilled his duties as a clerk-typist but also conducted a weekly class in music appreciation and led a glee club. In an article that appeared in *Etude* magazine (June 1947) he told Anthony Drummond: "I would not have given up my service in World War II for anything," adding that servicemen "were the greatest audience in the world." In 1946 he was discharged from military service with the rank of staff sergeant and was awarded three bronze stars.

(Continued next page)

PENNARIO, LEONARD—*Continued*

When Leonard Pennario gave his first New York recital on November 6, 1946 at Town Hall, he encountered a mixed reception from the critics. Although they found imagination and technical facility in his playing, they sensed an immature lack of discipline and restraint, "a tendency to overdrive, to sacrifice everything else to speed and brilliance" (New York *Post*, November 7, 1946).

Three years later the pianist was again charged with immaturity by the music critics. Arthur V. Berger of the New York *Herald Tribune* (January 12, 1949) criticized him for over-pedaling, rhythmic distortion, and "ostensible appeals for audience response," but he also admitted that Pennario had achieved an astonishing dexterity. "Mr. Pennario has fingers second to none," commented a New York *Times* critic (December 17, 1952) after a Carnegie Hall recital, "but the artist played the sonata as if he had not the faintest idea what it was about." Meanwhile Pennario became a popular performer in both the United States and Europe, in spite of the continuing criticism that he lacked depth of interpretation. In 1947 he gave fifty-eight concerts in the United States. At the end of his second European tour, in 1952, he played to a packed concert hall in Paris.

At the Berkshire Festival in 1958, Pennario played the Liszt E-Flat Concerto with the Boston Symphony Orchestra under Charles Münch —the same concerto with which he had created such a sensation in his New York debut fifteen years before. Edward Downes of the New York *Times* (August 4, 1958) found it a "well-combed, well-bred, overcautious performance." This criticism must have had a novel ring in Pennario's ears; he had for so long been looked upon as a brilliant virtuoso who lacked restraint and depth.

Neither the old criticism of excessive virtuosity nor the new criticism of insufficient virtuosity was leveled at Pennario for his performance at Carnegie Hall on February 8, 1959. *Musical America* (March 1959) called his interpretation of Rachmaninoff's Concerto No. 2 in C Minor "a performance as notable for its sensitive awareness of musical values as it was for the ease with which he handled its enormous technical difficulties."

For Capitol Records Leonard Pennario has recorded over twenty albums, including his notable interpretations of concertos by Rachmaninoff, Liszt, and Grieg. In the motion picture *September Affair* Joan Fontaine, as a concert pianist, went through the motions at the keyboard, but it was Leonard Pennario whom audiences heard on the sound track. For the film *Julie* Pennario composed the theme music, "Midnight on the Cliffs." He has also composed several classical and popular works including: *Concerto for Piano and Orchestra* (1940); *March of the Lunatics* (1941); and *Fireflies* (1942). He is a member of the American Society of Authors, Composers, and Publishers (ASCAP).

The personable concert pianist is six feet tall, has black hair, brown eyes, and weighs 165 pounds. He plays golf and enjoys bridge, Scrabble and the theater. A talented linguist, he speaks French, Spanish, and some Italian. His religious affiliation is Roman Catholic. The conductor Dimitri Mitropoulos once said of Pennario: "Collaboration with this young musician has been one of the happiest experiences of my life. I say musician because, although he possesses the technique necessary to virtuosity, he possesses what is more important—a soul."

References

Etude 65 :305 Je '47 pors

Ewen, David ed. Living Musicians 1st sup. Wilson '57 por

Who's Who in America, 1950-51

PERCY, CHARLES H(ARTING) Sept. 27, 1919- Business executive; political leader

Address: b. Bell & Howell Co., 7100 McCormick Rd., Chicago 45, Ill.; h. 40 Devonshire Lane, Kenilworth, Ill.

During the last decade youthful Charles H. Percy has directed the vast expansion program of the Bell & Howell Company of Chicago, the world's leading manufacturer of motion-picture equipment and a principal producer of other sight and sound devices. At the age of twenty-nine, Percy succeeded Joseph H. McNabb as president of Bell & Howell, after having served with the company since 1936.

Acting on his belief that business leaders should take a part in politics, Percy has for some time been active in the affairs of the Republican party. In February 1959 he was appointed to head the party's Committee on Program and Progress, which was charged with drafting a statement of long-range policies and objectives. A "modern" Republican, Percy advocates free trade through the reduction of tariffs.

The son of Edward H. and Elizabeth (Harting) Percy, Charles Harting Percy was born in Pensacola, Florida on September 27, 1919 and grew up in the Chicago area. His father was office manager for the Bell & Howell Company, a firm established in 1907 by Donald H. Bell and Albert S. Howell for the manufacture of movie projectors. At the age of five Percy began earning money by selling magazines; at the age of seven he won a Y.M.C.A. salesmanship award. For a time, while he was attending New Trier High School in Winnetka, Illinois, he held four jobs at once.

Later, at the University of Chicago, where he was a scholarship student, Percy operated a business which grossed $150,000 a year by selling food, coal, furniture, and linen to fraternity houses and university residences. He was called "the richest kid who ever worked his way through college" by Robert M. Hutchins, then president of the university (*Time*, May 11, 1959). Percy also found time to serve as president of Alpha Delta Phi, Inter-Fraternity Council, and Owl and Serpent, an honorary society;

as captain of the water polo team; and university marshal to President Hutchins. He was awarded the B.A. degree in 1941.

Joining the students' co-operative training program of Bell & Howell in 1936 at $12 a week, Percy worked in almost every department during summer vacations from the university. Assigned in 1937 to analyze administrative practices, he drew up a detailed efficiency-building program which attracted the interest of president Joseph H. McNabb.

In the following summer Percy was a sales apprentice; he also did sales-promotion work for the Crowell-Collier Publishing Company in 1939. When he was graduated from the University of Chicago, he joined the company on a full-time basis and became manager of the company's newly created war co-ordinating department. This unit manufactured lenses, gun sights, radar devices, and other optical and electrical equipment for scientific warfare. In recognition of his efficiency in filling war contracts, Percy was named a director and assistant secretary.

In addition to working in a war industry, Percy contributed to the war effort by enlisting in the United States Navy as an apprentice seaman; he later became a commissioned officer. For his administration of Naval Air Mobile Trainees (Ordnance) units he received a commendation from Rear Admiral V. H. Ragsdale. Percy, who attained the rank of lieutenant (s.g.), was discharged in 1945.

While serving in the Navy, Percy had studied the causes of strikes in West Coast industries in his spare time. When he returned to Bell & Howell, he was promoted to the post of corporate secretary, with responsibility for industrial relations and foreign manufacturing programs. From 1946 to 1948 he took a number of courses at the Chicago-Kent College of Law.

On January 12, 1949, after the death of McNabb, Charles H. Percy was elected president of Bell & Howell. At the age of twenty-nine, he was probably the youngest chief executive officer of any major corporation in the United States. As corporate secretary, Percy had insisted that employees be given a sense of importance and belonging to the company. As president, he introduced profit sharing, greater promotion possibilities, and the establishment of boards and committees on which management and employees have discussed research, merchandising, economy, and plant safety.

To the executives he gave genuine power, on the assumption that "responsibility brings out the best in people" (*Time*, May 11, 1959). Executives are encouraged to participate in public affairs, are given free copies of Plato, Rousseau, and John Dewey, and are required to attend discussion groups with university professors and such figures as Henry Cabot Lodge and Paul Hoffman.

The company earmarked a large amount of its working capital for research to develop cameras that would be cheaper and easier to operate. A camera priced at $39.95 was the result. (Before Percy became president, the least expensive Bell & Howell camera sold at $89.) The company also began to manufacture microfilm equipment and discontinued the prac-

CHARLES H. PERCY

tice of fair trade. Within the first two years after Percy became head of the firm, sales rose from about $13,000,000 in 1948 to over $22,000,000 in 1951.

In 1952 Bell & Howell introduced a Filmosound magnetic recording projector which enabled amateurs to add sound to their own movies. In 1954 the firm acquired the Three Dimension Company of Chicago, described as the "world's foremost manufacturer of slide-projectors"; it also annexed the De Vry Corporation, commercial versions of whose joint Army-Navy heavy-duty sound projector are now used in television, education, and business. That year Bell & Howell received an honorary Oscar from the Academy of Motion Picture Arts and Sciences for its pioneering in producing movie equipment that made modern motion-picture techniques possible.

An 8mm. home movie camera, containing an electric eye that uses only the energy of solar or light rays to adjust the opening of its lens, was released for sale by Bell & Howell in 1957. Another new Bell & Howell project is an automatic remote-control slide-projector. In 1958 sales of the company rose to a record high of $59,014,500. New products, developed in the last five years, account for 82 per cent of the total 1958 sales.

For years Percy has taken an interest in Republican politics, believing that the responsibility of business leaders goes beyond "making products for a profit." As a member of the Republican national finance committee and as president of the United Republican Fund of Illinois, Percy has helped to raise large sums of money for the Republican cause. In 1956 he was chosen to attend Presidential inauguration ceremonies in Peru and Bolivia as the personal representative of President Dwight D. Eisenhower, with the rank of Special Ambassador.

(Continued next page)

PERCY, CHARLES H.—*Continued*

An advocate of Eisenhower's reciprocal trade program, Percy has said that "a liberalized trade policy . . . will make industry in this country more efficient" and that "political friendships through the centuries have always followed the trade lanes" (*Atlantic Monthly,* June 1955). Percy has always championed free trade, although he operates in an industry that faces the challenge of imports.

With Meade Alcorn, chairman of the Republican National Committee, Percy proposed the formation of a Republican Committee on Program and Progress to promulgate the party's principles and aims during the next fifteen years. The suggestion was unanimously endorsed by the Republican National Committee, and a committee composed of forty-four members representing "all segments of Republican party thinking" was announced on February 25, 1959, with Charles Percy as chairman. He promised reports that, by avoiding platitudes and formulating a clear statement, would attract independents and "discerning Democrats" to the Republican cause when national elections came around in 1960. When the first of the four reports was completed, it was eulogized by Roscoe Drummond, who wrote in the New York *Herald Tribune* (October 7, 1959): "The Percy committee report is obviously not the final answer to the Republican party's need for a restatement of program and goals, but it is an eminently good beginning. . . . It's worth reading—and pondering."

Numerous honors have been conferred on Charles H. Percy during the last ten years. In 1949 he was named one of the ten outstanding young men by the United States Junior Chamber of Commerce. He has received the University of Chicago Alumni Association's Citation for Public Service, the World Trade Award, the Management Award of the National Sales Executives, Inc., and the Thirteenth Annual Award of the Foreign Traders Association.

Charles H. Percy was a trustee of the Illinois Institute of Technology from 1950 to 1954. He was chairman of the Chicago branch of the National Conference of Christians and Jews in 1951. He is currently a chairman of the Ford Foundation's Fund for Adult Education, a member of a special studies project of the Rockefeller Brothers Fund, and a trustee of the University of Chicago.

On June 12, 1943 Charles H. Percy was married to Jeanne Valerie Dickerson. They became the parents of twin daughters, Valerie Jeanne and Sharon Lee, and a son, Roger. After his first wife died in 1948, Percy married Loraine Diane Guyer on August 27, 1950. By this marriage he has a daughter, Gail, and a son, Mark. The Percys, who are Christian Scientists, begin each day by reading the Bible and singing hymns.

Because it takes too much spare time that he could spend with his family, Percy seldom plays golf these days. He plays tennis with his children and takes to the water in a small aluminum boat with an outboard motor. Photography, skiing, swimming, fishing, and hunting remain among his outdoor activities.

References

Forbes 77:25 My 15 '56 por
N Y Times p20 F 26 '59 por
N Y World-Telegram p16 Ja 25 '55; p30 Ag 21 '58 por
Murrow, E. R., ed. This I Believe (1954)
Who's Who in America, 1958-59
World Biography (1954)

PETERSON, ROGER TORY Aug. 28, 1908- Ornithologist; author; lecturer; artist
Address: b. c/o Houghton Mifflin Co., 2 Park St., Boston, Mass.; h. Old Lyme, Conn.

The growing popularity of bird watching as a hobby in the United States may in large measure be attributed to Roger Tory Peterson, an ornithologist whose writings and paintings have led to his being compared to John James Audubon. Peterson also teaches the enjoyment of nature study through his lectures, films, and photographs. Although he is best known for his work on birds, including *Birds Over America* (1948) and *A Bird Watcher's Anthology* (1957), he is a naturalist with knowledge of many subjects and the editor of Houghton Mifflin Company's Field Guide Series.

Roger Tory Peterson was born in Jamestown, New York on August 28, 1908, the son of Charles Gustav and Henrietta (Bader) Peterson. His father had come to the United States at the age of four from Värmland, Sweden. At the time of Roger's birth, he was a craftsman in the Art Metal Construction Company, one of Jamestown's office equipment factories.

When Roger Peterson was in the seventh grade, his science teacher, Miss Blanche Hornbeck, organized an Audubon Junior Club. As a result, the eleven-year-old boy, who had earlier been troublesome in school, acquired an absorbing interest in birds, which he feels "stemmed from the fact that these winged creatures were symbols of freedom in his maladjusted youth" (*Natural History,* May 1956).

In order to study birds he often made field trips around Lake Chautauqua, near Jamestown. His illustrations of what he found revealed ability in drawing, and after leaving high school he attended the Art Students League of New York City, in 1927-28, and the National Academy of Design in New York, from 1929 to 1931. John Sloan and Kimon Nicolaides were among his teachers. In 1931, when the depression ended his art training, he took a position as instructor in science and art at the Rivers School in Brookline, Massachusetts, where he remained until 1934.

During these years of teaching Peterson continued to pursue bird identification as a hobby and became expert in the subject. Encouraged by his friend William Vogt, the well-known ecologist, Peterson wrote magazine articles on recognizing birds and later put his methods in book form with his own illustrations. His *Field*

Guide to the Birds; Giving Field Marks of All Species Found in Eastern North America was published by Houghton Mifflin in 1934.

An immediate success, the book won for Peterson the highest award in the field of ornithology, the Brewster Memorial Medal, conferred by the American Ornithologists Union because of the manual's original contribution to the subject of bird identification and because it had interested many people in birds. At least a third of a million copies of *Field Guide to the Birds* have been sold. In his second revised edition, in 1947, Peterson made extensive changes and increased the number of illustrations, especially those in color. A New York *Times* reviewer (September 21, 1947) thought the new field guide "easily the best of its kind ever put together."

Peterson's first book led to his becoming education director in 1934 of the National Audubon Society in New York. One of his duties was to rewrite the Junior Audubon leaflets that had first interested him in birds. From 1934 to 1943 he was also art editor of *Audubon Magazine,* of which he is at present a contributing editor. In his free time he wrote *A Field Guide to Western Birds* (Houghton Mifflin, 1941).

In World War II the methods used by the Army and Navy in teaching plane spotting were influenced by Peterson's system of bird identification, which is based on shape, pattern, and distinguishing marks or characteristic features. Peterson, himself, served from 1943 to 1945 in the Army Engineer Corps at Fort Belvoir, Virginia, where he prepared technical manuals on defusing land mines, building bridges, and other subjects. Toward the close of the war he was assigned to the Air Corps to study the effects of D.D.T.

Since the war Peterson has traveled in many parts of Europe and the United States and in Central America and Africa to collect material and take pictures for his articles and books and for his lectures for the Audubon Screen Tour. Among the magazines in which his articles, photographs, and paintings have appeared are *Life, Audubon Magazine, Nature Magazine,* and *National Geographic Magazine.*

Birds Over America (Dodd, 1948), another account of Peterson's bird hunts, has 150 photographs. It was described in the *Saturday Review of Literature* (December 11, 1948) as combining "the knowledge and experience of the professional with the innocence and fresh delight of the amateur." His *How to Know the Birds* (Houghton, 1949) is illustrated with his own line drawings and silhouettes. Peterson, whose prints of birds decorate the walls of many homes, has also illustrated several books about birds by other authors.

As editor since 1946 of Houghton Mifflin Company's Field Guide Series, he has become known for his work in several branches of natural history, including minerals, flowers, trees, mammals, and reptiles. He also reveals himself as a naturalist with many interests besides birds in *Wildlife in Color* (Houghton, 1951), sponsored by the National Wildlife Federation in Washington, D.C.

ROGER TORY PETERSON

When traveling in Europe and preparing books on birds of Europe, Peterson had been assisted by his friend James Fisher, the British ornithologist, whom Peterson invited on a tour of North America. The two men set out from Newfoundland on April 1953, went south along the Appalachian highlands and East Coast to the Florida keys, across the Gulf States to Mexico, and up the Pacific coast to the seal islands of Alaska. Their account of their 100-day, 30,000-mile journey is given in *Wild America* (Houghton, 1955), which, Edwin Way Teale observed, "is a bountiful book both in text and illustrations, the latter superb examples of Mr. Peterson's scratchboard art. It is a long book, but not too long. The reader ends with the feeling of having been one of the party, of having joined two fortunate naturalists during great days of their lives" (New York *Times,* October 16, 1955).

Eighty-four selections from the writings of great naturalists and explorers like Darwin, Thoreau, and Burroughs make up *The Bird Watcher's Anthology* (Harcourt, 1957), which Peterson compiled and edited. David McCord recommended it in *Saturday Review* (December 7, 1957): "I can think of no higher praise than to say that it has in its own way something of the magic of de la Mare's *Come Hither*: in other words, it is a creative work controlled and informed by the editor. It has vitality and excitement. . . . It is a beautiful book."

For exemplary nature writing, Peterson was awarded the John Burroughs Medal in 1952. He received an honorary D.Sc. degree in 1952 from Franklin and Marshall College. He was a delegate to the eleventh International Ornithological Congress in Basel, Switzerland in 1954. He is a director of the National Audubon Society, a Fellow of the American Ornithologists Union and the Linnaean Society of New York, and a member of the American Nature Study

PETERSON, ROGER TORY—*Continued*

Society (former president), the British Ornithologists Union, and other organizations. His clubs are the Nuttall (Cambridge, Massachusetts), Cosmos, Baird, Biologists Field, and Century Association.

Roger Tory Peterson was married on July 29, 1943 to Barbara Coulter, who had been employed in the film and photography department of the National Audubon Society. They have two sons, Tory and Lee. (His first marriage, on December 19, 1936 to Mildred Warner Washington, ended in divorce.) Peterson's house, on a fifty-five-acre estate in Old Lyme, Connecticut, is close to a forest where many birds and other wildlife find a home. In *Natural History* (May 1956) Cedric Larson noted Peterson's "almost boyish enthusiasm for his work" and pictured him as a man who "loves nature in a philosophical way, yet . . . sees natural phenomena in a lucid, objective, and realistic manner."

References

    Twentieth Century Authors (First Supplement, 1955)
    Who Knows—and What (1954)
    Who's Who in America, 1958-59
    World Biography (1954)

PEVSNER, ANTOINE (pĕfs'nĕr) Jan. 18, 1886- Sculptor; artist

Address: b. 25 rue Edgar Quinet, Malakoff (Seine), France; h. 5 rue Jean Sicard, Paris 15°, France

From his early experiments with motion and space to his full development as a giant of modern sculpture and painting, Pevsner has charted new paths in the world of art. With his brother, Naum Gabo, he founded the constructivist school, and his works in glass, bronze, brass, and other metals are in the permanent collections of many of the world's principal museums.

"We realize our constructions in such a way that the air penetrating them becomes an integral part of the work," Pevsner and Gabo have written of their constructivist art. "We use space as a new plastic element, a substance which ceases, for us, to be an abstraction, and becomes a malleable matter. . . . Moreover, our constructions carry their own shadows and light . . . while they augment the variations of color thanks to materials of different tones."

Antoine Pevsner was born in Orel, Russia on January 18, 1886 to Agrippine-Fanny (Osersky) and Boris Pevsner. His father was an industrialist interested in copper refining. His two elder brothers became engineers and his younger brother, Naum, who changed his surname to Gabo, is an equally well-known sculptor.

With encouragement from his family, Pevsner, at the age of sixteen, went to study at the School of Beaux Arts in Kiev. The instruction that he received interested him less than the Pechersky Monastery and the city's

medieval art with its inverted perspective, which conveyed mobility by the arrangement of planes instead of figures in action. At the Academy of Beaux Arts in St. Petersburg, Pevsner was again disappointed academically, but profoundly impressed by the Russian and Byzantine icons and architecture that he saw in his travels.

Attracted by the art of impressionism, cubism, and Fauvism, Pevsner left for Paris in 1911. He was stirred by the beauty of the Eiffel Tower and by paintings to which he was exposed. Following a brief return to Russia, Pevsner again visited Paris in 1913. Through his friendship with Alexander Archipenko and Amedeo Modigliani, he was inspired to paint his first abstract canvas, *Study of a Head.*

In 1915 Pevsner joined his brother, Naum Gabo, who was in Oslo, Norway. It was there that Pevsner painted *Carnival* and *The Absinthe,* which now hang in the Moscow State Museum of Modern Western Art. He was drawn to sculpture and with Gabo he experimented in creating a new art, which, they explained, would be "capable of utilizing emptiness and liberating us from the compact mass."

Like many contemporary Russian artists, Pevsner and Gabo returned home after the Bolshevik Revolution, which in its first phase was an important stimulus to experimentation in the arts. Pevsner was appointed a professor of the School of Beaux Arts in Moscow. But by 1920 the Soviet state was demanding the subservience of art to political ideology. In bitter opposition, the brothers Pevsner and Gabo exhibited their work independently and issued the "Constructivist Manifesto" in 1920. It claimed for art an autonomous validity as an expression of man's search for higher truth and announced their intention to continue to work in constructivism.

When Soviet artists organized the First Russian Art Exhibition in Berlin, the brothers used the showing as a pretext to escape from the Soviet regime. Since then Pevsner has lived in Paris and became a French citizen in 1930. In the Berlin show the brothers' work indicated an almost complete departure from representation and tradition in sculpture. Their constructions are related to the world of machinery and architecture instead of to nature. No longer statues, the constructivist sculptures are pictures in three-dimensional space liberated from gravity and mass. Thus, the artist is free to react to landscapes, panoramas, and architecture rather than somatic forms.

The lyrical constructivism of Pevsner and Gabo was brought to a large audience when they were commissioned by Sergei Diaghilev to create the sets for the ballet *La Chatte* in 1927. Several years later Pevsner and Gabo became leaders in the international movement in nonfigurative art. In 1933 Pevsner wrote his manifesto, "Nonfigurative Art," which appeared in *Abstraction-Création.* During the war he worked in seclusion in his Paris studio.

"Developable surfaces" became Pevsner's primary technique after 1940. By a process of extreme heat over a period of several months, rods of copper, bronze, or brass are soldered together at different angles to create curves and arcs. Oxidized to various tones of red, silver, blue, and gold, "they shimmer with light, capturing and channeling it along the curved surface even as the curves 'capture' their enclosed space. In these works Pevsner most fully realizes his aim of making light and space 'malleable' and 'concrete'" (*Arts,* February 1957).

A new art group, Réalités Nouvelles, was organized by Pevsner, Albert Gleizes, and Auguste Herbin in 1946 and held its first show in 1947. In 1953 Pevsner was elected vice-president of the Salon des Réalités Nouvelles, and in 1956 he was elected honorary president of Réalités Nouvelles. In some of his recent creations Pevsner has further developed and changed his style. His sheets of metal are now rolled and turned into bristling and pointed shapes. Their symmetry does not prevent them from having a contorted, unconstructivist violence.

The use of simultaneity in Pevsner's art is "an insistent, repetitious projection of similar forms set at precise spatial intervals, and this manner of building a surface through a series of simultaneous elements is a constant element in his work. The heads in his figurative pieces give an impression of kinesthetic motion through this echoing plastic interval rather than by implying an object viewed from several angles at once" (*Arts,* February 1957).

"Our guiding idea has been a synthesis of the plastic arts, painting, sculpture and architecture," Pevsner and Gabo wrote in 1947. "Our principles, published in our youth at Moscow in the form of a manifesto in 1920, have remained at the base of our work: Art should be based on two fundamental elements, space and time. Volume is not the sole spatial expression. Kinetic and dynamic elements can permit the expression of real time; static rhythms are insufficient. Art must cease to be imitative in order to discover new forms."

Some of Pevsner's more important exhibitions have been held in galleries in New York, Paris, Stockholm, Zurich, Antwerp, and Amsterdam. His work is housed in the permanent collections of leading museums in the United States and in Europe, including the Museum of Modern Art in New York, Musée National d'Art Moderne in Paris, and the Tate Gallery in London.

In 1920 Antoine Pevsner was married to Virginie de Voinoff-Chilingarian, a singer. After having interviewed Pevsner in Paris early in 1957, Rosamond Bernier described him as "a small slight man with the high forehead and the pallor of an indoor intellectual—receding grey hair, the ghost of a white moustache hardly visible."

Clement Greenberg has called the art of Pevsner "a challenge in its totality—not only in its aesthetic, but also in what it says. The term 'heroic' seems very applicable when we see how greatly this artist risks being misunderstood in his passionate and rigorous endeavor to persuade us to change the world so

Sabine Weiss, Paris
ANTOINE PEVSNER

that it will correspond to our true and not our rationalized desires" (*Nation,* April 17, 1948).

References

Art N 47:22+ Mr '58 por
Drouin, R. ed. A. Pevsner (1947)
Naum Gabo and A. Pevsner (Museum of Modern Art, 1948)

PHILLIPS, MRS. ROBERT J(OHN) Feb. 17, 1903- Organization official
Address: b. League of Women Voters of the United States, 1026 17th St., N.W., Washington 6, D.C.; h. Dunham Rd., St. Charles, Ill.

The League of Women Voters of the United States, a nonpartisan organization, has been promoting effective and intelligent political participation since 1920. It has done this by disseminating facts and studies on candidates and current problems and by taking positive positions on important issues without commenting on personalities and parties. Under the presidency of Mrs. Robert J. Phillips, who was elected to head the 128,000-member organization on April 24, 1958, the group has given strong support to the mutual security program of the United States, foreign economic and technical assistance, active participation by the United States in the United Nations, and examination of the coverage of the Federal loyalty-security program with a view toward limiting it to sensitive jobs.

Active in the league since 1926, Mrs. Phillips has held various posts in its Illinois and national organizations. She believes that the group must foster an emphasis upon "individual responsibility for civic work in the community."

Mrs. Phillips was born Ruth Louise Schertz on February 17, 1903 in Fairbury, Illinois to Joseph B. Schertz, a farmer, and the former

Bradford Bachrach

MRS. ROBERT J. PHILLIPS

Mary Louise Hostettler. She has a sister, Mrs. J. Y. Masterson, an elementary school teacher in Fairbury. Her brother, Carl A. Schertz, was killed in World War II.

At Fairbury Township High School Ruth was a member of the Drama Club. Following her graduation in 1921, she attended Knox College in Galesburg, Illinois, where she was elected to the student council board and the Women's Self-Governing Board and was president of the Y.W.C.A. and the Mortar Board (1926). The B.A. degree was conferred upon her in 1926. While still in her senior year, Ruth Schertz joined the League of Women Voters and after her graduation became a staff member of the organization in Illinois. She has said that her parents influenced her in the choice of her career.

On June 16, 1928 she was married to Robert John Phillips. Mrs. Phillips remained in her job until her first child was born in 1933, and then continued as a member of the league. When the family moved to Elgin, Illinois, she was instrumental in organizing a local league in that city and also served on its board. Later the family moved to Glen Ellyn; she joined the league there and was voters' service chairman and president. She is now 'a member of the Geneva-St. Charles league.

In Glen Ellyn Mrs. Phillips worked to develop the league position and its relations with the Du Page County board of supervisors. In the late 1930's, she recalls, "we made a detailed plan for regular visits at county board meetings, just to learn how local government functioned. This was the beginning of a 'Go-See' project which blossomed into the establishment of one of the first county health units in Illinois, the solicitation of league-trained women to man its advisory council, and the establishment of a relationship of mutual help and understanding between a group of elected offi-

cials and an organization working in the public interest." She has said, "The results which came from a step-by-step steady building upon facts will never fail to impress me."

In the Illinois league Mrs. Phillips served as a member of its board from 1945, was vice-president (1945 to 1949), treasurer (1949 to 1953), and president (1953 to 1957). She was appointed to the national board in May 1957. Elected national president on April 24, 1958, Mrs. Phillips succeeded Mrs. John G. Lee (see *C.B.*, July 1950) on the following day for a two-year term.

An outgrowth of the National American Woman Suffrage Association, the league came into being when, in 1921, the adoption of the Nineteenth Amendment to the Constitution left the suffrage group with no further reason for existence. The paramount need then was the fostering of political education; for this purpose the league was founded. It is a volunteer organization whose officers serve without compensation. The present annual budget of approximately $1,300,000 is expended only on league work and staff members. It is "nonpartisan. It takes action in support of or in opposition to selected governmental issues, but it does not support or oppose candidates nor support or oppose political parties" (*Facts about the League of Women Voters*, 1958). However, the league does encourage individual members and the public to participate in the affairs of the party of their preference.

The *National Voter*, a monthly, and *Report from the Hill*, a monthly issued only during sessions of Congress, and many pamphlets are published by the league; it also distributes film strips. These contain information on issues to help the electorate cast an informed vote on candidates. At election time the league conducts meetings where members of the public can hear and question the various candidates, and it works to get out the vote. The organization now numbers 128,000 members in 1,056 local leagues in the forty-nine states, Hawaii, and the District of Columbia. The Carrie Chapman Catt Memorial Foundation was established by the league to educate foreign women visiting the United States in democratic techniques and citizenship so that they may practise these in their native countries.

The league takes its positions on important issues only after careful research and study of facts and has a record of success in helping to accomplish many of the proposals it espouses. For example, in the decade from 1937 to 1947 the league was in the forefront in developing the civil service system of the federal government (*Ten Eventful Years*, 1947). It spearheaded reform of the Food and Drug Act and supported several measures embodied in the Social Security Act, entry of displaced persons, and civilian control of atomic energy. The league has also worked for improvements in municipal government organization, public schools, housing, health services, tax systems, state constitutions, state legislative procedures, and child welfare laws.

In 1959 it is devoted to the principle of international cooperation; self-government for the

District of Columbia and extension of national suffrage to its citizens; those national water policies and practices which promote coordinated administration, equitable financing, and regional and river basins planning; legal protection of citizens in their right to vote; protection of minority groups against discrimination; removal of legal and administrative discriminations against women; and fiscal and monetary policies that promote a stable and expanding economy.

Mrs. Robert J. Phillips' community interests extend beyond league affairs; she has served on the village board of Glen Ellyn (1941-45) and been active in the Community Chest, P.T.A., Girl Scouts, and Y.W.C.A. Her hobbies are spectator sports, bridge, gardening, reading, the theatre, and, of course, the league, which, she believes, is "recreation in the fullest meaning—creating anew." She has hazel eyes, gray hair, formerly dark-brown, weighs 120 pounds, and stands five feet three inches.

Ruth and Robert Phillips have two children, Carol (Mrs. Gary E. Brown) and David B. Phillips. In early 1958 the family's 100-year-old home, "Windswept," set on six acres of land near Chicago, burned to the ground. A new house is now being built to replace it.

PHILLIPS, RUTH *See* Phillips, Mrs. Robert J.

PHOUI SANANIKONE (pwē să-nǎn′ē-kōn) Sept. 6, 1903- Premier of Laos
Address: b. National Assembly, Vientiane, Laos

Since he became Premier in August 1958, Phoui Sananikone has been trying to defend the newly attained independence of Laos in Southeast Asia from Communist penetration and corrupt officialdom. In January 1959 he was given special powers in order to cope with Communist subversion and invasion and to develop his backward nation. Earlier, Phoui Sananikone was Premier in 1950-51, held various cabinet posts, was President of the National Assembly, a leader of the resistance movement during World War II, and served as a government administrator.

Phoui Sananikone was born in Vientiane, the capital of Laos, on September 6, 1903. After his graduation at the age of twenty from Pavie College in Laos he entered government work. When he scored the highest mark in competitive tests similar to American civil service examinations, he was appointed a district administrator. Then, in 1941 he was named Governor of the province of Upper Mekong in Northern Laos. Before the Japanese invaded his country in World War II, he had reached the rank of *Chaokhoueng,* the highest classification for government administrators in Laos.

As Laotian deputy commander against the Japanese during World War II, he led the resistance movement in northern Laos. In 1945 French troops were forced to retreat from Laos, and Phoui had to leave the country with them. He went first to China, then later to Calcutta, India. The French returned to Laos when the

Leo Rosenthal

PHOUI SANANIKONE

Japanese government surrendered in the summer of 1945.

Laos is a monarchy with a dynasty that dates back to the fourteenth century. The country accepted French protection in 1893 and became a member of the French Indochinese Union in 1899. On May 11, 1947 Laos became a constitutional monarchy, with King Sisavang Vong (see *C.B., April 1954*) reigning but not ruling. Several of the King's sons by his fifteen wives are playing significant roles in politics. Prince Souvanna Phouma leads the conservatives, while his half-brother Prince Souphanou Vong leads Neo Lao Haksat, a communist party.

Laos, Cambodia, and Vietnam became Associated States within the French Union by the treaty of July 19, 1949. This agreement was followed by the Lao-French Association and Friendship Treaty signed on October 22, 1953 which granted Laos complete control over its international and external affairs. Leaving administrative service, Phoui Sananikone entered politics in 1947. In August he was elected to the First National Assembly, representing the province of Paksé. He became President of the Assembly in December 1947 and was re-elected to that position in 1948 and 1949.

Prince Souvannarath, as the first Premier, appointed Phoui to his cabinet in March 1947 as Minister of Education, Health, and Social Welfare, and he served until March 1949.

When King Sisavang Vong named Phoui Sananikone to form a government in February 1950, the new Premier immediately increased taxation to ease the financial crisis brought about by the gradual withdrawal of the French. Before this time France had underwritten 70 per cent of the expenses of the government. Phoui Sananikone also presided over the Laos delegation at the Inter-States Conference in Pau, France in July 1950.

(Continued next page)

PHOUI SANANIKONE—*Continued*

Re-elected to the Assembly in August 1951 as deputy from the province of Vientiane, he continued as Prime Minister until October, when his government resigned. He again scored a victory at the polls in 1955. In the years between 1951 and 1958, he was Deputy Premier and held various portfolios: Interior, National Defense, and Youth and Sport, 1951 to 1954; Interior and Foreign Affairs, March to November 1954; Foreign Affairs, December 1954 to August 1958.

Because of their poverty and vulnerable position, the Indochinese states had been the target of Communist military operations for almost eight years, beginning in 1945. On July 21, 1954 the Communist Vietminh forces and French Union commanders concluded a cease-fire agreement. On that day the Laotian government and the Vietminh also signed a truce. As a result of these agreements, an International Commission was formed to supervise the armistice in this area.

However, the Pathet Lao army, a local Communist group, continued to terrorize Laos. On September 18 the group raided Phoui Sananikone's home and killed Minister of Defense Kou Voravong who was visiting there. Pathet Lao and Laotian officials reached a cease-fire treaty on October 11, 1955. Most rebel troops were integrated into the Royal Laotian Army, and Samneua and Phongsaly, two northern provinces which they held, were relinquished on November 19, 1957. At that time a coalition government, with pro-Communist ministers, was sworn into office.

Laos is the poorest and least populated of the Indochinese states. Although its nearly 90,000 square miles make it roughly equivalent to the British Isles in size, its population only numbers 3,000,000. It has few developed resources. A nation of high mountains, heat-baked plateaus, and narrow tropical valleys, Laos exports about $3,000,000 worth of cattle, teak, benzoin, and opium by expensive transportation and must import $31,000,000 worth of food and other items.

The United States extended approximately $45,000,000 worth of aid in each of the years of 1955, 1956, and 1957, and about $35,000,000 in 1958. The General Accounting Office of the United States released a report on November 8, 1958 which charged that this assistance program had been hampered by profiteering and mismanagement. After a two-year investigation, a House of Representatives Government Operations subcommittee asserted in 1959 that the aid project gave Laos more assistance than its economy could absorb; excessive grants doubled the cost of living from 1953 to 1958; much of the waste stemmed from maintaining a 25,000-troop army when a 13,000-man force would suffice; and there had been much speculation, profiteering, and corruption (New York *Times,* June 15, 1959). United States foreign aid was again granted to Laos in 1959.

The founder of the Independent party in Laos, Phoui Sananikone served as its president until it merged with the right-wing Nationalist party and became the Rally of the Lao People,

a conservative coalition group. Prince Souvanna Phouma resigned as Premier in 1958 to become president of the party, and Phoui became vice-president. In the 1958 elections, the party controlled thirty-six of the fifty-nine seats in the National Assembly. Neo Lao Haksat, formerly the Pathet Lao party, won one third of the seats.

On August 18, 1958 a non-Communist government headed by Phoui Sananikone was approved. The Prime Minister assured his nation that he would resist all Communist attempts at subversion, remain faithful to the free world, and "pursue a policy of strict austerity and combat corruption" (New York *Herald Tribune,* September 2, 1958). He instituted a currency reform which "brought a halt to the scandalous abuse of U.S. aid" (*Time,* January 26, 1959).

At the beginning of 1959, it was reported that Communist North Vietnamese troops had penetrated nine miles into Laos territory. As a result, Phoui asked for special powers to carry out a program including a commission to alter the constitution; improvement of conditions in rural areas; agricultural and economic development; construction of roads, schools, wells, and small dams; extension of health services; and an attempt to settle the border troubles with North Vietnam on the basis of peaceful co-existence.

By a vote of 28 to 16 in the National Assembly, Phoui Sananikone was authorized on January 15, 1959 to reorganize his cabinet and to govern for a year by decree and without interference from the legislature. The Assembly gave him what amounted to quasi-dictatorial rights in order to deal with Communism and other problems (Washington *Post and Times Herald,* June 3, 1959). Thereupon, Phoui Sananikone dissolved the Assembly and on January 24 formed a new government including several army officers.

Phoui Sananikone renounced in the following month the 1954 Geneva agreements because the International Commission had failed to maintain peace. He said that Laos would depend directly on the U.N. to arbitrate and prevent disputes. On May 17, 1959 a hard core Pathet Lao battalion of 750 men surrendered after refusing to be integrated into the army. The battalion had wanted to keep its identity as a unit under its own commander. Prince Souphanou Vong was placed under house arrest and later arrested for subversion. Intermittent guerrilla attacks increased in 1959 and became a large-scale rebellion.

Phoui Sananikone was married to Nang Sida in 1925. Their son, Viengkeo, is deceased. He is six feet tall, handsome, stocky, and muscular. His decorations include the Grand Cross of the Royal Order of the Million Elephants and the White Parasol, Ordre du Règne en Vermeil, Grand Cross of the Royal Order of Cambodia, Commander of the French Legion of Honor, and French Croix de Guerre with palms.

Reference

International Year Book and Statesmen's Who's Who, 1959

PIEL, GERARD Mar. 1, 1915- Publisher
Address: b. 415 Madison Ave., New York 17;
h. 320 Central Park West, New York 25

For a century *Scientific American* chronicled
for the layman the progress of the industrial
revolution in the United States. In 1948 the
magazine was taken over by three men, still in
their thirties, who transformed the magazine
into the leading nontechnical journal of the
atomic revolution.

One of the three men was Gerard Piel, who
was born March 1, 1915, in Woodmere, Long
Island, the son of William F. J. and Loretto
(Scott) Piel. His father was the late president
of Piel Brothers, and he was the grandson of
Michael Piel, co-founder of the Brooklyn
brewery. One of six children, he was encouraged by his father—whom he has described
as "a very literary and cultured intellectual"—
to become a writer.

Piel attended Andover and Harvard, where
he majored in history, and became for a time
business manager of the *Harvard Advocate*. He
and four other editorial officers resigned, however, after they published two articles condemned by the police as obscene. All copies of
the issue were destroyed, and the group was
reprimanded by an assistant district attorney
as "inexperienced boys, suffering from delusions of grandeur."

At Harvard Piel was also a member of the
wrestling team. A Phi Beta Kappa student, he
was graduated *magna cum laude* in 1937. Soon
after, on February 4, 1938, he was married to
Mary Tapp Bird of Tenafly, New Jersey, who
was descended from a colonel in the American
Revolution.

Piel had spent a summer working as a cub
reporter on the Grand Forks (North Dakota)
Herald. He likes to tell the story of how he
convinced the publisher that he should write
some creative news stories. "I was given an
assignment to look at the potato crops in the
Red River Valley. I wrote a story telling what
a splendidly big crop of potatoes was growing
there. It started an uproar among the farmers,
who accused the paper of being in league with
the potato buyers to depress the price of
potatoes."

After graduation, Piel worked briefly for the
J. Sterling Getschal agency. Then he went to
Time, Inc., as an office boy and two years later
became science editor of *Life* magazine. Although he had never taken a science course in
college, he read many books and magazines on
the subject, and made the department one of the
most respected on the magazine.

In the process, Piel came to the conclusion
that although a large market for science reporting existed, there was no publication to which
the layman and nonspecialist could turn for
scientific information. Together with Dennis
Flanagan, who was war and technology editor
at *Life,* and Donald H. Miller, Jr., a management consultant and close friend of both, he
conceived the idea of a magazine to meet that
need.

In 1945 Piel left *Life* to work for Henry J.
Kaiser (about whom he had written a long *Life*

GERARD PIEL

article in 1942) as an assistant in guiding the
company through the trials of postwar reorganization. "It was a year and a half postgraduate
course in business," Piel said. During this
period he and his two collaborators held conferences and did research on the technical problems of producing their projected magazine.

In 1947 the three organized a management
partnership, and Piel, who had left Kaiser, set
out to get financial backing. He said he did not
have "a dime of capital to invest at the beginning"—neither he nor any of his family is active
in the Piel Brothers brewery. During the long
search for capital he turned out a number of
articles for *Life* and other magazines.

After more than a year he had raised
$450,000, mainly from Lessing J. Rosenwald, a
former board chairman of Sears, Roebuck;
John Hay Whitney (who recently bought the
New York *Herald Tribune*); and Frasier W.
McCann of the Woolworth family. A large
number of small backers included Bernard
Baruch, Gerard Swope (a past president of
General Electric), and Royal Little, board chair-
man of Textron.

For slightly under $40,000 Piel and his two
partners purchased *Scientific American* in January 1948. Once highly respected, it still enjoyed a good reputation, but had gone steadily
downhill. Of the 40,000 remaining subscriptions, only about 2,000 were paid, and the one
advertiser cancelled on their first day.

The magazine they had visualized would draw
on leading scientists as writers, with the editors
as journalistic middlemen to make their work
understandable to both the technical specialist
and the intelligent layman. At first it was difficult to get some scientists to co-operate.

"Their ideas have so often been misrepre-
sented or oversimplified by reporters," Piel said,
"that they've become very shy of the press."
Scientists who knew him from his days at

PIEL, GERARD—*Continued*

Life magazine were the first to submit contributions. Since then many scientists have joined his roster, among them seventeen Nobel prize winners.

In the first year 3,500,000 promotional pieces were mailed out In the first two years the magazine required five financings totaling $1,000,000. Advertising went up to forty-five pages per issue, each year revenues more than doubled, and the break-even point was passed in January 1951. In 1952 revenues passed $1,000,000, and by 1958 circulation reached 168,649. Nearly all the subscribers were men: engineers, scientists, industrial executives, researchers, teachers, and students.

In March 1950 Piel again encountered the censorship he had known as a college undergraduate. The Atomic Energy Commission held that material in an article about the hydrogen bomb violated security. A representative of the commission went to the plant where the magazine was printed and supervised the destruction of printed copies, proofs, plates, and Linotype slugs, in which the offending material appeared.

The article, with the deletions insisted upon by the commission, was published in the April 1950 issue. It had been written by Dr. Hans A. Bethe, Cornell University physics professor who was from 1943 to 1946 chief of the theoretical physics division of the Los Alamos Scientific Laboratory.

Piel strongly protested the commission's action. Much of the material deleted, he said, was either declassified or had never been classified, and much of it had been widely disseminated in the press. "Strict compliance with the commission's policies," he said "would mean that we could not teach physics."

Later that month Piel told a meeting of the American Society of Newspaper Editors in Washington, D. C.: "Secrecy has poisoned the relations of the A.E.C with the scientific community of America" The New York *Times,* commenting editorially on the speech, said (May 7, 1950) : "He discussed the need and the dangers of secrecy without heat and with good sense."

In May 1956 Piel testified before a House government information subcommittee in Washington on governmental handling and suppression of the results of scientific research. He cited the long history of simultaneous scientific discovery to show the fallacy of national security through secrecy. Enemy scientists may be held back, he said, but "they will ultimately discover these things on their own."

At the tenth annual Roosevelt Day dinner of the New York State Americans for Democratic Action on February 1, 1958, he restated the theme. "In our obsession with secrecy during the past fifteen years we have surely disrupted the work of American scientists," he said, "but we have not prevented scientists in other countries from discovering the secrets we were trying to hide."

Gerard Piel is a slender, athletic, and high-keyed man, who moves quickly. Soft-spoken and self-confident, he is resourceful when facing taxing situations. Although he seldom lapses into profanity, he likes to tell stories, especially those that exploit his ability to imitate accents.

On June 24, 1956, Piel was married for the second time, to Miss Eleanor Virden of Santa Monica, California, a Los Angeles trial lawyer. They live in New York, in a four-room penthouse apartment. He has two sons by his first marriage—Jonathan, twenty, and Samuel, eighteen—who attend Harvard.

In 1956 Piel received an honorary Doctor of Science degree from Lawrence College in Appleton, Wisconsin. He is a member of the board of trustees of the American Museum of Natural History, a director of the American Civil Liberties Union, and a Fellow of the American Academy of Arts and Sciences. He belongs to the Engineers Club and the Harvard Club of New York City.

References

Christian Sci Mon p13 Ap 16 '53
Newsweek 39:59 Mr 31 '52
Ptr Ink 265:75+ O 10 '58
Who's Who in America, 1958-59

PIRE, (DOMINIQUE) GEORGES (HENRI), REV. (pir) Feb. 10, 1910- Dominican priest

Address: b. 35 Rue du Marché, Huy, Belgium; h. 28 Plaine de la Sarte, Huy, Belgium

Since 1949 Father Georges Pire, a tall, white-cassocked Dominican priest from Belgium, has dedicated himself to the cause of giving the refugees of Europe a new start in life through shelter, land, and work. For his achievement the Nobel Committee in Oslo, Norway awarded him the 1958 Nobel Peace Prize in November 1958. Carrying a stipend of $41,250, the award is given annually to whoever "shall have most or best promoted the fraternity of nations." Simple and self-effacing, Father Pire claims to be no more than "a man looking at his brothers and trying hard to get men to look at *their* brothers."

In 1949 Father Pire founded a charitable organization called Aid to Displaced Persons, which tries to rehabilitate the so-called "hard core" or "residue" of refugees from Eastern Europe who are unable to immigrate to Western Europe because of age, illness, or other disabilities. The program works in three ways: West European families are encouraged to sponsor (by corresponding with and helping) refugee families; homes for aged refugees are established; and "European Villages" are built near large cities to give refugee families the normal life not possible in camps for displaced persons.

In his labors Father Pire is guided by the principles that love is the most important thing on earth; that each human being has an infinite value; that strength lies in unity; that there is too much *talking about* Europe and not enough action; and that one must not destroy, but construct.

Dominique Georges Henri Pire was born in Dinant, Belgium on February 10, 1910 to Georges and Françoise (Laurent) Pire. His father was a local official. He has one brother, Charles, and two sisters, Bertha and Nellie. He first studied classics and philosophy at the Collège de Bellevue at Dinant, and when he was eighteen entered the Dominican monastery of La Sarte in Huy, Belgium. From 1932 to 1936 he attended the Dominican university in Rome, the Collegio Angelico, from which he received the Doctor of Sacred Theology degree in 1936 for his study of the influence of Stoicism on early Christian thought. He had been ordained in 1934. He studied social and political science for a year at the University of Louvain in Belgium, and in 1937 began teaching moral philosophy and sociology at the Huy monastery. He also served as curé to the impoverished agricultural laborers of the parish of La Sarte. In 1938 he established an organization to help the poor children of Belgium.

When the Nazis overran his native country at the beginning of World War II, Father Pire joined the underground. He served as a chaplain for the resistance movement, and helped to establish an escape system for downed Allied fliers and an intelligence service for the Allied countries. For his work he was awarded the Belgian War Cross, with palms, the Medal of Resistance, and the Medal of National Reconnaissance.

After World War II Father Pire began setting up camps for French and Belgian refugee children. A turning point came in his life on February 27, 1949 when he heard Colonel Edward F. Squadrille, a young American official with the United Nations Relief and Rehabilitation Agency, give a talk about the plight of Europe's displaced persons. Before the colonel left, he gave the names of forty-seven displaced persons living in the Tyrol; everybody in his audience took one of the names and promised to write.

In April 1949 Father Pire visited the Austrian camps for displaced persons which that spring sheltered around 60,000 refugees. He tried to obtain information about the refugees and also looked for friends who would establish and maintain contact with them. Out of this grew the so-called "sponsoring" movement which in 1958 numbered about 15,000 persons in twenty countries who were "sponsoring" about 15,000 refugees. The simple formula that Father Pire prescribed was: "A little time, packages, money, and much love." Soon he established a home for aged refugees in Huy, then three more homes in other towns in Belgium. Before long he saw that material means alone could not cure the deep-seated psychological malady of the refugees.

He found that the displaced "suffer from a 'rusting of the soul,' from a total uprooting, not only from their own countries, but from the world of men." His idea was to build special "European Villages" for the displaced persons, a community which would not be separate, a "potential ghetto," but a "neighborhood glued onto a city."

The first of these villages, consisting of twenty houses, was constructed in 1956 at Aix-la-Chapelle, Germany. There the displaced persons were able to form their own community,

Wide World

REV. GEORGES PIRE

perform their own communal tasks, and assume their own communal responsibilities, instead of depending on handouts from reluctant countries. Similar communities were built at Augsburg, Germany, and Bregenz, Austria. Another was started near Brussels in March 1958 and still another in the Saar in September 1958. Two others have been planned. The sixth village, to be erected in Germany, will be named in memory of Anne Frank, who died at fifteen in a concentration camp at Bergen-Belsen. About 800 persons now inhabit the five "European Villages" which are in existence.

Father Pire's master organization, known as Aid to Displaced Persons, has self-governing national sections in West Germany, Austria, Belgium, France, Luxembourg, and Switzerland; there are national secretariats in Denmark, Italy, and the Netherlands. Because the work is supported by private contributions "from the hearts of men," the movement is popularly called "Europe of the Heart." In 1958 $10,500,000 was spent in support of the activities for the refugees.

Father Pire feels that "the West has no reason to be proud of what it has done for the refugees. The various countries have been preoccupied with the problem of able-bodied workers and the official international agencies have been of great help to those refugees who qualified for entry into Western nations. However, the ineligible were forgotten. And even for those selected, such were the criteria employed . . . that in many cases the refugees were given the cruel choice of emigrating alone . . . or remaining behind with their families to waste away slowly." To these people he devoted his energies and love.

On November 10, 1958 the Nobel Committee of the Norwegian Parliament announced that the 1958 Nobel Peace Prize had been awarded to Father Pire for his humanitarian work. The

PIRE, GEORGES, REV.—*Continued*

award money of $41,250 he planned to use toward the construction of two refugee camps. "Apart from the cash value, important though it is for my organization," the priest said, "I appreciate the moral credit attached to the reward. I am filled with pride and humility."

The New York *Times* (November 11, 1958) wrote: "By awarding the Nobel Peace Prize to Father Pire for his humanitarian work the Norwegian committee has focused international attention upon this much-needed activity. One result should be greater support for such efforts to help the tragic victims of the spread of Communist domination." The newspaper also commented that the Belgian priest had worked so anonymously and humbly that neither his country's embassy in Washington, D.C., nor its mission to the United Nations in New York could provide information about him. In the ceremonies in Oslo, Norway in early December 1958 Father Pire was presented with the prize.

Father Pire has dark hair and brown eyes; he is six feet tall and weighs 200 pounds. For recreation, he grows cactus and listens to the only luxury in which he has ever invested: a pet canary. He is godfather of one of the children of Colonel Edward F. Squadrille, whose speech in 1949 started him on his mission. At the priory in Huy where he has lived for thirty years, it was said that he discharged the usual religious duties, led a monastic life, and went on preaching.

In an address Father Pire delivered at the University of Oslo on October 21, 1958, he said that his work went beyond the nation and beyond the confessional. "I therefore hold no hidden mysterious mandate from a church or a country. I am bound by no border, belong to no political party and have my name on no list. I do not even take time to be anti-communistic. I am simply pro-human." Like Anne Frank, whose portrait he has hung in his office to give him an example of courage, he believes in "sharing the riches of the heart."

References

America 100:230 N 22 '58
Jubilee 6:28+ D '58 por
Life 45:149+ N 24 '58 por
N Y Times p13 N 11 '58
Time 72:24 N 24 '58 por
U S News 45:20 N 21 '58 por

POITIER, SIDNEY (pwoi-tyā') Feb. 20, 1924- Actor

Address: c/o Baum-Newborn Associates, 574 5th Ave., New York 36

From the beginning of his screen career nine years ago Sidney Poitier has displayed an exceptional talent that promises to place him in the front rank of Negro actors in the world today. In spite of the limited casting opportunities that the Hollywood film industry offers the serious Negro actor, he has established his reputation on the strength of his acting alone. For his performance in *The Defiant Ones* (1958), Poitier is the first of his race to be nominated as the best actor by the Academy of Motion Picture Arts and Sciences.

Poitier also appeared in *Cry, the Beloved Country* (1952), *The Blackboard Jungle* (1955), and other motion pictures. Before going to Hollywood he appeared on Broadway and played in productions of the American Negro Theatre in New York. When *A Raisin in the Sun* opened on Broadway in March 1959, he created the role of William Lee Younger.

The youngest of eight children of Reginald and Evelyn (Outten) Poitier, Sidney Poitier was born on February 20, 1924 in Miami, Florida. In his infancy he was taken to his parents' tomato farm on Cat Island in the Bahama Islands, where he was educated by private tutors. He later attended Western Senior High School and Governor's High School, both in Nassau. During the depression Poitier was forced to leave school and go to work; the demand for tomatoes had decreased, and his father, who had become a victim of rheumatism and arthritis, was unable to work.

At the age of fifteen Poitier returned to Miami, where he stayed with his married brother Cyril. Although he had to contend with a West Indian accent which made him almost unintelligible, he managed to find work as a messenger for a drugstore. The color line is clearly drawn in Nassau, but it was in Florida as a teen-ager that Poitier really first became conscious of the "barbed wire" that surrounds the white world. "My life was full of frustration and confusion," he recalls. "I experienced tremendous loneliness as a result of realizing for the first time that I couldn't trust adults" (New York *Times Magazine*, January 25, 1959).

Wanting to come to New York, but not having the funds for transportation, Poitier "rode the rails" and reached the Harlem section of New York City with $1.50 in his pocket. For a while he worked as a dishwasher and slept on a roof across from the Capitol Theatre. After the attack on Pearl Harbor, he enlisted in the United States Army. He was trained to be a physiotherapist, served with the 1267th Medical Detachment, and was discharged in 1945.

Back in New York, Poitier held a series of menial jobs, and found none of them satisfying. When he read a story in the Amsterdam *News* that the American Negro Theatre was looking for actors, he decided to apply. His audition was unfavorable, and director Frederick O'Neal made it clear that Poitier lacked the required talents.

Determined to become an actor, Poitier bought a radio and spent much of the next six months listening to cultivated voices and improving his enunciation of words. When he returned to the American Negro Theatre, O'Neal gave him acting lessons in exchange for doing backstage chores. As a member of the group, he alternated with Harry Belafonte in the leading role of *Days of Our Youth* and portrayed a butler in *Strivers Road* and Boris

Kolyenkov in *You Can't Take It with You.* He also appeared in *Rain, Freight, The Fisherman, Hidden Horizon,* and *Riders to the Sea.*

In 1946 Poitier was hired by James Light at $75 a week to play Polydorus in an all-Negro production of *Lysistrata.* It closed after four performances. After having appeared in various roles in the Broadway production of *Anna Lucasta* in 1948, he interpreted the leading male character, Rudolph, when the show went on the road.

In 1949 Poitier made his first film appearance, in an Army Signal Corps documentary called *From Whom Cometh My Help.* He made his Hollywood film debut in *No Way Out* (1950), giving a performance which moved Howard Barnes to the comment (New York *Herald Tribune,* August 17, 1950) that "Poitier is particularly good as the doctor who had to hurdle both his color and the exacting demands of his profession."

Other motion pictures in which Poitier has appeared are *Cry, the Beloved Country* (1952), *Red Ball Express* (1952), *Go, Man, Go* (1954), *Goodbye, My Lady* (1956), *Edge of the City* (1957), and *Band of Angels* (1957). In *Blackboard Jungle* (1955), a movie dealing with juvenile delinquency in the New York schools, he played the part of a gifted student whose truculence creates havoc in every classroom. Later, through the efforts of a teacher, he directs his energies toward constructive ends.

In *Something of Value* (1957), a film based on the novel by Robert Ruark, Poitier played a young Negro in Kenya torn between his respect for the British family with whom he grew up and his allegiance to the Mau Mau. *Newsweek* (May 13, 1957) called Poitier's acting the one startling performance in the picture.

In another film dealing with African nationalism, *The Mark of the Hawk* (1958), Poitier portrayed Oban, a cultured native leader who has to choose between violent and nonviolent methods in order to achieve self-rule for his country.

The Defiant Ones (1958) is about a pair of convicts, one a white man, the other a Negro, who escape from a prison van, but are shackled together. Hating each other at first, they learn eventually to respect one another. The movie is based on the belief that "brotherhood and the mutual respect of man for man is a desirable goal, regardless of race or color," observed the *Saturday Review* (July 26, 1958). It went on to praise Poitier's performance for its "dignity, power, and overwhelming conviction."

Poitier believes that the film has universal applicability because "whether we like it or not, we are chained together, and if one of us drowns the other one is going down, too" (*Ebony,* October 1958). For his acting in *The Defiant Ones* Poitier received the Silver Bear award at the Berlin film festival of 1958. The picture won the New York Film Critics' award and was named to six of the "ten-best" lists. In the film adaptation of the George Gershwin-Du Bose Heyward opera, *Porgy and Bess,* scheduled to be released in

United Artists Corp.

SIDNEY POITIER

1959, Poitier takes the stellar role of Porgy, which is sung by Robert McFarren.

On Broadway Poitier starred in Lorraine Hansberry's drama, *A Raisin in the Sun.* The play, which opened on March 11, 1959 depicts the problems of a Negro family in Chicago who are trying to cross the boundary line that separates lower-class status from the middle class. As the highstrung son, Poitier has to decide whether he will compromise himself to pander to his family's material needs or whether he will stand firm for freedom and dignity. In the New York *Times* (March 12, 1959) Brooks Atkinson wrote: 'Mr. Poitier is a remarkable actor with enormous power that is always under control. . . . He is as eloquent when he has nothing to say as when he has a pungent line to speak." He left the cast of *A Raisin in the Sun* on August 29, 1959.

When acting, Poitier has said, "all that matters to me is what I get out of a part. . . . I don't mean money . . . what I want is the kind of role that makes me feel worth-while. I will work anywhere—movies, theater, TV—provided the material has texture, quality, something good to say about life" (*Newsweek,* May 13, 1957).

Sidney Poitier and Juanita Hardy, formerly a dancer, were married on April 29, 1950 and have three daughters, Beverly, Pamela, and Sherry. Tall and lean in appearance, Poitier has said he is "blessed with a kind of physical averageness that fits Negroes" between eighteen and forty. He has a twelve-room house in Mount Vernon, New York in an interracial community. There, the Poitiers hold open house every Saturday and Sunday for their neighbors. Poitier's parents now live in Nassau in a house which he built for them.

When asked about his politics, Poitier said: "I have no politics, but I am a Negro. For this reason, I try to do and say nothing that

POITIER, SIDNEY—*Continued*

might be a step backward. I believe in integration, though I'd rather call it equality of opportunity. . . . Two years ago I had ulcers, a worry bug about my future, my family's future, the future of my race . . . but . . . I found I could learn to accept what I had to accept and to try to change what I wanted to change. Now? I 'dig' my work" (*Newsweek,* May 13, 1957).

References

Los Angeles Times p1 Ag 31 '58 por
International Motion Picture Almanac, 1959
Who's Who in Colored America, 1950

POPE JOHN XXIII *See* John XXIII, Pope

POWELL, BENJAMIN E(DWARD) Aug. 28, 1905-   Librarian; organization official
Address: b. American Library Association, 50 E. Huron St., Chicago 11, Ill.; Duke University Library, Durham, N.C.; h. 3609 Hathaway Rd., Hope Valley, Durham, N.C.

Climaxing more than two decades of professional activity with the American Library Association, Dr. Benjamin E. Powell of Duke University will be installed as president of the more than 20,000-member organization at its seventy-eighth annual conference, to be held in July 1959 in Washington, D.C. He succeeds Emerson Greenaway, director of the Free Library of Philadelphia (see *C.B., July 1958*). During the 1958-59 term, Dr. Powell served as president-elect of the ALA and also as its vice-president. Since 1946 he has been the librarian of Duke University in Durham, North Carolina.

Previously Dr. Powell had held other positions at that library and had been the librarian of the University of Missouri in Columbia, Missouri. He received the Bachelor of Library Science degree in 1930 from Columbia University in New York City, several years after his graduation from Duke University, and was awarded the Ph.D. degree in 1946 from the Graduate Library School of the University of Chicago. He has been active in the American Library Association and in other library organizations, and has exhibited a special interest in Americana and American regional history.

Benjamin Edward Powell, the son of Willis Warren and Beatrice (Franklin) Powell, was born in Sunbury, North Carolina, on August 28, 1905. He is of English and Welsh ancestry. His family settled in eastern North Carolina in the early eighteenth century, and his father, a farmer, was for many years county commissioner there. He has three brothers: Ferrell Franklin, Willis Warren, Jr., and Curtis Vance; and two sisters, Mrs. Margaret Lee Powell Brooks and Mrs. Mildred Powell Russell.

After his graduation from the Sunbury High School in 1922, Powell entered Duke Univer-

sity in Durham, North Carolina, where he majored in history. He was a varsity half-miler. He received the A.B. degree from Duke in 1926. An interest in libraries had led him to inquire about part-time work as a student assistant in the university library, and he worked there during his junior and senior years. This experience convinced him that he should make librarianship his career, but after his graduation from college, he taught and coached athletics in the Bethel (North Carolina) High School for a year, until a full-time position on the Duke University Library staff became available.

Encouragement from the librarian, Joseph P. Breedlove, and from the reference librarian, Louis T. Ibbotson, now the librarian of the University of Maine, had helped him to reach this decision. Returning to Duke, he rejoined, for one year, Quincy Mumford, now Librarian of Congress, with whom he had worked as a student assistant. From 1927 to 1928 he was an assistant in the circulation department of the Duke University Library, and in 1928 became head of that department. During 1929 and 1930 he served as a part-time assistant in the reference department of the New York Public Library, while studying at Columbia University, from which he received the Bachelor of Library Science degree in 1930.

Upon his return to the Duke University Library in 1930, Powell was made the head of the reference and circulation departments; he served in this capacity from 1930 to 1934 and from 1935 to 1937. He did part-time graduate study at Duke in American history and literature from 1935 to 1937. He then accepted a position as acting librarian of the University of Missouri in Columbia in 1937, and in the following year became the librarian. There he developed the library's book collections and helped to build up the size of the staff.

Meanwhile, he had been doing graduate work at the University of Chicago. From 1934 to 1935 he had studied there, and he had received a fellowship from the Graduate Library School for 1937 and 1938, when he was appointed to head the library at the University of Missouri. His work at Chicago was continued only when he could get away from his duties at Missouri. In 1946 he was awarded the Ph.D. degree from the Graduate Library School of the University of Chicago; his thesis topic was the development of libraries in Southern state universities up to 1920.

Powell's appointment as librarian of the Duke University Library came in 1946. This library had, at the end of 1956, a total of 1,268,871 volumes and an annual circulation of 341,513 books. It has a number of departmental libraries and special collections, including a manuscript collection particularly useful for research on the South. Its newspaper library specializes in newspapers from the American South, Germany, and Great Britain.

Over the years Powell has been active in the American Library Association. He was a member of the divisional relations committee from 1941 to 1948 and its chairman during the three years from 1945 to 1948. He served on the nominating committee from 1945 to 1946 and on the council from 1947 to 1954. For the four years from 1948 to 1952, he was a member of the board of resources of American libraries, and the board's chairman from 1950 to 1952.

He became chairman of the subcommittee on co-operative microfilm projects in 1950 (serving until 1954) and a member of the friends of libraries committee in 1952 (serving until 1954). He was made chairman of the joint committee on government publications in 1953, and a member of the constitution and bylaws committee in 1954 (serving until 1956). He began to serve on the executive board of the ALA in 1956, and was elected chairman of the committee on public documents in 1956 and chairman of the committee on reorganization in 1957.

At the July 1958 meeting of the ALA in San Francisco, Powell was elected vice-president for the 1958-59 term and president-elect, to serve during the 1959-1960 year. He will be installed as president in July 1959, succeeding Emerson Greenaway. The American Library Association, which was founded in 1876 and maintains headquarters in Chicago, is composed of over 20,000 librarians in the United States and Canada. The president of ALA is chosen by mail ballot a little over a year in advance of installation.

Dr. Powell has also taken part in the activities of other library associations of which he is a member. He was president of the Missouri Library Association (1938-39), and held various positions in the Association of College & Reference Libraries, including secretary (1940 to 1944), chairman of the nominating committee (1944-45), director (1946-47), vice-president (1947-48), and president (1948-49). He served on the executive board of the Southeastern Library Association from 1950 to 1954 and was acting chairman in 1951-52.

The North Carolina Library Association made Dr. Powell a member of its executive board in 1952 for a two-year term, and he was chairman in 1947 and 1948 of the co-operative committee on library building plans. He became a member of the advisory committee of the Association of Research Libraries in 1950 and served until 1955.

His articles on books and libraries have appeared in such periodicals as the *Wilson Library Bulletin, Missouri Library Association Quarterly, Southeastern Librarian, College & Research Libraries, Library Journal,* and the *ALA Bulletin.*

He belongs to the Torch Club, the Rotary Club, and the Hope Valley Country Club, and holds membership in the State Historical Society of Missouri, the North Carolina Literary and Historical Association, the Southern Historical Association, and the Roanoke Island Historical Association. He was on the board of directors of the Durham Community Chest in 1953 and 1954. His fraternities are Sigma Nu and Phi Beta Kappa.

Benjamin E. Powell married Betsy Graves, a teacher and interior decorator from Scottsbluff, Nebraska, on March 6, 1940. They have one daughter, Lisa Holland. He has brown hair

BENJAMIN E. POWELL

and brown eyes; he is five feet eleven inches tall and weighs 165 pounds. He is a Democrat and a Methodist. For recreation he enjoys playing handball and golf.

References

College & Research Libraries 7:264+ Jl '46

Directory of American Scholars (1942)
Who's Who in America, 1958-59
Who's Who in Library Service (1955)

POWER, TYRONE May 5, 1914-Nov. 15, 1958 Actor; starred in more than forty motion pictures and many stage plays. See *Current Biography* (December) 1950.

Obituary

N Y Times p 1+ N 16 '58

PRAEGER, FREDERICK A(MOS) Sept. 16, 1915- Publisher
Address: b. Frederick A. Praeger, Inc., 15 W. 47th St., New York 36; h. 225 E. 46th St., New York 17

In an era when experts claim that $1,000,000 are required to organize a publishing house, Frederick A. Praeger has directed the company which bears his name to a position of pre-eminence within nine years on an initial capital outlay in 1950 of $4,000. His firm has attained leadership in the fields of international relations, Russian history, the U.S.S.R., world communism, military science, and art. Notable among the approximately 450 titles it has issued are *Picasso* (1956), a study by Frank Elgar and Robert Maillard; *The New Class* (1957), by Milovan Djilas; and *The Naked God* (1957) by Howard Fast.

(Continued next page)

New York Times Studio

FREDERICK A. PRAEGER

Referring to the goals of his company, Praeger says that his enterprise has the "opportunity of providing information to an enlightened citizenry, of providing weapons in the intellectual and cultural battle between freedom and totalitarianism, of providing knowledge of, and intellectual stimulation to, the military establishment of the free world, and of assisting in the constant interchange of ideas which are the result of scholarly research conducted on an international level."

Praeger believes that the determination to seek out truth and to defend it can give a book explosive force. Literature not only can explore the dynamics of international relations, but can also form a bridge between nations. Thus, book production and distribution is to Praeger a dedicated profession, and he has chosen as his publishing slogan "books that matter."

Frederick Amos Praeger, the only child of Max Meyer and Manya (Foerster) Praeger was born in Vienna, Austria on September 16, 1915. In the following year his father bought the Viennese publishing firm of R. Loewit Verlag and its bookstore. He soon established a branch in Leipzig, Germany, and for a time he was also managing director of the Austrian branch of the Ullstein concern and managing director of a newspaper in Vienna. After the rise of Adolf Hitler, these businesses were confiscated.

Important early factors in the formation of his character and the choice of his career, Frederick A. Praeger recalls, were the "atmosphere of books at home and in my father's firm, my father's capacity to derive pleasure from producing and merchandising books, his tolerant and unprejudiced attitude toward life and people."

From 1933 to 1938 Praeger attended the faculty of law and political science of the University of Vienna. He also studied at the Sorbonne in Paris in 1934. Considered one of Austria's best runners in this period, he was Vienna's interscholastic champion in the 100, 200, and 400 meter races and was a member of relay teams that made national records. For three years beginning in 1935 he was associate editor of R. Loewit Verlag, and he also worked part time as a sports writer.

In 1938, soon after Germany annexed Austria, Praeger came to the United States. Arriving with very little money, he immediately began to work and held some thirty positions in twenty states. After being employed in such jobs as furniture mover and short-order cook, he became a jewelry salesman and later assistant merchandising manager of a chain of jewelry stores in Kansas City, Kansas.

Joining the United States Army as a private during World War II, Praeger became a research and editorial assistant at the Command and General Staff School in Fort Leavenworth, Kansas. Later, he was a military intelligence instructor specializing in German Army organization and tactics. Assigned to an intelligence unit of Combat Command A of the Sixth Armored Division, he participated in five European campaigns and received the Bronze Star and a field commission as a second lieutenant.

When the war ended Praeger was in Thuringia, Germany, where he took charge of the German and Austrian desk at the intelligence branch of the G-2 division in General Dwight D. Eisenhower's Frankfurt am Main headquarters. From there he went to Berlin as editor of the *Intelligence Summary* of the information control division. Transferred to Hesse, Germany, Praeger served with the Military Government with the rank of first lieutenant. Following his discharge he was civilian head of the publications branch, information control division of the Military Government in Hesse from 1946 to 1948.

In retrospect, Praeger states that this assignment fulfilled his aspiration to work for the establishment of "cultural bridges between America and Germany, to contribute to the understanding of national character and cultural dynamics, and to assist in establishing a regenerated, vigorous cultural life after the holocaust of the war."

On his return to the United States, Praeger founded a book exporting business. Then, in 1950 with $4,000 borrowed from friends, he published two British analyses of international law. Although these sold only about 1,500 copies each, they provided the necessary foundation for Praeger's company. His basic formula is to publish books that interest him. In addition to being president of Frederick A. Praeger, Inc., he is also president of Inter Books, Inc., a subsidiary which manages some of the activities of the Praeger firm abroad.

When Praeger read that former Vice-President Milovan Djilas of Yugoslavia could not find a publisher for a manuscript he had written, he sent Djilas an offer to print the work. Djilas sent part of the manuscript to Praeger; the remainder he had to smuggle out of Yugoslavia because he was under arrest at the time. The book appeared under the Praeger imprint in 1957 as *The New Class; An Analysis of the Communist System*. In his best-selling volume Djilas claimed that the Communist bureaucracy has superseded the landholders and capitalists as a parasitic class of exploiters.

For outstanding creative publishing in obtaining and offering the Djilas work the R. R. Bowker Company presented Praeger with the Carey-Thomas Award in 1957. In accepting the prize, Praeger stated that the book marked for him the fulfillment of a "professional dream of glory. I wanted to find an intellectual weapon of enormous explosive force, preferably written from inside the Communist orbit by a man . . . with a great name, integrity and determination to seek out truth and defend it—a weapon in the form of a book which could . . . be effective in areas such as the Soviet orbit and the neutralist and uncommitted countries."

For consenting to the publication of his book, Djilas was sentenced to seven years of strict imprisonment on October 5, 1957. At that time he was already serving a three-year prison term. Praeger retained the American attorney Joseph L. Rauh, Jr., to aid Djilas at his hearing in October 1957, but Rauh was unable to obtain a visa.

In 1957 Praeger engaged in a similar venture when he published Howard Fast's *The Naked God; The Writer and the Communist Party*. In it the American novelist recanted his former beliefs and analyzed his experiences in the Communist party. Fast, a Stalin Prize winner, who had joined the Communist party in 1943, resigned shortly before he wrote *The Naked God*.

Another major area of activities for the Praeger firm is the field of art. *Picasso; A Study of his Work by Frank Elgar; A Biographical Study by Robert Maillard* was published by Praeger in 1956. It contains reproductions in six colors and in black and white. An illustrated catalogue in the book lists the artist's principal paintings in chronological order. The total printing of some 38,000 copies was sold.

In September 1958 Praeger contracted with the Whitney Museum of American Art to be the sole publisher and distributor of the museum's books. The Whitney-Praeger publications for 1959 are *Four American Expressionists: Doris Caesar, Chaim Gross, Karl Knaths, Abraham Rattner* and *Zorach,* both by Lloyd Goodrich and John I. H. Baur.

During 1959 the Praeger concern is also issuing the *West Point Atlas of American Wars*. Consisting of text and about 400 colored maps of all battles in which the United States participated, the book was compiled at the United States Military Academy under the editorship of Colonel Vincent J. Esposito.

On May 8, 1946 Frederick Praeger married Cornelia E. Blach. They have two daughters, Claudia Elizabeth and Andrea Maxine. Praeger is five feet eight inches tall, weighs 175 pounds, and has brown hair and brown eyes. He has no religious or political affiliations. His avocational interests are skiing, tennis, swimming, and art. Praeger is a member of the American Council on Germany and the American Academy of Political and Social Science.

To be a publisher, Praeger has said, "means to be a maid of all work—dreamer of dreams, creator of ideas, efficiency expert, financial wizard, salesman, fund raiser, art director, psychiatrist, editor, architect, co-ordinator, stamp-licker, air-conditioning machine repairman, head coach, and probably twenty-seven more functions and professions. In order to be successful and reasonably happy in one's job, one probably has to be more than just a little bit crazy, and it is certain that one must have detachment from one's madness, and the ability to do mad things with integrity, and with a rather ruthless sense of perfection."

References

N Y Herald Tribune p17 O 16 '57 por
Who's Who in America (sup Jl '54)

PREMINGER, OTTO (LUDWIG) Dec. 5, 1906- Motion-picture director and producer; stage director; actor
Address: b. Carlyle Productions, Inc., 780 Gower St., Hollywood 38, Calif.

A pioneer in making controversial motion pictures, Otto Preminger has more than once ignored Hollywood taboos and has helped to relax the production code of the Motion Picture Association of America. Some of his important films are *The Moon is Blue, The Man with the Golden Arm,* and *Porgy and Bess.* He began his career in the theater in Vienna before he directed and acted in Broadway productions. Preminger, whose independent Carlyle Productions, Inc., plans a $12,500,000 filming schedule for 1959-60, has said that "all this talk about the movies going to pieces is nonsense."

Otto Ludwig Preminger was born on December 5, 1906 in Vienna, Austria, the son of Dr. Marc and Josefa Preminger. His father was an attorney, and Otto planned for a law career, to comply with his parents' wishes. His personal interest lay in the theater, however, and despite his law studies he made his stage debut when he was seventeen, playing Lysander in Max Reinhardt's production of *A Midsummer Night's Dream* at Vienna's Theater in der Josefstadt.

Associated with stock companies during his summer vacations, Preminger staged and acted in plays by Shakespeare, Goethe, and Schiller. While still a law student, he formed his own company, the Comedie, in Vienna. European producers leased their theaters on a long-term basis, rather than renting them for one production in the American fashion. Preminger's first such venture was successful enough to justify a second, the Schauspiel Haus, with a 3,000-seat capacity. Meanwhile he completed his law studies, graduating from the University of Vienna with an LL.D. in 1928.

At twenty-two years of age, Preminger was hired by Max Reinhardt to be a producer-director of the Theater in der Josefstadt. There,

OTTO PREMINGER

Preminger staged plays ranging from Greek classics to adaptations of such contemporary American hits as *The Front Page* and *Men in White*. He worked with such actresses as Hedy Lamarr and Luise Rainer, who later became Hollywood stars.

Partly because of attractive American offers and partly because of the political climate in Europe, Preminger immigrated to the United States in 1935. His first American assignment was *Libel*, which he staged for Gilbert Miller on Broadway. It opened on December 20, 1935 and ran for 159 performances. Then he went to Hollywood at the request of Joseph M. Schenck of the Twentieth Century-Fox Film Corporation.

After directing two minor motion pictures, Preminger returned to the legitimate theater. He staged a revival of Sutton Vane's *Outward Bound*, which was presented on December 22, 1938 and ran for nineteen months; Clare Boothe Luce's anti-Nazi play *Margin for Error*, which opened on November 3, 1939 and in which he also took the leading role; Catherine Turney's and Jerry Horwin's comedy, *My Dear Children*, which had its première on January 31, 1940 and starred John Barrymore in his last stage play; and Howard Koch's and John Huston's play about Woodrow Wilson, *In Time to Come* (which opened on December 28, 1941). From 1938 to 1941 he taught direction and production at the Yale University Drama School.

With Twentieth Century-Fox he signed a long-term contract in 1941 to produce, direct, and act in motion pictures. Because of his German accent he was cast as a Nazi during World War II; he played a Nazi officer in *The Pied Piper* (1942) and directed and starred in the movie version of *Margin for Error* (1943). With Bob Hope he appeared in MGM's *They Got Me Covered* (1943).

When *Laura,* a mystery drama starring Gene Tierney, was released in 1944, the critics and the movie industry began to look upon Preminger as an outstanding Hollywood talent. Alton Cook (New York *World-Telegram,* October 11, 1944) found it the "stunning surprise of the season . . . a deft masterpiece of the stealthy arts," adding that Preminger "finally makes it clear that he is one of Hollywood's great craftsmen among directors." The film won Preminger a nomination for an Academy of Motion Picture Arts and Sciences award.

Other films Preminger made for Twentieth Century-Fox were: *In the Meantime, Darling* (1944), *A Royal Scandal* (1945), *Fallen Angel* (1946), *Centennial Summer* (1946), *Daisy Kenyon* (1947), *Whirlpool* (1950), *Where the Sidewalk Ends* (1950), and *The Thirteenth Letter* (1951). When *Forever Amber,* a screen version of Kathleen Winsor's novel about a Restoration trollop, was released in 1947, Francis Cardinal Spellman and the Roman Catholic Legion of Decency placed it in the "condemned" category. The film was banned in Providence, Rhode Island; Rochester, New York prohibited it and later lifted the restriction; and showing of the film on Sundays was proscribed in Massachusetts. Preminger left Twentieth Century-Fox and formed his own company, Carlyle Productions, Inc., in 1951.

On Broadway in 1951 Preminger staged F. Hugh Herbert's lightweight comedy, *The Moon Is Blue,* which had its première on March 8. It had a successful run of 924 performances and went on tour, but it did not become a *cause célèbre* until Preminger adapted the play, in an almost unchanged version, for the screen in 1953. The Motion Picture Association of America's Production Code Administration refused to stamp it with its approval; the Roman Catholic Legion of Decency and state censors of Maryland and Kansas condemned it because of its offhand treatment of sex. Several local censorship boards banned it as obscene. The controversy went on until the United States Supreme Court in 1955 held that local censors could not prohibit its performance.

Preminger followed this venture with his all-Negro production of *Carmen Jones,* released through Fox in 1954, and *The Man with the Golden Arm,* released through United Artists in 1955. Because the latter film dealt with narcotics addiction, it was not sanctioned by the Motion Picture Association of America's Production Code Administration. After state censors had banned parts of the film, the Maryland Court of Appeals reversed this action in 1956. Preminger's pioneering movies and Supreme Court decisions, among other factors, led to a liberalization of the motion picture code in 1956.

In addition to making independent productions, Preminger also continued to work for the major studios. He directed *Angel Face* (1953) for RKO Pictures Corporation, *River of No Return* (1954) for Twentieth Century-Fox, and *The Court-Martial of Billy Mitchell* (1955) for Warner Brothers Pictures, Inc. He also performed his traditional Nazi role as the prison commandant in *Stalag* 17 (1953) and staged a television spectacular for NBC-TV in 1954.

After a well-publicized talent hunt conducted in the United States, Canada, and Europe, Preminger selected the seventeen-year-old American girl Jean Seberg to star in his movie adaptation of Bernard Shaw's *Saint Joan.* The film met with a mixed reception when it was shown in 1957. John Beaufort (*Christian Science Monitor,* July 2, 1957) remarked: "Perhaps the law that protects public monuments should be extended to include literary treasures."

Preminger then cast Miss Seberg in the film adaptation of Françoise Sagan's best-selling novel, *Bonjour Tristesse.* After it was released by United Artists in 1958, he directed *Porgy and Bess* for Sam Goldwyn. *Porgy and Bess,* based on the George Gershwin-Du Bose Heyward opera, is Preminger's second all-Negro motion picture. It was first exhibited in 1959.

It was announced in early 1959 that Preminger had bought the rights to four novels for filming by Carlyle Productions, to be made in the following two years at a cost of $12,500,000. These were Evelyn Piper's *Bunny Lake is Missing,* Leon M. Uris' *Exodus,* Pierre Boulle's *The Other Side of the Coin,* and Robert Traver's *Anatomy of a Murder.*

Otto Preminger and the Hungarian actress Marion Mill were married on August 3, 1942. After this marriage ended, he took Mary Gardner for his second wife on December 4, 1951. She divorced him on March 10, 1959. A large man (six feet tall, 170 pounds), Preminger has blue eyes and "a pinkish bald head, a strong Viennese accent, and a fancy for Picassos" (Don Ross, New York *Herald Tribune,* January 12, 1958). He became an American citizen in 1943.

As the "heart, hands, and brain of Carlyle Productions," commented *Newsweek* (April 8, 1957), "Preminger is a man of many roles. As a director, shouting a stream of ill-tempered commands, he seems driven by his own squad of Furies. As a producer, however, he has all the sober qualities of a stock-market analyst. . . Though he flourishes in an industry which is notoriously sensitive to criticism, he has deliberately nurtured a reputation for controversy in his career as an independent moviemaker." Preminger has said: "What good are successes if you don't have a failure once in a while? If a picture doesn't make money or win critical raves, I'm not upset. I've had most of my satisfaction while making it."

References

Newsweek 46:66+ D 26 '55 por
International Motion Picture Almanac, 1959
Preminger, M. M. All I Want Is Everything (1957)
Who's Who in America, 1958-59

PRESLEY, ELVIS (ARON) Jan. 8, 1935-
Singer; actor
Address: b. c/o Thomas A. Parker, P.O. 417, Madison, Tenn.

Out of the hillbilly tunes, Negro blues, and gospel songs of the American South has developed the unique singing style of Elvis Presley. His guitar strumming and bodily gyrations have brought him the adulation of millions of teen-age fans, who have purchased his recordings of such tunes as "Blue Suede Shoes" and "Hound Dog" in astronomical quantities. Presley first came to fame in 1956 when the quaking rhythms of rock 'n' roll began to pour from the jukeboxes of the United States. After he had conquered the recording industry, Presley performed on television, and became a box-office hit when he starred in several Hollywood motion pictures. In 1959 he is serving in the United States Army in Europe.

Elvis Aron Presley, who is of Irish descent, was born in Tupelo, Mississippi on January 8, 1935 to Vernon Elvis and Gladys Presley. His twin brother, Jessie Garon, the only other child in the family, died at birth. Vernon Presley, who worked as a cotton farmer, carpentry foreman, and factory worker, built his own home for his ardently religious family. Elvis had his first singing experiences in the choir of the local church of the Assembly of God and later at revivals and camp meetings. While still in elementary school he entered an amateur singing contest sponsored by WELO radio station and the Mississippi-Alabama Fair, in which he won fifth prize.

The boy received his first guitar as a birthday present when he was about twelve. He taught himself to strum chords, although even now he cannot read music, and learned hillbilly tunes and Negro blues songs by listening to phonograph records. Moving with his family to

Wide World

ELVIS PRESLEY

PRESLEY, ELVIS—*Continued*

Memphis, Tennessee in 1949, he attended the L.C. Humes High School, from which he was graduated in June 1953. He then became a truck driver for the Crown Electric Company, and at night studied to be an electrician.

That summer, Presley went to the Sun Record Company, which has a department that cuts personal records; there he paid $4 to make a recording of "My Happiness" and "That's When Your Heartaches Begin" as a present for his mother. Sam Phillips, the president of the Sun Record Company, which specializes in hillbilly music, heard the performance and later signed a contract with Presley.

A year later Presley made his first commercial coupling, "That's All Right, Mama" and "Blue Moon of Kentucky" for Sun. The record was heard over the radio program of Memphis disc jockey Dewey Phillips in the summer of 1954. That night, Phillips played each side seven times in response to forty-seven telephone calls and seventeen telegrams. In the following week Memphis stores sold some 6,000 copies of the record.

As a result of this initial success, impresario Colonel Thomas A. Parker signed Presley for a personal-appearance tour as The Hillbilly Cat. He also performed weekly on *Louisiana Hayride* over station KWKH in Shreveport, Louisiana. In the autumn of 1955 Presley was booked for a disc-jockey's convention in Nashville, Tennessee. By this time he had developed his own style of "rock 'n' roll," a variety of popular music which combines highly emotional, primitive, revivalist, and hillbilly elements.

At the convention his singing impressed RCA Victor talent scout Steve Sholes, who induced his firm to buy Presley's contract and five master discs from the Sun company for $35,000. In addition, RCA Victor paid Presley $5,000. He used the money to buy the first of several Cadillacs.

RCA Victor pressed all five of Presley's records under its own label and released them simultaneously. Within three months Presley discs accounted for more than half of the firm's popular-music production, and he was engaged for his first national TV appearance on Jackie Gleason's *Stage Show*. He sang "Heartbreak Hotel," and the record of this tune became the number one recording in the United States in popularity, selling over 1,000,000 copies within several weeks. By May 1956 seven of RCA Victor's fifteen best-selling popular discs had been recorded by Presley.

Throughout 1956 Presley luxuriated in a popularity seldom equaled in American entertainment. He earned $50,000 for three spots on the Ed Sullivan television program, and signed a seven-year movie contract with Hal Wallis Productions. But Presley made his strongest impact in his personal appearances, mainly upon impressionable audiences of teen-age girls.

"They get set off by shock waves of hysteria," reported a *Life* writer (August 27, 1956), "going into frenzies of screeching and wailing, winding up in tears." Carlton Brown, writing in *Coronet* (September 1956), described Presley's stage presence in these words: "The ir-

regular stress on syllables gave the song an urgent jerkiness that the singer's actions carried out visually. His legs spread in a straddling stance, he whacked his feet . . . like a cowboy riding a bronco with a rock-and-roll buck." It was these supplementary body movements which drew condemnation from the press.

"His movements and motions during his performance, described as a 'strip-tease with clothes on,' were not only suggestive, but downright obscene," according to an editorial in the Roman Catholic publication *America* (June 23, 1956), which concluded: "If the agencies would stop handling such nauseating stuff, all the Presleys of our land would soon be swallowed up in the oblivion they deserve."

Far from being "swallowed up," Presley had earned an estimated $1,000,000 by the end of 1956. Exploiting the boom, his business managers were preparing to sell between $19,000,000 and $24,000,000 worth of merchandise under Presley's name. The merchandise included such items as a Hound-Dog-Orange lipstick, named after a Presley hit song.

Love Me Tender, Presley's first film, was released by Twentieth Century-Fox Film Corporation in November 1956 and was followed by Paramount's *Loving You*, in July 1957. For his third film, MGM's *Jailhouse Rock* (November 1957), Presley earned $250,000 plus 50 per cent of the net profits. If Presley's motion pictures have not been artistic triumphs, all have been profitable.

Presley's career was interrupted when he was inducted into the army on March 24, 1958. After receiving basic training and advanced instruction in tank corps activities at Fort Hood, Texas, he was assigned to the 3d Armored Division in Germany as a truck and jeep driver. He maintains a seven-room house in Germany, which he shares with his father and grandmother, but performs the normal duties of an enlisted soldier.

Military service does not seem to have diminished Presley's popularity with his teen-age following. His most recent film, *King Creole*, was released in July 1958, and his recordings, which are still being released, command a high place on lists of best-selling discs. In 1958, although he was serving in the army, Presley earned about $2,000,000, largely from his records and his movies.

Elvis Presley weighed 185 pounds and stood six feet one inch in height when he was drafted into the United States Army. He is a "lanky, loose-jointed, sullenly handsome youth with sideburns" in civilian life. He has a classic Barrymore profile, wavy brown hair, blue eyes, and long, thick eyelashes. He dresses flamboyantly for his stage appearances and tends to be ill at ease when not performing. He neither smokes nor drinks. In addition to strumming a guitar, he plays the piano. Presley bought his family a seven-room ranchhouse in Memphis and persuaded his father to retire at the age of thirty-nine. His hobbies are sports cars, motorcycles, collecting teddy bears, swimming, water skiing, boxing, and football.

Having made twenty-one records which sold more than 1,000,000 copies each, and having consistently topped popularity polls in 1956, 1957, and 1958, Elvis Presley has often been the subject of speculation as to the source of his success. Perhaps the most penetrating analysis was written by James and Annette Baxter in *Harper's Magazine* (January 1958):

"Admonished that there were those who found his hip-swiveling offensive, Elvis is said to have replied, 'I never made no dirty body movements.' And this is believeable; Elvis moves as the spirit moves him; it all comes naturally. . . . But Presley's stunning rapport with his own generation is something more than the ageless call of the wild. . . . In the backwoods heterodoxies of Elvis the [teen-ager] recognizes a counterpart to his own instinctive rebellion . . . in his voice the teen-ager hears intimations of a world heavily weighted with real emotion."

References

Colliers 138:109+ O 26 '56 pors
Coronet 40:153+ S '56 por
Harper 214:86 Ap '57
Life 41:101+ Ag 27 '56; 44:117+ Ap 7 por; 45:77+ O 6 '58 pors
Look 20:82+ Ag 7; 9+ N 13 '56; 22: 113+ D 23 '58 pors

International Motion Picture Almanac, 1959

Who's Who in Rock 'n' Roll (1958)

PROFUMO, JOHN D(ENNIS) Jan. 30, 1915- British Minister of State for Foreign Affairs

Address: h. 3 Chester Terrace, London N.W. 1, England

As British Minister of State for Foreign Affairs, John D. Profumo has a role in determining British foreign policy second only to the Foreign Secretary, Selwyn Lloyd. Profumo was appointed to this post on January 16, 1959, succeeding Commander Allan Noble. Although only forty-four, Profumo has been in political office for almost twenty years. He served most recently as Parliamentary Under Secretary of State for Foreign Affairs. Previously, he was Parliamentary Under Secretary of State for the Colonial Office and Joint Parliamentary Secretary of the Ministry of Transport and Civil Aviation. Since 1950 he has represented Stratford-on-Avon in the House of Commons.

In May 1959 Profumo announced in the House of Commons that the British government had decided to sell jet bombers and tanks to Iraq, rather than force Premier Abdul Karim Kassem to rely on the Soviet Union for his supply of arms. This move, which has met with considerable Laborite criticism, is generally viewed as a "calculated risk" which may enable Britain to keep some influence in the strategic and oil-rich Middle East.

John Dennis Profumo was born on January 30, 1915, the eldest son of Baron Albert Profumo, King's Council. He was educated at Harrow and at Brasenose College, Oxford University. Profumo took his degree in agriculture and political economy and after his graduation

British Inf. Services

JOHN D. PROFUMO

took a trip around the world, during which he visited China, Japan, the United States, and the Soviet Union.

His first political position was the chairmanship of the West Midlands Federation of the Junior Imperial League (now the Young Conservatives Organization). At the age of twenty, he was named chairman of the East Fulham Conservative and Unionist Association. At a by-election in 1940, when he was twenty-five years old, he was elected a Member of Parliament for the district of Kettering with a majority of 11,298 votes.

Before World War II, Profumo had joined the Northamptonshire Yeomanry (Territorial Army), and after the hostilities broke out he served with his regiment until 1941. During that year he was appointed air liaison officer with the rank of captain. (Profumo was a qualified pilot who flew his own plane and was a member of the Oxford University Air Squadron.) Two years later, in 1943, he was promoted to the rank of major and served throughout the North African campaign. He next served on the staff of Field Marshal Alexander as a lieutenant colonel. Profumo was awarded the Order of the British Empire (Military Division) and the American Bronze Star in 1944.

During his military service, John Profumo kept his seat in Parliament, where he had the distinction of being the youngest member in the House of Commons. Making a special effort to represent the views and problems of the armed forces, he made a speech in 1944 that attracted particular attention. He had flown to London from the Italian front to open a debate on demobilization and home leave for men and women overseas. He took exception when the government, in formulating plans for demobilization, refused to give preference to those who had served overseas.

(Continued next page)

PROFUMO, JOHN D.—*Continued*

In 1945 John Profumo lost his Kettering seat at the general election. He was sent to Japan as chief of staff of the British military and diplomatic mission, serving as deputy to Sir Charles Gairdner, the Prime Minister's personal representative to General Douglas MacArthur. Promoted to brigadier, Profumo remained in this post until the end of 1947, when he returned to England to resume his political activities. For the next two years he served as broadcasting adviser at the central office of the Conservative party.

In 1948 Profumo became the Conservative candidate for the newly constituted Stratford-on-Avon division of Warwickshire. He won the seat in the 1950 general election. Two years later he was appointed Joint Parliamentary Secretary of the Ministry of Transport and Civil Aviation. Shortly after Prime Minister Harold Macmillan's government was formed in 1957, John Profumo was named Parliamentary Under Secretary of State for the Colonies. He visited a number of British territories and colonies, including Mauritius, Kenya, and Gibraltar, and in the spring of 1958 he represented the United Kingdom when Princess Margaret inaugurated the legislature of the Federation of the West Indies. Later in 1958 he was the first minister from the Colonial office to visit the Seychelles Islands in the Indian Ocean.

During a debate in the House of Commons on the question as to whether Cyprus should be partitioned or united with Greece, Profumo declared that partition, although not an ideal solution, was "possible" (New York *Times,* July 16, 1957). In November 1958 John Profumo became Under Secretary of State to the Foreign Office. Less than three months later, Commander Allan Noble (see *C.B.,* May 1957) resigned from his post as Minister of State for Foreign Affairs, and John D. Profumo became his successor. The appointment was announced publicly on January 16, 1959.

As Minister of State for Foreign Affairs, Profumo is subordinate to the British Foreign Secretary, Selwyn Lloyd. He does, however, occupy a seat in the Privy Council. According to the New York *Times* (January 17, 1959) Profumo's appointment came at a time when the personnel of the Foreign Office were under sharp criticism for their "apparent ignorance of the course of the Castro revolution in Cuba."

On May 11, 1959, Profumo told the House of Commons that the British Government had agreed to authorize sale to the government of Iraq of "a reasonable quantity" of aircraft, tanks, and other arms. He pointed out that ever since the July 1958 revolution in which pro-Western King Faisal was overthrown, the Russians had been "extremely busy" sending weapons to Iraq. "I really don't think" he continued, "that forcing General Kassem to rely solely on the Soviet bloc for arms would contribute to the stability of the Middle East, which is our sole aim" (New York *Times,* May 12, 1959). Profumo added that British au-

thorization of the arms sale had been approved in advance by the United States, and by Iran, Jordan, and Turkey, three unfriendly neighbors of Iraq.

British criticism of the arms sale was largely based on the pro-Communist leanings of the Kassem government. Such a sale, the opposition argued, would also imply hostility toward President Gamal Abdel Nasser's government, the anti-Communist United Arab Republic. This would be unfortunate, since a British mission was in Cairo at that time, trying to improve Anglo-Egyptian relations. Profumo, however, told the House of Commons that the British Government was not convinced that Kassem's regime was wholly pro-Communist; the arms sale would, he hoped, "allow General Kassem to maintain an independent line of action" (New York *Times,* May 12, 1959).

Commenting on Profumo's announcement, Dana Adams Schmidt of the New York *Times* (May 17, 1959) said: "Thus the British . . . are gambling for the preservation of their remaining stake in the Middle East. . . . Certainly no alternative to this British gambit has been offered by Washington."

In 1954 John Dennis Profumo married Valerie Hobson, the British stage and screen actress who has starred in many motion pictures, including *Kind Hearts and Coronets* and *Great Expectations.* They have a son who was born in October 1955. Profumo lists his favorite recreations as hunting, motion picture photography, and flying. His clubs are the Carlton and Boodle's. Profumo is the fifth baron of the late United Kingdom of Italy.

Reference

Who's Who, 1959

QUARLES, DONALD A(UBREY) July 30, 1894-May 8, 1959 United States Deputy Secretary of Defense (since 1957); Secretary of the Air Force (1955-57); Assistant Secretary of Defense for Research and Development (1953-55); vice-president of Western Electric Company (1952-53); engineer. See *Current Biography* (November) 1955.

Obituary

N Y Times p1+ My 9 '59

RAINS, ALBERT (M.) Mar. 11, 1902- United States Representative from Alabama

Address: b. House Office Bldg., Washington, D.C.; h. Gadsden, Ala.

The author of Democratic housing bills for nearly a decade, Congressman Albert Rains is serving as chairman of the housing subcommittee of the House Banking and Currency Committee. Rains, who has represented Alabama's Fifth District since 1945, numbers agriculture, foreign aid, and Social Security among his principal legislative interests. He began his career as a schoolteacher and later became one of Alabama's leading attorneys.

Albert M. Rains, the son of a farmer, was born in Groveoak, De Kalb County, Alabama on March 11, 1902. He received his early education at public schools there and at Snead Seminary, Boaz, Alabama. After attending Alabama State Teachers College in Jacksonville, Rains taught in a high school in his native county. Later, he studied law at the University of Alabama near Tuscaloosa and was admitted to the bar of his state in 1928. With his brother Will, he established the law firm of Rains & Rains, in Gadsden. He also served as deputy solicitor for Etowah County from 1930 to 1935 and as city attorney for Gadsden from 1935 to 1944.

Making his first bid for elective office in 1936, Rains challenged United States Representative Joe Starnes in the Democratic primary and lost by about 2,000 votes. In 1942 he was elected to his state's House of Representatives. There, he won substantial labor support by his opposition to the Bradford bill which required all unions to make detailed financial statements to the state.

After serving a two-year term in the Alabama lower chamber, Rains defeated Representative Starnes in the Democratic primary of May 2, 1944 and was unopposed in the November election for the Fifth District's seat in Congress. In explaining his victory over Starnes, Rains stated: "It was just a case where I convinced the people that I would work for them in all matters affecting their interests" (*PM*, May 23, 1944). In his freshman term he was named to the House Banking and Currency Committee and its housing subcommittee, and later to the Joint Committee on Defense Production. The latter is charged with overseeing defense stock-piling and with exploring economic problems related to the nation's security.

During his Congressional career, Rains has devoted much time to securing better housing and more public housing. He opposed the Wolcott housing bill in June 1948 which made no provision for public housing and proposals made in May 1951 and March 1952 to limit public housing to 5,000 units for each year. In April 1953 he supported a measure extending the public housing program. Assailing the administration housing program of 1957 as "pitifully inadequate," Rains introduced a bill to supply $1 billion of National Life Insurance reserves for the purchase of veterans' mortgages in order to ease the shortage of housing credit.

Amendments to housing acts which Rains introduced in 1958 would authorize the federal housing commissioner to purchase insured mortgages for purposes of avoiding foreclosures in cases where the mortgagee is in financial straits for reasons beyond his control; would make available loans for housing to be used by student nurses and interns at nonprofit hospitals; and would grant loans to educational institutions and hospitals to build classroom buildings and other educational facilities.

The Rains omnibus housing bill of 1959 provides for public housing, slum clearance, urban renewal, college housing, and housing for the elderly. The measure won House approval on May 21. A compromise proposal,

Wide World

ALBERT RAINS

appropriating $1.3 billion for the government's various housing programs, was passed by the Senate on June 22 and by the House on June 23. After this proposal and a second housing bill were vetoed, a third compromise measure was enacted in September 1959.

Important legislative bills presented by Congressman Rains included an amendment to the Federal Deposit Insurance Act to raise the amount of insured bank deposits from $5,000 to $10,000 and amendments to liberalize the Social Security Act.

With other members of his subcommittee, Rains traveled to New Jersey, Oklahoma, and Texas to examine the condition of houses bought with loans guaranteed by the Veterans Administration and the Federal Housing Administration. The subcommittee heard many complaints about defectively built and badly planned houses. However, Rains, who reported that 45,000,000 Americans lived in houses built with the assistance of the VA and FHA, stated that the veterans' housing plan had been successful despite the "laxness, laziness and carelessness" reported to the subcommittee (New York *Times,* February 12, 1952).

Four years later Rains and his group conducted another investigation of housing problems. This covered areas in New York and New Jersey, in the Midwest, the West Coast, and the Southern states. The study indicated to Rains and the subcommittee that the government slum clearance program was being jeopardized by "roadblocks and strangling red tape," and that the urban renewal program was "hopelessly bogged in administrative bungling" (New York *Times,* February 5, 1956).

Like many of his Southern colleagues in Congress, Rains is especially concerned with federal legislative attempts to promote civil rights. He opposed the anti-poll tax bill (June 1945 and July 1947), the voluntary compliance Fair Employment Practice Com-

RAINS, ALBERT—*Continued*

mission bill (February 1950), the Powell amendment to restrict federal aid to non-segregated schools (July 1956), and the civil rights bills (July 1956 and June 1957).

Rains supported the states' rights bills of July 1958 which provided that no act of Congress could nullify state laws on any subject unless it is so specified or unless there is an irreconcilable conflict between a state and federal law. In March 1956 Rains joined about 100 other Congressmen in signing a Southern manifesto which decried the Supreme Court's desegregation decisions and declared that they were resulting in "chaos and confusion in the states principally affected."

As a representative of a predominantly agricultural community, Rains favored high-level farm supports in measures voted upon in June 1952, May 1955, and April 1956. He opposed flexible farm price props in July 1954. On measures affecting the interests of workingmen Representative Rains voted to raise the income tax exemption for each individual (March 1954), to increase unemployment compensation benefits (July 1954), and to raise the minimum wage to $1 an hour (July 1955). He did, however, favor overriding President Truman's veto of the Taft-Hartley bill (June 1947).

On other domestic issues he favored a constitutional amendment giving the House the right to participate in treaty ratification (March 1945), price control extension (May 1945), a new steam plant for the Tennessee Valley Authority (June 1948), repeal of the federal margarine tax (April 1949), Natural Gas Act exemptions (August 1949), increasing funds for public power (April 1953), and the Department of Defense reorganization bill (June 1958). He opposed limiting the Presidency to two terms (February 1947) and private power development on the Niagara River in New York (July 1953).

For many years Rains has been a consistent supporter of foreign aid programs. He voted for the British loan (July 1946), Greek-Turkish aid (May 1947), Korean-Formosan economic aid (February 1950), and the mutual security acts (June 1956 and May 1958). However, in a newsletter of June 19, 1959 he notified his constituents that he was for all foreign aid cuts and that he hopes to see the aid program abolished in the next few years. "The program . . . has largely served the purpose for which it was intended. Our friends and allies are making economic progress. . . . Our public debt exceeds the combined debts of all those countries which we are helping and so, it is only reasonable, that this kind of aid . . . must after a whole decade approach some end."

Albert M. Rains married Allison Blair on December 29, 1939. Rains is a past district governor of the Alabama Lions Clubs, a counselor of the Lions International, a past president of the Etowah County Bar Association, past president of the Etowah County chapter of the Alabama League of Young Democrats, and a member of the First Baptist Church in Gadsden. Congressman Rains, who has earned the sobriquet "silver-tongued orator," is in frequent demand as a speaker.

References

Biographical Directory of the American Congress, 1774-1949 (1950)
Congressional Directory (1959)
Who's Who in America, 1958-59

RAMA RAU, SANTHA (rä'mä rou săn'thä)
Jan. 24, 1923- Author
Address: b. c/o Harper & Brothers, 49 E. 33d St., New York 16; c/o Helen Strauss, William Morris Agency, Inc., 1740 Broadway, New York 19

Reprinted from the *Wilson Library Bulletin* June 1959.

The books of Santha Rama Rau have vividly interpreted the traditions and problems of the Orient to Western readers. Born in India, but raised and educated in England and the United States, Miss Rama Rau combines sympathy for her native land with an understanding of Occidental views. Through her writing, she has helped to level the barriers between nations.

Vasanthi Rama Rau was born in Madras, India on January 24, 1923. Of Brahman families, her mother, the former Dhanvanthi Handoo, was from southwest India, and her father, Sir Benegal Rama Rau, from South Panara. Sir Benegal, a former diplomat, represented his country in London, the Union of South Africa, Japan, and the United States. Prior to his retirement in 1957 he was governor of the Reserve Bank of India. Lady Rama Rau has devoted herself to social work and among other achievements initiated the scheme of mobile medical units to tour small villages. She is president of India's Family Planning Association.

Santha Rama Rau began her travels at the age of six, attending school in London where her father was stationed. For the next ten years she continued her studies in England, finally leaving St. Paul's Girls' School, London in 1939. Summer holidays were spent in whatever country her parents were living; and in 1939, visiting her family in South Africa, she was unable to return to England on the outbreak of war.

So with her mother and sister she went back to India at the age of sixteen to discover her heritage in that richly varied land. There she met Madame Sarojini Naidu, poet and first woman president of the Indian National Congress, who encouraged her to write.

For the next two years Miss Rama Rau toured India, wrote for Indian magazines, gave occasional talks for All-India Radio, and recorded her impressions, which were included in her first book, *Home to India* (1944; Left Book Club choice). Isabelle Mallet said of it in the New York *Times Book Review*: "The book is touched with humor and a certain shrewdness in appraising fellow-Indians and their governors . . . indeed [it is] a plea for Indian nationalism."

Before the book was written, however, Miss Rama Rau went to the United States, to Wellesley College in Massachusetts, where she majored in English, starred in productions of the Shakespeare Society, and was on the board of the college magazine. She spent her vacations as a writer on the overseas program of the Office of War Information in New York. She graduated with a B.A. degree in 1944.

Returning to India in 1945, she worked as an editor on the magazine *Trend* in Bombay and continued writing for other magazines. In the summer of 1947 she went to Tokyo as hostess for her father, India's first Ambassador to Japan. Bored with the endless round of diplomatic entertainment, she volunteered to teach English to Japanese girls at Mrs. Motoko Hani's Freedom School. Her interest in Japanese life was appreciated: Japanese friends and acquaintances entertained her in their homes and took her about. She developed a keen interest in Japanese theater and met its actors and dancers. In arranging for her students to see a Kabuki performance, she met Faubion Bowers, American censor of the Japanese theater under occupation.

In the spring of 1948, Miss Rama Rau, an American newspaperwoman, a young Englishman, and Faubion Bowers began a tour of China, Indochina, Siam, and Indonesia. Bowers' facility in languages and his interest in the national theaters opened many doors. And whenever Miss Rama Rau identified herself as an Indian, Asian esteem for Gandhi and the Indian struggle for independence helped to make rough ways smooth.

Her account of this journey and of her life in Japan, *East of Home* (1950), "enables one to see Asia as a whole. . . . But its main value lies in the fact that an Asian writes about Asia," declared Nayantara Sahgal in the *Saturday Review of Literature*.

Miss Rama Rau and Faubion Bowers were married on October 20, 1951, and they continued to travel. She wrote of their tours in her succeeding books, much of the material appearing first in magazines such as *Holiday*. *This Is India* (1954) describes "places to see and people to watch . . . with graceful descriptions of the cultural treasures India has in store," said Vera M. Dean in the New York *Herald Tribune Book Review*.

Her first novel, *Remember the House* (1956), was a British Book Society recommendation. Maurice Richardson commented in *New Statesman and Nation* on "its documentary quality," saying that "as a picture of a particular stratum of Indian society, the Bombay smart set, uneasy despite independence, it is vivid and instructive."

A return to Asia with her husband and young son, Jai Peter, resulted in a fourth travel guide, *View to the Southeast* (1957; British Book Society recommendation) which again reveals her deep interest in human beings and their folk arts.

Santha Rama Rau has recently dramatized E. M. Forster's novel *A Passage to India* and has written a series of six articles on Russia for *Holiday* which appeared in book form in March 1959 as *My Russian Journey*. She is at work on a second novel.

Lotte Jacobi

SANTHA RAMA RAU

Miss Rama Rau is an attractive woman with black eyes and gray-black hair. She never tires of traveling. Her favorite place to visit is Bali ("Nobody in Bali is without friends"). Her favorite city is Madras, "with Tokyo and New York running a close second." Her favorite books are Flaubert's *Madame Bovary*, Turgenev's *First Love*, and Murasaki's *The Tale of Genji*. Her favorite sport is swimming—she always comments on fine beaches. She thoroughly appreciates the friendly Balinese farewell, "Safety in going."

References

New Yorker 26:26+ Ja 6 '51
Current Biography Yearbook, 1945
Rama Rau, Santha East of Home
  (1950); Home to India (1944)
Who's Who in America (sup Je-Ag '58)

RANKIN, J(AMES) LEE July 8, 1907-
United States government official; lawyer

Address: b. Department of Justice, Washington 25, D.C.; h. 600 Juniper Lane, Falls Church, Va.

As Solicitor General of the United States, J. Lee Rankin has pleaded cases for the federal government before the United States Supreme Court involving Communist party membership, passport rights of American citizens, states' ownership of oil-rich lands on the continental shelf, and federal control over natural gas used in interstate commerce. Before his appointment in 1956 as Solicitor General, Rankin had been an assistant attorney general in charge of the Justice Department's office of legal counsel and had presented the government's views in the school segregation case. For a number of years earlier he had practised law in Lincoln, Nebraska, where he was politically active for the Republican party.

(Continued next page)

J. LEE RANKIN

James Lee Rankin was born in Hartington, Nebraska on July 8, 1907, the son of Herman P. and Lois (Gable) Rankin. He attended grade school in Lincoln, Nebraska, and was graduated from the Lincoln High School. In Lincoln he also attended the University of Nebraska, which granted him an A.B. degree in 1928 and an LL.B. degree in 1930. During his college years he was interested in printing and operated not only Linotype machines but presses.

After his admission to the Nebraska bar in 1930, Rankin began to practise law in Lincoln with the firm of Beghtol, Foe and Rankin (subsequently Beghtol and Rankin), and became a member of the firm in 1935. Rankin, a Republican, began to take an active interest in politics, and he managed Thomas E. Dewey's primary campaign for the United States Presidency in 1940 in Nebraska. Eight years later he was responsible for Dewey's Presidential electoral campaign in that state. Dewey was defeated, but he carried Nebraska by 40,000 votes. When Dwight D. Eisenhower ran for the nation's highest office in 1952, Rankin headed the Eisenhower committee in Nebraska.

Following the election of Eisenhower to the United States Presidency in 1952, Rankin was appointed assistant attorney general in charge of the office of legal counsel of the Department of Justice and took office on January 28, 1953. Influential in his appointment was Herbert Brownell, Jr., an old friend and fellow Nebraskan who had been made United States Attorney General. As assistant attorney general in charge of the office of legal counsel, Rankin drafted Justice Department documents and was chief adviser to the Attorney General in the formulation of legal policy. He had a major hand in drafting legal opinions requested by President Eisenhower, Secretary of State John Foster Dulles, and other high officials of the executive branch.

Arguing for the United States government in the basic case that led to the Supreme Court ruling against school segregation, Rankin appeared before the court in December 1953, after the government had been asked to express its views as "a friend of the court," and supported the Negro plaintiffs' arguments against the principle of "separate but equal facilities" laid down by the United States Supreme Court in the case of *Plessy* v. *Ferguson* in 1896. The federal government argued that school segregation based on race or color was unconstitutional under the Fourteenth Amendment and that the Supreme Court had ample power and a firm obligation to decide that the segregation was unconstitutional.

Rankin "has given a good account of himself," the Washington *Post and Times Herald* (August 16, 1956) later noted, "Though he is not well known to the public or the bar outside the Department, his associates know him as a hardworking and able lawyer who is at home with the most intricate and involved legal problems." He wrote a memorandum, published in the *Department of State Bulletin* (April 4, 1955), on the question of trading in surplus agricultural commodities with Soviet bloc countries. He also made an official study for Eisenhower on the Presidential succession problem in 1956.

President Eisenhower announced the appointment of Rankin to the post of Solicitor General of the United States on August 14, 1956, to succeed Simon E. Sobeloff, who had recently been confirmed as a judge of the United States Court of Appeals for the Fourth Circuit. Rankin took the oath of office on the following day on a recess appointment and at that time Attorney General Brownell praised him for showing "superb professional competence" in his previous post. Some observers felt that Rankin's appointment might not be confirmed by the Senate because of his stand on the civil rights issue and his role in the administration's court fight for school desegregation, but his nomination was passed by the Senate on May 28, 1957.

As Solicitor General, Rankin has what has been called the "aristocrat of legal jobs." He has charge of the government briefs and arguments in all the cases before the Supreme Court, and he is appeal attorney for the federal government. He decides what cases lost by the government should be taken to the courts of appeals or to the Supreme Court. Only the Attorney General can overrule his decisions.

During the 1956-57 court term he presented the federal view in the first Supreme Court test of the right of witnesses to refuse to tell Congressional committees the names of others linked with Communist activities; he pleaded that the conviction of John T. Watkins for contempt of Congress should be sustained. Rankin argued the government's side of the appeals of Junius Irving Scales and Claude Mack Lightfoot, testing the constitutionality of the membership clause of the Smith Act, and the appeal of Mrs. Antonia Sentner, questioning whether or not an alien awaiting deportation can be required to leave the Communist party.

Later he argued that the government can deny passports to American citizens solely on the basis of confidential information in order to protect foreign relations. He contended successfully for the government position in 1957 that United States Army Specialist 3/c William S. Girard, accused of killing a Japanese woman in Japan, should be surrendered for trial by a Japanese court. Over several years he has pleaded for the government in the Supreme Court case involving the extent of the Gulf states' ownership of the mineral-rich lands along the continental shelf.

He has argued the case about Panama Canal tolls; the question of the Swiss holding company, Interhandel; the right of a federal agency to license a firm for building dams in Hell's Canyon; and several cases involving federal control over natural gas used in interstate commerce, including the "Memphis" case. For the government he decided in January 1958 not to appeal a judge's decision on material for the Kinsey Institute seized by the Customs Bureau, and thus accepted a new legal standard for obscenity.

Again concerned with the racial segregation issue, Rankin filed a brief on August 28, 1958 before the Supreme Court, which was then hearing arguments relating to a district court order postponing the Little Rock, Arkansas, school integration program. He attributed tension in the schools to violence caused by people opposed to the Supreme Court's 1954 anti-segregation decision. If children are taught that "the courts will bow" to violence, he said, "you destroy the whole educational process then and there." He urged that children be taught to respect constitutional rights—"not just the rights that I like and want for me, or that you like and want for you, but all of them for every man and woman" (New York *Times,* August 29, 1958).

Rankin's article "Federal Wages and Hours Act" appeared in the *Nebraska Law Bulletin* in December 1939, and his review of Lloyd W. Kennedy's book *Federal Income Taxation of Trusts and Estates* (1948) was published in the *Nebraska Law Review* of May 1949.

He belongs to the American and Nebraska bar associations, the Association of the Bar of the City of New York, the American Law Institute, and the American Judicature Society. He is a member of Phi Delta Phi fraternity; his clubs are the University and the Country (Lincoln). From 1928 to 1933 Rankin held a commission as a second lieutenant in the United States Army Reserves. He is a Congregationalist.

The New York *Times* (May 29, 1957) wrote: "A rugged Midwestern independence is a Rankin trait. He is married to Gertrude Carpenter, a boyhood sweetheart. Her family owned a large paper company. Undoubtedly money could have been found to buy the young couple an automobile. But until he could pay for a car with his own money, Rankin did without one." Their marriage took place on September 4, 1931. The Rankins have two sons and a daughter: James Lee, Jr., Roger Carpenter, and Sara Elizabeth. Riding is a favorite recreation of Rankin, who owns a ranch at Fort Pierre in South Dakota, where he raises Morgan horses and Hereford cattle. He also plays the piccolo, grows roses in his Virginia home, is an enthusiastic amateur photographer, and keeps a kennel full of dogs.

References

N Y Times p20 Ag 1 '55; p1+ Ag 8 '56; p14 My 29 '57
Newsweek 41:31 Mr 2 '53
U S News 41:20 Ag 24 '56
Washington (D.C.) Post p22 Ag 9 '56; p2 Ag 15 '56
Martindale-Hubbell Law Directory. 1958
Who's Who in America, 1958-59

REDFIELD, ROBERT Dec. 4, 1897-Oct. 16, 1958 Anthropologist; authority on Middle American folk culture; associated with the University of Chicago since 1927. See *Current Biography* (December) 1953.

Obituary

N Y Times p29 O 17 '58

REED, DANIEL A(LDEN) Sept. 15, 1875-Feb. 19, 1959 Representative from New York for more than forty years; former chairman of the House Ways and Means Committee. See *Current Biography* (May) 1953.

Obituary

N Y Times p25 F 20 '59

RENAULT, MARY Author
Address: b. c/o Pantheon Books, 333 6th Ave., New York 14

"Mary Renault" is the pseudonym used by a British novelist who is familiar to American readers mainly for her skillful and imaginative reconstruction of the ancient past in two novels, *The Last of the Wine* (Pantheon, 1956) and *The King Must Die* (Pantheon, 1958), a Book-of-the-Month Club selection for midsummer, 1958. *Return to Night* (Morrow, 1947), an earlier novel set in the contemporary scene, achieved considerable attention when it won the M.G.M. prize of $150,000.

Born in London, England, Mary Renault is the eldest daughter of a doctor. On her father's side she is descended from the French Huguenots who were driven out of their native land by the Edict of Nantes in 1685. Her mother was a descendant of the English Puritan divine, Richard Baxter. Miss Renault's earliest memory is of a Zeppelin raid during World War I, an experience she recalls now as "a splendid firework display." An imaginative child, she decided to become a writer at the age of eight and promptly launched her career by composing one chapter of a Western on the blank pages of a grocer's order book.

After preparing at boarding school near Bristol, Mary Renault studied for an Honours degree in English literature at Oxford University. During her university days she wrote and published a considerable amount of verse. At

MARY RENAULT

the time she left Oxford, Miss Renault decided, she writes, "that my experience of life was largely derived from other people's books, which were good because their writers had got it at first hand." She turned, therefore, to nursing, and enrolled as a probationer nurse at a large voluntary hospital, where for three years she wrote nothing except sketches for the nurses' Christmas concerts.

Mary Renault accomplished her first serious writing in spare moments snatched from nursing and other jobs, among them one as a matron in a girls' boarding school. Her first novel, *The Purposes of Love* (Longmans, 1939), published in America as *Promise of Love* (Morrow, 1939), was set in an English provincial hospital and drew upon the author's experience as a nurse. The book sold well in England where it was a Book Society recommendation. American reviewers welcomed it as a sound and serious achievement. E. H. Walton, in the New York *Times* (March 12, 1939), called it "an unusually excellent first novel," adding that "there is a fusion between background and personal drama, between inner and outer reality, which enriches and dignifies both."

The success of this first book encouraged Miss Renault to make writing her career, but the outbreak of World War II forced a drastic revision of her plans. Her second novel, a love story, *Kind Are Her Answers* (Longmans; Morrow, 1940), appeared during the week of the Dunkirk evacuation, and she immediately returned to hospital nursing. She remained a nurse throughout the war, specializing in neurosurgical work under the late Professor Sir Hugh Cairns.

The Friendly Young Ladies (Longmans, 1944) was her first postwar novel; it appeared in the United States as *The Middle Mist* (Morrow, 1945). This was a psychological study of three young women and their emotional entanglements, with much of the action taking place on a houseboat on the Thames. Critics generally found it a well-conceived, perceptive work, though some of them objected to the complications and subtleties of the plot and style. The London *Times Literary Supplement* (September 2, 1944) wrote: "Miss Renault has many gifts, but as yet seems unable, except in flashes, to use them with restraint and imaginative sincerity."

Return to Night (Longmans; Morrow, 1947) was the fourth of Miss Renault's books to appear in the United States. Originally entitled "The Sacred River," the book was renamed by M.G.M. when selected as the winner of its $150,000 prize contest of 1946. (The two earlier winners had been *Green Dolphin Street* by Elizabeth Goudge and *Before the Sun Goes Down* by Elizabeth Metzger Howard.) Although *Return to Night* was never made into a film, the publicity it received as the winner of this largest financial award in the field of literature brought Miss Renault's name to the attention of the American reading public. Orville Prescott (New York *Times,* April 29, 1947) called it "a mature and adroit novel of considerable interest." As in her first novel, the action takes place in a hospital in a small English town. Its heroine is a brilliant young doctor who falls in love with a patient some years her junior. Her struggle to help him achieve maturity and win independence from his domineering mother is the substance of the story. Miss Renault has written two other novels on contemporary themes—*The Charioteer* (Longmans, 1953) and *The North Face* (Longmans, Morrow, 1948).

Since the end of the war she has traveled extensively in France, Italy, Africa, Greece, and the Aegean Islands. "Of all these places I have found Greece incomparably the most moving and memorable," she writes. Greece—specifically Athens during the Third Peloponnesian War— is the scene of her first historical novel, *The Last of the Wine*. Woven into the fabric of this fictitious story are real figures—Socrates, Alcibiades, Phaedo. The soundness of Miss Renault's scholarship and the vividness of her imagination, enabling her to recreate the ancient scene with color and authentic flavor, won her high critical praise both in England and in the United States. The London *Times Literary Supplement* (June 29, 1956) called *The Last of the Wine* "a superb historical novel."

The idea for *The King Must Die* originated in a trip Miss Renault made to Crete. Visiting the Palace of Knossos, she was fascinated by the ruins of the Minoan art and culture. As she writes in the *Book-of-the-Month Club News* (July 1958): "Later I began thinking about Theseus and wondered what it was like for a simple Bronze Age warrior to be confronted with this sophisticated metropolis."

In *The King Must Die* she takes her legendary hero Theseus on a journey from Troizen, his birthplace, to the matriarchal society of Eleusis where he takes part in the ritual slaying of the king and becomes king himself; to Athens where he makes himself known to his father King Aigeus; and to Crete to which he volunteers to go as one of the sacrificial victims of the Minotaur. Here he participates in the dangerous but highly developed art of the bull-dance, and ultimately by his skill and shrewd intelligence, saves himself and his comrades from death. The bibliography appended to the novel ranges from Plutarch's *Life of Theseus* to the recently discovered translations of Mino-an texts by Michael Ventris and J. Chadwick in their *Documents in Mycenaean Greek.*

The main achievement of the book, Maurice Dolbier remarked in the New York *Herald Tribune* (July 14, 1958), is its "remarkable accomplishment in transmuting the findings and the theories of many branches of historical science into pure fictional gold."

Of Miss Renault's art as an historical novelist, the classical scholar, Moses Hadas, wrote: "In *The Last of the Wine* . . . Miss Renault showed how certain personal relationships and the practice of infanticide which we find distasteful and abhorrent could be an integral element in the luminous period of the Peloponnesian War. . . . In *The King Must Die* she contributes a greater increment to our knowledge of our past and ourselves by clarifying grimmer and more horrifying elements in the mistier antecedents of the classical efflorescence—which did not spring fully formed like Athena from the head of Zeus" (New York *Herald Tribune Book Review,* July 13, 1958).

Mary Renault has made her permanent home in Durban, South Africa, since the end of World War II. She lives with a friend whom she met when they were both taking nurses' training in London. Miss Renault has found South Africa an excellent field of study for an historical novelist, because, she writes, "one can find preserved in it so many stages of human history, some so old as to be, like the coelocanth, almost living fossils." She is a member of the Union Federal party which is opposed to *apartheid* and other racial policies of the South African government. Miss Renault is five feet, seven inches tall, of average weight, and has dark hair and blue eyes. She is unmarried. Her favorite authors are Plato and Sir Thomas Malory.

References

Book-of-the-Month Club News p4+ Jl '58 por
N Y Herald Tribune Bk R p2 Jl 27 '58 por
N Y Times Bk R p8 Jl 20 '58

RENOIR, JEAN (rĕ-nwàr') Sept. 15, 1894-
Film writer; director

Address: h. 9370 Santa Monica Blvd., Beverly Hills, Calif.

Like his famous father, Jean Renoir has spent most of his life trying to record visual beauty. He began his career as a ceramist and since 1924 has been directing and writing motion pictures. At their best his films combine the pictorial with the dramatic in a way that is audacious and exciting. The film for

Warner Bros.

JEAN RENOIR

which he is best known in the United States is perhaps *The River,* filmed in India in 1950. *La Grande Illusion,* which Renoir wrote and directed in France in 1937, was in 1958 selected by an international jury as one of the twelve great motion pictures of all time.

Jean Renoir was born in Paris on September 15, 1894, the second son of Pierre Auguste and Aline (Charigot) Renoir. His father was the great French impressionist painter, several of whose canvases depict a child with long red hair —Jean. With his brothers, Pierre and Claude, he grew up in the company of the most talented writers and artists in France.

He attended the Collège Sainte-Croix de Neuilly and received a Bachelor of Arts degree from the University of Aix-en-Provence in 1913. He was commissioned a lieutenant of cavalry in 1914, was seriously wounded in the trenches, twice decorated, and reassigned to the flying corps. Military service had a profound effect on his career. During his convalescence he saw his first motion pictures (as many as eight a day), and his later military service obliged him to fly over the front lines, filming enemy installations. He turned the horror he felt at what he saw into account in the making of such films as *La Grande Illusion.*

After his discharge in 1918, Renoir turned first to ceramics. He never considered painting. "How could I?" he said (*Newsweek,* April 14, 1958). "I still don't believe I'd have the spiritual strength to paint, after my father." His ceramics showed the family genius and today are included in outstanding collections throughout the world. He pursued this vocation until 1923.

Renoir entered the film industry as a ceramist, when he made several figurines for experimental films. He then turned to script writing and directing. In 1924 he directed *La Fille de l'Eau,* then *La Petite Marchande d'Allumettes,* which

RENOIR, JEAN—Continued

tried to duplicate on the screen the light and shadow effects of his father's impressionistic paintings.

With his own motion-picture company in Paris, Renoir turned to realism with the filming of Émile Zola's Nana in 1926. Although the critics were enthusiastic, the public did not accept the film, and Renoir turned to box-office entertainment to recoup his losses. Le Bled, Tournoi dans la Cité, Tire au Flanc, and On Purge Bébé were not artistic successes, but proved Renoir to be a good commercial director.

In 1929, with his finances again sound (On Purge Bébé was filmed in four days at a cost of 200,000 francs; it grossed five times that amount), Renoir secretly filmed La Chienne, a grim story of prostitution. Its première in Nancy provoked riots, and Renoir's backers withdrew their support. He managed to raise funds to make La Nuit du Carrefour, an innocuous detective story by Georges Simenon, and found a new backer.

Supported by playwright Marcel Pagnol, Renoir filmed Toni, a tragedy whose success enabled him to make La Crime de M. Lange and Flaubert's Madame Bovary in 1935. Both were mass-audience pictures of average quality. Again Renoir turned to stark realism with The Lower Depths, and again the public rioted at its première. Only when it was awarded the Louis Delluc prize (1936), a French critics' prize for the best movie of the year, was the film released to the general public.

Meanwhile, Renoir in 1937 wrote and filmed La Grande Illusion (Grand Illusion), an anti-war film which brought Erich von Stroheim back to the screen. In many respects a landmark in film history, the movie contained dialogue in three languages, and abounded in intellectual discussion. An international jury in 1958 chose it as one of the twelve greatest motion pictures ever made.

This work of art was followed by a mediocre historical romance, La Marseillaise, and then by the daring La Bête Humaine (The Human Beast). One observer remarked: "It is characteristic of Renoir's career to follow a success with a failure. Up to the present he has with fair regularity taken two steps forward and one back. With his latest production, La Bête Humaine, however, he has leaped into the realm that approaches classic perfection in film. Renoir as a director has attained full stature" (Richard Rene Plant, Theatre Arts, June 1939).

Renoir fled France before the invading German Army in 1939. He came to the United States with his family in 1941, and was later naturalized as an American citizen. He quickly adapted himself to Hollywood, causing critic Howard Barnes to comment that Renoir's first American film, Swamp Water, had "no more Gallic flavor than pone and corn whiskey" (New York Herald Tribune, November 17, 1941).

Among Renoir's films in his first Hollywood decade were The Southerner (the story of a sharecropper, which was banned in Tennessee) in 1943, The Diary of a Chambermaid in 1946, and The Woman on the Beach in 1947. He became an enthusiastic convert to the American policy of going on location to make movies. "What justifies trips to location is not what you see later on the screen," he has said (in Theatre Arts, August 1951), "but the effect on the people who make the film. . . . The use of location brings a different spirit." True to this policy, Renoir in 1950 made two 12,000-mile excursions to India to film The River on location in Calcutta.

"Renoir has recorded what he found, in color, with an almost mystic admiration for the natural beauties of his locale," wrote Otis L. Guernsey, Jr., in the New York Herald Tribune (September 16, 1951). "Atmosphere, texture, and line are the most striking qualities. It is a truly wonderful sequence of pictures that Renoir has worked out in 'The River'."

Using much the same pictorial technique, Renoir in 1953 filmed The Golden Coach in Rome. The movie starred Anna Magnani, and was an attempt, Renoir explained, to revive classical theater ideas on the motion-picture screen by presenting a play within a play. "On the whole," observed one critic (New York Herald Tribune, January 22, 1954), "his magic trick does not come off."

Renoir stepped out of his movie-making role in 1954 to direct a production of Shakespeare's Julius Caesar for the 2,000th anniversary of the founding of the city Arles by Caesar. He then produced his first original play, Orvet, which was performed at the Théâtre de la Renaissance, Paris, in May 1955. Described as "imaginative, appealing, and uncynical," the play starred Leslie Caron, for whom Renoir had written the script. In the next year, he wrote, directed, and produced French Cancan, followed in 1957 by Paris Does Strange Things. Both movies were filmed in Paris.

At the 1959 Venice Film Festival Le Testament du Docteur Cordelier, a TV movie by Renoir, was exhibited. It is a modern version of the story of Dr. Jekyll and Mr. Hyde.

Renoir is "a huge man with thinning hair, thick hands, and a button nose," according to Gordon Allison in Theatre Arts (August 1951). "Life runs around inside Renoir like a squirrel." He is a Chevalier in the Legion of Honor and holds the Croix de Guerre for his service in World War I. For his films he was awarded the International prize (Venice Film Festival) in 1951. He is a Roman Catholic. He married Andrée Madeleine Heuschling in 1920 and has one son, Alain, by his first wife. The marriage was later dissolved, and he married Dido Freire on February 6, 1944. Though he speaks English with an accent, he writes it with facility and has contributed articles to several American publications.

Dividing his time between Europe and the United States, and between the stage and the screen, Renoir does not believe that motion pictures should be narrowly regional. "Today the field to work in is the world," he has said. "No more only America, only Italy, only France. It's the world."

References

Life 32:90+ My 19 '52 por
Theatre Arts 23:429+ Je '39; 35:18+ Ag '51 por
Dictionnaire Biographique Français Contemporain (1954)
Who's Who in America, 1958-59
Who's Who in France (1955-56)

REUSS, HENRY S(CHOELLKOPF)

(rois) Feb. 22, 1912- United States Representative from Wisconsin; lawyer

Address: b. House Office Bldg., Washington, D.C.; 735 N. Water St., Milwaukee 2, Wis.; h. 1035 E. Ogden Ave., Milwaukee 2, Wis.; 6448 Brooks Lane, Bethesda 16, Md.

"Yes, there are modern Democrats, and I hope I am one of them," said Representative Henry S. Reuss in 1958. "To the modern Democrat a stable dollar is a goal no less imperative than full employment. . . . He is the most vigorous supporter of the last practitioners of competitive enterprise, the small businessman, and the family-sized farmer" (New York *Herald Tribune,* October 12, 1958).

A Milwaukee lawyer who attracted attention in 1952 with an aggressive pre-primary campaign against Senator Joseph R. McCarthy, Reuss was first elected to the House of Representatives in November 1954. He is a member of the House Banking and Currency and Government Operations Committees and the Joint Economic Committee.

The grandson of an 1848 German immigrant who became president of a large banking house in Wisconsin, Henry Schoellkopf Reuss was born in Milwaukee, Wisconsin on February 22, 1912 to Gustav A. and Paula (Schoellkopf) Reuss. After attending the Milwaukee public schools, where he played basketball, baseball, and football, Reuss studied at Cornell University. He received his A.B. in 1933. At Cornell he edited a college publication, and, arguing that the nation ought not to "change horses" in a depression, came out for Herbert Hoover in 1932. Reuss received his LL.B. from the Harvard Law School in 1936.

Admitted to the Wisconsin bar in 1936, Reuss began the private practice of law in Milwaukee. In 1939 and 1940 he served as assistant corporation counsel for Milwaukee County, and in 1941 and 1942 as assistant general counsel for the Office of Price Administration in Washington.

Entering the United States Army as a private in January 1943, Reuss was commissioned a second lieutenant in the following November. He saw active duty with the 63rd and 75th Infantry Divisions in France and Germany, and by the end of the war in Europe had been promoted to a captaincy. He was awarded the Bronze Star for action in the Rhine crossing and three bronze battle stars.

Wide World

HENRY S. REUSS

From June to December 1945 Reuss headed the price control division of the Office of Military Government for Germany. He then returned to Milwaukee and resumed his law practice. He served also as a director (and later president) of the White Elm Nursery Company of Hartland, Wisconsin, as director of the Marshall and Ilsley Bank at Milwaukee, and of the Niagara Share Corporation, Buffalo, New York.

Reuss, who had been a Willkie Republican in 1940, ran for mayor of Milwaukee as a nonpartisan in 1948, but lost to the Socialist candidate Frank Zeidler by a close margin. In 1948 he began four years on the advisory committee of the National Resources Board at Washington, and in 1949 he went to Paris as deputy general counsel for the Marshall Plan.

As special prosecutor for the Milwaukee County Grand Jury, Reuss conducted an investigation of corruption and graft in 1950. In the same year, running as a Democrat, he lost an election for Attorney General of Wisconsin. Reuss later attributed his switch to the Democratic party to his growing belief that Republican Senator Joseph McCarthy was "a disgrace to Wisconsin" (New York *Post,* November 21, 1954).

In July 1951 Reuss and three other Democrats organized an anti-McCarthy movement which they called "Operation Truth." A loudspeaker truck and a caravan of automobiles toured the rural areas of Wisconsin, where opposition to the Republican Senator had been practically nonexistent. In November Reuss started a campaign to be chosen candidate for the United States Senate in the Democratic primary the next year. By 1952 he had visited all of Wisconsin's seventy-one counties, frequently giving his campaign speeches in German.

(Continued next page)

REUSS, HENRY S.—*Continued*

"In challenging McCarthy," Reuss declared, "I am not simply saying that I, as a Democrat, disagree with him. My deep opposition to what he stands for is above any partisanship. We can root out Communists and subversives without tearing up the Bill of Rights" (New York *Post,* June 29, 1952). Adopting a fairly conservative position on the question of inflation, Reuss said that "the only way to stop inflation in the long run is to bring national supply and demand into balance." In foreign affairs he advocated the "Dean Acheson-Averell Harriman approach." In the Democratic primary Reuss lost to former Wisconsin Attorney General Thomas E. Fairchild, who was defeated by McCarthy in November.

Reuss in 1953 won his first elective office, membership on the Milwaukee School Board. In November 1954 he ran against the incumbent Republican Charles J. Kersten, a staunch McCarthyite, for United States Representative of the Fifth Wisconsin District. He defeated Kersten by a margin of 6000 votes.

Taking office in the Eighty-fourth Congress in January 1955, Reuss was assigned to the House Banking and Currency Committee and the Government Operations Committee. He soon made himself known in the legislative chamber. In March 1955, in connection with renewal of the Reciprocal Trade Agreements Act, he introduced a bill which would have given priority in government contracts to industries injured by import competition. In the same month he led a group of twenty freshman Democrats who, looking ahead to the Bandung Conference, called on the administration to provide greater aid to the Asian-African countries.

Having earlier accused the Department of the Interior of "subverting fifty years of good conservation practices," Reuss sponsored a bill in July 1955 to deny Secretary of the Interior Douglas McKay the right to dispose of any of the national wild-life refuges without the approval of Congress. For aid to the aged, he offered in February 1956 a bill to create a Federal Bureau of Older Persons. In March 1956 he advanced legislation to protect tribal interests in the timber on Wisconsin's Menominee Indian Reservation. In the same month he sponsored a bill to extend the G.I. loan program. In June 1956 he proposed restrictions on the spending of government-owned foreign currency by traveling Congressmen, and in August he protested against an Internal Revenue Service ruling which denied teachers tax deductions for training course expenses.

Representative Reuss greatly increased his majority at the election of November 1956, when he defeated his Republican opponent, Russell Wirth, Jr., by 118,603 votes to 86,764. During the 1957 session of the Eighty-fifth Congress he introduced legislation to establish and extend a national wilderness preservation system and to safeguard the Fish and Wildlife Service from the "spoils system." In February 1957 he voted for the Benson Soil Bank plan, and pushed through an amendment limiting payments to any one farmer. About

a year later he made an unsuccessful attempt to sue the Secretary of Agriculture for misinterpretation of this amendment. He requested in February 1957 the investigation which ultimately resulted, in May 1958, in the indictment of five large drug firms on charges of conspiracy to fix prices for Salk polio vaccine.

Having decided, in 1957, against candidacy for either the United States Senate or the governorship of Wisconsin, Reuss was reelected to the House in November 1958 by 104,374 votes to 45,901 for Otto R. Werkmeister, a Republican. As a member of the Joint Economic Committee in the Eighty-sixth Congress, he announced in January 1959 that he would co-sponsor a bill permitting the President's Council of Economic Advisers to demand public justification of any wage or price increases that might threaten economic stability. In March he assailed the financing of the national debt through commercial banks as "highly undesirable and potentially inflationary" (New York *Herald Tribune,* March 28, 1959). In April he was one of ten Democratic Representatives who, with six members of the British Parliament, suggested that the United Nations take over the policing of all Berlin.

In the three Congresses of which he has been a member Reuss has consistently supported the annual Mutual Security Acts. Although he voted in January 1957 for authorization of the Eisenhower Doctrine, he criticized in July 1958 the landing of troops in Lebanon. He favors rigid farm price supports, has voted for postal pay raises but not for increased rates, and opposed in November 1955 the exempting of natural gas from federal regulation. He has consistently supported the School Construction Aid and Civil Rights bills; he voted for the Powell Amendment in July 1956; in July 1958 and again in June 1959 he voted against the Smith bill, which provided that a federal law cannot be construed to nullify a state law on the same subject, except when Congress has specified its intention to pre-empt the field of legislation involved.

In July 1959 Reuss made a proposal, introduced as an amendment to a House Ways and Means Committee interest-rate bill, which was designed to assist the Treasury Department in the management of the national debt. The amendment advises (but does not require) the Federal Reserve Board to increase the national money supply by purchasing long-term government bonds rather than by lowering bank reserve requirements. William McChesney Martin, Jr., chairman of the Federal Reserve Board, attacked the Reuss amendment as inflationary.

Henry S. Reuss married Margaret Magrath of Winnetka, Illinois on October 24, 1942. They have four children: Christopher, Michael, Jacqueline, and Anne. Peter Edson of the New York *World-Telegram and Sun* (May 26, 1952) described him as being "tall, broadshouldered, square-jawed and fair-complexioned." Robert Spivack of the New York *Post* (June 29, 1952) characterized him as being "dignified, soft-spoken, and reasonable."

A former lecturer (1950 and 1951) at Wisconsin State College, the Congressman is vice-chairman of the Junior Bar Association of Milwaukee, chairman of the constitution and citizenship committee of Milwaukee County, a director of the Foreign Policy Association, and vice president of the Chi Psi Alumni Association. In 1956 he became alumni overseer for the *Harvard Law Review*.

References

N Y Herald Tribune II p3 Ja 13 '52 por
N Y Post Mag p2 Je 29 '52 por
N Y World-Telegram p14 My 26 '52 por
Congressional Directory (1959)
Who's Who in America, 1958-59
Who's Who in the Midwest (1956)

RHOADS, C(ORNELIUS) P(ACKARD)
June 20, 1898-Aug. 13, 1959 Physician; director of Sloan-Kettering Institute for Cancer Research since 1945; scientific director of Memorial Center for Cancer and Allied Diseases since 1953; specialized in pathology. See *Current Biography* (March) 1953.

Obituary

N Y Times p17 Ag 15 '59

RICHARDS, VINCENT Mar. 20, 1903-Sept. 28, 1959 Former tennis player; won Olympic tennis title (1924) and many other championships; member of Davis Cup teams. See *Current Biography* (July) 1947.

Obituary

N Y Times p39 S 29 '59

RITCHIE, JEAN Dec. 8, 1922- Folk singer; folklorist; author
Address: b. Oxford University Press, 417 Fifth Ave., New York 16; h. 7-A Locust Avenue, Port Washington, N.Y.

The delicate, clear, and untrained voice of Jean Ritchie has brought America's heritage of folk music to many Americans and Europeans who had been unaware that this heritage existed. Her records, recitals, and radio and TV appearances have made her one of the best-known folk singers in the country, and her *Singing Family of the Cumberlands* has given equal publicity to the Ritchie family.

A folklorist and writer as well as a singer, Miss Ritchie received a Fulbright grant in 1952. It enabled her to travel through the British Isles, tracking down the sources of the songs that her family sang in the Cumberlands, and comparing the versions she found with those she learned as a child. At the first annual Newport Folk Festival, held in Rhode Island in July 1959, Miss Ritchie endeared herself to an audience of thousands with the simplicity, directness, and sincerity of her singing as she accompanied herself on the dulcimer.

JEAN RITCHIE

Jean Ritchie was born in Viper, Kentucky, on December 8, 1922, the daughter of Balis W. and Abigail (Hall) Ritchie. She was the youngest of fourteen children, of whom three brothers and eight sisters are still living. The family was reared in mountain poverty, in a three-room house where the girls shared one room, the boys another, and parents and "the least ones" occupied the third room.

The Ritchies preserved a treasure of folk songs which provided their entertainment and eased their work. Some of the songs had been brought from England by Jean's great-great-grandfather; others came into the family by adoption. "Because we Ritchies loved to sing so well," she recalls, "we always listened to people singing songs we didn't know, and we caught many good ones that way."

Alan Lomax ("the ballad hunter") once paid tribute to this treasure by saying, "Ballad singing, like talent for music in general, often runs in families. . . . There are the Smiths of the Shenandoah Valley, who have spread the ballads west from Virginia to Kansas. And in Kentucky, two of the great ballad singing families are the Combses of Knott County and the Ritchies of Perry County."

Mr. Ritchie had been a schoolteacher, but had turned to farming when deafness forced him to quit his profession. By the time she was ten, Jean, like all her brothers and sisters, was a full-time worker in the fields. Although the crop yield was poor, Mr. Ritchie "always could think of one more scheme to make some money in a genteel way," and most of the children received good educations.

Jean attended local schools, graduating from Viper High School in 1940. She attended Cumberland College in Williamsburg, Kentucky, for a teaching course, and then transferred to the University of Kentucky in Lexington. Since the wartime emergency had caused a serious short-

RITCHIE, JEAN—*Continued*

age of teachers in the mountain communities, she interrupted her studies in 1942 in order to teach.

At nineteen, she was the sole instructor in an elementary school of fifty students at Little Leatherwood Creek, Cornettsville, Kentucky. After that year, she combined teaching with her studies, and one of her assignments was the instruction of crippled children in their mountain homes. This was the first time she used her folk songs in connection with her work.

At the University of Kentucky, where she majored in social work, Jean worked as assistant to the head of her department. In addition, she was a member of the YWCA, the glee club, and the literary society, Chi Delta Phi. She was graduated Phi Beta Kappa in 1946 with a B.A. degree, and then returned to Perry County as supervisor of the county's elementary schools.

One of her accomplishments there was the introduction of folk singing in the schools. She was trying to arrest the trend away from native music which had begun when radios were introduced into the mountains. "I can remember a time," she wrote later, "some few years there, when we in our family didn't near sing our own songs like we used to." There was so much new entertainment that "we just about quit gathering to talk and sing."

In 1947, over her father's protests, Miss Ritchie accepted a job as music counselor for the Henry Street Settlement in New York. She worked in the settlement's summer camp at Echo Hill Farm, near Yorktown Heights, and in the autumn transferred to the city. Thus she was able to combine her profession as social worker with her love of singing to the music of her Kentucky dulcimer.

This instrument, which she often played at work and at small gatherings, is a three-stringed affair shaped like a half-pear. Two strings are tuned in C and yield an identical bagpipe-like note when strummed. The third string is fretted and tuned in G, and carries the melody. The dulcimer is held in the player's lap.

"Although I started out to be a social worker (my upbringing and religious training had inspired me with a desire to do something good and worthwhile, if possible, for people in need of help in our mountains), I was able to continue in this field for three years only," Miss Ritchie has said. "At the Henry Street Settlement in New York, where I had come to gain practical experience, I began singing my old-fashioned family songs at friends' parties, then for schools and colleges, and found out two things: 1. The world was genuinely interested in my songs and tales from the Kentucky Mountains—more so than in my ability as a social worker; 2. I was much better, and more at ease, at performing than at teaching."

Miss Ritchie worked at the Henry Street Settlement for two years, until gradually her singing became a full-time occupation. She met folklorist Alan Lomax, and appeared with his group on radio. In 1948 she sang at the folk night of the Contemporary Music Festival at Columbia University, and the following winter appeared at New York's Town Hall.

Her first solo performance was in the spring of 1950 at the Greenwich Mews Playhouse. During the same year she sang every Sunday night on a folk song program over radio station WNYC. For the following two years she was occupied as a radio performer, recording artist, recitalist at schools and colleges, and supervisor of informal summer music camps.

The United States Educational Commission in 1952 awarded Miss Ritchie a Fulbright scholarship so that she could trace the origins of Appalachian folk songs in the British Isles. With her husband, photographer George Pickow, she traveled through England, Ireland, and Scotland. While abroad, she appeared at the Royal Albert Hall, on the BBC and Radio Erin, and made folk records for His Master's Voice and Argo in London.

Returning to the United States in 1953, Miss Ritchie finished work on the three literary projects she had begun earlier. Oxford University Press in 1952 had published her first book, *The Swapping Song Book*, which contained twenty-one folk songs for children. Each ballad was accompanied by a story of mountain customs and a photograph by Miss Ritchie's husband.

Broadcast Music Incorporated published *A Garland of Mountain Song* in 1953. It was a prelude and musical companion to her family portrait, *Singing Family of the Cumberlands*, released by the Oxford University Press in 1955. Some forty-two songs with music were included in this volume, which was cordially welcomed by critics for its simplicity and honesty.

"She writes as she sings—naturally and with an instinctive sense for rhythms," noted Carl Carmer in the New York *Herald Tribune* (February 20, 1955). "The Ritchies are no ordinary family, and their story makes for extraordinary reading," said Oscar Brand in the *Saturday Review* (February 19, 1955), adding that the songs were "woven through the narrative like the golden threads in some ancient tapestry."

Jean Ritchie married George Pickow on September 29, 1950. They have two sons, Jonathan Balis and Peter Ritchie Pickow. Feeling that she must give her spare time to her home and small children, she is continuing to only a limited extent her public appearances and her writing. Her fourth book, *From Fair to Fair*, was scheduled for publication in 1960 by Henry Z. Walck, Incorporated.

A tall woman, Miss Ritchie likes to design and make her own clothes, the better to suit her stature and personality. In public she usually wears a full skirt and a peasant blouse. She likes folk dancing, square dancing, boating, hiking, and family outings. She is five feet eight inches tall, weighs 160 pounds, has blue eyes, and hair that has been described as golden red.

Although she came to her profession by accident, Miss Ritchie regards it as a rewarding one. "Our country is at last grown-up enough to begin to care about its heritage and folk culture," she explains. "I can remember being ashamed to sing an old ballad for fear people would laugh at me. This is passing, in all parts of America. We're old enough not only to *have* a past, but to cherish its teachings."

References

    Am Girl 34:25+ Ag '51 por
    Cosmop 135:62+ Jl '53 por

    Ritchie, Jean   Singing Family of the Cumberlands (1955)

    Who's Who of American Women (1958-59)

ROBARDS, JASON (NELSON), JR. July 26, 1922- Actor

Address: b. c/o Peter Witt Associates, 37 W. 57th St., New York 19

After a decade of relative obscurity as an actor in stock companies, radio soap operas, and television, Jason Robards, Jr., came into prominence when he appeared in an off-Broadway revival of Eugene O'Neill's *The Iceman Cometh* in 1956. Later that year he was acclaimed for his acting in the Broadway production of O'Neill's *Long Day's Journey Into Night*, in which he appeared with Fredric March, Florence Eldridge, and Bradford Dillman.

For his performance as Manley Halliday in Budd Schulberg's *The Disenchanted* in 1958-59, Robards received an American National Theatre Academy (ANTA) Award and an American Theater Wing Antoinette Perry Award. He was named by the *Variety* poll of New York drama critics as the best male performer in a straight play. Robards' style of acting has been called "classical"; he is not a "method" actor like Marlon Brando and other alumni of the Actors Studio in New York City.

The son of Jason Nelson Robards, Sr., and Hope (Glanville) Robards, Jason Nelson Robards, Jr., was born on July 26, 1922. His father, a prominent actor in motion pictures and the theater, was appearing in a revival of Frank Bacon's and Winchell Smith's *Lightnin'* when Jason Robards, Jr., was born in Chicago, Illinois.

When Jason was five years old his parents were divorced. Robards, Sr., went to Hollywood, where he made about 175 movies, and Robards, Jr., lived with his father and stepmother in a large house in Beverly Hills. Indifferent to acting, the younger Robards avoided the profession because he had sensed its insecurity. "When I was twelve," he remembers, "Dad came on lean days and we moved to a less flashy house . . . with . . . a big lot nearby, where we played ball as much as we could" (*New Yorker,* January 3, 1959).

At Hollywood High School Robards joined the track, football, baseball, and basketball teams, and decided he wanted to become a professional athlete. Graduated in 1939, he went on active duty in 1940 with the United States Naval Reserve as an apprentice seaman. Serving in the Pacific Theater of Operations, Ro-

JASON ROBARDS, JR.

bards took part in thirteen major engagements. Once, near Guadalcanal, the ship he was on was sunk.

Before he was discharged in 1946 with the rank of radioman first class, Robards read some plays by Eugene O'Neill, and told his father that he wanted to become an actor after all. Robards, Sr., advised his son to enroll in the American Academy of Dramatic Arts. Entering the academy in 1946, Robards, Jr., attended classes for about eight months.

The director José Quintero, who met Robards in 1952, assigned him the male lead in Victor Wolfson's *American Gothic,* which opened in November 1953 at the off-Broadway Circle in the Square. As Ed Moody, an insensitive and unhappy young husband, Robards turned in what several reviewers called a striking and effective performance.

Robards achieved his first triumph in May 1956, when he appeared in a revival of Eugene O'Neill's *The Iceman Cometh* at the Circle in the Square under the direction of José Quintero. In O'Neill's tragedy, which suggests that no man can face life without sham dreams and empty hopes, Robards played Hickey, the salesman who forces each character to accept death. He ultimately emerges as a lunatic and murderer. "Mr. Robards plays with chilling authority," Wolcott Gibbs wrote in the *New Yorker* (May 26, 1956). "I left sad that Mr. O'Neill was not alive to witness it, because it was so clearly what he intended but never got."

The high artistic level of this revival of *The Iceman Cometh* led Carlotta O'Neill, the playwright's widow, to ask José Quintero to direct the American production of *Long Day's Journey Into Night.* Although O'Neill had finished his somber and autobiographical drama in 1941, he had asked that it be withheld from the public until twenty-five years after his death (which occurred in 1953). By action of his

ROBARDS, JASON, JR.—*Continued*

widow, however, the play had its successful world première on February 10, 1956, at the Royal Dramatic Theater in Stockholm, Sweden.

The Broadway production of *Long Day's Journey Into Night* opened on November 7, 1956, starring Fredric March and Florence Eldridge, with Jason Robards, Jr., as James Tyrone, Jr. Again demonstrating his special affinity for O'Neill, Robards gave what *Variety* (November 14, 1956) called "a scorching, expertly-pyramided portrayal of the sneering, contradictory and somehow sympathetic older brother." Walter Kerr in the New York *Herald Tribune* (November 8, 1956) wrote: "Mr. Robards lurches into the final scene with his hands, his mouth, and his mind wildly out of control, cracks himself in two as he pours out every tasteless truth that is in him, and subsides at last into the boozy sleep of the damned. The passage is magnificent."

The New York Drama Critics Circle voted *Long Day's Journey Into Night* the best play of the 1956-57 season. The judges of the Pulitzer Prize committee honored it with its drama award for 1957. Under the auspices of the United States Department of State and ANTA, the play was presented in Paris during the summer of 1957, with its original cast. José Quintero remarked of Robards' performance in Paris: "He was an especial sensation. Personally, I think he is the greatest young actor in the world" (*Cue,* August 10, 1957).

In March 1958, several weeks before the play closed, Robards left the cast. During the summer of 1958 he appeared with the Stratford Shakespearean Festival in Stratford, Ontario, Canada. He took the roles of Hotspur (Harry Percy) in *Henry IV, Part One* and Polixenes, the King of Bohemia, in *The Winter's Tale.* His "loud, American voice" and non-metrical delivery of Shakespeare provoked considerable controversy. Some reviewers found his performance lusty and stimulating, but the majority agreed with Gerald Weales (*Reporter,* September 4, 1958), who said "I have to admit that he is impossible as a Shakespearean actor." Undiscouraged, in the summer of 1959 Robards played Macbeth to Siobhan McKenna's Lady Macbeth at the Cambridge Drama Festival in Massachusetts. Not all the critics were kind.

For the first time Jason Robards, Sr., and Jason Robards, Jr., acted together in Budd Schulberg's and Harvey Breit's *The Disenchanted,* which opened on December 3, 1958. The elder Robards portrayed Burt Seixas, a publisher, and Robards, Jr., in his first starring Broadway role, played Manley Halliday, an exhausted and defeated writer. Halliday, whose character was modeled on that of F. Scott Fitzgerald, writes a trashy movie script for money, although he believes that "every time a man betrays his total gift, the universe fails." Reviewing the play, Brooks Atkinson commented in the New York *Times* (December 4, 1958): "Mr. Robards catches a whole lifetime in a performance that is open and sincere and touching. . . . As the publisher, Jason Robards,

Sr., gives an affectionate performance that is also first-rate."

Other members of the cast of *The Disenchanted* referred to the father and son team as "Big J" and "Little J." "I'm getting a big kick out of working with Dad in this play," Robards, Jr., said. "He has always been a great audience. He was blind for eight years, until 1956, when he had a couple of operations and got his sight back. All the time he used to listen to me on the radio and on TV, and he gave me a lot of wonderful advice" (*New Yorker,* January 3, 1959). After 189 performances, *The Disenchanted* ended its run on May 16, 1959.

Playing a Hungarian freedom fighter, Jason Robards made his motion-picture debut in *The Journey,* released in February 1959. After the shooting of the film was over, Robards said: "I still prefer the theater to the movies. Once you're on, nobody can say 'cut it.' You're out there on your own, and there's always that thrill of a real live audience" (*Newsweek,* December 15, 1958).

In another medium—television—Robards appeared as Robert Jordan in a dramatization of Hemingway's *For Whom the Bell Tolls* on *Playhouse 90* on two successive Thursday evenings in March 1959. Maria Schell, Eli Wallach, Maureen Stapleton, and Nehemiah Persoff also appeared in the three-hour adaptation, which was produced by Fred Coe and directed by John Frankenheimer. The $300,000 record-breaking budget for the production proved to be more generous than the reviews it received from the critics.

Jason Robards, Jr., and Eleanor Pitman, an actress, were married on May 7, 1948. The marriage ended in divorce. By his first wife, Robards has three children: Jason Nelson 3d, Sarah Louise, and David. In 1959 he was married for a second time, to the former Rachel Taylor. The actor has said that his wife is the "second Rachel Robards in our family. The first Rachel [Donelson] Robards married Andrew Jackson" (New York *Post,* May 20, 1959). Robards is six feet tall, weighs 156 pounds, and has deep-set hazel eyes and dark brown hair speckled with gray. He has been described as "lantern-jawed," "craggy-faced," and "convivial." His favorite hobby is cooking. His club is the Players, and he serves on the board of the American Academy of Dramatic Arts.

One of the roles that Robards would most like to play is that of the song-and-dance man, Harry Van, in Robert Sherwood's *Idiot's Delight.* "I'd even like to be in a musical," he has revealed. "Believe it or not, I can sing. However, I'll settle for playing the title role in O'Neill's one-acter, 'Hughie'" (*Newsweek,* December 15, 1958).

References

Coronet 45:10 My '59 por
N Y World-Telegram Mag p1 Ja 31 '59 por
Washington (D.C.) Post p7B F 3 '59
Who's Who in America (sup Je-Ag '59)

ROCKEFELLER, DAVID June 12, 1915-
Banker; philanthropist
Address: b. Chase Manhattan Bank, 18 Pine St.,
New York 5; 30 Rockefeller Plaza, New York
20; h. 146 E. 65th St., New York 21

In keeping with an historic family tradition
distinguished by achievements in industry, finance, and social welfare, David Rockefeller
has made noteworthy contributions of his own
and has participated with his brothers and sister
in several joint enterprises in business and
philanthropy. He has been vice-chairman since
1957 of the board of directors of Chase Manhattan Bank in New York City and has taken
particular interest in Manhattan redevelopment
projects.

The youngest of five sons, David Rockefeller
was born on June 12, 1915 in New York City
to John D. Rockefeller, Jr. (see *C.B.,* July
1941) and Abby Greene (Aldrich) Rockefeller.
His brothers are John D. 3d (see *C.B.,* June
1953), Nelson A. (see *C.B.,* March 1951), Laurance S., and Winthrop. He has one sister,
Mrs. Abby Rockefeller Mauzé. Their grandfather was John D. Rockefeller, Sr., whose
investments, largely in the oil industry, had
made him one of the richest men in the world

The Rockefeller children were taught that
their enormous wealth was a public responsibility, to be used as much for the benefit of others
as for themselves. For twelve years David
Rockefeller attended the Lincoln School of Columbia University's Teachers College. He received the B.S. degree from Harvard University in 1936, and after taking graduate courses
in economics at Harvard and studying for a
year in England at the London School of Economics, he entered the University of Chicago,
which granted him the Ph.D. degree in 1940.
His doctoral dissertation was entitled *Unused
Resources and Economic Waste* (1941).

To gain firsthand experience in city government Rockefeller worked without salary for
eighteen months, during 1940 and 1941, as one
of sixty "interns" in the administration of New
York City's Mayor Fiorello La Guardia. He
left the mayor's office in October 1941 to become assistant to Mrs. Anna Rosenberg, federal defense co-ordinator for New York state.
Enlisting as a private in the Army in 1942, he
attended Officers Candidates School and then
served in North Africa and France before his
discharge with the rank of captain in 1945. He
was awarded the Legion of Merit, the Commendation Ribbon, and the French Legion of
Honor.

In 1946 David Rockefeller joined the staff of
the Chase National Bank of New York, of
which his uncle, Winthrop W. Aldrich (see
C.B., March 1953), was chairman of the board
from 1933 until his resignation in 1952 to accept the appointment of United States Ambassador to Great Britain. Rockefeller's first position was as assistant manager in the foreign
department. He was promoted in 1947 to assistant cashier, in 1948 to second vice-president,
and in 1949 to vice-president. As supervisor of
the bank's business in Latin America, he di-

DAVID ROCKEFELLER

rected the establishment of new branches in
Cuba, Puerto Rico, and Panama, and in 1950
he founded the Chase quarterly economic publication, *Latin American Business Highlights.*

Appointed a senior vice-president of Chase
National Bank in 1952, he assumed responsibility for customer relations in the New York
City area and for the economic research department. When Chase National and the Bank of
Manhattan merged in March 1955, David
Rockefeller was made executive vice-president
of the Chase Manhattan Bank and given charge
of the bank's development department. Since
January 1, 1957 he has been vice-chairman of
the board of directors, with the responsibility
for the over-all administration and planning
functions of Chase Manhattan, which is the
largest bank in New York City and the second
largest in the nation.

He is also vice-chairman of the board of
directors of Chase International Investment
Corporation, a foreign-financing subsidiary
wholly owned by the Chase Manhattan Bank.
His other business affiliations include director-
ships in B. F. Goodrich Company, Punta Alegre
Sugar Corporation, American Overseas Finance
Corporation, and the Laboratory for Electronics,
Inc.

As a businessman, David Rockefeller has
been described as a "restless seeker for new
ways of combining the gratification of public
service with the imperatives of private profit"
(Arnold Beichman, *Christian Science Monitor,*
April 25, 1958). According to *Newsweek*
(April 28, 1958), he is "conservative." In a
speech in October 1956 before the American
Life Convention, he warned of the dangers of
overexpansion and praised the tight-credit policy of the Federal Reserve.

An internationalist, he is much concerned
with the role of the bank in furthering American private investments in underdeveloped

ROCKEFELLER, DAVID—*Continued*

countries and he believes that the United States has a vital interest in Latin America and the Middle East. "It is not consistent with our national objectives to see the rest of the world on a low standard of living," he said recently; "it is not consistent either morally or with our own economic well-being" (*Christian Science Monitor,* April 25, 1958). During the spring of 1958 he led an eleven-member American delegation to a conference of businessmen in Bonn, Germany to discuss common problems of American and European industry.

One of the Rockefeller philanthropic undertakings in which David Rockefeller has an especially important part is the Rockefeller Institute for Medical Research, which was founded in 1901 by John D. Rockefeller, Sr., and is one of the world's leading medical research institutions. David Rockefeller has been a member of the board since 1940; in 1950 he succeeded his father as president and in 1953 he became chairman. Four new buildings, costing more than $5,000,000, were completed in January 1958 on the Rockefeller Institute's campus along the East River in Manhattan.

Since 1940 the Rockefeller brothers have channeled most of their philanthropic activity through the Rockefeller Brothers Fund (not to be confused with the Rockefeller Foundation), which their sister also supports. David Rockefeller is a trustee of the fund. It was reported in June 1958 that grants of $3,870,981 (made to 110 organizations) during 1957 had brought the fund's total seventeen-year outlay up to $15,111,168. During 1958 the fund won headline attention in the national press through the publication of a series of special studies project reports on military, economic, educational, and other problems facing the United States.

In other Rockefeller enterprises David Rockefeller is director of Rockefeller Brothers, Inc., a management and investment company established in 1946; Rockefeller Center, Inc.; and International Basic Economy Corporation Research Institute.

Urban development is another of David Rockefeller's interests. In 1947 he helped create and was made president of Morningside Heights, Inc., an organization of fourteen New York City educational, religious, medical, and welfare institutions (including Columbia University) formed "to promote the improvement and redevelopment of Morningside Heights as an attractive residential, educational and cultural community." He is· currently chairman of the board of this nonprofit corporation whose achievements in physical and social rehabilitation have set a pattern for work in community betterment. He is also chairman of the Downtown-Lower Manhattan Association, Inc., which is planning a large redevelopment program for the southern part of New York City. A sixty-story headquarters building for the Chase Manhattan Bank, to cost $120,000,000, is currently under construction in this area.

Positions that David Rockefeller fills in other organizations include vice-chairman of the business and finance committee of the Mayor's Advisory Committee in New York City, member of the Westchester County Planning Commission, member of the United Nations advisory board of the staff pension fund, trustee of Carnegie Endowment for International Peace, director and vice-president of the Council on Foreign Relations, Inc., and trustee and chairman of the executive committee of International House, New York. He is an overseer of Harvard University and a trustee of the University of Chicago and of the Museum of Modern Art in New York. His clubs are the Harvard, University, Century, Links, and Knickerbocker, all in New York.

It was primarily for public service that David Rockefeller received an honorary LL.D. degree from Columbia University in 1954. He has also been awarded the 1953 World Brotherhood Award of the Jewish Theological Seminary of America for contributions to the ideal of human fellowship, the Citizens Budget Commission's medal for high civic service (1956), and the Medal of Honor of the Saint Nicholas Society of the City of New York for outstanding service to the city (1956).

David Rockefeller married Margaret McGrath on September 7, 1940, and is the father of six children: David, Abby A., Neva, Margaret, Richard G., and Eileen M. He has called himself "an enthusiastic Republican" (New York *Times,* November 22, 1957). In keeping with his internationalism, he has learned Spanish, French, and German. A champion of the values of the liberal arts, he has pointed out that "the conduct of modern enterprise is so complex that a person who knows and understands something about philosophy, literature, the arts and history, is the type of person who is most likely to succeed in business" (*Christian Science Monitor,* April 25, 1958).

He collects beetles as a hobby; another of his recreations is boating. He has a home in Pocantico Hills, New York and Seal Harbor, Maine as well as in Manhattan.

References

Fortune 51:138+ F; 114+ Mr '55 pors
Holiday 24:27+ Ag; 72+ S; 52+ O; 86+ N '58 pors
Business Executives of America (1950)
Morris, Joe Alex Those Rockefeller Brothers (1953)
Who's Who in America, 1958-59
World Biography (1954)

ROCKEFELLER, LAURANCE S(PELMAN) May 26, 1910- Business executive; conservationist; philanthropist

Address: b. 30 Rockefeller Plaza, New York 20; h. 834 5th Ave., New York 21

The particular fields of activity in which Laurance S. Rockefeller has distinguished himself from the other members of his famous family are conservation and aeronautics. Besides directing a number of his own enterprises, he collaborates on several philanthropic and commercial undertakings with his brothers:

John D. 3d (see *C.B.*, June 1953), Nelson A. (see *C.B.*, March 1951), Winthrop, and David (see *C.B.*, March 1959). His sister, who also participates in some of the joint projects, is Mrs. Abby Rockefeller Mauzé

Laurance Spelman Rockefeller, born in New York City on May 26, 1910, is the third son of John D. Rockefeller, Jr. (see *C.B.*, July 1941) and Abby Greene (Aldrich) Rockefeller and is the grandson of the wealthy oil magnate John D. Rockefeller, Sr. At home—in Manhattan or at Pocantico Hills, New York or at Seal Harbor, Maine—the Rockefeller children were taught thrift, self-reliance, and a sense of public obligation.

Like all his brothers except John, Laurance Rockefeller attended the Lincoln School of Teachers College at Columbia University. His interest in conservation was acquired early in life, as a result of trips made with his father and brothers. "Father, as his father had done with him, took us on these trips," Laurance Rockefeller said recently "not only for the thrill young boys would get from such journeys but also to inspire in us a portion of his own deep love for wilderness beauty and his interest in its protection." At Princeton University he majored in philosophy, earning his B.A. degree in 1932.

Since boyhood he had shown a liking for machinery and aeronautics. Applying this interest to business ventures, he provided financial backing in 1938 when Eddie Rickenbacker became president of Eastern Air Lines, of which Laurance Rockefeller is a director. He was a director of the McDonnell Aircraft Corporation (1941-42), vice-president of Air Youth of America (1938-42), director of the National Aeronautics Association (1942-44), and director of Inter-American Escadrille, formed in 1939 to encourage private flying in the Americas. He has also helped support the work of the Flight Safety Foundation.

Soon after the United States had entered World War II, he joined the Navy, serving from February 1942 until he went on inactive duty in November 1945 in the rank of lieutenant commander. His war assignment for the most part was with the Navy's bureau of aeronautics, for which he dealt with airplane production problems on the West Coast as a liaison officer. Because of his record in the field of aviation, he was appointed to a two-year term, beginning in 1946, as a member of the New York City Airport Authority.

Also in early 1946 Laurance Rockefeller became president of the Rockefeller Brothers, Inc., an enterprise formed to investigate and finance new business projects. Many of the ventures of this company have been in aviation, electronics, and housing. Since 1936 he has been a director of another family enterprise, Rockefeller Center, Inc., in New York and has served from 1953 to 1956 and since 1958 as chairman of this huge business and entertainment center which occupies about twelve and a half acres in the heart of Manhattan. It had been developed by John D. Rockefeller, Jr., over a period of years, beginning in the 1930's, and is reportedly worth some $150,000,000.

Gábor Éder

LAURANCE S. ROCKEFELLER

In collaboration with his brothers, Laurance Rockefeller has also been active in the International Basic Economy Corporation, which has provided capital to develop resources in Puerto Rico and Venezuela, among other Latin American countries. For the nonprofit Rockefeller Brothers Fund, he has served as vice-president and trustee and was a member of the panel which prepared the fund's Special Studies Project Report on the military aspects of international security, made public in January 1958.

His business affiliations include directorships in International Nickel Company of Canada, Olin Mathieson Chemical Corporation, and Filatures et Tissages Africains. Since 1954 he has held an interest in Nuclear Development Associates, an engineering corporation for designing reactors and other nuclear apparatus; and since 1957 he has been a director of the Vitro Corporation of America, engaged in technological activities, particularly in nuclear energy and metallurgy. He is also a member of the New York Stock Exchange. A few of the projects that Rockefeller helped finance are the Viking Rocket, the Banshee fighter, and a parachute that operates on the principle of the helicopter.

Conservation is the field with which Laurance Rockefeller's name is perhaps most closely associated. He is trustee and president of Jackson Hole Preserve, a nonprofit corporation which his father set up in 1940 to aid in conserving areas of natural beauty and to make such places available to the public. The organization takes its name from the Jackson Hole country of northwest Wyoming, whose preservation is one of its primary objectives. It also owns the Grand Teton Lodge Company, which provides facilities for visitors to the Grand Teton National Park in Wyoming.

(Continued next page)

ROCKEFELLER, LAURANCE S.—Cont.

Through Laurance Rockefeller's efforts and largely with his funds, Jackson Hole Preserve began in 1954 to acquire land on the island of St. John in the Virgin Islands. He later gave the land to the United States National Park Service for the creation, in 1956, of the Virgin Islands National Park to preserve the unspoiled beauty of the island. Resort facilities on St. John are operated on a nonprofit basis by the Caneel Bay Plantation, of which Laurance Rockefeller is chairman of the board of directors.

In late 1958 Rockefeller opened a 1,200-acre tourist project on Dorado Beach, some twenty miles west of San Juan, in Puerto Rico in connection with that country's economic expansion program. He has said that his aim in developing the $11,000,000 resort was "to bring people close to nature in a harmonious setting" (*Life*, January 5, 1959). He expects eventually to recover his investment by selling real estate near the hotel's spectacular golf course, built on a former swamp.

More simply for purposes of conservation, in October 1951 Laurance Rockefeller, who is commissioner and secretary of the Palisades Interstate Park Commission, purchased the Donderberg Mountain on the Hudson River and presented it to the Palisades Interstate Park. He is a director of the Hudson River Conservation Society, trustee of the Conservation Foundation, trustee of the American committee of International Wildlife Protection, and trustee and vice-president of the New York Zoological Society. President Eisenhower appointed him in 1958 as chairman of the Outdoor Recreation Resources Review Commission, established by Congress to make recommendations on the recreation resources of the country.

Actively interested in cancer research, Laurance Rockefeller is chairman of the executive committee of the Memorial Center for Cancer and Allied Diseases in New York and a trustee and member of the executive committee of the center's affiliate, Sloan-Kettering Institute for Cancer Research. His positions in other nonbusiness organizations include those of chairman of the advisory council of the department of philosophy of Princeton University and trustee of the Alfred P. Sloan Foundation, the Institute of Defense Analyses, the national board of the Y.W.C.A., and the National Geographic Society.

He is a member of the advisory council of the Naval Air Reserve and the Institute of Aeronautical Sciences, and he belongs to the River, Princeton, University, Downtown Association, Brook, Seawanhaka Yacht, Sleepy Hollow, and Knickerbocker clubs. In 1950 he was awarded Belgium's Commandeur de l'Ordre Royal du Lion.

Laurance S. Rockefeller married Mary French on August 15, 1934; their children are Laura Spelman, Marion French, Lucy Aldrich, and Laurance. The family enjoys outdoor sports, and Rockefeller operates his own airplane and PT boat. *Newsweek* (April 28, 1958) pictures him as a "bold enterpreneur . . . urbane, assured, and highly articulate" who finds that "there is a great personal satisfaction in taking major risks and seeing, in a remarkably high number of cases, success."

References

Fortune 51:138+ F; 114+ Mr '55 pors
Holiday 24:27+ Ag; 72+ S; 52+ O; 86+ N '58
Business Executives of America (1950)
Morris, Joe Alex Those Rockefeller Brothers (1953)
Who's Who in America, 1958-59
Who's Who in Commerce and Industry (1958)
World Biography (1954)

ROCKEFELLER, WINTHROP May 1, 1912- Business executive; gentleman farmer; philanthropist
Address: "Winrock Farm," Morrilton, Ark.

The five grandsons of John D. Rockefeller, who organized the Standard Oil trust, are concerned with spending the many millions they inherited in socially useful ways. Winthrop Rockefeller works toward this goal by co-operating with his brothers in such enterprises as the Rockefeller Brothers Fund and Colonial Williamsburg. Besides these family interests, Winthrop Rockefeller has tried to help the industrial development of the state of Arkansas, to promote the cause of racial integration through the National Urban League, and to demonstrate the feasibility of applying modern scientific procedures to agriculture on his model farm in Arkansas.

The second youngest child of Abby Greene (Aldrich) and John D. Rockefeller, Jr., (see *C.B.*, July 1941), Winthrop Rockefeller was born on May 1, 1912 in New York City. He, his sister, now Mrs. Abby Rockefeller Mauzé, and his brothers, John D. 3d (see *C.B.*, June 1953), Nelson A. (see *C.B.*, March 1951), Laurance S. (see *C.B.*, June 1959), and David (see *C.B.*, March 1959), were raised in New York, Seal Harbor, Maine, and on the family estate at Pocantico Hills, New York. Their deeply religious home environment emphasized thrift, the rights of others, the intrinsic enjoyments and rewards of work, the stewardship of wealth, and civic responsibility.

Winthrop was educated at the Lincoln School of Columbia University's Teachers College and the Loomis School in Windsor, Connecticut; during his school years he held various part-time jobs. In 1931 he entered Yale University, but he lost interest in his studies and left, without graduating, in 1934. Then, as a trainee in the Texas oil fields for the Humble Oil & Refining Company he dug pits and cleaned stills. He is the only Rockefeller brother who has ever been employed in hard manual labor.

During 1937-38 Rockefeller studied finance at the Chase National Bank in New York, and in the following year he served as executive vice-president of the Greater New York Fund. He returned to the oil business in 1939, in the foreign department of the Socony-Vacuum Oil Company, where he was interested in the company's human relations problems. Joe Alex Morris noted in *Those Rockefeller Brothers* (1953): "He became an industrial relations consultant for Rockefeller Center, Inc. He formed and became chairman of Air Youth of America. . . . He became, in 1940, a director of the executive board of the National Urban League to deal with social problems of Negroes in urban areas."

In January 1941, almost a year before the attack on Pearl Harbor, Winthrop Rockefeller enlisted as a private in the Army and a year later entered Officers Candidates School He fought with the 77th Division in the invasions of Guam, Leyte, and Okinawa. Badly burned in combat and suffering also from jaundice, he was sent home in 1945 for a period of hospitalization. Before his separation from the service in 1946 as a lieutenant colonel, he made a nation-wide survey of veterans' readjustment problems for the United States War Department. He received the Bronze Star with two oak leaf clusters and the Purple Heart.

At the end of the war Rockefeller returned to Socony-Vacuum, but resigned in 1951 after failing to convince the firm of the importance of reforming its labor policies. He then became chairman of the board of Ibec Housing Corporation, an affiliate of the International Basic Economy Corporation, founded by Nelson A. Rockefeller and his brothers in 1949 to further economic development in various parts of the world. The purpose of Ibec was to meet the needs of low-cost housing, and it has developed a poured-in-place method of construction which it has used in developments in Norfolk (Virginia), El Salvador, and on a larger scale in Puerto Rico and elsewhere.

Persuaded in part by his friend Frank Newell, whom he had met in the Army, Winthrop Rockefeller moved in 1953 from New York to Morrilton, Arkansas, where he purchased 900 acres on Petit Jean Mountain, sixty-five miles northwest of Little Rock. Soon after, he acquired some pure-bred Santa Gertrudis cattle from the King Ranch in Texas. This was the beginning of Winrock Farm, in which by 1956 he had invested some $2,000,000 and which has been developed into a model 3,500-acre cattle farm. Rockefeller is trying not only to improve this breed of cattle, but also to demonstrate successful farming methods through soil and water conservation, irrigation, and other scientific procedures. It is open to the public, and some 60,000 people visit it each year.

Rockefeller has also contributed his bounty to the educational, civic, health, and cultural undertakings of his adopted state of Arkansas. One of his many projects was the establishment of a model school system in Morrilton to which he gave $2,500,000 with the understanding that it would be integrated. His stepchildren attend the schools in the system.

In 1955 Rockefeller was appointed by Governor Orval E. Faubus to the chairmanship of the Arkansas Industrial Development Com-

WINTHROP ROCKEFELLER

mission. Besides offering his own financial assistance, Winthrop Rockefeller made speeches throughout the state to appeal for aid in developing Arkansas' natural resources and wrote a series of articles for the *Christian Science Monitor* (December 20, 21, 22, 1956).

Rockefeller's name was frequently mentioned in the press during the Little Rock school integration dispute in the fall of 1957, since his views on race prejudice were well known. In one of his few public statements on the issue he said that he believed "first and foremost in the Constitution of the United States and the law and order which it establishes" and expressed concern that the crisis had hurt the campaign to attract industry to Arkansas (Washington *Post and Times Herald*, October 6, 1957). Later, in September 1958, he said that Southern communities were responsible for the lowering of educational standards in integrated schools, because they had never faithfully applied the separate-but-equal mandate (New York *Times*, September 12, 1958).

In his other activities in Arkansas, Winthrop Rockefeller is chairman of the advisory committee of the University of Arkansas College of Medicine and a member of the board of the Arkansas Livestock Show Association and of the Arkansas General Assembly committee on vocational education. He is a director of the Union National Bank of Little Rock, chairman of Winrock Enterprises, Inc., and director of the Pulaski county chapter of the American Red Cross.

One of the Rockefeller family projects with which Winthrop is often identified is Colonial Williamsburg, a re-creation begun in the 1920's by John D. Rockefeller, Jr., of the eighteenth century Virginia colony capital. In April 1953 Winthrop Rockefeller succeeded his brother John D. 3d as chairman of the board of trustees of Colonial Williamsburg, Inc., and the board of directors of Williamsburg Resto-

ROCKEFELLER, WINTHROP—*Cont.*

ration, Inc. One of his first acts as head of the project was to desegregate inns and restaurants there.

By appointment of President Eisenhower in 1954, he was a member of the Jamestown-Williamsburg-Yorktown Celebration Commission to arrange ceremonies for the 350th anniversary in 1957 of the founding of Jamestown. In other family organizations he is a director of Rockefeller Center and Rockefeller Brothers, Inc., a corporation which invests in such fields as aviation, rocketry, housing, food production, and disease control. He is a founding trustee of Rockefeller Brothers Fund, a philanthropic enterprise. Through the latter the brothers sponsor such projects as the special studies entitled *America at Mid-Century* and have made grants of approximately $12,000,000 since 1940.

Before he moved to Arkansas, Winthrop Rockefeller was chairman of the board of trustees of New York University-Bellevue Medical Center. He is at present a trustee of the National Fund for Medical Education, Industrial Relations Counselors, and the Loomis School. He belongs to the Santa Gertrudis Breeders International Association and Delta Kappa Epsilon; and his clubs are the Yale, Links, and Union in New York and the Little Rock Country in Arkansas, among others. He is a Baptist and a Republican. Like his brothers and sister, Winthrop Rockefeller is interested in art, and his collection includes paintings by Henri Matisse and Maurice Utrillo.

On February 14, 1948 Winthrop Rockefeller married Mrs. Barbara "Bobo" (Paul) Sears. They have a son, Winthrop Paul Rockefeller. They were separated in 1949 and were divorced on August 3, 1954, when Mrs. Rockefeller accepted a $6,393,000 financial settlement (New York *Times,* March 22, 1958). Winthrop Rockefeller's second wife, whom he married on June 11, 1956, is Jeanette (Edris) Rockefeller, the mother of a son and a daughter by a previous marriage.

Tall and husky, Winthrop Rockefeller stands at six feet three inches and weighs 235 pounds. Some acquaintances find him to be the most "convivial" of the brothers. "The people of Arkansas wish Winthrop Rockefeller had been born quintuplets," Arkansas' former Governor Francis A. Cherry said in 1955 (Washington *Post and Times Herald,* October 4, 1957). "We haven't many rich people in this state but we have plenty rich enough to do the things Winthrop has done. The difference is that he does them."

References

Fortune 51:138+ F, 114+ Mr '55 pors
Holiday 24:27+ Ag; 72+ S; 52+ O; 86+ N '58
Newsweek 51:24+ Ap 28 '58 pors
Business Executives of America (1950)
Who's Who in America, 1958-59
World Biography (1954)

RODRÍGUEZ, JORGE ALESSANDRI
See Alessandri, Jorge

RODZINSKI, ARTUR Jan. 2, 1894-Nov. 27, 1958 Conductor; directed the New York Philharmonic-Symphony Orchestra and Chicago Symphony Orchestra, among others. See *Current Biography* (August) 1940.

Obituary

N Y Times p27 N 28 '58

RONCALLI, ANGELO GIUSEPPE *See* John XXIII, Pope

ROSE, ALEX Oct. 15, 1898- Labor union official
Address: b. United Hatters, Cap and Millinery Workers International Union, 245 Fifth Avenue, New York 16

The president of the United Hatters, Cap and Millinery Workers International Union is Alex Rose, who has been characterized in the New York *Post* as a man who wears two hats, both of which fit. He is, on one hand, an influential labor leader whose ideas are both daring and practical, and on the other, an adroit politician who has proved his ability in New York state politics, first with the now defunct American Labor party and, since 1944, with the Liberal party, of which he is vice-chairman. He has been president of his small but influential union since 1950, when he succeeded Max Zaritsky.

Alex Rose was born Olesh Royz in Warsaw, Poland, on October 15, 1898, to Hyman and Faiga (Halpern) Royz. His father was a well-to-do tanner, and Olesh grew up in pleasant surroundings, untouched by trade unionism or political activity. He completed high school in Warsaw, but, as a Jew, could not go on to a higher education in his native land. In 1913, accompanied by relatives, he immigrated to America with hopes of becoming a doctor.

When World War I broke out, his parents could no longer send him money, and Rose was forced to take a job as a millinery operator. The pay amounted to $6 a week. Before long, he was making $30 a week, and, later in 1914, he took out his first union card with the Millinery Workers Union, one of the unions that later joined together to form the United Hatters, Cap and Millinery Workers International Union. He became the recording secretary of Local 24 of the Millinery Workers Union in 1916, his first union position.

In 1918, Rose, who had been active in the Labor Zionist Organization, enlisted in the "Jewish Legion" of the British Army, serving as a private in Palestine, Egypt, and Syria. He returned to America in 1920, and again became active in trade unionism. By 1924, he was secretary-treasurer of Local 24, a post he won in a bitter election fight against a candidate backed by Communists, and by 1927 he was vice-president of the International Union.

From the early 1920's, Rose's role in the union, and later in politics, has been one of outspoken and usually effective opposition to Communists and labor racketeers. Writing in the New York *Herald Tribune* on September 1, 1958, M. Jay Racusin said: "It has been his boast that he has cleansed the union of all hoodlum and racketeering elements and Communists." Against these opponents, Rose seems to have won more battles than he has lost.

His first brush with the Communists came in 1921 when he returned from the Middle East (by way of London) to find that Local 24 had fallen under Communist control. Under Rose's leadership, an unofficial anti-Communist club, "The Millinery Club," was organized. After three years of hectic union politics, the club loosened the hold of the Communists on the local and achieved final victory when Rose was elected secretary-treasurer.

His stand against labor racketeers in the hat industry brought Rose a visit from a pair of notorious hoodlums in 1927, when "Little Augie" Orgen and "Legs" Diamond ordered him to call off a strike against a firm under their protection "or else." Fortunately for Rose, "Little Augie" was liquidated in a gang war not too long afterwards. In 1932 two thugs beat Rose up in the lobby of his apartment house. "In those days," Rose recalls, "I had a gun in my pocket and for months slept every night in a different hotel" (New York *Post*, September 7, 1958).

Rose's fight against union gangsters did not end with the 1930's. On June 7, 1953, Rose called for the establishment within the American Federation of Labor of a special "department of justice" to ferret out union racketeers. Again, on June 5, 1956, Rose recommended the creation by the AFL-CIO of a "Labor FBI" to expose and expel racketeers in the labor movement. Because of his opposition to racketeering, Rose was chosen to head the Appeals Committee at the 1957 convention of AFL-CIO. The committee was responsible for the expulsion of the International Brotherhood of Teamsters from the AFL-CIO.

Long a believer in political action on the part of labor, Rose in 1936 plunged into the politics of New York state when he helped to organize the American Labor party. Until 1944 he served as state secretary and executive director of the party. In that year, since the Communists had won the intraparty fight for control, he cut off all relations with the American Labor party; with David Dubinsky, John F. Childs, Adolf Berle, George Counts, and others he founded the Liberal party of the state of New York as a "competitive threat" to the two major parties. "We negotiate with the Democrats and with the Republicans to get the best possible terms for the community," says Rose (New York *Post*, September 7, 1958). He has been vice-chairman and the leading political strategist in the Liberal party since 1944.

The United Hatters of North America, composed mainly of Yankee and Irish craft unionists, merged with the Cloth Hat, Cap,

ALEX ROSE

and Millinery Workers, made up mostly of East European Jewish immigrants, in 1934. The new organization, numbering about 40,000 members, has been a model union from its inception, in spite of its heterogeneous composition.

Rose's climb to the top in the union was confirmed on March 25, 1950, when its executive board unanimously selected Rose as the new president. This move was tantamount to election, for the other nominees withdrew to endorse Rose, who was subsequently elected at a convention held in New York City on May 4.

Since taking over as president, Rose has guided his union through a successful forty-five-week strike against the Hat Corporation of America at Norwalk, Connecticut, in 1953-54, and a short national strike against 400 cap manufacturing firms in 1958. He is even better known for setting many precedents in co-operation between union and management.

Shortly before he became union president, Rose wrote a guest column for the New York *World-Telegram* on August 25, 1949. In it he declared that "the class struggle is a thing of the past in my union and in many others. . . . Our union has demonstrated its willingness and capacity to render constructive service in stabilizing our industry."

As examples of this "constructive service," Rose and the Hatters Union can point to the following: In 1954 the union lent the Kartiganer Hat Corporation $250,000 in order to keep the firm's plants operating and to preserve the jobs of 1,050 union workers; in December 1955, a union loan of $25,000 enabled the Berne Hat Company of Baltimore to resume operations under the name of the Baltimore Hat Company, after it had been forced to close down; in June 1958, the Hatters Union announced that it had purchased a building in the middle of New York's millinery

ROSE, ALEX—*Continued*

district for $1,500,000 and had taken a $2,000,000 mortgage on another building, to prevent a number of millinery companies from being dispossessed and from suffering excessive rent increases.

The Hatters Union in January 1959 began to invest in the 103-year-old Merrimac Hat Corporation of Amesbury, Massachusetts, to prevent its liquidation and to save 325 union jobs. The total investment eventually reached $435,000. The union became the largest stockholder in the company, and Rose became a member of the company's board of directors. The firm began operating under union control on February 2, 1959, and by July 11 the hat firm had made a profit of nearly $70,000 in contrast to a loss of $144,195 in the same five months of 1958. An editorial writer for the New York *Times* (January 26, 1959) observed: "Karl Marx must be turning in his grave." All in all, the Hatters Union has spent $6 million to increase jobs, revive faltering enterprises, and combat hatlessness among American males.

Alex Rose, the man instrumental in launching many of these projects, is a soft-spoken six-footer. He married the former Elsie Shapiro on July 7, 1920. They have two married children, Mrs. Carmy Schwartz and Herbert Rose, a lawyer, and several grandchildren. For relaxation, Rose enjoys classical music and an occasional game of chess. But the New York *Post* (September 7, 1958) quoted a friend of Rose as saying that "for relaxation, Alex works."

References

N Y Herald Tribune p40 Mr 26 '50; p5 S 1 '58
N Y Post Mag p2 S 7 '58
N Y Times p52 Mr 26 '50
Who's Who in American Jewry, 1938-39

RÖSSEL, AGDA (VIOLA JÄDER-STRÖM) (rŭs"l) Nov. 4, 1910- Swedish Permanent Representative to the United Nations

Address: b. Permanent Mission of Sweden to the United Nations, 8 E. 69th St., New York 21; h. 604 Park Ave., New York 21

On August 8, 1958, when Mrs. Agda Rössel presented her credentials as Swedish Permanent Representative to the United Nations, she became the first woman to head a delegation to the international organization. Mrs. Rössel, who succeeds Dr. Gunnar V. Jarring, holds the rank of Ambassador. She has served at the United Nations since 1951, representing her nation at the General Assembly and on several commissions. After World War II she established vocational guidance centers in Austria and Germany to aid displaced teen-agers, and she headed a Swedish government program for the resettlement of many refugees from the devastation of war and Nazism.

Agda Viola Jäderström was born on November 4, 1910 in Gällivare, Sweden, a small mining town north of the Arctic Circle. Her parents were Emil Jäderström, a railroad conductor, and Nina (Lindström) Jäderström. She attended schools in Gällivare and nearby Malmberget, and was fascinated by books and learning.

The circumstances of her girlhood made Agda Rössel sensitive to the needs of others at an early age. She was compelled to leave the Malmberget school during her second year when her mother became critically ill. Remaining at home, Agda cooked and cared for a household of seven people. When she was able to continue her education after three years, she studied nursing. Again her education was interrupted; this time Agda herself fell ill.

After she recovered she decided to move to Stockholm and devote herself to social service. While attending the Socialinstitutet i Stockholm, she worked with the city's welfare department and made psychiatric studies at the Långholmen prison. As early as 1932 she began to develop anti-Nazi views.

After her graduation in 1939 she worked in the personnel department of a Stockholm restaurant chain for two years and then was a business agent for the telephone operators' union. In 1943 she joined the wartime Labor Committee and was responsible for recruiting women workers to substitute for men who had been drafted into the armed services. In that year Miss Jäderström was married to James Rössel, a Swedish journalist.

During World War II Mrs. Rössel took a course designed for training persons who wanted to help reconstruct and rehabilitate Europe after the war. It was organized by such prominent Swedes as Count Folke Bernadotte and Mrs. Alva Myrdal. When hostilities ended, Mrs. Rössel, who had become chief of international activities of the Swedish Save-the-Children Federation, went to displaced persons' camps in Austria and Germany. There she set up vocational guidance hostels for young people between fourteen and eighteen years of age.

"There were hundreds of thousands of these young people, and we had enough money only for twelve hostels accommodating 1,200," Mrs. Rössel has said (New York *Post*, August 17, 1958). "It was a very small action in itself. We just started it . . . like small lamps set out in the dark . . . and then it grew." These activities of Mrs. Rössel were later taken over by the International Labor Organization, the United Nations Educational, Scientific, and Cultural Organization, and the United Nations International Children's Emergency Fund (now United Nations Children's Fund).

In the meantime, starting in 1938, refugees from Nazi persecution looked for asylum in neutral Sweden. When she returned to Sweden, Mrs. Rössel, as an executive of the Swedish government's Labor Market Board, helped to bring 10,000 Greek, Yugoslav, Italian, and Turkish refugees to the country. Especially interested in the sick, she arranged for the entry of 1,000 tuberculosis victims and their families. They were given medical care, employment, and the opportunity to become Swedish citizens.

In addition to her other activities, Mrs. Rössel helped to found the Swedish Central Organization of Salaried Employees in the early 1940's and was a member of its board from 1942 to 1956. From 1948 to 1952 she was president of the Swedish Federation of Business and Professional Women; two years later she became acting president of the International Federation of Business and Professional Women. She was a member of the board of the National Society for the Combating of Cancer and a member of the Association of Swedish Government Officials.

Mrs. Rössel first came to the United Nations in 1951 when she was selected to represent Sweden on the Human Rights Commission. At that time she was one of the three female members of the commission. She soon became known for her cogent arguments. Discussing the drafting of the United Nations covenant on human rights, Mrs. Franklin D. Roosevelt of the United States and Madame Hansa Mehta of India claimed that the word "women" should be retained in an article dealing with the right to "just and favorable conditions of work."

In opposition, Mrs. Rössel maintained that women were covered by article I of the covenant which reads "without distinction of any kind such as race, color, sex." Mentioning women in one article and not in others, in Mrs. Rössel's view, could lead to the interpretation that only men were being referred to when women were not specifically mentioned. She was equally quick to object to the statement that working mothers cannot be good mothers, and pointed out the feasibility of being both a good worker and a good parent.

Mrs. Rössel represented Sweden on the Human Rights Commission until 1953, and during 1952 and from 1954 to 1957 she was also a member of the Swedish delegation to the General Assembly. In 1953 she became a member of the Commission on the Status of Women and served as its chairman from 1956 to 1958.

The highest distinction that Mrs. Rössel has yet received at the United Nations came to her on July 1, 1958, when she was appointed as Sweden's Permanent Representative, with the rank of Ambassador. She presented her letters of credence to United Nations Secretary General Dag Hammarskjöld on August 8.

Agda Rössel is "an ambassador who also happens to be stunningly attractive, blond, blue-eyed, tall, and trim—a description which can be applied to very few persons in the history of diplomacy" (New York *Post*, August 17, 1958). She is also known for her good taste in clothes. Now divorced, Mrs. Rössel was married from 1943 to 1951 to James Rössel, a Swedish journalist. She has two children, Robert and Marianne.

The Ambassador writes and speaks English fluently. She has written several articles and monographs, some of which appeared in the

United Nations

AGDA RÖSSEL

official publications of the International Labor Organization. In her spare time she enjoys the theater, music, ballet, visiting art museums, and reading novels, poetry, and nonfiction.

References

N Y Post Mag p2 Ag 17 '58 por
N Y Times p3 Ag 9 '58 por

ROUECHÉ, BERTON (rōō-shā') Apr. 16, 1911- Author; journalist
Address: b. c/o The New Yorker, 25 W. 43d St., New York 36; h. Stony Hill Rd., Amagansett, N.Y.

Reprinted from the *Wilson Library Bulletin* Nov. 1959.

For his "narratives of medical detection" in the *New Yorker* Berton Roueché has received the 1952 Lasker Foundation Award for Medical Reporting and the 1957 award given annually by the Physician's Council for Information on Child Health (specifically, for his article on aspirin poisoning in *The Incurable Wound*). The Mystery Writers of America also bestowed on him in 1954 a Raven or special award, equivalent to their "Edgar" statuette, for *Eleven Blue Men, and Other Narratives of Medical Detection* as the best book in the mystery field outside the regular categories of crime novels and crime reporting. "These narratives [in *Eleven Blue Men*] are notable for a style which might be envied by true-crime and fiction writers alike," remarked Lenore Glen Offord in the San Francisco *Chronicle*.

A native of Missouri, Berton Roueché received his education and his training in journalism in that state. He was born in Kansas City on April 16, 1911, the son of Clarence Berton Roueché, a merchant whose great-

Hans Namuth

BERTON ROUECHÉ

grandfather came to the United States in the early nineteenth century from Alsace-Lorraine, and Nana (Mossman) Roueché, who was of Scottish descent.

After graduation in 1929 from Southwest High School, Berton Roueché went to Columbia to attend the University of Missouri. Here he majored in English and was granted the Bachelor of Journalism degree in 1934. He went to work as a reporter, rewrite man, and feature writer on the Kansas City *Star*, St. Louis *Globe-Democrat*, and St. Louis *Post-Dispatch*. Since 1944 he has been a staff member of the *New Yorker* magazine.

"Mr. Roueché writes in the demure, almost monotonous prose style that is common to many contributors to the *New Yorker*," wrote Bruce Bliven when he reviewed Roueché's *Eleven Blue Men* (Little, 1954). On the book Bliven commented: "His very colorlessness is reassuring to hypochondriacal readers, who cannot hear of any disease without developing the symptoms." This verdict was challenged by R. J. Dubos, who said of the same book in the New York *Times Book Review* that "he writes in the lively style . . . of the magazine and makes exciting adventure even of the most medical aspects of his tales."

A year after joining the staff of the *New Yorker*, Roueché wrote his first book, a psychological horror story. *Black Weather*'s (Reynal, 1945) scene is a "mildewed (and horror-ridden) rooming house, [with] a Poesque landlady as his villainess, and a neurotic young couple as his victims," according to the New York *Times Book Review*, which made the reservation—frequent thereafter — that "sometimes we are reminded that the novelist (who is also a *New Yorker* editor) has absorbed the style of that magazine through all his pores. The general reader may find that his characters resemble ectoplasm rather than people." The

New Yorker itself, though its book columns usually give little attention to books by staff members, commented that "he leads up quite convincingly to a situation as hopeless as it is inevitable. A quiet but successful first try."

Roueché's reporting on odd or unusual occupations carried on by people of independent or retiring disposition also has its admirers. *The Greener Grass, and Some People Who Found It* (Harper, 1948) is a brief collection of articles from the "Reporter at Large" columns of the *New Yorker*, describing his visits to a mink ranch, a sugarbush, a vineyard, duck and other farms, a monastery, and Shaker village. The *Saturday Review of Literature* recommended the book to "people who enjoy reading about other people," and *Library Journal* thought it would be useful in vocational guidance collections. *The Last Enemy* (Grove, 1956) is a novel, which was published as a paperback.

The Incurable Wound, and Further Narratives of Medical Detection (Little, 1958) is a second collection of cases similar to those in *Eleven Blue Men*. "Written in fascinating style, combining a unique degree of skill in crime reporting with the objectivity of a research scientist and suspense of a detective narrative," said the Chicago *Sunday Tribune*. "The achievement is particularly significant in that these narratives deal with public health rather than clinical medicine and surgery," added the New York *Times Book Review*. "Ten Feet Tall," one of the medical narratives describing the negative effects of cortisone, was made into a motion picture entitled *Bigger than Life* (1956), starring James Mason as the victim of euphoria. *The Delectable Mountains and Other Narratives* (Little, 1959) continues the vocational researches begun in *The Greener Grass*.

Roueché's impersonal style of reporting also appears in his answers to questionnaires. To queries about "favorite author, book, or books" and "favorite recreation, sports," he replied, "No comment." He is a Presbyterian, belongs to no clubs, and is affiliated with no political party. He has brown eyes and black hair, weighs 145 pounds, and lacks an inch of being six feet in height.

On October 28, 1936 Berton Roueché was married to Katherine Eisenhower. The Roueché family, which includes a son, Bradford, now lives on Stony Hill Road in Amagansett, on the south shore of Long Island, within commuting distance of the *New Yorker* offices in New York City.

ROUNTREE, WILLIAM M(ANNING)
Mar. 28, 1917- United States Ambassador to Pakistan

Address: American Embassy, Karachi, Pakistan

Having served as United States Assistant Secretary of State for three years, on August 17, 1959 William M. Rountree assumed the duties of Ambassador to Pakistan. He succeeded James M. Langley.

Crises in the chronically troubled Middle East were the main targets for the diplomatic skill of William M. Rountree after he became Assistant Secretary of State for Near Eastern, South Asian, and African Affairs in August 1956. He helped to guide the United States government in its stand on several conflicts of international importance, including those in Egypt (on the Suez Canal issue), Iraq, Jordan, Lebanon, and Cyprus.

Because of Rountree's key role in the conduct of American foreign relations, he often appeared before committees of the Senate and the House of Representatives, and he was a chief consultant to the Secretary of State on policy decisions affecting vital areas of the world.

William Manning Rountree was born on March 28, 1917 in Swainsboro, Georgia, the youngest of seven children—four boys and three girls—of William Manning and Clyde (Branan) Rountree. His father, who died when William Rountree was an infant, had been a farmer and county official. The boy attended public schools in Atlanta and at Technical High School played in the band.

Just after graduation in 1935 Rountree went north to Washington, D.C. There he enrolled as an evening student at Columbus University and secured a position as a junior employee with the United States Treasury Department. In six years he earned his bachelor of laws degree. Meanwhile, he had advanced through a series of fiscal jobs, including those of accountant and auditor. In 1941, the year he finished law school, Rountree became a budget officer and assistant in the Lend-Lease Administration.

During three years (1942-45) of wartime service in Cairo, Egypt, Rountree was assistant to the director of American Economic Operations in the Middle East. It was in that post that he developed a particular interest in international relations. In the year following World War II (1945-46) Rountree served as administrative officer for the Anglo-American Committee of Inquiry on Palestine and Related Problems.

Joining the State Department in September 1946, Rountree was appointed special assistant to the director of the office of Near Eastern and African affairs. In 1947 he became special assistant for economic affairs, and during that year he was also named a member of the American economic mission to Greece which conducted a survey just before the establishment of the United States aid program to that country. For over a year, beginning in mid-1948, he held the position in Athens of special assistant to the American Ambassador to Greece.

When he returned to Washington in October 1949, he was assigned to the State Department's office of Greek, Turkish, and Iranian affairs, where he advanced from special assistant to deputy director and in August 1950 to director. Two years later, in June, he became deputy chief of mission and counselor of the American Embassy at Ankara, Turkey, and from 1953 to

Department of State
—Whit Keith, Jr.

WILLIAM M. ROUNTREE

1955 served as deputy chief of mission of the American Embassy at Tehran, Iran, achieving the personal rank of minister in 1954.

In November 1955 Rountree was appointed Deputy Assistant Secretary of State for Near Eastern, South Asian, and African Affairs. The following July President Eisenhower sent his name to the United States Senate in nomination for the post of Assistant Secretary of State for that area, and Rountree was sworn into office in August. He headed, therefore, one of the regional bureaus that are an important part of the core of the State Department organization. One of Rountree's chief duties had been to meet regularly with the Secretary of State on matters relating to the Middle East and the other areas of Africa and Asia for which he was responsible—mostly to supply up-to-date information that might affect policy decisions.

Although newspaper readers frequently saw his name in reports of White House meetings, Congressional hearings, or visits to the United States by foreign dignitaries, William M. Rountree was relatively unknown to the general public until quite recently. His two-day visit to Iraq in December 1958 became front-page news in the United States and abroad because of violent anti-American demonstrations which threatened him in Baghdad.

The incident occurred during the Assistant Secretary's fact-finding tour of the Middle East, where he was scheduled to meet with United States diplomats and heads of government in Lebanon, Jordan, Iraq, Greece, and the United Arab Republic. Rountree made the two-week tour soon after a period of crises in the Middle East, following by two months the evacuation of American and British forces from Lebanon and Jordan, and by five months the

ROUNTREE, WILLIAM M.—*Continued*

military revolution in which Brigadier General Abdul Karim Kassem seized the government of Iraq.

Back in Washington later in December, Rountree said the "unhappy incident" had been "highly organized by certain elements" which he declined to identify. (Other officials termed them pro-Communist.) "But I want to emphasize," he added, "that I was welcomed by the government and the security protection they gave me was very adequate. Afterward we had useful and friendly discussions" (*Christian Science Monitor,* December 22, 1958).

American policy in the Middle East was the subject of an address that Rountree made before the National Conference on the Middle East in Dallas, Texas in May 1957. While affirming that the United States wanted to support the development of independent nations, he pointed out that in some Middle East countries extreme or "negative" nationalism had taken an anti-Western form. He further noted the readiness of the Soviet Union to take advantage of several major intra-area disputes in promoting international Communism.

In a statement in May 1958 before the Senate Committee on Foreign Relations, Rountree said, "In summing up the state of our relations with [the Near East, South Asia, and Africa], I would offer you the analogy of a spectrum. At one end are our very friendly relationships with those close allies associated with us in mutual-security arrangements. At the other end, through various gradations, are those few countries that still misconstrue our motives. It is, of course, not a full spectrum—far from it—for there are no Soviet satellites" (*United States Department of State Bulletin,* June 2, 1958).

In 1954 Rountree received the Department of State Superior Service Award. In 1957 he was given the National Civil Service League Career Service Award. According to a profile in the New York *Herald Tribune* (December 11, 1958), "He has earned the reputation of being able to slice through the blubber of bureaucracy to the heart of a problem. He is straightforward; polite, not blunt. . . . His travels throughout the world have washed away the Georgian drawl from an accent which now could be called cosmopolitan." He has been described elsewhere as "never loquacious."

On July 8, 1946 William M. Rountree married Suzanne McDowall, and they have a daughter Susan, eleven years old. He is tall (six feet one inch) and weighs 190 pounds. His hair and eyes are brown, and he wears horn-rimmed glasses. A member of the Kenwood Country Club in Washington, he names golf as a favorite recreation ("when I have time"). He is a Protestant.

References

N Y Herald Tribune p3 D 11 '58 por

Department of State Biographic Register, 1958

Who's Who in America, 1958-59

ROWANS, VIRGINIA *See* Tanner, Edward Everett, 3d

RUBOTTOM, R(OY) R(ICHARD), JR.

Feb. 13, 1912- United States government official
Address: b. c/o Department of State, Washington, D.C.; h. 4543 Klingle St., N.W., Washington, D.C.; Corsicana, Tex.

The guiding principle of R. R. Rubottom, Jr., Assistant Secretary of Inter-American Affairs, has been that the future of the United States depends upon the economic prosperity and political stability of its neighbors. In September 1957 he was appointed to his present post, succeeding Henry Holland. For his twelve years of outstanding achievement in the United States Foreign Service, he has received the Department of State's Superior Service Award (1952) and the National Civil Service League's Civil Service Award (1957). A specialist in Latin American problems, he has spent most of his diplomatic service in that area, except for three years in Spain.

Roy Richard Rubottom, Jr., the only son among the three children of Jennie Eleanor (Watkins) and Roy Richard Rubottom, was born on February 13, 1912 in Brownwood, Texas. After being educated in Brownwood public schools, he entered Southern Methodist University in Dallas, Texas in 1928 on a freshman scholarship.

As an undergraduate, Rubottom majored in journalism, received the Student Activity Scholarship, edited the college newspaper, and was elected president of his class. He was also chosen for membership in the Lambda Chi Alpha and Sigma Delta fraternities. He received the B.A. degree in 1932 and pursued graduate work at Southern Methodist.

In 1933 Rubottom completed the requirements for the M.A. degree in international relations. For three years beginning in 1938, he continued graduate study at the University of Texas in Austin. He concentrated on Latin American affairs, in which he had first become interested when he was studying Spanish in high school. However, he was never able to devote the time to fulfill the prerequisites for the Ph.D. degree.

From 1933 to 1935 Rubottom worked as a traveling secretary for Lambda Chi Alpha, advising chapters throughout the country on their various problems. Although he wanted to follow a career in educational administration, jobs that paid well were scarce. Rubottom was forced to become a kitchen equipment salesman with the Century Metalcraft Corporation in Chicago. Later, he turned to selling oil field equipment for the Guyberson Corporation in Dallas, Texas. He left the selling field in 1937 when he was appointed assistant dean of student life at the University of Texas. There he was concerned primarily with the administration of extracurricular activities.

Six months before the outbreak of World War II, Rubottom received a naval commission as a lieutenant, j.g. He was then stationed in the United States for a year and a half. Sent to Mexico as a naval liaison officer, he worked with Mexican authorities who were servicing

Pacific-bound United States ships. In 1945 he was assigned to Asunción, Paraguay as the naval attaché of the United States Embassy.

Following his discharge in 1946 in the rank of commander, he accepted a position as a vice-president of the State National Bank in Corsicana, Texas. At this small bank Rubottom acquired a background in economics which was to prove useful in his work with United States foreign aid programs. While with the bank he took a special Foreign Service exam for war veterans with experience in international affairs. He was appointed to the Foreign Service on April 10, 1947, at the age of thirty-five.

After spending two months at the Foreign Service Institute in Washington, Rubottom was sent to the United States Embassy in Bogotá, Colombia, where he served first as second secretary and later as consul. In 1948 he was appointed secretary of the American delegation to the Ninth International Conference of American States which was assembled in Bogotá.

Two years later Rubottom was transferred to the State Department as officer in charge of Mexican affairs. Appointed deputy director of the office of Middle American affairs in 1951, he was responsible for the negotiation of a migrant labor agreement and a lend-lease settlement, both with Mexico.

Promoted to the directorship of the Middle American office in 1952, he headed the American delegation to a conference in Caracas, Venezuela. There he arranged for revising a 1939 trade treaty between the two countries which had been rendered obsolete by the vast changes in economic conditions that had occurred. The new agreement reduced duties up to 50 per cent on oil imported from Venezuela in return for a Venezuelan reduction of tariffs on $154,000,000 worth of United States commodities.

The next assignment for Rubottom came in 1953 as first secretary of the United States Embassy in Madrid. With the consummation of the Spanish-United States military and economic agreements in late 1953, Rubottom was named deputy director of the United States economic and technical aid mission in 1954 and advanced to the post of director in the following year.

Recalled to Washington in 1956, he was appointed Deputy Assistant Secretary of State for Inter-American Affairs. The following year he was appointed Assistant Secretary of State. In this post he is chief of the bureau of Inter-American affairs, and thus supervises the activities of four subdivisional offices: Middle American affairs, South American affairs, Inter-American regional political affairs, and Inter-American regional economic affairs. Among his specific duties in directing foreign relations in this part of the world is supervising United States embassies, maintaining relations with Latin American representatives in Washington, initiating and co-ordinating policy in regard to the Inter-American system, and carrying out policies concerning Puerto Rico.

In 1957 Rubottom said in a speech at Harvard University that the United States carries on trade with Latin America amounting to $7.5 billion a year, often exceeding its trade in all

Department of State

R. R. RUBOTTOM, JR.

other areas of the world; United States investments in Latin America are about $9 billion; and that there had been a great increase in loans to countries of that region (*United States Department of State Bulletin*, September 30, 1957).

Economic crises and resulting political instability in Latin America are major problems with which Rubottom must contend. For the past few years prices of many Latin American exports have declined. Consequently, these countries have increased commercial debts and restricted imports, thus lowering the standard of living. Many of these nations have also suffered severe inflation and have failed to attract investment from domestic and foreign companies.

When Rubottom accompanied Vice-President Richard M. Nixon on his tour of eight South American countries in 1958, he witnessed anti-American rioting in Peru and Venezuela. The participants in these violent demonstrations attributed the deplorable economic conditions in their countries to United States policies and voiced their dissatisfaction with alleged United States cordiality to Latin American dictators. Some observers believed that the riots were instigated by Communists, and Rubottom said that they obscured the warmth with which the majority of Latin Americans received the mission.

A few months later, Rubottom accompanied Dr. Milton S. Eisenhower on a fact-finding trip to Central America. In agreement with Dr. Eisenhower and Vice-President Nixon, the Assistant Secretary feels that there should be a distinction between United States treatment of Latin American dictators and democratic leaders.

The United States must continue to adhere to its policies of recognizing dictatorships and non-intervention, Rubottom has said, but, he has

RUBOTTOM, R. R., JR.—*Continued*

added, dictators should be denied United States government decorations and the warm welcome accorded to the leaders of the democracies. This nonintervention policy was most recently exemplified in the United States' "hands-off" policy toward the new Cuban government headed by Fidel Castro in its executions of alleged war criminals of the regime of Fulgencio Batista.

Although Rubottom stresses the mutual dependence of the United States and Latin America, he opposes increasing assistance programs, is against commodity agreements which would control the prices of exports, and insists that "competitive free enterprise . . . through its role in trading and investment is doing and will do far more than any government can" (*United States Department of State Bulletin*, September 30, 1957).

Anti-United States sentiments in Latin America were again apparent in March 1959 when rioting in Bolivia broke out following statements in a *Time* magazine article which reportedly offended Bolivian sovereignty. Violence forced the American Embassy to be closed for several days.

R. R. Rubottom, Jr., met Billy Ruth Young at the University of Texas where she was the secretary to the university president. They were married on December 23, 1938 and have three children, Eleanor Ann, Frank Richard, and John William. The entire family speaks Spanish fluently. Rubottom has blue eyes, brown hair, stands almost six feet tall, and weighs 190 pounds. He is a Methodist. His clubs are the Metropolitan and Congressional Country. Golf is his major form of recreation. He received the Distinguished Alumnus Award from Southern Methodist University in 1958.

References

Department of State Biographic Register, 1958
Who's Who in America, 1958-59

RUDKIN, MRS. HENRY ALBERT *See* Rudkin, Margaret

RUDKIN, MARGARET (FOGARTY)
Sept. 14, 1897- Bakery executive
Address: b. Pepperidge Farm, Inc., Westport Ave., Norwalk, Conn.; h. Sturgis Highway, Fairfield, Conn.

Pepperidge Farm, Inc., of which Mrs. Margaret Rudkin is the founder and director, makes bread and other bakery products for those people who like the quality of homemade food and are willing to pay for it. The family company, with its headquarters in Norwalk, Connecticut, was started in 1937 by Mrs. Rudkin after she had begun baking bread for one of her sons who needed a special diet. As the firm expanded, it included not only bread in its list of products, but also rolls, herb-seasoned stuffing, cookies, and frozen pastries.

Now there are three bakeries: in Norwalk, Connecticut; Downington, Pennsylvania; and Downers Grove, Illinois. Several grist mills stone-grind the flour for the products, and the bread is kneaded by hand by the women employees at the baking plants. Mrs. Rudkin's husband and two of her three sons are active in the firm. She was presented in 1955 with the distinguished award to industry by the thirty-second Women's International Exposition of the Women's National Institute.

Margaret Fogarty, the daughter of Joseph J. and Margaret (Healy) Fogarty, was born in New York City on September 14, 1897. She has four brothers and sisters. Until she was twelve years old, the family lived with her grandmother in a brownstone house, on the site of Tudor City. After the death of her grandmother, they moved out to Flushing, where she attended the public schools and was graduated as valedictorian of her class.

For the next two years she worked as a bookkeeper in a bank in Flushing, and then was made a teller. After four years in this position, she became a "customer's woman" for the now dissolved brokerage firm of McClure, Jones & Co., where she met Henry Albert Rudkin, who was one of the partners. They were married on April 8, 1923, and lived for the next five years in New York City. In 1928 they bought land in Fairfield, Connecticut, and built a Tudor-style house. They moved there in the following year, and named it Pepperidge Farm, because there was an old pepperidge tree on the property.

When one of her sons had asthma and was kept on a special diet, he needed to eat homemade bread. "I had never baked bread in my life," Mrs. Rudkin has recalled. "They say life begins at forty—well, that's how old I was when I baked that first loaf. I just turned to the reliable *Boston Cookbook,* and started following directions. And then, suddenly, I seemed to remember the way my grandmother did it when I was six years old." Her son's physician asked her if she would make bread for some of his other patients, which she did. One day, in the fall of 1937, when she had some extra bread, she asked her grocer to sell it for her.

It sold very quickly, and Mrs. Rudkin then included several other local stores and the exclusive Charles and Company of New York City in her bread deliveries. She asked several women to help her in her kitchen, and converted the stables and part of the garage on the farm into a bakery. After a year, she was baking 4,000 loaves a week. As the firm expanded into an empty service station in Norwalk, Connecticut, Mrs. Rudkin added the production of melba toast and pound cake.

Mrs. Rudkin contracted to use the facilities of several mills for the grinding of the flour, including the Wayside Mill at South Sudbury, Massachusetts, and supplied her own top-grade wheat, bought in Minneapolis. Now the whole wheat flour used in the bread is ground at five different old-time grist-mills in the East. When building a new plant at Downers Grove in Illinois, the firm also built a mill, using large buhrstones and constructing it on the principles of the older mills. The Pepperidge company also uses slow-aged unbleached white flour.

The other ingredients of the bread include 93-score sweet creamery butter, fresh whole milk, yeast, water, salt, honey, and cane syrup. No yeast foods or commercial shortenings are ever used. The dough is mixed in small batches, and is cut and kneaded by hand. The bread loaf is wrapped by machines. It was only after much pressure that a modern bread slicer was introduced, as Mrs. Rudkin believes that old-fashioned bread should be cut just before it is eaten.

In 1956 Mrs. Rudkin began marketing a new line of delicate luxury cookies made from recipes long highly regarded in Belgium. She obtained the use of the recipes and the production data under an agreement with the House of Delacre (a Belgian bakery firm), after looking all over Europe for good cookies. The Pepperidge firm added a wing to the Downington (Pennsylvania) bakery, and imported a 150-foot oven from Belgium, with which to manufacture the cookies. The firm entered the frozen food field in the fall of 1958 with a new pastry line, including puff pastry desserts, and is in the process of perfecting frozen, uncooked patty shells.

The various products are sold throughout the United States, through mail-order shipments to stores where there are no distributors, and deliveries to out-of-town distributors. The firm does very little advertising, but has become successful by letting the products stand on their own merits and on the word-of-mouth reputation they receive.

Over 80 per cent of the stock in the firm is owned by the Rudkin family, and no figures are published on the gross income or profits of the company. Mrs. Rudkin handles the production and personnel end of the business; Mr. Rudkin has the responsibility of its general financial policy and of the marketing, sales, shipping, accounting, and purchasing of raw material and equipment problems. The Pepperidge firm employs about 600 persons, two-thirds of whom are women.

Mr. and Mrs. Rudkin have three sons: Henry Albert, Jr.; William Lincoln; and John Mark. All three attended Yale, and two of the sons, Henry and William, are vice-presidents of the Pepperidge Farm company. For recreation Mrs. Rudkin enjoys baking bread and pies at her home and testing new recipes. She collects antique bread boards. Her husband used to play polo and was president of the Fairfield Hunt Club for several years. In 1953 they bought an old Rudkin family farm in the village of Bagenalstown in Ireland, where they have gone during vacations.

References

Am Home 45:64+ Ap '51
Christian Sci Mon p14 Mr 24 '55
Coronet 34:61+ Ag '53
N Y Herald Tribune p25 N 18 '49
N Y Times III p3 D 4 '49
New Yorker 24:38+ My 22 '48

MARGARET RUDKIN

Newsweek 20:68+ S 21 '42
Read Digest 35:102+ D '39
Time 50:82+ Jl 14 '47
Who's Who in America, 1958-59
Who's Who in Commerce and Industry (1957)
Who's Who in the East (1957)
Who's Who of American Women, 1958-59

RUMMEL, JOSEPH F(RANCIS), ARCHBISHOP Oct. 14, 1876- Roman Catholic prelate
Address: b. 7845 Walmsley Ave., New Orleans, La.; h. 2809 Carrolton Ave., New Orleans, La.

When the United States Supreme Court ruled in May 1954 that segregation in the public school system was unconstitutional, it found an ally in Archbishop Joseph F. Rummel of New Orleans. Leader of the largest Roman Catholic flock in the deep South, Archbishop Rummel stated that the Supreme Court's ruling was "thoroughly in accord with the principles and teachings of the Catholic Church." A vigorous champion of the rights of the Negro, Archbishop Rummel has denounced racial segregation as "morally wrong and sinful."

Known as the "Archbishop of Catholic Action," the forthright prelate has often taken a stand that has brought him into the newspaper headlines. As builder and administrator, he has perhaps accomplished more during his tenure than any of his predecessors during the past century. His goal is the eventual integration of the 184 Catholic elementary and high schools in his archdiocese.

Joseph Francis Rummel was born on October 14, 1876 in Steinmanern, Baden, Germany, the only child of Gustave and Teresa (Bollweber) Rummel. His father was a shoemaker. At the

Wide World

ARCHBISHOP JOSEPH F. RUMMEL

age of six, Joseph came to America with his parents, who settled in Yorkville, the large German community on Manhattan's upper East Side.

Quickly hurdling the language barrier, Joseph attended St. Boniface school and at the age of twelve decided to study for the priesthood. He attended St. Mary's College, North East, Pennsylvania and received his B.A. degree from St. Anselm's College, in Manchester, New Hampshire in 1896. From that year until 1899 he studied at St. Joseph's Seminary in Yonkers, New York. While a student at St. Joseph's, he was selected to study at the North American College in Rome. He was ordained in Rome on May 24, 1902 by Pietro Cardinal Respighi, vicar general to his Holiness, Pope Leo XIII. Remaining in Rome after his ordination, he continued his studies at the North American College and received his doctorate in sacred theology in 1903.

Returning to New York City in 1903, Father Rummel was assigned as assistant at the Church of St. Joseph in Yorkville, where he remained until 1907. After having been a curate for four years, he became a pastor. From Yorkville he went to St. Peter's Church in Kingston, New York, where he stayed until 1915. He then served as pastor of the Parish of St. Anthony of Padua, Bronx, New York from 1915 to 1924 and as pastor of the Parish of St. Joseph of the Holy Family in Harlem from 1924 to 1928. In addition, he served as dean of Ulster and Sullivan counties from 1912 to 1915 and as executive secretary of the German Relief Committee (1923-24). On April 24, 1924 he was named papal chamberlain and given the title of Very Reverend Monsignor.

During his four years at the Parish of St. Joseph of the Holy Family in Harlem, Rummel saw the problems of the American Negro from a pastor's point of view at the parish level. He recalls that "Negroes were just beginning to move into Harlem in large numbers at that time. . . . The neighborhood was still predominantly white, but Negroes were on the increase. Already they were attending masses and sending children to our school" (Washington *Post and Times Herald,* February 23, 1956).

For four years in Harlem, Monsignor Rummel taught the Negro and white members of his parish how to work together. His talents for teaching, organizing, integrating, and building proved effective. On March 30, 1928 Monsignor Rummel was elevated to the bishopric, and on May 29, 1928 he was consecrated Bishop by Patrick Joseph Cardinal Hayes. He was assigned to the See of Omaha and in 1935 he was elevated to Archbishop and assigned to the Metropolitan See of New Orleans.

Archbishop Rummel's see is a vast one. The 12,000-square-mile archdiocese of New Orleans is the largest in the deep South. Archbishop Rummel is also titular head of Catholics in Alabama, Louisiana, Arkansas, Mississippi, and part of Florida. More than 50 per cent of the South's Catholics live in Louisiana. Statistics for 1956 indicated that 549,371 Catholics live in the archdiocese and that one out of every five is a Negro.

The parochial school system of New Orleans is the state's largest single school unit. Forty of its 184 Catholic elementary and high schools are for Negro children (New York *Times,* August 25, 1957).

The problems that confronted the Archbishop of New Orleans were also vast. Southerners were emotionally committed to segregation as a way of life, and this commitment was backed by legal sanction. But Archbishop Rummel had become the leading voice in the archdiocese insisting that segregation was morally, legally, and socially wrong. In 1953 he abolished segregation in all Catholic churches in his archdiocese and ordered that Negroes no longer be barred from parish organizations. They were no longer required to sit in separate pews or to wait at the end of the line to receive Holy Communion.

After the 1954 Supreme Court decision which ordered integration of Negroes and whites in the public schools, Archbishop Rummel began to take decisive action. In October 1955 he suspended services at the Roman Catholic Mission of St. Cecilia at Jesuit Bend, fifteen miles south of New Orleans, when its parishioners refused to permit Reverend Gerald Lewis, a young Negro priest, to say Sunday Mass.

Archbishop Rummel called the incident "a violation of the obligation of reverence and devotion which Catholics owe every priest of God, regardless of race, color, or nationality." He reduced services at two other nearby missions and announced the suspension and reduction would remain in effect "until the members of those communities express their willingness to accept for service in these churches whatever priest or priests we find it possible to send them" (New York *Herald Tribune,* October 15, 1955.)

Attracting national attention for his action, Archbishop Rummel also received commendation from the Vatican. Its official newspaper, *L'Osservatore romano* (October 17, 1955), called the actions of the parishioners blasphemous and voiced "Christian pride" in the American prelate. The Archbishop reopened the mission in April 1958.

In February 1956, four days after a special three-man federal court, declaring all Louisiana school segregation laws unconstitutional, issued a court order to carry out the Supreme Court decision, Archbishop Rummel issued a pastoral letter to be read at all masses in the archdiocese denouncing racial segregation as "morally wrong and sinful." He announced also that integration in the archdiocesan schools would be effected, advancing reasons from the moral and dogmatic teachings of the Church.

When the Supreme Court rendered its decision on segregation in the schools, the strongly prosegregational Louisiana Legislature passed provisions which enabled the state to exercise its police rights to continue segregation. On the same day in February 1956 that the three-man special federal court declared all segregation laws in Louisiana unconstitutional and instituted its court order to desegregate, three Catholic members of the Legislature, in an effort to halt integration, proposed extending the state's police power to Catholic schools.

Archbishop Rummel acted promptly. An editorial in *Catholic Action of the South,* the official weekly publication of the Archdiocese of New Orleans, warned the Roman Catholic legislators of the state that they faced automatic excommunication if they "worked for or voted for" laws continuing to segregate the state's parochial schools. The editorial also said that the excommunication could be incurred by "those who directly or indirectly impede the exercise of ecclesiastical jurisdiction either of the internal or the external forum, and for this purpose have recourse to a lay authority."

Despite legislative opposition and the resistance from White Citizens' Councils and the Association of Catholic Laymen, Archbishop Rummel confirmed his intention to continue to organize a program of gradual integration, one grade at a time, in the schools of the archdiocese. He was not intimidated by the actions of the Association of Catholic Laymen, which in 1957 appealed to Pope Pius XII to halt integration.

Archbishop Joseph F. Rummel has been frequently honored. He has received honorary degrees from St. Anselm's College, Creighton University, Loyola University of the South, Duquesne University, and Fordham University. Often commended by groups outside the Church, he was cited in January 1956 for "outstanding contribution to interracial understanding" by the Chicago *Defender,* a Negro daily newspaper.

As Archbishop of New Orleans, Rummel is *ipso facto* president of all Roman Catholic churches and religious charitable institutions in his archdiocese. Though suffering from glaucoma, which is sapping his eyesight, he is a member of the board of the New Orleans chapter of the American Red Cross, the New Orleans Eye, Ear, Nose, and Throat Hospital, the New Orleans Cancer Society, and the Catholic University of America in Washington, D.C.

References

N Y Times p16 O 15 '55
Washington (D.C.) Post p14 F 23 '56
American Catholic Who's Who, 1958-59
International Who's Who, 1958
Who's Who in America, 1958-59

SACHS, CURT June 29, 1881-Feb. 5, 1959 German-born musicologist; author; lectured at New York University and New York Public Library. See *Current Biography* (August) 1944.

Obituary

N Y Times p25 F 6 '59

SAINT-GAUDENS, HOMER (SCHIFF) Sept. 28, 1880-Dec. 8, 1958 Art authority; stage director; magazine editor; director of fine arts at the Carnegie Institute in Pittsburgh (1922-50). See *Current Biography* (October) 1941.

Obituary

N Y Times p58 D 9 '58

SANANIKONE, PHOUI *See* Phoui Sananikone

SCHLEIN, MIRIAM June 6, 1926- Author *Address*: h. Murray St., Westport, Conn.

Reprinted from the *Wilson Library Bulletin* Apr. 1959.

Children love the books of Miriam Schlein, because she has retained the faculty for seeing everyday things through the eyes of a child.

The daughter of Dr. William and Sophie (Bigleisen) Schlein, Miriam Schlein was born in Brooklyn, New York on June 6, 1926. She went coasting and skating in Prospect Park and rode her bicycle to the water front to see the tugboats and the big ships from other lands. She loved the zoo and her pets—which may be why many of her books tell of animals.

Miriam graduated from Manual Training High School in Brooklyn, then received her B.A. degree in English and psychology from Brooklyn College in 1947. She held a variety of jobs, all having to do with writing—advertising, radio continuity, secretary to a juvenile book editor. When she was in the children's department of Simon & Schuster she realized she wanted to devote all her time to writing. She herself, when young, loved the Doctor Dolittle books and Kipling's *Just So Stories.* The late Margaret Wise Brown, whom, she believes, is "the finest juvenile writer of our time," influenced her own work. Of adult books her

Bernard Cole

MIRIAM SCHLEIN

favorites are *War and Peace, Moby Dick,* and Harriette Arnow's *The Dollmaker* (Macmillan, 1954).

First of Miriam Schlein's books was *A Day at the Playground* (Little Golden Books, 1951). Then came a series published by William R. Scott, interpreting abstract concepts in terms a child can grasp. *Shapes* (1952) deals with roundness as compared with squareness. She says the idea came to her when she saw the round afternoon sun framed in her car window. Ellen Lewis Buell commented in the New York *Times Book Review*: "This is a brilliant little book which will help to train a youngster's eye and make him sharply aware of form and design." It is written in a lilting style that tots love.

Similarly, the idea of relative speeds inspired *Fast is not a Ladybug* (1953) which won the Boys' Club of America Junior Award. *Heavy is a Hippopotamus* (1954) explains the idea of weight. *It's About Time* (1955), which *Christian Science Monitor* voted "a chucklesome book," is recommended for kindergarten to fourth grade by the *Library Journal.*

William R. Scott also published a number of Miriam Schlein's stories about children and animals. *Go with the Sun* (1952) tells of a little boy who decides not to go south with the birds after all. *The Four Little Foxes* (1953) was a Junior Literary Guild selection. *Elephant Herd* (1954), another Junior Literary Guild choice, has, said New York *Herald Tribune Book Review,* "a worthwhile moral . . . as to why not to run away."

When Will the World Be Mine? (1953) was called by *New Yorker* "a poetic book about a baby snowshoe rabbit." *Lazy Day* came in 1955, as did *Big Talk,* a dialogue between an over-ambitious kangaroo and his mother. "Fine for reading aloud and remembering by heart," wrote Marjorie Fisher in the New York *Times Book*

Review. Little Rabbit, the Big Jumper (1957) concerns another boastful baby. *The Big Cheese* (1958) is the story of a gullible peasant carrying a cheese for the king, but on his way he meets too many cheese lovers.

Miss Schlein's other main publisher is Abelard-Schuman. *The Sun Looks Down* (1954) explains the idea of parents' protection. L. S. Bechtel, in New York *Herald Tribune Book Review,* believes it has "a mixture of treatments which prevents its being an artistic whole. But it is far more stimulating than the many realistic . . . books we forget after one look."

Little Red Nose (1955), an honor book at the New York *Herald Tribune* Spring Book Festival, contains illustrations by Roger Duvoisin and describes how a little boy feels when spring comes. This one has been translated into German, as has *Oomi, the New Hunter* (1955), a book for eight-to-twelve-year olds. *Deer in the Snow* (1956) tells how two children and their parents feed hungry deer until spring. In *The Bumblebee's Secret* (1958) creatures large and small follow a bumblebee out of curiosity. "For the youngest by far the most attractive book," according to the New York *Herald Tirbune Book Review,* is *Home: The Tale of a Mouse* (1958).

Amazing Mr. Pelgrew (1957), in which a small boy wonders what his grown-up friend does in the city, was another Junior Literary Guild selection. Entirely different is *A Bunny, a Bird, a Funny Cat* (1957)—explaining in pictures and a brief text how to make a flower, draw a horse, a man, a bunny. *The Raggle Taggle Fellow* (1959) is described by Virginia Kirkus as "a delightful new twist to an old pattern."

Three other publishers have also brought out books by Miss Schlein. Of *How Do You Travel?* (Abingdon, 1954) *Library Journal* said: "Some words need explanation . . . and some pages appear cluttered, but to have such a variety in a preschool book is refreshing." The Nashville *Tennesseean* commented that *Henry's Ride* (Abingdon, 1956) will mean special delight for the three-to-seven-year-old set.

Something for Now, Something for Later (Harper, 1956) tells of two farmers: Homer has a bumper crop of corn; Perry plants an orchard with cherry seedlings. *City Boy, Country Boy* (Childrens Press, 1955), a Junior Literary Guild choice for children from three to six, "brings most of the wonder of both lives to the young reader" (San Francisco *Chronicle*). *Herman McGregor's World* (1958) was published by Albert Whitman, as were *Here Comes Night* (1957) and *Puppy's House* (1955).

Miriam Schlein is brown-eyed, brown-haired, five feet four inches tall. She is of the Jewish faith. She was married in 1954 to Harvey Weiss, a sculptor and illustrator of several of her books. Both enjoy tennis, sailing, skiing. Their daughter, Elizabeth, was born in April 1957 and occupies most of her mother's time not devoted to writing. Their home is in Westport, Connecticut.

Reference

Who's Who of American Women (1958-59)

SCHORR, DANIEL (LOUIS) (shŏr) Aug. 31, 1916- Radio and television correspondent
Address: b. Columbia Broadcasting System, 485 Madison Ave., New York 22; h. 1387 Jessup Ave., New York 52

As radio and television news correspondent for the Columbia Broadcasting System, Daniel Schorr has brought the American public on-the-spot coverage from the U.S.S.R., the Netherlands, Venezuela, Costa Rica, Panama, and Capitol Hill. While serving in Moscow for two years he interviewed Premier Nikita S. Khrushchev in his first American telecast, seen in the United States on June 2, 1957. Schorr was twice honored by the Dutch government for his dispatches from Holland and received citations in 1957 and 1958 from the Overseas Press Club of America. Excluded from the Soviet Union in December 1957, Schorr is reporting in 1959 from Warsaw, Poland.

Daniel Louis Schorr was born in New York City on August 31, 1916, the son of Louis and Tillie (Godiner) Schorr. He has one brother, Alvin, now a social worker employed by the federal government; his father is a real estate dealer in New York. Daniel attended public elementary schools and the De Witt Clinton High School, where he worked on the staff of the student newspaper, *Clinton News,* and year-book, *The Clintonian.*

Following his graduation in 1933, Schorr majored in sociology at City College of the City of New York. There, he continued his journalistic interests by writing for *The Campus,* the undergraduate newspaper, and working as a cub reporter for the *Bronx Home News* (1934-35) and the Jewish Telegraphic Agency. He received his bachelor's degree in 1939.

After he completed his college courses, Schorr stayed on at the Jewish Telegraphic Agency as its assistant editor. In 1941 he joined the staff of Aneta (Dutch) News Agency as news editor. He left this post in 1943 to be inducted into the United States Army. Assigned to Intelligence, Schorr was stationed in San Antonio, Texas until his discharge in 1945 with the rank of sergeant.

His observations of the discrimination against Mexican-Americans in Texas formed the basis of an essay which appeared in the *New Republic* (September 30, 1946). As a free lance, Schorr also contributed articles to the New York *Times, PM,* and *Cosmopolitan.* After his release from military service, he returned to Aneta and was sent to Holland to head its European service.

Schorr became a free-lance correspondent in 1948, covering the Low Countries for the *Christian Science Monitor* and the London *Daily Mail.* His headquarters were in Amsterdam, but in June and July of 1948 he toured strife-torn Indonesia as a guest of the Dutch government. Several newspaper articles and a special radio series for the Columbia Broadcasting System resulted from the visit.

Among the stories which Schorr covered in the Low Countries were the abdication of Queen Wilhelmina in 1948, the attempt of Leopold III of Belgium to return to the throne in 1950,

DANIEL SCHORR

and the establishment of European Coal and Steel Community headquarters in Luxembourg City in 1952. In 1949 he sent a dispatch to the *Christian Science Monitor,* describing how the Dutch village of Borculo raised relief funds for Warren, Arkansas, which had been struck by a tornado. The aid was a token repayment of flood relief which had come to that town in 1925. The article was judged the story most conducive to understanding between Holland and the United States; for it Schorr received in 1950 the first William the Silent Award, which consisted of $2,500 and a gold medal.

From 1950 to 1953 Schorr continued his work in Holland as a correspondent for the New York *Times.* The climax of this overseas tour came in 1953 when floods inundated Holland. At this time he made as many as four broadcasts daily for CBS news. "Because the floods left me emotionally exhausted," he said later, "and because I found a new excitement in electronic journalism," he returned to the United States later that year.

As Washington correspondent for CBS News Schorr reported from Capitol Hill. He was also selected for special foreign assignments. In March 1954 he covered the tenth Inter-American Conference in Caracas, Venezuela; in January 1955 he gave a firsthand account of the rebel invasion in Costa Rica and events following the assassination of Panama's President José Antonio Remón; and in May 1955 he made a survey of refugee camps in Europe and the Near East. While on the latter mission, Schorr was again honored by Holland. Queen Juliana created him an Officer of the Order of Orange-Nassau, the first time that the honor was conferred upon an American journalist.

In September 1955 Schorr was sent by CBS News to cover the visit of West German Chancellor Konrad Adenauer to Moscow. Although his visa was valid for only one week, he

SCHORR, DANIEL—Continued

remained to open the first CBS news bureau in Moscow and in December 1955 was granted permanent accreditation by the Soviet government. Except for annual year-end visits to the United States, Schorr was stationed in Moscow until December 1957.

When Schorr first arrived in the Soviet capital, he was the second American radio, and television correspondent in the city. He found his colleague, Irving R. Levine of NBC, using a standard broadcasting studio for his dispatches, while Schorr was assigned to a telephone booth in Moscow's Central Telegraph Office. Schorr requested equal facilities. The Soviet officials filled the request by assigning Levine to the telephone booth, also, and thereafter the broadcasts of both networks went out from the makeshift studio. Although the correspondents draped their booth with velvet, their broadcasts often carried background murmurs from a newspaperman who was telephoning his story in the next booth.

Under such conditions, a Moscow assignment was the "most difficult and least rewarding" foreign post, according to Anne W. Langman in the *Nation* (February 2, 1957). She quoted Schorr as saying: "No correspondent in Moscow thinks he knows the truth. We're looking at Russia through a cloudy, sometimes broken piece of glass. . . . Nobody in Russia ever gives a straight answer to anything."

Perhaps in an attempt to interview the one man who might give a "straight answer" Daniel Schorr arranged for Soviet Premier Khrushchev to make his first television appearance on an American network. The interview was filmed on May 28, 1957 by a CBS crew flown from the United States and Britain and was broadcast over *Face the Nation* on June 2, attracting considerable comment in the American press.

Until this time, Schorr had been remarkably exempt from criticism by the Soviet press. During the World Festival of Youth and Students in August, however, he was singled out by *Komsomolskaya Pravda* as a "provocateur" and "adventurer" for his comments on the festival delegates, and a caricature depicted him as carrying a huge "smearpot" around Moscow. He was not allowed to return after his year-end visit to the United States in December.

Schorr, who had left his personal belongings in Moscow, waited six months for his re-entry permit. Finally, in the summer of 1958, the United States Department of State was informed by the Soviet Embassy in Washington that Schorr had been excluded. No reason was offered, but Schorr believes that the action resulted from his participation in a special broadcast concerning the Hungarian rebellion.

After several temporary assignments for CBS, including one as United Nations correspondent, Schorr gave up hope of returning to Russia when the CBS Moscow bureau was ordered closed on October 8, 1958, following a telecast of *The Plot to Kill Stalin* on September 25. Schorr then left on a tour of Poland and Yugoslavia. After a brief return to the United

States, he was sent in April 1959 to open a CBS bureau in Warsaw, Poland and received a special assignment to cover the Big Four Foreign Ministers' conference in May and June.

Schorr is a large man, standing five feet eleven inches and weighing 185 pounds; he has brown hair and brown eyes. He is unmarried, has no political or religious affiliation, and plays chess and tennis for recreation. He is a member of the Overseas Press Club of America in New York; and of the National Press Club, the Overseas Writers, Congressional Radio-TV Correspondents' Association, and State Department Correspondents' Association in Washington, D.C.

Like most foreign correspondents, Schorr is a versatile newsman. He must be adept with recording equipment for radio interviews, with a still camera for news events, and with a motion-picture camera for television programs. As a writer, he is a frequent contributor of articles and book reviews to national publications.

References

    Washington (D.C.) Post p3G Ap 27 '58 por

    Who's Who in Foreign Correspondence, 1956-57

SERLING, ROD Dec. 25, 1924- Television and film writer

Address: b. Columbia Broadcasting System, 485 Madison Ave., New York 22

Television writers have traditionally worked in anonymity, writing their dramas for an ephemeral audience that views them only once. One exception is Rod Serling, whom Harriet Van Horne of the New York *World-Telegram and Sun* has called "television's only angry young man." Author of more than 100 television plays, he was the first video dramatist to have one of his works produced a second time by popular demand. He is also one of the few who have had their dramas published in book form and made into motion pictures.

Serling has come to the top of his profession in a remarkably short span of time. He was born in Syracuse, New York, on December 25, 1924, the son of a wholesale butcher. He grew up in Binghamton, New York, and attended local public schools; he was president of his high school class and editor of the student newspaper. After his graduation in 1942, he enlisted in the United States Army as a paratrooper.

Serling's first fighting during World War II was as an amateur boxer; he won seventeen of his eighteen military bouts. Then he was transferred to the Pacific theater of operations. He was severely wounded in the Philippines campaign during his three years overseas. After the war, he enrolled at Antioch College in Yellow Springs, Ohio, under the "GI Bill" scholarship program. He began to write radio dramas while an undergraduate.

In 1950, when he was a senior at Antioch, Serling won second prize in a *Dr. Christian* script contest sponsored by the Columbia Broadcasting System. His prize included $500 and a trip to New York City with all expenses paid for Serling and his wife, a fellow student at Antioch. This success confirmed his ambition to be a script writer, and after his graduation in June 1950 he continued to write radio dramas.

Since his first forty free-lance scripts were all rejected, Serling was forced to find a salaried job to support his family. He worked first as a script writer for radio station WLW in Cincinnati, Ohio, then moved to television station WKRC-TV in the same city. Meanwhile, he had sold two scripts to the *Grand Central Station* program over CBS radio. Three more radio sales followed.

Serling made his breakthrough as a free lance in 1951, when he was twenty-six years old. He sold a television drama to the *Lux Video Theatre* series, and quickly followed this by selling ten more scripts to the same program. He earned $5,000 from his first successful season as a free lance, 1951-1952, and doubled that in the following year. He left his studio script-writing job in the spring of 1953.

A year later, after again doubling his previous season's earnings, Serling moved with his family to Westport, Connecticut, in order to be near the television centers in New York City. A one-hour drama by Rod Serling about life in the top echelons of big business, entitled *Patterns*, was telecast by the *Kraft Theatre* over NBC-TV on January 12, 1955.

Patterns was greeted by a New York *Times* critic as "one of the high points in the TV medium's evolution." It was telecast again on February 9, literally by popular demand, the first drama in the history of American television to receive a second production. Serling by this time had sold ninety scripts to the major networks in four years; suddenly he was one of the best-known writers in the business.

In April 1955 Serling signed a first-purchase-rights contract with CBS-TV. In the same month *The Rack* was telecast by the *US Steel Hour* on ABC-TV. Although this story of an American officer on trial for collaborating with the enemy was not an award winner, it enhanced Serling's growing reputation as a dramatist of merit, both in its original form and as a motion picture.

His scripts were now selling as fast as he could write them, for a total of twenty dramas telecast in 1955. In five days, from November 23 to November 28, three of his one-hour dramas were before the camera, while Serling himself was in Hollywood to write a screenplay for Metro-Goldwyn-Mayer. Before 1955 was finished he had also adapted *Patterns* and *The Strike* for filming by United Artists. Perhaps inevitably, the critics noticed decline in quality in many of Serling's video plays.

"From 'Patterns' on, I suffered what every writer's suffered from a single big success," he later said (New York *Times,* December 2, 1956). ". . . So much of what I put on after that was dictated by economic considerations, too. I had to live. Unlike a legitimate-theater man, I don't have eighteen months to three years for another success. I've got three weeks."

ROD SERLING

The motion-picture version of *Patterns,* with a screenplay by Rod Serling, was released in March 1956. Although several critics pronounced it "thin," "self-conscious," and "cliché-ridden," others agreed with A. H. Weiler (New York *Times,* March 28, 1956), who wrote that "Mr. Serling has given us a creative, frightening, and often moving portrait of familiar and rare executives caught in mahogany-paneled 'jungles' with their teeth, hearts and minds bared. . . . The movie has given 'Patterns' wider physical scope, but it has not glossed over its terrible truths."

A Serling drama entitled *Requiem for a Heavyweight* inaugurated the *Playhouse 90* series on October 11, 1956. A critical success, it re-established Serling's reputation as a top-flight video dramatist, and was purchased for the movies and the legitimate stage. With *The Rack, Old MacDonald Had a Curve,* and *Patterns,* it was also published in book form in *Patterns* (Simon and Schuster, 1957).

"The drama of television is such a fleeting thing," wrote critic Cecil Smith of the collection (Los Angeles *Times,* December 8, 1957), ". . . that some readers may be surprised that the plays of this little electronic theater . . . stand up with some of the best dramatic writing of our time. . ."

Among the Serling dramas which attracted notable attention in recent years were *The Comedian* in 1957, *A Town Has Turned to Dust* and *The Time Element* in 1958, and *The Rank and File* in 1959. Serling signed a new one-year contract with CBS-TV in mid-1958, but later in the year decided to write less for television, because of the censorship encountered by some of his scripts. Both *A Town Has Turned to Dust,* with its lynch-mob theme, and *The Rank and File,* dealing with corruption in labor unions, went through extensive revisions before they were accepted.

(Continued next page)

SERLING, ROD—*Continued*

Weary of the struggle with the censors, Serling switched from controversial dramas to fantasy in the autumn of 1959, when *Twilight Zone,* his series of filmed science-fiction programs exploring the quirks of man's imagination, opened on CBS-TV. "I simply got tired of battling," he told Harriet Van Horne of the New York *World-Telegram and Sun* (September 25, 1959). "You always have to compromise lest somebody—a sponsor, a pressure group, a network censor—gets upset. Result is that you settle for second best. It's a crime, but scripts with social significance simply can't be done on TV." In estimating his talents, he has said: "I don't have the imagination most writers have. I don't have Paddy Chayefsky's gift for back-fence observation" (*Newsweek,* December 12, 1955).

Like other video dramatists before him, Serling turned to Hollywood, moving there in 1958. He wrote a script for United Artists and signed a contract with Metro-Goldwyn-Mayer to write one screenplay a year for three years.

Serling holds many awards for his television dramas, including three "Emmy" trophies from the National Academy of Television Arts and Sciences, and two Sylvania "best drama" awards. To keep up his prolific output, he has abandoned typewriters in favor of recording machines; he usually works from 8 A.M. until noon, but will continue until midnight if he "feels driven."

Serling is married to the former Carol Kramer, and has two daughters, Jody and Nan; the family now lives in California. For recreation, Serling builds model airplanes and goes water-skiing. He is a small man, standing five feet five inches tall and weighing 137 pounds. "His nose might be described as hawklike," wrote Gilbert Millstein in the New York *Times* (December 2, 1956), "his eyebrows are black and beetling, and his mouth is usually composed purposefully and dramatically, thus giving him a facial expression of unusual intensity." Serling has more tersely described himself as looking "like a Sicilian boxer."

Serling views the world with intensity, and pugnacity, too. "Our society is a man-eat-man thing on every possible level," he has said (*Time,* June 30, 1958). With such uncompromising dramas as *Patterns, Requiem for a Heavyweight,* and *The Comedian,* he has brought his hard view to bear in a medium which too often is noted for the flabbiness of its approach.

References

Cosmop 145:41 Ag '58 por
N Y Times Mag p24+ D 2 '56 por
Newsweek 46:107 D 12 '55
Vogue 129:138 Ap 1 '57 por

SETTLE, MARY LEE July 29, 1918-
Author

Address: h. 808 Middle Rd., Charleston, W.Va.

Reprinted from the *Wilson Library Bulletin* Feb. 1959.

Mary Lee Settle is at work on a projected four-volume novel on the settlement of West Virginia from 1754 to the present. *O Beulah Land* (Viking, 1956), the first and so far only published book of the tetralogy, has elicited almost breathless praise from reviewers: "a novel of incomparable literary beauty" (Boston *Sunday Herald*)—"deserves serious consideration as a work of art" (*Saturday Review*)—"a dramatic talent of high order" (Nashville, Tennessee, *Banner*).

Miss Settle's goal in *O Beulah Land* is to describe the social, political, and economic background of the settlers' struggle in West Virginia in the twenty years between 1754 and 1774. Because of this approach—similar to that of the cultural anthropologist—Miss Settle's work "ranks far above the formula-ridden and sensational historical novels that have misinterpreted American history in recent years" (*Saturday Review*).

Mary Lee Settle was born at Charleston, West Virginia July 29, 1918. Her parents were Joseph Edward Settle, a civil engineer, and the former Rachel Tompkins, both of English and Scottish descent. She grew up chiefly in her mother's family home in Cedar Grove, West Virginia, and in Greenbriar County, West Virginia and in Kentucky. In 1936 she was graduated from Charleston High School, going on to Sweet Briar College in Virginia, although she took no degree.

Nevertheless, her stay at Sweet Briar shaped her future. A teacher, Joseph Dexter Bennett, appreciating her talent, advised her to write. "I tried to escape the effects of this suggestion," she says, "but did not succeed." At this stage of her career, she was a chronic verse writer; she had, indeed, broken into print with a poem at nine, but in her own judgment, this output was "very bad."

Eager to take an active part in World War II, Miss Settle went to England in 1942, joining the WAAF's. She remained there after the war and married Douglas Newton, the English poet and journalist. During the fourteen years she made England her home, Miss Settle traveled in France and Italy, finding Rome "the most beautiful city in the world." During these years abroad, she continued her writing: articles for the Office of War Information in London, editorial and writing duties for *Harper's Bazaar.* She also served as English correspondent for *Flair,* and she did one motion-picture scenario.

In 1954, Harper & Brothers published her first novel, *Love Eaters,* which was also released in England. Well received in both England and the United States, this book describes the emotional and professional tensions found in an amateur theatrical group of an Allegheny coal town. The London *Times Literary Supplement* declared: "Miss Lee Settle's book is uncomfortably alive with the antipathies of small-town American society, which she analyzes in the vigorous and rhythmic idiom of American speech, and, although this writer is a relentless analyst, the effect . . . is a compassionate one."

Soon after this success came *Kiss of Kin* (Harper, 1955) which also was published in England. The *Saturday Review* summed up both the negative and positive reaction to this story

Henry Ries

MARY LEE SETTLE

of a dying matriarch who had tried to force her unpleasant heirs to observe the Golden Rule: "Miss Settle's writing is quick and deft. Sometimes she touches only the surface of events and not all her characters are equally palpable; but taken as a unit, this second novel is a fine achievement."

Much of the three years of research for *O Beulah Land* was done in the British Museum Library, "because no libraries were kept in West Virginia at the time of the story." This novel of the Virginia frontier centers around Jonathan Lacey, a Virginia-wilderness-country gentleman in the years just before the American Revolution. After his service at the Battle of Little Meadows in 1775, Johnny scouts and surveys far into the mountains. He leads a heterogeneous group of early Americans westward with him to claim and clear his bounty land in the undefended King's Part of the colony beyond the Proclamation Line. It is on this land, called Beulah by Preacher Jeremiah, that Johnny proves his strength.

The author explained her approach to history in this novel: "It is not, I believe, what actually happens in any given period, but what the people believe at the time it is happening, which influences the future as handed down opinions, colorings, prejudices and habits." Fanny Butcher said of the book in the Chicago *Sunday Tribune*: "Like a tapestry, it is episodic . . . its threads are brilliantly colored, its individual scenes dramatic. It has, of course, one quality which no tapestry can have—a voice, and, if any one characteristic of *O Beulah Land* is outstanding, its voice, its language, is that quality."

Miss Settle's favorite authors are Tolstoy, Hardy, Conrad, Twain. For relaxation, she says, "I like to hunt, be in the woods, prefer trotting to any other form of racing." Historic research is both her hobby and vocation, and she likes to sing hymns.

Miss Settle is five feet eight inches tall and weighs 140 pounds. She has slightly wavy brown hair and brown eyes. She is a Democrat and an Episcopalian. Now divorced, Miss Settle lives in Charleston, West Virginia, where she is a member of the Edgewood Country Club. For the year 1957-58 she was awarded a John Simon Guggenheim Fellowship. At present she is working on the second volume of the proposed tetralogy, to be called "Know Nothing," a novel she says, "tracing through three brothers the growth of tension and cultural clash which resulted in the war between the states."

Reference

Mlle 40:85 Ja '55 por

SHAVER, DOROTHY July 29, 1897-June 28, 1959 Business executive; president of Lord & Taylor department store since 1945; opened branch stores. See *Current Biography* (January) 1946.

Obituary

N Y Times p1+ Je 29 '59

SHULMAN, MAX Mar. 14, 1919- Humorist

Address: b. c/o Harold Matson, 30 Rockefeller Plaza, New York 20; h. River Lane, Westport, Conn.

Variously described as "a satiric genius," a "master of undergraduate humor," a "cultured Perelman," and "an outrageous punster," Max Shulman, the American humorist, has been an entrepreneur in what he calls "the durable joke business" since 1942. He has written several best-selling novels, including *Rally Round the Flag, Boys!* and two long-running plays, *Barefoot Boy With Cheek* and *The Tender Trap*.

Every week Shulman regales American undergraduates with his syndicated humor column, "On Campus," which advertises Marlboro cigarettes. He has published over 100 of his stories in such mass-circulation magazines as *Saturday Evening Post, Cosmopolitan, Collier's,* and *Good Housekeeping*. He has also written scripts for motion pictures.

Max Shulman was born in St. Paul, Minnesota on March 14, 1919 to Abraham and Bessie (Karchmer) Shulman. His father was a house painter. Shulman has one sister, Esther. He attended Central High School in St. Paul, and was active on the school paper. After his graduation in 1936 he entered the University of Minnesota as a journalism major. While in college he edited *Ski-U-Mah,* the campus humor magazine, and wrote a column for the college newspaper, the Minnesota *Daily,* in which he carried on a playful feud with another columnist, Thomas Heggen, who later wrote *Mister Roberts.* Shulman showed some of his pieces to Sinclair Lewis, who said "first go to work in a grocery store." Since Shulman had already worked in a grocery store, he decided to go ahead with his writing.

(Continued next page)

Washington Post

MAX SHULMAN

An editor from Doubleday, Doran & Company encouraged Shulman to write his first book, *Barefoot Boy With Cheek*. It was published by Doubleday in 1943, the year after he was graduated from college. The book is a frivolous lampoon of college life, dedicated (among others) to the employees of the bureau of weights and standards. Its plot concerns the dilemma of Asa Hearthrug, a freshman, who is torn between Yetta Samovar, a campus leftist, and Noblesse Oblige, a sorority girl. *Barefoot Boy With Cheek* sold 33,000 copies in its hard cover edition, and still flourishes as a paperback, especially in college towns. Shulman's next novel, *The Feather Merchants* (1944) satirized the civilian home front during World War II.

Entering the United States Army Air Force in June 1942 as a private, Shulman served until 1946, when he was discharged with the rank of technical sergeant. "The only time I ever got emotional," he has confessed (New York *Sun*, February 28, 1947), "was when I went into the Army. I just knew I'd be killed, and I ended up writing training manuals for the air forces."

Shulman's next novel, *The Zebra Derby* (1946), recounted the further adventures of Asa Hearthrug, home from the Army and looking for work in the "brave new plastic world." "It is satiric fiction exploring the rehabilitation of the ex-serviceman," wrote Russell Maloney (New York *Times Book Review*, February 17, 1946). "His history of Bonanza, the wartime boom, is a sociological study worthy of the Lynds."

"It is absolutely impossible to describe the effect that Max Shulman has achieved," observed Clip Boutell (New York *Post*, January 14, 1946) in reviewing *The Zebra Derby*. "There are laughs on every page. Among the

subjects dealt with are reconversion . . . door-to-door selling, the new cars, Communism, surplus war materials, the press, and the GI's return to college. There are absurd and completely delightful fables tossed off in passing. . . . He is, perhaps, closest to S. J. Perelman. Nothing is sacred to either of these humorists, nothing impossible, nothing ever very probable. They both like puns, funny names . . . and both are satirists of no mean ability." *The Zebra Derby* was also notable for containing twenty-four characters named Max.

Shulman collaborated with producer George Abbott to turn *Barefoot Boy With Cheek* into a Broadway musical comedy which opened on April 3, 1947 and ran until July 5, 1949. Billy Redfield played the role of Asa Hearthrug, Nancy Walker was Yetta Samovar, and Red Buttons was Shyster Fiscal. Shulman told an interviewer that he rewrote the show nine times. "Every time I watch a player cross the stage," he said, "I think of a funnier line to put in his mouth. It's driving Mr. Abbott crazy!" (New York *Sun*, February 28, 1947). Most of the Broadway critics found *Barefoot Boy With Cheek* more full of exuberance than originality. Robert Coleman in the New York *Mirror* pointed out that the musical "lacks some of the novel's subtlety and suavity, but packs plenty of rousing, irresistible hilarity."

With Robert Paul Smith, Shulman collaborated on a Broadway comedy, *The Tender Trap*, which opened on October 13, 1954. It dealt with the amatory problems of a New York bachelor, and starred Robert Preston, Kim Hunter, and Ronny Graham. It ran for 102 performances, was published in a Fireside Theatre edition in 1955, and has since proved a favorite with little theater groups. The motion picture based on the play, released by Metro-Goldwyn-Mayer in 1955, starred Frank Sinatra and Debbie Reynolds, with Celeste Holm and David Wayne in supporting roles.

In August 1957 Doubleday & Company published Shulman's novel, *Rally Round the Flag, Boys!* Set in a fictitious town in Fairfield County, Connecticut, the satire tells what happens to the citizenry when the United States Army installs a guided missile station. Al Morgan, who reviewed the book for the New York *Herald Tribune* (August 11, 1957) said: "Max Shulman, the master of undergraduate humor, the outrageous pun, and the verbal caricature, has dropped all his many talents into the hopper and come up with what is, by a very wide margin, the funniest novel of the year." The book sold over 100,000 copies and Twentieth Century-Fox Film Corporation made a film adapted from it, starring Paul Newman and Joanne Woodward.

The CBS television network announced in the spring of 1959 that it would produce a new comedy series in the fall, written by Max Shulman and based on the adventures of Dobie Gillis, the teen-age hero of a number of Shulman's magazine stories. Dobie Gillis is also the hero of a new Shulman novel, *I Was a Teen-Age Dwarf*, published on August 25, 1959 by Bernard Geis Associates, a new publishing house. Shulman is enthusiastic about the new firm, which publishes under the imprint of Star Press Books. "Standard publishers," he says, "are inclined to treat authors like second-class citizens—the ink-stained wretch, you know. The publishing business is a hard one but it's been kept small because the publishers haven't been thinking big. They stay old-fashioned. This bunch is going to run a darned interesting experiment. I hope it works" (New York *Herald Tribune,* March 22, 1959).

Although Max Shulman once saw himself as "squat" and "moon-faced" (*Collier's,* July 24, 1948) a reporter for the New York *Sun* in the same period described him as "young and refreshingly humble... very handsome in a harmless sort of way" (February 28, 1947). He has hazel eyes and brown hair, is five feet six inches tall, and weighs 145 pounds. He is a Democrat. He belongs to the Authors Guild, the Dramatists Guild, and the Writers Guild of America. He permits himself a game of croquet or snooker pool occasionally, but thinks that strenuous exercise is "bad for the tissues." When asked by a young reporter if he would write his earlier works differently if he had to do them again, Shulman replied, "Yes, I would have put in a new ribbon." Asked about his writing habits, he said that he always writes the first draft in the sand with a pointed stick; *Rally Round the Flag, Boys!* was about six and a half miles long. His advice to young writers is—"marry money."

Max Shulman and Carol Rees were married on December 21, 1941. They have four children: Daniel, Max, Jr., Peter, and Martha. The Shulman family lives in Connecticut, in what Shulman describes as a rambling house which sits on two acres of land and 100,000 moles. In 1958 Shulman was one of six Minnesotans who were honored by having one of the state's lakes named after them. According to the humorist, Lake Shulman looks like its namesake, small and round.

References

> Time 55:99 Ap 10 '50 por
> Warfel, Harry R. American Novelists of Today (1951)
> Who's Who in America, 1958-59

SIQUEIROS, (JOSÉ) DAVID ALFARO
(sē-kě'ē-rōs) Dec. 29, 1896- Mexican painter
Address: Calle Queretaro 180, Mexico City 7, D.F., Mexico

The "shouting walls" of the three great Mexican muralists, David Alfaro Siqueiros, Diego Rivera, and José Clemente Orozco, still exhort Mexican workers and tourists. But of the triumvirate of proletarian artists which came into prominence during the 1930's only Siqueiros is still alive. "With the death of Orozco," noted Bernard S. Myers in *Mexican Painting In Our Time* (Oxford, 1956), "Siqueiros emerged in the 1950's as the outstanding muralist in Mexico and one of its pre-eminent easel painters as well. . . . Whatever the disagree-

DAVID ALFARO SIQUEIROS

ment with his social philosophy [he is an avowed Communist] many things for which he fought in mural art are gradually coming to pass." The famous muralist is frequently the center of artistic storms.

José David Alfaro Siqueiros was born in Chihuahua, state of Chihuahua, Mexico on December 29, 1896 to Cypriano Alfaro and Teresa Siqueiros de Alfaro. His father, of Portuguese descent, was a celebrated lawyer and wit, and the most influential person in his life. He has a sister, Luz, and a brother, Jesús, an actor. His family was noted "for its vitality and longevity," according to MacKinley Helm, author of *Modern Mexican Painters* (Harper, 1941). Siqueiros "began going to jail at the age of thirteen, in defense of his principles... and the prisons [of Mexico] are delightfully informal."

Siqueiros attended the parochial Colegio Franco Ingles from 1907 to 1911 and then entered the San Carlos Academy of Fine Arts. His attachment to the principles of Karl Marx began there in 1910, during a student strike. He soon started to use his paintings as vehicles of social protest. Joining the forces of General Manuel Diéguez (foe of Pancho Villa) in 1913, he became the general's messenger and rose to the rank of captain, which he held until 1919. Siqueiros was then sent to Madrid and Paris as military attaché to the Mexican legations there.

While in Europe (1919-22) he wrote a "Manifesto to the Painters of America," which he published in the first issue of *Vida Americana.* In it he declared the New World's freedom from the Old. In another publication, *Revista Americana,* he urged Mexican artists to exploit their native culture and traditions.

Called back to Mexico in 1922 by José Vasconcelos, Minister of Education, Siqueiros was commissioned to paint murals at the National

SIQUEIROS, DAVID ALFARO—Cont.

Preparatory School. He used encaustic—pigments mixed with hot wax—in his frescoes *Angels of Freedom* and *Burial of a Worker*. "His strong plastic statement of classic Mexican forms—brown naked giants against a brown background," observed Virginia Stewart in *45 Contemporary Mexican Artists* (Stanford University Press, 1951), "was reflected in many subsequent works by other painters." (These murals were mutilated during a student riot in 1924.)

As secretary general of the Painters' Syndicate, he published, with Diego Rivera and Xavier Guerrero, its newspaper, *El Machete*. After this syndicate was dissolved in 1924, Siqueiros went to Guadalajara and painted murals at the university there. He helped to organize the Alliance of Paint Workers, established the Jalisco Mining Federation, and published the anticlerical paper *El 130*. He made his first trip to Moscow in 1927 as chairman of a delegation of Mexican miners. In 1928 he became secretary of the General Confederación Sindical Unitaria de Mexico and, using literary and graphic material by the workers, he published the magazine *El Martillo* (The Hammer).

Most of Siqueiros' oils during 1930 were painted in a Taxco jail. He used cheap paints, and he was supplied with wood and stones for engravings and lithographs by William Spratling. In 1931 Siqueiros met the Russian motion picture director Sergei Eisenstein, from whom he learned the relation of psychology, chemistry, and biology to the plastic arts. He painted portraits of the American poet Hart Crane and the American composer George Gershwin.

Because of his political views, Siqueiros was ousted from Mexico in 1932. He went to Los Angeles, California, where he taught and painted murals at the Chouinard Art Institute. One of these was *The Struggle*. He was compelled to leave the United States when his mural, the *Crucifixion*, at the Plaza Arts Center, provoked a storm of criticism. It depicted a Latin American figure, bound to a cross surmounted by the American eagle. (Authorities later covered the mural with whitewash.) One of his murals, *Portrait of Mexico*, painted on the wall of a motion picture director's Hollywood house, expressed opposition to Mexico's former President Plutarco Elías Calles. For this reason Siqueiros was not allowed to return home at that time.

Consequently, Siqueiros went to South America. In 1933 he painted, alfresco, in Buenos Aires "an extraordinary and advanced decoration called *Plastic Study*. Using mechanical instruments, he painted walls, floor, and ceiling, attempting to develop a dynamic geometrical composition with architectural qualities" (Agustín Velázquez Chávez in *Contemporary Mexican Artists*, Covici, 1937). In 1934 he lectured in Rio de Janeiro and in the same year held an exhibit in New York City at the Delphic Studios. His first work using Duco paint as a medium on three-ply board instead of canvas was exhibited at the Mexican Art Gallery in July 1935. Continuing to experiment, he

added to homemade pigments ground whalebone for durability. One of his theories was that a painting should be a composite image of a motion picture.

Deeply concerned with the Loyalist cause in Spain, he went there in 1937 and fought in the Civil War, serving as a lieutenant colonel in the Spanish Republican Army. In 1939 he founded the pro-Loyalist review, *Documental*, for Spanish residents in Mexico.

The Museum of Modern Art in New York included five of Siqueiros' paintings in its "Twenty Centuries of Mexican Art" exhibition, held in 1940, and bought them for its permanent collection: *Proletarian Victim* (1933), *Collective Suicide* (1936), *Echo of a Scream* (1937), *The Sob* (1939), and *Ethnography* (1939). It also owns some of his prints and lithographs. In 1949 it purchased his painting *Hands*. The Pierre Matisse Gallery in New York exhibited his work in 1940. Also in 1940 he completed his mural *The Trial of Fascism* at the Electrical Syndicate in Mexico City; its textures include cement, sand, steel, iron, and sprayed-on paint. His painting *Sunrise at Mexico* is in the International Business Machines collection.

Arrested on suspicion of plotting an attack upon Leon Trotsky, the anti-Stalinist Russian revolutionist, who was living in a suburb of Mexico City in 1940, Siqueiros maintained that he was innocent and was released. With his wife, Angelica, he went to Chile and later to Cuba. He did not return to Mexico until 1944.

Siqueiros shared with another Mexican painter, Rufino Tamayo (see *C.B.,* March 1953), an exhibition in New York City at the Knoedler Galleries in 1945. Henry McBride (New York *Sun,* November 10, 1945) commented. "His specialty is anguish.... But he is a strong painter, suitable for museums rather than for private consumption, for no one cares to live continually with anguish."

Competing in the Biennale in Venice, Italy in 1950, Siqueiros won second prize. (Henri Matisse won first.) In the following year his mural *Cuauhtémoc* (the last Aztec ruler) was unveiled at the Palace of Fine Arts in Mexico City. His other mural there is *New Democracy.* Recent Siqueiros murals include those at the University of Mexico (1952), University of Morelia (1953), and the Social Security Administration building in Mexico City (1954).

Once Siqueiros has completed the planning of a large mural, he welcomes assistance. In 1955 he supervised the work done on a mural of more than 3,000 square yards in a Warsaw sports stadium. He employed twenty painters and five sculptors, using a new "paint sculpture" technique.

Upon his return in December 1955 from a visit to the Soviet Union, Siqueiros criticized both Russian and Mexican art. "Art in the U.S.S.R. and in Poland," he asserted, "is not really popular because it tends toward academism and is groping for form." Equally critical of art in other countries, he has said that "Picasso leans toward decadence in art," and that "in Italy, art today is seen only in commercial advertisements."

David Alfaro Siqueiros married Angelica Arenal in 1931. His present wife is named Adriana. He is very tall, weighs about 180 pounds, and has green eyes and black hair. His hobbies are pistol shooting and reading. Frequently attacked by the conservative press of Mexico, he was dubbed "El Coronelazo" (The Big Colonel), "a sarcastic appellation he has used with pride ever since then."

References

Newsweek 50:100+ O 28 '57 por

Mérida, Carlos Modern Mexican Artists (1937)

Myers, Bernard S. Mexican Painting In Our Time (1956)

Schmeckebier, Laurence E. Modern Mexican Art (1939)

World Biography (1948)

V. J. SKUTT

SKUTT, V(ESTOR) J(OSEPH) Feb. 24, 1902- Insurance company executive

Address: b. Mutual of Omaha, 33d & Farnam, Omaha, Neb.; h. 400 N. 62d St., Omaha, Neb.

In the home office building of Mutual of Omaha, a local landmark because of its pyramidal shape and pink Kasota stone, V. J. Skutt, as the president and chairman of the board of directors, heads a company that celebrated its fiftieth anniversary in 1959. Popularly known as "V.J.," he is generally regarded as the leading advocate of voluntary health insurance in America. During his ten years of command at Mutual of Omaha, he has seen his company grow into the largest purveyor of health and accident insurance in the world.

Born in Deadwood, South Dakota on February 24, 1902, Vestor Joseph Skutt is the son of Roy N. and Catherine (Gorman) Skutt. Growing up in the Black Hills area, he attended public and private schools in Deadwood and near Rapid City. He spent much of his youth traveling through the South Dakota ranch country with his father, who was an agent for the Equitable Life Insurance Company of New York. Remembering the ranchers for their neighborliness when anybody was injured or fell ill, he has tried to instill the same attitude into the business affairs of Mutual of Omaha.

After graduating from Sturgis High School, Skutt decided to study at Creighton University in Omaha. Since he had no funds for the fare, he took a job as a cattle tender on the railroad from Deadwood to Omaha. At Creighton University, Skutt studied law. He received his LL.B. degree in 1923 and in the same year was admitted to the Nebraska state bar. Immediately after his graduation, he joined the Equitable agency. In 1924 he came to Mutual, like many other graduates of Creighton, and has remained there ever since.

When Skutt joined Mutual, the company, which was then known as the Mutual Benefit Health & Accident Association, was only fifteen years old. It had been founded in 1909 by Dr. C. C. Criss, who, as a young medical student, had seen families impoverished by illness and accident. Dr. Criss established a plan which sponsored income-protection insurance.

In 1924 Skutt entered the legal department of Mutual in Omaha. Two years later he became legal counsel for the Southwestern division with headquarters in Dallas. After four years, he returned to the home office in Omaha. Continuing with the legal department, he also traveled for the expanding company. In 1935 he was named vice-president of the United Benefit Life Insurance Company, a Mutual affiliate, which had been formed in 1926 to broaden the line of coverage. Skutt was appointed to help United re-insure the American Life Insurance Company of Colorado and the Cedar Rapids Life Insurance Company of Cedar Rapids, Iowa.

V. J. Skutt was named a director and executive vice-president of Mutual in 1947. Two years later, when Dr. Criss retired, he was elected president. When the Companion Life Insurance Company was formed in 1949, he was named president and director of that Mutual subsidiary. He still heads that company.

Finding that most people could not remember the cumbersome name of the Mutual Benefit Health & Accident Association, Skutt copyrighted a nickname, Mutual of Omaha, and, determining to make it a household word, advertised widely in all media. Now that the company has policyholders numbering more than 7,000,000 and 10,000 representatives throughout the world, he feels he has accomplished his goal. But he also feels that he has built a company to fill a human need.

As the president of Mutual of Omaha, Skutt has dedicated himself to proving that socialized medicine in the United States is not needed. He believes that "voluntary health insurance is basically the American system of free enterprise in action," and that it reflects the American way of life (New York *Times*, March 8, 1959).

(Continued next page)

SKUTT, V. J.—*Continued*

Working six or seven days a week and on vacations, Skutt has helped to build Mutual of Omaha into the largest health and accident insurance company in the world. He has convinced the company that policies should be noncancellable, and has written income-protection policies to cover the entire family. He believes that policy clauses should be liberally interpreted in the payment of claims. Since Skutt became president, Mutual of Omaha has paid out $750,-000,000 in claims. In October 1958 it became the first company to pay out $1 billion in health and accident benefits in the first fifty years of its existence.

Annual premium income has also risen. When Skutt became president, the premium income was $77,000,000. In 1958 it was $187,000,000. Skutt's associates attribute the success of Mutual of Omaha to his progressive ideas about liberal benefits.

When the Federal Trade Commission indicted health and accident insurance companies a few years ago for misleading advertising and then dropped its cases for lack of jurisdiction, Skutt was not satisfied with a victory won on a technicality. He continued the investigation, in effect, in his own company by sending questionnaires to Mutual's policyholders. Of the more than 350,000 replying, 96.4 per cent expressed satisfaction with Mutual's overall service.

Using both the company plane and commercial airlines, Skutt flies about 100,000 miles a year. As air-minded as its president, Mutual has become a leader in travel insurance. Its coin-operated vending machines for air travel policies are installed in most major airports in the United States and in thirty-seven foreign countries. Mutual bought the Tele-trip Policy Company, Inc., of Washington, and established this division in 1953. Mutual's risk per plane is re-insured, beyond the first quarter-million dollars, with Lloyd's of London.

In addition to his posts at Mutual of Omaha and at the Companion Life Insurance Company of New York, Skutt holds membership on the board of directors of the Omaha National Bank and of several companies and foundations. He serves on numerous boards, councils, and committees, including President Eisenhower's Committee on Youth Fitness.

Six feet tall and weighing 175 pounds, Skutt looks like "a man who has just come from his Bond Street tailor, and he has the distinguished air of a Dean Acheson or a Sir Anthony Eden. His hair has gone from gray to white. . ." (Omaha *World-Herald Sunday Magazine,* March 15, 1959). In 1950 he established the Criss Award, in memory of Mutual's founder Dr. C. C. Criss, which is given every year to the person or persons making the greatest contribution to public health and/or safety during the preceding twelve months.

Many honors have been bestowed upon Skutt. In 1959 he was elected president of the Health Insurance Association of America. In 1950 he received the Harold R. Gordon Memorial for outstanding contributions to the health and accident insurance industry. In 1957 he was awarded the B'nai B'rith citation for Americanism by the local chapter of the organization, for having served as chairman of the 100th anniversary of the incorporation of the city of Omaha. In 1958 Omaha University conferred an honorary Doctor of Laws degree on Skutt.

Vestor Joseph Skutt was married to Angela Anderson on June 8, 1926. Their children are Thomas James, Joseph, and Sally Jane (Mrs. John F. Desmond, Jr.). The Skutts live in a ten-room house in a residential district of Omaha. In the little time that he can spare for recreation, Skutt enjoys golfing, fishing, and hunting. He belongs to the Omaha, Nebraska, and American bar associations, the Omaha Club, the Omaha Country Club, the Omaha Athletic Club, Rotary, and the legal fraternity Delta Theta Phi, among other organizations. He is a Roman Catholic.

References

American Catholic Who's Who, 1958 and 1959

Who's Who in America, 1958-59

Who's Who in Commerce and Industry (1957)

SLICHTER, SUMNER H(UBER) Jan. 8, 1892-Sept. 27, 1959 Economist; Lamont University Professor at Harvard University since 1940; author of many books, including *What's Ahead for American Business* (1951). See *Current Biography* (June) 1947.

Obituary

N Y Times p39 S 29 '59

SMITH, COURTNEY (CRAIG) Dec. 20, 1916- College president
Address: b. Swarthmore College, Swarthmore, Pa.; h. 324 Cedar Lane, Swarthmore, Pa.

When Courtney Smith was made ninth president of Swarthmore College in 1953, at the age of thirty-six, he became one of the youngest college presidents in the United States. Resigning his position as assistant professor of English at Princeton University, he succeeded John W. Nason, who left Swarthmore to be head of the Foreign Policy Association.

Swarthmore, a small college by deliberate policy, has some 900 students and 100 faculty members who are guided by the religious and ethical principles of the Religious Society of Friends, which founded the college in 1864. Although nonsectarian in control, it remains strongly Quaker in tradition and atmosphere.

Courtney Craig Smith was born in Winterset, Iowa, on December 20, 1916, the son of Samuel Craig Smith—a lawyer and banker—and Florence Myrtle (Dabney) Smith. With his two brothers and a sister, he was reared in the Midwest, receiving his early education in the public schools there. As a student in Roosevelt High School in Des Moines, Iowa, he was elected to the National Honor Society and was made an officer of the student council. He was also a member of the debating team and the tennis team. When he was graduated in 1934, his high scholarship assured his admittance to Harvard University.

At Harvard, where he majored in English literature, Smith's academic abilities were balanced by a proficiency in sports—especially squash and tennis. To earn his way, he waited on tables and worked as a library assistant. During summers he was a co-director of European tours. He won the Jonathan Brown Bright, Isham Carpenter, Saltonstall, and John Appleton Haven scholarships and prizes and was elected to Phi Beta Kappa. On receiving the A.B. degree *magna cum laude* in 1938, he was awarded a Rhodes Scholarship. In 1938-39, just before the outbreak of World War II, he studied at Merton College, Oxford University, England.

English literature was Smith's major study at Oxford, as it had been at Harvard. In deciding to become an English teacher, he had been encouraged by his sister and two of his teachers, Miss Ida T. Jacobs of Roosevelt High School and Professor James B. Munn of Harvard. Smith returned to Harvard for further graduate work, and for the four years beginning in 1939 he also held the posts of teaching fellow and tutor in English at the university. He received the M.A. degree in 1941 and the Ph.D. degree in 1944. His special interests were in the field of seventeenth century literature and of American literature.

On completion of his graduate studies he served in the United States Navy for two years (1944-46), advancing in rank from ensign to lieutenant (j.g.) in the Naval Reserve. He was assigned to Pensacola, Florida as liaison officer for Negro personnel at the Naval Air Station and as a staff member of the *Commander,* Naval Air Training Bases.

In 1946 Smith was appointed instructor in English at Princeton University. He became assistant professor in 1948 and remained in that position until 1953. Along with teaching, he carried the responsibilities of bicentennial preceptor at Princeton from 1951 to 1953 and was director of the National Woodrow Wilson Fellowship Program in 1952-53.

With his election to succeed John W. Nason as president of Swarthmore College in 1953, Smith turned his attention wholly to the administrative side of higher education. At Smith's inauguration in October, Nason introduced him as "an administrator with an instinctive flair for asking the right questions and arriving at the right decision."

Smith's inaugural address reflected his sympathy with the principles of the Quaker tradition at Swarthmore. Discussing the problems that education faces in a period of Congressional investigation and threats to civil liberties, he pointed out that the public regards colleges as "the haven of halfbacks, drum majorettes, Junior Proms, dormitory raiders, and absentminded yet cunningly conspiratorial professors." He stressed the need, therefore, for teaching the public an understanding of academic freedom. "We must resist . . . every effort to suppress free thought or free speech, just as the Society

Orren Jack Turner

COURTNEY SMITH

of Friends, known first as the "Friends of Truth," have from their very beginnings three hundred years ago resisted every form of suppression and insisted on the importance of questioning the accepted and of trying out new ways of doing things."

In this address and also in a speech at the forum of the Tuition Plan in February 1955, Smith explained that the liberal function of a college in reassessing the old and discovering the new is balanced by its conservative function of "preserving and passing on the inherited wisdom of the ages." He charged in the latter speech that colleges had "stooped to a good deal of education by façade—playing up our Gothic or Georgian dormitories, and our football teams, and our not always uncalculating honorary degrees." He suggested that a college be judged "by the extent to which it is willing to stick out its neck to be free" (New York *Herald Tribune,* February 13, 1955).

Swarthmore was among several colleges that opposed an antisubversion provision of the National Defense Education Act of 1958. In commenting on the necessity of the students' signing a non-Communist or "disclaimer" affidavit and taking an oath of allegiance to the United States to qualify for a loan, Dr. Smith said, "The whole thing is sheer nonsense. You don't start out on such an act by saying you don't trust your students, by asking a seventeen-year-old freshman to take an oath."

Shortly before being chosen president of Swarthmore, Dr. Smith had been named American secretary of the Rhodes Scholarship Trust. In January 1953 he replaced Frank Aydelotte, whom he had assisted for several years. (Aydelotte himself was president of Swarthmore from 1921 to 1940.) The position entails the responsibility of directing the choice of American college students for Rhodes Scholarships to

SMITH, COURTNEY—Continued

Oxford. Smith is also on the board of directors of the Association of American Rhodes Scholars.

Since late 1953 Smith has been a director of the John and Mary R. Markle Foundation of New York. This foundation supports charitable and medical research projects, awarding five-year grants to physicians in United States and Canadian medical schools to assist them in special research. Also, in 1953, he was made a trustee for the Eisenhower Fellowship Program.

In other educational affiliations, Smith is an associate trustee of the University of Pennsylvania, a member of the board of overseers of Harvard University, and a Fellow of the Society for American Studies. He is a member of the American Association of University Professors, the Modern Language Association, the Harvard Club of Philadelphia, and the University Club of New York.

Courtney Smith and his wife, the former Elizabeth Bowden Proctor of Boston, who were married on October 12, 1939, have three children—Courtney Craig, Jr., Elizabeth Bowden, and Carol Dabney. Smith is six feet tall, weighs 165 pounds, and has brown hair and brown eyes. Sports remain among his chief nonacademic interests. He belongs to the Rolling Green Golf Club and may be seen occasionally also on the tennis court.

References

N Y Times p34 O 18 '53
Who's Who in America, 1958-59
Who's Who in the East, 1957
World Biography (1954)

SMITH, DICK June 26, 1922- Make-up artist

Address: b. c/o National Broadcasting Co., 30 Rockefeller Plaza, New York 20; h. 209 Murray Ave., Larchmont, N.Y.

As make-up director for the National Broadcasting Company for fourteen years and television's first important make-up artist, Dick Smith has developed many new materials and shades of color and has pioneered in such techniques as the use of foam latex and plastics in unusual quick changes for both color and black-and-white TV shows. One of his most challenging assignments was for NBC's "live" presentation in 1957 of *Victoria Regina*, in which audiences saw actress Claire Bloom as the Queen age from twenty-two to eighty during the one-hour program.

Richard Emerson Smith, of English descent, was born on June 26, 1922 to Richard Roy and Coral Loetta (Brown) Smith in Larchmont, New York. His mother was the author of a cookbook on leftovers, the first to be published in both England and the United States. His father founded a publishing company which issued the literary newspaper *American Spectator* and numerous well-known trade books. Dick Smith is distantly related to Ralph Waldo Emerson. He has a half brother by his mother's former marriage.

During his college preparatory years at Wooster School in Danbury, Connecticut, Dick Smith's main extrascholastic activities were in arts and crafts. Upon his graduation in 1940 he entered Yale University as a premedical student, with dentistry his intended profession, and he majored in zoology. Attending Yale is a family tradition: his father had been a member of the class of 1908. Smith, who was studying on a partial scholarship, also supplemented his income by working as a printer for the Branford College press.

While at Yale, Smith first became interested in theatrical make-up. In his sophomore year he discovered a book on the tricks of make-up used by Hollywood experts during the filming of *The Hunchback of Notre Dame* and *Dr. Jekyll and Mr. Hyde*. He soon began to do make-up for the Yale drama group and, as he puts it: "I decided that I would make a career of it when I got out of college" (Miami *Herald* Sunday magazine supplement, January 19, 1958).

Smith was in the ROTC at Yale and after taking an accelerated course attended Officers Candidates School. In 1943 he received his B.A. degree from Yale and in the same year entered the United States Army to serve as a corporal in the field artillery. He advanced to the rank of second lieutenant before being discharged in 1945.

From time to time after leaving the Army Smith found work with small theatrical groups. He was also employed briefly at the Museum of Natural History in New York City. There "the only thing I did on my own," he recalls, "was to clean a plaster tree trunk." Learning that the National Broadcasting Company wanted to hire a make-up artist for its TV division, Smith applied for the position and in 1945 became the first staff make-up artist in television. NBC now employs eight or nine make-up specialists regularly and for shows with large casts calls in free lances. It is estimated that in the New York area there are only about seventy-five well-qualified men in the theatrical make-up field.

Since 1945 Smith has worked with many famous theatrical figures who have appeared on television. Among these have been Audrey Hepburn in *Mayerling* and José Ferrer in *Cyrano de Bergerac*. Smith was also in charge of TV make-up for the Democratic National Convention in 1948 and made up James A. Farley and Franklin D. Roosevelt, Jr., among other political personalities.

Although Smith was familiar with both theater and movie techniques of make-up artistry, he found that because of particular technical problems (such as heat from strong lights for cameras), he had to develop new methods of using them and also to create new techniques and materials of his own. In his own words: "For one thing, the equipment and a number of the men working it were new. Make-up that would go well in a theater had to be changed because of the many closeups that were being used in television. The lights in use then, although dramatic, were sometimes harsh, and consequently different methods of make-up had

DICK SMITH

to be devised to overcome this obstacle" (*Miami Herald* Sunday magazine supplement, January 19, 1958).

In his department at NBC, Smith has filing cabinets full of small boxes bearing labels such as "veins," "noses," "eyelids," "eye bag fillers," "horns," "moles," "third eyes," "bruises," "cauliflower ears," "scars," "nose plugs," and "face lifts." Most of these items are made from whipped-up foam latex, put into an oven and baked with great care. Smith explained how to make wrinkles: "It's simple. We stipple a special latex formula on with a sponge, then while it's drying, we stretch the actor's own skin—you know, maybe pull it up from the cheekbones. We use a hair dryer to dry the latex quickly and when we let go of the real skin, the face will be as wrinkled as a prune. If we want deeper wrinkles, we just add another layer of liquid latex" (New York *Sunday News*, July 13, 1958).

"I must be perfectly honest," Smith said on one occasion. "Foam latex was used by the films before I used it on TV, but they are so secretive about it that you have to rediscover it on your own." He has also used Koroseal Flexible Holding Compound as a substitute for latex, and liquid vinyl compounds for creating bald heads. Frequently Smith works out his own formulas from existing formulas.

In much demand as an expert in the art of make-up for women generally, Smith has been interviewed a number of times for magazine articles on beauty advice to women. *Vogue* (October 15, 1957), for example, quoted him: "Start off by spotting your worst feature. Then try to see the whole. Take a good front-back-and-side look at your hair, remembering that it makes the shape of the head. Then the two features to concentrate on are the eyes and mouth, they're the most revealing of character,

the areas where make-up can do the most to put your best face forward." He has generally recommended that women experiment with lighter, more pastel tones of lipstick and rouge, and he has pointed out that to use make-up skillfully, women must practise for hours.

On January 10, 1944 Dick Smith married Jocelyn De Rosa, then secretary to the curator of the film library of the Museum of Modern Art in New York. They have two sons, Douglas Todd and David Emerson. Smith has brown hair and brown eyes, is five feet nine and a half inches tall, and weighs 165 pounds. He is a Democrat and be belongs to the Society of Make-up Artists. Deeply interested in sculpturing and painting, he thinks that given the time and opportunity, sculpturing could have an important place in his future. He is said to be very tactful and seems to have little difficulty with even the most temperamental performers.

SMITH, RED Sept. 25, 1905- Sports writer
Address: b. New York Herald Tribune, 230 W. 41st St., New York 36; h. 4 Cedar Tree Lane, Wire Mill Rd., Stamford, Conn.

Ranking as one of the most literate of all American writers on sports and one of the most widely syndicated sports columnists in the United States at the present time, Red Smith of the New York *Herald Tribune* has come a long way from his start as a cub reporter on the Milwaukee *Sentinel* in 1927. His daily column, *Views of Sport*, is syndicated in about 100 newspapers, his articles appear in leading magazines, and he has won the Grantland Rice Memorial Award for outstanding sports writing. Some of his admirers, aware of his respect for the written word and his pawky sense of humor, believe that he can stand comparison with Grantland Rice, Ring Lardner, and other notable predecessors.

Walter Wellesley Smith was born on September 25, 1905 (or, as he puts it, "about eleven million words ago") in Green Bay, Wisconsin to Walter Philip and Ida (Richardson) Smith. His father was a prosperous dealer in wholesale produce. After attending the Green Bay schools, Smith entered the University of Notre Dame. After his graduation in 1927, he obtained his first newspaper assignment as a writer of general news for the Milwaukee *Sentinel*. He remained in Milwaukee a year and in 1928 moved to St. Louis.

Frank Sullivan, the humorist, once remarked (*PM*, June 1, 1947) that Red Smith "fell in love *in* St. Louis, but not *with* St. Louis." Sullivan was referring to the fact that Red Smith met Catherine Cody in St. Louis and married her there in 1933. In St. Louis he worked for the old *Star* (now the *Star-Times*), first as a copyreader, then as a sports writer.

At the *Star*, Smith was looked upon as only a middling copyreader, and when the entire sports staff was fired, Smith was the logical choice to move into one of the vacancies. He remained with the *Star* until 1936, when he moved to the Philadelphia *Record*, where he wrote a sports

New York Herald Tribune—Don Rice
RED SMITH

column under his own by-line, for which he was paid $120 a week.

While working on the Philadelphia *Record,* Smith was noticed by Stanley Woodward, then sports editor of the New York *Herald Tribune,* and now with the Newark *Star-Ledger.* Woodward called Smith "the best newspaper writer in the country" (*Newsweek,* October 10, 1949) and when Smith was about to join the staff of the *Herald Tribune* said: "In him the best attributes of the 'gee whiz' and 'aw nuts' schools are mingled" (New York *Herald Tribune,* September 1, 1945).

When Red Smith joined the *Herald Tribune* on September 24, 1945, he began writing *Views of Sport.* He has continued in that assignment ever since, turning out six columns a week, forty-eight weeks a year. Each column consists of about 800 words, and it takes Smith around three hours to write one. "It comes out in little drops of blood," he says.

The big spectator sports about which Red Smith most enjoys writing are baseball, football, boxing, and horse racing. He can work up no enthusiasm for basketball, but his apathy does not prevent him from producing an excellent column on the sport when the occasion demands.

Two books have grown out of Smith's daily columns in the *Herald Tribune. Out of the Red* was published by Alfred A. Knopf in 1950, with illustrations by the noted sports cartoonist, Willard Mullin. This was followed in 1954 by *Views of Sport,* also published under the Knopf imprint. Both books are samplings of Smith's most successful columns. Some of the essays in *Out of the Red* have been used as texts by students of English at Columbia University (*Look* magazine, April 25, 1951).

Away from his *Herald Tribune* desk, Smith has found time to contribute to some of the country's leading magazines, including *Sports Illustrated,* the *Saturday Evening Post,* and the now defunct *Collier's.* Oddly enough, Smith at first showed little promise in the field about which he now writes so well. His own athletic career was limited to a single one-mile race while a student at Notre Dame.

Smith appears occasionally on television. In 1955 he was signed to narrate a series of twenty-six television programs relating to little-known aspects of sports throughout the world, and on January 30, 1959 he appeared on Edward R. Murrow's *Person to Person* on CBS-TV.

From time to time, the need to fill his *Views of Sport* columns has taken Red Smith to many cities throughout the world. His superiors at the *Herald Tribune* have been generous with travel time, and he has used it to advantage: for a trip to the Soviet Union, to Los Angeles for the opening game of the transplanted Brooklyn Dodgers, and to Mexico City for an international golf tournament. While in Mexico, Smith wrote a column about basketball (New York *Herald Tribune,* December 11, 1958), in which he set out to prove that the sport was invented by the Mexicans and not by the American, Dr. James Naismith, as previously believed by the faithful. The column represented Red Smith at the top of his "tongue-in-cheek" form.

After being at the *Herald Tribune* for only a few months, Smith won the first of several awards during his membership on the staff. The National Headliners Club, sponsored by the Press Club of Atlantic City, honored him with one of its 1945 awards in journalism for a consistently outstanding sports column.

The award of which Red Smith is proudest, however, came to him in 1956 when he was chosen to receive the second Grantland Rice Memorial Award for outstanding sports writing in the Rice tradition. The award covered the period from July 13, 1955 to July 13, 1956. In presenting the award on November 1, 1956, Devereux Milburn, Jr., president of the Sportsmanship Brotherhood, said: "Breakfast without [reading] Red Smith is like champagne without bubbles."

Red Smith is the first to admit that he is scarcely the athletic type. He has described himself as a "seedy amateur with watery eyes behind glittering glasses, a retiring chin, a hole in his frowzy haircut, and a good deal of dandruff on his shoulders" (*Newsweek,* April 21, 1958). A writer for *Newsweek* had been more objective years earlier when he said that Smith was "scrawny, a little man with pale hair and gaunt features. His thinning hair is only slightly red. He is a chain smoker [whose] movements are quick. He's neat but casual, with a taste for sports jackets" (*Newsweek,* October 10, 1949).

While conducting interviews with sports celebrities, Smith refuses to take notes; he is convinced that note-taking "hampers the flow of conversation." Instead he relies on the tenacity of his memory and his knack for picking out a key phrase from a conversation and developing it.

On February 11, 1933 Walter Wellesley Smith married Catherine Cody of St. Louis. They have two children, Catherine, and Terence Fitzgerald. They make their home in Stamford, Connecticut in a seven-room house of the Cape Cod type, on a half-acre plot of land. The swimming pool Smith refers to as "the smallest in Connecticut." Smith writes his column at home and telephones it in to the office.

Explaining his delight in fishing for relaxation, Smith says: "I never played golf and when I was young enough to play tennis, any girl could beat me." Of his work, he states: "I've never heard of a better way to make a living."

References

Look 15:31 Ap 24 '51 por
Newsweek 51:77+ Ap 21 '58 por; 34:62 O 10 '49 por
Time 60:82+ My 15 '50 por
Who's Who in America, 1958-59

SMITH, RICHARD EMERSON See Smith, Dick

SMITH, SIDNEY (EARLE) Mar. 8, 1897-Mar. 17, 1959 Canadian Secretary of State for External Affairs since 1957; president of the University of Manitoba (1934-44) and president of the University of Toronto (1945-57). See Current Biography (January) 1955.

Obituary

N Y Times p37 Mr 18 '59

SMITH, WALTER WELLESLEY See Smith, Red

SPEARE, ELIZABETH GEORGE Nov. 21, 1908- Author
Address: h. 40 Chamberlain Rd., Wethersfield, Conn.

Reprinted from the Wilson Library Bulletin Apr. 1959.

Winner of the 1958 Newbery award for the most distinguished contribution of the year to American literature for boys and girls is Elizabeth George Speare. She received the Newbery medal for her book The Witch of Blackbird Pond (Houghton), an historical novel set in her own home town, Wethersfield, Connecticut.

Elizabeth George was born in Melrose, Massachusetts on November 21, 1908, the daughter of Harry Allan George, an engineer, and the former Demetria Simmons. Her paternal grandparents were Baptist missionaries to Burma. "I had an exceptionally happy home," Mrs. Speare says. "My mother was a very wonderful woman of great understanding."

After a year at Smith College, Northampton, Massachusetts, she went to Boston University in Massachusetts, where she was graduated in 1930 and received her master's degree in 1932. While still in college she drifted into teaching and

taught English until 1935. The following year she married Alden Speare, an industrial engineer. They have two children, Alden, Jr., a student at Cornell University, and Mary, who attends the Chaffee School for Girls in Windsor, Connecticut.

"I began to write from the age of eight on," Mrs. Speare recalls. "I filled volumes of brown notebooks with poetry and stories, all more incredibly naïve than any child could write today." Even with a growing family she found time for some writing, and in 1950 she began again in earnest. A small writers' club that still meets once a month was the stimulus Mrs. Speare needed.

She began with articles and sold them to Better Homes and Gardens, Woman's Day, Parents Magazine, among others. One that appeared in American Heritage in June 1957 was later produced on television. It tells the story of the famous Smith sisters of Glastonbury, Connecticut. The spinsters refused to pay their taxes, and the town seized their cows and land. They got the land back, but forfeited their right to vote.

One day while reading a history of the Connecticut River, Mrs. Speare stumbled upon an actual diary, A Narrative of the Captivity of Mrs. Johnson, first published in 1796. She continued her research and found a collection of rare books at Trinity College, Hartford, Connecticut. "Susanna Johnson's account of the carefree party on the night before the Indian raid quickened my imagination," Mrs. Speare wrote later, "especially her comment that 'a spruce young spark tarried with my sister Miriam.' The hint of an interrupted romance was irresistible." The result was an absorbing historical novel, Calico Captive (Houghton, 1957), most of which probably happened.

The Horn Book called the writing vivid, adding, "This is superior historical fiction." The New York Herald Tribune Book Review said: "It is that rarity in historical novels, one that does not seem to be written to provide 'background' but to tell a good story. . . ." It was selected as one of the Notable Children's Books of 1957 by the children's services division of the American Library Association.

On March 20, 1959 Mrs. Speare's second book, The Witch of Blackbird Pond, was awarded the thirty-eighth Newbery Medal, with "an almost unprecedented unanimity," on one ballot. It is the story of young Kit, an orphan reared in Barbados, who came to New England in the bleak days of 1687 to live with an aunt, and of her friendship with a old Quaker woman, thought by the town to be a witch. Kit, too, is suspect and brought to trial. The New York Times Book Review called the book ". . . topflight historical romance . . . a lively plot and excellent characterization." Saturday Review said it was "an outstanding historical novel," and the San Francisco Chronicle used the same adjective—outstanding.

Each book took a year and a half to write. "I love research, especially in the historical field," Mrs. Speare admits frankly. "Often I work hours and hours on one little detail." She went to Montreal to check details for Calico

ELIZABETH GEORGE SPEARE

Captive, but the work on her second book was close to home, for the setting is Wethersfield, a suburb of Hartford, where the Speares live in a two-story, yellow house.

Unlike *Calico Captive,* the award book is entirely imaginary and completely original, although the author studied the historical records of Wethersfield closely before writing it. She writes: "For example, the witchcraft hearing in this story normally would have been held in the magistrate's house. Checking with John Willard, an authority on local history, I learned that the magistrate at that time was Major Talcott, whose home was across the river in what is now Glastonbury but then was a part of Wethersfield. So I changed the setting to the Town House, which is mentioned in Stiles' *History.*"

Mrs. Speare has brown eyes and a ready smile. Her hair is gray. Her teaching these days is confined to Sunday school in the Congregational church that the family attends. She likes autobiography and reads a good deal of modern theology, but says she cannot keep her mind on a murder mystery. She loves to ski, although nowadays she goes along chiefly as a spectator, is good at picnics, loves to cook and to talk to people. "I also love sitting in a boat in the Maine wilderness while my husband fishes," she adds. "I owe a great deal to his encouragement. He listens to and criticizes the manuscript in progress."

For the past six years she has been associated with a research project at the University of Connecticut in Storrs in the area of work simplification for the rehabilitation of handicapped homemakers. And of course she is at work on a third novel, also historical.

References

Hartford (Conn) N 1 '58 por
Worcester (Mass) Sunday Telegram Ja 4 '59 por

STAMOS, THEODOROS (stá'môs) Dec. 31, 1922- Artist
Address: b. André Emmerich Gallery, 17 E. 64th St., New York 21; h. East Marion, N.Y.

The name of Theodoros Stamos has frequently been linked with that of William Baziotes and of Adolph Gottlieb as the "poetic symbolists" among the New York group of abstract expressionist painters. His lyrical abstractions, with their suggestive and subtle arrangements of color, texture, and light, are organic or biomorphic rather than geometrical in form. Using a landscape or natural object as a starting point, Stamos attempts to capture the essential mood rather than the content of nature in his work. As one critic has stated, his paintings "are not objects, but states or conditions, like weathers." Among Stamos' better-known pictures are *Nautical Warrior, Sounds in the Rock, The Emperor Plows the Fields, Echo, Symbolic Landscape,* and the *Tea House* series.

Since his first one-man show in 1943, Stamos has had eleven solo exhibitions in New York. He is one of the seventeen abstract artists represented in the Museum of Modern Art's "New American Painting" show, which in 1958 won applause during its tour of leading European museums.

Theodoros Stamos was born in New York City on December 31, 1922. He is one of the six children of Theodoros and Stamatina (Apostolakos) Stamatelos, Greek emigrants from Sparta, where his father had worked as a fisherman. Young Stamos received his education at Stuyvesant High School in New York. At the age of fourteen, he took a sheaf of drawings to the American Artists School and was awarded a scholarship which enabled him to attend night classes under Simon Kennedy. At first, Stamos specialized in sculpture, and since the students there worked in clay directly from the model, he never had formal instruction in drawing. One of his earliest sculptures is the *Young Torso* of 1938.

Around 1937 Stamos began to paint at home, and he was encouraged in his work by Joseph Solman, who was one of his teachers. The year 1939 marked his graduation from high school, and, according to Thomas Hess (*Art News,* February 1947), that same year he was expelled from art school "for political activities." At this time he abandoned sculpture and devoted his spare time entirely to painting. In order to support himself, he worked at a variety of jobs —as a teletype operator, book salesman, enamel polisher, stock clerk in a beauty supply house, tourist guide, caster, prism grinder, florist, hat blocker, printer, and maker of picture frames. A spleen operation disqualified him for service in the Army during World War II.

Stamos' early pictures were painted in a semiprimitive style; the subjects were either imaginary Greek scenes or landscapes along the New Jersey Palisades. Then, to quote Hess, "the large, simple, thickly painted shapes gave way to thinly painted, patterned works, which were strongly influenced by Milton Avery," such as the *Portrait of Dikran Kelekian* (1942).

Stamos' first one-man show in New York, which opened at the Wakefield Gallery at the end of November 1943, consisted of "naïve and decorative" oils, based on stories his mother had told him, and pastels (executed during the summer of 1943 at Rockport, Massachusetts) with "bold simplifications approaching the abstract." The reviewer for the New York *Times* found his work possessed "strength and originality."

Almost simultaneously with his first exhibition, Stamos began to evolve the characteristic style that established his reputation as one of the most promising of younger artists. Retaining the large, patterned forms, he started to paint the flotsam and jetsam cast up on beaches —starfish, shells, stones, sea anemones, driftwood, coils of rope, and desiccated roots. The first pictures were almost entirely realistic, but gradually he began to distort these forms and arrange them into abstract and symbolic patterns. When his new work was shown at the Mortimer Brandt Gallery in May 1945, several critics noted resemblances between his *Dying Bird on White Beach* and *Little Bird on Rock* and the paintings of Morris Graves. In April 1946 Stamos' work was again presented at the Brandt Gallery, in a joint show with Giglio Dante, and a critic for *Art News* (April 1946) observed that the artist's "quiet poetic quality" was well projected by "restrained colors and knowing textural contrasts."

In 1947 Stamos traveled to New Mexico and the Pacific Northwest. His pictures shown at the Betty Parsons Gallery in February of that year were described as "ideographs." To the reviewer for *Art Digest* (February 15, 1947) it seemed that what made these "abstract interpretations of natural objects" distinctive was "their paint quality and haunting color—low-keyed beauty of a subtle, sensuous nature." Sam Hunter, after viewing the seventeen canvases that made up Stamos' next show at the Parsons Gallery, a year later, judged the work "occasionally precious, often contrived, but for all that imaginative and personal" (New York *Times,* February 1, 1948).

On Stamos' return from a European trip in 1948-49, during which he visited France, Sparta, and the Red Sea, he exhibited his new pictures at the Parsons Gallery in April 1949. "Here in a precise and witty imagery, moon-like, floral, or altar forms rise quietly before backgrounds that become earth and sky in poetic, borderless landscapes," wrote Elaine de Kooning (*Art News,* May 1949). The following December marked the first showing of Stamos' work in watercolor and mixed medium. His next exhibition opened at the Parsons Gallery in January 1951. The reviewer for *Art Digest* (January 15, 1951) commented that the painter relied less upon evocative forms and more upon "the reverie-inducing possibilities of color alone, in amorphous drifts."

When Stamos' paintings were presented at the Parsons Gallery in February 1952, James Fitzsimmons (*Art Digest,* March 1, 1952) found they had "a new vigor and austerity, a sense of structure, a substantiality" not always seen in the earlier work. "This is achieved

THEODOROS STAMOS

with black—with a few sweeping strokes of black cutting across areas of smoky color." Another *Art Digest* (January 15, 1953) critic noted further consolidation in Stamos' next show at the Parsons Gallery in January 1953. "When the artist shifted his interest from earth and growth symbols in densely textured enclosed areas to spare open structures, it was as if he began to look up from the ground and out into space. Since abandoning his mystical references to the womb, both biological and geological, Stamos has had a year in which to gain spontaneity, directness, and authority."

"I am concerned with the idea of a thing," Stamos has explained about his painting. "I work with an idea—like a screen door or a tea ceremony—until I have exhausted it." Thus many of his canvases are united in series. Those he exhibited at the Parsons Gallery in January 1956 were grouped in two series: one derived from his Long Island environment of potato fields, trees, and the sea; the other based on a terrace overlooking the Red Sea. Eleven of Stamos' most recent pictures were displayed at the André Emmerich Gallery in April 1958. Commenting that the new work was transitional, the New York *Times* (April 6, 1958) reviewer continued: "The titles, such as *Sun Forest* and *Solstice,* seem to indicate an inspiration in nature for this work with its floating color, but it seems at one and the same time to have abandoned certain more formal aspects of past work and to be reaching forward toward something new, something of more cosmic implication."

Outside New York, Stamos has had solo exhibitions at the Duncan Phillips Gallery in Washington, D.C. (1950, 1954) and at the Philadelphia Art Alliance (1957). He has participated in national group shows at the Whitney Museum of American Art, Pennsylvania

STAMOS, THEODOROS—*Continued*

Academy of Fine Arts, and Carnegie Institute. His work is represented in the permanent collections of a number of American museums and universities, as well as in the Tel-Aviv Museum in Israel and the Museum of Modern Art in Rio de Janeiro.

Stamos received the Tiffany Fellowship in 1951 and a fellowship from the American Academy of Arts and Letters five years later. He has served as an instructor in art at Black Mountain College (1950) and at the Cummington (Massachusetts) School of Art (1952-53). The painter has three sons—Jason, Damon, and Socrates. In an interview for the New York *Times* (January 20, 1956), Dore Ashton described Stamos as follows: "He speaks haltingly, with a frown, his arched brows raised high over black eyes that fix the listener intently, and with his mouth hidden beneath a dense shelf of mustache. He gives one the impression of grave fierceness, but he often laughs, a high, full laugh." As a hobby, Stamos collects Tiffany glass and bentwood chairs. "I live in the country, really," he told Dore Ashton, "and I do most of my work there, or at least most of my thinking. I walk, fish, and I garden a lot. . . . I'm interested in Oriental philosophy, but only for myself, not to talk about."

References

Art N 45:34 F '47 por
N Y Times p21 Ja 20 '56 por
Baur, J. I. H. Nature in Abstraction (1958)
Seuphor, M. Dictionary of Abstract Painting (1957)
Who's Who in America, 1958-59
Who's Who in American Art (1956)

STAPLETON, MAUREEN 1925(?)- Actress

Address: b. c/o Actors Equity Association, 226 W. 47th St., New York 36

In the American theater Maureen Stapleton is recognized as one of the leading interpreters of heroines in plays by Tennessee Williams. A strong impetus was given to her acting career when she played the role of Serafina delle Rose in *The Rose Tattoo* in the original Broadway production in 1951; her performance in this part won for her an Antoinette Perry (Tony) Award from the American Theatre Wing. She had leading roles in Williams' short play 27 *Wagons Full of Cotton* and in his *Orpheus Descending* in 1956.

During the 1958-59 Broadway season she won other laurels for her performance as Ida in a play by S. N. Behrman entitled *The Cold Wind and the Warm*. She made her motion picture debut early in 1959 in *Lonelyhearts,* Dore Schary's film version of Nathanael West's novel, for which she was nominated by the Academy of Motion Picture Arts and Sciences as the best supporting actress.

Maureen Stapleton was born in Troy, New York about 1925, of Irish parentage. She attended Catholic Central High School, where she was "a persistent performer in all the ambitious theatrical efforts of the dramatic society" (*Cue*, March 17, 1951). After graduation she worked for the State Arsenal, which manufactured weapons for the government. When she had saved $100 she went to New York, in September 1943. Her first job was as a billing machine operator at the Hotel New Yorker, working from 11 P.M. to 7 A.M. These hours enabled her to take daytime classes in acting at Frances Robinson Duff's studio and later at Herbert Berghof's studio. Early in 1944 she was one of fourteen girls lecturing at the Chrysler Exhibit of War Weapons.

Describing her acting classes, she told Helen Ormsbee of the New York *Herald Tribune* (February 18, 1951): "'It was a whole new world. In Troy I used to go to movies and dream of being a star, with money and lovely clothes. But in this new world I learned other values—integrity in acting, for instance. . . . Herbert Berghof gave us all a love of the theater." In the summer of 1945 twenty-two of Berghof's students each contributed $150 and started a summer stock company at Blauvelt, New York. They called the venture the Greenbush Summer Theatre. Miss Stapleton played minor parts, ranging from the grandmother in *Over Twenty-one* to the bear in *Noah*. The next summer she acted in a stock company in Mount Kisco, New York.

On her return to New York she assisted Berghof in some of his classes. She telephoned Guthrie McClintic when she heard that he was casting *Playboy of the Western World*. He gave her a small role, and after understudying the part of Pegeen Mike, she played it for a week, opposite Burgess Meredith. She played a bit part with Katharine Cornell in *Antony and Cleopatra* and on tour in *The Barretts of Wimpole Street*. In *Detective Story* she was one of the crowd.

She became a charter member of the Actors Studio, where she studied first with Robert Lewis and later with Lee Strasberg. During the 1949-50 season she appeared as Melvyn Douglas' wife in *The Bird Cage* by Arthur Laurents. In between stage jobs she lived on her savings and on unemployment insurance. She also modeled for artists Raphael Soyer and Reginald Marsh.

In 1951 Cheryl Crawford asked Miss Stapleton to read for the role of Serafina delle Rose, the Sicilian-American heroine of Tennessee Williams' play *The Rose Tattoo*. After six readings, she was chosen to play the role. Her Italian accent in the play was taught to her by Italian-speaking members of the cast. When the play opened on February 3, her family from Troy were proud members of the audience. "I remember, though," Miss Stapleton said, "how they used to keep asking me if I hadn't had enough of this notion about being an actress, but I always told them, 'No.' Even if things hadn't turned out so wonderfully for me, I'd still be saying, 'No'" (New York *Herald*

Tribune, February 18, 1951). A week after the show opened, the names of Maureen Stapleton and Eli Wallach, another featured player in *The Rose Tattoo,* were put up in lights at the Martin Beck Theatre.

In the opinion of Otis L. Guernsey, Jr. (New York *Herald Tribune,* February 5, 1951), "Miss Stapleton's Serafina is an acting gem . . . [her] performance rises to crescendos of hysteria, but it is equally well modulated during her reluctant affair with the truck driver. Her vivid acting is a superb illumination of a vivid part." *The Rose Tattoo* ran on Broadway for 306 performances and was then made into a motion picture starring Anna Magnani.

"Somehow I never make the movie," Miss Stapleton told William Peper (New York *World-Telegram and Sun,* January 21, 1959). She was referring to the film *Baby Doll,* with Carroll Baker in the role which Miss Stapleton had played in 1955 on Broadway in Williams' *27 Wagons Full of Cotton,* a play which served as a basis for the controversial movie. Richard Watts, Jr. (New York *Post,* May 1, 1955) wrote: "I believe the finest and truest performance [of the season] is being given by Miss Stapleton. . . . With rare insight, subtlety and understanding she is able to reveal the wife's absurdity and her desperate pathos. It is a portrayal that is both merciless and deeply sympathetic. It is a masterpiece of acting."

During the 1953 season Miss Stapleton had played in George Tabori's short-lived drama, *The Emperor's Clothes,* and then she replaced Beatrice Straight in the feminine lead opposite Arthur Kennedy in the revival of Arthur Miller's play *The Crucible.* In 1954 she played in *The Sea Gull* at the Phoenix Theatre.

When Tennessee Williams' play *Orpheus Descending* opened at the Martin Beck Theatre on March 21, 1956, the critics had more praise for Miss Stapleton's performance as Lady Torrance, proprietress of a dry-goods store, than for the play. "Her fiercely intelligent eyes always carry conviction," observed Walter Kerr (New York *Herald Tribune,* March 22, 1957); "you're sure that she does know and feel everything the author says she knows and feels."

In *The Cold Wind and the Warm,* which opened on December 8, 1958 at the Morosco Theatre in New York, Maureen Stapleton played opposite Eli Wallach. "Cast as a matchmaker with a practical head and a warm heart, Miss Stapleton has added another interesting dimension to an already distinguished career. She has something pungent to say about everything, and her malapropisms . . . are often exceedingly funny," noted Richard P. Cooke (*Wall Street Journal,* December 10, 1958). On March 21, 1959 *The Cold Wind and the Warm* closed.

For her performance as Sadie Burke in the NBC-TV production of *All the King's Men* (May 1958), Maureen Stapleton won a Sylvania Award. Her other television roles have included the mother in *H.R. 8438—The Story of a Lost Boy* (June 1956) and Rachel in *Andrew Jackson* (December 1956). With Jason Robards, Jr., and Maria Schell, she appeared

MAUREEN STAPLETON

in the three-hour television adaptation of Ernest Hemingway's novel *For Whom the Bell Tolls* in March 1959 on *Playhouse 90.* She was much praised for her interpretation of Pilar, a gypsy woman.

A great admirer of Tennessee Williams, she thinks that the critics who complain of too much morbidity in his plays do not understand how real and universal are the characters he portrays. The roles which she has depicted, she believes, are wonderfully complex and exciting for an actress.

When Miss Stapleton was interviewed on April 18, 1957 by Mike Wallace on *Night Beat* she told him that she had been undergoing psychiatric treatment for over two years because she felt that her life was "so disorganized." She said that she has gradually learned that her responsibilities are to her husband—Max—and to her two children, and to the play in which she is appearing, and that she must not spread her energies over too large an area. "I love parties, and people, and going out socially," she said, "but I realize that first things must come first." She further revealed that she despises housework and would like to have her home so simple and uncluttered that it could be cleaned with a hose. It makes her "nervous to see little things being dusted endlessly." She also intensely dislikes kitchens and the preparation of food.

"Although softly young-looking at thirty-one and not unpretty offstage," Frances Herridge commented a few years ago (New York *Post,* April 8, 1957), "Maureen Stapleton projects an earthy blowziness across the footlights that better suits a middle-aged woman." She has hazel eyes and black hair, and her weight may vary between 125 and 155 pounds.

In 1949 Maureen Stapleton married Max Allentuck, who is general manager for Kermit Bloomgarden. The marriage was terminated by

STAPLETON, MAUREEN—*Continued*

divorce. They have two children, a daughter, Cathy, and a son, Danny. According to the *New Yorker* (February 24, 1951), apart from her family a major off-stage interest is reading movie magazines.

References

Cue 20:12 Mr 17 '51 por
N Y World-Telegram p9 Mr 16 '57
New Yorker 26:19+ F 24 '51

STAPP, JOHN PAUL July 11, 1910- Physician

Address: b. Aero Medical Laboratory, Wright Air Development Center, Wright-Patterson Air Force Base, Ohio; h. 210 Countryside Dr., Knollwood, Dayton 32, Ohio

Chief of the Aero Medical Laboratory at Wright-Patterson Air Force Base in Ohio, Dr. John Paul Stapp is conducting tests to determine how much human beings can endure when they pioneer along the new frontiers of space that have been opened up by aviation and rocketry. Trained as a physician and biophysicist, he has become prominent for his analysis of the effects on the human body of crashes and decelerations. He often used himself as the subject of his experiments.

Dr. Stapp has used animals and human beings in a variety of decelerating devices to provide criteria for air and ground vehicle safety design, for tolerance limits of trajectories of ejection seats and escape capsules on supersonic jets, and for impact forces expected in space ballistic flight. In 1959 he served as president of the American Rocket Society.

Born on July 11, 1910 in Bahia (now spelled Baía), Brazil, John Paul Stapp is the son of Reverend and Mrs. Charles Franklin Stapp. His

U. S. Air Force

DR. JOHN PAUL STAPP

father, who was president of the American Baptist College in Bahia, was a teacher and missionary. Reared in Brazil, the boy spoke only Portuguese until he was six, had only a few playmates besides his three younger brothers, and was educated under the supervision of his parents.

His father frowned upon the boy's early interest in biology, and he warned the mission doctor not to show him the medical books he was eager to see (*Time,* September 12, 1955). The boy was sent to the United States in 1922 in order to complete a formal high school education. Enrolled at the San Marcos Academy in Texas, he proved to be a good student. He joined the track team, acted with the dramatic club, played the bassoon in the band and orchestra, and served as associate editor of the school paper.

In 1927 Stapp matriculated at Baylor University in Waco, Texas, majoring in English literature. He received only a small allowance from his parents which he supplemented by working as a salesman for a cooking-utensil firm and later as a field man for a biological-supply company. At the end of his sophomore year, the accidental death of a young cousin by fire caused him to reconsider his choice of profession. "It was the first time I had seen anyone die," says Stapp. "I decided right then that I wanted to be a doctor" (*Time,* September 12, 1955). He then concentrated on zoology and chemistry courses during his junior and senior years. Again, at Baylor, Stapp played in the orchestra and band and ran with the track team.

After receiving the B.A. degree in 1931, Stapp continued his studies at Baylor, performing the duties of a teaching assistant at the same time. He earned the M.A. *cum laude* in the following year. Although medical school was still his goal, he postponed his entrance in order to help meet his brothers' college expenses. From 1932 to 1934 he was an instructor in zoology and chemistry at Decatur Baptist College in Texas. When he was awarded a fellowship at the University of Texas in Austin, Stapp studied for a doctorate in biophysics. He completed his dissertation, entitled "Biodetric Currents in Living Tissue Layers," in 1939, and a Ph.D. degree was conferred on him the following year.

At the age of twenty-nine, Stapp entered the University of Minnesota Medical School as a teaching fellow. He completed his training in 1943 and then served a one-year internship at St. Mary's hospital in Duluth. The M.D. degree was awarded to Stapp in 1944, and in October of that year he was inducted into the Medical Corps as a first lieutenant. He served at several Air Forces bases as a general medical officer, but after V-J day he became especially interested in the field of aero medicine. Having completed the course for flight surgeon in the School of Aviation Medicine in 1945, he was assigned to the Aero Medical Laboratory, Holloman Air Force Base, Alamogordo, New Mexico as a project officer.

During World War II jet pilots flew at great heights and at unprecedented speeds with some unusual medical results. "Aviation medicine," reported *Time* (September 12, 1955), "was faced with new and fascinating problems, and doctors were desperately trying to find the answers." As a project officer, Stapp conducted his research in the air under the strenuous and dangerous conditions experienced by pilots. On one assignment Dr. Stapp spent sixty-four and one half hours in the air at stratospheric altitudes testing a liquid oxygen, emergency breathing system. He recommended preventive measures for high-altitude bends, chokes, gas pains, and dehydration.

Dr. Stapp's next assignment was to Edwards Air Force Base, California, in 1947, where he organized an aero medical facility laboratory. He began working with *Gee-Whizz*, a rocket-propelled sled on rails, also called a decelerator, which had a maximum speed of about 200 miles per hour. Simulating air crashes, Stapp carried out experiments with the sled to ascertain how much deceleration ("slowdown") shock the human body can endure.

One of his first jobs was to collect information for improving the design of aircraft safety harnesses. Stapp used a dummy for thirty-two trial runs before attempting his first rocket sled ride at a speed of ninety miles per hour on December 10, 1947. The following day he doubled his speed.

"The unit by which Stapp measures the force of the jolts he experiences on his sled is called a g. One g equals your own weight—or one force of gravity" (*Collier's*, June 25, 1954). By May 1948 Dr. Stapp had taken sixteen rides in his sled and subjected himself to a deceleration shock of thirty-five times the pull of gravity, though it was thought the human body could not take more than eighteen g's. Stapp also calculates the severity of the jolt by the time it takes to build up to the maximum number of g's. He believes that with proper precautions "abrupt decelerations of more than 50 g's can be taken without injury or even loss of consciousness, and impacts of more than 100 g's can be survived—if the build-up rate is below 1,000 g's per second" (*Collier's*, June 25, 1954).

The Air Force transferred Colonel Stapp to Wright-Patterson Air Force Base in 1951. Two years later he was ordered to Holloman Air Force Base, where he guided balloon probes of the upper atmosphere and conducted studies in biodynamics. Stapp put into use a new rocket sled capable of doing up to 750 miles per hour and decelerations up to 150 g's.

In December 1954 he set a record land speed of 632 miles per hour which was equal to more than 1,000 miles per hour at a jet's normal cruising altitude of 35,000 feet. This record run, which was part of an extensive program to judge the effects of bailing outs at supersonic speeds, was intended to test "exposure to wind blast and effects of instant stops at high speed" (New York *Herald Tribune,* December 28, 1954).

After having taken part in twenty-nine decelerations and wind blast experiments, Colonel Stapp was grounded by the Air Force because "he had become too valuable to be risked in further high-speed flights" (New York *Times,* June 17, 1956). Stapp had sustained many injuries during his experiments, including broken arms, fractured ribs, concussions, and retinal hemorrhages.

"When I complete the program, I'll have a perfect graph of the survivable force limits of the human body," says Stapp. He hopes that his "experiments may take some of the danger out of flying through development of new protective devices" (*Collier's,* June 25, 1954). Among the suggestions offered by Stapp are shoulder harnesses to supplement lap safety belts and seats facing the rear which are more firmly anchored to the floor.

Now chief of the Aero Medical Laboratory of Wright Air Development Center, Colonel Stapp directs research and development in aviation and space life sciences. He feels that man is physically capable of reaching the moon but is totally unprepared psychologically. A motion picture, based on Dr. Stapp's heroic experiments, was made by Twentieth Century-Fox Film Corporation in 1956 and entitled *On the Threshold of Space.*

A prolific author, Dr. Stapp has written on aero medical subjects for scientific journals. He became a diplomate of the American Board of Preventive Medicine in 1955, and he was awarded an honorary D.Sc. degree by Baylor University the following year. He has received the National Air Council Award (1951), Legion of Merit (1952), Cheney Award of the Air Force (1955), among others.

The American Rocket Society elected Dr. Stapp to serve as its president in 1959, succeeding George P. Sutton. In 1957 he was named a vice-president of the Aerospace Medical Association, of which he was a Fellow in 1951. Other professional organizations to which Stapp belongs are the American Medical Association, American College of Preventive Medicine, and the bioastronautics committee of the Armed Forces-National Research Council.

Described as having the misleading "paunch of a country doctor, the ramrod posture of a professional soldier and the relentless curiosity of a dedicated scientist," John Paul Stapp is a stocky, bespectacled Air Force hero. He is five feet eight inches tall, weighs 173 pounds, and has curly brown hair and brown eyes. Stapp knows five languages, and when he is away from his work he is often absent-minded. In politics he is a Democrat and in religion, a Protestant. His favorite forms of relaxation are gardening, cooking Chinese and Mexican specialties, and listening to his high-fidelity set. Mrs. Stapp, whom he married on December 23, 1957, is the former Lillian Lanese, a soloist with the Ballet Theatre.

References

N Y Sunday News p82 F 20 '55 por
Read Digest 67:86 D '55
Scholastic 67:6 Ja 12 '56 por
American Men of Science vol I (1955)

STELLA, ANTONIETTA   Mar. 15, 1929-
Singer
Address: c/o Rasponi Associates, 667 Madison Ave., New York 21

The dramatic soprano Antonietta Stella, who has won recognition for her rich vocalism and expressive acting in opera houses from Milan to Tokyo, began her career only eight years ago. She made her debut with the Rome Opera House in 1951, first appeared at La Scala in Milan in 1953, and made her bow at the Metropolitan Opera House in New York in 1956 in *Aïda*. The management of the Metropolitan Opera House honored her in 1959 when it

ANTONIETTA STELLA

chose her to sing Leonora in *Il Trovatore* at the opening of the season on October 26, 1959. Miss Stella includes over fifty roles in her repertory, some of them in works by less-celebrated composers like Marcello and Stradella, but she is best known in the United States for her interpretation of Verdi and Puccini heroines.

Antonietta Stella was born on March 15, 1929 in Perugia, Italy. At the age of seven or eight she learned arias she heard over the radio, and began to take lessons when she was ten. At fifteen she entered the Conservatorio Francesco Morlacchi in Perugia, where she studied voice with Maestro Aldo Zeetti. She won a contest four years later at Bologna and took first prize in the Spoleto Operatic Festival in 1949.

It was as Leonora in Verdi's *La Forza del Destino* that Miss Stella made her professional debut, at the Rome Opera House on January 27, 1951. Her performance was much praised, and famous Italian singers who came to the United States that year spread her reputation by word of mouth as one of the great European sopranos. In the months that followed she sang leading roles from Verdi's *Simone Boccanegra*

and other operas. She was soon engaged by opera companies in Verona, Palermo, Torino, and Genoa, and in 1953 was invited to sing Desdemona in Verdi's *Otello* at La Scala in Milan. That same year she undertook the leading feminine role in Verdi's *Aroldo* at the Maggio Musicale in Florence; she also appeared at opera houses in Germany, Argentina, Brazil, Cuba, Puerto Rico, Japan, and Portugal. Her performance in *Aïda* at the Royal Opera in Covent Garden in London in 1954 was acclaimed by the music critics.

On November 13, 1956 Antonietta Stella sang for the first time at the Metropolitan Opera House, again in *Aïda*. Most of the New York music critics commended her for her stage presence, dramatic ability, and the sweeping range of her voice. A few wished for more finesse in her delivery. Howard Taubman (New York *Times,* November 14, 1956) remarked: "This was an Aïda well above the average. It would be a pity, however, if Signorina Stella were content with where she is now. She could become an outstanding soprano if she took the trouble to refine her singing."

Just three days later Miss Stella appeared as Leonora, the unhappy beloved of the troubadour Manrico, in Verdi's *Il Trovatore*. Her velvety pianissimos, tonal appeal, variations in color and volume, and lyrical passages, especially in the convent scene, won high critical praise. Robert Coleman of the New York *Sunday Mirror* (November 18, 1956) wrote: "In this young Italian soprano Rudolf Bing has popped up with a personality calculated to pack the big house whenever she appears. Antonietta has the face, figure, and voice to become the Met's new glamor girl."

When Miss Stella opened the season at Milan's La Scala in *Aïda* on December 7, 1956, some critics found her work disappointing. Returning to the Metropolitan Opera House in February 1957, she sang the title role in Puccini's *Tosca*. She was especially applauded for her intense acting in the second-act scene with Scarpia, the lecherous head of the secret police. After coaxing, pleading, and threatening, she kills Scarpia once she has obtained the official document she wants from him. At the end of the opera she captivated the audience with the athleticism with which she undertook the suicide leap from the rampart of San Angelo.

In the following month Miss Stella sang her first Elizabeth in Verdi's *Don Carlos* at the Metropolitan. In this role her confident technique and beautiful tone coloring were regarded as the finest since the revival of the opera in 1950. The New York *Times* (March 30, 1957) reviewer said that "her voice is exceptionally large-sized—large enough to soar over the combined voices of Jerome Hines, Robert Merrill, and Irene Dalis in the third-act quartet."

During the 1957-58 season Miss Stella added two roles to her repertory at the Metropolitan Opera House. The first was that of Violetta in *La Traviata*. The music critics were enthusiastic about her interpretation of Verdi's consumptive courtesan. Francis D. Perkins (New York *Herald Tribune,* November 21, 1957) said she presented an "integrated personality and revealed the character's emotions vividly both in its vocal and visual aspects." He was particularly impressed by her "array of color which formed a continuous spectrum and carried expressive conviction in the wide span of moods Violetta is called upon to reveal."

Her second role that was new to her New York repertory was that of Cio-Cio-San in *Madama Butterfly*. On February 19, 1958 Miss Stella headed the cast of the Metropolitan Opera House's first new production of this opera in thirty-four years; it was staged by Yoshio Aoyama with scenic designs and costumes by Motohiro Nagasaka. The soprano had worked with Aoyama, through a French interpreter, for many weeks to master the movements and make-up of the young Japanese girl. She not only kept her singing delicate and restrained, but ran about the stage with tiny steps, frequently genuflecting. "I worked especially hard," she later explained, "to understand and accept the strict discipline of . . . Japanese gestures" (*HiFi & Music Review*, November 1958). Before this performance Miss Stella had been considered mainly a singer of Verdi operas, with Tosca her only regular Puccini role.

Antonietta Stella performs at the Metropolitan Opera House for only part of the season; she devotes the rest of it to appearances at La Scala and other opera houses throughout the world. During the summer of 1957 she appeared at the Hollywood Bowl in California and with the Cincinnati Summer Opera at the Zoo. She was chosen to sing in the Italian centennial celebration for Puccini in the summer of 1959.

Angel Records and Columbia Records have made the operatic performances of Antonietta Stella available on long-playing discs. For Angel she has recorded the role of Violetta in *La Traviata*; for Columbia she has made *Tosca, La Bohème,* and Donizetti's *Linda di Chamounix,* in which she sings her first coloratura role. Columbia recorded the operas at the Teatro di San Carlo in Naples.

Antonietta Stella and her husband, Giuseppe Trepiccioni, make their permanent home in an apartment in Rome. The singer is five feet seven inches tall and weighs 146 pounds. Her hair is brown, and some observers have compared her eyes to those of the women who sat for the portraits of the Italian masters. She has acquired a reputation for serenity and calmness, and for an aloofness from the broils between prima donnas that sometimes enliven the opera houses. She told a reporter for *Newsweek* (November 26, 1956): "I sometimes have to make myself nervous before a performance. If you are too tranquil, it is no good." Envisioning the ideal prima donna, Miss Stella said: "She should have the voice of Muzio, the beauty of Sophia Loren, and the magnetism of Magnani."

The dramatic soprano plays the piano with the confidence of an expert and studies architecture with the interest of an amateur. She likes to read, collect antiques and eighteenth century British prints, attend the movies, drive an automobile, and cook. She has discovered that opera demands more from a singer than a trained and beautiful voice; it also requires acting ability. "The funniest thing of opera," she has said, "is its artificiality: the ridiculous gesture, the pompous manner. As a girl I used to howl with laughter at them" (*HiFi & Music Review,* November 1958).

References

Christian Sci Mon p15 D 20 '57 por
Mus Courier 155:12 Ap '57 por
Opera N 21:8+ F 18 '57 pors

STEWART, POTTER Jan. 23, 1915- Associate Justice of the Supreme Court of the United States

Address: b. Supreme Court Bldg., 1 First St., N.E., Washington 25, D.C.

In the fall of 1958 President Dwight D. Eisenhower named Potter Stewart as the successor to Associate Justice Harold H. Burton of the United States Supreme Court. Stewart had been a judge on the United States Court of Appeals for the Sixth Circuit since 1954. Before that, he had practised law in New York City and in Cincinnati, where he had served two terms on the City Council. As the fifth Eisenhower appointee to the Supreme Court and as a new justice at the time when the court was under attack for some of its decisions, Stewart was asked whether he was a liberal or a conservative. He replied: "I just don't know what I am. I'd like to be thought of as a lawyer." His political affiliation is with the Republican party.

Potter Stewart was born in Jackson, Michigan, on January 23, 1915, one of the three children of James Garfield and Harriet (Loomis) Potter. His father, who died in the spring of 1959, had been Mayor of Cincinnati from 1938 to 1947 and a judge of the Ohio Supreme Court since 1947. His brother, Zeph Stewart, is a professor of classics at Harvard University. His sister, Irene, is Mrs. John C. Taylor. They were brought up in Cincinnati, Ohio.

After his graduation from Hotchkiss School in Lakeville, Connecticut in 1933, Potter Stewart entered Yale University. There he majored in English literature and was chairman of the *Yale Daily News.* He was elected to Phi Beta Kappa and received the B.A. degree *cum laude* in 1937. During the summer he had worked as a cub reporter on the Cincinnati *Times-Star.* He has said that he voted for President Franklin D. Roosevelt in the 1936 election because of his humanitarian efforts and his social security and security exchange reforms. For a year following Stewart's graduation, he studied international law at Cambridge University in England as a Henry Fellow.

Returning to New Haven, he entered the Yale Law School. He won the moot court competition, was made an editor of the *Yale Law Journal,* was made a member of the Order of Coif, and was granted an LL.B. degree in 1941. After a year as an associate with the law firm of Debevoise, Stevenson, Plimpton & Page in New York City, Stewart was called into active service as an ensign with the United States

Ackad
ASSOCIATE JUSTICE POTTER STEWART

Naval Reserve. During World War II he saw three years of sea duty on an oil tanker in the Atlantic and the Mediterranean. He won three battle stars and rose to the rank of lieutenant.

At the end of the war Stewart returned to his position with the New York law firm. While there, he participated in the campaign against the election of United States Representative Vito Marcantonio. In 1947 he decided to move back to Cincinnati and became an associate with the firm of Dinsmore, Shohl, Sawyer & Dinsmore. In 1951 he was made a partner.

He was elected in 1949 to the City Council of Cincinnati and was re-elected two years later. He served as Vice-Mayor of Cincinnati in 1952-53. While on the council, he consistently voted for urban redevelopment housing projects. According to the Washington *Post and Times Herald* (October 12, 1958), Stewart in 1953 "fiercely attacked" two members of the City Planning Commission, "accusing them of concealing information concerning the then Planning Director, who admitted former Communist affiliations." He supported the Presidential drives of his friend, the late Senator Robert A. Taft, in 1948 and 1952, and worked for the campaign of Dwight D. Eisenhower in 1952 and 1956.

When a vacancy occurred on the United States Court of Appeals for the Sixth Circuit (Ohio, Michigan, Kentucky, and Tennessee), President Eisenhower appointed Stewart, who took the oath of office and assumed his duties as a circuit judge on June 1, 1954. While on this court, Stewart took part in 296 decisions and dissented in ten. In a case involving the Hillsboro, Ohio public schools, he concurred in a majority opinion which ordered desegregation.

In a dissenting opinion, he argued against depriving a labor union of access to the National Labor Relations Board because a union

official might have filed a false non-Communist affidavit (the United States Supreme Court later upheld his position). Judge Stewart in other cases insisted on fair procedure in prosecuting accused criminals. As a visiting judge in New York on the Court of Appeals for the Second Circuit, he wrote the opinion which affirmed the criminal contempt conviction of Marie Torre, a New York *Herald Tribune* columnist who refused to disclose her sources when questioned as a witness in a libel suit.

On October 14, 1958 Stewart was named by President Eisenhower to succeed Harold H. Burton as an associate justice of the Supreme Court of the United States. Stewart was sworn into office and took his seat that day, as a recess appointee. His nomination was formally submitted to the United States Senate on January 17, 1959. During the hearings held on his nomination by the Senate Judiciary Committee, whose chairman is Senator James O. Eastland (Democrat of Mississippi), Stewart was questioned closely about his views on the Supreme Court's 1954 school integration decision and other recent controversial rulings.

The committee approved his nomination, and the United States Senate confirmed it on May 5, 1959 by a vote of seventy to seventeen. The opposition votes were cast by Southern Democrats, who appeared to be registering their resentment against the 1954 desegregation decision of the Supreme Court. Justice Stewart took the oaths of office on May 15, 1959. During the annual term of the court, he heard cases ranging from commerce and natural gas questions to admiralty ones, and wrote eighteen opinions, dissents, separate concurrences, and other miscellaneous memoranda.

Stewart concurred in a court holding that in certain cases the federal and state governments can prosecute a person for the same criminal act. Justice Stewart wrote the court's majority opinion that the state of New York had no power to bar the showing of the film *Lady Chatterley's Lover*. He held with the majority of the court in finding that city inspectors might search a private home for unsanitary conditions without first obtaining a search warrant. He was also in the majority in the Barenblatt and Uphaus cases, which upheld the right of state governments and the House Committee on Un-American Activities to demand punishment for persons defying their investigations into Communism.

Other government positions which Stewart has held include membership on the Committee for the White House Conference on Education in 1954-55 and membership on the committee on court administration of the Judicial Conference of the United States from 1955 to 1958. He belongs to the American, Ohio, Cincinnati, and City of New York bar associations, the American Law Institute, and the American Judicature Society. He serves on the Yale Law School executive committee. He is a member of Delta Kappa Epsilon and Phi Delta Phi. His clubs in Cincinnati are the Camargo, Cincinnati, Commercial, Commonwealth, and University. His church affiliation is with the Episcopal Church. He was awarded an honorary LL.D. degree by Yale University in 1959.

Potter Stewart and Mary Anne Bertles were married on April 24, 1943. They have three children: Harriet Potter, Potter, Jr., and David Bertles. The Associate Justice has brown eyes and brown hair; he is five feet and eleven inches tall and weighs 160 pounds. For recreation he enjoys fishing and golf. Justice Stewart has said that the quality a judge needs, above all others, is fairness: "Fairness is really what justice is."

References

Bsns W p28 O 11 '58
Christian Sci Mon p1+ O 8 '58
N Y Herald Tribune p12, p22 O 8 '58;
 II p2 O 12 '58
N Y Times p26 O 8 '58
N Y World-Telegram p9 O 8 '58
Newsweek 52:38 O 20 '58
Reporter 20:31+ F 5 '59
Time 72:24 O 20 '58
U S News 47:76 Jl 13 '59
Washington (D.C.) Post pF6, pA22 O 12 '58

Who's Who in America, 1958-59

Wide World

CHIVU STOICA

STOICA, CHIVU Aug. 8, 1908- Premier of Romania
Address: b. Office of the President of the Council of Ministers, Bucharest, Romania

As Premier of Romania (President of the Council of Ministers), Chivu Stoica has headed since October 1955 a government controlled by a single political organization, the Romanian Communist party, under the leadership of First Secretary Gheorghe Gheorghiu-Dej (see *C.B.,* October 1958). Although Stoica's post is therefore considered secondary in power, he is by no means a figurehead in ruling this "docile" U.S.S.R. satellite, whose government was supported by Soviet Army occupation troops from its establishment soon after World War II until the summer of 1958. Ranking high also in his country's Communist party (since 1948 called the Romanian Workers' party), Stoica is deputy chairman of the Politburo of the party's Central Committee. He has served since 1946 in the Grand National Assembly (parliament), to which he was most recently re-elected to a four-year term in February 1957.

Chivu Stoica was born into a peasant family in Smeieni, a village in the Buzău district of Romania, on August 8, 1908. During his youth he worked as an apprentice in a railroad company and later was employed in metallurgical factories in Bucharest. He joined the Communist Youth Organization in 1929 and the Romanian Communist party in 1930. Shortly afterward he began working at the Grivitza Railroad Shop.

Like Gheorghiu-Dej, Stoica took part in organizing the historic Grivitza railway workers' strike of 1933. He was arrested and sentenced to fifteen years at hard labor in prison, and during part of World War II, in which Romania fought on the side of the Fascist nations, he was interned in the concentration camp at Târgu-Jiu. His release from prison came soon after the invasion of Romania by the Soviet Union Army in August 1944 and the *coup d'état* which permitted the inclusion of Communists in the government, thus preparing the way for eventual establishment of a Communist rule.

Assigned to industrial-labor relations work for the Romanian Communist party, Stoica helped organize the General Confederation of Labor, of which from 1945 to 1947 he was a vice-president. He was elected a member of the party's Central Committee and its Politburo in 1945. (At the congress of the party in 1948 he was demoted to candidate member of the Politburo, but was restored to full membership in 1952.) He ran successfully on the Communist ticket in 1946 for the Grand National Assembly, to become one of many Communist deputies whose victory in the election strengthened the Communist-dominated government of Premier Petru Groza (who died in 1958). Stoica was re-elected to the Romanian national legislature in 1948, 1952, and 1957.

From late 1946 to April 1948 Stoica was general manager of the Romanian Railways Administration. On April 13, 1948, some months after the proclamation of a People's Republic by the Groza government, Romania adopted a new constitution, broadly patterned on that of the Soviet Union. In the Groza Cabinet, Stoica held the position of Minister of Industry from April 1948 to November 1949. When this ministry was divided to form the Ministry of Light Industry and the Ministry of Metal and Chemical Industries, he became head of the latter department and served from November 1949 until May 1952. Through these offices he therefore played a substantial part in Romania's postwar industrialization program and its nationalization of industry.

A conflict within the Romanian Communist party led to an important governmental reorganization in June 1952, which resulted in the

STOICA, CHIVU—*Continued*

ouster of Ana Pauker, a Vice-Premier and Minister of Foreign Affairs, and in the proclamation of Gheorgiu-Dej as Premier in place of Groza, who was made President of the People's Republic. Stoica filled the office of Minister of Metallurgical Industry in Gheorghiu-Dej's Cabinet from October 1953 to October 1955. He was a Vice-President of the Council of Ministers from March 1950 to August 1954, when he was named first Vice-President of the council.

In accordance with the post-Stalin principle of collective leadership, Gheorghiu-Dej in April 1954 gave up his office of Secretary General (later First Secretary) of the Romanian Communist party to serve only as Premier. The following October, when he was restored to the top political position in the country, he turned over the Premiership to Stoica. In March 1957 Stoica was re-elected Premier by the Grand National Assembly resulting from the one-party parliamentary election of the preceding month, which had been a "99 per cent" victory for the Communists. He immediately announced a Cabinet reshuffle and the reduction of the number of ministries from thirty to sixteen.

Before and after becoming Premier, Chivu Stoica made many trips to the Soviet Union and Communist countries of Eastern Europe. As head of an economic delegation to Moscow in November-December 1956, during the revolution in Hungary, he signed a joint statement with Premier Nikolai A. Bulganin for increased economic co-operation between Romania and the U.S.S.R. and also gave full endorsement to the use of Soviet military forces against the Hungarian rebels. Stoica visited Moscow again in November 1957 and May 1958 for meetings with top-ranking leaders of other Communist countries.

Romania's relations with the Soviet satellite nations of eastern Europe are governed by its participation in the Warsaw Pact (officially known as the Warsaw Treaty of Friendship, Cooperation, and Mutual Assistance), created in 1955 as a Communist counterpart of the North Atlantic Treaty Organization. In January 1956 Stoica headed the Romanian delegation to the meeting in Prague of the political consultative committee of the member nations of the treaty. During a visit to Berlin the following year he signed with East German Premier Otto Grotewohl a declaration stating that in the event of an attack Romania and East Germany would assist each other on the basis of the Warsaw Pact.

Taking its direction from the Soviet Union, Romania in 1956 had re-established with Yugoslavia diplomatic relations broken since Tito's repudiation by the Cominform in 1948. Premier Stoica proposed in September 1957 that a conference be held of Romania, Bulgaria, Greece, Albania, Turkey, and Yugoslavia "to attain collective cooperation between the Balkan states for the purpose of safeguarding peace in this region as well as for the prosperity and progress of the peoples" (*Manchester Guardian,* September 18, 1957). Some of the nations re-

jected the proposal; others responded with reservations. In his first interview for an American newspaper, Stoica later told Elie Abel of the New York *Times* (February 27, 1958) that he would continue his efforts to bring about a Balkan conference.

On a very rare appearance from behind the Iron Curtain, Stoica paid a state visit to Indian Prime Minister Jawaharlal Nehru in New Delhi in March 1958. He is married and has a daughter; little else is generally known about him aside from the official acts that he performs as Premier. He is bald and stocky and speaks in a subdued manner. Elie Abel noted that during his interview of February 1958 he "expanded cheerfully" on his written replies to questions submitted in advance and that he "did not rule out any questions put to him orally." His decorations include the Order of the Star of the Romanian People's Republic and the Order of the State Banner of the Korean People's Republic.

Reference

International Who's Who, 1958

STONE, ABRAHAM Oct. 31, 1890-July 3, 1959; Urologist; world leader in birth control, marriage counseling, and population problems; a founder of a marriage consultation center which became a national model; author. See *Current Biography* (March) 1952.

Obituary

N Y Times p15 Jl 4 '59

STOUT, RUTH A(LBERTINE) 1910-
Educator; organization official
Address: h. 1614 Jewell Ave., Topeka, Kan.

"Education cannot be separated from scientific or social progress," Ruth Stout, president of the National Education Association for 1958-59, recently stated. ". . . When we speak of a good teacher these days, we speak also of a well-informed participating member of the community. We speak not of a public servant, but of a public leader. I am proud to be a part of this down-to-earth transition to a space age. To me it also represents a coming of age for the profession of teaching."

Ruth Stout had been vice-president during the 1957-58 term and was elected on July 4, 1958 to head the NEA, the world's largest educational organization, with 616,000 members in the United States and its territories. Miss Stout is also director of field programs of the Kansas State Teachers' Association. She has taught for over twenty years in high schools and colleges, and holds a Ph.D. degree from the University of Minnesota.

Ruth Albertine Stout was born in 1910 in Topeka, Kansas, the child of A. J. and Emma M. (Ahrens) Stout. She was raised in Topeka, where her father was the superintendent of schools, and was graduated from the Topeka High School in 1927. She then entered the University of Kansas in Lawrence, was on the honor roll for four years, and received the A.B. degree with honors in English in 1931. She became a member of Pi Lambda Theta, Delta Kappa Gamma, Tau Delta Pi, Nonoso, American College Quill Club, MacDowell Arts Society, and the Kansas Women's Dinner Club.

After teaching English and physical education for four years in the Clay County Community High School in Kansas, she returned to the University of Kansas and received her M.A. degree there in 1935 with a thesis entitled "The Utilization of Sports References by Representative Elizabethan Dramatists." For a number of years she alternated between teaching in the winter and studying during the summer at Columbia University, Northwestern University, the University of Chicago, and the University of Minnesota.

From 1935 to 1936 she taught English, speech, debating, and dramatics at the Clay County Community High School and for the next ten years, from 1936 to 1946, she was an instructor in English, debating, and radio at the Topeka High School. During the spring of 1946 she was, in addition, a part-time instructor in English at Washburn Municipal University in Topeka. Later she taught at the university on a full-time basis, as an instructor in English from 1946 to 1949 and an assistant professor from 1949 to 1953. She also was associate dean of students from 1946 to 1950 and dean of students from 1950 to 1953.

Returning to the University of Minnesota, she took graduate courses during the two years from 1951 to 1953, and she received the Ph.D. degree in 1957. Her thesis dealt with selective admissions and retention practices in college and university programs of teacher education. Part of it was published in the *Journal of Teacher Education* in September 1957.

Over the years she has been active in a number of professional organizations. She was on the salary committee of the Topeka Teachers Association for two years and served as president of the Topeka High School Teacher's Guild for a year. Long a prominent member of the Kansas State Teachers' Association, she was president in 1947-48, and a member of the board of directors in 1948 and 1949, the state resolutions committee in 1948 and 1949, the code of ethics committee in 1948 and 1949, the convention planning committee from 1948 to 1950, the committee on committees from 1948 to 1949, the subcommittee on articulation of general education and common learnings from 1949 to 1950, and the commission on teacher education and professional standards from 1946 to the present (chairman since 1949). She is now director of field programs of the association.

In 1944 and from 1947 to 1951 Miss Stout was a state delegate to the conventions of the National Education Association, which has a membership of 616,000 teachers, principals, supervisors, and superintendents from the United States and its territories. Overall policy for the NEA is made by an elected representative assembly of about 600 delegates from state, territorial, and affiliated teacher organizations.

RUTH A. STOUT

Between sessions, work is carried on by a board of directors and an executive council.

At the centennial convention of the NEA in 1957, Lyman V. Ginger was elected the ninety-sixth president, and Miss Stout, vice-president, for the 1957-58 term. At the 1958 convention, held in Cleveland, Ohio, Miss Stout was named president for a term of one year. Walter Eshelman was elected vice-president. Among the resolutions approved by the delegates were measures calling for Federal aid to education, higher teacher salaries, and reducing the voting age to eighteen years. Another resolution urged Americans to approach the problems of integration in the public schools "with the spirit of fair play, good will, and respect for law."

Speaking at the convention on the subject of a longer school year and teacher opposition to year-'round operation of the schools, Miss Stout said: "If children can profit by a longer school year, then the school year should be extended. If teachers are to be paid on a twelve-month basis, then they should be willing to give service, although I would hate to see a teacher actually teach for eleven months steadily." Among the current projects of the NEA are a study of the problems of education of the gifted student and a research program on juvenile delinquency, intended primarily for the benefit of classroom teachers.

Other organizations in which Miss Stout has participated are the American Association of University Women, American Association of Colleges for Teacher Education, North Central Association, National School Public Relations Association, Kansas Association of Teachers of English, and National Council of Teachers of English.

She has helped with several state government projects on education. She was made a member of the advisory council on education to the State Department of Education in Kansas in

STOUT, RUTH A.—*Continued*

April 1950, is a member of the committee on accreditation, and from 1948 to 1950 was a member of the subcommittee on in-service growth. In connection with the Governor's Conference on Education (Kansas), she served on the planning committee and as vice-chairman of the 1948 conference, as general chairman of the 1950 conference, and as a member of the planning committee for the 1952 conference.

Her articles and speeches have appeared in many professional magazines and publications, including the *Journal of the National Education Association, Personnel and Guidance Journal, Yearbook of the American Association of Colleges for Teacher Education, Bulletin of the Kansas Association of Teachers of English, Kansas Teacher, Kansas Speech Journal,* and *Journal of Teacher Education.*

For recreation she gardens and draws house and building plans. She has hazel eyes and gray hair, is five feet ten inches tall, and weighs 135 pounds. Her political affiliation is with the Republican party. She served on the board of education of the First Methodist Church of Topeka from 1946 to 1953 and as assistant in the Sunday school library from 1947 to 1953.

References

N Y Herald Tribune II p3 Jl 6 '58
Nat Educ Assn J 47 :361 S '58

STURGES, PRESTON Aug. 29, 1898-Aug. 6, 1959 Motion-picture director and producer; author; noted for his ludicrous, satirical comedies; wrote Broadway hit *Strictly Dishonorable* (1929-30); won an Oscar for *The Great McGinty* (1940); also wrote and directed the movie *The Miracle of Morgan's Creek* (1944). See *Current Biography* (April) 1941.

Obituary

N Y Times p23 Ag 7 '59

STURZO, LUIGI Nov. 26, 1871-Aug. 8, 1959 Italian priest; political leader; author; anti-Fascist; founder of a political group in 1919 which became Christian Democratic party after World War II; appointed Senator for life in 1952. See *Current Biography* (February) 1946.

Obituary

N Y Times p89 Ag 9 '59

SWING, JOSEPH M(AY) Feb. 28, 1894- United States government official; former Army officer

Address: b. 119 D St., N.E., Washington 25, D.C.; h. 5609 Pioneer Lane, Washington 16, D.C.

Administration of the complex McCarran-Walter Immigration and Nationality Act of 1950 dealing with the admission, exclusion, deportation, and naturalization of aliens is the responsibility of Joseph M. Swing, who has been Commissioner of Immigration and Nat-

uralization since May 1954. He succeeded Argyle R. Mackay, who stayed on as Deputy Commissioner. About two months earlier Lieutenant General Swing had retired from his position of Commanding General of the Sixth Army at San Francisco after a military career of almost forty years.

Joseph May Swing was born on February 28, 1894 in Jersey City, New Jersey, one of three sons of Mary Ann (Snellgrove) and Joseph Swing, a contractor. His brothers are William Snellgrove and George Snellgrove. He received his elementary and secondary education in the Jersey City public schools, and in 1911 was graduated from Newark's Barringer High. He then entered the United States Military Academy at West Point, New York in the same class as Dwight D. Eisenhower. In 1915 he was graduated with a B.S. degree in military science and engineering and commissioned a second lieutenant in the Field Artillery.

The following year Swing went on the punitive expedition to Mexico against Pancho Villa under the leadership of General John J. Pershing. After the United States entered World War I in 1917 he was sent to France as a major in the Field Artillery with the 1st Division. He later became an aide-de-camp to the Chief of Staff, General Peyton C. March.

When Swing returned to the United States in May 1919, he joined the 19th Field Artillery at Fort Myer, Virginia. Two years later he was sent to Hawaii, where he commanded the 1st Battalion of the 11th Field Artillery at Schofield Barracks, and in 1925 he returned to the mainland to assume command of the 9th Field Artillery Battalion at Fort Des Moines, Iowa. The next year he was graduated with honors from the Field Artillery School at Fort Sill, Oklahoma, and in 1927 he was graduated from the Command and General Staff School.

From 1927 to 1931 Swing was on duty in the office of the Chief of Field Artillery in Washington, D.C., and in 1933 he became chief of its war plans section. Two years later he was graduated from the Army War College in Washington, D.C. before being assigned to the 6th Field Artillery at Fort Hoyle, Maryland.

Sent next to Texas, Swing was division chief of the 2d Division at Fort Sam Houston from 1938 to 1940 in the rank of lieutenant colonel. In later assignments he took command of the 82d Field Artillery Regiment of the 1st Cavalry Division at Fort Bliss, Texas and then of the 1st Cavalry Division Artillery. As a brigadier general, in 1941 Swing organized the division artillery of the 82d Division at Camp Claiborne, Louisiana; and in 1943, as a major general, he activated the 11th Airborne Division at Camp Mackall, North Carolina.

The latter division, which Swing was to command for the remainder of World War II, proved that an entire division could be moved to its objective by air and that it could also be indefinitely supplied by airlift. Swing successfully used the airlift method in attacks on Leyte and on Nasagbu and Tagaytay Ridge in the Philippines.

After the Japanese surrender Swing's division was the first United States unit to occupy

Japan. For some years he was responsible for the island of Hokkaido and the northern part of Honshu. He then commanded I Corps with headquarters in Kyoto, Japan from February 1948 until he returned to the United States in 1949 and assumed command of the Artillery Center and the Artillery School at Fort Sill, Oklahoma. The following year he became the commandant of the Army War College at Fort Leavenworth, Kansas, and on August 1, 1951 he took command of the Sixth Army at San Francisco, California.

On February 28, 1954 Swing retired from active service with the rank of lieutenant general, and in May of that year he was appointed Commissioner of Immigration and Naturalization by President Eisenhower. The Immigration and Naturalization Service is part of the Department of Justice.

One of Swing's most striking successes in his first civilian post was Operation Wetback. This project, begun one month after he came into office, was aimed at stopping the seasonal illegal flow of Mexican farm laborers into the United States. Swing reorganized the border patrol to achieve more flexibility in the movement of task forces along the border, and he set up a plan for shipping into the interior of Mexico those wetbacks who were caught rather than just a few hundred feet across the border as had been previously done. This discouraged many from trying to come into the United States.

In 1956 Swing prepared for President Eisenhower proposals for the liberalization of the quota system in the immigration laws. The present system favors immigrants from northern European countries and severely restricts those from other parts of the world. The minor changes permitted by Congress in 1957, however, fell far short of those proposed by the administration.

More successful with other innovations, Swing made important changes in the Immigration and Naturalization Service. The main feature of his reorganization was the decentralization of the service's activities which he felt would speed procedures, set up closer supervision of the work, and delegate additional authority to the field.

Swing is credited with correcting several major defects in the agency's treatment of aliens. Immigration officers, many of whom lacked the necessary education and training, had been making decisions on whether a deportable alien would be subject to physical persecution if shipped back to his land of origin. Special inquiry officers had served as both prosecutor and judge in deportation hearings.

Under Swing's new system special inquiry officers with wide experience and a legal education were chosen to judge whether aliens would suffer persecution if deported. He stopped the automatic arrest of aliens served with deportation notices and called for special examining officers to present the government's case in deportation hearings. Furthermore, he restricted the use of secret information in deportation cases.

Commissioner Swing has also been active in carrying out President Eisenhower's plan to

LIEUT. GEN. JOSEPH M. SWING (RET.)

simplify air travel between the United States and its closest neighbors. In order to meet the complaints of air-line passengers over delays incidental to their arrival in the United States, Swing instituted a plan whereby United States immigration officers would process the passengers at their point of departure while they were waiting for their planes. This arrangement has been tried in Bermuda, Montreal, and Cuba.

From time to time Commissioner Swing has had to defend himself against Congressional criticism. In July 1956, for instance, when questioned by a subcommittee of the House Government Operations Committee, he testified that he made hunting trips to Mexico and Canada largely at government expense, but that the trips were part of his authorized business and were arranged to establish friendly relations with officials of those countries.

Notwithstanding this criticism, Congress in May 1958 voted to raise Commissioner Swing's salary from $17,500 to $20,000 a year. In commending the House of Representatives for its approval of the raise, Democratic Representative Francis E. Walter, co-author of the Immigration and Nationality Act and an opponent of proposed administration changes, nevertheless praised Swing for the progress he had made since taking office.

Swing's awards include the Distinguished Service Medal, the Silver Star with two oak leaf clusters, the Legion of Merit, the Bronze Star Medal with one cluster, the Air Medal with one cluster, the French Legion of Honor, and the Philippine Legion of Honor with the grade of chief commander.

Joseph M. Swing married Josephine Mary March, who is a daughter of General Peyton C. March, on July 8, 1918. They have a son, Joseph March Swing, and a daughter, Mrs. Mary Ann Mitchell. The white-haired commissioner has blue eyes, is six feet tall, and weighs

SWING, JOSEPH M.—*Continued*

178 pounds. He belongs to the Army and Navy Club in Washington, D.C. and the Bohemian Club in San Francisco. He is a Republican, and he attends the Reformed Church of America. Golf and hunting are his sports.

References

Gen Army 1:23+ Ag '53 por
N Y Times p23 Ap 29 '54 por; p12 Ap 25 '58 por
Who's Who in America, 1958-59

TANNER, EDWARD EVERETT, 3D
May 18, 1921- Author

Address: b. Harcourt, Brace & Co., Inc., 750 3d Ave., New York 17

Edward Everett Tanner 3d is the author of one of the most successful novels of recent years, and once had three books on the best-selling lists at the same time, but has yet to sign any of his books with his own name. He is better known as Patrick Dennis (author of *Auntie Mame* and coauthor of *Guestward Ho!*) or Virginia Rowans (author of *The Loving Couple*).

These pseudonyms originated in a desire for privacy which is unusual in the publishing world. Only in 1955 was Tanner's identity revealed to the general public, which was then buying 20,000 copies a week of his latest book. At the time he was promotion manager of *Foreign Affairs*.

Edward Everett Tanner 3d was born in Chicago, Illinois on May 18, 1921. He likes to remark that the event took place in the "same hospital, same room, same bed as Cornelia Otis Skinner—different time." Tanner's father was a stockbroker, who sent the boy to various private schools in Chicago and Evanston, Illinois. It was reported by *Look*

EDWARD EVERETT TANNER 3d

(January 20, 1959) that he was expelled from some of them.

Adopting his first alias while he was still a schoolboy, Tanner ignored his given names in favor of Patrick. It was under this name that, after leaving the last in his series of private schools, Tanner went to work for the Stebbins Hardware Company and then as a bookstore clerk in Chicago for Columbia Educational Books, Inc. He left this job for military service in World War II.

As a member of the American Field Service, Tanner served as an ambulance driver in Arabia, North Africa, Italy, and France. He was attached to the armed forces of seven nations—Great Britain, Australia, Union of South Africa, New Zealand, Greece, Poland, and France. His contact with French soldiers inspired the luxuriant beard he still affects. He was twice wounded during his military service, although not seriously, and at one time suffered from amnesia—which he claims to have enjoyed.

Following his discharge in 1945, Tanner settled in New York City which since then has been his home almost without interruption. After jobs as an account executive with Franklin Spier, Inc., an advertising agency, and as advertising manager for Creative Age Press, he became promotion director of *Foreign Affairs* magazine. He worked for *Foreign Affairs* until January 1, 1956.

Anonymous from the start of his literary career, Tanner began to write as a reviser of other people's books and as a ghost writer. As he had done in school, he continued to use Patrick Tanner as his preferred name in private life when he signed checks and transacted personal business. His multiple aliases have caused considerable confusion.

His wife, Louise Stickney Tanner, has told how Tanner's bank regularly sent a duplicate set of statements to their home, believing that Edward Everett and Patrick Tanner were separate individuals. "Until his $5.00 nest egg was demolished by service charges," she wrote, "he was probably the only living American to have a joint bank account with himself" (*Vogue*, November 1, 1956).

When Tanner submitted his first manuscript to a publisher, he gave the publisher a list of twenty pseudonyms which he thought acceptable. Of these the firm chose Virginia Rounds, which was slightly altered to avoid confusion with the cigarettes of the same name. When *Oh, What a Wonderful Wedding* (Crowell, 1953) was published, it was signed by Virginia Rowans.

"Miss Rowans," said Jane Cobb in the New York *Times Book Review* (June 28, 1953), "writes with a fine feminine realism and few of the foibles of our competitive society escape her." Joanna Spencer in the New York *Herald Tribune Book Review* (April 19, 1953) observed that sometimes "her efforts are too hysterical to produce anything but strain, and part of the time they are unpleasantly malicious. In between these exaggerations, however, there is a great deal of very funny and knowledgeable satire."

A year later, Tanner published *House Party* (Crowell, 1954) under the same pseudonym. This story of a socialite's weekend party on Long Island received more favorable attention from the critics.

Before either of these novels had been published, Tanner had created *Auntie Mame; An Irreverent Escapade in Biography*. After spending years in developing the plot, he wrote the book in ninety days. Three years passed before he could interest a publisher in *Auntie Mame*. Finally, it was released under the imprint of the Vanguard Press in 1955.

Auntie Mame appeared under the pseudonym of Patrick Dennis, the nephew of the middle-aged terror of Beekman Place. He told the story of his socialite relative's rampages at home and abroad to a public that was more than willing to listen. *Auntie Mame* was an immediate success. For more than two years the book led the best-selling lists and sold over 2,000,000 copies in the original, translations, and paperback editions.

In his review Robert W. Henderson noted: "The humor, broad at times, is coupled with satire on phony *avant garde* intellectuals, racial prejudices as evident in suburban communities, and snobbism in general" (*Library Journal*, January 1, 1955).

Auntie Mame was adapted for a Broadway production which, starring Rosalind Russell, enjoyed a run from October 3, 1956 to June 28, 1958. Miss Russell played the same role in a film version which was released on December 4, 1958. Beatrice Lillie starred in a London production of the American hit. But the great popularity of *Auntie Mame* brought about the loss of Tanner's cherished privacy.

"I always wanted to and did keep my identity private," he told reporter Martha MacGregor (New York *Post*, August 24, 1958). "I have my own life . . . and nobody cared who I was until that fine publication, *Time* magazine, decided the world couldn't live another hour without knowing." He was referring to a story in the July 4, 1955 edition.

In quick succession after *Auntie Mame* came two more Tanner books, *Guestward Ho! As Indiscreetly Confided to Patrick Dennis* (by Patrick Dennis and Mrs. Barbara C. Hooton, Vanguard, 1956) and *The Loving Couple* (by Virginia Rowans, Crowell, 1956). By the end of the year, these two books shared space on the lists of best sellers with *Auntie Mame*.

Tanner's next book, *The Pink Hotel* (Putnam, 1957), was the result of a collaborative effort, appearing under the double authorship of Patrick Dennis and Dorothy Erskine. This was followed by *Around the World with Auntie Mame* (Harcourt, 1958), which had sold over 130,000 copies by the spring of 1959. Tanner has also contributed articles and short stories to national magazines. Since 1957 he has been the drama critic of the *New Republic;* his reviews are the first of his writings to be printed under his own name.

Edward Everett Tanner 3d married writer Louise Stickney on December 30, 1948. They have two children, Michael and Elizabeth, and live in a redecorated town house in Manhattan.

Their home is furnished with Directoire and Queen Anne pieces and Tanner's collection of antique chime clocks. Apart from the clocks, Tanner enjoys small parties and listening to music.

Tanner is tall and lean and as bearded as a poilu; he dresses like "a refugee from the British Foreign Office" (*Time*, July 15, 1957). Concerning some of America's idolatries he says: "We make a fetish of youth. We're too conscious of publicity and of beauty. Nobody is all that young, all that newsworthy, all that attractive. People are people—and they deserve it" (New York *Post*, August 24, 1958).

References

Mademoiselle 44:67+ Ja '57 por
Vogue 127:98+ F 15 '56 por

TATUM, EDWARD L(AWRIE) Dec. 14, 1909- Geneticist; biochemist

Address: b. Rockefeller Institute for Medical Research, York Ave. and 66th St., New York 21; h. 445 E. 68th St., New York 21

For discovering "that genes act by regulating specific chemical processes," Dr. Edward L. Tatum has won a place among the Nobel laureates of the world. He was co-recipient of one half of the prize for 1958 in medicine and physiology with Dr. G. W. Beadle of the California Institute of Technology (see *C.B.*, April 1956), with whom he conducted joint research on the pink bread mold, *Neurospora crassa*. The other half of the $41,420 award was bestowed on Dr. Joshua Lederberg of Stanford University. Since January 1957 Tatum has been a member and professor of the Rockefeller Institute for Medical Research in New York City.

Edward Lawrie Tatum was born in Boulder, Colorado on December 14, 1909, one of the three children of Dr. Arthur Lawrie and Mabel (Webb) Tatum. His parents communicated to their children a strong feeling for learning and a life of service. His mother was one of the first women graduates of the University of Colorado and the elder Tatum, who held both M.D. and Ph.D. degrees, was a professor of pharmacology at the University of Wisconsin. A brother, Dr. Howard J. Tatum, is an obstetrician and gynecologist on the staff of the medical school of the University of Oregon, and his sister, Mrs. A. F. Rasmussen, is married to a member of the faculty of the University of California Medical School.

Although he is now a geneticist, Tatum's training was mainly in the related sciences. As an undergraduate at the University of Wisconsin in Madison, he majored in chemistry, receiving the A.B. degree in 1931. Research for his master's degree, conferred the next year, was completed in the field of microbiology, and his doctoral dissertation was written under Professor William H. Peterson, a noted biochemist. After receiving the Ph.D. degree in 1934, Tatum worked for one year as a research assistant in biochemistry. He was awarded a

Rockefeller Institute

EDWARD L. TATUM

General Education Board Fellowship for study in bacteriological chemistry at the University of Utrecht in the Netherlands during 1936-37.

Upon returning to the United States in 1937 Dr. Tatum was appointed a research associate at Stanford University in California. His early experiments involved the nutritional requirements and metabolic activity of insects, and he worked primarily with the small fruit fly Drosophila melanogaster, which had become standard in laboratory use for geneticists. By 1939 Tatum had established that the Drosophila larvae needed three factors supplied by yeast for normal growth and development in addition to the carbohydrates, amino acids, and known vitamin requirements. He also conducted research on the vitamin B requirements of the fruit fly, and his projects on the development of eye colors in Drosophila proved that "under suitable conditions certain bacteria synthesize a substance which has v+ hormone." With Dr. Beadle he isolated and identified kynurenine as an eye-color hormone in Drosophila.

In 1940 Dr. Tatum and Dr. G. W. Beadle, then a professor on the Stanford faculty and now chairman of the division of biology at the California Institute of Technology, decided to use Neurospora crassa for their experiments. This pink bread mold is a simple organism to handle since it can manufacture food from a mixture of mineral salts, sugar, and a vitamin known as biotin, and it reproduces both sexually and nonsexually, thus providing a mold with the same heredity when needed. Tatum and Beadle wanted to modify Neurospora genes to obtain strains of the organism which would differ chemically from the normal mold. "They irradiated mold with X rays to induce mutations. Then they gathered spores formed by sexual reproduction and laid them out on a sheet of agar jelly containing the minimum nutrients that natural wild mold requires" (Time, July 14, 1958).

The startling results of their research were reported in 1941, the same year that Tatum was promoted to assistant professor at Stanford. The two scientists found that some spores did not show any obvious mutation and continued to thrive normally; others died, possibly as a result of too much irradiation; a third category lived, but did not develop properly. These spores were nurtured with vitamins, amino acids, and other chemical nutrients in an effort to promote growth. On the 299th attempt Tatum and Beadle found an ailing spore that would grow when given vitamin B-6 (pyridoxine). An X-ray-damaged gene was held responsible for the spore's impaired biochemical processes: its inability to produce the necessary enzyme to manufacture the B-6. The experiments further demonstrated that when a normal mold and one with an altered gene mated, the latter transmitted its need for a dietary supplement in the proper Mendelian ratio.

The studies conducted by Tatum and Beadle at Stanford "correlated the biochemical nutritional requirements and the genetic changes and established that genes acted by regulating specific chemical processes" (New York Times, October 31, 1958). They demonstrated further that impairment of a specific gene resulted in a hereditary disturbance of metabolic activity. They gave "genetics a new exactness and [turned] it into a predominantly chemical science" (Time, November 10, 1958).

During World War II the advances made by the two geneticists were put to practical use in speeding up the production of penicillin and they have been responsible for introducing new methods for assaying vitamins and amino acids in foods and tissues.

The research on Neurospora was followed by a study of the effect of biochemical mutations on nutritional deficiencies of the bacteria Escherichia coli. Dr. Tatum continued his research in this field at Yale University, where he was appointed an associate professor of botany in 1945 and a full professor of microbiology the following year. His findings, published in the Proceedings of the National Academy of Sciences (August 1945), demonstrated that "growth-factor requirements in bacteria result from heritable changes analagous to true gene mutations." In 1946 Tatum and Joshua Lederberg, now head of genetics at Stanford's medical school, enlarged their study of bacteria with mutation-caused deficiencies. Their joint research showed that a strain of Escherichia could reproduce sexually, a process characteristic of higher forms of life. By crossing strains of the bacteria (an act known as genetic recombination), it was possible to obtain offspring having a new combination of hereditary factors. The Tatum-Lederberg research expanded the field of study pertaining to the genetic and physiological processes in bacteria and has shed some light on the characteristics of some virus forms.

Leaving Yale University in 1948, Tatum returned to Stanford University as professor of biology. He became professor of biochemistry and head of the department in 1956. Since January 1, 1957 he has been a member and professor of the Rockefeller Institute, "studying the genetics and metabolism of bacteria, yeast and molds. His aim is a clear understanding, at the molecular level, of how genes determine the characteristics of living organisms" (New York *Times,* January 13, 1957).

Dr. Tatum, who was named to the editorial board of *Science* in 1957, has been a frequent contributor to scientific journals, in which his laboratory work has been fully described and documented. He served in 1944 as a civilian with the Office of Scientific Research and Development. He belongs to the National Academy of Sciences, American Philosophical Society, and the National Science Foundation, among other organizations. He is also a member of the research advisory committees of the National Foundation and the American Cancer Society. The American Chemical Society honored him in 1953 with the Remsen Award for his contributions to biochemical genetics and for his "classic discovery" (with Joshua Lederberg) of "bi-parental inheritance and sexual reproduction in bacteria."

Blue-eyed and fair-complexioned Edward L. Tatum stands six feet tall and is ruggedly built. By his first marriage, to June Alton on July 28, 1934, he has two daughters—Margaret Carol and Barbara Ann. He is now married to the former Viola Kantor. His recreations are swimming, ice skating, and photography. In his youth he played the French horn and the trumpet and he is still an enthusiastic musician.

References

N Y Times p11 O 31 '58
N Y World-Telegram p1+ O 30 '58 por
Nature 179:290+ F 9 '57

American Men of Science vol I (1955)
Who's Who in America, 1958-59

TAUBMAN, (HYMAN) HOWARD July 4, 1907- Journalist; author

Address: b. c/o The New York Times, Times Sq., New York 36; h. 41 W. 83d St., New York 24; Danbury, Conn.

As music critic for the New York *Times,* Howard Taubman has reviewed concerts at Carnegie Hall, the Metropolitan Opera House, and Town Hall, and important musical events and festivals all over the world. He became the music critic in 1955, after twenty years as music editor and almost five years as a member of the music department. In addition to his reviews, he has written six books, including a biography of Arturo Toscanini, and numerous articles, which have appeared in such periodicals as *Musical America, Atlantic Monthly, Theatre Arts,* and the New York *Times Magazine.*

Hyman Howard Taubman, the son of Max and Etta (Shubert) Taubman, was born in New York City on July 4, 1907. He is the eldest of five children, having three younger

New York Times Studio

HOWARD TAUBMAN

brothers and a sister. At the DeWitt Clinton High School in New York he worked on the school newspaper, *Arista,* and took part in the student government. He took private musical instruction in piano. After his graduation from high school, he entered Cornell University in Ithaca, New York, where he held a tuition scholarship that he had won through competitive examinations.

At Cornell Taubman worked in the college infirmary to earn extra money, and also served as a campus correspondent for the New York *Post.* For six months he was forced to leave Cornell because of lack of funds and to work on the *Post*'s copy desk, but he later returned to his studies in English and the arts. He won a New York *Times* current events contest, was elected to Phi Beta Kappa, and received his B.A. degree from Cornell in 1929.

The New York *Times* city editor, David H. Joseph, gave Taubman a position as reporter on the Brooklyn-Queens section in June 1929. His first assignments included coverage of a Swedenborgian conclave, checking the effects of the Eighth Avenue subway excavations on Prospect Park (this story won commendations from Adolph S. Ochs, publisher of the *Times*), and describing the investigations of Brooklyn magistrates. When a replacement was needed in the music department in September 1930, Taubman accepted the position.

According to A. H. Weiler in *Times Talk* (June 1954), "The results of a balanced blend of musical background and reportorial ability were almost immediately apparent and Taubman has been running amuck in constructive style ever since. Word about the 'Met,' the Philharmonic, Beethoven and boogie-woogie began escaping the inside pages and landing up front with remarkable regularity. In one week in 1935, for example, one upheaval at the Metropolitan

TAUBMAN, HOWARD—*Continued*

Opera occasioned by the departure of the famed Gatti-Casazza found Taubman providing the *Times* with five successive, exclusive stories, three of which rated page one."

When Taubman accompanied the Metropolitan Opera Company on its first visit to Toronto, he discovered that the Toronto Orchestra was barred from performing in the United States because of restrictions in the McCarran-Walter Immigration and Nationality Act. He got the story to the New York *Times* before the Toronto press could publish anything about the situation.

From 1944 to 1945 Taubman was a staff member on the Mediterranean edition of the G.I. overseas newspaper, *Stars and Stripes*. He continued to send in stories to the *Times* during his Army service and rose in rank from private to sergeant. He covered the German surrender in Italy, wrote a series on the Italian underground, later reprinted in the *Times*, and, in what was perhaps his proudest accomplishment, prepared a long obituary on Franklin D. Roosevelt, when *Stars and Stripes* was caught without one just before going to press.

After the war, Taubman returned to New York and his regular work for the *Times*. He had become music editor in September 1935, and after twenty years in this position, he was named, in September 1955, the music critic. He succeeded Olin Downes, who died on August 22, 1955. Since then he has been directing the work of his department, reviewing musical events, and writing articles for various national magazines.

In recent years Taubman has reported on musical events abroad. In 1958 he spent four months in Europe, including Russia, and sent back to the *Times* articles which covered the music festivals, studied the status of the artist in the Soviet Union, and assessed the advantage that the government-subsidized arts enjoy in Europe in comparison with arts in the United States.

Over the years Taubman has written six books on music and musicians, and helped in the writing of others. His first book, published by Scribner's in 1938, was called *Opera—Front and Back*. The critic for the Boston *Transcript* (June 18, 1938) wrote that it is "eminently readable, full of entertaining stories and good, sound criticism of an institution which badly needs it." Peter Bowdoin in New York *Herald Tribune Books* (March 13, 1938) commented: "The book is liberally supplied with anecdotes, some of them indisputably authentic, others more or less open to question. However, books of this sort are not likely to be unduly sensitive to the chilling irony of fact and seldom can be added with security to one's reference library."

In 1939 *Music as a Profession* appeared with the Scribner imprint. In it Taubman wrote: "If this book can clear away some of the illusions and give a few elementary tips to aspirants for a musical career or to their parents or vocational counselors, it will have served a fundamental purpose. If it succeeds in discouraging some prospects from trying music as a career

and turning them to a field where there is more assurance of a living, it will have served a useful purpose. If it amuses and casts a little light on the odd mixture that human beings make of art in business and business in art, it will have served at least as an informative and entertaining chronicle."

John Erskine noted in New York *Herald Tribune Books* (November 19, 1939) that "the tone of his book is good-humored and courteous, but having some rather hard information to convey, he lets us discover it between the lines." Of Taubman's next book, *Music on My Beat; An Intimate Volume of Shop Talk* (Simon & Schuster, 1943), R. B. Cochrane wrote: "An extremely readable volume for the casual concert-goer. There is nothing pedantic about his gay quips, his chatty anecdotes (though some of the latter are warmed over), and his earnest passion for music for its own sake" (New York *Herald Tribune Weekly Book Review*, January 2, 1944).

Mixed reviews greeted Taubman's *The Maestro, The Life of Arturo Toscanini* (Simon & Schuster, 1951). The *New Yorker* (September 15, 1951) commented that "his style is dull, but enough of his idol's *brio* comes through to make an exciting book." B. H. Haggin turned in a dissenting report for the *Nation* (September 29, 1951).

Erich Leinsdorf, writing in the *Saturday Review of Literature* (March 31, 1951), found that Taubman had done "an admirable piece of work" and that the book was "alive, accurate, and objective." Ernest Newman in the New York *Times Book Review* (March 25, 1951) remarked: "His factual material goes down to 1950, and his book is based, so far as the shrewd and candid psychological study of the subject is concerned, on a close acquaintance with the great man. . . . The whole fascinating true story, which we would pronounce to be largely fictive if it were told of some musician of a century ago, can now be read in Taubman's glowing but shrewdly balanced record."

Taubman's other books are *How to Build a Record Library* (Hanover House, 1953; second edition, 1955) and *How to Bring up Your Child to Enjoy Music* (Hanover House, 1958). He helped Giulio Gatti-Casazza write his *Memories of the Opera*, published by Scribner's in 1941, and aided in the editing of a chapter in *The Roosevelt I Knew* (Viking Press, 1946), by Frances Perkins.

Hyman Howard Taubman married Nora Stern, a teacher, on July 3, 1934. They have two sons: William C. and Philip M. Taubman. He has brown eyes and gray hair; he is five feet six inches tall and weighs 155 pounds. For recreation he plays tennis. He is a member of the Dutch Treat Club in New York. In May 1958 Temple University awarded him an honorary Doctor of Music degree.

References

N Y Times p18 S 16 '55
Times Talk 7:2+ Je '54

Who's Who in America, 1958-59
Who's Who in the East (1955)

TAYLOR, MYRON C(HARLES) Jan. 18, 1874-May 6, 1959 Former United States Presidential representative to the Vatican (1939-50); board chairman and chief executive officer, United States Steel Corporation (1932-38); lawyer. See *Current Biography* (January-February) 1940.

Obituary

N Y Times p1+ My 7 '59

TAYLOR, ROBERT LEWIS Sept. 24, 1912- Author; journalist
Address: b. The New Yorker, 25 W. 43d St., New York 36

George Cserna

ROBERT LEWIS TAYLOR

When *The Travels of Jaimie McPheeters* was awarded a Pulitzer Prize for fiction in May 1959, Robert Lewis Taylor, its author, had been a professional writer for nearly thirty years. A productive author, Taylor has had nine books published, all of them under the imprint of Doubleday & Company, Inc., and is working on his tenth. He has written numerous profiles, feature articles, and short stories for the *New Yorker, Saturday Evening Post, Life, Collier's,* and other magazines.

Born Robert Taylor in Carbondale, Illinois on September 24, 1912, Taylor is the son of Roscoe Aaron and Mabel (Bowyer) Taylor. After attending local public schools, he enrolled at Southern Illinois University in 1929, and transferred to the University of Illinois the following year. He did his first professional writing while an undergraduate at the state university.

After his graduation with a Bachelor of Arts degree in 1933, Taylor left for a bicycle tour through six countries of Europe. He returned to the United States in 1934 and was hired as the editor of the Carbondale weekly newspaper, which, he has said (New York *Herald Tribune,* October 8, 1950), "was devoted mostly to libel. But it was a pleasant, cheerful sort of libel, and the townspeople came to enjoy it."

Taylor was soon seized by the urge to travel again, however, and after one year on the Carbondale newspaper he sailed for Tahiti. He lived in various places in Polynesia during 1935, supporting himself by writing articles for the *American Boy* magazine. Moving on to New Zealand, the Fiji Islands, and Honolulu, he completed his Pacific tour by a brief engagement as a reporter for the Honolulu *Advertiser.*

During his year in Polynesia, Taylor came to respect the natives deeply. He later declared (New York *Herald Tribune,* October 8, 1950) that "the primitive peoples of the globe ought to be sending missionaries up here rather than receiving ours with gullible cordiality." He returned to the United States in 1936, tried without success to find a job in New York City, and then went back to the Midwest.

He was hired as a reporter by the St. Louis *Post-Dispatch* and worked for the newspaper during the next three years. In 1939 his stories won for him the runner-up award, general reporting division, in an annual competition sponsored by Sigma Delta Chi, the honorary journalism fraternity. Taylor was hired the same year by the *New Yorker* as a "Profile" writer.

Taylor added the "Lewis" to his professional name when he joined the magazine, in order to avoid being confused with the cartoonist R. Taylor, who was also on the staff, and with the movie actor of the same name. He was being published in the *Saturday Evening Post* and *Reader's Digest* in addition to the *New Yorker,* which ran thirteen of his biographical features during his first two years on the staff.

Joining the United States Navy in 1942, Taylor served on active duty until 1946, when he was discharged with the rank of lieutenant commander. He wrote military training manuals and continued to write for the *New Yorker* from notes sent to him. "It was a nifty arrangement," he later remarked (*Saturday Review of Literature,* February 14, 1948). "They did the leg work and I did the writing."

Taylor returned to his full-time writing career in 1946. He wrote several short stories in addition to his magazine articles and finished a fantasy novel about six people who survived a world catastrophe. When the book, *Adrift in a Boneyard,* was published by Doubleday in 1947, it received mixed reviews. "Fortunately," wrote Spencer Klaw (New York *Herald Tribune,* May 11, 1947), "we know Mr. Taylor can do a lot better."

In 1948 Doubleday published *Doctor, Lawyer, Merchant, Chief,* a collection of Taylor's magazine pieces. The book included eleven profiles from the *New Yorker,* and one each from the *Saturday Evening Post, Life,* and *Redbook,* plus some fiction and travel "casuals" drawn from his experiences in the South Pacific. It was the biographies, however, that attracted the attention of the critics.

"To these diverse personalities," wrote H. W. Wind in the *Saturday Review* (February 28, 1948), "Mr. Taylor brings a very genuine en-

TAYLOR, ROBERT LEWIS—*Continued*
thusiasm and a really eclectic intelligence.
When Taylor writes about his Iranian expert,
for instance, he persuades you that he has been
hanging around Teheran all his life, but this is
impossible since he has obviously spent good
portions around bowling alleys, Ebbets Field,
and Rumania."

Before the publication of this book, Taylor
had been commissioned by the *Saturday Evening Post* to write the life story of W. C.
Fields, replacing Gene Fowler, an old friend of
the comedian, on the assignment. Taylor spent
the summer of 1948 in California doing research, and after a total of three years' part-
time work the series was published by the
Saturday Evening Post in May, June, and July
1949.

Doubleday published the material in book
form the same year with the title, *W. C. Fields;
His Follies and Fortunes*. Meanwhile the prolific Taylor was finishing two more books
which were published by Doubleday in 1950.
Professor Fodorski was a satire about a refugee civil engineer who became a football enthusiast; *The Running Pianist* was another
collection of Taylor's biographies and short
stories.

Again on commission by the *Saturday Evening Post,* Taylor spent 1951 in England,
gathering material for an anecdotal biography
of Winston Churchill. The *Saturday Evening
Post* published the series in eight parts in early
1952; it was condensed in the *Reader's Digest*
that August, and published in book form by
Doubleday with the title, *Winston Churchill;
An Informal Study of Greatness.*

For his seventh venture into book publication, Taylor again turned to fiction. "He does
not try to tell a coherent story," complained
a New York *Times* critic (February 21, 1954)
when *The Bright Sands* was published by
Doubleday. But a *Time* reviewer contended
(February 22, 1954) that the novel offered
"a good share of laughs, plus a steady run of
chuckles and a warm feeling for the human
race."

The setting of *The Bright Sands* was Cape
Cod; for some years Taylor and his family had
lived at Cape Cod in the summer and in Clearwater, Florida, in the winter. At Clearwater,
the winter home of the Ringling Brothers circus, Taylor observed the lives of circus people.
This curiosity resulted in the material for a
series of *New Yorker* articles and a book,
Center Ring; The People of the Circus (Doubleday, 1956).

Taylor's most recent and most successful
book was *The Travels of Jaimie McPheeters,*
which Doubleday published in 1958. Based on
the journals of Dr. Joseph Middleton, this
picaresque novel recounted the adventures of
fourteen-year-old Jaimie McPheeters and Sar-
dius McPheeters, his father, during the California Gold Rush of 1849. The book was
awarded the 1958 Pulitzer Prize for fiction,
and was purchased for a film by Metro-
Goldwyn-Mayer.

"To write this hilarious and hair-raising fiction," said Walter Havighurst in the New York
Herald Tribune (April 6, 1958), "Mr. Taylor

has ransacked a whole shelf of Western Americana. . . . It adds up to a rich and racy volume. . . . The Gold Rush belonged to America's
years of growing, and here it is set down as
a great lark, to renew the youth and restless-
ness of any reader."

Taylor married Judith Martin on February 3,
1945, and has two children, Martin Lewis and
Elizabeth Ann Taylor. He is a member of
Delta Tau Delta fraternity and is a boating
enthusiast during his Cape Cod summers and
Florida winters.

Taylor has frequently been commended for
bringing humor back to American literature.
An appraisal written of him in 1948 still seems
valid: "He looks at the world literally with
amused eyes, and talks in an understated voice,
not taking himself or anything else—except the
art of being funny—seriously" (*Saturday Review of Literature,* February 14, 1948).

References

N Y Herald Tribune Bk R p25 O 8 '50
N Y Times p36 My 5 '59 por
Sat Eve Post 221:152 Je 4 '49; 224:160
Ap 12 '52 pors
Sat R Lit 31:10 F 14 '48 por
Who's Who in America, 1958-59

TELLO (BAURRAUD), MANUEL Nov.
1, 1898- Mexican Secretary of Foreign Affairs
Address: b. Ministry of Foreign Affairs, Mexico City, D.F., Mexico

When the emergency conference of foreign
ministers of the twenty-one American republics
was called in August 1959, Manuel Tello, Mexican Secretary of Foreign Affairs, helped to
draft a compromise plan for coping with recent
crises in the Caribbean area. The plan revives
the Organization of American States' Inter-
American Peace Committee, to which Tello
was elected as vice-chairman, to study cases of
aggression and intervention in the Western
Hemisphere.

A member of Mexico's Foreign Service for
some thirty years, Dr. Tello was appointed to
his present post in late 1958, after having held
the same position from 1952 to 1953 and after
having served as Acting Secretary of Foreign
Affairs from 1948 to 1952. As Ambassador to
the United States for five years beginning in
1953, he won a reputation for improving Amer-
ican-Mexican relations. Later, in October 1959,
he was called upon to make further use of his
experience when he accompanied Adolfo López
Mateos on an official visit to the United States.

Manuel Tello Baurraud was born on November 1, 1898 in Zacatecas, Mexico to Mariano
Tello and María Baurraud de Tello. He was
educated at the Instituto Científico in Zacatecas
and the Liceo Católico and Colegio Civil, both
in Querétaro. For law studies he attended the
Escuela Nacional de Jurisprudencia of the Universidad Nacional Autónoma de México and the
Escuela Libre de Derecho. He also concentrated in the humanities at the Universidad
Nacional Autónoma de México.

Deciding to enter the Foreign Service of his
country in 1924, Tello was appointed vice-con-

sul at Brownsville and Laredo, Texas. This was followed by minor diplomatic assignments in Antwerp, Hamburg, Berlin, Yokohama, and Houston, Texas. Transferred to Geneva, Switzerland in 1934, he headed Mexican consular services there.

As a member of his country's delegation, Tello attended an international conference on political refugees in Germany and Austria, held in 1938. Then, in 1939, he was named secretary general and alternate delegate of the Mexican delegation to the League of Nations, and in the following year he became chief of the delegation. In the League he was active on international bodies concerned with labor, drug traffic, public education, rights of minors, and other social problems.

Recalled to Mexico, Tello was named in 1942 director general of political affairs in the Foreign Service. His next post was that of assistant to the Secretary of Foreign Affairs, beginning in 1943. Two years later he became Assistant Secretary of Foreign Affairs in charge of diplomatic dispatches. While serving in this post he was secretary general of the Conference on Inter-American Problems of War and Peace, held in Mexico in 1945, and a delegate to the United Nations Conference on International Organization, held in San Francisco later that year.

President Miguel Alemán appointed Tello Acting Secretary of Foreign Affairs in 1948 and Secretary three years later. Secretary Tello led the Mexican delegation to the meeting of Foreign Ministers of American Republics, which took place in Washington in March and April 1951.

While in the post of Secretary, Tello submitted a formula for resolving the deadlock on the exchange of prisoners in the Korean armistice in 1952. Alemán, who had conceived the plan, was a nominee for the Nobel Peace Prize that year. The plan provided that prisoners who desired repatriation be granted it immediately; those who rejected repatriation would be granted asylum by various U.N. member nations; and those who requested asylum would later be repatriated at their discretion. These recommendations were in part incorporated into the Korean armistice agreement of 1953.

After Miguel Alemán was succeeded in the Presidency by Adolfo Ruiz Cortines in December 1952, Tello was appointed Ambassador to the United States in February 1953. During his tenure in Washington Tello had a hand in renewing, on several occasions, the 1951 Mexican-United States itinerant labor treaty. The most recent renewal of the treaty, concluded in August 1958, permits some 400,000 Mexican laborers to enter the United States temporarily for work on American farms. One continuing difficulty, however, has been the large number of wetbacks, or migrant workers, who ford the Rio Grande River to enter the United States illegally.

In 1958 Tello was confronted with the United States Tariff Commission's finding that the continuation of the present level of lead and zinc imports would injure the American industry, which leads the world. As representative of another important producer of raw lead and

MANUEL TELLO

zinc, Dr. Tello immediately pointed to the adverse effect that the lowering of imports would have on the Mexican economy.

He stated: "There can be no doubt that the lead and zinc industry of the United States is going through a difficult situation. But the same thing may be said, and surely to a greater degree, regarding this industry's situation in other countries, especially Mexico. . . . The solution lies basically in the adoption of international formulas which would permit the strengthening [of the industry] in all countries" (New York Times, April 26, 1958).

When a new administration, headed by Adolfo Lopez Mateos, came into power in Mexico, Manuel Tello was appointed to the office of Secretary of Foreign Affairs. Succeeding Luis Padilla Nervo, Dr. Tello was sworn into office on December 1, 1958.

Secretary of Foreign Affairs Tello attended the fifth meeting of foreign ministers of the twenty-one member nations of the Organization of American States, which was convened in Santiago, Chile on August 12, 1959. In an atmosphere surcharged with tension, conferees listened to charges from Cuba that the Dominican Republic was involved in counterrevolutionary activities in Cuba, while Haiti claimed that it had been invaded by alleged Cuban rebels. As the spokesman for Mexico, Tello declared that under no circumstances could Mexico commit itself to any position that would undermine the principle of nonintervention, even in the case of a nation opposed to Mexican institutions, beliefs, and way of life. "We do not want to launch into the winds of the future a boomerang which could, in time, return to hurt our people" (Mexico, August 22, 1959). He also said that Mexico, which is dedicated to democratic representative government, believes in nonaggression and the right of man to exercise his political and other liberties.

(Continued next page)

TELLO, MANUEL—*Continued*

At the end of the conference the foreign ministers issued an agreement, which Tello helped to draft. It revived the Inter-American Peace Committee to study intervention or aggression in American states "at the request of governments or on its own initiative . . . subject to the express consent" of nations in whose territories inquiries will be made. The conclusions of the committee will be submitted to the eleventh conference of the Organization of American States, scheduled for early 1960. Secretary Tello was elected vice-chairman of the Inter-American Peace Committee.

Dr. Manuel Tello and Senorita Guadalupe Macias were married in 1934. Their five children are Manuel, Marilupe, Carlos, Enrique, and Alejandro. The Ambassador is of medium height and has dark-brown hair and brown eyes. In his hours spent away from official duties he enjoys art and books. For his twenty-five years' work in the Foreign Service he was awarded the Medalla del Servicio Exterior Mexicana. He also holds many honors from the countries in which he represented Mexico. Dr. Milton S. Eisenhower has described him as a "distinguished and able statesman, not given to overstatement."

References

Américas 6:40 F '54 pors
International Who's Who, 1958
International Year Book and Statesmen's Who Who, 1958
Who's Who in Latin America Pt 1 (1946)
World Biography (1948)

TEMPLEWOOD, SAMUEL JOHN GURNEY HOARE, 1ST VISCOUNT Feb. 24, 1880-May 7, 1959 Former British cabinet member (intermittently from 1923 to 1940); Ambassador to Spain (1940-44); Conservative Member of Parliament for Chelsea (1910-44). See *Current Biography* (Hoare) (October) 1940.

Obituary

N Y Times p21 My 9 '59

THADDEN-TRIEGLAFF, REINOLD (LEOPOLD ADOLPH LUDWIG) VON (tă' dĕn trēg' lăf) Aug. 13, 1891- German lay church leader

Address: 19 Magdeburger Strasse, Fulda, Germany

Since the end of World War II only one national organization, the German Evangelical Kirchentag, has succeeded in bridging the East-West zonal division within Germany. The Kirchentag (church day), a movement of Protestant laymen, was founded by Dr. Reinold von Thadden-Trieglaff, its president, in 1949. It has sponsored mass rallies in various sections of the country that have attracted hundreds of thousands of Christians.

Von Thadden, who has suffered from the tyranny of both Nazism and Communism, regards the Kirchentag as a challenge to the church to meet its responsibility not only in matters of spiritual welfare, but also in politics, economics, international relations, and all other areas of secular life. He is a member of the central committee of the World Council of Churches.

For some six centuries the von Thadden family had been landlords in the section of Pomerania where Reinold Leopold Adolph Ludwig von Thadden-Trieglaff was born on August 13, 1891. His birthplace, Mohrungen, was then in East Prussia and is now a part of Poland. He is the son of Baron Adolph von Thadden-Trieglaff, a district administrator, and of Ehrengard (von Gerlach) Thadden-Trieglaff. His great-grandfather, Baron Adolph Ferdinand von Thadden, was a leader in the Protestant church revival and missionary movement of his day.

Spending his childhood on the family estates, Reinold von Thadden-Trieglaff often accompanied his father on horseback to inspect their farms. After attending school in Gryfice, Pomerania, he studied law at the Sorbonne in Paris and then at the universities of Leipzig, Munich, and Greifswald. For his Doctor of Jurisprudence degree, conferred in 1920, he submitted a thesis on international law and the League of Nations.

Von Thadden had begun his career in the Prussian administrative service and for a brief time was a member of the state parliament. Interested in the problems of the common man, he found an opportunity to put his social theories into practice by working at the settlement house of Dr. Friedrich Siegmund-Schultze in the slums of Berlin. However, he was soon required to return home to manage his family estate, which had come close to bankruptcy.

Since his university days when he had attended international conferences of the Christian Student Movement, von Thadden had been concerned with church affairs and interdenominational activities. He became president in 1928 of the German Christian Student Movement and in 1929 vice-president of the Pomeranian Provincial Synod and a member of the Prussian General Synod in Berlin. During the 1930's, while Adolph Hitler's movement was gaining power, von Thadden worked with religious groups to combat Nazism. He was president of the Free Confessional Synod of Pomerania in 1934 and a member of the Prussian and Reich Brotherhood Councils. Beginning in 1936 he served for thirteen years as vice-president of the World Christian Student Federation.

As a member of the laity, von Thadden had an influential part in preparing the memorandum of the Confessional Church sent to Hitler in 1936 in protest against faking of elections, detention without trial in concentration camps, and other Nazi barbarities. The German laity chose him to be its spokesman at the World Conference on Life and Work at Oxford, England in 1937, but his imprisonment by the Gestapo both in Berlin and Stettin prevented him from attending the conference.

Even during his service as a major in the German Army in World War II, von Thadden opposed Nazism. When the Germans occupied Belgium, he was governor and commander from 1942 to 1944 of the district around Louvain. He worked to protect churches and schools, to prevent shooting of hostages, and to save Belgian students from deportation to Germany. (In gratitude for his efforts the city of Louvain honored him at a public reception in 1947). Before the end of the war, in early 1945, he was dismissed from the army as politically unreliable.

Meanwhile, his sister, Elisabeth von Thadden, denounced to the Gestapo as an anti-Nazi sympathizer, had been executed in 1944. Reinold von Thadden's three oldest sons—Dietrich, Leopold, and Bergislav—also died in the war, while fighting on the Russian front. When von Thadden returned home to Pomerania at the end of the war, just as the Russians were seizing the estates east of the Oder River, he was arrested by the Soviet NKVD (state police) as a member of the *Junker* class and a former army officer.

For some nine months von Thadden was imprisoned in concentration camps in the Arctic region of Russia. There prisoners of various faiths and nationalities turned to him to conduct religious services. In discussing with them the spiritual problems of everyday life, he discovered many needs that the church had tended to ignore—needs which became the subjects of future Kirchentag rallies. "It was a confessional church on the border of Asia," he later wrote, "desperate men forgetting their material distress in their worship of God. A fountain of life in the middle of a world of misery, hopelessness, and death" (quoted by Robert Merrill Bartlett in *They Stand Invincible*, Crowell, 1959).

After his release in late 1945 von Thadden returned to Berlin, where he was given medical treatment for illnesses resulting from privation in concentration camps, and was reunited with his wife and two surviving sons. He went to Switzerland in 1946 to help establish the World Council of Churches in Geneva and to assist in the work of its Ecumenical Institute at Château de Bossey, which offered training to those wanting to help war victims. For two years he traveled in Italy, France, Egypt, Belgium, and other countries to talk with prisoners of war and aid in their rehabilitation. He also took part in setting up evangelical academies in Germany to teach responsibilities in citizenship and rebuilding the country.

The first assembly of the World Council of Churches was held in Amsterdam in the summer of 1948. Dr. von Thadden attended as a German lay delegate and was appointed to the central committee of the council to plan for Protestant co-operative activities on a worldwide basis. From 1948 to 1954 he was chairman of the council's Ecumenical Institute. In the postwar years he also became a member of the German-French Brotherhood Council, the working group for Christian Responsibility for European Cooperation, and chairman of the Mutual Trust Council of Evangelical Students' Community in Germany.

Karl Heuer, Hanover

REINOLD VON THADDEN-TRIEGLAFF

To encourage Protestant laymen to assume responsibility in all areas of public life, in 1949 von Thadden called together German Christians for a conference in Hanover. The response to this first German Evangelical Kirchentag was so favorable that the following year he organized a mass rally at Essen which directed its attention to the needs of refugees and which attracted over 150,000 laymen from all parts of Germany.

Subsequent annual Kirchentags were held in Berlin, Stuttgart, and Hamburg. At the Kirchentag in Leipzig in East Germany in 1954 more than 650,000 people attended the final open-air rally. Full-scale meetings have since been called only every two years—in Frankfurt am Main in 1956 and in Hamburg in 1958. The idea of the Kirchentag has spread to other countries. Meetings similar to those that von Thadden organizes in Germany have been held in France, Scotland, Denmark, and Indonesia.

In 1952 von Thadden visited the United States to give a series of lectures sponsored by the World Council of Churches. He also attended United States conferences of the council in 1954 and 1956. In much of his writing and speaking he shows himself to be a practical man who is concerned with direct action rather than with dogma or abstract religious concepts. His article "The Kirchentag and the Renewal of the Church" (*Ecumenical Review*, July 1957) underscored the Kirchentag's concern not only with Bible study and theological matters, but with discussion of "the burning East-West problem, the possibility of real peace, the racial question, the pressing need for social reform, and the recovery and development of democratic civic consciousness."

Dr. von Thadden's books include *Das Laienamt der Kirche* (1936), *Jüngerschaft* (1937), *Kirche im Kampf* (1947), *Auf velorenem Posten?* (1948), and *Der junge Bismarck*. He is

THADDEN-TRIEGLAFF, REINOLD, VON—*Continued*

coeditor of *Zeitwende*. He has honorary doctoral degrees from the universities of Kiel (1948), Aberdeen (1953), Chicago (1954), Paris (1959), and Wittenberg College in Springfield, Ohio (1955). The German Federal Republic awarded him the Grand Cross of Merit in 1955.

Reinold von Thadden-Trieglaff married Baroness Elisabeth Freiin von Thüngen in 1921. He is pictured in *They Stand Invincible* as "still a round-faced, clear-eyed man with the gift of friendship, a dynamo of power and energy, whose hoarse voice, a reminder of his suffering, speaks unremittingly for international goodwill."

> *References*
>
> Time 59:63+ Mr 10 '52 por
> Bartlett, Robert Merrill They Dared to Believe (1952); They Stand Invincible (1959)
> Wer ist Wer? (1958)
> Who's Who in Germany (1956)
> World Biography (1954)

THOMAS, DANNY Jan. 6, 1914- Actor

Address: b. 228 S. Beverly Drive, Beverly Hills, Calif.

Over forty-four million Americans watch the antics of Danny Thomas and his television family each week over CBS-TV, thereby giving him the title of "America's favorite television comedian." Although he has had a television show since 1953, it is only since 1957, when its title was changed from *Make Room for Daddy* (ABC-TV) to *The Danny Thomas Show* (CBS-TV), that it has achieved such popularity.

ABC-TV

DANNY THOMAS

Thomas began his career in burlesque houses, beer taverns, and radio. He has performed in leading night clubs in the United States, has starred in several motion pictures, and sold numerous records. During World War II he traveled in Europe and the Far East with USO troupes, entertaining the Allied soldiers.

Danny Thomas is the name used professionally by Amos Jacobs, who was born in Deerfield, Michigan on January 6, 1914 to Charles and Margaret Christen (Simon) Jacobs. His parents were immigrants from Lebanon and his father was a laborer. Danny was the fifth of ten children. When he was very young, the family moved to Toledo, Ohio where Danny attended the public schools.

As a boy, Danny Thomas got his first taste of show business when he worked in a burlesque theater as a candy butcher. Later, he earned pocket money by singing and clowning at banquets. At sixteen, he quit Woodward High School in Toledo, determined to make entertainment his career. After trying without success to work as a comedian, he secured employment as a punch press operator and as a night watchman. For a time, he even played semiprofessional basketball.

When he was about twenty years old, Thomas obtained a job in Detroit, Michigan as master of ceremonies on a radio program called *The Happy Hour Club*. While working on this show, he met a young Italian-American singer, Rose Marie Cassaniti, whom he later married. After a successful engagement on the radio program, he was offered steady employment as master of ceremonies in Bert's Beer Garden in Detroit. According to Earl Eby, a former actor who knew Thomas in those days, "Detroit [was] the birthplace of the Thomas cult. Danny's fans followed him from saloon to saloon there when he was poor but locally famous" (*Look,* December 24, 1957).

Shortly after his marriage in 1936, the comedian lost his job. It was so difficult to find work at that time that Thomas considered giving up show business. In desperation, he prayed to Saint Jude, the patron saint of the hopeless. The following day he was offered a job in Chicago, which proved to be the turning point in his career.

In Chicago Thomas played in several radio serials and was then booked to play at a new night club, the 5100 Club. Before his opening, he decided to change his name to "Danny Thomas," using the first names of two of his brothers. Danny Thomas was an immediate success. For the next three years he played to capacity audiences, while his salary rose from $50 to $500 weekly.

In 1943, when the comic made his first New York night club appearance at La Martinique, a delegation of Chicago fans chartered special transportation to New York to watch him perform. While appearing as a guest on New York radio shows, he was heard by Fanny Brice and engaged for her program; for it, he created the character of Jerry Dingle. The following year Thomas went to Europe with the Marlene Dietrich unit of the USO, and later took his own troupe to the Pacific area. After the war ended, he returned to Chicago for a successful appearance at the Chez Paree, then moved to Beverly Hills, California with his family.

His first motion-picture role was in *The Unfinished Dance* (1947). Bosley Crowther of the New York *Times* (October 31, 1947) reported: "Danny Thomas . . . might better be done without. He only adds more cuteness. . . ." His notices were more favorable for *I'll See You In My Dreams* (1951). Otis L. Guernsey of the New York *Herald Tribune* (December 7, 1951) commented: "The comedian, in his first starring role, gets a quiet authority into his role of an impetuous, unhandsome, sensitive fellow. . . ." Among the other motion pictures Danny Thomas has appeared in are: *The Big City* (1948), *Call Me Mister* (1951), and *The Jazz Singer* (1953).

Between his motion-picture roles the comedian toured the United States, appearing in such night clubs and theaters as Ciro's in Hollywood and the Roxy in New York. He made frequent appearances on television on the *All-Star Revue* and the *Colgate Comedy Hour*. In 1953 he launched a situation comedy series over the ABC-TV network called *Make Room for Daddy*. The series, about an entertainer who wants to have more time to devote to his family, stems from Thomas' own domestic situation. After many years of traveling the night club circuit, the comedian discovered that his children hardly knew him. Thomas called on a producer and asked if he could find a show that would keep him at home. Recognizing a situation that was made to order for television, the producer devised *Make Room for Daddy*.

After four years on the ABC-TV network, Danny Thomas moved his show to the CBS-TV network. The format remained the same, but the title was changed to *The Danny Thomas Show*. During its first year on CBS-TV (1957-58) *The Danny Thomas Show* gained considerable popularity. The Nielsen rating rose from 137 to a place among the top ten television shows in the country, and *Time* magazine (April 21, 1958) called Thomas "the U.S.'s currently favorite tele-comedian." His associates on the program are Marjorie Lord, Sherry Jackson, Rusty Hamer and Angela Cartwright, who make up Danny's television family. His own company, Materto Productions, produces *The Danny Thomas Show* and *The Real McCoys* and holds an interest in other programs.

Not forgetting the time when he was out of work and prayed to Saint Jude for help, Danny Thomas has devoted much of his time to raising money for a children's hospital in honor of the saint. The comedian consulted the late Samuel Cardinal Stritch, and Memphis, Tennessee was selected as the site for the hospital. In November 1958 Thomas dedicated the site for Saint Jude Hospital for Children in Memphis.

Among the many awards he has received are: the *Variety* and *Billboard* awards (1948), the *Box Office* blue ribbon (1948, 1952), the Mt. Sinai Heart of Gold award (1949), the TV "Emmy" award for *Make Room for Daddy* (1954), and a special medal from Pope Pius XII, presented on the occasion of his becoming a Knight of Malta.

George Jessel called Danny Thomas "the only inheritor of the great tradition of American style humor that grew up at the Palace Theatre" (*Collier's*, June 14, 1952).

Danny Thomas was married to Rose Marie Cassaniti on January 15, 1936. They have three children, Margaret Julia, Theresa Cecelia, and Charles Anthony. Thomas is five feet eleven inches tall, weighs about 176 pounds and has black eyes and dark hair. A prominent feature of his appearance is his large nose. *Time* magazine (April 21, 1958) quotes the comedian as saying: "If you're going to have a nose, you ought to have a real one." The Thomas family lives in a large house of the Spanish type in Beverly Hills, California, where Thomas indulges in his favorite recreation of making furniture with his power tools. His religion is Roman Catholic.

References

Colliers 117:54+ Ap 20 '46; 129:24+ Je 14 '52 pors
Look 21:106+ D 24 '57 pors
Time 71:39+ Ap 21 '58 por
Who's Who in America, 1958-59
Wood, C. TV Personalities (1956)

THOMPSON, FRANK, JR. July 26, 1918- United States Representative from New Jersey; lawyer
Address: b. House Office Bldg., Washington, D.C.; h. Mountainview Rd., Trenton, N.J.; 3709 Lyons Lane, Alexandria, Va.

Known to some of his colleagues as the "culture-vulture" because of the legislation he has sponsored in education and the arts, Frank Thompson, Jr., has been United States Representative for New Jersey's Fourth District since 1955. A member of the House Education and Labor Committee, he co-sponsored in January 1959 a multibillion-dollar, aid-to-education bill drafted by the National Education Association. In association with Senator J. William Fulbright, he secured in 1958 enactment of a bill providing for the setting up of a national cultural center in Washington. A lawyer and a Democrat, Representative Thompson was minority leader of the New Jersey House of Assembly at the time of his first election to Congress.

Born to Frank Thompson and the former Beatrice Jamieson at Trenton, New Jersey on July 26, 1918, Frank Thompson, Jr., is the son of a newspaperman, the brother of a newspaperman, and the nephew of another, Frank Jamieson, now an adviser to New York's Governor Nelson A. Rockefeller. Another uncle, Crawford Jamieson, was a New Jersey Democratic leader and state senator. Thompson picked up his skill in public relations, his news sense, and his flair for politics in his immediate family circle.

Educated in the parochial and public schools of Trenton, Thompson entered Wake Forest College at Winston-Salem in North Carolina, where he studied the liberal arts, and where, following his graduation, he stayed on to study law. He received his LL.B. degree from Wake

Wide World

FRANK THOMPSON, JR.

Forest in 1941. He earned money through high school and college by playing jazz in a small musical combination.

Leaving school in 1941, Thompson served for nearly seven years in the United States Navy. As a World War II naval officer, he commanded the USS LCL(L) 428 and the LCI (Rocket) Squadrons 63 and 48 in the Pacific Theater. He was decorated with the Bronze Star, Gold Star, and Secretary of the Navy's Commendation Medal. Released from active duty in 1948, he was admitted to the New Jersey bar in the same year. He then became a partner in the firm of Thompson and Convery in Trenton.

Seeking election to the New Jersey House of Assembly in November 1949, Thompson won without difficulty in Democratic and industrial Trenton. In his first year he served as assistant minority leader in the Assembly. When war broke out in Korea, he saw active duty as the commanding officer of Naval Reserve Battalion 4-22, and on January 1, 1952 he completed a seventeen-month tour of duty on the staff of the commander, Eastern Sea Frontier. He is a commander in the United States Naval Reserve.

Returning to civilian life, Thompson was minority leader of the Assembly in the 1954 session. In the April 1954 primaries he won the Democratic nomination for United States Representative from the Fourth New Jersey District. This consists of Mercer County (in which Trenton is located) and the adjacent Burlington County. (The incumbent, Representative Charles R. Howell, sought election to the Senate.)

Self-styled "a New Deal-Fair Deal Democrat of the Adlai Stevenson school," Thompson stressed during his campaign the need for a genuine bipartisan foreign policy, a critical look at the Eisenhower military policy, and drastic revision of the Taft-Hartley Law. Although he won at the November election by 71,762 votes

to 51,910 for his Republican opponent, Thompson did not resign his seat in the New Jersey House of Assembly until January 1955.

Thompson voted with the Republicans to override successfully the veto by Democratic Governor, Robert B. Meyner, of a bill to exempt members of the Christian Science faith from physical examinations in public schools. He was thereupon stripped of his powers, though not his title, as minority leader

On taking his seat in the Eighty-fourth Congress in January 1955, Thompson was assigned to the Education and Labor and Administration committees. He promptly introduced a bill whereby a college education would be made available to a wider range of promising students through a program of federal aid.

In June 1955 Thompson submitted a bill to grant the National Music Council a Congressional charter; in August he proposed the creation of an advisory committee on cultural exchange and the repeal of the federal tax on concert and theater tickets. He also presented in 1955 bills to provide for the establishment of a federal advisory committee on the arts within the Department of Health, Education, and Welfare, as well as the working out of plans for a civic and cultural center in Washington. The latter failed of enactment in 1955 and again in 1956.

"Representative Thompson," reported Leslie Judd Portner in the Washington *Post and Times Herald* (July 15, 1956) "has introduced eight bills this year that are directly concerned with the arts. . . . His most outstanding achievement has been the passage of his bill (H.R. 11923) providing for 'the conferring of an award to be known as the Medal for Distinguished Civilian Service' in twelve fields of endeavor, among them the arts."

Other bills which Thompson introduced in 1956 were designed to assure protection of historic buildings and to provide for the construction of a new home for the Court of Claims, in order that the existing building could be used to house the entire National Collection of Fine Arts. As representative of the district in which Princeton University is situated, Thompson in April 1956 defended the right of a campus society to invite Alger Hiss for a speaking engagement, although he thought they were using bad judgment. In 1956 he tried to include a cultural plank in the Democratic national platform. With Senator Jacob K. Javits, Republican of New York, and Senator Paul H. Douglas, Democrat of Illinois, Thompson has consistently supported legislation to ease the tariff laws on art, including modern art.

During his years in Congress Thompson has taken an internationalist position. He favored a three-year reciprocal trade renewal bill (February 1955), a $3.4 billion appropriation for the Mutual Security program (July 1956), the Eisenhower Middle East Doctrine (January 1957), and increasing United States subscriptions to the International Monetary Fund and the International Bank for Reconstruction and Development (March 1959).

On military matters he supported the Department of Defense Reorganization Act (July 1958), extending the draft (February 1959), and authorizing $1.2 billion for military construction (April 1959). He voted "yea" on the civil rights bills of 1956 and 1957. His vote was "nay" on the Powell amendment to the school construction bill prohibiting federal funds to states not complying with Supreme Court decisions (July 1956). However, after the amendment was adopted he voted for the school construction bill itself (July 1956). He was opposed to killing the school construction bill of July 1957.

In regard to other domestic policies he voted to increase Congressional salaries to $25,000 (February 1955), restore rigid farm price supports (May 1955), liberalize the Social Security Act (July 1955), raise the minimum wage to $1 an hour (July 1955), build 45,000 public housing units in 1956 (August 1955), construct the Colorado River storage project (March 1956), grant statehood to Alaska (May 1958), authorize the Tennessee Valley Authority to issue $750,000,000 of revenue bonds to finance new power facilities (May 1959), and confer statehood on Hawaii (March 1959). He was opposed to eliminating a $20 income tax cut (February 1955) and Natural Gas Act exemptions (July 1955).

In November 1956 Thompson was re-elected by a slightly reduced majority. In July 1957 he praised the rulings of Chief Justice Earl Warren and suggested that the Democrats seriously consider nominating Warren for the Presidency in 1960. Thompson introduced in April 1958 a bill calling for a three-year expenditure of $1.5 billion for school construction, but this measure failed to pass the House committee. He finally won his battle for a cultural center at Washington on August 22, 1958, when his bill for its authorization passed the House, after a similar bill, sponsored by Senator J. William Fulbright of Arkansas, had been adopted in the upper chamber.

In January 1959 Thompson took over from Representative Lee Metcalf of Montana (who had moved to the Ways and Means Committee) the sponsorship of a bill drafted by the National Education Association to provide $1.1 billion in federal aid for school construction and teachers' salaries the first year, gradually raising it to $5 billion annually. At about the same time Thompson introduced a bill "to amend last year's National Defense Education Act, reinstating scholarships . . . and deleting the loyalty oath requirement for college students accepting federal loans."

Frank Thompson, Jr., married Evelina Gleaves Van Metre on January 10, 1942. They have two daughters, Anne Gleaves and Evelina Porter. Six feet three inches tall and weighing 185 pounds, Thompson has the physical attributes of a fighter. The art in which he is most interested is music, and his taste ranges from jazz to opera. He is a member of the New Jersey and Mercer County bar associations, the Naval Reserve Association, and the Navy League. His club is the Carteret in Trenton.

References

N Y Times p26 O 10 '56 por; p18 O 6 '58 por; p22 Ja 12 '59 por
Congressional Directory (1958)
Who's Who in America, 1958-59

THOMPSON, KAY Entertainer; author

Address: b. Eloise, Ltd., Hotel Plaza, New York 19

When Simon and Schuster published *Eloise in Moscow* on October 30, 1959, it was exploiting a market which showed no trace of a recession. The fourth volume about the fiendish child who lives in New York's Hotel Plaza, the book immediately promised the same success as the earlier best sellers and the Eloise dolls, fashions, and phonograph records which preceded it.

Eloise, the *enfant terrible*, is the creation of Kay Thompson, who first courted success as a piano prodigy with the St. Louis Symphony. She tried again as a vocalist on radio, and then went to Hollywood for a career as writer and arranger for film musicals. In 1947 she went on the road with her own night club act. The tour ended before the creation of Eloise in 1955, although Miss Thompson has since managed to combine her new profession with appearances on television, a movie, and the writing of popular songs.

Kay Thompson was born in St. Louis, Missouri, the daughter of a local jeweler. She early showed promise as a pianist; she started to play the piano when she was four, and at sixteen played Franz Liszt with the St. Louis Symphony. Shortly afterward, she appeared as featured vocalist with a local dance band.

"I was a stage-struck kid," she recalled (in *Time*, November 10, 1947), "and I got out of St. Louis fast." She went to California in 1929, when she was seventeen. Her first employment was as a diving instructor, but soon she was on the radio as a vocalist with the Mills Brothers. Later she joined Fred Waring's band in New York as a singer and arranger, "and was a brilliant success at both," according to writer Cynthia Lindsay (*McCall's*, January 1957). She decided to produce her own radio show, which was aired over the CBS network under the name *Kay Thompson and Company*, with Jim Backus as collaborator.

"We were an instantaneous flop," Miss Thompson said (in *McCall's*, January 1957). "After this show I came to a serious decision. I had to be an actress and I had to be alone. So I went to Hollywood, where I was neither."

Unable to earn a performer's role, Miss Thompson signed a contract with Metro-Goldwyn-Mayer studios as an arranger and composer. Beginning in 1942, she worked with MGM choreographer Robert Alton on such films as *The Ziegfeld Follies*, *The Harvey Girls*, and *The Kid From Brooklyn*. She re-

KAY THOMPSON

mained with the studio for four years, until she created her own night club routine with Alton's assistance.

The show opened at Ciro's night club in Hollywood in 1947 and was successful enough to be taken on the road. That autumn she opened in Chicago and in February 1948 she moved to Miami for a $15,000-a-week engagement. When she played the new Le Directoire night club in New York City, her verve kept the show going until 1953.

"She is witty, friendly, an accomplished musician, very agreeable to look at, and hardworking as a woodpecker," remarked a writer for *Harper's Magazine* (July 1948). The show consisted largely of sophisticated songs, backed up by the Williams Brothers (Richard, Robert, Donald, and Andrew), whose contribution to the routine was to "dance and sing and fall on their faces and mug," according to the same reviewer. "The effect," he added, "was a combination of ballet, barber shop, roughhouse and penthouse that never for a moment got out of hand, but always seemed as if it might."

Another writer (Harold Clurman in the *New Republic,* July 19, 1948) saw Miss Thompson as a "brief and abstract chronicle" of America. "The approach to the audience is erect and direct with a kind of horizontal thrust like a lightning-fast projectile," he wrote. "There is punishment in the pleasure, but it is all so neatly done that we cannot protest; we can only admire. Efficiency is the ultimate beauty of our society."

After a six-year tour, the act was disbanded in the summer of 1953. Miss Thompson amused herself by redecorating her Beverly Hills home and designing fashion slacks for long-legged women, a line called "Kay Thompson Fancy Pants." Then she created a one-woman show which opened at New York's Hotel Plaza in January 1954. Playing the role of an "outrageously blasé hostess," she entertained imagi-

nary cocktail guests for forty minutes nightly. The routine was applauded, but destined for a shorter life than her earlier show. Eloise provided the interruption.

"Eloise's birth was unexpected," said Maurice Dolbier in the New York *Herald Tribune* (October 12, 1958). "At rehearsals of her hotel and night club act with the Williams Brothers, Miss Thompson prized punctuality in herself and expected it from others. Then, one day, she was late. In a high, childish voice that she had never used before, she made her apology. One of her co-workers said, 'Who are you, little girl?' Miss Thompson replied, 'I am Eloise. I am six.' The others joined in the game, each assuming a juvenile identity, and it became a regular rehearsal pastime."

Later, when Miss Thompson was performing her new act at the Plaza's Persian Room, a friend introduced her to an illustrator who might be able to bring Eloise to life. The artist was Hilary Knight. She gave Knight a few lines to work with, and they became collaborators after he sent her a Christmas card containing his idea of what Eloise looked like. Miss Thompson took a three-month furlough from her show to write the book. *Eloise* was released by Simon & Schuster in November 1955, and had sold 150,000 copies by the time its sequel, *Eloise in Paris,* was published two years later. Also published by Simon & Schuster, the second volume had 100,000 copies in print within a week of publication day (November 14, 1957).

"Eloise is rawther unique," explained a writer in *Publishers' Weekly* (December 16, 1957). "As everyone who can read must know by [now], Eloise is an overprivileged six-year-old, the terror of the Hotel Plaza in New York. She is also ill-mannered, ill-tempered and ugly. But she has her charm. She often means well, and her mother neglects her. Even though you know that you would do the same thing if she were yours, you can't help finding this appealing."

By the time the Paris volume appeared, Eloise was a minor industry. In addition to the books (joined in September 1958 by *Eloise at Christmastime,* Random House), Miss Thompson created the firm of Eloise, Ltd., with headquarters appropriately located at the Hotel Plaza. Among its products are a phonograph record, "Absolutely Christmas Time," and a set of French postcards suitable for Eloise fans. Eloise has also inspired merchandise ranging from little-girl fashions to dolls and an Emergency Hotel Kit for itinerant six-year-olds.

Miss Thompson has not devoted all her time to Eloise, however. In 1956 she appeared with Audrey Hepburn and Fred Astaire in the motion picture *Funny Face.* The following year she created and starred in a television "spectacular" on NBC-TV, October 15, 1957, which John Crosby in the New York *Herald Tribune* (October 16, 1957) characterized as "an almost unqualified disaster." More recently, she composed a hit song, "Promise Me Love," which was recorded by Andy Williams, and co-starred with Margaret Lockwood and Trevor Howard in a British television series, *Riverside 1.*

Unmarried, Miss Thompson has been described (in *American Magazine,* April 1956) as a "tall, slender, silver blonde whose particular appeal . . . is an explosively zany style" which has served her well in her several careers.

"She doesn't think her diversity of talent is unusual," wrote Cynthia Lindsay (*McCall's,* January 1957). "'If artistically you are able to do one thing,' she says, 'you are more than likely able to do them all.' When asked her plans for the future, she says, 'The thing that comes up next is what I'll do next.'"

References
Harper 197:117+ Jl '48
McCalls 84:6+ Ja '57 por
N Y Herald Tribune Bk R p2 O 12 '58
    por
Pub W p16+ D 16 '57

TIZARD, SIR HENRY (THOMAS) Aug. 23, 1885-Oct. 9, 1959 British physicist; chief scientific adviser to the British government; contributed to the development of radar in air defense during World War II. See *Current Biography* (January) 1949.

Obituary

N Y Times p21 O 10 '59

TOBÉ *See* Davis, Tobé Coller

TOPPING, NORMAN (HAWKINS) Jan. 12, 1908- University president; scientist
Address: b. University of Southern California, University Park, Los Angeles 7, Calif.; h. 243 S. Muirfield Rd., Los Angeles, Calif.

The president of the University of Southern California, Dr. Norman Topping, is distinguished nationally for his research and administrative work in medicine and education. Succeeding Dr. Fred D. Fagg, Jr., Dr. Topping returned to his alma mater to take office on September 2, 1958 as the seventh president of the seventy-eight-year-old university, one of the oldest private institutions of higher learning in the West and, with an enrollment of more than 17,000 students in its sixteen colleges and professional schools, also one of the largest.

The son of a company physician at the lead mines in southeast Missouri, Norman Hawkins Topping was born on January 12, 1908, in the town of Flat River, Missouri, to Dr. Moses H. and Charlotte Amanda (Blue) Topping. The family (he has two sisters) later moved to the West coast, where he was graduated from Los Angeles High School in 1926. For his college training he first attended the University of Washington in Seattle, Washington, transferred to the University of California at Los Angeles for one year's study, and later entered the University of Southern California. Here he earned the B.A. degree in 1933 and the M.D. degree in 1936.

Univ. of Southern California
DR. NORMAN TOPPING

In that year he began sixteen years of medical research with the United States Public Health Service. After fulfilling his internship in its marine hospitals at San Francisco and Seattle, he was commissioned a medical officer in the United States Public Health Service. Following a brief tour of duty at the San Pedro (California) Quarantine Station, in 1937 he became a member of the staff of the National Institutes of Health at Bethesda, Maryland, the research arm of the United States Public Health Service.

During the next eleven years (1937-48) Dr. Topping studied viral and rickettsial diseases, and for the last two years of that period he was assistant chief of the division of infectious diseases of the National Institutes of Health. The term "rickettsial" refers to the family *Rickettsia* (named after Howard Taylor Ricketts, who died of the typhus fever that he was engaged in studying); this family includes the microorganism, standing between viruses and bacteria in size, which causes Rocky Mountain spotted fever when carried by infected ticks. Another microorganism in the same family causes typhus fever. It was Dr. Topping who developed the first effective treatment for Rocky Mountain spotted fever.

Reportedly the only researcher who ever survived an accidental infection of this fatal disease, which is characterized by violent headaches, chills, fever, and the breaking out of red spots over the body, he worked tirelessly to produce a serum. Its success was an important step forward in medical progress because this disease, carried by the wood tick in the West and the dog tick in the East, attacks at least 1,000 people a year. The serum is made by injecting vaccinated rabbits with ground-up ticks, then drawing off their blood, which is rich in antibodies.

(Continued next page)

TOPPING, NORMAN—*Continued*

Dr. Topping has written a number of published research articles on rickettsial diseases, including "Complement-fixation in Rickettsial Diseases" (*American Journal of Public Health,* January 1942; with Ida Albertina Bengston) and "Rocky Mountain Spotted Fever" (*Veterans Administration Technical Bulletin,* March 18, 1949). During World War II he was a consultant to the Army and the Navy as a member of the United States Typhus Commission.

From 1948 to 1952 Dr. Topping had the dual office of assistant surgeon general of the Public Health Service and associate director of the National Institutes of Health, devoting most of his time to the administration of the extensive research program of the N.I.H. (See his article "The Federal Government Looks at Medical Research," *American Journal of Tropical Medicine,* May 1950.) Two new institutes were authorized in 1950, the Institute on Neurological Diseases and Blindness and the Institute on Arthritis and Metabolic Diseases. These would assist, he declared, in the concentrated drive of researchers to prevent crippling diseases rather than to spend most of their efforts in repair work.

Having headed experts who conducted research on the common cold since January 1947, Dr. Topping stated their indeterminate conclusions in a question-and-answer interview in *United States News & World Report* of December 7, 1951. "We have learned a lot about the common cold, yet relatively speaking, we know very little. . .," he observed. "Despite considerable progress in virus research," the specific cold virus was not yet isolated and identified.

In *Science* magazine (December 26, 1947) Dr. Topping had described the successful isolation of the infectious agent for *one* type of cold, in his work with Dr. Leon T. Atlas on experiments with nasal washings. He reported that the study of cold vaccines (thoroughly pursued since 1932) had been abandoned and that there was considerable evidence that antihistamines had no specific effect on colds. Undiscouraged by the failure to find a cure or preventive for the common cold, "an acute infectious disease that is transmitted from person to person," Dr. Topping emphasized his faith in the value of "fundamental research."

Dr. Topping entered the field of educational administration in 1952 as vice-president for medical affairs at the University of Pennsylvania. In January 1958 he announced the Pennsylvania Plan to Develop Scientists in Medical Research, which would provide fellowships to medical graduates for advanced studies. "The freedom of the world may very well depend upon the recognition that we must have enough basic research. We can have it only if we maintain a steady and increasing flow of competent, well-trained young scientists from our universities," the veteran researcher stated (New York *Times,* January 22, 1958).

Selected from some 200 candidates for the presidency of the University of Southern California, Dr. Topping was installed in traditional ceremonies on October 23, 1958. The university is currently undergoing a $6,000,000 construction program, part of a long-range $75,000,000 expansion project begun in 1955 and scheduled for completion in 1980, the university's centennial.

While Topping believes that the university's "biggest object should be to see that the graduate is a well-rounded individual," he has indicated that he favors some form of special instruction for those students who excel in one subject but are only fair in others. He emphasized that "parents should realize that a college education for their offspring is one of the best investments that can be made."

Among the organizations with which Dr. Topping has been associated are the American Society of Tropical Medicine (president in 1949-50), the American Foundation for Tropical Medicine (member of the board of directors), National Foundation for Infantile Paralysis (chairman since 1956 of the committee on virus research and epidemiology). He is also a member of many medical groups and has received the award of the Washington Academy of Science, the Bailey K. Ashford Award of the American Society of Tropical Medicine, and the medal of the United States Typhus Commission.

He was a member of the Armed Forces Epidemiology Board from 1950 to 1956, and he has served on the Interdepartmental Committee for Scientific Research and Development appointed by the President of the United States, the committee on medical science of the Research and Development Board of the Department of Defense, the American Public Health Association's subcommittee on control of communicable diseases, and as chairman of the health committee for Foreign Operations Administration. Dr. Topping was the public health member of a medical mission sent to Germany by the Unitarian Church in 1951. He was appointed to a commission that reviewed the effectiveness of the governmental process of the Commonwealth of Pennsylvania, and he was on the advisory committee to that state's Secretary of Welfare.

Dr. Norman Topping is five feet eleven inches tall, weighs 185 pounds, and has brown hair and gray eyes. He belongs to the Army and Navy Club in Washington, D.C., the Kenwood Country Club in Bethesda, and the Philadelphia Country Club, and he names golf and photography as his favorite recreations. He married Helen Rummens, a graduate of the University of California at Los Angeles, on September 2, 1930. They have a son, Brian, and a daughter, Linda E. Topping.

References

Collier's 107:53+ My 17 '41 por
American Men of Science vol II (1955)
Who's Who in America, 1958-59
World Biography (1954)

TOURÉ, SÉKOU (tōō-rā' sā-kōō') Jan. 9, 1922- President of Guinea; labor organizer

Address: Le Palais du Gouvernement, Conakry, Guinea

As the advocate of secession from France, Sékou Touré, then Premier of French Guinea with a background of trade unionism, effected a dramatic change in his country's status. His was the only French territory to vote *"non"* in the September 1958 referendum on France's proposed constitution. Guinea automatically gained independence, and Touré, the idol of the populace, became President of the new republic, which was proclaimed on October 2, 1958.

Sékou Touré was born on January 9, 1922, in the village of Faranah, situated on the bank of the Niger River deep in the interior of Guinea. He was one of seven children of Alpha and Aminata Touré, peasant farmers of the Malinké tribe. He claims to be descended from the native hero, Samory Touré, who fought in a last-ditch struggle against the French until his capture in 1898.

Touré was raised as a Moslem, the predominating religion in Guinea. He attended the school of Koranic studies in the town of Kankan and a French primary school. In 1936 he went to Conakry, the capital city, where he attended the Georges Poiret Technical College. He was expelled at the age of fifteen for taking part in a food strike, but he continued his education on his own, by correspondence and by questioning his friends about their studies. He is fluent in French, his native Malinké, and the Soussou dialect of the coast; in all three he is a spellbinding orator.

In 1940 Touré entered the employ of a business firm, Niger Français. The following year he passed an examination qualifying him for administrative work in the Post and Telecommunications Department. He showed a strong interest in the labor movement and good organizing ability; he formed connections with the Confédération Générale de Travail (CGT), the Communist-dominated French labor organization. In 1945 he became secretary general of the Post and Telecommunications Workers' Union and helped to found the Federation of Workers' Unions of Guinea, co-ordinating local unions with ties to the World Federation of Trade Unions, which was under Communist auspices and of which Touré was to become vice-president.

Touré is widely reported to have made a tour behind the Iron Curtain in 1945, visiting Moscow and Warsaw and attending the Institute of Economic Studies in Prague. He has denied this, stating, "I've never been north or east of Brussels" (New York *Times,* October 19, 1958).

Subsequently assigned to the Colonial Treasury Office, Touré became secretary general of the Treasury employees' union. His union activities distressed his supervisors, who regarded him as a troublemaker. He became involved in African politics in 1946, when the African Democratic Rally (RDA) was organized under the leadership of Félix Houphouet-Boigny of the Ivory Coast.

French Embassy Press & Inf. Division

SÉKOU TOURÉ

In 1948 Touré was elected secretary general of the Territorial Union of the CGT. In that year, addressing the twenty-seventh congress of the CGT, he stated that African workers chose without hesitation to side with the anti-imperialist, democratic camp rather than with the imperialist, exploiting powers. He was named secretary general of the co-ordinating committee of the CGT for French West Africa and Togoland in 1950.

Besides being active in labor unions, Touré held a number of government positions. He served in the Guinean Legislative Assembly in 1950, became territorial councilor for Beyla in Guinea in 1953, and was chosen mayor of Conakry in 1955. After two defeats in previous elections he won a seat in the National Assembly in Paris in 1956. His maiden speech captured the attention of an audience which had been indifferent when he started.

When the RDA had begun to function openly in Guinea, in 1950, Touré declared that he had broken with the Communists. While he is believed to have undeniable sympathies in this direction, some nationalists have considered him not far enough to the Left. In recent years African nationalism rather than Marxism has seemed to be his guiding force, and he is expected to accept any aid toward that goal. Since 1952 he has been secretary general of the Guinea Democratic party (the local branch of the RDA).

By 1956 the RDA had become very strong. Its rise was violent; opposition was smothered; homes of opponents were sometimes burned. Touré could not stop the bloodshed in Conakry in October 1956 when RDA members clashed with mutually hostile tribes. He was booed by RDA Leftists in 1957 for advocating the inclusion of twelve Europeans on the electoral lists; they allowed three Europeans and three

TOURÉ, SÉKOU—*Continued*

of mixed descent. The RPF group (followers of Charles de Gaulle), locally known as the Action Démocratique et Sociale, had been gaining adherents in Africa, reflecting the rapid growth of the *petit blanc* population in the towns.

After being elected president of the CGT in Africa in 1956, Touré became an organizer of the General Labor Union of Negro Africa (UGTAN), founded independently of the CGT at Cotonou, Dahomey, in 1957. In that year he was named territorial councilor of Conakry, grand councilor for French West Africa, and, as a result of the new French *Loi-cadre,* Vice-President of the Governmental Council of Guinea, which was equivalent to Prime Minister under the French governor. An advocate of "direct action," he abolished the tribal chieftaincies, which he considered corrupt, and established more than 4,000 village councils, elected by universal suffrage.

When Premier de Gaulle toured Africa in August 1958, he found a generally favorable attitude toward his proposed constitution; a negative vote would mean severing political and economic ties with France. In Guinea, however, he encountered opposition. At a rally Touré echoed the cry of African students: "We prefer poverty in liberty to riches in slavery." Touré broke with the RDA and Houphouet-Boigny on this issue. Stating at his party congress that the proposed constitution granted Africa neither liberty of action nor equality with France, that it was the old French Union rebaptized, "old merchandise with a new label," Touré urged a vote of *"non."* Ninety-five per cent of the electorate on September 28, 1958 opposed the constitution. Ties with France were automatically severed, and on October 2 Guinea officially proclaimed itself a republic, with Touré as President.

Guinea found itself in economic straits without France's aid. The latter had been pouring in funds for economic development and had planned, in particular, to construct the Konkouré Dam to provide cheap hydroelectric power which would have permitted Guinea to do its own processing of bauxite resources into aluminum. Touré intends to carry out this project, stating that "we will build it with our hands, if necessary" (*Manchester Guardian,* January 7, 1959).

In November 1958 Touré visited nearby Ghana, which had won independence from Great Britain in 1957, and conferred with its Prime Minister, Kwame Nkrumah. An announcement was made that the two countries planned to unite as the nucleus of a United States of Africa, taking their inspiration from the thirteen American colonies. Ghana lent the new republic $28,000,000. It was eventually decided that Guinea, which contemplated entering the sterling area, would remain in the franc zone, and agreements with France for technical and administrative co-operation and cultural exchange were signed on January 7, 1959.

Touré has been married twice; his second wife, Andrée, is the daughter of a French father and a Malinké mother. He is known to

Guineans as "the Elephant" because he is strong and dignified. He has instituted a program of compulsory work and a one-party system which he describes as "total democracy." Philosophical theory does not interest him, nor does trade unionism divorced from the machinery of government. Although he has prefaced political meetings with prayer, he does not commit himself on his religious views. "I am all faiths," he has said. "As President, I am everybody" (*Time,* February 16, 1959).

References

Figaro S 29 '58
Manchester Guardian p8 Ja 8 '59
N Y Herald Tribune p10 O 1 '58 por
N Y Times p8 S 30 '58 por
U S News 45:22 O 10 '58
Thompson, Virginia and Adloff, Richard French West Africa (1958)

TUCKER, HENRY ST. GEORGE, BISHOP July 16, 1874-Aug. 8, 1959 Clergyman; president of Federal Council of the Churches of Christ in America (1942-44); presiding bishop of Protestant Episcopal Church of the United States (1938-46). See *Current Biography* (September) 1943.

Obituary

N Y Times p88 Ag 9 '59

TUNNARD, CHRISTOPHER July 7, 1910-Regional and city planner; landscape designer; university professor

Address: b. School of Architecture and Design, Yale University, New Haven, Conn.; h. 251 E. Rock Rd., New Haven, Conn.

Widely recognized for his concept of the "linear" or "regional" city, Christopher Tunnard, the authority on urban planning, directs the graduate program in city planning at the Yale University School of Architecture and Design. There he and his associates are making an extended study of the "Atlantic urban region"—Tunnard's name for a 600-mile strip which runs along the Atlantic seaboard from Norfolk, Virginia to Portland, Maine. According to Tunnard, this is only one of several in the United States which are rapidly developing into vast urban units.

To his research studies at Yale Professor Tunnard brought an impressive background of education and experience in landscape architecture, regional planning, and landscape design. He has written several authoritative books in his subject fields, including *Gardens in the Modern Landscape, The City of Man,* and *American Skyline.*

Christopher Tunnard was born in Victoria, British Columbia, Canada on July 7, 1910 to Christopher Coney and Madeline (Kingscote) Tunnard. He received his early education in Canada, where he attended St. Michaels School and Victoria College of the University of British Columbia.

In 1928 Tunnard went to England to study at Westminster Technical Institute in London and at the College of the Royal Horticultural Society, Wisley, England, from which he received a diploma in 1930. After graduation, he took a position as draftsman-designer for P. S. Cane, a London firm (1932-34).

From 1934 to 1937 Tunnard maintained a private practice as a landscape designer and site planner near London at St. Ann's Hill, Surrey. He moved his office to London in 1937, and continued to work there for the next two years. During this period he wrote his first book, *Gardens in the Modern Landscape* (Chemical Publishing Company, 1938).

In 1939 Tunnard was invited to Harvard as visiting lecturer in the Graduate School of Design. There he focused his attention almost exclusively on landscape design and city planning. Appointed a Wheelwright Traveling Fellow in Architecture at Harvard University in 1943, he held the fellowship until he went to Yale University in 1945 as assistant professor of city planning. He was advanced to the rank of associate professor in 1948 and in 1957 he was named director of the graduate program in city planning at Yale.

In 1941 Tunnard was associated with a group of architects who designed a defense housing project in Stamford, Connecticut. From 1942 to 1943 he served with the Royal Canadian Engineers. After his medical discharge, he helped make plans for the postwar rebuilding of London, when he acted as chairman of the town planning committee of the Modern Architectural Research Society of London.

Always in demand as a visiting lecturer at various colleges and universities, Tunnard has fulfilled engagements at the Massachusetts Institute of Technology (1948-49), North Carolina State College (1950-51), the University of Minnesota (1953), the University of Winnipeg (1958), and at Clemson College, North Carolina (1958).

Through his writings and lectures, Professor Tunnard is making the American public increasingly aware of the development of huge super cities. In "America's Super Cities," an article he wrote for *Harper's Magazine* (August 1958), he claims that between one-sixth and one-quarter of the total American population and half of the economic power in the entire world is concentrated in a 600-mile strip along the Atlantic seaboard. He calls this strip a "super city" of "staggering" character.

In another article, "Super City on the Seaboard" (*Rotarian* magazine, February 1959), Tunnard cites other great regional urban areas, including a group of cities dominated by steel: Pittsburgh, Youngstown, Canton, Akron, and Cleveland. Still others cluster around Detroit, Chicago, and Los Angeles. A new strip, he says, appears to be joining Chicago and Detroit. He maintains that these areas have many common problems which enforce the necessity to think in terms of regional rather than unit planning.

Christopher Tunnard's devotion to the importance of art in modern urban planning is clearly

CHRISTOPHER TUNNARD

stated in *The City of Man* (Scribner's, 1953). He observes: "We are now under a new obligation which is based on a change in the world situation. . . . It is now quite obvious that the hand of the artist has become necessary in order to remove from the city areas of ugliness as well as misery and to replace them with the useful and the beautiful or the city will not function in the way that we desire. It has been discovered, rather late in the day, that the aesthetic is intimately related to the economic function in urban planning."

As director of the graduate program in city planning at Yale, Tunnard is making a special study of regional planning with a large grant from the Rockefeller Foundation. He believes that this study will encourage city planners in all parts of the world to investigate the problem of how to avoid the destruction of landscape by more creative designing of urban areas.

Tunnard does not concentrate all of his energy on the rapidly growing industrial urban areas of the United States. He headed a field study of the town of Monroe, Connecticut which demonstrated that one of the state's woodland towns was in danger of being destroyed because of lack of planning. As a result of this study, a planning board was established in the town; it is serving as a model for other communities faced with the same situation.

In his study of the town of Monroe Tunnard repeated his conviction that planners can no longer think of a state simply as a state but as part of a vast urban region which needs to be considered as a unit.

This concept of regional planning has caught the attention of business, industry, and government. Tunnard's talent for thinking on a large scale about the problems of America's mush-

TUNNARD, CHRISTOPHER—*Continued*

rooming metropolitan areas has been translated into action on the part of private agencies, industries, and city planning commissions.

In addition to *Gardens in the Modern Landscape* and *The City of Man,* Tunnard has written (in conjunction with Henry Hope Reed) *American Skyline,* published first in a hardcover edition by Houghton Mifflin in 1955, then released as a paperback by Mentor Books in 1956. With J. N. Pearce he edited a series of papers collected into a volume entitled *City Planning at Yale,* issued in 1954 by the Yale University department of architecture graduate program in city planning

Christopher Tunnard has received several honors, special grants, and citations. He won a special award for excellence in landscape design at the Paris Exposition of 1937. In 1939 he was named honorary secretary of the Institute of Landscape Artists. A Guggenheim Fellowship in 1950 enabled him to visit many of the cities in the United States in preparation for writing his book on city planning, *The City of Man.* He was appointed a Fulbright Fellow in 1956 and used the grant to attend the Institut d'Urbanism of the University of Paris.

On June 9, 1945 Christopher Tunnard married Lydia Evans of Boston, Massachusetts. They have one son, Christopher. When not traveling, meeting with city and regional officials, or teaching at Yale or elsewhere, Tunnard relaxes at his home in New Haven. He has been a naturalized American citizen since 1949.

Reference

Who's Who in America, 1958-59

TURECK, ROSALYN Dec. 14, 1914- Pianist

Address: b. c/o Ibbs & Tillett, Ltd., 120 Wigmore St., London, W.1, England; Concert Associates, Inc., 36 W. 57th St., New York 19

Although the American pianist Rosalyn Tureck has been recognized all over the world as an authoritative interpreter of the music of Johann Sebastian Bach, it was not until the 1958-59 season that she received enthusiastic responses from large audiences in the United States. In December 1958 she was the first woman to direct the New York Philharmonic-Symphony Orchestra.

Miss Tureck, who has played a significant role in bringing contemporary music to the concert stage, spent a number of years teaching at Columbia University, the Juilliard School of Music, and other institutions. "The music of Bach," she has said, "is so universal in its human meaning and so all-embracing in its musical structures that for the receptive mind it illuminates all other music, including contemporary music. The artist need never feel limited with Bach as the fountainhead."

Rosalyn Tureck was born in Chicago on December 14, 1914. Her parents, Samuel and Monya (Lipson) Tureck, were of Turkish and Russian origin and came to the United States

early in this century. All the members of her immediate family, including her sisters Margaret and Sonya, have been amateur musicians from early childhood. Rosalyn's musical instruction began early, and, in addition to the piano, she studied the harpsichord, clavichord, and organ.

At the age of ten, after having made her public debut with two solo piano recitals in Chicago, Rosalyn began lessons under Sophia Brilliant-Liven. In 1926 she performed with the Chicago Symphony Orchestra. In the Greater Chicago Piano Playing Tournament, in which 15,000 children were entered, she won first place. She then made a short concert tour, after which her parents decided that Rosalyn should mature normally at home and continue her studies instead of embarking upon a career as a child prodigy.

Her next teacher was Jan Chiapusso, the Dutch-Italian pianist and Bach specialist, with whom she began to study at fourteen. After a year of study she gave two all-Bach concerts in Chicago. At sixteen she won a four-year fellowship to the Juilliard School of Music's Graduate School in New York, where one of her instructors was Olga Samaroff.

During her second year of study at Juilliard, Miss Tureck discovered that she would have to revise all her views on music completely. "There was no one to tell me what to do," she has said in describing this critical turning point. "My conviction sprang from within myself. I had to chop down every tree." Her methods of practice and research became painstaking; she developed a new technique for each composition. In the same year she learned to play Bach's "Goldberg" Variations in two weeks, to be told later by the president that the work was unsuited to the piano. "Luckily," she has said, "I did not know." She has recorded the "Goldberg" Variations, and the work is now an important part of her repertoire.

Graduated, *cum laude,* from Juilliard in 1935, Miss Tureck began seven years of teaching on the faculty of the Philadelphia Conservatory of Music. She appeared in her first New York concert at Carnegie Hall, interpreting Brahm's Concerto in B-Flat Major with the Philadelphia Orchestra. Her series of six all-Bach recitals at Town Hall, during which she played the complete forty-eight preludes and fugues of the *Well-Tempered Clavier,* the "Goldberg" Variations, and miscellaneous works, was an outstanding musical event of 1937. In later New York recitals she broadened her repertoire to include selections from Beethoven, Brahms, Sibelius, and Paul Nordoff, the contemporary American composer and teacher. In 1937 she began her annual concert tours of the United States and Canada.

In the 1930's Miss Tureck won several contests and awards: the Schubert Memorial Contest in 1935, National Federation of Music Clubs Contest in 1935, Phi Beta Award in 1936, and Town Hall Endowment Award in 1938.

In 1944 and from 1946 to 1954 she presented an annual series of Bach concerts in New York and in the last three of these years she dedicated many recitals to contemporary music. During this period she continued to teach: at the Mannes School of Music from 1940 to 1944; at Juilliard from 1943 to 1955; at Teachers College of Columbia University from 1944 to 1955; and at the School of General Studies of Columbia University from 1944 to 1955.

Miss Tureck has often appeared in concerts as a soloist with American symphony orchestras. Among them are the New York Philharmonic-Symphony Orchestra, Chicago Symphony Orchestra, Philadelphia Orchestra, Minneapolis Symphony Orchestra, and the Rochester Philharmonic Orchestra.

Reviews of Miss Tureck's performances were consistently good. Virgil Thomson (New York *Herald Tribune,* November 13, 1945) praised her intelligent and impassioned interpretation, excellent technique, and beautiful sense of rhythm. "The secret of her work at its best," he wrote, "seems to be that her passionate nature finds its completest expression in works that demand by their own nature an objective approach." He found, however, that she had no ease; "corseted music" was her forte, but the elegant neo-Romanticism of Aaron Copland and the urbanity of Mozart were foreign to her.

In 1947 Miss Tureck made her first European tour, when she presented all-Bach recitals in Copenhagen and Stockholm and over the facilities of the British Broadcasting Corporation. In 1953 and 1954 she played in various parts of the British Isles. The critic of the London *Times* (October 19, 1954) said: "The encomiums she has received are not exaggerated: she plays the piano beautifully and Bach authentically. She demolishes our cherished purism and proves the piano a better instrument than a harpsichord, and better for Bach."

When she returned to the United States she found her audiences were smaller and less responsive than those in Europe, although the music critics continued their glowing reports. Again in Europe in 1955, she gave recitals in the Netherlands and Germany, and played the "Goldberg" Variations to a capacity audience at the Edinburgh Festival; London's Wigmore Hall was sold out at her appearance there, including seats on the stage, and the Royal Festival Hall, with over 3,000 seats, was filled to capacity.

She remained in Europe and toured extensively in 1956, performing English and American works at the Venice Contemporary Music Festival and Bach selections at the Edinburgh and Scheveningen (the Netherlands) festivals. At Copenhagen she was soloist and director with the Collegium Musicum Chamber Orchestra and played to capacity audiences at the Concertgebouw of Amsterdam and the Royal Festival Hall in London.

In 1957 she toured Italy, Scandinavia, Great Britain, Ireland, and Switzerland, and performed at the Holland Festival. She was soloist-director in 1958 with the Philharmonia Orchestra of London in a series of three

ROSALYN TURECK

concerts covering all Bach's Concerti for One Clavier. After appearances at the Bach Festival in June and the Brussels World's Fair in July, she played in South Africa.

In the 1958-59 season she returned to the United States for a tour and made her first appearance at Town Hall. On December 18, 19, 20, and 21 she was the soloist and conductor of the New York Philharmonic in performances of Bach's D Minor and G Minor Concerti. This was unprecedented; no woman had ever conducted the Philharmonic before. In directing the orchestra, Miss Tureck believes that she can achieve a broad and deliberate, rather than a feathery and ice-edged manner. She attempts to capture the stylistic and emotional essence of the music instead of emphasizing the instruments. At rehearsals she provides the orchestra with her own printed editions of the scores, and she writes her own program notes.

The artistry of Rosalyn Tureck is available on long-playing records. Her interpretation of the entire Bach *Clavierübung* was recorded by the British company known as His Master's Voice; some of these records have been made available in the United States by Capitol Records. Other Bach performances by Miss Tureck have been released by Allegro and Decca Records.

Miss Tureck has brown eyes, brown hair, is five feet two inches tall, and weighs 125 pounds. Fond of animals, she has a dog named Billy Budd after Benjamin Britten's opera. For relaxation she reads and listens to lieder, modern music, jazz, and compositions by Beethoven and Schubert. Usually nervous before a concert, she rehearses on the piano she will use. Often she practises twelve hours a day, with intervals when she does not touch the keys. The sculptor, Sir Jacob Epstein, has

TURECK, ROSALYN—*Continued*

executed a head of Miss Tureck, the first in a sculpture collection in the Royal Festival Hall. Since 1956 she has lived in a mansion in London.

References

Time 70:68 Jl 29 '57 por
Who's Who, 1959
Who's Who in America, 1956-57

URIS, LEON (MARCUS) Aug. 3, 1924-
Author; scenarist
Address: b. c/o Columbia Pictures Corp, 711 5th Ave., New York 22; h. 5078 Amestoy, Encino, Calif.

Reprinted from the *Wilson Library Bulletin* Dec. 1959.

Author of *Exodus* (Doubleday, 1958), a best-selling novel of modern Israel and the Jewish people which was a Book-of-the-Month Club alternate selection a year after publication, Leon Uris remarked after his first successful novel, *Battle Cry* (Putnam, 1953), that he had been a "working stiff" all his life. He wishes to correct the mistaken impression that he is either Greek-born or Palestinian-born, or that he died

LEON URIS

of cancer after returning to the South Pacific. Leon Marcus Uris was born in Baltimore, Maryland, on August 3, 1924, the second child of William Uris, a paper hanger of Polish stock who is now a storekeeper, and Anna (Blumberg) Uris.

At the age of six Leon wrote an operetta inspired by the death of his dog, and he has continued to write ever since when not occupied with warfare and travel. He attended John Bartram High School in Philadelphia, but left in his last year at seventeen to join the Marines.

(He has also attended Baltimore City College.)

First stationed in New Zealand, he later went through the Guadalcanal and Tarawa campaigns. Transferred to San Francisco to recuperate from malaria, he fell in love with his sergeant and married her—Marine Sergeant Betty Beck (Women's Reserves). With their three children, Karen, Mark, and Michael, they live in Encino, California.

After his marriage Uris held a job with the San Francisco *Call-Bulletin* as manager of the home-delivery district, with thirty-eight newsboys. In 1950 he wrote a "nasty piece" in *Esquire* about the method used to choose the All-American football team (his first sale) and then decided to start a novel about the Marine Corps. "My guiding thought throughout," he told Bernard Kalb of *Saturday Review,* "was that the real Marine story had not been told."

"If *Battle Cry* is not an original work of the imagination, it is probably out of all World War II novels about Marines, the most intimate and accurate account of the way Marines were trained to fight and the way they did fight," said the New York *Times Book Review* critic, while the Chicago *Sunday Tribune* thought that "the United States marines will be as proud to claim this book by one of their own as they are to claim their illustrious title. It is first rank war fiction." The film version, for which Uris wrote the scenario, was curiously softened; as Bosley Crowther remarked when it was released in 1955, "The war is kept to a minimum. Somebody might get killed."

For the background of *The Angry Hills* (Random House, 1955) Uris drew on a diary of an uncle, formerly a member of the volunteer Palestinian Brigade that fought in Greece. David Dempsey in the New York *Times Book Review* called it a "competently plotted . . . slam-bang adventure story." The next year, after completing the screenplay for the successful film, *Gunfight at the O.K. Corral* (1957), Uris started research for *Exodus,* reading 300 books on Israel and the Middle East. After visiting Denmark, Italy, Cyprus, and Iran, he set up his home base at the Accadia Hotel near Tel Aviv in March 1956.

In the next months he traveled 12,000 miles inside Israel, going through Arab and Jewish towns, over 100 frontier farms, and many cooperative settlements. About 1,200 interviews gave him 1,000 pages of notes and many thousands of feet of taped conversations. Mrs. Uris with the three children had joined him, but had to leave on an hour's notice when the brief Sinai campaign broke out. Before rejoining his family in Rome, Uris filed three reports as a war correspondent, also visiting Gaza and United Nations refugee camps. They returned to America, broke, and Uris set to work to boil down a million and a half words to 626 printed pages.

" 'Exodus' is overwritten and perhaps overwrought," wrote Herbert Kupferberg in the New York *Herald Tribune Book Review.* "But it can be searing in its intensity and illuminating in its insight." "If Mr. Uris sometimes lacks tone as a novelist, if his central figures are social types rather than individual portraits, there is also a kind of 'underground power' in his writing," said Maxwell Geismar in the *Saturday Review*. *Exodus* brought its author numerous awards and citations. The film version, with a scenario by Uris, is being produced and directed by Otto Preminger.

In 1959 he signed with Columbia Pictures Corporation for what is believed to be the "first multiple-book deal in the movie industry," according to Murray Schumach (New York *Times*, August 23, 1959). "He will produce the movies made from four of his novels. Mr. Uris has not yet written any of the books in the package and Columbia signed without seeing a word of manuscript." This is particularly gratifying to Uris since he was once discharged while doing the film adaptation of his novel *The Angry Hills*, because, he was told, he "did not understand the characters." (This film had been first exhibited in 1959.)

Uris enjoys tennis, his sons' H.O. miniature toy trains, and all spectator sports; likes John Steinbeck's *Tortilla Flat* and the work of Clifford Odets. Blue-eyed, with black hair turning gray, he is five feet nine inches in height and weighs 169 pounds. His Hebrew name, "Yerushalmi," means "Man of Jerusalem."

References

Lib J 78:370 F 15 '53
N Y Herald Tribune Bk R p2+ Ag 16 '59 por
Sat R 36:16 Ap 25 '53

URRUTIA LLEO, MANUEL (ōō-rōō′ tē ä lyĕ ō′) Dec. 8, 1901- Former Provisional President of Cuba; former judge

Address: c/o Herminia Lleo Vda Urrutia, Heredia 36 y Lacret, Vibora, Havana, Cuba

Formally proclaimed on January 2, 1959, Manuel Urrutia Lleo served as Provisional President of Cuba. He was inaugurated after a civil war lasting two years, which ended when President Fulgencio Batista resigned and fled. Urrutia, a former judge of the urgency court at Santiago de Cuba, had been selected for the post by Fidel Castro, who had led the successful rebel forces. Together with Castro, who now holds the office of Premier, and a cabinet, President Urrutia was expected to govern by decree for a period of eighteen months to two years. After that time, free elections are promised. In July 1959, however, Castro charged Urrutia with actions that "border on treason" and the latter resigned as Provisional President.

Manuel Urrutia Lleo was born on December 8, 1901 at Yaguajay, Las Villas Province to Manuel Urrutia and Herminia Lleo de Urrutia. His father, who died when the boy was ten months old, was an army officer who participated in the revolt which culminated in the Spanish-American War. His mother, now eighty years old, raised money and performed medical duties in Remedios, Las Villas Province for the revolutionary movement. She was later a schoolteacher. Urrutia has one sister, Alicia Urrutia de Gaycalbo.

With the assistance of scholarships and money earned from menial jobs, Urrutia was

Wide World

MANUEL URRUTIA LLEO

able to attend school and received a law degree in 1923 from the University of Havana. He then won a competitive civil service examination and was appointed municipal judge for Jiguaní in Oriente Province in 1928. He later held similar posts in Cienfuegos in Las Villas Province and in Los Arabos in Matanzas Province.

"His courage and idealism have been long demonstrated in his judicial career" (New York *Times*, January 3, 1959). Reportedly, under the repressive regime of Gerardo Machado in 1932 orders had been issued to take three allegedly rebel brothers at night from Los Arabos to San José de los Ramos and shoot them en route. Instead, Urrutia put them on a crowded daytime train. The brothers were later captured and executed, and the judge was compelled to go into hiding.

Following the overthrow of Machado in 1933, Urrutia was "restored to the judiciary in Matanzas with a two-grade promotion" (New York *Times*, January 3, 1959). In 1949 he was appointed a judge of the urgency court at Santiago de Cuba, the capital of Oriente Province. When former President Batista returned to power by a *coup d'état* in 1952, Urrutia remained a member of the urgency court. Each year he submitted a thesis to the Supreme Court of Cuba which contended that Batista had "no legal right to power" (New York *Times*, January 3, 1959).

An unsuccessful attempt to provoke a general uprising against Batista was made on July 26, 1953 when a group of young men headed by Fidel Castro attacked the Moncada Barracks at Santiago de Cuba. Cases of subversion and conspiracy came within the jurisdiction of the urgency courts. When eighty-six rebels were found dead in the Moncada Barracks, Urrutia was ordered to investigate the situation. "The judge found the fully

URRUTIA LLEO, MANUEL—*Continued*

dressed bodies actually had wounds indicating that the men had been riddled while captive and naked. He ordered photographs and reports, which went into the court record" said Dr. Charles A. Santos Buch, New York adviser to the Civic Resistance Movement (New York *Times*, January 3, 1959).

Fidel Castro (see *C.B.*, July 1958), who was captured and imprisoned, was released in 1955 in a general amnesty. He then went into exile in New York City and Mexico. On December 2, 1956 he returned to Cuba as leader of eighty-two youthful rebels. The group suffered heavy casualties on landing, but the survivors became the nucleus of a rebel army fighting the Batista regime.

Urrutia became a national symbol of opposition to repressive government on May 11, 1957 when, as presiding judge of a three-member urgency court, he voted to acquit 150 youths charged with rebellion. "The country is in a state of agitation and . . . it is necessary that tranquility be restored," he declared. However, citing Article 40 of the Cuban constitution, he stated that "adequate resistance for the protection of guaranteed individual rights is legitimate." His two colleagues voted to convict forty of the defendants.

Two days later, procedure for Urrutia's removal from the bench was begun by the Ministry of Justice. His home was attacked and nearly burned. In November 1957 he was "retired" on pension. In the following month he went into voluntary exile in the United States, where he lived first in Miami, Florida and later in Woodside, Queens County, New York.

On December 13 a spokesman for Castro released a twelve-page letter from the rebel leader urging the Council for Cuban Liberation, which represented seven anti-Batista groups some of which were lukewarm to Castro, to designate this "honest judge" as Provisional President when Batista had been overthrown. This now famous letter split Castro's opposition. Castro "believes that I am absolutely impartial among all those that are fighting against Batista," Urrutia later explained to Mike Wallace (New York *Post*, April 7, 1958).

Arriving in New York City early in January 1958, Urrutia declared that Batista should be "legally tried for usurpation of power" and urged United Nations action to find the existing government in violation of the 1948 Declaration of Human Rights. At a press conference later in the month he charged that Batista had encouraged gambling as "one way of corrupting the people" and affirmed his belief in its "absolute repression" in Cuba. Later, despite a reputation as an opponent of violence, he was quoted as saying that when Batista had finally fallen "after rivers of blood have flown," there would be mass trials of Batista henchmen.

On August 12, 1958, following the union of all anti-Batista factions under the so-called Caracas Pact, the rebel radio announced that Urrutia had been named president of a "Republic in Arms" which would operate from Venezuela until the liberation of Cuba had been achieved. This was followed by an offensive carried out by the Fidelistas which cut Cuba into two parts.

At Havana on January 1, 1959 Batista resigned and fled to the Dominican Republic. Urrutia had meanwhile returned to Cuba in November 1958, and at Santiago de Cuba on January 2, 1959 he was proclaimed by Castro as Provisional President. Taking the oath of office on January 3 and appointing several cabinet ministers, Urrutia named Castro the commander in chief of the armed forces.

Arriving in Havana on January 5, President Urrutia took up residence in the Presidential Palace and announced the appointment of Dr. José Miró Cardona, president of the Havana Bar Association, as Premier. He also cancelled a martial law proclamation earlier decreed and announced that free elections would be held within eighteen months to two years.

The Cuban Parliament was dissolved, the urgency courts abolished, and government by decree proclaimed on January 6. It was also made public that legislative functions would be exercised by the Provisional President and the cabinet. On the following day the United States recognized the new regime, which undertook to honor its international and financial obligations.

The provisional government drew world attention and much criticism when it carried out mass executions of alleged war criminals. It also enacted legislation authorizing the confiscation of property owned by officials of the Batista regime. Some of the problems facing the new leaders are labor difficulties, unemployment, and a treasury depleted by the huge military costs and widespread corruption of the ousted government. To strengthen the position of the present rule, Castro became Premier on February 16, succeeding Miró Cardona.

On February 11 Urrutia stated that increased foreign investments would be welcomed. It is estimated that American companies now have over $1 billion invested in Cuba (Miami *Herald*, February 12, 1959). However, during the revolution Castro and his supporters had promised nationalization of some industries. This commitment was reflected in the temporary assumption of control by government of the Cuban Telephone Company in March and the immediate reduction of rates. The firm exercises a monopoly on the island, and 65 per cent of its stock is owned by the International Telephone & Telegraph Corporation.

Although Urrutia favored the total repression of gambling, opposition to this policy developed. At the end of January a compromise was reached whereby a three-member commission would draft a new law permitting the reopening of casinos "under respectable businessmen" with patronage limited to foreigners and wealthy Cubans. Castro favored the compromise in the interests of tourism, the second most important industry after sugar growing, because 10,000 workers depend upon it. It was also announced that the Cuban Communist party, which had been outlawed under Batista, would be permitted to reorganize as a legal political party. At the time of Dr. Urrutia's resignation, one of the charges brought against him was that he delayed the resumption of gambling.

Manuel Urrutia Lleo and the former Esperanza Llaguno Aguirre were married in 1936 and have two sons, Alejandro Rubio and Jorge, and a daughter, Victoria Esperanza. Urrutia is short and stocky and wears a mustache and dark glasses. He likes to study the career of the Cuban revolutionary José Martí.

References

Miami News Ja 2 '59
N Y Herald Tribune p4 Ja 2 '59 por; p3 Ja 3 '59 por
Newsday p50 Ja 15 '59 por
U S News 46:19 Ja 16 '59

VAN ALLEN, JAMES A(LFRED) Sept 7, 1914- Physicist; university professor

Address: b. State University of Iowa, Iowa City, Iowa; h. 131 Ferson Ave., Iowa City, Iowa

State University of Iowa

JAMES A. VAN ALLEN

Chairman of the physics department at the State University of Iowa and one of the United States' outstanding younger scientists, Dr. James Alfred Van Allen has taken part in virtually every aspect of high-altitude research and rocket development. He tested the first captured German V-2 rockets and helped to invent the Aerobee rocket. To conduct experiments on the intensity of cosmic ray particles he ventured from the equator to the poles and developed the "rockoon" technique, a combined rocket and balloon device, to increase scientific accuracy and decrease the costs. Plans for the International Geophysical Year (1957-58) were born in his home, and he has been a leading figure in the American satellite program as chief of the internal instrumentation section.

In outspoken criticism of the American space program, he had led a group of scientists in an appeal for the creation of a national space establishment with an appropriation of one billion dollars a year for ten years. The purpose of the agency would be pioneering in a program of study for outer space, directed toward asserting "United States leadership in space research by 1960" (New York *Times,* December 29, 1957). (A step was made toward fulfilling this proposal when the United States Aeronautics and Space Administration was created in July 1958.)

Born on September 7, 1914 in Mount Pleasant, Iowa, James Alfred Van Allen is the son of Alfred Morris Van Allen, an attorney, and Alma E. (Olney) Van Allen. He was educated in the local elementary school and at Mount Pleasant High School, where he was named class valedictorian when he graduated in 1931.

At Iowa Wesleyan College in Mount Pleasant Van Allen studied physics and chemistry under Dr. Thomas Poulter, who encouraged his students to undertake individual and original experimentation. As a freshman Van Allen prepared research instruments for the Byrd Antarctic Expedition of which Poulter was a member. After receiving his B.S. degree *summa cum laude* in 1935, Van Allen continued his studies in nuclear physics at State University of Iowa, Iowa City. He was awarded the M.Sc. degree in 1936 and the Ph.D. degree three years later.

Van Allen was a research fellow and physicist with the Carnegie Institution in Washington from 1939 to 1942. During World War II he joined the U.S. Naval Reserve and advanced from lieutenant (j.g.) to lieutenant commander. He worked at the Ordnance Bureau on proximity fuses for naval artillery shells and was stationed for a time in the Pacific, where he won four combat stars and other citations.

Upon his return to civilian life in 1946 the young scientist was appointed head of high-altitude research at the Applied Physics Laboratory at Johns Hopkins University in Baltimore. He supervised tests of captured German V-2 rockets and led in developing the Aerobee rocket, a smaller, less complex version of the V-2, for use in probing the upper atmosphere. Late in 1946 Van Allen announced that a V-2 rocket, traveling at 5,450 feet per second, had reached a height of 114 miles, the greatest altitude yet achieved by a man-made object up to that time. Soon jet-propelled rockets containing magnetometers and sensitive photographic equipment were penetrating the upper atmosphere at a height of 250 miles.

Dr. Van Allen was appointed to his present position as professor and head of the physics department at State University of Iowa January 1, 1951. Teaching duties did not restrict other scientific activities. He supervised several ground and shipboard launchings of Aerobee rockets to collect data on cosmic radiation, and during the summers from 1952 to 1955 he supervised naval expeditions to study cosmic

VAN ALLEN, JAMES A.—Continued

ray intensity near the geomagnetic north pole, an area where cosmic rays are not deflected from striking the earth, and are thus brought within the field of measurement. In 1956 Professor Van Allen was general director of a series of cosmic ray experiments conducted in Iowa, Texas, and Minnesota. The following year his staff collected information on cosmic ray particles in the upper atmosphere near the equator. On an expedition to the Greenland-Baffin Island area in August 1957, he carried out the first-known rocket flight through a "visible aurora."

In all of these experiments Van Allen and his associates used the "rockoon," or balloon-assisted take-off technique that he has developed. This launching method uses a balloon to carry the rocket to an altitude of ten to fifteen miles where reduced air pressure triggers an automatic device hurtling the rocket into space on its own power. "This costs only a fraction of the amount needed to build a rocket that can lift the same payload from the ground, since the rockoon does not have to push through the denser portions of the atmosphere" (New York Times, March 27, 1958).

Like the satellites which have succeeded them, the rockets contained Geiger counters, magnetometers, and radio transmitters to relay data on cosmic radiation. At the completion of his expedition to the geomagnetic pole in the summer of 1952, Van Allen expressed complete satisfaction with his invention. During the summer of 1953 the rockets reached an altitude of 64.4 miles, and the Iowa scientists gathered enough information to conclude that primary radiation (low-energy atomic nuclei) bombarded the earth only near the geomagnetic north pole (New York Times, September 27, 1953). The rockoon ceiling was later increased to eighty-five miles.

Dr. Van Allen was one of a small group of influential scientists who initiated plans for a world-wide scientific investigation of the earth. The suggestion to combine aspects of the earth sciences in a single international study was made in Van Allen's home on April 5, 1950 while he entertained Professor Sydney Chapman, renowned British geophysicist. The proposal culminated in plans for the International Geophysical Year (1957-58), of which the single most spectacular phase was the satellite program.

When the United States announced that it would launch an artificial "moon," Van Allen was named a member of the supervising technical panel. In January 1956 he was appointed head of the working group on internal instrumentation "to survey all proposed experiments to be carried within the 'moons' and to make recommendations on the most practical design of the satellites" (Congressional Record, February 6, 1958).

The United States Army launched its first earth satellite on January 31, 1958. Van Allen and his staff had supervised plans for the satellite's basic design in the laboratories at the State University of Iowa and had developed the essential cosmic ray recording equipment contained in the baby "moon." The satellite also held the "Van Allen package" of instruments to measure micrometeorites and the temperature within the satellite.

Two weeks after the launching, Van Allen wrote, "Explorer I is making possible the most comprehensive survey ever undertaken of cosmic ray intensity in outer space. The earth's bulge at the equator is being measured more precisely than ever before. We are learning more about the earth's magnetic field, more about the amount of meteoric dust in space and more about the density of the atmosphere at various altitudes. The satellite is transmitting valuable data about its own temperature." Admitting that the information gathered by one satellite was limited, Van Allen pointed out that "it is only by building our knowledge fact by fact that we will lay the groundwork for the more practical discoveries that lie ahead" (Life, February 17, 1958).

Explorer II (launched unsuccessfully on March 5, 1958) and Explorer III (sent aloft on March 26, 1958) contained "an ingenious magnetic tape-recorder . . . no bigger than a king-size pack of cigarettes" designed under Dr. Van Allen's supervision at the State University of Iowa laboratories. Invented to transmit data on cosmic ray bombardment collected on its orbit around the globe, the recorder which has a built-in "memory" can "play back two hour's worth of information in a mere six seconds," upon command from a ground radio station. This prevents the loss (as in Explorer I) of 90 per cent of the data which had been sent out over oceans and remote areas where signals were unheard (New York Times, March 27, 1958).

The successful firing of Explorer IV was announced by Van Allen shortly after the satellite had entered its orbit on July 26, 1958. It was sent aloft "to conduct experiments involving the intense, mysterious radiation that bombarded Explorers I and III" (New York Times, July 27, 1958). The satellite confirmed the existence of the radiation band starting in some areas at an altitude of 250 miles above the earth. The moon-probe rocket, Pioneer, launched on October 11, 1958, also carried a radiation-measuring tube designed by State University of Iowa scientists. The instruments on Pioneer, which traveled a third of the way to the moon, indicated that radiation intensity decreased at extreme altitudes. Later, Van Allen concluded that there are two radiation bands encircling the earth, one nearer and the other farther away.

A prolific writer, Van Allen has prepared more than fifty articles on cosmic rays, nuclear and atmospheric physics, and the use of rockets in high-altitude research. He was the editor of Scientific Uses of Earth Satellites (University of Michigan Press, 1956), and he contributed a chapter entitled "The Nature and Intensity of Cosmic Radiation" to Physics and Medicine of the Upper Atmosphere (1952).

Among Van Allen's professional organizations are the American Physical Society (Fellow) and the American Geophysical Union. He has been chairman of an independent group of scientists known as the Rocket and Satellite Research Panel since 1947 and a member of the National Advisory Committee for Aeronautics and the space science board of the National Academy of Sciences-National Research Council. In 1948 he was honored by the American Rocket Society for his accomplishments in high-altitude research. He was the recipient of a Guggenheim fellowship in 1951 and in the summer of 1953 he was co-organizer of an international conference on upper-atmospheric research sponsored by the Royal Society of London. During the academic year 1953-54 Van Allen directed the experimental instrumentation program for Project Sherwood at the James Forrestal Research Center, as research associate at Princeton University in New Jersey.

James A. Van Allen is of medium height and build and has short dark hair and dark eyes. He married Abigail Fithian Halsey on October 13, 1945. They have a son, Thomas Halsey, and three daughters, Cynthia Olney, Margo Isham, and Sarah Halsey. Van Allen is a Presbyterian. His principal form of relaxation is making things in his woodworking shop.

References

N Y Herald Tribune p17 Mr 27 '58 por
N Y Times p15 Mr 27 '58 por
American Men of Science vol I (1955)
Who's Who in America, 1958-59

VAN BEINUM, EDUARD *See* Beinum, Eduard van

VANCE, HAROLD S(INES) Aug. 22, 1890-Aug. 31, 1959 United States government official; commissioner of Atomic Energy Commission since 1955; president of Studebaker Corporation (1948-54). See *Current Biography* (May) 1949.

Obituary

N Y Times p29 S 1 '59

VERA-ELLEN Feb. 16, 1926- Dancer; actress
Address: b. c/o Actors' Equity Association, 6636 Hollywood Blvd., Los Angeles, Calif.

Equally proficient in tap, toe, acrobatic, and dramatic dancing, Vera-Ellen is one of the most versatile dancers in motion pictures. Some critics believe that in her pleasing appearance, vibrancy, and technical skill she is as fine a dancing partner as any that Fred Astaire and Gene Kelly have had on the screen. Danny Kaye and Donald O'Connor are among the other Hollywood stars with whom she has performed in the course of dancing, singing, and acting in more than a dozen musical comedies.

The only child of Martin F. and Alma (Westmeyer) Rohe was born in Cincinnati, Ohio, on February 16, 1926, and given the

Metro-Goldwyn-Mayer
VERA-ELLEN

name of Vera-Ellen because, as she herself has explained, "My mother saw the hyphenated name on a theatre marquee in a dream several nights before I was born" (quoted by Sidney Skolsky, New York *Post*, October 24, 1954). Her father was a piano tuner. A frail child, Vera-Ellen began taking dancing lessons at the age of ten to help improve her health. She attended classes at the Hessler Dancing Studios and the Norwood View High School in Cincinnati.

While still in her teens, Vera-Ellen went to New York as a delegate to a convention of the Dancing Teachers of America. She made use of the opportunity to try out for a *Major Bowes Amateur Hour* program, and as a result was signed up for a tour with a Major Bowes unit which appeared in a number of cities, including St. Louis, Pittsburgh, Washington, Baltimore, Philadelphia, and Boston.

Returning to New York, Vera-Ellen persuaded her mother to join her. Mrs. Rohe became secretary at the Sonia Serova School of Dancing, where Vera-Ellen continued her studies. Among early engagements which the dancer obtained were those as a Rockette at Radio City Music Hall, at Billy Rose's Casa Manana night club in a specialty dance, and with Ted Lewis' band in a song-and-dance offering.

Work in Broadway musicals came next, starting with a dancing bit and one line to speak in *Very Warm for May*, which had its première on November 17, 1939. She was then engaged for a specialty number in *Higher and Higher*, opening on April 4, 1940. Later in the year, on October 30, she gave her first performance in *Panama Hattie*, in which she had the dancing lead. Beginning on June 3, 1942 in the role of Minerva in *By Jupiter*, she danced opposite Ray Bolger. During her fifth Broadway show, a revival of *A Connecticut*

VERA-ELLEN—*Continued*

Yankee, which opened on November 17, 1943, she came to the attention of Samuel Goldwyn. A motion-picture contract resulted, and the Rohe family moved to Hollywood.

Vera-Ellen's entrance into motion pictures was auspicious. She appeared opposite Danny Kaye in *The Wonder Man* (1945) and was well received by the critics. "A pert and chic new dancer," wrote the New York *Times* reviewer, who "dances with captivating rhythm" (June 9, 1945). "A fine young hoofer who can handle lines as well," *Variety* commented (April 25, 1945).

Dancing again with Danny Kaye the following year, in the *Kid from Brooklyn,* Vera-Ellen won further excellent notices. The *Christian Science Monitor* review (April 17, 1946) referred to her as "a sprite of a performer" and called her contribution to the picture "outstanding," while other critics found her "spectacular" and "ecstatic."

In her third motion picture, *Three Little Girls in Blue* (1946), a favorably reviewed Twentieth Century-Fox film, Vera-Ellen's singing was praised along with her dancing. Another Twentieth Century-Fox production, *Carnival in Costa Rica* (1947), did not fare so well, despite a cast which included Dick Haymes, Cesar Romero, and Celeste Holm, in addition to Vera-Ellen. Howard Barnes of the New York *Herald Tribune* (March 29, 1947) described the film as "a florid and witless extravagance," adding that "of the principals, Vera-Ellen alone succeeds in capturing fleeting attention by the sheer bounce of her hoofing and make-believe."

Released from her contract with Goldwyn following these four pictures, the dancer felt that she was in a slump. "I decided that when Hollywood hit a depression," she later said, "the studio wouldn't put a specialty artist under contract. I was known only for my dancing, so I went to work on everything I could think of that might help . . . singing, dramatic courses, dancing in every form, speaking voice" (New York *Herald Tribune,* September 26, 1949). During this free-lance period, she worked for different studios, but not in the type of role that suited her. She was about to return to New York and the Broadway stage when Metro-Goldwyn-Mayer engaged her for the ballet "Slaughter on Tenth Avenue," which was a feature of the film *Words and Music,* starring Gene Kelly. For her work in the picture, released in 1948, Vera-Ellen received a seven-year contract with MGM.

The successor to this film was *On the Town* (1949), another Gene Kelly-Vera-Ellen comedy. The New York *Times* review (December 9, 1949) referred to the two as "deliciously coupled in the singing and dancing of 'Main Street' and a new Leonard Bernstein ballet, 'A Day in New York.'" At the same time the *Herald Tribune* critic commented that Vera-Ellen's solo work was "the show's dancing sensation."

Love Happy, a film presented by Mary Pickford in which Vera-Ellen appeared with Ilona Massey and the three Marx brothers, followed in 1950. In the same year MGM released *Three Little Words,* which teamed Vera-Ellen with Fred Astaire. A dance pantomime in which the two portrayed the domestic life of a pair of married dancers brought the comment from the New York *Times* critic, "The hyphenated young lady beautifully complements her partner in this imaginative, exquisitely conceived and executed number" (August 10, 1950). "Vera-Ellen, with this picture, becomes the undisputed première-danseuse of the screen," *Variety's* reviewer wrote on July 12, 1950. "She matches Astaire tap for tap in their terping duets, which is no mean achievement, and looks to be possibly the best partner he's ever had."

Also in 1950 during a visit to England, Vera-Ellen danced in the British-made film *Happy Go Lovely,* in which she, David Niven, and Cesar Romero shared the honors. Describing the film as a "featherweight" musical, Bosley Crowther of the New York *Times* spoke of "a certain limpid charm" in it "due in the main, we would reckon, to Vera-Ellen's youthfulness and grace" (July 26, 1951). The same critic had additional praise for the dancer in her next picture, *The Belle of New York* (1952), in which she was co-starred with Fred Astaire. "Add to the list of young ladies who have danced on the screen with Fred Astaire the name of Vera-Ellen, and mark it with a star," he wrote. "For this agile and twinkling charmer, who accompanied the ageless Mr. A. in his latest if not his greatest Metro musical . . . is as graceful and pleasing a dancer as any that has gone before."

Heading the cast with Ethel Merman and Donald O'Connor, Vera-Ellen was next seen in *Call Me Madam* (1953), Twentieth Century-Fox's film version of the Howard Lindsay-Russel Crouse musical comedy. For Paramount Pictures she appeared with Bing Crosby, Danny Kaye, and Rosemary Clooney in *White Christmas* (1954), filmed in Technicolor and VistaVision.

In the role of a Vermont girl visiting Scotland, Vera-Ellen starred in her second British-made musical, *Let's Be Happy* (1957), an Allied Artists release based on the play *Jeannie* by Aimee Stuart. Discussing the picture with Sheilah Graham in early 1957, she said, "I had more dialogue in it than I ever had before. I like to dance but I'm less interested in just being a dancer. I want to do some dramatic stories in television. Or situation comedies." Among several TV programs on which Vera-Ellen has danced are the *Colgate Variety Hour* (July 1955) and the *Perry Como Show* (November 1958).

Vera-Ellen has been married twice. Her first husband was Robert Hightower, a dancer. On November 19, 1954, at St. Paul's Lutheran Church in San Fernando Valley, California, she was married to Victor Rothschild. The dancer has light-brown hair and brown eyes is five feet four and a half inches in height, and weighs about 105 pounds. Her hobbies are swimming, riding, sailing, and charcoal drawing.

References

N Y Herald Tribune p22 D 4 '56 por
N Y Sunday Mirror p48 F 17 '57
San Francisco Sunday Chronicle (This World) p14 Jl 5 '53 por
International Motion Picture Almanac, 1957

VERONESE, VITTORINO (vä″rō-nā′sâ vĕt-tô′rī-nō) Mar. 1, 1910- United Nations organization official; lawyer
Address: b. UNESCO, Place de Fontenoy, Paris 7°, France; h. 21 Via Cadlolo, Rome, Italy

The first Italian citizen to head any United Nations agency and the first Continental European to occupy his position, Dr. Vittorino Veronese became the new Director General of the United Nations Educational, Scientific, and Cultural Organization on December 5, 1958. Dr. Luther H. Evans, his predecessor, hailed him as a man "profoundly attached to the spiritual values which must guide the action of UNESCO." Dr. Veronese will hold his present position for a term of six years.

Because Dr. Veronese is a militant Roman Catholic and a confirmed anti-Communist, the Soviet Union opposed his candidacy vigorously, as did some of the underdeveloped countries which feared that as a former professor and a European intellectual, he would stress cultural programs at the expense of technical assistance. But, with the support of the United States, he was elected by a margin of nearly three to one, and thus became the fourth man to hold the $20,000-a-year post of Director General of UNESCO.

Vittorino Veronese was born on March 1, 1910 in Vicenza, Italy, in the countryside near Venice. His parents are Bartolomeo and Dirce (Muzolon) Veronese. He studied at the University of Padua, where he received a Doctorate of Law degree when he was only twenty years old. For ten years he practised law, and then became a professor at the Institute of Social Sciences at the Athenaeum Angelicum in Rome. He also served as a captain in the infantry reserve.

Since Dr. Veronese did not support the Mussolini regime, he was shut out from the official life of Italy before 1944. During this period he devoted himself to a study of social and educational problems, particularly in the area of international co-operation.

During the Mussolini dictatorship Dr. Veronese also joined the Catholic Movement of University Graduates, a group of anti-fascist intellectuals who were dedicated to intellectual freedom. Many of Italy's future leaders, including Alcide de Gasperi, who became Premier in 1946, participated in the movement. In 1939 Veronese became central secretary of the group, and for some time he edited *Studium,* its democratically oriented review.

VITTORINO VERONESE

In 1944, after the fall of fascism, Dr. Veronese became secretary general of the Catholic Institute of Social Work (ICAS), and served as its president from 1944 until 1952. During the same period he served as secretary general and president of the Catholic Action movement in Italy.

In addition to being active in religious organizations, Dr. Veronese has had a distinguished career in the field of finance. An able administrator, he served the Italian government as commissioner of the Central Credit Institute, and later as its president from 1945 until 1952. The President of Italy appointed him chairman of the Public Works Credit Association in 1952. He has also served as vice-president of the Catholic Bank of Venice and as a member of the board of directors of the Bank of Rome.

Ever since Italy joined UNESCO in 1948, Dr. Veronese has attended every general session as a member of the Italian delegation. In 1952 he served as a member of a UNESCO committee which was set up to deliberate on the right to participate in cultural life, and in the same year he was unanimously elected a member of the UNESCO Executive Board.

While on the Executive Board, Dr. Veronese originated the idea of holding a series of "informal" meetings to study the reorganization of UNESCO. A much-heralded result was the "Major Projects" program, which is now the main way in which UNESCO achieves its aims. The three major projects on which UNESCO is now concentrating are directed toward the expansion of primary education in Latin America, the reclamation of arid lands through scientific research, and the promotion of mutual understanding between East and West.

(Continued next page)

VERONESE, VITTORINO—*Continued*

In 1954 Veronese was unanimously re-elected to the Executive Board. He narrowly missed being elected its chairman, tying Dr. Muldaliar of India for that position. But Dr. Muldaliar was selected by drawing lots, and Dr. Veronese served instead as vice-chairman for 1955-56. He was unanimously elected chairman for the following term, 1957-58.

At its September 1958 meeting the Executive Board of UNESCO nominated Veronese as its candidate for Director General, thereby touching off a controversy which at one point forced the Soviet Union into the anomalous position of supporting Dr. Luther H. Evans of the United States for a second term, after the United States had switched its support to Dr. Veronese.

In spite of the opposition of some of the underdeveloped Asian and African countries, as well as that of Russia, Veronese won the support of Latin American and European countries in addition to that of the United States. The final vote in his favor was 55-20, with four countries abstaining.

As the fourth Director General since UNESCO's inception in 1945, Dr. Veronese succeeded Julian Huxley of Great Britain (a noted scientist and brother of the novelist Aldous Huxley), Jaime Torres Bodet of Mexico (a cabinet minister), and his immediate predecessor, Dr. Luther H. Evans of the United States (former Librarian of Congress).

In his inaugural address on December 5, 1958, Dr. Veronese tried to quiet the fears of underdeveloped countries that he would ignore technical aid. "Assistance to scientific and cultural cooperation is not to the prejudice of technical assistance," he said, "but, on the contrary, lends it impetus." He went on: "It is one of UNESCO's main duties to convince specialists that their research work must have a bearing on technical assistance, even when it is not directly associated with it."

Dr. Veronese also called upon UNESCO to rise above the political differences of its members and to maintain a neutral position with respect to their competing ideologies. "Education, science and culture are the freest of all human activities," he said, "and should be the most independent." He warned, however, that UNESCO could not ignore the moral misgivings of the contemporary world and the search for a new social ethic. "Impartiality does not mean indifference," he said.

As Director General of UNESCO, Dr. Veronese heads an organization which has eighty-one members and six associates. He must administer its 1959-60 budget of $25,907,463, in addition to the $4,300,000 which is UNESCO's share of the United Nations Technical Assistance Program. UNESCO's program in member states is carried out only at the request of their governments and with their co-operation. It is estimated that UNESCO will have sent 300 experts to more than fifty countries in 1959.

Besides working for UNESCO, Dr. Veronese has been active in many religious and cultural organizations and has taken part in many international congresses. Since 1951 he has served as president, then honorary president, of the Association of Refugee Intellectuals in Italy. He was vice-president of the Italian delegation to the Social Conference of the European Movement (Rome, 1950) and deputy to the Italian delegation at the second congress of the Latin Union (Madrid, 1954).

Dr. Veronese is on the board of directors of the Italian Society for International Organizations, the executive committee of the Union of International Associations (Brussels), and the board of governors of the "Premi Roma" foundation for young people and the Italian-African Institute. A member of the editorial board of the review, *Africa,* Dr. Veronese is also a member of the European Cultural Society (Venice) and the Group of Twenty of the European Cultural Center (Geneva). His varied activities have been officially recognized by the Italian government, which has awarded him the Gold Medal for Service to Culture. He has also received several foreign decorations.

Vittorino Veronese and Maria Petrarca were married in 1939. In his rare moments of leisure Dr. Veronese likes to explore the historical monuments of Rome with his wife and seven children. Listening to classical music is another of his off-duty pleasures. Medium in height and bespectacled, he would be inconspicuous among the other members at UNESCO meetings if he were not so fond of wearing tweedy sport coats.

References

N Y Times p8 D 6 '58 por
UNESCO Courier 11:33+ D '58 por
Chi è ? (1957)
Panorama Biografico degli Italiani d'Oggi (1956)
Who's Who in Italy, 1957-58

VERWOERD, H(ENDRIK) F(RENSCH)

(fär-vo̅o̅rt') Sept. 8, 1901- Prime Minister of the Union of South Africa
Address: b. Union Bldgs., Pretoria, South Africa; h. Libertas, Pretoria, South Africa

The cause of Afrikaner nationalism was substantially advanced in September 1958 with the election of Dr. H. F. Verwoerd as leader of the Nationalist party and, therefore, Prime Minister of the Union of South Africa. He had previously served for a little over seven years as Minister of Native Affairs and is regarded as the architect of the apartheid doctrine of complete racial segregation. As Prime Minister in succession to the late Johannes Gerhardus Strijdom, he is furthermore pledged to making South Africa eventually a republic, probably independent of the British Commonwealth of Nations, of which it is now a member. Verwoerd, who is also a psychologist, sociologist, and farmer, was the editor during World War II of the Johannesburg newspaper, *Die Transvaler.*

Hendrik Frensch Verwoerd, born on September 8, 1901, spent only one year in his native city of Amsterdam in the Netherlands before his parents, Wilhelm Johannes and Anna Verwoerd, took him to South Africa. He has a brother, Len, a plant pathologist and farmer, and a sister, Hendrika (now Mrs. J. Cloete). Reared in the Cape Province, he went to school at Wynberg near Cape Town until his father, who later owned a book and newspaper firm, became a Dutch Reformed Church missionary and moved his family to Bulawayo in Southern Rhodesia.

At the Milton High School in Bulawayo the boy made above-average marks. He also attended school at Brandfort in the Orange Free State before entering the University of Stellenbosch in the Cape Province. While specializing at Stellenbosch in psychology and philosophy, Verwoerd engaged in various sports and became chairman of the Union Debating and Philosophical Society and of the Students' Representative Council. He was awarded his B.A. degree in 1921 and remained to study for his M.A. degree in psychology and philosophy, writing theses on certain thought processes and on the problem of values. In 1923 he was appointed a lecturer in logic and psychology at Stellenbosch.

During 1926-27 Verwoerd engaged in research work at three German universities—Hamburg, Leipzig, and Berlin—and also visited the United States. At the Leipzig psychological laboratory he conducted in 1926 the investigation described in his articles "The Distribution of 'Attention' and Its Testing" and "Effects of Fatigue in the Distribution of Attention" (*Journal of Applied Psychology,* October and December 1928).

For his Ph.D. degree he submitted the thesis *Experimental Study of the Blunting of the Emotions,* published in book form in the Annals of the University of Stellenbosch series. He was promoted at Stellenbosch to professor of applied psychology and became head of his department in 1928. For the four years beginning in 1933 he occupied the chair of professor of sociology and social work, and in 1935-36 he was the chief organizer of the National Conference on the Poor White Problem, becoming chairman of its continuation committee.

Dr. Verwoerd served on Cape Town organizations for housing and common charities (1932), unemployment (1933), and for the people of mixed race called Coloreds (1936). He led a small group of Stellenbosch professors during 1936 in a protest against the admission to South Africa of Jewish refugees from Germany.

In 1937 a new Afrikaans-language daily, *Die Transvaler,* was established in Johannesburg as a Nationalist party organ. Dr. Verwoerd became its editor in chief and remained so until 1948. Throughout World War II *Die Transvaler* "triumphantly headlined every Nazi victory" (*Time,* September 15, 1958). When Verwoerd sued the rival Johannesburg *Star* for libel in asserting that his "spiritual home was nearer to Berchtesgaden" than South Africa, he lost his case (New York *Times,* September 3, 1958). He was the author of a proposed republican constitution for South Africa pub-

State Information Office,
Pretoria

H. F. VERWOERD

lished in 1942, and in 1947 his newspaper "boycotted" the tour of the Union by the British Royal Family.

As vice-chairman of the Witwatersrand Nationalist party, Verwoerd worked hard for the victory that the Nationalists won at South Africa's first postwar general election, on May 26, 1948. He himself, however, was defeated in his attempt to represent the Alberton district of the Transvaal in Parliament. A coalition of the Nationalist and Afrikaner parties (which later merged) gained control of the House of Assembly, and in June the Union's first Nationalist government was formed, with Daniel François Malan as Prime Minister.

Later in the year Verwoerd ran successfully for the Senate, and in 1950 he joined Malan's cabinet as Minister of Native Affairs. In this position, which he occupied for the next eight years, he was the chief planner of apartheid, the policy of total segregation of the races in a country with a population of 3,000,000 white persons and about three times that number of native Africans.

"In its ultimate form," stated Professor L. Gray Cowan of Columbia University in an article on Africa in *Information Please Almanac, 1959,* "the policy of apartheid is envisaged as total separation of the races by removing the Bantus from those areas presently occupied by Europeans. They would be forced to live in reserved areas which would be under African forms of local government."

One of several major enforcement laws passed since 1950 is the Bantu Education Act (1954), which transferred the control of education of Africans from the provinces to the Minister of Native Affairs. Dr. Verwoerd was "instrumental in closing 5000 Protestant mission schools to Negroes and in enacting legisla-

VERWOERD, H. F.—*Continued*

tion to stop Africans from worshipping in white churches" (Washington *Post and Times Herald*, September 3, 1958).

At the same time he has been responsible for many improvements in Negro housing, hospitals, and schools, spending large sums of money on Bantu developments. "Then, too," John Hughes pointed out in the *Christian Science Monitor* (October 17, 1958), "there can be no doubting the sincerity of his belief that ultimately his actions will benefit the African people as a whole."

In certain extremist quarters Dr. Verwoerd was even accused of being "soft" towards the natives, and about a month before the general election of April 16, 1958 he asked to be relieved of his portfolio of Native Affairs. After eight years as a Senator he won election to the Assembly in the Heidelberg district of the Transvaal. At the April election the Nationalists under Johannes Gerhardus Strijdom (who had succeeded Malan as Prime Minister in 1954) gained a majority of 43 in the House of Assembly, the largest they had ever enjoyed.

Prime Minister Strijdom died on August 24, 1958. A week later, at a party caucus at Cape Town, Dr. Verwoerd was elected leader of the Nationalists over both Acting Prime Minister Charles R. Swart and Interior Minister Theophilus E. Donges. Sworn in as Prime Minister on September 3, Verwoerd stated in a press conference later that his government was dedicated to making South Africa a republic, but refused to discuss the date.

Hendrik Frensch Verwoerd and Elizabeth Schoombee were married on January 5, 1927 and are the parents of seven children: Wilhelm Johannes, Anna, Daniel Wynand, Elsabet, Hendrik Frans, Christiaan Andries, and Wynand Schoombee. He is a member of the Dutch Reformed Church. Of striking appearance, he is six feet one inch tall, weighs 215 pounds, and has gray eyes and graying hair. The zeal and energy with which he works suggest a driving sense of mission and self-confidence. Personal courage is said to be another of his prominent characteristics.

References

Christian Sci Mon p1 S 2 '58 por
Manchester Guardian p7 S 3 '58
N Y Post p67 S 17 '58 por
Toronto Globe and Mail Mag p15 S 27 '58 por
International Who's Who, 1958
South Africa Who's Who, 1956

VON THADDEN-TRIEGLAFF, REINOLD *See* Thadden Trieglaff, Reinold von

WALKER, ERIC A(RTHUR) April 29, 1910- University president; electrical engineer.
Address: b. The Pennsylvania State University, University Park., Pa.; h. 777 West Park Ave., College Park, Pa.

As president of Pennsylvania State University in University Park since 1956, Eric A. Walker has been studying and dealing with its various problems, and, he says, "doing all I can to solve them to the complete satisfaction of every public to which this university is responsible." Succeeding Milton S. Eisenhower, Walker became the twelfth president in the history of the land-grant institution, which was founded in 1855. He has had a long career in education, as a teacher of electrical engineering, and has also devoted much of his time to industry and government. He was born in England, came to the United States in 1923, and was naturalized in 1937.

Eric Arthur Walker was born in Long Eaton, England, on April 29, 1910, the son of Arthur and Violet Elizabeth (Haywood) Walker. He has two brothers, Frank and Alan, now both residents of the United States. His father, a lace designer, moved his family to Saskatchewan in Canada to escape the postwar economic conditions in England. From the age of ten to thirteen, Eric worked as a cook's helper in a construction camp in northwestern Canada and helped his father to build a homestead there. He then accepted an invitation to go to Pennsylvania to live with his aunt, Mrs. Bessie Warfield, at Wrightsville.

There he resumed his schooling, working meanwhile in a York County foundry before and after school hours and in a bridge construction firm during the summer. He was graduated second in his class at the Wrightsville High School in 1928; his extracurricular activities were editing the school newspaper, playing basketball, and track. A high school biology teacher, Miss Adelaide Hawk, first interested him in science and encouraged him to go to college. He accepted a scholarship to Harvard College and began his higher education with $300 of his own. At Harvard he worked at a variety of odd jobs and dropped athletics for lack of time and money. He was awarded a B.S. degree from Harvard in 1932, a master's degree in business administration in 1933, and a doctorate in engineering in 1935.

Walker's teaching career began at Tufts College in Medford, Massachusetts in 1933, where he gave courses in mathematics and electrical engineering until 1940 and served as chairman of the department of electrical engineering from 1938 to 1940. He conducted research for the Doble Engineering Company, Medford Hillside, Massachusetts, from 1935 to 1939. Joining the faculty of the University of Connecticut in Storrs in 1940, he taught electrical engineering and established courses for a special war-training program.

After the United States had entered World War II, Walker was called to Harvard as a research associate of the Underwater Sound Laboratory at Cambridge, Massachusetts, in 1942. Later he was promoted to assistant director and then associate director of the laboratory, where he had charge of the development of ordnance weapons. The homing torpedoes, used successfully against the German submarines, were developed in the laboratory.

For his work, Walker was awarded the Naval Ordnance Development Award and also a Presidential Certificate of Merit.

At the end of World War II Walker began his association with Pennsylvania State University as a professor and head of the department of electrical engineering. According to the September 1956 issue of the *Journal of the Acoustical Society of America,* "in 1945, through the efforts of Dr. Walker and the late Dr. Harry P. Hammond, then dean of the College of Engineering and Architecture, arrangements were completed to establish the Ordnance Research Laboratory at Pennsylvania State University.... The laboratory is engaged in the research and development of new weapons for the Navy."

He was named dean of the College of Engineering and Architecture at the university in 1951. According to the *Journal of the Acoustical Society of America* (September 1956), "Dr. Walker expanded the work in engineering to include the construction of a research reactor and a computation center; the development of a program in engineering science for training outstanding students who wish to enter the fields of research development and other creative aspects of engineering; the development of two-year curriculums leading to associate degrees to train engineering helpers; and the establishment of a co-operative program with six liberal arts colleges to enable students to begin their college programs at these colleges, near their homes, and then transfer to Pennsylvania State University to train in one of several fields of engineering."

Walker was named to the newly created post of vice-president of the university, effective July 1, 1956. The president, Milton S. Eisenhower, gave notice of his resignation on June 11, 1956, and Walker was appointed on June 29 to succeed him. "That," Walker once remarked, "made me probably the only vice-president of anything with a term of office of minus-two days." Actually, his inauguration took place on October 3, 1956.

One of the problems facing Pennsylvania State University is its ability to assume its fair share of the load when the college enrollment rush begins. "Mounting costs and diminishing endowments may make it impossible for the private colleges and universities to expand," he points out. "In Pennsylvania, that would bring chaos unless the State University were prepared to undertake the job." The university's enrollment on campus and in undergraduate centers is over 15,000 students and is expected to rise soon to over 25,000.

Over the years Walker has often been associated with the federal government. He was a civilian with the Office of Scientific Research and Development in 1944 and was consultant to the National Research Council from 1949 to 1950. He is a former chairman and member of the National Research Council's committee on undersea warfare. He was executive secretary of the Defense Department's Research and Development Board from 1950 to 1951 and was chairman of the National Science Foundation's advisory committee for engineering from 1951

ERIC A. WALKER

to 1953. He has been a member of the Naval Research Advisory Committee and the United States Army's Scientific Advisory Board.

President Dwight D. Eisenhower appointed Walker vice-chairman of the Committee for the Development of Scientists and Engineers in 1956 and general chairman of the Conference on Technical and Distribution Research for the Benefit of Small Business in 1957. He became a member, board of visitors, United States Naval Academy in 1958. Among his other activities have been chairmanship of the Engineering College Research Council from 1952 to 1954 and the directorship of a comprehensive study of the nation's needs for research in engineering in 1956 for the American Society for Engineering Education. He initiated the Conference on the Administration of Research in 1947 and attended in 1954 the founding of its international counterpart, the International Symposium on Research Organization and Management, at Nancy, France.

Walker's articles have been published in such periodicals as the *Journal of Engineering Education, American Journal of Physics, Junior College Journal,* and the *Bulletin* of Pennsylvania State College. With E. W. Jones he wrote *The Physical Bases of Electrical Engineering,* published in 1946 by Pennsylvania State College. He is a registered professional engineer in Pennsylvania and Connecticut, and has been an electrical engineering consultant for many years. Among his fields of special interest are instrumentation by electronics; acoustics in fluid; high-voltage insulation; electrostatics precipitation; and the application of acoustics in fluids and solids, and to precipitation, coagulation, mixing and shaking problems.

Temple University and Lehigh University awarded Walker honorary LL.D. degrees in 1957. He is a Fellow of the Acoustical Society of America, American Institute of Electrical

WALKER, ERIC A.—*Continued*

Engineers, and the American Physical Society. He is a member of the Institute of Radio Engineers, American Institute of Physics, American Society for Engineering Education (vice-president, 1952 to 1954), Newcomen Society, Sigma Xi, and Tau Beta Pi. He is a Republican and a Methodist. His club is the Cosmos in Washington, D.C.

Eric Arthur Walker married Josephine Schmeiser of Wapello, Iowa, on December 10, 1937. They have two children: Gail and Brian. For recreation he enjoys participating in such sports as golf, tennis, and squash; playing the organ; fishing; and collecting stamps (with special emphasis on plate blocks, first day covers, and mint sheets). He is a member of the American Philatelic Society. Walker is currently serving his second term on the Borough Council in State College, Pennsylvania. "Public service," he has said, "is a civic duty. I like to feel that I am doing my part."

References

Acous Soc Am J 28:993+ S '56
N Y Herald Tribune p18 Jl 1 '56
N Y Times p8 My 10 '51; p68 S 30 '56
Penn State Alumni News 43:2+ O 1 '56
American Men of Science vol 1 (1955)
Who Knows—and What (1949)
Who's Who in America, 1958-59
Who's Who in the East (1955)

WALKER, FRANK C(OMERFORD) May 30, 1886-Sept. 13, 1959 Former United States Postmaster General (1940-45); chairman, Democratic National Committee (1943-44); lawyer; businessman. See *Current Biography* (October) 1940.

Obituary

N Y Times p29 S 14 '59

WALL, ART(HUR JONATHAN), JR. Nov. 25, 1923- Golfer

Address: b. Pocono Manor Golf Club, Pocono Manor, Pa.; h. Honesdale, Pa.

In one of the most sensational events of the 1959 year in golf, Art Wall, Jr., a journeyman professional golfer with a few major tournament victories to his credit, leaped into prominence in April with a come-from-behind win in the time-honored Masters Tournament in Augusta, Georgia. Before 25,000 fans and millions more who watched the action on television, Wall shot a pressure-packed 66 over the final 18 holes to finish with a four-round total of 284, taking the $15,000 first-prize money. He followed his Masters win with second-place finishes in the Tournament of Champions, the Canadian Open, and the Insurance City golf tournament. In July he beat Dow Finsterwald in an 18-hole play-off to capture first place and $9,000 in the Buick Open at Grand Blanc, Michigan. A nation-wide poll of sports writers

and sports broadcasters named Wall "professional golfer-of-the-year" for 1959 in October 1959.

Arthur Jonathan Wall, Jr., was born on November 25, 1923 in Honesdale, Pennsylvania, the son of a representative to the Pennsylvania legislature. As a boy, he went for instruction to nearby Pocono Manor Golf Club, which he now represents as a traveling professional. He was considered something of a golf prodigy and at the age of twelve sank his first hole in one (he now has well over thirty).

By the time he entered Duke University at Durham, North Carolina, Wall was almost certain he wanted to play golf as a profession. But because he wanted a solid preparation for earning a living in another field, he majored in business administration. His roommate at Duke was Mike Souchak, who has since become an outstanding professional golfer in his own right. He beat Wall in the 1959 Tournament of Champions in Las Vegas, Nevada.

Wall first caught the attention of golf fans in 1943 when as a nineteen-year-old amateur he won the Pan-American Open. His studies at Duke were interrupted by World War II, and he served three years with the Air Force before returning to the university. He graduated in 1949. Wall had captained the Duke golf team in his senior year, and a university official has recalled, "We always knew Art would be great. He had all the shots even when he was in school here. . . . We figured he was good for three points in any important match" (*Christian Science Monitor*, April 30, 1954).

A few months after Wall had won the Pennsylvania Amateur title in 1949, he turned professional. "There was," he said, "the feeling that no matter how many tournaments I won as an amateur, they weren't apt to mean too much because most of the first-rate, experienced golfers turn pro. And I just had to see if I could play the game well enough to keep up with the pros" (*Christian Science Monitor*, May 1, 1959).

For a while Wall appeared to have chosen the wrong profession. It was two years before he received his first tournament checks, in the Anthracite, Pennsylvania and Fort Jackson, South Carolina tourneys, minor ones at best. In 1952 Wall's highest finish was at the Greensboro (North Carolina) Open, where he placed sixth. In 1953, however, he began to live up to the great things predicted of him. In eleven of his seventeen tournament appearances he finished high on the list of winners and in the Fort Wayne (Indiana) Open capped his achievements of the year with a play-off victory over Cary Middlecoff.

His first major tournament win came in April 1954, when he shot a 278 at Las Vegas to capture the Tournament of Champions by six strokes over his nearest rival. The win was worth $10,000 to him. Wall's conquest was produced by rounds of 69, 66, 70, and 73.

Two years later in the Fort Wayne Open, Wall scored his next major victory. He broke a three-way tie on the first hole of a sudden-death play-off. There was another dry spell of a year before he broke through again, capturing the Pensacola (Florida) Open with a final

Wide World

ART WALL, JR.

round of 66 and a 72-hole total of 273. In 1958 he also scored only one major win, that in the Rubber City tournament at Akron, Ohio. He beat Finsterwald on the second hole in a sudden-death play-off.

Wall's workmanlike but far from impressive record did little to prepare golf fans for his sudden blossoming in 1959. "For nine years, though winning his share of tournaments and more than his share of prize money, this quiet but articulate golfer has been one of the overlooked members of the professional circuit," Gwilym Brown wrote in *Sports Illustrated* (April 13, 1959). "Then this year, at 35, Wall seems abruptly to have reached his competitive maturity. He barely lost the Los Angeles Open to Ken Venturi's final round 63 . . . , won the Bing Crosby Invitation, finished second in tournaments at Phoenix and Tucson [Arizona] before winning the Azalea Open [at Wilmington, North Carolina] just before the Masters."

Wall's play in the Masters had enough drama to please even the most blasé golf follower. He shot a first-round 73, good only for a nine-way tie for tenth place. His second round was a mediocre 74, which placed him well back from the lead, in a seven-way tie for twenty-first. He picked up in the third round, shooting a 71, but at the end of fifty-four holes he was no better than thirteenth, six strokes off the lead.

Pacing the players into the final round were Arnold Palmer and Stan Leonard, both with 212. Middlecoff was a stroke back. And here Wall began his astonishing stretch run. He shot a closing 66, which included eight birdies, five of them in the last six holes. His 284 total beat Middlecoff by one stroke. His victory boosted his total winnings for 1959 to $33,000, the largest amount ever won by a professional golfer at that point in the year.

Wall's golf is distinguished on two points. He has been called the "Master of Concentration" and uses what is called a "baseball grip" on the club. Of the first, he said, "If you use good judgement you reduce your margin of error to one thing, faulty stroking." He added that how to think was the most important part of golf (New York *World-Telegram and Sun*, April 8, 1959).

Of the baseball grip, in which the hands are placed next to each other on the golf shaft, Wall wrote in *Golf Digest*, "I think that anyone who would like more power would be wise to try [it]. I personally think my hands are stronger and my swing is freer with this grip. The baseball grip is the perfectly natural way to hold a club. That's why I started using it, and I'll never change" (quoted in *Christian Science Monitor*, April 15, 1959).

Art Wall, Jr., is six feet tall and weighs 165 pounds. He is married and is a father. He avoids habits such as drinking and smoking that are generally considered hazardous to an athlete.

References

Christian Sci Mon p7 Ap 30 '54; p19 My 1 '59 por
N Y World-Telegram p34 Ap 8 '59
Sport Illus 10:16+ Ap 13 '59 por; 10: 38+ Ap 20 '59 por

WALLACH, ELI Dec. 7, 1915- Actor
Address: b. c/o Actors' Equity Association, 226 W. 47th St., New York 36; h. 135 MacDougal St., New York 12

A product of the Actors Studio in New York which has trained many stage and screen stars in the Stanislavski method, Eli Wallach has reached prominence on Broadway, in Hollywood films, and on television within the past six years. New York audiences have seen him in *Mr. Roberts, The Rose Tattoo, The Teahouse of the August Moon, Camino Real,* and *The Cold Wind and the Warm;* while movie viewers have acclaimed his roles in *Baby Doll* and *The Lineup.*

Eli Wallach was born in Brooklyn, New York on December 7, 1915 to Abraham and Bertha (Schorr) Wallach. His brother and two sisters became teachers, and other members of his family chose professions in law and medicine. "Being an actor to them is like joining the Foreign Legion," Wallach told Cecil Smith (Los Angeles *Times*, November 17, 1957). He was graduated from Erasmus High School and then attended the University of Texas. After receiving the B.A. degree in 1936, he returned to New York and earned the M.Sc. degree in education at City College of New York in 1938.

Deciding not to teach, Wallach turned to studying acting at the Neighborhood Playhouse School of the Theatre in New York, where he received a two-year scholarship. He had appeared in plays in grade school and later in a boys' club play when he was fourteen. His

Friedman—Abeles

ELI WALLACH

dramatic training was interrupted by World War II, and he served for several years in the Medical Corps of the United States Army.

On November 8, 1945 Wallach made his first professional stage appearance, at the Belasco Theatre as the crew chief in *Skydrift*. He subsequently appeared with Eva Le Gallienne's American Repertory Theatre on Broadway during 1946 and 1947, playing in *Androcles and the Lion, Henry VIII, Yellow Jack, Winterset,* and other dramas. Whenever he had no theatrical commitments he acted in Equity Library productions.

Still, Wallach felt that he was getting nowhere. "I had put in an application to become a postman," he has recalled (Los Angeles *Times,* November 17, 1957). "Then Joshua Logan came to a play I directed and listened to me make a speech before the curtain. I got the speech bollixed up and it was pretty funny and Logan gave me a part in *Mr. Roberts.*" In January 1949 Wallach succeeded Ted Kazanoff as Stefanowski in the play.

He kept this role until February 1951 when he was chosen to portray the Sicilian lover in Tennessee Williams' *The Rose Tattoo,* opposite Maureen Stapleton (see *C.B.,* May 1959). "Eli Wallach quit a good job in *Mister Roberts* for this new adventure," noted Ward Morehouse (New York *World-Telegram and Sun,* February 10, 1951). "He is a skillful and ingratiating performer."

"Wallach . . . must be given a large share of the interpretive honors," commented Otis L. Guernsey, Jr. (New York *Herald Tribune,* February 5, 1951). "As the fellow whose name means 'Eat a horse' in Italian, he makes a nice adjustment between nobility and buffoonery. His Mangiacavallo attracts great sympathy as well as loud laughter as he voices his despair at his own shortcomings and yet fills the stage

with an irresistible humanity." For this performance Wallach received four awards in 1951: the Donaldson, Drama Critics, Theatre, and Antoinette Perry (Tony) as the best featured actor.

After playing in *The Rose Tattoo* for the Broadway run and on tour, Wallach portrayed Kilroy in Tennessee Williams' *Camino Real.* He declined the role of Maggio in the motion picture *From Here to Eternity* (which won Frank Sinatra an Academy Award), even though he liked the part, since he had a moral obligation to appear in the Williams play. It ran for only sixty performances, from March 19 to May 9, 1953. Most of the critics thought the "poetic experiment" unsuccessful, but Brooks Atkinson in the New York *Times* (March 20, 1953) considered that, "as theatre, 'Camino Real' is an eloquent and rhythmic as a piece of music . . . the great mass of it is lucid and pertinent. . . . Wallach's good-humored, colloquial portrait of Kilroy, the American boy, is excellent."

Subsequent roles which he played successively on Broadway were the Dauphin in *The Lark,* opposite Julie Harris; Julien in *Mademoiselle Colombe,* also opposite Julie Harris; Sakini, replacing David Wayne in 1955 as the Okinawan interpreter in *The Teahouse of the August Moon* (Wallach had played this role in the London production in 1954); and Bill Walker in *Major Barbara* in 1956-57. In an off-Broadway production in early 1958 he was a doddering husband of ninety-five in Eugene Ionesco's play *The Chairs.* Then as a young intellectual, Willie Lavin, he played opposite Maureen Stapleton in *The Cold Wind and the Warm.* Adapted by S. N. Behrman from autobiographical sketches, it opened at the Morosco Theatre on December 8, 1958. Many newspaper reviews called attention to Wallach's subtlety in handling the complexity of his role.

When director Elia Kazan cast Wallach as Silva Vacarro in the Warner Brothers motion picture *Baby Doll* (written by Tennessee Williams and based on his short play *27 Wagons Full of Cotton*), he predicted that Wallach would be "the screen's most exciting actor" (New York *Mirror,* December 13, 1956). The picture proved highly controversial, was condemned by some church groups, and defended by others. The critics joined in praising Wallach's interpretation of the "tough and angry Sicilian." "He establishes himself as a top player," noted *Variety* (December 5, 1956). "His performance has many fine shades of emotion and violence," observed William K. Zinsser (New York *Herald Tribune,* December 23, 1956).

In the Columbia Pictures film *The Lineup,* Wallach played what Joe Hyams (New York *Herald Tribune,* October 31, 1957) called the most violent nonchalant murderer he had ever seen. Hyams predicted that Wallach would be the screen's newest villain. When he asked Wallach how he was able to bring such vicious reality to his performance, Wallach replied: "I make up imaginary circumstances, but I draw on remembered emotions . . . like recalling being so annoyed by a mosquito you wanted to kill it." Although he has lectured in Rome on the Stanislavski method (he is a charter member of the Actors Studio), Wallach conceded that he found it difficult to use in films. "I have great respect for the moving picture medium," he said, "because you have to act scenes separately without continuity."

Among Wallach's television roles are Albert Anastasia for a *Climax* presentation (March 1958); Poskrebyshev, Stalin's right-hand aide, in *The Plot to Kill Stalin*, produced on *Playhouse 90* (September 1958); and the gypsy Rafael in *For Whom the Bell Tolls*, also on *Playhouse 90* (March 1959). For the BBC-TV in London he appeared as George Simon in *Counsellor at Law* (December 1957) and as Tom in *The Glass Menagerie* (December 1957).

Near the beginning of his career while acting in an off-Broadway Tennessee Williams play called *This Property Is Condemned*, Eli Wallach met actress Anne Jackson. They were married on March 5, 1948. They also appeared together in 1953 in Percy MacKaye's *The Scarecrow* and in 1957 in Shaw's *Major Barbara* when she replaced Glynis Johns. They have a son, Peter David, and two daughters, Roberta and Katherine.

Of sturdy build, Eli Wallach enjoys all active sports, and he set up gymnastic apparatus in his dressing room to exercise during the run of *The Rose Tattoo*. His hobbies are woodworking and collecting antiques. He has said that he would not want to live anywhere but in New York, because his roots are too deeply imbedded there, although he likes acting in Hollywood and London occasionally. He has told newspaper interviewers that he would like to play Iago in *Othello*.

References

Los Angeles Times V p1 N 17 '57 por
N Y Post p36 Ja 13 '58 por
Who's Who in the Theatre (1957)

WALWORTH, ARTHUR (CLARENCE, JR.) July 9, 1903- Writer
Address: h. 100 Homer St., Newton Centre, Mass.

The 1959 Pulitzer Prize for biography went to Arthur Walworth for the first volume of his work on Woodrow Wilson, entitled *Woodrow Wilson; American Prophet*. This was published together with the second volume, *Woodrow Wilson; World Prophet*, by Longmans, Green & Company in 1958, after Walworth had engaged in ten years of research. For sixteen years Walworth worked for the publishing house of Houghton Mifflin in Boston. A specialist in the history of the relationship between the United States and the Far East, Walworth is the author of *Black Ships off Japan; The Story of Commodore Perry's Expedition*, published by Alfred A. Knopf in 1946. He has also written *School Histories at War* (Harvard, 1938) and *Cape Breton* (Longmans, 1948).

Arthur Clarence Walworth, Jr., the son of Arthur and Ruth (Lippincott) Walworth, was born in Newton, Massachusetts on July 9, 1903.

Sargent Studio

ARTHUR WALWORTH

His father, a civil engineer who designed cooling systems, later became president of the Vulcan Radiator Company. Walworth has one sister, Mrs. Robert Ross, of Duxbury, Massachusetts. He grew up in Newton, attended Phillips Academy in the town of Andover, Massachusetts, from which he was graduated in 1921. He played intramural baseball at Andover, and was particularly impressed by the well-known teacher of English, Claude M. Fuess.

Like his father, Walworth went to Yale, where he majored in English and was an editor of the *Yale Daily News*. At Yale, he says, he was much influenced by "the stimulating course in Modern European History that was given by Professor (later President) Charles Seymour while I was an undergraduate. Also the teaching of John M. Berdan and other teachers of English." Walworth received a B.A. degree from Yale in 1925.

After graduation Walworth went to China, where he taught English and modern European history at the college of Yale-in-China at Changsha. While teaching history, he found his students' questions about Western imperialism particularly penetrating. Walworth also traveled in Japan for six weeks in 1925, and on his way home from China spent three weeks in India and a few weeks in Italy, France, Switzerland, and England. He has never been back to the Eastern Hemisphere.

From 1927 to 1943 Walworth worked in the educational department of the Houghton Mifflin Company in Boston, doing selling, advertising, and editorial work. One of his achievements was the preparation of a revised edition of *China's Story; In Myth, Legend, and Annals* by William Elliot Griffis, which Houghton published in 1935. Walworth added three chapters to this edition of a book which Houghton had

WALWORTH, ARTHUR—Continued

first published in 1911. The new edition was generally considered a timely and interesting work on China for the uninitiated.

In 1938 the Harvard University Press published Walworth's *School Histories at War: A Study of the Treatment of our Wars in the Secondary School History Books of the United States and in those of its Former Enemies.* This scholarly, readable treatise was welcomed by educational journals as a valuable antidote to chauvinistic propaganda. At the end of 1943 Walworth left Houghton Mifflin, in order to work for the Office of War Information as a writer in the overseas branch.

After the war Walworth began to devote his full time to writing. His next book, *Black Ships off Japan; The Story of Commodore Perry's Expedition,* was published by Alfred A. Knopf in 1946. "The Perry story appealed to me," Walworth says, "as a chronicle of the first meeting, *en masse,* of men from the Western Hemisphere with men of Japan." To write the story of the opening of Japan to Western trade, the author used official records, private letters, Japanese accounts of the expedition, and an unpublished diary written against Perry's orders by one of his sailors. Published soon after the holocausts of Hiroshima and Nagasaki, the book had a timeliness which, in addition to its entertaining style, made it a considerable success. "At last," announced a headline in the New York *Herald Tribune Weekly Book Review* (April 7, 1946), "the full romantic, bizarre, amusing, shocking record."

Walworth's next work was a travel book, *Cape Breton, Isle of Romance,* published by Longmans, Green in 1948. The writer had made several trips to Nova Scotia and Cape Breton, and his book is a useful guide whose "best bits," according to Larry Nixon (*Saturday Review of Literature,* July 31, 1948), "come when the writer forgets hard-to-please people and tells of his own personal joys and his own delight at the escape from modernism that is found in this most interesting land."

For the next ten years Walworth worked on his biography of Woodrow Wilson. Among the new sources he used were the diaries of the official interpreter for the Paris Peace Conference, the complete private papers of Wilson's confidential stenographer, and the important additions Mrs. Wilson had recently made to the Wilson Collection in the Library of Congress. He also interviewed and corresponded with members of the Wilson family and other people important in Wilson's life and public career. *Woodrow Wilson; American Prophet* covers the President's life through his first administration; the second volume deals with his re-election, World War I, the peace negotiations, and the League of Nations.

Reviews were not unanimously favorable. Some critics felt that Walworth had overstressed the prophetic element in Wilson's personality and that he had bypassed important aspects of the political background. Most of them, however, agreed with J. M. Blum, who commented in the *Yale Review* (June 1958) that the biography "never smells of the lamp.

The author is particularly successful in catching the spirit of his subject, in revealing his passions and his fulfillments, his extraordinary capacity for love, for hate, for self-mastery, and for self-delusion." "Mr. Walworth's is not the last life of Woodrow Wilson that will be written," wrote Erwin D. Canham (*Christian Science Monitor,* February 20, 1958). "But it may well be one of the most careful, perceptive, and interesting among them. His style is agreeably free from pedantry. The greatness of the subject gives it grandeur and sweep." *Woodrow Wilson; American Prophet* won the Pulitzer Prize for the best biography of 1958.

In 1959 Walworth was working on a study of the American diplomatic mission to the Paris Peace Conference. As in his researches on the relationship between feudal Japan and the industrial West, the subject appealed to him as an example of diplomatic adventure between continents.

In addition to his other travels, Arthur Walworth, Jr., has visited Colombia and the Panama Canal Zone. His favorite recreation is summer camping at Medomak Camp at Washington, Maine; he enjoys coaching boys in chess, sailing, and tennis. He belongs to the First Baptist Church of Newton Centre and is an independent in politics: He is a trustee of the Yale-in-China Association.

"My methods of work," says Arthur Walworth, Jr., "are very prosaic, and my diversions unexciting. I'd much prefer that readers should be interested in my books rather than in me."

WARNER, W(ILLIAM) LLOYD Oct. 26, 1898- University professor; anthropologist

Address: b. 5835 S. Kimbark Ave., Chicago 37, Ill.; h. "Dune Acres," Chesterton, Ind.

In the forefront of sociologists who have applied the research methods of cultural anthropology to the complex problems of contemporary society, W. Lloyd Warner, professor of sociology and anthropology at the University of Chicago, has made significant contributions to the understanding of present-day American culture. He has taken a special interest in the study of class structure, symbol systems, and motivation, and he has made mobility in small-town social status and in the ranks of industrial leaders the subject of several books. Currently he is taking part in a project to study managerial employees of the federal government in somewhat the same manner that he has studied business executives.

Through such mass media as the Luce publications, the findings contained in Warner's Yankee City Series volumes have become known to the general public. These sociological analyses of life in a typical American community have been praised for their careful documentation and thorough research. In his publications both for the scholar and the general reader, Warner's conclusions are sometimes controversial, always thought-provoking.

One of three children (a boy and two girls) of William Taylor and Clara Belle (Carter) Warner, William Lloyd Warner was born in Redlands, California on October 26, 1898. He grew up also in the district around Los Angeles, lived for a time in Whittier, and was graduated from San Bernardino High School in 1917. Then after serving during 1917-18 as a private in the infantry of the United States Army, he entered the University of California in Berkeley and received his B.A. degree in 1925.

Warner's major subject at the university had been anthropology. Pursuing this interest after graduation, he began field research on Australian aborigines in 1926 under a Rockefeller Foundation fellowship. During the period from 1927 to 1929 he made a second expedition, this time for the Australian National Research Council. In his book *A Black Civilization; A Social Study of an Australian Tribe* (Harper, 1937) Warner gave an integrated picture of the Murngin society, employing a number of the various approaches of the different schools of anthropology. L. S. Cottrell, Jr., commented: "Sociologists will find the book a significant contribution to functional theory of social dynamics" (*American Journal of Psychology*, January 1938).

While taking graduate courses at Harvard University, Warner was an instructor and then assistant professor of social anthropology at the university and Radcliffe College from 1929 to 1931. He also taught at Harvard's Graduate School of Business Administration. In 1935 he became associate professor of anthropology and sociology at the University of Chicago, where he has had the rank of professor since 1941. He serves also as a member of the executive committee of the university's committee on human development. During summers he sometimes lectures at other universities, including Columbia in 1936 and California at Los Angeles in 1942.

Throughout his many years of teaching Warner has also been occupied with research on the social life of communities in New England, the South, and the Midwest, with special attention to racial relationships, class structure, and symbolic behavior. His studies have been reported in some twenty or more publications and their influence, according to Alain Touraine, "has already given rise to a vast movement of concrete research on contemporary American life" (*American Journal of Sociology*, March 1954).

In co-operation with a group of social anthropologists Warner has had a major part in preparing the Yankee City Series, published by the Yale University Press. Each volume in the projected six-volume series deals with an important aspect of life in a representative American town, a small industrial community in New England, called, for the purpose of the study, Yankee City. The five volumes that have appeared so far are *The Social Life of a Modern Community* (with Paul S. Lunt, 1941), *The Status System of a Modern Community* (with Lunt, 1942), *The Social Systems of American Ethnic Groups* (with Leo Srole, 1945), *The Social System of the Modern Factory; The Strike: A Social Analysis* (with J. O. Low, 1947), and *The Living and the Dead* (1959). The last-named volume investigates the mean-

Fabian Bachrach
W. LLOYD WARNER

ings and social functions of certain contemporary American symbol systems—political and historical, sacred and patriotic, those of the elite and commoner, of the living and the dead, and others.

As a result of his research on social structure and status, Warner defined three major classes (lower, middle, and upper) with two divisions (upper and lower) for each. His findings and interpretations in regard to the characteristics of these classes, their status symbols, and the movement from one level to another are presented not only in the Yankee City Series but also in *Democracy in Jonesville; A Study in Quality and Inequality* (with associates; Harper, 1949) and in *Social Class in America; A Manual of Procedure for the Measurement of Social Status* (with Marchia Meeker and Kenneth Eells; Science Research Associates, 1949). The latter book, reprinted by Peter Smith Publishers in 1957, is based upon about twenty years of research on social classes in American communities of less than 20,000 population. In collaboration with Mildred Hall Warner, he also wrote *What You Should Know about Social Class* (Science Research Associates, 1953).

Much of Warner's work, particularly his discussions of methodology and interpretation of material, require from the reader some training in social science. In 1953, however, he presented a concise summary and popularization of the main conclusions of his research in *American Life: Dream and Reality* (University of Chicago Press). The book is a revised form of his *Structure of American Life*, published the preceding year by the University of Edinburgh Press. "The book will help a large audience to become more conscious of the society in which it lives," Alain Touraine observed, "to cast healthy doubts on myths which fail to correspond to surrounding realities, and to fill the

WARNER, W. LLOYD—*Continued*

large gap which exists between ideology and actual behavior. Few books from this point of view are more provocative than *American Life"* (*American Journal of Sociology,* March 1954).

Also influential in applying techniques of social science to the field of marketing, consumer motivation, and related subjects, Warner was a cofounder, with Burleigh B. Gardner, in 1946 of the Chicago motivational research firm, Social Research, Inc. The overseas division of this organization opened a branch in Hamburg, Germany in 1959 to aid German industries in analyzing their products and markets from a psychological point of view.

In another area of industrial research, Warner has made comprehensive sociological studies of the careers of 8,000 leaders in all types of American business and industrial enterprise from every region of the United States. With James C. Abegglen as co-author, he presented his findings in *Big Business Leaders in America* (Harper, 1955) and the companion volume for scholars, *Occupational Mobility in American Business and Industry, 1928-52.* The authors concluded that vertical mobility in occupations has become more fluid and flexible during the past quarter of a century. Although sons with fathers at the elite levels in business still have greater opportunity, competitive forces that stress individual achievement are stronger today than in previous generations.

"Some of [the authors'] conclusions seem a little on the complacent side, perhaps as a concession to the business groups that sponsored the study," A. H. Raskin wrote in the *Saturday Review* (January 21, 1956), "but their total analysis is a valuable contribution to an improved understanding of the men who shape our economic destines."

It was announced in mid-1958 that the University of Chicago and Cornell University, under a grant from the Carnegie Corporation of New York, would undertake a three-and-a-half-year study of 20,000 executives in the federal government. The project is directed by Warner, Paul P. Van Riper of Cornell University, and Norman H. Martin of the University of Chicago. A principal question to be answered by the survey is: "In the light of the social characteristics, training and attitudes of public executives, to what extent can we expect our national administrative establishment to act in accord with the fundamental desires of the American voting public?" (New York *Times,* July 27, 1958).

Professor W. Lloyd Warner received an honorary M.A. degree from Trinity College, Cambridge University, England in 1954. He is a member of the American Anthropological Association, American Sociological Society, the Society for Research in Child Development, the Society for Applied Anthropology, and Sigma Xi.

Warner's wife, Mildred Hall Warner of Oak Park, Illinois, has shared in his work. They were married on January 10, 1932 and have two daughters, Ann Covington (Mrs. Michael Arlen) and Caroline Ranghild, and a son, William Taylor. Warner has blue eyes and brown hair, weighs 205 pounds, and is six feet two inches tall. His church is the Congregational, and in political elections he votes as an independent.

References

American Men of Science vol III (1956)
Leaders in Education (1948)
Who's Who in America, 1958-59
Who's Who in Chicago and Illinois (1950)

WEIS, MRS. CHARLES W(ILLIAM), JR. (wīs) July 8, 1901- United States Representative from New York

Address: b. House Office Bldg., Washington 25, D.C.; h. 1063 Thomas Jefferson St., N.W., Washington, D.C.; 1099 East Ave., Rochester 7, N.Y.

One of seventeen women currently serving in the United States House of Representatives, Mrs. Charles W. Weis, Jr., was elected in November 1958 from New York's Thirty-eighth District to take the seat vacated by Kenneth B. Keating. Since 1935 she has been active in the Republican party in New York state and since 1954 has been a member of the executive committee of the Republican National Committee. Her primary interests are in good government and a balanced budget.

Jessica McCullough Weis, one of two daughters of Jessie (Martin) and Charles H. McCullough, Jr., was born in Chicago, Illinois on July 8, 1901. When she was still a young girl her family moved to Buffalo, New York where her father was president of the Lackawanna Steel Company. She was educated in Buffalo schools; at Miss Wright's School in Bryn Mawr, Pennsylvania, from which she was graduated in 1916; and at Mme. Rieffel's French School in New York City in 1916-17.

On September 24, 1921 she married Charles William Weis, Jr., and moved to Rochester, New York, where her husband was a stockbroker and the chairman of the Specher Lithograph Corporation. Although her husband and three children took up most of her time, Mrs. Weis was able to participate in the social and civic activities of Rochester. In 1923 she founded the Chatterbox Club, a primarily social organization which devoted some time to charity. She was a member of the Rochester Junior League, of which she became vice-president in 1935.

That same year Mrs. Weis entered politics. Upset by "those who worried about the New Deal and didn't do anything about it" (Washington *Post and Times Herald,* February 7, 1954), she accepted Monroe County Republican leader Thomas E. Broderick's appointment as vice-chairman of the local citizens finance committee. In 1936 she organized motor caravans in support of Presidential nominee Alfred M. Landon. Although Landon was badly defeated by Franklin D. Roosevelt, Mrs. Weis was rewarded the following year with advancement to vice-chairman of the Monroe County Republican Committee, a position in which she worked for sixteen years.

Having quickly become known outside her own county, Mrs. Weis was appointed to the New York State Republican Committee's executive committee in 1938 and also was named vice-president of the National Federation of Republican Women's Clubs. In 1940 she became both the federation's second president and a delegate at large to the Republican National Convention. She attended the 1940, 1944, 1948, 1952, and 1956 conventions and was vice-chairman of the New York delegation four times.

During World War II Mrs. Weis took time from her political activities to work with the Red Cross blood bank program and the Rochester Canteen, of which she was chairman. She stepped up her political work in the 1948 Presidential election. At the Republican National Convention she seconded the nomination of Thomas E. Dewey for the Presidency and later was named associate campaign manager for the Dewey-Warren ticket. She was the first woman ever appointed to that position in a Presidential campaign.

Although Mrs. Weis helped to plan campaign strategy for both men's and women's activities, she made a special effort to arouse the reportedly lagging interest of women in the contest. She used campaign literature which stressed the Republican party's intention to appoint women to important government positions.

For the next ten years politics continued to be a major interest of Mrs. Weis. In 1954 she was appointed by President Eisenhower to the national advisory board of the Federal Civil Defense Administration and the same year was named by the State Department as an adviser to the American delegate to the Inter-American Commission of Women. In 1956 she headed the program-planning committee which streamlined the G.O.P. convention in San Francisco.

After the nomination in August 1958 of Kenneth B. Keating as Republican candidate for the United States Senate, Mrs. Weis decided to campaign for the seat in the House of Representatives that Keating would vacate. The district that she sought to represent includes the industrial eastern half of Monroe County and agricultural Wayne County. Mrs. Weis, traveling in a "land cruiser" equipped with bunks and kitchenette, covered the entire district and stopped at virtually every store, factory, fertilizer plant, and shopping center. The approximately 26,000-vote majority with which she defeated Democrat Alphonse L. Cassetti in November 1958 proved that she succeeded.

Mrs. Weis, who was assigned to the Government Operations and District of Columbia Committees, insists that she has "no violent axes to grind" (Rochester *Democrat and Chronicle*, February 13, 1959). Maintaining that she plans during her first year to learn the techniques of government, she has introduced relatively few bills.

These include proposals to encourage competition in procurement by the armed services "to better insure that [her] district receives an equitable share of defense contracts"; to prohibit state taxation on income derived exclusively in interstate commerce; to amend the Social Security Act so as to remove the limitation upon the amount of outside income which

Wide World

MRS. CHARLES W. WEIS, JR.

an individual may earn while receiving benefits; and to prohibit discrimination on account of sex in payment of wages by employers having employees engaged in interstate commerce. She has also proposed an amendment to the Constitution prohibiting discrimination on account of sex.

Mrs. Weis adheres closely to President Eisenhower's political philosophy of economy in government and a balanced budget. Insisting that "we simply have got to forego all but the most vitally important expenditures until we can put our house in order" (Rochester *Times-Union*, June 10, 1959), she has consistently opposed the "spenders."

During the first session of the Eighty-sixth Congress (1959). Mrs. Weis voted "nay" on a veterans housing bill which would increase the amount that the Veterans Administration can draw from the Treasury for direct loans (February); on the airport construction bill (March); and on a bill which authorized TVA to issue up to $750,000,000 worth of revenue bonds to finance new power facilities (May). She also opposed the housing bill (June) and a proposed increase in federal water pollution grants (June).

As a representative of a partially agricultural district, Mrs. Weis has affirmed support for Eisenhower's proposal to change the structure of the farm program. She approved a bill to continue the program which would encourage farmers to plant less than their acreage allotments (August 1959), and in June 1959 she appeared before the Senate Committee on Labor and Public Welfare in behalf of the fruit growers of her district to urge that special exemptions granted to that industry under the Fair Labor Standards Act be continued.

On other domestic issues coming before the House in 1959 the New York Representative supported the extension of the military draft

WEIS, MRS. CHARLES W., JR.—*Cont.*

(February), Hawaiian statehood (March), authorization of $180,500,000 for the National Aeronautics and Space Administration (May), an extension of the Renegotiation Act of 1951 which would enable the government to recapture excessive profits made in defense procurement contracts (May), the Landrum-Griffin labor bill (August), and the revised housing bill (August).

Because she feels that an important function of a representative is to inform the constituents, Mrs. Weis sends out periodic newsletters on major legislative issues and appears regularly on a Rochester television and radio program in which she interviews prominent political personalities.

Mrs. Weis's husband died on July 19, 1958. She has a son, Charles McCullough Weis, and two daughters, Jessica Weis Warren and Joan Weis Jameson. The New York Congresswoman, whose friends call her Judy, has gray eyes and gray hair, is five feet eight inches tall, and weighs 135 pounds. She is an effective public speaker and has long been active in welfare and philanthropic work in Rochester. She served in 1939-40 as president of the women's board of the Genesee Hospital and is a member of the Rochester Convalescent Hospital for Children and the Rochester Christmas Bureau. She also belongs to the Rochester Museum and the Rochester Business and Professional Women's Club. She is an Episcopalian. When she has time Mrs. Weis enjoys reading, gardening, bridge, and needle point.

References

N Y Herald Tribune p7 N 6 '58 por
N Y Times p28 Ja 23 '43 por
Washington (D.C.) Post p28 F 7 '54 por
Congressional Directory (1959)
Who's Who in America, 1958-59
Who's Who in United States Politics (1952)
Who's Who of American Women, 1958-59

WEIS, JESSICA MCCULLOUGH *See* Weis, Mrs. Charles W., Jr.

WELENSKY, SIR ROLAND *See* Welensky, Sir Roy

WELENSKY, SIR ROY Jan. 20, 1907-

Prime Minister of the Federation of Rhodesia and Nyasaland

Address: Wallace Ave., Broken Hill, Northern Rhodesia; Arcturus Rd., Greendale, Salisbury, Southern Rhodesia

One of the principal architects of the Federation of Rhodesia and Nyasaland, which came into being in August 1953, and its Prime Minister since November 1956, Sir Roy Welensky has been called a "crucial" statesman in the British Commonwealth. At a conference sched-

uled to be held some time in 1960 it is expected that he will ask full Commonwealth status for the federation that he heads. Welensky, who terms himself a "Socialist Conservative," had been a locomotive fireman and engineer and a trade union official before entering politics in 1938 as a candidate for election to the Northern Rhodesian Legislative Council. In the matter of race relations he has been called "a middle-of-the-road white paternalist who often finds himself caught between racial extremes" (New York *Times,* March 24, 1959).

"As you know, I do not have a drop of English blood in my veins, but if there is one thing I stand for . . . it is a belief in the British Empire." These words were written to a friend some years ago by Sir Roy Welensky, whose father, Michael Welensky, was a Jew from Vilna in Poland, and whose mother, Leah Welensky, came of South African Dutch stock. The youngest of their thirteen children, he was born on January 20, 1907 at Salisbury, Southern Rhodesia, where his father was running a saloon and boarding house. Although Roland was the name given Welensky at his christening, he has always been called Roy.

Welensky spent his childhood at Johannesburg in the Transvaal and at Salisbury, where he entered a government school at the age of seven. His mother died when he was eleven. At fourteen he left school to earn his own living and help support his aged father. "For two years," Don Taylor noted in his biography *The Rhodesian* (Museum Press, 1955), "the young Rhodesian roamed around the country in carefree style. He worked not only as a barman, but also as a butcher, a baker, a clerk to a second hand dealer, a 'kaffir storekeeper,' and a mines storekeeper."

In 1924, when Welensky was seventeen, he went to live with an aunt at Bulawayo in Southern Rhodesia. Through her husband he got a job as a fireman on Rhodesian Railways. He was promoted to engine driver when he was twenty-one and in 1933 was transferred to Broken Hill in Northern Rhodesia, his permanent home ever since. For a time he fought as a professional boxer and from 1925 to 1927 held the heavyweight boxing championship of the Rhodesias.

At the time of Welensky's arrival at Broken Hill the racial doctrines of Nazism were rife among railway workers, and the half-Jewish newcomer's locomotive was once defaced with anti-Semitic scrawls. He decided to combat the evil through what Don Taylor described as "trade unionism on the long-tried British model." Accepting the chairmanship of the almost defunct local branch of the Railway Workers' Union, he gained several concessions for the workers in negotiations and was elected to his union's national council.

In 1935 Welensky became politically active as a supporter of Stewart Gore-Browne, one of seven successful candidates for election to the North Rhodesian Legislative Council. They were pledged to press not only for changes in the local constitution, giving greater voice to the white settlers, but also for amalgamation with Southern Rhodesia. (A British protectorate since 1924, when administration was taken over from the South African Company founded by Cecil Rhodes, Northern Rhodesia was largely controlled by the Colonial Office in London, acting through a Governor who appointed the majority of the members of both the Legislative and Executive Councils). Welensky became an "unofficial" (i.e., elected) member of the Legislative Council in 1938 and of the Executive Council in 1940.

Although the administration of Northern Rhodesia had passed from the South African Company, the latter continued to monopolize the protectorate's vast mineral resources. Strikes and rioting in the copper belt early in 1940 brought the appointment first of a wartime Manpower Committee, of which Welensky became a member, and afterward a Parliamentary commission of enquiry headed by Sir John Forster.

As a member of Forster's commission, Welensky supported proposals by Gore-Browne for the formation of African regional and representative councils. Nevertheless, when Welensky formed the Northern Rhodesian Labour party in 1941, it was pledged to protect the security of the white worker against cheap black competition. From 1941 until the end of World War II, Welensky served as Northern Rhodesia's Director of Manpower; he was a member of the Strauss Railway Arbitration Tribunal in 1943 and in 1946 served on the Grant Tribunal. During the latter year he succeeded Gore-Browne as chairman of the Unofficial Members Association.

Visiting London in 1949, Welensky was primarily responsible for securing an important economic agreement which provided that the British South Africa Company give 20 per cent of its mineral royalties to the Northern Rhodesian government until 1986. After that year the rights would be transferred to the government.

For some time Welensky had been working with Sir Godfrey Huggins (later Lord Malvern), the Prime Minister of the self-governing colony of Southern Rhodesia (see *C.B.*, November 1956), for a closer political association of the two Rhodesias. A scheme for a "Capricorn Federation" had already been rejected by the ruling British Labour party, many members of which feared white domination of the Africans, but the return of the Conservatives to power in 1950 brought the appointment as Colonial Secretary of Oliver Lyttelton, who favored the principle of federation.

Plans for a federation of the Rhodesias and adjacent Nyasaland were discussed in London in 1950 and 1951 and in the latter year also at a Closer Association Conference at Victoria Falls on the Zambezi, where Welensky headed the Northern Rhodesian delegation. A constitution was approved by the British Parliament in March 1953 and later ratified through a plebiscite in Southern Rhodesia and by the Legislative Councils in Northern Rhodesia and Nyasaland. The constitution provided for a Federal Assembly consisting of thirty-five members, nine of whom (six Africans and three whites) represented African interests. Contrary to the hopes of both Huggins and Welensky, dominion

John Akester

SIR ROY WELENSKY

status was not conferred on the federation, and both Northern Rhodesia and Nyasaland remained protectorates.

Sir Roy Welensky (he was knighted by Queen Elizabeth II in June 1953) served as Minister of Transport, Communications and Posts in the interim government headed by Sir Godfrey Huggins which functioned until the first federal election, on December 15, 1953. At this election the new Federal party, formed by Huggins and Welensky and dedicated to "racial partnership," won twenty-four of the twenty-six election seats. The Confederate party, favoring the total segregation doctrine of South African Prime Minister Daniel François Malan (apartheid), won only one.

When the Assembly convened in February 1954 and Huggins was confirmed as Prime Minister, Welensky was named Deputy Prime Minister. He continued also as Minister of Transport until November 1956. At that time Huggins (now Lord Malvern) resigned as Prime Minister, and Welensky took office as Prime Minister, Minister of External Affairs, and Minister of Defence. In June 1959 he relinquished the Defence portfolio.

During 1957 the British government agreed to a conference in 1960 on greater independence, and possibly full Commonwealth status, for the Rhodesia-Nyasaland federation. Also in 1957 the federal constitution was amended to increase the Assembly from thirty-five to fifty-nine members and eventually eliminate racial representation. A new federal election, held in November 1958, resulted in a landslide victory for Sir Roy's United Federal party. In the balloting for Northern Rhodesia's first elected multiracial Legislative Council in March 1959, however, the United Federal party failed to win a clear majority.

(Continued next page)

WELENSKY, SIR ROY—*Continued*

In the spring of 1959 serious rioting by natives broke out in Nyasaland, which is overwhelmingly Negro, in protest against continued federation. Sir Roy explained in the Federal Assembly that nationalism in Nyasaland had been deeply affected by the All-Africa People's Conference in Ghana in December 1958. "This is a multi-racial country," he stated, "and the Europeans have no intention of being pushed out or massacred" (New York *Times,* April 8, 1959).

Lady Welensky is the former Elizabeth Henderson. Married March 21, 1928, the Welenskys have one son and one daughter, Joan Leah, now Mrs. Dennis Bridge. Sir Roy, who stands more than six feet tall and weighs 320 pounds, is a "bulky, ruddy, tufty-browed man . . . noted for a blunt outspokenness" (*Christian Science Monitor*). He is also described as "a man of real charm [who] makes it clear he wants very much to be liked" (New York *Times*). Music, gardening, and shooting are among his diversions. In March 1959 he was made Knight Commander of the Order of St. Michael and St. George.

References

> Christian Sci Mon p9 My 28 '53; p9 D 27 '56 por
> Life 34:57+ My 4 '53 pors
> N Y Times p16 Mr 24 '59
> Toronto Globe and Mail Globe Mag p7 Ja 10 '59 por
> Central and East African Who's Who (1955)
> Gunther, J. Inside Africa (1955)
> International Who's Who, 1958
> International Year Book and Statesmen's Who's Who, 1958
> Kelly's Handbook to the Titled, Landed and Official Classes, 1958
> South African Who's Who, 1958
> Who's Who, 1958

WELLS, AGNES (ERMINA) Jan. 4, 1876-July 6, 1959 Educator; mathematician; astronomer; dean of women at Indiana University (1918-38); chairman, National Woman's party (1949-51). See *Current Biography* (November) 1949.

Obituary

> N Y Times p29 Jl 8 '59

WHITE, W(ILLIAM) WILSON Feb. 23, 1906- Former United States government official; lawyer
Address: h. Lynnebrook Lane, Philadelphia 18, Pa.

"The field of race relations is one where mutual understanding is of the highest importance," said W. Wilson White, when he was Assistant Attorney General in charge of the new civil rights division of the United States Department of Justice. "Feelings run so high that if some one can moderate differences, he can often come up with the right answer. Often, if people feel they can get a fair shake, troubles can be resolved."

His appointment to the civil rights division was made by President Dwight D. Eisenhower in December 1957, soon after William P. Rogers became Attorney General. The Senate delayed confirmation of White's nomination until August 1958. Previously White had been Assistant Attorney General in charge of the Justice Department's office of legal counsel and, earlier, United States attorney for eastern Pennsylvania. On September 28, 1959 White resigned as Assistant Attorney General in charge of civil rights to return to the private practice of law.

William Wilson White was born in Philadelphia, Pennsylvania on February 23, 1906, the son of Thomas Raeburn and Elizabeth (Wilson) White. His father, a member of the Philadelphia firm of White, Williams & Scott, is still a practising lawyer and has been active in civic and Republican affairs in that city. Raised as a Quaker, White was graduated from the Germantown Friends School in 1923. He was granted the A.B. degree from Harvard College in 1930 and three years later, the LL.B. degree with honors from the University of Pennsylvania Law School, where he was editor in chief of the *Law Review*.

After his admission to the Pennsylvania bar in 1933, he joined his father's firm, White, Williams & Scott, in Philadelphia. There he specialized in corporation law and spent much time in trial courts. When the United States entered World War II, he became a lieutenant in the Navy and subsequently served as commander of a submarine chaser on the West coast and as executive officer of a troopship in the Pacific Ocean. He was discharged with the rank of commander in 1946 and returned to his law practice in Philadelphia.

In April 1953 President Dwight D. Eisenhower appointed White to be United States attorney for the Eastern District of Pennsylvania. He found that post "absolutely fascinating" and, according to the New York *Times* (August 19, 1958), established an outstanding record by cleaning up a backlog of more than 2,000 criminal cases and disposing of 3,000 civil cases in his four years there. He handled several cases of police mistreatment of minorities and tried to solve them by mediation. "We were able to work most of them out in conference," he explained once, "and never actually had them to trial."

The most publicized case that he prosecuted was the seventy-one-day trial in 1954 of nine Communists in the Philadelphia area accused of conspiracy to teach and advocate the overthrow of the United States government by force. He won the case, which he later described as "a grueling grind." The nine were convicted by a jury of seven women and five men on August 13, 1954; four were given three-year sentences and five were given two-year terms in June 1955. White had asked for maximum sentences of five years' imprisonment and fines of $10,000 each under the Smith Act.

President Eisenhower nominated White on February 27, 1957 to succeed J. Lee Rankin as an Assistant Attorney General. He assumed this position on March 25, 1957, taking charge of the office of legal counsel within the United States Department of Justice at a salary of $22,000 a year. This office had the task of preparing the legal documents surrounding the dispatch of Federal troops to enforce desegregation in Central High School in Little Rock, Arkansas in the fall of 1957. White drafted the Presidential proclamation and executive orders dealing with the crisis.

After Congress passed the Civil Rights Act of 1957, President Eisenhower selected White to head the newly created civil rights division of the Department of Justice. He took office on December 9, 1957 as Assistant Attorney General in charge of the division under a recess appointment. The nomination for his permanent appointment was submitted to the Senate in January 1958. Hearings were held by the Senate Judiciary Committee, headed by Senator James O. Eastland, Democrat of Mississippi, one of the leading Congressional opponents of civil rights action.

When questioned by the Judiciary Committee about his views on civil rights, White said that he could make no precise commitments and would be guided entirely by circumstances. "But," he added, "I can say categorically that it is not the program of the Justice Department to enforce school integration at the point of a bayonet" (New York *Herald Tribune,* August 7, 1958). He refused, however, to rule out the possibility that troops might again be called out to ensure school integration. After a six-month delay, arising from the opposition of Southern leaders to White because of his drafting of the legal bases for use of federal troops in the Little Rock conflict, his nomination was passed on by the Judiciary Committee and confirmed by the Senate on August 18, 1958 by a vote of 56 to 20.

The civil rights division was authorized by Congress to bring civil suits against anyone who tries to prevent a United States citizen from voting for racial or color reasons. It will also handle the enforcement of other civil rights statutes. In line with his ideal of moderation, White announced that he would appoint some Southerners to his legal staff of sixty, "to get their point of view and that of their part of the country" (New York *Herald Tribune,* August 7, 1958).

The United States government tested its power under the 1957 Civil Rights Act for the first time in September 1958 by asking a federal district court to grant an injunction against the registrars of Terrell County, Georgia, to bar them from preventing qualified Negroes from registering to vote. The Justice Department suit accused the registrars of refusing to allow Negro college graduates to register to vote on grounds that they could not read correctly. White said that a study by the civil

W. WILSON WHITE

rights division had begun in April 1958 and had covered registration activities in the county for the past two years. On April 16, 1959 a Macon, Georgia federal judge held unconstitutional the provision of the 1957 Civil Rights Act which granted the federal government the right to sue for injunctions against encroachments on Negro voting rights.

His article "In Defense of the Grand Jury" appeared in the *Pennsylvania Bar Association Quarterly* in April 1954. White is a member of the American, Pennsylvania, and Philadelphia bar associations and belongs to the Order of the Coif, Phi Kappa Sigma society and Philadelphia Cricket Club. He was director of the world affairs council of the American Legion from 1949 to 1950 and is a former judge advocate of the legion.

W. Wilson White married Mary Lowber Sailer on December 27, 1932. They have three sons: William Wilson, Welsh Strawbridge, and Alexander Strawbridge. He became an Episcopalian at the time of his marriage. The New York *Times* (August 19, 1958) wrote: "A pleasant man of medium height, White has gracious manners. His rather severe face lights up when he smiles. In a conversation he looks directly at a person out of dark-brown eyes." For recreation he enjoys playing golf, gardening, and making cabinets and tables. He lives in a contemporary contour house at the edge of a hill on Lynnebrook Lane in the Chestnut Hill section of Philadelphia.

An indefatigable worker, White often stays on a difficult job until midnight and through weekends. His theory is: "You've got to like what you're doing. You've got to be willing to give it all the time it needs. It's the only way to get the job done right." The Washington *Post and Times Herald* (August 14, 1958)

WHITE, W. WILSON—*Continued*

commented that White's "legal ability, his integrity and his devotion to duty have been generally recognized."

References

N Y Herald Tribune p3 Ag 7 '58 por
N Y Post p18 S 22 '58 por
N Y Times p21 Ag 19 '58
U S News 43:19 N 29 '57; 45:12 Ag 29 '58

Martindale-Hubbell Law Directory, 1958
Who's Who in America, 1958-59

WHYTE, WILLIAM H(OLLINGS-WORTH), JR. Oct. 1, 1917- Writer; editor

Address: b. Fortune, 9 Rockefeller Plaza, New York 20; h. 180 E. 75th St., New York 21

In his books and articles William H. Whyte, Jr., assistant managing editor of *Fortune* magazine, has analyzed and criticized the customs of American corporations and suburbia which orient the life of an executive toward the values of the group rather than of the individual. Simon & Schuster published Whyte's *Is Anybody Listening?* in 1952 (written with the editors of *Fortune*) and *The Organization Man* in 1956, for which he was honored with the American Library Association Liberty and Justice Award of $5,000 the following year.

His articles have appeared in *Fortune, Harper's Magazine, Life, Encounter, Saturday Review,* and *Reader's Digest,* sometimes under the pseudonym of Otis Binet Stanford. In 1953 he received the Benjamin Franklin Magazine Writing Award. Some of his articles have been reprinted in book collections. Whyte joined *Fortune* in 1946 and assumed his present position there in 1953.

WILLIAM H. WHYTE. JR.

William Hollingsworth Whyte, Jr., the son of William Hollingsworth and Louise Troth (Price) Whyte, was born in West Chester, Pennsylvania on October 1, 1917. His father was in railroading. He has a brother, Robert Whyte. He attended St. Andrew's School in Middletown, Delaware, where he was editor of the school newspaper. He was graduated in 1935. At Princeton University he won an undergraduate playwriting contest, was on the editorial staff of the *Nassau Lit,* and became a member of the Quadrangle Club. He was granted the A.B. degree, *cum laude,* in 1939, after majoring in English.

From 1939 to 1940 he was an apprentice at the Vick School of Applied Merchandising and then was associated with the Vick Chemical Company until 1941, when in October he entered the United States Marine Corps. He joined the 1st Marine Division, rising to the rank of captain and served in Europe and the Pacific during the course of World War II. Later he was attached to the chief intelligence section of the Marine Corps Staff and Command School at Quantico in Virginia. He was discharged from the service in October 1945.

Joining the editorial staff of *Fortune* in June 1946, Whyte became an associate editor of the magazine in 1948 and assistant managing editor in 1953. He headed the *Fortune* study on communications from 1949 to 1951. His articles for *Fortune* have dealt with many aspects of the modern American corporation and its executives, covering such topics as sabbaticals for businessmen, the language of advertising, the wives of management, the fallacies of personality testing, and the high-pressured lives of executives.

Some of his articles have been reprinted in *Prize Articles, 1954; The Benjamin Franklin Magazine Awards administered by the University of Illinois* (Urbana, 1954), edited by Llewellyn Miller; *Explorations: Reading, Thinking, Discussions, Writing* (New York, 1956), edited by T. C. Pollock and others; *Meaning in Reading* (New York, 1956), edited by J. H. Wise and others; *Readings for Thought and Expression* (New York, 1956), edited by S. S. Morgan and others; and *Readings in Social Science* (Michigan State University, 1958).

Is Anybody Listening? How and Why U.S. Business Fumbles When It Talks with Human Beings (1952) was written by Whyte and the editors of *Fortune,* with drawings by Robert Osborn. In the New York *Times Book Review* (April 6, 1952), D. L. Cohn wrote: "This is an inquiry . . . into a massive failure of American business; namely, the failure to 'sell' free enterprise to the people. It is the more grievous because presently business is concerned more with selling itself than with selling merchandise. And it is phenomenal, since its failure flows from no deep-seated antipathy of the people to business but from the inability of business to talk humanity to human beings." Excerpts from the book were printed in *Life* on January 7, 1952.

After three years of reading, interviewing and writing, Whyte finished *The Organization Man,* published by Simon & Schuster in 1956. The Anchor Books paperback edition had extended to 225,000 copies in four printings by the end of 1958. In this book Whyte studies the ideology, training, and neuroses of the men who give their allegiances as employees to The Organization, of which the complex business corporation is an example. This type of collectivization is also seen in education, in the church, in research foundations, in medicine, and in all parts of American society.

The book postulates that the old "Protestant Ethic" of individual independence, self-reliance, and ambition is being replaced in modern America with a new "Social Ethic," which makes morally legitimate the pressures of society against the individual, by promoting the belief in the group as the source of creativity, the belief in belongingness as the ultimate need of the individual, and the belief in the application of science to achieve that belongingness. No longer is the brilliant individual who achieves greatness in spite of the opposition of society a hero. Today the team player is the ideal. The cult of the group can be pleasant and comforting, he observes, but also flat, unenterprising, tyrannical, and imposing a dreary conformity.

At the end of his book Whyte writes that men "must *fight* The Organization. Not stupidly, or selfishly, for the defects of individual self-regard are no more to be venerated than the defects of co-operation. But fight he must, for the demands for his surrender are constant and powerful, and the more he has come to like the life of organization the more difficult does he find it to resist these demands, or even to recognize them. It is wretched, dispiriting advice to hold before him the dream that ideally there need be no conflict between him and society. There always is; there always must be. Ideology cannot wish it away; the peace of mind offered by organization remains a surrender, and no less so for being offered in benevolence. That is the problem."

C. Wright Mills commented that Whyte "has the patience carefully to analyze malarkey; the writing skill to make details so fascinating the reader overlooks his inattention to their fuller meaning. His belief in the value of the individual mind lends an edge to his work, and makes his description of the ethos of the technician in America today among the best available" (New York *Times Book Review,* December 9, 1956). In summing up the book, Orville Prescott wrote: "When adjustment to others and to the organization becomes the supreme virtue, Whyte asks, what will become of the individual soul and the health of the nation? Other than pious hopes for a renewed emphasis on our traditional belief in the individual's superiority to society, Whyte has no answer" (New York *Times,* December 14, 1956).

At a ceremony in New York the American Library Association on April 25, 1957 presented the first ALA Liberty and Justice Book Awards of $5,000 each to three writers, one of whom was Whyte for *The Organization Man.* These awards, set up by the Fund for the Republic, are given for books which "make distinguished contributions to the American tradition of liberty and justice." Whyte's book won for him in the category of Contemporary Affairs and Problems (nonfiction). Judges for this category were Herbert Brucker, editor of the Hartford (Connecticut) *Courant,* Justice William O. Douglas of the United States Supreme Court, and Margaret Chase Smith, United States Senator from Maine.

During the winter and spring of 1957-58 a series of articles by the editors appeared in *Fortune* dealing with problems arising from the rapid and chaotic growth of cities and suburbs in the United States. The series was published in book form by Doubleday & Company in 1958 under the title of *The Exploding Metropolis,* with an introduction by Whyte, who also wrote two of the articles, "Are Cities Un-American?" and "Urban Sprawl." In the latter he challenges communities to face the urgent threat of the metropolitan sprawl and suggests that by a state-financed program, communities can reserve open space now by buying land outright or buying the development rights to it.

William H. Whyte served on the board of trustees of St. Andrew's School in Middletown, Delaware and is a trustee of the Episcopal Church School Foundation. He has hazel eyes and brown hair; he weighs 170 pounds and is five feet eleven inches tall. He is an Episcopalian and a Democrat. He is a member of the National Society for the Study of Communication, and his club is the Princeton in New York.

Reference

Who's Who in America, 1958-59

WIGGEN, HENRY W. *See* Harris, Mark

WIGGLESWORTH, RICHARD B(OW-DITCH) Apr. 25, 1891- United States Ambassador to Canada

Address: American Embassy, Ottawa, Canada; h. 203 Adams St., Milton, Mass.

Appointed United States Ambassador to Canada on October 29, 1958, Richard B. Wigglesworth of Massachusetts assumed his first diplomatic post after thirty years of continuous membership in the United States House of Representatives and on the House Appropriations Committee. He made his mark as "chairman or the most influential member of the subcommittees that fixed the budget allocations for the military defense of the United States and for the collective security of the West" (Arthur Krock, New York *Times,* June 26, 1958). In his ambassadorial assignment he succeeded Livingston T. Merchant.

Richard Bowditch Wigglesworth was born in Boston, Massachusetts on April 25, 1891, one of the six children of the late George and Mary Catherine (Dixwell) Wigglesworth. His father, a lawyer and financier with extensive textile interests, was sixth in descent from Edward

Harris & Ewing

RICHARD B. WIGGLESWORTH

Wigglesworth who came to Charlestown, Massachusetts in 1638. His mother was a granddaughter of Nathaniel Bowditch, mathematician and navigator, and a sister-in-law to Oliver Wendell Holmes.

After being graduated in 1908 from Milton Academy in Massachusetts, Wigglesworth entered Harvard College, where he was an All-American football quarterback and an outfielder on the baseball team. He received the B.A. degree in 1912. For a short time in the following year he was private secretary to W. Cameron Forbes, Governor-General of the Philippine Islands, before entering Harvard Law School.

Having earned his LL.B. degree and admission to the Massachusetts bar in 1916, Wigglesworth practised law in Boston. In his free time, he was a quarterback and backfield coach with Percy Haughton's football team. During World War I, Wigglesworth served with the United States Army in France as captain of Battery E and later as commanding officer, First Battalion, 303d Field Artillery, 76th Division. After his return to civilian life, he was legal adviser to the United States Assistant Secretary of the Treasury in charge of foreign loans and railway payments and secretary of the World War Foreign Debt Commission (1922-24). From 1924 to 1927 he was assistant to the agent general for reparations payments at Berlin. Then in 1927 he was appointed representative and general counsel for organizations created under the Dawes plan.

Wigglesworth was in Paris in 1928 when he accepted the Republican nomination for United States Representative of the Fourteenth Massachusetts District. He was nominated both for the unexpired term of the late Louis A. Frothingham, a Republican, and for the regular term beginning in 1929. Unopposed at the November 6, 1928 election, he immediately took the oath of office. Through the reapportionment resulting

from the 1930 census, Wigglesworth's district, which includes Quincy, Brockon, Milton, and part of Boston, became the Thirteenth District.

At the beginning of his Congressional career, Wigglesworth was assigned to the House Appropriations Committee, the only permanent committee on which he ever served. With two other minority members of the Appropriations Committee, he issued a report on relief spending which suggested that no federal appropriation be "used for competition with private business" (Arthur Krock, New York *Times*, May 12, 1938). In 1940 he was made chairman of the speakers' bureau of the Republican National Committee.

In the summer of 1943 Wigglesworth called unsuccessfully for a Rules Committee investigation of charges by Vice-President Henry A. Wallace that Secretary of Commerce Jesse H. Jones was "hamstringing the Board of Economic Warfare." As one of the two Republican members of a special House committee investigating the Federal Communications Commission, he said in 1944 that the Roosevelt Administration had "from the first" sought to "sabotage" its investigation. In the Republican-controlled Eightieth Congress, Wigglesworth headed an Appropriation subcommittee concerned with FCC funds.

While serving on the Joint Committee on Reduction of Nonessential Federal Expenditures in 1947, Wigglesworth had a hand in writing the "legislative budget" which recommended a $6 billion reduction in the Truman administration estimates. As head of an Appropriations subcommittee study of the Veterans Administration's budget, Wigglesworth asserted that $493,000,000 could be cut from the VA's appropriation of $6.9 billion without contracting its services. Nevertheless, the agency received the $6.9 billion appropriation.

When a $56 billion armed services appropriation bill was under consideration by the House, Wigglesworth called the sum a "down payment on tragic errors in judgment made at Teheran, Yalta, and Potsdam" (New York *Times*, August 9, 1951). In 1953, when the Republican party controlled Congress, Wigglesworth served as chairman of the Appropriations subcommittee on armed services, and, a year later, was floor manager during the $28.6 billion defense appropriation bill. A slightly higher figure was passed in June.

During his long Congressional tenure some votes cast by Wigglesworth on significant financial issues included a "yea" to reduce federal spending by $600,000,000 (May 1950), a "yea" to increase the debt limit to $290 billion (July 1953), and "nay" to an additional $99,000,000 to the Department of Defense's appropriation in order to retain Army strength at 900,000 troops (June 1958).

On labor legislation he voted for the employment-production bill (December 1945), the full-employment bill (February 1946), overriding the veto of the Taft-Hartley bill (June 1947), using the Taft-Hartley Law in the steel strike (June 1952), and the temporary unemployment compensation act (May 1958). He opposed raising unemployment benefits in July 1954. Regarding civil rights proposals, he favored the anti-poll tax bill (June 1945), the school construction aid bill and its Powell amendment (July 1956), and the civil rights bill (June 1957).

On other domestic issues he approved the creation of a permanent committee on un-American activities (January 1945), a two-term limit for the Presidency (February 1947), quit-claim offshore oil bill (April 1953), atomic energy bill (July 1954), Social Security amendments (July 1955), and Department of Defense reorganization bill (June 1958).

Congressman Wigglesworth cast negative votes on the WPA bill (January 1939), termination of price controls (June 1952), increasing Congressional salaries (February 1955), and Alaska statehood bill (May 1958).

In foreign policy he favored the lend-lease appropriation (March 1941), a $1.3 billion contribution to UNRRA (December 1945), a $3.7 billion loan to Great Britain (July 1946), Greek-Turkish aid bill (May 1947), Korea-Formosa economic aid bill (February 1950), Eisenhower Middle East Doctrine (January 1957), and Mutual Security appropriation (August 1957). He opposed the arms embargo (November 1939), revision of the Neutrality Act (November 1939), guarantees for American capital abroad (July 1950), and cutting European economic aid by $350,000,000 (August 1951).

Representative Wigglesworth won his last election in November 1956 when he defeated Democrat Richard E. McCormick by 109,950 votes to 87,719. On June 9, 1958 the Congressman announced that he would not seek re-election.

On October 29, 1958, a week after United States Ambassador Livingston T. Merchant had been recalled from Ottawa to resume the post of United States Assistant Secretary of State for European Affairs, President Eisenhower announced the recess appointment of Richard B. Wigglesworth as United States Ambassador to Canada.

Commenting on the appointment, the Toronto *Globe and Mail* (November 1, 1958) noted that, while the new envoy was "not a career diplomat in the sense that Mr. Merchant is," he "brings considerable intellectual ability to his task which will help him overcome quickly the initial obstacles of an unfamiliar role." The *Globe and Mail* also pointed out Wigglesworth's initial opposition in May 1954 to the construction of the St. Lawrence Seaway because of the economic threat it posed to the port of Boston and its railroads. On December 15, 1958 Wigglesworth presented his letters of credence to Governor-General Vincent Massey.

Richard Bowditch Wigglesworth and Florence Joyes Booth of Louisville, Kentucky were married April 30, 1931 and have three daughters, Ann Joyes, Mary Dixwell, and Jane Booth. Ambassador Wigglesworth is an enthusiastic yachtsman. His church is the Unitarian. He belongs to various veterans' organizations and bar associations.

References

N Y Sun p17 Ag 3 '43
Biographical Directory of the American Congress, 1774-1949 (1950)
Who's Who in America, 1958-59

WILDE, FRAZAR B(ULLARD) Jan. 26, 1895- Insurance executive
Address: b. Connecticut General Life Insurance Co., 900 Cottage Grove Rd., Bloomfield, Conn.; h. 65 Walbridge Rd., West Hartford 7, Conn.

In the twenty-three years that Frazar B. Wilde has been its president, the Connecticut General Life Insurance Company has grown from a regional organization to the nation's third largest insurance concern owned by stockholders, with assets of nearly $2 billion. A pioneer in group insurance for airlines, Wilde has done much to advance life insurance in the United States, and in 1958 he was president of the Life Insurance Association of America. Wilde was appointed in May 1958 to the chairmanship of a twenty-five-member commission on money and credit, organized by the nonpartisan Committee for Economic Development to undertake a "full-fledged study of the nation's monetary structure." According to *Business Week* (May 31, 1958), it is "the most important commission on money problems in fifty years."

Of old New England ancestry, Frazar Bullard Wilde was born on January 26, 1895 in Boston, Massachusetts and was brought up in Hartford, Connecticut, where his father, Edwin F. Wilde, was for many years in charge of the local office of Lee, Higginson and Company. A graduate of the Hartford Public High School, the younger Wilde worked as a newspaper reporter before joining the Connecticut General Life Insurance as an office boy in 1914.

The company, of which Robert W. Huntington became president in 1901, had been organized in 1865 to provide life insurance for persons of substandard health. Its accident department dates from 1912, and a year later, when group insurance was "still a pioneering idea," the company wrote its first group life case, covering employees of the Hartford *Courant*.

Wilde's long period of employment in the insurance firm was interrupted only by military service. He was called to active duty with Troop B of the Connecticut National Guard on the Mexican border in 1915, was commissioned a first lieutenant in 1917, and as a field artillery officer saw World War I service with the AEF in Europe. Returning to Connecticut General in 1919, he worked briefly as a traveling auditor before being put in charge of the company's new claims department. He was

Karsh, Ottawa

FRAZAR B. WILDE

promoted to secretary of the accident department in 1925 and to secretary of the company in 1927.

With another company official, George Bulkley, he made a comprehensive aerial inspection in 1928 of the first airline operating between Chicago and Detroit. As a result of their report, Connecticut General "pioneered in offering crews and passengers standard-rate insurance" (*Fortune*, September 1957), and today two thirds of the nation's airlines carry Connecticut General group insurance. In 1932 Wilde became vice-president in charge of the agency department and secretary.

Elected president of Connecticut General in February 1936, when Robert W. Huntington moved up to the chairmanship of the board, the forty-one-year-old Frazar Wilde was one of the youngest men to head an American insurance concern. As a vice-president he had, despite the depression, "deliberately accelerated" a program calling for complete modernization of all the company's offices.

By the end of his first five years as president the number of field offices had increased to sixty-one. Under Wilde the company adopted in the 1940's a social service called "estate planning," whereby a Connecticut General representative could help his client plan his entire financial outlay. In the field of group insurance the company introduced a program to help the employee better understand his benefits.

During the ten years preceding the end of World War II "the company's insurance in force . . . doubled from $1,056,560,000 to $2,-102,820,000" (*Fortune*, September 1957). By 1947 it had become clear that a new wing added in 1938 to the Hartford headquarters would not meet the needs of steady expansion. Company officials decided to move the home office to the country and in 1950 acquired a tract of 200

(later increased to 300) acres at Bloomfield, about five miles out of Hartford. Here was erected the "new, sleek $19,000,000 complex of buildings" (*Fortune*) to which headquarters were transferred in 1957. President Wilde himself helped to plan the new office, which includes an assembly-line system for processing policies, tennis courts for employees, a swan lake, and courtyards designed by Isamu Noguchi.

The Life Insurance Association of America of which Wilde was president for 1958 was established in 1906, along with the American Life Convention of which Wilde was president in 1952. Both have "the general objectives of performing functions useful to the business as a whole" (*Encyclopaedia Britannica*), the former representing in the main the larger companies. Wilde has served as a member of L.I.A.A. and A.L.C. joint committees relating to inflation control, economic policy, government employee group insurance and monetary affairs, and was a founder (1939) and the first chairman of the Institute of Life Insurance for the promotion of "better public relations and popular understanding of the business."

Wilde is a director of two industrial concerns, the Emhart Manufacturing Company (glass containers and other products) of Hartford and the Plax Corporation, and is a member of the taxation committee of the National Association of Manufacturers. As chairman of the research and policy committee of the Committee for Economic Development, a privately financed "nonprofit, nonpolitical economic research and educational organization of 150 businessmen and educators," Wilde headed a body which in September 1954 recommended a new federal budget policy "aimed at surpluses in good times, deficits in depressions and long-time debt reduction" (New York *Times,* September 26, 1954).

In April 1956 Wilde announced the undertaking of an intensive study exploring the consequence to the United States of "a persistent inflationary policy." Early in December 1957 the program subcommittee of the research and policy committee recommended a national farm program calling for a retirement policy in regard to poor farm land and gradual removal of farm price and income supports. Four months later the committee recommended a temporary 20 per cent reduction in personal income taxes should the recession deepen.

A $500,000 grant from the Ford Foundation in November 1957 preceded the announcement by the Committee for Economic Development on May 28, 1958 that it had formed a twenty-five-member commission, with Wilde as chairman, to make a three-year over-all study of the nation's public and private monetary policies. This commission on money and credit has been described as the "most important . . . on money problems" since the Aldrich Commission, whose findings in 1911 led to the establishment of the Federal Reserve System (*Business Week,* May 31, 1958).

Frazar B. Wilde was for ten years a member or chairman of the town finance committee of

West Hartford; is a founder and past president of the Governmental Research Institute of Hartford; was the chairman in 1955 of Connecticut's Highway Financing Advisory Committee and a member of the Highway Financing Study Commission. In activities outside his home state he has been an adviser to the board of governors of the Federal Reserve Board, is a panel member of the Special Studies Project of the Rockefeller Brothers Fund, Inc., and was recently elected to the board of directors of the Flight Safety Foundation, Inc.

He has received honorary degrees from Trinity and Hillyer colleges and from Wesleyan University. He is a member of the advisory committee of Rensselaer Polytechnic Institute and chairman of the board of trustees of Connecticut College. He has also been active on behalf of the Hartford Hospital and the Greater Hartford Y.M.C.A., and he is a trustee of the Wadsworth Atheneum and a vestryman of St. John's Church.

Mrs. Wilde is the former Mildred Taylor; the Wildes have two sons (Watrous and Frazar, Jr.), two daughters (Mrs. Earl Schultz and Mrs. Roger H. Dickinson), and several grandchildren. "Wilde's hobbies," states the New York *Times* (May 29, 1958), "are sailing, hiking and nature-watching. His forty-foot cutter, the *Pilgrim,* takes him each summer to Maine, where he has a summer place on Casco Bay."

References

Weekly Underwriter 134:300 F 8 '56 por

Poor's Register of Directors and Executives (1958)

Who's Who in America, 1958-59

Who's Who in Insurance, 1958

Who's Who in New England (1949)

WILKINS, SIR (GEORGE) HUBERT Oct. 31, 1888-Dec. 1, 1958 Polar explorer and geographer; made ten expeditions to the arctic and Antarctica. See *Current Biography* (January) 1957.

Obituary

N Y Times p1+ D 2 '58

WILKINS, J(ESSE) ERNEST Feb. 1, 1894-Jan. 19, 1959 Former United States Assistant Secretary of Labor (1954-58); practised law in Chicago (1921-54); first Negro to hold a sub-cabinet post. See *Current Biography* (December) 1954.

Obituary

N Y Times p35 Ja 20 '59

WILSON, ANGUS (FRANK JOHN-STONE-) Aug. 11, 1913- Author
Address: b. 02 Grenville House, Dolphin Square, London, S.W. 1, England; h. Woodside, Bradfield St. George, Bury St. Edmunds, Suffolk, England

Since 1949 the British writer Angus Wilson has produced three volumes of short stories, three novels, a play, a critical examination of the works of Zola, and a sketch about the 1920's. For these books he has been praised on both sides of the Atlantic as one of the most important literary discoveries to come out of postwar England. If some critics hint that the honor is slightly diminished by the fact that the front rank of British novelists is somewhat depleted, others concede that his malicious irony, his razor-edged phrases, and his satiric and probing appraisals of contemporary life show the touch of a genuine craftsman.

Angus Frank Johnstone-Wilson was born on August 11, 1913 in Bexhill, Sussex, the youngest of the six sons of William and Maude (Caney) Johnstone-Wilson. His mother had come from Durban, Natal, South Africa and after World War I the family lived there for three years. From that sojourn the small boy derived his permanent love of the heat of the sun and his hatred of racism.

Back in England, Angus was sent to Westminster School in 1927 as a day boy, and during the next four years lived in private hotels, an experience he later drew upon for his knowledge of the shadier side of life. At Merton College, Oxford he studied medieval history, and earned his bachelor of arts degree in 1935. Wilson says that he enjoyed his stay at the Oxford of the 1930's, much as it may be derided today. In the next two years he held a succession of odd jobs, including tutoring, secretarial work, judging folk-dancing, secretarial work, catering and running a restaurant, and acting as social organizer. In 1937 he joined the staff of the Department of Printed Books at the British Museum.

After working in the Foreign Office from 1942 to 1946, Wilson returned to the British Museum, where he was charged with the task of replacing as many as possible of the 300,000 books destroyed by bombing. In 1949 he was appointed deputy superintendent of the Reading Room, a post he held until 1955, when his literary success enabled him to devote full time to writing.

Angus Wilson began to write in 1946. He has said: "It had always been my intention not to write books. I used to say that too many people wrote, and I still do." But during the war he suffered a nervous breakdown, and feeling the need for an additional interest in life, he began to write stories during his week ends.

The Wrong Set was an immediate success in both Great Britain and in the United States, where it was published by William Morrow & Company in 1950. In the Chicago *Sunday Tribune* (March 19, 1950), Paul Engle said: "It's the most delightful and disturbing book of stories I've seen in a long time."

The reviewer for *Time* magazine (April 10, 1950) termed *The Wrong Set* "thirteen remarkably unpleasant stories" and described Wilson as a man with "large, sad, slightly protuberant eyes, the mournful, darkling air of most younger British writers and a considerable reputation

Paul Moor

ANGUS WILSON

in some unexpected quarters." The critic thought that Wilson's compassion and economy of phrasing redeemed the pathological atmosphere of the collection.

When Wilson's next collection of short stories, *Such Darling Dodos,* was published in Great Britain in 1950, the London *Tribune* predicted that a better collection would probably not be printed that year. The American edition was published by William Morrow & Company in 1951, followed in 1952 by Wilson's *Emile Zola; An Introductory Study of His Novels.*

Wilson's first novel, *Hemlock and After,* provoked favorable comment on both sides of the Atlantic. William Peden in the *Saturday Review* (October 4, 1952) believed that it established Angus Wilson as one of the major English fiction writers of the decade. The novel deals with the moral and physical decay of Bernard Sands, a celebrated, middle-aged novelist who has obtained a government subsidy with which he has set up a retreat for young writers. As he dominates the grotesques who make up the cast of minor characters, Sands becomes increasingly obsessed with an awareness of evil and his own irresponsibility. Ernest Jones in the *Nation* (October 11, 1952) downgraded the novel for its spasmodic movement of plot, weak ending, and minor characterization, but endorsed its brilliant analysis of homosexual society and magnificent portrayal of the British middle class.

For Whom the Cloche Tolls; A Scrapbook of the Twenties received comparatively little critical notice when it was published in the United States in 1953. This held true of Wilson's play, *The Mulberry Bush,* which was produced in London in 1956, but has not yet found an American publisher.

Both American and British critics called Wilson's second novel, *Anglo-Saxon Attitudes,* a triumph. The central figure is Gerald Middleton, an elderly historian, who has long sus-

pected that a renowned archaeological discovery of 1912 was a hoax. Wilson plagues Middleton with shocks and misfortunes and surrounds him with a gallery of rogues. The "attitudes" of the title, explained James Gray in the *Saturday Review* (October 6, 1956), "are those that dramatize Anglo-Saxon morality.... No novelist has ever written about the academic world with so fine a respect, edged with so sharp an irony."

By the time his third collection of short stories, *A Bit Off the Map,* was published, Wilson had become, according to Martha Bacon, "a well-fixed star in the system of contemporary literature" (New York *Herald Tribune Book Review,* November 17, 1957). She pointed out that although Wilson's viewpoint is sad and harsh, his voice "always hits the middle of the note." When another novel, *The Middle Age of Mrs. Eliot* (Viking, 1959), was issued, most critics agreed with John Wain (*New Yorker,* April 11, 1959) that it "is not a successfully executed novel, but it is a serious and courageous book."

Angus Wilson admits that his fiction has often been criticized for its savage character portrayal and its unsavory collection of characters, but attributes this to his realistic approach to his materials. He claims that "if the novel is to recover from the anemia which has beset it since the 1920's, it must once more cover a wide, social canvas." In an article, "The Revolt of Samuel Butler," published in the *Atlantic Monthly* in November 1957 he says that "young writers today are in revolt against what they feel to be the solemnity, the self-satisfaction and the decay of the established order."

Speaking before a large audience of delegates to an international literary conference in London on July 10, 1956, Wilson urged them not to talk down to mass audiences, "not to be the schoolmaster, or, most dangerously, the highbrow clown."

Critics have compared Angus Wilson to a number of writers, including Evelyn Waugh, Aldous Huxley, and Charles Dickens. Kingsley Amis instituted a new comparison when he commented in the *New Republic* (October 15, 1956): "May he take his place, not as our Galsworthy or our George Eliot between whom he seems at present to be uncertainly hovering, but as our Thackeray."

For recreation, Wilson enjoys travel, conversation, gardening, cookery, and reading history. After the publication of *Anglo-Saxon Attitudes* he spent some time in Toulouse, France, and during 1957 visited Japan for two months. He has contributed reviews and articles to many British periodicals and has often broadcast over the BBC.

References

N Y Herald Tribune Bk R p3 O 5 '52
N Y Times p10 Jl 11 '56; p31 O 4 '56
Nation 175:331 O 11 '52
New Yorker 32:176 O 6 '56
Sat R 39:22 O 6 '56
Twentieth Century Authors (First Supplement, 1955)
Who's Who, 1958

WILSON, SLOAN May 8, 1920- Author
Address: h. High Ridge, Pound Ridge, N.Y.

By 1959 "the man in the gray flannel suit," a phrase deriving from the title of a best-selling novel of a few years earlier, had come to stand for a state of mind and a part of American folklore. For many readers it was the definitive epithet for the commuting suburbanite, the status-hungry conformist from Madison Avenue. The novel most responsible for spawning a host of books about anxiety in the executive suites was *The Man in the Gray Flannel Suit* (1955) by Sloan Wilson, sometime journalist, editor, publicist, and assistant professor of English. Wilson has also written poetry, articles for newspapers and magazines, and two other novels, *Voyage to Somewhere* (1946) and *A Summer Place* (1958).

An advocate of raising the standards of American education and of integrating the public schools, Wilson served on the staff of the National Citizens Commission for the Public Schools (1949-52) and the White House Conference on Education (1955).

Sloan Wilson was born in Norwalk, Connecticut on May 8, 1920, one of the three children (two sons and a daughter) of Albert Frederick and Ruth (Danenhower) Wilson. Both parents were authors: his father, a professor, wrote a novel and several other books; his mother wrote a number of studies on sociological and psychological subjects, among them *Jim Crow Joins Up; A Study of Negroes in the Armed Forces of the United States* ('1944).

During his childhood Sloan and his family lived in various cities on the Atlantic seaboard. He was educated at Phillips Exeter Academy in Exeter, New Hampshire and was graduated in 1937 from the Adirondack-Florida School of Onchiota, New York and Coconut Grove, Florida. Entering Harvard College in 1938, Wilson majored in philosophy and psychology and composed fiction and poetry for a Harvard literary magazine. In the summer months he operated an eighty-seven-foot commercial schooner which took groups of students to Cuba and Nova Scotia.

His education was interrupted in 1942 when he joined the United States Coast Guard with the rank of ensign. He commanded a small craft in the North Atlantic and South Pacific and was discharged as a lieutenant in 1945. Military service provided him with background material for his first published work, the poem "The Soldiers Who Sit," and his first novel, *Voyage to Somewhere* (Wyn, 1946).

After being discharged Wilson returned to Harvard and received the B.A. degree in 1946. He then was a cub reporter for a year with the Providence (Rhode Island) *Bulletin* and *Journal* and a researcher for two years with *Time* magazine. Leaving *Time* in 1949, Wilson worked with the National Citizens Commission for the Public Schools, established by President Truman and headed by Roy E. Larsen, president of Time, Inc. In a series of conferences and study groups the commission discussed such problems facing educators as inadequate facilities, overcrowding, and the shortage of teachers.

Philippe Halsman

SLOAN WILSON

In 1952 Wilson became assistant professor of English and director of information services at the University of Buffalo in New York. Three years later he was appointed assistant director of the White House Conference on Education, an assemblage of educators concerned with problems arising from increased public and private school enrollments. The conferees recommended government subsidies to higher education and increased federal aid for public schools. Wilson has strongly supported both these measures.

After the White House Conference ended, Wilson became education editor of *Parents' Magazine* in December 1955; he also became education editor of the New York *Herald Tribune* in August 1956. In his articles he wrote about the unprecedented increase in the number of students on all levels; the increased costs of obtaining and offering education; the teacher shortage; and the Supreme Court's 1954 decision which held that public school segregation is unconstitutional. He became a stern critic of Congressional reluctance to authorize funds for public schools and of the federal Office of Education (New York *Herald Tribune*, September 2, 1956).

Writing in the New York *Herald Tribune* (August 26, 1956), Wilson took the position that because the South had never enforced the separate-but-equal mandate of the Supreme Court, integration in the public schools would result in lowering of standards, making the "present generation of white children in the South pay for the sins of their forefathers." To counteract this situation he urged that federal aid be granted to Southern communities that end segregation in their schools. Integration must be "not only a matter of civil rights and psychological adjustment and the enforcement of the law, it must also be an act of

WILSON, SLOAN—*Continued*

creation—the creation of vast new school facilities in the South." In the fall of 1956 Wilson covered the integration crisis at Clinton, Tennessee.

In order to devote more of his time to writing, Wilson resigned from his post at *Parents' Magazine* in February 1957 and from the New York *Herald Tribune* ten months later. He found time, however, to conduct a survey on education for *Life* and his summary appeared in an article, "It's Time to Close Our Carnival" (March 24, 1958).

Wilson found that the schools have been overcrowded for years; classes are held in shacks and hallways; most teachers are grossly underpaid and many are unqualified and incompetent; the schools emphasize elective courses rather than traditional disciplines; there is little provision for brilliant students; educators have been debating for a quarter of a century on whether to help a child in his social adjustment or to teach him something; and the standards of education are shockingly low.

While holding various jobs Wilson has been writing in the evenings and on weekends, just as he had done during his service with the Coast Guard. "Writers usually make miserable employees," he has remarked, "and institutions which put up with them ought to get all possible credit." While in military service he wrote the poem "The Soldiers Who Sit," which was published by the *New Yorker* on January 6, 1945. It has been widely reprinted, and formed the basis of two radio programs.

Voyage to Somewhere (Wyn, 1946), Wilson's first novel, was largely autobiographical. It told about the novice crew of a small supply ship in the Pacific during World War II which rescues a sister ship during a typhoon. Because its publication coincided with the appearance of a spate of war novels, *Voyage to Somewhere* did not receive the attention it deserved and sold only about 1,600 copies. "It is one of the few honest and straightforward sea books that have come out of the war," commented Lincoln Colcord (New York *Herald Tribune Weekly Book Review*, December 29, 1946). "It bears every evidence of a slice out of life, a glimpse of native realism."

The Man in the Gray Flannel Suit (Simon & Schuster, 1955), which was serialized in part in *Collier's*, met with instant success. The Literary Guild chose it for its August 1955 selection, and Pocket Books issued it in a paperbound edition. Its hero, Thomas Rath, is a Korean war veteran who is dissatisfied with suburbia and the ethos of Madison Avenue. In writing the novel Wilson used the flash back technique and a number of Korean war sequences. Some critics compared its style to that of J. P. Marquand. A screenplay by Nunnally Johnson based on the book was filmed in 1956 by Twentieth Century-Fox Film Corporation with Gregory Peck in the leading role.

According to Wilson (New York *Post,* June 5, 1958), the characters of his novel *A Summer Place* (a Ridge Press Book published by Simon & Schuster, 1958) are obsessed with proving their worth in terms of making money and achieving status and have no clear answers to moral questions. He attempted to convey his belief that "we're all headed for the grave. This is the only thing you can definitely know, in a cold intellectual sense . . . and I can think of no way to prove that life is worth living." The book contains a seriocomic characterization of "antipeople people," that is, those who do not wish to associate with members of minority groups or the poor.

Some of the reviewers did not interpret *A Summer Place* in Wilson's terms. The *New Yorker* (April 12, 1958) called it a "conventional and fattily written novel dealing with a couple of middle-class Eastern families and a steady, worried round of adultery, alcoholism, divorce, and premature marriage, all of which is settled in a firm, rose-colored way." Ben Ray Redman (*Saturday Review,* May 3, 1958) noted that its style will be "pleasantly familiar to lovers of radio serials." The story of *A Summer Place,* whose film rights were purchased by Warner Brothers, appeared in serial form in *McCall's* and was the Literary Guild selection for May 1958.

While still in college Sloan Wilson and Elise Pickhardt were married on February 4, 1941; they have two daughters, Lisa and Rebecca, and a son, David Sloan. The novelist is five feet ten and one-half inches tall, weighs 185 pounds, and has blue eyes, and blond hair. His hobbies are sailing and reading. He is a Democrat and a member of the Harvard Club of New York. Wilson is more intent upon expressing emotions than ideas. Working "disorderly and passionately," he types "ten or twenty very sloppy pages," then edits them with a pencil. His ambition is to write a series of novels with the "social insight of Marquand and the power of Hemingway" (*Cosmopolitan,* August 1958).

Sloan Wilson has become sensitive to the charge, often made by some of his critics, that he has hit the jackpot by writing upper middle-class soap operas. He says: "I think the criticism that I most resent is the accusation of pandering to the public taste. I don't know what the public's taste is, and I don't think any one does. The only thing I can write about is what is preoccupying me. I can't separate writing from life" (New York *Herald Tribune,* April 13, 1958).

References

N Y Herald Tribune Bk R p2 Ap 13 '58
Who's Who in America (sup Je-Ag '56)
Who's Who in the East (1957)

WOOLLEN, EVANS, JR.

WOOLLEN, EVANS, JR. Mar. 15, 1897-Jan. 25, 1959 Indianapolis banker; president of the American Bankers Association (1948-49). See *Current Biography* (December) 1948.

Obituary

N Y Times p29 Ja 26 '59

WRIGHT, FRANK LLOYD June 8, 1869-
Apr. 9, 1959 Architect; pioneer in functional
and "organic" architecture; conceived plans for
Imperial Hotel in Tokyo (1915-22), Falling
Water House in Bear Run, Pennsylvania
(1936), Solomon R. Guggenheim Museum in
New York (1952-59); author; teacher. See
Current Biography (November) 1952.

Obituary

N Y Times p1+ Ap 10 '59

WU, CHIEN SHIUNG (wōō chĕn shōōng)
May 29, 1912 (?) Physicist; university professor

Address: b. Columbia University, New York
27; h. 15 Claremont Ave., New York 27

In a citation read at the graduation exercises
of Princeton University in June 1958, Dr.
Chien Shiung Wu, a professor at Columbia
University, was called "the world's foremost
female experimental physicist." She has won
this distinction by her significant contributions
to the research of nuclear forces and structure
and, in particular, for her work in overthrowing the principle of parity. This law, regarded
as basic to physics for the last thirty years,
held that a phenomenon of nature looks the
same whether observed directly or through a
mirror, with left and right reversed.

Theorists Tsung Dao Lee and Chen Ning
Yang suggested that the parity principle was
unacceptable when dealing with weak interactions of subatomic particles. Dr. Wu devised
and conducted experiments with cooled-down
radioactive Cobalt 60 that proved the Lee-Yang
hypothesis.

The success of Professor Wu's research on
the parity question has opened new fields for
investigation. "With these new developments,"
says Chien Shiung Wu, "physicists are now
viewing Nature with a new understanding. . . .
When we arrive at this understanding, we shall
marvel how neatly all the elementary particles
fit into the Great Scheme. Indeed, how deeply
privileged our generation is to have been challenged with this fascinating task."

Chien Shiung Wu was born on May 29, 1912
(some sources give 1915) in Liu Ho, China,
the daughter of a school principal whom she
describes as being "always ahead of his time—
questioning, learning." She and her two
brothers read a great deal. "It was a wonderfully happy life," she says. "I had a fortunate
and happy childhood." She went to secondary
school in Soochow, where she learned English
and decided to become a physicist.

During the early years of the Chinese-Japa-
nese war she matriculated at the National Central University at Nanking, and in spite of the
upheaval of the invasion she completed her education and received a Bachelor of Science degree in 1936. The same year she came to the
United States to do graduate work at the University of California under Ernest O. Lawrence, winner of the 1939 Nobel Prize in phys-

CHIEN SHIUNG WU

ics for the invention of the atom-smashing
cyclotron. For her distinguished work as a
graduate student, Dr. Wu was elected to Phi
Beta Kappa.

After taking her Ph.D. degree in 1940, Dr.
Wu taught at Smith College and Princeton
University. She joined the scientific staff of
the Division of War Research at Columbia
University in March 1944 and worked on radiation detection. After the war she stayed on at
Columbia as a research associate; in 1952 she
became an associate professor of physics and
a full professor in 1959.

Dr. Wu has devoted a considerable portion
of her career to a study of nuclear forces and
structure, in particular, beta disintegration. In
view of this background she was invited by Dr.
Tsung Dao Lee, a colleague on the Columbia
faculty, and Dr. Chen Ning Yang of the Institute for Advanced Study at Princeton to conduct experiments designed to disprove a basic
law of physics, the principle of conservation of
parity. Accepted as a bulwark of physics since
1925, the parity principle maintained that in
nature there is no intrinsic difference between
right and left. The concept was "so solidly
bolstered by experimental data that few scientists would question its verity" (New York
Herald Tribune, December 29, 1957). The
parity law was not successfully challenged until
Dr. Lee and Dr. Yang offered their revolutionary conclusions to the world in the summer of
1956.

Though they recognized that parity held for
all strong and electro-magnetic interactions, the
two physicists were convinced that the principle
was not valid when dealing with weak interactions of sub-atomic particles. Lee and Yang,
the theoretical physicists, suggested several
tests to recognize the right and left "handed-

WU, CHIEN SHIUNG—Continued

ness" of particles, and Dr. Wu, the experimental physicist, then engaged in the actual proof.

Dr. Wu conducted her parity experiments with a select group of scientists from the National Bureau of Standards. They cooled radioactive Cobalt 60 to 0.01° above absolute zero (about 459 degrees below zero Fahrenheit). The low temperature minimized the random thermal movements of the cobalt nuclei, making it possible to record the disintegration of the radioactive atoms without other effects occurring simultaneously. "The essence of the experiment," Dr. Wu told a scientific audience, "was to line up the spins of the Cobalt 60 nuclei along the same axis and then to determine whether the beta particles were emitted preferentially in one direction or the other along the axis." If the electrons had shot off in equal numbers in both directions along the spin axes of the lined up nuclei, the parity law would have been sustained. "The results," according to Chien Shiung Wu, "showed that the electrons were emitted preferentially in the direction opposite to that of nuclear spin and therefore conclusively proved that the beta decay of Cobalt 60 behaves like a left-handed screw."

Recalling the hectic last weeks of experimentation, Dr. Wu says "it was like a nightmare. I wouldn't want to go through them again." The success of these investigations, however, brought world-wide acclaim to Dr. Wu as well as to Dr. Lee and Dr. Yang. When scientists at the University of Chicago and at Columbia University confirmed that this screw sense observed in beta decay exists in many other weak interactions, the parity law was completely shattered. "This small, modest woman," commented the writer of a New York Post profile (January 22, 1959) "was powerful enough to do what armies can never accomplish: she helped destroy a law of nature. And laws of nature, by their very definition, should be constant, continuous, immutable, indestructible."

The total significance of Dr. Wu's investigations is still uncertain. "We have no idea now what they will lead to," she says. "The sudden liberation of our thinking on the very structure of the physical world has been overwhelming." Subsequent investigations by other researchers have shown that the Wu results with Cobalt 60 hold true for all weak interactions, none of which shows parity conservation. "In place of parity conservation," states Dr. Wu, "there may be a deeper symmetry connecting, for the first time, space and electric charge." Whatever the consequences of the abolition of parity, scientists agree that the Lee-Yang-Wu research is perhaps "the most important development in nuclear physics since the actual unleashing of atomic energy" (New York Post, January 22, 1959).

A singular honor was bestowed on Dr. Wu in 1958 when she was made the first woman to receive the Research Corporation Award, given annually to an outstanding scientist. It was probably the first time, as Dr. Wu remarked in her acceptance speech, that the award was made "not for establishing a law, but for overthrowing it."

Another "first" for Dr. Wu came in June 1958 when Princeton University named her as the first woman to receive an honorary degree of Doctor of Science. For her successful collaboration with Dr. Lee and Dr. Yang, Dr. Wu was congratulated for proving "the unwisdom of underestimating the powers of a woman. By her decisive demonstration that the law of the conservation of parity is no longer tenable, she has decisively reasserted the principle of intellectual parity between women and men" (New York Times, June 18, 1958). As another result of her important work, Dr. Wu was elected to the National Academy of Sciences, the seventh woman to be so honored in its history.

Petite and feminine, Dr. Wu has warm and expressive eyes and long black hair which she fashions into a bun at her neck. Although she became a United States citizen in 1954, she still wears slit-skirted Chinese clothes. She remains modest and reticent about her scientific accomplishments. When discussing her profession, Dr. Wu explained "there was nothing unusual about women students in China, then as now. There are more women, proportionately, studying science and engineering in China, than here in the United States" (New York Post, January 22, 1959).

Though completely dedicated to her work, Dr. Wu has managed to combine a career with family life. She is married to Dr. Luke Chialiu Yuan, also a physicist, and has an eleven-year-old son. Despite her son's scholastic prowess in a school in France, Dr. Wu is somewhat concerned that he is losing his grasp of the Chinese language.

"Science is not static," Dr. Wu said in an address to the National Science Award students in Washington in March 1958, "but ever-growing and dynamic. . . . It is the courage to doubt what has long been established, the incessant search for its verification and proof that pushed the wheel of science forward."

References

N Y Post p48 Ja 22 '59 por
Yost, Edna Women of Modern Science (1959)

YOST, CHARLES W(OODRUFF) Nov. 6, 1907- United States Ambassador to Morocco
Address: b. American Embassy, Rabat, Morocco

The second United States Ambassador to Morocco, a country which won back its unity and independence from France and Spain in 1956, is Charles W. Yost, who was appointed to his present post in July 1958. Like his predecessor, Cavendish W. Cannon, now retired, he has been regarded as one of the State Department's ablest trouble-shooters. Morocco is the site of important American air bases established under an agreement with France in 1951. An immediate task confronting Ambassador Yost has been negotiating the time and terms of eventual withdrawal of United States forces from these bases.

Charles Woodruff Yost, the only child of Nicholas Doxtater Yost, a lawyer, and Gertrude A. (Cooper) Yost, was born on November 6, 1907 in Watertown, New York. He prepared for college at the Hotchkiss School, Lakeville, Connecticut, where his extracurricular activities included dramatics and debating as well as writing for the school magazine. Graduated from Hotchkiss in 1924, he entered Princeton University, majored in history, worked on the *Daily Princetonian,* and during one vacation made the "cross-continental trip in an ancient Dodge" that resulted in his short story "Holiday," published in *Scribner's Magazine* of July 1930.

Leaving Princeton with the A.B. degree in 1928, Yost studied for one year at the École des Hautes Études Internationales of the University of Paris. He also visited the Soviet Union and the Balkans before his return to the United States to receive his appointment on December 16, 1930 as a foreign service officer. In deciding to make his career in the field of international relations he had been encouraged by former Secretary of State Robert Lansing and Ambassador J. Butler Wright.

Assigned, two days after his appointment, as a vice-consul at Alexandria, Egypt, Yost served until February 1932, when he entered the Foreign Service School. He was reassigned as vice-consul at Warsaw, Poland in July 1932, but resigned from the Foreign Service in August 1933, following his engagement to a Polish girl, Irena Oldakowska. (They were married September 8, 1934.) Yost, who has published short stories and articles in *Harper's Magazine* and *Scribner's Magazine* and articles in various newspapers, was occupied as a free-lance journalist during the next two years.

In 1935 he returned to government service, working briefly in the Resettlement Administration before being appointed divisional assistant in the State Department in August 1935. The following month he received the assignment of assistant chief of the State Department's new office of arms and munitions control, established to "carry out the registration of manufacturers and the issuance of export and import licenses under the direction of the Munitions Control Board . . . set up under the authority of the Neutrality Act" (New York *Times,* September 22, 1935).

Yost was appointed assistant chief of the division of exports and defense aid in October 1941. He represented the State Department on the policy committee of the Board of Economic Warfare in 1941-42, and in June 1942 was named assistant chief of the division of special research. He became divisional assistant in the division of European affairs in September 1943, and executive secretary of the policy coordination committee in February 1944. As assistant to the chairman of the United States delegation, Yost attended the United Nations Conference on International Organization at San Francisco

Department of State

CHARLES W. YOST

in the spring of 1945 and in July 1945 served as secretary general of the United States delegation to the Potsdam Conference.

While on a temporary assignment later in 1945 as United States political adviser to the Commanding General of the India-Burma theater, Yost observed at Bangkok the negotiations for a peace treaty between Great Britain and Siam (Thailand). In January 1946 when the United States and Siam resumed diplomatic relations after a lapse of four years, Yost was named chargé d'affaires at Bangkok.

A few months later he was sent to Czechoslovakia as counselor and first secretary of the American Embassy in Prague; from there he was detailed in October to act as political adviser to the United States delegation to the U.N. General Assembly. In 1947 he began a two-year period as counselor of the American Legation in Vienna. He then returned to Washington and in 1949-50 directed the office of European affairs in the State Department. His next post was minister-counselor at the American Embassy in Athens. He left Greece in 1953 for Austria, where he served for a year as Deputy High Commissioner in Vienna and United States representative on the Allied Council for Austria.

In August 1954 Charles W. Yost became the first United States minister to the kingdom of Laos, one of the three Indochinese states that had just been accorded sovereignty under the terms of a peace settlement reached in Geneva. (Cambodia and Vietnam were the others.) About a year later the United States "put its diplomatic relations with Laos on an ambassadorial plane . . . in the face of Communist efforts to overthrow the royal government" (New York *Herald Tribune,* August 11, 1955). At the same time Yost was named Ambassador.

(Continued next page)

YOST, CHARLES W.—*Continued*

Next sent to Paris, he was counselor and deputy chief of mission with the rank of minister at the United States Embassy from August 1956 until the end of 1957. By a recess appointment announced by President Dwight D. Eisenhower on December 26, 1957, Yost was made Ambassador to Syria. He served only until the last week of February 1958, when United States recognition of the merging of Egypt and Syria as the United Arab Republic brought about his departure from Damascus. Then for several months Yost was occupied as a member of the State Department's policy planning staff in Washington. On July 7, 1958 Eisenhower nominated him to succeed Cavendish W. Cannon as United States Ambassador to Morocco. This appointment was confirmed by the Senate nine days later.

In 1951, when Morocco was still a protectorate of France and Spain, the United States contracted with France for the use of air bases at Benguérir, Nouaseur, Boulhaut, and Sidi Slimane and of a naval air station at Port-Lyautey. The United States, which has invested about $1 billion in these military installations, continued to occupy the bases after Morocco had gained its sovereignty in 1956.

"Young Moslem activists in Morocco found the United States bases a convenient weapon to use against King Mohammed V's moderate regime," *Time* stated (October 6, 1958). Ambassador Yost arrived in Morocco in August 1958 and had barely handed his credentials to the King before the Moroccan government yielded to political pressure to the extent of preventing the unloading of an American ship bearing munitions. "Moroccans sympathetic to the United States [were] privately urging that it negotiate an agreement to evacuate air bases here as the surest means of retaining them," Thomas F. Brady disclosed (New York *Times,* August 12, 1958).

By mid-September 1958 Ambassador Yost and Premier Ahmed Balafrej were holding meetings designed to reach an understanding on the bases. It was unofficially reported that Yost proposed evacuating the bases at the end of seven years and that Moroccan officials pressed for a more immediate withdrawal. While negotiations between the two countries were in progress, political unrest in Morocco led to the resignation of Premier Balafrej on December 3, 1958.

Three children, Nicholas, Casimir, and Felicity, have been born to Charles W. and Irena (Oldakowska) Yost. The Ambassador has blue eyes and blond hair, is five feet eleven inches in height and 130 pounds in weight. His church is the Presbyterian. He belongs to the University Club in Washington and the Automobile Club of France. Swimming, tennis, and writing are his favorite recreations.

References

N Y Times p10 D 25 '57 por
U S News 44:16+ Ja 3 '58 por
Department of State Biographic Register (1957)
Who's Who in America, 1958-59

YOUNG, STEPHEN M(ARVIN) May 4, 1890- United States Senator; lawyer

Address: b. Senate Office Bldg., Washington 25, D.C.; h. 2527 P St., N.W., Washington, D.C.

The subject of much controversy in the Eighty-sixth Congress, United States Senator Stephen M. Young, Democrat of Ohio, has been called a "precedent-shattering" Congressman, "freshman iconoclast," a "conscientious American," a "foe of capitalism," and an "important liberal Democrat." He was elected to a six-year term on November 4, 1958, defeating the incumbent, Republican John W. Bricker.

When Young voluntarily disclosed his financial holdings, he set off a debate in the American press. He also disposed of some sugar and air-line stocks which he thought might hamper his work on the Senate Agricultural and Forestry Committee and the Aeronautical and Space Sciences Committee.

First elected as Ohio's United States Representative-at-Large in 1932, Young was returned by his constituents in 1934, 1940, and 1948. For many years he had been a trial counsel in Cleveland. He served in both World Wars in the United States Army, and he was Allied military governor of the province of Reggio nell'Emilia, Italy in 1945.

Stephen Marvin Young was born on a farm in Norwalk, Ohio on May 4, 1890 to Stephen M. and Belle M. (Wagner) Young. His father was a judge in Huron County. After attending Norwalk High School, Stephen studied at Kenyon College in Gambier, Ohio. He then was transferred to Adelbert College and later entered the Franklin Thomas Backus School of Law, both divisions of Western Reserve University in Cleveland. In 1912 he received the LL.B. degree. During military operations on the Mexican border in 1916 he saw action with the Third Ohio Infantry, and in World War I he served with the Field Artillery.

Entering politics, Young was a member of the Ohio General Assembly for two terms (1913-17). He was then successively assistant prosecuting attorney of Cuyahoga County (1917-19); chief criminal prosecuting attorney there (1919-20); member of the Ohio Commission on Unemployment Insurance (1931-32); and special counsel to Ohio's Attorney General (1937-39). In 1922 he was Democratic nominee for attorney general and in 1930 and 1936 a candidate for the Democratic nomination as Governor.

Young was elected as Representative-at-Large to the Seventy-third, Seventy-fourth, Seventy-seventh, and Eighty-first Congresses. He did not succeed in his attempt at re-election in 1942.

On major domestic legislation in the Eighty-first Congress Young supported rent control extension (March 1949), repeal of federal margarine taxes (April 1949), and reducing federal spending by $600,000,000 (May 1950). He opposed the coalition (as opposed to the Truman) bill to repeal the Taft-Hartley Act (May

1949), Natural Gas Act exemptions (August 1949), and the coalition (versus Truman) minimum-wage bill (August 1949).

In the field of foreign relations Young voted for extending the Trade Agreements Act (February 1949), continuing the Marshall Plan (April 1949), cutting military aid to European countries by 50 per cent (August 1949), and providing guarantees for United States foreign investments (July 1950).

In 1942 Young volunteered for military service and was sent to North Africa and Italy. He won a commendation from General Mark W. Clark, the Bronze Star, and other citations. Following the armistice Young was the Allied military governor of the Italian province of Reggio nell'Emilia, and he was awarded the Order of the Crown of Italy. In 1946 he returned to the practice of law in Cleveland.

One of the surprises of the November 4, 1958 election occurred when Young defeated John W. Bricker, a veteran of thirteen years in the United States Senate. Young, who won 1,652,211 votes to 1,497,199 for his opponent, had campaigned as a Fair Dealer with the support of organized labor.

In the Eighty-sixth Congress Senator Young was assigned to the Aeronautical and Space Sciences, the Agriculture and Forestry, and the Public Works Committees. In one of his first speeches on the floor of the Senate, Young urged repeal of the 10 per cent excise tax on telephone calls. He explained that this tax is classified as a luxury tax, but telephone service is a necessity.

Although members of Congress are not required to reveal their stockholdings, Senator Young disclosed his shortly after taking office. Valued at about $270,000, his portfolio now includes stock in thirteen oil companies, the Monsanto Chemical Company, Radio Corporation of America, W.R. Grace & Company, and United Fruit Company.

"Young's philosophy has often been pro-labor," noted the Associated Press (*Miami Herald,* June 4, 1959). In his Straight From Washington letter to his constituents (February 2, 1959) Young wrote: "The labor movement in the United States has 16,000 full-time paid national and international officials, and more than 400,000 local union officers . . . 'labor racketeers' and 'union goons' refers to perhaps forty trade union officers against whom Senate and House Committees, in five years, have uncovered dishonest actions."

Since becoming a Senator in January 1959 the voting record indicates that on foreign policy matters Young favored an amendment increasing the United States subscription to the International Monetary Fund and the International Bank for Reconstruction and Development (March).

On defense measures he favored extending the draft (March) and authorizing $485,300,000 in fiscal 1960 for the National Aeronautics and Space Administration (June). In the field of taxation Young supported an amendment to

Fabian Bachrach

STEPHEN M. YOUNG

repeal the 4 per cent tax credit on dividend income (June), a measure denying tax deductions on certain entertainment, gift, and travel expenses (June), and a proposal to reduce the depletion allowance on oil and gas wells (June).

Senator Young is five feet eight inches tall and weighs 152 pounds. His eyes are brown and his hair is gray. "He walks in a choppy side-to-side motion. His trim . . . [figure] and clear skin, kept that way by tennis and gym workouts, give him an amazingly youthful look for his sixty-nine years." Other forms of relaxation that he enjoys are swimming and watching TV westerns. He says that he will retire when his term ends in 1965, and he has no need to cultivate votes for re-election.

Stephen M. Young and Ruby Louise Dawley were married on January 18, 1911. They had two sons, Stephen M. Young, Jr., who died in 1958, and Richard Dawley Young, and one daughter, Marjorie L. (Mrs. Robert R. Richardson). Mrs. Young died in October 1952. On March 28, 1957 he married Rachel Louise Bell.

Senator Young's religious affiliation is Methodist. In 1933 he was awarded the honorary Master of Civil Law degree by Kenyon College.

References

Congressional Directory (1959)
Who's Who in America, 1950-51

ZAROUBIN, GEORGI N(IKOLAE-VICH) 1900-Nov. 24, 1958 Soviet diplomat; Ambassador to the United States (1952-58). See *Current Biography.* (Apr.) 1953.

Obituary

N Y Times p29 N 26 '58

ZERBE, KARL (zĕr'bĕ) Sept. 16, 1903-
Artist

Address: b. Art Department, Florida State University, Tallahassee, Fla.; h. 1807 Ataphanene St., Tallahassee.

The German-born expressionist painter Karl Zerbe is noted for his symbolic still lifes, city landscapes, and figure studies of circus performers and angels, with their brilliant color, complex design, and dramatic intensity. He settled in the United States in 1934 when his first one-man show was presented in New York, at the Marie Sterner Gallery.

His revival of the ancient encaustic method, by which colors are mixed with hot wax and afterwards baked into the canvas, may well be his "most lasting contribution to modern art." As head of the department of painting at the School of the Museum of Fine Arts, Boston, from 1937 to 1954, Zerbe exercised an important influence on the younger generation of artists in that city. At present he is professor of art at Florida State University in Tallahassee.

KARL ZERBE

Karl Zerbe was born in Berlin, Germany on September 16, 1903, the son of Karl Henrich and Maria (Krammer) Zerbe. A year later the family moved to Paris, where his father was an executive in an electrical supply concern. They returned to Germany in 1914 and lived in Frankfurt throughout World War I, in which the elder Zerbe was killed. After several years as a chemistry student in the technical Hochschule at Friedberg, Karl in 1920 began working in an architect's office in Munich. At the same time, he studied at Debichitz Art School with Josef Eberz and Karl Caspar, the latter being a follower of the Norwegian expressionist, Edvard Munch. Later Zerbe took courses at the Munich Academy of Art.

Zerbe's first one-man show was held in 1922 at the Gurlitt Gallery, in Berlin. The following year he was awarded a traveling scholarship by the city of Munich, which enabled him to live and travel in Italy for three years. He came under the influence of the *Neue Sachlichkeit,* "New Objectivity," movement in postwar German painting. In reaction against the extreme subjectivity of the expressionists, this group of artists, headed by Otto Dix, Alexander Kanoldt, Karl Mense, Georg Schrimpf, and Fritz Burman, concentrated upon the objective, material world, which they depicted with meticulous realism.

In 1926 Zerbe was given a full-scale solo exhibition at the Gaspari Gallery in Munich, and his work was acquired by the Staedel Institute in Frankfurt and the National Gallery in Berlin. By this time, Zerbe had become interested in the expressive spirit of such contemporaries as Oskar Kokoschka, the early George Grosz, and the sculptor Wilhelm Lehmbruck, and he aligned himself in both his brushwork and color with the expressionist tradition.

The first showing of Zerbe's paintings in the United States was in a group exhibition of foreign artists at the Golz Gallery in 1933. After the Nazis seized power and denounced all modern art as *Kulturbolschewismus,* Zerbe came to the United States in 1934 and settled in Boston. His first American one-man shows were presented that same year at the Marie Sterner Gallery, in New York ("a deft and sensitive painter" was *Art Digest's* verdict), and at the Germanic Museum of Harvard University. Zerbe's work at this time consisted almost exclusively of landscapes and flower pieces painted in gouache.

In the opinion of H. W. Janson (*Parnassus*), a greater concern with structural clarity began to appear in Zerbe's pictures after 1936, as the result of "a newly acquired sympathy with the heritage of cubism." Zerbe spent the summers of 1935 and 1938 painting in France, and in Mexico in 1936 and 1937. Solo exhibitions of his work were displayed at the Marie Sterner Gallery in 1935 and 1937 and at the Grace Horne Galleries, in Boston, in 1938.

Meanwhile, Zerbe was appointed to the faculty of the Fine Arts Guild, in Cambridge, Massachusetts in 1935. Two years later, he became head of the department of drawing and painting at the School of the Museum of Fine Arts, in Boston. He was soon recognized as the leader of the so-called "Boston school of expressionists," which included such artists as Jack Levine, Hyman Bloom, and David Aronson (who served as Zerbe's assistant at the Museum School).

During 1939 he experimented with encaustic, a process used in the Greco-Egyptian mummy portraits of the second century, B.C. whereby the wax medium is heated on an electric palette. Dry color is then added to the molten wax, which may be applied to either a hot or cold panel. In fifteen months of experimentation, Zerbe developed encaustic to a high degree of flexibility. Since the mixture is burned into the panel, the distinctive luminosity of the colors is sealed in, and they will not darken with time.

Among his earliest encaustic paintings were *Plaster of Paris, The Striped Dress,* and a series of harlequins, shown at a one-man exhibition at the Buchholz Gallery in 1941. The New York *Herald Tribune* reviewer of Zerbe's next solo show, at the Downtown Gallery in 1943, observed that the artist had begun "a new and inventive style of painting, partly realistic and partly fanciful." Three years later another one-man show at the Downtown Gallery, included his encaustics *At Night, Gilded Acrobat,* and *Woman on the Trapeze.* The critics commented on Zerbe's fondness for symbols of mortality and his growing preoccupation with the human form. Emily Genauer (New York *World-Telegram,* November 2, 1948) noted its "more opulent color and a new emotional intensity."

In 1949, Zerbe was forced to abandon his encaustic technique, since he found that he was suffering from an allergy, which was attributed to the wax or the procedure as a whole. He took a trip to Italy and returned with a few paintings in polymer tempera, a new medium which had been developed by one of his former students, Alfred Duca. This is made by mixing polyvinyl acetate, a bland white plastic, with softener and ammonia, to which dry pigment is then added. Zerbe frequently mixes in mica to build up the surface texture. The result is a fast-drying medium capable of withstanding all temperature changes. Examples of Zerbe's work in polymer tempera were included in a retrospective exhibition at the Institute of Contemporary Art in Boston in 1951, and in his solo exhibition at the Downtown Gallery.

In 1954 Zerbe joined the faculty of Florida State University, in Tallahassee, as professor of art. That same year the Alan Gallery gave him one-man shows in January and December. The former exhibition was entitled "The Face of the City." *Time's* critic noted that the paintings were "markedly more abstract than his earlier work," their architectural construction being "expressed in long, vertical-lined backgrounds."

Twelve of Zerbe's gouaches and temperas were exhibited at the Nordness Gallery in April 1958. Their themes were divided between allegories of good and evil angels in conflict, and mask-like images inspired by the totem carvings of the Pacific Northwest Indians. According to Stuart Preston (New York *Times*), the "inscrutability of symbolical subject matter and maximum elaboration of paint handling" gave the new work "the rich, rigid, hieratic look of Byzantine mosaics."

Among the prizes Zerbe has received are the John Barton Paine Medal of the Virginia Museum of Fine Arts (for *The Storm*) in 1942; the Walter F. Blair Purchase Prize (for *Still Life with Mirror*) and Norman Wait Harris Silver Medal, from the Art Institute of Chicago, in 1944 and 1946, respectively; the third prize at the 1948 "Painting in the United States" show at the Carnegie Institute (for *The Actors*); the Henry Schiedt Memorial Prize of the Pennsylvania Academy, in 1949;

the Philadelphia Watercolor Prize, in 1950; and the grand prize at the Boston Art Festival, in 1953.

Works by Zerbe are represented in the permanent collections of major museums and galleries throughout the United States.

He became an American citizen in 1939. He holds membership in the College Art Association and the Society of American Graphic Artists, and in April 1957 was elected president of the Artists Equity Association. He was married to Marion S. Koegel on September 2, 1936, and they have a daughter, Maria Carolina. A documentary color film, *Encaustic by Zerbe,* was produced by Roy Flynn in 1957. In Tallahassee, the artist finds time to participate in community and campus events. He is an avid concertgoer and bird watcher.

References

Art N 50:26-9 F '52 por
Parnassus 13:65-9 F '41
Who's Who in America, 1958-59
Who's Who in American Art (1956)

ZILBOORG, GREGORY Dec. 25, 1890-Sept. 17, 1959 Psychiatrist; psychoanalyst; private practitioner in New York since 1931; was secretary to Russian Ministry of Labor (1917); translated into English and wrote books on psychiatry and other topics; was clinical professor at New York Medical College. See *Current Biography* (September) 1941.

Obituary

N Y Times p31 S 18 '59

ZIRATO, BRUNO Sept. 27, 1884- Former orchestra manager

Address: b. c/o Philharmonic-Symphony Society of New York, 113 W. 57th St., New York 19; h. 171 W. 57th St., New York 19

For twenty-eight years only a small number of the music lovers who crowded the concerts of the Philharmonic-Symphony Society of New York knew of the man who played a major part in the business and other practical operations that made the concerts possible. He is Bruno Zirato, the former managing director (1956-59), who has been associated with the society since 1927.

On the eve of Zirato's retirement in May 1959 Leonard Bernstein, the orchestra's conductor, presented him to a standing, cheering audience in New York's Carnegie Hall as the man "nobody in the world of music will ever forget—a warm, lovable man, so much in love with music." Zirato is continuing his dedication to music and the Philharmonic as consultant to the society's board of directors.

Bruno Zirato was born in Calabria, Italy, on the Strait of Messina across from Sicily, on September 27, 1884. His father was John Zirato, a magistrate, and his mother was Josephina (Lazzarini) Zirato. There were also four daughters in the family. He was ten years old when his family took him to Rome to live.

BRUNO ZIRATO

His devotion to music and musicians began there, and he has vivid memories of the nights when he was smuggled into the opera under the cloak of one of his uncles.

With high ambitions for his son, Zirato's father hoped that after his graduation from the Rome Institute of Technology in 1901, Bruno would study law. Aspiring, however, to become a journalist, he tried his mettle first with one of Rome's great newspapers, *Il Giornale d'Italia.* While on the staff, he learned the techniques of publishing as well as writing for a newspaper. To this day he prides himself on his ability to read type backward, as it appears on the stone on which the paper is made up. Later Zirato moved on to become assistant music critic for several Roman newspapers.

Zirato then went to Paris, with the intention of studying journalism for a year at the Sorbonne. A few days after his arrival he met an American doctor who talked enthusiastically of the opportunities in his own country and persuaded Zirato to make a trip to the United States. The two sailed on the SS *Philadelphia* and in August 1912 arrived in New York. There the American abruptly left his Italian acquaintance, who found himself alone in the city with rapidly diminishing funds and very little knowledge of English.

For the next three years Zirato supported himself in part by making sales of articles to Italian-language newspapers, giving lessons in Italian at 75 cents an hour, and coaching singers in Italian pronunciation. From 1913 to 1915 he found employment as a lecturer at New York University's summer sessions and for the city's board of education.

A turning point in Zirato's life came in 1915 when he was working as a member of a committee to organize a fund-raising bazaar at Grand Central Palace. His job of persuading

celebrities to appear at booths where sales needed boosting led to his meeting Metropolitan Opera tenor Enrico Caruso. The next day, after they had talked together about Italy and music, the star engaged him to handle correspondence and other secretarial matters. Zirato, who remained with the singer for six years, also became his personal representative and a buffer between the singer and the public. Caruso died in 1921, and Zirato devoted the next year to writing *Enrico Caruso, a Biography* (Little, 1922), with the late Pierre V. R. Key, then manager of *Musical Digest.*

From 1922 to 1928 Zirato was business manager of *Musical Digest.* During this period he was New York representative of the San Francisco and Los Angeles opera companies, of La Scala in Milan, and Teatro Colón in Buenos Aires. He was also personal representative of conductors and singers of the Metropolitan Opera Company, including Lily Pons, Grace Moore, Ezio Pinza, and many others.

When Arturo Toscanini became principal conductor of the New York Philharmonic-Symphony Orchestra in the late 1920's, the board of directors of the Philharmonic-Symphony Society decided to appoint an Italian-speaking liaison official to handle matters between Toscanini and the Philharmonic management. Zirato was selected for the position and given the title of special representative of the society for Toscanini. He carried out this assignment for three years and was a member of the managerial staff in charge of the European tour which the orchestra made in 1930 under Toscanini's direction. In a resolution of May 29, 1931 the orchestra board paid this tribute to Zirato: "It was through the instrumentality of Mr. Zirato that the society was able to finish the season without losing the services of Maestro Toscanini."

With his appointment in 1931 to the post of assistant manager, Zirato began his twenty-eight years of service in the higher echelons of Philharmonic management. His chief was Arthur Judson, who had taken part in organizing the Columbia Broadcasting Company in 1927 and two years later was the principal organizer of Columbia Concerts, Inc. (later Columbia Artists Management, Inc.). Zirato's activities in the musical field were further broadened when he was chosen in 1936 to be vice-president of Columbia Artists Management. For twenty years in this post, before resigning in 1956, he played an active part in shaping the careers of many young artists.

Meanwhile, the orchestra's board of directors advanced Zirato to co-manager with Judson in 1947. Eight years later, in the last year of his tenure as co-manager, the Philharmonic, under Zirato's personal supervision, made its first tour to the West Coast during May and June. In September Zirato fulfilled his plans for the orchestra's first tour of the British Isles and the Continent since the tour under Toscanini in 1930.

In September 1956, upon the retirement of Judson as co-manager, the directors of the Philharmonic gave Zirato a title not previously used in the society—managing director. Zirato retired from this position at the end of the 1958-59 season, on May 31, 1959.

During the years of Zirato's directorship attendance at Philharmonic concerts had showed marked increases. In 1957, with Zirato as principal representative of the society, major union contracts were negotiated, one with local 802 of the American Federation of Musicians; the other with the American Guild of Musical Artists (AGMA). With Zirato as chairman of the Orchestra Managers Committee for all major orchestras in the United States, a four-year contract was worked out with the American Society of Composers, Authors and Publishers (ASCAP). Zirato also handled the negotiation of the Philharmonic's contracts with CBS radio from the first Philharmonic broadcasts through twenty-eight succeeding years.

Bruno Zirato was married on June 15, 1921 to Nina Morgana, at that time a soprano at the Metropolitan Opera. They have a son, Bruno. Zirato became a naturalized United States citizen in 1917. Impressive in appearance, Zirato is six feet two inches tall, weighs 230 pounds, and has brown eyes and gray hair. He now considers journalism his avocation and contributes articles to newspapers and magazines in the United States and Italy. He is a Republican and a Catholic. His favorite recreation is gardening. Although he has devoted most of his life to music and musicians he plays no musical instrument. "The only instrument I play," he is quoted as saying in the *New Yorker* (March 29, 1958), "is the cash register."

References

Mus Am 76:14 O '56 por
N Y Herald Tribune p19 S 19 '56 por
N Y Times II p11 My 3 '59
New Yorker 34:24 Mr 29 '58
Who's Who in America, 1958-59
Who's Who in New York, 1952

BIOGRAPHICAL REFERENCES

Consulted by the research staff of CURRENT BIOGRAPHY.

American Architects Directory, 1956
American Bar, 1959
American Catholic Who's Who, 1958 and 1959
American Medical Directory, 1958
American Men in Government (1949)
American Men of Science vols 1-3 (1955-56)
American Women, 1939-40
America's Young Men, 1938-39
ASCAP Biographical Dictionary of Composers, Authors, and Publishers (1952)
Asia Who's Who, 1958
Author's & Writer's Who's Who (1948-49)

Baker, T. ed. Biographical Dictionary of Musicians (1940)
Baseball Register, 1959
Bénézit, E. ed. Dictionnaire Peintres, Sculpteurs, Dessinateurs et Graveurs (1948-55)
Biographical Directory of the American Congress, 1774-1949 (1950)
Biographical Encyclopedia of Pakistan, 1955-56
Biographic Directory of the USSR (1958)
Burke's Landed Gentry (1952)
Burke's Peerage, Baronetage, and Knightage, 1953
Business Executives of America (1950)

Canadian Who's Who, 1955-57
Catholic Who's Who, 1952
Chemical Who's Who, 1956
Chi è? (1957)
China Yearbook, 1958-59
Chujoy, A. ed. Dance Encyclopedia (1949)
Congressional Directory (1959)
Congressional Quarterly Almanac, 1958

Davidson, G. Opera Biographies (1955)
Department of State Biographic Register, 1959
Dictionnaire Biographique des Artistes Contemporains, 1910-30
Dictionnaire Biographique Français Contemporain (1954)

Dictionnaire National des Contemporains (1936)
Directory of American Judges (1955)
Directory of American Scholars (1957)
Directory of Medical Specialists (1951)
Directory of Medical Women, 1949
Directory of the American Political Science Association, 1953

Ewen, D. ed. Composers of Today (1936); Living Musicians (1940; First Supplement, 1957); Men and Women Who Make Music (1949); European Composers Today (1954)

Grove's Dictionary of Music and Musicians (1955)

Hindustan Year-Book & Who's Who, 1954
Hoehn, M. A. ed. Catholic Authors (1952)
Hvem er Hvem? 1955

Indian and Pakistan Year Book and Who's Who, 1948
International Motion Picture Almanac, 1959
International Press Who's Who; New Zealand, 1938
International Television Almanac, 1959
International Who's Who, 1959
International Who's Who in World Medicine, 1947
International World Who's Who (1949)
International Year Book and Statesmen's Who's Who, 1959
Italian-American Who's Who (1946)

Japan Biographical Encyclopedia & Who's Who (1958)
Japan Who's Who, 1950-51
Junior Book of Authors (1956)

Kelly's Handbook to the Titled, Landed and Official Classes, 1957-58
Kraks Blaa Bog, 1954
Kürschners, Deutscher Gelehrten-Kalender, 1954

Leaders in Education (1948)

Martindale-Hubbell Law Directory, 1959
Middle East, 1958

Nalanda Year-Book and Who's Who in India and Pakistan, 1958
National Cyclopædia of American Biography current vols A-H (1926-52)
New Century Cyclopedia of Names (1954)

Österreicher der Gegenwart (1951)

Panorama Biografico degli Italiani d'Oggi (1956)

Quem é Alguém (1947)
Quien es Quien en la Argentina, 1958-59
Quien es Quien en Venezuela, Panama, Ecuador, Colombia, 1952

Radio and Television Who's Who, 1954
Religious Leaders of America, 1941-42

Slavonic Encyclopedia (1949)

Thompson, O. ed. International Cyclopedia of Music and Musicians, 1956
Turkin, H., and Thompson, S. C. Official Encyclopedia of Baseball (1959)
Twentieth Century Authors (1942; First Supplement, 1955)

Vem är Det, 1959
Vem och Vad, 1948

Warfel, H. R. American Novelists of Today (1951)
Webster's Biographical Dictionary (1956)

Wer ist Wer? (1958)
Who is Who in Music (1951)
Who Knows—and What (1954)
Who's Who, 1959
Who's Who in Advertising, 1957
Who's Who in America, 1958-59
Who's Who in American Art, 1956
Who's Who in American Education, 1955-56
Who's Who in Art, 1958
Who's Who in Australia, 1955
Who's Who in Austria, 1957-1958
Who's Who in Belgium (1959)
Who's Who in British Science, 1953
Who's Who in Canada, 1956-57
Who's Who in Central and East-Europe, 1935-36
Who's Who in Chicago and Illinois (1950)
Who's Who in Colored America, 1950
Who's Who in Commerce and Industry (1959)
Who's Who in Engineering, 1959
Who's Who in France, 1959-60
Who's Who in France (Paris), 1953-54
Who's Who in Germany (1956)

Who's Who in Government (1932-33)
Who's Who in Insurance, 1959
Who's Who in Italy, 1957-58
Who's Who in Labor (1946)
Who's Who in Latin America Pts 1-7 (1946-51)
Who's Who in Library Service (1955)
Who's Who in Modern China (1955)
Who's Who in New England (1949)
Who's Who in New York, 1952
Who's Who in New Zealand, 1956
Who's Who in Philosophy (1952)
Who's Who in Railroading in North America (1959)
Who's Who in Switzerland: 1955
Who's Who in the East (1959)
Who's Who in the Midwest (1956)
Who's Who in the Nation's Capital, 1938-39
Who's Who in the South and Southwest (1959)
Who's Who in the Theatre (1957)
Who's Who in the United Nations (1951)
Who's Who in the West (1958)

Who's Who in U.A.R. and the Near East, 1959
Who's Who in United States Politics (1952)
Who's Who in World Aviation and Astronautics (1958)
Who's Who in World Jewry (1955)
Who's Who Israel, 1958
Who's Who of American Women, 1958-59
Who's Who of Southern Africa, 1959
Wie is Dat? (1956)
Winchester's Screen Encyclopedia (1948)
Women Lawyers in the United States (1957)
Women of Achievement (1940)
Wood, C. TV Personalities vols 1-3 (1955-57)
World Biography (1954)
World Diplomatic Directory, 1951

Yost, E. American Women of Science (1943)

PERIODICALS AND NEWSPAPERS CONSULTED

NOTE: Most of the publications below are listed in Wilson Company periodical indexes found in most libraries. For addresses, subscription price, etc., consult your librarian.

ALA Bul—American Library Association Bulletin
Am Artist—American Artist
Am Assn Univ Women J—Journal of the American Association of University Women
Am Bar Assn J—American Bar Association Journal
Am Hist R—American Historical Review
Am Mag—American Magazine (discontinued)
Am Mercury—American Mercury
Am Pol Sci R—American Political Science Review
Am Scholar—American Scholar
Am Sociol R—American Sociological Review
Am W—American Weekly
America—America
Américas—Américas (incorporating Bul Pan Am Union)
Ann Am Acad—Annals of the American Academy of Political and Social Science
Arch Forum—Architectural Forum, the Magazine of Building
Arch Rec—Architectural Record
Archaeology—Archaeology: A Magazine Dealing with the Antiquity of the World
Art N—Art News
Arts—Arts
Arts & Arch—Arts & Architecture
Atlan—Atlantic Monthly
Aviation W—Aviation Week

Barrons—Barron's
Bet Hom & Gard—Better Homes & Gardens
Book-of-the-Month Club N—Book-of-the-Month Club News
Books Abroad—Books Abroad
Bsns W—Business Week
Bul Atomic Sci—Bulletin of the Atomic Scientists

Can Hist R—Canadian Historical Review
Cath World—Catholic World
Chem & Eng N—Chemical and Engineering News
Christian Cent—Christian Century
Christian Sci Mon—Christian Science Monitor
Colliers—Collier's (discontinued)
Commonweal—Commonweal
Cong Digest—Congressional Digest
Cong Q—Congressional Quarterly Weekly Report
Coronet—Coronet
Cosmop—Cosmopolitan
Cue—Cue
Cur Hist—Current History

Dance Mag—Dance Magazine

Ed—Education
Ed & Pub—Editor & Publisher
Ed Res Reports—Editorial Research Reports
Etude—Etude (discontinued)

Facts on File—Facts on File
For Affairs—Foreign Affairs
For Policy Bul—Foreign Policy Bulletin
Forbes—Forbes
Fortune—Fortune

Gen Army—Generals of the Army and the Air Force and Admirals of the Navy (discontinued)
Good H—Good Housekeeping

Harper—Harper's Magazine
Holiday—Holiday
House & Gard—House & Garden

Illus London N—Illustrated London News
Ind Woman—Independent Woman. Continued as National Business Woman

J Am Med Assn—Journal of the American Medical Association

Ladies Home J—Ladies' Home Journal
Lib J—Library Journal
Life—Life
Look—Look

McCalls—McCall's
Macleans Mag—Maclean's Magazine
Mag Wall St—Magazine of Wall Street and Business Analyst
Manchester Guardian—Manchester Guardian
Mlle—Mademoiselle
Mus Am—Musical America
Mus Courier—Musical Courier
Mus Mod Art—Museum of Modern Art Bulletin

NEA J—Journal of the National Education Association
N Y Herald Tribune—New York Herald Tribune
N Y Herald Tribune Bk R—New York Herald Tribune Book Review
N Y Post—New York Post
N Y Times—New York Times
N Y Times Bk R—New York Times Book Review
N Y Times Index—New York Times Index
N Y Times Mag—New York Times Magazine
N Y World-Telegram—New York World-Telegram and Sun
Nat Bsns Woman—National Business Woman
Nat Geog Mag—National Geographic Magazine
Nation—The Nation
Nations Bsns—Nation's Business
Nature—Nature
New Engl Q—New England Quarterly
New Repub—New Republic
New Statesm—New Statesman
New Yorker—New Yorker
Newsweek—Newsweek

Opera N—Opera News

Pol Sci Q—Political Science Quarterly
Pop Mech—Popular Mechanics Magazine
Pop Phot—Popular Photography
Pop Sci—Popular Science Monthly
Ptr Ink—Printers' Ink
Pub W—Publishers' Weekly

Read Digest—Reader's Digest
Reporter—The Reporter
Rotarian—Rotarian

Sat Eve Post—Saturday Evening Post
Sat Night—Saturday Night
Sat R—Saturday Review
Sch & Soc—School and Society
Sci Am—Scientific American
Sci Mo—Scientific Monthly
Sci N L—Science News Letter
Science—Science
Spec—Spectator
Sports Illus—Sports Illustrated
Sr Schol—Senior Scholastic

Theatre Arts—Theatre Arts
This Week—This Week Magazine
Time—Time
Times Lit Sup—London Times Literary Supplement
Toronto Globe and Mail—Toronto Globe and Mail
Toronto Globe and Mail Globe Mag—Toronto Globe and Mail Globe Magazine
Travel—Travel

U N R—United Nations Review
U S Dept State Bul—United States Department of State Bulletin
U S News—United States News & World Report

Variety—Variety
Vital Speeches—Vital Speeches of the Day
Vogue—Vogue

Washington (D.C.) Post—Washington Post and Times Herald
Wilson Lib Bul—Wilson Library Bulletin
Womans Home C—Woman's Home Companion (discontinued)

Yale R—Yale Review

NECROLOGY

This is a list of biographees' obituaries which are in the Yearbook, including those of late 1958. Deaths which occurred in late 1959 are recorded in the early 1960 issues of CURRENT BIOGRAPHY.

Adrian (biog 1941)
Anderson, Sir Kenneth A. N. (biog 1943)
Anderson, Maxwell (biog 1953)
Antheil, George (biog 1954)
Araki, Eikichi (biog 1952)
Ashida, Hitoshi (biog 1948)

Badger, Oscar C. (biog 1949)
Bandaranaike, S. W. R. D. (biog 1956)
Barrymore, Ethel (biog 1941)
Beard, Mary (biog 1941)
Beinum, Eduard van (biog 1955)
Bell, Bernard Iddings, Rev. Dr. (biog 1953)
Bell, Bert (biog 1950)
Benoit-Lévy, Jean (biog 1947)
Berger, Meyer (biog 1943)
Berggrav, Eivind, Bishop (biog 1950)
Berkson, Seymour (biog 1949)
Bloch, Ernest (biog 1953)
Blücher, Franz (biog 1956)
Bowditch, Richard L. (biog 1953)
Brunauer, Esther C. (biog 1947)

Chandler, Raymond (biog WLB 1946)
Costello, Lou (biog 1941)
Craigie, Sir Robert (biog 1942)

Dallas, C. Donald (biog 1949)
De Mille, Cecil B. (biog 1942)
Derwent, Clarence (biog 1947)
Donovan, William J. (biog 1954)
Dulles, John Foster (biog 1953)
Duplessis, Maurice (biog 1948)

Enckell, Carl J. A. (biog 1950)
Epstein, Sir Jacob (biog 1945)

Feldmann, Markus (biog 1956)
Flexner, Abraham (biog 1941)
Fox, Genevieve (biog WLB 1949)
Fredenthal, David (biog 1942)
Frost, Frances Mary (biog WLB 1950)
Frothingham, Channing (biog 1948)
Frye, Jack (biog 1945)
Furey, Warren W. (biog 1950)

Gamble, Ralph A. (biog 1953)
Gordon, Thomas S. (biog 1957)
Griswold, Oscar W. (biog 1943)
Grosz, George (biog 1942)
Guerrero, José Gustavo (biog 1947)
Guest, Edgar A. (biog 1941)
Guffey, Joseph F. (biog 1944)
Gwenn, Edmund (biog 1943)

Halsey, William F., Jr. (biog 1942)
Hatoyama, Ichiro (biog 1955)
Helburn, Theresa (biog 1944)
Herzog, Isaac Halevi, Rabbi (biog 1959)
Hilaly, Ahmed Naguib (biog 1952)
Hines, Duncan (biog 1946)
Hoppe, Willie (biog 1947)
Humphrey, Doris (biog 1942)

Irons, Ernest E. (biog 1949)
Ironside, William Edmund Ironside, 1st Baron (biog 1940)

Johnson, Edward (biog 1943)

Kelly, Joe (biog 1945)
Kettering, Charles Franklin (biog 1951)
Key, William S. (biog 1943)
King, Samuel Wilder (biog 1953)
Kitson, Harry Dexter (biog 1951)

Landowska, Wanda (biog 1945)
Leahy, William D. (biog 1941)
Lemkin, Raphael (biog 1950)
L'Esperance, Elise (biog 1950)
Litchfield, P. W. (biog 1950)

McKay, Douglas (biog 1949)
Malan, Daniel François (biog 1949)
Mallory, C. C. (biog 1956)
Manuilsky, Dmitri Z. (biog 1948)
Marshall, George C. (biog 1947)
Martin, Harry (biog 1948)
Martinu, Bohuslav (biog 1944)
May, Andrew Jackson (biog 1941)
Meyer, Eugene (biog 1941)
Mooney, Edward, Cardinal (biog 1946)
Mosher, A. R. (biog 1950)

Nelson, Donald M. (biog 1941)
Noble, Edward J. (biog 1944)
Norton, Mary T. (biog 1944)

Ogburn, William F. (biog 1955)
Ott, Mel (biog 1941)

Parkinson, Thomas I. (biog 1949)
Pauli, Wolfgang (biog 1946)
Power, Tyrone (biog 1950)

Quarles, Donald A. (biog 1955)

Redfield, Robert (biog 1953)
Reed, Daniel A. (biog 1953)
Rhoads, C. P. (biog 1953)
Richards, Vincent (biog 1947)
Rodzinski, Artur (biog 1940)

Sachs, Curt (biog 1944)
Saint-Gaudens, Homer (biog 1941)
Shaver, Dorothy (biog 1946)
Slichter, Sumner H. (biog 1947)
Smith, Sidney (biog 1955)
Stone, Abraham (biog 1952)
Sturges, Preston (biog 1941)
Sturzo, Luigi (biog 1946)

Taylor, Myron C. (biog 1940)
Templewood, Samuel John Gurney Hoare, 1st Viscount (biog 1940)
Tizard, Sir Henry (biog 1949)
Tucker, Henry St. George, Bishop (biog 1943)

Vance, Harold S. (biog 1949)

Walker, Frank C. (biog 1940)
Wells, Agnes (biog 1949)
Wilkins, Sir Hubert (biog 1957)
Wilkins, J. Ernest (biog 1954)
Woollen, Evans, Jr. (biog 1948)
Wright, Frank Lloyd (biog 1952)

Zaroubin, Georgi N. (biog 1953)
Zilboorg, Gregory (biog 1941)

CLASSIFICATION BY PROFESSIONAL FIELD—1959

Advertising

Alberti, Jules

Agriculture

Morse, True D.
Rockefeller, Winthrop

Archaeology

Jacopi, Giulio

Architecture

Belluschi, Pietro
Gruen, Victor
Tunnard, Christopher

Art

Archambault, Louis
Bazin, Germain
Brooks, James
Buffet, Bernard
Conrad, Barnaby, Jr.
Dreyfuss, Henry
Evatt, Harriet (WLB)
Gottlieb, Adolph
Hartford, Huntington, 2d
Lasker, Mrs. Albert D.
Morgan, Lucy
Osborn, Robert C.
Peterson, Roger Tory
Pevsner, Antoine
Siqueiros, David Alfaro
Stamos, Theodoros
Zerbe, Karl

Aviation

Felt, Harry D.
Norstad, Lauris
Stapp, John Paul

Business

Alberti, Jules
Alessandri, Jorge
Bache, Harold L.
Barton, Robert B. M.
Boone, Pat
Carter, John
Cresap, Mark W., Jr.
Davis, Nathanael V.
Davis, Tobé Coller
Donner, Frederic G.
Dreyfuss, Henry
Fuller, Margaret H.

Fuoss, Robert M.
Hartford, Huntington, 2d
Hope, Stanley C.
Innocenti, Ferdinando
Jordan, B. Everett
Kahane, Melanie
Kerr, James W.
McCone, John A.
McDonnell, William A.
Mason, Norman P.
Mueller, Frederick H.
Nickerson, Albert L.
Obolensky, Serge
Olivetti, Adriano
Paxton, Robert
Percy, Charles H.
Rockefeller, David
Rockefeller, Laurance S.
Rockefeller, Winthrop
Rudkin, Margaret
Skutt, V. J.
Wilde, Frazar B.

Dance

Bowers, Faubion
Bruhn, Erik
Vera-Ellen

Diplomacy

Barros Hurtado, César
Beale, Howard
Beam, Jacob D.
Bonsal, Philip Wilson
Chagla, Mahomed Ali Currim
Chapman, Daniel A.
Hill, Robert C.
Jernegan, John D.
John XXIII, Pope
Kennan, George F.
Knuth-Winterfeldt, Kield Gustav, Count
Lindt, Auguste R.
Münnich, Ferenc
Rountree, William M.
Tello, Manuel
Wigglesworth, Richard B.
Yost, Charles W.

Education

Arendt, Hannah
Bailar, John C., Jr.
Barros Hurtado, César
Bazin, Germain
Belluschi, Pietro
Bissell, Claude T.
Brinton, Crane
Brooks, James
Buechner, Frederick (WLB)
Carr, Emma P.

Chamberlain, Francis L.
Chapman, Daniel A.
Clark, Charles E.
Dunton, A. Davidson
Evans, Herbert M.
Fels, William C.
French, Robert W.
Galbraith, John Kenneth
Gifford, Chloe
Harrelson, Walter, Rev. Dr.
Harris, Mark (WLB)
Hatfield, Mark O.
Hayakawa, S. I.
Hevesy, George de
Jacopi, Giulio
Johnson, Wendell
Killian, James R., Jr.
Krutch, Joseph Wood
Kuiper, Gerard P.
Kunitz, Stanley
Lederberg, Joshua
Lorge, Irving
McCall, Duke K., Rev. Dr.
MacLeish, Archibald
Morgan, Lucy
Powell, Benjamin E.
Smith, Courtney
Stout, Ruth A.
Tatum, Edward L.
Topping, Norman
Tunnard, Christopher
Van Allen, James A.
Veronese, Vittorino
Verwoerd, H. F.
Walker, Eric A.
Warner, W. Lloyd
Wilson, Sloan
Wu, Chien Shiung
Zerbe, Karl

Engineering

Froehlich, Jack E.
Killian, James R., Jr.

Fashion

Davis, Tobé Coller
Kahane, Melanie
Thompson, Kay

Finance

Bache, Harold L.
Donner, Frederic G.
Fleming, Donald M.
Franke, William B.
Kuzmin, Iosif I.
Latham, Dana
McDonnell, William A.
Miller, Lee P.
Rockefeller, David
Wilde, Frazar B.

Government— Foreign

Akihito, Crown Prince of Japan
Alessandri, Jorge
Ayub Khan, Mohammad
Beale, Howard
Bolz, Lothar
Chagla, Mahomed Ali Currim
Chapman, Daniel A.
Chen Yi
Debré, Michel
Dunton, A. Davidson
Eghbal, Manouchehr
Endeley, E. M. L.
Fischer, Carlos L.
Fleming, Donald M.
Fulton, E. D.
Hees, George
Jacopi, Giulio
Karami, Rashid
Kassem, Abdul Karim
Knuth-Winterfeldt, Kield Gustav, Count
Kozlov, Frol R.
Kuzmin, Iosif I.
Lee Kuan Yew
López Mateos, Adolfo
Malraux, André
Manley, Norman W.
Manning, Ernest
Mattei, Enrico
Mboya, Tom
Münnich, Ferenc
Olivetti, Adriano
Pant, Govind Ballabh
Phoui Sananikone
Profumo, John D.
Rössel, Agda
Stoica, Chivu
Tello, Manuel
Touré, Sékou
Urrutia Lleo, Manuel
Verwoerd, H. F.
Welensky, Sir Roy

Government— United States

Beam, Jacob D.
Bonsal, Philip Wilson
Brown, Newell
Clapp, Verner W.
Clark, Charles E.
Coffin, Frank M.
Dodd, Thomas J.
Dryden, Hugh L.
Egan, William Allen
Finnegan, Joseph F.
Franke, William B.
French, Robert W.
Galbraith, John Kenneth
Granahan, Kathryn E.
Hart, Philip A.
Hatfield, Mark O.
Hill, Robert C.
Jernegan, John D.
Jones, Roger W.

Jordan, B. Everett
Killian, James R., Jr.
Latham, Dana
Lawrence, David L.
McCone, John A.
Malone, Ross L.
Mason, Norman P.
Mitchell, William L.
Morgan, Thomas E.
Morse, True D.
Mueller, Frederick H.
O'Brien, Leo W.
Rains, Albert
Rankin, J. Lee
Reuss, Henry S.
Rountree, William M.
Rubottom, R. R., Jr.
Stewart, Potter
Swing, Joseph M.
Thompson, Frank, Jr.
Weis, Mrs. Charles W., Jr.
White, W. Wilson
Wigglesworth, Richard B.
Yost, Charles W.
Young, Stephen M.

Industry

Barton, Robert B. M.
Cresap, Mark W., Jr.
Davis, Nathanael V.
Donner, Frederic G.
Dreyfuss, Henry
Fuller, Margaret H.
Hope, Stanley C.
Innocenti, Ferdinando
Kuzmin, Iosif I.
Mattei, Enrico
Mueller, Frederick H.
Nickerson, Albert L.
Olivetti, Adriano
Paxton, Robert
Percy, Charles H.
Rockefeller, Laurance S.

International Relations

Barros Hurtado, César
Beale, Howard
Beam, Jacob D.
Bonsal, Philip Wilson
Chagla, Mahomed Ali Currim
Chapman, Daniel A.
Chen Yi
Fisk, James Brown
Hill, Robert C.
Jernegan, John D.
Joyce, J. Avery
Kennan, George F.
Lindt, Auguste R.
Mboya, Tom
Münnich, Ferenc
Norstad, Lauris
Profumo, John D.
Rössel, Agda
Rountree, William M.
Rubottom, R. R., Jr.

Tello, Manuel
Veronese, Vittorino
Welensky, Sir Roy
Wigglesworth, Richard B.
Yost, Charles W.

Journalism

Clurman, Harold
De Vries, Peter (WLB)
Fleeson, Doris
Fuoss, Robert M.
Golden, Harry
Gordimer, Nadine (WLB)
Goren, Charles H.
Krutch, Joseph Wood
Levine, Irving R.
Mannes, Marya
O'Brien, Leo W.
Piel, Gerard
Rouché, Berton (WLB)
Schorr, Daniel
Smith, Red
Taubman, Howard
Whyte, William H., Jr.
Wilson, Sloan

Labor

Brown, Newell
Endeley, E. M. L.
Finnegan, Joseph F.
Livingston, John W.
McDevitt, James L.
Mboya, Tom
Rose, Alex
Touré, Sékou
Welensky, Sir Roy

Law

Beale, Howard
Chagla, Mahomed Ali Currim
Clark, Charles E.
Coffin, Frank M.
Dodd, Thomas J.
Finnegan, Joseph F.
Fleming, Donald M.
Fulton, E. D.
Hart, Philip A.
Joyce, J. Avery
Latham, Dana
Lee Kuan Yew
Lipsky, Eleazar (WLB)
Mahan, John W.
Malone, Ross L.
Manley, Norman W.
Moore, Preston J.
Rankin, J. Lee
Stewart, Potter
Urrutia Lleo, Manuel
White, W. Wilson
Young, Stephen M.

Library Service

Adkinson, Burton W.
Brigham, Clarence S.
Clapp, Verner W.

Francis, Frank
Fuller, Margaret H.
MacLeish, Archibald
Powell, Benjamin E.

Literature

Baldwin, James (WLB)
Buechner, Frederick (WLB)
Carter, John
Cheney, Brainard (WLB)
Coker, Elizabeth Boatwright (WLB)
Conrad, Barnaby, Jr.
De Vries, Peter (WLB)
Dürrenmatt, Friedrich
Evatt, Harriet (WLB)
Gordimer, Nadine (WLB)
Grau, Shirley Ann (WLB)
Hansberry, Lorraine
Harris, Mark (WLB)
Herold, J. Christopher (WLB)
Hilliard, Jan (WLB)
Hunter, Kermit
Ionesco, Eugène
Kerouac, Jack
Krutch, Joseph Wood
Kubly, Herbert
Kunitz, Stanley
Lipsky, Eleazar (WLB)
MacLeish, Archibald
McMinnies, Mary (WLB)
Malraux, André
Mannes, Marya
Newman, Bernard
Osborne, John
Pasternak, Boris
Peare, Catherine Owens (WLB)
Rama Rau, Santha (WLB)
Renault, Mary
Roueché, Berton (WLB)
Schlein, Miriam (WLB)
Settle, Mary Lee (WLB)
Shulman, Max
Speare, Elizabeth George (WLB)
Tanner, Edward Everett, 3d
Taylor, Robert Lewis
Thompson, Kay
Uris, Leon (WLB)
Wilson, Angus
Wilson, Sloan

Medicine

Chamberlain, Francis L.
Eghbal, Manouchehr
Endeley, E. M. L.
Evans, Herbert M.
Gundersen, Gunnar
Lasker, Mrs. Albert D.
Lederberg, Joshua
Morgan, Thomas E.
Roueché, Berton (WLB)
Stapp, John Paul
Tatum, Edward L.
Topping, Norman

Military

Anderson, William R.
Ayub Khan, Mohammad
Felt, Harry D.
Hodes, Henry I.
Norstad, Lauris
Stapp, John Paul
Swing, Joseph M.

Motion Pictures

Andrews, Dana
Boone, Pat
Coe, Fred
Curtis, Tony
Daly, James
Field, Betty
Ford, Glenn
Fresnay, Pierre
Hartford, Huntington, 2d
Hawkins, Jack
Hayes, Peter Lind
Houseman, John
Loren, Sophia
MacLaine, Shirley
Monroe, Marilyn
Murray, Don
Newman, Paul
Paar, Jack
Paige, Janis
Poitier, Sidney
Preminger, Otto
Presley, Elvis
Renoir, Jean
Robards, Jason, Jr.
Stapleton, Maureen
Tanner, Edward Everett, 3d
Thomas, Danny
Thompson, Kay
Uris, Leon (WLB)
Vera-Ellen
Wallach, Eli

Music

Boone, Pat
Bowers, Faubion
Clark, Dick
Garner, Erroll
Lenya, Lotte
Malbin, Elaine
Niles, John Jacob
Paige, Janis
Pennario, Leonard
Presley, Elvis
Ritchie, Jean
Stella, Antonietta
Taubman, Howard
Thompson, Kay
Tureck, Rosalyn
Zirato, Bruno

Nonfiction

Arendt, Hannah
Barros Hurtado, César
Bazin, Germain

Bowers, Faubion
Brigham, Clarence S.
Brinton, Crane
Carter, John
Clurman, Harold
Conrad, Barnaby, Jr.
Galbraith, John Kenneth
Gheerbrant, Alain
Golden, Harry
Goren, Charles H.
Hayakawa, S. I.
Johnson, Wendell
Joyce, J. Avery
Kennan, George F.
Krutch, Joseph Wood
Kubly, Herbert
Levine, Irving R.
Lorge, Irving
Malraux, André
Mannes, Marya
Newman, Bernard
Obolensky, Serge
Peare, Catherine Owens (WLB)
Peterson, Roger Tory
Rama Rau, Santha (WLB)
Ritchie, Jean
Roueché, Berton (WLB)
Shulman, Max
Taubman, Howard
Taylor, Robert Lewis
Walworth, Arthur
Warner, W. Lloyd
Whyte, William H., Jr.

Organizations

Adkinson, Burton W.
Allen, Martha F.
Bailar, John C., Jr.
Chamberlain, Francis L.
Clapp, Verner W.
Daniels, Grace B.
Fuller, Margaret H.
Gifford, Chloe
Gundersen, Gunnar
Hope, Stanley C.
Klopsteg, Paul E.
Livingston, John W.
McDevitt, James L.
McDonnell, William A.
Mahan, John W.
Malone, Ross L.
Miller, Lee P.
Moore, Preston J.
Parsons, Mrs. William Barclay
Phillips, Mrs. Robert J.
Powell, Benjamin E.
Stout, Ruth A.
Veronese, Vittorino

Philosophy

Arendt, Hannah
Krutch, Joseph Wood

Politics— Foreign

Alessandri, Jorge
Ayub Khan, Mohammad
Barros Hurtado, César
Beale, Howard
Bolz, Lothar
Chen Yi
Debré, Michel
Eghbal, Manouchehr
Endeley, E. M. L.
Fischer, Carlos L.
Fleming, Donald M.
Fulton, E. D.
Gandhi, Indira
Hees, George
Karami, Rashid
Kassem, Abdul Karim
Kozlov, Frol R.
Kuzmin, Iosif I.
Lee Kuan Yew
López Mateos, Adolfo
Malraux, André
Manley, Norman W.
Manning, Ernest
Mboya, Tom
Münnich, Ferenc
Olivetti, Adriano
Pant, Govind Ballabh
Phoui Sananikone
Profumo, John D.
Stoica, Chivu
Touré, Sékou
Urrutia Lleo, Manuel
Verwoerd, H. F.
Welensky, Sir Roy

Politics— United States

Brown, Newell
Coffin, Frank M.
Dodd, Thomas J.
Egan, William Allen
Granahan, Kathryn E.
Hart, Philip A.
Hatfield, Mark O.
Jordan, B. Everett
Lawrence, David L.
Morgan, Thomas E.
O'Brien, Leo W.
Percy, Charles H.
Phillips, Mrs. Robert J.
Rains, Albert
Reuss, Henry S.
Rose, Alex
Thompson, Frank, Jr.
Weis, Mrs. Charles W., Jr.
Wigglesworth, Richard B.
Young, Stephen M.

Publishing

Fuoss, Robert M.
Golden, Harry
Herold, J. Christopher (WLB)
Piel, Gerard
Praeger, Frederick A.

Radio

Boone, Pat
Dunton, A. Davidson
Grauer, Ben
Hayes, Peter Lind
Houseman, John
Levine, Irving R.
Paar, Jack
Schorr, Daniel

Religion

Buechner, Frederick (WLB)
Harrelson, Walter, Rev. Dr.
Herzog, Isaac Halevi, Rabbi
Janssens, John Baptist, Very Rev.
John XXIII, Pope
McCall, Duke K., Rev. Dr.
Manning, Ernest
Pire, Georges, Rev.
Rummel, Joseph F., Archbishop
Thadden-Trieglaff, Reinold von

Science

Adkinson, Burton W.
Bailar, John C., Jr.
Carr, Emma P.
Dryden, Hugh L.
Evans, Herbert M.
Fisk, James Brown
Froehlich, Jack E.
Fuller, John L.
Hevesy, George de
Killian, James R., Jr.
Klopsteg, Paul E.
Kuiper, Gerard P.
Lasker, Mrs. Albert D.
Lederberg, Joshua
Lovell, Bernard
McCone, John A.
Peterson, Roger Tory
Piel, Gerard
Stapp, John Paul
Tatum, Edward L.
Van Allen, James A.
Walker, Eric A.
Wu, Chien Shiung

Social Science

Arendt, Hannah
Barros Hurtado, César
Brigham, Clarence S.
Brinton, Crane
Galbraith, John Kenneth
Gheerbrant, Alain
Hayakawa, S. I.
Johnson, Wendell
Kennan, George F.
Lorge, Irving
Veronese, Vittorino
Verwoerd, H. F.
Warner, W. Lloyd

Social Service

Allen, Martha F.
Lasker, Mrs. Albert D.
Lindt, Auguste R.
Murray, Don
Parsons, Mrs. William Barclay
Pire, Georges, Rev.
Rockefeller, David
Rockefeller, Laurance S.
Rockefeller, Winthrop
Rössel, Agda

Sports

Banks, Ernie
Conrad, Barnaby, Jr.
Goren, Charles H.
Heiss, Carol E.
Jensen, Jackie
Johansson, Ingemar
Olmedo, Alex
Smith, Red
Wall, Art, Jr.

Technology

Adkinson, Burton W.
Dryden, Hugh L.
Froehlich, Jack E.
Innocenti, Ferdinando
Kerr, James W.
Killian, James R., Jr.
Klopsteg, Paul E.
Piel, Gerard
Van Allen, James A.
Walker, Eric A.

Television

Boone, Pat
Clark, Dick
Coe, Fred
Daly, James
Dunton, A. Davidson
Grauer, Ben
Hayes, Peter Lind
Houseman, John
Levenson, Sam
Levine, Irving R.
MacLaine, Shirley
Malbin, Elaine
Newman, Paul
Paar, Jack
Paige, Janis
Robards, Jason, Jr.
Schorr, Daniel
Serling, Rod
Smith, Dick
Stapleton, Maureen
Thomas, Danny
Thompson, Kay
Wallach, Eli

Theater

Andrews, Dana
Bowers, Faubion
Browne, Coral
Clurman, Harold
Coe, Fred
Daly, James
De Vries, Peter (WLB)
Dürrenmatt, Friedrich
Field, Betty

Ford, Glenn
Fresnay, Pierre
Hansberry, Lorraine
Hartford, Huntington, 2d
Hawkins, Jack
Hayes, Peter Lind
Houseman, John
Hunter, Kermit
Ionesco, Eugène
Kubly, Herbert
Lenya, Lotte

Murray, Don
Neville, John
Newman, Paul
Osborne, John
Paige, Janis
Poitier, Sidney
Preminger, Otto
Robards, Jason, Jr.
Shulman, Max
Stapleton, Maureen
Tanner, Edward Everett, 3d
Wallach, Eli

CUMULATED INDEX—1951-1959

This is a nine-year cumulation of all names which have appeared in CURRENT BIOGRAPHY from 1951 through 1959. The dates after names indicate monthly issues and/or Yearbooks in which biographies and obituaries are contained.

For the index to 1940-1950 biographies, see CURRENT BIOGRAPHY 1950 Yearbook.

Aaltonen, Wäinö (Waldemar) Jun 54

Aandahl, Fred G(eorge) Sep 58

Aaron, Hank See Aaron, Henry May 58

Aaron, Henry (Louis) May 58

Abbé Pierre See Pierre, Abbé Nov 55

Abbell, Maxwell biog Jul 51 obit Sep 57

Abbott, Edith biog Sep 41 obit Oct 57

Abdullah al-Salim al Subah, Sir, Sheikh of Kuwait Jul 57

Abdullah ibn Hussein, King of Jordan biog Jun 48 obit Sep 51

Abdullah, Seif-ul-Islam, Prince See Seif-ul-Islam Abdullah, Prince biog Dec 47 obit Sep 55

Abdullah, Mohammad Nov 52

Abelson, Nat(han) Nov 57

Abend, Hallett (Edward) biog Sep 42 obit Feb 56

Abercrombie, Sir (Leslie) Patrick biog Apr 46 obit Jun 57

Abrahams, Peter (Henry) (WLB) Yrbk 57

Abrams, Benjamin Sep 54

Abrams, Harry N(athan) Jun 58

Abul Kalam Azad, Maulana biog Jul 42 obit May 58

Achelis, Elisabeth Jun 54

Acker, Achille (H.) van May 58

Adamic, Louis biog Yrbk 40 obit Oct 51

Adams, Arthur S(tanton) Jan 51

Adams, Diana Apr 54

Adams, Edith Feb 54

Adams, Sir Grantley H(erbert) Sep 58

Adams, John Cranford Sep 58

Adams, Sherman Nov 52

Adams, Stanley Feb 54

Addams, Charles (Samuel) Jan 54

Addis Ababa, Duca d' See Badoglio, Pietro biog Oct 40 obit Jan 57

Adenauer, Konrad Apr 58

Adkins, Bertha S(heppard) May 53

Adkinson, Burton W(ilbur) Jun 59

Adler, Julius Ochs biog Jun 48 obit Dec 55 Yrbk 56

Adler, Mortimer J(erome) Sep 52

Adrian, E(dgar) D(ouglas) Adrian, 1st Baron Feb 55

Adrian, (Gilbert) biog Feb 41 obit Nov 59

Afro Nov 58

Aga Khan, The (Aga Sultan Sir Mahomed Shah) biog May 46 obit Sep 57

Ahlgren, Mildred Carlson See Ahlgren, Mrs. O. A. Jul 52

Ahlgren, Mrs. Oscar A(lexander) Jul 52

Ahmad, King of the Yemen Mar 56

Ahmadu, Alhaji, Sardauna of Sokoto; Awolowo, Obafemi; and Azikiwe, Nnamdi Jul 57

Akihito, Crown Prince of Japan Apr 59

Ala, Hussein May 51

Alberghetti, Anna Maria Jan 55

Albert, Carl (Bert) Jun 57

Albert, Eddie Jan 54

Alberti, Jules (Robert) Jul 59

Albion, Robert Greenhalgh May 54

Albright, Tenley Sep 56

Albright, William F(oxwell) Sep 55

Alcorn, (Hugh) Meade (Jr.) May 57

Aldrich, Richard (Stoddard) Jun 55

Aldrich, Winthrop W(illiams) Mar 53

Aldridge, John W(atson) (WLB) Yrbk 58

Alessandri (Rodríguez), Jorge May 59

Alexander, Archie A. biog Jun 55 obit Mar 58

Alexander, Madame (Beatrice) Sep 57

Alexander, Holmes (Moss) Sep 56

Alexander, Madame See Alexander, Madame (Beatrice) Sep 57

Alexanderson, Ernst F(redrik) W(erner) Sep 55

Alexei, Patriarch of Russia Mar 53

Al-Hassan, Prince See al-Hassan, Prince of the Yemen Feb 57

Ali, Chaudhri Mohamad Feb 56

Ali, Mohammed Oct 52

Al Kuwatly, Shukri See Kuwatly, Shukri al May 56

Allen, (Andrew) Ralph Jul 58

Allen, Ethan (Nathan) Mar 54

Allen, Fred biog Feb 41 obit May 56

Allen, Gracie See Burns, G. and Allen, G. Mar 51

Allen, Helen Howe See Howe, H. (WLB) Yrbk 54

Allen, Martha F(rances) Oct 59

Allen, Ralph See Allen, (Andrew) Ralph Jul 58

Allen, Raymond B(ernard) Mar 52

Allen, Stephen Valentine See Allen, S. Jul 51

Allen, Steve Jul 51

Allen, Mrs. Steve See Meadows, Jayne May 58

Allen, William L. Sep 53

Allen, William M(cPherson) Mar 53

Allison, John M(oore) Mar 56

Allman, David B(acharach) Feb 58

Allott, Gordon (Llewellyn) May 55

Allyn, Stanley C(harles) Mar 56

Allyson, June Jan 52

Almond, Edward M(allory) Mar 51

Almond, J(ames) Lindsay, Jr. Mar 58

Alonso, Alicia Jul 55

Alphand, Hervé Nov 51

Al-Shabandar, Moussa See Shabandar, Moussa Feb 56

Alsop, Joseph W(right), Jr. and Stewart (Johonnot Oliver) Oct 52

Alsop, Stewart See Alsop, Joseph W., Jr. Oct 52

Alstadt, W(illiam) R(obert) Jul 58

Alston, Walter (Emmons) Jun 54

Alvarez, Walter C(lement) Sep 53

Ambedkar, B(himrao) R(amji) biog Nov 51 obit Feb 57

Amery, L(eopold Charles Maurice) S(tennett) biog Jul 42 obit Nov 55 Yrbk 56

Ames, Louise See Ilg, Frances L. Sep 56

Amis, Kingsley (William) (WLB) Yrbk 58

Amory, Derick Heathcoat Apr 58

Amrit Kaur, Rajkumari See Kaur, Rajkumari Amrit Oct 55

Anderson, Carl D(avid) Jan 51

Anderson, Erica (Kellner Collier) Feb 57

Anderson, Gaylord W(est) Feb 53

511

Anderson, Howard (Richmond) Jan 55

Anderson, Sir John See Waverley, John Anderson, 1st Viscount biog Jul 41 obit Mar 58

Anderson, John W(illiam) Jul 53

Anderson, Sir Kenneth A(rthur) N(oel) biog Feb 43 obit Jul 59

Anderson, Leroy Sep 52

Anderson, Maxwell biog Sep 53 obit May 59

Anderson, R(obert) B(ernerd) Jun 53

Anderson, Robert (Woodruff) Sep 54

Anderson, Samuel W(agner) Jun 54

Anderson, Sigurd Sep 53

Anderson, Victor E(manuel) Sep 56

Anderson, William R(obert) Apr 59

Andrade, Victor (Manuel) Feb 53

Andresen, August H(erman) biog Feb 56 obit Mar 58

Andrewes, Sir William (Gerrard) Sep 52

Andrews, Bert biog Sep 48 obit Oct 53

Andrews, (Carver) Dana Oct 59

Andrews, Julie Jul 56

Andrews, Roy Chapman Jul 53

Andrews, Stanley Jun 52

Andrews, T(homas) Coleman Apr 54

Angeles, Victoria de los Feb 55

Angle, Paul M(cClelland) Jul 55

Angoff, Charles (WLB) Yrbk 55

Anouilh, Jean Apr 54

Anspach, Charles L(eroy) Sep 56

Antheil, George biog Jul 54 obit Apr 59

Antoine Jun 55

Araki, Eikichi biog Oct 52 obit Apr 59

Aramburu, Pedro Eugenio Jan 57

Arbenz Guzman, Jacobo Sep 53

Arcaro, Eddie Sep 58

Arcaro, George Edward See Arcaro, Eddie Sep 58

Archambault, Louis (De Gonzague Pascal) Sep 59

Archipenko, Alexander Sep 53

Arciniegas, Germán May 54

Ardalan, Ali Gholi Apr 54

Arden, Elizabeth Jul 57

Arden, Eve Sep 53

Areilza, José María de, Count of Motrico Apr 55

Arendt, Hannah May 59

Arlen, Harold Jul 55

Armand, Louis; Etzel, Franz; and Giordani, Francesco Sep 57

Armas, Carlos Castillo See Castillo Armas, Carlos biog Jan 55 obit Sep 57

Armitage, Kenneth Apr 57

Armour, Richard (Willard) Nov 58

Armstrong, Edwin Howard biog Apr 40 obit Mar 54

Armstrong, George E(llis) Apr 52

Armstrong, Harry G(eorge) Jul 51

Armstrong, J(ames) Sinclair Mar 58

Arnaz, Desi See Ball, L. and Arnaz, D. Sep 52

Arnon, Daniel I(srael) Jun 55

Arnow, Harriette (Louisa) Simpson (WLB) Yrbk 54

Aron, Raymond (Claude Ferdinand) Jun 54

Aronin, Jeffrey Ellis Jan 55

Aronson, J(ohn) Hugo Feb 54

Arp, Hans See Arp, J. May 54

Arp, Jean May 54

Asaf Ali biog Jun 47 obit May 53

Asakai, Koichiro Sep 57

Ascoli, Max Feb 54

Asgeirsson, Asgeir Sep 52

Ashida, Hitoshi biog Jun 48 obit Sep 59

Ashmore, Harry S(cott) Sep 58

Ashton, Frederick May 51

Asimov, Isaac (WLB) Yrbk 53

Assis Chateaubriand (Bandeira de Mello, Francisco de) Jun 57

Astin, Allen V(arley) May 56

Astor, John Jacob May 54

Aswell, James biog (WLB) Yrbk 51 obit Apr 55

Atkinson, Joseph Hampton May 56

Atkinson, Oriana (Torrey) (WLB) Yrbk 53

Atwood, Donna May 54

Auchincloss, Louis (WLB) Yrbk 54

Auriol, Jacqueline Sep 53

Austin, Margretta (Stroup) Feb 54

Avenol, Joseph (Louis Anne) biog Jan-Feb 40 obit Oct 52

Averoff-Tositsas, Evangelos May 57

Avery, Milton (Clark) Jun 58

Avila Camacho, Manuel biog Sep 40 obit Dec 55 Yrbk 56

Awolowo, Obafemi See Ahmadu, Alhaji, Sardauna of Sokoto Jul 57

Aydelotte, Frank biog Apr 52 obit Feb 57

Ayub Khan, Mohammad Apr 59

Azikiwe, Nnamdi See Ahmadu, Alhaji, Sardauna of Sokoto Jul 57

Azuma IV, Tokuho Apr 54

Babb, James T(inkham) Jul 55

Babson, Naomi Lane (WLB) Yrbk 52

Bacharach, Bert(ram Mark) Dec 57

Bachauer, Gina Jun 54

Bache, Harold L(eopold) May 59

Backman, Jules Apr 52

Backstrand, C(lifford) J(ulius) Feb 54

Bacon, Francis Feb 57

Bacon, Leonard biog Jun 41 obit Mar 54

Bacon, Selden D(askam) May 52

Badger, Oscar C(harles) biog May 49 obit Feb 59

Badoglio, Pietro biog Oct 40 obit Jan 57

Bailar, John C(hristian), Jr. Jul 59

Bailey, Consuelo Northrop Jun 54

Bailey, L(iberty) H(yde) biog Jun 48 obit Mar 55

Bailey, Pearl (Mae) Jun 55

Baird, Bil and Cora Mar 54

Baker, George T(heodore) Jun 53

Baker, Louise (WLB) Yrbk 54

Baker, Nina Brown biog (WLB) Yrbk 47 obit Nov 57

Bakke, E(dward) Wight Sep 53

Bakshi Ghulam Mohammad Jun 56

Balanchine, George Jun 54

Baldwin, James (Arthur) (WLB) Yrbk 59

Balenciaga, (Cristóbal) May 54

Ball, Lucille and Arnaz, Desi Sep 52

Ball, Stuart S(coble) Jul 52

Ball, Zachary (WLB) Yrbk 53

Ballantine, Ian (Keith) May 54

Balmain, Pierre (Alexandre) Jul 54

Bandaranaike, S(olomon) W(est) R(idgeway) D(ias) biog Sep 56 obit Nov 59

Bankhead, Tallulah (Brockman) Jan 53

Banks, Ernest See Banks, Ernie May 59

Banks, Ernie May 59

Bannister, Constance Jul 55

Bannister, Roger (Gilbert) Apr 56

Barbieri, Fedora Feb 57

Barcelona, Count of See Juan Carlos, Count of Barcelona Oct 51

Bard, Mary (Ten Eyck) (WLB) Yrbk 56

Bardeen, John Sep 57

Barkley, Alben W(illiam) biog Jan 49 obit Jul 56

Barlow, Howard Jul 54

Barnes, Albert C(oombs) biog Mar 45 obit Sep 51

Barnes, Henry A. Jun 55

Barnes, Margaret Campbell (WLB) Yrbk 53

Barnes, Stanley N(elson) Sep 53

Barnes, Wendell B(urton) Jun 57

Barnhart, Clarence L(ewis) Sep 54

Barrault, Jean-Louis and Renaud, Madeleine Mar 53

Barrett, Frank A. Jul 56

Barros Hurtado, César Jan 59

Barrymore, Ethel biog Mar 41 obit Sep 59

Barrymore, Lionel biog Jul 43 obit Jan 55

Blücher, Franz biog Jan 56 obit Jun 59

Blume, Peter Mar 56

Blundell, Michael Mar 54

Blunt, Katharine biog Dec 46 obit Oct 54

Boatner, Haydon L(emaire) Jul 52

Bob and Ray See Elliott, Bob Oct 57

Bogart, Humphrey biog May 42 obit Mar 57

Boggs, Hale See Boggs, (Thomas) Hale Apr 58

Boggs, J(ames) Caleb Jul 56

Boggs, (Thomas) Hale Apr 58

Boheman, Erik (Carlson) Mar 51

Bohrod, Aaron Feb 55

Boigny, Félix Houphouet- See Houphouet-Boigny, Félix Oct 58

Bok, William Curtis May 54

Boles, Ewing T(homas) Apr 53

Boles, Paul Darcy (WLB) Yrbk 56

Bolt, Richard H(enry) Jun 54

Bolte, Charles L(awrence) Jan 54

Bolton, Frances P(ayne Bingham) Apr 54

Bolz, Lothar Sep 59

Bond, Horace Mann Mar 54

Bonner, Herbert C(ovington) Jul 56

Bonner, Paul Hyde (WLB) Yrbk 55

Bonomi, Ivanoe biog Aug 44 obit May 51

Bonsal, Philip Wilson Jun 59

Bonsal, Stephen biog Aug 45 obit Jul 51

Boone, J(oel) T(hompson) Mar 51

Boone, Pat Jul 59

Booth, Shirley Apr 53

Borberg, William biog Nov 52 obit Sep 58

Borden, Neil H(opper) May 54

Borgese, G(iuseppe) A(ntonio) biog Dec 47 obit Jan 53

Borgnine, Ernest Apr 56

Born, Max May 55

Borne, Mortimer Apr 54

Borst, Lyle B(enjamin) Jul 54

Bosustow, Stephen Jun 58

Bothe, Walther (Wilhelm Georg) biog May 55 obit Apr 57

Bourgès-Maunoury, Maurice (Jean-Marie) Jul 57

Bourguiba, Habib ben Ali Sep 55

Boutelle, Richard S(chley) Sep 51

Bovet, Daniele Jan 58

Bowater, Sir Eric (Vansittart) Sep 56

Bowditch, Richard L(yon) biog Jul 53 obit Nov 59

Bowen, Ira Sprague Jun 51

Bowers, Claude G(ernade) biog Sep 41 obit Mar 58

Bowers, Faubion Sep 59

Bowers, Mrs. Faubion See Rama Rau, Santha (WLB) Yrbk 59

Bowles, Chester (Bliss) Jan 57

Boyd, Alan T. Lennox- See Lennox-Boyd, Alan T. Jun 56

Boyer, Harold Raymond Feb 52

Boyer, M(arion) W(illard) Jan 51

Brackett, Charles Feb 51

Brackman, Robert Jul 53

Bradbury, Ray (Douglas) Jun 53

Braddock, Bessie See Braddock, E. M. Jul 57

Braddock, E(lizabeth) M(argaret Bamber) Jul 57

Bradley, Preston, Rev. Dr. Mar 56

Bragdon, Helen D(alton) Feb 51

Brahdy, Mrs. Leopold See Rees, Mina S. Nov 57

Brailowsky, Alexander Jun 56

Brancusi, Constantin biog Sep 55 obit Jun 57

Brando, Marlon Apr 52

Brandt, Willy Jun 58

Braniff, T(homas) E(lmer) biog Apr 52 obit Mar 54

Bransome, Edwin D(agobert) Apr 52

Brattain, Walter H(ouser) Sep 57

Braun, (Joachim) Werner Jun 57

Braun, Wernher von See Von Braun, W. Jan 52

Breckinridge, Aida de Acosta Jun 54

Breech, Ernest R(obert) Sep 55

Brennan, William J(oseph), Jr. Jun 57

Brentano (di Tremezzo), Heinrich von Feb 55

Brenton, W(oodward) Harold Jan 53

Breslin, Howard (Mary) (WLB) Yrbk 58

Brewer, Roy M(artin) Sep 53

Brice, Fanny biog Jun 46 obit Jul 51

Brick, John (WLB) Yrbk 53

Brickell, (Henry) Herschel biog Nov 45 obit Jul 52

Bricker, John W(illiam) Jul 56

Bridgman, P(ercy) W(illiams) Apr 55

Brier, Howard M(axwell) (WLB) Yrbk 51

Briggs, James E(lbert) Jun 57

Brigham, Clarence S(aunders) Jul 59

Brind, Sir (Eric James) Patrick Nov 52

Briney, Nancy (Wells) Jan 54

Briney, Mrs. Paul See Briney, N. (W.) Jan 54

Brinton, (Clarence) Crane Jun 59

Briscoe, Robert May 57

Britton, Edgar C(lay) Apr 52

Bro, Margueritte Harmon (WLB) Yrbk 52

Brod, Mrs. Albert Thomas See Hagy, Ruth Geri Oct 57

Brode, Wallace R(eed) Jun 58

Broglie, Louis (Victor Pierre Raymond), Prince de Sep 55

Bromfield, Louis biog Jul 44 obit May 56

Bronowski, J(acob) Sep 58

Brooke-Popham, Sir Robert (Moore) biog Oct 41 obit Jan 54

Brooks, C(harles) Wayland biog Sep 47 obit Mar 57

Brooks, D(avid) W(illiam) Jun 51

Brooks, James (D.) Feb 59

Brooks, Overton Jun 57

Brophy, Thomas D'Arcy Sep 52

Brosio, Manlio (Giovanni) Sep 55

Brossard, Edgar B(ernard) Jul 54

Brouwer, Dirk Mar 51

Browdy, Benjamin G. Jul 51

Brown, Alberta L(ouise) May 58

Brown, Charles R(andall) Jul 58

Brown, Harrison (Scott) Jul 55

Brown, Irving (Joseph) Jul 51

Brown, Lewis H(erold) biog Oct 47 obit Mar 51

Brown, Newell Sep 59

Browne, Coral (Edith) Dec 59

Brownell, Herbert, Jr. Feb 54

Brownell, Samuel Miller Feb 54

Brownson, Charles B(ruce) Jul 55

Broz, Josip See Tito Mar 55

Brubeck, Dave Mar 56

Brucker, Wilber M(arion) Sep 55

Bruhn, Erik (Belton Evers) Apr 59

Brunauer, Esther C(aukin) biog Nov 47 obit Sep 59

Brundage, Percival F(lack) Apr 57

Brunner, Edmund de S(chweinitz) Sep 58

Brunner, Jean Adam biog Sep 45 obit Jun 51

Bruns, Franklin R(ichard), Jr. May 54

Brunsdale, (Clarence) Norman Sep 54

Bryan, Ernest R(owlett) biog Jul 50 obit Feb 55

Brynner, Yul Sep 56

Bryson, Lyman (Lloyd) Sep 51

Buber, Martin Jun 53

Buchanan, Frank biog Feb 51 obit May 51

Buchanan, Wiley T(homas), Jr. Nov 57

Bucher, Walter H(erman) Feb 57

Buck, Gene biog Feb 41 obit May 57

Buck, Paul H(erman) Jul 55

Buck, Pearl (Sydenstricker) Jul 56

Budenz, Louis F(rancis) Jun 51

Buechner, (Carl) Frederick (WLB) Yrbk 59

Buffet, Bernard Apr 59

Buford, John Lester Apr 56

Bugher, John C(lifford) Apr 53

Buley, R(oscoe) Carlyle Jul 51

Bulganin, Nikolai A(leksandrovich) Feb 55

Bullard, Sir Edward (Crisp) Sep 54

Chandler, Mrs. Norman See Chandler, Dorothy Buffum Jul 57

Chandler, Raymond biog (WLB) Yrbk 46 obit Jun 59

Chanel, Gabrielle (Bonheur) Sep 54

Chapman, Albert K(inkade) Sep 52

Chapman, Charles F(rederic) May 58

Chapman, Daniel A(hmling) Apr 59

Chapman, Gilbert W(hipple) Jun 57

Chapman, Helen Louise Busch See Chapman Mrs. T. S. Apr 55

Chapman, Sydney Jul 57

Chapman, Mrs. Theodore S. Apr 55

Charisse, Cyd Jan 54

Charles-Roux, François (-Jules) Jan 52

Charlesworth, James C(lyde) Sep 54

Charques, Dorothy (Taylor) (WLB) Yrbk 58

Charques, Mrs. Robert Denis See Charques, Dorothy (WLB) Yrbk 58

Chase, Edna Woolman biog Nov 40 obit Jun 57

Chase, Mrs. Hamilton See Seton, A. (WLB) Yrbk 53

Chase, Harry Woodburn biog Jun 48 obit Jun 55

Chase, Joseph Cummings May 55

Chase, William C(urtis) Nov 52

Chastain, Madye Lee (WLB) Yrbk 58

Chateaubriand, Assis See Assis Chateaubriand Jun 57

Chaudhri Mohamad Ali See Ali, Chaudhri Mohamad Feb 56

Chauncey, Henry Jul 51

Chayefsky, Paddy Sep 57

Chelf, Frank L(eslie) Jun 52

Chen Yi Oct 59

Cheney, Brainard (Bartwell) (WLB) Yrbk 59

Chennault, Claire L(ee) biog Oct 42 obit Oct 58

Cherry, Francis A(dams) Jul 54

Cherwell, Frederick Alexander Lindemann, 1st Viscount biog Mar 52 obit Sep 57

Chevrier, Lionel Jun 52

Chiang Ching-kuo Sep 54

Chiang Kai-shek May 53

Chidlaw, Benjamin W(iley) Mar 55

Chifley, Joseph B(enedict) biog Aug 45 obit Jul 51

Childs, Richard S(pencer) Sep 55

Chiperfield, Robert B(ruce) Sep 56

Chipp, Mrs. Rodney Duane See Hicks, Beatrice A. Jan 57

Chirico, Giorgio de Jan 56

Chou En-lai Jul 57

Christenberry, Robert K(eaton) Mar 52

Christians, Mady biog May 45 obit Dec 51

Christopher, George Feb 58

Christopher, George T. biog Nov 47 obit Jul 54

Chubb, L(ewis) Warrington biog Feb 47 obit May 52

Church, Frank (Forrester) Mar 58

Church, Mrs. Marguerite Stitt Feb 51

Churchill, (Clementine Ogilvy Hozier Spencer), Lady Jul 53

Churchill, Gordon (Minto) Sep 58

Churchill, Sarah May 55

Churchill, Sir Winston (Leonard Spencer) Jul 53

Churchill, Mrs. Winston (Leonard Spencer) See Churchill, (C.O. H.S.), Lady Jul 53

Chute, Charles Lionel biog Sep 49 obit Jan 54

Cicognani, Amleto Giovanni, Archbishop Jul 51

Cisler, Walker (Lee) Sep 55

Claire, Ina May 54

Clapp, Verner W(arren) Mar 59

Clark, Bennett Champ biog Nov 41 obit Sep 54

Clark, Charles E(dward) Jul 59

Clark, Dick May 59

Clark, Dorothy Park See Mc-Meekin, Isabel McLennan (WLB) Yrbk 57

Clark, Mrs. Edward R. See Mc-Meekin, Isabel McLennan (WLB) Yrbk 57

Clark, Eugenie Sep 53

Clark, John Apr 52

Clark, J(oseph) J(ames) Jan 54

Clark, Joseph S(ill), Jr. Jun 52

Clark, Leonard (Francis) biog Jan 56 obit Sep 57

Clark McMeekin See McMeekin, Isabel McLennan (WLB) Yrbk 57

Clark, Paul F(oster) Apr 55

Clark, Robert L(incoln) Nov 52

Clark, Sydney (Aylmer) Sep 56

Clayton, P(hilip Thomas) B(yard), Rev. May 55

Clement, Frank G(oad) Jul 55

Clements, Earle C. Sep 55

Cliburn, Van Sep 58

Clift, David H(orace) Jun 52

Clift, Montgomery Jul 54

Cline, John Wesley Jun 51

Clooney, Rosemary Feb 57

Clurman, Harold (Edgar) Feb 59

Clyde, George D(ewey) Jul 58

Coanda, Henri (-Marie) Jul 56

Cobb, Ty(rus Raymond) Sep 51

Coblentz, Stanton A(rthur) Jun 54

Coblentz, W(illiam) W(eber) Mar 54

Cobo, Albert E(ugene) biog Nov 51 obit Dec 57 Yrbk 58

Coca, Imogene Apr 51

Cochran, Sir Charles Blake biog Oct 40 obit Mar 51

Cochrane, Edward L(ull) Mar 51

Cocke, C(harles) Francis Mar 52

Cocke, Erle, Jr. Jan 51

Cockrell, Ewing May 51

Coe, Fred(erick) Jan 59

Coffin, Frank M(orey) Apr 59

Coffin, Henry Sloane, Rev. Dr. biog Apr 44 obit Jan 55

Cohen, Barbara and Roney, Marianne May 57

Cohu, La Motte T(urck) Apr 51

Coit, Margaret Louise June 51

Coker, Elizabeth Boatwright (WLB) Yrbk 59

Coker, Mrs. James Lide, 3d See Coker, Elizabeth Boatwright (WLB) Yrbk 59

Colbert, Lester L(um) Apr 51

Cole, Albert M(cDonald) Jan 54

Cole, Nat King Feb 56

Cole, W(illiam) Sterling Mar 54

Coleman, J(ames) P(lemon) Sep 56

Coleman, John S(trider) biog Apr 53 obit Jul 58

Coleman, Lonnie (WLB) Yrbk 58

Colina, Rafael de la Jan 51

Collet, John C(askie) biog Feb 46 obit Feb 56

Collier, Constance biog Jul 54 obit Jun 55

Collins, LeRoy See Collins, (Thomas) LeRoy Jun 56

Collins, Seaborn P. Apr 55

Collins, (Thomas) LeRoy Jun 56

Colman, Ronald (Charles) biog Jul 43 obit Sep 58

Colvin, Mrs. D(avid) Leigh biog Dec 44 obit Jan 56

Comber, Elizabeth (Chow) See Han Suyin (WLB) Yrbk 57

Comber, Mrs. Leonard See Han Suyin (WLB) Yrbk 57

Compton, Arthur H(olly) Sep 58

Compton, Karl T(aylor) biog Mar 41 obit Sep 54

Compton, Wilson (Martindale) Apr 52

Conan Doyle, Adrian (Malcolm) See Doyle, A. (M.) C. Sep 54

Conant, James Bryant Feb 51

Concheso, Aurelio Fernández biog May 42 obit Jan 56

Conley, Eugene (Thomas) Jul 54

Connell, Arthur J(oseph) Feb 54

Conner, Nadine Jan 55

Connolly, Maureen (Catherine) Nov 51

Conrad, Barnaby, Jr. Sep 59

Conroy, Pat(rick Dominic) Jul 54

Cook, Donald Jul 54

Cook, Donald C(larence) May 52

Cooke, (Alfred) Alistair Jun 52

Cooley, Harold D(unbar) Mar 51

Coolidge, Elizabeth Sprague biog Aug 41 obit Jan 54

Deasy, Mary (Margaret) (WLB) Yrbk 58

Déat, Marcel biog Jan 42 obit May 55

Debré, Michel (Jean Pierre) May 59

De Broglie, Louis, Prince See Broglie, Louis, Prince de Sep 55

DeButts, Harry A(shby) Apr 53

De Chirico, Giorgio See Chirico, Giorgio de Jan 56

DeCoursey, Elbert Sep 54

De Galard Terraube, Geneviève See Galard Terraube, G. de Oct 54

De Gasperi, Alcide See Gasperi, A. de biog Dec 46 obit Oct 54

De Givenchy, Hubert See Givenchy, H. (J. T.) de May 55

De Hevesy, George See Hevesy, George de Apr 59

Dehler, Thomas Jul 55

Dejong, Meindert (WLB) Yrbk 52

De Kauffmann, Henrik See Kauffmann, Henrik Apr 56

De Kiewiet, Cornelis W(illem) Jul 53

De Kleine, William biog Apr 41 obit Dec 57 Yrbk 58

De Kooning, Willem Jun 55

De La Colina, Rafael See Colina, R. de la Jan 51

De la Guardia, Ernesto, Jr. See Guardia, Ernesto de la, Jr. Jan 57

DeLany, Walter S(tanley) Dec 52

De Lima, Sigrid (WLB) Yrbk 58

Della Casa, Lisa Jul 56

Dello Joio, Norman Sep 57

Del Monaco, Mario See Monaco, Mario del Feb 57

De los Angeles, Victoria See Angeles, V. de los Feb 55

De Mille, Cecil B(lount) biog May 42 obit Mar 59

DeMott, Richard H(opper) Feb 51

De Moya, Manuel A. See Moya, Manuel A. de Nov 57

Dendramis, Vassili biog Jun 47 obit Jul 56

Denebrink, Francis C(ompton) Feb 56

Denham, R(obert) N(ewton) biog Oct 47 obit Sep 54

Deniel, Enrique, Cardinal Pla y See Pla y Deniel, E., Cardinal Feb 55

Dennis, Patrick See Tanner, Edward Everett, 3d May 59

De Onís, Harriet See Onís, Harriet de Apr 57

Der Harootian, Koren Jan 55

Derthick, L(awrence) G(ridley) Apr 57

Derwent, Clarence biog Nov 47 obit Nov 59

Desai, Morarji (Ranchhodji) Sep 58

De Sapio, Carmine G(erard) Sep 55

De Sica, Vittorio Jul 52

Dessès, Jean Jan 56

De Valera, Eamon Sep 51

Dever, Paul A(ndrew) biog May 49 obit Jul 58

Deviny, John J(oseph) biog Sep 48 obit Apr 55

De Voto, Bernard biog Sep 43 obit Jan 56

De Vries, Peter (WLB) Yrbk 59

Dewey, John biog Aug 44 obit Jul 52

De Wohl, Louis (WLB) Yrbk 55

Dexheimer, W(ilbur) A(pp) Feb 55

D'Harnoncourt, René Sep 52

Dhebar, U(chharangrai) N(avalshanker) Jun 55

Dial, Morse G(rant) Mar 56

Dibelius, Otto (Friedrich Karl), Bishop May 53

Dickey, John Sloan Apr 55

Dickinson, Robert L(atou) biog Mar 50 obit Jan 51

Dickson, Marguerite (Stockman) biog (WLB) Yrbk 52 obit Jan 54

Didrikson, Babe (Mildred) See Zaharias, Babe Didrikson biog Apr 47 obit Dec 56

Diefenbaker, John G(eorge) May 57

Diem, Ngo Dinh See Ngo-dinh-Diem Mar 55

Dietrich, Marlene Jun 53

Diggs, Charles C(ole), Jr. Jul 57

Dillon, C(larence) Douglas Apr 53

DiMaggio, Joe Jul 51

DiMaggio, Joseph Paul See DiMaggio, J. Jul 51

Dingell, John D(avid) biog Mar 49 obit Nov 55 Yrbk 56

Dior, Christian biog Oct 48 obit Jan 58

Dirksen, Everett M(cKinley) Sep 57

DiSalle, Michael V(incent) Jan 51

Disney, Doris Miles (WLB) Yrbk 54

Disney, Walt Apr 52

Ditchy, Clair W(illiam) Mar 54

Dix, Dorothy biog Jan-Jun 40 obit Feb 52

Dixon, Sir Pierson (John) Sep 54

Djilas, Milovan Sep 58

Djuanda Apr 58

Doan, Leland I(ra) Oct 52

Dobbs, Mattiwilda Sep 55

Docking, George Jun 58

Dodd, Alvin E(arl) biog Nov 47 obit Jul 51

Dodd, Thomas J(oseph) Sep 59

Dodge, Cleveland E(arl) Mar 54

Dodge, David (Francis) (WLB) Yrbk 56

Dolan, D(aniel) Leo Sep 56

Dolbier, Maurice (Wyman) (WLB) Yrbk 56

Domagk, Gerhard (Johannes Paul) Mar 58

Donegan, Horace W(illiam) B(aden), Rt. Rev. Jul 54

Donnelly, Phil M. Jun 56

Donnelly, Walter J(oseph) Sep 52

Donner, Frederic G(arrett) Jan 59

Donovan, William J(oseph) biog Sep 54 obit Apr 59

Dooley, Thomas A(nthony) Jul 57

Doolittle, James H(arold) Mar 57

Dooyeweerd, H(erman) Sep 58

Dorsey, Jimmy biog Apr 42 obit Sep 57

Dorsey, Tommy biog Apr 42 obit Feb 57

Doughton, Robert L(ee) biog Jul 42 obit Dec 54 Yrbk 55

Douglas, Arthur F(iske) biog Nov 50 obit May 56

Douglas, James H(enderson), Jr. Sep 57

Douglas, Kirk Mar 52

Douglas, Marjory Stoneman Jul 53

Douglas, Thomas C(lement) Jul 57

Dowling, Robert W(hittle) Oct 52

Downes, Olin biog Mar 43 obit Oct 55

Downs, Robert B(ingham) Jun 52

Doyle, Adrian (Malcolm) Conan Sep 54

Draper, William H(enry), Jr. Mar 52

Dressen, Charles Walter See Dressen, C. Jul 51

Dressen, Chuck Jul 51

Dreyfus, Camille (Edouard) biog May 55 obit Dec 56 Yrbk 57

Dreyfus, Pierre Jul 58

Dreyfuss, Henry Oct 59

Drum, Hugh A(loysius) biog Jul 41 obit Nov 51

Dryden, Hugh L(atimer) Apr 59

Dubilier, William Sep 57

Dubinsky, David Jun 57

Du Bois, Guy Pène biog Oct 46 obit Oct 58

Dubos, René J(ules) Oct 52

Duchin, Eddy biog Jan 47 obit Mar 51

Dufek, George J(ohn) Mar 57

Duffy, Bernard C(ornelius) Jul 52

Dufy, Raoul (Ernest Joseph) biog Mar 51 obit May 53

Duggar, Benjamin Minge biog Nov 52 obit Nov 56

Du Jardin, Rosamond (Neal) (WLB) Yrbk 53

Faubus, Orval E(ugene) Oct 56
Faulkner, Nancy (WLB) Yrbk 56
Faulkner, William Jan 51
Faure, Edgar Feb 52
Faust, Clarence H(enry) Mar 52
Fawzi, Mahmoud Dec 51
Fechteler, William M(orrow) Sep 51
Feininger, Andreas (Bernhard Lyonel) Oct 57
Feininger, Lyonel (Charles Adrian) biog Jul 55 obit Mar 56
Feinsinger, Nathan P(aul) May 52
Feisal II, King of Iraq biog Jul 55 obit Oct 58
Feldmann, Markus biog Jun 56 obit Jan 59
Felix, Robert H(anna) Apr 57
Feller, Abraham H(oward) biog Nov 46 obit Jan 53
Fellini, Federico Jun 57
Fellows, Harold E(verett) Feb 52
Fels, William C(arl) Apr 59
Felt, Harry D(onald) Mar 59
Feltin, Maurice, Cardinal May 54
Felton, Ralph A(lmon) Sep 57
Ferguson, Harry (George) Mar 56
Ferguson, Malcolm P(hilip) May 57
Fergusson, Erna (WLB) Yrbk 55
Fermi, Enrico biog Oct 45 obit Jan 55
Fermi, Mrs. Enrico See Fermi, Laura May 58
Fermi, Laura (Capon) May 58
Fermor, Patrick Leigh (WLB) Yrbk 55
Fernandel Oct 55
Ferren, John (Millard) Jul 58
Ferrer, José (Pepe) Figueres See Figueres Ferrer, J. (P.) Oct 53
Ferrier, Kathleen biog Oct 51 obit Dec 53
Feynman, R(ichard) P(hillips) Oct 55
Field, Betty Sep 59
Field, Henry Mar 55
Field, Marshall, 3d biog Mar 52 obit Jan 57
Fields, Dorothy Feb 58
Fields, Herbert biog Feb 58 obit Jun 58
Figueres Ferrer, José (Pepe) Oct 53
Figueroa, Ana Feb 52
Filho, Joao Café See Café Filho, J. (F.C.) Jan 55
Fine, John S(ydney) Sep 51
Finet, Paul Sep 51
Fingesten, Peter Oct 54
Finkelstein, Louis, Rabbi Mar 52
Finley, David E(dward) Feb 51
Finnegan, Joseph F(rancis) Apr 59
Finney, Gertrude E(lva Bridgeman) (WLB) Yrbk 57
Finney, Mrs. John Montfort See Finney, Gertrude E. (WLB) Yrbk 57
Finnie, Mrs. Haldeman See Holt, Isabella (WLB) Yrbk 56

Fischer, Carlos L. Feb 59
Fischer, John May 53
Fisher, Eddie Oct 54
Fisher, Harry L(inn) Oct 54
Fisk, James Brown Jan 59
Fitzgerald, Ella Oct 56
Fitz Gerald, Leslie M(aurice) Sep 54
Flaherty, Robert (Joseph) biog Mar 49 obit Sep 51
Flandin, Pierre-Étienne biog Jan 41 obit Oct 58
Fleck, Sir Alexander Apr 56
Fleck, Jack Sep 55
Fleeson, Doris May 59
Fleischmann, Manly Jul 51
Fleming, Sir Alexander biog Apr 44 obit May 55
Fleming, Donald M(ethuen) Feb 59
Fleming, (Jiles) Berry (WLB) Yrbk 53
Fleming, John A(dam) biog May 40 obit Oct 56
Fleming, Philip Bracken biog Apr 40 obit Dec 55 Yrbk 56
Flemming, Arthur S(herwood) Jun 51
Fletcher, C(yril) Scott Feb 53
Flexner, Abraham biog Jun 41 obit Nov 59
Florence, Fred F(arrel) Jun 56
Flynn, Edward J(oseph) biog Sep 40 obit Oct 53
Fogarty, Anne Oct 58
Foot, Sir Hugh (Mackintosh) Oct 53
Forbes, B(ertie) C(harles) biog Mar 50 obit Jul 54
Forbes, John J. (V.) Apr 52
Ford, Benson Feb 52
Ford, Glenn Jun 59
Ford, Tennessee Ernie Mar 58
Forssmann, Werner (Theodor Otto) Mar 57
Forsyth, W(illiam) D(ouglass) Apr 52
Foss, Joe See Foss, Joseph Jacob Oct 55
Foss, Joseph Jacob Oct 55
Fowler, Henry H(amill) Sep 52
Fowler, R(obert) M(acLaren) Oct 54
Fox, Genevieve (May) biog (WLB) Yrbk 49 obit Dec 59
Foyle, Gilbert (Samuel) and William Alfred Jun 54
Foyle, William Alfred See Foyle, G. (S.) and W. A. Jun 54
Franca, Celia May 56
France, Pierre Mendès- See Mendès-France, P. Oct 54
Francis, Arlene May 56
Francis, Frank (Chalton) Jul 59
Franck, James May 57
Franco (y Bahamonde), Francisco Mar 54
Frank, Jerome N(ew) biog Apr 41 obit Mar 57

Frank, Lawrence K(elso) and Mary (Hughes) Jan 58
Frank, Mary See Frank, Lawrence K. Jan 58
Franke, William B(irrell) Sep 59
Frankenberg, Mrs. Lloyd See MacIver, L. (N.) Nov 53
Frankfurter, Felix Jul 57
Fraser, Ian Forbes Jun 54
Fraser, James Earle biog Jul 51 obit Jan 54
Fraser, Peter biog May 42 obit Jan 51
Fraser, Sir Robert (Brown) Oct 56
Frear, J(oseph) Allen, Jr. Oct 54
Fredenthal, David biog Sep 42 obit Jan 59
Frederick, Pauline Oct 54
Frederika (Louise), Consort of Paul I, King of the Hellenes Jan 55
Freehafer, Edward G(eier) Jun 55
Freeman, Lucy (Greenbaum) Oct 53
Freeman, Orville L(othrop) Jun 56
Freitag, Walter biog Jan 54 obit Oct 58
French, Paul Comly May 51
French, Robert W(arren) Oct 59
Fresnay, Pierre Feb 59
Friday, William (Clyde) Apr 58
Friendly, Fred W. Sep 57
Froehlich, Jack E(dward) Jul 59
Frondizi, Arturo Oct 58
Frost, Frances Mary biog (WLB) Yrbk 50 obit Apr 59
Frost, Leslie M(iscampbell) Oct 53
Frothingham, Channing biog Mar 48 obit Nov 59
Fruehauf, Roy (August) Feb 53
Fry, Christopher Feb 51
Frye, Jack biog Apr 45 obit Apr 59
Fuchs, Sir Vivian E(rnest) Oct 58
Fuentes, Miguel Ydígoras, See Ydígoras Fuentes, Miguel Nov 58
Fujiyama, Aiichiro Apr 58
Fulbright, J(ames) William Oct 55
Fuller, Charles E(dward), Rev. Dr. Dec 51
Fuller, John L(angworthy) Mar 59
Fuller, Margaret H(artwell) Jun 59
Fulton, E(dmund) D(avie) Jan 59
Funk, Charles Earle biog Jun 47 obit Jul 57
Funk, Wilfred (John) Jan 55
Funston, G(eorge) Keith Jul 51
Fuoss, Robert M(artin) Feb 59
Furcolo, (John) Foster Jan 58
Furey, Warren W(illiam) biog May 50 obit Jan 59
Furman, N(athaniel) Howell Dec 51
Furnas, Clifford Cook Oct 56

Graham, Frank P(orter) Jul 51
Graham, Virginia Oct 56
Graham, William Franklin, Rev. Apr 51
Graham, Winston (WLB) Yrbk 55
Granahan, Kathryn E(lizabeth) Oct 59
Granik, (S.) Theodore Dec 52
Grant, Gordon (Hope) Jun 53
Grant, Hilda Kay See Hilliard, Jan (WLB) Yrbk 59
Grantham, Sir Alexander (William George Herder) May 54
Granville, William Spencer Leveson-Gower, 4th Earl biog Sep 50 obit Sep 53
Grau, Shirley Ann (WLB) Yrbk 59
Grauer, Ben(jamin Franklin) Jul 59
Grauer, Mrs. Ben(jamin Franklin) See Kahane, Melanie Jul 59
Graves, Alvin C(ushman) Dec 52
Graves, Morris (Cole) Jul 56
Gray, Carl R(aymond), Jr. biog Mar 48 obit Feb 56
Graziani, Rodolfo biog Apr 41 obit Mar 55
Grebe, John J(osef) Oct 55
Greco, José Mar 52
Grede, William J(ohn) Feb 52
Green, Dwight H(erbert) biog Apr 48 obit Apr 58
Green, Edith S(tarrett) May 56
Green, William biog Mar 42 obit Jan 53
Greenaway, Emerson Jul 58
Greenbaum, Lucy See Freeman, L. (G.) Oct 53
Greene, Mrs. Stephen See de Lima, Sigrid (WLB) Yrbk 58
Greenstreet, Sydney (Hughes) biog May 43 obit Mar 54
Greenwood, Arthur biog Oct 40 obit Sep 54
Greenwood, Joan May 54
Gregg, Hugh Jan 54
Gregg, Milton F(owler) Oct 55
Gregory, Paul Apr 56
Grenfell, Joyce (Irene) Mar 58
Grewe, Wilhelm (Georg) Oct 58
Grey, J(ames) D(avid) Sep 52
Grieder, Naomi Lane Babson See Babson, N. L. (WLB) Yrbk 52
Griffin, Bernard (William), Cardinal biog Oct 46 obit Oct 56
Griffin, John D(ouglas Morecroft) May 57
Griffin, Marvin See Griffin, (Samuel) Marvin Jun 56
Griffin, R(obert) Allen Feb 51
Griffin, (Samuel) Marvin Jun 56
Griffith, Clark (Calvin) biog Jun 50 obit Jan 56
Griffiths, Mrs. Hicks G(eorge) See Griffiths, Martha W(right) Oct 55
Griffiths, Martha W(right) Oct 55
Griswold, Dwight P(almer) biog Dec 47 obit Jun 54

Griswold, Erwin N(athaniel) Oct 56
Griswold, Oscar W(oolverton) biog Sep 43 obit Dec 59
Grogan, John Joseph Dec 51
Gromyko, Andreï A(ndreevich) Oct 58
Gronchi, Giovanni Oct 55
Gropius, Walter (Adolf) Mar 52
Gross, Ernest A(rnold) Feb 51
Gross, Robert E(llsworth) Jan 56
Grossinger, Jennie Oct 56
Grosz, George biog Apr 42 obit Oct 59
Grouès, Henri Antoine See Pierre, Abbé Nov 55
Gruen, Victor (David) Mar 59
Guardia, Ernesto de la, Jr. Jan 57
Gueden, Hilde Apr 55
Guerrero, José Gustavo biog Jan 47 obit Jan 59
Guest, Edgar A(lbert) biog Sep 41 obit Nov 59
Guffey, Joseph F. biog Mar 44 obit May 59
Guggenheim, Harry F(rank) Oct 56
Guggenheim, Mrs. Harry F(rank) See Patterson, Alicia Nov 55
Guillaume, Augustin (Léon) Jan 52
Guinzburg, Harold K(leinert) Jul 57
Gumpert, Martin Dec 51
Gundersen, Gunnar Feb 59
Guptill, Arthur L(eighton) biog Mar 55 obit May 56
Guthrie, (William) Tyrone Jul 54
Guzman, Jacobo Arbenz See Arbenz Guzman, J. Sep 53
Gwenn, Edmund biog Sep 43 obit Nov 59
Gyalpo Wangchuk See Wangchuk, Jigme Dorji, Druk Gyalpo of Bhutan Oct 56
Györgyi, Albert Szent- See Szent-Györgyi, A. (von N.) Jan 55

Haakon VII, King of Norway biog May 40 obit Dec 57
Haas, Francis J(oseph), Bishop biog Aug 43 obit Oct 53
Haber, Heinz Dec 52
Hackett, Albert See Goodrich, Frances and Hackett, Albert Oct 56
Hackett, Mrs. Albert See Goodrich, Frances and Hackett, Albert Oct 56
Hackworth, Green H(aywood) Jan 58
Hafstad, Lawrence R(andolph) Oct 56
Hagen, John P(eter) Oct 57
Hagerty, James C. Mar 53
Hagy, Ruth Geri Oct 57
Hahn, Otto Mar 51

Haile Selassie I, Emperor of Ethiopia Oct 54
Hailsham, Lord See Hailsham, Quintin McGarel Hogg, 2d Viscount Sep 57
Hailsham, Quintin McGarel Hogg, 2d Viscount Sep 57
Haley, Andrew G(allagher) Oct 55
Halim, Mustafa (Ahmed) Ben Sep 56
Hall, Fred(erick Lee) Oct 55
Hall, Joyce C(lyde) May 53
Hall, Leonard W(ood) Jul 53
Hall, Marjory (WLB) Yrbk 57
Hall, Raymond S(tewart), Rev. Dr. Oct 53
Hall, William Edwin Jan 54
Halley, Rudolph biog Jun 53 obit Jan 57
Halligan, William J(oseph) Oct 57
Hallinan, Vincent (W.) Oct 52
Hallstein, Walter Oct 53
Halpert, Edith Gregor Jul 55
Halpert, Mrs. Samuel See Halpert, Edith Gregor Jul 55
Halsey, William F(rederick), Jr. biog Dec 42 obit Nov 59
Hamblet, Julia E. Oct 53
Hamlin, Talbot (Faulkner) biog Oct 54 obit Dec 56 Yrbk 57
Hammarskjöld, Dag (Hjalmar Agne Carl) May 53
Hammon, William McDowell Sep 57
Hammond, Caleb D(ean), Jr. Apr 56
Hammond, E(dward) Cuyler Jun 57
Hammond, Godfrey Oct 53
Hammond-Innes, Ralph See Innes, (R.) H. (WLB) Yrbk 54
Hampden, Walter (Dougherty) biog May 53 obit Sep 55
Han Suyin (WLB) Yrbk 57
Hancher, Virgil M(elvin) Feb 57
Hancock, John M(ilton) biog Apr 49 obit Dec 56 Yrbk 57
Handlin, Oscar Jul 52
Handy, Thomas T(roy) Sep 51
Handy, W(illiam) C(hristopher) biog Mar 41 obit Jun 58
Hannagan, Steve biog Aug 44 obit Mar 53
Hannah, John A(lfred) Oct 52
Hannikainen, Tauno (Heikki) Jul 55
Hansberry, Lorraine Sep 59
Hansen, H(ans) C(hristian Svane) Mar 56
Harber, W. Elmer Mar 51
Hardie, S(teven) J(ames) L(indsay) Jul 51
Harding, Allan Francis See Harding, Sir J. Oct 52
Harding, Sir John Oct 52
Hardy, Porter, Jr. May 57
Hare, Raymond A(rthur) Jul 57
Harlan, John Marshall May 55

Hoad, Lew(is A.) Sep 56

Hoare, Sir Samuel John Gurney, 2d Baronet See Templewood, Samuel John Gurney Hoare, 1st Viscount biog Oct 40 obit Jul 59

Hobbs, Leonard S(inclair) Oct 54

Hobby, Oveta Culp Feb 53

Hobby, Mrs. William (Pettus) See Hobby, O. C. Feb 53

Hodes, Henry I(rving) Feb 59

Hodges, Luther H(artwell) Jul 56

Hodgson, W(illiam) R(oy) biog May 46 obit Apr 58

Hoegh, Leo A(rthur) Jul 56

Hoey, Clyde R(oark) biog Oct 49 obit Jul 54

Hoffman, Joseph G(ilbert) May 58

Hofmann, Hans Oct 58

Hofstadter, Richard Oct 56

Hogan, Frank S(mithwick) Sep 53

Hogg, Quintin See Hailsham, Quintin McGarel Hogg, 2d Viscount Sep 57

Holaday, William M(arion) May 58

Holden, William Jun 54

Holder, Geoffrey Oct 57

Holenstein, Thomas (Emil Leo) May 58

Holifield, Chet (Chester Earl) Oct 55

Holland, (George) Kenneth Mar 52

Hollenbeck, Don biog Feb 51 obit Sep 54

Holliday, Judy Apr 51

Hollister, John B(aker) Oct 55

Holm, Hanya Jul 54

Holmes, (Elias) Burton biog May 44 obit Oct 58

Holmes, Robert D(enison) Jul 58

Holt, Cooper T. Jul 57

Holt, Hamilton biog Dec 47 obit May 51

Holt, Isabella (WLB) Yrbk 56

Home, Alexander Frederick Douglas-Home, 14th Earl of Feb 58

Homer, Arthur B(artlett) Jul 52

Honegger, Arthur biog Apr 41 obit Feb 56

Honeywell, Annette Jul 53

Hood, Clifford F(iroved) Apr 53

Hook, Sidney Oct 52

Hooper, C(laude) E(rnest) biog Apr 47 obit Feb 55

Hoopes, Darlington Sep 52

Hooton, Earnest Albert biog Yrbk 40 obit Jun 54

Hoover, Herbert (Clark), Jr. Oct 54

Hope, Bob Oct 53

Hope, Clifford R(agsdale) May 53

Hope, Leslie Townes See Hope, B. Oct 53

Hope, Stanley C. May 59

Hopkins, John Jay biog Mar 54 obit Jul 57

Hoppe, Willie biog Jun 47 obit Apr 59

Horder, Thomas J(eeves) Horder, 1st Baron biog Jul 44 obit Oct 55

Hore-Belisha, Leslie Hore-Belisha, 1st Baron biog Jul 41 obit May 57

Hormel, Jay C(atherwood) biog Jul 46 obit Oct 54

Horne, John E(lmer) Dec 52

Horner, H(orace) Mansfield Oct 55

Horney, Karen biog Aug 41 obit Jan 53

Hornsby, Rogers Sep 52

Horsbrugh, Florence Feb 52

Horthy de Nagybánya, Nicholas biog Oct 40 obit Apr 57

Horwich, Frances (Rappaport) Oct 53

Horwich, Mrs. Harvey L. See Horwich, F. (R.) Oct 53

Hosmer, (Chester) Craig May 58

Houphouet-Boigny, Félix Oct 58

Houseman, John Jul 59

Houser, Theodore V. Mar 57

Houtte, Jean van Mar 52

Hovde, Bryn(jolf) J(acob) biog Jan 46 obit Oct 54

Howard, Mrs. Charles P(agelsen) Jul 53

Howard, Elizabeth (WLB) Yrbk 51

Howard, Katherine (Montague) G(raham) See Howard, Mrs. C. P. Jul 53

Howe, Helen (WLB) Yrbk 54

Howell, Charles R(obert) Feb 54

Howley, Christine Wetherill See Leser, Tina Jun 57

Howorth, Mrs. Joseph Marion See Howorth, L. S. Oct 51

Howorth, Lucy Somerville Oct 51

Howrey, Edward F. Jul 53

Hruska, Roman Lee Jul 56

Hubbard, Margaret Ann (WLB) Yrbk 58

Huck, Arthur Feb 57

Hudleston, Edmund C(uthbert) May 51

Hudson, Robert S(pear) Hudson, 1st Viscount biog Nov 42 obit Apr 57

Huggins, Sir Godfrey See Malvern, Godfrey Huggins, 1st Viscount Nov 56

Hughes, Rowland R(oberts) biog Feb 56 obit Jun 57

Hulcy, Dechard A(nderson) Sep 51

Hull, Cordell biog Aug 40 obit Oct 55

Hull, John E(dwin) Apr 54

Hull, Josephine (Sherwood) biog Oct 53 obit May 57

Hume, Edgar Erskine biog Aug 44 obit Mar 52

Humphrey, Doris biog Apr 42 obit Mar 59

Humphrey, George M(agoffin) Feb 53

Humphrey, Helen F(lorence) Nov 52

Hunt, Sir (Henry Cecil) John; Hillary, Sir Edmund (Percival); and Tenzing Norkey Oct 54

Hunt, Herold C(hristian) May 56

Hunt, Sir John See Hunt, Sir (H. C.) J.; Hillary, Sir E. (P.); and Tenzing Norkey Oct 54

Hunt, Lester C(allaway) biog Mar 51 obit Sep 54

Hunt, Mabel Leigh (WLB) Yrbk 51

Hunter, Croil Jul 51

Hunter, Evan (WLB) Yrbk 56

Hunter, Kermit (Houston) May 59

Hunter, Kim May 52

Huntington, Anna Hyatt Oct 53

Huntington, Mrs. Archer M(ilton) See Huntington, A. H. Oct 53

Huntley, Chester Robert See Huntley, Chet Oct 56

Huntley, Chet Oct 56

Hurd, Peter Oct 57

Hurley, Laurel Jun 57

Hurley, Roy T. Jun 55

Hurok, S(olomon) Apr 56

Hurtado, César Barros See Barros Hurtado, César Jan 59

Hussein I, King of Hashemite Jordan Jul 55

Hussein, Ahmed Mar 56

Hussein, Taha Oct 53

Hutcheson, William L(evi) biog Sept 43 obit Jan 54

Hutchins, Robert Maynard Feb 54

Hutchinson, Paul biog Dec 49 obit Jun 56

Hutchison, (William) Bruce Oct 56

Hyatt, Anna See Huntington, A. H. Oct 53

Ibáñez (del Campo), Carlos Dec 52

Ibarra, José María Velasco See Velasco Ibarra, J. M. Nov 52

Ibn Saud, King of Saudi Arabia biog Feb 43 obit Jan 54

Ickes, Harold L(e Claire) biog Jul 41 obit Mar 52

Idell, Albert E(dward) biog Oct 43 obit Oct 58

Idriss Senussi I, King of Libya Jan 56

Ilg, Frances L(illian) and Ames, Louise (Bates) Sep 56

Impellitteri, Vincent R(ichard) Feb 51

Ingalls, (Mildred Dodge) Jeremy (WLB) Yrbk 54

Inge, William (Motter) Jun 53

Ingram, Jonas H(oward) biog Apr 47 obit Oct 52

Innes, (Ralph) Hammond (WLB) Yrbk 54

Kearns, Nora Lynch Sep 56
Keck, Mrs. George Fred See Keck, L. L. Mar 54
Keck, Lucile L(iebermann) Mar 54
Kee, Elizabeth (Frazier) Jan 54
Kee, John biog Jun 50 obit Jun 51
Kee, Mrs. John See Kee, E. (F.) Jan 54
Keenan, Joseph B(erry) biog Sep 46 obit Feb 55
Keeney, Barnaby C(onrad) Mar 56
Keeny, Spurgeon M(ilton) Jan 58
Keith, Harold (Verne) (WLB) Yrbk 58
Keller, James (Gregory), Rev. Oct 51
Kelley, Augustine B(ernard) biog Apr 51 obit Feb 58
Kelly, Emmett Jul 54
Kelly, E(verett) Lowell Mar 55
Kelly, Grace (Patricia) Mar 55
Kelly, Joe biog Jun 45 obit Jul 59
Kelly, Judith biog Oct 41 obit Jul 57
Kelly, Mervin J(oe) Oct 56
Kelly, Nancy Jun 55
Kelly, Mrs. Norman H. See Kelly, Regina Z. (WLB) Yrbk 56
Kelly, Regina Z(immerman) (WLB) Yrbk 56
Kelly, Walt(er Crawford) Oct 56
Kelsen, Hans Sep 57
Kemsley, James Gomer Berry, 1st Viscount Jan 51
Kennan, George F(rost) Jan 59
Kennedy, Robert F(rancis) Feb 58
Kennedy, Stephen P(atrick) Jun 56
Kennelly, Ardyth (WLB) Yrbk 53
Kennon, Robert F(loyd) Oct 54
Kenny, Elizabeth biog Oct 42 obit Jan 53
Kenyatta, Jomo Oct 53
Kerouac, Jack Nov 59
Kerr, Sir Archibald (John Kerr) Clark See Inverchapel of Loch Eck, A. J. K. C. K., 1st Baron biog Dec 42 obit Sep 51
Kerr, James W(inslow) Oct 59
Kerr, Jean (Collins) Jul 58
Kerr, Walter F(rancis) Oct 53
Kerr, Mrs. Walter F(rancis) See Kerr, Jean Jul 58
Kersten, Charles J. Sep 52
Kessler, Henry H(oward) Oct 57
Kestnbaum, Meyer May 53
Ketcham, Hank Jan 56
Kettering, Charles Franklin biog Dec 51 obit Feb 59
Key William S(haffer) biog Jul 43 obit Mar 59
Keyhoe, Donald E(dward) Jun 56
Keys, David A(rnold) Oct 58
Khan, Aga See Aga Khan, The biog May 46 obit Sep 57

Khan, Liaquat Ali biog Jun 48 obit Dec 51
Khan, Mohammad Ayub See Ayub Khan, Mohammad Apr 59
Khoman, Thanat Mar 58
Khoury, Bechara El- Dec 51
Khrushchev, Nikita S(ergeyevich) Jul 54
Kiam, Omar biog Dec 45 obit May 54
Kiewiet, Cornelis W(illem) de See de Kiewiet, C. W. Jul 53
Kilday, Paul J(oseph) Oct 58
Kilgallen, Dorothy, and Kollmar, Dick Feb 52
Kilgore, Harley M(artin) biog Jun 43 obit May 56
Killian, James R(hyne), Jr. May 59
Killion, George (Leonard) Nov 52
Kim Il Sung Sep 51
Kimball, Dan A(ble) Sep 51
Kimball, Lindsley F(iske) Jul 51
Kimble, George H(erbert) T(inley) Oct 52
Kimpton, Lawrence A(lpheus) Jun 51
Kindelberger, J(ames) H(oward) Mar 51
Kinder, Katharine L(ouise) May 57
Kiner, Ralph (McPherran) May 54
King, Cecil R(hodes) Feb 52
King, Ernest Joseph biog Feb 42 obit Sep 56
King, Martin Luther, Jr., Rev. May 57
King, Samuel Wilder biog Oct 53 obit Jun 59
Kinnear, Helen (Alice) Apr 57
Kinsey, Alfred C(harles) biog Jan 54 obit Oct 56
Kiphuth, Robert J(ohn) H(erman) Jun 57
Kirby, Rollin biog Dec 44 obit Jun 52
Kirk, Grayson L(ouis) May 51
Kirkus, Virginia Jun 54
Kirstein, Lincoln (Edward) Dec 52
Kishi, Nobusuke Jun 57
Kissinger, Henry A(lfred) Jun 58
Kitchell, Iva Dec 51
Kitson, Harry Dexter biog Apr 51 obit Nov 59
Kitt, Eartha Apr 55
KleinSmid, Rufus B(ernhard) von Jun 58
Kleist, Paul Ludwig (Ewald) von biog Jul 43 obit Jan 55
Kleitman, Nathaniel Oct 57
Klopsteg, Paul E(rnest) May 59
Kluckhohn, Clyde (Kay Maben) Nov 51
Klumpp, Theodore G(eorge) Oct 58
Knaths, (Otto) Karl Jul 53
Knight, Frances G(ladys) Oct 55
Knight, Goodwin (Jess) Jan 55

Knight, O(rie) A(lbert) Jun 52
Knight, Ruth Adams (Yingling) (WLB) Yrbk 55
Knoll, Hans G(eorge) biog May 55 obit Dec 55
Knopf, Mrs. Alfred A. Jul 57
Knopf, Blanche (Wolf) See Knopf, Mrs. Alfred A. Jul 57
Knopf, Mrs. Hans See Vanderbilt, A. Feb 54
Knorr, Nathan H(omer) Feb 57
Knox, Ronald (Arbuthnott), Msgr. biog Jul 50 obit Nov 57
Knuth-Winterfeldt, Kield Gustav, Count Sep 59
Knutson, Coya Mar 56
Knutson, Harold biog Jan 47 obit Oct 53
Koch, Fred(erick Henry), Jr. Oct 53
Kohler, Walter J(odok), Jr. Jan 53
Kokoschka, Oskar Oct 56
Kollmar, Dick See Kilgallen, D. and Kollmar, D. Feb 52
Kollmar, Richard Tompkins See Kilgallen, D. and Kollmar, D. Feb 52
Kollmar, Mrs. Richard Tompkins See Kilgallen, D. and Kollmar D. Feb 52
Kollontay, Alexandra (Mikhailovna) biog Oct 43 obit Apr 52
Komarovsky, Mirra Oct 53
Konev, Ivan S(tepanovich) Jan 56
Konstantinu, Mrs. Ilias See Clark, E. Sep 53
Konstanty, Casimer James See Konstanty, J. Apr 51
Konstanty, Jim Apr 51
Kooning, Willem de See de Kooning, W. Jun 55
Köprülü, (Mehmet) Fuat Jun 53
Korda, Sir Alexander biog Sep 46 obit Mar 56
Körner, Theodor biog Jul 51 obit Mar 57
Korngold, Erich W(olfgang) biog Mar 43 obit Feb 58
Kotelawala, Sir John (Lionel) Oct 55
Kotschnig, Walter M(aria) Oct 52
Koussevitzky, Serge biog Nov 40 obit Jul 51
Kovacs, Ernie Feb 58
Kozlov, Frol R(omanovich) Nov 59
Kraft, Ole Björn Feb 53
Kramer, Stanley (E.) May 51
Kramm, Joseph Jul 52
Krasna, Norman May 52
Krautter, Elisa Bialk See Bialk, E. (WLB) Yrbk 54
Krebs, H(ans) A(dolf) Mar 54
Krebs, Richard Julius Herman See Valtin, J. biog Apr 41 obit Jan 51
Krekeler, Heinz L(udwig) Dec 51
Kress, Samuel H(enry) biog Oct 55 obit Nov 55

Marsh, Reginald biog Sep 41 obit Sep 54

Marshall, David (Saul) Jul 56

Marshall, George C(atlett) biog Mar 47 obit Dec 59

Marshall, Mrs. Peter See Marshall, (S.) C. (W.) Jan 55

Marshall, Rosamond (Van der Zee) biog Aug 42 obit Feb 58

Marshall, S(amuel) L(yman) A(t-wood) Nov 53

Marshall, (Sarah) Catherine (Wood) Jan 55

Marshall, Thurgood Nov 54

Martel, Sir Giffard Le Quesne biog Jul 43 obit Nov 58

Martin, A(rcher) J(ohn) P(orter) Nov 53

Martin, Fletcher Feb 58

Martin, Glenn L(uther) biog Feb 43 obit Feb 56

Martin, Harry (Leland, Jr.) biog Jun 48 obit Mar 59

Martin, John Bartlow (WLB) Yrbk 56

Martin, Paul (Joseph James) Dec 51

Martin, Thomas E(llsworth) Mar 56

Martin, Walter B(ramlette) Nov 54

Martin, William C(lyde), Bishop Apr 53

Martin, William McChesney, Jr. May 51

Martínez Trueba, Andrés Nov 54

Martini, Mrs. Fred See Martini, Helen Jul 55

Martini, Helen (Frances Theresa) Jul 55

Martino, Gaetano May 56

Martinu, Bohuslav biog Nov 44 obit Nov 59

Martland, Harrison Stanford biog Nov 40 obit Jun 54

Marx, Elizabeth Lisl Weil See Weil, Lisl Jan 58

Marzotto, Gaetano, Count Jul 53

Masina, Giulietta Apr 58

Mason, Noah (Morgan) Nov 57

Mason, Norman P(eirce) Jun 59

Massey, Vincent Oct 51

Massigli, René (Lucien Daniel) May 56

Masters, Kelly Ray See Ball, Z. (WLB) Yrbk 53

Mateos, Adolfo López See López Mateos, Adolfo Mar 59

Mates, Leo Nov 56

Mather, Kirtley F(letcher) Jan 51

Mathewson, Lemuel Dec 52

Mathias, Robert Bruce Sep 52

Matisse, Henri (Emile Benoit) biog Jun 53 obit Jan 55

Matskevich, Vladimir V(ladimirovich) Nov 55

Matsudaira, Koto Nov 58

Matta (Echaurren, Roberto Antonio Sebastian) Nov 57

Mattei, Enrico Apr 59

Matthews, Francis P(atrick) biog Sep 49 obit Dec 52

Matthews, W(ilmot) Donald Sep 52

Mattson, Henry (Elis) Jan 56

Mature, Victor Dec 51

Maunoury, Maurice Bourgès- See Bourgès-Maunoury, Maurice Jul 57

Maverick, Maury biog Mar 44 obit Sep 54

Maximos, Demetrios biog Mar 48 obit Dec 55

Maxwell, David F(arrow) Jun 57

May, Andrew Jackson biog Apr 41 obit Nov 59

Maybank, Burnet R(hett) biog Apr 49 obit Nov 54

Mayer, Jane See Jaynes, C. (WLB) Yrbk 54

Mayer, Louis B(urt) biog Jun 43 obit Jan 58

Maynor, Dorothy Dec 51

Mayo, Charles W(illiam) Nov 54

Mays, Ewing W(oodrow) Jan 52

Mays, Willie May 55

Maza (Fernández), José Nov 55

Mboya, Thomas Joseph See Mboya, Tom Jun 59

Mboya, Tom Jun 59

Mead, Margaret May 51

Meader, George Jul 56

Meadows, Audrey May 58

Meadows, Jayne May 58

Meany, George Mar 54

Mechem, Edwin L(eard) Jul 54

Medaris, John B(ruce) Feb 58

Medina Angarita, Isaías biog Mar 42 obit Nov 53

Mehta, G(aganvihari) L(allubhai) Nov 52

Melas. George V(ictor) Jul 56

Mendelsohn, Eric biog Nov 53 obit Nov 53

Menderes, Adnan Nov 54

Mendès-France, Pierre Oct 54

Menon, K(umara) P(admanabha) S(ivasankara) Mar 57

Menon, V(engalil) K(rishnan) Krishna See Krishna Menon, V. K. Mar 53

Menshikov, Mikhail A(lekseevich) May 58

Menzel, Donald H(oward) Apr 56

Mercer, Samuel A(lfred) B(rowne), Rev. Dr. Feb 53

Merchant, Livingston T(allmadge) Nov 56

Merck, George W(ilhelm) biog Dec 46 obit Jan 58

Merman, Ethel May 55

Merriam, Charles E(dward) biog Feb 47 obit Feb 53

Merrill, Charles E(dward) biog Apr 56 obit Dec 56

Merrill, Frank (Dow) biog Jul 44 obit Feb 56

Merrill, Robert Mar 52

Merz, Charles Nov 54

Meyer, Eugene biog Sep 41 obit Oct 59

Meyer, Jean Nov 55

Meyer, K(arl) F(riedrich) Mar 52

Meyner, Robert B(aumle) Apr 55

Middlecoff, (Emmett) Cary Jul 52

Mies van der Rohe, Ludwig Oct 51

Mikhaïlov, Nikolaï A(leksandrovich) Nov 58

Mikoyan, Anastas I(vanovich) May 55

Millar, Kenneth (WLB) Yrbk 53

Mille, Cecil B. de See De Mille, Cecil B. biog May 42 obit Mar 59

Miller, Edward G(odfrey), Jr. Jun 51

Miller, Gilbert (Heron) Apr 58

Miller, Irving Nov 52

Miller, J. Cloyd Dec 51

Miller, Lee P(feiffer) Jul 59

Miller, Marshall E. Oct 53

Miller, Mildred Jun 57

Miller, Mitch(ell William) Jul 56

Milles, Carl (Wilhelm Emil) biog Dec 52 obit Nov 55

Millett, John D(avid) Feb 53

Milligan, Mary Louise May 57

Millikan, Robert A(ndrews) biog Jun 52 obit Feb 54

Millikin, Eugene D(onald) biog Apr 48 obit Oct 58

Mills, Wilbur D(aigh) Nov 56

Mindszenty, József, Cardinal Jan 57

Miner, Tony See Miner, W. (C.) Feb 53

Miner, Worthington (C.) Feb 53

Minor, Robert biog Apr 41 obit Jan 53

Miranda, Carmen biog Jun 41 obit Oct 55

Mirvish, Robert F(ranklin) (WLB) Yrbk 57

Mirza, Iskander May 56

Mistral, Gabriela biog Feb 46 obit Mar 57

Mitchell, Howard (Bundy) May 52

Mitchell, James P(aul) Sep 55

Mitchell, Stephen A(rnold) Oct 52

Mitchell, William D(e Witt) biog Jan 46 obit Nov 55

Mitchell, William L(loyd) Nov 59

Mitropoulos, Dimitri Mar 52

Mizner, Elizabeth Howard See Howard, E. (WLB) Yrbk 51

Mohammad, Bakshi Ghulam See Bakshi Ghulam Mohammad Jun 56

Mohammed V, King See Sidi Mohammed, Sultan of Morocco Oct 51

Mohammed Zahir Shah Mar 56

Mohammed, Ghulam biog Jul 54 obit Nov 56

Newman, Bernard (Charles) Apr 59

Newman, J(ames) Wilson Apr 55

Newman, Paul Nov 59

Newsom, Carroll Vincent Apr 57

Newsom, Herschel D(avis) Apr 51

Newton, Eric Feb 56

Ney, Hubert Nov 56

Ngawang Lobsang Yishey Tenzing Gyatso See Dalai Lama Jul 51

Ngo-dinh-Diem Mar 55

Niall, Michael See Breslin, Howard (WLB) Yrbk 58

Niarchos, Stavros (Spyros) May 58

Nichols, William I(chabod) Jun 58

Nichols, William T(homas) Oct 53

Nicholson, Ben Jan 58

Nicholson, Margaret Nov 57

Nickerson, Albert L(indsay) Nov 59

Nicolet, Marcel Nov 58

Niebuhr, Reinhold, Rev. Dr. Nov 51

Nielsen, A(rthur) C(harles) Dec 51

Niles, John Jacob Nov 59

Niven, David Mar 57

Nixon, Richard M(ilhous) Jun 58

Nizer, Louis Nov 55

Nkrumah, Kwame Jul 53

Noble, Allan (Herbert Percy) May 57

Noble, Edward J(ohn) biog Jan 44 obit Mar 59

Nobs, Ernst biog Sep 49 obit Jun 57

Nolan, Lloyd Nov 56

Noon, Malik Firoz Khan Jun 57

Nordhoff, Heinz Nov 56

Norgay, Tenzing See Hunt, Sir (H. C.) J.; Hillary, Sir E. (P.); and Tenzing Norkey Oct 54

Norodom Sihanouk, King of Cambodia Mar 54

Norstad, Lauris Feb 59

North, Andrew See Norton, Andre Jan 57

North, John Ringling Jun 51

Norton, Alice Mary See Norton, Andre Jan 57

Norton, Andre Jan 57

Norton, Mary T(eresa Hopkins) biog Nov 44 obit Nov 59

Norwich, Alfred Duff Cooper, 1st Viscount biog Aug 40 obit Mar 54

Notman, J(ames) Geoffrey Jan 58

Novaes (Pinto), Guiomar Jun 53

Novak, Kim Apr 57

Novotný, Antonín May 58

Nu, Thakin Dec 51

Nu, U See Nu, T. Dec 51

Nuckols, William P(reston) May 52

Nufer, Albert F. biog Mar 55 obit Jan 57

Nuñez Portuondo, Emilio Apr 57

Nuri as-Said biog Jun 55 obit Oct 58

Nutting, (Harold) Anthony Feb 55

Nyborg, Victor H(ugo) Feb 54

Nyrop, Donald W(illiam) Jun 52

Nystrom, Paul H(enry) Mar 51

Oberth, H(ermann Julius) Apr 57

Obolensky, Serge Oct 59

O'Brian, Hugh Jul 58

O'Brien, Leo W(illiam) Jun 59

O'Connor, Donald May 55

O'Connor, Flannery (WLB) Yrbk 58

Odría (Amoretti), Manuel A(polinario) Nov 54

Oettinger, Katherine Brownell Nov 57

Ogburn, Charlton Feb 55

Ogburn, William F(ielding) biog Feb 55 obit Jul 59

Ogden, C(harles) K(ay) biog Jan 44 obit Jun 57

Ogilvie, Elisabeth (May) (WLB) Yrbk 51

O'Gorman, Juan Nov 56

O'Hara, Maureen Feb 53

Oïstrakh, David (Fyodorovich) Mar 56

O'Konski, Alvin E(dward) Nov 55

Oliphant, Marcus L(aurence Elwin) Dec 51

Olivetti, Adriano Jan 59

Ollenhauer, Erich Jan 53

Olmedo, Alex Dec 59

Olmedo y Rodríguez Alejandro See Olmedo, Alex Dec 59

Olmsted, Frederick Law biog Jun 49 obit Mar 58

Olson, Harry F(erdinand) Nov 55

O'Malley, Walter F(rancis) Mar 54

O'Meara, Walter (Andrew) (WLB) Yrbk 58

O'Neal, Edward A(sbury) biog Sep 46 obit May 58

O'Neil, Thomas F(rancis) Nov 55

O'Neill, C. William Jul 58

O'Neill, J(ohn) E(dward) Jun 52

Onís, Harriet (Vivian Wishnieff) de Apr 57

Onsager, Lars Apr 58

Orlando, Vittorio Emanuele biog Feb 44 obit Jan 53

Orton, Helen Fuller biog Jan 41 obit Apr 55

Orville, Howard T(homas) May 56

Osborn, Robert C(hesley) Jun 59

Osborne, John (James) Jun 59

Ott, Mel(vin Thomas) biog Jul 41 obit Jan 59

Ötüken, Adnan Jun 54

Oursler, Fulton biog Oct 42 obit Jul 52

Overholser, Winfred Nov 53

Owen, Ruth Bryan See Rohde, R. B. O. biog Dec 44 obit Oct 54

Owens, James Cleveland See Owens, Jesse Nov 56

Owens, Jesse Nov 56

Paar, Jack (Harold) Apr 59

Paasikivi, Juho Kusti biog May 44 obit Feb 57

Pacelli, Eugenio See Pius XII, Pope biog Mar 50 obit Dec 58

Pacheco e Chaves, Joao Nov 54

Packard, Vance (Oakley) Apr 58

Packer, Fred L(ittle) biog Jul 52 obit Feb 59

Paddleford, Clementine (Haskin) Feb 58

Padover, Saul K(ussiel) Oct 52

Page, Geraldine Nov 53

Pagnol, Marcel (Paul) Mar 56

Paige, Janis Jan 59

Paige, Leroy (Robert) Sep 52

Paige, Satchel See Paige, L. (R.) Sep 52

Paley, William S(amuel) Dec 51

Palmer, Hazel Jun 58

Palmer, Lilli May 51

Pant, Govind Ballabh Jan 59

Pantaleoni, Mrs. Guido See Pantaleoni, Helenka Nov 56

Pantaleoni, Helenka (Tradeusa Adamowski) Nov 56

Papagos, Alexander biog Nov 51 obit Dec 55

Parker, Buddy Dec 55

Parker, Cola G(odden) Sep 56

Parker, John J(ohnston) biog Dec 55 obit May 58

Parker, Raymond K(lein) See Parker, Buddy Dec 55

Parker, Roy H(artford) Oct 51

Parkes, Henry Bamford Mar 54

Parkinson, Thomas I(gnatius) biog Apr 49 obit Sep 59

Parnis, Mollie May 56

Parrish, Wayne W(illiam) Nov 58

Parrish, Mrs. Wayne William See Knight, Frances G. Oct 55

Parsons, Harriet (Oettinger) Jan 53

Parsons, Rose Peabody See Parsons, Mrs. William Barclay Dec 59

Parsons, Mrs. William Barclay Dec 59

Partridge, Earle E(verard) Apr 55

Pascal, Gabriel biog Jan 42 obit Sep 54

Pasquel, Jorge biog Jul 46 obit May 55

Pasternak, Boris (Leonidovich) Feb 59

Pastore, John O(rlando) Apr 53

Pasvolsky, Leo biog May 45 obit Jun 53

Pate, Maurice Jun 51

Pate, Randolph McC(all) Sep 58

Quarles, Donald A(ubrey) biog Nov 55 obit Jul 59

Quill, Michael J(oseph) Mar 53

Quinn, Anthony (Rudolph Oaxaca) Dec 57

Quinn, William F(rancis) Nov 58

Quintero, José (Benjamin) Apr 54

Quirino, Elpidio biog Sep 48 obit May 56

Quo Tai-chi biog May 46 obit Apr 52

Raab, Julius Apr 54

Rabaut, Louis Charles Jan 52

Raborn, William Francis, Jr. Jul 58

Rackmil, Milton R. Nov 52

Raddall, Thomas (Head) (WLB) Yrbk 51

Radhakrishnan, Sir Sarvepalli Jun 52

Raedler, Dorothy (Florence) Dec 54

Rahman, Abdul, Paramount Ruler of Malaya Dec 57

Rahman, Abdul, Prince Dec 57

Rainier III, Prince of Monaco Nov 55

Rains, Albert (M.) Sep 59

Ralls, Charles C. Jan 51

Rama Rau, Lady (Benegal) See Rau, D. (H.) R. Apr 54

Rama Rau, Santha (WLB) Yrbk 59

Ramo, Simon and Wooldridge, Dean E(verett) Apr 58

Ramsey, DeWitt C(linton) Jan 53

Ramspeck, Robert (C. Word) Jun 51

Rance, Sir Hubert Elvin Dec 53

Rand, William M(cNear) May 53

Randall, Clarence B(elden) Jun 52

Randall, Mrs. J. G. See Randall, Ruth Painter (WLB) Yrbk 57

Randall, Ruth (Elaine) Painter (WLB) Yrbk 57

Randers, Gunnar Jan 57

Randolph, A(sa) Philip Oct 51

Rankin, J(ames) Lee Feb 59

Rankin, K(arl) L(ott) Apr 55

Rao, Shanta Dec 57

Rapacki, Adam Jul 58

Rappard, William E(mmanuel) biog Oct 51 obit Jul 58

Rasmussen, Gustav biog Dec 47 obit Nov 53

Rassweiler, Clifford F(red) Oct 58

Rathbone, Basil Mar 51

Rathbone, Monroe J(ackson) Mar 57

Rattigan, Terence (Mervyn) Dec 56

Rau, Sir Benegal Narsing biog Dec 51 obit Feb 54

Rau, Lady (Benegal) Rama See Rau, D. (H.) R. Apr 54

Rau, Dhanvanthi (Handoo) Rama Apr 54

Rawalt, Marguerite Mar 56

Rawlings, Marjorie Kinnan biog Jul 42 obit Feb 54

Razmara, Ali biog Oct 50 obit Mar 51

Reavey, Mrs. George See Pereira, I. R. Nov 53

Redfield, Robert biog Dec 53 obit Jan 59

Redpath, Anne Jan 57

Reed, Daniel A(lden) biog May 53 obit Apr 59

Reed, Ralph T(homas) Apr 51

Rees, Edward H(erbert) Jan 58

Rees, Mina S(piegel) Nov 57

Reese, Everett D. Mar 54

Reichstein, Tadeus Feb 51

Reid, Helen Rogers May 52

Reid, Mrs. Ogden Mills See Reid, H. R. May 52

Reid, Ogden R(ogers) Feb 56

Reid, Whitelaw Dec 54

Reinartz, F(rederick) Eppling Rev. Dr. Jul 53

Reiner, Fritz Dec 53

Remorino, Jerónimo Sep 51

Renaud, Madeleine See Barrault, J. L. and Renaud, M. Mar 53

Renault, Mary Jan 59

Renner, Karl biog Sep 45 obit Jan 51

Renoir, Jean Dec 59

Reshevsky, Samuel Feb 55

Resnik, Regina Jan 56

Reuss, Henry S(choellkopf) Oct 59

Reuter, Ernst biog Oct 49 obit Dec 53

Reuther, Victor (George) Dec 53

Revelle, Roger (Randall) Mar 57

Revercomb, (William) Chapman Jun 58

Reynolds, Albert Pierce See Reynolds, A. Jun 52

Reynolds, Allie Jun 52

Reynolds, R(ichard) S(amuel), Sr. biog Feb 53 obit Oct 55

Rhoads, C(ornelius) P(ackard) biog Mar 53 obit Nov 59

Rhyne, Charles S(ylvanus) May 58

Ribicoff, Abraham A. Jun 55

Rice, Grantland biog Sep 41 obit Sep 54

Rich, Daniel Catton Dec 55

Richard, Maurice (Joseph Henri) Dec 58

Richards, Dickinson W(oodruff) Mar 57

Richards, James P(rioleau) Sep 51

Richards, John S(tewart) Jun 55

Richards, Robert E(ugene), Rev. Jun 57

Richards, Vincent biog Jul 47 obit Dec 59

Richards, Wayne E. Jul 54

Richardson, Seth (Whitley) biog Feb 48 obit May 53

Ritchie, Jean Oct 59

Richter, Conrad (Michael) Jun 51

Rickenbacker, Eddie See Rickenbacker, E. V. Feb 52

Rickenbacker, Edward Vernon Feb 52

Rickover, Hyman G(eorge) May 53

Riddell, R(obert) Gerald biog Sep 50 obit Apr 51

Riddleberger, James W(illiams) May 57

Ridenour, Nina Apr 51

Riebel, John P(aul) Jan 57

Riesenberg, Felix, Jr. (WLB) Yrbk 57

Riesman, David, (Jr.) Jan 55

Riiser-Larsen, Hjalmar Nov 51

Riley, Susan B. Feb 53

Riley, William E(dward) Nov 51

Rincón de Gautier, Felisa See Gautier, Felisa Rincón de Oct 56

Rinehart, Stanley M(arshall), Jr. Dec 54

Ripley, Elizabeth (Blake) (WLB) Yrbk 58

Ritchard, Cyril Jan 57

Riter, Henry G., 3d biog Oct 55 obit Sep 58

Ritner, Ann (Gilliland) (WLB) Yrbk 53

Ritter, Thelma Dec 57

Rivera, Diego biog Jul 48 obit Feb 58

Rives, Hallie Erminie (WLB) biog Yrbk 56 obit Yrbk 56

Robards, Jason (Nelson), Jr. Oct 59

Robb, Inez (Callaway) Dec 58

Robbins, Frederick C. See Enders, J. F. Jun 55

Robbins, William J(acob) Feb 56

Robens, Alfred Jun 56

Roberts, C(harles) Wesley Apr 53

Roberts, Dennis J(oseph) Dec 56

Roberts, Dorothy James (WLB) Yrbk 56

Roberts, Goodridge See Roberts, (William) Goodridge May 55

Roberts, Owen J(osephus) biog Oct 41 obit Jul 55

Roberts, Robin (Evan) Dec 53

Roberts, (William) Goodridge May 55

Robertson, Norman A(lexander) Dec 57

Robertson, Reuben B(uck), Jr. Dec 55

Robertson, R(obert) B(lackwood) May 57

Robertson, Walter S(pencer) Dec 53

Robinson, Boardman biog Dec 41 obit Oct 52

Sarnoff, Robert W(illiam) Dec 56
Sarton, George (Alfred Léon) biog Jul 42 obit May 56
Saud, King of Saudi Arabia Apr 54
Saulnier, Raymond J(oseph) Dec 57
Saunders, Hilary A(idan) St. George biog Jun 43 obit Feb 52
Saunders, Robert (Hood) biog Dec 51 obit Mar 55
Savitt, Dick See Savitt, R. Jun 52
Savitt, Richard Jun 52
Sawyer, Helen (Alton) Oct 54
Sayegh, Fayez A(bdullah) Jul 57
Sayre, Francis B(owes), Jr., Very Rev. Dec 56
Sayre, Morris biog Jan 48 obit Apr 53
Scarbrough, (Lawrence) Roger Lumley, 11th Earl of Jan 58
Scelba, Mario May 53
Schachter, Mrs. Jules See Edwards, J. Oct 53
Schäffer, Fritz Mar 53
Schärf, Adolf Oct 57
Scherman, Thomas (Kielty) Dec 54
Schiaparelli, Elsa Nov 51
Schildkraut, Joseph Apr 56
Schindler, John A(lbert) biog Mar 56 obit Jan 58
Schlein, Miriam (WLB) Yrbk 59
Schnabel, Artur biog Jul 42 obit Sep 51
Schneider, Alma K(ittredge) Dec 54
Schneider, Mrs. Daniel Jacob See Schneider, A. K. Dec 54
Schneider, Hannes biog Mar 41 obit Jun 55
Schneirla, T(heodore) C(hristian) Dec 55
Schnurer, Carolyn (Goldsand) Mar 55
Schnurer, Mrs. Harold T(eller) See Schnurer, C. (G.) Mar 55
Schoeppel, Andrew F. Mar 52
Schönberg, Arnold biog Apr 42 obit Sep 51
Schoonover, Lawrence (Lovell) (WLB) Yrbk 57
Schorr, Daniel (Louis) Sep 59
Schorr, Friedrich biog Jul 42 obit Jun 54
Schottland, Charles I(rwin) Dec 56
Schram, Emil May 53
Schreiber, J.-J. Servan- See Servan-Schreiber, J.-J. Jan 55
Schreiber, (Karl Rudolf) Walther biog Feb 54 obit Sep 58
Schriever, Bernard A(dolf) Oct 57
Schulberg, Budd (Wilson) May 51
Schumacher, Kurt biog Feb 48 obit Oct 52
Schwartz, Maurice Feb 56
Schwarzkopf, Elisabeth Dec 55

Schwebel, Stephen M(yron) Jul 52
Scoggin, Margaret C(lara) Jul 52
Scott, (Guthrie) Michael, Rev. Apr 53
Scott, W(illiam) Kerr biog Apr 56 obit Jul 58
Scribner, Fred C(lark), Jr. Dec 58
Sears, Robert R(ichardson) Jul 52
Seaton, Fred(erick) A(ndrew) Nov 56
Sebald, William J(oseph) Oct 51
Sebrell, W(illiam) H(enry), Jr. May 51
Sedgman, Francis Arthur See Sedgman, F. Nov 51
Sedgman, Frank Nov 51
Seefried, Irmgard Feb 56
Segni, Antonio Dec 55
Segura, Francisco Sep 51
Seif al-Islam al-Hassan, Prince See al-Hassan, Prince of the Yemen Feb 57
Seif-ul-Islam Abdullah, Prince biog Dec 47 obit Sep 55
Seifert, Elizabeth (WLB) Yrbk 51
Seifert, Shirley (Louise) (WLB) Yrbk 51
Seitz, Frederick Apr 56
Seixas, E(lias) Victor, Jr. Jul 52
Selassie See Haile Selassie I, Emperor of Ethiopia Oct 54
Selinko, Annemarie Jan 55
Seltzer, Louis B(enson) Dec 56
Selye, Hans (Hugo Bruno) Jun 53
Semenov, Nikolai N(ikolaevich) Mar 57
Sen, B(inay) R(anjan) Dec 52
Senanayake, Don Stephen biog Apr 50 obit May 52
Senanayake, Dudley (Shelton) Dec 52
Serling, Rod Dec 59
Serov, Ivan A(leksandrovich) Dec 56
Serratosa Cibils, Joaquin Feb 54
Servan-Schreiber, J(ean)-J(acques) Jan 55
Seton, Anya (WLB) Yrbk 53
Settle, Mary Lee (WLB) Yrbk 59
Sforza, Carlo, Count biog Jun 42 obit Oct 52
Shabandar, Moussa (Mahmoud Al-) Feb 56
Shafer, Paul W(erntz) biog Jul 52 obit Oct 54
Shafik, Doria (Ahmad) May 55
Shahn, Ben(jamin) Dec 54
Shantz, Bobby See Shantz, R. C. Apr 53
Shantz, Robert Clayton Apr 53
Shapiro, Harry L(ionel) Dec 52
Shapley, Harlow Dec 52
Shaver, Dorothy biog Jan 46 obit Sep 59
Shaw, Ralph R(obert) Jun 56
Shay, Edith (WLB) Yrbk 52

Shay, Frank biog (WLB) Yrbk 52 obit Mar 54
Shea, Andrew B(ernard) Jan 57
Shearing, George (Albert) Apr 58
Sheen, Fulton J(ohn), Bishop Jan 51
Shehu, Mehmet Feb 58
Shellabarger, Samuel biog May 45 obit May 54
Shelly, Mary Jo(sephine) Oct 51
Shelly, Warner S(woyer) Feb 52
Shelton, James E(rrett) Feb 51
Shepherd, Lemuel C(ornick), Jr. Feb 52
Shepilov, Dmitri Trofimovitch Dec 55
Sherman, Forrest P(ercival) biog Mar 48 obit Sep 51
Sherman, Henry C(lapp) biog Jan 49 obit Dec 55
Sherwood, Robert E(mmet) biog Jan-Jun 40 obit Jan 56
Shidehara, Kijuro biog Apr 46 obit Apr 51
Shield, Lansing P(eter) Jun 51
Shields, James P. biog Mar 51 obit Sep 53
Shigemitsu, Mamoru biog Jun 43 obit Mar 57
Shimkin, Leon May 54
Shinn, Everett biog May 51 obit Jun 53
Shippen, Katherine B(inney) (WLB) Yrbk 54
Shivers, Allan Oct 51
Shockley, William Dec 53
Shoemaker, Samuel M(oor), Rev. Dr. Apr 55
Shoriki, Matsutaro Feb 58
Short, Dewey Dec 51
Short, Hassard biog Nov 48 obit Dec 56
Short, Joseph (Hudson, Jr.) biog Feb 51 obit Nov 52
Shull, Martha A(rvesta) Apr 57
Shulman, Harry biog Apr 52 obit May 55
Shulman, Irving (WLB) Yrbk 56
Shulman, Max Oct 59
Shuman, Charles B(aker) Feb 56
Shvernik, Nikolai (Mikhailovich) Oct 51
Sidi Mohammed, Sultan of Morocco Oct 51
Siepi, Cesare Dec 55
Sigerist, Henry Ernest biog Sep 40 obit Jun 57
Sikorsky, Igor I(van) Dec 56
Siles Zuazo, Hernán Sep 58
Sillcox, Lewis K(etcham) Dec 54
Silva, Vieira da See Vieira da Silva Dec 58
Silva de Santolalla, Irene See Santolalla, Irene Silva de Dec 56
Silvers, Phil Dec 57
Simkhovitch, Mary (Melinda) K(ingsbury) biog Mar 43 obit Dec 51

Sterling, J(ohn) E(wart) Wallace Jan 51

Stern, Arthur Cecil Apr 56

Sterne, Hedda Mar 57

Sterne, Maurice biog Apr 43 obit Oct 57

Stevens, George (Cooper) Apr 52

Stevens, Robert T(en Broeck) Jul 53

Stevens, Roger L(acey) Dec 55

Stevenson, Elizabeth (WLB) Yrbk 56

Stewart, Potter Dec 59

Stine, Charles Milton Altland biog Jan-Jun 40 obit Sep 54

Stirnweiss, George (Henry) biog Mar 46 obit Dec 58

Stoessel, Mrs. Henry Kurt See Chastain, Madye Lee (WLB) Yrbk 58

Stoica, Chivu Jan 59

Stokes, Richard R(apier) biog Sep 51 obit Oct 57

Stokes, Thomas L(unsford, Jr.) biog May 47 obit Sep 58

Stokowski, Leopold (Anton Stanislaw) Jul 53

Stolk, William C. Mar 53

Stolz, Mary Slattery (WLB) Yrbk 53

Stone, Abraham biog Mar 52 obit Oct 59

Stone, Edward D(urell) Jun 58

Storey, Robert G(erald) Nov 53

Stout, Ruth A(lbertine) Jan 59

Stout, William Bushnell biog Mar 41 obit May 56

Strachan, Paul A(mbrose) Jan 52

Stranahan, Frank (Richard) Sep 51

Strasberg, Susan (Elizabeth) May 58

Stratemeyer, George E(dward) Feb 51

Stratton, William G(rant) Apr 53

Straus, Jack I(sidor) Mar 52

Straus, Michael W(olf) Jun 52

Straus, Oskar biog Mar 44 obit Mar 54

Straus, Roger W(illiams) biog Jul 52 obit Oct 57

Strauss, Franz Josef Feb 57

Strauss, J(acobus) G(ideon) N(el) Jan 51

Stravinsky, Igor (Fëdorovich) Apr 53

Street, James (Howell) biog (WLB) Yrbk 46 obit Nov 54

Streibert, Theodore C(uyler) Feb 55

Streuli, Hans Apr 57

Strijdom, Johannes Gerhardus biog May 56 obit Nov 58

Stritch, Samuel (Alphonsus), Cardinal biog Apr 46 obit Sep 58

Stroessner, Alfredo Dec 58

Struble, Arthur D(ewey) Nov 51

Struther, Jan biog Jan 41 obit Oct 53

Stuhlinger, Ernst Nov 57

Stump, Felix B(udwell) Jan 53

Sturges, Preston biog Apr 41 obit Oct 59

Sturgis, Samuel D(avis), Jr. Jan 56

Sturzo, Luigi biog Feb 46 obit Nov 59

Subah, Abdullah al-Salim al, Sheikh See Abdullah al-Salim al Subah, Sir, Sheikh of Kuwait Jul 57

Sucksdorff, Arne (Edvard) Apr 56

Sugrue, Thomas (Joseph) biog Jun 48 obit Feb 53

Suhr, Otto (Ernst Heinrich Hermann) biog Apr 55 obit Nov 57

Suhrawardy, H(ussain) S(haheed) Apr 57

Sullivan, A(loysius) M(ichael) Dec 53

Sullivan, Brian Dec 57

Sullivan, Ed(ward Vincent) Sep 52

Sullivan, Francis L(oftus) biog Jun 55 obit Jan 57

Sullivan, Gael (E.) biog May 47 obit Jan 57

Sullivan, Henry J. Jun 58

Sullivan, Mrs. John B(erchmans) See Sullivan, L. (A.) K. Dec 54

Sullivan, Leonor (Alice) K(retzer) Dec 54

Sultan of Morocco See Sidi Mohammed, Sultan of Morocco Oct 51

Sultan of Oman See Said bin Taimur, Sultan of Muscat and Oman Oct 57

Sumac, Yma Dec 55

Summerfield, Arthur E(llsworth) Sep 52

Sumner, (Bertha) Cid Ricketts (WLB) Yrbk 54

Sumner, Mrs. G. Lynn See Picken, M. B. Dec 54

Sumner, James B(atcheller) biog Jan 47 obit Oct 55

Suslov, Mikhail A(ndreyevich) Feb 57

Sutherland, Graham (Vivian) Jan 55

Sutton, George P(aul) Jul 58

Suyin, Han See Han Suyin (WLB) Yrbk 57

Suzuki, Daisetz T(eitaro) Oct 58

Svanholm, Set (Karl Viktor) Dec 56

Sveda, Michael Dec 54

Sweeney, James Johnson Mar 55

Swigert, Ernest G(oodnough) Oct 57

Swing, Joseph M(ay) Apr 59

Swings, Paul See Swings, P. (F. F.) Dec 54

Swings, Pol(idore F. F.) Dec 54

Swirbul, Leon A. Apr 53

Swope, Gerard biog Sep 41 obit Feb 58

Swope, Herbert Bayard biog Nov 44 obit Sep 58

Syme, John P(rescott) Mar 57

Symes, James M(iller) Dec 55

Symington, (William) Stuart Jul 56

Synge, Richard L(aurence) M(illington) Nov 53

Szent-Györgyi, Albert (von Nagyrapolt) Jan 55

Szigeti, Joseph Mar 58

Szyk, Arthur biog Nov 46 obit Oct 51

Taber, Gladys (Leonae Bagg) (WLB) Yrbk 52

Taffin de Givenchy, Hubert See Givenchy, H. (J. T.) de May 55

Taft, Robert A(lphonso) biog May 40 Apr 48 obit Oct 53

Talal, former King of Jordan Jan 52

Talbert, Billy Mar 57

Talbert, William F(ranklin) See Talbert, Billy Mar 57

Talbott, Harold E(lstner) biog Jul 53 obit May 57

Talbott, Philip M. Apr 58

Tallamy, Bertram D(alley) May 57

Tallant, Robert biog (WLB) Yrbk 53 obit Jun 57

Tallchief, Maria Nov 51

Tamayo, Rufino Mar 53

Tandy, Jessica Mar 56

Tani, Masayuki May 56

Tanner, Edward Everett, 3d May 59

Tassigny, Jean (Joseph Marie Gabriel) de Lattre de See Lattre de Tassigny, J. (J. M. G.) de biog Jan 45 obit Feb 52

Tata, J(ehangir) R(atanji) D(adbhoy) Dec 58

Tatum, Edward L(awrie) Mar 59

Taubman, (Hyman) Howard Apr 59

Taylor, Elizabeth Jul 52

Taylor, Francis Henry biog Jan-Feb 40 obit Feb 58

Taylor, John W(ilkinson) Jan 54

Taylor, Myron C(harles) biog Jan-Feb 40 obit Jul 59

Taylor, Robert May 52

Taylor, Robert Lewis Dec 59

Taylor, Mrs. William Bolling See Young, M. Jun 52

Tchelitchew, Pavel biog Mar 43 obit Oct 57

Teague, Olin E(arl) Mar 52

Tebaldi, Renata Apr 55

Tebbel, John (William) (WLB) Yrbk 53

Teitgen, Pierre-Henri Jan 53

Teller, Edward Dec 54

Tello, Manuel (Baurrad) Dec 59

Templer, Sir Gerald (Walter Robert) Jul 52

Verwoerd, H(endrik) F(rensch) Mar 59

Victor, Sally (Josephs) Apr 54

Vidor, King (Wallis) Feb 57

Vieira da Silva, (Maria Helena) Dec 58

Vigneaud, Vincent du See du Vigneaud, Vincent Jan 56

Villon, Jacques Jan 56

Vinson, Fred(erick) M(oore) biog Aug 43 obit Nov 53

Viscardi, Henry, Jr. Jan 54

Vishinskii, Andrei (IAnuar'evich) biog May 44 obit Jan 55

Vogel, Herbert D(avis) Dec 54

Vogt, William Mar 53

Von Braun, Wernher Jan 52

Von Brentano, Heinrich See Brentano (di Tremezzo), H. von Feb 55

Von Eckardt, Felix See Eckardt, Felix von Jan 56

Von Einem, Gottfried See Einem, G. von Jul 53

Von Heidenstam, Rolf See Heidenstam, Rolf von biog Oct 51 obit Oct 58

Von Karajan, Herbert See Karajan, Herbert von Oct 56

Von Kármán, Theodore May 55

Von KleinSmid, Rufus B. See KleinSmid, Rufus B. von Jun 58

Von Kleist, Paul Ludwig See Kleist, P. L. (E.) von biog Jul 43 obit Jan 55

Von Mannerheim, Carl Gustaf Emil, Baron See Mannerheim, C. G. E., Baron von biog Apr 40 obit Feb 51

Von Neumann, John biog Jul 55 obit Apr 57

Von Rundstedt, Karl (Rudolf Gerd) See Rundstedt, K. (R. G.) von biog Nov 41 obit Apr 53

Von Szent-Györgyi, Albert See Szent-Györgyi, A. (von N.) Jan 55

Von Thadden-Trieglaff, Reinold See Thadden-Trieglaff, Reinold von Jul 59

Voorhees, Tracy S(tebbins) Feb 57

Voronoff, Serge biog Jan 41 obit Oct 51

Vukmanović-Tempo, Svetozar (N.) Dec 58

Vyshinsky, Andrei See Vishinskii, Andrei (IAnuar'evich) biog May 44 obit Jan 55

Wadsworth, James J(eremiah) Jun 56

Wadsworth, James W(olcott) biog Jul 43 obit Sep 52

Wagner, J(ohn) Addington May 56

Wagner, Robert F(erdinand) biog May 41 obit Jun 53

Wagner, Robert F(erdinand, Jr.) Feb 54

Wainwright, Jonathan M(ayhew) biog May 42 obit Nov 53

Wakehurst, John de Vere Loder, 2d Baron Dec 54

Wald, Jerome Irving See Wald, J. May 52

Wald, Jerry May 52

Walden, Amelia Elizabeth (WLB) Yrbk 56

Walker, E(dward) Ronald Dec 56

Walker, Eric A(rthur) Mar 59

Walker, Frank C(omerford) biog Oct 40 obit Nov 59

Walker, John May 57

Walker, Norma Ford Oct 57

Walker, Paul A(tlee) May 52

Walker, Ralph (Thomas) Dec 57

Walker, Walton H(arris) biog Sep 50 obit Jan 51

Walker, Waurine (Elizabeth) Feb 55

Wall, Art(hur Jonathan), Jr. Dec 59

Wallace, DeWitt and Lila (Bell) Acheson May 56

Wallace, Mrs. DeWitt See Wallace, DeWitt and Lila Acheson May 56

Wallace, Lila (Bell) Acheson See Wallace, DeWitt and Lila Acheson May 56

Wallace, Mike Jul 57

Wallach, Eli May 59

Wallenstein, Alfred (Franz) Apr 52

Waller, Fred(eric) biog Feb 53 obit Jul 54

Wallop, (John) Douglass (WLB) Yrbk 56

Walsh, Mrs. Richard J(ohn) See Buck, Pearl Jul 56

Walter, Francis E(ugene) Jun 52

Walton, Ernest Thomas Sinton Mar 52

Walworth, Arthur (Clarence, Jr.) Dec 59

Wambaugh, Sarah biog Apr 46 obit Jan 56

Wampler, (ElRey) Cloud Dec 52

Wan (Waithayakon), Prince Jun 54

Wang, Ping-nan Dec 58

Wangchuk, Jigme Dorji, Druk Gyalpo of Bhutan Oct 56

Warburton, Herbert B(irchby) Nov 51

Waring, Roane biog Dec 43 obit Dec 58

Warne, William E(lmo) Nov 52

Warner, Edward P(earson) biog Oct 49 obit Sep 58

Warner, Harry M(orris) biog Jan 45 obit Oct 58

Warner, W(illiam) Lloyd Dec 59

Warren, Avra M(ilvin) biog Feb 55 obit Mar 57

Warren, Earl Jan 54

Warren, Leonard Dec 53

Washburn, Gordon Bailey Dec 55

Waterman, Alan T(ower) Jun 51

Waters, Ethel Mar 51

Watkins, Shirley (WLB) Yrbk 58

Watson, Burl S(tevens) Apr 57

Watson, John B(roadus) biog Oct 42 obit Dec 58

Watson, Lucile Dec 53

Watson, Thomas J(ohn), Sr. biog Jul 50 obit Sep 56

Watson, Thomas J(ohn), Jr. Feb 56

Watt, Donald (Beates) Jan 58

Waugh, Samuel C(lark) Dec 55

Waverley, John Anderson, 1st Viscount biog Jul 41 obit Mar 58

Wayne, David Jun 56

Wayne, John Feb 51

Weafer, Elizabeth Jan 58

Weafer, Mrs. Eugene C(lyde) See Weafer, Elizabeth Jan 58

Weaver, Sylvester L(aflin), Jr. Jan 55

Weaver, Warren Apr 52

Webb, Aileen O(sborn) Dec 58

Webb, Jack (Randolph) May 55

Webb, Maurice biog May 50 obit Sep 56

Webb, Mrs. Vanderbilt See Webb, Aileen O. Dec 58

Webster, H(arold) T(ucker) biog Mar 45 obit Nov 52

Wechsberg, Joseph Apr 55

Wedgwood, C(icely) V(eronica) Jan 57

Weede, Robert Feb 57

Weeks, Sinclair Mar 53

Weil, Frank L(eopold) biog Feb 49 obit Jan 58

Weil, Lisl Jan 58

Weil, Richard, Jr. biog Jul 51 obit Jul 58

Weir, Ernest T(ener) biog Jun 41 obit Oct 57

Weis, Mrs. Charles W(illiam), Jr. Dec 59

Weis, Jessica McCullough See Weis, Mrs. Charles W., Jr. Dec 59

Weizmann, Chaim biog Nov 42 Nov 48 obit Dec 52

Welch, Joseph N(ye) Jun 54

Welensky, Sir Roland See Welensky, Sir Roy Jul 59

Welensky, Sir Roy Jul 59

Welk, Lawrence Feb 57

Welker, Herman biog Feb 55 obit Jan 58

Weller, Thomas H. See Enders, J. F. Jun 55

Wellman, Manly Wade (WLB) Yrbk 55

Wells, Agnes (Ermina) biog Nov 49 obit Oct 59

Welman, Joseph C(larence) May 58

ADDENDA

BRIGHAM, CLARENCE S. Retired on October 21 after fifty-one years as librarian, director, and president of the American Antiquarian Society and was succeeded by Carleton R. Richmond. Page 43

PHOUI SANANIKONE. Resigned as Premier of Laos on December 30 and was succeeded by Thao Kou Abhay, who headed a caretaker government. Page 359